Collins

— POCKET —

Thai
Dictionary

ไทย-อังกฤษ อังกฤษ-ไทย

HarperCollins Publishers
Westerhill Road
Bishopbriggs
Glasgow
G64 2QT
Great Britain

First Edition 2012

© HarperCollins Publishers 2012

Reprint 10 9 8 7 6 5 4 3 2 1

ISBN 978-0-00-745422-8

www.collinslanguage.com

A catalogue record for this book is
available from the British Library

Typesetting by Davidson Publishing
Solutions, Glasgow and Lingea s.r.o.

Printed in India by
Gopsons Papers Ltd

Acknowledgements

We would like to thank those authors and
publishers who kindly gave permission
for copyright material to be used in the
Collins Word Web. We would also like
to thank Times Newspapers Ltd for
providing valuable data.

Series Editor
Rob Scriven

Managing Editor
Ruth O'Donovan

Project Manager
Morven Dooner

Editor
Susie Beattie

Contributors
Nitchaya Boonma
Wannaporn Rienjang

For the Publisher
Lucy Cooper
Kerry Ferguson
Elaine Higgleton
Susanne Reichert

สารบัญ   CONTENTS

บทนำ

เรารู้สึกยินดีที่คุณตัดสินใจซื้อพจนานุกรมไทย-อังกฤษ อังกฤษ-ไทย ฉบับนี้ และหวังว่าคุณจะพอใจ
และได้รับประโยชน์จากการใช้งานพจนานุกรมที่บ้าน ในวันหยุด หรือที่ทำงาน

INTRODUCTION

We are delighted that you have decided to buy this Thai-English, English-Thai dictionary and hope that you will enjoy and benefit from using it at home, on holiday or at
work.

คำย่อ		**ABBREVIATIONS**
คุณศัพท์	*adj*	adjective
กริยาวิเศษณ์	*adv*	adverb
อุทาน	*excl*	exclamation
บุพบท	*prep*	preposition
สรรพนาม	*pron*	pronoun
นาม	*n*	noun
เพศหญิง	*f*	feminine
เพศชาย	*m*	masculine
ไม่มีเพศ	*nt*	neuter
พหูพจน์	*pl*	plural
กริยา	*v*	verb
อกรรมกริยา	*vi*	intransitive verb
สกรรมกริยา	*vt*	transitive verb

THAI PRONUNCIATION

Thai is a tonal language with 5 tonal sounds and 4 tonal marks. Intonation of a syllable is determined by a combination of the class of consonants, the type of syllables (open or closed), the tonal marks, and the length of the vowel. Instead of using characters from the International Phonetic Alphabet to illustrate how Thai words are pronounced, this dictionary provides romanized transcriptions for all Thai words, phrases and translations to show you exactly how to pronounce things correctly.

VOWELS

The Thai language has two different types of vowels: short and long. Short vowels are cut off at the end and long vowels are more drawn out. A short vowel sound is represented by a single letter or a single letter followed by a colon, while a long vowel sound is shown by a double letter or a combination of two letters.

Short and Long vowels

Vowel	Equivalent English Pronunciation
a	**a**way
aa	**fa**ther
i	t**i**p
ii	b**ee**
u	g**oo**d
uu	r**u**le
e	g**e**t
ee	p**a**le
o	b**oa**t
oo	g**o**
o	**aw**kward
o	f**o**r
a:	h**a**zard
ae	h**a**ng
u:	th**e**
ur	b**ur**n

CONSONANTS

There are 20 different consonant sounds in Thai. The following list shows those Thai consonants that are pronounced in the same way as in English:

Thai character	Explanation
ก	Pronounced as in 'golf'.
จ	Pronounced as in 'John'.
ซ	Pronounced as in 'song'.
ญ	Pronounced as in 'yummy'.
ฎ	Pronounced as in 'door'.
ฑ	Pronounced as in 'Tom'.
ณ	Pronounced as in 'Name'.
บ	Pronounced as in 'Born'.
ฝ	Pronounced as in 'Funny'.
ม	Pronounced as in 'Mother'.
ย	Pronounced as in 'Young'.
ร	Pronounced as in 'Run'.
ล ฬ	Pronounced as in 'Lean'.
ว	Pronounced as in 'Wing'.
ห	Pronounced as in 'Happy'.

There are a few Thai sounds which can be difficult to pronounce:

ฏ	A hard t/d sound. Pronounced as in 'style'.
ป	A hard p/b sound. Pronounced as in 'Nappy'.
ฉ	Pronounced as in 'chin'.
ง	Nasal sound. Pronounced as in 'singing'.

Thai people often do not differentiate between the sounds 'r' and 'l': they are pronounced in the same tone. Unlike in English, the 'ng' sound is often used at the beginning of Thai words, rather than at the end.

ENGLISH PRONUNCIATION

The International Phonetic Alphabet is used to show how English words are pronounced in this dictionary.

STRESS
การออกเสียงภาษาอังกฤษ

VOWELS

	ตัวอย่างภาษาอังกฤษ	คำอธิบาย
[ɑ:]	father	เสียงสระ "อา" ในภาษาไทย เช่น มา
[ʌ]	but, come	เสียงสระ "อะ, อ้-" ในภาษาไทย เช่น วัน
[æ]	man, cat	เสียงสระ "แอะ" และ "แอ" ในภาษาไทย เช่น แสง
[ə]	father, ago	เสียงสระ "เออะ" ในภาษาไทย เช่น เลอะ
[ɜ:]	bird, heard	เสียงสระ "เออ" ในภาษาไทย เช่น เธอ
[ɛ]	get, bed	เสียงสระ "เอะ" ลดรูป เช่น เล็ง
[ɪ]	it, big	เสียงสระ "อิ" ในภาษาไทย เช่น มิ
[i:]	tea, see	เสียงสระ "อี" ในภาษาไทย เช่น ตี
[ɒ]	hot, wash	เสียงสระ "เอาะ" ในภาษาไทย เช่น เลาะ
[ɔ:]	saw, all	เสียงสระ "ออ" ในภาษาไทย เช่น ลอม
[ʊ]	put, book	เสียงสระ "อุ" ในภาษาไทย เช่น ลุ
[u:]	too, you	เสียงสระ "อู" ในภาษาไทย เช่น หรู

DIPHTHONGS

	ตัวอย่างภาษาอังกฤษ	คำอธิบาย
[aɪ]	fly, high	เสียงสระ "อาย" ในภาษาไทย เช่น สาย
[aʊ]	how, house	เสียงสระ "อาว" ในภาษาไทย เช่น น้าว
[ɛə]	there, bear	เสียงสระ "แอ" ในภาษาไทย เช่น แล
[eɪ]	day, obey	เสียงสระ "เอ" ในภาษาไทย เช่น เลน
[ɪə]	here, hear	เสียงสระ "เอีย" ในภาษาไทย เช่น เลียน
[əʊ]	go, note	เสียงสระ "โอ" ในภาษาไทย เช่น โล้
[ɔɪ]	boy, oil	เสียงสระ "ออย" ในภาษาไทย เช่น ลอย
[ʊə]	poor, sure	เสียงสระ "อ้ว" ในภาษาไทย เช่น มัว

CONSONANTS

	ตัวอย่างภาษาอังกฤษ	คำอธิบาย
[b]	**b**ig, lo**bb**y	เสียง "บ" ในภาษาไทย เช่น บัว ดาบ
[d]	men**d**e**d**	เสียง "ด" ในภาษาไทย เช่น เด็ด
[g]	**g**o, **g**et, bi**g**	เสียง "ก" เป็นเสียงหยุดและก้อง
[dʒ]	**g**in, **j**u**dg**e	เสียง "จ" เป็นเสียงกักเสียดแทรกและก้อง
[ŋ]	si**ng**	เสียง "ง" ในภาษาไทย สงฆ์
[h]	**h**ouse, **h**e	เสียง "ฮ" ในภาษาไทย เช่น ฮา
[j]	**y**oung, **y**es	เสียง "ย" ในภาษาไทย เช่น ยาย
[k]	**c**ome, mo**ck**	เสียง "ค" เมื่อเป็นพยัญชนะต้น เช่น โค และ "ก" เมื่อเป็นพยัญชนะท้าย เช่น นก
[r]	**r**ed, t**r**ead	เสียง "ร" ในภาษาไทย เช่น ร้อน
[s]	**s**and, ye**s**	เสียง "ซ" เมื่อเป็นพยัญชนะต้น เช่น ซา และ "ส" เมื่อเป็นพยัญชนะท้าย เป็นเสียงเสียดแทรกและไม่ก้อง
[z]	ro**s**e, **z**ebra	เสียง "ซ" เมื่อเป็นพยัญชนะต้น เช่น ซา และ "ส" เมื่อเป็นพยัญชนะท้าย เป็นเสียงเสียดแทรกและก้อง
[ʃ]	**sh**e, ma**ch**ine	เสียง "ช" เป็นเสียงเสียดแทรกและไม่ก้อง
[tʃ]	**ch**in, ri**ch**	เสียง "ช" เป็นเสียงกักเสียดแทรกและไม่ก้อง
[v]	**v**alley	เสียง "ว" เป็นเสียงเสียดแทรกและก้อง
[w]	**w**ater, **wh**ich	เสียง "ว" เป็นเสียงเปิด
[ʒ]	vi**s**ion	เสียง "ช" เป็นเสียงเสียดแทรกและก้อง
[θ]	**th**ink, my**th**	เสียง "ธ" เป็นเสียงเสียดแทรกและไม่ก้อง
[ð]	**th**is, **th**e	เสียง "ธ" เป็นเสียงเสียดแทรกและก้อง

NUMBERS		ตัวเลข
zero	0	ศูนย์ [sun]
uno	1	หนึ่ง [nueng]
two	2	สอง [song]
three	3	สาม [sam]
four	4	สี่ [si]
five	5	ห้า [ha]
six	6	หก [hok]
seven	7	เจ็ด [chet]
eight	8	แปด [paet]
nine	9	เก้า [kao]
ten	10	สิบ [sip]
eleven	11	สิบเอ็ด [sip et]
twelve	12	สิบสอง [sip song]
thirteen	13	สิบสาม [sip sam]
fourteen	14	สิบสี่ [sip si]
fifteen	15	สิบห้า [sip ha]
sixteen	16	สิบหก [sip hok]
seventeen	17	สิบเจ็ด [sip chet]
eighteen	18	สิบแปด [sip paet]
nineteen	19	สิบเก้า [sip kao]
twenty	20	ยี่สิบ [yi sip]
twenty-one	21	ยี่สิบเอ็ด [yi sip et]
twenty-two	22	ยี่สิบสอง [yi sip song]
twenty-three	23	ยี่สิบสาม [yi sip sam]
thirty	30	สามสิบ [sam sip]
thirty-one	31	สามสิบเอ็ด [sam sip et]
forty	40	สี่สิบ [si sip]
fifty	50	ห้าสิบ [ha sip]
sixty	60	หกสิบ [hok sip]
seventy	70	เจ็ดสิบ [chet sip]
eighty	80	แปดสิบ [paet sip]
ninety	90	เก้าสิบ [kao sip]
one hundred	100	หนึ่งร้อย [nueng roi]

one hundred and ten	110	หนึ่งร้อยสิบ [nueng roi sip]
two hundred	200	สองร้อย [song roi]
two hundred and fifty	250	สองร้อยห้าสิบ [song roi ha sip]
one thousand	1,000	หนึ่งพัน [nueng pan]
one million	1,000,000	หนึ่งล้าน [nueng lan]

DAYS OF THE WEEK วันในสัปดาห์

Monday	วันจันทร์ [wan chan]
Tuesday	วันอังคาร [wan ang khan]
Wednesday	วันพุธ [wan phut]
Thursday	วันพฤหัสบดี [wan pha rue hat sa bo di]
Friday	วันศุกร์ [wan suk]
Saturday	วันเสาร์ [wan sao]
Sunday	วันอาทิตย์ [wan a thit]

MONTHS เดือน

January	มกราคม [mok ka ra khom]
February	กุมภาพันธ์ [kum pha phan]
March	มีนาคม [mi na khom]
April	เมษายน [me sa yon]
May	พฤษภาคม [phrue sa pa khom]
June	มิถุนายน [mi thu na yon]
July	กรกฎาคม [ka ra ka da khom]
August	สิงหาคม [sing ha khom]
September	กันยายน [kan ya yon]
October	ตุลาคม [tu la khom]
November	พฤศจิกายน [phrue sa chi ka yon]
December	ธันวาคม [than wa khom]

THAI–ENGLISH
ไทย–อังกฤษ

ก

ก็ [ko] ถ้าไม่...ก็... [tha mai...ko...] *pron*
either (.. or)

กก [kok] *n* ต้นไม้จำพวกอ้อหรือกก [ton mai
cham phuak o rue kok] *n* reed

กงสุล [kong sun] *n* consul; สถานกงสุล [sa
than kong sun] *n* consulate

กฎ [kot] *n* กฎจราจรว่าด้วยการใช้ทางหลวง
[kod ja ra jon wa duai kan chai thang
luang] *n* Highway Code; ฉันเสียใจมาก
ฉันไม่รู้กฎข้อบังคับ [chan sia jai mak
chan mai ru kot kho bang khap] I'm
very sorry, I didn't know the
regulations

กฎระเบียบ [kot ra biap] *n* regulation

กฎหมาย [kot mai] *n* law; ร่างกฎหมาย
[rang kot mai] *n* bill (legislation); การออก
กฎหมาย [kan ok kot mai] *n*
legislation; ที่ถูกกฎหมาย [thii thuk kot
mai] *adj* legal

กด [kot] *v* press

กดขี่ [kot khi] กดขี่รังแก [kot khii rang
kae] *v* bully

กดดัน [kot dan] *n* กดดันให้ทำ [kot dan
hai tham] *v* pressure; ภาวะถูกกดดัน
[pha wa thuk kot dan] *adj* stressed

กติกา [ka ti ka] การทำผิดกติกา [kan

tham phit ka ti ka] *n* foul

ก้น [kan] *n* bottom, bum

กบ [kop] *n* frog; ลูกกบ [luk kop] *n*
tadpole; กบไสไม้ [kop sai mai] *n* plane
(tool)

กรกฎ [ko ra kot] *n* ราศีกรกฎ [ra si ko ra
kot] *n* Cancer (star sign)

กรกฎาคม [ka ra ka da khom] เดือน
กรกฎาคม [duean ka ra ka da khom] *n*
July

กรง [krong] *n* cage

กรงเล็บ [krong lep] *n* claw

กรณี [ko ra ni] กรณีใด ๆ [ko ra nii dai
dai] *adv* anyhow; คดี กรณี [kha di, ko
ra nii] *n* case

กรด [krot] *n* acid

กรน [kron] *v* snore

กรมธรรม์ [krom ma than] กรมธรรม์
ประกัน [krom ma than pra kan] *n*
insurance policy

กรรไกร [kan krai] *npl* clippers, scissors;
กรรไกรตัดเล็บ [kan krai tat lep] *npl* nail
scissors

กรรเชียง [kan chiang] ท่าว่ายน้ำแบบตี
กรรเชียง [tha wai nam baep ti kan
chiang] *n* backstroke

กรรมกร [kam ma kan] *n* labourer

กรรมการ [kam ma kan] *n* referee;
กรรมการตัดสิน [kam ma kan tat sin] *n*
umpire; กรรมการผู้จัดการ [kam ma kan
phu chat kan] *n* managing director

กรรมการผู้จัดการ [kam ma kan phu
chat kan] กรรมการผู้จัดการที่นี่ชื่ออะไร?
[kam ma kan phu jat kan thii nii chue
a rai] What is the name of the
managing director?

กรรมพันธุ์ [kam ma phan] เป็นกรรมพันธุ์
[pen kam ma phan] *adj* hereditary

กรวด [kruat] *n* pebble; ก้อนกรวด [kon
kraut] *n* gravel; กรวดทราย [kraut sai] *n*
grit

กรวย [kruai] *n* cone, funnel

กรอ [kro] กรอเทปกลับ [kro thep klap] *v*
rewind

กรอก [krok] v fill in

กรอง [krong] v filter; เครื่องกรอง [khrueang krong] n filter; ที่กรอง [thii krong] n sieve

กรอบ [krop] adj crisp; กรอบรูป [krop rup] n frame; อย่างกรอบ [yang krop] adj crispy

กรอบรูป [krop rup] n picture frame

กระจก [kra chok] n mirror; กระจกสี [kra jok sii] n stained glass; กระจกหน้ารถ [kra jok na rot] n windscreen

กระจาย [kra chai] vt spread ▷ n การกระ จาย [kan kra chai] n spread ▷ adj ซึ่ง แพร่กระจายได้ [sueng phrae kra jai dai] adj contagious

กระจายเสียง [kra chai siang] เครื่อง กระจายเสียง [khrueang kra jai siang] n loudspeaker; กระจายเสียง เผยแพร่ [kra jai siang phoei prae] v broadcast

กระชอน [kra chon] n colander

กระชับ [kra chap] adj compact; สั้น กระชับ [san kra chap] adj concise

กระเช้า [kra chao] กระเช้าไฟฟ้า [kra chao fai fa] n ski lift

กระซิบ [kra sip] v whisper

กระดาน [kra dan] n board (wood); แผ่น กระดานหก [phaen kra dan hok] n seesaw; กระดานสีขาว [kra dan sii kao] n whiteboard

กระดานโต้คลื่น [kra dan to khluen] n surfboard; เล่นกระดานโต้คลื่น [len kra dan to khuen] v surf; การเล่น กระดานโต้คลื่น [kan len kra dan to khuen] n surfing; ผู้เล่นกระดานโต้คลื่น [phu len kra dan to khluen] n surfer

กระดาษ [kra dat] n paper; กระดาษเขียน [kra dat khian] n writing paper; กระดาษแข็ง [kra dat khaeng] n cardboard

กระดาษชำระ [kra dat cham ra] n toilet paper; ไม่มีกระดาษชำระ [mai mii kra dat cham ra] There is no toilet paper

กระดาษทิชชู [kra dat thit chu] n tissue (paper)

กระดุม [kra dum] n button; กระดุมข้อมือ เสื้อเชิร์ต [kra dum kho mue suea shoet] npl cufflinks

กระดูก [kra duk] n bone; กระดูกเชิงกราน [kra duk choeng kran] n pelvis; กระดูก ไหปลาร้า [kra duk hai pla ra] n collarbone; กระดูกสันหลัง [kra duk san lang] n backbone

กระดูกสันหลัง [kra duk san lang] n spine

กระเด็น [kra den] สาดกระเด็น [sat kra den] v splash

กระโดด [kra dot] v leap, jump; กีฬา กระโดดค้ำถ่อ [ki la kra dot kham tho] n pole vault; กระโดดโลดเต้น [kra dot lot ten] vt skip; กระโดดสูง [kra dot sung] n high jump; ฉันจะไปกระโดดหน้าผาสูงได้ที่ ไหน? [chan ja pai kra dot na pha sung dai thii nai] Where can I go bungee jumping?

กระต่าย [kra tai] n rabbit; กระต่ายป่า [kra tai pa] n hare

กระติก [kra tik] กระติกน้ำร้อนหรือน้ำเย็น [kra tik nam ron rue nam yen] n flask, Thermos®

กระตือรือร้น [kra tue rue ron] adj energetic, enthusiastic, keen ▷ n activity; ความกระตือรือร้น [khwam kra tue rue ron] n enthusiasm

กระตุ้น [tra tun] สิ่งกระตุ้น [sing kra tun] n incentive; กระตุ้นให้เกิดความรู้สึกในทาง สวยงาม [kra tun hai koed khwam ru suk nai thang suai ngam] adj sensuous; ซึ่งกระตุ้นความรู้สึกทางเพศ [sueng kra tun khwam ru suk thang phed] adj erotic

กระถาง [kra thang] กระถางต้นไม้ [kra thang ton mai] n plant pot

กระโถน [kra thon] กระโถนสำหรับเด็กเล็ก [kra thon sam rap dek lek] n potty; คุณ มีกระโถนเด็กไหม? [khun mii kra thon dek mai] Do you have a potty?

กระทบ [kra thop] v affect; ผลกระทบ [phon kra thop] n effect, impact

กระทรวง [kra suang] n ministry

(government)

กระท่อม [kra thom] n cottage, hut; กระท่อมที่ใกล้ที่สุดบนเขาอยู่ที่ไหน? [kra thom thii klai thii sud bon khao yu thii nai] Where is the nearest mountain hut?

กระทะ [kra tha] n pan; กระทะทอด [kra tha thot] n frying pan

กระทา [kra tha] n นกกระทา [nok kra tha] n partridge

กระทำ [kra tham] v act; การกระทำ [kan kra tham] n act, action; การกระทำผิดกฎหมาย [kan kra tham pit kot mai] n offence

กระทืบ [kra thuep] กระทืบ เหยียบ [kra thuep, yiab] vt stamp

กระทุง [kra thung] นกกระทุง [nok kra thung] n pelican

กระเทียม [kra thiam] n garlic; มีกระเทียมอยู่ในนี้บ้างไหม? [mii kra thiam yu nai nii bang mai] Is there any garlic in it?

กระบวนการ [kra buan kan] กระบวนการเผาผลาญอาหาร [kra buan kan phao phlan a han] n metabolism

กระบอก [kra bok] กระบอกสูบ [kra bok sub] n cylinder

กระบอกฉีด [kra bok chit] n syringe

กระบองเพชร [kra bong phet] n cactus

กระบือ [kra bue] n buffalo

กระเบื้อง [kra bueang] n tile; กระเบื้องหินชนวน [kra bueang hin cha nuan] n slate; ที่ปูด้วยกระเบื้อง [thii pu duai kra bueang] adj tiled

กระป๋อง [kra pong] กระป๋องสเปรย์ [kra pong sa pre] n canister; ที่เปิดกระป๋อง [thii poet kra pong] n can-opener, tin-opener; ที่บรรจุในกระป๋อง [thii ban chu nai kra pong] adj canned

กระปุก [kra puk] กระปุกใส่สตางค์ที่เป็นรูปหมู [kra puk sai sa tang thii pen rup mu] n piggybank

กระเป๋า [kra pao] n pocket; เงินติดกระเป๋า [ngoen tit kra pao] n pocket money; สำนักงานที่เก็บกระเป๋าที่ถูกทิ้งไว้ [sam nak ngan thii kep kra pao thii thuk thing wai] n left-luggage office; กระเป๋า ถุง [kra pao, thung] n bag; กระเป๋าน้ำร้อน [kra pao nam ron] n hot-water bottle; ที่เรียกเก็บกระเป๋าเดินทาง [thii riak kep kra pao doen thang] n baggage reclaim

กระเป๋าสตางค์ [kra pao sa tang] ฉันทำกระเป๋าสตางค์หาย [chan tham kra pao sa tang hai] I've lost my wallet

กระโปรง [kra prong] n skirt; กระโปรงสั้น [kra prong san] n miniskirt; กระโปรงสั้นแค่เข่าจับจีบลายตาใส่ทั้งชายและหญิงในสก็อตแลนด์ [kra prong san khae khao chap chip lai ta sai thang chai lae ying nai sa kot land] n kilt; กระโปรงชั้นในผู้หญิง [kra prong chan nai phu ying] n underskirt

กระพริบ [kra prip] กระพริบตา [kra phrip ta] vi blink

กระพือ [kra phue] กระพือปีก [kra phue piik] v flap

กระเพาะปัสสาวะ [kra pho pat sa wa] n bladder; โรคกระเพาะปัสสาวะ [rok kra phao pat sa wa] n cystitis

กระรอก [kra rok] n squirrel

กระวนกระวาย [kra won kra wai] adj nervous

กระสอบ [kra sop] n sack (container)

กระสับกระส่าย [kra sap kra sai] adj edgy

กระสา [kra sa] นกกระสา [nok kra sa] n heron; นกกระสา [nok kra sa] n crane (bird)

กระสุน [kra sun] n bullet; ที่ใส่กระสุน [thii sai kra sun] n magazine (ammunition); ปลอกกระสุนปืน [plok kra sun puen] n cartridge

กระแส [kra sae] กระแสไฟ [kra sae fai] n current (electricity); กระแสไฟดูด [kra sae fai dut] n electric shock; กระแสลม [kra sae lom] n draught

กระแสน้ำ [kra sae nam] มีกระแสน้ำไหม? [mii kra sae nam mai] Are there currents?

กระแสรายวัน [kra sae rai wan] บัญชี

กระแสรายวัน [ban chi kra sae rai wan] n current account

กระหายน้ำ [kra hai nam] ความกระหายน้ำ [khwam kra hai nam] n thirst; ที่กระหายน้ำ [thii kra hai nam] adj thirsty

กระโหลก [kra lok] กะโหลกศีรษะ [ka lok sii sa] n skull

กรัม [kram] น้ำหนักเป็นกรัม [nam nak pen kram] n gramme

กราฟ [krap] n graph

กราฟฟิก [krap fik] ภาพกราฟฟิก [phap kraf fik] npl graphics

กริ๊ก [krik] เสียงดังกริ๊ก [siang dang krik] n click; เกิดเสียงดังกริ๊ก [koet siang dang krik] v click

กริ่ง [kring] กริ่งประตู [kring pra tu] n doorbell

กริยา [ka ri ya] รูปกริยาที่ตั้งต้นด้วย [rup ka ri ya thii tang ton duai to] n infinitive

กรีก [krik] เกี่ยวกับแบบกรีกและโรมัน [kiao kap baep krik lae ro man] adj classical; แห่งประเทศกรีก [haeng pra tet krik] adj Greek; ชาวกรีก [chao kriik] n Greek (person)

กรีฑา [kri tha] การแข่งขันกรีฑาห้าประเภท [kan khaeng khan krii tha ha pra phet] n pentathlon

กรีด [krit] เขากรีดตัวเอง [khao krit tua eng] He has cut himself

กรีดร้อง [krit rong] v scream; การกรีดร้อง [kan krit rong] n scream

กรีนแลนด์ [krin laen] ประเทศกรีนแลนด์ [pra tet krin laen] n Greenland

กรุณา [ka ru na] excl please; คุณกรุณาพูดช้ากว่านี้ได้ไหม? [khun ka ru na phut cha kwa nii dai mai] Could you speak more slowly, please?; คุณกรุณาพูดดังกว่านี้ได้ไหม? [khun ka ru na phut dang kwa nii dai mai] Could you speak louder, please?; คุณกรุณาพูดย้ำอีกทีได้ไหม? [khun ka ru na phut yam ik thii dai mai] Could you repeat that, please?

กรุ๊ป [krup] กรุ๊ปทัวร์ [krup thua] n guided tour

กลไก [kon kai] กลไกการทำงานของเครื่องจักร [kon kai kan tham ngan khong khrueang chak] n mechanism

กลม [klom] adj round; รูปทรงกลม [rup song klom] n round (series); ก้อนกลมเล็ก ๆ [kon klom lek lek] n pellet; อ้วนกลม [uan klom] adj chubby

กลยุทธ์ [kon la yut] เกี่ยวกับยุทธวิธีหรือกลยุทธ์ [kiao kap yut tha wi thi rue kon la yut] adj strategic

กล้วย [kluai] n banana

กล้วยไม้ [kluai mai] ต้นกล้วยไม้ [ton kluai mai] n orchid

กลวิธี [kon wi thi] n technique

กลอง [klong] n drum; กลองที่มีเสียงต่ำ [klong thii mii siang tam] n bass drum; คนตีกลอง [khon ti klong] n drummer

กล่อง [klong] n box; หีบ ลัง กล่อง [hip, lang, klong] n chest (storage); กล่องใส่สายชนวน [klong sai sai cha nuan] n fuse box; กล่องใส่ดินสอ [klong sai din so] n pencil case

กล้อง [klong] เลนส์ของกล้องที่ขยายปรับภาพโดยรักษาโฟกัสเดิมไว้ [len khong klong thii kha yai prab phap doi rak sa fo kas doem wai] n zoom lens; โทรศัพท์ที่มีกล้องถ่ายรูปในตัว [tho ra sap thii mii klong thai rup nai tua] n camera phone; กล้องส่องทางไกล [klong song thang klai] n binoculars; กล้องฉันติดขัด [klong chan tit khat] My camera is sticking

กล้องจุลทรรศน์ [klong chun la that] n microscope

กล้องดิจิตัล [klong di chi tan] มีเม็มเมอร์รี่การ์ดสำหรับกล้องดิจิตัลไหม? [mii mem moe ri kaat sam rap klong di gi tal mai] A memory card for this digital camera, please

กล้องวีดีโอ [klong wi di o] ขอเทปสำหรับกล้องวีดีโอได้ไหม? [kho thep sam rap klong wi di o dai mai] Can I have a tape for this video camera, please?

กล้องส่องทางไกล [klong song thang klai] n telescope

กล่องเสียง [klong siang] โรคกล่องเสียงอักเสบ [rok klong siang ak sep] n laryngitis

กลอน [klon] กลอนหรือเพลงง่าย ๆ สำหรับเด็ก [klon rue pleng ngai ngai sam rup dek] n nursery rhyme; กลอนประตู [klon pra tu] n bolt

กล่อม [klom] เพลงร้องกล่อมเด็ก [phleng rong klom dek] n lullaby

กลอุบาย [kon u bai] ซึ่งมีกลอุบาย [sueng mii kon u bai] adj shifty

กลัดกลุ้ม [klat klum] v fret

กลั่น [klan] โรงกลั่น [rong klan] n refinery; โรงกลั่นน้ำมัน [rong klan nam man] n oil refinery; โรงงานต้มและกลั่นเหล้า [rong ngan tom lae klan lao] n brewery

กลั่นแกล้ง [klan klaeng] v pick on

กลับ [klap] กลับไป [klap pai] v go back; กลับไปสภาพเดิม [klap pai sa phap doem] adv back; กลับมา [klap ma] v come back, get back; เราควรกลับมาที่รถเมื่อไร? [rao khua klap ma thii rot muea rai] When should we be back on board?

กลัว [klua] adj afraid ▷ v fear; การกลัวที่อยู่ในที่แคบ [kan klua thii yu nai thii khaep] adj claustrophobic; ความกลัว [khwam klua] n fear; น่าสะพึงกลัว [na sa phueng klua] adj dreadful

กล้า [kla] v dare

กลาง [klang] ระหว่างกลาง [ra wang klang] adj intermediate; ขนาดกลาง [kha nat klang] adj medium-sized; ความเป็นกลาง [khwam pen klang] n neutral; คุณมีขนาดกลางไหม? [khun mii kha nat klang mai] Do you have a medium?

กลางคืน [klang khuen] n night; โรงเรียนในตอนเย็นหรือกลางคืน [rong rian nai ton yen rue klang khuen] n night

school; กะกลางคืน [ka klang khuen] n nightshift; ชุดกลางคืน [chut klang khuen] n evening dress; ตอนกลางคืน [ton klang khuen] at night

กลางแจ้ง [klang chaeng] adv out-of-doors; ที่อยู่กลางแจ้ง [thii yu klang chaeng] adj outdoor

กลางวัน [klang wan] เวลากลางวัน [we la klang wan] n daytime; ฉันว่างตอนอาหารกลางวัน [chan wang ton a han klang wan] I'm free for lunch

กล้ามเนื้อ [klam nuea] n muscle; เกี่ยวกับกล้ามเนื้อ [kiao kap klam nuea] adj muscular; การชักกระตุกของกล้ามเนื้อ [kan chak kra tuk khong klam nuea] n spasm

กลายเป็น [klai pen] v become

กล่าว [klao] กล่าวถึง [klao thueng] v mention; บอกกล่าว [bok klao] v notify, state

กล่าวหา [klao ha] v accuse; การกล่าวหา [kan klao ha] n accusation; ข้อกล่าวหา [kho klao ha] n allegation, charge (accusation); ซึ่งถูกกล่าวหา [sueng thuk klao ha] adj alleged

กล้าหาญ [kla han] adj brave, courageous, daring; ความกล้าหาญ [khwam kla han] n bravery, courage, nerve (boldness)

กลืนกลืน [klam kluen] vi swallow

กลิ้ง [kling] vi roll

กลิ่น [klin] n odour, scent, smell; ได้กลิ่น [dai klin] vt smell; มีกลิ่น [mii klin] adj smelly; กลิ่นหอม [klin hom] n aroma; มีกลิ่นแปลก ๆ [mii klin plaek plaek] There's a funny smell

กลีบ [klip] กลีบดอกไม้ [klip dok mai] n pedal

กลืน [kluen] กลืน, ดูดกลืน, ฝืนทน [kluen, dut kluen, fuen thon] vt swallow; การกลืนน้ำลาย [kan kluen nam lai] n swallow

กลุ่ม [klum] n group; กลุ่ม สมาคม [klum, sa ma khom] n association; กลุ่ม หมู่

คณะ [klum, moo ka na] *n* collective; กลุ่ม พวง รวง เครือ [klum, phuang, ruang, khruea] *n* bunch; มีส่วนลดสำหรับ กลุ่มต่าง ๆ หรือไม่? [mii suan lot sam rap klum tang tang rue mai] Are there any reductions for groups?

กลุ่มน้อย [klum noi] คนกลุ่มน้อย [khon klum noi] *n* minority

กลูโคส [klu khos] *n* glucose

ก๋วยเตี๋ยว [kuai tiao] เส้นก๋วยเตี๋ยว [sen kuai tiao] *npl* noodles

กว่า [kwa] เกินกว่า [koen kwa] *conj* than

กวาง [kwang] *n* deer; เนื้อกวาง [nuea kwang] *n* venison; กวางขนาดใหญ่แถบ ขั้วโลกเหนือ [kwang kha nat yai thaep khua lok nuea] *n* reindeer

กว้าง [kwang] *adj* broad, wide; ความกว้าง [khwam kwang] *n* width

กว้างขวาง [kwang khwang] *adj* extensive ▷ *adv* wide; อย่างกว้างขวาง [yang kwang khwang] *adv* extensively

กวาด [kwat] *v* sweep

กวี [ka wi] *n* poet

กษาปณ์ [ka sap] โรงกษาปณ์ [rong ka sap] *n* mint (coins)

ก่อกวน [ko kuan] การก่อกวน [kan ko kuan] *n* mischief

ก่อการจลาจล [ko kan cha la chon] *v* riot

ก่อการร้าย [ko kan rai] ลัทธิก่อการร้าย [lat thi ko kan rai] *n* terrorism; การถูก โจมตีจากผู้ก่อการร้าย [kan thuk chom ti chak phu ko kan rai] *n* terrorist attack; ผู้ก่อการร้าย [phu ko kan rai] *n* terrorist

กอง [kong] *n* heap, pile; กองระเกะระกะ [kong ra ke ra ka] *n* clutter; กองขึ้นมา [kong khuen ma] *n* pile-up; กองดิน [kong din] *n* drift

กองทัพ [kang thap] *n* army; กองทัพเรือ [kong thap ruea] *n* navy; กองทัพอากาศ [kong thap a kat] *n* Air Force

กองทุน [kong thun] *npl* funds

กอด [kot] *vt* hug; กอดด้วยความรักใคร่ [kot duai khwam ruk khrai] *v* cuddle ▷ *n* การกอด [kan kot] *n* hug; การกอดด้วย

ความรักใคร่ [kan kot duai khwam ruk kai] *n* cuddle

ก่อน [kon] *adv* before; เมื่อก่อนนี้ [muea kon nii] *adv* formerly; ก่อนเวลาที่กำหนด ไว้ [kon we la thii kam not wai] *adj* early; ก่อนหน้านั้น [kon na nan] *adv* earlier; ก่อนห้าโมง [kon ha mong] before five o'clock

ก้อน [kon] *n* lump; ก้อนสต๊อค [kon sa tok] *n* stock cube; ก้อนกลมเล็ก ๆ [kon klom lek lek] *n* pellet

กอล์ฟ [kop] เป้ารองรับลูกกอล์ฟในการตี [pao rong rap luk kolf nai kan ti] *n* tee; ไม้ตีกอล์ฟ [mai ti kolf] *n* golf club (game); สโมสรกอล์ฟ [sa mo son kolf] *n* golf club (society); ฉันจะเล่นกอล์ฟได้ที่ ไหน? [chan ja len kof dai thii nai] Where can I play golf?

กอริลล่า [ko lil la] ลิงกอริลล่า [ling ko ril la] *n* gorilla

ก่อวินาศกรรม [ko wi nat sa kam] *v* sabotage; การก่อวินาศกรรม [kan ko wi nat sa kam] *n* sabotage

ก่อสร้าง [ko sang] การก่อสร้าง [kan ko sang] *n* construction; ช่างก่อสร้าง [chang ko sang] *n* builder; บริเวณที่ ก่อสร้าง [bo ri wen thii ko sang] *n* building site

กะ [ka] กะกลางคืน [ka klang khuen] *n* nightshift

กะทันหัน [ka than han] อย่างกะทันหัน [yang ka than han] *adv* suddenly

กะรัต [ka rat] *n* carat

กะหล่ำ [ka lam] *n* cabbage; ลูกกะหล่ำเล็ก [luk ka lam lek] *npl* Brussels sprouts

กะหล่ำปลี [ka hlam pli] สลัดกะหล่ำปลีใส่ มายองเนส [sa lat ka lam plii sai ma yong nes] *n* coleslaw

กักกัน [kak kan] สถานกักกันเพื่อป้องกันการ แพร่ของเชื้อโรค [sa than kak kan phuea pong kan kan prae khong chuea rok] *n* quarantine

กักขัง [kak khang] ผู้ถูกกักขังในคุก [phu thuk kak khang nai khuk] *n* inmate

กังวล [kang won] *adj* concerned; เป็นห่วง
กังวล [pen huang kang won] *adj*
worried; ความกังวล [khwam kang won]
n concern; ความวิตกกังวล [khwam wi
tok kang won] *n* anxiety

กังหันลม [kang han lom] *n* windmill

กัญชา [kan cha] *n* cannabis, grass
(*marijuana*), marijuana

กัด [kat] *v* bite, sting; รอยกัด [roi kat] *n*
bite; ฉันถูกกัด [chan thuk kat] I have
been bitten

กันชน [kan chon] *n* bumper

กันน้ำ [kan nam] ที่กันน้ำได้ [thii kan
nam dai] *adj* waterproof

กันเปื้อน [kan puean] ผ้ากันเปื้อนเด็ก [pha
kan puean dek] *n* bib

กันย์ [kan] ราศีกันย์ [ra si kan] *n* Virgo;
ราศีกันย์ [ra si kan] *n* Pisces

กันยายน [kan ya yon] เดือนกันยายน
[duean kan ya yon] *n* September

กับ [kap] ร่วมกับ [ruam kap] *prep* with

กับข้าว [kap khao] *n* dish (*food*); ตำรา
กับข้าว [tam ra kap khao] *n* recipe

กับดัก [kap dak] *n* trap

กัปตัน [kap tan] *n* captain

กัมพูชา [kam phu cha] เกี่ยวกับประเทศ
กัมพูชา [kiao kap pra thet kam phu
cha] *adj* Cambodian; ชาวกัมพูชา [chao
kam phu cha] *n* Cambodian (*person*);
ประเทศกัมพูชา [pra tet kam phu cha] *n*
Cambodia

กัมมันตภาพรังสี [kam man ta phap
rang si] เกี่ยวกับกัมมันตภาพรังสี [kiao
kap kam man ta phap rang sii] *adj*
radioactive

กัวเตมาลา [kua te ma la] ประเทศ
กัวเตมาลา [pra tet kua te ma la] *n*
Guatemala

กา [ka (kaa)] กาต้มน้ำ [ka tom nam] *n*
kettle; กาน้ำชา [ka nam cha] *n* teapot;
นกกา [nok ka] *n* crow

กางเกง [kang keng] *npl* trousers; สายโยง
กางเกง [sai yong kang keng] *npl* braces;
สายที่แขวนกางเกง [sai thii khwaen

kang keng] *npl* suspenders; กางเกงใน
สตรี [kang keng nai sa tree] *npl*
knickers

ก๊าซ [kas] *n* gas; ก๊าซที่บรรจุในภาชนะเล็ก ๆ
ใช้เมื่อไปตั้งแคมป์ [kas thii ban chu nai
pha cha na lek lek chai muea pai tang
khaem] *n* camping gas; ก๊าซธรรมชาติ
[kas tham ma chat] *n* natural gas

กาตาร์ [ka ta] ประเทศกาตาร์ [pra tet ka
ta] *n* Qatar

ก้าน [kan] ก้านโลหะที่ใช้ตรวจว่าน้ำมันอยู่
ในแท็งค์เท่าไหร่ [kan lo ha thii chai
truat wa mii nam man yu nai thaeng
thao rai] *n* dipstick

กานพลู [kan phlu] *n* clove

กานา [ka na] เกี่ยวกับชาวกานา [kiao kap
chao ka na] *adj* Ghanaian; ชาวกานา
[chao ka na] *n* Ghanaian; ประเทศกานา
[pra tet ka na] *n* Ghana

กาบอน [ka bon] ประเทศกาบอน [pra tet
ka bon] *n* Gabon

กาฝาก [ka fak] ไม้จำพวกกาฝากขึ้นตาม
ต้นไม้ [mai cham phuak ka fak khuen
tam ton mai] *n* mistletoe

กาแฟ [ka fae] *n* coffee; เมล็ดกาแฟ [ma
let ka fae] *n* coffee bean; โต๊ะกาแฟ [to
ka fae] *n* coffee table; ร้านกาแฟ [ran ka
fae] *n* café; ขอกาแฟหนึ่งที่ [kho ka fae
nueng thii] A coffee, please

กายกรรม [kai ya kam] นักกายกรรม [nak
kai ya kam] *n* acrobat

กายบริหาร [kai bo ri han] *npl*
gymnastics; นักกายบริหาร [nak kai bo
ri han] *n* gymnast

กายภาพบำบัด [kai ya phap bam bat]
การทำกายภาพบำบัด [kan tham kai ya
phap bam bat] *n* physiotherapy; นัก
กายภาพบำบัด [nak kai ya phap bam
bat] *n* physiotherapist

การ [kan] การเลือกตั้ง [kan lueak tang] *n*
election; การศึกษา [kan suek sa] *n*
education

การกระทำ [kan kra tham] ผลของการ
ระทำ [phon khong kan kra tham] *npl*

repercussions

การแข่งขัน [kan khaeng khan] การแข่งขันกีฬารอบรองชนะเลิศ [kan khaeng khan ki la rop rong cha na loet] *n* semifinal

การโฆษณาชวนเชื่อ [kan kho sa na chuan chuea] *n* propaganda

การเงิน [kan ngoen] *n* finance; เกี่ยวกับการเงิน [kiao kap kan ngoen] *adj* fiscal; ทางการเงิน [thang kan ngoen] *adj* financial

การ์ด [kat] การ์ดบันทึกความจำของคอมพิวเตอร์ [kat ban thuek khwam cham khong khom pio toe] *n* memory card; ขอการ์ดโทรศัพท์หนึ่งใบ [kho kat tho ra sap nueng bai] A phonecard, please!; ฉันใช้การ์ดเบิกเงินสดที่เครื่องเบิกเงินได้ไหม? [chan chai kaat boek ngoen sot thii khrueang boek ngoen dai mai] Can I use my card with this cash machine?

การเดินทาง [kan doen thang] ฉันไม่มีประกันการเดินทาง [chan mai mii pra kan kaan doen thang] I don't have travel insurance

การ์ตูน [ka tun] *n* cartoon; หนังสือการ์ตูน [nang sue ka tun] *n* comic strip

การแต่งกาย [kan taeng kai] มีแบบอย่างการแต่งกายหรือไม่? [mii baep yang kan taeng kai rue mai] Is there a dress code?

การนำกลับมาใช้อีก [kan nam klap ma chai ik] *n* recycling

การบ้าน [kan ban] *n* homework

การประท้วง [kan pra thuang] เพราะมีการประท้วง [khro mii kan pra thuang] because of a strike

การเมือง [kan mueang] หลักการและข้อคิดเห็นทางการเมือง [lak kan lae kho kit hen thang kan mueang] *npl* politics; ที่เกี่ยวกับพรรคการเมืองหรือรัฐบาล [thii kiao kap phak kan mueang rue rat tha ban] *adj* political; นักการเมือง [nak kan mueang] *n* politician

การศึกษา [kan suek sa] ใบรับรองผลการศึกษา [bai rap rong phon kan suek sa] *n* transcript; การศึกษาผู้ใหญ่ [kan suek sa phu yai] *n* adult education; ปีการศึกษา [pi kan suek sa] *n* academic year

การแสดง [kan sa daeng] *n* showing; การแสดงการขี่ม้าวิ่งข้ามสิ่งกีดขวาง [kan sa daeng kan khi ma wing kham sing kit khwang] *n* show-jumping

การหยุดชะงัก [kan yut cha ngak] *n* hold-up

กรุณา [ka ru na] ความเมตตากรุณา [khwam met ta ka ru na] *n* kindness

กาว [kao] *n* glue

ก้าว [kao] *n* step; ก้าวเดิน [kao doen] *n* footstep, pace

ก้าวร้าว [kao rao] *adj* aggressive

ก้าวหน้า [kao na] *v* advance; ความก้าวหน้า [khwam kao na] *n* advance, progress; ทำให้เจริญก้าวหน้า [tham hai cha roen kao na] *v* bring forward

กำกับ [kam kap] กำกับดูแลโดยรัฐ [kam kap du lae doi rat] *v* nationalize

กำจัด [kam chat] คุณกำจัดคราบนี้ได้ไหม? [khun kam chat khrap nii dai mai] Can you remove this stain?

กำเนิด [kam noet] จุดกำเนิด [chut kam noet] *n* origin; ที่เป็นมาโดยกำเนิด [thii pen ma doi kam noet] *adj* born; ทำให้กำเนิดมาจากเซลล์เดียวกัน [tham hai kam noet ma chak sel diao kan] *v* clone

กำบัง [kam bang] หลบ กำบัง ป้องกัน ปกปิด เหมือนกับมีฉากกั้น [lop, kam bang, pong kan, pok pit muean kap mii chak kan] *v* screen (off); ที่กำบัง [thii kam bang] *n* shelter

กำปั้น [kam pan] *n* fist

กำพร้า [kam phra] ลูกกำพร้า [luk kam phra] *n* orphan

กำแพง [kam phaeng] *n* wall

กำมะหยี่ [kam ma yi] ผ้ากำมะหยี่ [pha kam ma yi] *n* velvet

กำเริบ [kam roep] อาการที่โรคกำเริบอีก [a kan thii rok kam roep ik] *n* relapse

กำไร [kam rai] ได้กำไร [dai kam rai] *vt*

gain; มีกำไรงาม [mii kam rai ngam] *adj* lucrative; ที่ได้ผลกำไร [thii dai phon kam rai] *adj* profitable

กำลัง [kam lang] *n* force; กำลังคน [kam lang kon] *n* manpower; กำลังดำเนินอยู่ [kam lang dam noen yu] *dv* on; อย่างมีกำลัง [yang mii kam lang] *adv* strongly

กำลังใจ [kam lang chai] *n* morale; ให้กำลังใจ [hai kam lang jai] *v* encourage; หมดกำลังใจ [mot kam lang jai] *adj* depressing; การให้กำลังใจ [kan hai kam lang jai] *n* encouragement

กำหนด [kam not] กำหนดการเดินทาง [kam not kan doen thang] *n* itinerary; ขายก่อนหมดวันที่กำหนด [khai kon mot wan thii kam nod] *n* sell-by date; ถึงกำหนด [thueng kam not] *adj* due

กำหนดการ [kam not kan] *n* agenda

กิจกรรม [kit cha kam] ในระหว่างเวลาที่มีกิจกรรมน้อย [nai ra wang we la thii mii kit cha kam noi] *adv* off-season; ที่มีกิจกรรมที่เกิดขึ้นน้อย [thii mii kit cha kam thii koet khuen noi] *adj* off-season; วันหยุดท่องเที่ยวที่มีกิจกรรม [wan yut thong thiao thii mii kit cha kam] *n* activity holiday; มีกิจกรรมกลางแจ้งอะไรบ้าง? [mii kit cha kam klang chaeng a rai bang] What outdoor activities are there?

กิจวัตร [kit cha wat] กิจวัตรประจำ [kit ja wat pra cham] *n* routine

กิน [kin] ซึ่งกินได้ [sueng kin dai] *adj* edible; มีที่กินอาหารบนเรือไหม? [mii thii kin a han bon ruea mai] Is there somewhere to eat on the boat?; คุณอยากกินอะไรไหม? [khun yak kin a rai mai] Would you like something to eat?

กินี [ki ni] ประเทศกินี [pra tet ki ni] *n* Guinea

กิ๊บ [kip] กิ๊บติดผม [kip tit phom] *n* hairgrip

กิโล [ki lo] *n* kilo

กิโลเมตร [ki lo met] *n* kilometre; ตัวย่อของกิโลเมตรต่อชั่วโมง [tua yo khong ki lo met to chau mong] *abbr* km/h

กี่ [ki] มีสถานีจอดกี่แห่งที่จะไป... [mii sa tha ni jot ki haeng thii ja pai…] How many stops is it to…?; รถโดยสารคันสุดท้ายมากี่โมง? [rot doi san khan sut thai ma ki mong] What time is the last bus?

กีดกัน [kit kan] การกีดกันทางเพศ [kan kit kan thang phet] *n* sexism

กีดกั้น [kit kan] เครื่องกีดกั้นที่ต้องแสดงตั๋วก่อนผ่านเข้าไป [khrueang kit kan thii tong sa daeng tua kon phan khao pai] *n* ticket barrier

กีดขวาง [kit khwang] *v* block; สิ่งกีดขวาง [sing kit khwang] *n* barrier, block (*obstruction*); ที่กีดขวาง [thii kit khwang] *adj* blocked

กีตาร์ [ki ta] *n* guitar

กีวี [ki wi] ผลกีวี [phon ki wi] *n* kiwi

กีฬา [ki la] *n* sport; ในด้านกีฬา [nai dan ki la] *adj* athletic; กีฬาเล่นโดยใช้ลูกบอลโยนกับกำแพง [ki la len doi chai luk bal yon kap kam phaeng] *n* handball; กีฬาเน็ตบอลมีสองทีม ๆ ละเจ็ดคน [ki la net bal mii song thim thim la chet kon] *n* netball; มีอุปกรณ์กีฬาอะไรบ้าง? [mii up pa kon ki la a rai bang] What sports facilities are there?

กุ้ง [kung] *n* prawn, shrimp; กุ้งชนิดหนึ่งคล้ายกุ้งก้ามกราม [kung cha nit nueng khlai kung kam kram] *n* crayfish; กุ้งชุบแป้งทอด [kung chup paeng thot] *npl* scampi; กุ้งทะเลขนาดใหญ่ [kung tha le kha nat yai] *n* lobster

กุญแจ [kun chae] *n* key (*for lock*), lock (*door*); ใส่กุญแจ [sai kun jae] *vt* lock; ไขกุญแจ [khai kun jae] *v* unlock; กุญแจเลื่อน [kun jae luean] *n* spanner; ใส่กุญแจประตูไม่ได้ [sai kun jae pra tu mai dai] The door won't lock

กุมภ์ [khum] ราศีกุมภ์ [ra si kum] *n* Aquarius

กุมภาพันธ์ [kum pha phan] เดือนกุมภาพันธ์ [duean kum pha phan] *n* February

กุศล [ku son] ร้านการกุศล [ran kan ku

son] n charity shop; การกุศล [kan ku son] n charity

กุหลาบ [ku lap] ต้นกุหลาบ [ton ku lap] n rose

กู้ [ku] เงินกู้ [ngoen ku] n loan

กูยานา [ku ya na] ประเทศกูยานา [pra tet ku ya na] n Guyana

เกณฑ์ [ken] n criterion

เก็บ [kep] v stock, store, keep; เรียกเก็บเงิน [riak kep ngoen] vt charge (price); เก็บเงิน [kep ngoen] v save up; เก็บไว้ที่เดิม [kep wai thii doem] v put back; ขอฉันเก็บไว้ได้ไหม? [kho chan kep wai dai mai] May I keep it?

เก็บเกี่ยว [kep kiao] v harvest; การเก็บเกี่ยว [kan kep kiao] n harvest

เกม [kem] เกมโดมิโน [kem do mi no] npl domino, dominoes; เกมบิงโก [kem bing ko] n bingo

เกมส์ [kem] n game; เกมส์คอมพิวเตอร์ [kem khom phio toe] n computer game, PlayStation®; เกมส์ที่เล่นบนกระดาน [kem thii len bon kra dan] n board game; เกมส์พนันรูเลทท์ [kem pha nan ru let] n roulette

เกราะ [kro] เสื้อเกราะ [suea kro] n armour

เกรียง [kriang] n trowel

เกรียม [kriam] เกรียมจากการถูกแดดมากเกินไป [kriam chak kan thuk daet mak koen pai] adj sunburnt; ผิวเกรียมจากการถูกแดดมากเกินไป [phio kriam chak kan thuk daet mak koen pai] n sunburn

เกรี้ยวกราด [kriao krat] การมีอารมณ์เกรี้ยวกราด [kan mii a rom kriao krat] n tantrum

เกเร [ke re] adj mischievous

เกล็ด [klet] n scale (tiny piece)

เกล็ดหิมะ [klet hi ma] n snowflake

เกลียด [kliat] v hate; ความเกลียด [khwam kliat] n hatred; ฉันเกลียด... [chan kliat...] I hate...

เกลียดชัง [kliat chang] v loathe

เกลียว [kliao] แป้นเกลียวของสลัก [paen kliao khong sa lak] n nut (device); คลาย

เกลียว [khlai kliao] v unscrew

เกลือ [kluea] n salt; ช่วยส่งเกลือให้หน่อย [chuai song kluea hai noi] Pass the salt, please

เกวียน [kwian] เกวียน รถเข็น [kwian, rot khen] n cart

เกษตรกรรม [ka set tra kam] การเกษตรกรรม [kan ka set tra kam] n agriculture, farming; ที่เกี่ยวกับเกษตรกรรม [thii kiao kap ka set tra kam] adj agricultural

เกษียณ [ka sian] v retire; คนชราเกษียณผู้รับบำนาญ [khon cha ra ka sian phu rap bam nan] n old-age pensioner; ฉันเกษียณแล้ว [chan ka sian laeo] I'm retired

เกสร [ke son] ละอองเกสรดอกไม้ [la ong ke son dok mai] n pollen

เก่า [kao] มองดูเก่า [mong du kao] adj shabby; ซึ่งใช้จนเก่า [sueng chai chon kao] adj worn

เก้า [kao] number nine; ลำดับที่เก้า [lam dap thii kao] n ninth; ที่เก้า [thii kao] adj ninth

เก่าแก่ [kao kae] โบราณ แบบดั้งเดิม แบบเก่าแก่ [bo ran, baep dang doem, baep kao kae] adj traditional

เกาลัด [kao lat] ลูกเกาลัด [luk kao lat] n chestnut

เก้าสิบ [kao sip] number ninety

เกาหลี [kao li] เกี่ยวกับเกาหลี [kiao kap kao lii] adj Korean; เกาหลีเหนือ [kao lii nuea] n North Korea; ชาวเกาหลี [chao kao lii] n Korean (person)

เกาหลีใต้ [kao hli tai] ประเทศเกาหลีใต้ [pra tet kao lii tai] n South Korea

เก้าอี้ [kao i] n chair (furniture); เก้าอี้เข็นสำหรับคนป่วยหรือคนพิการ [kao ii khen sam rap khon puai rue khon phi kan] n wheelchair; เก้าอี้เด็ก [kao ee dek] n highchair; เก้าอี้โยก [kao ii yok] n rocking chair; คุณมีเก้าอี้สำหรับเด็กไหม? [khun mii kao ii sam rap dek mai] Do you have a high chair?

เกาะ [ko] *n* island; เกาะมาดากัสการ์ใน
มหาสมุทรอินเดีย [ko ma da kas ka nai
ma ha sa mut in dia] *n* Madagascar;
เกาะกลางทะเลทราย [ko klang tha le sai]
n desert island; เกาะตาฮิติทางตอนใต้ของ
มหาสมุทรแปซิฟิก [ko ta hi ti thang ton
tai khong ma ha sa mut pae si fik] *n*
Tahiti

เกิด [koet] เริ่ม ลงมือ ทำให้เกิด [roem, long
mue, tham hai koet] *vi* start; เกิดซ้ำ ๆ
[koet sam sam] *adj* recurring; แรกเกิด
[raek koet] *adj* newborn; เกิดอะไรขึ้น?
[koet a rai khuen] What happened?

เกิดขึ้น [koet khuen] *v* happen, occur;
เกิดขึ้นตลอดเวลา [koet khuen ta lot we
la] *adv* constantly; ไม่น่าจะเกิดขึ้น [mai
na ja koet khuen] *adj* unlikely; สิ่งที่เกิด
ขึ้นหรือทำขึ้นเพียงครั้งเดียว [sing thii koet
khuen rue tham khuen phiang khrang
diao] *n* one-off; เกิดขึ้นเมื่อไร? [koet
khuen muea rai] When did it happen?

เกิน [koen] จำนวนที่เกิน [cham nuan thii
koen] *n* surplus; ซึ่งมากเกินความจำเป็น
[sueng mak koen khwam cham pen]
adj excessive

เกินไป [koen pai] มันเล็กเกินไป [man lek
koen pai] It's too small; มันใหญ่เกินไป
[man yai koen pai] It's too big; มี...ในนี้
มากเกินไป [mii...nai nii mak koen pai]
There's too much... in it

เกียจคร้าน [kiat khran] *adj* idle

เกียร์ [kia] *n* gear (equipment); เกียร์รถ
[kia rot] *n* gear (mechanism); กระปุกเกียร์
[kra puk kia] *n* gear box, gear stick; การ
เปลี่ยนเกียร์ [kan plian kia] *n* gearshift;
เกียร์ไม่ทำงาน [kia mai tham ngan] The
gears are not working, The gears don't
work

เกียรติ [kiat] ความมีเกียรติ [khwam mii
kiat] *n* dignity

เกียรติยศ [kiat ti yot] *adj* glorious ▷ *n*
honour

เกี่ยวกับ [kiao kap] *prep* about,
concerning, regarding; เกี่ยวกับ

เครื่องจักรกล [kiao kap khrueang chak
kon] *adj* mechanical; คุณมีใบปลิวเกี่ยว
กับ...บ้างไหม? [khun mii bai plio kiao
kap...bang mai] Do you have any
leaflets about...?

เกี่ยวข้อง [kiao khong] เลือกที่จะไม่
เกี่ยวข้องด้วย [lueak thii ja mai kiao
khong duai] *v* opt out; ไม่เกี่ยวข้องกัน
[mai kiao khong kan] *adj* irrelevant;
ความเกี่ยวข้องกันของสิ่งของหรือบุคคล
[khwam kiao khong kan khong sing
khong rue buk kon] *n* relation

เกี่ยวเนื่อง [kiao nueang] ที่เกี่ยวเนื่อง
[thii kiao nueang] *adj* associate

เกี้ยวพาราสี [kiao pha ra si] *v* flirt

เกือก [kueak] เกือกม้า [kueak ma] *n*
horseshoe

เกือบ [kueap] *adv* nearly; เกือบจะไม่
[kueap ja mai] *adv* hardly

เกือบจะ [kueap cha] *adv* almost

เกือบไม่พอ [kueap mai pho] *adv* barely

แก่ [kae] *adj* old; แก่กว่า [kae kwa] *adj*
elder; แก่ที่สุด [kae thii sut] *adj* eldest

แก้ [kae] *v* undo; แก้ห่อออก [kae ho ok] *v*
unwrap; แก้ปัญหา [kae pan ha] *v* solve;
แก้ปัญหา [kae pan ha] *v* settle

แก้ไข [kae khai] เปลี่ยนแปลงแก้ไข [plian
plaeng kae khai] *v* modify; แก้ไขให้ถูก
ต้อง [kae khai hai thuk tong] *v* correct;
แก้ไขให้ถูกต้อง [kae khai hai thuk tong]
v rectify

แกง [kaeng] *n* curry; เครื่องแกงที่เป็นผง
[khrueang kaeng thii pen phong] *n*
curry powder

แก๊สน้ำตา [kaet nam ta] *n* teargas

แก้ตัว [kae tua] *v* defend, excuse; ข้อ
แก้ตัว [kho kae tua] *n* excuse

แกน [kaen] แกน เพลา [kaen, phlao] axle

แก้ผ้า [khae pha] *v* strip

แก้ม [kaem] *n* cheek; โหนกแก้ม [nok
kaem] *n* cheekbone; ครีมหรือแป้งสีทา
แก้ม [khrim rue paeng sii tha kaem] *n*
blusher

แกมเบีย [kaem bia] ประเทศแกมเบีย [pra

tet kaem bia] n Gambia

แกรนิต [krae nit] หินแกรนิต [hin krae nit] n granite

แกล้ง [klaeng] v pretend; แกล้งตั้งใจทำ [klaeng tang jai tham] v bluff; การแกล้ง ตั้งใจทำบางสิ่ง [kan klaeng tang jai tham bang sing] n bluff

แก้ว [kaeo] n glass; แก้วเจียระไน [kaew chia ra nai] n crystal; แก้วไวน์ [kaew wine] n wineglass; ฉันขอแก้วสะอาดหนึ่ง ใบได้ไหม? [chan kho kaew sa aat nueng bai dai mai] Can I have a clean glass, please?

แกว่ง [kwaeng] vi swing; แกว่งไปมา [kwaeng pai ma] v sway; โยก แกว่ง เขย่า [yok, kwaeng, kha yao] v rock; การแกว่งไปมา [kan kwaeng pai ma] n swing

แกะ [kae] n lamb, sheep; เนื้อแกะ [nuea kae] n mutton; แกะตัวเมียที่โตเต็มที่ [kae tua mia thii to tem thii] n ewe; หนัง แกะ [nang kae] n sheepskin

แกะสลัก [kae sa lak] vt carve

แก้แค้น [kae khaen] การแก้แค้น [kan kae khaen] n revenge

โกโก้ [ko ko] ผงโกโก้ [phong ko ko] n cocoa

โกง [kong] โกงกิน [kong kin] adj bent (dishonest); การโกง [kan kong] n fraud; การโกง การหลอกลวง การต้มตุ๋น [kan kong, kan lok luang, kan tom tun] n rip-off

โกดัง [ko dang] โกดังสินค้า [ko dang sin ka] n warehouse

โกน [kon] v shave; โฟมโกนหนวด [fom kon nuat] n shaving foam; ไม่โกนหนวด เครา [mai kon nuat khrao] adj unshaven; ครีมโกนหนวด [khrim kon nuat] n shaving cream

โกรธ [krot] adj angry, furious, mad (angry); โกรธง่าย [krot ngai] adj irritable; โกรธฉุนเฉียว [krot chun chiao] adj cross; ความโกรธ [khwam krot] n anger

โกลาหล [ko la hon] ความยุ่งเหยิง ความ โกลาหล สถานการณ์สับสนวุ่นวาย [khwam yung yoeng, khwam ko la hon, sa than na kan sap son wun wai] npl shambles

โกหก [ko hok] v lie, lie down; การโกหก [kan ko hok] n lie; คนโกหก [khon ko hok] n liar

โกหร่าน [ko ha ran] คัมภีร์โกหร่าน [kham phii ko ran] n Koran

ใกล้ [klai] adj close, near ▷ adv about; ใน ระยะเวลาอันใกล้ [nai ra ya we la an klai] adv near; อยู่ใกล้ [yu klai] adj close by; ฉันจะไปสถานีรถไฟใต้ดินที่ใกล้ที่สุดได้ อย่างไร? [chan ja pai sa tha ni rot fai tai din thii klai thii sut dai yang rai] How do I get to the nearest tube station?

ใกล้เคียง [klai khiang] adv nearby; บริเวณใกล้เคียง [bo ri wen klai khiang] n vicinity; บริเวณที่ใกล้เคียง [bo ri wen thii klai khiang] n proximity

ใกล้ชิด [klai chit] adj intimate; อย่างใกล้ ชิด [yang klai chit] adv closely

ไก่ [kai] n chicken; แม่ไก่ [mae kai] n hen; ไก่ตัวผู้ [kai tua phu] n cock; ไก่ที่ มีอายุน้อยกว่าหนึ่งปี [kai thii mii a yu noi kwa nueng pi] n cockerel

ไก่งวง [kai nguang] n turkey

ไกด์ [kait] ไกด์พาเที่ยวเริ่มเวลาเท่าไร? [kai pha thiao roem we la thao rai] What time does the guided tour begin?; มี ไกด์ทัวร์เป็นภาษาอังกฤษไหม? [mii kai tua pen pha sa ang krit mai] Is there a guided tour in English?; มีไกด์ที่พูดภาษา อังกฤษไหม? [mii kai thii phut pha sa ang] Is there a guide who speaks English?

ไกล [klai] adj remote ▷ adv far; ไกลกว่า [klai kwa] adv further; ห่างไกล [hang klai] adv distant, far; ความห่างไกล [khwam hang klai] n distance; ป้ายรถ โดยสารอยู่ไกลแค่ไหน? [pai rot doi san yu klai khae nai] How far is the bus stop?

บ

ขจัด [kha chat] v eliminate

ขณะ [kha na] ในขณะนั้น [nai kha na nan] adv then; ชั่วขณะหนึ่ง [chua kha na nueng] n while

ขณะที่ [kha na thi] adv meanwhile ▷ conj while; เมื่อหรือขณะที่ [muea rue kha na thii] conj when; ขณะที่ ดังที่ เนื่องจาก [kha na thii, dang thii, nueang chak] conj as

ขน [khon] เต็มไปด้วยขน [tem pai duai khon] adj hairy; ขนนก [khon nok] n feather

ขนม [kha nom] ขนมเค้ก [kha nom khek] n cake; ขนมแพนเค้ก [kha nom phaen khek] n pancake; ขนมแอปเปิ้ลพาย [kha nom ap poen phai] n apple pie

ขนมปัง [kha nom pang] n bread; เครื่อง ปิ้งขนมปัง [khrueang ping kha nom pang] n toaster; ร้านขายขนมปัง [ran khai kha nom pang] n bakery; ก้อน ขนมปัง [kon kha nom pang] n loaf; คุณ อยากได้ขนมปังไหม? [khun yak dai kha nom pang mai] Would you like some bread?

ขนลุก [kha nom luk] npl goose pimples

ขนส่ง [khon song] v transport, carry; สินค้าที่ขนส่ง [sin kha thii khon song] n freight; การขนส่ง [kan khon song] n transit, transport; การขนส่งมวลชน [kan khon song muan chon] n public transport

ขนสัตว์ [khon sat] n fur; เสื้อผ้าที่ทำจากขน สัตว์ [suea pha thii tham chak khon sat] npl woollens; ขนสัตว์ เช่น ขนแกะ และสัตว์อื่น ๆ [khon sat chen khon kae lae sat uen uen] n wool; ขนสัตว์นุ่มที่ได้ จากแพะ [khon sat num thii dai chak phae] n cashmere

ขนาด [kha nat] n size; การวัดขนาด [kan wat kha nat] n dimension; ขนาดกลาง [kha nat klang] adj medium-sized; ฉัน ขนาดเบอร์สิบหก [chan kha nat boe sip hok] I'm a size 16

ขนาน [kha nan] adj parallel

ขบขัน [khop khan] ความขบขัน [khwam khop khan] n fun; ตลกขบขัน [ta lok khop khan] adj humorous

ขบวน [kha buan] ขบวนแห่ [kha buan hae] n parade; ขบวนที่เคลื่อนที่ไป [kha buan thii khluean thii pai] n procession

ขม [khom] adj bitter

ขมขื่น [khom khuen] รู้สึกขมขื่น [ru suk khom khuen] v resent; ความรู้สึกโกรธ และขมขื่น [khwam ru suek krot lae khom khuen] n venom

ข่มขืน [khom khuen] n rape (sexual attack) ▷ v rape; คนที่ข่มขืน [khon thii khom khuen] n rapist; ฉันถูกข่มขืน [chan thuk khom khuen] I've been raped

ข่มขู่ [khom khu] ข่มขู่คุกคาม [khom khu khuk kham] v intimidate; คนข่มขู่เพื่อ ชิงทรัพย์ [khon khom khu phuea ching sap] n mugger

ข่มใจ [khom chai] การข่มใจตัวเอง [kan khom jai tua eng] n self-control

ข่มเหง [khom heng] v abuse; การข่มเหง [kan khom heng] n abuse

ขมิ้น [kha min] n cumin

ขโมย [kha moi] *n* burglar, thief; เครื่อง
กันขโมย [khrueang kan kha moi] *n*
burglar alarm; การลักขโมยของในร้าน
[kan lak ka moi khong nai ran] *n*
shoplifting; การขโมยเอกลักษณ์ [kan
kha moi ek ka lak] *n* identity theft

ขยะ [kha ya] *n* garbage, litter, refuse,
rubbish; ขยะไปรษณีย์อิเล็กทรอนิกส์ [kha
ya prai sa nii i lek thro nik] *n* spam; คน
เก็บขยะ [khon kep kha ya] *n* dustman;
ตะกร้าใส่ขยะ [ta kra sai kha ya] *n*
wastepaper basket; เราจะทิ้งขยะได้ที่
ไหน? [rao ja thing kha ya dai thii nai]
Where do we leave the rubbish?

ขยะแขยง [kha ya kha yaeng] ซึ่งน่า
ขยะแขยง [sueng na kha ya kha yaeng]
adj disgusted; ที่ทำให้ขยะแขยง [thii
tham hai kha ya kha yaeng] *adj*
horrifying; น่าขยะแขยง [na kha ya kha
yaeng] *adj* repulsive

ขยับ [kha yap] ย้าย ขยับ [yai, kha yap] *vi*
move; เขาขยับขาไม่ได้ [khao kha yap
kha mai dai] He can't move his leg

ขยับเขยื้อน [kha yap kha yuean]
อุปกรณ์ต่าง ๆ ในรถขยับเขยื้อนไม่ได้ [up
pa kon tang tang nai rot kha yap kha
yuean mai dai] The controls have
jammed

ขยาย [kha yai] เครื่องขยายเสียง
[khrueang kha yai siang] *n* amplifier;
การขยาย [kan kha yai] *n* enlargement;
การขยายออก [kan kha yai ok] *n*
extension

ขยิบตา [kha yip ta] *v* wink

ขยี้ [kha yi] ขยี้ให้ดับ [kha yii hai dab] *v*
stub out

ขรุขระ [khru khra] *adj* bumpy

ขลิบ [khlip] *v* trim

ขลุ่ย [khlui] *n* flute

ขวด [khuat] *n* bottle, jar; สว่านเปิดจุกขวด
[sa wan poet chuk khaut] *n* corkscrew;
ขวดแยม [khaut yaem] *n* jam jar; ขวด
ชนิดหนึ่งที่ใส่น้ำดื่มหรือไวน์เพื่อเสิร์ฟที่โต๊ะ
อาหาร [khaut cha nit nueng thii sai

nam duem rue wai phuea soep thii to
a han] *n* carafe; ไวน์แดงหนึ่งขวด [wine
daeng nueng khaut] a bottle of red
wine

ขวดนม [khuat nom] ขวดนมเด็ก [khaut
nom dek] *n* baby's bottle

ขวบ [khuap] เขาอายุสิบขวบ [khao a yu
sip khuap] He is ten years old

ขวา [khwa] ขับทางด้านขวามือ [khap
thang dan khwa mue] *n* right-hand
drive; ด้านขวามือ [dan khwa mue] *adj*
right-hand; ทางขวา [thang khwa] *adj*
right (not left); เลี้ยวขวา [liao khwa]
Turn right

ขวาง [khwang] ขวางทาง [khwang
thang] *v* obstruct

ขว้าง [khwang] *v* fling, pitch; การขว้าง
[kan khwang] *n* cast

ขวาน [khwan] *n* axe

ขอ [kho] ขอให้ทำ [kho hai tham] *v* ask
for; ขอความช่วยเหลือ [kho khwam
chuai luea] *v* resort to; ขอตั๋วสองใบ
[kho tua song bai] I'd like two tickets,
please

ข้อ [kho] ข้อแก้ตัว [kho kae tua] *n*
excuse; ข้อลูกโซ่ [kho luk so] *n* link;
ข้อสอบ [kho sop] *n* exam

ข้อเขียน [kho khian] คำพูดหรือข้อเขียนที่
แสดงเชาวน์ปัญญา [kham phut rue kho
khian thii sa daeng chao pan ya] *n* wit

ข้อความ [kho khwam] *n* note (message);
แฟ้มในเครื่องคอมพิวเตอร์ใช้เก็บข้อความที่
ส่งทางอีเล็กโทรนิค [faem nai khrueang
khom phio toe chai kep kho khwam
thii song thang i lek tro nik] *n* inbox;
ระบบการส่งข้อความทางโทรศัพท์ [ra bop
kan song kho khwam thang tho ra
sap] *n* MMS; ระบบอีเล็คทรอนิกส์ที่ส่งผ่าน
และเก็บข้อความทางโทรศัพท์ [ra bop e lek
tro nik thii song phan lae kep kho
khwam thang tho ra sap] *n* voicemail

ข้อคิดเห็น [kho khit hen] การให้ข้อคิด
เห็น [kan hai kho kit hen] *n* remark;
ข้อคิดเห็นที่มีประโยชน์ [kho kit hen thii

mii pra yot] *v* tip (*suggestion*)

ของ [khong] *prep* of; ของแท้ [khong thae] *adj* authentic; ของหวาน [khong wan] *n* dessert; ของผู้ซึ่ง [khong phu sueng] *pron* whose

ของเก่า [khong kao] *n* antique; ร้านขายของเก่า [ran khai khong kao] *n* antique shop; ของเก่าที่ไม่ต้องการแล้ว [khong kao thii mai tong kan laeo] *n* junk

ของขวัญ [khong khwan] *n* gift, present (*gift*); ร้านขายของขวัญ [ran khai khong khwan] *n* gift shop; บัตรของขวัญ [bat khong khwan] *n* gift voucher; ฉันกำลังหาของขวัญสักชิ้นหนึ่งให้เด็ก [chan kam lang ha khong khwan sak chin nueng hai dek] I'm looking for a present for a child

ของเขา [khong khao] *adj* his; ของเขาผู้ชาย [khong khao phu chai] *pron* his

ของแข็ง [khong khaeng] ชิ้นหรือของหรือวัสดุที่เป็นของแข็ง [chin rue khong rue wat sa du thii pen khong khaeng] *n* block (*solid piece*)

ของคาว [khong khao] ที่เป็นของคาว [thii pen khong khao] *adj* savoury

ของคุณ [khong khun] *adj* your (*singular*) ▷ *pron* yours (*singular*)

ของใคร [khong khrai] *pron* whose

ของฉัน [khong chan] *adj* my ▷ *pron* mine

ของชำ [khong cham] ร้านขายของชำ [ran khai khong cham] *n* grocer's; คนขายของชำ [khon khai khong cham] *n* grocer; อาหารและสิ่งอื่น ๆ ขายที่ร้านขายของชำ [a han lae sing uen uen khai thii ran khai khong cham] *npl* groceries

ของใช้ [khong chai] ของใช้บนเตียงนอนเช่น ผ้าห่ม ฟูก [khong chai bon tiang non chen pha hom fuk] *npl* bedclothes

ของที่ทำด้วยมือ [khong thi tham duai mue] เป็นของที่ทำด้วยมือหรือเปล่า? [pen khong thii tham duai mue rue plao] Is this handmade?

ของที่ระลึก [khong thi ra luek] *n* memento, souvenir; คุณมีของที่ระลึกไหม? [khun mii khong thii ra luek mai] Do you have souvenirs?

ของฝาก [khong fak] ฉันจะซื้อของฝากได้ที่ไหน? [chan ja sue khong fak dai thii nai] Where can I buy gifts?

ของพวกเขา [khong phuak khao] *adj* their ▷ *pron* theirs

ของพวกคุณ [khong phuak khun] *adj* your (*plural*) ▷ *pron* yours (*plural*)

ของพวกท่าน [khong phuak than] *adj* your (*singular polite*) ▷ *pron* yours (*singular polite*)

ของมัน [khong man] *adj* its

ของมีค่า [khong mi kha] ฉันเก็บของมีค่าไว้ที่ไหนได้? [chan kep khong mii kha wai thii nai dai] Where can I leave my valuables?; ฉันอยากวางของมีค่าไว้ในตู้นิรภัย [chan yak wang khong mii kha wai nai tu ni ra phai] I'd like to put my valuables in the safe

ของเรา [khong rao] *adj* our; ของเราเอง [khong rao eng] *pron* ours

ของเล่น [khong len] *n* toy; ของเล่นเด็กที่เขย่ามีเสียงรัว [khong len dek thii kha yao mii siang rua] *n* rattle

ของหลอน [khong hlon] *adj* her ▷ *pron* hers

ของหวาน [khong wan] *n* pudding, sweet ▷ *npl* afters

ของเหลว [khong leo] *n* liquid; เครื่องทำให้เป็นของเหลว [khrueang tham hai pen khong leo] *n* liquidizer

ข้อตกลง [kho tok long] *n* agreement

ข้อต่อ [kho to] *n* joint (*meat*); โรคข้อต่ออักเสบ [rok kho to ak sep] *n* arthritis; ข้อต่อสำหรับเครื่องอัดน้ำมันหรือน้ำ [kho to sam rap khrueang at nam man rue nam] *n* hose

ข้อทาน [kho than] *n* beggar

ข้อเท้า [kho thao] *n* ankle

ขอโทษ [kho thot] *excl* pardon?, sorry! ▷ *v* apologize; คำขอโทษ [kham kho thot] n apology

ขอบ [khop] n edge, margin, rim; ระบาย
ขอบ [ra bai khop] n fringe; ขอบหน้าต่าง
ส่วนล่าง [kop na tang suan lang] n
windowsill; ขอบถนน [kop tha non] n
kerb

ขอบเขต [khop khet] n border,
boundary, circuit, extent, range
(limits); ขอบเขตของการเล่นกีฬาบางอย่าง
[kop khet khong kan len ki la bang
yang] n touchline

ขอบคุณ [khop khun] excl thanks! ▷ v
thank; สบายดี ขอบคุณ [sa bai di, kop
khun] Fine, thanks; ขอบคุณมาก [kop
khun mak] Thank you very much; ฉัน
ไม่ดื่ม ขอบคุณ [chan mai duem kop
khun] I'm not drinking, thank you

ขอบตา [khop ta] n ที่วาดขอบตา [thii wat
kop ta] n eyeliner

ขอบฟ้า [khop fa] n horizon

ขอผิดพลาด [kho phit phlat] มันมีข้อผิด
พลาด [man mii kho phit phlat] It's
faulty

ข้อมือ [kho mue] n wrist

ข้อมูล [kho mun] n information; ใส่ข้อมูล
ส่วนบุคคล [sai kho mun suan buk
khon] v blog; สำนักงานข้อมูล [sam nak
ngan kho mun] n information office;
สถิติ ข้อมูล [sa thi ti, kho mun] npl
data; ฉันอยากได้ข้อมูลเกี่ยวกับ... [chan
yak dai kho mun kiao kap...] I'd like
some information about...

ขอร้อง [kho rong] v beg; คำขอร้อง [kham
kho rong] n appeal

ข้ออ้าง [kho ang] n pretext

ขัง [khang] ห้องเล็กในห้องขัง [hong lek
nai hong khang] n cell

ขัด [khat] การขัดให้ขึ้นเงา [kan khat hai
khuen ngao] n polish; ขัดให้ขึ้นเงา [khat
hai khuen ngao] v polish; ยาขัดรองเท้า
[ya khat rong thao] n shoe polish

ขัดขวาง [khat kwang] การขัดขวาง [kan
khat khwang] n inhibition

ขัดแย้ง [khat yaeng] v contradict; ความ

ขัดแย้ง [khwam khat yaeng] n conflict,
contradiction; ความขัดแย้งกัน [khwam
khat yaeng kan] n disagreement

ขัน [khan] อารมณ์ขัน [a rom khan] n
humour

ขับ [khap] v drive; การสอบขับรถ [kan sop
khap rot] n driving test; การขับ [kan
khap] n drive, steering; การขับด้านซ้าย
[kan khap dan sai] n left-hand drive;
คุณขับรถเร็วเกินไป [khun khap rot reo
koen pai] You were driving too fast

ขับขี่ [khap khi] ใบขับขี่ [bai khap khi] n
driving licence; ใบขับขี่ของฉัน
หมายเลข... [bai khap khi khong chan
mai lek...] My driving licence number
is...; ฉันไม่มีใบขับขี่ในตอนนี้ [chan mai
mii bai khap khii nai ton nii] I don't
have my driving licence on me

ขับรถ [khap rot] ครูสอนขับรถ [khru son
khap rot] n driving instructor; บทเรียน
สอนขับรถ [bot rian son khap rot] n
driving lesson; เขาขับรถเร็วเกินไป [khao
khap rot reo koen pai] He was driving
too fast

ขั้วโลก [khua lok] n pole; เกี่ยวกับขั้วโลก
[kiao kap khua lok] adj polar; มหาสมุทร
ขั้วโลกเหนือ [ma ha sa mut khua lok
nuea] n Arctic Ocean; หมีขั้วโลก [mii
khua lok] n polar bear

ขา [kha] n leg; ต้นขา [ton kha] n thigh;
เธอทำขาเธอเจ็บ [thoe tham kha thoe
chep] She has hurt her leg; ฉันขยับขาไม่
ได้ [chan kha yap kha mai dai] I can't
move my leg

ขากรรไกร [kha kan krai] n jaw

ข้าง [khang] เคลื่อนไปด้านข้าง [khluean
pai dan khang] adv sideways; ข้างๆ
[khang khang] prep beside

ข้างๆ [khang khang] prep next to

ข้างทาง [khang thang] n layby

ข้างนอก [khang nok] adj outside ▷ n
outside

ข้างใน [khang nai] n inner

ข้างบน [khang bon] adv upstairs

ขาด [khat] *adj* absent; การขาด [kan khat] *n* lack; ขาดหรือแตกอย่างฉับพลัน [khat rue taek yang chap phlan] *vt* snap; จำนวนที่ขาดไป [cham nuan thii khat pai] *n* shortfall

ขาดแคลน [khat khlaen] การขาดแคลน [kan khat khlaen] *n* shortage; ความขาดแคลนอาหาร [khwam khaat khlaen a han] *n* famine

ขาด ช่วงเวลา [khat chuang we la] การขาด ช่วงเวลาที่ไม่อยู่ [kan khat, chuang we la thii mai yu] *n* absence

ขาดอาหาร [khat a han] การขาดอาหาร [kan khat a han] *n* malnutrition

ขานชื่อ [khan chue] การขานชื่อ [kan khan chue] *n* roll call

ข้าม [kham] *prep* across ▷ *vt* cross; การข้าม [kan kham] *n* crossing; ข้ามประเทศ [kham pra tet] *n* cross-country; ทางเดินข้าม [thang doen kham] *n* pedestrian crossing; รถหนึ่งคันกับผู้โดยสารสี่คนข้ามฝั่งไปราคาเท่าไร? [rot nueng khan kap phu doi san si khon kham fang pai ra kha thao rai] How much is the crossing for a car and four people?; การข้ามฝั่งเจอพายุทะเล [kan kham fang choe pha yu tha le] The crossing was rough

ขาย [khai] *vt* sell; ราคาขาย [ra kha khai] *n* selling price; การขาย [kan khai] *n* sale; การขายสินค้าราคาพิเศษ [kan khai sin kha ra kha phi set] *n* special offer; คุณขายการ์ดโทรศัพท์ไหม? [khun khai kaat tho ra sap mai] Do you sell phone cards?

ขายปลีก [khai phlik] *v* retail; ราคาขายปลีก [ra kha khai plik] *n* retail price; การขายปลีก [kan khai plik] *n* retail; ผู้ขายปลีก [phu khai plik] *n* retailer

ขายส่ง [khai song] โดยการขายส่ง [doi kan khai song] *adj* wholesale; การขายส่ง [kan khai song] *n* wholesale

ข้าราชการ [kha rat cha kan] ข้าราชการพลเรือน [kha rat cha kan phon la ruean] *n* civil servant

ขาว [khao] สีขาว [sii khao] *adj* white; กระดานสีขาว [kra dan sii kao] *n* whiteboard; ทาให้ขาว [tha hai khao] *v* whitewash; เป็นขาวกับดำ [pen khao kap dam] in black and white

ข่าว [khao] *npl* news; หัวข่าว [hua khao] *n* headline; หัวข้อข่าว [hua kho khao] *n* lead (*position*); คนส่งข่าว [khon song khao] *n* messenger; จะมีข่าวเมื่อไร? [ja mii khao muea rai] When is the news?

ข้าว [khao] *n* rice; รำข้าว [ram khao] *n* bran; ข้าวซ้อมมือ [khao som mue] *n* brown rice; ข้าวบาร์เลย์ [khao ba le] *n* barley

ข้าวโพด [khao pot] *n* corn, maize; แป้งข้าวโพด [paeng khao phot] *n* cornflour; ข้าวโพดหวาน [khao phot wan] *n* sweetcorn; ข้าวโพดคั่ว [khao phot khua] *n* popcorn

ข่าวลือ [khao lue] *n* rumour

ข่าวสาร [khao san] *n* message; หน้าแรกของข่าวสารขององค์การหรือบุคคล [na raek khong khao san khong ong kan rue buk khon] *n* home page

ข้าวสาลี [khao sa li] *n* wheat; คนที่แพ้อาหารที่ทำจากข้าวสาลี [khon thii pae a han thii tham chak khao sa lii] *n* wheat intolerance

ข้าวโอ๊ต [khao ot] *npl* oats; ข้าวโอ๊ตบดหยาบ ๆ [khao oat bot yab yab] *n* oatmeal; อาหารเช้าที่ทำจากข้าวโอ๊ตที่ใส่น้ำหรือนม [a han chao thii tham chak khao ot thii sai nam rue nom] *n* porridge

ขิง [khing] *n* ginger

ขี่ [khi] การขี่ม้า [kan khi ma] *n* horse riding, riding; การขี่จักรยาน [kan khi chak kra yan] *n* cycling; ขี่ เช่นขี่ม้า ขี่จักรยานหรือจักรยานยนต์ [khi chen khi ma khi chak kra yan rue chak kra yan yon] *n* ride

ขี้เกียจ [khi kiat] *adj* lazy

ขี้ขลาด [khi khlat] คนขี้ขลาด [khon khii khlat] *n* coward; อย่างขี้ขลาด [yang khii khlad] *adj* cowardly

ขีด [khid] ขีดฆ่า [khit kha] *v* cross out

ขีดเส้นใต้ [khit sen tai] *v* underline

ขีดออก [khit ok] ทำเครื่องหมายขีดออก [tham khrueang mai khit ok] *v* tick off

ขีปนาวุธ [khi pa na wut] *n* missile

ขี้ผึ้ง [khi pheung] *n* ointment, wax

ขี่ม้า [khi ma] การขี่ม้าขึ้นไปในระยะทางชัน และลำบาก [kan khi ma khuen pai nai ra ya thang chan lae lam bak] pony trekking; เราไปขี่ม้าได้ไหม? [rao pai khi ma dai mai] Can we go horse riding?; ไปขี่ม้ากันเถอะ [pai khi ma kan thoe] Let's go horse riding

ขี้เลื่อย [khi lueai] *n* sawdust

ขี้เหนียว [khi niao] *adj* stingy

ขึ้น [khuen] *v* get on; ในทิศทางขึ้น [nai thit thang khuen] *adv* up; ขึ้นไป [khuen pai] *v* go up; ขึ้นไปทางเหนือ [khuen pai thang nuea] *adv* upwards

ขึ้นทะเบียน [khuen tha bian] การขึ้น ทะเบียน [kan khuen tha bian] *n* registration

ขึ้นอยู่กับ [khuen yu kap] *v* depend, rely on

ขุด [khut] *vt* dig; เครื่องมือที่ใช้ในการขุด [khrueang mue thii chai nai kan khut] *n* digger; สถานที่ที่ขุดเอาหินออกมา [sa than thii thii khut ao hin ok ma] *n* quarry

ขุ่นเคือง [khun khueang] ซึ่งทำให้ขุ่น เคือง [sueng tham hai khun khueang] *adj* offensive; ทำให้ขุ่นเคือง [tham hai khun khueang] *v* offend

ขู่ [khu] การขู่ว่าจะเปิดโปงความลับ [kan ku wa ja poet pong khwam lap] *n* blackmail

ขู่เข็ญ [khu khen] *v* threaten; การขู่เข็ญ [kan ku khen] *n* threat; ที่ขู่เข็ญ [thii khu khen] *adj* threatening

ขูด [khut (khuut)] ขูดออก [khud ok] *v* grate, scratch

ขูดเลือด [khut lueat] หักหลัง ขูดเลือด [hak lang, khut lueat] *adj* extortionate

เขต [khet] *n* district, precinct, region; เกี่ยวกับเขตนั้น ๆ [kiao kap khet nan nan] *adj* regional; เขตเลือกตั้ง [khet lueak tang] *n* constituency, ward *(area)*; เขตที่มีคนอยู่อาศัย [khet thii mii khon yu a sai] *n* neighbourhood

เขตร้อน [khet ron] เกี่ยวกับเขตร้อน [kiao kap khet ron] *adj* tropical

เข็ม [khem] *n* needle; เข็มเครื่องหมาย [khem khrueang mai] *n* badge; เข็มหัว ใหญ่ [khem hua yai] *n* thumb tack; เข็ม ถัก [khem thak] *n* knitting needle; คุณมี เข็มกับด้ายไหม? [khun mii khem kap dai mai] Do you have a needle and thread?

เข้ม [khem] ทำให้สีเข้มขึ้น [tham hai sii khem khuen] *adj* tinted

เข็มกลัด [khem klat] *n* brooch, clasp, safety pin; ฉันอยากได้เข็มกลัด [chan yak dai khem klat] I need a safety pin

เข้มข้นมาก [khem khon mak] การทำให้ มีความเข้มข้นมากขึ้น การย่อความ [kan tham hai mii khwam khem khon mak khuen, kan yo khwam] *n* condensation

เข็มขัด [khem khat] *n* belt; เข็มขัดชูชีพ [khem khat chu chip] *n* lifebelt; เข็มขัด นิรภัย [khem khat ni ra phai] *n* safety belt, seatbelt

เข้มแข็ง [khem khaeng] ความเข้มแข็ง [khwam khem khaeng] *n* strength

เข้มงวด [khem nguat] *adj* strict

เข็มทิศ [khem thit] *n* compass

เข็มหมุด [khem mut] *n* drawing pin, pin

เขม่า [kha mao] เขม่า เขม่าถ่านหิน [kha mao, kha mao than hin] *n* soot

เขย [khoei] ลูกเขย [luk khoei] *n* son-in-law; พี่เขยหรือน้องเขย [phi khoei rue nong khoei] *n* brother-in-law

เขย่า [kha yao] โยก แกว่ง เขย่า [yok, kwaeng, kha yao] *v* rock

เขย่าขวัญ [kha yao khwan] *adj* thrilling; เรื่องเขย่าขวัญ [rueang kha yao khwan] *n* thriller; น่าเขย่าขวัญ [na kha yao khwan] *adj* nerve-racking

เขลา [khlao] *adj* ignorant

เขา [khao] *n* horn; เขาเตี้ย ๆ [khao tia tia] *n* hill; เขาผู้ชาย [khao phu chai] *pron* he, him; เดินเขา [doen khao] *n* hill-walking

เข่า [khao] *n* knee

เข้า [khao] *vt* enter; เข้าไป [khao pai] *v* go in; เข้าไปใน [khao pai nai] *v* get into; เข้าไปได้ [khao pai dai] *v* access

เข้าใกล้ [khao klai] *v* approach

เข้าคุก [khao khuk] เอาเข้าคุก [ao khao khuk] *v* jail

เข้าใจ [khao chai] *v* understand; เข้าใจได้ [khao jai dai] *adj* understandable; เข้าใจถ่องแท้ [khao jai thong thae] *v* master; ความเข้าใจ [khwam khao jai] *n* comprehension; คุณเข้าใจไหม? [khun khao jai mai] Do you understand?

เข้าใจผิด [khao chao phit] *v* misunderstand; การเข้าใจผิด [kan khao jai phit] *n* misunderstanding; ซึ่งเข้าใจผิด [sueng khao jai phit] *adj* mistaken; ซึ่งทำให้เข้าใจผิด [sueng tham hai khao jai phit] *adj* misleading

เข้านอน [khao non] เราเข้านอนแล้วเมื่อคุณกลับมา [rao khao non laeo muea khun klap ma] We'll be in bed when you get back

เข้ามา [khao ma] ให้เข้ามา [hai khao ma] *v* let in

เข้าร่วม [khao ruam] *v* attend, join; ผู้เข้าร่วม [phu khao ruam] *n* joiner; ผู้เข้าร่วมการแข่งขัน [phu khao ruam kan khaeng khan] *n* racer; ฉันเข้าร่วมกับคุณได้ไหม? [chan khao ruam kap khun dai mai] Can I join you?

เขินอาย [khoen ai] *v* blush

เขี่ย [khia] ที่เขี่ยบุหรี่ [thi khia bu ri] *n* ashtray

เขียน [khian] *v* write; เขียนลง [khian long] *v* write down; เขียนหวัด ๆ [khian wat wat] *v* scribble; เขียนอักษรย่อ

[khian ak son yo] *v* initial; คุณกรุณาเขียนให้ได้ไหม? [khun ka ru na khian hai dai mai] Could you write it down, please?

เขียว [khiao] เขียวซอุ่ม [kheo cha um] *adj* lush; สีเขียว [sii khiao] *adj* green *(colour)*; สีเขียว [sii khiao] *adj* green

เขื่อน [khuean] *n* dam, embankment

แขก [khaek] แขกที่มาเยี่ยม [khaek thii ma yiam] *n* guest; การรับรองแขก [kan rap rong khaek] *n* hospitality

แข็ง [khaeng] *adj* firm, hard *(firm, rigid)*, solid, stiff

แข่ง [khaeng] สนามแข่ง [sa nam khaeng] *n* racecourse; สนามแข่งม้า [sa nam khaeng ma] *n* racehorse; การแข่งม้า [kan khaeng ma] *n* horse racing

แข็งแกร่ง [khaeng kraeng] ความทรหดอดทน ความแข็งแกร่งที่ยืนหยัดอยู่ได้นาน [khwam tho ra hot ot thon, khwam khaeng kraeng thii yuen yat yu dai nan] *n* stamina

แข่งขัน [khaeng khan] *v* compete; การแข่งขัน [kan khaeng khan] *n* competition, contest, match *(sport)*, rivalry, tournament; การแข่งขันรอบก่อนรองชนะเลิศ [kan khaeng khan ron kon rong cha na loet] *n* quarter final; การแข่งขันกีฬาานาชาติโดยเฉพาะกีฬาฟุตบอล [kan khaeng khan ki la na na chat doi cha po ki la fut ball] *n* World Cup

แข่งม้า [khaeng ma] ฉันอยากดูแข่งม้า [chan yak du khaeng ma] I'd like to see a horse race

แข่งเรือ [khaeng ruea] เราจะไปเล่นแข่งเรือได้ที่ไหน? [rao ja pai len khaeng ruea dai thii nai] Where can we go rowing?

แข็งแรง [khaeng raeng] *adj* strong; แข็งแรงขึ้น [khaeng raeng khuen] *v* strengthen

แขน [khaen] *n* arm; แขนสั้น [khaen san] *adj* short-sleeved; ฉันขยับแขนไม่ได้

[chan kha yap khaen mai dai] I can't move my arm

แขนเสื้อ [khaen suea] *n* sleeve; ไม่มีแขน เสื้อ [mai mii khaen suea] *adj* sleeveless

แขวน [khwaen] *v* suspend, hang; ไม้ แขวนเสื้อ [mai khwaen suea] *n* coathanger

โขมย [kha moi] การโขมย [kan kha moi] *n* theft

โขยกเขยก [kha yok kha yaek] เดินโขยก เขยก [doen kha yok kha yek] *v* limp

ไข [khai] ไขกุญแจ [khai kun jae] *v* unlock

ไข่ [khai] *n* egg; ไข่เจียว [khai chiao] *n* omelette; ไขแดง [khai daeng] *n* egg yolk, yolk; ไข่ขาว [khai khao] *n* egg white; คุณทำอาหารที่ไม่มีไข่ได้ไหม? [khun tham a han thii mai mii khai dai mai] Could you prepare a meal without eggs?

ไข้ [khai] ไข้มาลาเรีย [khai ma la ria] *n* malaria; ไข้ละอองฟาง [khai la ong fang] *n* hay fever; การเป็นไข้ [kan pen khai] *n* fever; เขามีไข้ [khao mii khai] He has a fever

ไขข้อ [khai kho] โรคไขข้ออักเสบ [rok khai kho ak sep] *n* rheumatism

ไขควง [khai khuang] *n* screwdriver

ไข่ดิบ [khai dip] ฉันทานไข่ดิบไม่ได้ [chan than khai dip mai dai] I can't eat raw eggs

ไขมัน [khai man] *n* fat; เป็นไขมันลื่น [pen khai man luen] *adj* greasy; ไขมันใน เส้นเลือด [khai man nai sen lueat] *n* cholesterol; ส่วนที่เป็นไขมันของนมซึ่ง ลอยขึ้นมาบนผิวนม [suan thii pen khai man khong nom sueng loi khuen ma bon phio nom] *n* cream

ไข่มุก [khai muk] *n* pearl

ไขรากสาดน้อย [khai rak sat noi] *n* typhoid

ไขว้เขว [khai kheo] ทำให้ไขว้เขว [tham hai khwai khwe] *v* distract

ไขสันหลัง [khai san lang] *n* spinal cord

ไข้หวัด [khai wat] ไข้หวัดใหญ่ [khai wat yai] *n* flu, influenza; ไข้หวัดนก [khai wat nok] *n* bird flu

ไข้หวัดใหญ่ [khai wat yai] ฉันเป็นไข้หวัด ใหญ่ [chan pen khai wat yai] I've got flu; ฉันเป็นไข้หวัดใหญ่เมื่อเร็ว ๆ นี้ [chan pen khai wat yai muea reo reo nii] I had flu recently

ด้านใดด้านหนึ่ง [khon thii mii chue siang nai dan dai dan nueng] *n* star (*person*); คนนำทาง [khon nam thang] *n* guide

คนไข้ [khon khai] ตึกคนไข้ [tuek khon khai] *n* ward (*hospital room*)

ค้นคว้า [khon kwa] การค้นคว้า [kan khon khwa] *n* research

คนงาน [khon ngan] *n* workman; คนงานเหมือง [khon ngan mueang] *n* miner

คนป่วย [khon puai] *n* patient

คนแปลกหน้า [khon plaek na] *n* stranger

ค้นพบ [khon phop] *v* discover, find out

คนพิการ [khon phi kan] มีห้องน้ำสำหรับคนพิการไหม? [mii hong nam sam rap khon phi kan mai] Are there any toilets for the disabled?; คุณมีเก้าอี้เข็นคนพิการไหม? [khun mii kao ii khen khon phi kan mai] Do you have wheelchairs?; คุณมีสิ่งอำนวยความสะดวกอะไรบ้างสำหรับคนพิการ? [khun mii sing am nuai khwam sa duak a rai bang sam rap khon phi kan] What facilities do you have for disabled people?

คนรับใช้ [khon rap chai] *n* servant

ค้นหา [khon ha] *v* search; ระบบการค้นหาทางโดยใช้ดาวเทียม [ra bop kan khon ha thang doi chai dao thiam] *abbr* GPS; การค้นหา [kan khon ha] *n* search; ค้นหาศัพท์หรือข้อมูล [khon ha sap rue kho mun] *v* look up

คม [khom] แหลม คม [laem, khom] *adj* sharp

ครบครัน [khrop khran] *adj* equipped

ครบถ้วน [khrop thuan] สิ่งที่ครบถ้วน [sing thii khrop thuan] *n* whole

ครบรอบ [krop rop] การครบรอบหนึ่งร้อยปี [kan khrop rop nueng roi pi] *n* centenary

ครรภ์ [khan] ทารกในครรภ์ [tha rok nai khan] *n* foetus

ครองชีพ [khrong chip] มาตรฐานการครองชีพ [mat tra than kan khrong

---

ก

คงอยู่ [khong yu] *adj* intact ▷ *v* remain; ที่ยังคงอยู่ [thii yang khong yu] *adj* persistent

คณะ [kha na] *n* party (*group*); กลุ่ม หมู่ คณะ [klum, moo ka na] *n* collective; คณะเดินทาง [kha na doen thang] *n* expedition; คณะลูกขุน [kha na luk khun] *n* jury

คณิตศาสตร์ [kha nit ta sat] *npl* mathematics; เกี่ยวกับคณิตศาสตร์ [kiao kap kha nit ta sat] *adj* mathematical; วิชาคณิตศาสตร์ [wi cha kha nit ta sat] *npl* maths

คด [khot] คดงอ [khot ngo] *adj* bent (*not straight*)

คดโกง [khot kong] การคดโกง [kan khot kong] *n* cheat

คดี [kha di] คดี กรณี [kha di, ko ra nii] *n* case

คติพจน์ [kha ti phot] *n* proverb

คน [khon] *n* human being ▷ *vt* stir; คนเก็บเงินบนรถประจำทาง [khon kep ngen bon rot pra cham thang] *n* bus conductor; คนเก็บขยะ [khon kep kha ya] *n* dustman; คนเดินหนังสือ [kon doen nang sue] *n* courier; คนที่มีชื่อเสียงใน

chip] n standard of living; ค่าครองชีพ [kha khrong chiip] n cost of living

ครอบครอง [khrop khrong] การครอบครอง [kan khrop khrong] n takeover

ครอบครัว [khrop khrua] n family, household; ที่ทำเองในครอบครัว [thii tham eng nai khrop khrua] adj home-made; ฉันมาที่นี่กับครอบครัว [chan ma thii ni kap khrob khrua] I'm here with my family

ครอบคลุม [khrop khlum] ที่ครอบคลุม [thii khrop khlum] adj comprehensive

ครอบงำ [khrop ngam] การครอบงำจิตใจ [kan khrop ngam jit jai] n obsession

ครั้ง [khrang] สองครั้ง [song khrang] adv twice

ครั้งแรก [khrang raek] นี่เป็นการเดินทางครั้งแรกของฉันที่จะไป... [ni pen kan doen thang khrang raek khong chan thii ja pai…] This is my first trip to…

ครั้งหนึ่ง [khrang nueng] adv once

ครัว [khrua] n kitchen; ครัวสำเร็จรูปที่สร้างติดไว้กับที่ [khrua sam ret rup thii sang tit wai kap thii] n fitted kitchen

คราง [khrang] v groan

คราด [khrat] n rake

คราบ [khrap] เป็นคราบ [pen khrap] v stain; คุณกำจัดคราบนี้ได้ไหม? [khun kam chat khrap nii dai mai] Can you remove this stain?; นี่คือคราบกาแฟ [ni khue khrap ka fae] This stain is coffee

คราบเปื้อน [khrap puean] น้ำยากำจัดคราบเปื้อน [nam ya kam chat khrab puean] n stain remover

คร่ำเคร่ง [khlam khleng] adj intensive

คริกเก็ต [khrik ket] กีฬาคริกเก็ต [ki la khrik ket] n cricket (game)

คริสต์ [khrit] สมาชิกของนิกายหนึ่งในศาสนาคริสต์ [sa ma chik khong ni kai nueng nai sat sa na kris] n Presbyterian; คริสต์ศาสนิกชน [khrit sat sa nik ka chon] n Christian

คริสต์มาส [kris mat] n Christmas, Xmas; ละครที่มีพื้นฐานมาจากเทพนิยายแสดงช่วง

คริสต์มาส [la khon thii mii phuen than chak thep ni yai sa daeng chuang khris mas] n pantomime; คืนก่อนวันคริสต์มาส [khuen kon wan khris mas] n Christmas Eve; ต้นคริสต์มาส [ton khris mas] n Christmas tree; เมอรี่คริสต์มาส [moe ri khris mas] Merry Christmas!

คริสต์ศักราช [khrit sak ka rat] AD; ตัวย่อของก่อนคริสต์ศักราช [tua yo khong kon khrit sak ka rat] abbr BC

คริสต์ศาสนา [khrit sat sa na] พระในคริสต์ศาสนา [phra nai khris sat sa na] n vicar

ครีม [khrim] n cream; ครีมโกนหนวด [khrim kon nuat] n shaving cream; ครีมหรือแป้งสีทาแก้ม [khrim rue paeng sii tha kaem] n blusher; ครีมกันแสงอาทิตย์ [khrim kan saeng a thit] n sunblock

ครีมนวด [khrim nuat] คุณขายครีมนวดไหม? [khun khai khrim nuat mai] Do you sell conditioner?

ครึ่ง [khrueng] adj half ▷ adv half; ครึ่งเทอม [khrueng thoem] n half-term; ครึ่งเวลา [khrueng we la] n half-time; ครึ่งราคา [khrueng ra kha] adj half-price; เวลาสองโมงครึ่ง [we la song mong khrueng] It's half past two

ครึ่งวงกลม [khueng wong klom] n semicircle

ครู [khru] n teacher; ครูใหญ่ [khru yai] n head (principal), headteacher; ครูสอนขับรถ [khru son khap rot] n driving instructor; ครูสอนนักเรียน [khru son nak rian] n schoolteacher; ฉันเป็นครู [chan pen khru] I'm a teacher

คฤหาสน์ [ka rue hat] คฤหาสน์หลังใหญ่ [kha rue hat lang yai] n stately home

คลอง [khlong] n canal

คล่องแคล่ว [khlong khlaeo] adj active; พูดหรือเขียนได้อย่างคล่องแคล่ว [phut rue khian dai yang klong khaeo] adj fluent

คลอด [khlot] การลาหยุดหลังคลอด [kan la yut lang khlot] n maternity leave; ฉัน

จะคลอดภายในห้าเดือน [chan ja khlot phai nai ha duen] I'm due in five months

คลอรีน [khlo rin] n chlorine

คลัง [khlang] คลังสินค้า [khlang sin kha] n stock

คลั่ง [khlang] คนคลั่ง [khon khlang] n maniac

คลั่งไคล้ [khlang khlai] adj devoted; ความคลั่งไคล้ [khwam khlang khlai] n mania; ผู้คลั่งไคล้ [phu khlang khlai] n fanatic

คลัทช์ [khlut] คลัทช์ในรถยนต์ [khlat nai rot yon] n clutch

คลับ [khlap] คลับวัยรุ่นที่จัดให้มีกิจกรรมเพื่อ ความบันเทิง [khlap wai run thii chat hai mii kit cha kam phuea khwam ban thoeng] n youth club; มีคลับดี ๆ อยู่ ที่ไหน? [mii khlap di di yu thii nai] Where is there a good club?

คลาน [khlan] v crawl

คลาย [khlai] คลายเกลียว [khlai kliao] v unscrew

คล้าย [khlai] v resemble

คล้ายคลึง [khlai khlueng] adj similar; ความคล้ายคลึง [khwam khlai khlueng] n resemblance, similarity

คลาสสิก [klat sik] adj classic

คลำ [khlam] v grope

คลินิค [kli nik] n clinic

คลิป [khlip] คลิปติดกระดาษ [khlip tit kra dat] n paperclip

คลี่ [khli] คลี่ออก [khlii ok] v unwind

คลื่น [khluen] n wave; คลื่นซึนามิเกิดจาก แผ่นดินไหวใต้ทะเล [khluen sue na mi koet chak phaen din wai tai tha le] n tsunami; คลื่นที่ซัดฝั่ง [khluen thii sat fang] n surf; ช่วงความยาวคลื่น [chuang khwam yao khluen] n wavelength

คลื่นไส้ [khluen sai] adj sick; อาการ คลื่นไส้ [a kan khluen sai] n nausea

คลุม [khlum] v cover

คลุมเครือ [khlum khluea] adj vague; พูด คลุมเครือ [phut khlum khruea] v waffle

ควบคุม [khuap khum] v contain, control; เข้าควบคุม [khao khuap khum] v take over; การควบคุม [kan khuap khum] n curb; การควบคุมดูแล [kan khuap khum du lae] n control

ควบม้า [khuap ma] v gallop; การควบม้า [kan khuap ma] n gallop

ควบรวม [khwuap ruam] การควบรวม [kan khuap ruam] n merger

ควัน [khwan] n smoke; ควันจากท่อไอเสีย [khwan chak tho ai sia] npl exhaust fumes; ควันพิษ [khwan phit] npl fumes

คว้า [khwa] v grasp, snatch

ความ [khwam] ความพยายาม [khwam pha ya yam] n effort

ความกดดัน [khwam kot dan] n pressure

ความคิด [khwam khit] n idea, thought; ในความคิดของ [nai khwam kit khong] prep considering; ความคิดสร้างสรรค์ [khwam kit sang san] n innovation; ความคิดหรือกิจกรรมที่สัมพันธ์กัน [khwam kit rue kit cha kam thii sam phan kan] n complex

ความคิดเห็น [khwam kit hen] n opinion, point, view; แสดงความคิดเห็น [sa daeng khwam kit hen] v comment; การแสดงความคิดเห็น คำวิจารณ์ [kan sa daeng khwam kit hen, kham wi chan] n commentary; การสำรวจความคิดเห็น [kan sam ruat khwam kit hen] n opinion poll

ความจริง [khwam ching] n reality, truth; ใกล้เคียงความจริง [klai khiang khwam ching] adj realistic; การพูดเกิน ความจริง [kan phut koen khwam ching] n exaggeration

ความจำ [khwam cham] n memory; การ์ดบันทึกความจำของคอมพิวเตอร์ [kat ban thuek khwam cham khong khom pio toe] n memory card

ความจุ [khwam chu] ความจุ ปริมาตร [khwam ju, pa ri mat] n volume

ความดัน [khwam dan] ความดันโลหิต

[khwam dan lo hit] *n* blood pressure; ความดันยางควรเป็นเท่าไร? [khwam dan yang khuan pen thao rai] What should the tyre pressure be?

ความบันเทิง [khwam ban thoeng] มีความบันเทิงอะไรบ้างที่นั่น? [mii khwam ban thoeng a rai bang thii nan] What entertainment is there?

ความเป็นเจ้าของ [khwam pen chao khong] *n* possession

ความเป็นอยู่ [kham pen yu] *n* living

ความผิด [khwam phit] *n* guilt; ผู้กระทำความผิด [phu kra tham khwam phit] *n* culprit

ความเย็น [khwam yen] *n* cold

ความร้อน [khwam ron] เครื่องอัตโนมัติสำหรับควบคุมความร้อน [khrueang at ta no mat sam rap khuap khum khwam ron] *n* thermostat; ระบบทำความร้อน [ra bop tham khwam ron] *n* central heating; อุณหภูมิความร้อนของโลกที่เพิ่มขึ้น [un ha phum khwam ron khong lok thii poem khuen] *n* global warming

ความรัก [khwam rak] *n* love

ความรู้ [khwam ru] *n* knowledge; ให้ความรู้ [hai khwam ru] *adj* informative; มีความรู้ [mii khwam ru] *adj* knowledgeable; ความรู้ทั่วไป [khwam ru thua pai] *n* general knowledge

ความรู้สึก [khwam ru suek] *n* emotion, feeling, sense; ไม่แสดงอารมณ์และความรู้สึก [mai sa daeng a rom lae khwam ru suek] *adj* reserved; ความรู้สึกหมดแรงและสูญเสียทิศทางเพราะการเดินทางระหว่างเวลาที่ต่างกัน [khwam ru suek mot raeng lae sun sia thit thang phro kan doen thang ra wang we la thii tang kan] *n* jet lag; ความรู้สึกผิดชอบชั่วดี [khwam ru suek phit chop chua dii] *n* conscience

ความเร็ว [khwam reo] *n* speed; แผ่นที่บอกอัตราความเร็ว [phaeng thii bok at tra khwam reo] *n* speedometer; การ

เพิ่มความเร็ว [kan poem khwam reo] *n* acceleration; อัตราความเร็ว [at tra khwam reo] *n* speed limit, speeding

ความแรง [khwam raeng] ความแรงไฟฟ้าเท่าไร? [khwam raeng fai fa thao rai] What's the voltage?

ความลับ [khwam lap] *n* secret; เป็นความลับ [pen khwam lap] *adj* secret; ที่เป็นความลับ [thii pen khwam lap] *adj* confidential

ความสะอาด [khwam sa ad] เราต้องทำความสะอาดบ้านก่อนออกไปไหม? [rao tong tham khwam sa at baan kon ok pai mai] Do we have to clean the house before we leave?; ฉันจะทำความสะอาดได้ที่ไหน? [chan ja tham khwam sa aat dai thii nai] Where can I get this cleaned?; ฉันอยากทำความสะอาดเสื้อผ้าพวกนี้ [chan yak tham khwam sa aat suea pha phuak nii] I'd like to get these things cleaned

ความสัมพันธ์ทางเพศ [khwam sam phan thang phet] การมีความสัมพันธ์ทางเพศ [kan mii khwam sam phan thang phet] *n* sexual intercourse

ความสามารถ [khwam sa mat] ไม่มีความสามารถ [mai mii khwam sa mat] *adj* incompetent; ความสามารถทางจิต [khwam sa mat thang chit] *n* mentality

ความสามารถพิเศษ [khwam sa mat phi set] *n* talent; ซึ่งมีความสามารถพิเศษ [sueng mii khwam sa maat phi set] *adj* talented

ความหมาย [khwam mai] *n* meaning

ความหลัง [khwam lang] สิ่งเตือนความหลัง [sing tuean khwam lang] *n* reminder

ความเห็น [khwam hen] ซึ่งลงความเห็นแล้ว [sueng long khwam hen laeo] *adj* decisive; ทัศนคติ ความเห็น [that sa na kha ti, khwam hen] *n* attitude

คว่ำ [khwam] *v* capsize

คอ [kho] *n* neck, throat

ค็อกเทล [kok tel] คุณขายค็อกเทลไหม? [khun khai khok then mai] Do you sell cocktails?

คอกม้า [khok ma] n stable

คอเคเซีย [kho khe sia] เทือกเขาในคอเคเซีย [thueak khao nai kho khe chia] n Caucasus

คองโก [khong ko] ประเทศคองโก [pra tet khong ko] n Congo

คูอด [khot] ปลาคอด [pla khot] n cod

ค้อน [khon] n hammer

คอนกรีต [khon krit] n concrete

ค่อนข้าง [khon khang] adv rather

ค่อนข้างจะ [khon khang cha] adv quite

คอนแทคเลนส์ [kon thak len] ฉันใส่ คอนแทคเลนส์ [chan sai khon thaek len] I wear contact lenses; น้ำยาล้าง คอนแทคเลนส์ [nam ya lang khon thaek len] cleansing solution for contact lenses

คอนแท็คเลนส์ [khon taek len] npl contact lenses

คอนเสิรต [kon soet] n concert; มีการ แสดงคอนเสิร์ตดี ๆ บางไหม? [mii kan sa daeng khon soet di di bang mai] Are there any good concerts on?; คืนนี้มีการ แสดงอะไรที่หอแสดงคอนเสิร์ต? [khuen nii mii kan sa daeng a rai thii ho sa daeng khon soet] What's on tonight at the concert hall?; ฉันจะซื้อตั๋วคอนเสิร์ตได้ที่ ไหน? [chan ja sue tua khon soet dai thii nai] Where can I buy tickets for the concert?

คอมพิวเตอร์ [kom pio toe] เกมส์ คอมพิวเตอร์ [kem khom phio toe] n computer game; เครื่องคอมพิวเตอร์ [khrueang khom phio toe] n computer; เครื่องคอมพิวเตอร์ส่วนตัว [khrueang khom phio toe suan tua] n PC; คอมพิวเตอร์ฉันไม่ทำงาน [khom phio toe chan mai tham ngan] My computer has frozen

คอมมิวนิสต์ [khom mio nit] n communist; เกี่ยวกับคอมมิวนิสต์ [kiao

kap khom mio nis] adj communist; ระบบคอมมิวนิสต์ [ra bop khom mio nis] n communism

คอย [khoi] v hang on; รอคอย [ro khoi] v wait for, wait up

ค่อยเป็นค่อยไป [khoi pen phoi pai] adj gradual; อย่างค่อยเป็นค่อยไป [yang khoi pen khoi pai] adv gradually

คอสโซโว [kot so wo] ประเทศคอสโซโว [pra tet kos so vo] n Kosovo

คอสตาริกา [kot sa ta ri ka] ประเทศคอสตา ริก้า [pra tet kos ta ri ka] n Costa Rica

คะแนน [kha naen] n mark, score (game/ match); การให้คะแนน [kan hai kha naen] v mark (grade); คะแนนเท่ากัน [kha naen thao kan] v draw (tie); ทำคะแนน [tham kha naen] v score

คัดค้าน [khat khan] ความรู้สึกคัดค้าน [khwam ru suek khat khan] n objection

คัดเลือก [khat lueak] v elect; การคัดเลือก [kan khat lueak] n selection

คัน [khan] v itch; มีอาการคัน [mii a kan khan] adj itchy; คันบังคับเครื่องบิน [khan bang khap khrueang bin] n joystick; ขาฉันคัน [kha chan khan] My leg itches

คันเบ็ด [khan bet] n fishing rod

คันเร่ง [khan reng] n accelerator

คับ [khap] คับแน่น [khap naen] adj tight

คัมภีร์ [kham phi] คัมภีร์โกหร่าน [kham phii ko ran] n Koran; คัมภีร์ไบเบิล [kham phii bai boen] n Bible

คัสตาร์ด [cus tat] n custard

ค่า [kha] การลดค่าเงิน [kan lot kha ngen] n devaluation; ค่าเล่าเรียน [kha lao rian] npl tuition fees; ค่าเข้า [kha khao] n entrance fee; เก็บค่าระยะการเดินทาง ไหม? [kep kha ra ya kan doen thang mai] Is there a mileage charge?

ค่าขาย [kha khai] การค้าขาย [kan ka khai] n trade

ค่าเข้า [kha khao] ต้องเสียค่าเข้าเท่าไรเพื่อ เข้าข้างใน? [tong sia kha khao thao rai phuea khao khang nai] How much does it cost to get in?

คาง [khang] n chin, shin

ค้าง [khang] เงินค้างชำระ [ngoen kang cham ra] npl arrears; เราตั้งค่ายค้างคืนที่ นี่ได้ไหม? [rao tang khai khang khuen thii ni dai mai] Can we camp here overnight?; ฉันต้องนอนค้างคืนไหม? [chan tong non khang khuen mai] Do I have to stay overnight?

ค้างคก [khang khok] n toad

ค้างคาว [khang khao] n bat (mammal)

ค้างคืน [khang khuen] ฉันจอดค้างคืนที่นี่ ได้ไหม? [chan jot khang khuen thii ni dai mai] Can I park here overnight?

คางทูม [khang thum] โรคคางทูม [rok khang thum] n mumps

ค่าจอง [kha chong] มีค่าจองหรือไม่? [mii kha chong rue mai] Is there a booking fee?

ค่าจ้าง [kha chang] n wage; ไม่ได้ค่าจ้าง [mai dai kha chang] adj unpaid; ได้รับ ค่าจ้างน้อยไป [dai rap kha chang noi pai] adj underpaid; ค่าจ้างในระหว่างที่ลา ป่วย [kha chang nai ra wang thii la puai] n sick pay

ค่าเช่า [kha chao] ค่าเช่าสนามเทนนิสเป็น จำนวนเท่าใด? [kha chao sa nam then nis pen cham nuan thao dai] How much is it to hire a tennis court?

ค่าใช้จ่าย [kha chai chai] ค่าใช้จ่ายใน การดำเนินธุรกิจ [kha chai chai nai kan dam noen thu ra kit] npl overheads; ช่วยกันออกค่าใช้จ่าย [chuai kan ok kha chai jai] v club together

คาซัคสถาน [kha sak sa than] ประเทศคา ซักสถาน [pra tet kha sak sa than na] n Kazakhstan

คาด [khat] คาดว่า [khat wa] v expect

คาดคะเน [khat kha ne] v guess; การคาด คะเน [kan khat kha ne] n guess

คาดคิด [khat khit] ไม่คาดคิดมาก่อน [mai khat kit ma kon] adj unexpected; อย่าง ไม่คาดคิดมาก่อน [yang mai khat kit ma kon] adv unexpectedly

คาดหวัง [khat wang] โดยคาดหวังสิ่งที่ดี [doi khat wang sing thii di] adj optimistic

คาถา [kha tha] มนตร์คาถา [mon kha tha] n spell (magic)

คาทอลิค [ka tho lik] นิกายคาทอลิค [ni kai kha tho lik] adj Catholic; ผู้นับถือ นิกายคาทอลิค [phu nap thue ni kai kha tho lik] n Catholic

ค่าธรรมเนียม [kha tham niam] ค่า ธรรมเนียมในการเข้า [kha tham niam nai kan khao] n admission charge; ค่า ธรรมเนียมธนาคาร [kha tham niam tha na khan] npl bank charges

คานรับน้ำหนัก [khan rap nam nak] ลำแสง, คานรับน้ำหนัก รอยยิ้มกว้าง [lam saeng, khan rap nam nak, roi yim kwang] n beam

ค่าบริการ [kha bo ri kan] มีค่าบริการเพิ่ม จากค่าอาหารหรือไม่? [mii kha bo ri kan poem chak kha a han rue mai] Is there a cover charge?; รวมค่าบริการหรือเปล่า? [ruam kha bo ri kan rue plao] Is service included?

ค่าบสมุทร [khap sa mut] n peninsula

ค่าปรับ [kha prup] ค่าปรับเท่าไร? [kha prap thao rai] How much is the fine?; ฉันจ่ายค่าปรับที่ไหน? [chan chai kha prap thii nai] Where do I pay the fine?

คาเฟ่ [kha fe] อินเตอร์เนตคาเฟ่ [in ter net kha fe] n cybercafé

คาเฟอีน [kha fe in] สารคาเฟอีน [san kha fe in] n caffeine; ที่ไม่มีคาเฟอีน [thii mai mii kha fe in] adj decaffeinated

ค่าไฟ [kha fai] เราต้องจ่ายค่าไฟเพิ่มไหม? [rao tong chai kha fai poem mai] Do we have to pay extra for electricity?; รวมค่าไฟด้วยหรือไม่? [ruam kha fai duai rue mai] Is the cost of electricity included?

ค่าย [khai] n camp; ไปค่าย [pai khai] v camp; การไปค่าย [kan pai khai] n camping; ชาวค่าย [chao khai] n camper

คาร์เนชั่น [kha ne chan] ดอกคาร์เนชั่น [dok kha ne chan] *n* carnation

คาร์บอน [kha bon] *n* carbon; คาร์บอนที่แต่ละคนใช้ในชีวิตประจำวันส่งไปในบรรยากาศของโลก [kha bon thii tae la khon chai nai chi wid pra cham wan song pai nai ban ya kat khong lok] *n* carbon footprint

คาร์โบไฮเดรท [ka bo hai dret] *n* carbohydrate

คาราเต้ [kha ra te] มวยคาราเต้ [muai kha ra te] *n* karate

คาราเมล [ka ra mel] *n* caramel

คาราวาน [kha ra wan] รถคาราวาน [rot kha ra van] caravan; ที่จอดรถคาราวาน [thii jot rot kha ra wan] *n* caravan site; เราจอดรถคาราวานของเราที่นี่ได้ไหม? [rao jot rot kha ra van khong rao thii ni dai mai] Can we park our caravan here?

ค่าแลก [kha laek] ค่าแลกเท่าไร? [kha laek thao rai] What's the commission?; คุณเก็บค่าแลกไหม? [khun kit kha laek mai] Do you charge commission?

คาวบอย [khao boi] *n* cowboy

ค่าโอน [kha on] มีค่าโอนไหม? [mii kha on mai] Is there a transfer charge?

คำ [kham] *n* word; คำแนะนำสั่งสอน [kham nae nam sang son] *npl* instructions; คำกำกับนามที่ขึ้นต้นด้วยสระ [kham kam kap nam thii khuen ton duai sa ra] *art* an; คำขอร้อง [kham kho rong] *n* appeal; คำเดียวทั้งหมด [kham diao thang mot] all one word

คำกริยา [kham ka ri ya] *n* verb

คำขาด [kham khat] *n* ultimatum

คำตอบ [kham top] *n* reply, response; คำตอบที่แก้ปัญหา [kham top thii kae pan ha] *n* solution

คำถาม [kham tham] *n* query, question; ตัวย่อของคำถามที่ถามบ่อย ๆ [tua yo khong kham tham thii tham boi boi] *abbr* FAQ

คำนวณ [kham nuan] *v* calculate; การคำนวณ [kan kham nuan] *n* calculation; คิดคำนวณ [khit kham nuan] *v* figure out

คำนับ [kham nap] *v* bow, salute

คำแปล [kham plae] คำแปลที่เขียนไว้ข้างล่างในภาพยนตร์ [kham plae thii khian wai khang lang nai phap pa yon] *npl* subtitles; ที่มีคำแปลเขียนไว้ข้างล่างในภาพยนตร์ [thii mii kham plae khian wai khang lang nai phap pha yon] *adj* subtitled

คำพูด [kham phut] คำพูดหรือข้อเขียนที่แสดงเชาวน์ปัญญา [kham phut rue kho khian thii sa daeng chao pan ya] *n* wit; ซึ่งใช้คำพูดอย่างมีสติปัญญาและตลก [sueng chai kham phut yang mii sa ti pan ya lae ta lok] *adj* witty

คำศัพท์ [kham sap] *n* vocabulary; ซอฟต์แวร์ของคอมพิวเตอร์ที่ใช้สำหรับตรวจคำศัพท์ [sop wae khong khom phio toe thii chai sam rap truat kham sap] *n* spellchecker

คำสอน [kham son] คำสอนของพระเยซู [kham son khong phra ye su] *n* gospel

คำสั่ง [kham sang] *n* command, order; คำสั่งห้าม [kham sang ham] *n* ban

คำสุภาพ [kham su phap] คำสุภาพสำหรับเรียกผู้ชาย [kham su phap sam rap riak phu chai] *n* sir

คำอุทาน [kham u than] คำอุทานแสดงความรังเกียจหรือไม่พอใจ [kham u than sa daeng khwam rang kiat rue mai pho jai] *excl* ugh

คิด [khit] *v* think; แก้ปัญหาหรือวางแผนโดยการคิดไตร่ตรอง [kae pan ha rue wang phaen doi kan kit trai trong] *v* work out; มีอยู่แต่ในความนึกคิด [mii yu tae nai khwam nuek kit] *adj* imaginary; คิดเกินราคา [khit koen ra kha] *v* overcharge

คิดถึง [khit thueng] คิดถึงบ้าน [khit thueng baan] *adj* homesick; ที่คิดถึงความคิดของผู้อื่น [thii kit thueng khwam kit khong phu uen] *adj* considerate

คิดเห็น [khit hen] ข้อคิดเห็น [kho khit hen] *n* comment

คิปเปอร์ [kip poe] ปลาคิปเปอร์ [pla khip poe] *n* kipper

คิว [khio] เข้าคิว [khao khio] *v* queue

คิ้ว [khwio] *n* eyebrow

คิวบา [khio ba] เกี่ยวกับประเทศคิวบา [kiao kap pra thet khio ba] *adj* Cuban; ชาวคิวบา [chao khio ba] *n* Cuban; ประเทศคิวบา [pra tet khio ba] *n* Cuba

คีม [khim] *npl* pliers

คื่นช่าย [khuen chai] ผักคื่นช่าย [phak khuen chai] *n* celery

คืน [khuen] เงินที่จ่ายคืน [ngoen thii chai khuen] *n* repayment; ให้คืน [hai khuen] *v* give back; ใช้เงินคืน [chai ngoen khuen] *v* reimburse; คืนละเท่าไร? [khuen la thao rai] How much is it per night?

คืนนี้ [khuen ni] *adv* tonight

คือ [khue] เป็น อยู่ คือ [pen, yu, khue] *v* be; ตัวย่อของคือ [tua yo khong khue] *abbr* i.e.

คุก [khuk] *n* jail; คุกใต้ดินในปราสาท [khuk tai din nai pra sat] *n* dungeon; ผู้ถูกกักขังในคุก [phu thuk kak khang nai khuk] *n* inmate

คุกเข่า [khuk khao] *v* kneel; คุกเข่าลง [khuk khao long] *v* kneel down

คุกคาม [khuk kham] ข่มขู่คุกคาม [khom khu khuk kham] *v* intimidate

คุณ [khun] *pron* you (*singular*); ตัวคุณเอง [tua khun eng] *pron* yourself (*intensifier*); ตัวคุณเอง [tua khun eng] *pron* yourself; แล้วคุณล่ะ? [laeo khun la] And you?

คุณค่า [khun kha] *n* value; มีคุณค่าที่น่าสังเกต [mii khun kha thii na sang ket] *adj* remarkable; คนที่ไม่มีคุณค่า [khon thii mai mii khun kha] *n* punk; ที่ไม่มีคุณค่า [thii mai mii khun kha] *adj* worthless

คุณภาพ [khun na phap] *n* quality

คุณลักษณะ [khun na lak sa na] *n* character

คุณสมบัติ [khun na som bat] *n* qualification; ไม่มีคุณสมบัติ [mai mii khun som bat] *adj* unfit; มีคุณสมบัติ [mii khun som bat] *v* qualify; ที่มีคุณสมบัติ [thii mii khun na som bat] *adj* qualified

คุ้นเคย [khun khoei] *adj* familiar; ไม่รู้จักคุ้นเคย [mai ru chak khun khoei] *adj* unfamiliar

คุม [khum] ผู้คุมสอบ [phu khum sob] *n* invigilator

คุ้มกัน [khum kan] คนคุ้มกัน [khon khum kan] *n* bodyguard

คุมกำเนิด [khum kam noet] การคุมกำเนิด [kan khum kam noet] *n* birth control; การคุมกำเนิด [kan khum kam noet] *n* contraception; ยาหรือสิ่งที่ใช้คุมกำเนิด [ya rue sing thii chai khum kham noet] *n* contraceptive

คุ้มครอง [khum khrong] การคุ้มครอง [kan khum khrong] *v* custody, escort

คุย [khui] ห้องคุย [hong khui] *n* chatroom; การพูดคุยกันเล่น ๆ [kan phut khui kan len len] *v* chat; คุยเล่น [khui len] *v* chat

คู [khu] *n* trench; คูน้ำ [khu nam] *n* ditch; คูน้ำรอบปราสาทหรือเมือง [khu nam rop pra saat rue mueang] *n* moat

คู่ [khu] *n* couple, pair; ห้องคู่ [hong khu] *n* twin room; คู่สมรส [khu som rot] *n* partner; คู่ต่อสู้ [khu to su] *n* adversary

คู่กันกับ [khu kan kap] *prep* along

คู่แข่ง [khu khaeng] *n* rival; ที่เป็นคู่แข่งกัน [thii pen khu khaeng kan] *adj* rival

คูณ [khun] *v* multiply; การคูณ [kan khun] *n* multiplication

คู่มือ [khu mue] หนังสือคู่มือ [nang sue khu mue] *n* handbook, manual

คู่รัก [khu rak] *n* lover

คูเวต [khu wet] เกี่ยวกับคูเวต [kiao kap khu wet] *adj* Kuwaiti; ชาวคูเวต [chao khu wet] *n* Kuwaiti; ประเทศคูเวต [pra tet khu wet] *n* Kuwait

คู่หมั้น [khu man] คู่หมั้นหญิง [khu man ying] n fiancée; คู่หมั้นชาย [khu man chai] n fiancé

เค้ก [khek] เค้กชั้นก้อนใหญ่ [khek chan kon yai] n gateau; เค้กที่ฟู [khek thii fu] n sponge (cake); ขนมเค้ก [kha nom khek] n cake

เคนยา [ken ya] จากเคนยา [chak ken ya] adj Kenyan; ชาวเคนยา [chao ken ya] n Kenyan; ประเทศเคนยา [pra tet ken ya] n Kenya

เคบิน [khe bin] ห้องเคบิน [hong khe bin] n cabin; ห้องเคบินหมายเลข 5 อยู่ที่ไหน? [hong khe bin mai lek ha yu thii nai] Where is cabin number five?

เคเบิล [khe boen] โทรทัศน์ที่รับระบบการส่งสัญญาณด้วยสารเคเบิล [tho ra tat thii rap ra bop kan song san yan duai sai khe boen] n cable television; รถที่เคลื่อนที่โดยสายเคเบิล [rot thii khluean thii doi sai khe boen] n cable car

เคเบิ้ล [khe boen] สายเคเบิ้ล [sai khe boel] n cable

เค็ม [khem] เกี่ยวกับน้ำเค็ม [kiao kap nam khem] adj saltwater; ซึ่งมีรสเค็ม [sueng mii rot khem] adj salty; อาหารเค็มเกินไป [a han khem koen pai] The food is too salty

เคมี [khe mi] วิชาเคมี [wi cha ke mii] n chemistry

เคย [khoei] คุณเคยไปที่...ไหม? [khun khoei pai thii…mai] Have you ever been to...?; ฉันไม่เคยไป... [chan mai khoei pai…] I've never been to...; ฉันไม่เคยดื่มไวน์ [chan mai khoei duem wine] I never drink wine

เคยชิน [khoei chin] ความเคยชิน [khwam khoei chin] n habit

เคร่งขรึม [khreng khruem] adj grim, serious

เคร่งครัด [khreng khrat] adj stark; ความเคร่งครัด [khwam khreng khrat] n austerity; อย่างเคร่งครัด [yang khreng khrat] adv strictly

เครดิต [khre dit] บัตรเครดิต [bat khre dit] n credit card

เครา [khrao] n beard; เคราแข็งสองข้างปาก [khrao khaeng song khang pak] npl whiskers; ที่เต็มไปด้วยหนวดเครา [thii tem pai duai nuat khrao] adj bearded

เคราะห์ร้าย [khro rai] ผู้เคราะห์ร้าย [phu khrao rai] n victim; อย่างเคราะห์ร้าย [yang khrao rai] adv unfortunately

เครียด [khriat] v stress; ความเครียด [khwam khriat] n stress

เครือ [khruea] กลุ่ม พวง รวง เครือ [klum, phuang, ruang, khruea] n bunch

เครือข่าย [khruea khai] n network, Net; เครือข่ายคอมพิวเตอร์ทั่วโลก ๒ [khruea khai khom phio toe thua lok song] Web 2.0; ระบบเครือข่ายที่ใช้ประโยชน์ของเทคโนโลยีของอินเตอร์เน็ต [ra bop khruea khai thii chai pra yot khong thek no lo yii khong in toe net] n intranet; ฉันไม่ได้รับเครือข่าย [chan mai dai rap khruea khai] I can't get a network

เครื่อง [khrueang] เครื่องเล่นซีดี [khrueang len si di] n CD player; เครื่องเล่นดีวีดี [khrueang len di vi di] n DVD player; เครื่องเป่า [khrueang pao] n dryer; เครื่องขยายเสียง [khrueang kha yai siang] n amplifier; เครื่องจักร [khrueang chak] n machine, machinery; เครื่องที่ต่อกับทีวีใช้เล่นวิดีโอเกมส์ [khrueang thii to kap thii wii chai len vi di o kem] n games console; เครื่องฟังดนตรีเอ็มพี ๔ [khrueang fang don trii em phi si] n MP4 player

เครื่องเขียน [khrueang khian] n stationery; ร้านขายเครื่องเขียน [ran khai khrueang khian] n stationer's

เครื่องคิดเลข [khrueang kit lek] เครื่องคิดเลขฉบับกระเป๋า [khrueang kit lek cha bap kra pao] n pocket calculator

เครื่องจักร [khrueang chak] ผู้ควบคุมเครื่องจักร [phu khuap khum khrueang chak] n operator

เครื่องฉาย [khrueang chai] เครื่องฉาย

แผ่นใสสไลด์ [khrueang chai phaen sa lai]
n projector

เครื่องฉายภาพ [khrueang chai phap]
เครื่องฉายภาพบนผนังหรือจอ [khrueang
chai phap bon pha nang rue cho] n
overhead projector

เครื่องช่วยฟัง [khrueang chuai fang]
ฉันมีเครื่องช่วยฟัง [chan mii khrueang
chuai fang] I have a hearing aid

เครื่องชั่ง [khrueang chang] npl scales

เครื่องใช้ [khrueang chai] n appliance;
เครื่องใช้ในห้องน้ำ เช่น สบู่ ยาสระผม
ยาสีฟัน เป็นต้น [khrueang chai nai hong
nam chen sa bu ya sa phom ya sii fan
pen ton] npl toiletries

เครื่องซักผ้า [khrueang sak pha] n
washing machine; เครื่องซักผ้านี้ทำงาน
อย่างไร? [khrueang sak pha nii tham
ngan yang rai] How does the washing
machine work?; เครื่องซักผ้าอยู่ที่ไหน?
[khrueang sak pha yu thii nai] Where
are the washing machines?

เครื่องดนตรี [khrueang don tri] n
musical instrument; เครื่องดนตรีชนิด
หนึ่งคล้ายไวโอลินแต่มีขนาดใหญ่กว่าและมี
เสียงต่ำกว่า [khrueang don tri cha nit
nueng khlai wai o lin tae mii kha naat
yai kwa lae mii siang tam kwa] n viola;
เครื่องดนตรีประเภทเป่า [khrueang don tri
pra phet pao] n woodwind; เครื่องดนตรี
ประเภทเป่าชนิดหนึ่ง [khrueang don tri
pra phet pao cha nit nueng] n clarinet,
oboe

เครื่องดื่ม [khrueang duem] n drink;
เครื่องดื่มเหล้าผสมน้ำผลไม้ [khrueang
duem lao pha som nam phon la mai] n
cocktail; เครื่องดื่มซึ่งไม่ใช่เหล้า
[khrueang duem sueng mai chai lao] n
soft drink; เครื่องดื่มที่มีแอลกอฮอล์
[khrueang duem thii mii aen ko ho] n
booze; คุณมีเครื่องดื่มไม่มีแอลกอฮอล์อะไร
บ้าง? [khun mii khrueang duem mai
mii aen ko ho a rai bang] What
non-alcoholic drinks do you have?

เครื่องดูดฝุ่น [khrueang dut fun] n
vacuum cleaner

เครื่องแต่งกาย [khrueang taeng kai] n
dress

เครื่องถ้วยชาม [khrueang thuai cham]
เราอยากได้เครื่องถ้วยชามเพิ่มอีก [rao yak
dai khrueang thuai cham poem ik] We
need more crockery

เครื่องทำความร้อน [khrueang tham
khwam ron] เครื่องทำความร้อนไม่ทำงาน
[khrueang tham khwam ron mai
tham ngan] The heating doesn't work;
ฉันเปิดเครื่องทำความร้อนไม่ได้ [chan poet
khrueang tham khwam ron mai dai] I
can't turn the heating on; ฉันปิดเครื่อง
ทำความร้อนไม่ได้ [chan pit khrueang
tham khwam ron mai dai] I can't turn
the heating off

เครื่องทำน้ำร้อน [khrueang tham
khwam ron] เครื่องทำน้ำร้อนทำงาน
อย่างไร? [khrueang tham nam ron
tham ngan yang rai] How does the
water heater work?

เครื่องเทศ [khrueang thet] n spice;
เครื่องเทศสีแดงอ่อนใส่อาหาร [khrueang
tet sii daeng on sai a han] n paprika

เครื่องโทรสาร [khrueang thro ra san] มี
เครื่องโทรสารที่ฉันจะใช้ได้ไหม? [mii
khrueang tho ra san thii chan ja chai
dai mai] Is there a fax machine I can
use?; คุณมีเครื่องโทรสารไหม? [khun mii
khrueang tho ra san mai] Do you have
a fax?

เครื่องนอน [khrueang non] n bedding

เครื่องบิน [khrueang bin] n aircraft,
plane (aeroplane); เรือหรือเครื่องบินที่เดิน
ทางประจำเส้นทาง [ruea rue khrueang
bin thii doen thang pra cham sen
thang] n liner; เครื่องบินเจ็ท [khrueang
bin chet] n jet; เครื่องบินเจ็ทขนาดใหญ่
มาก [khrueang bin chet kha nat yai
mak] n jumbo jet; เครื่องบินฉันออกจาก...
[khrueang bin chan ok chak...] My
plane leaves at...

เครื่องเบิกเงิน [khrueang bek ngoen] เครื่องเบิกเงินกลืนการ์ดฉันไป [khrueang boek ngoen kluen kat chan pai] The cash machine swallowed my card

เครื่องแบบ [khrueang baep] n uniform; เครื่องแบบนักเรียน [khrueang baep nak rian] n school uniform

เครื่องประดับ [khrueang pra dap] n accessory, ornament

เครื่องปรับอากาศ [khrueang prap a kat] เครื่องปรับอากาศไม่ทำงาน [khrueang prap a kat mai tham ngan] The air conditioning doesn't work

เครื่องปั่น [khrueang pan] เครื่องปั่นผ้าให้ แห้ง [khrueang pan pha hai haeng] n spin dryer

เครื่องปั้นดินเผา [khrueang pan din phao] n pottery

เครื่องปั๊ม [khrueang pum] n pump

เครื่องปิ้ง [khrueang ping] เครื่องปิ้ง ขนมปัง [khrueang ping kha nom pang] n toaster

เครื่องเป่าผม [khrueang pao phom] ฉัน อยากได้เครื่องเป่าผม [chan yak dai khrueang pao phom] I need a hair dryer

เครื่องพิมพ์ [khrueang phim] n printer (machine); มีเครื่องพิมพ์สีไหม? [mii khrueang phim sii mai] Is there a colour printer?

เครื่องพิมพ์ดีด [khrueang phim dit] n typewriter

เครื่องมือ [khrueang mue] n apparatus, equipment, tool; เครื่องมือที่ใช้ในการขุด [khrueang mue thii chai nai kan khut] n digger; ชุดเครื่องมือ [chut khrueang mue] n kit

เครื่องยนต์ [khrueang yon] n motor; ช่าง เครื่องยนต์ [chang khrueang yon] n motor mechanic

เครื่องเรือน [khrueang ruean] n furniture; ซึ่งมีเครื่องเรือนพร้อม [sueng mii khrueang ruean phrom] adj furnished

เครื่องส่งเสียง [khrueang song siang] มี

เครื่องส่งเสียงไหม? [mii khrueang song siang mai] Is there an induction loop?

เครื่องสำอาง [khrueang sam ang] npl cosmetics; ที่ร้านขายยาหรือเครื่องสำอาง [thii ran khai ya rue khrueang sam ang] n chemist('s)

เครื่องสำอาง [khrueang sam ang] n make-up; เครื่องสำอางใช้ทาขนตา [khrueang sam ang chai tha khon ta] n mascara

เครื่องหมาย [khrueang mai] n tick; เข็ม เครื่องหมาย [khem khrueang mai] n badge; เครื่องหมาย : [khrueang mai:] n colon; เครื่องหมาย มักใช้ในคอมพิวเตอร์ [khrueang mai mak chai nai khom phio toe] n backslash; ฉันหา เครื่องหมาย@ ไม่ได้ [chan ha khrueang mai @ mai dai] I can't find the @ sign

เครื่องหมายการค้า [khrueang mai kan kha] n trademark

เครื่องหมาย คำถาม [khrueang mai kham tham] เครื่องหมายคำถาม [khrueang mai kham tham] n question mark

เครื่องหยอดเหรียญ [khrueang yot rian] เครื่องหยอดเหรียญสำหรับเล่นพนัน [khrueang yot rian sam rap len pha nan] n slot machine

เครื่องอบ [khrueang op] เครื่องอบผ้าให้ แห้ง [khrueang op pha hai haeng] n tumble dryer

เครือญาติ [khruea yat] n relative

เคล็ด [khlet] ทำให้เคล็ด [tham hai khlet] v sprain; อาการเคล็ด [a kan khlet] n sprain

เคลื่อน [khluean] เคลื่อน เปลี่ยนตำแหน่ง [khluean plian tam naeng] vi move; เคลื่อนไปข้างหน้า [khluean pai khang na] v move forward; เคลื่อนไปด้านข้าง [khluean pai dan khang] adv sideways

เคลื่อนที่ [khluean thi] เคลื่อนที่อย่างเสียง ดัง [khluean thii yang siang dang] vi crash; ขบวนที่เคลื่อนที่ไป [kha buan thii khluean thii pai] n procession; ที่

เคลื่อนที่ได้ [thii khluean thii dai] *adj* removable

เคลื่อนย้าย [khluean yai] *v* remove, shift; เคลื่อนย้ายจากที่หนึ่งไปอีกที่หนึ่ง [khluean yai chak thii nueng pai ik thii nueng] *adj* migrant; การเคลื่อนย้าย [kan khluean yai] *n* removal; การเคลื่อนย้าย การย้าย [kan khluean yai, kan yai] *n* shift

เคลื่อนไหว [khlluean wai] เคลื่อนไหวไม่ได้ [khluean wai mai dai] *adj* paralysed; เคลื่อนไหวช้ากว่าผู้อื่น [khluean wai cha kwa phu uen] *v* lag behind; ไม่มีการเคลื่อนไหว [mai mii kan khluean wai] *adj* motionless; เธอเคลื่อนไหวไม่ได้ [thoe khluean wai mai dai] She can't move

เคลือบ [khueap] เครื่องเคลือบดินเผา [khrueang khlueap din phao] *n* china; สิ่งเคลือบ [sing khlueap] *n* enamel

เคอร์ฟิว [koe fio] มีเคอร์ฟิวไหม? [mii khoe fio mai] Is there a curfew?

เคาน์เตอร์ [kao toe] *n* counter; เคาน์เตอร์ที่ขายของ [khao toe thii khai khong] *npl* stands

เคารพ [khao rop] *v* respect; เป็นที่เคารพบูชา [pen thii khao rop bu cha] *adj* holy; ความเคารพ [khwam khao rop] *n* respect; ความเคารพนบนอบที่เป็นผลมาจากความสำเร็จ [khwam khao rop nop nop thii pen phon ma chak khwam sam ret] *n* prestige

เคารพนับถือ [khao rom nap thue] ซึ่งเป็นที่เคารพนับถือ [sueng pen thii khao rop nap thue] *adj* prestigious

เคาะ [kho] *v* knock, knock *(on the door etc.)*; การเคาะ [kan kho] *n* knock; การตบเบา ๆ การเคาะเบา ๆ การตีเบา ๆ [kan top bao bao, kan kho bao bao, kan ti bao bao] *n* tap

เคี่ยว [khiao] เคี่ยวอาหาร [khiao a han] *adj* poached *(simmered gently)*

เคี้ยว [khiao] *v* chew

แค็ตตาล็อก [kaet ta lok] ฉันอยากได้แค็ตตาล็อก [chan yak dai khat ta lok] I'd like a catalogue

แคนาดา [khae na da] *adj* เกี่ยวกับประเทศแคนาดา [kiao kap pra thet khae na da] *adj* Canadian ▷ *n* ชาวแคนาดา [chao khae na da] *n* Canadian; ประเทศแคนาดา [pra tet khae na da] *n* Canada

แคนารี [kae na ri] ไวน์จากหมู่เกาะแคนารี่ [wine chak mu ko khae na ri] *n* canary; หมู่เกาะแคนารี่ [mu kao khae na ri] *npl* Canaries

แคนู [khae nu] เรือแคนู [ruea khae nu] *n* canoe; การเล่นเรือแคนู [kan len ruea khae nu] *n* canoeing; เราจะไปเล่นเรือแคนูได้ที่ไหน? [rao ja pai len ruea khae nu dai thii nai] Where can we go canoeing?

แคบ [khaep] *adj* narrow; การกลัวที่อยู่ในที่แคบ [kan klua thii yu nai thii khaep] *adj* claustrophobic

แคมเมอรูน [kaem moe run] ประเทศแคมเมอรูน [pra thet khaem moe run] *n* Cameroon

แคร่ [khrae] แคร่เลื่อนยาวติดกับรองเท้าใช้เล่นหิมะ [krae luean yao tit kap rong thao chai len hi ma] *n* ski

แครนเบอรี่ [khraen boe ri] ลูกแครนเบอรี่ [luk khraen boe ri] *n* cranberry

แครอท [kae rot] *n* carrot

แคระ [khrae] คนแคระ [khon khrae] *n* dwarf

แคริเบียน [mae ri bian] เกี่ยวกับประเทศในทะเลแคริเบียน [kiao kap pra thet nai tha le khae ri bian] *adj* Caribbean; ชาวแคริเบียน [chao khae ri bian] *n* Caribbean

แคลเซียม [khaen siam] *n* calcium

แค่ไหน [khae nai] ใช้เวลานานแค่ไหนที่จะไปที่...? [chai we la nan khae nai thii ja pai thii…] How long will it take to get to…?; อยู่ไกลแค่ไหน? [yu klai khae nai] How far is it?

แค่เอื้อม [khae ueam] *adj* nearby

โค้ก [khok] *n* Coke®

โคเคน [kho khen] *n* crack *(cocaine)*

โค้ง [khong] โค้งตัว [khong tua] v bend over; โครงสร้างที่มีรูปโค้ง [khrong sang thii mii rup khong] n arch; ของที่มีรูป ร่างโค้งเหมือนตะขอ [khong thii mii rup rang khong muean ta kho] n crook

โค้ท [khot] เสื้อโค้ทกันหนาว [suea khot kan nao] n overcoat

โค่น [khon] โค่นต้นไม้ [khon ton mai] v cut down

โคม [khom] โคมไฟ [khom fai] n lampshade

โคมไฟ [khom fai] โคมไฟข้างเตียงนอน [khom fai khang tiang non] n bedside lamp; โคมไฟไม่ทำงาน [khom fai mai tham ngan] The lamp is not working

โครง [khrong] โครงยกพื้นที่ใช้สำหรับสร้าง หรือซ่อมตึกหรือสถานที่ต่าง ๆ [khrong yok phuen thii chai sam rap sang rue som tuek rue sa than thii tang tang] n scaffolding

โครงกระดูก [khlong kra duk] n skeleton

โครงการ [khrong kan] n project; หนังสือ โครงการ [nang sue khrong kan] n prospectus

โครงงาน [khrong ngan] n layout

โครงสร้าง [khrong sang] n frame, structure; เปลี่ยนโครงสร้างใหม่ [plian khrong sang mai] v restructure; โครงสร้างพื้นฐานเช่น ถนน สะพาน [khrong sang phuen than chen tha non sa phan] n infrastructure; ที่เกี่ยว กับโครงสร้าง [thii kiao kap khrong sang] adj constructive

โครเมี่ยม [khro miam] แผ่นโครเมี่ยม [phaen khro miam] n chrome

โครเอเชีย [khro e chai] เกี่ยวกับประเทศ โครเอเชีย [kiao kap pra thet khro e chia] adj Croatian; ชาวโครเอเชียน [chao khro e chian] n Croatian (person); ประเทศโครเอเชีย [pra tet khro e chia] n Croatia

โคลน [khlon] n mud; เต็มไปด้วยโคลน [tem pai duai khlon] adj muddy

โคลัมเบีย [ko lam bia] เกี่ยวกับประเทศ โคลัมเบีย [kiao kap pra thet kho lam bia] adj Colombian; ชาวโคลัมเบีย [chao kho lam bia] n Colombian; ประเทศ โคลัมเบีย [pra tet kho lam bia] n Colombia

โควตา [kho ta] n quota

ใคร [khrai] pron who, whom; ใครสักคน [khrai sak khon] pron anyone; ใครก็ได้ [khrai ko dai] pron anybody; ไม่มีใคร [mai mii khrai] pron no one, nobody; ฉันกำลังพูดกับใคร? [chan kam lang phut kap khrai] Who am I talking to?

ไครกีสถาน [khrai ki sa than] ประเทศไค รกีสถาน [pra tet khai ki sa than] n Kyrgyzstan

ฆ ง

ฆ่า [kha] v kill; การฆ่าหมู่ [kan kha mu] n
massacre; ฆ่าโดยการบีบคอ [kha doi kan
bip kho] v strangle; ผู้ฆ่า [phu kha] n
killer

ฆ่าเชื้อ [kha chuea] นมผ่านการฆ่าเชื้อ
[nom phan kan kha chuea] n UHT milk

ฆ่าเชื้อโรค [kha chuea rok] ที่ผ่านการฆ่า
เชื้อโรค [thii phan kan kha chuea rok]
adj pasteurized

ฆาตกร [kha ta kon] n murderer

ฆาตกรรม [ka ta kam] v murder; การ
ฆาตกรรม [kan khat ta kam] n murder

ฆ่าตัวตาย [kha tua tai] การฆ่าตัวตาย
[kan kha tua tai] n suicide

ฆ่าเวลา [kha we la] ฆ่าเวลาโดยการทำ
อะไรที่ไม่สำคัญ [kha we la doi kan tham
a rai thii mai sam khan] v mess about

เมฆ [mek] มีเมฆมาก [mii mek mak] adj
overcast

โฆษก [kho sok] n spokesman,
spokesperson; โฆษกหญิง [kho sok
ying] n spokeswoman

โฆษณา [kho sa na] n advert; โฆษณาเล็ก
ๆ [khot sa na lek lek] npl small ads;
โฆษณาคั่นรายการ [khot sa na khan rai
kan] n commercial break

งงงวย [ngong nguai] ทำให้งงงวย [tham
hai ngong nguai] adj baffled, puzzling

แจ้ง [chaeng] เราตองแจ้งกับตำรวจ [rao
tong chaeng kap tam ruat] We will
have to report it to the police

งดงาม [ngot ngam] สวยงดงาม [suai
ngot ngam] adj picturesque

งบ [ngop] งบประมาณ [ngop pra man] n
budget

งบดุล [ngop dun] n balance sheet; งบดุล
ธนาคาร [ngop dun tha na khan] n bank
balance

งบประมาณ [ngop pra man] ปีงบประมาณ
[pi ngop pra man] n financial year,
fiscal year

ง่วงนอน [nguang non] adj sleepy

งวด [nguat] เงินที่จ่ายเป็นงวด [ngoen thii
chai pen nguat] n instalment

งอ [ngo] v bend; คดงอ [khot ngo] adj
bent (not straight)

งอกงาม [ngok ngam] เติบโต งอกงาม
[toep to, ngok ngam] vi grow

ง่วงเงีย [nguang ngia] adj drowsy

งา [nga] งาช้าง [nga chang] n ivory

งาน [ngan] n job; ไม่มีงาน [mai mii
ngan] adj jobless; ไม่มีงานทำ [mai mii

ngan tham] *adj* unemployed; หน่วย
จัดหางาน [nuai chat ha ngan] *n* job
centre; งานศิลปะ [ngan sin la pa] *n*
work of art

งานเลี้ยง [ngan liang] งานเลี้ยงของหนุ่ม
โสดก่อนวันแต่งงาน [ngan liang khong
num sot kon wan taeng ngan] *n* stag
night; งานเลี้ยงอาหารค่ำ [ngan liang a
han kham] *n* dinner party; จัดงานเลี้ยง
[chat ngan liang] *v* party

งานศิลปะ [ngan sin la pa] งานศิลปะที่ทำ
ด้วยมือ [ngan sin la pa thii tham duai
mue] *n* craft

งานอดิเรก [ngan a di rek] *n* pastime

งาม [ngam] ความงาม [khwam ngam] *n*
beauty

ง่าย [ngai] *adj* easy, simple; ทำให้ง่ายขึ้น
[tham hai ngai khuen] *v* simplify; อย่าง
ง่าย ๆ [yang ngai ngai] *adv* simply; อย่าง
ง่าย ๆ อย่างสบาย ๆ [yang ngai ngai,
yang sa bai sa bai] *adj* easy-going

งีบหลับ [ngip lap] *v* doze, snooze; การงีบ
หลับ [kan ngib lap] *n* nap, snooze; งีบ
หลับไป [ngip lap pai] *v* doze off

งุนงง [ngun ngong] งุนงงอย่างที่สุด [ngun
ngong yang thii sut] *adj* bewildered

ง่มงาม [ngum ngam] *adj* awkward,
clumsy

งู [ngu] *n* snake; งูกะปะ [ngu ka pa] *n*
rattlesnake

เงา [ngao] *n* shadow; ใส่น้ำมันชักเงา [sai
nam man chak ngao] *v* varnish; ซึ่งเป็น
มันเงา [sueng pen man ngao] *adj* shiny;
น้ำมันชักเงา [nam man chak ngao] *n*
varnish

เงิน [ngoen] *n* money, silver; เกี่ยวกับเงิน
ตรา [kiao kap ngoen tra] *adj* monetary;
เครื่องคิดเงิน [khrueang kit ngoen] *n*
cash register; เงินเฉพาะจำนวนที่ให้
ธนาคารจ่าย [ngoen cha pho cham nuan
thii hai tha na khan chai] *n* standing
order; เงินทุน [ngoen thun] *n* grant; เจ้า
หน้าที่การเงิน [chao na thii kan ngoen] *n*
cashier; ถุงเงิน [thung ngoen] *n* purse;

ฉันไม่มีเงิน [chan mai mii ngoen] I have
no money

เงินเดือน [ngoen duean] *n* salary; ซึ่งให้
เงินเดือนสูง [sueng hai ngoen duean
sung] *adj* well-paid

เงินทอน [ngoen thon] เสียใจด้วย ฉันไม่มี
เงินทอน [sia jai duai chan mai mii
ngoen thon] Sorry, I don't have any
change; คุณมีเงินทอนสำหรับธนบัตรใบนี้
ไหม? [khun mii ngen thon sam rap
tha na bat bai nii mai] Do you have
change for this note?; คุณมีเศษเงินทอน
ไหม? [khun mii set ngen thon mai] Do
you have any small change?

เงินทุน [ngoen thun] จัดหาเงินทุนให้
[chat ha ngen thun hai] *v* finance

เงินฝาก [ngoen fak] บัญชีเงินฝาก [ban
chi ngoen fak] *n* account (*in bank*)

เงินเฟ้อ [ngoen foe] ภาวะเงินเฟ้อ [pha wa
ngoen foe] *n* inflation

เงินสด [ngoen sot] ฉันไม่มีเงินสด [chan
mai mii ngoen sot] I don't have any
cash

เงียบ [ngiap] *adj* quiet, silent; ความเงียบ
[khwam ngiap] *n* silence; ซึ่งเงียบสงบ
และผ่อนคลาย [sueng ngiap sa ngob lae
phon khlai] *adj* restful; อย่างเงียบ [yang
ngiap] *adv* quietly; ฉันอยากได้ห้องเงียบ ๆ
[chan yak dai hong ngiap ngiap] I'd like
a quiet room

เงื่อน [nguean] *n* knot

เงื่อนไข [nguean khai] สภาวะ เงื่อนไข [sa
pha wa, nguean khai] *n* condition; ที่
เป็นเงื่อนไข [thii pen nguean khai] *adj*
conditional; ที่ไม่มีเงื่อนไข [thii mai mii
nguean khai] *adj* unconditional

เงื่อนงำ [nguean ngam] *n* clue

โง่ [ngo] *adj* daft, dumb, silly, stupid; คน
โง่ [khon ngo] *n* fool, idiot, twit; ความโง่
เขลา [khwam ngo khlao] *n* ignorance

โง่เขลา [ngo khlao] *adj* senseless

จ

จงรักภักดี [chong rak phak di] ความ
จงรักภักดี [khwam chong rak phak dii]
n loyalty

จงอย [cha ngoi] จะงอยปากนก [cha ngoi
pak nok] *n* beak

จด [chot] จดลง [chot long] *v* jot down;
จดลงไป [chot long pai] *v* note down

จดหมาย [chot mai] *n* letter *(message)*,
mail, post *(mail)*; เพื่อนทางจดหมาย
[phuean thang chot mai] *n* penfriend;
มีจดหมายถึงฉันบ้างไหม? [mii chot mai
thueng chan bang mai] Is there any
mail for me?

จตุรัส [cha tu rat] สี่เหลี่ยมจตุรัส [si liam
chat tu rat] *n* square

จนกระทั่ง [chon kra thang] *conj* till,
until; จนกว่า จนกระทั่ง [chon kwa, chon
kra thang] *prep* till

จนกว่า [chon kwa] *prep* until; จนกว่า จน
กระทั่ง [chon kwa, chon kra thang] *prep*
till

จนมุม [chon mum] สภาพที่จนมุม [sa
phap thii chon mum] *n* stalemate

จบ [chop] *vt* finish ▷ *n* ตอนจบ [ton job] *n*
end, ending, finish ▷ *adj* ที่จบสิ้น [thii
job sin] *adj* over

จม [chom] *vi* sink; จมน้ำ [chom nam] *v*
drown

จมูก [cha muk] *n* nose; รูจมูก [ru cha
muk] *n* nostril

จรจัด [chon chat] คนจรจัด [khon chon
chat] *n* tramp *(beggar)*

จรวด [cha ruat] *n* rocket

จระเข้ [cha ra ke] *n* alligator, crocodile

จราจร [cha ra chon] เจ้าหน้าที่การจัดการ
จราจร [chao na thii kan chat kan cha
ra chon] *n* traffic warden; สัญญาน
จราจร [san yan cha ra chon] *npl* traffic
lights

จริง [ching] *adj* genuine; โดยแท้จริง [doi
thae ching] *adj* indeed; ไม่มองดูสภาพ
จริง [mai mong du sa phap ching] *adj*
unrealistic; ความจริง [khwam ching] *n*
fact

จริงจัง [ching chang] อย่างจริงจัง [yang
ching chang] *adv* seriously

จริงใจ [ching chai] *adj* sincere; ไม่จริงใจ
[mai ching jai] *adj* insincere; อย่าง
จริงใจ [yang ching jai] *adv* sincerely

จริยธรรม [cha ri ya tham] ตามหลัก
จริยธรรม [tam lak cha ri ya tham] *adj*
ethical

จลาจล [cha la chon] การจลาจล [kan cha
la chon] *n* riot

จอ [cho] จอภาพแบน [cho phap baen] *n*
flat-screen

จอง [chong] *v* book; สำนักงานจอง [sam
nak ngan chong] *n* booking office; การ
จอง [kan chong] *n* reservation; การจอง
ล่วงหน้า [kan chong luang na] *n*
booking

จ้อง [chong] *v* stare

จ้องมอง [chong mong] *v* gaze

จอด [chot] *v* park; การนำเครื่องบินลงจอด
[kan nam khrueang bin long jod] *n*
landing; จอดเรือ [jot ruea] *v* moor

จอภาพ [cho phap] โปรแกรมรักษาจอภาพ
[pro kraem rak sa cho phap] *n*
screen-saver; จอภาพแบน [cho phap
baen] *n* plasma screen

จอร์เจีย [cho chia] เกี่ยวกับจอร์เจีย [kiao kap cho chia] *adj* Georgian; ประเทศจอร์เจีย [pra tet chor chia] *n* Georgia (*country*)

จอร์เจียน [cho chian] ชาวจอร์เจียน [chao cho chian] *n* Georgian (*inhabitant of Georgia*)

จอร์แดน [cho daen] เกี่ยวกับประเทศจอร์แดน [kiao kap pra thet cho daen] *adj* Jordanian; ชาวจอร์แดน [chao cho daen] *n* Jordanian; ประเทศจอร์แดน [pra tet chor daen] *n* Jordan

จั๊กจี้ [chak ka chi] จั๊กจี้ได้ง่าย [chak ka chi dai ngai] *adj* ticklish; ทำให้จั๊กจี้ [tham hai chak ka chi] *v* tickle

จักรกล [chak kon] เกี่ยวกับเครื่องจักรกล [kiao kap khrueang chak kon] *adj* mechanical

จักรพรรดิ [chak kra phat] *n* emperor

จักรยาน [chak kra yan] *n* bicycle, bike, cycle (*bike*); เส้นทางขี่จักรยาน [sen thang khi chak kra yan] *n* cycle path; มือถือสำหรับเลี้ยวรถจักรยาน [mue thue sam rap liao rot chak kra yan] *npl* handlebars; การขี่จักรยาน [kan khi chak kra yan] *n* cycling; ไปขี่จักรยานกันเถอะ [pai khi chak kra yan kan thoe] Let's go cycling

จักรยานยนต์ [chak kra yan yon] รถจักรยานยนต์ [rot chak kra yan yon] *n* motorbike

จักรเย็บผ้า [chak yep pha] *n* sewing machine

จักรราศี [chak kra ra si] *n* zodiac

จักรวาล [chak kra wan] *n* universe

จังหวะ [chang wa] *n* rhythm; เต้นรำจังหวะวอลทซ [ten ram chang wa walt] *v* waltz

จังหวัด [chang wat] ศาลากลางจังหวัด [sa la klang changhwat] *n* town hall

จัด [chat] การแสดง การจัดวาง [kan sa daeng, kan chat wang] *v* display; การจัด [kan chat] *v* format; การจัดประเภท [kan chat pra phet] *n* assortment, sort; ฉันต้องจัดกระเป๋าเดี๋ยวนี้ [chan tong chat kra pao diao nii] I need to pack now

จัดการ [chat kan] *v* deal with, handle, manage, organize, direct ▷ *n* การจัดการแข่งขันใหม่ [kan chat kan khaeng khan mai] *n* replay; ตารางจัดการหมายถึงโปรแกรมคอมพิวเตอร์ประเภทหนึ่ง [ta rang chat kan mai thueng pro kraem khom phio toe pra pet nueng] *n* spreadsheet ▷ *adj* ที่จัดการได้ [thii chat kan dai] *adj* manageable

จัดเตรียม [chat triam] *vt* arrange; การจัดเตรียม [kan chat triam] *n* arrangement; วาง จัดเตรียม ตั้งเวลา ตั้งระบบ [wang, chat triam, tang we la, tang ra bop] *vt* set

จัดแสง [chat saeng] การจัดแสง [kan chat saeng] *n* lighting

จัดหา [chat ha] *v* provide, supply; สิ่งที่จัดหาให้ [sing thii chat ha hai] *n* supplies, supply; จัดหาเงินทุนให้ [chat ha ngen thun hai] *v* finance; จัดหาให้ [chat ha hai] *v* provide for

จันทร์ [chan] วันจันทร์ [wan chan] *n* Monday

จันทร์เทศ [chan thet] ต้นจันทร์เทศ [ton chan tet] *n* nutmeg

จับ [chap] การจับ การยึด [kan chap, kan yued] *n* seizure; จับได้ ฉวยจับ [chap dai, chuai chap] *vt* catch; จับฉวย [chap chuai] *v* grab

จับกุม [chap khum] *v* arrest, capture; การจับกุม [kan chap kum] *n* arrest

จับผิด [chap phit] จ้องจับผิด [chong chap phit] *v* nag

จ่า [cha] *n* sergeant; สิบโท จ่าอากาศโท [sip tho, cha a kaat tho] *n* corporal

จ้า [cha] สว่างจ้า [sa wang cha] *adj* bright

จาก [chak] *prep* from; มาจาก [ma chak] *v* come from; การจากกัน [kan chak kan] *n* parting; จากไป [chak pai] *adj* go off, gone

จากนั้นมา [chak nan ma] *adv* since

จ้าง [chang] ลูกจ้าง [luk chang] *n*

employee; การว่าจ้าง [kan wa chang] n
employment; นายจ้าง [nai chang] n
employer

จางหาย [chang hai] ละลาย ทำให้
หลอมละลาย [la lai, tham hai lom la lai]
vt melt

จาน [chan] n dish (plate), plate; เครื่องล้าง
จาน [khrueang lang chan] n
dishwasher; หน่วยจานบันทึก [nuai
chan ban thuek] n disk drive; จานรอง
[chan rong] n saucer; มีอะไรอยู่ในจานนี้?
[mii a rai yu nai chan nii] What is in
this dish?

จานบิน [chan bin] ตัวย่อของจานบินของ
มนุษย์ต่างดาว [tua yo khong chan bin
khong ma nut tang dao] abbr UFO

จาม [cham] v sneeze

จาไมก้า [cha mai ka] เกี่ยวกับจาไมก้า
[kiao kap cha mai ka] adj Jamaican;
ชาวจาไมก้า [chao cha mai ka] n
Jamaican

จ่าย [chai] vi pay; ได้จ่ายแล้ว [dai chai
laeo] adj paid; สามารถจ่ายได้ [sa maat
chai dai] v afford; การจ่าย [kan chai] n
pay; มีการจ่ายเพิ่มหรือไม่? [mii kan chai
poem rue mai] Is there a supplement
to pay?

จ่ายยา [chai ya] สั่งจ่ายยา [sang chai ya]
v prescribe

จารกรรม [cha ra kam] n espionage

จารึก [cha ruek] ข้อความที่จารึก [kho
khwam thii cha ruek] n inscription

จำ [cham] v remember; จำได้ [cham dai]
v recognize; ซึ่งสามารถจำได้ [sueng sa
maat cham dai] adj recognizable

จำกัด [cham kat] v crack down on,
restrict; ขีดจำกัด [khit cham kat] n
limit

จำนวน [cham nuan] ค้นพบจำนวนที่
แน่นอน [khon phop cham nuan thii
nae non] v quantify; คนหรือสิ่งของ
จำนวนมาก [khon rue sing khong cham
nuan mak] pron many; จำนวนเงินที่เป็น
หนี้ธนาคาร [cham nuan ngen thii pen

nii tha na khan] n overdraft

จำนวนหนึ่ง [cham nuan nueng] pron
any

จำนอง [cham nong] v mortgage; การ
จำนอง [kan cham nong] n mortgage

จำนำ [cham nam] โรงรับจำนำ [rong rap
cham nam] n pawnbroker

จำแนก [cham naek] จำแนกความแตกต่าง
[cham naek khwam taek tang] v
distinguish

จำเป็น [cham pen] adj necessary; ไม่
จำเป็น [mai cham pen] adj
unnecessary; ความจำเป็น [khwam
cham pen] n necessity; อย่างจำเป็น
[yang cham pen] adv necessarily

จำพวก [cham phuak] n kind

จำลอง [cham long] สภาวะเหมือนจริงที่
จำลองโดยทางเทคนิคคอมพิวเตอร์ [sa pha
wa muean ching thii cham long doi
thang tek nik khom phio toe] n virtual
reality; ของจำลอง [khong cham long] n
replica; ที่จำลองขึ้น [thii cham long
khuen] adj mock

จำเลย [cham loei] n defendant

จำหน่าย [cham nai] ผู้แทนจำหน่าย [phu
thaen cham nai] n distributor

จิ้งจก [ching chok] สัตว์ประเภทจิ้งจกอาศัย
ได้ทั้งบนบกและในน้ำ [sat pra phet ching
chok a sai dai thang bon bok lae nai
nam] n newt

จิ้งจอก [ching chok] สุนัขจิ้งจอก [su nak
ching chok] n fox

จิงโจ้ [ching cho] n kangaroo

จิ้งหรีด [ching rit] n cricket (insect)

จิต [chit] เกี่ยวกับจิต [kiao kap chit] adj
psychological; ความสามารถทางจิต
[khwam sa mat thang chit] n
mentality; ช่วงเวลาที่เจ็บป่วยทางจิต
[chuang we la thii chep puai thang
chit] n nervous breakdown

จิตใจ [chit chai] n mind; ยาที่ทำให้จิตใจ
สงบ [ya thii tham hai chit jai sa ngop]
n tranquillizer

จิตแพทย์ [chit ta phaet] จิตแพทย์ [chit

ta phaet] *n* psychiatrist

จิตรกร [chit ta kon] *n* painter

จิตวิทยา [chit wit tha ya] *n* psychology; ที่เกี่ยวกับจิตวิทยา [thii kiao kap chit ta wit tha ya] *adj* psychiatric; นักจิตวิทยา [nak chit ta wit tha ya] *n* psychologist

จินตนาการ [chin ta na kan] *n* imagination; ทำให้จินตนาการจินตนาการเห็น [tham hai chin ta na kan chin ta na kan hen] *v* visualize; อยู่ในจินตนาการ [yu nai chin ta na kan] *adj* unreal

จิ้ม [chim] การจิ้มน้ำจิ้ม [kan chim nam chim] *n* dip *(food/sauce)*

จี้ [chi] จี้ห้อยคอ [chi hoi kho] *n* locket, pendant

จีน [chin] ชาวจีน [chao chin] *n* Chinese *(person)*; ที่เกี่ยวกับชาติจีน [thii kiao kap chat chin] *adj* Chinese; ประเทศจีน [pra tet chin] *n* China

จีบ [chip] รอยจีบ [roi chip] *n* plait

จุด [chut] *n* dot; มหัพภาค จุด [ma hup phak chut] *n* full stop; จุดด่างพร้อย [chut dang phroi] *n* spot *(blemish)*; จุดที่เล็กที่สุดที่รวมกันเป็นภาพ [chut thii lek thii sut thii ruam kan pen phap] *n* pixel

จุดไฟ [chut fai] *v* light

จุดสุดยอด [chut sut yot] จุดสุดยอดของความรู้สึกทางเพศ [chut sut yot khong khwam ru suek thang phet] *n* orgasm

จุดหมาย [chut mai] *n* aim; ไร้จุดหมาย [rai chut mai] *adj* pointless; จุดหมายปลายทาง [chut mai plai thang] *n* destination

จุ่ม [chum] *vt* dip

จู้จี้ [chu chi] *adj* bossy, fussy

จู่โจม [chu chom] *v* raid; การจู่โจม [kan chu chom] *n* raid

จูบ [chup] *v* kiss; การจูบ [kan chup] *n* kiss

เจ [che] อาหารนี้เหมาะสำหรับพวกกินเจไหม? [a han nii mao sam rap phuak kin che mai] Is this suitable for vegans?

เจ็ด [chet] *number* seven; ลำดับที่เจ็ด [lam dap thii chet] seventh; ที่เจ็ด [thii chet] *adj* seventh

เจ็ดสิบ [chet sip] *number* seventy

เจตนา [chet ta na] *adj* intentional; ไม่ได้เจตนา [mai dai chet ta na] *adj* unintentional

เจตนาร้าย [chet ta na rai] *n* spite; ซึ่งมีเจตนาร้าย [sueng mii chet ta na rai] *adj* spiteful

เจ็ทสกี [chet sa ki] ฉันจะเช่าเจ็ทสกีได้ที่ไหน? [chan ja chao chet sa ki dai thii nai] Where can I hire a jet-ski?

เจ็บ [chep] หูเจ็บ [hu chep] *n* earache; คนเจ็บ [khon chep] *n* invalid; ความเจ็บ [khwam chep] *n* sore; เขาทำแขนตัวเองเจ็บ [khao tham khaen tua eng chep] He has hurt his arm

เจ็บปวด [chep puat] *adj* painful, sore ▷ *v* ache; ความเจ็บปวด [khwam chep puat] *n* ache, pain

เจ็บป่วย [chep puai] ความเจ็บป่วย [khwam chep puai] *n* illness, sickness; ช่วงเวลาที่เจ็บป่วยทางจิต [chuang we la thii chep puai thang chit] *n* nervous breakdown

เจริญ [cha roen] ทำให้เจริญก้าวหน้า [tham hai cha roen kao na] *v* bring forward; พัฒนา เจริญ เติบโต [phat ta na, cha roen, toep to] *vi* develop

เจริญเติบโต [cha roen toep to] *v* grow up; ปลูก ทำให้เจริญเติบโต [pluk, tham hai cha roen toep to] *vt* grow

เจริญรอยตาม [cha roen roi tam] *v* take after

เจริญรุ่งเรือง [cha roen rung rueang] ความเจริญรุ่งเรือง [khwam cha roen rung rueang] *n* prosperity

เจล [chel] เจลใส่ผม [chen sai phom] *n* hair gel; เจลสำหรับแต่งผม [chen sam rap taeng phom] *n* gel; เจลอาบน้ำ [chen aap nam] *n* shower gel

เจอเรเนียม [choe re niam] ต้นเจอเรเนียมมีดอกสีชมพูหรือสีม่วง [ton choe re niam mii dok sii chom phu rue sii muang] *n* geranium

เจ้าของ [chao khong] *n* owner; เจ้าของและผู้จัดการบาร์ [chao khong lae phu chat kan ba] *n* publican; เจ้าของร้าน [chao khong ran] *n* shopkeeper; เจ้าของที่ดิน [chao khong thii din] *n* landowner; ฉันขอพูดกับเจ้าของได้ไหม? [chan kho phut kap chao khong dai mai] Could I speak to the owner, please?

เจ้าชาย [chao chai] *n* prince

เจ้าชู้ [chao chu] คนเจ้าชู้ [khon chao chu] *n* flirt

เจ้านาย [chao nai] *n* boss, master

เจ้าเนื้อ [chao nuea] *adj* plump

เจ้าบ่าว [chao bao] *n* bridegroom, groom (*bridegroom*); เพื่อนเจ้าบ่าว [phuean chao bao] *n* best man

เจ้าแผ่นดิน [chao phaen din] *n* monarch

เจ้าพ่อ [chao pho] *n* godfather (*criminal leader*)

เจ้าภาพ [chao phap] *n* host (*entertains*)

เจ้าเล่ห์ [chao le] *adj* cunning

เจ้าสาว [chao sao] *n* bride; เพื่อนเจ้าสาว [phuean chao sao] *n* bridesmaid

เจ้าหญิง [chao ying] *n* princess

เจ้าหน้าที่ [chao na thi] *adj* official; เจ้าหน้าที่เรือนจำ [chao na thii ruean cham] *n* prison officer; เจ้าหน้าที่การเงิน [chao na thii kan ngoen] *n* cashier; เจ้าหน้าที่การจัดการจราจร [chao na thii kan chat kan cha ra chon] *n* traffic warden

เจาะ [cho] *v* pierce, prick, drill; เจาะรู [jo ru] *v* bore (*drill*); การเจาะ [kan jo] *n* piercing, puncture; ที่ถูกเจาะ [thii thuk jo] *adj* pierced

เจิดจ้า [choet cha] เจิดจ้า สว่างไสว [choet cha, sa wang sa wai] *adj* vivid

เจือจาง [chue chang] *v* dilute; เจือจางอ่อนแอ [chuea chang, on ae] *v* faint; ทำให้เจือจาง [tham hai chuea chang] *adj* diluted

แจ๊กเก็ต [chaek ket] เสื้อแจ๊กเก็ต [suea chaek ket] *n* jacket; เสื้อแจ๊กเก็ตกีฬาหรือโรงเรียน [suea chaek ket ki la rue rong rian] *n* blazer

แจกจ่าย [chaek chai] *v* distribute, give out

แจกัน [chae kan] *n* vase

แจ็คเกต [chaek ket] เสื้อแจ็คเก็ตมีหมวกคลุมหัวกันลมและฝน [suea chaek ket mii muak khlum hua kan lom lae fon] *n* cagoule

แจ้ง [chaeng] แจ้งให้ทราบ [chaeng hai sap] *v* inform; แจ้งออก [chaeng ok] *v* check out; การแจ้งล่วงหน้า [kan chaeng luang na] *n* notice (*termination*)

แจ๊ส [chaes] ดนตรีแจ๊ส [don tree jas] *n* jazz

โจมตี [chom ti] *vt* attack; การโจมตี [kan chom ti] *n* attack; การซุ่มโจมตี [kan sum chom ti] *n* ambush; การถูกโจมตีจากผู้ก่อการร้าย [kan thuk chom ti chak phu ko kan rai] *n* terrorist attack

โจร [chon] *n* robber; โจรปล้นจี้ [chon plon chi] *n* hijacker

โจรสลัด [chon sa lat] *n* pirate

ใจกลาง [chai klang] ใจกลางเมือง [jai klang mueang] *n* town centre

ใจกว้าง [chai kwang] *adj* broad-minded, generous; ความมีใจกว้าง [khwam mii jai kwang] *n* generosity

ใจแคบ [chai khaep] *adj* narrow-minded

ใจจดใจจ่อ [chai chot chai cho] *adj* preoccupied

ใจดี [chai di] *adj* kind; คนใจดี [khon jai dii] *adj* good-natured; อย่างใจดี [yang jai di] *adv* kindly; คุณใจดีมาก [khun jai di mak] That's very kind of you

ใจลอย [chai loi] *adj* absent-minded

ฉ

[khuen nii rong nang mii nang a rai chai] What's on tonight at the cinema?

ฉายา [cha ya] *n* alias

ฉิ่ง [ching] *npl* cymbals

ฉีก [chik] *v* tear, rip; ฉีกออก [chiik ok] *v* tear up

ฉีด [chit] *v* inject; ฉีดวัคซีน [chiit wak sin] *v* vaccinate

ฉีดยา [chit ya] การฉีดยา [kan chit ya] *n* injection; กรุณาฉีดยาให้ฉัน [ka ru na chit ya hai chan] Please give me an injection; ฉันอยากฉีดยาแก้ปวด [chan yak chit ya kae puat] I want an injection for the pain

ฉุกเฉิน [chuk choen] การจอดลงอย่างฉุกเฉินของเครื่องบิน [kan jod long yang chuk choen khong khrueang bin] *n* emergency landing; ทางออกฉุกเฉิน [thang ok chuk choen] *n* emergency exit; ภาวะฉุกเฉิน [pha wa chuk choen] *n* emergency; ร้านขายยาร้านไหนมีบริการขายฉุกเฉิน? [ran khai ya ran nai mii bo ri kan khai chuk choen] Which pharmacy provides emergency service?

ฉุนเฉียว [chun chiao] โกรธฉุนเฉียว [krot chun chiao] *adj* cross; ฉุนเฉียวโกรธง่าย [chun chiao krot ngai] *adj* touchy

เฉพาะ [cha pho] เฉพาะบุคคล [cha pho buk khon] *adj* individual; ลักษณะเฉพาะ [lak sa na cha pho] *adj* unique

เฉลี่ย [cha lia] โดยเฉลี่ย [doi cha lia] *adj* average; ค่าเฉลี่ย [kha cha lia] *adj* average, mean

เฉลียว [cha liao] เฉลียวฉลาด [cha liao cha lat] *adj* clever

เฉลียวฉลาด [cha liao cha lat] *adj* ingenious, wise; สติปัญญา ความเฉลียวฉลาด [sa ti pan ya, khwam cha liao cha lat] *n* wisdom

เฉา [chao] เหี่ยวเฉา [hiao chao] *v* wilt

เฉื่อยชา [chueai cha] *adj* passive

ฉกฉวย [chok chuai] *v* seize

ฉนวน [cha nuan] ฉนวนกันความร้อน [cha nuan kan khwam ron] insulation

ฉบับ [cha bap] *n* version

ฉลอง [cha long] *v* celebrate; การฉลอง [kan cha long] *n* celebration; การฉลองครบรอบปี [kan cha long khrop rob pi] *n* anniversary

ฉลาก [cha lak] การขายตั๋วจับฉลากที่มีสิ่งของเป็นรางวัลมากกว่าเงิน [kan khai tua chab cha lak thii mii sing khong pen rang wan mak kwa ngen] *n* raffle; ฉลากติด สติ๊กเกอร์ [cha lak tit, sa tik koe] *n* sticker

ฉลาด [cha lat] *adj* intelligent; เฉลียวฉลาด [cha liao cha lat] *adj* clever; ไม่ฉลาด [mai cha lat] *adj* unwise; ฉลาดมาก [cha lat mak] *adj* brainy

ฉลาดแกมโกง [cha lat kaem kong] ซึ่งมีเล่ห์เหลี่ยม อย่างฉลาดแกมโกง [sueng mii le liam, yang cha lat kaem kong] *adj* sly

ฉลาม [cha lam] *n* shark

ฉัน [chan] *pron* I, me; ตัวของฉัน [tua khong chan] *pron* myself

ฉาย [chai] คืนนี้โรงหนังมีหนังอะไรฉาย?

ช

ชก [chok] v punch; การชก [kan chok] n punch (blow)

ชกมวย [chok muai] การชกมวย [kan chok muai] n boxing

ชดเชย [chot choei] v compensate; การชดเชย [kan chot choei] n compensation

ชน [chon] vi clash; ไชโย ชนแก้ว [chai yo chon kaew] excl cheers!; การชน [kan chon] n bump, crash; การชนกัน [kan chon kan] n collision

ชนชั้น [chon chan] ชนชั้นกลาง [chon chan klang] adj middle-class; ชนชั้นผู้รับจ้าง [chon chan phu rap chang] adj working-class

ชนชาติ [chon chat] เกี่ยวกับลัทธิชนชาติ [kiao kap lat thi chon chat] adj racist

ชนบท [chon na bot] n countryside; ในชนบท [nai chon na bot] adj rural; คนที่ไปเดินในชนบท [khon thii pai doen nai chon na bot] n rambler

ชนวน [cha nuan] สายชนวน [sai cha nuan] n fuse; กลองใส่สายชนวน [klong sai sai cha nuan] n fuse box; กระเบื้องหินชนวน [kra bueang hin cha nuan] n slate

ชนะ [cha na] v conquer, win; ตำแหน่งชนะเลิศ [tam naeng cha na loet] n championship; ผู้ชนะ [phu cha na] n winner; ผู้ชนะเลิศ [phu cha na loet] n champion

ชนะเลิศ [cha na loet] การแข่งขันรอบก่อนรองชนะเลิศ [kan khaeng khan rop kon rong cha na loet] n quarter final; การแข่งขันกีฬารอบรองชนะเลิศ [kan khaeng khan ki la rop rong cha na loet] n semifinal; ผู้รองชนะเลิศ [phu rong cha na loet] n runner-up

ชนิด [cha nit] n species

ชม [chom] ผู้ชม [phu chom] n audience, spectator; ผู้ดู ผู้ชมเช่น ผู้ชมรายการโทรทัศน์ [phu du, phu chom chen phu chom rai kan tho ra tat] n viewer

ชมเชย [chom choei] v compliment; การชมเชย [kan chom choei] n rave; คำชมเชย [kham chom choei] n compliment; ที่ชมเชย [thii chom choei] adj complimentary

ชมพู [chom phu] ซึ่งมีสีชมพู [sueng mii sii chom phu] adj pink

ชรา [cha ra] เกี่ยวกับคนชรา [kiao kap khon cha ra] adj geriatric; สถานดูแลคนชรา [sa than du lae khon cha ra] n nursing home; คนชรา [khon cha ra] n geriatric

ช่วง [chuang] ช่วงเวลาพัก [chuang we la phak] n interval; ช่วงหยุดพักอาหารกลางวัน [chuang yut phak a han klang wan] n lunch break; ช่วงวัยรุ่น [chuang wai run] npl adolescence

ช่วงเวลา [chuang we la] n duration, spell (time)

ช่วย [chuai] vt help; การให้ความช่วยเหลือทางโทรศัพท์ [kan hai khwam chuai luea thang tho ra sap] n helpline; ความช่วยเหลือ [khwam chuai luea] n help; ช่วยด้วย [chuai duai] excl help!; ขอคนมาช่วยเร็วหน่อย [kho khon ma chuai reo noi] Fetch help quickly!

ช่วยชีวิต [chuai chi wit] v save; การช่วย

ชีวิต [kan chuai chi wit] *n* rescue

ช่วยเหลือ [chuai luea] *v* rescue; เงินช่วย
เหลือ [ngoen chuai luea] *n* subsidy; ให้
ความช่วยเหลือในด้านการเงิน [hai khwam
chuai luea nai dan kan ngoen] *v*
subsidize; ไม่ช่วยเหลือ [mai chuai luea]
adj unhelpful; หน่วยบริการช่วยเหลือใกล้
ที่สุดอยู่ที่ไหน? [nuai bo ri kan chuai
luea klai thii sut yu thii nai] Where is
the nearest mountain rescue service
post?

ชวเลข [cha wa lek] *n* shorthand

ช่อ [cho] ช่อดอกไม้ [cho dok mai] *n*
bouquet

ช็อกโกแลต [chok ko laet] *n* chocolate;
ช็อกโกแลตที่รสค่อนข้างขมและมีสีดำ [chok
ko laet thii rot khon khang khom lae
mii sii dam] *n* plain chocolate;
ช็อกโกแลตนม [chok ko laet nom] *n* milk
chocolate

ช่อง [chong] *n* aperture, channel; ช่องที่
แคบและยาว [chong thii khaep lae yao]
n slot

ช่องแคบ [chong khaep] *n* pass (*in
mountains*)

ช่องว่าง [chong wang] *n* blank, gap

ช้อน [chon] *n* spoon; เต็มช้อน [tem chon]
n spoonful; มีด ช้อนและส้อม [miit chon
lae som] *n* cutlery; ช้อนโต๊ะ [chon to] *n*
tablespoon; ฉันขอช้อนสะอาดหนึ่งคันได้
ไหม? [chan kho chon sa aat nueng
khan dai mai] Could I have a clean
spoon, please?

ชอบ [chop] *v* like; ไม่ชอบ [mai chop] *v*
dislike; การชอบมากกว่า [kan chop mak
kwa] *n* preference; คนหรือสิ่งของที่ชอบ
เป็นพิเศษ [khon rue sing khong thii
chop pen phi set] *n* favourite; ฉันไม่
ชอบ... [chan mai chop...] I don't like...

ชอล์ก [chok] *n* chalk

ชะงัก [cha ngak] การหยุดชะงัก [kan yut
cha ngak] *n* hitch, interruption; ติด
ชะงัก [tit cha ngak] *adj* stuck; ทำให้หยุด
ชะงัก [tham hai yut cha ngak] *v*
interrupt

ชะโงก [cha ngok] ชะโงกออกไป [cha
ngok ok pai] *v* lean out

ชะตากรรม [cha ta kam] *n* destiny

ชะแลง [cha laeng] *n* lever

ชัก [chak] อาการชักของลมบ้าหมู [a kan
chak khong lom ba mu] *n* epileptic fit

ชักกระตุก [chak kra tuk] การชักกระตุก
ของกล้ามเนื้อ [kan chak kra tuk khong
klam nuea] *n* spasm

ชักโครก [chak khrok] *v* flush; ห้องน้ำกด
ชักโครกไม่ลง [hong nam kot chak
khrok mai long] The toilet won't flush

ชักจูง [chak chung] *v* persuade; ซึ่งชักจูง
ได้ [sueng chak chung dai] *adj*
persuasive

ชักชวน [chak chuan] ชักชวนให้เข้าร่วม
[chak chuan hai khao ruam] *v* rope in

ชักช้า [chak cha] ทำให้ชักช้า [tham hai
chak cha] *v* hold up

ชักเย่อ [chak ka yoe] *n* tug-of-war

ชั่ง [chang] ชั่งน้ำหนัก [chang nam nak] *v*
weigh

ชัด [chat] เห็นได้ชัด [hen dai chat] *adj*
obvious; เห็นชัด [hen chat] *v* stand out;
อย่างเห็นได้ชัด [yang hen dai chat] *adv*
obviously

ชัดเจน [chat chen] *adj* apparent, clear;
ซึ่งไม่ชัดเจน [sueng mai chat chen] *adj*
unclear; อย่างชัดเจน [yang chat chen]
adv apparently, clearly

ชัดแจ้ง [chat chen] *adj* blatant

ชัน [chan] สูงชัน [sung chan] *adj* steep;
ชันมากไหม? [chan mak mai] Is it very
steep?

ชั้น [chan] *n* layer; ระดับชั้น [ra dap chan]
n grade; ชั้นล่าง [chan lang] *n* ground
floor; ชั้นรอง [chan rong] *adj*
second-rate

ชั้นใน [chan nai] เสื้อชั้นในสตรี [suea
chan nai sa trii] *n* bra

ชั้นเรียน [chan rian] *n* class; ชั้นเรียนใน
เวลาเย็น [chan rian nai we la yen] *n*
evening class

ชั้นวาง [chan wang] *n* shelf

ชัยชนะ [chai cha na] ความยินดีจาก ชัยชนะ [khwam yin dii chak chai cha na] *n* triumph; ชัยชนะในการสงคราม [chai cha na nai kan song khram] *n* victory; ซึ่งมีชัยชนะ [sueng mii chai cha na] *adj* winning

ชั่ว [chua] ชั่วร้าย [chua rai] *adj* evil

ชั่วขณะ [chua kha na] *n* moment

ชั่วคราว [chua khrao] *adj* provisional, temporary; การหยุดชั่วคราว [kan yut chua khrao] *n* suspension; พนักงาน ชั่วคราว [pha nak ngan chua khrao] *n* temp

ชั่วครู่ [chua khru] *adj* momentary

ชั่วโมง [chua mong] *n* hour; ครึ่งชั่วโมง [khrueng chau mong] *n* half-hour; ชั่วโมงเร่งด่วน [chau mong reng duan] *n* rush hour; ชั่วโมงเยี่ยม [chau mong yiam] *npl* visiting hours; ชั่วโมงละ เท่าไร? [chau mong la thao rai] How much is it per hour?

ชั่วร้าย [chua rai] *adj* sinister, vile, wicked; ความชั่วร้าย [khwam chua rai] *n* vice; ตัวชั่วร้าย [tua chua rai] *n* villain

ชา [cha] *adj* numb; เวลาดื่มน้ำชา [we la duem nam cha] *n* teatime; กาน้ำชา [ka nam cha] *n* teapot; ชาสมุนไพร [cha sa mun phrai] *n* herbal tea

ช้า [cha] *adj* late *(delayed)*, slow; แล่นช้า ลง [laen cha long] *v* slow down; ทำให้ ช้า [tham hai cha] *n* setback; อย่างช้า ๆ [yang cha cha] *adv* slowly; เรามาช้าสิบ นาที [rao ma cha sip na thi] We are ten minutes late

ช่าง [chang] เกี่ยวกับวิชาช่าง [kiao kap wi cha chang] *adj* technical; ช่างเครื่อง [chang khrueang] *n* mechanic; ช่าง เครื่องยนต์ [chang khrueang yon] *n* motor mechanic; คุณส่งช่างมาได้ไหม? [khun song chang ma dai mai] Can you send a mechanic?

ช้าง [chang] *n* elephant; สัตว์ขนาดใหญ่ คล้ายช้างขนยาว งาโค้งยาวสูญพันธุ์ไปแล้ว [sat kha nat yai khlai chang khon yao nga khong yao sun phan pai laeo] *n* mammoth

ช่างพูด [chang phut] *adj* talkative

ช่างไม้ [chang mai] *n* carpenter; ที่เกี่ยว กับช่างไม้ [thii kiao kap chang mai] *n* carpentry

ชาด [chat] ประเทศชาดในอัฟริกา [pra tet chad nai af ri ka] *n* Chad

ชาติ [chat] เพลงชาติ [phleng chat] *n* national anthem; มีใจรักชาติ [mii jai rak chat] *adj* patriotic; คนรักชาติ [khon rak chat] *n* nationalist

ชาตินิยม [chat ni yom] *n* nationalism

ชาน [chan] ชานบ้าน [chaan baan] *n* porch; นอกชาน [nok chan] *n* patio

ชานชาลา [chan cha la] รถไฟจะออกจาก สถานีที่ชานชาลาไหน? [rot fai ja ok chak sa tha ni thii chan cha la nai] Which platform does the train leave from?

ชานเมือง [chan mueang] *n* suburb ▷ *npl* outskirts

ชาม [cham] *n* bowl

ชาย [chai] เด็กชาย [dek chai] *n* boy; ชาย โสด [chai sot] *n* bachelor; ผู้ชาย [phu chai] *n* chap

ชายทะเล [chai tha le] *n* seaside

ชายฝั่ง [chai fang] *n* coast, shore; หน่วย รักษาการณ์ตามชายฝั่งทะเล [nuai rak sa kan tam chai fang tha le] *n* coastguard; ชายฝั่งทะเล [chai fang tha le] *n* seashore

ชายหาด [chai hat] *n* beach; เราอยู่ห่าง จากชายหาดมากแค่ไหน? [rao yu hang chak chai hat mak khae nai] How far are we from the beach?; ฉันจะไปที่ ชายหาด [chan ja pai thii chai hat] I'm going to the beach; ชายหาดอยู่ไกลแค่ ไหน? [chai hat yu klai khae nai] How far is the beach?

ชาร์จ [chat] ไม่เก็บไฟที่ชาร์จไว้ [mai kep fai thii chat wai] It's not holding its charge; ไม่ชาร์จไฟ [mai chat fai] It's not charging; ฉันจะชาร์จไฟใส่โทรศัพท์

มือถือได้ที่ไหน? [chan ja chat fai sai tho ra sap mue thue dai thii nai] Where can I charge my mobile phone?

ชาว [chao] ชาวต่างชาติ [chao tang chat] n foreigner; ชาวประมง [chao pra mong] n fisherman

ชำนาญ [cham nan] ไม่มีความชำนาญ [mai mii khwam cham nan] adj unskilled; ความชำนาญในการทำสิ่งที่ยาก [khwam cham nan nai kan tham sing thii yak] n know-how; ความชำนาญ พิเศษ [khwam cham nan phi set] n speciality

ชำระล้าง [cham ra lang] v rinse; การ ชำระล้าง [kan cham ra lang] n rinse

ชำเลือง [cham lueang] การชำเลือง [kan cham lueang] n glance; ชำเลืองดู [cham lueang du] v glance

ชิงทรัพย์ [ching sap] คนข่มขู่เพื่อชิงทรัพย์ [khon khom khu phuea ching sap] n mugger; ทำร้ายเพื่อชิงทรัพย์ [tham rai phuea ching sap] v mug

ชิด [chit] ชิดกัน [chit kan] adv close

ชิ้น [chin] n slice; เศษชิ้นเล็กชิ้นน้อย [set chin lek chin noi] n scrap (small piece); ชิ้นส่วน [chin suan] n piece; ชิ้นปลาหรือ เนื้อที่ไม่มีกระดูก [chin pla rue nuea thii mai mii kra duk] n fillet

ชิ้นเอก [chin ek] งานชิ้นเอก [ngan chin ek] n masterpiece

ชิม [chim] v taste; ขอฉันชิมได้ไหม? [kho chan chim dai mai] Can I taste it?

ชิมแปนซี [chim paen si] ลิงชิมแปนซี [ling chim paen si] n chimpanzee

ชิลี [chi li] เกี่ยวกับประเทศชิลี [kiao kap pra thet chi li] adj Chilean; ชาวชิลี [chao chi li] n Chilean; ประเทศชิลี [pra tet chi li] n Chile

ชิอะ [chi a] นิกายชิอะ [ni kai chi a] adj Shiite

ชี้ [chi] vi point; เครื่องชี้นำ [khrueang chii nam] n indicator; การชี้ตัว [kan chii tua] n identification

ชี้ตัว [chi tua] v identify

ชี้บอก [chi bok] v indicate

ชีพจร [chip pha chon] n pulse

ชีว [chi wa] เกี่ยวกับชีวสถิติวิทยา [kiao kap chi wa sa thi ti wit tha ya] adj biometric

ชีวเคมี [chi wa ke mi] n biochemistry

ชีววิทยา [chi wa wit tha ya] n biology; ทางชีววิทยา [thang chi wa wit tha ya] adj biological

ชีวิต [chi wit] n life; มีชีวิต [mii chi wit] v alive; ซึ่งช่วยชีวิต [sueng chuai chi wit] adj life-saving; ที่มีชีวิตชีวา [thii mii chi wit chi wa] v live

ชีวิตชีวา [chi wit chi wa] ไม่มีชีวิตชีวา [mai mii chi wit chi wa] adj drab

ชื้น [chuen] adj damp, humid, moist; ความชื้น [khwam chuen] n humidity, moisture

ชื่นชม [chuen chom] v admire; ความ ชื่นชม [khwam chuen chom] n admiration; น่าชื่นชมยินดี [na chuen chom yin dii] adj delighted

ชื่อ [chue] n name; ชื่อเล่น [chue len] n nickname; ชื่อสกุลของหญิงก่อนแต่งงาน [chue sa kun khong ying kon taeng ngan] n maiden name; ชื่อจริง [chue chring] n first name; คุณชื่ออะไร? [khun chue a rai] What's your name?

ชื่อเรื่อง [chue rueang] n title

ชื่อเสียง [chue siang] n fame, reputation; มีชื่อเสียง [mii chue siang] adj famous; คนที่มีชื่อเสียงในด้านใดด้าน หนึ่ง [khon thii mii chue siang nai dan dai dan nueng] n star (person); ที่มีชื่อ เสียง [thii mii chue siang] adj well-known

ชุด [chut] n set; รายการอาหารเป็นชุด [rai kan a han pen chut] n set menu; ชุด แต่งงาน [chut taeng ngan] n wedding dress; ชุดแฟนซี [chut faen si] n fancy dress

ชุดชั้นใน [chut chan nai] ชุดชั้นในของ สตรี [chut chan nai khong sa tree] n lingerie; ชุดชั้นในของผู้หญิง [chut chan nai khong phu ying] *n* slip (*underwear*); แผนกชุดชั้นในอยู่ที่ไหน? [pha naek chut chan nai yu thii nai] Where is the lingerie department?

ชุดนอน [chut non] *npl* pyjamas

ชุมชน [chum chon] *n* community

ชุมนุม [chum num] การชุมนุม [kan chum num] *n* rally; ชุมนุม จัดให้พบกัน [chum num, chat hai phop kan] *vi* meet

ชูชีพ [chu chip] เรือชูชีพ [ruea chu chip] *n* lifeboat; เสื้อชูชีพ [suea chu chip] *n* life jacket; เข็มขัดชูชีพ [khem khat chu chip] *n* lifebelt

เช็ก [chek] ชาวเช็ก [chao chek] *n* Czech (*person*)

เช็ค [chek] เช็คเดินทาง [chek doen thang] *n* traveller's cheque; เช็คเปล่า [chek plao] *n* blank cheque; เช็คไปรษณีย์ [chek prai sa ni] *n* postal order; มีคนขโมยเช็คเดินทางของฉัน [mii khon kha moi chek doen thang khong chan] Someone's stolen my traveller's cheques

เช็คอิน [chek in] ฉันเช็คอินอย่างช้าที่สุดได้เมื่อไร? [chan chek in yang cha thii sut dai muea rai] When is the latest I can check in?; ฉันไปเช็คอินเที่ยวบินไป...ได้ที่ไหน? [chan pai chek in thiao bin pai…dai thii nai] Where do I check in for the flight to…?; ฉันต้องเช็คอินเมื่อไร? [chan tong chek in muea rai] When do I have to check in?

เช็ด [chet] เช็ดให้สะอาด [chet hai sa at] *v* wipe up; เช็ดทำความสะอาดด้วยไม้ถูพื้น [chet tham khwam sa at duai mai thu phuen] *v* mop up; เช็ดออก [chet ok] *v* wipe

เช่น [chen] ตัวย่อของตัวอย่างเช่น [tua yo khong tua yang chen] *abbr* e.g.

เช่นกัน [chen kan] *adv* also; ไม่เช่นกัน [mai chen kan] *adv* either (*with negative*)

เช่นนี้ [chen ni] *adj* such

เชสเนีย [ches nia] ประเทศเชสเนีย [pra tet ches nia] *n* Chechnya

เชอร์รี่ [choe ri] ผลเชอร์รี่ [phon choe ri] *n* cherry

เชอรี่ [choe ri] เหล้าเชอรี่ [lao choe ri] *n* sherry

เช่า [chao] *v* hire, lease, rent; รถเช่า [rot chao] *n* car hire, car rental, hired car, rental car; สัญญาเช่า [san ya chao] *n* lease; การเช่ารถ [kan chao rot] *n* hire car; ฉันจะเช่าไม้เล่นได้ที่ไหน? [chan ja chao mai len dai thii nai] Where can I hire a racket?

เช้า [chao] เวลาเช้า [we la chao] *n* morning; อาหารเช้า [a han chao] *n* breakfast; เช้านี้ [chao nii] this morning

เชาวน์ปัญญา [chao pan ya] คำพูดหรือข้อเขียนที่แสดงเชาวน์ปัญญา [kham phut rue kho khian thii sa daeng chao pan ya] *n* wit

เชิง [choeng] เชิงเทียน [choeng thian] *n* candlestick

เชิงกราน [choeng kran] กระดูกเชิงกราน [kra duk choeng kran] *n* pelvis

เชิญ [choen] *v* invite; คุณใจดีมากที่เชิญเรา [khun jai di mak thii choen rao] It's very kind of you to invite us; คุณใจดีมากที่เชิญฉัน [khun jai di mak thii choen chan] It's very kind of you to invite me

เชียร์ [chia] การส่งเสียงเชียร์ [kan song siang chia] *n* cheer

เชี่ยวชาญ [chiao chan] ความเชี่ยวชาญ [khwam chiao chan] *n* skill; ผู้เชี่ยวชาญ [phu chiao chan] *n* expert, specialist; ผู้เชี่ยวชาญในวิชาชีพ [phu chiao chan nai wi cha chip] *n* professional

เชื่อ [chuea] *vt* believe; ซึ่งไม่น่าเชื่อว่าเป็นจริง [sueng mai na chuea wa pen ching] *adj* unbelievable

เชื้อ [chuea] เชื้อแบคทีเรีย [chuea baek thi ria] *npl* bacteria

เชือก [chueak] *n* rope, string; เชือกบังเหียน [chueak bang hian] *npl* reins;

เชือกผูกรองเท้า [chueak phuk rong thao] *n* shoelace

เชื่อง [chueang] *adj* tame; ไม่เชื่อง [mai chueang] *adj* wild

เชื่อใจ [chua chai] ความเชื่อใจ [khwam chua jai] *n* confidence (*secret*), trust; ความไว้เนื้อเชื่อใจ [khwam wai nuea chua jai] *n* confidence (*trust*)

เชื้อชาติ [chua chat] *n* race (*origin*); เกี่ยวกับเชื้อชาติ [kiao kap chua chat] *adj* ethnic; ที่เกี่ยวกับเชื้อชาติ [thii kiao kap chua chat] *adj* racial

เชื้อเชิญ [chua choen] การเชื้อเชิญ [kan chua choen] *n* invitation

เชื่อโชคลาง [chua chok lang] ซึ่งเชื่อ โชคลาง [sueng chua chok lang] *adj* superstitious

เชื่อถือ [chue thue] เชื่อถือได้ [chua thue dai] *adj* faithful, reliable; ความน่า เชื่อถือ [khwam na chua thue] *n* credit; น่าเชื่อถือ [na chua thue] *adj* credible, reputable

เชื้อเพลิง [chua phloeng] *n* fuel

เชื่อฟัง [chue fung] *adj* obedient ▷ *v* obey; ไม่เชื่อฟัง [mai chua fang] *v* disobey; ซึ่งไม่เชื่อฟัง [sueng mai chua fang] *adj* disobedient

เชื่อม [chueam] *v* link (up); ที่เชื่อมตรงกับ อินเตอร์เน็ต [thii chueam trong kap in toe net] *adv* online

เชื่อมต่อ [chueam to] เชื่อมต่อกับ อินเตอร์เน็ตแบบไร้สาย [chueam to kap in toe net baep rai sai] *n* WiFi; ขณะเชื่อมต่อ กับอินเตอร์เน็ต [kha na chueam to kap in toe net] *adv* online

เชื่อมั่น [chua man] ความเชื่อมั่น [khwam chua man] *n* belief; ซึ่งเชื่อมั่น ในตัวเอง [sueng chua man nai tua eng] *adj* self-assured

เชื้อโรค [chue rok] *n* germ; โปรตีนต่อต้าน เชื้อโรคในร่างกาย [pro tin to tan chuea rok nai rang kai] *n* antibody; ระบบต่อ ต้านเชื้อโรค [ra bop to tan chuea rok] *n* immune system; สารที่ใช้ฆ่าเชื้อโรค

[san thii chai kha chuea rok] *n* disinfectant

เชื้อสาย [chue sai] เชื้อสายวงศ์ตระกูล [chua sai wong tra kun] *adj* pedigree

แช่ [chae] *v* soak

แช่แข็ง [chae khaeng] ตู้แช่แข็ง [tu chae khaeng] *n* freezer; ปลาสดหรือแช่แข็ง? [pla sot rue chae khaeng] Is the fish fresh or frozen?; ผักต่าง ๆ สดหรือแช่แข็ง? [phak tang tang sot rue chae khaeng] Are the vegetables fresh or frozen?

แชมเปญ [chaem pen] *n* champagne

โชค [chok] *n* luck

โชคชะตา [chok cha ta] *n* fate

โชคดี [chok di] *adj* fortunate, lucky ▷ *adv* luckily; อย่างโชคดี [yang chok di] *adv* fortunately

โชคร้าย [chok rai] *adj* unlucky; ความโชค ร้าย [khwam chok rai] *n* misfortune

โชว์ [cho] เราจะไปดูโชว์ได้ที่ไหน? [rao ja pai du cho dai thii nai] Where can we go to see a show?

ใช่ [chai] *excl* yes

ใช้ [chai] *v* spend, use; ใช้เงินคืน [chai ngoen khuen] *v* reimburse; ใช้เวลา [chai we la] *vt* take (*time*); ใช้ไปโดย เปล่าประโยชน์ [chai pai doi plao pra yot] *v* waste

ใช้จ่าย [chai chai] ใช้จ่ายสุรุ่ยสุร่าย [chai chai su rui su rai] *v* squander; การใช้ จ่ายเงิน [kan chai chai ngen] *n* expenditure; ค่าใช้จ่าย [kha chai chai] *npl* charge (*price*), cost, expenses

ไชโย [chai yo] ไชโย ชนแก้ว [chai yo chon kaew] *excl* cheers!

ซ

ซอง [song] *n* sachet; ซองจดหมาย [song chot mai] *n* envelope

ซ่อน [son] ซ่อน ซุกซ่อน [son, suk son] *vt* hide; ซ่อน ปกปิด [son, pok pit] *vi* hide

ซอฟแวร [sof wae] ซอฟแวร์ของคอมพิวเตอร์ที่ใช้สำหรับตรวจคำศัพท์ [sop wae khong khom phio toe thii chai sam rap truat kham sap] *n* spellchecker; ซอฟแวร์ที่บันทึกดนตรีลงในซีดี [sop wae thii ban thuek don tree long nai si di] *n* CD burner

ซ่อม [som] การซ่อม [kan som] *n* repair; การซ่อมถนน [kan som tha non] *npl* roadworks; ร้านซ่อมเก้าอี้คนพิการอยู่ใกล้ที่สุดอยู่ที่ไหน? [ran som kao ii khon phi kan yu klai thii sut yu thii nai] Where is the nearest repair shop for wheelchairs?

ซ่อมแซม [som saem] *v* mend, repair, fix; ซ่อมแซมโดยการเย็บ [som saem doi kan yep] *v* sew up; ซ่อมแซมให้สู่สภาพเดิม [som saem hai su sa phap doem] *v* restore

ซอส [sot] ซอสมะเขือเทศ [sos ma khuea tet] *n* tomato sauce

ซอส [sot] ซ้อสมะเขือเทศ [sos ma khuea tet] *n* ketchup

ซัก [sak] การซักเสื้อผ้า [kan sak suea pha] *n* washing; ซักด้วยเครื่องซักผ้าได้ [sak duai khrueang sak pha dai] *adj* machine washable; ฉันจะซักผ้าได้ที่ไหน? [chan ja sak pha dai thii nai] Where can I do some washing?

ซักถาม [sak tham] *v* query

ซักผ้า [sak pha] มีร้านซักผ้าเล็ก ๆ อยู่ใกล้ที่นี่ไหม? [mii ran sak pha lek lek yu kai thii ni mai] Is there a launderette near here?; มีบริการซักผ้าไหม? [mii bo ri kan sak pha mai] Is there a laundry service?

ซักแห้ง [sak haeng] การซักแห้ง [kan sak haeng] *n* dry-cleaning; ที่ร้านซักแห้ง [thii ran sak haeng] *n* dry-cleaner's; ฉันต้องการซักแห้ง [chan tong kan sak haeng] I need this dry-cleaned

ซับซ้อน [sap son] *adj* complex

ซาก [sak] ซากศพ [saak sop] *n* corpse

ซากปรักหักพัง [sak prak hak phang] *n* ruin, wreckage

ซานมาริโน [san ma ri o] ประเทศซานมาริโน [pra tet san ma ri no] *n* San Marino

ซ้าย [sai] ไปทางซ้าย [pai thang sai] *adv* left; มือซ้าย [mue sai] *adj* left-hand; การขับด้านซ้าย [kan khap dan sai] *n* left-hand drive; เลี้ยวซ้าย [liao sai] Turn left

ซาร์ดีน [sa din] ปลาซาร์ดีน [pla sa din] *n* sardine

ซาลามิ [sa la mi] ไส้กรอกซาลามิ [sai krok sa la mi] *n* salami

ซาอุดิอาระเบีย [sa u di a ra bia] เกี่ยวกับประเทศซาอุดิอาระเบีย [kiao kap pra thet sa u di a ra bia] *adj* Saudi, Saudi Arabian; ชาวซาอุดิอาระเบีย [chao sa u di a ra bia] *n* Saudi; ประเทศซาอุดิอาระเบีย [pra tet sa u di a ra bia] *n* Saudi Arabia

ซาฮารา [sa ha ra] ทะเลทรายซาฮารา [tha le sai sa ha ra] *n* Sahara

ซ้ำ [sam] เกิดซ้ำ ๆ [koet sam sam] *adj* recurring; การกระทำซ้ำ [kan kra tham sam] *n* repeat; พูด เขียนทำซ้ำ [phut khian tham som] v repeat

ซ้ำซาก [sam sak] ที่ทำซ้ำซาก [thii tham sam sak] adj repetitive; น่าเบื่อหน่าย เพราะซ้ำซาก [na buea nai phro sam sak] adj monotonous

ซิกข์ [sik] เกี่ยวกับศาสนาซิกข์ [kiao kap sat sa na sik] n Sikh; ชาวศาสนาซิกข์ [chao sat sa na sik] n Sikh

ซิการ์ [si ka] n cigar

ซิป [sip] n zip; รูดซิป [rut sip] vi zip (up); รูดซิปออก [rut sip ok] v unzip

ซิมบับเว [sim bap we] เกี่ยวกับประเทศ ซิมบับเว [kiao kap pra thet sim bap we] adj Zimbabwean; ชาวซิมบับเว [chao sim bap we] n Zimbabwean; ประเทศ ซิมบับเว [pra tet sim bab we] n Zimbabwe

ซี่โครง [si khrong] เนื้อติดซี่โครง [nuea tit si khrong] n rib

ซีด [sit] ซีดเผือด [sid phueat] adj pale

ซีดี [si di] n CD; เครื่องเล่นซีดี [khrueang len si di] n CD player; ซีดี-รอม [si di -rom] n CD-ROM; ซีดีจะเสร็จเมื่อไร? [si di ja set muea rai] When will the CD be ready?

ซีเมนต์ [si men] n cement; ส่วนผสมของ ปูนขาวหรือซีเมนต์กับน้ำและทราย [suan pha som khong pun khao rue si men kap nam lae sai] n mortar (plaster)

ซีเรีย [si ria] เกี่ยวกับประเทศซีเรีย [kiao kap pra thet si ria] adj Syrian; ชาวซีเรีย [chao si ria] n Syrian; ประเทศซีเรีย [pra tet si ria] n Syria

ซี่ล้อ [si lo] ซี่ล้อรถ [si lo rot] n spoke

ซีอิ๊ว [si io] น้ำซีอิ๊ว [nam si io] n soy sauce

ซึ่งทำงาน [sueng tham ngan] ซึ่งทำงาน อิสระไม่ได้รับเงินเดือนประจำ [sueng tham ngan it sa ra mai dai rap ngoen duean pra cham] adv freelance

ซึนามิ [sue na mi] คลื่นซึนามิเกิดจากแผ่น ดินไหวใต้ทะเล [khluen sue na mi koet chak phaen din wai tai tha le] n tsunami

ซื้อ [sue] v buy, purchase; ได้ซื้อ [dai sue]

adj bought; สามารถซื้อได้ [sa maat sue dai] adj affordable; ผู้ซื้อ [phu sue] n buyer; ฉันจะซื้อตั๋วได้ที่ไหน? [chan ja sue tua dai thii nai] Where do I buy a ticket?

ซื้อของ [sue khong] การซื้อของ [kan sue khong] n shopping; คำพูดเพื่อซื้อของ [kham phut phuea sue khong] Shopping phrases

ซื้อขาย [sue khai] การซื้อขาย [kan sue khai] n deal; การซื้อขายหุ้นของบริษัท [kan sue khai hun khong bo ri sat] n buyout

ซื้อเชื่อ [sue chuea] การซื้อเชื่อ [kan sue chuea] n credit

ซื่อสัตย์ [sue sat] adj honest, truthful; ไม่ ซื่อสัตย์ [mai sue sat] adj dishonest, unfaithful; ความซื่อสัตย์ [khwam sue sat] n honesty; อย่างซื่อสัตย์ [yang sue sat] adv honestly

ซุกซน [suk son] adj naughty

ซุกซ่อน [suk son] ซ่อน ซุกซ่อน [son, suk son] vt hide

ซุป [sup] n broth, soup; ซุปประจำวันคือ อะไร? [sup pra cham wan khuea a rai] What is the soup of the day?

ซุปเปอร์มาร์เก็ต [sup poe ma ket] ฉันต้อง มองหาซุปเปอร์มาร์เก็ต [chan tong mong ha sup poe ma ket] I need to find a supermarket

ซุปเปอร์มาร์เก็ต [sup poe ma ket] n supermarket

ซุ่ม [sum] การซุ่มโจมตี [kan sum chom ti] n ambush

ซูดาน [su dan] เกี่ยวกับประเทศซูดาน [kiao kap pra thet su dan] adj Sudanese; ชาว ซูดาน [chao su dan] n Sudanese; ประเทศซูดาน [pra tet su dan] n Sudan

เซ [se] v stagger

เซ็น [sen] ฉันเซ็นชื่อที่ไหน? [chan sen chue thii nai] Where do I sign?

เซ็น [sen] เซ็นลงทะเบียนเพื่อรับเงินสวัสดิการ [sen long tha bian phuea rap ngoen sa wat sa di kan] v sign on

เซ็นชื่อ [sen chue] v sign

เซ็นติเกรด [sen ti kret] องศาเซ็นติเกรด [ong sa sen ti kret] n degree centigrade

เซนติเมตร [sen ti met] n centimetre

เซเนกัล [se ne kan] เกี่ยวกับสาธารณรัฐเซเนกัล [kiao kap sa tha ra na rat se ne kal] adj Senegalese; สาธารณรัฐเซเนกัลในอัฟริกา [sa tha ra na rat se ne kal nai af ri ka] n Senegal; ชาวเซเนกัล [chao se ne kal] n Senegalese

เซรามิค [se ra mik] adj ceramic

เซลเซียส [sen siat] องศาเซลเซียส [ong sa sel sias] n degree Celsius

เซลล์ [sel] ทำให้กำเนิดมาจากเซลล์เดียวกัน [tham hai kam noet ma chak sel diao kan] v clone

เซโล [se lo] ไวโอลินเซโล [vi o lin che lo] n cello

เซอร์เบีย [soe bia] adj เกี่ยวกับเซอร์เบีย [kiao kap soe bia] adj Serbian ▷ n ชาวเซอร์เบีย [chao soe bia] n Serbian (person); ประเทศเซอร์เบีย [pra tet soe bia] n Serbia

แซ็กโซโฟน [saek so fon] n saxophone

แซนด์วิช [san wit] ขนมปังแซนด์วิช [kha nom pang saen wit] n sandwich; คุณมีขนมปังแซนด์วิชอะไรบ้าง? [khun mii kha nom pang saen wit a rai bang] What kind of sandwiches do you have?

แซมเบีย [saem bia] เกี่ยวกับประเทศแซมเบีย [kiao kap pra tet saem bia] adj Zambian; ชาวแซมเบีย [chao saem bia] n Zambian; ประเทศแซมเบีย [pra tet saem bia] n Zambia

แซลมอน [saen mon] ปลาแซลมอน [pla sael mon] n salmon

โซ่ [so] n chain; ฉันต้องใส่โซ่กันหิมะหรือไม่? [chan tong sai so kan hi ma rue mai] Do I need snow chains?

โซดา [so da] น้ำโซดา [nam so da] n sparkling water; วิสกี้กับโซดาหนึ่งแก้ว [wis ki kap so da nueng kaeo] a whisky and soda

โซเดียมไบคาร์บอเนต [so diam bai kha bo net] สารโซเดียมไบคาร์บอเนต [san so diam bi kha bo net] n bicarbonate of soda

โซน [son] โซน แถบ เขต [son, thaep, khet] n zone

โซมาเลีย [so ma lia] เกี่ยวกับประเทศโซมาเลีย [kiao kap pra thet so ma lia] adj Somali; ชาวโซมาเลีย [chao so ma lia] n Somali (person); ประเทศโซมาเลีย [pra tet so ma lia] n Somalia

ไซโคลน [sai khlon] พายุหมุนไซโคลน [pha yu mun sai khlon] n cyclone

ไซบีเรีย [sai bi ria] ประเทศไซบีเรีย [pra tet sai bi ria] n Siberia

ไซปรัส [sai prat] เกี่ยวกับประเทศไซปรัส [kiao kap pra thet sai bras] adj Cypriot; ชาวไซปรัส [chao sai pras] n Cypriot (person); ประเทศไซปรัส [pra tet sai pras] n Cyprus

ฌ   ญ

ฌาปนกิจ [cha pa na kit] โรงงานประกอบ
พิธีฌาปนกิจศพ [rong ngan pra kop phi
ti cha pa na kit sop] *n* funeral parlour

ญาติ [yat] เป็นญาติกัน [pen yat kan] *adj*
related; ญาติที่ใกล้ที่สุด [yat thii klai
thii sut] *n* next-of-kin; ญาติพี่น้องที่มา
จากการแต่งงาน [yat phi nong thii ma
chak kan taeng ngan] *npl* in-laws
ญี่ปุ่น [yi pun] เกี่ยวกับญี่ปุ่น [kiao kap yi
pun] *adj* Japanese; ชาวญี่ปุ่น [chao yi
pun] *n* Japanese (*person*); ประเทศญี่ปุ่น
[pra tet yii pun] *n* Japan

ฐ ณ

ฐาน [than] ฐานข้อมูล [tan kho mun] *n* database

ฐานทัพ [than thap] พื้นฐาน ฐานทัพ [phuen than, than thap] *n* base

ณ ที่นี้ [na thi ni] *n* present (*time being*)

ดนตรี [don tri] n music; เล่นดนตรี [len don trii] play (music); เสียงดนตรี [siang don trii] n melody; เกี่ยวกับดนตรี [kiao kap don tree] adj musical; เราจะฟังดนตรีสดได้ที่ไหน? [rao ja fang don trii sot dai thii nai] Where can we hear live music?

ดม [dom] ดมกลิ่น [dom klin] vi smell

ดลใจ [don chai] ซึ่งดลใจ [sueng don jai] adj moving

ดวงตราไปรษณียกร [duang tra prai sa ni] n stamp

ดวงอาทิตย์ [duang a thit] เกี่ยวกับดวงอาทิตย์ [kiao kap duang a thit] adj solar

ด่วน [duan] คุณจัดการให้มีเงินส่งมาด่วนได้ไหม? [khun chat kan hai mii ngoen song ma duan dai mai] Can you arrange to have some money sent over urgently?; ฉันต้องการโทรด่วน [chan tong kan tho duan] I need to make an urgent telephone call

ด้วยกัน [duai kan] อยู่ด้วยกัน [yu duai kan] v live together; เราใช้แท็กซี่ไปด้วยกันได้ [rao chai thaek si pai duai kan dai] We could share a taxi

ดอก [dok] ดอกเดซี่ [dok de si] n daisy; ดอกแดฟโฟดิลมีสีเหลือง [dok daef fo dil

mii sii lueang] n daffodil

ดอกเบี้ย [dok bia] n interest (income); อัตราดอกเบี้ย [at tra dok bia] n interest rate

ดอกไม้ [dok mai] n blossom, flower; ร้านดอกไม้ [ran dok mai] n florist; กลีบดอกไม้ [klip dok mai] n pedal; ช่อดอกไม้ [cho dok mai] n bouquet

ดอกไม้ไฟ [dok mai fai] npl fireworks

ด้อย [doi] ด้อยกว่า [doi kwa] adj inferior; ผู้ด้อยกว่า [phu doi kwa] n inferior

ด้อยพัฒนา [doi phat tha na] ประเทศที่ด้อยพัฒนา [pra tet thii doi phat ta na] n Third World

ดอลล่าร์ [don la] คุณรับดอลล่าร์ไหม? [khun rap don la mai] Do you take dollars?

ดอลล่าร์ [don la] เงินดอลลาร์ [ngoen don la] n dollar

ดัก [dak] ที่ดักแมลง [thii dak ma laeng] n stick insect

ดักฟัง [dak fung] adj bugged

ดัง [dang] adj loud; เสียงดังมาก [siang dang mak] adj deafening; อย่างดัง [yang dang] adv aloud

ดั้งเดิม [dang doem] แบบดั้งเดิม [baep dang doem] adj primitive; โบราณ แบบดั้งเดิม แบบเก่าแก่ [bo ran, baep dang doem, baep kao kae] adj traditional

ดังที่ [dang thi] ขณะที่ ดังที่ เนื่องจาก [kha na thii, dang thii, nueang chak] conj as

ดังนั้น [dang nan] adv consequently ▷ conj so (that)

ดัช [dat] เกี่ยวกับดัช [kiao kap dat] adj Dutch; ชาวดัช [chao dat] n Dutch; ผู้หญิงชาวดัช [phu ying chao dat] n Dutchwoman

ดัชนี [dut cha ni] n index (numerical scale)

ดัด [dat] การดัดผม [kan dat phom] n perm; ผมฉันเป็นผมดัด [phom chan pen phom dat] My hair is permed

ดัน [dan] คุณช่วยดันรถหน่อยได้ไหม?

[khun chuai dan rot noi dai mai] Can
you give me a push?

ดับ [dap] ขยี้ให้ดับ [kha yii hai dab] v
stub out

ดับเพลิง [dap phloeng] เครื่องดับเพลิง
[khrueang dap phloeng] n
extinguisher; เครื่องดับเพลิง [khrueang
dap phloeng] n fire extinguisher; เจ้า
หน้าที่ดับเพลิง [chao na thii dap
phloeng] n fireman

ดับไฟ [dap fai] การดับไฟ [kan dap fai] n
blackout

ด่างพร้อย [dang phroi] จุดด่างพร้อย
[chut dang phroi] n spot (blemish)

ดาดฟ้า [dat fa] ดาดฟ้าเรือ [dat fa ruea] n
deck; เราขึ้นไปบนดาดฟ้าเรือได้ไหม? [rao
khuen pai bon dat fa ruea dai mai] Can
we go out on deck?

ด้าน [dan] n side; ด้านวิชาการ [dan wi
cha kan] adj academic; ที่อยู่คนละด้าน
[thii yu khon la dan] adv opposite

ด้านลบ [dan lop] ที่เป็นด้านลบ [thii pen
dan lop] adj negative

ดาบ [dap] n sword

ด้าม [dam] n handle

ด้าย [dai] n thread; คุณมีเข็มกับด้ายไหม?
[khun mii khem kap dai mai] Do you
have a needle and thread?

ดารา [da ra] เป็นดารานำแสดง [pen da ra
nam sa daeng] v star; ดาราภาพยนตร์
[da ra phap pha yon] n film star

ดาราศาสตร์ [da ra sat] n astronomy

ดาว [dao] n star (sky); ดาวหาง [dao hang]
n comet

ดาวเคราะห์ [dao khro] ดาวเคราะห์เก้าดวง
[dao khrao kao duang] n planet

ดาวเทียม [dao thiam] n satellite; ระบบ
การค้นหาทางโดยใช้ดาวเทียม [ra bop kan
khon ha thang doi chai dao thiam]
abbr GPS; จานดาวเทียม [chan dao
thiam] n satellite dish

ดาวเรือง [dao rueang] ต้นไม้ประเภทดาว
เรือง [ton mai pra phet dao rueang] n
marigold

ดำ [dam] adj black; คนดำ [khon dam] n
Niger; เป็นขาวกับดำ [pen khao kap
dam] in black and white

ดำน้ำ [dam nam] v dive; การดำน้ำ [kan
dam nam] n dive, diving; การดำน้ำด้วยถัง
ออกซิเจน [kan dam nam duai thang ok
si chen] n scuba diving; ชุดดำน้ำ [chut
dam nam] n wetsuit; ฉันอยากไปดำน้ำ
[chan yak pai dam nam] I'd like to go
diving

ดำน้ำตื้น [dam nam tuen] ฉันอยากไปดำ
น้ำตื้น [chan yak pai dam nam tuen] I'd
like to go snorkelling

ดำเนิน [dam noen] กำลังดำเนินอยู่ [kam
lang dam noen yu] dv on; ดำเนินต่อไป
[dam noen to pai] vt carry on,
continue; ดำเนินต่อไปใหม่ [dam noen
to pai mai] v resume; เขาดำเนินกิจการ
โรงแรม [khao dam noen kit cha kan
rong raeng] He runs the hotel

ดำเนินการ [dam noen kan] v execute;
การดำเนินการ [kan dam noen kan] npl
operation (undertaking), proceedings;
การติดต่อทางธุรกิจ การดำเนินการทางธุรกิจ
[kan tit to thang thu ra kit, kan dam
noen kan thang thu ra kit] n
transaction; ดำเนินการต่อไป [dam noen
kan to pai] v go on

ดำเนินชีวิต [dam noen chi wit] v live

ดิจิตัล [di chi tal] โทรทัศน์ดิจิตัล [tho ra
tat di chi tal] n digital television; กล้อ
งดิจิตัล [klong di chi tan] n digital
camera; นาฬิกาดิจิตัล [na li ka di chi
tal] n digital watch

ดิน [din] n dirt, soil; ดินเหนียว [din niao]
n clay

ดินเผา [din phao] เครื่องเคลือบดินเผา
[khrueang khlueap din phao] n china

ดินสอ [din so] n pencil; กล่องใส่ดินสอ
[klong sai din so] n pencil case; ดินสอสี
[din so sii] n crayon; ที่เหลาดินสอ [thii
lao din so] n pencil sharpener

ดิบ [dip] adj raw

ดิสก์ [disk] แผ่นดิสก์ [phaen dis] n

compact disc, disk

ดิสโก้ [dit sa ko] การเต้นดิสโก้ [kan ten dis ko] n disco

ดิสค์ [disk] แผ่นดิสค์ [phaen dis] n disc

ดี [di] adj fine, good, nice, well; มาตรฐานที่ดีกว่า [mat tra than thii di kwa] adv better; การทำให้ดีขึ้น [kan tham hai di khuen] n improvement; ดีเลิศ [di loet] adj ideal

ดีเจ [di che] abbr DJ

ดีใจ [di chai] adj glad

ดีซ่าน [di san] โรคดีซ่าน [rok di san] n jaundice

ดีเซล [di sel] น้ำมันดีเซล [nam man di sel] n diesel; กรุณาเติมดีเซลเป็นเงิน... [ka ru na toem di sel pen ngeg...]... worth of diesel, please

ดีด [dit] ตี ดีด ปะทะ [ti, diit, pa tha] strike

ดีบุก [di buk] n tin

ดีวีดี [di wi di] n DVD; เครื่องเล่นดีวีดี [khrueang len di vi di] n DVD player; ซอฟแวร์ที่ทำให้บันทึกลงในดีวีดีได้ [sop wae thii tham hai ban thuek long nai di wi di dai] n DVD burner

ดึก [duek] อยู่ดึก [yu duek] v stay up

ดึง [dueng] vt pull; การดึงและบิดอย่างแรง [kan dueng lae bit yang raeng] n wrench; ดึงและบิดอย่างแรง [dueng lae bit yang raeng] v wrench; ดึงลง [dueng long] v pull down

ดึงดูด [dueng dut] มีเสน่ห์ดึงดูด [mii sa ne dueng dut] adj attractive; การดึงดูดความสนใจ [kan dueng dud khwam son jai] n attraction; ดึงดูดความสนใจ [dueng dut khwam son jai] v attract

ดื่ม [duem] vt drink; การดื่มเหล้ามากเกินไป [kan duem lao mak koen pai] n binge drinking; การดื่มอวยพร [kan duem uai pon] n toast (tribute); ดื่มอัลกอฮอล์แล้วขับรถ [duem aen ko ho laeo khap rot] n drink-driving; คุณอยากดื่มอะไร? [khun yak duem a rai] What would you like to drink?

ดื้อ [due] adj stubborn; หัวดื้อ [hua due] adj bigheaded

ดื้อดึง [due dueng] adj obstinate

ดุ [du] ดุว่า [du wa] v scold, tell off

ดุร้าย [du rai] adj fierce

ดุลยพินิจ [dun ya phi nit] การใช้ดุลยพินิจ [kan chai dun la ya phi nit] n discretion

ดุเหว่า [du wao] นกดุเหว่า [nok du wao] n blackbird

ดู [du (duu)] เฝ้าระวังดู [fao ra wang du] v watch out; การดูนก [kan du nok] n birdwatching; ชำเลืองดู [cham lueang du] v glance; มีอะไรให้ดูที่นั่น? [mii a rai hai du thii nan] What is there to see here?

ดูด [dud] v suck; ตัวดูดอากาศเข้าลูกสูบ [tua dut a kaat khao luk sup] n carburettor; ยี่ห้อเครื่องดูดฝุ่น [yi ho khrueang dut fun] n Hoover®

ดูดฝุ่น [dud fun] v hoover, vacuum

ดูถูก [du thuk] v insult; การดูถูก [kan du thuk] n insult

ดูแล [du lae] v care, look after; กำกับดูแลโดยรัฐ [kam kap du lae doi rat] v nationalize; การควบคุมดูแล [kan khuap khum du lae] n control; การดูแล [kan du lae] n care; ฉันอยากได้คนดูแลเด็ก ๆ คืนนี้ [chan yak dai khon du lae dek dek khuen nii] I need someone to look after the children tonight

เด็ก [dek] n child, kid; เด็กหนุ่ม [dek num] n lad; เด็กชาย [dek chai] n boy; เด็กประจำ [dek pra cham] n boarder; เด็กคนนี้อยู่ในหนังสือเดินทางเล่มนี้ [dek khon nii yu nai nang sue doen thang lem nii] The child is on this passport

เด้ง [deng] vi bounce

เดซี [de si] ดอกเดซี่ [dok de si] n daisy

เด็ดเดี่ยว [det diao] adj determined; ความเด็ดเดี่ยวแน่นอน [khwam det diao nae non] n resolution

เด่น [den] adj distinctive; จุดเด่น [chut den] n highlight

เดนมาร์ก [den mak] เกี่ยวกับชาวเดนมาร์ก [kiao kap chao den mak] *adj* Danish; ชาวเดนมาร์ก [chao den mak] *n* Dane; ประเทศเดนมาร์ก [pra tet den mak] *n* Denmark

เดิน [doen] *v* march, walk; เดินเขา [doen khao] *n* hill-walking; เดินโขยกเขยก [doen kha yok kha yek] *v* limp; เดินไปโดยไม่มีจุดหมาย [doen pai doi mai mii chut mai] *v* wander; ฉันเดินไปได้ไหม? [chan doen pai dai mai] Can I walk there?

เดินขบวน [doen kha buan] การเดินขบวน [kan doen kha buan] *n* march

เดินเครื่อง [doen khrueang] วิ่ง วิ่งหนี เปิดเครื่อง เดินเครื่อง [wing, wing nii, poet khrueang, doen khrueang] *vi* run

เดินทาง [doen thang] *v* commute, travel; เริ่มเดินทาง [roem doen thang] *v* set off, start off; เริ่มออกเดินทาง [roem ok doen thang] *v* set out; เช็คเดินทาง [chek doen thang] *n* traveller's cheque; การประกันเดินทาง [kan pra kan kan doen thang] *n* travel insurance; ผู้เดินทาง [phu doen thang] *n* commuter, traveller; ฉันเดินทางคนเดียว [chan doen thang khon diao] I'm travelling alone

เดินเรือ [doen ruea] การเดินเรือ [kan doen ruea] *n* sailing

เดิม [doem] กลับไปสภาพเดิม [klap pai sa phap doem] *adv* back

เดี่ยว [diao] *adj* single; เตียงเดี่ยว [tiang diao] *n* single bed; ห้องเดี่ยว [hong diao] *n* single, single room; การเล่นเดี่ยว [kan len diao] *npl* singles

เดียวดาย [diao dai] *adj* lonesome

เดี๋ยวนี้ [diao ni] *adv* now

เดือด [dueat] เดือดแล้ว [dueat laeo] *adj* boiled; เดือดจนล้น [dueat chon lon] *v* boil over; กำลังเดือด [kam lang dueat] *adj* boiling

เดือดดาล [dueat dan] ความเดือดดาล [khwam dueat dan] *n* rage

เดือน [duean] *n* month; เดือนเมษายน [duean me sa yon] *n* April; เดือนมกราคม [duean mok ka ra khom] *n* January; เดือนมิถุนายน [duean mi thu na yon] *n* June; หนึ่งเดือนมาแล้ว [nueng duean ma laeo] a month ago

แดง [daeng] *adj* red; แดงน้ำตาล [daeng nam tan] *adj* ginger; สีแดงสด [sii daeng sot] *adj* scarlet; หน้าหรือผิวแดง [na rue phio daeng] *n* flush

แดด [daet] สีไหม้เกรียมของผิวหนังจากการตากแดด [sii mai kriam khong phio nang chak kan tak daet] *n* tan; ผิวหนังเป็นสีน้ำตาลเนื่องจากตากแดด [phio nang pen sii nam tan nueang chak tak daet] *n* suntan; มีแดดออก [mii daet ok] It's sunny

แดฟโฟดิล [daep fo dil] ดอกแดฟโฟดิลมีสีเหลือง [dok daef fo dil mii sii lueang] *n* daffodil

โดดเด่น [dot den] ซึ่งโดดเด่น [sueng dot den] *adj* striking

โดดเดี่ยว [dot diao] *adj* isolated, stranded

โดนัท [do nat] ขนมโดนัท [kha nom do nat] *n* doughnut

โดมินิกันรีพับลิค [do mi ni kan ri phap blik] ประเทศโดมินิกันรีพับลิค [pra tet do mi ni kan ri phap lik] *n* Dominican Republic

โดมิโน [do mi no] เกมโดมิโน [kem do mi no] *npl* domino, dominoes

โดย [doi] *prep* by

โดยเฉพาะ [doi cha pho] *adj* particular, specific ▷ *adv* exclusively; โดยเฉพาะอย่างยิ่ง [doi cha pho yang ying] *adv* especially, particularly

โดยทาง [doi thang] *prep* via

โดยลำพัง [doi lam phang] *adj* alone

โดยสาร [doi san] การโดยสารไปด้วย [kan doi san pai duai] *n* lift (*free ride*); ค่าโดยสาร [kha doi san] *n* fare; ผู้โดยสาร [phu doi san] *n* passenger; มีรถโดยสารไปในเมืองไหม? [mii rot doi san pai nai mueang mai] Is there a bus to the city?

โดยสิ้นเชิง [doi sin choeng] *adv* totally

ได้ [dai] *v* get, get *(to a place)*; ได้กำไร [dai kam rai] *vt* gain; ได้คืนมาอีก [dai khuen ma ik] *v* regain; ที่สามารถทำได้ [thii sa maat tham dai] *adj* capable

ไดโนเสาร์ [dai no sao] *n* dinosaur

ได้เปรียบ [dai priap] ความได้เปรียบ [khwam dai priap] *n* advantage

ได้ผล [dai phon] ได้ผลดี [dai phon di] *adj* effective; อย่างได้ผล [yang dai phon] *adv* effectively

ได้ยิน [dai yin] *v* hear; การได้ยิน [kan dai yin] *n* hearing; พลาด ไม่เห็น ไม่เข้าใจ ไม่ได้ยิน [phlat, mai hen, mai khao jai, mai dai yin] *vt* miss

ไดร์เชอรี่ [dai choe ri] ขอไดรเชอรี่หนึ่ง แก้ว [kho drai choe ri nueng kaeo] A dry sherry, please

ได้รับ [dai rap] *v* obtain, receive; ได้รับ รายได้ [dai rap rai dai] *v* earn; ผู้ได้รับ [phu dai rap] *n* receiver *(person)*, recipient

ไดอารี่ [dai a ri] ไดอารี่เล่มใหญ่ [dai a ri lem yai] *n* personal organizer

ต

ตก [tok] เธอตกลงมา [thoe tok long ma] She fell

ตกกระ [tok kra] *npl* freckles

ตกใจ [tok chai] *v* shock; สั่น ทำให้สั่น ทำให้ตกใจและสะเทือนใจ [san, tham hai san, tham hai tok jai lae sa thuean jai] *vt* shake; ความตกใจ [khwam tok jai] *n* fright, shock; ซึ่งตกใจสุดขีด [sueng tok jai sut khit] *adj* shocking

ตกตะลึง [tok ta lueng] ทำให้ตกตะลึง เพราะความกลัว [tham hai tok ta lueng phro khwam klua] *adj* petrified

ตกต่ำ [tok tam] การตกต่ำทางเศรษฐกิจ [kan tok tam thang set tha kit] *n* recession

ตกแต่ง [tok taeng] ช่างตกแต่ง [chang tok taeng] *n* decorator; ตกแต่งใหม่ [tok taeng mai] *v* redecorate; นักตกแต่ง ภายใน [nak tok taeng phai nai] *n* interior designer

ตกปลา [tok pla] *vi* fish; การตกปลา [kan tok pla] *n* angling, fishing; นักตกปลา [nak tok pla] *n* angler; ขอเราตกปลาที่นี่ ได้ไหม? [kho rao tok pla thii nii dai mai] Can we fish here?

ตกลง [tok long] ไม่ตกลงใจ [mai tok long

jai] *adj* undecided; คุณตกลงไหม? [khun tok long mai] Are you alright?

ตกหลุมรัก [tok lum rak] *v* fall for

ต้น [tan] ต้นเมเปิล [ton me poel] *n* maple; ต้นเฟอร์ [ton foe] *n* fir (tree); ต้นเดือนมิถุนายน [ton duean mi thu na yon] at the beginning of June

ต้นฉบับ [ton cha bap] *n* text

ต้นไม้ [ton mai] *n* tree; หัวของต้นไม้ [hua khong ton mai] *n* bulb (*plant*); ต้นไม้เลื้อยชนิดหนึ่งมีกลิ่นหอม [ton mai lueai cha nit nueng mii klin hom] *n* honeysuckle

ต้นหอม [ton hom] *n* spring onion

ต้นอ่อน [ton on] *npl* sprouts

ตบ [top] *v* slap; การตบเบา ๆ การเคาะเบา ๆ การตีเบา ๆ [kan top bao bao, kan kho bao bao, kan ti bao bao] *n* tap

ต้ม [tom] *vt* boil

ต้มตุ๋น [tom tun] การโกง การหลอกลวง การต้มตุ๋น [kan kong, kan lok luang, kan tom tun] *n* rip-off

ตรง [trong] *adj* direct; เครื่องทำผมให้ตรง [khrueang tham phom hai trong] *npl* straighteners; โดยตรง [doi trong] *adv* directly; ไม่ตรง [mai trong] *adj* indirect; ฉันต้องการเดินทางสายตรง [chan tong kan doen thang sai trong] I'd prefer to go direct

ตรงกันข้าม [trong kan kham] การตรงกันข้าม [kan trong kan kham] *n* contrary; ที่อยู่ตรงกันข้าม [thii yu trong kan kham] *adj* opposite

ตรงข้าม [trong kham] *prep* opposite; ด้านตรงข้าม [dan trong kham] *n* reverse; ฝ่ายตรงข้าม [fai trong kham] *n* opponent, opposition

ตรงต่อเวลา [trong to we la] ที่ตรงต่อเวลา [thii trong to we la] *adj* punctual

ตรงไป [trong pai] ที่ตรงไป [thii trong pai] *adj* straight; อย่างตรงไป [yang trong pai] *adv* straight on

ตรงไปตรงมา [trong pai trong ma] *adj* straightforward; อย่างตรงไปตรงมา [yang trong pai trong ma] *adv* frankly

ตรงเวลา [trong we la] *adj* on time; ที่ตรงเวลา [thii trong we la] *adj* prompt; อย่างตรงเวลา [yang trong we la] *adv* promptly

ตรวจ [truat] *vt* check; การตรวจ [kan truat] *n* check; การตรวจเลือด [kan truat lueat] *n* blood test; คุณช่วยตรวจดูน้ำได้ไหม? [khun chuai truat du nam dai mai] Can you check the water, please?

ตรวจตรา [truat tra] *v* supervise; การดูแลตรวจตรา [kan du lae truat tra] *n* oversight (*supervision*)

ตรวจภายใน [truat phai nai] การตรวจภายใน [kan truat phai nai] *n* smear test

ตรวจสอบ [truat sop] *v* examine; การตรวจสอบบัญชี [kan truat sob ban chii] *n* audit; ตรวจสอบบัญชี [truat sop ban chii] *v* audit; ตรวจสอบอย่างละเอียด [truat sop yang la iad] *v* inspect

ตรอก [trok] *n* alley, lane, lane (*driving*)

ตระกร้า [tra kra] *n* basket; ตะกร้าใส่ขยะ [ta kra sai kha ya] *n* wastepaper basket

ตระกูล [tra kun] เชื้อสายวงศ์ตระกูล [chuea sai wong tra kun] *adj* pedigree

ตระเตรียม [tra triam] การตระเตรียม [kan tra triam] *n* preparation

ตระหนก [tra nak] *adj* apprehensive

ตระหนัก [tra nak] *v* realize; ตระหนักรู้ [tra nak ru] *adj* aware

ตระหนี่ [tra ni] *adj* thrifty; คนตระหนี่ [khon tra nii] *n* miser

ตรา [tra] *n* brand

ตราประทับ [tra pra thap] *n* seal (*mark*); ตราประทับบนไปรษณียภัณฑ์ [tra pra thap bon prai sa ni phan] *n* postmark

ตรี [tri] ปริญญาตรี [pa rin ya tree] *abbr* BA

ตลก [ta lok] *adj* funny; เรื่องตลก [rueang ta lok] *n* joke; ละครตลก [la khon ta lok] *n* comedy; หนังสือตลก [nang sue ta lok] *n* comic book

ตลอด [ta lot] *adv* ever

ตลอดไป [ta lot pai] *adv* forever

ตลอดเวลา [ta lot we la] เกิดขึ้นตลอดเวลา [koet khuen ta lot we la] *adv* constantly; ที่เกิดขึ้นตลอดเวลา [thii koet khuen ta lot we la] *adj* constant

ตลาด [ta lat] *n* market; การทำการตลาด [kan tham kan ta lat] *n* marketing; ตลาดสินค้า [ta lat sin kha] *n* marketplace; มีตลาดเมื่อไร? [mii ta lat muea rai] When is the market on?

ตลาดหลักทรัพย์ [ta lad hlak sap] *n* stock exchange

ตลาดหุ้น [ta lad hun] *n* stock market

ตลิ่ง [ta ling] *n* bank (ridge)

ต่อ [to] *prep* per ▷ *v* connect; ตัวแตน ตัวต่อ [tua taen, tua to] *n* wasp

ต้อ [to] *n* cataract (eye)

ต้อง [tong] *v* have to, must

ต้องการ [tong kan] *v* demand, need, require, want; ความต้องการ [khwam tong kan] *n* demand, need, requirement, wish; ต้องการอย่างมาก [tong kan yang mak] *adj* demanding; คุณต้องการอะไรบ้างไหม? [khun tong kan a rai bang mai] Do you need anything?

ต่อต้าน [to tan] *prep* against ▷ *v* oppose, resist; ระบบต่อต้านเชื้อโรค [ra bop to tan chuea rok] *n* immune system; การต่อต้าน [kan to tan] *n* resistance; ซึ่งต่อต้าน [sueng to tan] *adj* opposing

ตอน [ton] *n* episode; ตอนบ่าย [ton bai] *n* afternoon; ที่เป็นตอน ๆ [thii pen ton ton] *n* serial

ตอนเช้า [ton chao] ในตอนเช้า [nai ton chao] in the morning; ฉันป่วยตั้งแต่ตอนเช้า [chan puai tang tae ton chao] I've been sick since this morning

ตอนนี้ [ton ni] ฉันจ่ายตอนนี้หรือจ่ายทีหลัง? [chan chai ton nii rue chai thii lang] Do I pay now or later?

ตอนบ่าย [ton bai] ในตอนบ่าย [nai ton bai] in the afternoon

ตอนเย็น [ton yen] ในตอนเย็น [nai ton yen] in the evening; มีอะไรทำที่นั่นในตอนเย็น? [mii a rai tham thii nan nai ton yen] What is there to do in the evenings?

ต้อนรับ [ton rap] *v* welcome; การต้อนรับ [kan ton rap] *n* welcome; พบโดยบังเอิญ ต้อนรับ [phop doi bang oen, ton rab] *vt* meet

ต่อนหลัง [ton lang] *adv* later

ต่อเนื่อง [to nueang] *adj* continual; สิ่งที่ต่อเนื่องกัน [sing thii to nueang kan] *n* series; การพัฒนาต่อเนื่อง [kan phat ta na to nueang] *n* process; ซึ่งต่อเนื่องกัน [sueng to nueang kan] *adj* continuous

ตอบ [top] *v* answer, respond; ให้คำตอบ [hai kham top] *v* reply; คำตอบ [kham top] *n* answer

ต่อไป [to pai] *adj* next; เรือลำต่อไปล่อง ไป...เมื่อไร? [ruea lam to pai long pai... muea rai] When is the next sailing to...?; รถโดยสารคันต่อไปที่จะไป...เดินทาง เมื่อไร? [rot doi san khan to pai thii ja pai...doen thang muea rai] When is the next bus to...?

ต่อม [tom] *n* gland

ต่อมทอนซิล [tom thon sin] *npl* tonsils; ภาวะต่อมทอนซิลอักเสบ [pha wa tom thon sil ak sep] *n* tonsillitis

ต่อย [toi] แผลถูกแมลงกัดต่อย [phlae thuk ma laeng kat toi] *v* sting; ต่อยจนล้มลุก ไม่ขึ้น [toi chon lom luk mai khuen] *v* knock out; ฉันถูกต่อย [chan thuk toi] I've been stung

ต่อรอง [to rong] *v* negotiate; การต่อรอง [kan to rong] *npl* bargain, negotiations; ต่อรองราคา [to rong ra kha] *v* haggle; ผู้ต่อรอง [phu to rong] *n* negotiator

ต่อสู้ [to su] *v* fight, scrap; การต่อสู้ [kan to su] *n* fight, fighting, scrap (dispute); คู่ต่อสู้ [khu to su] *n* adversary

ต่อสู้กับ [to su kap] *prep* versus

ต่ออายุ [to a yu] ซึ่งต่ออายุใหม่ได้ [sueng

to a yu mai dai] *adj* renewable

ตะกละ [ta kla] ซึ่งตะกละมาก [sueng ta kla mak] *adj* ravenous

ตะกั่ว [ta kua] *n* lead *(metal)*, pewter; ไร้สารตะกั่ว [rai san ta kua] *adj* lead-free; น้ำมันไร้สารตะกั่ว [nam man rai san ta kua] *n* unleaded, unleaded petrol

ตะเกียง [ta kiang] *n* lamp

ตะเกียบ [ta kiap] *npl* chopsticks

ตะแกรง [ta klaeng] *n* grid

ตะโกน [ta kon] *v* shout; การตะโกน [kan ta khon] *n* shout; ตะโกน ร้อง [ta khon, rong] *v* yell; ตะโกนใส่ [ta khon sai] *v* slag off

ตะขอ [ta kho] *n* hook; ของที่มีรูปร่างโค้งเหมือนตะขอ [khong thii mii rup rang khong muean ta kho] *n* crook

ตะเข็บ [ta khep] *n* seam

ตะคิว [ta khio] ฉันเป็นตะคิวที่ขา [chan pen ta khio thii kha] I've got cramp in my leg

ตะไคร้ [ta khrai] พืชตะไคร่น้ำ [phuet ta khrai nam] *n* moss

ตะไบ [ta bai] *n* file *(tool)* ▷ *v* file *(smoothing)*; ตะไบขัดเล็บ [ta bai khat lep] *n* nailfile

ตะปู [ta pu] *n* nail; ตะปูควง [ta pu khuang] *n* screw

ตะลึง [ta lueng] ตกตะลึง [tok ta lueng] *adj* stunned

ตะวันตก [ta wan tok] ซึ่งเกี่ยวกับทางทิศตะวันตก [sueng kiao kap thang thit ta wan tok] *adj* west; ซึ่งเคลื่อนไปทางตะวันตก [sueng khluean pai thang ta wan tok] *adj* westbound; ซึ่งอยู่ไปทางทิศตะวันตก [sueng yu pai thang thit ta wan tok] *adj* western

ตะวันออก [ta wan ok] เกี่ยวกับทิศตะวันออก [kiao kap thit ta wan ok] *adj* east, eastern; กลุ่มประเทศในเอเชียตะวันออก [klum pra tet nai e chia ta wan ok] *n* Far East; ซึ่งเดินทางไปทางด้านตะวันออก [sueng doen thang pai thang dan ta wan ok] *adj* eastbound

ตะวันออกกลาง [ta wan ok klang] *n* Middle East

ตัก [tak] *n* lap

ตักเตือน [tak tuean] การตักเตือน [kan tak tuean] *n* caution

ตั๊กแตน [tak ka taen] *n* grasshopper

ตั้ง [tang] ซึ่งตั้งอยู่ [sueng tang yu] *adj* situated; ตั้งขึ้น [tang khuen] *v* put up; ที่ตั้งขึ้น [thii tang khuen] *adv* upright

ตั้งครรภ์ [tang khan] *adj* pregnant

ตั้งใจ [tang chai] ไม่ได้ตั้งใจ [mai dai tang jai] *adv* inadvertently; การตั้งใจ [kan tang jai] *n* concentration; ความตั้งใจ [khwam tang jai] *n* attention, intention

ตั้งแต่ [tang tae] *prep* since; ฉันป่วยตั้งแต่วันจันทร์ [chan puai tang tae wan chan] I've been sick since Monday

ตั้งเป้า [tang pao] *v* aim

ตั้งหลักฐาน [tang lak than] *v* settle down

ตัณหา [tan ha] *n* lust

ตัด [tat] *v* cut; การตัด [kan tat] *n* cutting; การตัดไฟชั่วคราว [kan tat fai chua khrao] *n* power cut; การตัดผม [kan tat phom] *n* haircut; ฉันถูกตัดสาย [chan thuk tat sai] I've been cut off

ตัดขาด [tat khat] ตัดขาดจากกัน [tat khat chak kan] *v* disconnect

ตัดสิน [tat sin] *v* judge; การตัดสิน [kan tat sin] *n* arbitration; คำตัดสินของคณะลูกขุน [kham tat sin khong kha na luk khun] *n* verdict; ตัดสินลงโทษ [tat sin long thot] *v* sentence

ตัดสินใจ [tat sin chai] *v* decide; การตัดสินใจ [kan tat sin jai] *n* decision; ตัดสินใจผิด [tat sin jai phit] *v* misjudge

ตัดเสื้อ [tat suea] ช่างตัดเสื้อ [chang tat suea] *n* tailor

ตัดหญ้า [tat ya] *v* mow

ตัน [tan] ทางตัน [thang ton] *n* dead end

ตับ [tap] *n* liver; โรคตับอักเสบ [rok tap ak sep] *n* hepatitis; ฉันกินตับไม่ได้ [chan kin tab mai dai] I can't eat liver

ตับอ่อน [tap on] สารชนิดหนึ่งสกัดจากตับอ่อน [san cha nit nueng sa kat chak tap on] *n* insulin

ตั๋ว [tua] *n* ticket; เครื่องกีดกั้นที่ต้องแสดงตั๋วก่อนผ่านเข้าไป [khrueang kit kan thii tong sa daeng tua kon phan khao pai] *n* ticket barrier; เครื่องขายตั๋ว [khrueang khai tua] *n* ticket machine; สำนักงานขายตั๋ว [sam nak ngan khai tua] *n* ticket office; เครื่องขายตั๋วไม่ทำงาน [khrueang khai tua mai tham ngan] The ticket machine isn't working

ตัวต่อ [tua to] ตัวต่อสำหรับสร้างเป็นภาพ [tua to sam rap sang pen phap] *n* jigsaw

ตัวตุ่น [tua tun] *n* mole *(mammal)*

ตัวแทน [tua thaen] *n* agent, delegate; เป็นตัวแทน [pen tua taen] *adj* represent, representative; ตัวแทนสำนักงานท่องเที่ยว [tua thaen sam nak ngan thong thiao] *n* travel agent; ที่สำนักงานตัวแทนท่องเที่ยว [thii sam nak ngan tua taen thong thiao] *n* travel agent's

ตัวย่อ [tua yo] ตัวย่อของเร็วที่สุดเท่าที่จะเป็นไปได้ [tua yo khong reo thii sut thao thii ja pen pai dai] *adv abbr* asap; ตัวย่อของเตียงนอนและอาหารเช้า [tua yo khong tiang non lae a han chao] *n* B&B; ตัวย่อของก่อนคริสต์ศักราช [tua yo khong kon khrit sak ka rat] *abbr* BC

ตัวร้อน [tua ron] ฉันอยากได้อะไรสักอย่างสำหรับตัวร้อน [chan yak dai a rai sak yang sam rap tua ron] I'd like something for a temperature

ตัวเลข [tua lek] *n* figure, number; ซึ่งส่งรับข้อมูลโดยใช้ตัวเลข [sueng song rap kho mun doi chai tua lek] *adj* digital

ตัวเลือก [tua lueak] ซึ่งมีตัวเลือก [sueng mii tua lueak] *adv* alternatively; ที่มีตัวเลือก [thii mii tua lueak] *adj* alternative

ตัวอย่าง [tua yang] *n* example, instance, sample; ซึ่งเป็นตัวอย่าง [sueng pen tua yang] *adj* typical; ตัวย่อของตัวอย่างเช่น [tua yo khong tua yang chen] *abbr* e.g.

ตัวเอก [tua ek] *n* lead *(in play/film)*

ตัวเอง [tua eng] ตัวย่อของทำด้วยตัวเอง [tua yo khong tham duai tua eng] *abbr* DIY; ที่เป็นของตัวเอง [thii pen khong tua eng] *adj* own; ช่วยตัวเอง [chuai tua eng] Help yourself!

ตา [ta] *n* eye, grandpa; เปลือกตา [plueak ta] *n* eyelid; สิ่งที่ใช้ปิดตา [sing thii chai pit ta] *n* blindfold; ขนตา [khon ta] *n* eyelash; มีบางอย่างอยู่ในลูกตาฉัน [mii bang yang yu nai luk ta chan] I have something in my eye

ตาก [tak] มีที่ไหนที่ฉันจะตากผ้าได้ไหม? [mii thii nai thii chan ja tak pha dai mai] Is there somewhere to dry clothes?

ตากอากาศ [tak a kat] สถานที่ตากอากาศ [sa than thii tak a kaat] *n* resort

ตาไก่ [ta kai] *n* ring binder

ตาข่าย [ta khai] ตาข่ายดักสัตว์ [ta khai dak sat] *n* net

ต่าง [tang] ต่างกัน [tang kan] *adj* different; ต่างชนิด [tang cha nit] *adj* various

ต่างก็ไม่ [tang ko mai] *adv* neither ▷ *pron* neither

ต่างชาติ [tang chat] ชาวต่างชาติ [chao tang chat] *n* foreigner

ต่างด้าว [tang dao] คนต่างด้าว [khon tang dao] *n* alien

ต่างต่างนานา [tang tang na na] *adj* varied

ต่างประเทศ [tang pra thet] เกี่ยวกับต่างประเทศ [kiao kap tang pra thet] *adv* foreign, overseas; ไปต่างประเทศ [pai tang pra tet] *n* abroad *(go abroad)*; ต่างประเทศ [tang pra thet] *adv* abroad; ฉันจะโทรศัพท์ไปต่างประเทศได้ที่ไหน? [chan ja tho ra sap pai tang pra tet dai thii nai] Where can I make an international phone call?

ต่างหาก [tang hak] ขอนมต่างหาก [kho nom tang hak] with the milk separate

ตาบอด [ta bot] ตาบอดสี [ta bot sii] *adj* colour-blind; ฉันตาบอด [chan ta bot] I'm blind

ตาปลา [tok pla] ตาปลาบนเท้า [ta pla bon thao] *n* bunion

ตาม [tam] *vt* follow; ที่จะตามมา [thii ja tam ma] *adv* next

ตามเข็ม [tam khem] ตามเข็มนาฬิกา [tam khem na li ka] *adv* clockwise

ตามใจ [tam chai] ทำให้เสียหาย ตามใจจน เสียคน [tham hai sia hai, tam jai chon sia khon] *vt* spoil

ตามทัน [tam than] *v* catch up; ไล่ตามทัน [lai tam than] *v* overtake

ตามที่ [tan thi] *prep* according to

ตามนั้น [tam nan] *adv* accordingly

ตามลำดับ [tam lam dap] *adv* respectively; เหตุการณ์ที่เกิดขึ้นตามลำดับ [het kan thii koet khuen tam lam dap] *n* sequence

ตาย [tai] *v* die; เพิ่งตาย [phoeng tai] *adj* late (dead); ความตาย [khwam tai] *n* death; ซึ่งทำให้ถึงตาย [sueng tham hai thueng tai] *adj* fatal

ตาราง [ta rang] *n* chart; ตารางเวลา [ta rang we la] *n* timetable; ตารางรายการ [ta rang rai kan] *n* table (chart); ตาราง จัดการหมายถึงโปรแกรมคอมพิวเตอร์ ประเภทหนึ่ง [ta rang chat kan mai thueng pro kraem khom phio toe pra pet nueng] *n* spreadsheet

ตารางเวลา [ta rang we la] *n* schedule

ตาเหล่ [ta le] *v* squint

ตาฮิติ [ta hi ti] เกาะตาฮิติทางตอนใต้ของ มหาสมุทรแปซิฟิก [ko ta hi ti thang ton tai khong ma ha sa mut pae si fik] *n* Tahiti

ต่ำ [tam] *adj* low ▷ *adv* low; ต่ำสุด [tam sut] *adj* bottom; ต่ำกว่า [tam kwa] *v* lower; ต่ำกว่ากำหนดอายุ [tam kwa kam not a yu] *adj* underage

ตำนาน [tam nan] *n* legend, mythology

ตำรวจ [tam ruat] *n* cop, police; สถานี ตำรวจ [sa tha ni tam ruat] *n* police station; ตำรวจหญิง [tam ruat ying] *n* policewoman; ตำรวจชาย [tam ruat chai] *n* policeman; เรียกตำรวจ [riak tam ruat] Call the police

ตำรา [tam ra] ตำรากับข้าว [tam ra kap khao] *n* recipe; ตำราอาหาร [tam ra a han] *n* cookbook

ตำราเรียน [tam ra rian] *n* textbook

ตำหนิ [tam ni] *n* fault (defect) ▷ *v* blame; สะอาดไม่มีตำหนิ [sa at mai mii tam ni] *adj* spotless; การตำหนิ คำติเตียน [kan tam hni, kham ti tian] *n* blame

ตำแหน่ง [tam naeng] *n* placement, position, post (position), rank (status); ลดตำแหน่ง [lot tam naeng] *v* relegate; ตำแหน่งชนะเลิศ [tam naeng cha na loet] *n* championship; ตำแหน่งว่าง [tam naeng wang] *n* vacancy

ติด [tit] ใช้กาวติด [chai kao tit] *v* glue; การหนีบติดกัน [kan niip tit kan] *n* clip; การติดเชื้อโรค [kan tit chuea rok] infection; ฉันติดคุณเท่าไร? [chan tit khun thao rai] What do I owe you?

ติดใจ [tit chai] น่าติดใจ [na tit jai] *adj* gripping

ติดเชื้อ [tit chuea] มันติดเชื้อไหม? [man tit chuea mai] Is it infectious?

ติดต่อ [tit to] *v* contact; การติดต่อ [kan tit to] *n* contact; การติดต่อสื่อสาร [kan tit to sue san] *n* communication; การ ติดต่อกันทางจดหมาย [kan tit to kan thang chot mai] *n* correspondence; เรา จะต้องติดต่อใครถ้าเกิดปัญหา? [rao ja tong tit to khrai tha koet pan ha] Who do we contact if there are problems?

ติดตาม [tit tam] *v* pursue; แสวงหาติดตาม [sa waeng ha tit tam] *v* go after; การ ติดตาม [kan tit tam] *n* pursuit; ติดตาม จนพบ [tit tam chon phop] *v* track down

ติดอ่าง [tit ang] *v* stutter

ติเตียน [ti tian] การตำหนิ คำติเตียน [kan tam hni, kham ti tian] *n* blame

ตี [ti] *v* beat (strike), hit; ตี ตีด ปะทะ [ti,

diit, pa tha] strike; การตี [kan ti] *n* hit;
การตี [kan ti] *n* beat, percussion

ตีลังกา [ti lang ka] การตีลังกาโดยไม่ใช้มือ
[kan ti lang ka doi mai chai mue] *n*
aerial

ตึก [tuek] ช่วงตึก [chuang tuek] *n* block
(buildings); ตึก อาคาร [tuek, a khan] *n*
building; ตึกกระฟ้า [tuek ra fa] *n*
skyscraper;...อยู่ที่ตึกไหน? [...yuu thii
tuek nai] Which ward is... in?

ตึง [tueng] *adj* tense

ตึงเครียด [tueng khriat] *adj* stressful,
uptight ▷ *n* tense; ความตึงเครียด
[khwam tueng khriat] *n* strain, tension

ตื่น [tuen] *adj* awake; การนอนตื่นสายใน
ตอนเช้า [kan non tuen sai nai ton chao]
n have a lie-in, lie in; ตื่นขึ้น [tuen
khuen] *v* wake up; ปลุก ทำให้ตื่น [pluk,
tham hai tuen] *v* awake

ตื้น [tuen] *adj* shallow

ตื่นตัว [tuen tua] *adj* alert

ตื่นเต้น [tuen ten] ความตื่นเต้น [khwam
tuen ten] *n* thrill; ตื่นเต้นดีใจ [tuen ten
di jai] *adj* excited; ที่รู้สึกตื่นเต้น [thii ru
suek tuen ten] *adj* thrilled

ตื่นนอน [tuen non] คุณตื่นนอนกี่โมง?
[khun tuen non kii mong] What time
do you get up?

ตุ๊กตา [tuk ka ta] *n* doll; ตุ๊กตาหมี [tuk ka
ta mii] *n* teddy bear

ตุ๋น [tun] *v* simmer

ตุ้ม [tum] ตุ้มหู [tum hu] *n* earring

ตุรกี [tu ra ki] เกี่ยวกับตุรกี [kiao kap tu ra
ki] *adj* Turkish; ชาวตุรกี [chao tu ra ki] *n*
Turk; ประเทศตุรกี [pra tet tu ra ki] *n*
Turkey

ตุล [tun] ราศีตุล [ra si tun] *n* Libra

ตุลาคม [tu la kan] เดือนตุลาคม [duean tu
la khom] *n* October; วันอาทิตย์ที่สาม
ตุลาคม [wan a thit thii sam tu la
khom] It's Sunday third October

ตู้ [tu] *n* cupboard; ตู้เสบียงบนรถไฟ [tu sa
biang bon rot fai] *n* dining car; ตู้เก็บ
เครื่องใช้หรือภาชนะที่ใช้ในการรับประทาน

อาหาร [tu kep khrueang chai rue pha
cha na thii chai nai kan rap pra than a
han] *n* sideboard; ตู้เก็บอาหาร [tu kep a
han] *n* larder

ตู้โชว์ [tu cho] หน้าต่างตู้โชว์ของร้านค้า
[na tang tu cho khong ran ka] *n* shop
window

ตู้นิรภัย [tu ni ra phai] *n* safe; ฉันมีของใน
ตู้นิรภัย [chan mii khong nai tu ni ra
phai] I have some things in the safe; ฉัน
อยากวางเครื่องประดับไว้ในตู้นิรภัย [chan
yak wang khrueang pra dap wai nai tu
ni ra phai] I would like to put my
jewellery in the safe

ตูนีเซีย [tu ni sia] เกี่ยวกับตูนีเซีย [kiao
kap tu ni sia] *adj* Tunisian; ชาวตูนีเซีย
[chao tu ni sia] *n* Tunisian; ประเทศตูนี
เซีย [pra tet tu ni sia] *n* Tunisia

ตู้ปลา [tu phla] *n* aquarium

ตู้เย็น [tu yen] *n* fridge, refrigerator; ตู้เย็น
ขนาดเล็กในห้องพักโรงแรม [tu yen kha
naat lek nai hong phak rong raeng] *n*
minibar

ตู้เสื้อผ้า [tu suea pha] *n* wardrobe

เตน [ten] เต้นเป็นจังหวะ [ten pen chang
wa] *v* throb; การเต้นแอร์โรบิค [kan ten
ae ro bik] *npl* aerobics

เต็นท์ [ten] *n* tent; ไม้ค้ำเต็นท์ [mai kham
tent] *n* tent pole; ตอกหมุดสำหรับเต็นท์
[tok mut sam rap tent] *n* tent peg; เรา
อยากได้ที่ตั้งเต็นท์ [rao yak dai thii tang
tent] We'd like a site for a tent

เต้นระบำ [ten ra bam] การเต้นระบำเปลื้อง
ผ้า [kan ten ra bam plueang pha] *n*
strip; นักเต้นระบำเปลื้องผ้า [nak ten ra
bam plueang pha] *n* stripper

เต้นรำ [ten ram] *v* dance; เต้นจังหวะ
วอลทซ์ [ten ram chang wa walt] *v*
waltz; การเต้นรำ [kan ten ram] *n*
dance, dancing; การเต้นรำโดยใช้รองเท้า
เคาะพื้นเป็นจังหวะ [kan ten ram doi chai
rong thao kho phuen pen chang wa] *n*
tap-dancing; เราจะไปเต้นรำได้ที่ไหน?
[rao ja pai ten ram dai thii nai] Where

can we go dancing?

เต็ม [tem] *adj* full; เต็มช้อน [tem chon] *n* spoonful

เต็มใจ [tem chai] ไม่เต็มใจ [mai tem jai] *adj* reluctant; ความไม่เต็มใจ [khwam mai tem jai] *n* grudge; อย่างเต็มใจ [yang tem jai] *adv* willingly

เต็มที่ [tem thi] *adj* sheer; อย่างเต็มที่ [yang tem thii] *adv* fully

เตรียม [triam] *v* prepare; ที่เตรียมไว้ [thii triam wai] *adj* prepared

เตะ [te] *vt* kick; เตะเริ่ม [te roem] *v* kick off; เตะฟรีในฟุตบอล [te frii nai fut bal] *n* free kick; การเตะ [kan te] *n* kick

เตา [tao] เตาหุงอาหาร [tao hung a han] *n* cooker; เตาทำอาหาร [tao tham a han] *n* stove; เตาทำอาหารที่ใช้แก๊ส [tao tham a han thii chai kaes] *n* gas cooker

เต่า [tao] *n* tortoise, turtle

เตาผิง [tao phing] ชั้นที่อยู่เหนือเตาผิง [chan thii yu nuea tao phing] *n* mantelpiece

เตารีด [tao rit] ฉันอยากได้เตารีด [chan yak dai tao riit] I need an iron

เตาอบ [tao op] *n* oven; เหมาะกับการใช้ใน เตาอบ [mo kap kan chai nai tao op] *adj* ovenproof

เติบโต [toep to] เติบโต งอกงาม [toep to, ngok ngam] *vi* grow; ความเติบโต [khwam toep to] *n* growth; พัฒนา เจริญ เติบโต [phat ta na, cha roen, toep to] *vi* develop

เติม [toem] *vt* fill; เติมเชื้อเพลิง [toem chuea phloeng] *v* refuel; เติมให้เต็ม [toem hai tem] *v* fill up, refill; บัตรเติม [bat toem] *n* top-up card; ช่วยเติมให้เต็ม ด้วย [chuai toem hai tem duai] Fill it up, please

เตียง [tiang] เก้าอี้นวมที่นั่งในเวลากลางวัน และเป็นเตียงเวลากลางคืน [kao ii nuam thii nang nai we la klang wan lae pen tiang we la klang khuen] *n* sofa bed; เตียงเดี่ยว [tiang diao] *n* single bed; เตียง สำหรับเด็ก [tiang sam rap dek] *n* cot;

เตียงไม่สบาย [tiang mai sa bai] The bed is uncomfortable

เตือน [tuean] *v* alert, remind, warn; สิ่ง เตือนความหลัง [sing tuean khwam lang] *n* reminder; การเตือน [kan tuean] *n* warning; การเตือนล่วงหน้า [kan tuean luang na] *n* premonition

เตือนภัย [tuean phai] เครื่องสัญญาณเตือน ภัย [khrueang san yan tuean phai] *n* smoke alarm; สัญญาณเตือนภัยปลอม [san yan tuean phai plom] *n* false alarm

แต่ [tae] *conj* but

แตก [taek] เรือแตก [ruea taek] *n* shipwreck; เศษเล็ก ๆ ที่แตกออก [set lek lek thii taek ok] *n* splinter; แตกหัก [taek hak] *adj* broke, broken; ฉันทำ หน้าต่างแตก [chan tham na tang taek] I've broken the window

แตกต่าง [taek tang] ความแตกต่าง [khwam taek tang] *n* contrast, difference; จำแนกความแตกต่าง [cham naek khwam taek tang] *v* distinguish

แตกแยก [taek yaek] *v* break up

แตกร้าว [taek rao] *vi* crack

แต่ก่อน [tae kon] *adv* previously

แตงกวา [taeng kwa] *n* cucumber

แต่งกาย [taeng kai] เครื่องแต่งกาย [khrueang taeng kai] *n* costume

แต่งงาน [taeng ngan] *v* marry; แหวน แต่งงาน [waen taeng ngan] *n* wedding ring; แต่งงานใหม่ [taeng ngan mai] *v* remarry; ไม่แต่งงาน [mai taeng ngan] *adj* unmarried; ฉันแต่งงานแล้ว [chan taeng ngan laeo] I'm married

แต่งตั้ง [taeng tang] *v* appoint; การแต่งตั้ง [kan taeng tang] *n* appointment

แต่งตัว [taeng tau] แต่งตัวอย่างสวยงาม [taeng tua yang suai ngam] *v* dress up; โต๊ะแต่งตัว [to taeng tua] *n* dressing table; ได้แต่งตัวแล้ว [dai taeng tua laeo] *adj* dressed

แตงโม [taeng mo] *n* watermelon

แตน [taen] ตัวแตน ตัวต่อ [tua taen, tua

to] *n* wasp

แต้มต่อ [taem to] แต้มต่อของคุณเท่าไร? [taem to khong khun thao rai] What's your handicap?; แต้มต่อของฉันคือ... [taem to khong chan khue...] My handicap is...

แตร [trae] *n* trumpet; แตรทองเหลืองรูปร่าง โค้งงอ [trae thong lueang rup rang khong ngo] *n* French horn; แตรทอง เหลืองขนาดเล็ก [trae thong lueang kha nat lek] *n* cornet; แตรยาว [trae yao] *n* trombone

แต่ละ [tae la] *adj* each ▷ *pron* each

แตะพื้น [tae phuen] การบินลงแตะพื้น [kan bin long tae phuen] *n* touchdown

โต [to] ใหญ่โต [yai to] *adj* huge, massive; ยังไม่โตเต็มที่ [yang mai to tem thii] *adj* premature

โต้เถียง [to thiang] *v* argue; การโต้เถียง [kan to thiang] *n* argument

โต้แย้ง [to yaeng] ไม่อาจจะโต้แย้งได้ [mai at ja to yaeng dai] *adj* undisputed; ซึ่ง ก่อให้เกิดการโต้แย้ง [sueng ko hai koet kan to yaeng] *adj* controversial

โต้วาที [to wa thi] *v* debate; การโต้วาที [kan to wa tii] *n* debate

โต๊ะ [to] *n* desk, table (*furniture*); โต๊ะแต่ง ตัว [to taeng tua] *n* dressing table; โต๊ะ สอบถาม [to sop tham] *n* enquiry desk; โต๊ะกาแฟ [to ka fae] *n* coffee table; ขอ โต๊ะสำหรับสี่คน [kho to sam rap si kon] A table for four people, please

ใต้ [tai] ในทางภาคใต้ [nai thang phak tai] *adj* southern; ข้างใต้ [khang tai] *prep* underneath; ขั้วโลกใต้ [khua lok tai] *n* South Pole

ใต้ดิน [tai din] *adv* underground; ชั้น ใต้ดิน [chan tai din] *n* underground

ใต้น้ำ [tai nam] *adv* underwater

ไต [tai] *n* kidney

ไต [tai] ฉันอยากไปไต่ลงเขาโดยใช้เชือก [chan yak pai tai long khao doi chai chueak] I'd like to go abseiling

ไต่เขา [tai khao] การไต่เขา [kan tai khao] *n* mountaineering, rock climbing; ขึ้นม้า ไต่เขา [khuen ma, tai khao] *v* mount; นักไต่เขา [nak tai khao] *n* mountaineer

ไต่ถาม [tai tham] *v* inquire, question

ไตร่ตรอง [trai trong] แก้ปัญหาหรือ วางแผนโดยการคิดไตร่ตรอง [kae pan ha rue wang phaen doi kan kit trai trong] *v* work out

ไต่สวน [tai suan] การไต่สวน [kan tai suan] *n* enquiry

ไต้หวัน [tai hwan] ชาวไต้หวัน [chao tai wan] *n* Taiwanese; ที่เกี่ยวกับประเทศ ไต้หวัน [thii kiao kap pra tet tai wan] *adj* Taiwanese; ประเทศไต้หวัน [pra tet tai wan] *n* Taiwan

ถ

ถนน [tha non] n road, street; แผนที่ถนน
[phaen thii tha non] n street map,
street plan; ไฟถนน [fai tha non] n
streetlamp; ขอบถนน [kop tha non] n
kerb; คุณมีแผนที่ถนนของบริเวณนี้ไหม?
[khun mii phaen thii tha non khong
bo ri wen nii mai] Do you have a road
map of this area?

ถนัด [tha nat] ถนัดมือซ้าย [tha nat mue
sai] adj left-handed

ถ่มน้ำลาย [thom nam lai] v spit

ถล่ม [tha lom] แผ่นดินถล่ม [phaen din
tha lom] n landslide

ถลา [tha la] ถลาไปอย่างรวดเร็ว [tha la
pai yang ruat reo] vi dash; ทำให้ลื่นถลา
[tham hai luen tha la] v slide

ถ้วย [tuai] n cup; ถ้วยใส่ไข่ [thuai sai
khai] n eggcup; ถ้วยใหญ่มีหู [thuai yai
mii hu] n mug; ถ้วยชา [thuai cha] n
teacup; ขอกาแฟให้พวกเราอีกถ้วยได้
ไหม? [kho ka fae hai phuak rao ik
thuai dai mai] Could we have another
cup of coffee, please?

ถ้วยรางวัล [thuai rang wan] n trophy

ถอด [thot] v take off; ถอดเสื้อผ้า [thot
suea pha] v undress; ถอดปลั๊ก [thot

pluk] v unplug

ถอน [thon] ถอนเงินเกิน [thon ngoen
koen] adj overdrawn; ถอนคืน [thon
khuen] v withdraw; ถอนตำแหน่ง [thon
tam naeng] n withdrawal

ถอนหายใจ [thon hai chai] v sigh; การ
ถอนหายใจ [kan thon hai jai] n sigh

ถ่อมตัว [thom tua] adj humble, modest

ถอยกลับ [thoi klap] v reverse

ถอยหลัง [thoi lang] adv backwards ▷ v
back

ถัก [thak] vt knit; เข็มถัก [khem thak] n
knitting needle; การถัก [kan thak] n
knitting; การถักโครเชต์ [kan thak kro
chae] v crochet

ถักร้อย [thak roi] เย็บปักถักร้อย [yep pak
thak roi] v embroider

ถัง [thang] n bucket, pail; ถังใส่ขยะ
[thang sai kha ya] n litter bin; ถังใส่
ของเหลว [thang sai khong leo] n barrel;
ถังขนาดใหญ่บรรจุน้ำหรือก๊าซ [thang kha
naat yai ban chu nam rue kas] n tank
(large container)

ถัดไป [that pai] adj following

ถั่ว [thua] n bean, nut (food); เนยผสมถั่ว
ลิสงบด [noei pha som thua li song bod]
n peanut butter; การแพ้ถั่ว [kan phae
thua] n nut allergy; ถั่วเฮเซลนัท [thua
he sel nat] n hazelnut; คุณทำอาหารที่
ไม่มีถั่วได้ไหม? [khun tham a han thii
mai mii thua dai mai] Could you
prepare a meal without nuts?

ถั่วลิสง [thua li song] ฉันแพ้ถั่วลิสง [chan
pae thua li song] I'm allergic to
peanuts; นั่นมีถั่วลิสงไหม? [nan mii
thua li song mai] Does that contain
peanuts?

ถั่วเหลือง [thua lueang] n soya

ถ้า [tha] conj if; ถ้าไม่ [tha mai] conj
unless

ถาด [that] n tray

ถ่าน [than] n charcoal

ถ่านหิน [than hin] n coal; เหมืองถ่านหิน
[mueang than hin] n colliery; ถ่านหิน

เลน [than hin len] *n* peat

ถาม [tham] *v* ask; ถามคำถาม [tham kham tham] *v* enquire

ถ่าย [thai] การถ่ายเลือด [kan thai luead] *n* blood transfusion; ถ่ายสินค้า [thai sin ka] *v* unload

ถ่ายทอด [thai thot] การถ่ายทอด [kan thai thot] *n* relay

ถ่ายเท [thai the] อากาศไม่ถ่ายเท [a kaat mai thai the] *adj* stuffy

ถ่ายภาพ [thai phap] *v* photograph; การถ่ายภาพ [kan thai phap] *n* photography; การถ่ายภาพอย่างรวดเร็ว [kan thai phap yang ruad reo] *n* snapshot; ช่างถ่ายภาพ [chang thai phap] *n* photographer

ถ่ายรูป [thai rup] คุณช่วยถ่ายรูปให้เราได้ ไหม? [khun chuai thai rup hai rao dai mai] Would you take a picture of us, please?; ถ่ายรูปที่นี่ได้ไหม? [thai rup thii ni dai mai] Is it OK to take pictures here?

ถ่ายเลือด [thai lueat] การถ่ายเลือด [kan thai luead] *n* transfusion

ถ่ายสำเนา [thai sam nao] *v* copy; การ ถ่ายสำเนา [kan thai sam nao] *n* photocopy

ถ่ายหนัง [thai nang] ถ่ายหนังที่นี่ได้ไหม? [thai nang thii ni dai mai] Can I film here?

ถ่ายเอกสาร [thai ek ka san] เครื่องถ่าย เอกสาร [khrueang thai ek ka san] *n* photocopier; คุณถ่ายเอกสารนี้ให้ฉันได้ ไหม? [khun thai ek ka san nii hai chan dai mai] Can you copy this for me?; ฉัน จะถ่ายเอกสารได้ที่ไหน [chan ja thai ek ka san dai thii nai] Where can I get some photocopying done?

ถาวร [tha won] *adj* permanent; อย่าง ถาวร [yang tha won] *adv* permanently

ถ้ำ [tham] *n* cave

ถี่ [thi] ความถี่ [khwam thi] *n* frequency

ถี่ถ้วน [thi thuan] ละเอียดถี่ถ้วน [la iat thi thuan] *adj* thorough

ถึง [thueng] *prep* to; ไปถึง [pai thueng] *prep* reach; มาถึง [ma thueng] *v* arrive; การมาถึง [kan ma thueng] *n* arrival; เรา จะถึงที่...เวลาอะไร? [rao ja thueng thii... we la a rai] What time do we get to...?

ถึงแม้ว่า [thueng mae wa] *conj* although, though

ถือ [thue] *vt* hold; คุณช่วยถือนี้ให้ฉันได้ ไหม? [khun chuai thue nii hai chan dai mai] Could you hold this for me?

ถือตัว [thue tua] หยิ่งแบบถือตัว [ying baep thue tua] *adj* vain

ถือศีลอด [thue sin ot] เดือนถือศีลอดของ ชาวมุสลิม [duean thue sin ot khong chao mus sa lim] *n* Ramadan

ถุง [thung] กระเป๋า ถุง [kra pao, thung] *n* bag; ถุงเงิน [thung ngoen] *n* purse; ถุง ใส่ของ [thung sai khong] *n* carrier bag, shopping bag; ฉันไม่ต้องการถุง ขอบคุณ [chan mai tong kan thung kop khun] I don't need a bag, thanks

ถุงเท้า [thung thao] *n* sock

ถุงน่อง [thung nong] *n* stocking ▷ *npl* tights

ถุงนอน [thung non] *n* sleeping bag

ถุงน้ำ [thung nam] ถุงน้ำที่เกิดในร่างกาย คนหรือสัตว์ [thung nam thii koet nai rang kai khon rue sat] *n* cyst

ถุงน้ำดี [thung nam di] *n* gall bladder

ถุงมือ [thung mue] *n* glove; ถุงมือแบบสี่ นิ้วรวมกันแต่นิ้วโป้งแยกออก [thung mue baep mii si nio ruam kan tae nio pong yaek ok] *n* mitten; ถุงมือจับภาชนะร้อน จากเตาอบ [thung mue chap pha cha na ron chak tao op] *n* oven glove; ถุงมือยาง [thung mue yang] *npl* rubber gloves

ถุงยาง [thung yang] ถุงยางอนามัย [thung yang a na mai] *n* condom

ถู [thu] *v* rub; เช็ดทำความสะอาดด้วยไม้ถู พื้น [chet tham khwam sa at duai mai thu phuen] *v* mop up; ถูทำความสะอาด อย่างแรง [thu tham khwam sa aat yang raeng] *v* scrub

ถูก [thuk] ซึ่งมีราคาถูกและไม่ใช่ช่วงที่นิยม

[sueng mii ra kha thuk lae mai chai chuang thii ni yom] *adv* off-peak; อย่าง ถูก [yang thuk] *adj* cheap; มีตั๋วรถไฟ ราคาถูกไหม? [mii tua rot fai ra kha thuk mai] Are there any cheap train fares?

ถูกต้อง [tuk tong] *adj* correct, perfect, right (*correct*); ไม่ถูกต้อง [mai thuk tong] *adj* incorrect; ถูกต้องแม่นยำ [thuk tong maen yam] *adj* exact; อย่างไม่ถูก ต้อง [yang mai thuk tong] *adj* wrong; ชานชาลานี้ที่ถูกต้องไหมสำหรับรถไฟที่จะ ไป…? [chaan cha la nii thii thuk tong mai sam rap rot fai thii ja pai…] Is this the right platform for the train to…?

แถบ [thaep] แถบ เส้น ริ้ว [thaep, sen, rio] *n* bar (*strip*); โซน แถบ เขต [son, thaep, khet] *n* zone; ซึ่งเป็นแถบ [sueng pen thaep] *adj* striped

แถบผ้า [thaep pha] แถบผ้าคล้องคอสำหรับ แขวนมือหรือแขนที่บาดเจ็บ [thaep pha khlong kho sam rap khwaen mue rue khaen thii bat chep] *n* sling

แถบสี [thaep si] *n* stripe

แถลง [tha laeng] แถลงข้อความต่อ สาธารณะชน [tha laeng kho khwam to sa tha ra na chon] *v* issue; คุณมี สำนักงานแถลงข่าวไหม? [khun mii sam nak ngan tha laeng khao mai] Do you have a press office?

แถลงการณ์ [tha laeng kan] *n* statement

แถลงข่าว [tha laeng khao] การแถลงข่าว [kan tha laeng khao] *n* press conference

แถว [thaeo] *n* queue, rank (*line*), row (*line*); จัดแถว [chat thaeo] *v* rank; นี่เป็น ตอนท้ายของแถวใช่ไหม? [ni pen ton thai khong thaeo chai mai] Is this the end of the queue?

โถง [thong] ห้องโถง [hong thong] *n* hall; ทางเดินห้องโถง [thang doen hong thong] *n* hallway

ไถ [thai] *vt* plough; การไถ [kan thai] *n* plough

ไถตัว [thai tua] ค่าไถ่ตัว [kha thai tua] *n* ransom

ไถล [tha lai] ลื่นไถล [luen tha lai] *adj* slippery; ลื่นไถลไป [luen tha lai pai] *vi* slip; การลื่นไถล [kan luen tha lai] *n* slide

ท

ทดลอง [thot long] ระยะเวลาทดลอง [ra ya we la thot long] n trial period; ห้องทดลองทางวิทยาศาสตร์ [hong thot long thang wit tha ya sart] n laboratory; หลอดทดลอง [lot thot long] n test tube; ฉันขอทดลองได้ไหม? [chan kho thot long dai mai] Can I test it, please?

ทดสอบ [thot sop] v test; การทดสอบ [kan thot sob] n test; การทดสอบการแสดง [kan thot sop kan sa daeng] n audition

ทน [thon] v bear; ซึ่งไม่สามารถทนได้ [sueng mai sa maat thon dai] adj unbearable; ซึ่งทนไม่ได้ [sueng thon mai dai] adj intolerant

ทนทาน [thon than] ที่ทนทาน [thii thon than] adj tough

ทนาย [tha nai] ทนาย นิติกร [tha nai, ni ti kon] n attorney

ทนายความ [tha nai khwam] n lawyer, solicitor

ทบทวน [thop thuan] v revise; การทบทวน [kan thop thuan] n revision

ทแยงมุม [tha yaeng mum] adj diagonal

ทรง [song] ทรงผม [song phom] n hairdo, hairstyle

ทรงเกียรติ [song kiat] ความทรงเกียรติ [khwam song kiat] n glory

ทรงผม [song phom] ทรงผมหางม้าของเด็กผู้หญิง [song phom hang ma khong dek phu ying] n ponytail; ทรงผมของผู้ชายที่สั้นมาก [song phom khong phu chai thii san mak] n crew cut

ทรมาน [to ra man] v torture; การทรมาน [kan tho ra man] v torture; ความทรมาน [khwam tho ra man] n agony; ทนทุกข์ทรมาน [thon thuk tho ra man] v suffer

ทรยศ [tho ra yot] v betray

ทรหด [tho ra hot] ความทรหดอดทน ความแข็งแกร่งที่ยืนหยัดอยู่ได้นาน [khwam tho ra hot ot thon, khwam khaeng kraeng thii yuen yat yu dai nan] n stamina

ทรัพย์สมบัติ [sap som bat] n property; ทรัพย์สมบัติมากมาย [sap som bat mak mai] n fortune; ทรัพย์สมบัติส่วนตัว [sap som bat suan tua] n private property

ทรัพย์สิน [sap sin] ทรัพย์สินที่ดิน [sap sin thii din] n estate

ทรัพยากร [pha ya kon] n resource; ทรัพยากรธรรมชาติ [sap pha ya kon tham ma chaat] npl natural resources

ทราบ [sap] ฉันไม่ทราบ [chan mai sap] I don't know

ทราย [sai] n sand; หลุมทราย [lum sai] n sandpit; หินทราย [hin sai] n sandstone; กรวดทราย [kraut sai] n grit

ทรินิแดด [thri ni daet] สาธารณรัฐทรินิแดดและโทบาโก [sa tha ra na rat thri ni daet lae tho ba ko] n Trinidad and Tobago

ทฤษฎี [thrit sa di] n theory

ทวด [thuat] n great-grandfather, great-grandmother

ทวนเข็ม [thuan khem] ที่ทวนเข็มนาฬิกา [thii thuan khem na li ka] adv anticlockwise

ท่วม [thuam] vt flood

ท่วมท้น [thuam thon] ทำให้ท่วมท้นด้วยความรู้สึก ที่เสียหาย [tham hai thuam thon duai khwam ru suk thii sia hai] adj devastated

ทวีป [tha wip] *n* continent; ทวีปเอเชีย [tha wip e chia] *n* Asia; ทวีปยุโรป [tha wip yu rop] *n* Europe; ทวีปอเมริกาใต้ [tha wip a me ri ka tai] *n* South America

ทศนิยม [thot sa ni yom] เลขทศนิยม [lek thot sa ni yom] *adj* decimal

ทศวรรษ [thot sa wat] *n* decade

ทหาร [tha han] *n* soldier; สตรีที่รับ ราชการทหาร [sa tree thii rap rat cha kan tha han] *n* servicewoman; กอง ทหาร [kong tha haan] *npl* regiment, troops; กองทหารราบ [kong tha haan raap] *n* infantry

ท่อ [tho] *n* pipe; ท่อระบายน้ำ [tho ra bai nam] *n* drain, drainpipe; ท่อช่วยหายใจ ในน้ำ [tho chuai hai jai nai nam] *n* snorkel; ท่อประปา [tho pra pa] *n* plumbing

ทอง [thong] *n* gold; เหมือนทอง [muean thong] *adj* golden; เคลือบทอง [khlueap thong] *adj* gold-plated; เป็นสีทอง [pen sii thong] *adj* blonde

ท้อง [thong] *n* abdomen, belly, stomach, tummy; การตั้งท้อง [kan tang thong] *n* pregnancy; ช่องท้อง [chong thong] *adj* coeliac; ปวดท้อง [puat thong] *n* stomachache

ทองคำขาว [thong kham khao] *n* platinum

ท่องจำ [thong cham] *v* memorize

ทองแดง [thong daeng] *n* copper

ท้องถิ่น [thong thin] ประจำท้องถิ่น [pra cham thong thin] *adj* local; ภาษาท้อง ถิ่น [pha sa thong thin] *n* dialect; เรา อยากเห็นพืชของท้องถิ่น [rao yak hen phuet khong thong thin] We'd like to see local plants and trees

ท่องเที่ยว [thong thiao] สำนักงานการท่อง เที่ยว [sam nak ngan kan thong thiao] *n* tourist office; สำนักงานท่องเที่ยว [sam nak ngan thong thiao] *n* travel agency; หนังสือที่ให้ข้อมูลกับนักท่องเที่ยว [nang sue thii hai kho mun kap nak thong thiao] *n* guidebook; เที่ยวชมสถานที่และ สำนักงานท่องเที่ยว [thiao chom sa than thii lae sam nak ngan thong thiao] Sightseeing and tourist office

ท้องผูก [thong phuk] *adj* constipated; ฉันท้องผูก [chan thong phuk] I'm constipated

ท้องฟ้า [thong fa] *n* sky

ท้องร่วง [thong ruang] อาการท้องร่วง [a kan thong ruang] *n* diarrhoea; ฉันท้อง ร่วง [chan thong ruang] I have diarrhoea

ทองเหลือง [thong lueang] *n* brass

ทอด [thot] *v* fry; ซึ่งทอดในน้ำมัน [sueng thot nai nam man] *adj* fried; ทอดอาหาร ที่มีน้ำมันมาก [thot a han thii mii nam man mak] *v* deep-fry

ทอดทิ้ง [thot thing] *v* leave, neglect; ถูก ทอดทิ้ง [thuk thot thing] *adj* neglected

ท้อแท้ [tho thae] ท้อแท้ หงุดหงิด [tho thae, ngut ngit] *adj* frustrated

ทอน [thon] คุณมีเงินทอนสำหรับมิเตอร์จอด รถไหม? [khun mii ngen thon sam rap mi toe jot rot mai] Do you have change for the parking meter?

ท่อน้ำเสีย [tho nam sia] *n* sewer

ทอร์นาโด [tho na do] พายุทอร์นาโด [pha yu tho na do] *n* tornado

ท่อระบายน้ำ [tho ra bai nam] ท่อระบาย น้ำตัน [tho ra bai nam tan] The drain is blocked

ท่อไอเสีย [tho ai sia] *n* exhaust pipe; ควันจากท่อไอเสีย [khwan chak tho ai sia] *npl* exhaust fumes; อุปกรณ์ที่ช่วยลด สารเป็นพิษในท่อไอเสีย [up pa kon thii chuai lot san pen phit nai tho ai sia] *n* catalytic converter

ทะเบียน [tha bian] สำนักทะเบียน [sam nak tha bian] *n* registry office; ป้าย ทะเบียนรถ [pai tha bian rot] *n* number plate; ทะเบียนรถหมายเลข... [tha bian rot mai lek...] Registration number...

ทะเบียนสมรส [tha bian som rot] ใบ ทะเบียนสมรส [bai tha bian som rot] *n* marriage certificate

ทะเยอทะยาน [tha yoe tha yan] *adj* ambitious; ความทะเยอทะยาน [khwam tha yoe tha yan] *n* ambition

ทะเล [tha le] *n* sea; ระดับน้ำทะเล [ra dap nam tha le] *n* sea level; ชายฝั่งทะเล [chai fang tha le] *n* seashore; ทะเลเหนือ [tha le nuea] *n* North Sea

ทะเลทราย [tha le sai] *n* desert; เกาะกลาง ทะเลทราย [ko klang tha le sai] *n* desert island; ทะเลทรายซาฮารา [tha le sai sa ha ra] *n* Sahara; บริเวณอุดมสมบูรณ์ใน ทะเลทราย [bo ri wen u dom som bun nai tha le sai] *n* oasis

ทะเลเมดิเตอร์เรเนียน [tha le me di toe re nian] *n* Mediterranean; เกี่ยวกับทะเล เมดิเตอร์เรเนียน [kiao kap tha le me di toe re nian] *adj* Mediterranean

ทะเลสาบ [tha le sap] *n* lake

ทะเลาะ [tha lo] *v* quarrel; ทะเลาะกัน [tha lao kan] *v* fall out; ทะเลาะกัน [tha lao kan] *v* squabble

ทะเลาะวิวาท [tha lo wi wat] *v* row (*to argue*); การทะเลาะวิวาท [kan tha lo wi wat] *n* quarrel, row (*argument*)

ทักซิโด [tak si do] ชุดทักซิโด [chut thak si do] *n* tuxedo

ทักทาย [thak thai] *v* greet; คำทักทาย [kham thak thai] *n* greeting

ทั้งสอง [thang song] *pron* both; ไม่ใช่ทั้ง สอง [mai chai thang song] *conj* neither

ทั้งหมด [thang mot] *adj* all, complete, entire, whole ▷ *adv* altogether, overall; โดยทั้งหมด [doi thang mot] *adv* entirely; จำนวนทั้งหมด [cham nuan thang mot] *n* a lot; อย่างทั้งหมด [yang thang mot] *adv* completely; ขอทั้งหมด [kho thang mot] All together, please

ทัณฑ์บน [than bon] การพ้นโทษอย่างมี เงื่อนไขหรือทำทัณฑ์บนไว้ [kan phon thot yang mii nguean khai rue tham than bon wai] *n* parole

ทันที [than thi] *adj* immediate; โดยทันที [doi than thi] *adv* immediately; ซึ่ง กระทำเองโดยทันที [sueng kra tham eng doi than thi] *adj* spontaneous; ทันที ทันใด [than thii than dai] *adj* abrupt, instant, sudden

ทันสมัย [than sa mai] *adj* contemporary, cool (*stylish*), fashionable, up-to-date; ไม่ทันสมัย [mai than sa mai] *adj* unfashionable; ทำให้ทันสมัย [tham hai tan sa mai] *v* modernize, update

ทับ [thap] *n* forward slash

ทับทิม [thap thip] ผลทับทิม [phon thap thim] *n* pomegranate

ทัพพี [thap phi] *n* ladle

ทั่วไป [thua pai] โดยทั่วไป [doi thua pai] *adv* general, generally; ไม่เป็นไปตามกฎ ทั่วไป [mai pen pai tam kot thua pai] *adj* unconventional; พูดคลุมทั่ว ๆ ไป [phut khlum thua thua pai] *v* generalize

ทัวร์ [tua] กรุ๊ปทัวร์ [krup thua] *n* guided tour; ทัวร์ที่จัดแบบครบวงจร [thua thii chat baep khrop wong chon] *n* package tour; มีทัวร์เที่ยวชมสถานที่ในเมืองไหม? [mii thua thiao chom sa than thii nai mueang mai] Are there any sightseeing tours of the town?

ทัศนคติ [that sa na kha ti] *n* outlook, perspective, standpoint, viewpoint; ทัศนคติ ความเห็น [that sa na kha ti, khwam hen] *n* attitude

ทัศนวิสัย [that sa na wi sai] *n* visibility

ทัศนียภาพ [that sa ni ya phap] ทัศนียภาพที่อยู่ใกล้ที่สุด [that sa nii ya phap thii yu klai thii sut] *n* foreground

ทัสเมเนีย [tas me nia] รัฐทัสเมเนียใน ประเทศออสเตรเลีย [rat tas me nia nai pra tet os tre lia] *n* Tasmania

ทา [tha] ทาให้ขาว [tha hai khao] *v* whitewash

ท่า [tha] ท่าจอดเรือ [tha jot ruea] *n* marina

ทาก [thak] ตัวทากกินใบไม้ [tua thak kin bai mai] *n* slug

ทาง [thang] ไหล่ทาง [lai thang] *n* hard shoulder; ไปทาง [pai thang] *prep* towards; ครึ่งทาง [khrueng thang] *adv* halfway; เธอไม่ได้ให้ทาง [thoe mai dai hai thang] She didn't give way

ทางการ [thang kan] ไม่เป็นทางการ [mai pen thang kan] *adj* unofficial; ความเป็นทางการ [khwam pen thang kan] *n* formality

ทางข้าม [thang kham] ทางข้ามไฟที่มีสัญญาณโดยผู้ข้ามเป็นผู้กดปุ่ม [thang kham fai thii mii san yan doi phu kham pen phu kot pum] *n* pelican crossing

ทางเข้า [thang khao] *n* entrance, way in; ทางเข้าที่มีแกนหมุนให้ผ่านได้ทีละคน [thang khao thii mii kaen mun hai phan dai thi la khon] *n* turnstile

ทางเข้าออก [thang khao ok] คุณจัดให้มีทางเข้าออกสำหรับคนพิการไหม? [khun chat hai mii thang khao ok sam rap khon phi kan mai] Do you provide access for the disabled?; ทางที่เข้าออกได้ของเก้าอี้คนพิการอยู่ที่ไหน? [thang thii khao ok dai khong kao ii khon phi kan yu thii nai] Where is the wheelchair-accessible entrance?

ทางชัน [thang chan] ปีนขึ้นทางชันครั้งสุดท้ายเมื่อไร? [pin khuen thang chan khrang sut thai muea rai] When is the last ascent?

ทางเดิน [thang doen] *n* footpath, passage (*route*), path; ทางเดินเลียบชายทะเลที่สถานพักผ่อนชายทะเล [thang doen liap chai tha le thii sa than phak phon chai tha le] *n* promenade; ทางเดินเท้า [thang doen thao] *n* pavement, walkway; ทางเดินระหว่างที่นั่ง [thang doen ra wang thii nang] *n* aisle; ทางเดินนี้จะพาไปที่ไหน? [thang doen nii ja pha pai thii nai] Where does this path lead?

ทางม้าลาย [thang ma lai] *n* zebra crossing

ทางแยก [thang yaek] *n* joint (*junction*), junction; ทางแยกจากถนนใหญ่ [thang yaek chak tha non yai] *n* side street; เลี้ยวขวาที่ทางแยก [liao khwa thii thang yaek] Go right at the next junction; รถอยู่ที่ทางแยกหมายเลข... [rot yu thii thang yaek mai lek...] The car is near junction number...

ทางลัด [thang lat] *n* shortcut

ทางลาด [thang lat (thang laat)] *n* ramp

ทางเลือก [thang lueak] *n* alternative; ซึ่งเป็นทางเลือก [sueng pen thang lueak] *adj* optional

ทางหลวง [thang luang] *n* motorway; ถนนเชื่อมทางหลวง [tha non chueam thang luang] *n* slip road; มีด่านเก็บทางบนทางหลวงนี้ไหม? [mii dan kep thang bon thang luang nii mai] Is there a toll on this motorway?; รถติดมากบนทางหลวงหรือเปล่า? [rot tit mak bon thang luang rue plao] Is the traffic heavy on the motorway?

ทางออก [thang ok] *n* exit, way out; ทางออกฉุกเฉิน [thang ok chuk choen] *n* emergency exit; ทางออกทางไหนสำหรับ...? [thang ok thang nai sam rap...] Which exit for...?; ทางออกอยู่ที่ไหน? [thang ok yu thii nai] Where is the exit?

ทาเจคกิสถาน [tha chek ki sa than] ประเทศทาเจคกิสถาน [pra tet tha chek ki sa than] *n* Tajikistan

ท่าทาง [tha thang] *n* gesture; ลักษณะท่าทาง [lak sa na tha thang] *n* manner

ท้าทาย [tha thai] *v* challenge; การท้าทาย [kan tha thai] *n* challenge; ที่ท้าทาย [thii tha thai] *adj* challenging

ทาน [than] คุณทานอาหารหรือยัง? [khun than a han rue yang] Have you eaten?; คุณอยากทานอะไร? [khun yak than a rai] What would you like to eat?

ท่าน [than] *pron* you (*singular polite*); ตัวท่านเอง [tua than eng] *pron* yourself (*polite*)

ทานตะวัน [than ta wan] ดอกทานตะวัน [dok than ta wan] n sunflower

ท่ามกลาง [tham klang] prep among

ท้ายที่สุด [thai thi sut] adv ultimately

ทายาท [tha yat] n heir; ทายาทหญิง [tha yat ying] n heiress

ทารก [tha rok] เด็กทารก [dek tha rok] n baby; ทารกในครรภ์ [tha rok nai khan] n foetus

ทารุณ [tha run] การกระทำทารุณต่อเด็ก [kan kra tham tha run to dek] n child abuse

ท่าเรือ [tha rue] n harbour, jetty, port (ships), quay

ทาส [that] n slave

ทาสี [tha si] vt paint

ทำ [tham] v make, do; ตัวย่อของทำด้วยตัว เอง [tua yo khong tham duai tua eng] abbr DIY; ที่สั่งทำ [thii sang tham] adj customized; ที่ทำเองในครอบครัว [thii tham eng nai khrop khrua] adj home-made; มีอะไรทำบ้างที่นั่น? [mii a rai tham bang thii nan] What is there to do here?; คุณทำอะไร? [khun tham a rai] What do you do?; คุณทำอะไรเย็นนี้? [khun tham a rai yen nii] What are you doing this evening?

ทำความสะอาด [tham khwam sa ad] vt clean; ทำความสะอาดจนหมด [tham khwam sa aat chon mot] v clear up; ทำความสะอาดบ้านทั่วทั้งหลัง [tham khwam sa aat baan thua thang lang] n spring-cleaning

ทำงาน [tham ngan] v work; ใบอนุญาต ให้ทำงาน [bai a nu yat hai tham ngan] n work permit; ไม่ทำงาน [mai tham ngan] adv off; สถานที่ทำงาน [sa than thii tham ngan] n work station, workplace, workstation; เครื่องขายตั๋ว ทำงานอย่างไร? [khrueang khai tua tham ngan yang rai] How does the ticket machine work?

ทำแท้ง [tham thaeng] การทำแท้ง [kan tham thang] n abortion

ทำนอง [tham nong] n tune

ทำนาย [tham nai] v predict; ทำนายไม่ได้ [tham nai mai dai] adj unpredictable; พอที่จะทำนายได้ [pho thii ja tham nai dai] adj predictable

ทำผิด [tham phit] v mistake; การทำผิด เพราะสะเพร่า [kan tham phit phro sa phrao] n blunder

ทำไม [tham mai] adv why

ทำร้าย [tham rai] การทำร้าย [kan tham rai] v damage; การทำร้ายเพื่อปล้นทรัพย์ [kan tham rai phuea plon sab] n mugging; ทำร้ายเพื่อชิงทรัพย์ [tham rai phuea ching sap] v mug; ฉันถูกทำร้าย [chan thuk tham rai] I've been attacked

ทำลาย [tham lai] v destroy, sack; สิ่งที่ถูก ทำลายอย่างเสียหายยับเยิน [sing thii thuk tham lai yang sia hai yap yoen] n wreck; การทำลาย [kan tham lai] n destruction; การทำลายทรัพย์สิน [kan tham lai sap sin] n vandalism

ทำให้ดีขึ้น [tha hai di khuen] v improve

ทำอาหาร [tham a han] v cook; คุณทำ อาหารจานนี้อย่างไร? [khun tham a han chan nii yang rai] How do you cook this dish?

ทิ้ง [thing] v ditch, dump; โยนทิ้ง [yon thing] v throw away; ซึ่งออกแบบมาให้ ใช้แล้วทิ้ง [sueng ok baep ma hai chai laeo thing] adj disposable

ทิป [thip] เป็นเรื่องปรกติไหมถ้าจะให้เงิน ทิป? [pen rueang prok ka ti mai tha ja hai ngoen thip] Is it usual to give a tip?; ฉันควรให้เงินทิปเท่าไร? [chan khuan hai ngoen thip thao rai] How much should I give as a tip?

ทิวเขา [thio khao] n range (mountains)

ทิวทัศน์ [thio that] n scenery

ทิวลิป [thio lip] ดอกทิวลิป [dok thio lip] n tulip

ทิศ [thit] ทิศตะวันออก [thit ta wan ok] n east

ทิศทาง [thit thang] n direction; ทิศทาง

ต่าง ๆ [thit thang tang tang] *npl* directions; คุณวาดแผนที่บอกทิศทางให้ฉันได้ไหม? [khun wat phaen thii bok thit thang hai chan dai mai] Can you draw me a map with directions?

ทิศเหนือ [thit nuea] *n* north

ที่ [thi] *prep* at; ในที่ซึ่ง [nai thii sueng] *conj* where; ที่เก็บขนมปัง [thii kep kha nom pang] *n* bread bin; ที่เก็บน้ำ [thii kep nam] *n* reservoir; ที่ที่คนทำงาน [thii thii khon tham ngan] *n* workspace; ที่ว่างเหนือศีรษะ [thii wang nuea si sa] *n* headroom

ที่เก็บ [thi kep] *n* storage

ที่เขี่ยบุหรี่ [thi khia bu ri] ฉันขอที่เขี่ยบุหรี่ได้ไหม? [chan kho thii khia bu ri dai mai] May I have an ashtray?

ที่คั่น [thi khan] ที่คั่นหนังสือ [thii khan nang sue] *n* bookmark

ที่จอดรถ [thi chot rot] *n* parking

ที่จับ [thi chap] ที่จับหลุดออกมา [thii chap lut ok ma] The handle has come off; ที่จับประตูหลุดออกมา [thii chap pra tu lut ok ma] The door handle has come off

ที่ดิน [thi din] *n* land, plot (*piece of land*); คนที่ทำงานเกี่ยวกับขายบ้านและที่ดิน [khon thii tham ngan kiao kap khai baan lae thii din] *n* estate agent; ที่ดินและสิ่งปลูกสร้าง [thii din lae sing pluk sang] *npl* premises; ทรัพย์สินที่ดิน [sap sin thii din] *n* estate

ที่ใดที่หนึ่ง [thi dai thi nueng] *adv* somewhere

ที่ทำงาน [thi tham ngan] ฉันจะไปที่ทำงานคุณได้อย่างไร? [chan ja pai thii tham ngan khun dai yang rai] How do I get to your office?

ที่นอน [thi non] *n* mattress; ที่นอนเด็กที่หิ้วไปไหน ๆ ได้ [thii non dek thii hio pai nai nai dai] *n* carrycot; ที่นอนในเรือ [thii non nai ruea] *n* bunk; ที่นอนในเรือหรือรถไฟ [thii non nai ruea rue rot fai] *n* berth

ที่นั่ง [thi nang] ที่นั่งใกล้หน้าต่าง [thii nang klai na tang] *n* window seat; ที่นั่งในรัฐสภา [thii nang nai rat tha sa pha] *n* seat (*constituency*); ที่นั่งมีพนักพิงและที่วางแขน [thii nang mii pha nak phing lae thii wang khaen] *n* settee; เราขอที่นั่งด้วยกันได้ไหม? [rao kho thii nang duai kan dai mai] Can we have seats together?

ที่นั่น [thi nan] *adv* there; ฉันจะไปที่นั่นได้อย่างไร? [chan ja pai thii nan dai yang rai] How do I get there?

ที่นี่ [thi ni] *adv* here

ที่โน่น [thi non] อยู่ที่โน่น [yu thii non] It's over there

ที่ปัด [thi pat] ที่ปัดกระจก [thii pat kra chok] *n* windscreen wiper

ที่พัก [thi pak] ที่พักกางแรมที่ให้อาหารเช้า [thii phak kang raem thii hai a han chao] *n* bed and breakfast; ที่พักที่คนซื้อและใช้ตามเวลาที่กำหนดในแต่ละปี [thii phak thii khon sue lae chai tam we la thii kam not nai tae la pi] *n* timeshare; ที่พักอาหารเช้าและเย็น [thii phak a han chao lae yen] *n* half board

ที่เย็บกระดาษ [thi yep kra dat] *n* stapler

ที่รัก [thi rak] *n* darling; ซึ่งเป็นที่รักยิ่ง [sueng pen thii rak ying] *adj* dear (*loved*)

ที่แล้ว [thi laeo] ปีที่แล้ว [pi thii laeo] last year; วันเสาร์ที่แล้ว [wan sao thii laeo] last Saturday; อาทิตย์ที่แล้ว [a thit thii laeo] last week

ที่ว่าง [thi wang] *n* space

ทีวี [thi wi] *n* telly, TV; รายการทีวีที่แสดงสภาพความเป็นจริง [rai kan thii wii thii sa daeng sa phap khwam pen ching] *n* reality TV; รายการทีวีที่มีการพูดคุยกับแขกรับเชิญ [rai kan thii wii thii mii kan phut khui kap khaek rap choen] *n* chat show; ทีวีที่มีจอภาพแบน [tii wii thii mii cho phap baen] *n* plasma TV; มีทีวีในห้องไหม? [mii thii wii nai hong mai] Does the room have a TV?

ที่สุด [thi sut] *adj* extreme ▷ *adv* most

(superlative); ในที่สุด [nai thi sut] *adv* finally; ดีที่สุด [di thii sut] *adj* best; อย่างที่สุด [yang thii sut] *adv* extremely

ทีหลัง [thi lang] เราพบกันทีหลังดีไหม? [rao phop kan thi lang di mai] Shall we meet afterwards?; ฉันจ่ายตอนนี้หรือจ่ายทีหลัง? [chan chai ton nii rue chai thii lang] Do I pay now or later?

ที่ไหน [thi nai] *adv* where; ไม่มีที่ไหน [mai mii thii nai] *adv* nowhere; ที่ไหนก็ตาม [thii nai ko tam] *adv* anywhere; เราจะไป...ได้ที่ไหน? [rao ja pai...dai thii nai] Where can you go...?

ที่อยู่ [thi yu] *n* address (location), home address; คำย่อของที่อยู่ของเว็บไซต์บนอินเตอร์เน็ต [kham yo khong thii yu khong web sai bon in toe net] *n* URL; ที่อยู่ของเว็บบนระบบค้นหาและเข้าถึงข้อมูลบนอินเตอร์เน็ต [thii yu khong web bon ra bop khon ha lae khao thueng kho mun bon in toe net] *n* website; ที่อยู่ของข้อมูลที่เราจะหาได้ทางอินเตอร์เน็ต [thii yu khong kho mun thii rao ja ha dai thang in toe net] *n* web address; คุณจะช่วยเขียนที่อยู่ได้ไหม? [khun ja chuai khian thii yu dai mai] Will you write down the address, please?

ทึกทัก [thuek thak] ทึกทักเอา [thuek thak ao] *v* assume

ทึ่ง [thueng] น่าทึ่ง [na thueng] *adj* amazed

ทื่อ [thue] *adj* blunt

ทุก [thuk] *adj* every; ทุกเดือน [thuk duean] *adj* monthly; ทุกชั่วโมง [thuk chau mong] *adv* hourly; รถโดยสารวิ่งทุกยี่สิบนาที [rot doi san wing thuk yi sip na thi] The bus runs every twenty minutes

ทุกข์ [thuk] ทนทุกข์ทรมาน [thon thuk tho ra man] *v* suffer

ทุกข์ยาก [thuk yak] ความทุกข์ยาก [khwam thuk yak] *n* misery

ทุกคน [thuk khon] *pron* all, everybody, everyone

ทุกที่ [thuk thi] *adv* everywhere

ทุกวัน [thuk wan] *adj* daily

ทุกสิ่งทุกอย่าง [thuk sing thuk yang] *pron* everything

ทุกหนทุกแห่ง [thuk hon thuk haeng] *prep* throughout

ทุ่ง [thung] ทุ่งโล่ง [thung long] *n* moor

ทุ่งหญ้า [thung ya] *n* meadow

ทุจริต [thut cha rit] *adj* corrupt ▷ *v* cheat; การทุจริต [kan thut cha rit] *n* corruption; คนทุจริต [khon thut cha rit] *n* crook (swindler)

ทุน [thun] เงินทุน [ngoen thun] *n* grant; ทุนเล่าเรียน [thun lao rian] *n* scholarship

ทุ่น [thun] *n* buoy

ทุนนิยม [thun ni yom] ระบบทุนนิยม [ra bop thun ni yom] capitalism

ทุบ [thup] *v* thump

ทูต [thut] เกี่ยวกับการทูต [kiao kap kan thut] *adj* diplomatic; นักการทูต [nak kan thut] *n* diplomat

ทูน่า [tu na] ปลาทูน่า [pla thu na] *n* tuna

เท [the] *vt* pour

เทคโนโลยี [tek no lo yi] ทางเทคโนโลยี [thang thek no lo yii] *adj* technological

เทคโนโลยีสารสนเทศ [tek no lo yi sa ra son thet] ตัวย่อของเทคโนโลยีสารสนเทศ [tua yo khong thek no lo yii sa ra son tet] *abbr* IT

เทนนิส [then nis] *n* tennis; ไม้ตีเทนนิส [mai ti then nis] *n* tennis racket; สนามเทนนิส [sa nam then nis] *n* tennis court; ผู้เล่นเทนนิส [phu len then nis] *n* tennis player; เราอยากเล่นเทนนิส [rao yak len then nis] We'd like to play tennis

เทป [thep] เครื่องอัดเทป [khrueang at thep] *n* tape recorder; เทปใส [thep sai] *n* Sellotape®; ตลับเทป [ta lap thep] *n* cassette

เทพนิยาย [thep ni yai] นิทานเทพนิยาย [ni than thep ni yai] *n* fairytale

เทศกาล [thet sa kan] *n* festival; คืนวัน

ก่อนวันเทศกาล [khuen wan kon wan tet sa kan] *n* eve; วันเทศกาลสารภาพบาป [wan tet sa kan sa ra phap bap] *n* Shrove Tuesday

เทศนา [thet sa na] การเทศนา การให้ โอวาท [kan ted sa na, kan hai o wat] *n* sermon

เทศบาล [thet sa ban] สมาชิกสภาเทศบาล [sa ma chik sa pha tet sa ban] *n* councillor; บ้านของเทศบาล [baan khong tet sa ban] *n* council house

เทศมนตรี [thet sa mon tri] นายก เทศมนตรี [na yok tet sa mon tree] *n* mayor

เทอม [thoem] *n* semester; ครึ่งเทอม [khrueng thoem] *n* half-term

เทา [thao] สีเทา [sii thao] *adj* grey; ที่มีผม สีเทา [thii mii phom sii thao] *adj* grey-haired

เท่า [thao] เพิ่มเป็นสามเท่า [poem pen sam thao] *v* treble; สองเท่า [song thao] *adj* double

เท้า [thao] *n* foot ▷ *npl* feet; เท้าเปล่า [thao plao] *adv* barefoot; ส้นเท้า [son thao] *n* heel; ตาปลาบนเท้า [ta pla bon thao] *n* bunion; เท้าฉันเบอร์หก [thao chan boe hok] My feet are a size six

เท่ากัน [thao kan] ซึ่งเท่ากัน [sueng thao kan] *adj* equal; ทำคะแนนเท่ากัน [tham kha naen thao kan] *v* equalize

เท่ากับ [thao kap] *n* equivalent

เท่าเทียม [thao thiam] ความเท่าเทียม [khwam thao thiam] *n* equation; ทำให้ เท่าเทียมกัน [tham hai thao thiam kan] *v* equal

เท่านั้น [thao nan] *adv* only; เพียงเท่านั้น [phiang thao nan] *adj* mere, only

เท่าไร [thao rai] รูปภาพราคาเท่าไร? [rup phap ra kha thao rai] How much do the photos cost?; ราคาเท่าไรที่จะจอดรถ ที่พักกลางแจ้งสำหรับสี่คน? [ra kha thao rai thii ja jot rot thii phak klang chaeng sam rap si khon] How much is it for a camper with four people?; คุณ

คิดค่าแลกเท่าไร? [khun kit kha laek thao rai] How much do you charge?

เที่ยงคืน [thiang khuen] *n* midnight; เวลาหลังเที่ยงคืนถึงเที่ยงวัน [we la lang thiang khuen thueng thiang wan] *abbr* a.m.; เวลาเที่ยงคืน [we la thiang khuen] at midnight

เที่ยงตรง [thiang trong] ไม่เที่ยงตรง [mai thiang trong] *adj* inaccurate

เที่ยงวัน [thiang wan] *n* midday, noon; เวลาหลังเที่ยงคืนถึงเที่ยงวัน [we la lang thiang khuen thueng thiang wan] *abbr* a.m.; เวลาเที่ยงวัน [we la thiang wan] It's twelve midday; ตอนเที่ยงวัน [ton thiang wan] at midday

เทียน [thian] *n* candle; เชิงเทียน [choeng thian] *n* candlestick

เทียม [thiam] *n* artificial

เที่ยว [thiao] การไปเที่ยวนอกบ้านและนำ อาหารไปรับประทาน [kan pai thiao nok baan lae nam a han pai rap pra than] *n* picnic; ออกเที่ยวฟังความเห็น เที่ยวหาเสียง [ok thiao fang khwam hen, thiao ha siang] *v* canvass; เที่ยวให้สนุกนะ [thiao hai sa nuk na] Enjoy your holiday!

เที่ยวบิน [thiao bin] *n* flight; มีเที่ยวบิน ราคาถูกไหม? [mii thiao bin ra kha thuk mai] Are there any cheap flights?; ฉันตกเที่ยวบิน [chan tok thiao bin] I've missed my flight; ฉันอยากเปลี่ยนเที่ยวบิน ของฉัน [chan yak plian thiao bin khong chan] I'd like to change my flight

เทือกเขา [thueak khao] เทือกเขาแอลป์ [thueak khao aelp] *npl* Alps; เทือกเขา แอนดีส [thueak khao aen dis] *npl* Andes; เทือกเขาในคอเคเซีย [thueak khao nai kho khe chia] *n* Caucasus

แท้ [thae] โดยแท้จริง [doi thae ching] *adj* indeed; ของแท้ [khong thae] *adj* authentic

แท็กซี่ [taek si] รถแท็กซี่ [rot thaek si] *n* taxi; รถขับที่ใช้เป็นแท็กซี่ [rot khap thii chai pen thaek si] *n* minicab; คนขับรถ แท็กซี่ [khon khap rot thaek si] *n* taxi driver; ฉันต้องการแท็กซี่หนึ่งคัน [chan tong kan thaek si nueng khan] I need a taxi

แทง [thaeng] v stab ▷ vi stick

แท้ง [thaeng] การแท้งบุตร [kan thang but] n miscarriage; การทำแท้ง [kan tham thang] n abortion

แท้จริง [thae ching] adj real; โดยแท้จริง [doi thae ching] adj really, virtual; อย่างแท้จริง [yang thae ching] adv literally, truly

แทน [thaen] v stand for; แทนที่ [thaen thi] v instead; การทำหน้าที่แทน [kan tham na thii thaen] n replacement

แท่น [thaen] แท่นบูชา [thaen bu cha] n altar

แทนซาเนีย [than sa nia] เกี่ยวกับประเทศแทนซาเนีย [kiao kap pra thet thaen sa nia] adj Tanzanian; ชาวแทนซาเนีย [chao taen sa nia] n Tanzanian; ประเทศแทนซาเนีย [pra tet taen sa nia] n Tanzania

แทนที่ [than thi] v replace, substitute; คนหรือสิ่งที่เข้าแทนที่ [khon rue sing thii khao taen thii] n substitute

แทนที่จะ [thaen thi cha] prep instead of

แทนบูชา [thaen bu cha] n shrine

แทรกซึม [saek suem] ผู้แทรกซึม [phu saek suem] n mole (infiltrator)

แทรกเตอร์ [thraek toe] รถแทรกเตอร์ [rot traek toe] n tractor; รถแทรกเตอร์เกลี่ยดิน [rot traek toe klia din] n bulldozer

โทโก [to ko] สาธารณรัฐโทโก [sa tha ra na rat tho ko] n Togo

โทนิค [tho nik] ฉันจะดื่มยินกับโทนิค [chan ja duem yin kap tho nik] I'll have a gin and tonic, please

โทบาโก [tho ba ko] สาธารณรัฐทรินิแดดและโทบาโก [sa tha ra na rat thri ni daet lae tho ba ko] n Trinidad and Tobago

โทร [tho] v phone; โทรกลับ [tho klap] v call back, phone back, ring back; การโทรปลุก [kan to pluk] n alarm call; คุณอยากโทรกลับบ้านไหม? [khun yak tho

klap baan mai] Would you like to phone home?

โทรทัศน์ [tho ra that] n television; เครื่องโทรทัศน์วงจรปิด [khrueang tho ra tat wong chon pit] n monitor; โทรทัศน์สี [tho ra tat sii] n colour television; โทรทัศน์ดิจิตัล [tho ra tat di chi tal] n digital television; โทรทัศน์อยู่ที่ไหน? [tho ra tat yu thii nai] Where is the television?

โทรเลข [tho ra lek] n telegram; ฉันส่งโทรเลขจากที่นี่ได้ไหม? [chan song tho ra lek chak thii ni dai mai] Can I send a telegram from here?; ฉันจะส่งโทรเลขได้ที่ไหน? [chan ja song tho ra lek dai thii nai] Where can I send a telegram from?; ฉันอยากส่งโทรเลข [chan yak song tho ra lek] I want to send a telegram

โทรศัพท์ [tho ra thap] n phone, telephone; เสียงสายไม่ว่างของโทรศัพท์ [siang sai mai wang khong tho ra sap] n engaged tone; โทรศัพท์มือถือ [tho ra sap mue thue] n mobile phone; โทรศัพท์มือถือยี่ห้อหนึ่ง [tho ra sap mue thue yi ho nueng] n BlackBerry®; ฉันโทรศัพท์ไปต่างประเทศจากที่นี่ได้ไหม? [chan tho ra sap pai tang pra tet chak thii ni dai mai] Can I phone internationally from here?

โทรสาร [tho ra san] n fax; โทรสารคุณมีปัญหา [tho ra san khun mii pan ha] There is a problem with your fax; ฉันส่งโทรสารจากที่นี่ได้ไหม? [chan song tho ra san chak thii ni dai mai] Can I send a fax from here?; ฉันอยากส่งโทรสาร [chan yak song tho ra san] I want to send a fax

โทษ [thot] โทษทัณฑ์ทางกฎหมาย [thot than thang kot mai] n penalty

ไทย [thai] adj เกี่ยวกับประเทศไทย [kiao kap pra thet thai] adj Thai ▷ n ชาวไทย [chao thai] n Thai (person); ประเทศไทย [pra tet thai] n Thailand

ธ

ordinary; จะใช้เวลานานเท่าไรที่จะส่งแบบ
ธรรมดา? [ja chai we la nan thao rai
thii ja song baep tham ma da] How
long will it take by normal post?

ธรรมเนียม [tham niam] ค่าธรรมเนียม
[kha tham niam] *n* fee; ตามธรรมเนียม
ปฏิบัติ [tam tham niam pa ti bat] *adj*
formal

ธัญพืช [than ya puet] อาหารที่ประกอบ
ด้วยธัญพืชถั่วและผลไม้แห้ง [a han thii
pra kop duai than ya phuet thua lae
phon la mai haeng] *n* muesli

ธัญญาหาร [than ya han] อาหารเช้าที่ทำ
จากพืชพันธุ์ธัญญาหาร [a han chao thii
tham chak phuet phan than ya han]
npl cornflakes

ธัญพืช [tha ya phuet] ธัญพืชคล้ายข้าว
สาลี [than ya phuet khlai khao sa lii] *n*
rye; อาหารเช้าที่ทำจากธัญพืช [a han
chao thii tham chak than ya phuet] *n*
cereal

ธันวาคม [than wa khom] เดือนธันวาคม
[duean than wa khom] *n* December;
วันศุกร์ที่สามสิบเอ็ด ธันวาคม [wan suk
thii sam sip et than wa khom] on
Friday the thirty first of December

ธาตุ [that] ธาตุปรอท [that pa rot] *n*
mercury; ธาตุยูเรเนียม [that u re niam]
n uranium

ธารน้ำแข็ง [than nam khaeng] *n* glacier

อิเบต [thi bet] ชาวอิเบต [chao thi bet] *n*
Tibetan (*person*); ประเทศอิเบต [pra tet
thi bet] *n* Tibet; ภาษาอิเบต [pha sa thi
bet] *n* Tibetan (*language*)

ธุรกิจ [thu ra kit] *n* business; การเดินทาง
ไปทำธุรกิจ [kan doen thang pai tham
thu ra kit] *n* business trip; ธุรกิจการ
บันเทิง [thu ra kit kan ban thoeng] *n*
show business; นักธุรกิจชาย [nak thu
ra kit chai] *n* businessman; ฉันมาทำ
ธุรกิจที่นี่ [chan ma tham thu ra kit thii
ni] I'm here on business

เธอ [thoe] *pron* her, she

ธง [thong] *n* flag

ธนบัตร [tha na bat] *n* banknote, note
(*banknote*)

ธนาคาร [tha na kan] *n* bank (*finance*);
เครื่องกดเงินสดจากธนาคาร [khrueang
kot ngoen sot chak tha na khan] *n*
cash dispenser; ค่าธรรมเนียมธนาคาร
[kha tham niam tha na khan] *npl* bank
charges; งบดุลธนาคาร [ngop dun tha
na khan] *n* bank balance; มีธนาคารอยู่
ใกล้ที่นี่ไหม? [mii tha na khan yu klai
thii ni mai] Is there a bank nearby?

ธนู [tha nu] ลูกธนู [luk tha nu] *n* arrow;
ราศีธนู [ra si tha nu] *n* Sagittarius; คัน
ธนู [khan tha nu] *n* bow (*weapon*)

ธรณีวิทยา [tho ra ni wit tha ya] *n*
geology

ธรรมชาติ [tham ma chat] *adj* natural
▷ *n* nature; เหนือธรรมชาติ [nuea tham
ma chat] *adj* supernatural; ก๊าซ
ธรรมชาติ [kas tham ma chat] *n* natural
gas; ที่ไม่เป็นธรรมชาติ [thii mai pen
tham ma chaat] *adj* strained

ธรรมดา [tham ma da] พื้นฐาน ธรรมดา
[phuen than, tham ma da] *adj* basic;
อย่างธรรมดา [yang tham ma da] *adj*

น

นก [nok] *n* bird; ลูกไก่ ลูกนก [luk kai, luk nok] *n* chick; การดูนก [kan du nok] *n* birdwatching; นกกระสา [nok kra sa] *n* crane *(bird)*

นกกระจอกเทศ [nok kra chok thet] *n* ostrich

นกเค้าแมว [nok khao maeo] *n* owl

นกนางนวล [nok nang nuan] *n* seagull

นม [nom] *n* milk; หน้าอก นม [na ok, nom] *n* bust; นมผ่านการฆ่าเชื้อ [nom phan kan kha chuea] *n* UHT milk; ผลผลิตจากนม [phon pha lit chak nom] *n* dairy produce; คุณดื่มนมไหม? [khun duem nom mai] Do you drink milk?

นรก [na rok] *n* hell

นวด [nuat] การนวด [kan nuat] *n* massage

นวนิยาย [na wa ni yai] *n* fiction; นักแต่ง นวนิยาย [nak taeng na wa ni yai] *n* novelist; นวนิยายวิทยาศาสตร์ [na wa ni yai wit tha ya saat] *n* science fiction; นวนิยายวิทยาศาสตร์เรื่องสั้น [na wa ni yai wit tha ya saat rueang san] *n* scifi

นวล [nuan] เป็นสีนวล [pen sii nuan] *adj* cream

นอก [nok] ให้อยู่ข้างนอก [hai yu khang nok] *v* keep out; ข้างนอก [khang nok] *n* out, outdoors; นอกเวลา [nok we la] *adv* part-time

นอกจาก [nok chak] *prep* apart from, except, outside

นอกจากนี้ [nak chak ni] *adv* besides

นอกเมือง [nok mueang] *adj* suburban

น้อง [nong] น้องสะใภ้หรือพี่สะใภ้ [nong sa phai rue phii sa phai] *n* sister-in-law; พี่เขยหรือน้องเขย [phi khoei rue nong khoei] *n* brother-in-law; พี่ชายหรือน้อง ชาย [phi chai rue nong chai] *n* brother

น้องชาย [nong chai] พี่ชายน้องชายต่าง บิดา [phi chai nong chai tang bi da] *n* stepbrother

น้องสาว [nong sao] พี่สาวหรือน้องสาว [phi sao rue nong sao] *n* sister; พี่สาว น้องสาวต่างบิดา [phi sao nong sao tang bi da] *n* stepsister

นอน [non] *v* sleep; เวลานอน [we la non] *n* bedtime; นอนห้องเดียวกัน [non hong diao kan] *v* sleep together; นอนนานกว่า ปรกติ [non nan kwa prok ka ti] *v* sleep in; ฉันนอนไม่หลับเพราะเสียง [chan non mai lap phro siang] I can't sleep for the noise

นอนหลับ [non lap] การนอนหลับ [kan non lap] *n* sleep; ยานอนหลับ [ya non lap] *n* sleeping pill; คุณนอนหลับดีไหม? [khun non lap di mai] Did you sleep well?

น้อย [noi] *adj* few; จำนวนน้อย [cham nuan noi] *pron* few; จำนวนน้อยที่สุด [cham nuan noi thii sut] *n* minimum; ที่พบได้น้อย [thii phop dai noi] *adj* rare *(uncommon)*

น้อยๆ [noi noi] เล็ก ๆ น้อย ๆ [lek lek noi noi] *n* bit

นอร์เวย์ [no we] เกี่ยวกับนอร์เวย์ [kiao kap no we] *adj* Norwegian; ชาวนอร์เวย์ [chao no we] *n* Norwegian *(person)*; ประเทศนอร์เวย์ [pra tet nor we] *n* Norway

นัก [nak] นักเล่นกล [nak len kon] *n*

magician; นักโบราณคดี [nak bo ran kha di] *n* archaeologist; นักตกแต่งภายใน [nak tok taeng phai nai] *n* interior designer

นักกีฬา [nak ki la] *n* sportsman; มีน้ำใจเป็นนักกีฬา [mii nam jai pen nak ki la] *adj* sporty; นักกีฬาหญิง [nak ki la ying] *n* sportswoman

นักดนตรี [nak don tri] กลุ่มนักร้องหรือนักดนตรีสี่คน [klum nak rong rue nak don tree sii khon] *n* quartet; เราจะฟังนักดนตรีท้องถิ่นเล่นได้ที่ไหน? [rao ja fang nak don trii thong thin len dai thii nai] Where can we hear local musicians play?

นักเต้น [nak ten] นักเต้นระบำปลายเท้า [nak ten ra bam plai thao] *n* ballet dancer; นักเต้นบัลเล่ต์หญิง [nak ten bal le ying] *n* ballerina

นักแต่ง [nak taeng] นักแต่งนวนิยาย [nak taeng na wa ni yai] *n* novelist

นักแต่งเพลง [nak taeng phleng] *n* composer

นักท่องเที่ยว [nak thong thiao] นักท่องเที่ยวประเภทต่าง ๆ [nak thong thiao pra phet tang tang] Different types of travellers; นักท่องเที่ยวพิการ [nak thong thiao phi kan] Disabled travellers

นักธุรกิจ [nuk thu ra kit] ฉันเป็นนักธุรกิจหญิง [chan pen nak thu ra kit ying] I'm a businesswoman; ผมเป็นนักธุรกิจ [phom pen nak thu ra kit] I'm a businessman

นักบิน [nak bin] *n* pilot

นักบุญ [nak bun] *n* saint

นักร้อง [nak rong] *n* singer; กลุ่มนักร้องหรือนักดนตรีสี่คน [klum nak rong rue nak don tree sii khon] *n* quartet; นักร้องเดี่ยว [nak rong diao] *n* soloist; นักร้องรำทำกินเร่ตามถนน [nak rong ram tham kin re tam tha non] *n* busker

นักเรียน [nak rian] *n* pupil *(learner)*, student; เด็กนักเรียน [dek nak rian] *n* schoolchildren; เด็กนักเรียนชาย [dek nak rian chai] *n* schoolboy; นักเรียนทหาร [nak rian tha han] *n* cadet; ฉันเป็นนักเรียน [chan pen nak rian] I'm a student

นักศึกษา [nak suek sa] นักศึกษาระดับปริญญาตรี [nak suek sa ra dap pa rin ya tree] *n* undergraduate; นักศึกษาที่เรียนต่อจากปริญญาตรี [nak suek sa thii rian to chak pa rin ya tree] *n* postgraduate

นักสืบ [nak suep] *n* detective

นั่ง [nang] *vi* sit; นั่งลง [nang long] *v* sit down; ฉันสามารถนั่งได้ที่ใดบ้าง? [chan sa maat nang dai thii dai bang] Is there somewhere I can sit down?; ฉันจะนั่งได้ที่ไหน? [chan ja nang dai thii nai] Where can I sit down?

นั่งเล่น [nang len] ห้องนั่งเล่น [hong nang len] *n* living room, sitting room

นั่งสมาธิ [nang sa ma thi] การนั่งสมาธิ [kan nang sa ma thi] *n* meditation

นัด [nat] คุณมีนัดไหม? [khun mii nat mai] Do you have an appointment?; ฉันมีนัดกับ... [chan mii nat kap...] I have an appointment with...; ฉันขอนัดหมอได้ไหม? [chan kho nat mo dai mai] Can I have an appointment with the doctor?

นัดพบ [nat phop] การนัดพบตามเวลาที่นัดไว้ [kan nat phop tam we la thii nat wai] *n* rendezvous

นั่น [nan] *adj* that ▷ *pron* that; อันนั้น [an nan] *pron* that

นับ [nap] *v* count

นับถือ [nap thue] ความนับถือ [khwam nap thue] *n* regard; น่านับถือ [na nap thue] *adj* respectable

นา [na] ชาวนา [chao na] *n* farmer

นา [na] ป้า นา อาผู้หญิง [pa na a phu ying] *n* auntie; ป้า นา อาผู้หญิง [pa na a phu ying] *n* aunt

นาก [nak] ตัวนาก [tua nak] *n* otter

นากลัว [na klua] *adj* gruesome, spooky; ความนากลัว [khwam na klua] *n* horror; ที่นากลัว [thii na klua] *adj* scared; ทำให้

น่ากลัวมาก [tham hai na klua mak] *adj* terrified

น่าเกลียด [na kliat] *adj* ugly

นาง [nang] *n* Mrs

นางเงือก [nang ngueak] *n* mermaid

นางแบบ [nang baep] *n* model

นางพยาบาล [nang pha ya ban] *n* nurse

นางฟ้า [nang fa] *n* angel, fairy

นางสาว [nang sao] *n* Miss

น่าจะ [na cha] ไม่น่าจะเกิดขึ้น [mai na ja koet khuen] *adj* unlikely

น่าจะเป็นไปได้ [na cha pen pai dai] ความน่าจะเป็นไปได้ [khwam na ja pen pai dai] *n* probability; ที่น่าจะเป็นไปได้ [thii na ja pen pai dai] *adj* probable; อย่างน่าจะเป็นไปได้ [yang na ja pen pai dai] *adv* probably

น่าเชื่อ [na chuea] ไม่น่าเชื่อ [mai na chuea] *adj* incredible; มีความน่าเชื่อ [mii khwam na chuea] *adj* sensible

นาโต้ [na to] ตัวย่อขององค์การนาโต้ [tua yo khong ong kan na to] *abbr* NATO

นาที [na thi] *n* minute

น่าทึ่ง [na thueng] *adj* stunning

นาน [nan] ไม่นาน [mai nan] *adv* soon; นาน ๆ ครั้ง [nan nan khrang] rarely; ยาวนาน [yao nan] *adv* long; ใช้เวลานานเท่าไรในการซ่อม? [chai we la nan thao rai nai kan som] How long will it take to repair?

น่านฟ้า [nan fa] *n* airspace

นาม [nam] คำนำหน้านามชี้เฉพาะ [kham nam na nam chii cha pho] *art* the; คำนาม [kham nam] *n* noun

นามธรรม [nam ma tham] ที่เป็นนามธรรม [thii pen nam ma tham] *adj* abstract

นามบัตร [nam bat] คุณมีนามบัตรไหม? [khun mii nam bat mai] Do you have a business card?; ฉันขอนามบัตรคุณได้ไหม? [chan kho nam bat khun dai mai] Can I have your card?; นี่คือนามบัตรของฉัน [ni khue nam bat khong chan] Here's my card

นามแฝง [nam faeng] *n* pseudonym

นามสกุล [nam sa kun] *n* surname

นาย [nai] *n* Mr

นายก [na yok] นายกเทศมนตรี [na yok tet sa mon tree] *n* mayor

นายกรัฐมนตรี [na yok rat tha mon tri] *n* prime minister

นายพราน [nai phran] *n* hunter

นายพล [nai phon] *n* general

นายพลตำรวจ [nai pon tam ruat] *n* police officer

นายหน้า [nai na] *n* broker; นายหน้าขายหุ้น [nai na khai hun] *n* stockbroker

น่ารัก [na rak] *adj* cute, lovely

นาวิเกเตอร์ [na wi ke toe] เครื่องนำทางนาวิเกเตอร์ [khrueang nam thang, na wi ke toe] *n* sat nav

น่าสนใจ [na son chai] มีที่เดินที่น่าสนใจใกล้ ๆ บ้างไหม? [mii thii doen thii na son jai klai klai bang mai] Are there any interesting walks nearby?; คุณแนะนำที่ที่น่าสนใจที่จะไปได้ไหม? [khun nae nam thii thii na son jai thii ja pai dai mai] Can you suggest somewhere interesting to go?

น่าสังเกต [na sang ket] มีคุณค่าที่น่าสังเกต [mii khun kha thii na sang ket] *adj* remarkable

นาฬิกา [na li ka] *n* clock; สายนาฬิกา [sai na li ka] *n* watch strap; ตามเข็มนาฬิกา [tam khem na li ka] *adv* clockwise; นาฬิกาข้อมือ [na li ka kho mue] *n* watch

นำ [nam] *v* head, lead; นำไปคืน [nam pai khuen] *v* take back; นำมา [nam ma] *v* bring; นำกลับมา [nam klap ma] *v* bring back

น้ำ [nam] *n* water; หยดน้ำ [yot nam] *n* drip, drop; น้ำส้ม [nam som] *n* orange juice; น้ำที่หยดออกมาจากเนื้อ [nam thii yot ok ma chak nuea] *n* gravy

นำกลับมาใช้อีก [nam klap ma chai ik] *v* recycle

น้ำขึ้น [nam khuen] น้ำขึ้นเมื่อไร? [nam khuen muea rai] When is high tide?

น้ำขึ้นน้ำลง [nam khuen nam long]

ปรากฏการณ์น้ำขึ้นน้ำลง [pra kot kan nam khuen nam long] n tide

นำเข้า [nam khao] v import; การนำเข้า [kan nam khao] n import

น้ำแข็ง [nam khaeng] n ice; ก้อนน้ำแข็ง [kon nam khaeng] n ice cube; ขจัด น้ำแข็ง [kha chat nam khaeng] n de-icer; น้ำแข็งที่ผสมน้ำผลไม้ [nam khaeng thii pha som nam phon la mai] n sorbet; ขอน้ำแข็งด้วย [kho nam khaeng duai] With ice, please

น้ำค้าง [nam khang] น้ำค้างแข็ง [nam khang khaeng] n frost

น้ำเงิน [nam ngoen] สีน้ำเงินอมเขียว [sii nam ngoen om khiao] adj turquoise; น้ำเงินเข้ม [nam ngoen khem] adj navy-blue

น้ำใจ [nam chai] มีน้ำใจเป็นนักกีฬา [mii nam jai pen nak ki la] adj sporty

น้ำเชื่อม [nam chueam] n syrup, treacle

น้ำตก [nam tok] n waterfall; น้ำตกที่สูง ชัน [nam tok thii sung chan] n cataract (waterfall)

น้ำตา [nam ta] n tear (from eye)

น้ำตาล [nam tan] n sugar; ไม่มีน้ำตาล [mai mii nam tan] adj sugar-free; สี น้ำตาลอ่อน [sii nam tan on] adj beige; น้ำตาลไอซิ่งบนขนมเค้ก [nam tan ai sing bon kha nom khek] n frosting; ไม่ใส่ น้ำตาล [mai sai nam tan] no sugar

น้ำตาลเทียม [nam tan thiam] คุณมี น้ำตาลเทียมไหม? [khun mii nam tan thiam mai] Do you have any sweetener?

น้ำท่วม [nam thuam] n flood, flooding

น้ำทะเล [nam tha le] ความสูงเหนือพื้นดิน หรือเหนือน้ำทะเล [khwam sung nuea phuen din rue nuea nam tha le] n altitude

นำทาง [nam thang] v guide; เครื่อง นำทาง นาวิเกเตอร์ [khrueang nam thang, na wi ke toe] n sat nav; คน นำทาง [khon nam thang] n guide; คุณ ช่วยนำทางให้ฉันด้วยได้ไหม? [khun chuai nam thang hai chan duai dai mai] Can you guide me, please?

น้ำปรุงรส [nam prung rot] n sauce

น้ำผลไม้ [nam phon la mai] น้ำแข็งที่ ผสมน้ำผลไม้ [nam khaeng thii pha som nam phon la mai] n sorbet

น้ำผึ้ง [nam khueng] n honey; น้ำผึ้ง พระจันทร์ [nam phueng phra chan] n honeymoon

น้ำผึ้งพระจันทร์ [nam phueng phra chan] เรามาดื่มน้ำผึ้งพระจันทร์ที่นี่ [rao ma duem nam phueng phra chan thii ni] We are on our honeymoon

น้ำพุ [nam phu] n fountain

น้ำมะนาว [nam ma nao] ขอน้ำมะนาวหนึ่ง แก้ว [kho nam ma nao nueng kaew] A glass of lemonade, please

น้ำมัน [nam man] n grease, oil; โรงกลั่น น้ำมัน [rong klan nam man] n oil refinery; น้ำมันไร้สารตะกั่ว [nam man rai san ta kua] n unleaded, unleaded petrol; นี่คือคราบน้ำมัน [ni khue khrap nam man] This stain is oil

น้ำยา [nam ya] น้ำยาล้างเล็บ [nam ya lang lep] n nail-polish remover; น้ำยา ล้างจาน [nam ya lang chan] n washing-up liquid; น้ำยาล้างปาก [nam ya lang pak] n mouthwash

น้ำยาปรับผ้านุ่ม [nam ya prap pha num] คุณมีน้ำยาปรับผ้านุ่มไหม? [khun mii nam ya prab pha num mai] Do you have softener?

น้ำร้อน [nam ron] ไม่มีน้ำร้อน [mai mii nam ron] There is no hot water

น้ำแร่ [nam rae] น้ำแร่แบบไม่ซ่าหนึ่งขวด [nam rae baep mai sa nueng khaut] a bottle of still mineral water; น้ำแร่แบบ ซ่าหนึ่งขวด [nam rae baep sa nueng khaut] a bottle of sparkling mineral water; น้ำแร่หนึ่งขวด [nam rae nueng khaut] a bottle of mineral water

น้ำลาย [nam lai] n saliva; ผ้ากันน้ำลาย ของเด็ก [pha kan nam lai khong dek] n pinafore

น้ำสต๊อค [nam sa tok] อาหารนี้ทำในน้ำ สต๊อคเนื้อหรือเปล่า? [a han nii tham nai nam sa tok nuea rue plao] Is this cooked in meat stock?; อาหารนี้ทำในน้ำ สต๊อคปลาหรือเปล่า? [a han nii tham nai nam sa tok pla rue plao] Is this cooked in fish stock?

น้ำส้ม [nam som] n vinegar

น้ำสลัด [nam sa lat] น้ำสลัดชนิดหนึ่งทำ จากน้ำมัน น้ำส้มและเครื่องปรุงรส [nam sa lat cha nit nueng tham chak nam man nam som lae khrueang prung rot] n vinaigrette

น้ำหนัก [nam nak] n weight; หน่วยน้ำ หนักเท่ากับสองพันสองร้อยสี่สิบปอนด์ [nuai nam nak thao kap song phan song roi si sip pond] n ton; ชั่งน้ำหนัก [chang nam nak] v weigh; ที่มีน้ำหนักมากเกินไป [thii mii nam nak mak koen pai] adj overweight

น้ำหอม [nam hom] n perfume; น้ำหอม ปรับผิวหลังโกนหนวด [nam hom prap phio lang kon nuat] n aftershave

นิกาย [ni kai] สมาชิกของนิกายยะโฮวา วิทเนส [sa ma chik khong ni kai ya ho va wit nes] n Jehovah's Witness; ที่เกี่ยว กับนิกายโปรเตสแตนต์ [thii kiao kap ni kai pro tes taen] adj Methodist; นิกาย หนึ่งของศาสนาคริสต์ซึ่งเคร่งมาก [ni kai nueng khong sat sa na khris sueng khreng mak] n Quaker

นิคารากัว [ni kha ra kua] เกี่ยวกับนิคารากั ว [kiao kap ni kha ra kua] adj Nicaraguan; ชาวนิคารากัว [chao ni kha ra kua] n Nicaraguan; ประเทศนิคารากัว [pra tet ni kha ra kua] n Nicaragua

นิโคติน [ni kho tin] สารนิโคตินในยาสูบ หรือบุหรี่ [san ni kho tin nai ya sup rue bu ri] n nicotine

นิ่ง [ning] adj still

นิตยสาร [nit ta ya san] n magazine (periodical); นิตยสารในคอมพิวเตอร์ [nit ta ya san nai khom phio toe] n webzine; ฉันจะซื้อนิตยสารได้ที่ไหน?

[chan ja sue nit ta ya san dai thii nai] Where can I buy a magazine?

นิติกร [ni ti kon] ทนาย นิติกร [tha nai, ni ti kon] n attorney

นิทาน [ni than] นิทานเทพนิยาย [ni than thep ni yai] n fairytale; นิทานปรัมปรา [ni than pa ram pa ra] n myth; ผู้เล่า นิทาน [phu lao ni than] n teller

นินทา [nin tha] v gossip; การนินทา [kan nin tha] n gossip

นิยม [ni yom] เป็นที่นิยม [pen thii ni yom] adj popular; ไม่เป็นที่นิยม [mai pen thii ni yom] adj unpopular; ความนิยม [khwam ni yom] n popularity

นิยาม [ni yam] v define

นิยาย [ni yai] n novel

นิรนาม [ni ra nam] adj anonymous

นิรภัย [ni ra phai] เข็มขัดนิรภัย [khem khat ni ra phai] n safety belt, seatbelt; ถุงอากาศนิรภัย [thung a kaat ni ra phai] n airbag

นิรันดร [ni ran don] n eternity; ที่อยู่ชั่วนิ รันดร [thii yu chua ni ran] adj eternal

นิ้ว [nio] นิ้วในถุงน้ำดี [nio nai thung nam di] n gallstone

นิ้ว [nio] n inch; ลายพิมพ์นิ้วมือ [lai phim nio mue] n fingerprint; นิ้วเท้า [nio thao] n toe; นิ้วโป้ง [nio pong] n thumb

นิวเคลียร์ [nio klia] เกี่ยวกับนิวเคลียร์ [kiao kap nio khlia] adj nuclear

นิวซีแลนด์ [nio si laen] ชาวนิวซีแลนด์ [chao nio si laen] n New Zealander; ประเทศนิวซีแลนด์ [pra tet nio si laen] n New Zealand

นิเวศน์วิทยา [ni wet wit tha ya] n ecology; เกี่ยวกับนิเวศน์วิทยา [kiao kap ni wet wit tha ya] adj ecological

นี่ [ni] นี่คือ... [ni khue...] It's... (calling), This is... (calling)

นี้ [ni] adj this; อันนี้ [an nii] pron this; วัน เสาร์นี้ [wan sao nii] this Saturday

นีออน [ni on] ไฟนีออน [fai ni on] n fluorescent, neon

นุ่ม [num] น้ำยาปรับให้นุ่ม [nam ya prap

hai num] n conditioner; อ่อนนุ่ม [on num] adj soft

นุ่มนวล [num nuan] อย่างนุ่มนวล [yang num nuan] adv gently

เนคไท [nek thai] n tie

เน็ตบอล [net bon] กีฬาเน็ตบอลมีสองทีม ๆ ละเจ็ดคน [ki la net bal mii song thim thim la chet kon] n netball

เนเธอร์แลนด์ [ne thoe laen] ประเทศเนเธอร์แลนด์ [pra tet ne thoe laen] npl Netherlands

เน้น [nen] v emphasize, highlight; จุดเน้น [chut nen] n focus

เนปาล [ne pan] ประเทศเนปาล [pra tet ne pan] n Nepal

เนย [noei] n butter; เนยเหลวชนิดหนึ่ง [noei leo cha nit nueng] n cottage cheese; เนยเทียม [noei thiam] n margarine; เนยแข็ง [noei khaeng] n cheese

เนยแข็ง [noei khaeng] คุณมีเนยแข็งแบบ ไหน? [khun mii noei khaeng baep nai] What sort of cheese?

เนรเทศ [ne ra thet] เนรเทศออกจาก ประเทศ [ne ra thet ok chak pra thet] v deport

เน่า [nao] v rot; เหม็นเน่า [men nao] adj foul

เน่าเปื่อย [nao pueai] adj rotten ▷ v decay

เนิน [noen] ซึ่งเป็นเนิน [sueng pen noen] adv uphill

เนื้อ [nuea] n meat; เนื้อและผักชิ้นเล็กเสียบ ด้วยไม้เสียบแล้วย่าง [nuea lae phak chin lek siap duai mai siap laeo yang] n kebab; แฮมเบอร์เกอร์เนื้อ [haem boe koe nuea] n beefburger; ที่ร้านคนขายเนื้อ [thii ran khon khai nuea] n butcher's; คุณทานเนื้อไหม? [khun than nuea mai] Do you eat meat?

เนื่องจาก [nueang chak] conj since ▷ prep owing to; ขณะที่ ดังที่ เนื่องจาก [kha na thii, dang thii, nueang chak] conj as

เนื่องด้วย [nueang duai] เนื่องด้วยเหตุผล

บางอย่าง [nueang duai het phon bang yang] adv somehow

เนื้องอก [nue ngok] n tumour

เนื้อเพลง [nuea phleng] npl lyrics

เนื้อเยื่อ [nuea yuea] เนื้อเยื่อของคน สัตว์ และพืช [nuea yuea khong khon sat lae phuet] n tissue (anatomy)

เนื้อหา [nuea ha] เนื้อหาสาระ [nuea ha sa ra] n substance

แน่ใจ [nae chai] ไม่แน่ใจ [mai nae jai] adj unsure; ทำให้แน่ใจว่า [tham hai nae jai wa] v ensure

แน่น [naen] adj packed; คับแน่น [khap naen] adj tight; ติดแน่น [tit naen] adj fixed; ทำให้แน่นหรือตึงขึ้น [tham hai naen rue tueng khuen] v tighten

แน่นอน [nae non] adj certain, definite, sure; ความเด็ดเดี่ยวแน่นอน [khwam det diao nae non] n resolution; ความ แน่นอน [khwam nae non] n certainty; ความไม่แน่นอน [khwam mai nae non] n instability, uncertainty

แน่นอนใจ [nae non chai] ความไม่แน่นอน ใจ [khwam mai nae non jai] n suspense

แนบ [naep] การผูกติด สิ่งที่แนบมา [kan phuk tit, sing thii naep ma] n attachment

แนวดิ่ง [naeo ding] ซึ่งเป็นแนวดิ่ง [sueng pen naeo ding] adj vertical

แนวทาง [naeo thang] n trend; วิธีหรือ แนวทาง [wi thi rue naeo thang] n way

แนวนอน [naeo non] adj horizontal, reclining

แนวหน้า [naeo na] adj advanced

แนะนำ [nae nam] v advise, instruct, introduce, recommend, suggest; แนะนำให้รู้จัก [nae nam hai ru chak] v present; การแนะนำ [kan nae nam] n introduction, recommendation; คำ แนะนำ [kham nae nam] n advice, suggestion; คุณแนะนำไวน์ดี ๆ ได้ไหม? [khun nae nam wine di di dai mai] Can you recommend a good wine?

โน้ต [not] โน้ตเพลง [not phleng] *n* note (*music*)

โน้ตเพลง [not phleng] *n* score (*of music*)

โน้มน้าว [nom nao] *v* convince; ซึ่งโน้มน้าว [sueng nom nao] *adj* convincing

โน้มเอียง [nom iang] *v* tend; ความโน้มเอียง [khwam nom iang] *n* tendency

ใน [nai] *prep* in; ในบ้าน [nai baan] *adv* indoors; ข้างใน [khang nai] *prep* inside; ด้านใน [dan nai] *n* inside

ในฐานะ [nai tha na] *prep* as

ในทางกลับกัน [nai thang klap kan] *adv* vice versa

ในที่สุด [nai thi sut] *adv* eventually

ในนามของ [nai nam khong] *n* on behalf of

ในไม่ช้า [nai mai cha] *adv* presently, sooner

ในร่ม [nai rom] *adj* indoor

ไนจีเรีย [nai chi ria] เกี่ยวกับไนจีเรีย [kiao kap nai chi ria] *adj* Nigerian; ชาวไนจีเรีย [chao nai chi ria] *n* Nigerian; ประเทศไนจีเรีย [pra tet nai chi ria] *n* Nigeria

ไนโตรเจน [nai tro chen] *n* nitrogen

ไนท์คลับ [nait khlap] *n* nightclub

ไนลอน [nai lon] เส้นใยไนลอน [sen yai nai lon] *n* nylon; เวลโคร ไนลอนสองชิ้นที่ยึดสิ่งของให้ติดแน่น ใช้แทนซิป กระดุมและขอเกี่ยว [wel khro nai lon song chin thii yuet sing khong hai tit naen chai taen sip kra dum lae kho kiao] *n* Velcro®

 บ

บกพร่อง [bok phrong] ข้อบกพร่อง [kho bok phrong] *n* defect, flaw, shortcoming

บงการ [bong kan] *v* boss around; ควบคุมบงการ [khuap khum bong kan] *v* manipulate

บด [bot] *v* mince, grind; เครื่องบดถนน [khrueang bot tha non] *n* roller; บดละเอียด [bot la iat] *v* crush

บท [bot] บทเรียนสอนขับรถ [bot rian son khap rot] *n* driving lesson; บทสนทนา [bot son tha na] *n* conversation; บทของหนังสือหรืองานเขียน [bot khong nang sue rue ngan khian] *n* chapter

บทกวี [bot ka wi] *n* poem, poetry

บทเขียน [bot khian] บทเขียนวิจารณ์ [bot khian wi chan] *n* review

บทความ [bot khwam] *n* article

บทบาท [bot bat] หน้าที่หรือบทบาท [na thii rue bot bat] *n* role

บทเรียน [bot rian] *n* lesson

บทละคร [bot la khon] ผู้เขียนบทละคร [phu khian bot la khon] *n* playwright

บน [bon] *prep* on

บน [bon] *v* moan, mutter; การบ่น [kan bon] *n* grouse (*complaint*); บ่นด้วยความโกรธ [bon duai khwam krot] *v* growl

บรรจุ [ban chu] *vt* pack; การบรรจุลง [kan ban chu long] *n* download; บรรจุใหม่ [ban chu mai] *v* recharge; บรรจุลง [ban chu long] *v* download

บรรณาธิการ [ban na thi kan] *n* editor

บรรณารักษ์ [ban na rak] *n* librarian

บรรทัด [ban that] เส้นบรรทัด [sen ban that] *n* line

บรรทุก [ban thuk] รถบรรทุก [rot ban thuk] *n* lorry; น้ำหนักบรรทุก [nam nak ban thuk] *n* load; บรรทุกสินค้า [ban thuk sin kha] *v* load; มีเรือแฟร์รี่บรรทุกรถ ไป...ไหม? [mii ruea fae ri ban thuk rot pai...mai] Is there a car ferry to...?

บรรพบุรุษ [ban pha bu rut] *n* ancestor

บรรยากาศ [ban ya kat] *n* atmosphere

บรรยาย [ban yai] *v* lecture; รายงาน การ บรรยาย [rai ngan, kan ban yai] *n* account *(report)*; การบรรยาย [kan ban yai] *n* lecture; คำบรรยาย [kham ban yai] *n* speech

บรรลุ [ban lu] การบรรลุผลสำเร็จ [kan ban lu phon sam ret] *n* achievement

บรอดแบน [brot baen] *n* broadband

บรั่นดี [bran di] เหล้าบรั่นดี [lao bran di] *n* brandy; ฉันจะดื่มบรั่นดี [chan ja duem bran di] I'll have a brandy

บราซิล [bra sin] *adj* เกี่ยวกับประเทศบราซิล [kiao kap pra thet bra sil] *adj* Brazilian ▷ *n* ชาวบราซิล [chao bra sin] *n* Brazilian; ประเทศบราซิล [pra tet bra sil] *n* Brazil

บริกร [bo ri kan] บริกรหญิง [bo ri kon ying] *n* waitress; บริกรชาย [bo ri kon chai] *n* waiter; บริกรบนเครื่องบิน [bo ri kon bon khrueang bin] *n* steward

บริการ [bo ri kan] *v* serve; แบบบริการตัว เอง [baep bo ri kan tua eng] *adj* self-service; บริการรับใช้ในห้องของ โรงแรม [bo ri kan rap chai nai hong khong rong raeng] *n* room service; เรา ยังรอให้คุณมาบริการเรา [rao yang ro hai khun ma bo ri kan rao] We are still waiting to be served

บริจาค [bo ri chak] *v* donate; การบริจาค [kan bo ri chak] *n* contribution; ผู้ บริจาค [phu bo ri chak] *n* donor

บริบท [bo ri bot] *n* context

บริโภค [bo ri phok] ผู้บริโภค [phu bo ri phok] *n* consumer

บริเวณ [bo ri wen] *n* area; บริเวณใกล้เคียง [bo ri wen klai khiang] *n* vicinity; บริเวณ ที่ใกล้เคียง [bo ri wen thii klai khiang] *n* proximity; บริเวณที่รอบล้อม [bo ri wen thii rop lom] *npl* surroundings

บริษัท [bo ri sat] *n* company, firm; รถ บริษัท [rot bo ri sat] *n* company car; บริษัทละคร [bo ri sat la khon] *n* rep; บริษัทระหว่างประเทศ [bo ri sat ra wang pra tet] *n* multinational; ฉันอยากได้ ข้อมูลเกี่ยวกับบริษัทคุณ [chan yak dai kho mun kiao kap bo ri sat khun] I would like some information about the company

บริสุทธิ์ [bo ri sut] *adj* pure

บริหาร [bo ri han] เกี่ยวกับการบริหาร [kiao kap kan bo ri han] *adj* administrative; การบริหาร [kan bo ri han] *n* administration; การบริหาร [kan bo ri han] *n* running

บลอนด์ [blon] ผมฉันเป็นสีบลอนด์ตาม ธรรมชาติ [phom chan pen sii blon tam tham ma chaat] My hair is naturally blonde

บลูเบอร์รี่ [blu boe ri] ผลบลูเบอร์รี่ [phon blu boe ri] *n* blueberry

บวบ [buap] *n* courgette, zucchini; บวบ ฝรั่งขนาดใหญ่ [buap fa rang kha naat yai] *n* marrow

บวม [buam] *adj* swollen

บ่อ [bo] บ่อ เช่น บ่อแร่ บ่อน้ำมัน บ่อน้ำ [bo chen bo rae bo nam man bo nam] *n* well

บอก [bok] *vt* tell; การบอกใบ้ [kan bok bai] *n* hint; ซึ่งบอกเป็นนัย ๆ [sueng bok pen nai nai] *adj* subtle; บอกใบ้ [bok bai] *v* hint

บอด [bot] ตาบอด [ta bot] *n* blind

บ่อน [bon] บ่อนการพนัน [bon kan pha nan] *n* casino

บอบช้ำ [bop cham] ซึ่งบอบช้ำทางจิตใจ [sueng bop cham thang chit jai] *adj* traumatic

บ่อย [boi] *adv* often; บ่อย ๆ [boi boi] *adj* frequent; บ่อยขึ้น [boi khuen] *adv* more; รถโดยสารไป...บ่อยแค่ไหน? [rot doi san pai...boi khae nai] How often are the buses to...?

บอร์ดดิ้งการ์ด [bot ding kat] นี่คือบอร์ดดิ้ง การ์ดของฉัน [ni khue bot ding kaat khong chan] Here is my boarding card

บอลข่าน [bol khan] ประเทศในคาบสมุทร บอลข่าน [pra tet nai khap sa mut bon khan] *adj* Balkan

บอสซาวานา [bot sa wa na] ประเทศบอสซา วานา [pra tet bos sa wa na] *n* Botswana

บอสเนีย [bos nia] *adj* เกี่ยวกับประเทศ บอสเนีย [kiao kap pra thet bos nia] *adj* Bosnian ▷ *n* ชาวบอสเนีย [chao bos nia] *n* Bosnian (*person*); ประเทศบอสเนีย [pra tet bos nia] *n* Bosnia

บังกาโล [bang ka lo] *n* bungalow

บังคลาเทศ [bang kha la thet] ชาวบังคลา เทศ [chao bang khla tet] *n* Bangladeshi; ที่เกี่ยวกับประเทศบังคลาเทศ [thii kiao kap pra tet bang khla tet] *adj* Bangladeshi; ประเทศบังคลาเทศ [pra tet bang khla tet] *n* Bangladesh

บังคับ [bang khap] *v* force; ข้อบังคับ [kho bang khap] *n* discipline; คันบังคับเครื่อง บิน [khan bang khap khrueang bin] *n* joystick; ที่บังคับ [thii bang khap] *adj* compulsory

บังโคลน [bang khlon] บังโคลนรถ [bang khlon rot] *n* mudguard

บังตา [bang ta] *adj* blind

บังเหียน [bang hian] เชือกบังเหียน [chueak bang hian] *npl* reins

บังเอิญ [bang oen] เหตุบังเอิญ [het bang oen] *n* coincidence; เป็นเหตุบังเอิญ [pen het bang oen] *adj* accidental; โดย บังเอิญ [doi bang oen] *adj* accidentally, by chance, by accident, casual

บัญชาการ [ban cha kan] กองบัญชาการ [kong ban cha kaan] *npl* headquarters

บัญชี [ban chi] รายการของเงินที่หักบัญชี [rai kan khong ngoen thii hak ban chi] *n* debit; หักบัญชี [hak ban chi] *v* debit; หมายเลขบัญชี [mai lek ban chi] *n* account number

บัตร [bat] ตั๋วหรือบัตรที่ใช้แทนเงินในการซื้อ สินค้าที่ระบุ [tua rue bat thii chai thaen ngoen nai kan sue sin kha thii ra bu] *n* voucher; บัตรเล่นสกี [bat len sa ki] *n* ski pass; บัตรเครดิต [bat khre dit] *n* credit card; ฉันจะใช้บัตรเบิกเงินสดได้ไหม? [chan ja chai bat boek ngoen sot dai mai] Can I use my card to get cash?

บัตรเครดิต [bat khre dit] คุณรับบัตรเครดิต ไหม? [khun rap bat khre dit mai] Do you take credit cards?; ฉันจ่ายด้วยบัตร เครดิตได้ไหม? [chan chai duai bat khre dit dai mai] Can I pay by credit card?; ฉันจะเบิกเงินสดล่วงหน้าจากบัตรเครดิตของ ฉันได้ไหม? [chan ja boek ngoen sot luang na chak bat khre dit khong chan dai mai] Can I get a cash advance with my credit card?

บัตรเดบิต [bat de bit] คุณรับบัตรเดบิต ไหม? [khun rap bat de bit mai] Do you take debit cards?

บัตรผ่าน [bat phan] มีส่วนลดสำหรับบัตร ผ่านนี้หรือไม่? [mii suan lot sam rap bat phan nii rue mai] Is there a reduction with this pass?

บันได [ban dai] *n* ladder ▷ *npl* stairs; บันไดเลื่อน [ban dai luean] *n* escalator; บันไดทอดหนึ่ง [ban dai thot nueng] *n* staircase; บันไดพับได้ [ban dai phap dai] *n* stepladder

บั้นท้าย [ban thai] *npl* buttocks

บันทึก [ban thuek] *v* record; แผ่นบันทึก [phaen ban thuek] *n* floppy disk, hard disk; ลงบันทึกเข้า [long ban thuek khao] *v* log in; ลงบันทึกเปิด [long ban thuek poet] *v* log on

บันเทิง [ban thoeng] ธุรกิจการบันเทิง [thu ra kit kan ban thoeng] *n* show business; ผู้ให้ความบันเทิง [phu hai khwam ban thoeng] *n* entertainer

บัลลังก์ [ban lang] *n* throne

บัลเลต์ [bal le] รองเท้าบัลเลต์ [rong thao ban le] *npl* ballet shoes; นักเต้นบัลเลต์หญิง [nak ten bal le ying] *n* ballerina; ฉันจะซื้อตั๋วแสดงบัลเลต์ได้ที่ไหน? [chan ja sue tua sa daeng ban le dai thii nai] Where can I buy tickets for the ballet?

บ้า [ba] *adj* crazy; คนบ้า [khon ba] *n* lunatic, madman

บาง [bang] แบบบาง [baep bang] *adj* frail

บาง [bang] *adj* any

บางคน [bang khon] *pron* somebody, someone

บางครั้งบางคราว [bang khang bang khrao] *adv* occasionally, sometimes

บางที [bang thi] *adv* perhaps

บางเวลา [bang we la] *adv* sometime

บางส่วน [bang suan] *adv* partly ▷ *pron* some; ซึ่งเป็นบางส่วน [sueng pen bang suan] *adj* partial

บางสิ่ง [bang sing] *pron* something

บางแห่ง [bang haeng] *adv* someplace

บาดเจ็บ [bat chep] *v* wound, hurt; การทดเวลาบาดเจ็บ [kan thot we la bat chep] *n* injury time; ความบาดเจ็บ [khwam bat chep] *n* injury; ชนล้มและบาดเจ็บ [chon lom lae bat chep] *v* run over

บาดทะยัก [bat tha yak] โรคบาดทะยัก [rok bat tha yak] *n* tetanus; ฉันต้องฉีดกันบาดทะยัก [chan tong chiit kan bat tha yak] I need a tetanus shot

บาดแผล [bat phlae] *n* wound

บาทหลวง [bat luang] ตำแหน่งบาทหลวงที่ปกครองบาทหลวงอื่น ๆ [tam naeng bat luang thii pok khrong bat luang uen uen] *n* bishop

บ้าน [ban] *n* home, house; ไม่มีบ้าน [mai mii baan] *adj* homeless; คนที่ทำงานเกี่ยวกับขายบ้านและที่ดิน [khon thii tham ngan kiao kap khai baan lae thii din] *n* estate agent; งานบ้าน [ngan baan] *n* housework; คุณจะกลับบ้าน

เมื่อไร? [khun ja klap baan muea rai] When do you go home?

บานเกล็ด [ban klet] บานเกล็ดหน้าต่าง [baan klet na tang] *n* shutters

บานพับ [ban phap] *n* hinge

บาป [bap] *v* sin

บ่าย [bai] ตอนบ่าย [ton bai] *n* afternoon; พรุ่งนี้บ่าย [phrung nii bai] tomorrow afternoon

บาร์ [ba] *n* pub; เจ้าของและผู้จัดการบาร์ [chao khong lae phu chat kan ba] *n* publican; คนเฝ้าหน้าบาร์ที่กันไม่ให้คนเข้า [khon fao na bar thii kan mai hai khon khao] *n* bouncer; บาร์ ที่จำหน่ายเครื่องดื่ม {baa thii cham nai khrueang duem] *n* bar (*alcohol*)

บาร์เทนเดอร์ [ba ten doe] *n* bartender

บาร์บีคิว [ba bi kio] *n* barbecue; บริเวณที่บาร์บิคิวอยู่ที่ไหน? [bo ri wen thii bar bi khio yu thii nai] Where is the barbecue area?

บาร์เบโดส [ba be dos] ประเทศบาร์เบโดส [pra tet bar be dos] *n* Barbados

บาร์เลย์ [ba le] ข้าวบาร์เลย์ [khao ba le] *n* barley

บาร์เหริน [ba ha ren] ประเทศบาร์เหริน [pra tet bar ren] *n* Bahrain

บาสเกตบอล [bas ket bon] กีฬาบาสเกตบอล [ki la bas ket bal] *n* basketball

บาสค์ [bat] *adj* เกี่ยวกับชาวบาสค์ [kiao kap chao bas] *adj* Basque ▷ *n* ชาวบาสค์ [chao bas] *n* Basque (*person*); ภาษาบาสค์ [pha sa bas] *n* Basque (*language*)

บาฮามาส [ba ha mas] ประเทศบาฮามาส [pra tet ba ha mas] *npl* Bahamas

บำนาญ [bam nan] *n* pension; คนชราเกษียณผู้รับบำนาญ [khon cha ra ka sian phu rap bam nan] *n* old-age pensioner; ผู้รับบำนาญ [phu rap bam nan] *n* pensioner

บำบัดโรค [bam bat rok] การบำบัดโรค [kan bam bat rok] *n* therapy

บำรุง [bam rung] การบำรุงผิวหน้า [kan bam rung phio na] *n* facial

บิกินี่ [bi ki ni] n bikini

บิงโก [bing ko] เกมบิงโก [kem bing ko] n bingo

บิชอพ [bi chop] หัวหน้าของบิชอพ [hua na khong bi chop] n archbishop

บิด [bit] การดึงและบิดอย่างแรง [kan dueng lae bit yang raeng] n wrench; ดึงและบิด อย่างแรง [dueng lae bit yang raeng] v wrench; บิดเป็นเกลียว [bit pen kliao] vi twist

บิน [bin] vi fly; การบิน [kan bin] n fly; การ บินขึ้น [kan bin khuen] n takeoff; บินไป [bin pai] v fly away

บิล [bin] บิลเก็บเงินค่าโทรศัพท์ [bil kep ngoen kha tho ra sap] n phone bill; ใส่ ลงไปในบิลฉัน [sai long pai nai bil chan] Put it on my bill; ฉันขอบิลที่แสดงทุก รายการได้ไหม? [chan kho bil thii sa daeng thuk rai kan dai mai] Can I have an itemized bill?

บิลเลียด [bin liat] npl billiards; ไม้แทง บิลเลียด [mai thaeng bil liad] n cue (billiards)

บีช [bit] ต้นบีช [ton bit] n beech (tree)

บีตรูต [bit rut] หัวบีตรูต [hua bit rut] n beetroot

บีบ [bip] v squeeze

บีบคอ [bip kho] ฆ่าโดยการบีบคอ [kha doi kan bip kho] v strangle

บีบอัด [bip at] เครื่องบีบอัด [khrueang bip at] n press

บึง [bueng] n marsh; บึงน้ำเค็ม [bueng nam khem] n lagoon

บึ้ง [bueng] ทำหน้าบึ้ง [tham na bueng] v frown

บุ [bu] ผ้าบุคลุมเตียง [pha bu khlum tiang] n quilt

บุก [buk] บุกเข้าไป [buk khao pai] v break in, break in (on); บุกเข้ามาขโมยของ [buk khao ma kha moi khong] v burgle

บุกรุก [buk ruk] v invade; การบุกรุกเข้าไป [kan buk ruk khao pai] n break-in; ผู้ บุกรุก [phu buk ruk] n intruder

บุคคล [bu khon] n person; เฉพาะบุคคล [cha pho buk khon] adj individual; บุคคลที่ [buk khon thii] pron who; ฝ่าย บุคคล [fai buk khon] n personnel

บุคลิก [buk ka lik] บุคลิกลักษณะ [buk kha lik lak sa na] n personality

บุญคุณ [bun kun] ไม่สำนึกบุญคุณ [mai sam nuek bun khun] adj ungrateful; ซึ่งสำนึกในบุญคุณ [sueng sam nuek nai bun khun] adj grateful

บุตรบุญธรรม [but bun tham] การรับเลี้ยง บุตรบุญธรรม [kan rap liang but bun tham] n adoption

บุฟเฟต์ [bup fe] มีที่ทานอาหารแบบบุฟเฟต์ บนรถไฟไหม? [mii thii than a han baep buf fe bon rot fai mai] Is there a buffet car on the train?; ที่กินอาหารแบบบุฟเฟต์ อยู่ที่ไหน? [thii kin a han baep buf fe yu thii nai] Where is the buffet car?

บุ๋ม [bum] รอยบุ๋ม [roi bum] n dent

บุหรี่ [bu ri] n cigarette; ไฟที่จุดบุหรี่ [fai thii chut bu ri] n cigarette lighter; ที่ เขี่ยบุหรี่ [thi khia bu ri] n ashtray

บูชา [bu cha] v adore, worship; เป็นที่ เคารพบูชา [pen thii khao rop bu cha] adj holy; แท่นบูชา [thaen bu cha] n altar

บูดบึ้ง [but bueng] อารมณ์บูดบึ้ง [a rom but bueng] adj grumpy; อารมณ์บูดบึ้งไม่ พูดไม่จา [a rom but bueng mai phut mai cha] v sulk

บูท [but] รองเท้าบูท [rong thao but] n boot

บูท [but] ร้านที่เป็นบูทเล็ก ๆ [ran thii pen but lek lek] n kiosk; รองเท้าบูทยาง [rong thao but yang] npl wellies, wellingtons; ราคานี้รวมรองเท้าบูทไหม? [ra kha nii ruam rong thao but mai] Does the price include boots?

บูลกาเรีย [bul kae ria] ชาวบูลกาเรีย [chao bul ka ria] n Bulgarian (person); ที่เกี่ยว กับบูลกาเรีย [thii kiao kap bul ka ria] adj Bulgarian; ประเทศบูลกาเรีย [pra tet bul ka ria] n Bulgaria

เบญจมาศ [ben cha mat] ดอกเบญจมาศ [dok ben cha mat] n chrysanthemum

เบ็ดเตล็ด [bet ta let] adj miscellaneous

เบรค [brek] เบรคมือ [brek mue] n
handbrake; เบรคหรือเครื่องห้ามล้อ [brek
rue khrueang ham lo] n brake; ไฟเบรค
[fai brek] n brake light; เบรคไม่ทำงาน
[brek mai tham ngan] The brakes are
not working, The brakes don't work

เบรารัสเซี่ยน [brao rat sia] n ชาวเบรารัส
เซี่ยน [chao be ra ras sian] n
Belarussian (person); ภาษาเบรารัสเซี่ยน
[pha sa be ra ras sian] n Belarussian
(language)

เบรารุส [be ra rut] เกี่ยวกับชาวเบรารุส [kiao
kap chao be ra rus] n Belarussian; ประ
เทศเบรารุส [pra tet be ra rus] n Belarus

เบลเยี่ยม [ben yiam] adj เกี่ยวกับชาว
เบลเยี่ยม [kiao kap chao bel yiam] adj
Belgian ▷ n ชาวเบลเยี่ยม [chao bel yiam]
n Belgian; ประเทศเบลเยี่ยม [pra tet bel
yiam] n Belgium

เบสบอล [bes bon] หมวกแก๊ปสำหรับเล่น
เบสบอล [muak kaep sam rap len bes
bal] n baseball cap; กีฬาเบสบอล [ki la
bes bal] n baseball

เบอร์ [boe] รายการเบอร์โทรศัพท์ [rai kan
boe tho ra sap] n entry phone; โทรสาร
เบอร์อะไร? [tho ra san boe a rai] What is
the fax number?; โทรศัพท์เบอร์อะไร?
[tho ra sap boe a rai] What's the
telephone number?

เบอร์เกอร์ [boe koe] n burger

เบอร์รี่ [boe ri] ลูกเบอร์รี่เป็นลูกไม้ส่วนใหญ่
กินได้และมีลักษณะกลม [luk boe ri pen
luk mai suan yai kin dai lae mii lak sa
na klom] n berry

เบา [bao] adj light (not heavy)

เบาหวาน [bao hwan] โรคเบาหวาน [rok
bao wan] n diabetes; คนเป็นเบาหวาน
[khon pen bao wan] n diabetic; ซึ่งเป็น
เบาหวาน [sueng pen bao wan] adj
diabetic; ฉันเป็นเบาหวาน [chan pen bao
wan] I'm diabetic

เบาะ [bo] เบาะรอง [bo rong] n pad; เบาะ
พลาสติกที่เป่าให้พองลมได้ [bo phas tik
thii pao hai phong lom dai] n Lilo®

เบิก [boek] ฉันจะเบิกเงินสดล่วงหน้าจากบัตร
เครดิตของฉันได้ไหม? [chan ja boek
ngoen sot luang na chak bat khre dit
khong chan dai mai] Can I get a cash
advance with my credit card?; ฉันอยาก
เบิกสองร้อย... [chan yak boek song
roi...] I'd like two hundred...; ฉันอยาก
เบิกห้าร้อย... [chan yak boek ha roi...]
I'd like five hundred...

เบิร์ช [boet] ต้นไม้ชนิดหนึ่งชื่อต้นเบิร์ช [ton
mai cha nit nueng chue ton birch] n
birch

เบียด [biat] เบียดเข้าไป [biat khao pai] v
squeeze in

เบียดเสียด [biat siat] v squash

เบียร์ [bia] n beer; เบียร์สีอ่อนเก็บไว้ในถังบ่ม
[bia sii on kep wai nai thang bom] n
lager; เบียร์อีกแก้ว [bia ik kaew] another
beer; ขอเบียร์สด [kho bia sot] A draught
beer, please

เบื่อ [buea] adj fed up ▷ v bore (be dull);
เบื่อและไม่พอใจ [buea lae mai pho jai]
adj restless; ความเบื่อ [khwam buea] n
boredom; ทำให้เบื่อ [tham hai buea]
adj bored

เบื้องต้น [bueang ton] adj gross (income
etc.)

เบื่อหน่าย [buea nai] น่าเบื่อหน่ายเพราะ
ซ้ำซาก [na buea nai phro sam sak] adj
monotonous

แบคทีเรีย [bak thi ria] เชื้อแบคทีเรีย
[chuea baek thi ria] npl bacteria

แบ่ง [baeng] vt divide; แบ่งส่วน [baeng
suan] v share; แบ่งออก [baeng ok] v share
out; การแบ่ง [kan baeng] n division

แบ่งแยก [baeng yaek] การแบ่งแยก [kan
baeng yaek] n distinction; การแบ่งแยก
เพศ [kan baeng yaek phet] adj sexist

แบดมินตัน [bat min tan] n badminton

แบตเตอรี่ [bat toe ri] n battery; สายต่อ
หม้อแบตเตอรี่ [sai to mo baet toe ri] npl
jump leads; แบตเตอรี่เสีย [baet toe ri
sia] The battery is flat; คุณมีแบตเตอรี่
ไหม? [khun mii baet toe ri mai] Do you

have any batteries?

แบน [baen] จอภาพแบน [cho phap baen] n flat-screen; ยางรถฉันแบน [yang rot chan baen] I've a flat tyre

แบนโจ [baen cho] แบนโจ เครื่องดนตรี [baen jo khrueang don trii] n banjo

แบบ [baep] n pattern

แบบฉบับ [baep cha bap] ซึ่งเป็นแบบฉบับ [sueng pen baep cha bap] adj original

แบบฟอร์ม [baep fom] แบบฟอร์มใบสมัคร [baep fom bai sa mak] n application form; แบบฟอร์มสั่งซื้อ [baep fom sang sue] n order form; แบบฟอร์มการเรียกร้อง [baep fom kan riak rong] n claim form

แบบอย่าง [baep yang] ทำให้เป็นแบบอย่าง [tham hai pen baep yang] adj model

แบลคเคอแรนต์ [blaek koe raen] ผล แบลคเคอแรนต์ [phon blaek koe raen] n blackcurrant

โบกมือ [bok mue] v wave

โบกรถ [bok rot] โบกรถเพื่อนเดินทาง [bok rot phuean doen thang] v hitchhike

โบสถ์ [bot] โบสถ์เล็ก ๆ [bot lek lek] n chapel

โบนัส [bo nat] เงินโบนัส [ngoen bo nas] n bonus

โบราณ [bo ran] adj ancient; แบบโบราณ [baep bo ran] adj quaint; โบราณ แบบ ดั้งเดิม แบบเก่าแก่ [bo ran, baep dang doem, baep kao kae] adj traditional

โบราณคดี [bo ran kha di] นักโบราณคดี [nak bo ran kha di] n archaeologist; วิชาโบราณคดี [wi cha bo ran kha di] n archaeology

โบลิเวีย [bo li wia] ชาวโบลิเวีย [chao bo li wia] n Bolivian; ประเทศโบลิเวีย [pra thet bo li wia] n Bolivia

โบว์ [bo] โบว์หูกระต่าย [bo hu kra tai] n bow tie

โบว์ลิ่ง [bo ling] n bowling; เล่นเล่นโบว์ลิ่ง [len len bo ling] n bowling alley; โบว์ลิ่ง แบบตัวตั้งสิบตัว [bo ling baep tua tang sip tua] n tenpin bowling

โบสถ์ [bot] n church; โบสถ์ของศาสนายิว [bot khong sat sa na yio] n synagogue; เราไปเยี่ยมชมโบสถ์ได้ไหม? [rao pai yiam chom bot dai mai] Can we visit the church?

ใบ [bai] ใบเกิด [bai koet] n birth certificate; ใบแจ้งหนี้ [bai chaeng nii] n bill (account); ใบรายการส่งสินค้าที่แสดง ราคา [bai rai kan song sin ka thii sa daeng ra kha] n invoice

ใบ [bai] บอกใบ้ [bok bai] v hint

ใบปลิว [bai plio] แผ่นใบปลิว [phaen bai plio] n leaflet; คุณมีใบปลิวเป็นภาษา อังกฤษไหม? [khun mii bai plio pen pha sa ang krit mai] Do you have a leaflet in English?; คุณมีใบปลิวบ้างไหม? [khun mii bai plio bang mai] Do you have any leaflets?

ใบไม้ [bai mai] n leaf; ใบไม้หลายใบ [bai mai lai bai] npl leaves; ฤดูใบไม้ร่วง [rue du bai mai ruang] n autumn

ใบรับรอง [bai rap rong] ใบรับรองผลการ ศึกษา [bai rap rong phon kan suek sa] n transcript

ใบรับรองแพทย์ [bai rap rong phaet] n medical certificate

ใบเรือ [bai ruea] n sail

ใบสั่ง [bai sang] n parking ticket

ใบสั่งจ่ายยา [bai sang chai ya] n prescription

ใบเสร็จ [bai set] ฉันขอใบเสร็จรับเงิน [chan kho bai set rap ngoen] I need a receipt, please; ฉันอยากได้ใบเสร็จสำหรับประกัน [chan yak dai bai set sam rap pra kan] I need a receipt for the insurance

ใบเสร็จรับเงิน [bai set rap ngoen] n receipt

ใบหน้า [bai na] n face; เกี่ยวกับใบหน้า [kiao kap bai na] adj facial

ใบอนุญาต [bai a nu yat] คุณต้องมีใบ อนุญาตตกปลาไหม? [khun tong mii bai a nu yat tok pla mai] Do you need a fishing permit?

ไบเบิล [bai boen] คัมภีร์ไบเบิล [kham phii bai boen] n Bible

ป

ปก [pok] ปกเสื้อ [pok suea] n collar; ปก
หนังสือ [pok nang sue] n cover

ปกครอง [pok khrong] เจ้าหน้าที่ฝ่าย
ปกครอง [chao na thii fai pok khrong] n
magistrate; การปกครองโดยมีพระมหา
กษัตริย์เป็นประมุข [kan pok khrong doi
mii phra ma ha ka sat pen pra muk] n
monarchy; การปกครองตนเอง [kan pok
khrong ton eng] n autonomy; ฉันเป็นผู้
ปกครองเต็มเวลา [chan pen phu pok
khrong tem we la] I'm a full-time
parent

ปกป้อง [pok pong] ผู้ปกป้อง [phu pok
pong] n defender

ปกปิด [pok pit] หลบ กำบัง ป้องกัน ปกปิด
เหมือนกับมีฉากกัน [lop, kam bang, pong
kan, pok pit muean kap mii chak kan]
v screen (off); ซ่อน ปกปิด [son, pok pit]
vi hide

ปฏิทิน [pa ti thin] n calendar

ปฏิกรณ์นิวเคลียร์ [pa ti kon nio khlia]
เครื่องปฏิกรณ์นิวเคลียร์ [khrueang pa ti
kon nio khlia] n reactor

ปฏิกิริยา [pa ti ki ri ya] n reaction; มี
ปฏิกิริยา [mii pa ti ki ri ya] v react

ปฏิชีวนะ [pa ti chi wa na] ยาปฏิชีวนะ [ya

pa ti chi wa na] n antibiotic

ปฏิญาณ [pa ti yan] คำปฏิญาณ [kham pa
ti yan] n oath

ปฏิบัติ [pa ti bat] v behave, operate (to
function), treat; เหมาะสมที่จะปฏิบัติ [mo
som thii ja pa ti bat] adj practical; ที่
ปฏิบัติไม่ได้ [thii pa ti bat mai dai] adj
impractical; ปฏิบัติต่ออย่างไม่ดี [pa ti bat
to yang mai di] v ill-treat

ปฏิภาณ [pa ti phan] การมีไหวพริบหรือ
ปฏิภาณดี [kan mii wai phrip rue pa ti
phan dii] n tact

ปฏิวัติ [pa ti wat] เกี่ยวกับการปฏิวัติ [kiao
kap kan pa ti wat] adj revolutionary;
การปฏิวัติ [kan pa ti wat] n revolution

ปฏิเสธ [pa ti set] v deny, refuse, reject;
การปฏิเสธ [kan pa ti set] n refusal; คำ
ปฏิเสธ [kham pa ti set] n negative; ซึ่ง
ไม่อาจปฏิเสธได้ [sueng mai aat pa ti set
dai] adj undeniable

ปฐมพยาบาล [pa thom pha ya ban] การ
ปฐมพยาบาลเบื้องต้น [kan pa thom pha ya
baan bueang ton] n first aid; ชุด
ปฐมพยาบาล [chut pa thom pha ya
baan] n first-aid kit

ปรกติ [prok ka ti] adj normal; เป็นปรกติ
[pen prok ka ti] adj usual; โดยปรกติ [doi
prok ka ti] adv normally, regularly,
usually

ปรบมือ [prop mue] v applaud, clap; การ
ปรบมือแสดงความชื่นชม [kan prop mue
sa daeng khwam chuen chom] n
applause

ปรมาณู [po ra ma nu] เกี่ยวกับปรมาณู
[kiao kap pa ra ma nu] adj atomic;
ระเบิดปรมาณู [ra boet pa ra ma nu] n
atom bomb

ปรอท [prot] ธาตุปรอท [that pa rot] n
mercury; ปรอทวัดอุณหภูมิ [pa rot wat
un ha phum] n thermometer

ประกอบ [pra kop] ประกอบด้วย [pra kop
duai] adj included; ภาพประกอบ [phap
pra kop] n illustration

ประกอบด้วย [pra kop duai] v consist of

ประกัน [pra kan] v insure; ใบประกัน [bai pra kan] n insurance certificate; กรมธรรมประกัน [krom ma than pra kan] n insurance policy; การประกัน [kan pra kan] n insurance; ฉันขอประกันกระเป๋าเดินทางของฉันได้ไหม? [chan kho pra kan kra pao doen thang khong chan dai mai] Can I insure my luggage?

ประกายไฟ [pra kai phai] n spark

ประกาศ [pra kat] v announce, declare, notice; กระดานปิดประกาศ [kra dan pid pra kat] n bulletin board; การประกาศ [kan pra kat] n announcement; การประกาศข่าวมรณกรรม [kan pra kat khao mo ra na kam] n obituary

ประกาศนียบัตร [pra ka sa ni ya bat] n certificate, diploma

ประจำ [pra cham] เด็กประจำ [dek pra cham] n boarder; เป็นประจำ [pen pra cham] adj regular; โรงเรียนประจำ [rong rian pra cham] n boarding school

ประจำเดือน [pra cham duean] การมีประจำเดือน [kan mii pra cham duen] n menstruation; ช่วงวัยหมดประจำเดือน [chuang wai mot pra cham duen] n menopause

ประจำตัว [pra cham tua] บัตรประจำตัว [bat pra cham tua] n identity card

ประจำปี [pra cham pi] adj annual, yearly

ประจุ [pra chu] ประจุไฟฟ้า [pra chu fai fa] n charge (electricity)

ประชด [pra chot] การประชด [kan pra chot] n irony

ประชากร [pra cha kon] n population; การสำรวจจำนวนประชากร [kan sam ruat cham nuan pra cha kon] n census

ประชาชน [pra cha chuen] บัตรประจำตัวประชาชน [bat pra cham tua pra cha chon] abbr ID card

ประชาธิปไตย [pra cha thi pa tai] n democracy; เกี่ยวกับประชาธิปไตย [kiao kap pra cha thip pa tai] adj democratic

ประชาสัมพันธ์ [pra cha sam phan] npl public relations

ประชุม [pra chum] การประชุม [kan pra chum] n meeting; การประชุมประจำปี [kan pra chum pra cham pi] abbr AGM; ฉันอยากจัดให้การประชุมกับ... [chan yak chat hai kan pra chum kap...] I'd like to arrange a meeting with...

ประณีต [pra nit] สะอาดและประณีต [sa at lae pra nit] adj smart

ประดับ [pra dap] v decorate; การประดับเหรียญให้ [kan pra dap rian hai] n medallion

ประดิษฐ์ [pra dit] v invent; การประดิษฐ์ [kan pra dit] n invention; ผู้ประดิษฐ์ [phu pra dit] n inventor

ประตู [pra tu] n door, gate; รถยนต์ที่มีประตูหลัง [rot yon thii mii pra tu lang] n hatchback; คนเปิดประตูหน้าโรงแรมหรืออาคารต่าง ๆ [khon poet pra tu na rong raeng rue a khan tang tang] n doorman; ที่จับประตู [thii chap pra tu] n door handle; กรุณาไปที่ประตูโดยสารที่... [ka ru na pai thii pra tu doi san thii...] Please go to gate...

ประถม [pra thom] โรงเรียนชั้นประถม [rong rian chan pra thom] n primary school

ประถมศึกษา [pra thom suek sa] โรงเรียนระดับประถมศึกษา [rong rian ra dap pra thom suek sa] n elementary school

ประท้วง [pra thuang] n strike ▷ v protest; หยุดงานประท้วง [yut ngan pra thuang] strike (suspend work); การประท้วง [kan pra thuang] n demonstration, protest; คนที่หยุดงานประท้วง [khon thii yut ngan pra thuang] n striker

ประทัด [pra that] n cracker

ประทับใจ [pra thap chai] v impress; สิ่งที่ประทับใจ [sing thii pra thap jai] n impression; น่าประทับใจ [na pra thap jai] adj impressive; อย่างประทับใจ [yang pra thap jai] adj impressed

ประเทศ [pra thet] n country, nation;

เกี่ยวกับหลายประเทศ [kiao kap lai pra tet] *adj* multinational; ในประเทศ [nai pra tet] *adj* domestic; ระหว่างประเทศ [ra wang pra thet] *adj* international; ฉันจะซื้อแผนที่ของประเทศนี้ได้ที่ไหน? [chan ja sue phaen thii khong pra tet nii dai thii nai] Where can I buy a map of the country?

ประเทศโบลิเวีย [pra thet bo li wia] เกี่ยวกับประเทศโบลิเวีย [kiao kap pra thet bo li via] *adj* Bolivian

ประเทศโมร็อคโค [pra thet mo rok ko] *n* Morocco

ประธาน [pra than] ประธานกรรมการ [pra than kam ma kan] *n* chairman

ประธานาธิบดี [pra tha na thi bo di] *n* president

ประนาม [pra nam] *v* condemn

ประนีประนอม [pra ni pra nom] *v* compromise; การประนีประนอม [kan pra nii pra nom] *n* compromise

ประปา [pra pa] ช่างประปา [chang pra pa] *n* plumber; ท่อประปา [tho pra pa] *n* plumbing

ประพฤติ [pra pruet] ที่มีความประพฤติเรียบร้อย [thii mii khwam pra phruet riap roi] *adj* well-behaved; ประพฤติตัวไม่เหมาะสม [pra phruet tua mai mo som] *v* misbehave

ประพันธ์ [pra phan] นักประพันธ์ [nak pra phan] *n* author; นักประพันธ์ นักศิลปะหรืองานทางศิลปะที่ยอดเยี่ยมที่สุด [nak pra phan, nak sin la pa rue ngan thang sin la pa thii yot yiam thii sut] *n* classic

ประเพณี [pra phe ni] *n* tradition; เรื่องราวประเพณีและความเชื่อของผู้คน [rueang rao pra phe ni lae khwam chuea khong phu kon] *n* folklore; เกี่ยวกับประเพณีนิยม [kiao kap pra phe ni ni yom] *adj* conventional

ประภาคาร [pra pha khan] *n* lighthouse

ประเภท [pra phet] การจัดประเภท [kan chat pra phet] *n* assortment, sort;

ประเภทต่าง ๆ [pra phet tang tang] *n* variety

ประมง [pra mong] ชาวประมง [chao pra mong] *n* fisherman

ประมาณ [pra man] *adj* approximate ▷ *prep* around ▷ *v* estimate; โดยประมาณ [doi pra man] *adv* approximately

ประมุข [pra muk] การปกครองโดยมีพระมหากษัตริย์เป็นประมุข [kan pok khrong doi mii phra ma ha ka sat pen pra muk] *n* monarchy

ประมูล [pra mun] *vi* bid (*at auction*); การประมูล [kan pra mun] *n* auction, bid

ประเมิน [pra moen] ประเมินมากเกินไป [pra moen mak koen pai] *v* overestimate; ประเมินค่า จัดอันดับ [pra moen kha, chat an dap] *v* rate; ประเมินต่ำไป [pra moen tam pai] *v* underestimate

ประยุกต์ [pra yuk] ประยุกต์ใช้ [pra yuk chai] *v* apply

ประโยค [pra yok] *n* sentence (*words*)

ประโยชน์ [pra yot] *n* asset; เป็นประโยชน์ [pen pra yot] *adj* helpful; มีประโยชน์ต่อ [mii pra yot to] *v* benefit; ซึ่งไม่มีประโยชน์ [sueng mai mii pra yot] *adj* useless

ประวัติ [pra wat] ตัวย่อของประวัติส่วนตัว [tua yo khong pra wat suan tua] *abbr* CV; ประวัติส่วนตัว [pra wat suan tua] *n* curriculum vitae

ประวัติศาสตร์ [pra wat ti sat] *n* history; ก่อนประวัติศาสตร์ [kon pra wat ti sat] ÐÐ prehistoric; ที่เกี่ยวกับประวัติศาสตร์ [thii kiao kap pra wat ti saat] *adj* historical; นักประวัติศาสตร์ [nak pra wat ti saat] *n* historian

ประสบ [pra sop] ประสบ อดทน อดกลั้น [pra sop, ot thon, ot klan] *v* undergo

ประสบการณ์ [phra sop kan] *n* experience; ไม่มีประสบการณ์ [mai mii pra sop kan] *adj* inexperienced; ซึ่งมีประสบการณ์ [sueng mii pra sop kan] *adj* veteran; ที่มีประสบการณ [thii mii pra sop kan] *adj* experienced

ประสบความสำเร็จ [pra sop khwam sam ret] *v* succeed, triumph; ไม่ประสบความสำเร็จ [mai pra sop khwam sam ret] *adj* unsuccessful

ประสบผลสำเร็จ [pra sop phon sam ret] *adj* successful ▷ *v* achieve; อย่างประสบผลสำเร็จ [yang pra sop phon sam ret] *adv* successfully

ประสาท [pra sat] เกี่ยวกับโรคประสาท [kiao kap rok pra sat] *adj* neurotic; ยาระงับประสาท [ya ra ngap pra saat] *n* sedative

ประสานเสียง [pra san siang] คณะร้องเพลงประสานเสียง [kha na rong phleng pra san siang] *n* choir

ประสิทธิภาพ [pra sit thi phap] ไร้ประสิทธิภาพ [rai pra sit thi phap] *adj* inefficient; ซึ่งมีประสิทธิภาพ [sueng mii pra sit thi phap] *adj* efficient; อย่างมีประสิทธิภาพ [yang mii pra sit thi phap] *adv* efficiently

ประหยัด [pra yat] *adj* economical ▷ *v* economize; ชั้นประหยัด [chan pra yat] *n* economy class

ประหลาด [pra lat] *adj* peculiar; แปลกประหลาด [plaek pra lat] *adj* weird; คนที่แปลกประหลาด [khon thii plaek pra lat] *adj* eccentric

ประหลาดใจ [pra lat chai] ความประหลาดใจ [khwam pra lat jai] *n* surprise; ที่ประหลาดใจ [thii pra lat jai] *adj* astonished; ทำให้ประหลาดใจ [tham hai pra lat jai] *adj* amaze, surprised

ประหาร [pra han] การลงโทษประหารชีวิต [kan long thot pra han chi wit] *n* capital punishment; การประหารชีวิต [kan pra han chi wit] *n* execution

ปรัชญา [plat cha ya] *n* philosophy

ปรับ [prap] ค่าปรับ [kha prup] *n* fine

ปรับตัว [prap tua] *v* adapt, adjust; ที่ปรับตัวเข้ากับสถานการณ์ [thii prap tua khao kap sa tha na kan] *adj* flexible; ปรับตัวได้ [prap tua dai] *adj* adjustable

ปรับปรุง [prap prung] ปรับปรุงใหม่ [prap prung mai] *v* renovate; วิชาที่ปรับปรุงใหม่ [wi cha thii prap prung mai] *n* refresher course

ปรับเปลี่ยน [prap plian] การปรับเปลี่ยน [kan prap plian] *n* adjustment

ปรับอากาศ [prap a kat] ซึ่งได้ปรับอากาศ [sueng dai prap a kaat] *adj* air-conditioned

ปรัมปรา [pram pra] นิทานปรัมปรา [ni than pa ram pa ra] *n* myth

ปรากฏ [pra kot] ไม่ปรากฏชื่อ [mai pra kot chue] *adj* unidentified; การปรากฏตัว [kan pra kot tua] *n* appearance; ที่ปรากฏ [thii pra kot] *v* seem

ปรากฏการณ์ [pra kot ta kan] ปรากฏการณ์น้ำขึ้นน้ำลง [pra kot kan nam khuen nam long] *n* tide

ปรากฏตัว [pra kot tua] การปรากฏตัวของคนหรือสิ่งสำคัญ [kan pra kot tua khong khon rue sing sam khan] *n* advent

ปรารถนา [prat tha na] *v* desire

ปรารถนา [prat tha na] *v* fancy, wish; ความปรารถนา [khwam prat tha na] *v* desire

ปราศจาก [prat sa chak] *prep* without

ปราศจากเชื้อ [prat sa chak chuea] *adj* sterile; ทำให้ปราศจากเชื้อ [tham hai prat sa chak chuea] *v* sterilize

ปราศรัย [pra sai] คำปราศรัย [kham pra sai] *n* address *(speech)*

ปราสาท [pra sat] *n* castle; ปราสาททราย [pra saat sai] *n* sandcastle; เราไปเยี่ยมชมปราสาทได้ไหม? [rao pai yiam chom pra sat dai mai] Can we visit the castle?; ปราสาทเปิดให้สาธารณะชนเข้าชมไหม? [pra saat poet hai sa tha ra na chon khao chom mai] Is the castle open to the public?

ปริญญา [pa rin ya] การจบปริญญา [kan job pa rin ya] *n* graduation; ตัวย่อของปริญญาเอก [tua yo khong pa rin yaa ek] *n* PhD; ปริญญาตรี [pa rin ya tree] *abbr* BA

ปริญญาตรี [pa rin ya tri] นักศึกษาระดับ ปริญญาตรี [nak suek sa ra dap pa rin ya tree] *n* undergraduate

ปริมาณ [po ri man] ปริมาณสูงสุดที่รับได้ [pa ri man sung sut thii rap dai] *n* capacity; ปริมาณที่ขาด การขาดดุล [pa ri man thii khat, kan khat dun] *n* deficit; ปริมาณยาที่ให้แต่ละครั้ง [pa ri man ya thii hai tae la khrang] *n* dose

ปริมาตร [pa ri mat] ความจุ ปริมาตร [khwam ju, pa ri mat] *n* volume

ปริศนา [prit sa na] ปริศนาอักษรไขว้ [prit sa na ak son khwai] *n* crossword

ปรึกษา [pruek sa] *v* consult; การปรึกษา หารือ [kan pruek sa ha rue] *n* discussion; ปรึกษาหารือ [pruek sa ha rue] *v* discuss; ผู้ให้คำปรึกษา [phu hai kham pruek sa] *n* consultant (adviser)

ปรุง [prung] หนังสือการปรุงอาหาร [nang sue kan prung a han] *n* cookery book; การปรุงอาหาร [kan prung a han] *n* cookery

ปรุงรส [prung rot] การปรุงรส [kan prung rot] *n* seasoning

ปลด [plot] ปลดออกจากตำแหน่ง [plot ok chak tam naeng] *v* dismiss

ปลดเกษียณ [plot ka sian] *adj* retired; การปลดเกษียณ [kan plot ka sian] *n* retirement

ปลดปล่อย [plot ploi] *v* release; การปลด ปล่อย การปลดปล่อยเป็นอิสระ [kan plot ploi, kan plot ploi pen it sa ra] *v* release; การปลดปล่อยให้เป็นอิสระ [kan plot ploi hai pen it sa ra] *n* liberation

ปล้น [plon] *v* hijack, rob; การทำร้ายเพื่อ ปล้นทรัพย์ [kan tham rai phuea plon sab] *n* mugging; การปล้น [kan plon] *n* robbery; ฉันถูกปล้น [chan thuk plon] I've been robbed

ปลอก [plok] *n* collar, band, case; ปลอกหมอน [plok mon] *n* pillowcase

ปล่องไฟ [plong fai] *n* chimney

ปลอดภัย [plot phai] *adj* safe, secure;

ความปลอดภัย [khwam plot phai] *n* safety, security; ผู้คุ้มกันความปลอดภัย [phu khum kan khwam plot phai] *n* security guard; ปลอดภัยไหมที่จะว่ายน้ำที่ นี่? [plot phai mai thii ja wai nam thii ni] Is it safe to swim here?

ปลอม [plom] *adj* fake, false; ของปลอม [khong plom] *n* fake; ฟันปลอม [fan plom] *npl* dentures

ปลอมตัว [plom tua] *v* disguise

ปลอมแปลง [plom plaeng] *v* forge; การ ปลอมแปลง [kan plom plaeng] *n* forgery

ปล่อย [ploi] ปล่อยเรือลงน้ำเป็นครั้งแรก [ploi ruea long nam pen khrang raek] *vt* launch; ปล่อยฉันไว้ตามลำพัง [ploi chan wai tam lam phang] Leave me alone!

ปลั๊ก [plak] เสียบปลั๊ก [siap pluk] *v* plug in; ถอดปลั๊ก [thot pluk] *v* unplug; ปลั๊กตัว เมีย [plak tua mia] *n* socket; ปลั๊กสำหรับ ที่โกนหนวดไฟฟ้าอยู่ที่ไหน? [plak sam rap thii kon nuat fai fa yu thii nai] Where is the socket for my electric razor?

ปลั๊กไฟ [plak fai] *n* plug

ปลา [pla] *n* fish; คนขายปลา [khon khai pla] *n* fishmonger; ชิ้นปลาหรือเนื้อที่ไม่มี กระดูก [chin pla rue nuea thii mai mii kra duk] *n* fillet; ปลาเฮอริ่ง [pla hoe ring] *n* herring; คุณมีอาหารปลาอะไร บ้าง? [khun mii a han pla a rai bang] What fish dishes do you have?

ปลาย [plai] จุดปลายสุด [chut plai sut] *n* tip (end of object); ปลายเดือนมิถุนายน [plai duean mi thu ma yon] at the end of June

ปลายทาง [plai thang] ฉันอยากโทรศัพท์ เก็บเงินปลายทาง [chan yak tho ra sap kep ngoen plai thang] I'd like to make a reverse charge call

ปลายเท้า [plai thao] เดินด้วยปลายเท้า [doen duai plai thao] *n* tiptoe

ปลาวาฬ [pla wan] *n* whale

ปลาหมึก [pla muek] *n* squid; ปลาหมึก

ยักษ์ [pla muek yak] n octopus

ปลุก [pluk] การโทรปลุก [kan to pluk] n alarm call; ปลุก ทำให้ตื่น [pluk, tham hai tuen] v awake; ฉันจะปลุกคุณดีไหม? [chan ja pluk khun di mai] Shall I wake you up?

ปลูก [pluk] v plant; ปลูก ทำให้เจริญเติบโต [pluk, tham hai cha roen toep to] vt grow

ปลูกถ่ายอวัยวะ [pluk thai a wai ya wa] การปลูกถ่ายอวัยวะ [kan pluk thai a wai ya wa] n transplant

ปวด [puat] การปวดฟัน [kan puat fan] n toothache; ปวดหัว [puat hua] n headache; ปวดหลัง [puat lang] n back pain; มันปวด [man puat] It's sore

ปวดหัว [puat hua] ฉันอยากได้อะไรสัก อย่างเพื่อแก้ปวดหัว [chan yak dai a rai sak yang phuea kae puat hua] I'd like something for a headache

ป่วย [puai] adj ill; ฉันรู้สึกป่วย [chan ru suek puai] I feel ill

ป้องกัน [pong kan] v prevent, protect; หลบ กำบัง ป้องกัน ปกปิดเหมือนกับมีฉากกัน [lop, kam bang, pong kan, pok pit muean kap mii chak kan] v screen (off); การป้องกัน [kan pong kan] n defence, prevention, protection; การ ป้องกันตัวเอง [kan pong kan tua eng] n self-defence

ปอด [pot] n lung

ปอดบวม [phot buam] โรคปอดบวม [rok pot buam] n pneumonia

ปอนด์ [pon] เงินปอนด์ [ngoen pon] n pound

ป๊อปปี้ [pop pi] ดอกป๊อปปี้ [dok pop pi] n poppy

ป้อม [pom] n fort

ปะ [pa] แผ่นผ้าปะรูในเสื้อผ้า [phaen pha pa ru nai suea pha] n patch; ที่ได้รับการ ปะ [thii dai rap kan pa] adj patched

ปะการัง [pa ka rang] หินปะการัง [hin pa ka rang] n coral

ปะทะ [pa tha] ตี ดีด ปะทะ [ti, diit, pa

tha] strike; ปะทะกัน [pa tha kan] v collide

ปัก [pak] เย็บปักถักร้อย [yep pak thak roi] v embroider; การเย็บปักถักร้อย [kan yep pak thak roi] n embroidery

ปักกิ่ง [pak king] กรุงปักกิ่ง [krung pak king] n Beijing; ชาวปักกิ่ง [chao pak king] n Pekinese

ปัจจุบัน [pat chu ban] เหตุการณ์ปัจจุบัน [het kan pat chu ban] npl current affairs; ในปัจจุบัน [nai pat chu ban] adv currently; สถานภาพปัจจุบัน [sa tha na phap pat chu ban] n status quo

ปัญญา [pan ya] ซึ่งมีปัญญาสูง [sueng mii pan ya sung] adj intellectual; ผู้มีปัญญา สูง [phu mii pan ya sung] n intellectual

ปัญหา [pan ha] n problem, trouble; แก้ ปัญหา [kae pan ha] v solve; แก้ปัญหา [kae pan ha] v settle; คำตอบที่แก้ปัญหา [kham top thii kae pan ha] n solution; ไม่มีปัญหา [mai mii pan ha] No problem

ปัญหา ยุ่งยาก [pan ha yung yak] ปัญหา ยุ่งยาก [pan ha yung yak] n puzzle

ปัด [pat] ปัดฝุ่น [pat fun] vi dust

ปั่น [pun] เครื่องปั่น [khrueang pan] n blender; นมปั่น [nom pan] n milkshake

ปั้น [pun] รูปปั้น [rup pan] n sculpture; นักปั้น [nak pan] n sculptor

ปั้นจั่น [pan chan] n jack; ปั้นจั่นยกของ หนัก [pan chan yok khong nak] n crane (for lifting)

ปั่นป่วน [pan puan] ความปั่นป่วน [khwam pan puan] n turbulence

ปั๊ม [pum] ปั๊มน้ำมัน [pam nam man] n petrol station; มีปั๊มน้ำมันที่อยู่ใกล้ที่นี่ ไหม? [mii pam nam man thii yu klai thii ni mai] Is there a petrol station near here?; ปั๊มเลขสาม [pam lek sam] Pump number three, please

ปัสสาวะ [pat sa wa] น้ำปัสสาวะ [nam pat sa wa] n urine

ป่า [pa] n forest; สัตว์และพืชป่า [sat lae phuet pa] n wildlife; ป่าหนาทึบในเขต

ร้อนซึ่งมีฝนตกมาก [pa na thuep nai khet ron sueng mii fon tok mak] n rainforest; ป่าทึบ [pa thuep] n jungle

ป้า [pa] ป้า น้า อาผู้หญิง [pa na a phu ying] n auntie; ป้า น้า อาผู้หญิง [pa na a phu ying] n aunt

ปาก [pak] n mouth; น้ำยาล้างปาก [nam ya lang pak] n mouthwash

ปากกา [pak ka] n pen; ปากกาลูกลื่น [pak ka luk luen] n ballpoint pen; ปากกาลูกลื่นกลม [pak ka luk luen klom] n Biro®; ปากกาสะท้อนแสงที่ใช้เน้นข้อความให้เด่นชัด [pak ka sa thon saeng thii chai nen kho khwam hai den chat] n highlighter; คุณมีปากกาให้ฉันยืมไหม? [khun mii pak ka hai chan yuem mai] Do you have a pen I could borrow?

ปากีสถาน [pa ki sa than] เกี่ยวกับปากีสถาน [kiao kap pa ki sa than] adj Pakistani; ชาวปากีสถาน [chao pa ki sa than] n Pakistani; ประเทศปากีสถาน [pra tet pa ki sa than] n Pakistan

ปาฐกถา [pa tha ka tha] การแสดงปาฐกถา [kan sa daeng pa tha ka tha] n talk

ป่าเถื่อน [pa thuean] adj barbaric

ปานกลาง [pan klang] adj moderate

ปานามา [pa na ma] ประเทศปานามา [pra tet pa na ma] n Panama

ป่าไม้ [pa mai] n wood (forest)

ป้าย [pai] n sign; แถบป้ายบอกข้อมูล [thaep pai bok kho mun] n tag; ป้ายโฆษณา [pai khot sa na] n poster; ป้ายจราจร [pai cha ra chon] n road sign

ป้ายรถ [pai rot] ป้ายรถโดยสารประจำทาง [pai rot doi san pra cham thang] n bus stop

ปารากวัย [pa ra kwai] เกี่ยวกับปารากวัย [kiao kap pa ra kwai] adj Paraguayan; ชาวปารากวัย [chao pa ra kwai] n Paraguayan; ประเทศปารากวัย [pra tet pa ra kwai] n Paraguay

ปาล์ม [pam] ต้นปาล์ม [ton palm] n palm (tree)

ปาเลสไตน์ [pa les tai] เกี่ยวกับปาเลสไตน์ [kiao kap pa les tai] adj Palestinian; ชาวปาเลสไตน์ [chao pa les tai] n Palestinian; ประเทศปาเลสไตน์ [pra tet pa les tai] n Palestine

ปิงปอง [ping pong] การเล่นปิงปอง [kan len ping pong] n table tennis

ปิด [pit] v close, switch off, turn off, turn out, shut; เวลาปิด [we la pit] n closing time; ลงบันทึกปิด [long ban thuek pit] v log off; การปิด [kan pit] n closure; มันปิดไม่ได้ [man pit mai dai] It won't turn off

ปิดกั้น [pit kan] หยุด ระงับ ปิดกั้น [yut, ra ngab, pit kan] vt stop

ปิดตา [pit ta] เอาผ้าปิดตา [ao pha pit ta] v blindfold

ปิดบัง [pit bang] ซึ่งปิดบัง [sueng pit bang] adj hidden

ปิดผนึก [pit pha nuek] v seal

ปิติ [pi ti] น่าปิติยินดี [na pi ti yin dii] adj delightful

ปิรามิด [pi ra mit] n pyramid

ปี [pi] n year; ระยะเวลาหนึ่งพันปี [ra ya we la nueng phan pi] n millennium; การครบรอบหนึ่งร้อยปี [kan khrop rop nueng roi pi] n centenary; ซึ่งเกิดปีละครั้ง [sueng koet pi la khrang] adv annually; ปีหน้า [pi na] next year

ปี่ [pi] ปี่ใหญ่ [pi yai] n bassoon; ปี่สก๊อต [pi sa kot] npl bagpipes

ปีก [pik] n wing

ปีน [pin] v climb; การปีน [kan pin] n climbing; คนปีน [khon pin] n climber; ฉันอยากไปปีนเขา [chan yak pai pin khao] I'd like to go climbing

ปืน [puen] n gun, pistol; ปืนเล็กยาว [puen lek yao] n rifle; ปืนล่าสัตว์ [puen la sat] n shotgun; ปืนพกลูกโม่ [puen phok luk mo] n revolver

ปืนกล [puen kon] n machine gun

ปืนใหญ่ [puen yai] ปืนใหญ่ขนาดเล็ก [puen yai kha nat lek] n mortar (military)

ปุ่ม [pum] ฉันต้องกดปุ่มไหน? [chan tong

kot pum nai] Which button do I press?

ปุ๋ย [pui] n fertilizer; ถังปุ๋ยหมัก [thang pui mak] n septic tank

ปู [pu] n crab

ปู่ [pu] ปู่ ตา [pu ta] n granddad, grandfather; ปู่ ย่า ตา ยาย [pu ya ta yai] npl grandparents

ปูน [pun] ช่างปูน [chang pun] n bricklayer; ปูนฉาบผนัง [pun chap pha nang] n plaster (for wall)

ปูนขาว [pun khao] n lime (compound); ส่วนผสมของปูนขาวหรือซีเมนต์กับน้ำและ ทราย [suan pha som khong pun khao rue si men kap nam lae sai] n mortar (plaster)

เป้ [pe] เป้สะพายหลัง [pe sa phai lang] n rucksack

เป็ด [pet] n duck

เป็น [pen] เป็น อยู่ คือ [pen, yu, khue] v be

เป็นของ [pen khong] v belong

เป็นครั้งคราว [pen khrang khrao] ซึ่งเป็น ครั้งคราว [sueng pen khrang khrao] adj occasional

เป็นทางการ [pen thang kan] ไม่เป็น ทางการ [mai pen thang kan] adj informal

เป็นไปได้ [pen pai dai] adj likely; ความ เป็นไปได้ [khwam pen pai dai] n possibility, potential; ซึ่งเป็นไปได้ [sueng pen pai dai] adj feasible, possible; ตัวย่อของเร็วที่สุดเท่าที่จะเป็นไป ได้ [tua yo khong reo thii sut thao thii ja pen pai dai] adv abbr asap

เป็นไปไม่ได้ [pen pai mai dai] ที่เป็นไป ไม่ได้ [thii pen pai mai dai] adj impossible

เป็นมิตร [pen mit] adj sociable; ไม่เป็น มิตร [mai pen mit] adj unfriendly

เป็นลม [pen lom] v faint; เธอเป็นลม [thoe pen lom] She has fainted

เป็นหนี้ [pen ni] v owe

เปราะบาง [pro bang] adj fragile

เปรียบเทียบ [priap thiap] v compare; โดยเปรียบเทียบกับสิ่งอื่น [doi priap thiap kap sing uen] adv relatively; การเปรียบ เทียบ [kan priap thiap] n comparison; ที่เปรียบเทียบได้ [thii priap thiap dai] adv comparatively

เปรี้ยว [priao] มีรสเปรี้ยว [mee rot priao] adj sour

เปรู [pe ru] เกี่ยวกับเปรู [kiao kap pe ru] adj Peruvian; ชาวเปรู [chao pe ru] n Peruvian; ประเทศเปรู [pra tet pe ru] n Peru

เปล [ple] n hammock; เปลเด็ก [ple dek] n cradle; เปลหาม [phle ham] n stretcher

เปล่งเสียง [pleng siang] เปล่งเสียงแสดง ความยินดี [pleng siang sa daeng khwam yin dii] v cheer

เปลวไฟ [pleo fai] n blaze, flame; เปลวไฟ ที่จุดเตาแก๊ซ [pheo fai thii chut tao kaes] n pilot light

เปล่าเปลี่ยว [plao pliao] ความรู้สึกหรือ สภาพเปล่าเปลี่ยวอ้างว้าง [khwam ru suek rue sa phap plao pliao ang wang] n void

เปลี่ยน [plian] v switch, change, convert; เคลื่อน เปลี่ยนตำแหน่ง [khluean plian tam naeng] vi move; เปลี่ยน แลก เปลี่ยน [plian, laek plian] vt change; เปลี่ยนโครงสร้างใหม่ [plian khrong sang mai] v restructure; ฉันเปลี่ยนห้องได้ ไหม? [chan plian hong dai mai] Can I switch rooms?

เปลี่ยนแปลง [plian pleng] v vary; เปลี่ยนแปลงแก้ไข [plian plaeng kae khai] v modify; เปลี่ยนแปลงได้ตลอดเวลา [plian plaeng dai ta lot we la] adj variable; การเปลี่ยนแปลง [kan plian plaeng] n change, makeover, transition

เปลือก [plueak] n shell; เปลือกมะนาวหรือ ส้ม [plueak ma nao rue som] n zest (lemon-peel)

เปลือย [plueai] เปลือยกาย [plueai kai] adj naked, nude; คนเปลือยกาย [khon plueai kai] n nude, nudist

เปลือยเปล่า [pluea plao] adj bare

เปอร์เซ็นต์ [poe sen] *adv* per cent

เปอร์เชีย [poe sia] เกี่ยวกับเปอร์เชีย [kiao kap poe sia] *adj* Persian

เปอร์โตริโก [poe to ti ko] ประเทศเปอร์โตริโก [pra tet poe to ri ko] *n* Puerto Rico

เป่า [pao] *vi* blow; เครื่องเป่า [khrueang pao] *n* dryer; เครื่องเป่าผม [khrueang pao phom] *n* hairdryer; เครื่องดนตรีประเภทเป่า [khrueang don tri pra phet pao] *n* woodwind; ช่วยตัดและเป่าให้แห้ง [chuai tat lae pao hai haeng] A cut and blow-dry, please

เป้า [pao] เป้ารองรับลูกกอล์ฟในการตี [pao rong rap luk kolf nai kan ti] *n* tee

เป้าหมาย [pao mai] *n* goal, objective, target

เปิด [poet] *v* switch on, turn on, open; เปิดออก [poet ok] *adj* open; ลงบันทึกเปิด [long ban thuek poet] *v* log on; ชั่วโมงที่เปิด [chau mong thii poet] *npl* opening hours; เปิดหน้าต่างไม่ได้ [poet na tang mai dai] The window won't open; เปิดประตูไม่ได้ [poet pra tu mai dai] The door won't open; เปิดวันนี้ไหม? [poet wan nii mai] Is it open today?; มันเปิดไม่ได้ [man poet mai dai] It won't turn on

เปิดเผย [poet phoei] *v* disclose, reveal; เปิดเผยให้เห็น [poet phoei hai hen] *v* show up; ทำให้โล่ง เปิดเผยออกมา [tham hai long, poet phoei ok ma] *v* bare; พูดจาเปิดเผย [phud cha poet phoei] *adj* outspoken

เปียก [piak] *adj* wet; ทำให้เปียก [tham hai piak] *adj* soaked; ทำให้เปียกชุ่ม [tham hai piak chum] *v* drench

เปียกโชก [piak chok] *adj* soggy

เปียโน [pia no] *n* piano; นักเปียโน [nak pia no] *n* pianist

เปื้อน [phuean] ผ้ากันเปื้อน [pha kan puean] *n* apron

แป้ง [paeng] *n* flour, starch; แป้งข้าวโพด [paeng khao phot] *n* cornflour; แป้งที่ใช้เป็นฐานของขนมพาย [paeng thii chai pen than khong kha nom phai] *n* shortcrust pastry; แป้งผสมฟู่ที่มีแผ่นบางหลายชั้นซ้อนกัน [paeng pha som fu thii mii phaen bang lai chan son kan] *n* puff pastry

แปซิฟิก [pae si fik] มหาสมุทรแปซิฟิก [ma ha sa mut pae si fik] *n* Pacific

แปด [plaet] *number* eight; ที่แปด [thii paet] *n* eighth

แปดสิบ [paet sip] *number* eighty

แป้น [paen] แผงแป้นอักขระ [phaeng paen ak kha ra] *n* keyboard

แปรง [plraeng] *v* brush; แปรงแปรงผม [praeng praeng phom] *n* hairbrush; แปรงทำความสะอาดเล็บ [praeng tham khwam sa at lep] *n* nailbrush; แปรงทาสี [praeng tha sii] *n* paintbrush

แปรงสีฟัน [praeng si fan] *n* toothbrush

แปรรูป [prae rup] แปรรูปหน่วยราชการและรัฐวิสาหกิจให้เป็นเอกชน [prae rup nuai rat cha kan lae rat wi sa ha kit hai pen ek ka chon] *v* privatize

แปล [plae] *n* translate ▷ *v* interpret; แปลคำพูดด้วยการอ่านริมฝีปาก [plae kham phut duai kan an rim fi pak] *v* lip-read; การแปล [kan plae] *n* translation; ผู้แปล [phu plae] *n* translator; คุณกรุณาแปลนี้ให้ได้ไหม? [khun ka ru na plae ni hai dai mai] Can you translate this for me?

แปลก [plaek] *adj* odd, strange; แปลกจนไม่สามารถอธิบายได้ [plaek chon mai sa mat a thi bai dai] *adj* uncanny; แปลกประหลาด [plaek pra lat] *n* weird

แปลกใจ [plaek chai] ทำให้แปลกใจ [tham hai plaek jai] *v* astonish

แปลกประหลาด [plaek pra lat] ฉันไม่อยากได้อะไรที่แปลกประหลาดมากไป [chan mai yak dai a rai thii plaek pra lat mak pai] I don't want anything drastic

แปลงไฟ [plang fai] ตัวแปลงไฟ [tua plaeng fai] *n* adaptor

โป่ง [pong] โป่งหรือพองเหมือนถุง [pong

rue phong muean thung] *adj* baggy

โปรแกรม [pro kraem] โปรแกรมรักษา
จอภาพ [pro kraem rak sa cho phap] *n*
screen-saver; โปรแกรมคอมพิวเตอร์ [pro
kraem khom phio toe] *n* software;
โปรแกรมที่ใช้สำหรับเปิดดูเว็บไซด์ต่าง ๆ ที่
ใช้ภาษาไฮเปอร์เท็กซ์ [pro kraem thii
chai sam rap poet du web sai tang tang
thii chai pha sa hai poe thek] *n*
browser

โปร่งใส [prong sai] *adj* see-through,
transparent

โปรตีน [pro tin] *n* protein; โปรตีนเหนียวที่
พบในธัญพืช [pro tin niao thii phop nai
than ya phuet] *n* gluten

โปรตุเกส [pro tu ket] เกี่ยวกับชาวโปรตุเกส
[kiao kap chao pro tu ket] *adj*
Portuguese; ชาวโปรตุเกส [chao pro tu
ket] *n* Portuguese *(person)*; ประเทศ
โปรตุเกส [pra tet pro tu ket] *n* Portugal

โปรเตสแตนส์ [pro tet sa taen] ที่เกี่ยวกับ
นิกายโปรเตสแตนส์ [thii kiao kap ni kai
pro tes taen] *adj* Methodist

โปรแตสแตนต์ [pro tact sa taen] เกี่ยวกับ
นิกายหนึ่งของโปรแตตสแตนต์ [kiao kap ni
kai nueng khong pro tes taen] *adj*
Presbyterian

โปลิโอ [po li o] โรคโปลิโอ [rok po li o] *n*
polio

โปแลนด์ [po laen] ชาวโปแลนด์ [chao po
laen] *n* Pole, Polish; ที่เกี่ยวกับโปแลนด์
[thii kiao kap po laen] *adj* Polish;
ประเทศโปแลนด์ [pra tet po laen] *n*
Poland

โปสการ์ด [pos kat] คุณมีโปสการ์ดบ้าง
ไหม? [khun mii pos kart bang mai] Do
you have any postcards?; ฉันหา
โปสการ์ด [chan ha pos kaat] I'm looking
for postcards; ฉันขอซื้อแสตมป์สำหรับ
โปสการ์ดสี่ใบไป...ได้ไหม? [chan kho sue
sa taem sam rap pos kart sii bai pai...
dai mai] Can I have stamps for four
postcards to...

ไป [pai] ไป เคลื่อนไป ออกไป [pai,
khluean pai, ok pai] *vi* go; ไปเป็นเพื่อน
[pai pen phuean] *v* accompany; ไปเอา
มา [pai ao ma] *vt* fetch; เราจะไป... [rao
ja pai...] We're going to...

ไปกลับ [pai klap] ไปกลับในหนึ่งวัน [pai
klap nai nueng wan] *n* day return

ไปรษณีย์ [prai sa ni] *n* post office; เช็ค
ไปรษณีย์ [chek prai sa ni] *n* postal
order; ไปรษณีย์หญิง [prai sa ni ying] *n*
postwoman; รหัสไปรษณีย์ [ra hat prai
sa ni] *n* postcode; ไปรษณีย์เปิดเมื่อไร?
[prai sa ni poet muea rai] When does
the post office open?

ไปรษณียบัตร [prai sa ni ya bat] *n*
postcard

ไปรษณียภัณฑ์ [prai sa ni ya phan] ตรา
ประทับบนไปรษณียภัณฑ์ [tra pra thap
bon prai sa ni phan] *n* postmark

ผ

ผง [phong] *n* powder; เครื่องแกงที่เป็นผง [khrueang kaeng thii pen phong] *n* curry powder; ผงสีเหลืองอมส้มทำจากดอกโครคัส [phong sii lueang om som tham chak dok khro khas] *n* saffron

ผงซักฟอก [phong sak fok] *n* detergent, washing powder; คุณมีผงซักฟอกไหม? [khun mii phong sak fok mai] Do you have washing powder?

ผงฟู [phong fu] *n* baking powder

ผจญภัย [pha chon phai] การผจญภัย [kan pha chon phai] *n* adventure; ชอบผจญภัย [chop pha chon phai] *adj* adventurous

ผดุงครรภ์ [pha dung khan] นางพยาบาลผดุงครรภ์ [nang pha ya baan pa dung khan] *n* midwife

ผนัง [pha nang] กระดาษบุผนังหรือเพดาน [kra dat bu pha nang rue phe dan] *n* wallpaper

ผม [phom] *n* hair; เครื่องทำผมให้ตรง [khrueang tham phom hai trong] *npl* straighteners; เจลใส่ผม [chen sai phom] *n* hair gel; แปรงแปรงผม [praeng praeng phom] *n* hairbrush; ผมปลอมของชาย [phom plom khong chai] *n*

toupee; คุณแนะนำอะไรสำหรับผมฉัน? [khun nae nam a rai sam rap phom chan] What do you recommend for my hair?

ผมปลอม [phom plom] *n* wig

ผล [phon] เป็นผล [pen phon] *v* result in; ให้ผลตรงข้ามกับที่ตั้งใจไว้ [hai phon trong kham kap thii tang jai wai] *v* backfire; ตอบรับ: ผลตอบรับ [top rap : phon top rap] *n* feedback

ผลข้างเคียง [phon khang khiang] *n* side effect

ผลงาน [phon ngan] *n* performance (*functioning*)

ผลผลิต [phon pha lit] *n* crop, product; ผลผลิต ปริมาณผลผลิต [phon pha lit, pa ri man phon pha lit] *vi* return (*yield*); ผลผลิตจากนม [phon pha lit chak nom] *n* dairy produce; ผลผลิตต่าง ๆ จากนม [phon pha lit tang tang chak nom] *npl* dairy products

ผลไม้ [phon la mai] *n* fruit (*botany*), fruit (*collectively*); ร้านขายผักและผลไม้สด [ran khai phak lae phon la mai sot] *n* greengrocer's; สลัดผลไม้ [sa lat phon la mai] *n* fruit salad; สวนผลไม้ [suan phon la mai] *n* orchard

ผลรวม [phon ruam] *n* total

ผลลัพธ์ [phon lap] *n* consequence, outcome, result

ผลสำเร็จ [phon sam ret] การบรรลุผลสำเร็จ [kan ban lu phon sam ret] *n* achievement

ผลัก [phlak] *vt* push

ผลิดอก [phli dok] *v* flower

ผลิต [pha lit] *n* make ▷ *v* manufacture, produce, yield; การผลิต [kan pha lit] *n* production; การผลิตใหม่ [kan pha lit mai] *n* reproduction; ความสามารถในการผลิต [khwam sa mat nai kan pha lit] *n* productivity

ผลิตภัณฑ์ [pha lit ta phan] ผลิตภัณฑ์ที่ทำจากนม [pha lit ta phan thii tham chak nom] *n* dairy

ผสม [pha som] *vt* mix; เครื่องผสม [khrueang pha som] *n* mixer; การผสม [kan pha som] *n* mix; ที่ผสมกัน [thii pha som kan] *adj* mixed

ผสมพันธุ์ [pha som phan] *v* breed

ผ่อนคลาย [phon khlai] *v* relieve; การผ่อนคลาย [kan phon khlai] *n* relief; ซึ่งเงียบสงบและผ่อนคลาย [sueng ngiap sa ngob lae phon khlai] *adj* restful; ซึ่งช่วยให้ผ่อนคลาย [sueng chuai hai phon khlai] *adj* relaxing

ผอม [phom] *adj* thin; ผอมเพรียว [phom phriao] *adj* slender, slim; ผอมโยง [phom yong] *adj* lanky; ผอมมาก [phom mak] *adj* skinny

ผัก [phak] *n* vegetable; ร้านขายผักและผลไม้สด [ran khai phak lae phon la mai sot] *n* greengrocer's; ผักลีก [phak lik] *n* leek; ผักสวิดิเป็นหัว [phak sa wi di pen hua] *n* swede; มีผักรวมอยู่ในนี้ด้วยไหม? [mii phak ruam yu nai nii duai mai] Are the vegetables included?

ผักกาด [phak kat] ผักกาดที่ใส่ในสลัด [phak kaat thii sai nai sa lad] *n* lettuce

ผักโขม [phak khom] *n* spinach

ผ้า [pha] *n* cloth; กระดาษหรือผ้าเช็ดตัวเด็ก [kra dat rue pha chet tua dek] *n* baby wipe; ผ้าเช็ดหน้า [pha chet na] *n* handkerchief, hankie; ผ้าเช็ดจาน [pha chet chan] *n* dish towel, dishcloth; ผ้าคลุมไหล่ [pha khlum lai] *n* shawl; ผ้าปูที่นอน [pha pu thi non] *n* bed linen, fitted sheet, sheet

ผ้าขนหนู [pha khon nu] *n* towel; ผ้าขนหนูเช็ดตัว [pha khon nu chet tua] *n* bath towel

ผ้าขี้ริ้ว [pha khi rio] *n* rag

ผ้าเช็ดตัว [pha chet tua] ช่วยเอาผ้าเช็ดตัวมาให้ฉันอีกหลาย ๆ ผืน [chuai ao pha chet tua ma hai chan ik lai lai phuen] Please bring me more towels; ผ้าเช็ดตัวหมด [pha chet tua mot] The towels have run out

ผ้าเช็ดมือ [pha chet mue] *n* tea towel

ผ่าตัด [pha tat] *v* operate (*to perform surgery*); แพทย์ผ่าตัด [phaet pha tat] *n* surgeon; ห้องผ่าตัด [hong pha tat] *n* operating theatre; การผ่าตัด [kan pha tat] *n* surgery (*operation*)

ผ่าน [phan] เลยผ่าน [loei phan] *prep* past; เดินผ่านไป [doen phan pai] *v* go past; ส่งต่อไป [song to pai, song phan, song hai] *vi* pass; ฉันขอทางผ่านด้วย [chan kho thang phan duai] Please let me through

ผ้าใบ [pha bai] เก้าอี้ผ้าใบ [kao ii pha bai] *n* deckchair; เตียงผ้าใบน้ำหนักเบา [tiang pha bai nam nak bao] *n* camp bed; ผ้าใบอาบน้ำมันใช้ทำผ้าคลุมกันฝน [pha bai aap nam man chai tham pha khlum kan fon] *n* tarpaulin

ผ้าปูที่นอน [pha pu thi non] เราอยากได้ผ้าปูที่นอนเพิ่มอีก [rao yak dai pha pu thii non poem ik] We need more sheets; ผ้าปูที่นอนสกปรก [pha pu thii non sok ka prok] The sheets are dirty

ผ้าพันคอ [pha phan kho] *n* scarf

ผ้าพันแผล [pha phan phae] ฉันอยากได้ผ้าพันแผล [chan yak dai pha phan phlae] I'd like a bandage; ฉันอยากได้ผ้าพันแผลใหม่ [chan yak dai pha phan phlae mai] I'd like a fresh bandage

ผ้าห่ม [pha hom] *n* blanket, duvet; ผ้าห่มไฟฟ้า [pha hom fai fa] *n* electric blanket; เราต้องการผ้าห่มเพิ่มอีก [rao tong kan pha hom poem ik] We need more blankets; ช่วยเอาผ้าห่มมาให้ฉันอีกผืน [chuai ao pha hom ma hai chan ik phuen] Please bring me an extra blanket

ผ้าอนามัย [pha a na mai] *n* sanitary towel; ผ้าอนามัยแบบสอด [pha a na mai baep sot] *n* tampon

ผ้าอ้อม [pha om] ผ้าอ้อมเด็ก [pha om dek] *n* nappy

ผิด [phit] เกี่ยวกับความผิด [kiao kap khwam phit] *adj* guilty; ผิดกฎหมาย [phit kot mai] *adj* illegal; ผิดศีลธรรม

[phit sin la tham] *adj* immoral; คุณโทร
ผิดเบอร์ [khun tho phit boe] You have
the wrong number

ผิดกฎหมาย [phit kot mai] การกระทำผิ
ดกฎหมาย [kan kra tham pit kot mai] *n*
offence

ผิดชอบ [phit chop] ความรู้สึกผิดชอบชั่วดี
[khwam ru suek phit chop chua dii] *n*
conscience

ผิดธรรมดา [phit tham ma da] *adj*
extraordinary

ผิดปกติ [phit pok ka ti] ความผิดปกติใน
การอ่าน [khwam phit pok ka ti nai kan
aan] *n* dyslexia; มีอะไรผิดปรกติไหม?
[mii a rai phit prok ka ti mai] What's
wrong?

ผิดปรกติ [phit prok ka ti] *adj* abnormal,
unusual; ผิดปรกติและน่าตกใจ [phit prok
ka ti lae na tok jai] *adj* outrageous

ผิดพลาด [phit phlat] ขอผิดพลาด [kho
phit phlat] *n* error, fault *(mistake)*; ความ
ผิดพลาด [khwam phit phlat] *n*
mistake, slip-up; ความผิดพลาดเพราะ
ละเลยหรือไม่สังเกต [khwam phit phlat
phro la loei rue mai sang ket] *n*
oversight *(mistake)*

ผิดหวัง [phit wang] ความผิดหวัง
[khwam phit wang] *n*
disappointment; ซึ่งผิดหวัง [sueng phit
wang] *adj* disappointing; ที่ผิดหวัง [thii
phit hwang] *adj* disappointed

ผิว [phio] *n* complexion; ที่มีผิวสีแทน [thii
mii phio sii taen] *adj* tanned

ผิวปาก [phio pak] *v* whistle; การผิวปาก
[kan phio pak] *n* whistle

ผิวเผิน [phio phoen] ผิวเผิน ไม่ลึกซึ้ง ไม่
สำคัญ [phio phoen, mai luek sueng,
mai sam khan] *adj* superficial

ผิวหนัง [phio nang] *n* skin; ผิวหนังเป็นสี
น้ำตาลเนื่องจากตากแดด [phio nang pen
sii nam tan nueang chak tak daet] *n*
suntan

ผิวหน้า [phio na] *n* surface

ผี [phi] *n* ghost; ผีที่สูบเลือดคน [phi thii

sup lueat khon] *n* vampire

ผีเสื้อ [phi suea] *n* butterfly; หนอนผีเสื้อ
[non phi suea] *n* caterpillar; ผีเสื้อราตรี
ออกหากินกลางคืน [phi suea ra tree ok
ha kin klang khuen] *n* moth

ผึ้ง [phueng] *n* bee; ผึ้งมีขนตัวใหญ่
[phueng mii khon tua yai] *n*
bumblebee

ผื่น [phuen] ฉันมีผื่นคัน [chan mii phuen
khan] I have a rash

ผื่นคัน [phuen khan] *n* rash

ผู้ [phu] ผู้เห็นเหตุการณ์ [phu hen het
kan] *n* onlooker; ผู้เผด็จการ [phu pha
det kan] *n* dictator; ผู้แสวงหาที่ลี้ภัย
[phu sa waeng ha thii lii phai] *n*
asylum seeker; ผู้จ่าย [phu chai] *n*
dispenser; ผู้ติดยา [phu tit ya] *n* drug
addict; ผู้ผลิต [phu pha lit] *n* maker,
manufacturer

ผูก [phuk] ผูกให้แน่น [phuk hai naen] *v*
tie; คุณช่วยปรับที่ผูกข้อมือให้ฉันได้ไหม?
[khun chuai prap thii phuk kho mue
hai chan dai mai] Can you adjust my
bindings, please?; คุณช่วยผูกที่ผูกข้อมือ
ฉันให้แน่นขึ้นได้ไหม? [khun chuai phuk
thii phuk kho mue chan hai naen
khuen dai mai] Can you tighten my
bindings, please?

ผูกขาด [phuk khat] ระบบผูกขาด [ra bop
phuk khat] *n* monopoly

ผูกติด [phuk tit] การผูกติด สิ่งที่แนบมา
[kan phuk tit, sing thii naep ma] *n*
attachment

ผูกมัด [phuk mat] ข้อผูกมัด [kho phuk
mat] *n* bond

ผู้ขับขี่ [phu khap khi] *n* rider

ผู้เขียน [phu khian] ผู้เขียนบทละคร [phu
khian bot la khon] *n* playwright

ผู้คุ้มกัน [phu khum kan] ผู้คุ้มกันความ
ปลอดภัย [phu khum kan khwam plot
phai] *n* security guard

ผู้จัดการ [phu chat kan] *n* manager;
เจ้าของและผู้จัดการบาร์ [chao khong lae
phu chat kan ba] *n* publican; กรรมการผู้

จัดการ [kam ma kan phu chat kan] *n* managing director; ผู้จัดการหญิง [phu chat kan ying] *n* manageress; ฉันขอพูด กับผู้จัดการ [chan kho phut kap phu chat kan] I'd like to speak to the manager, please

ผู้ช่วย [phu chuai] *n* assistant; การเป็นผู้ ช่วยเลี้ยงเด็ก [kan pen phu chuai liang dek] *n* babysitting; ครูผู้ช่วยในห้องเรียน [khru phu chuai nai hong rian] *n* classroom assistant; ผู้ช่วยเลี้ยงเด็ก [phu chuai liang dek] *n* babysitter

ผู้ชาย [phu chai] *n* bloke, guy, male, man; ซึ่งเป็นของผู้ชาย [sueng pen khong phu chai] *adj* male; ผู้ชายที่แต่ง ตัวเป็นเพศตรงกันข้าม [phu chai thii taeng tua pen phet trong kan kham] *n* transvestite; อย่างผู้ชาย [yang phu chai] *adj* masculine

ผู้โดยสาร [phu doi san] ห้องพักสำหรับผู้ โดยสารที่จะเปลี่ยนเครื่องบิน [hong phak sam rap phu doi san thii ja plian khrueang bin] *n* transit lounge

ผู้ต้องสงสัย [phu tong song sai] *n* suspect

ผู้ติดยาเสพติด [phu tit ya sep tit] addict

ผู้ถือหุ้น [phu thue hun] *n* shareholder

ผู้ถูกขัง [phu thuk khang] *n* prisoner

ผู้แทน [phu thaen] ผู้แทนการขาย [phu thaen kan khai] *n* sales rep; ผู้แทน จำหน่าย [phu thaen cham nai] *n* distributor

ผู้นำ [phu nam] *n* leader

ผู้บริหาร [phu bo ri han] คณะผู้บริหาร [kha na phu bo ri han] *n* management

ผู้บังคับบัญชา [phu bang khap ban cha] *n* superior

ผู้ปกครอง [phu pok khrong] มีสิ่งอำนวย ความสะดวกสำหรับผู้ปกครองและเด็กไหม? [mii sing am nuai khwam sa duak sam rap phu pok khrong lae dek mai] Are there facilities for parents with babies?

ผู้เยาว์ [phu yao] *n* minor

ผู้สืบตำแหน่ง [phu suep tam naeng] *n* successor

ผู้แสดง [phu sa daeng] ผู้แสดงแทนในฉาก เสี่ยงอันตราย [phu sa daeng thaen nai chak siang an ta rai] *n* stuntman

ผู้หญิง [phu ying] *n* woman; เด็กผู้หญิงที่ มีพฤติกรรมคล้ายเด็กผู้ชาย [dek phu ying thii mii phruet ti kam khlai dek phu chai] *n* tomboy; คุณผู้หญิง [khun phu ying] *n* madam; ผู้หญิงที่รับอุ้มท้องแทน [phu ying thii rap um thong taen] *n* surrogate mother

ผู้ใหญ่ [phu yai] *n* adult, grown-up; เป็น ผู้ใหญ่ [pen phu yai] *adj* mature; นักเรียนผู้ใหญ่ [nak rian phu yai] *n* mature student

เผชิญหน้า [pha choen na] *v* face

เผด็จการ [pha det kan] ผู้เผด็จการ [phu pha det kan] *n* dictator

เผยแพร่ [phoei phrae] กระจายเสียง เผย แพร่ [kra jai siang phoei prae] *v* broadcast

เผ่า [phao] *n* tribe

เผาผลาญ [phao phan] กระบวนการเผา ผลาญอาหาร [kra buan kan phao phlan a han] *n* metabolism

เผาไหม้ [khao mai] เผาไหม้ทำลายลง [phao mai tham lai long] *v* burn down; ไหม้ เผาไหม้ [mai, phao mai] *n* burn; การติดเครื่อง [kan tit khrueang] *n* ignition

แผ่ [phae] แผ่ออกไป [phae ok pai] *v* spread out

แผง [phlaeng] แผงหน้าปัดรถยนต์ [phaeng na pat rot yon] *n* dashboard; แผงขายของ [phaeng khai khong] stall

แผ่น [phaen] แผ่นรองเมาส์ [phaen rong mao] *n* mouse mat; แผ่นดิสก์ [phaen dis] *n* compact disc; แผ่นบันทึก [phaen ban thuek] *n* floppy disk, hard disk

แผนก [pha naek] *n* department; แผนก ชุดชั้นในอยู่ที่ไหน? [pha naek chut chan nai yu thii nai] Where is the lingerie department?

แผนกฉุกเฉิน [pha naek chuk choen]
แผนกฉุกเฉินอยู่ที่ไหน? [pha naek chuk
choen yu thii nai] Where is casualty?;
ฉันต้องไปที่แผนกฉุกเฉิน [chan tong pai
thii pha naek chuk choen] I need to go
to casualty

แผนการ [phaen kan] n plan, scheme

แผ่นดิน [phaen din] แผ่นดินใหญ่ [phaen
din yai] n mainland; แผ่นดินถล่ม
[phaen din tha lom] n landslide

แผ่นดินไหว [phaen din wai] n
earthquake; คลื่นซึนามิเกิดจากแผ่นดิน
ไหวใต้ทะเล [khluen sue na mi koet
chak phaen din wai tai tha le] n
tsunami

แผนที่ [phaen thi] n map; แผนที่ถนน
[phaen thii tha non] n road map,
street map, street plan; สมุดแผนที่ [sa
mut phaen thii] n atlas; คุณมีแผนที่เส้น
ทางสกีไหม? [khun mii phaen thii sen
thang sa ki mai] Do you have a map of
the ski runs?

แผ่นพับ [phaen phap] n pamphlet; แผ่น
พับโฆษณา [phaen phap khot sa na] n
brochure

แผนภาพ [phaen phap] n diagram

แผ่นเสียง [phaen siang] ผู้จัดรายการ
ดนตรีแผ่นเสียง [phu chat rai kan don
tree phaen siang] n disc jockey

แผล [phlae] แผลเป็น [phlae pen] n scar;
แผลเปื่อย [phlae pueai] n cold sore,
ulcer; แผลถูกแมลงกัดต่อย [phlae thuk
ma laeng kat toi] v sting

โผล่ [phlo] ซึ่งโผล่อย่างฉับพลัน [sueng
phlo yang chap phlan] n pop-up

ไผ่ [phai] ต้นไผ่ [ton phai] n bamboo

ฝ

ฝน [fon] n rain; เสื้อกันฝน [suea kan fon]
n raincoat; ฝนตกหนักมาก [fon tok nak
mak] n downpour; ฝนที่เป็นกรด [fon
thii pen krot] n acid rain; คุณคิดว่าฝนจะ
ตกไหม? [khun kit wa fon ja tok mai]
Do you think it's going to rain?

ฝนตก [fon tok] v rain; ซึ่งมีฝนตก [sueng
mii fon tok] adj rainy; ฝนตกปรอย ๆ [fon
tok proi proi] n drizzle

ฝรั่งเศส [fa rang set] adj เกี่ยวกับชาว
ฝรั่งเศส [kiao kap chao fa rang set] adj
French ▷ n หญิงฝรั่งเศส [ying fa rang
set] n Frenchwoman; ชายฝรั่งเศส [chai
fa rang set] n Frenchman

ฝักบัว [fak bua] ฝักบัวรดน้ำต้นไม้ [fak bua
rot nam ton mai] n watering can; ห้อง
อาบน้ำฝักบัวสกปรก [hong aap nam fak
bua sok ka prok] The shower is dirty

ฝัง [fang] v bury

ฝั่ง [fang] เราขึ้นฝั่งตอนนี้ได้ไหม? [rao
khuen fang ton nii dai mai] Can we go
ashore now?

ฝังเข็ม [fang khem] การฝังเข็ม [kan fang
khem] n acupuncture

ฝัน [fan] v dream; ความฝัน [khwam fan]
n dream; ฝันร้าย [fan rai] n nightmare

ฝา [fa] ฝากระโปรงรถยนต์ [fa kra prong rot yon] *n* bonnet *(car)*; ฝาปิด [fa pit] *n* lid

ฝ่ามือ [fa mue] *n* palm *(part of hand)*

ฝ่าย [fai] ฝ่ายตรงข้าม [fai trong kham] *n* opponent, opposition; ฝ่ายบุคคล [fai buk khon] *n* personnel

ฝ้าย [fai] ผ้าฝ้าย [pha fai] *n* cotton

ฝี [fi] *n* abscess; ฉันมีฝี [chan mii fii] I have an abscess

ฝีมือ [fi mue] ช่างฝีมือ [chang fi mue] *n* craftsman

ฝึก [fuek] การฝึก [kan fuek] *n* training; ผู้ได้รับการฝึก [phu dai rap kan fuek] *n* trainee; ผู้ฝึก [phu fuek] *n* trainer

ฝึกงาน [fuek ngan] ผู้ฝึกงาน [phu fuek ngan] *n* apprentice

ฝึกซ้อม [fuek som] *v* practise, rehearse; การฝึกซ้อม [kan fuek som] *n* rehearsal; การฝึกซ้อมที่ทำเป็นประจำ [kan fuek som thii tham pen pra cham] *n* practice

ฝึกฝน [fuek fon] การฝึกฝน [kan fuek fon] *n* drill

ฝุ่น [fun] *n* dust; ซึ่งปกคลุมไปด้วยฝุ่น [sueng pok khlum pai duai fun] *adj* dusty; ที่ปัดฝุ่นพร้อมแปรง [thii pat fun phrom praeng] *n* dustpan

ฝูงชน [fung chon] *n* crowd; ซึ่งเต็มไปด้วยฝูงชน [sueng tem pai duai fung chon] *adj* crowded

ฝูงสัตว์ [fung sat] *n* flock, herd

เฝ้า [fao] *v* guard; เฝ้าระวังดู [fao ra wang du] *v* watch out; คุณเห็นคนเฝ้ารถไฟ ไหม? [khun hen khon fao rot fai mai] Have you seen the guard?

เฝ้าดู [fao du] *vt* watch

เฝือก [fueak] *n* splint

แฝด [faet] แฝดสาม [faer sam] *npl* triplets; คู่แฝด [khu faet] *n* twin

ไฝ [fai] *n* mole *(skin)*; ก้อนเล็ก ๆ ที่ขึ้นบน ผิวหนัง เช่น ไฝหรือหูด [kon lek lek thii khuen bon phio nang chen fai rue hut] *n* wart

พ

พจนานุกรม [phot cha na nu krom] *n* dictionary

พ่น [phon] *v* spray

พ้น [phan] พ้นกำหนดเวลา [phon kam not we la] *adj* overdue

พ้นโทษ [phon thot] การพ้นโทษอย่างมี เงื่อนไขหรือทำทัณฑ์บนไว้ [kan phon thot yang mii nguean khai rue tham than bon wai] *n* parole

พนักงาน [pha nak ngan] *n* staff *(workers)*; แอร์โฮสเตส [ae hot sa tet] *n* air hostess; พนักงานขาย [pha nak ngan khai] *n* sales assistant, salesperson; พนักงานขายหญิง [pha nak ngan khai ying] *n* saleswoman

พนักงานต้อนรับ [pha nak ngan ton rap] *n* receptionist

พนักงานหญิงบริการบนเครื่องบิน [pha nak ngan ying] air hostess

พนัน [pha nan] *vi* bet; เกมส์พนันรูเลททท์ [kem pha nan ru let] *n* roulette; เครื่อง หยอดเหรียญสำหรับเล่นการพนัน [khrueang yot rian sam rap len kan pha nan] *n* fruit machine; เครื่องหยอด เหรียญสำหรับเล่นพนัน [khrueang yot rian sam rap len pha nan] *n* slot machine

พบ [phop] ชุมนุม จัดให้พบกัน [chum num, chat hai phop kan] *vi* meet; พบเห็น [phop hen] *vt* spot; พบโดย บังเอิญ ตอนรับ [phop doi bang oen, ton rab] *vt* meet; เราจะพบกันได้ที่ไหน? [rao ja phop kan dai thii nai] Where can we meet?

พม่า [pha ma] เกี่ยวกับประเทศพม่า [kiao kap pra thet pha ma] *adj* Burmese; ชาว พม่า [chao pha ma] *n* Burmese (*person*); ประเทศพม่า [pra tet pha ma] *n* Burma, Myanmar

พยักหน้า [pha yak na] *v* nod

พยัญชนะ [pha yan cha na] ตัวพยัญชนะ [tua pha yan cha na] *n* consonant

พยากรณ์ [pha ya kon] การพยากรณ์ [kan pha ya kon] *n* forecast; การพยากรณ์ อากาศ [kan pha ya kon a kat] *n* weather forecast; พยากรณ์อากาศเป็น อย่างไร? [pha ya kon a kaat pen yang rai] What's the weather forecast?

พยางค์ [pha yang] *n* syllable

พยาธิ [pha yat] *n* worm

พยาน [pha yan] *n* witness; คุณเป็นพยาน ให้ฉันได้ไหม? [khun pen pha yan hai chan dai mai] Can you be a witness for me?

พยาบาล [pha ya ban] รถพยาบาล [rot pha ya ban] *n* ambulance; นางพยาบาล ผดุงครรภ์ [nang pha ya baan pa dung khan] *n* midwife; ฉันอยากพูดกับพยาบาล [chan yak phut kap pha ya baan] I'd like to speak to a nurse

พยายาม [pha ya yom] *v* attempt, struggle, try; ความพยายาม [khwam pha ya yam] *n* attempt, effort, struggle, try

พรม [phrom] *n* carpet; พรมที่ปูติดแน่น [phrom thii pu tit naen] *n* fitted carpet; พรมผืนเล็ก [phrom phuen lek] *n* rug

พรมแดน [phrom daen] เขตพรมแดน [khet phrom daen] *n* frontier

พรรคการเมือง [phak kan muang] พรรคการเมืองฝ่ายซ้าย [phak kan mueang fai sai] *adj* left-wing; พรรคการเมืองอนุรักษ์นิยม [phak kan mueang a nu rak ni yom] *adj* right-wing

พรสวรรค์ [pon sa wan] มีพรสวรรค์ [mii phon sa wan] *adj* gifted

พรหมจารีย์ [phrom ma chan] หญิงพรหม จารีย์ [ying prom ma cha ri] *n* virgin

พร้อม [phrom] *adj* ready; ซึ่งมีทุกอย่าง พร้อมในตัว [sueng mii thuk yang prom nai tua] *adj* self-contained; คุณพร้อม หรือยัง? [khun phrom rue yang] Are you ready?; ฉันพร้อมแล้ว [chan phrom laeo] I'm ready

พร้อมกัน [phrom kan] โดยเกิดขึ้นพร้อม กัน [doi koet khuen phrom kan] *adv* simultaneously; ที่พร้อมกัน [thii phrom kan] *adj* simultaneous

พระ [phra] *n* monk, priest; ที่อยู่ของพระ [thii yu khong phra] *n* monastery; พระ ในคริสต์ศาสนา [phra nai khris sat sa na] *n* vicar; พระในศาสนายิว [phra nai sat sa na yio] *n* rabbi

พระจันทร์ [phra chan] *n* moon; น้ำผึ้ง พระจันทร์ [nam phueng phra chan] *n* honeymoon; พระจันทร์เต็มดวง [phra chan tem duang] *n* full moon

พระเจ้า [phra chao] *n* god; ผู้เชื่อว่าพระเจ้า ไม่มีจริง [phu chuea wa phra chao mai mii ching] *n* atheist; พระเจ้าศาสนา อิสลาม [phra chao sat sa na is sa lam] *n* Allah

พระเจ้าแผ่นดิน [phra chao phaen din] *n* king

พระพุทธรูป [phra phut tha rup] *n* Buddha

พระมหากษัตริย์ [phra ma ha ka sat] การ ปกครองโดยมีพระมหากษัตริย์เป็นประมุข [kan pok khrong doi mii phra ma ha ka sat pen pra muk] *n* monarchy

พระเยซู [phra ye su] คำสอนของพระเยซู [kham son khong phra ye su] *n* gospel;

พระเยซูคริสต์ [phra ye su khris] *n* Christ, Jesus

พระราชวัง [phra rat cha wang] *n* palace; พระราชวังเปิดให้สาธารณะชนเข้าชมไหม? [phra rat cha wang poet hai sa tha ra na chon khao chom mai] Is the palace open to the public?; พระราชวังจะเปิดเมื่อไร? [phra rat cha wang ja poet muea rai] When is the palace open?

พระราชินี [phra ra chi ni] *n* queen

พระสันตะปาปา [phra san ta pa pa] พระสันตะปาปาหัวหน้าบิชชอปและผู้นำของนิกายโรมันคาทอลิค [phra san ta pa pa hua na bis chop lae phu nam khong ni kai ro man kha tho lik] *n* pope

พระอาทิตย์ [phra a thit] *n* sun

พระอาทิตย์ขึ้น [phra a thit khuen] *n* sunrise

พระอาทิตย์ตก [phra a thit tok] *n* sunset

พรายแสง [phrai saeng] พรายแสง ฉลาดเยี่ยม [phrai saeng, cha lat yiam] *adj* brilliant

พริก [phrik] *n* chilli

พริกไทย [prik thai] กระปุกบดพริกไทย [kra puk bod prik thai] *n* peppermill; พริกไทยป่น [phrik thai pon] *n* pepper

พรุ่งนี้ [phrung ni] *adj* tomorrow; เปิดพรุ่งนี้ไหม? [poet phrung nii mai] Is it open tomorrow?; คืนพรุ่งนี้ [khuen phrung nii] tomorrow night; ฉันโทรหาคุณพรุ่งนี้ได้ไหม? [chan tho ha khun phrung nii dai mai] May I call you tomorrow?

พฤติกรรม [phrue ti kam] *n* behaviour

พฤศจิกายน [prue sa chi ka yon] เดือนพฤศจิกายน [duean phruet sa chi ka yon] *n* November

พฤษภ [phruek sop] ราศีพฤษภ [ra si phrue sop] *n* Taurus

พฤษภาคม [prue sa pha khom] เดือนพฤษภาคม [duean phruet sa pha khom] *n* May

พฤหัสบดี [pha rue hat sa bo di] วันพฤหัสบดี [wan pha rue hat sa bo di] *n* Thursday

พลเมือง [phon la muang] *n* citizen; ความเป็นพลเมือง [khwam pen phon la mueang] *n* citizenship; พลเมืองอาวุโส [phon la mueang a wu so] *n* senior citizen

พลเรือน [phon la ruan] *n* civilian; เกี่ยวกับพลเรือน [kiao kap phon la ruean] *adj* civilian

พลัง [pha lang] เต็มไปด้วยพลังและความคิดสร้างสรรค์ [tem pai duai pha lang lae khwam kit sang san] *adj* dynamic

พลังงาน [pha lang ngan] *n* energy; หน่วยพลังงานความร้อน [nuai pha lang ngan khwam ron] *n* calorie; พลังงานแสงอาทิตย์ [pha lang ngan saeng a thit] *n* solar power

พลับพลา [phlap phla] *n* pavilion

พลัม [phlam] ลูกพลัม [luk phlam] *n* plum

พลั่ว [phlua] *n* shovel, spade

พลาด [phlat] *n* slip (*mistake*); พลาด ไม่เห็น ไม่เข้าใจ ไม่ได้ยิน [phlat, mai hen, mai khao jai, mai dai yin] *vt* miss

พลาสติก [phlas tik] ซึ่งทำด้วยพลาสติก [sueng tham duai phlat sa tik] *adj* plastic; ถุงพลาสติก [thung phas tik] *n* plastic bag, polythene bag; วัตถุพลาสติก [wat thu phlas tik] *n* plastic

พลาสเตอร์ [plas toe] *n* Elastoplast®; พลาสเตอร์ปิดแผล [plas toe pit phlae] *n* plaster (*for wound*)

พลิก [phlik] พลิกเอาด้านบนลงล่าง [phlik ao dan bon long lang] *adv* upside down; พลิกหงาย [phlik ngai] *v* turn up

พวก [phuak] สมัครพรรคพวก [sa mak phak phuak] *n* gang

พวกเขา [phuak khao] *pron* them, they; ด้วยตัวของพวกเขาเอง [duai tua khong phuak khao eng] *pron* themselves

พวกคุณ [phuak khun] *pron* you (*plural*); ตัวพวกคุณเอง [tua phuak khun eng] *pron* yourselves

พวกท่าน [phuak than] ตัวพวกท่านเอง [tua phuak than eng] *pron* yourselves

(polite)

พวกเรา [phuak rao] *pron* we; ตัวของพวก
เราเอง [tua khong phuak rao eng] *pron*
ourselves

พวง [phuang] กลุ่ม พวง รวง เครือ [klum,
phuang, ruang, khruea] *n* bunch

พวง [phuang] รถพ่วง [rot phuang] *n*
trailer

พวงมาลัยรถ [phuang ma lai] *n* steering
wheel

พหูพจน์ [pha hu phot] *n* plural

พอ [pho] แค่นั้นพอแล้ว ขอบคุณ [khae nan
pho laeo khop khun] That's enough,
thank you

พ่อ [pho] *n* dad, daddy, father; พ่อเลี้ยง
[pho liang] *n* stepfather; พ่อหรือแม่
[pho rue mae] *n* parent; พ่อหรือแม่ที่เลี้ยง
ลูกคนเดียว [pho rue mae thii liang luk
khon diao] *n* single parent

พอกัน [pho kan] อย่างพอ ๆ กัน [yang pho
pho kan] *prep* as

พ่อครัว [pho khrua] *n* cook; หัวหน้าพ่อ
ครัว [hua na pho khrua] *n* chef

พ่อค้า [pho kha] พ่อค้าขายผลิตภัณฑ์
ประเภทยาสูบ [pho kha khai pha lit ta
phan pra phet ya sup] *n* tobacconist's

พอง [phong] โป่งหรือพองเหมือนถุง [pong
rue phong muean thung] *adj* baggy; ที่
ทำให้พองได้ [thii tham hai phong dai]
adj inflatable

พอใจ [pho chai] *adj* pleased, satisfied;
เบื่อและไม่พอใจ [buea lae mai pho jai]
adj restless; ไม่น่าพอใจ [mai na pho jai]
adj unsatisfactory; ร้องแสดงความพอใจ
[rong sa daeng khwam pho jai] *v* purr;
ฉันไม่พอใจกับสิ่งนี้ [chan mai pho jai
kap sing nii] I'm not satisfied with this

พอใช้ได้ [pho chai dai] *adj* okay ▷ *adv*
pretty

พอดี [pho di] *vi* fit; ความพอดี [khwam
pho dii] *n* fit; ฉันใส่ไม่พอดี [chan sai
mai pho dii] It doesn't fit me

พอประมาณ [pho pra man] ความพอ
ประมาณ [khwam pho pra man] *n*
moderation

พอเพียง [pho phiang] *adj* enough; ไม่พอ
เพียง [mai pho phiang] *adj* skimpy;
จำนวนที่พอเพียง [cham nuan thii pho
phiang] *pron* enough; อย่างไม่พอเพียง
[yang mai pho phiang] *adv* scarcely

พ่อมด [pho mot] *n* sorcerer

พ่อแม่ [pho mae] *npl* parents

พ่อหม้าย [pho mai] *n* widower

พัก [phak] การหยุดพักระหว่างทาง [kan
yut phak ra wang thang] *n* stopover;
การพักอยู่ [kan phak yu] *n* stay; พักอยู่
[phak yu] *v* stay; คุณพักที่ไหน? [khun
phak thii nai] Where are you staying?

พักผ่อน [phak phon] *vi* relax, rest; สถาน
ที่ที่คนไปออกกำลังกายหรือพักผ่อน [sa
than thii thii khon pai ok kam lang
kai rue phak phon] *n* leisure centre;
การพักผ่อน [kan phak phon] *n*
relaxation, rest

พักอาศัย [phak a sai] เขตที่มีที่พักอาศัย
[khet thii mii thii phak a sai] *adj*
residential; ผู้พักอาศัย [phu phak a sai]
n resident

พังทลาย [phang tha lai] *v* collapse

พังพอน [phang phon] สัตว์คล้ายพังพอน
[sat khlai phang phon] *n* ferret

พัฒนา [phat tha na] การพัฒนา [kan
phat ta na] *n* development; การพัฒนา
ต่อเนื่อง [kan phat ta na to nueang] *n*
process; ประเทศที่กำลังพัฒนา [pra tet
thii kam lang phat ta na] *n* developing
country

พัดลม [phat lom] *n* fan; มีพัดลมในห้อง
ไหม? [mii phat lom nai hong mai]
Does the room have a fan?

พัน [phan] *v* wind (coil around); เศษหนึ่ง
ส่วนพัน [set nueng suan phan] *n*
thousandth; หนึ่งพัน [nueng phan]
number thousand; ที่หนึ่งพัน [thii
nueng phan] *adj* thousandth

พันธมิตร [phan tha mit] *n* alliance

พันธุ์ [phan] *n* breed; สายพันธุ์ [sai phan]
n gene; คนสัตว์หรือพืชที่เป็นพันธุ์ผสม

[khon sat rue phuet thii pen phan pha som] *n* mongrel

พันธุกรรม [phan thu kam] รหัสทางพันธุกรรม [ra hat thang phan tu kam] *n* DNA

พันธุ์ไม้ [phan mai] ชื่อพันธุ์ไม้ชนิดหนึ่ง [chue phan mai cha nit nueng] *n* hyacinth; พันธุ์ไม้มีหนามจำพวกหนึ่ง [phan mai mii nam cham phuak nueng] *n* thistle; พันธุ์ไม้ชนิดหนึ่งใช้ดอกทำอาหาร [phan mai cha nit nueng chai dok tham a han] *n* artichoke

พันธุศาสตร์ [pan thu sat] *n* genetics; เกี่ยวกับพันธุศาสตร์ [kiao kap phan thu sat] *adj* genetic; ซึ่งเปลี่ยนแปลงทางพันธุศาสตร์ [sueng plian plang thang phan tu sat] *adj* genetically-modified; ตัวย่อของแก้ไขเปลี่ยนแปลงเกี่ยวกับพันธุศาสตร์ [tua yo khong kae khai plian plang kiao kap phan thu sat] *abbr* GM

พันเอก [phan ek] *n* colonel

พับ [phap] *vt* fold; รอยพับ [roi phap] *n* fold; ที่พับเก็บได้ [thii phap kep dai] *adj* folding

พัสดุ [phat sa du] *n* parcel; ราคาส่งกล่องพัสดุใบนี้เท่าไร? [ra kha song klong phat sa du bai nii thao rai] How much is it to send this parcel?; ฉันอยากส่งกล่องพัสดุใบนี้ [chan yak song klong phat sa du bai nii] I'd like to send this parcel

พา [pha] คุณช่วยพาฉันไปที่อยู่ได้ไหม? [khun chuai pha chan pai thii u dai mai] Can you give me a lift to the garage?; คุณพาฉันไปโดยรถยนต์ได้ไหม? [khun pha chan pai doi rot yon dai mai] Can you take me by car?; ช่วยพาฉันไปใจกลางเมือง [chuai pha chan pai jai klang mueang] Please take me to the city centre

พาย [phai] *v* row (in boat); ขนมแอปเปิ้ลพาย [kha nom ap poen phai] *n* apple pie; ขนมพาย [kha nom phai] *n* pie; ขนมพายไส้ต่าง ๆ [kha nom phai sai tang tang] *n* tart

พ่ายแพ้ [phai phae] *vi* lose; ความพ่ายแพ้ [khwam phai phae] *n* defeat; ทำให้พ่ายแพ้ [tham hai phai phae] *v* beat (outdo), defeat; ทำให้พ่ายแพ้ไม่ได้ [tham hai phai phae mai dai] *adj* unbeatable

พายเรือ [phai ruea] *vt* paddle; ไม้พายเรือ [mai phai ruea] *n* paddle; การพายเรือ [kan phai ruea] *n* rowing

พายุ [pha yu] *n* storm; ลมพายุ [lom pha yu] *n* gale; ราวกับพายุ [rao kap pha yu] *adj* stormy; พายุเฮอริเคน [pha yu hoe ri khen] *n* hurricane; คุณคิดว่าจะมีพายุหรือไม่? [khun kit wa ja mii pha yu rue mai] Do you think there will be a storm?

พาราไกลดิ้ง [pha ra klai ding] คุณจะไปพาราไกลดิ้งได้ที่ไหน? [khun ja pai pha ra klai ding dai thii nai] Where can you go paragliding?

พาราเซทตามอล [pa ra set ta mon] ฉันอยากได้พาราเซทตามอล [chan yak dai pha ra set ta mon] I'd like some paracetamol

พาราเซลลิ่ง [pha ra sen ling] คุณจะไปพาราเซลลิ่งได้ที่ไหน? [khun ja pai pha ra sen ling dai thii nai] Where can you go para-sailing?

พาราฟิน [pha ra fin] *n* paraffin

พาสตา [pas ta] พาสตา อาหารจำพวกแป้ง [phas ta a han cham phuak paeng] *n* pasta; ฉันอยากได้พาสต้าเป็นรายการแรก [chan yak dai phas ta pen rai kan raek] I'd like pasta as a starter

พาสเตอร์ [pas toe] ผ้าพาสเตอร์ [pha phas toe] *n* Band-Aid®

พาสลี [phat sa li] พาสลี่ ผักใช้ปรุงอาหาร [phas li phak chai prung a han] *n* parsley

พาหนะ [pha ha na] พาหนะขนส่งสาธารณะ [pha ha na khon song sa tha ra na] *n* shuttle

พิการ [phi kan] *adj* disabled, handicapped; เก้าอี้เข็นสำหรับคนป่วยหรือคนพิการ [kao ii khen sam rap khon puai rue khon phi kan] n wheelchair; โรคอาการการพิการทางสมอง [rok a kan phi kan thang sa mong] n Down's syndrome; คนพิการ [khon phi kan] npl disabled

พิง [phing] v lean

พิจารณา [phi cha ra na] v regard, consider; คิดว่า พิจารณาว่า [khit wa, phi cha ra na wa] v reckon; พิจารณา ใหม่ [phi cha ra na mai] v reconsider

พิจารณาคดี [phi cha ra na kha di] การ พิจารณาคดี [kan phi cha ra na kha di] n trial

พิจิก [phi chik] ราศีพิจิก [ra si phi chik] n Scorpio

พิซซา [phit sa] n pizza

พิณ [phin] พิณตั้ง [phin tang] n harp

พิธี [phi thi] พิธีแมสในโบสถ์ [phi ti maes nai bot] n mass (church)

พิธีกร [phi thi kon] n compere

พิธีกรรม [phi thi kam] เกี่ยวกับพิธีกรรม [kiao kap phi thi kam] adj ritual; พิธีกรรมทางศาสนา [phi ti kam thang sat sa na] n ritual

พิธีการ [phi thi kon] n ceremony

พิธีแมส [phi thi maet] ทำพิธีแมสเมื่อไร [tham phi thi maes muea rai] When is mass?

พินัยกรรม [phi nai kam] n will (document)

พินาศ [phi nat] ทำให้พินาศ [tham hai phi nat] v ruin

พิพากษา [phi phak sa] การพิพากษา [kan phi phak sa] n sentence (punishment); ผู้พิพากษา [phu phi phak sa] n judge

พิพิธภัณฑ์ [phi phit tha phan] n museum; พิพิธภัณฑ์เปิดตอนเช้าไหม? [phi phit tha phan poet ton chao mai] Is the museum open in the morning?; พิพิธภัณฑ์เปิดตอนบ่ายไหม? [phi phit tha phan poet ton bai mai] Is the museum open in the afternoon?; พิพิธภัณฑ์เปิด วันอาทิตย์ไหม? [phi phit tha phan poet wan a thit mai] Is the museum open

on Sundays?

พิมพ์ [phim] v print, type; สิ่งพิมพ์ [sing phim] n print; การพิมพ์ผิด [kan phim phit] n misprint; ข้อมูลที่พิมพ์ออกจาก เครื่องคอมพิวเตอร์ [kho mun thii phim ok chak khrueang khom pio toe] n printout; ค่าพิมพ์ราคาเท่าไร? [kha phim ra kha thao rai] How much is printing?

พิราบ [phi rap] นกพิราบ [nok phi rap] n dove, pigeon

พิเศษ [phi set] adj special; เป็นพิเศษ [pen phi set] adj extra; การขายสินค้าราคา พิเศษ [kan khai sin kha ra kha phi set] n special offer; ดีเป็นพิเศษ [di pen phi set] adj exceptional

พิษ [phit] เลือดเป็นพิษ [lueat pen phit] n blood poisoning; มีพิษ [mii phit] adj toxic; ซึ่งเป็นพิษ [sueng pen phit] adj poisonous

พิสูจน์ [phi sut] v prove; ข้อพิสูจน์ [kho phi sut] n proof (for checking); พิสูจน์ว่ามี ความผิด [phi sut wa mii khwam phit] v convict; พิสูจน์ว่าถูกต้อง [phi sut wa thuk tong] v justify

พี่ [phi] น้องสะใภ้หรือพี่สะใภ้ [nong sa phai rue phii sa phai] n sister-in-law; พี่เขย หรือน้องเขย [phi khoei rue nong khoei] n brother-in-law; พี่ชายหรือน้องชาย [phi chai rue nong chai] n brother

พีช [phuet] ลูกพีช [luk phiit] n peach

พี่ชาย [phi chai] พี่ชายน้องชายต่างบิดา [phi chai nong chai tang bi da] n stepbrother

พี่น้อง [phi nong] npl siblings

พี่เลี้ยง [phi liang] พี่เลี้ยงดูแลเด็ก [phi liang du lae dek] n nanny

พี่สาว [phi sao] พี่สาวหรือน้องสาว [phi sao rue nong sao] n sister; พี่สาวน้องสาวต่าง บิดา [phi sao nong sao tang bi da] n stepsister

พึ่งพา [phueng pha] v lean on; พึ่งพาได้ [phueng pha dai] v count on

พืช [phuet] n plant; ใบพืชที่มีรสแรงใช้ทำ สลัดและสำหรับตกแต่งอาหาร [bai phuet thii mii rot raeng chai tham sa lat lae sam rap tok taeng a han] n cress; สัตว์และพืชป่า [sat lae phuet pa] n wildlife; พืชคล้ายหัวหอมมีก้านยาวสีเขียว [phuet khlai hua hom mii kan yao sii khiao] npl chives; เราอยากเห็นพืชของท้องถิ่น [rao yak hen phuet khong thong thin] We'd like to see local plants and trees

พืชผัก [phuet phak] n vegetation

พื้น [phuen] n floor; วางลงบนพื้น [wang long bon phuen] v ground

พื้นฐาน [phuen than] โครงสร้างพื้นฐาน เช่น ถนน สะพาน [khrong sang phuen than chen tha non sa phan] n infrastructure; โดยพื้นฐาน [doi phuen than] adv basically; สิ่งที่เป็นพื้นฐาน [sing thii pen phuen than] npl basics

พื้นดิน [phuen din] n ground

พื้นที่ [phuen thi] โครงยกพื้นที่ใช้สำหรับสร้างหรือซ่อมตึกหรือสถานที่ต่าง ๆ [khrong yok phuen thii chai sam rap sang rue som tuek rue sa than thii tang tang] n scaffolding; พื้นที่ลาดเอียง [phuen thii lat iang] n slope; พื้นที่บริการ [phuen thii bo ri kan] n service area

พื้นเมือง [phuen mueang] adj native

พื้นราบ [phuen rap] n plane (surface)

พุ่ง [phung] พุ่งไปอย่างรวดเร็ว [phung pai yang ruat reo] v plunge

พุ่งหลาว [phung lao] กีฬาพุ่งหลาว [ki la phung lao] n javelin

พุดดิ้ง [phut ding] ก้อนพุดดิ้ง [kon phut ding] n dumpling

พุดเดิ้ล [put doen] สุนัขพันธุ์พุดเดิ้ล [su nak phan put doen] n poodle

พุทธ [phut] เกี่ยวกับชาวพุทธ [kiao kap chao phut] adj Buddhist; ชาวพุทธ [chao phut] n Buddhist; ศาสนาพุทธ [sat sa na phut] n Buddhism

พุธ [phut] วันพุธ [wan phut] n Wednesday

พุพอง [phu phong] แผลพุพอง [phlae phu phong] n blister

พุ่มไม้ [phum mai] n bush (thicket),

shrub

พูด [phut] v say, speak; ไม่สามารถพูดได้ [mai sa mat phut dai] adj speechless; การพูด [kan phut] n saying; การพูดเกินความจริง [kan phut koen khwam ching] n exaggeration; มีใครที่นี่พูดภาษา...ไหม? [mii khrai thii ni phut pha sa...mai] Does anyone here speak...?

พูดติดอ่าง [put tit ang] v stammer

พูดเยาะเย้ย [put yo yoei] v scoff

เพ่ง [pheng] เพ่งความสนใจ [pheng khwam son jai] v concentrate

เพชร [pet] n diamond

เพชรพลอย [pet ploi] n gem, jewel; เครื่องเพชรพลอย [khrueang phet ploy] n jewellery; คนขายซื้อและซ่อมเครื่องเพชรพลอย [khon khai sue lae som khrueang phet ploi] n jeweller; ที่ร้านขายเครื่องเพชรพลอย [thii ran khai khrueang phet ploy] n jeweller's

เพดาน [phe dan] n ceiling; ห้องเพดาน [hong phe dan] n loft

เพ็นกวิน [pen kwin] นกเพ็นกวิน [nok phen kwin] n penguin

เพนิซิลิน [phen ni si lin] ฉันแพ้เพ็นนิซิลิน [chan phae phen ni si lin] I'm allergic to penicillin

เพนนี [pen ni] n penny

เพราะ [phro] prep due to; เพราะว่า [phro wa] conj because

เพราะฉะนั้น [phro cha nan] adv therefore

เพราะว่า [phro wa] conj that

เพลง [phleng] n song; เพลงร้องเดี่ยว [phleng rong diao] n solo; เพลงร้องกล่อมเด็ก [phleng rong klom dek] n lullaby; เพลงสำหรับวงดนตรีประสานเสียงขนาดใหญ่ [phleng sam rap wong don trii pra san siang kha nat yai] n symphony

เพลา [phlao] แกน เพลา [kaen, phlao] axle

เพลิดเพลิน [phloet phloem] ซึ่งสนุกสนานเพลิดเพลิน [sueng sa nuk sa nan phloet ploen] *adj* entertaining; ทำให้เพลิดเพลิน [tham hai phoet phloen] *v* entertain

เพศ [phet] *n* gender, sex; เรื่องทางเพศ [rueang thang phet] *n* sexuality; เกี่ยวกับเพศ [kiao kap phet] *adj* sexual; เกี่ยวกับเพศตรงข้าม [kiao kap phet trong kham] *adj* heterosexual

เพศสัมพันธ์ [phet sam phan] มีเพศสัมพันธ์กับคนหลายคน [mii phet sam phan kap khon lai khon] *v* sleep around

เพ้อเจ้อ [phoe choe] พูดเพ้อเจ้อ [phut phoe choe] *v* rave

เพาะกาย [pho kai] การเพาะกาย [kan po kai] *n* bodybuilding

เพาะปลูก [pho pluk] ที่เพาะปลูกและเลี้ยงสัตว์ [thii pho pluk lae liang sat] *n* farm

เพิง [phoeng] เพิงเก็บของ [phoeng kep khong] *n* shed

เพิ่ง [phoeng] *adv* just; ฉันเพิ่งมาถึง [chan phoeng ma thueng] I've just arrived

เพิ่ม [phoem] เพิ่มเป็นสามเท่า [poem pen sam thao] *v* treble; เพิ่มมากขึ้นทุกที [poem mak khuen thuk thi] *adv* increasingly; เพิ่มขึ้น [phoem khuen] *v* increase; มีส่วนที่ต้องจ่ายเพิ่มไหม? [mii suan thii tong chai poem mai] Is there a supplement to pay?

เพิ่มขึ้น [phoem khuen] การเพิ่มขึ้น [kan poem khuen] *n* increase

เพียง [phiang] เพียงเท่านั้น [phiang thao nan] *adj* mere

เพียงพอ [phiang pho] *adj* sufficient; ไม่เพียงพอ [mai phiang pho] *adj* inadequate, insufficient

เพี้ยน [phian] คนเพี้ยน [khon phian] *n* nutter

เพื่อ [phuea] *prep* for

เพื่อน [phuean] *n* friend, mate; เพื่อนเจ้าสาว [phuean chao sao] *n* bridesmaid; เพื่อนเจ้าบ่าว [phuean chao bao] *n* best man; เพื่อนเดินทาง [phuean doen thang] *n* companion; ฉันมาที่นี่กับเพื่อน ๆ [chan ma thii ni kap phuean

phuean] I'm here with my friends

เพื่อนบ้าน [phuean ban] *n* neighbour

แพ [phae] *n* raft

แพ้ [phae] *adj* allergic; การแพ้ถั่ว [kan phae thua] *n* nut allergy; คนแพ้อาหารที่ทำจากข้าวสาลี [khon thii pae a han thii tham chak khao sa lii] *n* wheat intolerance; ยาแก้แพ้ชนิดหนึ่ง [ya kae pae cha nit nueng] *n* antihistamine

แพง [phaeng] *adj* expensive; ไม่แพง [mai phaeng] *adj* inexpensive; ราคาแพงเกินไปสำหรับฉัน [ra kha phaeng koen pai sam rap chan] It's too expensive for me; ราคาค่อนข้างแพง [ra kha khon khang phaeng] It's quite expensive

แพทย์ [phaet] *n* doctor; เจ้าหน้าที่ทางการแพทย์ [chao na thii thang kan phaet] *n* paramedic; แพทย์ผ่าตัด [phaet pha tat] *n* surgeon; ห้องแพทย์ [hong phaet] *n* surgery (doctor's)

แพ้ท้อง [phae thong] *n* morning sickness

แพนเค้ก [paen khek] ขนมแพนเค้ก [kha nom phaen khek] *n* pancake

แพนด้า [paen da] หมีแพนด้า [mii phaen da] *n* panda

แพร์ [phae] ลูกแพร์ [luk pae] *n* pear

แพร่ [phrae] แพร่ไปทั่ว [prae pai thua] *adj* widespread; ซึ่งแพร่กระจายได้ [sueng phrae kra jai dai] *adj* contagious

แพะ [phae] *n* goat

โพรง [phlong] เป็นโพรง [pen phrong] *adj* hollow

โพรงกระดูก [phrong kra duk] โพรงกระดูกในศีรษะ [phrong kra duk nai si sa] *n* sinus

ไพ่ [phai] แต้มเอหรือเลขหนึ่งในการเล่นไพ่ [taem e rue lek nueng nai kan len pai] *n* ace; การเล่นไพ่ [kan len pai] *n* playing card

ไพลิน [phai lin] ไพลินสีน้ำเงินหรือสีฟ้าเข้ม [phai lin sii nam ngoen rue sii fa khem] *n* sapphire

ฟ

ฟกช้ำ [fok cham] แผลฟกช้ำ [phlae fok cham] n bruise

ฟรี [fri] adj free (no cost)

ฟลามิงโก [fla ming ko] นกฟลามิงโก [nok fla ming ko] n flamingo

ฟอก [fok] n bleach; ถูกฟอก [thuk fok] adj bleached

ฟอง [fong] n bubble; ฟองอาบน้ำ [fong aap nam] n bubble bath

ฟองน้ำ [fong nam] n sponge (for washing)

ฟ้องร้อง [fong rong] v charge (accuse), prosecute, sue

ฟักทอง [fak thong] n pumpkin

ฟัง [fang] v listen, listen to; เครื่องช่วยฟัง [khrueang chuai fang] n hearing aid; หู ฟัง [hu fang] npl earphones; ผู้ฟัง [phu fang] n listener

ฟัน [fan] n tooth ▷ v hack; เกี่ยวกับฟัน [kiao kap fan] adj dental; ไหมขัดฟัน [mai khat fan] n dental floss; หมอฟัน [mo fan] n dentist; ปวดฟันซี่นี้ [puat fan si nii] This tooth hurts

ฟันปลอม [fan plom] คุณซ่อมฟันปลอมฉัน ได้ไหม? [khun som fan plom chan dai mai] Can you repair my dentures?

ฟ้า [fa] สีฟ้า [sii fa] adj blue

ฟางข้าว [fang khao] n straw

ฟ้าร้อง [fa rong] เสียงและลักษณะแบบ ฟ้าร้อง [siang lae lak sa na baep fa rong] adj thundery; เสียงฟ้าร้อง [siang fa rong] n thunder; ฉันคิดว่าจะมีฟ้าร้อง [chan kit wa ja mii fa rong] I think it's going to thunder

ฟาโรห์ [fa ro] หมู่เกาะฟาโรห์ [mu kao fa ro] npl Faroe Islands

ฟ้าแลบ [pha laep] สายฟ้าแลบ [sai fa laep] n lightning

ฟาห์เรนไฮต์ [fa ren hai] องศาฟาห์เรนไฮต์ [ong sa fa ren hai] n degree Fahrenheit

ฟีจิ [fi ji] ประเทศฟีจิ [pra tet fi chi] n Fiji

ฟินแลนด์ [fin laen] เกี่ยวกับประเทศ ฟินแลนด์ [kiao kap pra thet fin laen] adj Finnish; ชาวฟินแลนด์ [chao fin laen] n Finn, Finnish; ประเทศฟินแลนด์ [pra tet fin laen] n Finland

ฟิล์ม [fim] ขอฟิล์มสี [kho fim sii] A colour film, please; คุณช่วยล้างฟิล์มได้ไหม? [khun chuai lang fim dai mai] Can you develop this film, please?; ฉันอยากได้ ฟิล์มสีสำหรับกล้องอันนี้ [chan yak dai fim sii sam rap klong an nii] I need a colour film for this camera

ฟิลิปปินส์ [fi lip pin] เกี่ยวกับชาวฟิลิปปินส์ [kiao kap chao fi lip pin] adj Filipino; หญิงชาวฟิลิปปินส์ [ying chao fi lip pin] n Filipino

ฟิวส์ [fio] กล่องฟิวส์อยู่ที่ไหน? [klong fio yu thii nai] Where is the fusebox?; คุณ ซ่อมฟิวส์ได้ไหม? [khun som fio dai mai] Can you mend a fuse?; ฟิวส์ขาด [fio khat] A fuse has blown

ฟิสิกส์ [fi sik] นักฟิสิกส์ [nak fi sik] n physicist; วิชาฟิสิกส์ [wi cha phi sik] npl physics

ฟื้น [fuen] หาย ฟื้น [hai, fuen] vi recover; ฟื้นขึ้นมา [fuen khuen ma] v come round; ฟื้นจากการเจ็บป่วย [fuen chak kan chep puai] n recovery

ฟุตบอล [fut bon] n football; เตะฟรีใน

ฟุตบอล [te frii nai fut bal] *n* free kick; กีฬาแข่งขันฟุตบอล [ki la khaeng khan fut bal] *n* football match; การแข่งขันกีฬานานาชาติโดยเฉพาะกีฬาฟุตบอล [kan khaeng khan ki la na na chat doi cha po ki la fut ball] *n* World Cup; มาเล่นฟุตบอลกัน [ma len fut bal kan] Let's play football

ฟุ่มเฟือย [fum fueai] *adj* extravagant

ฟู [fu] ออกเสียงฟู [ok siang fu] *adj* fizzy

เฟอร์ [foe] ต้นเฟอร์ [ton foe] *n* fir (tree)

เฟิร์น [foen] ต้นเฟิร์น [ton foen] *n* fern

แฟกซ์ [faek] ส่งแฟกซ์ [song fak] *v* fax

แฟชั่น [fae chan] *n* fashion

แฟน [faen] เสียใจด้วย ฉันมีแฟนแล้ว [sia jai duai chan mii faen laeo] Sorry, I'm in a relationship

แฟนซี [fan si] ชุดแฟนซี [chut faen si] *n* fancy dress

แฟ้ม [faem] แฟ้มเอกสาร [faem ek ka san] *n* file (folder); แฟ้มในเครื่องคอมพิวเตอร์ใช้เก็บข้อความที่ส่งทางอีเล็กโทรนิค [faem nai khrueang khom phio toe chai kep kho khwam thii song thang i lek tro nik] *n* inbox; จัดเข้าแฟ้ม [chat khao faem] *v* file (folder)

แฟร์รี่ [fae ri] เรือแฟร์รี่บรรทุกรถต่าง ๆ [ruea fae ri ban thuk rot tang tang] *n* car-ferry

แฟลช [flaet] ไฟแฟลชของกล้องถ่ายรูป [fai flaet khong klong thai rup] *n* flash; ไฟแฟลชไม่ทำงาน [fai flaet mai tham ngan] The flash is not working

โฟม [fom] โฟมโกนหนวด [fom kon nuat] *n* shaving foam

ไฟ [fai] *n* fire; เครื่องอัดไฟ [khrueang at fai] *n* charger; แสงไฟสว่างจ้าที่ใช้ในสนามกีฬาหรือนอกอาคาร [saeng fai sa wang cha thii chai nai sa nam ki la rue nok a khan] *n* floodlight; โคมไฟ [khom fai] *n* lampshade; ทางหนีไฟ [thang nii fai] *n* fire escape

ไฟฉาย [fai chai] *n* flashlight, torch; ไฟฉายที่มีแสงสว่างจ้ามาก [fai chai thii mii saeng sa wang cha mak] *n* spotlight

ไฟแช็ก [fai cheak] *n* lighter

ไฟแช็ค [fai chaek] คุณมีที่เติมก๊าซสำหรับไฟแช็คก๊าซของฉันไหม? [khun mii thii toem kas sam rap fai chaek kas khong chan mai] Do you have a refill for my gas lighter?

ไฟฟ้า [fai fa] *n* electricity; เสาไฟฟ้า [sao fai fa] *n* lamppost; เกี่ยวกับไฟฟ้า [kiao kap fai fa] *adj* electric, electrical; เครื่องกำเนิดไฟฟ้า [khrueang kam noet fai fa] *n* generator; ไม่มีไฟฟ้า [mai mii fai fa] There is no electricity

ไฟล์ [fai] พีดีเอฟไฟล์ [phi di ef fim] *n* PDF

ไฟไหม้ [fai mai] สัญญาณเตือนไฟไหม้ [san yan tuean fai mai] *n* fire alarm

ภ

ภรรยา [phan ra ya] n wife; สามีหรือ
ภรรยา [sa mii rue phan ra ya] n
spouse; อดีตภรรยา [a dit phan ra ya] n
ex-wife; นี่ภรรยาผมครับ [ni phan ra ya
phom krap] This is my wife
ภาค [phak] ภาคหรือกลุ่ม [phak rue klum]
n sector
ภาคภูมิใจ [phak phum chai] ความภาค
ภูมิใจ [khwam phak phum jai] n pride
ภาคเรียน [phak rian] n term (division of
year)
ภาชนะ [pha cha na] ภาชนะใส่ของ [pha
cha na sai khong] n container
ภาพ [phap] สัญลักษณ์ภาพ [san ya lak
phap] n icon; ห้องแสดงภาพ [hong sa
daeng phap] n gallery; จุดที่เล็กที่สุดที่รวม
กันเป็นภาพ [chut thii lek thii sut thii
ruam kan pen phap] n pixel; คุณช่วยใส่
ภาพพวกนี้ลงบนซีดีได้ไหม? [khun chuai
sai phap phuak nii long bon si di dai
mai] Can you put these photos on CD,
please?
ภาพพจน์ [phap phot] n image
ภาพยนตร์ [phap pha yon] n film, movie;
โรงภาพยนตร์ [rong phap pha yon] n
cinema; คำแปลที่เขียนไว้ข้างล่างใน
ภาพยนตร์ [kham plae thii khian wai
khang lang nai phap pa yon] npl
subtitles; ดาราภาพยนตร์ [da ra phap
pha yon] n film star; ที่มีคำแปลเขียนไว้
ข้างล่างในภาพยนตร์ [thii mii kham plae
khian wai khang lang nai phap pha
yon] adj subtitled
ภาพร่าง [phap rang] n sketch
ภาพวาด [phap wat] n painting
ภายใต้ [phai tai] adv underneath
ภายนอก [phai nok] adj exterior; ที่ใช้
ภายนอก [thii chai phai nok] adj
external
ภายใน [phai nai] adj internal ▷ adv
inside ▷ n interior ▷ prep within (space),
within (term); นักตกแต่งภายใน [nak tok
taeng phai nai] n interior designer
ภายหน้า [phai na] adj future
ภายหลัง [phai lang] prep after
ภารกิจ [pha ra kit] n task
ภารโรง [phan rong] n janitor
ภาระ [pha ra] n burden
ภาวะ [pha wa] ภาวะเงินเฟ้อ [pha wa
ngoen foe] n inflation; ภาวะไม่อยากหรือ
ทานอาหารไม่ได้ [pha wa mai yak rue
than a han mai dai] n anorexia;
ภาวะฉุกเฉิน [pha wa chuk choen] n
emergency
ภาษา [pha sa] n language; เจ้าของภาษา
[chao khong pha sa] n native speaker;
โรงเรียนสอนภาษา [rong rian son pha sa]
n language school; สามารถเขียนหรือพูด
ได้สองภาษา [sa maat khian rue phut
dai song pha sa] adj bilingual; คุณพูด
ภาษาอะไรบ้าง? [khun phut pha sa a rai
bang] What languages do you speak?
ภาษาศาสตร์ [pha sa sat] เกี่ยวกับ
ภาษาศาสตร [kiao kap pha sa sat] adj
linguistic; นักภาษาศาสตร์ [nak pha sa
saat] n linguist
ภาษี [pha si] n tax; สินค้าปลอดภาษี [sin
kha plot pha si] n duty-free; ที่ปลอดภาษี
[thii plot pha si] adj duty-free; ผู้เสีย
ภาษี [phu sia pha si] n tax payer

ภูเขา [phu khao] *n* mountain; เต็มไปด้วย
ภูเขา [tem pai duai phu khao] *adj*
mountainous; ภูเขาน้ำแข็งลอยอยู่กลาง
ทะเล [phu khao nam khaeng loi yu
klang tha le] *n* iceberg; ยอดสุดของภูเขา
[yot sut khong phu khao] *n* summit;
ฉันอยากได้ห้องที่มีวิวภูเขา [chan yak dai
hong thii mii wio phu khao] I'd like a
room with a view of the mountains
ภูเขาไฟ [phu khao fai] *n* volcano
ภูต [phut] *n* devil
ภูมิใจ [phum chai] *adj* proud
ภูมิประเทศ [phu mi prathet] *n*
landscape; สิ่งที่เป็นลักษณะเด่นของ
ภูมิประเทศ [sing thii pen lak sa na den
khong phu mi pra tet] *n* landmark
ภูมิภาค [phu mi phak] ฉันจะซื้อแผนที่ของ
ภูมิภาคนี้ได้ที่ไหน? [chan ja sue phaen
thii khong phu mi phak nii dai thii
nai] Where can I buy a map of the
region?
ภูมิศาสตร์ [phu mi sat] *n* geography
ภูมิหลัง [phum hlang] *n* background
เภสัชกร [phe sat cha kon] *n* pharmacist
โภชนาการ [pho cha na kan] *n* nutrition

ม

มกราคม [mok ka ra khom] เดือนมกราคม
[duean mok ka ra khom] *n* January
มงกุฎ [mong kut] *n* crown
มด [mot] *n* ant
มนตร์ [mon] มนตร์คาถา [mon kha tha] *n*
spell *(magic)*
มนุษย์ [ma nut] เกี่ยวกับมนุษย์ [kiao kap
ma nut] *adj* human; มนุษย์อวกาศ [ma
nut a wa kat] *n* astronaut
มนุษยชาติ [ma nut sa ya chat] *n*
mankind
มนุษย์ต่างดาว [ma nut tang dao] ตัวย่อ
ของจานบินของมนุษย์ต่างดาว [tua yo
khong chan bin khong ma nut tang
dao] *abbr* UFO
มนุษยธรรม [ma nut sa ya tham] มี
มนุษยธรรม [mii ma nut sa ya tham] *adj*
humanitarian
มนุษยศาสตร์ [ma nut sa ya sat] *n*
anthropology
มโนคติวิทยา [ma no kha ti wit tha ya]
n ideology
มโนภาพ [ma no phap] วาดมโนภาพ [wad
ma no phap] *v* imagine
มรณกรรม [mo ra na kam] การประกาศ
ข่าวมรณกรรม [kan pra kat khao mo ra

na kam] *n* obituary

มรดก [mo ra dok] *n* heritage, inheritance

มรรยาท [ma ra yat] *npl* manners

มรสุม [mo ra sum] ฤดูมรสุม [rue du mo ra sum] *n* monsoon

มลพิษ [mon la phit] การทำให้เป็นมลพิษ [kan tham hai pen mon la phit] *n* pollution; ที่เป็นมลพิษ [thii pen mon la phit] *adj* polluted; ทำให้เป็นมลพิษ [tham hai pen mon la phit] *v* pollute

ม่วง [muang] สีม่วงอ่อน [sii muang on] *adj* mauve; ที่มีสีม่วง [thii mii sii muang] *adj* purple; ที่มีสีม่วงอ่อน [thii mii sii muang on] *adj* lilac

ม้วน [muan] เครื่องม้วน [khrueang muan] *n* reel; โรลม้วนผม [rol muan phom] *n* curler; ม้วนกระดาษชำระ [muan kra dat cham ra] *n* toilet roll

มวย [muai] นักมวย [nak muai] *n* boxer

มวยปล้ำ [muai plam] การแข่งขันมวยปล้ำ [kan khaeng khan muai plam] *n* wrestling; นักมวยปล้ำ [nak muai plam] *n* wrestler

มหัพภาค [ma hap phak] มหัพภาค จุด [ma hup phak chut] *n* full stop

มหัศจรรย์ [ma hat sa chan] เรื่อง มหัศจรรย์ [rueang ma hat sa chan] *n* miracle

มหาวิทยาลัย [ma ha wit tha ya lai] *n* university; ตัวย่อของมหาวิทยาลัย [tua yo khong ma ha wit ta ya lai] *n* uni

มหาสมุทร [ma ha sa mut] *n* ocean; มหาสมุทรแปซิฟิก [ma ha sa mut pae si fik] *n* Pacific; มหาสมุทรแอตแลนติก [ma ha sa mut at laen tik] *n* Atlantic; มหาสมุทรขั้วโลกเหนือ [ma ha sa mut khua lok nuea] *n* Arctic Ocean

มหึมา [ma hue ma] *adj* mammoth; ที่ ใหญ่มหึมา [thii yai ma hu ma] *adj* enormous

มโหฬาร [ma ho lan] *adj* gigantic

มอง [mong] มองไปรอบ ๆ [mong pai rop rop] *v* look round; มองหา [mong ha] *v*

look for; มองข้าม [mong kham] *v* overlook

มองโกเลีย [mong ko lia] เกี่ยวกับ มองโกเลีย [kiao kap mong ko lia] *adj* Mongolian; ชาวมองโกเลีย [chao mong ko lia] Mongolian *(person)*; ประเทศ มองโกเลีย [pra tet mong ko lia] *n* Mongolia

มองในแง่ดี [mong nai ngae di] การมอง ในแง่ดี [kan mong nai ngae dii] *n* optimism; ซึ่งมองในแง่ดี [sueng mong nai ngae di] *adj* positive

มองโลกในแง่ดี [mong lok nai ngae di] ผู้มองโลกในแง่ดี [phu mong lok nai ngae di] *n* optimist

มองโลกในแง่ร้าย [mong lok nai ngae rai] คนมองโลกในแง่ร้าย [khon mong lok nai ngae rai] *n* pessimist; ที่มองโลก ในแง่ร้าย [thii mong lok nai ngae rai] *adj* pessimistic

มองหา [mong ha] เรากำลังมองหา... [rao kam lang mong ha...] We're looking for...

มองเห็น [mong hen] การมองเห็น [kan mong hen] *n* sight

มอเตอร์ไซด์ [mo toe sai] มอเตอร์ไซด์ ขนาดเล็ก [mo toe sai kha naat lek] *n* moped; รถมอเตอร์ไซด์ [rot mo toe sai] *n* motorcycle; นักขับมอเตอร์ไซด์ [nak khap mo toe sai] *n* motorcyclist; ฉัน อยากเช่ามอเตอร์ไซด์คันเล็กหนึ่งคัน [chan yak chao mo toe sai khan lek nueng khan] I want to hire a moped

มอบ [mop] ส่งมอบ [song mop] *vt* deliver

มอบหมาย [mop mai] งานที่ได้รับมอบหมาย [ngan thii dai rap mop mai] *n* assignment

มอบให้ทำแทน [mop hai tham thaen] *v* delegate

มอร์ฟีน [mo fin] *n* morphine

มอริชัส [mo ri chas] ชาวมอริชัส [chao mo ri chas] *n* Mauritius

มอริทาเนีย [mo ri tha nia] ประเทศมอริทา เนีย [pra tet mo ri tha nia] *n*

Mauritania

มอลโดวัน [mon do wan] ชาวมอลโดวัน [chao mol do wan] n Moldovan

มอลโดวา [mon do wa] เกี่ยวกับมอลโดวา [kiao kap mol do va] adj Moldovan; ประเทศมอลโดวาอยู่ในทวีปอัฟริกา [pra tet mol do va yu nai tha wip af ri ka] n Moldova

มอลตา [mon ta] เกี่ยวกับมอลตา [kiao kap mol ta] adj Maltese; ชาวมอลตา [chao mol ta] n Maltese (person); ประเทศมอลตา [pra tet mol ta] n Malta

มะกอก [ma kok] n olive; ต้นมะกอก [ton ma kok] n olive tree; น้ำมันมะกอก [nam man ma kok] n olive oil

มะกะโรนี [ma ka ro ni] npl macaroni

มะเขือ [ma khuea] มะเขือฝรั่งมีสีม่วงผลยาวใหญ่ [ma khuea fa rang mii sii muang phon yao yai] n aubergine

มะเขือเทศ [ma khuea thet] n tomato; ซ้อสมะเขือเทศ [sos ma khuea tet] n ketchup; ซอสมะเขือเทศ [sos ma khuea tet] n tomato sauce

มะเดื่อ [ma duea] ต้นหรือผลตระกูลมะเดื่อ [ton rue phon tra kun ma duea] n fig

มะนาว [ma nao] n lemon, lime (fruit); เปลือกมะนาวหรือส้ม [plueak ma nao rue som] n zest (lemon-peel); น้ำมะนาว [nam ma nao] n lemonade; ใส่มะนาว [sai ma nao] with lemon

มะพร้าว [ma phrao] n coconut

มะม่วง [ma muang] n mango

มะม่วงหิมพานต์ [ma muang him ma phan] เมล็ดมะม่วงหิมพานต์ [ma let ma muang him ma phan] n cashew

มะเร็ง [ma reng] n cancer (illness)

มะฮอกกานี [ma hok ka ni] ต้นมะฮอกกานี [ton ma hok ka ni] n mahogany

มัคคุเทศก์ [mak khu thet] n tour guide

มังกร [mang kon] n dragon; ราศีมังกร [ra si mang kon] n Capricorn

มั่งคั่ง [mang kang] ร่ำรวยมั่งคั่ง [ram ruai mang khang] adj wealthy; ความร่ำรวยมั่งคั่ง [khwam ram ruai mang khang] n wealth

มังสวิรัติ [mang sa wi rat] adj vegetarian; ผู้นับถือลัทธิมังสวิรัติ [phu nap thue lat thi mang sa wi rat] n vegan; มีร้านอาหารมังสวิรัติที่นี่ไหม? [mii ran a han mang sa wi rat thii ni mai] Are there any vegetarian restaurants here?; คุณมีอาหารมังสวิรัติไหม? [khun mii a han mang sa wi rat mai] Do you have any vegetarian dishes?

มัด [mat] มัดให้แน่น [mat hai naen] v tie up

มัดจำ [mat cham] ขอเงินมัดจำของฉันคืน [kho ngen mat cham khong chan khuen] Can I have my deposit back, please?; ค่ามัดจำเท่าไร? [kha mat cham thao rai] How much is the deposit?; ค่าวางมัดจำเท่าไร? [kha wang mat cham thao rai] How much is the deposit?

มัธยม [mat tha yom] โรงเรียนชั้นมัธยม [rong rian chan mat tha yom] n secondary school

มัน [man] pron it; มันบด [man bot] npl mashed potatoes; มันอบ [man op] n baked potato; ซึ่งเป็นมันเงา [sueng pen man ngao] adj shiny

มั่นคง [man khong] adj stable, steady; ไม่มั่นคง [mai man khong] adj insecure, unstable, unsteady; ความมั่นคง [khwam man khong] n stability

มั่นใจ [man chai] ให้ความมั่นใจ [hai khwam man jai] v assure; ความมั่นใจ [khwam man jai] n confidence (self-assurance); ที่ให้ความมั่นใจ [thii hai khwam man jai] adj reassuring

มันฝรั่ง [man fa rang] n potato; มันฝรั่งหั่นบางทอดกรอบ [man fa rang han bang thot krop] npl crisps; มันฝรั่งทอด [man fa rang thot] npl chips; มันฝรั่งอบทั้งลูก [man fa rang op thang luk] n jacket potato

มัมมี่ [mam mi] n mummy (body)

มัสตาร์ด [mat sa tat] ผงมัสตาร์ดใช้ปรุงอาหาร [phong mas tat chai prung a han] n mustard

มา [ma] v come; มาจาก [ma chak] v come from; ที่กำลังจะมาถึง [thii kam lang ja ma thueng] adj coming; ฉันจะไม่มา [chan ja mai ma] I'm not coming

ม้า [ma] n horse; เกือกม้า [kueak ma] n horseshoe; ม้าหรือม้าลายตัวเมีย [ma rue ma lai tua mia] n mare; ม้าพันธุ์เล็ก [ma phan lek] n pony

มาก [mak] adj much ▷ adv so; มากเกินไป [mak koen pai] adv grossly; มากกว่า [mak kwa] adj more; มากที่สุด [mak thii sut] adj most

มากมาย [mak mai] adj many, numerous; จำนวนมากมาย [cham nuan mak mai] n plenty

มาจอรั่ม [ma cho ram] ต้นมาจอรั่มมีใบหอมใช้ปรุงอาหารและใส่ในสลัด [ton ma cho ram mii bai hom chai prung a han lae sai nai sa lat] n marjoram

มาดากัสการ์ [ma da kat sa ka] เกาะมาดากัสการ์ในมหาสมุทรอินเดีย [ko ma da kas ka nai ma ha sa mut in dia] n Madagascar

มาตรฐาน [mat tra than] n standard; มาตรฐานการครองชีพ [mat tra than kan khrong chip] n standard of living; ซึ่งเป็นมาตรฐาน [sueng pen mat tra than] adj standard

มาตรา [mat tra] n clause

ม่าน [man] ม่านเกล็ดไม้รูดขึ้นลงได้ [man klet mai rut khuen long dai] n Venetian blind; ผ้าม่าน [pha man] n curtain

ม่านตา [man ta] n iris

ม้านั่ง [ma nang] n bench; ม้านั่งไม่มีพนัก [ma nang mai mii pha nak] n stool

มายองเนส [ma yong net] n mayonnaise

มายากล [ma ya kon] นักแสดงมายากล [nak sa daeng ma ya kon] n conjurer

ม้าโยก [ma yok] ม้าโยกไม้สำหรับเด็กนั่งเล่น [ma yok mai sam rap dek nang len] n rocking horse

มาร์กซ์ [mak] ลัทธิมาร์กซ์ [lat thi mark] n Marxism

มารดา [man da] เกี่ยวกับมารดา [kiao kap man da] adj maternal

มารยา [ma ra yat] ไม่มีเล่ห์เหลี่ยม ไม่มีมารยา [mai mii le liam, mai mii man ya] adj naive

มาราธอน [ma ra thon] การวิ่งแข่งมาราธอน [kan wing khaeng ma ra thon] n marathon

ม้าลาย [ma lai] n zebra; ม้าหรือม้าลายตัวเมีย [ma rue ma lai tua mia] n mare

มาลาเรีย [ma la ria] ไข้มาลาเรีย [khai ma la ria] n malaria

มาลาวี [ma la wi] ประเทศมาลาวี [pra tet ma la wi] n Malawi

มาเลเซีย [ma le sia] เกี่ยวกับประเทศมาเลเซีย [kiao kap pra thet ma le sia] adj Malaysian; ชาวมาเลเซีย [chao ma le sia] n Malaysian; ประเทศมาเลเซีย [pra tet ma le sia] n Malaysia

ม้าหมุน [ma mun] n merry-go-round

มิงค์ [ming] ตัวมิงค์ ขนใช้ทำเสื้อกันหนาว [tua ming khon chai tham sue kan nao] n mink

มิฉะนั้น [mi cha nan] conj otherwise

มิตร [mit] เป็นมิตร [pen mit] adj friendly; ไม่เป็นมิตร [mai pen mit] adj hostile; ที่เป็นมิตรกับสภาพแวดล้อม [thii pen mit kap sa phap waet lom] adj environmentally friendly

มิตรภาพ [mit tra phap] n friendship

มิติ [mi ti] สามมิติ [sam mi ti] adj three-dimensional

มิเตอร์ [mi toe] มิเตอร์จอดรถ [mi toe jot rot] n parking meter; มันมากกว่าบนมิเตอร์ [man mak kwa bon mi toe] It's more than on the meter; มิเตอร์แก๊สอยู่ที่ไหน? [mi toe kaes yu thii nai] Where is the gas meter?

มิถุน [mi thun] ราศีมิถุน [ra si mi thun] n Gemini

มิถุนายน [mi thu na yon] เดือนมิถุนายน [duean mi thu na yon] n June; ต้นเดือนมิถุนายน [ton duean mi thu na yon] at

the beginning of June; ตลอดเดือน
มิถุนายน [ta lot duen mi thu na yon] for
the whole of June

มิลลิเมตร [min li met] n millimetre

มิสซิสซิปปี้ [mit sit sip pi] ตัวย่อของแม่น้ำ
มิสซิสซิปปี้ในอเมริกา [tua yo khong mae
nam mis sis sip pi nai a me ri ka] abbr
MS

มี [mi] v have; มีผลใช้ได้ [mii phon chai
dai] n availability; มีอยู่ [mii yu] adj
available; คุณมี...บ้างไหม? [khun mii...
bang mai] Have you got any...?

มีค่า [mi kha] มีค่าเป็นเงินมาก [mii kha
pen ngoen mak] adj valuable; ของมีค่า
[khong mi kha] npl valuables

มีชีวิต [mi chi wit] v exist; มีชีวิตอยู่ต่อไป
[mii chi wid yu to pai] v live on

มีชีวิตชีวา [mi chi wit chi wa] adj lively
▷ v revive

มีชีวิตรอด [mi chi wit rot] v survive

มีชื่อเสียง [mi chue siang] adj renowned

มีด [mit] n knife; ใบมีด [bai mit] n blade;
มีด ช้อนและส้อม [miit chon lae som] n
cutlery; มีดเล็กที่พับได้ [miit lek thii
phap dai] n penknife

มีดโกน [mit kon] n razor; ใบมีดโกน [bai
mit kon] n razor blade; มีดโกนไฟฟ้า
[miit kon fai fa] n shaver

มีผลบังคับใช้ [mi phon bang khap] adj
valid

มีส่วนทำให้ [mi suan tham hai] v
contribute

มีส่วนร่วม [mi suan ruam] v participate;
เข้าไปมีส่วนร่วม [khao pai mii suan
ruam] v involve

มีนเมา [muen mao] adj tipsy

มืด [muet] adj dark

มือ [mue] n hand; ไม่ใช้มือ [mai chai
mue] adj hands-free; ที่ทำด้วยมือ [thii
tham duai mue] adj handmade

มื้อ [mue] มื้ออาหาร [mue a han] n meal;
อาหารมื้อหลัก [a han mue lak] n main
course

มือถือ [mue thue] โทรศัพท์มือถือ [tho ra

sap mue thue] n mobile phone; เบอร์มือ
ถือคุณเบอร์อะไร? [boe mue thue khun
boe a rai] What is the number of your
mobile?; เบอร์มือถือฉันเบอร์... [boe mue
thue chan boe...] My mobile number
is...

มือสอง [mue song] adj secondhand

มืออาชีพ [mue a chip] อย่างมืออาชีพ
[yang mue a chip] adv professionally

มุง [mung] ที่มุงด้วยจาก [thii mung duai
chak] adj thatched

มุ่ง [mung] มุ่งไปที่ [mung pai thii] v
point out

มุ่งเน้น [mung nen] v focus

มุ่งร้าย [mung rai] adj malicious ▷ v
spite; ที่มุ่งร้าย [thii mung rai] adj
malignant

มุม [mum] n angle, corner; มุมที่ถูกต้อง
[mum thii thuk tong] n right angle

มุมมอง [mum mong] n aspect

มุสลิม [mut sa lim] adj Muslim; เกี่ยวกับ
มุสลิม [kiao kap mus sa lim] adj
Moslem; ชาวมุสลิม [chao mus sa lim] n
Moslem, Muslim

มูล [mun] มูลสัตว์ [mun sat] n manure

มูลค่า [mun kha] n worth; มีมูลค่า [mii
mun kha] v cost

มูส [mus] มูสใส่ผมให้อยู่ทรง [mus sai
phom hai yu song] n mousse

เมกกะ [mek ka] กรุงเมกกะ [krung mek
ka] n Mecca

เม็กซิกัน [mek si kan] เกี่ยวกับเม็กซิกัน
[kiao kap mex si kan] adj Mexican; ชาว
เม็กซิกัน [chao mex si kan] n Mexican

เม็กซิโก [mek si ko] ประเทศเม็กซิโก [pra
tet mex si ko] n Mexico

เมฆ [mek] n cloud; ที่ปกคลุมด้วยเมฆ [thii
pok khlum duai mek] adj cloudy

เม็ด [met] เม็ดยี่หร่า [met yi ra] n fennel

เม็ดโลหิต [met lo hit] โรคที่มีเม็ดโลหิตขาว
มากเกินไป [rok thii mii met lo hit khao
mak koen pai] n leukaemia

เมตตา [met ta] ความเมตตา [kwam met
ta] n mercy; ความเมตตากรุณา [kwam

met ta ka ru na] *n* kindness

เมตตาปราณี [met ta pra ni] ไร้ความ
เมตตาปราณี [rai khwam met ta pra nii]
adj ruthless

เมตร [met] *n* metre; หน่วยวัดความยาวเป็น
เมตร [nuai wat khwam yao pen met] *n*
meter; ซึ่งวัดเป็นเมตร [sueng wat pen
met] *adj* metric

เม่น [men] *n* hedgehog

เมเปิล [mem mo ri kat] ต้นเมเปิล [ton me
poel] *n* maple

เม็มเมอร์รี่การ์ด [mem mo ri kat] มีเม็มเม
อร์รี่การ์ดสำหรับกล้องดิจิตัลไหม? [mii
mem moe ri kaat sam rap klong di gi
tal mai] A memory card for this digital
camera, please

เมรุ [men] *n* crematorium

เมล็ด [ma let] เมล็ดในของผลไม้ [ma let
nai khong phon la mai] *n* pip; เมล็ด
มะม่วงหิมพานต์ [ma let ma muang him
ma phan] *n* cashew; เมล็ดกาแฟ [ma let
ka fae] *n* coffee bean

เมล็ดพืช [ma let phuet] *n* seed

เมลอน [me lon] เมลอนเป็นผลไม้จำพวกแตง
[me lon pen phon la mai cham phuak
taeng] *n* melon

เมษ [met] ราศีเมษ [ra si met] *n* Aries

เมษายน [me sa yon] เดือนเมษายน [duean
me sa yon] *n* April

เมา [mao] *adj* drunk; เมาเครื่องบิน [mao
khrueang bin] airsick; เมาคลื่น [mao
khluen] *adj* seasick

เมารี [mao ri] เกี่ยวกับเมารี [kiao kap
mao ri] *adj* Maori; ชาวเมารี [chao mao
ri] *n* Maori (*person*); ภาษาเมารี [pha sa
mao ri] *n* Maori (*language*)

เมาส์ [maot] แผ่นรองเมาส์ [phaen rong
mao] *n* mouse mat

เมื่อ [muea] เมื่อหรือขณะที่ [muea rue kha
na thii] *conj* when

เมื่อก่อน [muea kon] *adj* previous

เมื่อคืนนี้ [muea khuen ni] last
night

เมือง [mueang] *n* city; เขตเมือง [khet
mueang] *n* town; ใจกลางเมือง [jai
klang mueang] *n* city centre, town
centre; ตัวเมือง [tua mueang] *adv*
downtown; ฉันจะซื้อแผนที่ของเมืองนี้
ได้ที่ไหน? [chan ja sue phaen thii
khong mueang nii dai thii nai] Where
can I buy a map of the city?

เมืองหลวง [muang luang] *n* capital

เมื่อเร็วๆนี้ [muea reo reo ni] *adv* lately

เมื่อไร [muea rai] เราจะถึงที่...เมื่อไร? [rao
ja thueng thii...muea rai] When does
it arrive in...?; คุณจะเสร็จเมื่อไร? [khun
ja set muea rai] When will you have
finished?

เมื่อวานซืน [muea wan suen] the day
before yesterday

เมื่อวานนี้ [muea wan ni] *adv* yesterday

เมื่อไหร่ [muea rai] *adv* when

แม่ [mae] *n* mother, mum, mummy
(*mother*); แม่เลี้ยง [mae liang] *n*
stepmother; แม่สามี [mae sa mii] *n*
mother-in-law; แม่อุปถัมป์ [mae up pa
tham] *n* godmother

แม็กเคอเริล [maek khoe ren] ปลา
แม็กเคอเริล [pla mak koe rel] *n* mackerel

แมกไพ [maek phai] นกแมกไพ [nok
maek phai] *n* magpie

แมงกระพรุน [maeng kra phrun] *n*
jellyfish; ที่นี่มีแมงกะพรุนไหม? [thii ni
mii maeng ka prun mai] Are there
jellyfish here?

แมงมุม [maeng mum] *n* spider; ใยแมงมุม
[yai maeng mum] *n* cobweb

แม่ชี [mae chi] *n* nun; สำนักแม่ชี [sam
nak mae chi] *n* convent

แม่นย่า [maen yam] *adj* accurate,
precise; ความแม่นย่า [khwam maen
yam] *n* accuracy; ถูกต้องแม่นย่า [thuk
tong maen yam] *adj* exact; อย่างแม่นย่า
[yang maen yam] *adv* accurately,
precisely

แม่น้ำ [mae nam] *n* river; ส่วนของแม่น้ำที่
ไหลแรงและเร็ว [suan khong mae nam

thii lai raeng lae reo] *npl* rapids; เราว่าย
น้ำในแม่น้ำได้ไหม? [rao wai nam nai
mae nam dai mai] Can one swim in the
river?

แม่บ้าน [mae ban] *n* housewife

แม่พิมพ์ [mae phim] *n* mould (*shape*)

แม่มด [mae mot] *n* witch

แมลง [ma leng] *n* bug, insect; แมลงตัว
เล็กคล้ายยุงกัดคนและสัตว์ [ma laeng tua
lek khlai yung kat khon lae sat] *n*
midge; แมลงปีกแข็ง [ma laeng pik
khaeng] *n* ladybird; แมลงปีกแข็ง เช่นตัว
ด้วง [ma laeng pik khaeng chen tua
duang] *n* beetle; มีแมลงในห้องฉัน [mii
ma laeng nai hong chan] There are
bugs in my room

แมลงป่อง [ma laeng pong] *n* scorpion

แมลงสาบ [ma laeng sap] *n* cockroach

แมว [maeo] *n* cat; ลูกแมว [luk maeo] *n*
kitten

แมวน้ำ [maeo nam] *n* seal (*animal*)

แมส [maet] พิธีแมสในโบถส์ [phi ti maes
nai bot] *n* mass (*church*)

แม่หม้าย [mae mai] *n* widow

แม่เหล็ก [mae lek] *n* magnet; ซึ่งมี
คุณสมบัติเป็นแม่เหล็ก [sueng mii khun
som bat pen mae lek] *adj* magnetic

โมฆะ [mo kha] ที่เป็นโมฆะ [thii pen mo
kha] *adj* void

โมซัมบิก [mo sam bik] ประเทศโมซัมบิก
[pra tet mo sam bik] *n* Mozambique

โมเด็ม [mo dem] *n* modem

โมเต็ล [mo ten] *n* motel

โมนาโค [mo na kho] ประเทศโมนาโค [pra
tet mo na kho] *n* Monaco

โมร็อคโค [mo rok kho] เกี่ยวกับโมร็อคโค
[kiao kap mo rok kho] *n* Moroccan;
ชาวโมร็อคโค [chao mo rok kho] *n*
Moroccan

โมเลกุล [mo le kun] *n* molecule

ไม่ [mai] *adv* not ▷ *excl* no!; ไม่ มักใช้คู่กับ
neither [mai mak chai khu kap
neither] *conj* nor; ไม่แม้แต่หนึ่ง [mai
mae tae nueng] *adj* no

ไม้ [mai] *n* wood (*material*); เนื้อหรือไม้ชิ้น
หนาสั้น [nuea rue mai chin na san] *n*
chunk; ไม้เป็นท่อน [mai pen thon] *n*
log; ไม้แขวนเสื้อ [mai khwaen suea] *n*
coathanger; จุกไม้ก๊อก [chuk mai kok]
n cork

ไม้กวาด [mai kwat] *n* broom

ไม้กอล์ฟ [mai kop] เขาให้เช่าไม้กอล์ฟ
ไหม? [khao hai chao mai kolf mai] Do
they hire out golf clubs?

ไม้กางเขน [mai kang khen] *n* cross; ไม้
กางเขนที่พระเยซูถูกตรึง [mai kang khen
thii phra ye su thuk trueng] *n* crucifix

ไม้แขวนเสื้อ [mai khwaen suea] *n*
hanger

ไม่ค่อย [mai khoi] ไม่ค่อยจะ [mai khoi
ja] *adv* seldom

ไม่ค่อย [mai khoi] ไม่ค่อยพบ [mai khoi
phop] *adj* scarce

ไม้ค้ำ [mai kham] ไม้ค้ำ เสาค้ำ ไม้เท้า
[mai kham, sao kham, mai thao] *n*
staff (*stick or rod*)

ไม่เคยมีมาก่อน [mai khoei ma kon] *adj*
unprecedented

ไมโครชิป [mai khro chip] แผ่นไมโครชิป
[phaen mai khro chip] *n* chip
(*electronic*); การฝังไมโครชิป [kan fang
mai khro chip] *n* silicon chip

ไมโครชิพ [maek phai] *n* microchip

ไมโครโฟน [mai khro fon] *n*
microphone, mike; มีไมโครโฟนไหม?
[mii mai khro fon mai] Does it have a
microphone?

ไมโครเวฟ [mai khro wep] เตาอบ
ไมโครเวฟ [tao op mai khro wep] *n*
microwave oven

ไม้จิ้มฟัน [mai chim fan] *n* toothpick

ไม่เช่นนั้น [mai chen nan] *adv*
otherwise

ไม้ดอก [mai dok] ไม้ดอกชนิดหนึ่งนิยมปลูก
ในสวนใบเหมือนหญ้าดอกเล็ก [mai dok
cha nit nueng ni yom pluk nai suan
bai muean ya dok lek] *n* crocus

ไม้เทนนิส [mai then nit] เขามีไม้เล่น

เทนนิสให้เช่าไหม? [khao mii mai len then nis hai chao mai] Do they hire out rackets?

ไม้เท้า [mai thao] *n* stick, walking stick; ไม้เท้าใช้พยุง [mai thao chai pha yung] *n* crutch; ไม้ค้ำ เสาค้ำ ไม้เท้า [mai kham, sao kham, mai thao] *n* staff *(stick or rod)*

ไม้บรรทัด [mai ban that] *n* ruler *(measure)*

ไม้พาย [mai phai] *n* oar; ไม้พายที่ใช้ทำอาหาร [mai phai thii chai tham a han] *n* spatula

ไม้พุ่ม [mai phum] *n* bush *(shrub)*; ไม้พุ่มสมุนไพร [mai phum sa mun phrai] *n* rosemary

ไม้มี [mai mi] ไม่มีสักสิ่ง [mai mii sak sing] *pron* none

ไม่มีทาง [mai mi thang] *adv* never

ไมล์ [mai] *n* mile; เครื่องวัดจำนวนไมล์ [khrueang wat cham nuan mai] *n* mileometer; ระยะทางเป็นไมล์ [ra ya thang pen mai] *n* mileage; ตัวย่อของไมล์ต่อชั่วโมง [tua yo khong mai to chau mong] *abbr* mph

ไม่เลื้อย [mai lueai] ไม้เลื้อยชื่อต้นไอวี่ [mai lueai chue ton ai vi] *n* ivy

ไม่ว่าจะ [mai wa cha] ไม่ว่าจะ...หรือไม่ [mai wa ja...rue mai] *conj* whether

ไม้เสียบ [mai siap] *n* skewer

ไม้หนีบ [mai nip] ไม้หนีบผ้า [mai nip pha] *n* peg

ไม้อัด [mai at] *n* plywood

ย

ยก [yok] ยกขึ้น [yok khuen] *v* lift, raise; คุณช่วยฉันยกกระเป๋าได้ไหม? [khun chuai chan yok kra pao dai mai] Can you help me with my luggage, please?

ยกน้ำหนัก [yok nam nak] การยกน้ำหนัก [kan yok nam nak] *n* weightlifting; ผู้ยกน้ำหนัก [phu yok nam nak] *n* weightlifter

ยกยอ [yok yo] *v* flatter; ที่ได้รับการยกยอ [thii dai rap kan yok yo] *adj* flattered

ยกย่อง [yok yong] *v* appreciate; พูดยกย่องตัวเองจนเกินไป [phud yok yong tua eng chon koen pai] *v* boast

ยกเลิก [yok loek] *v* abolish, give up, cancel; การยกเลิก [kan yok loek] *n* cancellation; ฉันต้องยกเลิกการ์ดของฉัน [chan tong yok loek kat khong chan] I need to cancel my card; ฉันอยากยกเลิกเที่ยวบินของฉัน [chan yak yok loek thiao bin khong chan] I'd like to cancel my flight

ยกเว้น [yok wen] ข้อยกเว้น [kho yok wen] *n* exception

ยน [yon] รอยยน [roi yon] *n* crease; อย่างยน [yang yon] *adj* creased

ยนต์ [yon] เรือยนต์ [ruea yon] *n*

motorboat; เครื่องยนต์ [khrueang yon] n engine

ยโส [ya so] หยิ่งยโส [ying ya so] adj arrogant

ย่อ [yo] การทำให้มีความเข้มข้นมากขึ้น การย่อความ [kan tham hai mii khwam khem khon mak khuen, kan yo khwam] n condensation; ตัวย่อ [tua yo] n acronym; ตัวย่อของ และอื่น ๆ [tua yo khong lae uen uen] abbr etc

ยอด [yot] ยอดสุดของภูเขา [yot sut khong phu khao] n summit; ยอดหลังคา [yot lang kha] n steeple

ยอดขาย [yot khai] n turnover

ยอดเยี่ยม [yod yiam] adj splendid

ยอน [yon] ย้อนรอยเดิม [yon roi doem] v retrace

ยอม [yom] ยอมให้เข้า [yom hai khao] v admit (allow in)

ย้อม [yom] v dye; การย้อม [kan yom] n dye; คุณช่วยยอมรากผมให้ฉันได้ไหม? [khun chuai yom rak phom hai chan dai mai] Can you dye my roots, please?; คุณช่วยย้อมผมให้ฉันได้ไหม [khun chuai yom phom hai chan dai mai] Can you dye my hair, please?

ยอมแพ้ [yom phae] v give in, surrender

ยอมรับ [yom rap] v accept; ไม่ยอมรับ [mai yom rap] v rule out; การยอมรับ [kan yom rap] n acknowledgement; ซึ่งไม่สามารถยอมรับได้ [sueng mai sa maat yom rap dai] adj unacceptable

ย่อย [yoi] v digest; การไม่ย่อยของอาหาร [kan mai yoi khong a han] n indigestion; การย่อย [kan yoi] n digestion

ย่อหน้า [yo na] n paragraph

ยักษ์ [yak] n giant

ยักไหล่ [yak lai] ยักไหล่เพื่อแสดงความไม่สนใจหรือไม่ทราบ [yak lai phuea sa daeng khwam mai son jai rue mai sap] v shrug

ยัง [yang] adv yet (with negative); ยังคง [yang khong] adv still

ยังแข็งแรง [yang khaeng raeng] v bear up

ยังคงอยู่ [yang khong yu] ที่ยังคงอยู่ [thii yang khong yu] adj remaining

ยับยั้ง [yap yang] อำนาจในการยับยั้ง [am nat nai kan yap yang] n veto

ยา [ya] n drug, medicine, pill; ร้านขายยา [ran khai ya] n pharmacy; คนขายยา [khon khai ya] n drug dealer; ที่ร้านขายยาหรือเครื่องสำอาง [thii ran khai ya rue khrueang sam ang] n chemist('s); ยาดับกลิ่น [ya dap klin] n deodorant; ยาที่อยู่ในหลอดเล็ก ๆ [ya thii yu nai lot lek lek] n capsule; ฉันได้รับยานี้ไปแล้ว [chan dai rap ya nii pai laeo] I'm already taking this medicine

ยา [ya] ปู่ ย่า ตา ยาย [pu ya ta yai] npl grandparents; ย่า ยาย [ya, yai] n grandma, grandmother; ยาย ย่า [yai, ya] n granny

ยาก [yak] adj difficult, hard (difficult); ความยากลำบาก [khwam yak lam bak] n difficulty; ยากเย็น [yak yen] adv hard; ยากที่จะเข้าใจ [yak thii ja khao jai] adj complicated

ยากจน [yak chon] adj poor; ความยากจน [khwam yak chon] n poverty

ยากันแมลง [ya kan ma laeng] คุณมียากันแมลงไหม? [khun mii ya kan ma laeng mai] Do you have insect repellent?

ยาคุมกำเนิด [ya khum kam noet] ฉันอยากได้ยาคุมกำเนิด [chan yak dai ya khum kam noet] I need contraception

ยาฆ่าแมลง [ya kha ma laeng] n pesticide

ยาง [yang] n rubber; ยางในของรถ [yang nai khong rot] n inner tube; ยางรัดผม [yang rat phom] n hairband; ยางรถ [yang rot] n tyre

ย่าง [yang] v grill; ซึ่งถูกย่าง [sueng thuk yang] adj grilled; อาหารย่าง [a han yang] n grill

ยางมะตอย [yang ma toi] n tarmac

ยางไม้ [yang mai] n resin

ยางรัด [yang rat] n rubber band

ยาชา [ya cha] n anaesthetic; ยาชาเฉพาะ
แห่ง [ya chaa cha pho haeng] n local
anaesthetic

ยาน [yan] หย่อนยาน [yon yan] adj flabby

ยานพาหนะ [yan pha ha na] n vehicle;
ตัวย่อของยานพาหนะที่สามารถบรรทุกของ
หนัก [tua yo khong yan pha ha na thii
sa maat ban thuk khong nak] abbr
HGV; ยานพาหนะที่เดินทางไปด้วยกัน [yan
pha ha na thii doen thang pai duai
kan] n convoy

ยานอวกาศ [yan a wa kat] n spacecraft

ยาบำรุง [ya bam rung] n tonic

ยาปฏิชีวนะ [ya pha ti chi wa na] ยา
ปฏิชีวนะชื่อเพนนิซิลิน [ya pa ti chi wa na
chue pen ni si lin] n penicillin

ยาพิษ [ya phit] วางยาพิษ [wang ya phit]
v poison

ยาม [yam] n guard

ยาย [yai] ปู่ ย่า ตา ยาย [pu ya ta yai] npl
grandparents; ย่า ยาย [ya, yai] n
grandma, grandmother; ยาย ย่า [yai,
ya] n granny

ย้าย [yai] การเคลื่อนย้าย การย้าย [kan
khluean yai, kan yai] n shift; การย้ายที่
อยู่ [kan yai thii yu] n move; ย้าย ขยับ
[yai, kha yap] vi move

ย้ายโอน [yai on] v transfer; การย้ายโอน
[kan yai on] n transfer

ยาว [yao] adj long; ความยาว [khwam
yao] n length; ยาวกว่า [yao kwa] adv
longer; ยาวนาน [yao nan] adv long

ยาสระผม [ya sa phom] n shampoo; คุณ
ขายยาสระผมไหม? [khun khai ya sa
phom mai] Do you sell shampoo?

ยาสลบ [ya sa lop] การวางยาสลบ [kan
wang ya sa lop] n general anaesthetic

ยาสีฟัน [ya si fan] n toothpaste

ยาสูบ [ya sup] ต้นยาสูบ [ton ya sup] n
tobacco; พ่อค้าขายผลิตภัณฑ์ประเภท
ยาสูบ [pho kha khai pha lit ta phan pra
phet ya sup] n tobacconist's

ยาเสพติด [ya sep tit] ทำให้ติดยาเสพติด
[tham hai tit ya sep tit] adj addicted; ผู้
ติดยาเสพติด [phu tit ya sep tit] n addict;
ยาเสพติดชนิดหนึ่ง [ya sep tit cha nit
nueng] n cocaine

ยิง [ying] vt shoot; การยิง [kan ying] n
shooting, shot

ยิ่ง [ying] หยิ่งแบบถือตัว [ying baep thue
tua] adj vain; ยิ่งไปกว่านั้น [ying pai kwa
nan] adv even

ยิ่งใหญ่ [ying yai] adj grand, great,
mega; ซึ่งปรากฏที่ยิ่งใหญ่ [sueng pra kot
thii ying yai] adj spectacular

ยินดี [yin di] แสดงความยินดี [sa daeng
khwam yin dii] v congratulate; การ
แสดงความยินดี [kan sa daeng khwam
yin dii] npl congratulations; ความปีติ
ยินดี [khwam pi ti yin dii] n pleasure; มี
ความยินดีที่ได้พบคุณ [mii khwam yin dii
thii dai phop khun] It was a pleasure
to meet you

ยินดีต้อนรับ [yin di ton rap] excl
welcome!

ยินยอม [yin yom] adj agreed; สัมปทาน
การยินยอม [sam pa than, kan yin yom]
n concession

ยิปซี [yip si] ชาวยิปซี [chao yip si] n
gypsy

ยิม [yim] โรงยิม [rong yim] n gym

ยิ้ม [yim] v smile; การยิ้มอย่างเปิดเผย [kan
yim yang poet phoei] n grin; ยิ้มยิงฟัน
[yim ying fan] v grin

ยิว [yio] เกี่ยวกับยิว [kiao kap yio] adj
Jewish; โบสถ์ของศาสนายิว [bot khong
sat sa na yio] n synagogue; สะอาดและดี
พอที่จะกินได้ตามกฎของอาหารยิว [sa at
lae di pho thii ja kin dai tam kot
khong a han yio] adj kosher

ยืน [yin] ฉันจะดื่มยินกับโทนิค [chan ja
duem yin kap tho nik] I'll have a gin
and tonic, please

ยีนส์ [yin] กางเกงยีนส์ [kang keng yin] npl
jeans; ผ้ายีนส์ [pha yin] npl denim,
denims

ยีราฟ [yi rap] *n* giraffe

ยีสต์ [yist] ยีสต์ เชื้อหมัก [yis, chuea mak] *n* yeast

ยี่สิบ [yi sip] *number* twenty; ลำดับที่ยี่สิบ [lam dap thii yi sip] *adj* twentieth

ยี่หร่า [yi ra] เม็ดยี่หร่า [met yi ra] *n* fennel

ยี่ห้อ [yi ho] *n* brand name

ยึด [yuet] การจับ การยึด [kan chap, kan yued] *n* seizure; ยึดแน่น [yuet naen] *v* hold on; ยึดทรัพย์ [yuet sap] *v* confiscate

ยึดครอง [yuet khrong] *v* occupy; การยึดครอง [kan yuet khrong] *n* occupation (invasion)

ยึดถือ [yuet thue] ผู้ยึดถืออุดมการณ์ [phu yuet thue u dom kan] *n* chauvinist

ยึด [yuet] คุณยึดผมฉันให้ตรงได้ไหม? [khun yuet phom chan hai trong dai mai] Can you straighten my hair?

ยึดหยุ่น [yuet yun] เวลาที่ยึดหยุ่นได้ [we la thii yuet yun dai] *n* flexitime; ไม่ยึดหยุ่น [mai yuet yun] *adj* inflexible; ความยึดหยุ่น [khwam yuet yun] *n* elastic

ยืน [yuen] *vi* stand; ยืนขึ้น [yuen khuen] *v* stand up

ยื่น [yuen] ยื่นออกมา [yuen ok ma] *v* stick out

ยืนยัน [yuen yan] *v* confirm, insist; การยืนยัน [kan yuen yan] *n* confirmation; ฉันยืนยันการจองด้วยจดหมาย [chan yuen yan kan chong duai chot mai] I confirmed my booking by letter

ยืนหยัด [yuen yan] *v* last; ยืนหยัดถึงที่สุด [yuen yat thueng thii sut] *v* persevere

ยืม [yuem] *v* borrow; คุณมีปากกาให้ฉันยืมไหม? [khun mii pak ka hai chan yuem mai] Do you have a pen I could borrow?

ยื้อยุด [yue yut] การยื้อยุดหยุดฝ่ายตรงข้ามในการครองลูกฟตบอลหรือรักบี้ [kan yue yut fai trong kham nai kan khrong luk fut bon rue rak bii] *n* tackle

ยุค [yuk] ยุคกลาง [yuk klang] *npl* Middle Ages

ยุคกลาง [yuk klang] เกี่ยวกับยุคกลาง [kiao kap yuk klang] *adj* mediaeval

ยุง [yung] *n* mosquito

ยุง [yung] *adj* busy

ยุ่งยาก [yung yak] การทำให้ยุ่งยาก [kan tham hai yung yak] *n* complication; ที่ยุ่งยาก [thii yung yak] *adj* puzzled; ทำให้ยุ่งยาก [tham hai yung yak] bother

ยุ่งเหยิง [yung yoeng] *adj* chaotic

ยุ่งเหยิง [yung yoeng] ความยุ่งเหยิง ความโกลาหล สถานการณ์สับสนวุ่นวาย [khwam yung yoeng, khwam ko la hon, sa than na kan sap son wun wai] *npl* shambles; ทำให้ยุ่งเหยิง [tham hai yung yoeng] *v* disrupt

ยุติ [yu ti] *adj* finished ▷ *v* call off; หยุด ยุติ เลิก [yut, yu ti, loek] *vi* stop

ยุติธรรม [yu ti tham] ไม่ยุติธรรม [mai yu ti tham] *adj* unfair; ความไม่ยุติธรรม [khwam mai yut ti tham] *n* injustice; ความยุติธรรม [khwam yut ti tham] *n* fairness, justice

ยุทธภัณฑ์ [yut tha phan] อาวุธยุทธภัณฑ์ [a wut yut tha phan] *n* ammunition

ยุทธวิธี [yut tha wi thi] *n* strategy ▷ *npl* tactics; เกี่ยวกับยุทธวิธีหรือกลยุทธ [kiao kap yut tha wi thi rue kon la yut] *adj* strategic; ปราศจากยุทธวิธี [prat sa chak yut tha wi thi] *adj* tactless

ยุโรป [yu rop] เกี่ยวกับดินแดนในยุโรปเหนือ [kiao kap din daen nai yu rop nuea] *adj* Scandinavian; เกี่ยวกับยุโรป [kiao kap yu rop] *adj* European; สหภาพยุโรป [sa ha phap yu rop] *n* European Union

ยูเครน [u khren] เกี่ยวกับประเทศยูเครน [kiao kap pra thet yu khren] *adj* Ukrainian; ชาวยูเครน [chao u khren] *n* Ukrainian (person); ประเทศยูเครน [pra tet yu khren] *n* Ukraine

ยูโด [yu do] กีฬายูโด [ki la yu do] *n* judo

ยูไนเต็ดอาหรับเอเมเรซ [u nai tet a rap e me ret] ประเทศยูไนเต็ดอาหรับเอเมเรซ [pra tet yu nai tet a rab e me ret] *npl* United Arab Emirates

ยูเรเนียม [u re niam] ธาตุยูเรเนียม [that u re niam] *n* uranium

ยูโร [yu ro] เงินยูโร [ngoen u ro] *n* euro

เย็น [yen] *adj* cold, cool (cold); เย็นเฉียบ [yen chiap] *adj* freezing; เย็นจัด [yen chat] *adj* icy; เย็นจัด [yen chat] *adj* frosty; เนื้อเย็น [nuea yen] The meat is cold

เย็บ [yep] *v* sew, stitch; เย็บปักถักร้อย [yep pak thak roi] *v* embroider; การเย็บ [kan yep] *n* sewing; ซ่อมแซมโดยการเย็บ [som saem doi kan yep] *v* sew up

เยเมน [ye men] ประเทศเยเมน [pra tet ye men] *n* Yemen

เยลลี่ [yen li] *n* jelly

เยอรมัน [yoe ra man] เกี่ยวกับเยอรมัน [kiao kap yoe ra man] *adj* German; ชาวเยอรมัน [chao yoe ra man] *n* German (person); ประเทศเยอรมัน [pra tet yoe ra man] *n* Germany

เย่อหยิ่ง [yoe ying] *adj* stuck-up

เยาว์วัย [yao wai] ยังเยาว์วัย [yang yao wai] *adj* immature

เยาะเย้ย [yo yoei] *v* mock

เยี่ยม [yiam] *adj* fabulous; มาเยี่ยม [ma yiam] *n* visit; การไปเยี่ยม [kan pai yiam] *n* visit; ชั่วโมงเยี่ยม [chau mong yiam] *npl* visiting hours

เยี่ยมชม [yiam chom] การเยี่ยมชม [kan yiam chom] *n* sightseeing; เรามีเวลาที่จะเยี่ยมชมเมืองไหม? [rao mii we la thii ja yiam chom mueang mai] Do we have time to visit the town?; เราจะเยี่ยมชมสถานที่อะไรได้บ้างที่นี่? [rao ja yiam chom sa than thii a rai dai bang thii ni] What sights can you visit here?

เยื่อ [yuea] เยื่อหุ้มสมองอักเสบ [yuea hum sa mong ak sep] *n* meningitis

เยือกแข็ง [yueak khaeng] สารต้านการเยือกแข็ง [san tan kan yueak khaeng] *n* antifreeze

แย่ [yae] แย่มาก [yae mak] *adj* awful; แย่ลง [yae long] *adj* worse; แย่กว่า [yae kwa] *adv* worse; สายตาของฉันแยลง [sai ta khong chan yae long] I'm visually impaired

แยก [yaek] *vt* split; แยกจาก [yaek chak] *adv* apart; แยกออก [yaek ok] *v* sort out; แยกออกไป [yaek ok pai] *v* exclude

แยกเขี้ยว [yaek khiao] *v* snarl

แย็บ [yaep] การแย็บ [kan yaep] *n* jab

แยม [yaem] *n* jam; แยมส้ม [yam som] *n* marmalade; ขวดแยม [khaut yaem] *n* jam jar

โยก [yok] โยก แกว่ง เขย่า [yok, kwaeng, kha yao] *v* rock

โยคะ [yo kha] *n* yoga

โยน [yon] *vt* throw; โยนเหรียญ [yon lian] *v* toss; โยนทิ้ง [yon thing] *v* throw away; โยนออกไป [yon ok pai] *v* throw out

ใย [yai] ใยแมงมุม [yai maeng mum] *n* cobweb; ใยไหมแก้ว [yai mai kaew] *n* fibreglass

ใยแมงมุม [yai maeng mum] *n* web

ร

รก [rok] สภาพรกรุงรัง [sa phap rok rung rang] *n* mess

รณรงค์ [ron na rong] การรณรงค์ [kan ron na rong] *n* campaign

รดน้ำ [rot nam] *v* water

รถ [rot] เรือหรือรถที่บรรทุกน้ำมันหรือ ของเหลวอื่น ๆ [ruea rue rot thii ban thuk nam man rue khong leo uen uen] *n* tanker; โรงรถ [rong rot] *n* garage; รถ เล็กไม่มีประตู [rot lek mai mii pra tu] *n* buggy; รถคันใหญ่ที่หรูหราโอ่อ่า [rot khan yai thii ru ra o a] *n* limousine; รถ ที่เคลื่อนที่โดยสายเคเบิล [rot thii khluean thii doi sai khe boen] *n* cable car; รถยนต์ที่มีประตูหลัง [rot yon thii mii pra tu lang] *n* hatchback; มีรถโดยสารไป... ไหม? [mii rot doi san pai…mai] Is there a bus to…?

รถเข็น [rot khen] *n* trolley; เกวียน รถเข็น [kwian, rot khen] *n* cart; รถเข็นเด็ก [rot khen dek] *n* pram, pushchair; รถเข็นใน ห้างสรรพสินค้า [rot khen nai hang sap pha sin ka] *n* shopping trolley

รถโคช [rot khot] รถโคชออกไปโดยไม่มี ฉัน [rot khot ok pai doi mai mii chan] The coach has left without me

รถชน [rot chon] มีรถชนกัน [mii rot chon kan] There's been a crash; มีคนถูกรถชน [mii khon thuk rot chon] Someone has been knocked down by a car

รถโดยสาร [rot doi san] รถโดยสารประจำ สนามบิน [rot doi san pra cham sa nam bin] *n* airport bus

รถถัง [rot thang] *n* tank *(combat vehicle)*

รถบรรทุก [rot ban thuk] คนขับรถบรรทุก [khon khap rot ban thuk] *n* truck driver

รถประจำทาง [rot pra cham thang] *n* bus; คนเก็บเงินบนรถประจำทาง [khon kep ngen bon rot pra cham thang] *n* bus conductor; รถประจำทางพาเที่ยวเมือง เมื่อไร? [rot pra cham thang pha thiao mueang muea rai] When is the bus tour of the town?

รถพยาบาล [rot pha ya ban] เรียกรถ พยาบาล [riak rot pha ya baan] Call an ambulance

รถไฟ [rot fai] *n* railway, train; เตียงนอน บนรถไฟ [tiang non bon rot fai] *n* couchette; สถานีรถไฟ [sa tha ni rot fai] *n* railway station; ห้องในรถไฟ [hong nai rot fai] *n* compartment; มี รถไฟสายตรงไหม? [mii rot fai sai trong mai] Is it a direct train?

รถไฟใต้ดิน [rot fai tai din] *n* subway; สถานีรถไฟใต้ดิน [sa tha ni rot fai tai din] *n* metro station, tube station

รถเมล [rot me] รถเมล์เล็ก [rot me lek] *n* minibus

รถยนต์ [rot yon] *n* car; คนขับรถยนต์ [khon khap rot yon] *n* motorist; ฝากระ โปรงรถยนต์ [fa kra prong rot yon] *n* bonnet *(car)*

รถสามล้อ [rot sam lo] *n* tricycle

รบ [rop] การหยุดรบ [kan yut rop] *n* ceasefire

รบกวน [rop kuan] *v* disturb, pester; ผู้ รบกวนความสุขของผู้อื่น [phu rop kuan khwam suk khong phu uen] *n* spoilsport

ร่ม [rom] *n* umbrella; ร่ม ที่ร่ม [rom, thii rom] *n* shade

รมควัน [rom khwan] *adj* smoked; เนื้อด้านหลังและส่วนนอกของหมูที่ใส่เกลือรมควัน [nuea dan lang lae suan nok khong mu thii sai kluea rom khwan] *n* bacon

ร่มชูชีพ [rom chu chip] *n* parachute

รวง [ruang] กลุ่ม พวง รวง เครือ [klum, phuang, ruang, khruea] *n* bunch

รวดเร็ว [ruat reo] *adj* quick; อย่างรวดเร็ว [yang ruat reo] *adv* fast, quickly

รวม [ruam] *v* add, mix up; รวมเข้าด้วยกัน [ruam khao duai kan] *v* merge; รวมกัน [ruam kan] *v* combine; รวมตัวกัน [ruam tua kan] *v* round up

ร่วม [ruam] การเกิดขึ้นร่วมกัน [kan koet khuen ruam kan] *n* conjunction; ที่อยู่ร่วมกันได้ [thii yu ruam kan dai] *adj* compatible

รวมกลุ่ม [ruam klum] การรวมกลุ่ม [kan ruam klum] *n* assembly

รวมกัน [ruam kan] การรวมกัน [kan ruam kan] *n* conjugation, union

ร่วมกัน [ruam kan] *adv* together

รวมทั้ง [ruam thang] *prep* including

ร่วมเพศ [ruam phet] ผู้ที่ชอบร่วมเพศกับเด็ก [phu thii chop ruam phet kap dek] *n* paedophile

ร่วมมือ [ruam mue] *v* collaborate; การร่วมมือกัน [kan ruam mue kan] *n* cooperation

รวย [ruai] *adj* rich

รส [rot] การปรุงรส [kan prung rot] *n* flavouring; ออกรส [ok rot] *adj* tasty; รสไม่ค่อยดี [rot mai khoi di] It doesn't taste very nice

รสจัด [rot chat] ที่มีรสจัด [thii mii rot chat] *adj* spicy; อาหารรสจัดเกินไป [a han rot chat koen pai] The food is too spicy

รสชาติ [rot chat] *n* flavour, taste; ซึ่งมีรสชาติอ่อน [sueng mii rot chat on] *adj* mild

รสนิยม [rot ni yom] ไม่มีรสนิยม [mai mii rot ni yom] *adj* tasteless; ความมีรสนิยมการออกแบบ [khwam mii rot ni yom, kan ok baep] *n* style; ซึ่งมีรสนิยม [sueng mii rot ni yom] *adj* tasteful

รหัส [ra hat] *n* code; เลขรหัสลับส่วนตัว [lek ra hat lap suan tua] *npl* PIN; รหัสไปรษณีย์ [ra hat prai sa ni] *n* postcode; รหัสมอร์ส [ra hat mos] *n* Morse; รหัสหมุนไปสหราชอาณาจักรคืออะไร? [ra hat mun pai sa ha rat cha a na chak khue a rai] What is the dialling code for the UK?

รอ [ro] *vi* wait; รอคอย [ro khoi] *v* wait for, wait up; ห้องที่ใช้นั่งรอ [hong thii chai nang ro] *n* waiting room; เราได้รอมาเป็นเวลานานมาก [rao dai ro ma pen we la nan mak] We've been waiting for a very long time

รอคอย [ro khoi] *v* long

รอง [rong] เป็นรอง [pen rong] *adj* minor; รองอาจารย์ใหญ่ [rong a chan yai] *n* deputy head; ชั้นรอง [chan rong] *adj* second-rate

ร้อง [rong] ร้องแสดงความพอใจ [rong sa daeng khwam pho jai] *v* purr; ร้องโหยหวน [rong hoi huan] *v* howl; ตะโกนร้อง [ta khon, rong] *v* yell

ร้องทุกข์ [rong thuk] *v* complain

รองเท้า [rong thao] *n* shoe; เชือกผูกรองเท้า [chueak phuk rong thao] *n* shoelace; ร้านขายรองเท้า [ran khai rong thao] *n* shoe shop; รองเท้าแตะ [rong thao tae] *n* flip-flops, sandal; รองเท้าฉันมีรู [rong thao chan mii ru] I have a hole in my shoe

ร้องเพลง [rong phleng] *v* sing; ร้องเพลงในคอ [rong phleng nai kho] *v* hum; การร้องเพลง [kan rong phleng] *n* singing; การร้องเพลงไปกับทำนองเพลงที่มีเนื้อร้องบนจอทีวี [kan rong phleng pai kap tham nong phleng thii mii nuea rong bon jo tii wii] *n* karaoke

ร้องรอย [rong roi] *n* trace

ร้องเรียน [rong rian] การร้องเรียน [kan

rong rian] *n* petition; ฉันจะร้องเรียนได้
กับใคร? [chan ja rong rian dai kap
khrai] Who can I complain to?; ฉันอยาก
ร้องเรียน [chan yak rong rian] I'd like to
make a complaint

ร้องไห้ [rong hai] *v* cry, weep; ร้องไห้
สะอึกสะอื้น [rong hai sa uek sa uen] *v*
sob

ร่อน [ron] เครื่องร่อน [khrueang ron] *n*
glider; เครื่องร่อน [khrueang ron] *n*
hang-gliding; การร่อน [kan ron] *n*
gliding

ร้อน [ron] *adj* hot; เครื่องทำความร้อน
[khrueang tham khwam ron] *n* heater,
heather; ร้อนและอบ [ron lae op] *adj*
stifling; ร้อนมาก [ron mak] *adj*
sweltering; มันร้อนไปหน่อย [man ron
pai noi] It's a bit too hot

ร้อนใน [ron nai] *n* heartburn

ร้อนลง [ron long] นำร้อนลง [nam ron
long] *vi* land

รอบ [rop] คุณพาเราดูรอบ ๆ ได้ไหม? [khun
pha rao du rop rop dai mai] Could you
show us around?

รอบๆ [rop rop] *adv* around

รอบคอบ [rop khop] ซึ่งทำอย่างรอบคอบ
[sueng tham yang rop khop] *adj*
deliberate; อย่างละเอียดรอบคอบ [yang
la iat rop khop] *adv* thoroughly; อย่าง
รอบคอบ [yang rop khop] *adv*
deliberately

รอบล้อม [rop lom] บริเวณที่รอบล้อม [bo ri
wen thii rop lom] *npl* surroundings

รอม [rom] ซีดี-รอม [si di -rom] *n*
CD-ROM

รอย [roi] รอยแตก [roi taek] *n* crack
(*fracture*); รอยกัด [roi kat] *n* bite; รอยจีบ
[roi chip] *n* plait

ร้อย [roi] ที่หนึ่งร้อย [thii nueng roi]
number hundred

รอยขวาน [roi khuan] *n* scratch

รอยฉีก [roi chik] *n* tear (*split*)

รอยเท้า [roi thao] *n* footprint

รอยโท [roi tho] นายร้อยโท [nai roi tho]

n lieutenant

รอยบุ๋ม [roi bum] ทำให้เป็นรอยบุ๋ม [tham
hai pen roi bum] *v* dent

รอยเปื้อน [roi puean] *n* smudge, stain

รอยย่น [roi yon] รอยย่นบนผิว [roi yon
bon phio] *n* wrinkle; ซึ่งมีรอยย่น [sueng
mii roi yon] *adj* wrinkled

รอยยิ้ม [roi yim] *n* smile; หน้าที่มีรอยยิ้ม
[na thii mii roi yim] *n* smiley

รอยยิ้มกว้าง [roi yim kwang] ลำแสง คาน
รับน้ำหนัก รอยยิ้มกว้าง [lam saeng, khan
rap nam nak, roi yim kwang] *n* beam

รอยเย็บ [roi yep] *n* stitch

ร้อยละ [roi la] อัตราร้อยละ [at tra roi la] *n*
percentage

ระเกะระกะ [ra ke ra ka] กองระเกะระกะ
[kong ra ke ra ka] *n* clutter

ระฆัง [ra khang] *n* bell; การตีระฆัง [kan ti
ra khang] *n* toll

ระงับ [ra ngap] หยุด ระงับ ปิดกั้น [yut, ra
ngab, pit kan] *vt* stop

ระดับ [ra dap] *n* level; ระดับชั้น [ra dap
chan] *n* grade; ระดับตามแนวราบ [ra dap
tam naeo rap] *adj* level

ระดับเสียง [ra dap siang] *n* pitch (*sound*)

ระนาด [ra nat] ระนาดฝรั่ง [ra nat fa rang]
n xylophone

ระบบ [ra bop] *n* system; ระบบเครือข่ายที่
ใช้ประโยชน์ของเทคโนโลยีของอินเตอร์เน็ต
[ra bop khruea khai thii chai pra yot
khong thek no lo yii khong in toe net]
n intranet; ระบบราชการ [ra bop rat cha
kan] *n* bureaucracy; ระบบการส่งข้อความ
ทางโทรศัพท์ [ra bop kan song kho
khwam thang tho ra sap] *n* MMS

ระบาด [ra bat] การแพร่ระบาดอย่างรวดเร็ว
[kan prae ra bat yang ruat reo] *n*
epidemic

ระบาย [ra bai] ระบาย ขอบ [ra bai khop] *n*
fringe; ระบายลม [ra bai lom] *v* wind
(*with a blow etc.*); ระบายออก [ra bai ok]
vt drain

ระบายอากาศ [ra bai a kat] การระบาย
อากาศ [kan ra bai a kat] *n* ventilation

ระบำ [ra bam] ระบำปลายเท้า [ra bam plai thao] *n* ballet; นักเต้นระบำปลายเท้า [nak ten ra bam plai thao] *n* ballet dancer

ระบุ [ra bu] *v* specify

ระเบิด [ra boet] *n* explosive ▷ *v* burst, explode; ลูกระเบิด [luk ra boet] *n* bomb; ระเบิดที่ตั้งเวลาได้ [ra boet thii tang we la dai] *n* time bomb; ระเบิดปรมาณู [ra boet pa ra ma nu] *n* atom bomb

ระเบียง [ra biang] *n* balcony, terrace; ราว ระเบียง [rao ra biang] *n* banister; คุณมี ห้องที่มีระเบียงไหม? [khun mii hong thii mii ra biang mai] Do you have a room with a balcony?; ฉันไปทานที่ระเบียงได้ ไหม? [chan pai than thii ra biang dai mai] Can I eat on the terrace?

ระเบียบ [ra biap] ไม่เป็นระเบียบเรียบร้อย [mai pen ra biap riap roi] *adj* untidy; ความเป็นระเบียบ [khwam pen ra biap] *v* order; ความไม่เป็นระเบียบ [khwam mai pen ra biap] *n* muddle

ระเบียบวินัย [ra biap wi nai] การทำให้มี ระเบียบวินัย [kan tham hai mii ra biap wi nai] *n* self-discipline

ระมัดระวัง [ra mat ra wang] *adj* careful, cautious ▷ *vi* mind; ไม่ระมัดระวัง [mai ra mat ra wang] *adj* careless; การระมัดระวัง ไว้ก่อน [kan ra mat ra wang wai kon] *n* precaution; อย่างระมัดระวัง [yang ra mat ra wang] *adv* carefully, cautiously

ระยะทาง [ra ya thang] ระยะทางเป็นไมล์ [ra ya thang pen mai] *n* mileage

ระยะเวลา [ra ya we la] *n* period, session; ระยะเวลาที่กำหนด [ra ya we la thii kam not] *n* term (*description*); ระยะเวลา ทดลอง [ra ya we la thot long] *n* trial period; ระยะเวลายาวนาน [ra ya we la yao nan] *n* cycle (*recurring period*)

ระหว่าง [ra wang] *prep* between; ใน ระหว่าง [nai ra wang] *prep* during; ใน ระหว่างนั้น [nai ra wang nan] *adv* meantime; ระหว่างกลาง [ra wang klang] *adj* intermediate

ระหว่างประเทศ [ra wang pra thet] บริษัท

ระหว่างประเทศ [bo ri sat ra wang pra tet] *n* multinational; ขอการ์ดโทรศัพท์ ระหว่างประเทศหนึ่งใบ [kho kat tho ra sap ra wang pra tet nueng bai] An international phone card, please

รัก [rak] *v* love; มีใจรักชาติ [mii jai rak chat] *adj* patriotic; ใช่ ฉันรักที่จะ... [chai chan rak thii ja...] Yes, I'd love to; ฉัน รัก... [chan rak...] I love...

รักใคร่ [rak khrai] เรื่องรักใคร่ [rueang rak khrai] *n* romance; เกี่ยวกับเรื่องรัก ใคร่ [kiao kap rueang rak khrai] *adj* romantic; ซึ่งรักใคร่ [sueng rak khrai] *adj* affectionate

รักบี้ [rak bi] กีฬารักบี้ [ki la rak bii] *n* rugby; การยื้อยุดหยุดฝ่ายตรงข้ามในการ ครองลูกฟุตบอลหรือรักบี้ [kan yue yut fai trong kham nai kan khrong luk fut bon rue rak bii] *n* tackle

รักแร้ [rak rae] *n* armpit

รักษา [rak sa] *v* heal, cure; ไม่สามารถ รักษาได้ [mai sa mat rak sa dai] *adv* terminally; รักษาไว้ที่ระดับปัจจุบัน [rak sa wai thii ra dap pat chu ban] *v* keep up, keep up with; การเก็บรักษา [kan kep rak sa] *n* reserve (*retention*)

รักษาการณ์ [rak sa kan] หน่วยรักษาการณ์ ตามชายฝั่งทะเล [nuai rak sa kan tam chai fang tha le] *n* coastguard

รักษาการแทน [rak sa kan thaen] *adj* acting

รัง [rang] *n* nest

รังเกียจ [rang kiat] ทำให้เป็นที่รังเกียจ [tham hai pen thii rang kiat] *adj* repellent; น่ารังเกียจ [na rang kiat] *adj* lousy, nasty, obnoxious, revolting

รังแก [rang kae] กดขี่รังแก [kot khii rang kae] *v* bully

รังไข่ [rang khai] รังไข่ของสตรี [rang khai khong sa tree] *n* ovary

รังควาน [rang khwan] การรังควาน [kan rang khwan] *n* harassment

รังแค [rang khae] *n* dandruff

รังสี [rang si] *n* radiation; รังสีแม่เหล็ก

ไฟฟ้าชนิดหนึ่งผ่านสิ่งของบางประเภทได้ [rang sii mae lek fai fa cha nit nueng phan sing khong bang pra phet dai] *n* X-ray; ถ่ายภาพด้วยรังสีเอ็กซ์ [thai phap duai rang sii ex] *v* X-ray

รัฐ [rat] กำกับดูแลโดยรัฐ [kam kap du lae doi rat] *v* nationalize

รัฐธรรมนูญ [rat tha tham ma nun] *n* constitution

รัฐบาล [rat tha ban] *n* government

รัฐมนตรี [rat tha mon tri] *n* minister (*government*); คณะรัฐมนตรี [kha na rat tha mon tree] *n* cabinet

รัฐศาสตร์ [rat tha sat] คณะรัฐศาสตร์ [kha na rat tha sat] *n* law school

รัฐสภา [rat tha sa pha] *n* parliament; ที่นั่งในรัฐสภา [thii nang nai rat tha sa pha] *n* seat (*constituency*)

รัดรูป [rat rup] *adj* skin-tight

รับ [rap] รับเอามา [rap ao ma] *v* adopt; การรับไว้ [kan rap wai] *adv* reception; การรับสมาชิกใหม่ [kan rap sa ma chik mai] *n* recruitment; คุณได้รับอีเมลล์ฉันไหม? [khun dai rap e mail chan mai] Did you get my email?

รับจ้าง [rap chang] รถรับจ้าง [rot rap chang] *n* cab; ชนชั้นผู้รับจ้าง [chon chan phu rap chang] *adj* working-class

รับประกัน [rap pra kan] *v* guarantee; การรับประกัน [kan rap pra kan] *n* guarantee, warranty

รับประทาน [rap pra than] *vt* eat; คนที่มารับประทานในร้านอาหาร [khon thii ma rap pra than nai ran a han] *n* diner

รับผิดชอบ [rap phit chop] ไม่รับผิดชอบ [mai rap phit chop] irresponsible; ความรับผิดชอบ [khwam rap phit chop] *n* responsibility; อย่างรับผิดชอบ [yang rap phit chop] *adj* responsible

รับมรดก [rap mo ra dok] *v* inherit

รับมือ [rap mue] *v* tackle; รับมือได้ [rap mue dai] *v* cope (with)

รับรอง [rap rong] หนังสือรับรอง [nang sue rap rong] *npl* credentials; การรับรองแขก

[kan rap rong khaek] *n* hospitality

รับเลี้ยง [rap liang] รับเลี้ยงเป็นลูก [rap liang pen luk] *adj* adopted; สถานรับเลี้ยงเด็ก [sa than rap liang dek] *n* nursery; การรับเลี้ยงบุตรบุญธรรม [kan rap liang but bun tham] *n* adoption

รัม [ram] เหล้ารัม [lao ram] *n* rum

รั่ว [rua] *vi* leak; การรั่ว [kan rua] *n* leak; เครื่องทำความร้อนรั่ว [khrueang tham khwam ron rua] There is a leak in the radiator; แท็งค์น้ำมันรั่ว [thang nam man rua] The petrol tank is leaking

รั้ว [rua] *n* fence, hedge; รั้วสำหรับแข่งกระโดดข้าม [rua sam rap khaeng kra dot kham] *n* hurdle

รัสเซีย [rut sia] *adj* เกี่ยวกับรัสเซีย [kiao kap ras sia] *adj* Russian ▷ *n* ชาวรัสเซีย [chao ras sia] *n* Russian (*person*); ประเทศรัสเซีย [pra tet ras sia] *n* Russia

รา [ra] *n* mould (*fungus*); ซึ่งปกคลุมด้วยรา [sueng pok khlum duai ra] *adj* mouldy

ราก [rak] *n* root

รากฐาน [rak than] *n* basis; รากฐานสิ่งก่อสร้าง [rak than sing ko sang] *npl* foundations; ซึ่งเป็นรากฐาน [sueng pen rak than] *adj* based

ราคา [ra kha] *n* price; มีราคาสูง [mii ra kha sung] *adj* dear (*expensive*); ราคาลดสำหรับนักเรียน [ra kha lot sam rap nak rian] *n* student discount; ราคาขาย [ra kha khai] *n* selling price

ราง [rang] *n* rail; รางอาหารหรือน้ำสำหรับสัตว์ [rang a han rue nam sam rap sat] *n* trough

ร่าง [rang] ร่างกฎหมาย [rang kot mai] *n* bill (*legislation*)

ร่างกาย [rang kai] *n* body, physical; เกี่ยวกับร่างกาย [kiao kap rang kai] *adj* physical

ร่างภาพ [rang phap] *v* sketch

รางวัล [rang wan] *n* award, prize, reward; ให้เงินรางวัล [hai ngoen rang wan] *vt* tip (*reward*); การให้เงินรางวัล [kan hai ngen rang wan] *n* tip (*reward*);

การให้รางวัล [kan hai rang wan] *n* prize-giving

ราชการ [rat cha kan] ระบบราชการ [ra bop rat cha kan] *n* bureaucracy; สตรีที่ รับราชการทหาร [sa tree thii rap rat cha kan tha han] *n* servicewoman; หน่วย สืบราชการลับ [nuai suep rat cha kan lap] *n* secret service

ราชวงศ์ [rat cha wong] เกี่ยวกับราชวงศ์ [kiao kap rat cha wong] *adj* royal

ราชอาณาจักร [rat cha a na chak] *n* kingdom

ราตรีสวัสดิ์ [ra tri sa wat] Good night

ร้าน [ran] *n* shop; เจ้าของร้าน [chao khong ran] *n* shopkeeper; ร้านเสริมสวย [ran soem suai] *n* beauty salon; ร้านรับ พนัน [ran rap pha nan] *n* betting shop; ร้านขายยา [ran khai ya] *n* pharmacy; ร้านอาหารที่นำเข้าจากต่างประเทศเช่น ไส้กรอก เนื้อรมควันและอื่น ๆ [ran a han thii nam khao chak tang pra tet chen sai krok nuea rom khwan lae uen uen] *n* delicatessen

ร้านค้า [ran kha] *n* store

ร้านอาหาร [ran a han] *n* restaurant

ราบ [rap] *adj* flat; ราบเรียบ [rap riap] *adj* plain; ที่ราบ [thii rap] *n* flat, plain

ราบรื่น [rap ruen] ไม่สนุก ไม่ราบรื่น [mai sa nuk, mai rap ruen] *adj* unpleasant

ราบเรียบ [rap riap] *adj* even

ร้าย [rai] เลวร้าย [leo rai] *adj* horrible; ชั่ว ร้าย [chua rai] *adj* evil; ร้านขายยาที่ใกล้ ที่สุดอยู่ที่ไหน? [ran khai ya thii klai thii sut yu thii nai] Where is the nearest chemist?

รายการ [rai kan] *n* list; ใบรายการส่งสินค้า ที่แสดงราคา [bai rai kan song sin ka thii sa daeng ra kha] *n* invoice; ไม่อยู่ใน รายการ [mai yu nai rai kan] *adj* unlisted; ลงรายการ [long rai kan] *v* list

รายการอาหาร [rai kan a han] ขอรายการ อาหาร [kho rai kan a han] The menu, please; คุณมีรายการอาหารเด็กไหม? [khun mii rai kan a han dek mai] Do

you have a children's menu?

รายงาน [rai ngan] *v* report; รายงาน การ บรรยาย [rai ngan, kan ban yai] *n* account (report); การรายงาน [kan rai ngan] *n* report; บัตรรายงาน [bat rai ngan] *n* report card; ฉันจำเป็นต้องมี รายงานของตำรวจสำหรับการประกัน [chan cham pen tong mii rai ngan khong tam ruat sam rap kan pra kan] I need a police report for my insurance

รายชื่อ [rai chue] รายชื่อและที่อยู่ของคนที่ ได้รับข่าวสาร โฆษณาและข้อมูลเป็นประจำ [rai chue lae thii yu khong khon thii dai rap khao san khot sa na lae kho mun pen pra cham] *n* mailing list; ราย ชื่อของคนที่รอคิวอยู่ [rai chue khong khon thii ro khio yu] *n* waiting list; สมุดรายชื่อ [sa mut rai chue] *n* directory

รายได้ [rai dai] *n* income ▷ *npl* earnings, proceeds, takings; รายได้ของรัฐที่ได้จาก การเก็บภาษีอากรและธรรมเนียม [rai dai khong rat thii dai chak kan kep pha si a kon lae tham niam] *n* revenue

ร้ายแรง [rai raeng] ที่ร้ายแรง [thii rai raeng] *adj* vicious; อยู่ในขั้นร้ายแรง [yu nai khan rai raeng] *n* terminal; มันร้าย แรงไหม? [man rai raeng mai] Is it serious?

รายละเอียด [rai la iad] *n* detail; ซึ่งมีราย ละเอียดมาก [sueng mii rai la iat mak] *adj* detailed; นี่คือรายละเอียดการประกัน ของฉัน [ni khue rai la iat kan pra kan khong chan] Here are my insurance details

ราว [rao] *n* rail ▷ *npl* railings; ราวระเบียง [rao ra biang] *n* banister; ราวตากผ้า [rao tak pha] *n* clothes line, washing line

ร้าว [rao] *adj* cracked

ราศี [ra si] ราศีกุมภ์ [ra si kum] *n* Aquarius; ราศีเมษ [ra si met] *n* Aries; ราศีมังกร [ra si mang kon] *n* Capricorn; ราศีมิถุน [ra si mi thun] *n* Gemini

ราสเบอรี่ [ras boe ri] ลูกราสเบอรี่ [luk ras

boe ri] n raspberry

ร่ำข้าว [ram khao] ซึ่งไม่ได้เอารำข้าวสาลี
ออก [sueng mai dai ao ram khao sa lii
ok] adj wholemeal

ร่ำคาญ [ram khan] การก่อให้เกิดความ
รำคาญ [kan ko hai koed khwam ram
khan] n nuisance; คำอุทานแสดงความ
รำคาญ [kham u than sa daeng khwam
ram khan] adj damn; ทำให้รำคาญ
[tham hai ram khan] adj annoy,
irritating

ร่ำรวย [ram ruai] ร่ำรวยมั่งคั่ง [ram ruai
mang khang] adj wealthy; ความร่ำรวย
มั่งคั่ง [khwam ram ruai mang khang] n
wealth; ซึ่งร่ำรวย [sueng ram ruai] adj
well-off

ริดสีดวงทวาร [rit si duang tha wan] npl
haemorrhoids; โรคริดสีดวงทวาร [rok rit
sii duang tha wan] npl piles

ริบบิ้น [rip bin] ริบบิ้น เส้นหรือแถบผ้ายาวที่
ใช้ผูกเพื่อประดับตกแต่ง [rip bin, sen rue
thaep pha yao thii chai phuk phuea
pra dap tok taeng] n ribbon

ริมฝีปาก [rim fi pak] n lip

ริเริ่ม [ri roem] การริเริ่ม [kan ri roem] n
initiative; ซึ่งมีความคิดริเริ่ม [sueng mii
khwam kit ri roem] adj creative

ริ้ว [rio] แถบ เส้น ริ้ว [thaep, sen, rio] n
bar (strip)

ริษยา [rit sa ya] v envy

รีด [rit] รีดด้วยเตารีด [riit duai tao riit] v
iron; ฉันจะรีดผ้าได้ที่ไหน? [chan ja riit
pha dai thii nai] Where can I get this
ironed?

รีดนม [rit nom] v milk

รีดผ้า [rit pha] การรีดผ้า [kan rit pha] n
ironing; ที่รีดผ้า [thii riit pha] n ironing
board

รีบ [rip] ความเร่งรีบ [khwam reng rip] n
hurry; วิ่งแข่ง รีบไป เคลื่อนไปอย่างรวดเร็ว
[wing khaeng, rip pai, khluean pai
yang ruat reo] vt run; อย่างรีบเร่ง [yang
rip reng] adv hastily; ฉันกำลังรีบ [chan
kam lang rip] I'm in a hurry

รื่นเริง [ruen roeng] adj jolly, merry

รื้อถอน [rue thon] v demolish

รุกล้ำ [ruk lam] adj poached (caught
illegally)

รุ้ง [rung] รุ้งกินน้ำ [rung kin nam] n
rainbow

รุงรัง [rung rang] สภาพรกรุงรัง [sa phap
rok rung rang] n mess

รุนแรง [run raeng] รุนแรงมาก [run raeng
mak] adj drastic; คนที่มีหัวรุนแรง [khon
thii mii hua run raeng] n extremist;
ความรุนแรง [khwam run raeng] n
violence

รู [ru] n hole; รูที่ให้น้ำไหลออก [ru thii hai
nam lai ok] n plughole

รู้ [ru] v know; รู้ล่วงหน้า [ru luang na] v
foresee; คนที่แกล้งทำเป็นรู้มากกว่าคนอื่น
[khon thii klaeng tham pen ru mak
kwa khon uen] n know-all; ตระหนักรู้
[tra nak ru] adj aware; คุณรู้ไหมว่าจะทำ
นี้ได้อย่างไร? [khun ru mai wa ja tham
ni dai yang rai] Do you know how to
do this?

รู้จัก [ru chak] เป็นที่รู้จัก [pen thii ru
chak] adj known; ไม่มีใครรู้จัก [mai mii
khrai ru chak] adj unknown; ไม่รู้จักคุ้น
เคย [mai ru chak khun khoei] adj
unfamiliar; คุณรู้จักเขาไหม? [khun ru
chak khao mai] Do you know him?

รูด [rut] รูดซิป [rut sip] vi zip (up); รูดซิป
ออก [rut sip ok] v unzip

รูป [rup] รูปวาด [rup wat] n drawing;
กรอบรูป [krop rup] n frame

รูปทรง [rup song] n form

รูปแบบ [rup baep] n format, type

รูปปั้น [rup pan] n statue

รูปภาพ [rup phap] n picture

รูปร่าง [rup rang] n shape

รูปวาด [rup wat] รูปวาดของคน [rup wat
khong khon] n portrait

รู้แล้วรู้รอด [ru laeo ru rot] v get over

รู้สึก [ru suek] v feel; รู้สึกตัว [ru suek tua]
adj conscious; การรู้สึกตัว [kan ru suk
tua] n consciousness; ที่ทำด้วยความรู้สึก

ในด้านดี [thii tham duai khwam ru suek nai dan di] *adj* conscientious; คุณรู้สึกอย่างไรตอนนี้? [khun ru suek yang rai ton nii] How are you feeling now?

รู้สึกตัว [ru suek tua] ไม่รู้สึกตัว [mai ru suek tua] *adj* unconscious

เร่ง [reng] เร่งให้เร็วขึ้น [reng hai reo khuen] *v* speed up; เร่งความเร็ว [reng khwam reo] *v* accelerate; การเร่ง [kan reng] *n* rush

เร่งด่วน [reng duan] ที่จำเป็นเร่งด่วน [thii cham pen reng duan] *adj* urgent

เร่งรีบ [reng rip] *v* hurry, hurry up; เคลื่อนหรือทำอย่างเร่งรีบ [khluean rue tham yang reng rip] *vi* rush; การเร่งรีบ [kan reng rip] *n* urgency

เรดาห์ [re da] *n* radar

เรร่อน [re ron] *vi* drift

เร็ว [reo] *adj* fast; เร่งให้เร็วขึ้น [reng hai reo khuen] *v* speed up; ตัวย่อของเร็วที่สุดเท่าที่จะเป็นไปได้ [tua yo khong reo thii sut thao thii ja pen pai dai] *adv abbr* asap; ฉันคิดว่านาฬิกาฉันเดินเร็ว [chan kit wa na li ka chan doen reo] I think my watch is fast

เร็วๆนี้ [reo reo ni] *adj* recent ▷ *prep* near; เมื่อเร็วๆนี้ [muea reo reo ni] *adv* recently; ในเร็ว ๆ นี้ [nai reo reo nii] *adv* shortly

เรอ [roe] *vi* burp; การเรอ [kan roe] *n* burp

เรา [rao] *pron* us

เราใจ [rao chai] น่าเร้าใจ [na rao jai] *adj* sensational

เริ่ม [roem] *v* begin; เริ่ม เริ่มทำ เริ่มต้น [roem, roem tham, roem ton] *vt* start; เริ่ม ลงมือ ทำให้เกิด [roem, long mue, tham hai koet] *vi* start; เริ่มเดินทาง [roem doen thang] *v* set off, start off; จะเริ่มเมื่อไร? [ja roem muea rai] When does it begin?

เริ่มต้น [roem ton] การเริ่มต้น [kan roem ton] *n* outset

เรียก [riak] *vt* call; เรียกโดยใช้เครื่องขยายเสียงหรือเครื่องส่งสัญญาณติดตามตัว [riak doi chai khrueang kha yai siang rue khrueang song san yan tit tam tua] *v* page; การเรียก การโทรศัพท์ [kan riak, kan tho ra sap] *n* call; ช่วยเรียกบริการรถเสียให้ด้วย [chuai riak bo ri kan rot sia hai duai] Call the breakdown service, please

เรียกร้อง [riak rong] *v* claim, request; แบบฟอร์มการเรียกร้อง [baep fom kan riak rong] *n* claim form; การเรียกร้อง [kan riak rong] *n* claim, request

เรียกหา [riak ha] *v* call for

เรียงความ [riang khwam] *n* essay

เรียน [rian] *v* learn, study; เรียนอย่างหนัก [rian yang nak] *v* swot; ห้องเรียน [hong rian] *n* classroom; การเรียนพิเศษแบบเข้ม [kan rian phi set baep khem] *n* tutorial; ฉันยังเรียนหนังสืออยู่ [chan yang rian nang sue yu] I'm still studying

เรียบ [riap] *adj* smooth; ราบเรียบ [rap riap] *adj* plain

เรียบร้อย [riap roi] *adj* neat; ไม่เป็นระเบียบเรียบร้อย [mai pen ra biap riap roi] *adj* untidy; จัดให้เป็นระเบียบเรียบร้อย [chat hai pen ra biap riap roi] *v* tidy up; ซึ่งไม่เรียบร้อยและสกปรก [sueng mai riap roi lae sok ka prok] *adj* messy

เรือ [rua] *n* boat, ship; เรือเร็ว [rua reo] *n* speedboat; เรือแคนู [rua khae nu] *n* canoe; เรือแตก [rua taek] *n* shipwreck; ลูกเรือ [luk rua] *n* crew, sailor; ตัวเรือ [tua rua] *n* hull; เรือลำแรกมาเมื่อไร? [rua lam raek ma muea rai] When is the first boat?

เรื่อง [rueang] เรื่องเล็ก ๆ น้อย ๆ [rueang lek lek noi noi] *n* trifle; เรื่องสอนใจ [rueang son jai] *n* moral; เรื่องตลก [rueang ta lok] *n* joke

เรื่องราว [rueang rao] *n* story; เรื่องราวที่ติดตามมา [rueang rao thii tit tam ma] *n* sequel; เรื่องราวประเพณีและความเชื่อของผู้คน [rueang rao pra phe ni lae khwam chuea khong phu kon] *n* folklore

เรื่องเล่า [rueang lao] n tale

เรื่องสั้น [rueang san] n short story

เรือชูชีพ [rua chu chip] เรียกเรือชูชีพ [riak rua chu chip] Call out the lifeboat!

เรือดำน้ำ [rua dam nam] n submarine

เรือนกระจก [ruean kra chok] เรือนกระจกสำหรับเก็บต้นไม้ [ruean kra chok sam rap kep ton mai] n conservatory; เรือนกระจกสำหรับปลูกต้นไม้ [ruean kra chok sam rap pluk ton mai] n greenhouse

เรื้อนกวาง [ruean kwang] โรคเรื้อนกวาง [rok ruean kwang] n eczema

เรือนจำ [ruan cham] n prison; เจ้าหน้าที่เรือนจำ [chao na thii ruean cham] n prison officer

เรือใบ [rua bai] n sailing boat; เรือใบสำหรับที่ใช้ท่องเที่ยวหรือแข่งเรือ [rua bai sam rap thii chai thong thiao rue khaeng rua] n yacht

เรื้อรัง [rue rang] adj chronic

แร่ [rae] ที่มีแร่ [thii mii rae] adj mineral; น้ำแร่ [nam rae] n mineral water

แรก [raek] adj initial; เป็นอันดับแรก [pen an dap raek] adj preceding; แต่แรก [tae raek] adv early; ตั้งแต่แรก [tang tae raek] adv initially

แรกเริ่ม [raek roem] โดยแรกเริ่ม [doi raek roem] adv originally

แรง [raeng] ฉันอยากได้อะไรที่แรงกว่านี้ [chan yak dai a rai thii raeng kwa nii] I need something stronger

แรง [raeng] นกแรง [nok raeng] n vulture

แรงกล้า [raeng kla] adj intense

แรงงาน [raeng ngan] n labour

แรงดัน [raeng dan] แรงดันไฟฟ้าที่มีหน่วยเป็นโวลต์ [raeng dan fai fa thii mii nuai pen volt] n voltage; หน่วยแรงดันไฟฟ้า [nuai raeng dan fai fa] n volt

แรงบันดาลใจ [raeng ban dan chai] n motivation, will (motivation); ซึ่งมีแรงบันดาลใจ [sueng mii raeng ban dan jai] adj motivated

แร่ธาตุ [rae that] n mineral

โรค [rok] n disease; เกี่ยวกับโรคประสาท [kiao kap rok pra sat] adj neurotic; โรคเลือดคั่งในสมอง [rok lueat khang nai sa mong] n multiple sclerosis; โรคเรื้อนกวาง [rok ruean kwang] n eczema; โรคกระเพาะปัสสาวะ [rok kra phao pat sa wa] n cystitis; โรคที่มีเม็ดโลหิตขาวมากเกินไป [rok thii mii met lo hit khao mak koen pai] n leukaemia; มีเชื้อไวรัสที่ทำให้เกิดโรคเอดส์ [mii chuea wai ras thii tham hai koet rok aid] adj HIV-positive

โรคจิต [rok chit] เป็นโรคจิต [pen rok chit] adj mental; โรคจิตชนิดหนึ่งที่มีสองบุคลิกในคนคนเดียว [rok chit cha nit nueng thii mii song buk kha lik nai khon khon diao] adj schizophrenic; โรงพยาบาลโรคจิต [rong pha ya baan rok chit] n mental hospital

โรคพิษสุนัขบ้า [rok phit su nak ba] n rabies

โรคหัด [rok hat] ฉันเป็นโรคหัดเมื่อเร็ว ๆ นี้ [chan pen rok hat muea reo reo nii] I had measles recently

โรคหืด [rok huet] ฉันทุกข์ทรมานด้วยโรคหืด [chan thuk tho ra man duai rok huet] I suffer from asthma

โรง [rong] โรงรถ [rong rot] n garage; โรงกลั่น [rong klan] n refinery; โรงกษาปณ์ [rong ka sap] n mint (coins); โรงเล่นกีฬาอยู่ที่ไหน? [rong len ki la yu thii nai] Where is the gym?

โรงกลั่น [rong klan] โรงกลั่นสุรา [rong klan su ra] n distillery

โรงงาน [rong ngan] n factory, plant (site/equipment); โรงงานต้มและกลั่นเหล้า [rong ngan tom lae klan lao] n brewery; ห้องทำงานในโรงงาน [hong tham ngan nai rong ngan] n workshop; ฉันทำงานในโรงงาน [chan tham ngan nai rong ngan] I work in a factory

โรงนา [rong na] n barn

โรงพยาบาล [rong pha ya ban] n

hospital, infirmary; โรงพยาบาลแม่และ
เด็ก [rong pha ya baan mae lae dek] n
maternity hospital; โรงพยาบาลโรคจิต
[rong pha ya baan rok chit] n mental
hospital; เราต้องพาเขาไปโรงพยาบาล
[rao tong pha khao pai rong pha ya
baan] We must get him to hospital

โรงรถ [rong rot] กุญแจดอกไหนเป็นกุญแจ
โรงรถ? [kun jae dok nai pen kun jae
rong rot] Which is the key for the
garage?

โรงเรียน [rong rian] n school; โรงเรียน
เด็กเล็ก [rong rian dek lek] n infant
school; โรงเรียนเด็กเล็กอายุ ๒ ถึง ๕ ปี
[rong rian dek lek a yu song thueng ha
pi] n nursery school; โรงเรียนในตอนเย็น
หรือกลางคืน [rong rian nai ton yen rue
klang khuen] n night school

โรงแรม [rong raem] n hotel; โรงแรมเล็ก
ๆ [rong raeng lek lek] n inn; บริการรับใช้
ในห้องของโรงแรม [bo ri kan rap chai
nai hong khong rong raeng] n room
service; เก้าอี้เข็นสามารถเข้าออกโรงแรม
ของคุณได้ไหม? [kao ii khen sa maat
khao ok rong raeng khong khun dai
mai] Is your hotel accessible to
wheelchairs?

โรงละคร [rong la kon] n theatre; มีการ
แสดงอะไรที่โรงละคร? [mii kan sa daeng
a rai thii rong la khon] What's on at
the theatre?

โรงละคร/โรงโอเปร่า [rong la khon/
rong o pe ra] Theatre/opera

โรงสี [rong si] n mill

โรงหนัง [rong nang] มีหนังอะไรฉายที่โรง
หนัง? [mii nang a rai chai thii rong
nang] What's on at the cinema?

โรงโอเปร่า [rong o pe ra] คืนนี้มีการแสดง
โอเปร่าอะไร? [khuen nii mii kan sa
daeng o pe ra a rai] What's on tonight
at the opera?

โรม [rom] ที่เกี่ยวกับโรม [thii kiao kap
rom] adj Roman

โรมัน [ro man] เกี่ยวกับแบบกรีกและโรมัน
[kiao kap baep krik lae ro man] adj
classical

โรมันคาทอลิค [ro man kha tho rik] ที่
เกี่ยวกับศาสนาโรมันคาทอลิค [thii kiao
kap sat sa na ro man kha tho lik] adj
Roman Catholic; ผู้นับถือนิกายโรมันคา
ทอลิค [phu nap thue ni kai ro man kha
tho lik] n Roman Catholic

โรมาเนีย [ro ma nia] เกี่ยวกับโรมาเนีย
[kiao kap ro ma nia] adj Romanian;
ชาวโรมาเนีย [chao ro ma nia] n
Romanian (person); ประเทศโรมาเนีย
[pra tet ro ma nia] n Romania

ไร่ [rai] บ้านไร่ [baan rai] n farmhouse

ไร้เดียงสา [rai diang sa] adj innocent; ไร้
เดียงสาอย่างเด็ก [rai diang sa yang dek]
adj childish

ไร้สาระ [rai sa ra] adj absurd; เรื่องไร้สาระ
[rueang rai sa ra] n nonsense

ฤ ล

ฤดู [rue du] *n* season; ฤดูใบไม้ร่วง [rue du bai mai ruang] *n* autumn; ฤดูมรสุม [rue du mo ra sum] *n* monsoon; ฤดูถือบวช โดยอดอาหารประจำปีก่อนวันอีสเตอร์ของ ชาวคริสต์ [rue du thue buat doi ot a han pra cham pi kon wan is toe khong chao khris] *n* Lent

ฤดูกาล [rue du kan] ตามฤดูกาล [tam rue du kan] *adj* seasonal; ฤดูกาลที่มีธุรกิจ มาก [rue du kan thii mii thu ra kit mak] *n* high season

ฤดูใบไม้ผลิ [rue du bai mai phli] *n* spring *(season)*, springtime

ฤดูร้อน [rue du ron] *n* summer; เวลาใน ฤดูร้อน [we la nai rue du ron] *n* summertime; วันหยุดในฤดูร้อน [wan yut nai rue du ron] *npl* summer holidays

ฤดูหนาว [rue du nao] *n* winter; กีฬาฤดู หนาว [ki la rue du nao] *npl* winter sports

ลง [long] ลงไป [long pai] *v* go down; ลง มา [long ma] *v* come down, descend; ขอให้ฉันลงจากรถ [kho hai chan long chak rot] Please let me off

ลงคะแนนเสียง [long kha naen siang] *v* vote; การลงคะแนนเสียง [kan long kha naen siang] *n* vote

ลงทะเบียน [long tha bian] *n* recorded delivery ▷ *v* register; เซ็นลงทะเบียนเพื่อ รับเงินสวัสดิการ [sen long tha bian phuea rap ngoen sa wat sa di kan] *v* sign on; ลงทะเบียนเพื่อเข้าพัก [long tha bian phuea khao phak] *v* check in; จะ ใช้เวลานานเท่าไรถ้าส่งแบบลงทะเบียน? [ja chai we la nan thao rai tha song baep long tha bian] How long will it take by registered post?

ลงทุน [long thun] *v* invest; การลงทุน [kan long thun] *n* investment; นักลงทุน [nak long thun] *n* investor

ลงโทษ [long thot] *v* penalize, punish; การลงโทษ [kan long thot] *n* punishment; การลงโทษประหารชีวิต [kan long thot pra han chi wit] *n* capital punishment

ลงมือ [long mue] เริ่ม ลงมือ ทำให้เกิด

[roem, long mue, tham hai koet] vi
start

ลด [lot] ลดราคา [lot ra kha] v knock
down; ลดตำแหน่ง [lot tam naeng] v
relegate; คุณช่วยลดเสียงลงได้ไหม?
[khun chuai lot siang long dai mai]
Please could you lower the volume?

ลดน้ำหนัก [lot nam nak] ควบคุมอาหาร
เพื่อลดน้ำหนัก [khuap khum a han
phuea lot nam nak] v diet

ลดลง [lot long] v decrease; การทำให้ลด
ลง [kan tham hai lot long] n reduction;
ทำให้ลดลง [tham hai lot long] v
diminish, reduce, turn down

ลดหลั่น [lot lun] ทำให้ลดหลั่นเป็นชั้น [tham
hai lot lan pen chan] adj terraced

ล้น [lon] ไหลบ่า ไหลล้น [lai ba, lai lon] vi
flood

ลบ [lop] prep minus ▷ v delete; ลบออก
[lop ok] v deduct, erase; ลบออกไป [lop
ok pai] v leave out, subtract

ลม [lom] n wind; ลมแรงพัดกะทันหัน [lom
raeng phat kra tan han] n gust; ลมพายุ
[lom pha yu] n gale

ลมบ้าหมู [lom ba mu] โรคลมบ้าหมู [rok
lom ba mu] n epileptic; อาการชักของลม
บ้าหมู [a kan chak khong lom ba mu] n
epileptic fit

ล้มละลาย [lom la lai] adj bankrupt

ล้มเลิก [lom loek] การล้มเลิก [kan lom
loek] n abolition

ลมหายใจ [lom hai chai] เครื่องวัดปริมาณ
แอลกอฮอล์จากลมหายใจ [khrueang wat
pa ri man aen ko ho chak lom hai jai]
n Breathalyser®

ล้มเหลว [lom leo] vi fail; ความล้มเหลว
[khwam lom leo] n failure, flop

ล้วงกระเป๋า [luang kra pao] นักล้วง
กระเป๋า [nak luang kra pao] n
pickpocket

ลวงตา [luang ta] ภาพลวงตา [phap luang
ta] n illusion

ล่วงเวลา [luang we la] n overtime

ล่วงหน้า [luang na] adv beforehand; จ่าย

ล่วงหน้า [chai luang na] adj prepaid

ลวด [luat] n wire; เส้นลวด [sen luat] n
barbed wire

ลวดเย็บกระดาษ [luat yep kra dat] n
staple (wire); ติดด้วยลวดเย็บกระดาษ [tit
duai luat yep kra daat] v staple

ลวดลาย [luat lai] ลวดลายที่ทำด้วยกระจกสี
[luat lai thii tham duai kra chok sii] n
mosaic

ล่อ [lo] n mule

ล้อ [lo] n wheel; ล้ออะไหล่ [lo a lai] n
spare wheel; การขับทั้งสี่ล้อ [kan khap
thang si lo] n four-wheel drive

ลอก [lok] การลอกเลียนแบบ [kan lok lian
baep] n imitation

ล็อกออน [lok on] ฉันล็อกออนไม่ได้ [chan
lok on mai dai] I can't log on

ล็อค [lok] ล็อคประตู [lok pra tu] Keep the
door locked; ฉันล็อคตัวเองออกนอกห้อง
[chan lok tua eng ok nok hong] I have
locked myself out of my room

ล็อคเกอร์ [lok koe] ตู้ล็อคเกอร์ [tu lok koe]
n locker; ตู้ล็อคเกอร์เก็บกระเป๋าเดินทาง [tu
lok koe kep kra pao doen thang] n
left-luggage locker; ล็อคเกอร์ของฉันอัน
ไหน? [lok koe khong chan an nai]
Which locker is mine?

ลอง [long] ลองสวมใส่ [long suam sai] v
try on; ลองดู [long du] v try out; คุณลอง
ใหม่อีกทีได้ไหม? [khun long mai ik thii
dai mai] Can you try again later?

ล่องเรือ [long ruea] การล่องเรือ [kan long
ruea] n cruise; เราจะล่องเรือเมื่อไร? [rao ja
long ruea muea rai] When do we sail?

ล่อใจ [lo chai] adj tempting; การล่อใจ
[kan lo jai] n temptation

ลอน [lon] หยักศก ที่เป็นลอน [yak sok, thii
pen lon] adj curly; ผมเป็นลอน [phom
pen lon] n curl

ลอนดอน [lon don] n London

ลอบ [lop] การลอบวางเพลิง [kan lop wang
phloeng] n arson

ล็อบบี้ [lop bi] ฉันจะไปพบคุณที่ล็อบบี้ [chan
ja pai phop khun thii lop bi] I'll meet

you in the lobby

ล้อม [lom] การปิดล้อม [kan pit lom] n
blockage

ล้อมรอบ [lom rop] prep round ▷ v
surround

ลอย [loi] ลอยบนผิวน้ำหรือในอากาศ [loi
bon phio nam rue nai a kaat] vi float;
สิ่งที่ลอยได้เช่นแพ [sing thii loi dai chen
phae] n float

ล้อเล่น [lo len] v kid

ล้อเลียน [lo lian] v mimic

ละ [la] ราคาห้องคนละเท่าไร? [ra kha hong
khon la thao rai] How much is it per
person?; ราคาห้องคืนละเท่าไร? [ra kha
hong khuen la thao rai] How much is it
per night?; ราคาห้องอาทิตย์ละเท่าไร? [ra
kha hong a thit la thao rai] How much
is it per week?

ละคร [la kon] n drama; โรงละครสัตว์
[rong la khon sat] n circus; ละครเพลง
[la khon phleng] n musical; ละครตลก
[la khon ta lok] n comedy

ละติน [la tin] ภาษาละติน [pha sa la tin] n
Latin

ละตินอเมริกา [la tin a me ri ka] n Latin
America

ละทิ้ง [la thing] v abandon

ละมั่ง [la mang] n antelope

ละเมอ [la moe] เดินละเมอ [doen la moe] v
sleepwalk

ละลาย [la lai] vt dissolve; ละลาย ทำให้
หลอมละลาย [la lai, tham hai lom la lai]
vt melt; ซึ่งสามารถละลายได้ [sueng sa
maat la lai dai] adj soluble; ตัวทำละลาย
[tua tham la lai] n solvent

ละเลย [la loei] v ignore; การละเลย [kan la
loei] n neglect

ละออง [la ong] ละอองของเหลว [la ong
khong leo] n aerosol

ละอองน้ำ [la ong nam] n spray

ละเอียด [la iat] ละเอียดถี่ถ้วน [la iat thi
thuan] adj thorough; ละเอียดอ่อน [la iat
on] adj delicate; อย่างละเอียดรอบคอบ
[yang la iat rop khop] adv thoroughly

ลักขโมย [lak kha moi] v steal

ลักเซมเบิร์ก [lak sem boek] ประเทศลัก
เซมเบิร์ก [pra tet lak sem boek] n
Luxembourg

ลักพาตัว [lak pha tua] v abduct, kidnap

ลักลอบนำเข้า [lak lop nam khao] v
smuggle; การลักลอบนำเข้า [kan lak lop
nam khao] n smuggling; ผู้ลักลอบนำเข้า
[phu lak lop nam khao] n smuggler

ลักษณะ [lak sa na] ลักษณะเฉพาะ [lak sa
na cha pho] adj unique; ลักษณะหน้าตา
[lak sa na na ta] n feature; ลักษณะ
ท่าทาง [lak sa na tha thang] n manner

ลัง [lang] หีบ ลัง กล่อง [hip, lang, klong]
n chest (storage)

ลังเล [lang le] adj indecisive; ลังเลใจ
[lang le jai] v hesitate; อย่างไม่ลังเล
[yang mai lang le] adv readily

ลัทธิ [lat thi] เกี่ยวกับลัทธิเสรีนิยม [kiao
kap lat thi se ri ni yom] adj liberal; เกี่ยว
กับลัทธิชนชาติ [kiao kap lat thi chon
chat] adj racist; ลัทธิมาร์กซ์ [lat thi
mark] n Marxism

ลับ [lap] หน่วยสืบราชการลับ [nuai suep
rat cha kan lap] n secret service; อย่าง
ลับ ๆ [yang lap lap] adv secretly

ลับสุดยอด [lap sut yot] adj top-secret

ลา [la (laa)] n donkey;
การลาหยุดหลังคลอด [kan la yut lang
khlot] n maternity leave

ลาก [lak] vt drag; ลากไป [lak pai] v tow
away

ลาก่อน [la kon] excl bye!, bye-bye!,
cheerio!, farewell!, goodbye!

ล่าง [lang] ข้างล่าง [khang laang] adv
beneath, downstairs; ข้างล่าง [khang
laang] adv downstairs; ชั้นล่าง [chan
lang] n ground floor

ล้าง [lang] เครื่องล้างจาน [khrueang lang
chan] n dishwasher; ล้างจาน [lang
chan] v wash up; ล้างออกไป [lang ok
pai] v wash; ฉันล้างมือได้ที่ไหน? [chan
lang mue dai thii nai] Where can I
wash my hands?

ล้างบาป [lang bap] การทำพิธีล้างบาปและ
ตั้งชื่อ [kan tham phi thii lang bap lae
tang chue] n christening; ผู้ทำพิธีล้าง
บาป [phu tham phi thi lang bap] n
Baptist

ล่าช้า [la cha] v delay; ความล่าช้า
[khwam la cha] n delay; ทำให้ล่าช้า
[tham hai la cha] adj delayed; เที่ยวบิน
ล่าช้า [thiao bin la cha] The flight has
been delayed

ลาดชัน [lat chan] ที่ลาดชันสำหรับฝึกเล่น
สกี [thii lat chan sam rap fuek len sa
ki] n nursery slope

ลาดตระเวน [lat tra wen] รถลาดตระเวน
[rot lay tra wen] n patrol car; การลาด
ตระเวน [kan lat tra wen] n patrol

ลาดเอียง [lat iang] พื้นที่ลาดเอียง [phuen
thii lat iang] n slope

ลาน [lan] ลานเล่นสเก็ต [lan len sa ket] n
skating rink; ลานเล่นสเก็ตน้ำแข็ง [lan
len sa ket nam khaeng] n rink; ลานน้ำ
แข็งเล่นสเก็ต [lan nam khaeng len sa
ket] n ice rink

ล้าน [lan] adj bald; หนึ่งล้าน [nueng lan] n
million; พันล้าน [phan lan] n billion

ลานบิน [lan bin] n runway

ลาป่วย [la puai] การลาป่วย [kan la puai]
n sick leave; ค่าจ้างในระหว่างที่ลาป่วย
[kha chang nai ra wang thii la puai] n
sick pay; จดหมายลาป่วยที่แพทย์เป็นผู้
เขียน [chot mai la puai thii phaet pen
phu khian] n sick note

ล่าม [lam] n interpreter; คุณช่วยเป็นล่าม
แปลให้เราได้ไหม? [khun chuai pen
laam plae hai rao dai mai] Could you
act as an interpreter for us, please?; ฉัน
ต้องการล่าม [chan tong kan lam] I need
an interpreter

ลามก [la mok] adj obscene; หนังสือ ภาพ
เรื่องเขียน หนังและศิลปะที่ลามก [nang
sue phap rueang khian nang lae sin la pa
thii la mok] n pornography; ตัวย่อของ
หนังสือ ภาพ เรื่องเขียน หนังและศิลปะที่
ลามก [tua yo khong nang sue phap

rueang khian nang lae sin la pa thii la
mok] n porn; ที่ลามก [thii la mok] adj
pornographic

ลาย [lai] ซึ่งมีลาย [sueng mii lai] adj
stripy; ที่มีลายตารางหมากรุก [thii mii lai
ta rang mak ruk] adj checked

ลายเซ็น [lai sen] n autograph, signature

ลายมือ [lai mue] n handwriting

ลายสก็อต [lai sa kot] adj tartan

ลาว [lao] ประเทศลาว [pra tet lao] n Laos

ลาวา [la wa] หินลาวา [hin la va] n lava

ลาเวนเดอร์ [la wen doe] ต้นลาเวนเดอร์
ดอกมีสีฟ้ามวง [ton la wen doe dok mii
sii fa muang] n lavender

ล้าสมัย [la sa mai] adj out-of-date; ที่ล้า
สมัย [thii la sa mai] adj obsolete

ล่าสัตว์ [la sat] v hunt; การล่าสัตว์ [kan la
sat] n hunting

ล่าสุด [la sut] adv last

ลาหยุด [la yut] การลาหยุด [kan la yut] n
leave; การลาหยุดของพ่อเพื่อเลี้ยงดูลูกแรก
เกิด [kan la yut khong pho phuea liang
du luk raek koet] n paternity leave

ลาออก [la ok] v resign

ล้ำค่า [lam kha] adj precious

ลำดับ [lam dap] v range; ที่ต่อเนื่องตาม
ลำดับ [thii to nueang tam lam dap] adj
consecutive

ลำต้น [lam ton] n trunk

ลำธาร [lam than] n stream

ลำบาก [lam bak] สภาวะลำบาก [sa pha
wa lam bak] n dilemma; ความยาก
ลำบาก [khwam yak lam bak] n
difficulty

ลำแสง [lam saeng] ลำแสง คานรับน้ำหนัก
รอยยิ้มกว้าง [lam saeng, khan rap nam
nak, roi yim kwang] n beam

ลำไส้ [lam sai] npl bowels

ล้ำหน้า [lam na] ที่อยู่ในตำแหน่งล้ำหน้า
[thii yu nai tam naeng lam na] adj
offside

ลำเอียง [lam iang] ไม่ลำเอียง [mai lam
iang] adj impartial; ซึ่งลำเอียง [sueng
lam iang] adj biased

ลิขสิทธิ์ [lik kha sit] n copyright

ลิคเตนสไตน์ [lik ten sa tai] ประเทศ ลิคเตนสไตน์ [pra tet lik ten sa tai] n Liechtenstein

ลิง [ling] n monkey; ลิงกอริลล่า [ling ko ril la] n gorilla; ลิงชิมแปนซี [ling chim paen si] n chimpanzee

ลิตร [lit] หน่วยวัดปริมาณ ๑ ลิตร [nuai wat pa ri man nueng lit] n litre

ลิทัวเนีย [li thua nia] เกี่ยวกับลิทัวเนีย [kiao kap li thua nia] adj Lithuanian; ชาวลิทัวเนีย [chao li thua nia] n Lithuanian (person); ประเทศลิทัวเนีย [pra tet li thua nia] n Lithuania

ลิ้น [lin] n tongue

ลิ้นชัก [lin chak] n drawer; กล่องหรือลิ้น ชักเก็บเงิน [klong rue lin chak kep ngen] n till; ลิ้นชักติด [lin chak tit] The drawer is jammed

ลินิน [li nin] ผ้าลินิน [pha li nin] n linen

ลิเบีย [li bia] เกี่ยวกับลิเบีย [kiao kap li bia] adj Libyan; ชาวลิเบีย [chao li bia] n Libyan; ประเทศลิเบีย [pra tet li bia] n Libya

ลิปสติก [lip sa tik] n lipstick

ลิฟต์ [lip] n lift (up/down); มีลิฟต์ไหม? [mii lift mai] Is there a lift?; ลิฟต์อยู่ ที่ไหน? [lift yu thii nai] Where is the lift?; คุณมีลิฟต์สำหรับเก้าอี้เข็นคนพิการ ไหม? [khun mii lift sam rap kao ii khen khon phi kan mai] Do you have a lift for wheelchairs?

ลิฟท์ [lip] มีลิฟท์ในตึกนี้ไหม? [mii lift nai tuek nii mai] Is there a lift in the building?

ลิลลี่ [lin li] ดอกไม้ชื่อลิลลี่ออฟเดอะแวลลี่ มีสี ขาวมีกลิ่นหอม [dok mai chue lil li of doe vael li mii sii khao mii klin hom] n lily of the valley; ดอกลิลลี่ [dok lil li] n lily

ลี้ภัย [li phai] การลี้ภัย [kan lii phai] n exile; ที่ลี้ภัย [thii lii phai] n asylum; ผู้ แสวงหาที่ลี้ภัย [phu sa waeng ha thii lii phai] n asylum seeker

ลึก [luek] adj deep; ความลึก [khwam

luek] n depth; อย่างลึกมาก [yang luek mak] adv deeply; น้ำลึกแค่ไหน? [nam luek khae nai] How deep is the water?

ลึกซึ้ง [luek sueng] ผิวเผิน ไม่ลึกซึ้ง ไม่ สำคัญ [phio phoen, mai luek sueng, mai sam khan] adj superficial

ลึกลับ [luek lap] ความลึกลับ [khwam luek lap] n mystery; ที่ลึกลับ [thii luek lap] adj mysterious

ลื่น [luen] v skid; ลื่นไถล [luen tha lai] adj slippery; ลื่นไถลไป [luen tha lai pai] vi slip; การลื่นไถล [kan luen tha lai] n slide; รถลื่น [rot luen] The car skidded

ลืม [luem] v forget; โรคลืม อัลไซเมอร์ [rok luem, al sai moe] n Alzheimer's disease; ไม่สามารถที่จะลืมได้ [mai sa mat thii ja luem dai] adj unforgettable; ที่ถูกลืม [thii thuk luem] adj forgotten; ฉันลืมกุญแจ [chan luem kun jae] I've forgotten the key

ลุก [luk] ลุกขึ้น [luk khuen] v get up; คุณ ช่วยพาฉันลุกขึ้นได้ไหม? [khun chuai pha chan luk khuen dai mai] Can you help me get on, please?

ลุกขึ้น [luk khuen] v rise; การลุกขึ้น [kan luk khuen] n rise

ลุง [lung] n uncle

ลู่ [lu] ลู่ที่ใช้แข่งขันความเร็ว [lu thii chai khaeng khan khwam reo] n racetrack

ลูก [luk] ลูกเลี้ยง [luk liang] n foster child; ลูกเรือ [luk ruea] n crew; ลูกเขย [luk khoei] n son-in-law; ลูก ๆ ของฉัน อยู่ในรถ [luk luk khong chan yu nai rot] My children are in the car

ลูกกวาด [luk kwat] npl sweets

ลูกเกด [luk ket] n currant, raisin; ลูกเกด ชนิดไม่มีเมล็ด [luk ket cha nit mai mii ma let] n sultana

ลูกขนไก่ [luk khon kai] n shuttlecock

ลูกข่าง [luk khang] n top

ลูกขุน [luk khun] คำตัดสินของคณะลูกขุน [kham tat sin khong kha na luk khun] n verdict; คณะลูกขุน [kha na luk khun] n jury

ลูกค้า [lik kha] n client, customer

ลูกชิ้น [luk chin] n meatball

ลูกโซ่ [luk so] ข้อลูกโซ่ [kho luk so] n link

ลูกดอก [luk dok] n dart; ลูกดอกหลายลูก [luk dok lai luk] npl darts

ลูกเต๋า [luk tao] npl dice

ลูกทุ่ง [luk thung] ดนตรีลูกทุ่ง [don tree luk thung] n folk music

ลูกบอล [luk bon] n ball (toy); ไม้ตีลูกบอล [mai ti luk bon] n bat (with ball)

ลูกบาศก์ [luk bat] n cube; ที่เป็นลูกบาศก์ [thii pen luk baat] adj cubic

ลูกบิด [luk bit] n knob

ลูกปัด [luk pat] n bead

ลูกโป่ง [luk pong] n balloon

ลูกพรุน [luk phrun] n prune

ลูกพี่ลูกน้อง [luk pi luk nong] n cousin

ลูกไม้ [luk mai] n lace

ลูกเรือ [lik ruea] n cabin crew, seaman

ลูกเลี้ยง [luk liang] ลูกเลี้ยงหญิง [luk liang ying] n stepdaughter; ลูกเลี้ยงที่ เป็นชาย [luk liang thii pen chai] n stepson

ลูกสูบ [luk sup] n piston; ตัวดูดอากาศเข้า ลูกสูบ [tua dut a kaat khao luk sup] n carburettor; วงแหวนอัดลูกสูบ [wong waen at luk sup] n gasket

ลูกเสือ [luk suea] n scout

ลูกเห็บ [luk hep] n hail

ลูกอม [luk om] n toffee

ลูบ [lup] การลูบหรือการสัมผัส [kan lub rue kan sam phat] n stroke (hit)

ลูบคลำ [lup khlam] สัมผัสหรือลูบคลำ [sam phat rue lup khlam] v stroke

เล็ก [lek] adj little, small; เล็กมาก [lek mak] adj miniature, minute, tiny; สิ่งที่มี ขนาดเล็กมาก [sing thii mii kha naat lek mak] n miniature; ทำให้เล็กลงที่สุด [tham hai lek long thii sut] v minimize; ห้องเล็กเกินไป [hong lek koen pai] The room is too small

เล็กๆ [lek lek] เล็ก ๆ น้อย ๆ [lek lek noi noi] n bit

เล็กน้อย [lek noi] adj some; เล็กน้อยมาก

[lek noi mak] adj slight; อย่างเล็กน้อย [yang lek noi] adv slightly

เล็กๆน้อยๆ [lek lek noi noi] เรื่องเล็ก ๆ น้อย ๆ [rueang lek lek noi noi] n trifle

เลข [lek] เครื่องคิดเลข [khrueang kit lek] n calculator

เลขา [le kha] ตัวย่อของเลขาส่วนตัว [tua yo khong le kha suan tua] abbr PA

เลขานุการ [le kha nu kan] n secretary

เลเซอร์ [le soe] แสงเลเซอร์ [saeng le soe] n laser

เล่น [len] เลนเล่นโบว์ลิ่ง [len len bo ling] n bowling alley

เล่น [len] vt play (in sport); เล่นใหม่ [len mai] v replay; เล่นดนตรี [len don trii] play (music); เวลาเล่น [we la len] n playtime

เล่นกล [len kon] นักเล่นกล [nak len kon] n juggler, magician

เล่นพนัน [len pha nan] v gamble

เลนส์ [len] เลนส์ของกล้องที่ขยายปรับภาพ โดยรักษาโฟกัสเดิมไว้ [len khong klong thii kha yai prab phap doi rak sa fo kas doem wai] n zoom lens; เลนส์ตา [len to] n lens; แว่นสองเลนส์ [waen song len] npl bifocals

เล็บ [lep] n nail; เล็บมือ [lep mue] n fingernail; แปรงทำความสะอาดเล็บ [praeng tham khwam sa at lep] n nailbrush; กรรไกรตัดเล็บ [kan krai tat lep] npl nail scissors

เล็ม [lem] ฉันขอเล็มผมได้ไหม? [chan kho lem phom dai mai] Can I have a trim?

เลย [loei] เลยออกไป [loei ok pai] prep beyond

เลว [leo] adj bad ▷ adv badly; เลวร้าย [leo rai] adj horrible; เลวที่สุด [leo thii sut] adj worst; คนเลว [khon leo] n brat

เลวร้าย [leo rai] อย่างเลวร้าย [yang leo

rai] *adv* awfully

เล่ห์ [le] เล่ห์อุบาย [le u bai] *n* scam

เล่ห์เหลี่ยม [le liam] *n* trick; ใช้เล่ห์เหลี่ยม [chai le liam] *v* trick; ไม่มีเล่ห์เหลี่ยม ไม่มี มารยา [mai mii le liam, mai mii man ya] *adj* naive; ซึ่งมีเล่ห์เหลี่ยม อย่างฉลาด แกมโกง [sueng mii le liam, yang cha lat kaem kong] *adj* sly

เล่าเรียน [lao rian] ค่าเล่าเรียน [kha lao rian] *npl* tuition fees

เลิก [loek] *vt* quit; หยุด ยุติ เลิก [yut, yu ti, loek] *vi* stop

เลิกจ้าง [loek chang] เลิกจ้างงาน [loek chang ngan] *v* lay off

เลิศ [loet] ดีเลิศ [di loet] *adj* ideal; อย่างดี เลิศ [yang di loet] *adv* ideally

เลีย [lia] *v* lick

เลี้ยง [liang] *v* breed; เลี้ยงให้ของ [liang hai khong] *n* treat; คนเลี้ยงแกะ [khon liang kae] *n* shepherd; คนเลี้ยงดูเด็ก [khon liang du dek] *n* au pair

เลี้ยงดู [liang du] *v* bring up; เลี้ยงดูเด็ก [liang du dek] *v* foster; การเลี้ยงดูอบรม สั่งสอน [kan liang du op rom sang son] *n* upbringing

เลียนแบบ [lian baep] *v* imitate; การลอก เลียนแบบ [kan lok lian baep] *n* imitation

เลี้ยว [liao] *vi* turn; เลี้ยวกลับ [liao klap] *v* turn back; การเลี้ยว [kan liao] *n* turn; การเลี้ยวกลับที่ทางเลี้ยวเป็นรูปตัวยู [kan liao klap thii thang liao pen rup tua u] *n* U-turn; เลี้ยวขวา [liao khwa] Turn right

เลือก [lueak] *v* choose, select, pick; เลือก ที่จะไม่เกี่ยวข้องด้วย [lueak thii ja mai kiao khong duai] *v* opt out; เลือกออก [lueak ok] *v* pick out; การเลือก [kan lueak] *n* choice, option, pick

เลือกตั้ง [lueak tang] เขตเลือกตั้ง [khet lueak tang] *n* constituency; การเลือกตั้ง [kan lueak tang] *n* election; การเลือกตั้ง ทั่วไป [kan lueak tang thua pai] *n* general election

เลือด [lueat] *n* blood; เลือดเป็นพิษ [lueat pen phit] *n* blood poisoning; เต็มไปด้วย เลือด [tem pai duai lueat] *adj* bloody; กลุ่มเลือด [klum lueat] *n* blood group; เลือดฉันกลุ่มโอ [lueat chan klum o] My blood group is O positive

เลือดกำเดา [lueat kam dao] เลือดกำเดา ออก [lueat kam dao ok] *n* nosebleed

เลือดออก [lueat ok] *vi* bleed

เลือน [luean] *v* fade

เลื่อน [luean] เลื่อนออกไป [luean ok pai] *v* postpone, put off; แคร่เลื่อนยาวติดกับ รองเท้าใช้เล่นหิมะ [krae luean yao tit kap rong thao chai len hi ma] *n* ski; เรา ไปเล่นเลื่อนบนหิมะได้ที่ไหน? [rao pai len luean bon hi ma dai thii nai] Where can we go sledging?

เลื่อนหิมะ [luean hi ma] *n* toboggan; เลื่อนหิมะขนาดใหญ่ [luean hi ma kha nat yai] *n* sledge; การเล่นเลื่อนหิมะ [kan len luean hi ma] *n* sledging; การเล่น เลื่อนหิมะ [kan len luean hi ma] *n* tobogganing

เลื่อมใส [lueam sai] เลื่อมใส ศรัทธา [lueam sai, sat tha] *vi* believe

เลื่อย [lueai] *n* saw

แลก [laek] สำนักงานแลกเงิน [sam nak ngan laek ngoen] *n* bureau de change; สำนักงานแลกเงินจะเปิดเมื่อไร? [sam nak ngan laek ngoen ja poet muea rai] When is the bureau de change open?; ฉันแลกเช็คที่นี่ได้ไหม? [chan laek chek thii ni dai mai] Can I cash a cheque?

แล็กเกอร์ [lak koe] น้ำมันแล็กเกอร์ [nam man laek koe] *n* lacquer

แลกเงิน [laek ngoen] ตั๋วแลกเงิน [tua laek ngoen] *n* draft

แลกเปลี่ยน [laek plian] *v* swap; เปลี่ยน แลกเปลี่ยน [plian, laek plian] *vt* change; การแลกเปลี่ยน [kan laek plian] *v* exchange; อัตราแลกเปลี่ยน [at tra laek plian] *n* exchange rate

แลตเวีย [laet wai] เกี่ยวกับประเทศแลตเวีย [kiao kap pra thet laet via] *adj* Latvian;

ชาวแลตเวีย [chao laet wia] *n* Latvian
(*person*); ประเทศแลตเวีย [pra tet laet via]
n Latvia

แล่นเรือ [laen ruea] *v* sail

แล้ว [laeo] *adv* already

และ [lae] *conj* and

โลก [lok] *n* earth, world; ลูกโลก [luk lok]
n globe; การกระจายไปทั่วโลก [kan kra
chai pai thua lok] *n* globalization; ทั่ว
โลก [thua lok] *adj* global

โลโก้ [lo ko] *n* logo

โล่ง [long] ทำให้โล่ง เปิดเผยออกมา [tham
hai long, poet phoei ok ma] *v* bare

โลชั่น [lo chan] *n* lotion; โลชั่นหลัง
อาบแดด [lo chan lang aap daet] *n* after
sun lotion; โลชั่นทำความสะอาด [lo chan
tham khwam sa at] *n* cleansing lotion

โลภ [lop] *adj* greedy

โลมา [lo ma] ปลาโลมา [pla lo ma] *n*
dolphin

โล่ห์ [lo] *n* shield

โลหะ [lo ha] *n* metal; เครื่องใช้ที่ทำด้วย
โลหะ [khrueang chai thii tham duai lo
ha] *n* hardware; โลหะแผ่น [lo ha
phaen] *n* foil; ร้านขายเครื่องใช้ที่ทำด้วย
โลหะ [ran khai khrueang chai thii
tham duai lo ha] *n* ironmonger's

โลหิต [lo hit] ความดันโลหิต [khwam dan
lo hit] *n* blood pressure

โลหิตจาง [lo hit chang] ที่เกี่ยวกับโรค
โลหิตจาง [thii kiao kap rok lo hit
chang] *adj* anaemic

ไล่ [lai] ไล่ตาม [lai tam] *v* chase; ไล่ตาม
ทัน [lai tam than] *v* overtake; การไล่
ตาม [kan lai tam] *n* chase

ไลบีเรีย [lai bi ria] เกี่ยวกับไลบีเรีย [kiao
kap lai bi ria] *adj* Liberian; ชาวไลบีเรีย
[chao lai bi ria] *n* Liberian; ประเทศ
ไลบีเรีย [pra tet lai bi ria] *n* Liberia

ไลแลค [lai laek] ดอกไลแลคมีสีม่วงแดงหรือ
ขาวมีกลิ่นหอม [dok lai laek mii sii
muang daeng rue khao mii klin hom]
n lilac

ไล่ออก [lai ok] *n* sack (*dismissal*) ▷ *v* expel

ว

วกวน [wok won] ทางวกวน [thang wok
won] *n* maze

วง [wong] วงดนตรี [wong don tri] *n* band
(*musical group*); วงดนตรีเครื่องเป่า [wong
don tree khrueang pao] *n* brass band

วงกลม [wong klom] *n* circle, round
(*circle*); ที่เป็นวงกลม [thii pen wong
klom] *adj* circular

วงดนตรี [wong don tri] วงดนตรีขนาด
ใหญ่ที่เล่นเพลงคลาสสิค [wong don tree
kha naat yai thii len phleng khlas sik]
n orchestra

วงเล็บ [wong lep] ในวงเล็บ [nai wong
lep] *npl* brackets

วงเวียน [wong wian] วงเวียนที่ต้องขับรถ
รอบ [wong wian thii tong khap rot rop]
n roundabout

วงแหวน [wong waen] ถนนวงแหวน [tha
non wong waen] *n* ring road; วงแหวน
อัดลูกสูบ [wong waen at luk sup] *n*
gasket

วน [won] วนไปวนมา [won pai won ma] *v*
go round

วนิลา [wa ni la] กลิ่นหรือรสวนิลา [klin
rue rot wa ni la] *n* vanilla

วรรค [wak] เครื่องหมายวรรคตอน

[khrueang mai wak ton] *n* apostrophe

วรรณคดี [wan na kha di] *n* literature

วลี [wa li] *n* phrase; หนังสือที่เกี่ยวกับวลี [nang sue thii kiao kap wa li] *n* phrasebook

วอลทซ์ [wolt] เต้นรำจังหวะวอลทซ์ [ten ram chang wa walt] *v* waltz; การเต้นรำ จังหวะวอลทซ์ [kan ten ram chang wa walt] *n* waltz

วอลนัท [won nat] ถั่ววอลนัทมีเปลือกแข็ง รอยหยักและทานได้ [thua wal nat mii plueak khaeng roi yak lae than dai] *n* walnut

วอลเลย์บอล [won le bon] กีฬาวอลเลย์บอล [ki la wal le bal] *n* volleyball

วัคซีน [wak chin] การฉีดวัคซีน [kan chit wak sin] *n* vaccination; ฉีดวัคซีน [chiit wak sin] *v* vaccinate; ฉันต้องฉีดวัคซีน [chan tong chiit wak sin] I need a vaccination

วัชพืช [wat cha phuet] *n* weed; ยากำจัด วัชพืช [ya kam chat wat cha phuet] *n* weedkiller

วัฒนธรรม [wat tha na tham] *n* culture; ทางวัฒนธรรม [thang wat tha na tham] *adj* cultural

วัณโรค [wan na rok] *n* tuberculosis; โรค วัณโรค [rok wan na rok] *n* TB

วัด [wat] *n* temple ▷ *v* gauge, measure; เครื่องวัด [khrueang wat] *n* gauge; การ วัด [kan wat] *npl* measurements; การ วัด [kan wat] *npl* scale (*measure*); คุณ ช่วยวัดตัวฉันได้ไหม? [khun chuai wat tua chan dai mai] Can you measure me, please?

วัตถุ [wat thu] วัตถุสิ่งของ [wat thu sing khong] *n* object

วัตถุประสงค์ [wat thu pra song] *n* purpose

วัน [wan] *n* day; แต่ละวัน [tae la wan] *adv* daily; วันเกิด [wan koet] *n* birthday; วัน เทศกาลสารภาพบาป [wan tet sa kan sa ra phap bap] *n* Shrove Tuesday; เป็นวันที่ อากาศดี [pen wan thii a kat di] What a

lovely day!

วันเกิด [wan koet] สุขสันต์วันเกิด [suk san wan koet] Happy birthday!

วันจันทร์ [wan chan] on Monday

วันที่ [wan thi] *n* date; ขายก่อนหมดวันที่ กำหนด [khai kon mot wan thii kam nod] *n* sell-by date; วันที่อะไร? [wan thii a rai] What is the date?; วันนี้วันที่ เท่าไร? [wan nii wan thii thao rai] What is today's date?

วันธรรมดา [wan tham ma da] วัน ธรรมดาตั้งแต่วันจันทร์ถึงวันศุกร์ [wan tham ma da tang tae wan chan thueng wan suk] *n* weekday

วันนี้ [wan ni] *adj* today; วันนี้คุณอยากทำ อะไร? [wan nii khun yak tham a rai] What would you like to do today?

วันพฤหัสบดี [wan pha rue hat sa bo di] on Thursday

วันพุธ [wan phut] on Wednesday

วันมะรืน [wan ma ruen] the day after tomorrow

วันศุกร์ [wan suk] on Friday

วันเสาร์ [wan sao] on Saturday; วันเสาร์ ต่าง ๆ [wan sao tang tang] on Saturdays

วันหยุด [wan yut] ช่วงวันหยุดหรือไม่ไป ทำงาน [chuang wan yut rue mai pai tham ngan] *n* time off; วันหยุดเพื่อระลึก ถึงการอพยพของชาวอียิปต์ [wan yut phuea ra luek thueng kan op pha yop khong chao i yip] *n* Passover; วันหยุดใน ฤดูร้อน [wan yut nai rue du ron] *npl* summer holidays

วันอังคาร [wan ang khan] on Tuesday

วันอาทิตย์ [wan a thit] on Sunday

วัย [wai] สูงวัย [sung wai] *adj* elderly; ซึ่ง มีวัยกลางคน [sueng mii wai klang khon] *adj* middle-aged; วัยเด็ก [wai dek] *n* childhood

วัยรุ่น [wai run] *n* adolescent, teenager; คลับวัยรุ่นที่จัดให้มีกิจกรรมเพื่อความบันเทิง [khlap wai run thii chat hai mii kit cha kam phuea khwam ban thoeng] *n* youth club; ช่วงวัยรุ่น [chuang wai run]

npl adolescence, teens

วัว [wao] เนื้อลูกวัว [nuea luk wua] *n* veal; เนื้อวัว [nuea wua] *n* beef; ลูกวัว [luk wua] *n* calf

วัสดุ [wat sa du] *n* material; ชิ้นหรือของหรือวัสดุที่เป็นของแข็ง [chin rue khong rue wat sa du thii pen khong khaeng] *n* block *(solid piece)*; วัสดุอะไร? [wat sa du a rai] What is the material?

ว่า [wa] ดุว่า [du wa] *v* scold, tell off; คุณจะว่าอย่างไรไหม? [khun ja wa yang rai mai] Do you mind?; ฉันไม่ว่าอย่างไร [chan mai wa yang rai] I don't mind

วาง [wang] *v* put; วาง จัดเตรียม ตั้งเวลา ตั้งระบบ [wang, chat triam, tang we la, tang ra bop] *vt* set; วางเข้าไปใน [wang khao pai nai] *v* put in; วางไว้ในตำแหน่ง [wang wai nai tam naeng] *vt* place; ช่วยวางมันลงที่นั่น [chuai wang man long thii nan] Put it down over there, please

ว่าง [wang] *adj* blank, vacant; เสียงสายไม่ว่างของโทรศัพท์ [siang sai mai wang khong tho ra sap] *n* engaged tone; เวลาว่าง [we la wang] *n* spare time; ตำแหน่งว่าง [tam naeng wang] *n* vacancy

ว่างงาน [wang ngan] เงินที่รัฐบาลให้กับคนว่างงานทุกเดือน [ngoen thii rat tha ban hai kap khon wang ngan thuk duean] *n* dole; การว่างงาน [kan wang ngan] *n* unemployment

วางใจ [wang chai] ไว้วางใจ [wai wang chai] *v* trust; ทำให้วางใจ [tham hai wang jai] *v* reassure

ว่างเปล่า [wang plao] *adj* empty; ทำให้ว่างเปล่า [tham hai wang plao] *vt* empty

วางผังเมือง [wang phang mueang] การวางผังเมือง [kan wang phang mueang] *n* town planning

วางแผน [wang phen] *v* plan, plot *(conspire)*, plot *(secret plan)*; การวางแผน [kan wang phaen] *n* planning; การวางแผนการอย่างลับ ๆ [kan wang phaen kan yang lap lap] *n* conspiracy

วางเพลิง [wang phloeng] การลอบวางเพลิง [kan lop wang phloeng] *n* arson

วางหู [wang hu] วางหูโทรศัพท์ [wang hu tho ra sap] *v* hang up

วาด [wat] ที่วาดขอบตา [thii wat kop ta] *n* eyeliner; วาดมโนภาพ [wad ma no phap] *v* imagine; วาดภาพ [wat phap] *vt* draw *(sketch)*

วาติกัน [wa ti kan] สำนักวาติกันที่เป็นที่ประทับของพระองค์สันตะปาปาในกรุงโรม [sam nak wa ti kan thii pen thii pra thap khong ong san ta pa pa nai krung rom] *n* Vatican

ว่ายน้ำ [wai nam] *vi* swim; สระว่ายน้ำ [sa wai nam] *n* baths, swimming pool; การว่ายน้ำ [kan wai nam] *n* swimming; การว่ายน้ำท่าผีเสื้อ [kan wai nam tha phii suea] *n* breaststroke; ไปว่ายน้ำกันเถอะ [pai wai nam kan thoe] Let's go swimming

วารสารศาสตร์ [wa ra san sat] *n* journalism

ว่าว [wao] *n* kite

ว้าวุ่น [wa wun] ที่ทำให้ว้าวุ่นใจ [thii tham hai wa wun jai] *adj* shaken

วิกฤต [wi krit] ช่วงวิกฤต [chuang wi krit] *n* crisis

วิกลจริต [wi kon cha rit] *adj* mad *(insane)*; ความวิกลจริต [khwam wi kon ja rit] *n* madness; ที่วิกลจริต [thii wi kon ja rit] *adj* insane

วิเคราะห์ [wi khro] *v* analyse; นักวิเคราะห์ระบบ [nak wi khrao ra bop] *n* systems analyst; ผลการวิเคราะห์ [phon kan wi khrao] *n* analysis

วิ่ง [wing] การแข่งวิ่งเร็วในระยะสั้น [kan khaeng wing reo nai ra ya san] *n* sprint; การวิ่ง [kan wing] *n* run, running; การวิ่งเหยาะ [kan wing yo] *n* jogging; ฉันจะวิ่งได้ที่ไหน? [chan ja wing dai thii nai] Where can I go jogging?

วิ่งแข่ง [wing khaeng] *vi* race

วิ่งเหยาะ [wing yo] *vi* jog

วิจัย [wi chai] การวิจัยตลาด [kan wi jai ta lad] *n* market research

วิจารณ์ [wi chan] *v* criticize; เกี่ยวกับการ วิจารณ์ สำคัญ [kiao kap kan wi chan, sam khan] *adj* critical; การแสดงความคิด เห็น คำวิจารณ์ [kan sa daeng khwam kit hen, kham wi chan] *n* commentary; การวิจารณ์ [kan wi chan] *n* criticism

วิชา [wi cha] วิชาเคมี [wi cha ke mii] *n* chemistry; วิชาโบราณคดี [wi cha bo ran kha di] *n* archaeology; วิชาที่ ปรับปรุงใหม่ [wi cha thii prap prung mai] *n* refresher course

วิชาการ [wi cha kan] ด้านวิชาการ [dan wi cha kan] *adj* academic

วิชาชีพ [wi cha chip] เกี่ยวกับวิชาชีพ [kiao kap wi cha chip] *adj* vocational; ผู้เชี่ยวชาญในวิชาชีพ [phu chiao chan nai wi cha chip] *n* professional

วิญญาณ [win yan] *n* soul, spirit

วิดพื้น [wit puen] การวิดพื้น [kan wit phuen] *n* press-up; การออกกำลังกายแบบ วิดพื้น [kan ok kam lang kai baep wid phuen] *n* push-up

วิตก [wi tok] ความวิตกกังวล [khwam wi tok kang won] *n* anxiety; วิตกกังวล [wi tok kang won] *vi* worry

วิตกกังวล [wi tok kang won] สาเหตุของ ความวิตกกังวล [sa het khong khwam wi tok kang won] *adj* worrying; ความหวาด กลัวหรือวิตกกังวล [khwam wat klua rue wi tok kang won] *n* panic

วิตามิน [wi ta min] *n* vitamin

วิถีทาง [wi thi thang] วิถีทางการดำเนิน ชีวิต [wi thi thang kan dam noen chi wit] *n* lifestyle

วิทยาเขต [wit tha ya khet] *n* campus

วิทยาลัย [wit tha ya lai] *n* college

วิทยาศาสตร์ [wit tha ya sat] ห้องทดลอง ทางวิทยาศาสตร์ [hong thot long thang wit tha ya sart] *n* laboratory; การนำเอา วิทยาศาสตร์มาใช้ในการปฏิบัติ [kan nam ao wit ta ya sat ma chai nai kan pa ti bat] *n* technology; ตัวย่อของห้องทดลอง ทางวิทยาศาสตร์ [tua yo khong hong thot long thang wit ta ya saat] *n* lab

วิทยุ [wit tha yu] *n* radio; เครื่องรับส่งวิทยุ มือถือ [khrueang rap song wit tha yu mue thue] *n* walkie-talkie; สถานีวิทยุ [sa tha ni wit tha yu] *n* radio station; ที่ ควบคุมด้วยวิทยุ [thii khuap khum duai wit tha yu] *adj* radio-controlled

วิธี [wi thi] *npl* means; วิธีหรือแนวทาง [wi thi rue naeo thang] *n* way

วิธีการ [wi thi kan] *n* method; วางวิธีการ ให้ [wang wi thi kan hai] *v* program

วินเซิฟ [win soep] คุณจะไปวินเซิร์ฟได้ที่ ไหน? [khun ja pai win soep dai thii nai] Where can you go surfing?; ฉัน อยากไปเล่นวินเซิร์ฟ [chan yak pai len vin serf] I'd like to go windsurfing

วินด์เซิร์ฟ [win soep] กีฬาวินด์เซิร์ฟ [ki la win serf] *n* windsurfing

วินัย [wi nai] ความตั้งใจและความมีวินัยที่นำ ตัวเองไปสู่ความสำเร็จ [khwam tang jai lae khwam mii wi nai thii nam tua eng pai su khwam sam ret] *n* willpower

วินิจฉัย [wi nit chai] การวินิจฉัยโรค [kan wi nit chai rok] *n* diagnosis

วิลล่า [win la] ฉันอยากเช่าวิลล่า [chan yak chao win la] I'd like to rent a villa

วิว [wio] เราอยากเห็นวิวที่น่าตื่นเต้น [rao yak hen wio thii na tuen ten] We'd like to see spectacular views; ฉันอยากได้ ห้องที่มีวิวทะเล [chan yak dai hong thii mii wio tha le] I'd like a room with a view of the sea

วิวัฒนาการ [wi wat tha na kan] *n* evolution

วิศวกร [wit sa wa kon] *n* engineer

วิศวกรรมศาสตร์ [wit sa wa kam ma sat] *n* engineering

วิเศษ [wi set] *adj* fantastic, magic, superb

วิสกี้ [wit sa ki] *n* whisky; เหล้าวิสกี้ที่ทำ

จากข้าวมอลต์ [lao wis ki thii tham chak khao malt whisky] *n* malt whisky; ฉันจะดื่มวิสกี้ [chan ja duem wis ki] I'll have a whisky; วิสกี้กับโซดาหนึ่งแก้ว [wis ki kap so da nueng kaeo] a whisky and soda

วิหาร [wi han] มหาวิหาร [ma ha wi han] *n* cathedral

วีซ่า [wi sa] วีซ่า เอกสารอนุมัติที่ประทับตราบนหนังสือเดินทาง [wi sa, ek ka san a nu mat thii pra thap tra bon nang sue doen thang] *n* visa; ฉันมีวีซ่าเข้าประเทศ [chan mii wi sa khao pra tet] I have an entry visa; นี่คือวีซ่าของฉัน [ni khue wi sa khong chan] Here is my visa

วีดีโอ [wi di o] ภาพหรือหนังในเทปวีดีโอ [phap rue nang nai thep wi di o] *n* video

วีดีโอเกมส์ [wi di o kem] เครื่องที่ต่อกับทีวีใช้เล่นวีดีโอเกมส์ [khrueang thii to kap wii chai len vi di o kem] *n* games console; ฉันเล่นวีดีโอเกมส์ได้ไหม? [chan len wi di o kem dai mai] Can I play video games?

วีรบุรุษ [wi ra bu rut] *n* hero

วีรสตรี [wi ra sa tri] *n* heroine

วุ่นวาย [wun wai] สับสนวุ่นวาย [sap son wun wai] *adj* upset; ความยุ่งเหยิง ความโกลาหล สถานการณ์สับสนวุ่นวาย [khwam yung yoeng, khwam ko la hon, sa than na kan sap son wun wai] *npl* shambles; ความวุ่นวาย [khwam wun wai] *n* fuss

เวทมนตร์ [wet mon] *n* magic; ซึ่งมีเวทมนตร์ [sueng mii wet mon] *adj* magical

เวที [we thi] เวทีการแสดง [we thi kan sa daeng] *n* stage; เวทีที่ยกพื้น [we thi thii yok phuen] *n* platform

เวเนซุเอลา [we ne su e la] ชาวเวเนซุเอลา [chao we ne su e la] *n* Venezuelan; ที่เกี่ยวกับเวเนซุเอลา [thii kiao kap we ne su e la] *adj* Venezuelan; ประเทศเวเนซุเอลา [pra tet ve ne su e la] *n* Venezuela

เว็บไซต์ [wep sait] คำย่อของที่อยู่ของเว็บไซต์บนอินเตอร์เน็ต [kham yo khong thii yu khong web sai bon in toe net] *n* URL; ผู้ดูแลเว็บไซต์ [phu du lae wep sai] *n* webmaster

เว็ปไซต์ [wep sait] ที่อยู่ของเว็ปไซต์คือ... [thii yu khong web sai khue...] The website address is...

เวลโคร [wen khro] เวลโคร ไนลอนสองชั้นที่ยึดสิ่งของให้ติดแน่น ใช้แทนชิป กระดุม และขอเกี่ยว [wel khro nai lon song chin thii yuet sing khong hai tit naen chai taen sip kra dum lae kho kiao] *n* Velcro®

เวลส์ [wel] เกี่ยวกับประชาชนและวัฒนธรรมเวลส์ [kiao kap pra cha chon lae wat tha na tham wel] *adj* Welsh; ชาวเวลส์ [chao wel] *n* Welsh; ประเทศเวลส์ที่รวมอยู่ในสหราชอาณาจักรอังกฤษ [pra tet wel thii ruam yu nai sa ha rat cha a na chak ang krit] *n* Wales

เวลา [we la] *n* time; เขตเวลาของโลกซึ่งมี ๒๔ เขต [khet we la khong lok sueng mii yi sip sii khet] *n* time zone; เครื่องจับเวลา [khrueang chap we la] *n* timer; เวลาเล่น [we la len] *n* playtime; ในระหว่างเวลาที่มีกิจกรรมน้อย [nai ra wang we la thii mii kit cha kam noi] *adv* off-season; ช่วงเวลาพัก [chuang we la phak] *n* interval; พ้นกำหนดเวลา [phon kam not we la] *adj* overdue; เวลาต่ำที่สุดเท่าไร? [we la tam thii sut thao rai] What's the minimum amount of time?

เวียดนาม [wiat nam] *adj* Vietnamese ▷ *n* Vietnamese (*language*), Vietnamese (*person*); ประเทศเวียดนาม [pra tet viat nam] *n* Vietnam

เวียน [wian] เวียนศรีษะ [wian si sa] *adj* dizzy; ฉันมีอาการเวียนศรีษะบ่อย [chan mii a kan wian sii sa boi] I keep having dizzy spells; ฉันรู้สึกเวียนศรีษะ [chan ru suek wian sii sa] I feel dizzy

เวียนศรีษะ [wian si sa] อาการเวียนศรีษะ

ทำให้ทรงตัวลำบาก [a kan wian si sa
tham hai song tua lam bak] *n* vertigo

แวง [waeng] เส้นแวง [sen waeng] *n*
longitude

แวดล้อม [waet lom] สภาวะแวดล้อม [sa
pha wa waet lom] *adj* environmental

แว่น [waen] แว่นสองเลนส์ [waen song
len] *npl* bifocals; แว่นขยาย [waen kha
yai] *n* magnifying glass

แว่นตา [waen ta] *npl* glasses, specs,
spectacles; แว่นตากันแดด [waen ta kan
daet] *npl* sunglasses; แว่นตากันลม/ ฝุ่น/
น้ำ [waen ta kan lom/ fun/ nam] *npl*
goggles; คุณซ่อมแว่นตาฉันได้ไหม?
[khun som waen ta chan dai mai] Can
you repair my glasses?

โวลต์ [wolt] แรงดันไฟฟ้าที่มีหน่วยเป็นโวลต์
[raeng dan fai fa thii mii nuai pen
volt] *n* voltage

ไว [wai] ซึ่งไวต่อสิ่งกระตุ้น [sueng wai to
sing kra tun] *adj* sensitive; ที่ไม่ไวต่อ
ความรู้สึกของผู้อื่น [thii mai wai to
khwam ru suek khong phu uen] *adj*
insensitive

ไว้ใจ [wai chai] ไว้ใจไม่ได้ [wai jai mai
dai] *adj* unreliable

ไว้ทุกข์ [wai thuk] การไว้ทุกข์ [kan wai
thuk] *n* mourning

ไวน์ [wai] *n* wine; แก้วไวน์ [kaew wine] *n*
wineglass; ไวน์แดง [wine daeng] *n* red
wine; ไวน์ของร้านอาหาร [wine khong
ran a han] *n* house wine; ไวน์เย็นไหม?
[wine yen mai] Is the wine chilled?

ไวยากรณ์ [wai ya kon] *n* grammar; ที่
เกี่ยวกับไวยากรณ์ [thii kiao kap wai ya
kon] *adj* grammatical

ไวรัส [wai ras] เชื้อไวรัส [chuea wai rat]
n virus; ยาต่อต้านไวรัส [ya to tan vai ras]
n antivirus

ไว้วางใจ [wai wang chai] ที่ไว้วางใจ
[thii wai wang jai] *adj* trusting

ไวโอลิน [wai o lin] เครื่องดนตรีชนิดหนึ่ง
คล้ายไวโอลินแต่มีขนาดใหญ่กว่าและมีเสียง
ต่ำกว่า [khrueang don tri cha nit nueng
khlai wai o lin tae mii kha naat yai
kwa lae mii siang tam kwa] *n* viola;
เครื่องดนตรีประเภทสีชนิดหนึ่ง ไวโอลิน
[khrueang don tri pra phet sii cha nit
nueng vi o lin] *n* violin; ไวโอลินเซโล [vi
o lin che lo] *n* cello

ศตวรรษ [sa ta wat] *n* century

ศพ [sop] ห้องเก็บศพ [hong kep sop] *n* morgue; หลุมฝังศพ [lum fang sop] *n* grave; งานศพ [ngan sop] *n* funeral

ศรัทธา [sat tha] เลื่อมใส ศรัทธา [lueam sai, sat tha] *vi* believe; ความศรัทธา [khwam sat tha] *n* faith

ศรีลังกา [si lang ka] ประเทศศรีลังกา [pra tet sri lang ka] *n* Sri Lanka

ศีรษะ [si sa] โพรงกระดูกในศีรษะ [phrong kra duk nai si sa] *n* sinus; กะโหลกศีรษะ [ka lok sii sa] *n* skull; ที่ว่างเหนือศีรษะ [thii wang nuea si sa] *n* headroom

ศอก [sok] ข้อศอก [kho sok] *n* elbow

ศักดิ์สิทธิ์ [sak sit] ผู้ที่เดินทางไปสถานที่ศักดิ์สิทธิ์ [phu thii doen thang pai sa than thii sak sit] *n* pilgrim

ศักราช [sak ka rat] คริสต์ศักราช [khrit sak ka rat] *abbr* AD

ศัตรู [sat tru] *n* enemy; ทำให้กลายเป็นศัตรู [tham hai klai pen sa tru] *v* antagonize

ศัลยกรรม [san ya kam] *n* operation (*surgery*); การผ่าตัดศัลยกรรมเสริมความงาม [kan pha tat san la ya kam soem khwam ngam] *n* cosmetic surgery;

ศัลยกรรมตกแต่ง [san la ya kam tok taeng] *n* plastic surgery

ศาล [san] *n* court; ศาลยุติธรรม [san yu thi tham] *n* tribunal

ศาลากลาง [sa la klang] ศาลากลางจังหวัด [sa la klang changhwat] *n* town hall

ศาสตราจารย์ [sat tra chan] *n* professor

ศาสนศาสตร์ [sat sa na] *n* theology

ศาสนา [sat sa na] *n* religion; เกี่ยวกับศาสนา [kiao kap sat sa na] *adj* religious, spiritual; เกี่ยวกับศาสนาซิกข์ [kiao kap sat sa na sik] *n* Sikh; เขตศาสนาที่มีโบสถ์และพระ [khet sat sa na thii mii bot lae phra] *n* parish

ศิลป์ [sin] *n* art

ศิลปะ [sin la pa] เกี่ยวกับศิลปะ [kiao kap sin la pa] *adj* artistic; โรงเรียนศิลปะ [rong rian sin la pa] *n* art school; ห้องแสดงงานศิลปะ [hong sa daeng ngan sin la pa] *n* art gallery

ศิลปิน [sin la pin] *n* artist

ศีรษะ [si sa] *n* head (*body part*)

ศีลธรรม [sin tham] เกี่ยวกับศีลธรรม [kiao kap sin la tham] *adj* moral; ผิดศีลธรรม [phit sin la tham] *adj* immoral

ศึกษา [suek sa] สถาบันศึกษา [sa tha ban suek sa] *n* academy; การศึกษา [kan suek sa] *n* education; การศึกษาระดับสูง [kan suek sa ra dap sung] *n* further education, higher education

ศุกร์ [suk] วันศุกร์ [wan suk] *n* Friday; วันศุกร์ที่สามสิบเอ็ด ธันวาคม [wan suk thii sam sip et than wa khom] on Friday the thirty first of December

ศุลกากร [sun la ka kon] *n* custom; เจ้าหน้าที่ศุลกากร [chao na thii sun la ka kon] *n* customs officer

ศูนย์ [sun] *n* nil, nought, zero; ศูนย์โทรศัพท์ [sun tho ra sap] *n* call centre; ศูนย์ขายต้นไม้และเครื่องมือในการทำสวน [sun khai ton mai lae khrueang mue nai kan tham suan] *n* garden centre; ศูนย์ดนตรี [sun don tree] *n* music centre

ศูนย์กลาง [sun klang] *n* centre; ที่เป็น

ศูนย์กลาง [thii pen sun klang] *adj*
central; ฉันจะไปที่ศูนย์กลางของ...ได้
อย่างไร? [chan ja pai thii sun klang
khong...dai yang rai] How do I get to
the centre of...?

ศูนย์การค้า [sun kan kha] *n* shopping
centre

ศูนย์สูตร [sun sut] เส้นศูนย์สูตร [sen sun
sut] *n* equator

เศรษฐกิจ [set tha kit] *n* economy; เกี่ยว
กับเศรษฐกิจ [kiao kap set tha kit] *adj*
economic; การตกต่ำทางเศรษฐกิจ [kan
tok tam thang set tha kit] *n* recession

เศรษฐศาสตร์ [set tha sat] นัก
เศรษฐศาสตร์ [nak set tha sat] *n*
economist; วิชาเศรษฐศาสตร์ [wi cha set
tha sat] *npl* economics

เศรษฐี [set thi] เศรษฐีเงินล้าน [set thi
ngoen lan] *n* millionaire

เศร้า [sao] *adj* sad, unhappy; ความเศร้าใจ
[khwam sao jai] *npl* blues; ยาต้านอาการ
เศร้าซึม [ya tan a kan sao suem] *n*
antidepressant; อย่างเศร้าใจ [yang sao
jai] *adv* sadly

เศร้าใจ [sao chai] *adj* gloomy

เศร้าโศก [sao sok] ความเศร้าโศก [khwam
sao sok] *n* grief

เศษ [set] เศษเล็กเศษน้อย [set lek set noi]
n crumb; เศษเล็ก ๆ ที่แตกออก [set lek lek
thii taek ok] *n* splinter; เศษชิ้นเล็กชิ้น
น้อย [set chin lek chin noi] *n* scrap
(*small piece*)

เศษหนึ่งส่วนสี่ [set nueng suan si] *n*
quarter

โศกนาฏกรรม [sok ka nat ta kam] *n*
tragedy

ส

สกปรก [sok ka prok] *adj* dirty; สกปรก
ที่สุด [sok ka prok thii sut] *adj* filthy; ซึ่ง
ไม่เรียบร้อยและสกปรก [sueng mai riap
roi lae sok ka prok] *adj* messy; ทำให้
สกปรก [tham hai sok ka prok] *v* mess
up; มันสกปรก [man sok ka prok] It's
dirty

สก็อตแลนด์ [sa kot laen] *adj* เกี่ยวกับ
สก็อตแลนด [kiao kap sa kot laen] *adj*
Scottish ▷ *n* หญิงชาวสก็อตแลนด์ [ying
chao sa kot laen] *n* Scotswoman; ชาย
ชาวสก็อตแลนด์ [chai chao sa kot laen] *n*
Scotsman

สกี [sa ki] เคลื่อนไปบนสกี [khluean pai
bon sa ki] *v* ski; การเล่นสกี [kan len sa
ki] *n* skiing; ที่ลาดชันสำหรับฝึกเล่นสกี
[thii lat chan sam rap fuek len sa ki] *n*
nursery slope; เล่นสกีน้ำที่นี่ได้ไหม? [len
sa ki nam thii ni dai mai] Is it possible
to go water-skiing here?

สกีน้ำ [sa ki nam] การเล่นสกีน้ำ [kan len
sa ki nam] *n* water-skiing

สกุลเงิน [sa kun ngoen] สกุลเงินของสห
ราชอาณาจักรอังกฤษ [sa kun ngoen
khong sa ha rat cha a na chak ang krit]
n sterling

155 | สเตริโอ [sa te ri o]

สเก็ต [sa ket] เล่นสเก็ต [len sa ket] v
skate; ลานเล่นสเก็ต [lan len sa ket] n
skating rink; ลานเล่นสเก็ตน้ำแข็ง [lan
len sa ket nam khaeng] n rink; เราจะเช่า
สเก็ตได้ที่ไหน? [rao ja chao sa ket dai
thii nai] Where can we hire skates?

สแกนดิเนเวีย [sa kaen di ne wia] กลุ่ม
ประเทศสแกนดิเนเวีย [klum pra tet sa
kaen di ne via] n Scandinavia

ส่ง [song] v send; ส่งแฟกซ์ [song fak] v
fax; ส่งให้ [song hai] v hand; ส่งมอบ
[song mop] vt deliver; ค่าส่งโทรสารราคา
เท่าไร? [kha song tho ra san ra kha
thao rai] How much is it to send a fax?

ส่งของ [song khong] ทำใบส่งของ [tham
bai song khong] v invoice

สงคราม [song khram] n war;
สงครามกลางเมือง [song khram klang
mueang] n civil war

สงฆ์ [song] สำนักสงฆ์ [sam nak song] n
abbey

สงบ [sa ngop] ความสงบเรียบร้อย [khwam
sa ngob riap roi] n peace; ซึ่งเงียบสงบ
และผ่อนคลาย [sueng ngiap sa ngob lae
phon khlai] adj restful; ที่มีอารมณ์สงบ
[thii mii a rom sa ngop] adj calm

สงบศึก [sa ngop suek] การสงบศึกชั่วคราว
[kan sa ngob suek chua khrao] n truce

สงวน [sa nguan] เขตสงวน [khet sa
nguan] n reserve (land)

สงสัย [song sai] adj dubious, suspicious
▷ v doubt, suspect, wonder; ไม่เป็นที่น่า
สงสัยใด ๆ ทั้งสิ้น [mai pen thii na song
sai dai dai thang sin] adv undoubtedly;
ความสงสัย [khwam song sai] n doubt;
ที่เป็นที่สงสัย [thii pen thii song sai] adj
doubtful

สงสาร [song san] v pity; ความสงสาร
[khwam song san] n pity; น่าสงสาร [na
song san] adj pathetic

ส่งเสริม [song some] v boost, promote;
การส่งเสริมสนับสนุน [kan song sem sa
nab sa nun] n promotion

ส่งเสียง [song siang] ส่งเสียงดังก้องวาน

[song siang dang kang wan] v ring; การ
ส่งเสียงเชียร์ [kan song siang chia] n
cheer

ส่งออก [song ok] v export; การส่งออก
[kan song ok] n export

สง่า [sa nga] สง่างาม [sa nga ngam] adj
magnificent

สง่างาม [sa nga ngam] อย่างสง่างาม
[yang sa ngan gam] adj graceful

สง่าผ่าเผย [sa nga pha phoei] ความสง่า
ผ่าเผย [khwam sa nga pha phoei] n
majesty

สด [sot] adj fresh; ไม่สด [mai sot] adj
stale; ปลาสดหรือแช่แข็ง? [pla sot rue
chae khaeng] Is the fish fresh or frozen?

สดชื่น [sot chuen] การทำให้สดชื่น [kan
tham hai sot chuen] npl refreshments;
ซึ่งทำให้สดชื่น [sueng tham hai sot
chuen] adj refreshing; ที่ทำให้รู้สึกสดชื่น
[thii tham hai ru suek sot chuen] adj
cheerful

สตรอเบอรี่ [sa tro boe ri] ผลสตรอเบอรี่
[phon sa tro boe ri] n strawberry

สตรี [sa tri] เกี่ยวกับสตรี [kiao kap sa tree]
adj female; สตรีที่ไม่ได้แต่งงาน [sa tree
thii mai dai taeng ngan] n spinster;
สตรีที่รับราชการทหาร [sa tree thii rap rat
cha kan tha han] n servicewoman

สติ [sa ti] มีสติรู้ตัว [mii sa ti ru tua] adj
self-conscious

สติ๊กเกอร์ [stik koe] ฉลากติด สติ๊กเกอร์
[cha lak tit, sa tik koe] n sticker

สติปัญญา [sa ti pan ya] n intelligence;
สติปัญญา ความเฉลียวฉลาด [sa ti pan ya,
khwam cha liao cha lat] n wisdom; ซึ่ง
ใช้คำพูดอย่างมีสติปัญญาและตลก [sueng
chai kham phut yang mii sa ti pan ya
lae ta lok] adj witty

สตูว์ [sa tu] n stew

สเต็ค [sa tek] เนื้อสเต็ค [nuea sa tek] n
steak

สเตริโอ [sa te ri o] มีระบบสเตริโอในรถ
ไหม? [mee ra bob sa toe ri o nai rot
mai] Is there a stereo in the car?

สเตอรอยด์ [sa toe roi] n steroid

สเตอริโอ [sa toe ri o] ระบบเสียงแบบ สเตอริโอ [ra bop siang baep sa toe ri o] n stereo; สเตอริโอส่วนตัว [sa toe ri o suan tua] n personal stereo

สถาน [sa than] สถานรับเลี้ยงเด็ก [sa than rap liang dek] n nursery; สถานดูแลคน ชรา [sa than du lae khon cha ra] n nursing home; สถานบำรุงสุขภาพ [sa than bam rung suk kha phap] n spa

สถานการณ์ [sa tha na kan] n situation ▷ npl circumstances; สถานการณ์ที่ได้รับ การจัดการ [sa tha na kan thii dai rap kan chat kan] n affair

สถานทูต [sa than thut] n embassy

สถานที่ [sa than thi] n location, place, spot (place); สถานที่เก็บเอกสารสำคัญ [sa than thii kep ek ka san som khan] n archive; สถานที่เกิด [sa than thii koet] n birthplace, place of birth; สถานที่เกิด เหตุ [sa than thii koet het] n scene

สถานทูต [sa than thut] ฉันต้องโทรหาส ถานทูตของฉัน [chan tong tho ha sa than thut khong chan] I need to call my embassy; ฉันอยากโทรไปที่สถานทูต ของฉัน [chan yak tho pai thii sa than thut khong chan] I'd like to phone my embassy

สถานบันเทิง [sa than ban thoeng] สถาน บันเทิงเวลากลางคืน [sa than ban thoeng we la klang khuen] n nightlife

สถานภาพ [sa tha na phap] สถานภาพ การแต่งงาน [sa tha na phap kan taeng ngan] n marital status; สถานภาพ ปัจจุบัน [sa tha na phap pat chu ban] n status quo

สถานะ [sa tha na] ฉันตกอยู่ในสถานะ ลำบาก [chan tok yu nai sa tha na lam bak] I am in trouble

สถานี [sa tha ni] n station; สถานีรถ โดยสารประจำทาง [sa tha ni rot doi san pra cham thang] n bus station; สถานี รถไฟ [sa tha ni rot fai] n railway station; สถานีรถไฟใต้ดิน [sa tha ni rot

fai tai din] n metro station, tube station; สถานีรถโดยสารอยู่ที่ไหน? [sa tha ni rot doi san yu thii nai] Where is the bus station?

สถานีตำรวจ [sa tha ni tam ruat] สถานี ตำรวจอยู่ที่ไหน? [sa tha ni tam ruat yu thii nai] Where is the police station?; ฉันมองต้องหาสถานีตำรวจ [chan mong tong ha sa tha ni tam ruat] I need to find a police station

สถานีรถไฟ [sa tha ni rot fai] วิธีไหนที่ดี ที่สุดที่จะไปสถานีรถไฟ? [wi thi nai thii di thii sut thii ja pai sa tha ni rot fai] What's the best way to get to the railway station?

สถาบัน [sa tha ban] n institution; สถาบันศึกษา [sa tha ban suek sa] n academy

สถาปนิก [sa tha pa nik] n architect

สถาปัตยกรรม [sa tha pat ta ya kam] n architecture; ซึ่งเป็นสถาปัตยกรรมที่แพร่ ในยุโรปตะวันตกตั้งแต่ศตวรรษที่ ๙ ถึง ๑๒ [sueng pen sa ta pat ta ya kam thii phrae nai yu rop ta wan tok tang tae sat ta wat thii thueng] adj Romanesque

สถิติ [sa thi ti] เกี่ยวกับชีวสถิติวิทยา [kiao kap chi wa sa thi ti wit tha ya] adj biometric; สถิติ ข้อมูล [sa thi ti, kho mun] npl data; ภาพแสดงสถิติรูปพาย [phap sa daeng sa thi ti rup phai] n pie chart

สน [son] ต้นสน [ton son] n conifer, pine

ส้น [son] ส้นเท้า [son thao] n heel; ที่มีส้น สูง [thii mii son sung] adj high-heeled; คุณใส่ส้นรองเท้านี้ได้ไหม? [khun sai son rong thao nii dai mai] Can you re-heel these shoes?

สนใจ [son chai] v interest; เกี่ยวกับเรื่องที่ ได้รับความสนใจในขณะนั้น [kiao kap rueang thii dai rap khwam son jai nai kha na nan] adj topical; เพ่งความสนใจ [pheng khwam son jai] v concentrate; มีความสนใจ [mii khwam son jai] adj interested; ขอโทษ ฉันไม่สนใจ [kho thot chan mai son jai] Sorry, I'm not interested

สนทนา [son tha na] การสนทนา [kan son tha na] n dialogue; บทสนทนา [bot son tha na] n conversation

สนธิสัญญา [son thi san ya] n treaty

สนับสนุน [sa nap sa nun] n backup ▷ v back up, support; การส่งเสริมสนับสนุน [kan song sem sa nab sa nun] n promotion; การสนับสนุน [kan sa nap sa nun] n support; ผู้สนับสนุน [phu sa nap sa nun] n supporter

สนาม [sa nam] n field; สนามเด็กเล่น [sa nam dek len] n playground; สนามเด็ก เล่น [sa nam dek len] n pitch (sport); สนามเทนนิส [sa nam then nis] n tennis court

สนามกอล์ฟ [sa nam kop] มีสนามกอล์ฟ สาธารณะใกล้ที่นี่ไหม? [mii sa nam kolf sa tha ra na klai thii ni mai] Is there a public golf course near here?

สนามกีฬา [sa nam ki la] สนามกีฬาที่มี อัฒจันทร์โดยรอบ [sa nam ki la thii mii at tha chan doi rop] n stadium; เราจะไป ที่สนามกีฬาได้อย่างไร? [rao ja pai thii sa nam ki la dai yang rai] How do we get to the stadium?

สนามบิน [sa nam bin] n airport; แท็กซี่ ไปสนามบินราคาเท่าไร? [thaek si pai sa nam bin ra kha thao rai] How much is the taxi to the airport?; ฉันจะไปสนามบิน ได้อย่างไร? [chan ja pai sa nam bin dai yang rai] How do I get to the airport?

สนามหญ้า [sa nam ya] n lawn

สนิม [sa nim] n rust; ที่เป็นสนิม [thii pen sa nim] adj rusty

สนุก [sa nuk] ไม่สนุก ไม่ราบรื่น [mai sa nuk, mai rap ruen] adj unpleasant; สวนสนุก [suan sa nuk] n fairground, funfair; น่าสนุก [na sa nuk] adj fun; เรา สนุกมาก [rao sa nuk mak] We are having a nice time

สนุกเกอร์ [sa nuk koe] n snooker

สนุกสนาน [sa nuk sa nan] v enjoy; สนุกสนานเฮฮา [sa nuk sa nan he ha] adj hilarious; ความสนุกสนาน [khwam sa nuk sa nan] n zest (excitement); ชอบเล่น สนุกสนาน [chop len sa nuk sa nan] adj playful

สบถ [sa bot] v swear; คำสบถ [kham sa bot] n swearword

สบาย [sa bai] ไม่สบาย [mai sa bai] adj unwell; ไม่ค่อยสบาย [mai khoi sa bai] adj poorly; สะดวกสบาย [sa duak sa bai] adj comfortable; เขาไม่สบาย [khao mai sa bai] He's not well

สบายใจ [sa bai chai] adj smug

สบู่ [sa bu] n soap; จานสบู่ [chan sa bu] n soap dish; ผงสบู่ [phong sa bu] n soap powder; ไม่มีสบู่ [mai mii sa bu] There is no soap

สปริง [sa pring] ลวดสปริง [luat sa pring] n spring (coil)

สปาเก็ตตี้ [sa pa ket ti] n spaghetti

สเปน [sa pen] adj เกี่ยวกับสเปน [kiao kap sa pen] adj Spanish ▷ n ชาวสเปน [chao sa pen] n Spaniard; ประเทศสเปน [pra tet sa pen] n Spain, Spanish

สเปรย์ [sa pre] สเปรย์ฉีดผม [sa pre chit phom] n hair spray

สภา [sa pha] สภาท้องถิ่น [sa pha thong thin] n council

สภากาชาด [sap ha ka chat] n Red Cross

สภาพ [su phap] สภาพไม่รู้สึกตัวของผู้ป่วย [sa phap mai ru suek tua khong phu puai] n coma; สภาพรกรุงรัง [sa phap rok rung rang] n mess; สภาพที่จนมุม [sa phap thii chon mum] n stalemate

สภาพแวดล้อม [sa phap waet lom] n environment, state; ที่เป็นมิตรกับสภาพ แวดล้อม [thii pen mit kap sa phap waet lom] adj environmentally friendly; ที่ไม่ ทำความเสียหายกับสภาพแวดล้อม [thii mai tham khwam sia hai kap sa phap waet lom] adj ecofriendly

สภาวะ [sa pha wa] สภาวะ เงื่อนไข [sa pha wa, nguean khai] n condition;

สภาวะเหมือนจริงที่จำลองโดยทางเทคนิค
คอมพิวเตอร์ [sa pha wa muean ching
thii cham long doi thang tek nik khom
phio toe] *n* virtual reality; สภาวะ
แวดล้อม [sa pha wa waet lom] *adj*
environmental

สภาวะฉุกเฉิน [sa pha wa chuk choen]
เป็นสภาวะฉุกเฉิน [pen sa pha wa chuk
choen] It's an emergency!

ส้ม [som] *n* mandarin *(fruit)*; ส้มชนิดหนึ่ง
[som cha nit nueng] *n* clementine; ต้น
ส้ม [ton som] *n* orange; ที่มีสีส้ม [thii mii
sii som] *adj* orange

สมควรได้รับ [som khuan dai rap] *v*
deserve

สมดุล [som dun] ความสมดุล [khwam
som dun] *n* balance; ซึ่งมีสัดส่วนสมดุลกัน
[sueng mii sat suan som dun kan] *adj*
symmetrical; ที่สมดุล [thii som dun]
adj balanced

สมบัติ [som bat] *n* treasure; สมบัติส่วนตัว
[som bat suan tua] *npl* belongings

สมบูรณ์ [som bun] โดยสมบูรณ์ [doi som
bun] *n* total; ไม่สมบูรณ์ [mai som boon]
adj incomplete; ความสมบูรณ์แบบ
[khwam som boon baep] *n* perfection

สมมุติ [som mut] *v* suppose; ตามที่สมมุติ
[tam thii som mut] *adv* supposedly; ถ้า
สมมุติว่า [tha som mut wa] *conj*
supposing

สมรส [som rot] คู่สมรส [khu som rot] *n*
partner

สมรู้ร่วมคิด [som ru ruam kit] ผู้สมรู้ร่วม
คิด [phu som ru ruam kit] *n*
accomplice

สมหวัง [som wang] *v* fulfil

สมเหตุสมผล [som het som phon] ไม่สม
เหตุสมผล [mai som het som phon] *adj*
unreasonable

สมอ [sa mo] สมอเรือ [sa mo ruea] *n*
anchor

สมอง [sa mong] *n* brain; เยื่อหุ้มสมอง
อักเสบ [yuea hum sa mong ak sep] *n*
meningitis; โรคเลือดคั่งในสมอง [rok

lueat khang nai sa mong] *n* multiple
sclerosis; โรคอาการพิการทางสมอง [rok a
kan phi kan thang sa mong] *n* Down's
syndrome

ส้มโอ [som o] ส้มโอฝรั่ง [som o fa rang] *n*
grapefruit

สมัคร [sa mak] แบบฟอร์มใบสมัคร [baep
fom bai sa mak] *n* application form; ใบ
สมัคร [bai sa mak] application; ผู้สมัคร
[phu sa mak] *n* applicant, candidate

สมัครใจ [sa mak chai] เสนอตัวโดยสมัคร
ใจ [sa noe tua doi sa mak jai] *v*
volunteer; โดยสมัครใจ [doi sa mak jai]
adj voluntary; อย่างสมัครใจ [yang sa
mak jai] *adj* voluntarily, willing

สมัครเล่น [sa mak len] มือสมัครเล่น [mue
sa mak len] *n* amateur

สมัยเก่า [sa mai kao] *adj* old-fashioned

สมัยใหม่ [sa mai mai] *adj* modern; ภาษา
สมัยใหม่ต่าง ๆ [pha sa sa mai mai tang
tang] *npl* modern languages

สมาคม [sa ma khom] สมาคม สโมสร [sa
ma khom, sa mo son] *n* club *(group)*;
กลุ่ม สมาคม [klum, sa ma khom] *n*
association

สมาชิก [sa ma chik] *n* member; เป็น
สมาชิกของ [pen sa ma chik khong] *v*
belong to; สมาชิกสภาเทศบาล [sa ma
chik sa pha tet sa ban] *n* councillor;
การเป็นสมาชิก [kan pen sa ma chik] *n*
membership; คุณต้องเป็นสมาชิกหรือไม่?
[khun tong pen sa ma chik rue mai]
Do you have to be a member?

สม่ำเสมอ [sa mam sa moe] ไม่สม่ำเสมอ
[mai sa mam sa moe] *adj* inconsistent,
irregular

สมุด [sa mut] สมุดแผนที่ [sa mut phaen
thii] *n* atlas; สมุดโทรศัพท์ [sa mut tho
ra sap] *n* phonebook, telephone
directory; สมุดโทรศัพท์ฉบับโฆษณาสินค้า
[sa mut tho ra sap cha bap khot sa na
sin ka] *npl* Yellow Pages®

สมุดภาพ [sa mut phap] album

สมุนไพร [sa mun phrai] *npl* herbs; ไม้

พุ่มสมุนไพร [mai phum sa mun phrai] *n* rosemary; สมุนไพรชนิดหนึ่งมีกลิ่นหอมใช้ อาหาร [sa mun phrai cha nit nueng mii klin hom chai a han] *n* tarragon; สมุนไพรอย่างหนึ่งเป็นหัวมีรสเผ็ด [sa mun phrai yang nueng pen hua mii rot phet] *n* horseradish

สโมสร [sa mo son] สโมสรกอล์ฟ [sa mo son kolf] *n* golf club (*society*); สมาคม สโมสร [sa ma khom, sa mo son] *n* club (*group*)

สรรพนาม [sap pha nam] *n* pronoun

สรรเสริญ [san soen] การสรรเสริญ [kan san sen] *v* praise

สร้อย [soi] สร้อยคอ [soi kho] *n* necklace

สร้อยข้อมือ [soi kho mue] กำไลหรือสร้อย ข้อมือ [kam lai rue soi kho mue] *n* bracelet

สระ¹ [sa ra] สระน้ำตื้น ๆ สำหรับเด็กเล็ก [sa nam tuen tuen sam rap dek lek] *n* paddling pool; สระว่ายน้ำ [sa wai nam] *n* baths, swimming pool; เป็นสระข้าง นอกใช่ไหม? [pen sa khang nok chai mai] Is it an outdoor pool?

สระ² [sa ra] เสียงสระ [siang sa ra] *n* vowel

สระน้ำ [sa nam] *n* pond, pool (*water*)

สระว่ายน้ำ [sa wai nam] มีสระว่ายน้ำเด็ก ไหม? [mii sa wai nam dek mai] Is there a children's pool?; มีสระว่ายน้ำไหม? [mii sa wai nam mai] Is there a swimming pool?; มีสระว่ายน้ำที่เด็ก ๆ จะลงแกว่งแขน ขาในน้ำไหม? [mii sa wai nam thii dek dek ja long kwaeng khaen kha nai nam mai] Is there a paddling pool for the children?

สร้าง [sang] *v* construct, create, build; สร้างใหม่ [sang mai] *v* rebuild; การสร้าง [kan sang] *n* creation; ซึ่งสร้างขึ้นมา [sueng sang khuen ma] *adj* man-made

สร้างสรรค์ [sang san] *adj* innovative; ความคิดสร้างสรรค์ [khwam kit sang san] *n* innovation

สรุป [sa rup] *v* summarize, conclude; ใจความสรุป [jai khwam sa rup] *n* summary; สรุปสาระ [sa rup sa ra] *v* sum up; การสรุป [kan sa rup] *n* conclusion

สลดใจ [sa lot chai] น่าสลดใจ [na sa lot jai] *adj* tragic

สละ [sa la] ยอมสละ [yom sa la] *v* part with

สละสิทธิ์ [sa la sit] *v* waive

สลัก [sa lak] *v* engrave; แป้นเกลียวของสลัก [paen kliao khong sa lak] *n* nut (*device*)

สลัด [sa lat] *n* salad; สลัดรวม [sa lat ruam] *n* mixed salad; สลัดกะหล่ำปลีใส่มา ยองเนส [sa lat ka lam plii sai ma yong nes] *n* coleslaw; สลัดผักสีเขียว [sa lat phak sii khiao] *n* green salad

สลับ [sa lap] ซึ่งสลับกัน [sueng sa lap kan] *adj* alternate

สลัว [sa lua] *adj* dim

สลาก [sa lak] *n* draw (*lottery*)

สลากกินแบ่ง [sa lak kin baeng] *n* lottery

สแลง [sa laeng] ภาษาสแลง [pha sa sa laeng] *n* slang

สโลวาเกีย [sa lo wa kia] เกี่ยวกับสาธารณ รัฐสโลวาเกีย [kiao kap sa tha ra na rat sa lo va kia] *adj* Slovak; ชาวสโลวาเกีย [chao sa lo wa kia] *n* Slovak (*person*); ประเทศสโลวาเกีย [pra tet sa lo va kia] *n* Slovakia

สโลเวเนีย [sa lo we nia] เกี่ยวกับ สาธารณรัฐสโลเวเนีย [kiao kap sa tha ra na rat sa lo ve nia] *adj* Slovenian; สาธารณรัฐสโลเวเนีย [sa tha ra na rat sa lo ve nia] *n* Slovenia; ชาวสโลเวเนียน [chao sa lo we nian] *n* Slovenian (*person*)

สวดมนต์ [suat mon] *v* pray; ผู้สวดมนต์ [phu suat mon] *n* prayer

สวน [suan] *n* garden; สวนสนุก [suan sa nuk] *n* fairground, funfair; สวน สาธารณะ [suan sa tha ra na] *n* park; สวนผลไม้ [suan phon la mai] *n* orchard; เราไปเยี่ยมชมสวนได้ไหม? [rao pai yiam chom suan dai mai] Can we visit the gardens?

ส่วน [suan] ส่วนหนึ่ง [suan nueng] n
part; ส่วนที่ตัดออก [suan thii tat ok] n
section

ส่วนเกิน [suan koen] เป็นส่วนเกิน [pen
suan koen] adj surplus

ส่วนตัว [suan tua] โดยส่วนตัว [doi suan
tua] adv personally; ไม่ใช่ส่วนตัว [mai
chai suan tua] adj impersonal; ความ
เป็นส่วนตัว [khwam pen suan tua] n
privacy; มีห้องน้ำส่วนตัวในห้องไหม? [mii
hong nam suan tua nai hong mai]
Does the room have a private
bathroom?

ส่วนบุคคล [suan bu khon] adj personal

ส่วนแบ่ง [suan baeng] n portion, share

ส่วนประกอบ [suan pra kop] n
component; เกี่ยวกับส่วนประกอบ [kiao
kap suan pra kop] adj component

ส่วนผสม [suan pha som] n ingredient,
mix-up, mixture; ส่วนผสมสำหรับแก้ไอ
[suan pha som sam rap kae ai] n cough
mixture; ส่วนผสมของแป้ง น้ำและอื่น ๆ
เช่นน้ำมัน น้ำตาลเพื่อทำขนมปัง [suan pha
som khong paeng nam lae uen uen
chen nam man nam tan phuea tham
kha nom pang] n dough; ส่วนผสมของ
ปูนขาวหรือซีเมนต์กับน้ำและทราย [suan
pha som khong pun khao rue si men
kap nam lae sai] n mortar (plaster)

ส่วนมาก [suan mak] adj major ▷ adv
mostly

ส่วนร่วม [suan ruam] การมีส่วนร่วม [kan
mii suan ruam] n communion; ซึ่งมี
ส่วนร่วมกัน [sueng mii suan ruam kan]
adj mutual

ส่วนลด [suan lot] มีส่วนลดให้คนพิการ
ไหม? [mii suan lot hai khon phi kan
mai] Is there a reduction for disabled
people?; มีส่วนลดสำหรับเด็กหรือไม่? [mii
suan lot sam rap dek rue mai] Are
there any reductions for children?; มี
ส่วนลดสำหรับนักเรียนหรือไม่? [mii suan
lot sam rap nak rian rue mai] Are there
any reductions for students?

ส่วนสนุก [suan sa nuk] n theme park;
ลานรถลื่นไถลสำหรับการเล่นของเด็กในสวน
สนุก [lan rot luen tha lai sam rap kan
len khong dek nai suan sa nuk] n
rollercoaster

ส่วนสัตว์ [suan sat] n zoo

ส่วนใหญ่ [suan yai] n majority; โดยส่วน
ใหญ่ [doi suan yai] adv mainly

สวม [suam] สวมใส่ [suam sai] vt wear

สวย [suai] adj pretty; สวยงดงาม [suai
ngot ngam] adj picturesque; สวยงาม
[suai ngam] adj elegant

สวยงาม [suai ngam] adj beautiful,
gorgeous; สถานที่สวยงาม [sa than thii
suai ngam] n beauty spot; อย่างสวยงาม
[yang suai ngam] adv beautifully,
prettily

สวรรค์ [sa wan] n heaven, paradise

สวัสดิการ [sa wat di kan] เซ็นต์ลงทะเบียน
เพื่อรับเงินสวัสดิการ [sen long tha bian
phuea rap ngoen sa wat sa di kan] v
sign on

สวัสดี [sa wat di] excl hello!, hi!

สว่าง [sa wang] adj light (not dark); แสง
สว่าง [saeng sa wang] n light; สว่างจ้า
[sa wang cha] adj bright; ฉันเอาไปดูตรง
ที่สว่างได้ไหม? [chan ao pai du trong
thii sa wang dai mai] May I take it over
to the light?

สว่างไสว [sa wang sa hwai] เจิดจ้า
สว่างไสว [choet cha, sa wang sa wai]
adj vivid

สวาซิแลนด์ [sa wa si laen] ประเทศ
สวาซิแลนด์ [pra tet sa wa si laen] n
Swaziland

สว่าน [sa wan] สว่านเปิดจุกขวด [sa wan
poet chuk khaut] n corkscrew; สว่าน
ชนิดที่ใช้กำลังอัดของอากาศ [sa wan cha
nit thii chai kam lang at khong a kaat]
n pneumatic drill

สวิตเซอร์แลนด์ [sa wit soe laen] เกี่ยวกับ
ชาวสวิตเซอร์แลนด์ [kiao kap chao sa wis
soe laen] n Swiss; ประเทศสวิตเซอร์แลนด์
[pra tet sa vis soe laen] n Swiss,

Switzerland

สวีเดน [sa wi den] เกี่ยวกับประเทศสวีเดน [kiao kap pra thet sa wi den] *adj* Swedish; ชาวสวีเดน [chao sa wi den] *n* Swede; ประเทศสวีเดน [pra tet sa wi den] *n* Sweden

สหพันธ์ [sa ha phan] *n* league

สหภาพ [sa ha phap] สหภาพยุโรป [sa ha phap yu rop] *n* European Union; ประเทศในกลุ่มสหภาพยุโรป [pra tet nai klum sa ha phap yu rop] *abbr* EU

สหภาพแรงงาน [sa ha phap raeng ngan] *n* trade union; สมาชิกสหภาพแรงงาน [sa ma chik sa ha phap raeng ngan] *n* trade unionist

สหรัฐอเมริกา [sa ha rat a me ri ka] *n* US; ตัวย่อของประเทศสหรัฐอเมริกา [tua yo khong pra tet sa ha rat a me ri ka] *n* USA; ประเทศสหรัฐอเมริกา [pra tet sa ha rat a me ri ka] *n* United States

สหราชอาณาจักร [sa ha rat cha a na chak] ชาวสหราชอาณาจักร [chao sa ha rat cha a na chak] *n* British; ประเทศสหราชอาณาจักร [pra tet sa ha rat cha a na chak] *n* Great Britain; ประเทศสหราชอาณาจักรอังกฤษ [pra tet sa ha rat cha a na chak ang krit] *n* Britain

สหราชอาณาจักรอังกฤษ [sa ha rat cha a na chak ang krit] ประเทศสหราชอาณาจักรอังกฤษ [pra tet sa ha rat cha a na chak ang krit] *n* United Kingdom

สอง [song] *num* two; ในลำดับที่สอง [nai lam dap thii song] *adv* secondly; ลำดับที่สอง [lam dap thii song] *n* second; สองเท่า [song thao] *adj* double; เวลาสองโมง [we la song mong] It's two o'clock

ส่อง [song] กล้องส่องทางไกล [klong song thang klai] *n* binoculars

ส่องเท่า [song thao] ทำเป็นสองเท่า [tham pen song thao] *vt* double

ส่องแสง [song saeng] ส่องแสงเจิดจ้า [song saeng chet cha] *v* glare; ส่องแสงวาบขึ้นมา [song saeng wab khuen ma] *vi* flash; ทำให้ส่องแสง [tham hai song saeng] *v* shine

สอดคล้อง [sot khlong] สอดคล้องกันพอดี [sot khlong kan pho dii] *v* coincide; ที่สอดคล้องกัน [thii sot khlong kan] *adj* consistent

สอดแนม [sot naem] การสอดแนม [kan sot naem] *n* spying

สอดรู้สอดเห็น [sot ru sot hen] *v* pry

สอน [son] *v* teach; การสอน [kan son] *n* teaching; การสอนพิเศษ [kan son phi set] *n* tuition; ที่เกี่ยวกับการเรียนการสอน [thii kiao kap kan rian kan son] *adj* educational

สอบ [sop] สอบใหม่ [sop mai] *v* resit; สอบผ่าน สอบไล่ได้ [sop phan, sop lai dai] *v* pass (an exam); การสอบ [kan sop] *n* examination

สอบถาม [sop tham] แบบสอบถาม [baep sop tham] *n* questionnaire; โต๊ะสอบถาม [to sop tham] *n* enquiry desk; สำนักงานที่คนไปสอบถาม [sam nak ngan thii khon pai sop tham] *n* inquiries office

สอบปากคำ [sop pak kham] *v* interrogate

สอบสวน [sop suan] การสอบสวน [kan sop suan] *n* inquiry; การสอบสวนสาเหตุที่เสียชีวิต [kan sop suan sa het thii sia chi wid] *n* inquest

ส้อม [som] มีด ช้อนและส้อม [miit chon lae som] *n* cutlery; ส้อมทานอาหาร [som than a han] *n* fork; ฉันขอส้อมสะอาดหนึ่งคันได้ไหม? [chan kho som sa aat nueng khan dai mai] Could I have a clean fork please?

สะกด [sa kot] การสะกดคำ [kan sa kot kham] *n* spelling; อ่านสะกดคำ [arn sa kot kham] *v* spell; คุณสะกดคำนี้อย่างไร? [khun sa kot kham nii yang rai] How do you spell it?

สะดวก [sa duak] *adj* convenient; ใช้สะดวก [chai sa duak] *adj* handy, user-friendly; ไม่สะดวก [mai sa duak] *adj* inconvenient; สะดวกสบาย [sa duak sa bai] *adj* comfortable

สะดวกสบาย [sa duak sa bai] ไม่สะดวก
สบาย [mai sa duak sa bai] *adj*
uncomfortable; ความสะดวกสบายสมัย
ใหม่ [khwam sa duak sa bai sa mai
mai] *npl* mod cons

สะดือ [sa due] *n* belly button, navel

สะดุ้ง [sa dung] *v* startle

สะดุด [sa dut] *v* stumble, trip (up)

สะท้อน [sa thon] เสียงสะท้อน [siang sa
thon] *n* echo; สะท้อนกลับ [sa thon klap]
v reflect; การสะท้อนกลับ [kan sa thon
klap] *n* reflection

สะเทือนใจ [sa thuean chai] สั่น ทำให้สั่น
ทำให้ตกใจและสะเทือนใจ [san, tham hai
san, tham hai tok jai lae sa thuean jai]
vt shake

สะบ้า [sa ba] กระดูกสะบ้าหัวเข่า [kra duk
sa ba hua khao] *n* kneecap

สะพาน [sa phan] *n* bridge; สะพานแขวน
[sa phan khwaen] *n* suspension
bridge; สะพานที่ยื่นออกไปในน้ำ [sa phan
thii yuen ok pai nai nam] *n* pier

สะพาย [sa phai] กระเป๋าสะพายหลัง [kra
pao sa phai lang] *n* backpack; การใส่
กระเป๋าสะพายหลัง [kan sai kra pao sa
phai lang] *n* backpacking; ผู้ใส่กระเป๋า
สะพายหลัง [phu sai kra pao sa phai
lang] *n* backpacker

สะเพร่า [sa phrao] การทำผิดเพราะสะเพร่า
[kan tham phit phro sa phrao] *n*
blunder

สะโพก [sa phok] *n* hip

สะใภ้ [sa phai] ลูกสะใภ้ [luk sa phai] *n*
daughter-in-law; น้องสะใภ้หรือพี่สะใภ้
[nong sa phai rue phii sa phai] *n*
sister-in-law

สะระแหน่ [sa ra nae] *n* peppermint; ใบ
สะระแหน่ [bai sa ra nae] *n* mint (herb/
sweet)

สะสม [sa som] *vt* collect; สิ่งที่สะสมไว้
[sing thii sa som wai] *n* collection; นัก
สะสม [nak sa som] *n* collector

สะอาด [sa ad] *adj* clean; สะอาดและประณีต
[sa at lae pra nit] *adj* smart; สะอาดไม่มี

ตำหนิ [sa at mai mii tam ni] *adj*
spotless; สิ่งที่ใช้ทำความสะอาดผิวหน้า
[sing thii chai tham khwam sa at phio
na] *n* cleanser; ห้องไม่สะอาด [hong mai
sa at] The room isn't clean

สะอิดสะเอียน [sa it sa ian] น่า
สะอิดสะเอียน [na sa it sa ian] *adj*
sickening

สะอึก [sa uek] *npl* hiccups

สะอึกสะอื้น [sa uek sa uean] ร้องไห้สะอึก
สะอื้น [rong hai sa uek sa uen] *v* sob

สัก [sak] รอยสัก [roi sak] *n* tattoo

สักการะ [sak ka ra] ซึ่งเป็นที่สักการะทาง
ศาสนา [sueng pen thii sak ka ra thang
sat sa na] *adj* sacred

สักหลาด [sak ka lat] สักหลาดที่เป็นริ้ว [sak
ka lat thii pen rio] *n* corduroy; ผ้า
สักหลาดอ่อน [pha sak ka lat on] *n*
flannel

สั่ง [sang] *v* order (command), order
(request); แบบฟอร์มสั่งซื้อ [baep fom
sang sue] *n* order form; ที่สั่งทำ [thii
sang tham] *adj* customized; ฉันไม่ได้สั่ง
[chan mai dai sang] This isn't what I
ordered

สังกะสี [sang ka si] *n* zinc

สังเกต [sang ket] *v* observe; การสังเกต
[kan sang ket] *n* notice (note); ช่าง
สังเกต [chang sang ket] *adj* observant;
ที่สังเกตเห็นได้ [thii sang ket hen dai]
adj noticeable

สังเกตการณ์ [sang ket kan] หอ
สังเกตการณ์ [ho sang ket kan] *n*
observatory; ผู้สังเกตการณ์ [phu sang
ket kan] *n* observer

สังคม [sang khom] *n* society; อยู่ร่วมกัน
ในสังคม [yu ruam kan nai sang khom]
adj social

สังคมนิยม [sang khom ni yom] ระบบ
สังคมนิยม [ra bop sang khom ni yom] *n*
socialism; ที่เป็นแบบสังคมนิยม [thii pen
baep sang khom ni yom] *adj* socialist;
นักสังคมนิยม [nak sang khom ni yom] *n*
socialist

สังคมวิทยา [sang khom wit tha ya] n
sociology

สังคมสงเคราะห์ [sang khom song khro]
การบริการสังคมสงเคราะห์ [kan bo ri kan
sang khom song khro] npl social
services; นักสังคมสงเคราะห์ [nak sang
khom song khro] n social worker

สั่งซื้อ [sang sue] การสั่งซื้อเป็นประจำ [kan
sang sue pen pra cham] n subscription

สังสรรค์ [sang san] v get together

สั่งสอน [sang son] คำแนะนำสั่งสอน
[kham nae nam sang son] npl
instructions; ผู้แนะนำสั่งสอน [phu nae
nam sang son] n instructor

สัญชาตญาณ [san chat ta yan] n
instinct; การรู้โดยสัญชาตญาณ [kan ru
doi san chat ta yan] n intuition

สัญชาติ [san chat] n nationality

สัญญลักษณ์ [san ya lak] n symbol;
สัญลักษณ์บนคอมพิวเตอร์แสดงให้เห็นจุดที่
พิมพ์ได้ [san ya lak bon khom phio toe
sa daeng hai hen chut thii phim dai] n
cursor; สิ่งที่ใช้เป็นสัญลักษณ์ [sing thii
chai pen san ya lak] n token; ภาษา
สัญญลักษณ์ [pha sa san ya lak] n sign
language

สัญญา [san ya] n contract ▷ v promise;
ให้คำมั่นสัญญา [hai kham man san ya]
v commit; สัญญาเช่า [san ya chao] n
lease; คำมั่นสัญญา [kham man san ya]
n promise

สัญญาณ [san yan] สัญญาณเตือนไฟไหม้
[san yan tuean fai mai] n fire alarm;
สัญญาณเตือนภัยปลอม [san yan tuean
phai plom] n false alarm; สัญญาณขอ
ความช่วยเหลือ [san yan kho khwam
chuai luea] n SOS

สัญญาณ [san yan] n signal; เสียงสัญญาณ
เตือนภัย [siang san yan tuean phai] n
siren; เครื่องส่งสัญญาณติดตามตัว
[khrueang song san yan tit tam tua] n
bleeper; เครื่องสัญญาณเตือนภัย
[khrueang san yan tuean phai] n
smoke alarm

สัญลักษณ์ [san ya lak] สัญลักษณ์ภาพ
[san ya lak phap] n icon

สัญญาณ [san yan] สัญญาณไม่ว่าง [san
yan mai wang] n busy signal

สัดส่วน [sat suan] n proportion; ทำให้ได้
สัดส่วนกัน [tham hai dai sat suan kan]
adj proportional

สัตว์ [sat] n animal; โรงละครสัตว์ [rong la
khon sat] n circus; ลูกสัตว์ [luk sat] n
litter (offspring); ลูกของสัตว์ [luk khong
sat] n cub

สัตว์ทะเล [sat tha le] สัตว์ทะเลพวกเดียวกับ
สิงโตทะเลและแมวน้ำ [sat tha le phuak
diao kap sing to tha le lae maeo nam]
n walrus

สัตว์น้ำ [sat nam] สัตว์น้ำประเภทมีเปลือก
[sat nam pra phet mii plueak] n
shellfish; ฉันแพ้สัตว์น้ำที่มีเปลือก [chan
phae sat nam thii mii plueak] I'm
allergic to shellfish

สัตว์ประหลาด [sat pra lat] n monster

สัตว์ป่า [sat pa] เราอยากเห็นสัตว์ป่า [rao
yak hen sat pa] We'd like to see wildlife

สัตวแพทย์ [sat phaet] n vet

สัตว์เลี้ยง [sat liang] n pet

สัตว์เลี้ยงลูกด้วยนม [sat liang luk duai
nom] n mammal; สัตว์เลี้ยงลูกด้วยนมที่
ใช้ฟันแทะ [sat liang luk duai nom thii
chai fan thae] n rodent

สัตว์เลื้อยคลาน [sat lueai khlan] n
reptile; สัตว์เลื้อยคลานเช่นจิ้งจกหรือตุ๊กแก
[sat lueai khlan chen ching chok rue
tuk kae] n lizard

สัตววิทยา [sat ta wa wit tha ya] n
zoology

สั่น [san] สั่น ทำให้สั่น ทำให้ตกใจและ
สะเทือนใจ [san, tham hai san, tham
hai tok jai lae sa thuean jai] vt shake;
สั่นเพราะหนาวหรือความกลัว [san phro
nao rue khwam klua] v shiver; สั่นระริก
ด้วยความกลัว [san ra rik duai khwam
klua] v shudder

สั้น [san] adj brief, short; แขนสั้น [khaen
san] adj short-sleeved; สั้นกระชับ [san

kra chap] *adj* concise; สายตาสั้น [sai ta san] *adj* near-sighted

สั่นคลอน [san khlon] *adj* shaky

สันนิษฐาน [san ni than] *v* presume

สั่นสะเทือน [san sa thuean] *v* tremble; สั่นสะเทือน หวั่นไหว [san sa thuean, wan wai] *vi* shake

สันหลัง [san lang] กระดูกสันหลัง [kra duk san lang] *n* backbone

สับ [sap] *v* chop; การสับ [kan sap] *v* chop

สับปะรด [sap pa rot] *n* pineapple

สับสน [sap son] *v* confuse; สับสนวุ่นวาย [sap son wun wai] *adj* upset; ความ สับสน [khwam sap son] *n* chaos, confusion; ความยุ่งเหยิง ความโกลาหล สถานการณ์สับสนวุ่นวาย [khwam yung yoeng, khwam ko la hon, sa than na kan sap son wun wai] *npl* shambles

สัปดาห์ [sap da] หนึ่งสัปดาห์ [nueng sap da] *n* week

สัมนา [sam ma na] การสัมนา [kan sam ma na] *n* conference

สัมปทาน [sam pa than] สัมปทาน การ ยินยอม [sam pa than, kan yin yom] *n* concession

สัมผัส [sam phat] *v* touch; สัมผัสหรือ ลูบคล่ำ [sam phat rue lup khlam] *v* stroke; การลูบหรือการสัมผัส [kan lub rue kan sam phat] *n* stroke (hit); ที่ถูกสัมผัส [thii thuk sam phat] *adj* touched

สัมพันธ์ [sam pan] สัมพันธ์กัน [sam phan kan] *adj* joint; ความสัมพันธ์ [khwam sam phan] *n* relationship; ความสัมพันธ์ กัน [khwam sam phan kan] *n* connection

สัมพันธมิตร [sam phan tha rat] *n* ally

สัมภาษณ์ [sam pat] *v* interview; การ สัมภาษณ์ [kan sam phat] *n* interview; ผู้ สัมภาษณ์ [phu sam phat] *n* interviewer

สัมฤทธิ์ [sam rit] ทองสัมฤทธิ์ [thong sam rit] *n* bronze

สาขา [sa kha] *n* branch

สาด [sat] สาดกระเด็น [sat kra den] *v* splash

สาธารณรัฐอัฟริกันกลาง [sa tha ra na rat ap fri kan klang] ประเทศสาธารณรัฐอัฟริ กันกลาง [pra tet sa tha ra na rat af ri kan klang] *n* Central African Republic

สาธารณรัฐ [sa tha ra na rat] *n* republic

สาธารณรัฐเช็ก [sa tha ra na rat chek] *n* Czech Republic; เกี่ยวกับสาธารณรัฐเช็ก [kiao kap sa tha ra na rat chek] *n* Czech

สาธารณรัฐทองกา [sa tha ra na rat thong ka] *n* Tonga

สาธารณะ [sa tha ra na] *n* public; ที่ สาธารณะ [thii sa tha ra na] *n* public

สาธิต [sa thit] การสาธิต [kan sa thit] *n* demo

สาปแช่ง [sap chaeng] คำสาปแช่ง [kham sap chaeng] *n* curse

สาม [sam] *number* three; เศษหนึ่งส่วนสาม [set nueng suan sam] *n* third; ในลำดับ สาม [nai lam dap sam] *adv* thirdly; ซึ่ง เป็นลำดับที่สาม [sueng pen lam dap thii sam] *adj* third; เวลาสามโมง [we la sam mong] at three o'clock, It's three o'clock

สามสิบ [sam sip] *number* thirty

สามเหลี่ยม [sam liam] *n* triangle

สามัญสำนึก [sa man sam nuke] *n* common sense

สามารถ [sa mat] *adj* able; ไม่สามารถที่จะ [mai sa mat thii ja] *adj* unable to; ไม่ สามารถอ่านและเขียนได้ [mai sa mat an lae khian dai] *adj* illiterate; สามารถ เขียนหรือพูดได้สองภาษา [sa maat khian rue phut dai song pha sa] *adj* bilingual

สามี [sa mi] *n* husband; แม่สามี [mae sa mii] *n* mother-in-law; สามีหรือภรรยา [sa mii rue phan ra ya] *n* spouse; อดีต สามี [a dit sa mii] *n* ex-husband; นี่สามี ดิฉันค่ะ [ni sa mii di chan kha] This is my husband

สาย [sai] *adv* late; สายเคเบิ้ล [sai khe boel] *n* cable; สายชนวน [sai cha nuan] *n* fuse; สายต่อหม้อแบตเตอรี่ [sai to mo baet toe ri] *npl* jump leads; รถไฟมาสาย ใช่ไหม? [rot fai ma sai chai mai] Is the train running late?

สายการบิน [sai kan bin] n airline

สายคาด [sai khat] n band (strip)

สายเคเบิล [sai khe boen] ปิดที่สายเคเบิล ใหญ่ [pit thii sai khe boen yai] Turn it off at the mains

สายตา [sai ta] n eyesight; สายตาสั้น [sai ta san] adj near-sighted; ซึ่งมีสายตาสั้น [sueng mii sai ta san] adj short-sighted; ผู้มีคุณสมบัติที่จะตรวจ ออกใบวัดและขายอุปกรณ์เกี่ยวกับสายตา [phu mii khun na som bat thii ja truat ok bai wat lae khai ub pa kon kiao kap sai ta] n optician

สายพาน [sai phan] สายพานในเครื่องยนต์ [sai phan nai khrueang yon] n fan belt; สายพานการขนส่ง [sai phan kan khon song] n conveyor belt

สายไฟ [sai fai] n flex; ที่ต่อสายไฟ [thii to sai fai] n extension cable

สายยาง [sai yang] n hosepipe

สายรัด [sai rat] n strap

สายวัด [sai wat] n tape measure

สายไหม [sai mai] ขนมสายไหม [kha nom sai mai] n candyfloss

สาร [san] สารโซเดียมไบคาร์บอเนต [san so diam bi kha bo net] n bicarbonate of soda; สารคาเฟอีน [san kha fe in] n caffeine; สารชนิดหนึ่งสกัดจากตับอ่อน [san cha nit nueng sa kat chak tap on] n insulin

สารกันบูด [san khan but] n preservative

สารคดี [sa ra kha di] n documentary

สารเคมี [san khe mi] n chemical

สารบัญ [sa ra ban] n index (list)

สารภาพ [sa ra phap] v admit (confess), confess, own up; คำสารภาพ [kham sa ra phap] n confession

สารภาพบาป [sa ra phap bap] วันเทศกาล สารภาพบาป [wan tet sa kan sa ra phap bap] n Shrove Tuesday

สารอาหาร [san a han] n nutrient

สาระ [sa ra] เนื้อหาสาระ [nuea ha sa ra] n substance; ที่ไร้สาระ [thii rai sa ra] adj

rubbish

สารานุกรม [sa ra nu krom] n encyclopaedia

สาวใช้ [sao chai] n maid; สาวใช้ทำความ สะอาดห้องนอน [sao chai tham khwam sa at hong non] n chambermaid

สาหร่าย [sa rai] สาหร่ายทะเล [sa rai tha le] n seaweed

สำคัญ [sam khan] adj chief, important; เกี่ยวกับการวิจารณ์ สำคัญ [kiao kap kan wi chan, sam khan] adj critical; เป็น เรื่องสำคัญ [pen rueang sam khan] v matter; ไม่สำคัญ [mai sam khan] adj trivial, unimportant

สำแดง [sam daeng] ฉันไม่มีอะไรที่ต้อง สำแดง [chan mai mii a rai thii tong sam daeng] I have nothing to declare; ฉันมีเหล้าที่จะต้องสำแดง [chan mii lao thii ja tong sam daeng] I have a bottle of spirits to declare; ฉันมีแอลกอฮอล์ตาม จำนวนที่อนุญาตที่ต้องสำแดง [chan mii aen ko ho tam cham nuan thii a nu yat thii tong sam daeng] I have the allowed amount of alcohol to declare

สำนัก [sam nak] สำนักแม่ชี [sam nak mae chi] n convent; สำนักสงฆ์ [sam nak song] n abbey; สำนักทะเบียน [sam nak tha bian] n registry office

สำนักงาน [sam nak ngan] n office; สำนักงานเก็บของหาย [sam nak ngan kep khong hai] n lost-property office; สำนักงานแลกเงิน [sam nak ngan laek ngoen] n bureau de change; สำนักงาน ใหญ่ [sam nak ngan yai] n head office; เที่ยวชมสถานที่และสำนักงานท่องเที่ยว [thiao chom sa than thii lae sam nak ngan thong thiao] Sightseeing and tourist office

สำนึก [sam nuek] ไม่สำนึกบุญคุณ [mai sam nuek bun khun] adj ungrateful; ซึ่งสำนึกในบุญคุณ [sueng sam nuek nai bun khun] adj grateful

สำนึกผิด [sam nuek phit] การสำนึกผิด [kan sam nuek phit] n remorse

สำเนา [sam nao] ฉบับสำเนา [cha bap sam nao] n copy (written text); ทำสำเนา [tham sam nao] n copy (reproduction)

สำรวจ [sam ruat] v explore; การสำรวจ [kan sam ruat] n survey; การสำรวจความคิดเห็น [kan sam ruat khwam kit hen] n opinion poll; การสำรวจความคิดเห็นจากคนส่วนมาก [kan sam ruat khwam kit hen chak kon suan mak] n poll

สำรอง [sam rong] v reserve; เก็บสำรองไว้ [kep sam rong wai] v stock up on; ไม่มีสำรอง [mai mii sam rong] v run out of; ห้องว่างหรือห้องสำรอง [hong wang rue hong sam rong] n spare room

สำเร็จ [sam ret] ความสำเร็จ [khwam sam ret] n success; ทำให้สำเร็จ [tham hai sam ret] v carry out

สำลี [sam li] n cotton wool; สำลีแคะหู [sam lii khae hu] n cotton bud

สำหรับ [sam rap] กุญแจดอกนี้สำหรับที่ไหน? [kun jae dok nii sam rap thii nai] What's this key for?; ฉันอยากจองโต๊ะสำหรับสองคนเวลาเจ็ดโมงครึ่ง [chan yak chong to sam rap song khon we la chet mong khrueng] I'd like to make a reservation for half past seven for two people

สิง [sing] ซึ่งสิงอยู่ [sueng sing yu] adj haunted

สิ่ง [sing] ไม่มีสักสิ่ง [mai mii sak sing] pron none; สิ่งกีดขวาง [sing kit khwang] n block (obstruction); สิ่งกระตุ้น [sing kra tun] n incentive

สิ่งก่อสร้าง [sing ko sang] สิ่งก่อสร้างสูงรูปกรวยที่เป็นส่วนหนึ่งของโบสถ์ [sing ko sang sung rup kruai thii pen suan nueng khong bot] n spire

สิ่งกีดขวาง [sing kit khang] n roadblock

สิ่งของ [sing khong] n pack, thing; รายการสิ่งของ [rai kan sing khong] n inventory; สิ่งของในรายการ [sing khong nai rai kan] n item; วัตถุสิ่งของ [wat thu sing khong] n object

สิ่งตีพิมพ์ [sing ti phim] n publication

สิงโต [sing to] n lion; สิงโตตัวเมีย [sing to tua mia] n lioness

สิ่งทอ [sing tho] ผ้าหรือสิ่งทอ [pha rue sing tho] n fabric; วัตถุดิบที่นำมาทำสิ่งทอ [wat thu dip thii nam ma tham sing tho] n textile

สิ่งที่ [sing thi] สิ่งที่ อันที่ [sing thii, an thii] pron which

สิ่งประดับ [sing pra dap] สิ่งประดับแวววาว [sing pra dap waeo wao] n tinsel

สิ่งปลูกสร้าง [sing pluk sang] ที่ดินและสิ่งปลูกสร้าง [thii din lae sing pluk sang] npl premises

สิ่งมีชีวิต [sing mi chi wit] n creature; สิ่งมีชีวิตเช่นพืชและสัตว์ [sing mii chi wit chen phuet lae sat] n organism; สิ่งมีชีวิตที่เกิดมาจากเซลล์เดียวกัน [sing mii chi wit thii koet ma chak sel diao kan] n clone; ซึ่งมาจากสิ่งมีชีวิต [sueng ma chak sing mii chi wit] adj organic

สิงห์ [sing] ราศีสิงห์ [ra si sing] n Leo

สิงหาคม [sing ha khom] เดือนสิงหาคม [duean sing ha khom] n August

สิ่งไหน [sing nai] อันไหน สิ่งไหน [an nai, sing nai] pron what

สิ่งอำนวยความสะดวก [sing am nuai khwam sa duak] npl amenities

สิทธิ [sit thi] n right; สิทธิของมนุษย์ [sit thi khong ma nut] npl human rights; สิทธิที่เท่ากันของพลเมือง [sit thi thii thao kan khong phon la mueang] npl civil rights; สิทธิผ่านทาง [sit thi phan thang] n right of way

สินค้า [sin kha] n cargo ▷ npl goods; ใบรายการส่งสินค้าที่แสดงราคา [bai rai kan song sin ka thii sa daeng ra kha] n invoice; สินค้าที่ขนส่ง [sin kha thii khon song] n freight; สินค้าปลอดภาษี [sin kha plot pha si] n duty-free

สินทรัพย์ [sin sap] n assets

สินบน [sin bon] การให้สินบน [kan hai sin bon] n bribery

สิ้นสุด [sin sut] ซึ่งไม่สิ้นสุด [sueng mai sin sut] adj endless; ทำให้สิ้นสุด [tham hai sin sut] *v* end

สิ้นหวัง [sin wang] ความสิ้นหวัง [khwam sin wang] *n* despair; ซึ่งสิ้นหวัง [sueng sin wang] *adj* desperate; อย่างสิ้นหวัง [yang sin wang] *adv* desperately

สิบ [sip] *number* ten; ที่สิบ [thii sip] *adj* tenth; อันดับที่สิบ [an dap thii sip] *n* tenth; เวลาสองโมงสิบนาที [we la song mong sip na thi] It's ten past two

สิบเก้า [sip kao] *number* nineteen; ที่สิบ เก้า [thii sip kao] *adj* nineteenth

สิบเจ็ด [sip chet] *number* seventeen; ที่สิบ เจ็ด [thii sip chet] *adj* seventeenth

สิบโท [sip tho] สิบโท จ่าอากาศโท [sip tho, cha a kaat tho] *n* corporal

สิบแปด [sip paet] *number* eighteen; ที่สิบ แปด [thii sip paet] *adj* eighteenth

สิบสอง [sip song] *number* twelve; ลำดับที่ สิบสอง [lam dap thii sip song] *adj* twelfth

สิบสาม [sip sam] *number* thirteen; ลำดับ ที่สิบสาม [lam dap thii sip sam] *adj* thirteenth

สิบสี่ [sip si] *number* fourteen; อันดับที่สิบสี่ [an dap thii sip si] *adj* fourteenth

สิบหก [sip hok] *number* sixteen; ที่สิบหก [thii sip hok] *adj* sixteenth

สิบห้า [sip ha] *number* fifteen; ลำดับที่สิบ ห้า [lam dap thii sip ha] *adj* fifteenth

สิบเอ็ด [sip et] *number* eleven; ที่สิบเอ็ด [thii sip et] *adj* eleventh

สิว [sio] *n* acne, pimple, zit; เต็มไปด้วยสิว [tem pai duai sio] *adj* spotty

สิ่ว [sio] *n* chisel

สี [si] *n* colour, paint; เป็นสีทอง [pen sii thong] *adj* blonde; เป็นสีนวล [pen sii nuan] *adj* cream; แปรงทาสี [praeng tha sii] *n* paintbrush; ที่เป็นสีเหลือง [thii pen sii lueang] *adj* yellow; เป็นสี [pen sii] in colour

สี่ [si] *number* four; อันดับที่สี่ [an dap thii si] *adj* fourth

สีแทน [si thaen] ที่มีผิวสีแทน [thii mii phio sii taen] *adj* tanned

สีน้ำ [si nam] *n* watercolour

สีสัน [si san] เต็มไปด้วยสีสัน [tem pai duai sii san] *adj* colourful

สีสิบ [si sip] *number* forty

สี่เหลี่ยม [si liam] เป็นสี่เหลี่ยมจัตุรัส [pen si liam chat tu rat] *n* square; รูปสี่เหลี่ยมผืน ผ้า [rup si liam phuen pha] *adj* oblong; สี่เหลี่ยมจตุรัส [si liam chat tu rat] *n* square

สี่เหลี่ยมผืนผ้า [si liam phuen pha] *n* rectangle; ที่เป็นสี่เหลี่ยมผืนผ้า [thii pen si liam phuen pha] *adj* rectangular

สืบ [suep] *vi* spy; นักสืบ [nak suep] *n* spy

สืบสวน [suep suan] การสืบสวน [kan suep suan] *n* investigation

สื่อมวลชน [sue muan chon] *npl* media

สื่อสาร [sue san] การสื่อสารทางไกลโดยใช้ เทคโนโลยี [kan sue san thang klai doi chai thek no lo yii] *npl* telecommunications; การติดต่อสื่อสาร [kan tit to sue san] *n* communication; ติดต่อสื่อสาร [tit to sue san] *v* communicate; สื่อสารลำบาก [sue san lam bak] Communication difficulties

สุก [suk] *adj* ripe; ไม่สุก [mai suk] *adj* rare *(undercooked)*; ที่สุกแล้ว [thii suk laeo] *adj* ready-cooked; ที่สุกมากเกินไป [thii suk mak koen pai] *adj* overdone

สุกร [su kon] *n* pork

สุข [suk] เป็นสุข [pen suk] *adj* happy; ความสุข [khwam suk] *n* happiness; ความสุขอันสุดยอด [khwam suk an sut yot] *n* bliss

สุขภาพ [suk kha phap] *n* health; มี สุขภาพดี [mii suk kha phap di] *adj* healthy; สถานบำรุงสุขภาพ [sa than bam rung suk kha phap] *n* spa; การตรวจ สุขภาพ [kan truat suk kha phap] *n* check-up

สุดท้าย [sut thai] *adj* final, last, ultimate; ที่สองจากที่สุดท้าย [thii song chak thii sut thai] *adj* penultimate; ที่สุดท้าย [thii sut thai] *adv* lastly; อัน สุดท้าย [an sut thai] *n* final; เรือลำสุดท้าย

มาเมื่อไร? [ruea lam sut thai ma muea rai] When is the last boat?

สุนัข [su nak] n dog; ลูกสุนัข [luk su nak] n puppy; สุนัขใหญ่ขนยาวที่ใช้เลี้ยงแกะ [su nak yai khon yao thii chai liang kae] n collie; สุนัขขนาดเล็กพันธุ์หนึ่งเมื่อ ก่อนใช้เป็นสุนัขล่าเนื้อ [su nak kha naat lek phan nueng muea kon chai pen su nak la nuea] n terrier; ฉันมีสุนัขนำทาง [chan mii su nak nam thang] I have a guide dog

สุนัขป่า [su nak pa] n wolf

สุภาพ [su phap] adj polite; ความสุภาพ อ่อนโยน [khwam su phap on yon] n politeness; อย่างสุภาพ [yang su phap] adv politely

สุภาพบุรุษ [su phap bu rut] n gentleman

สุภาพสตรี [su phap sa tri] n lady

สุ่ม [sum] โดยการสุ่ม [doi kan sum] adj random

สุรา [su ra] ร้านขายสุรา [ran khai su ra] n off-licence

สุริยะจักรวาล [su ri ya chak kea wan] ระบบสุริยะจักรวาล [ra bop su ri ya chak kra wan] solar system

สุรุ่ยสุร่าย [su rui su rai] ใช้จ่ายสุรุ่ยสุร่าย [chai chai su rui su rai] v squander

สุสาน [su san] n cemetery, graveyard; สุสานฝังศพ [su san fang sop] n tomb

สุเหร่า [su rao] n mosque; มีสุเหร่าอยู่ ที่ไหน? [mii su rao yu thii nai] Where is there a mosque?

สูง [sung] adj high, tall; สูงกว่า [sung kwa] adj upper; สูงวัย [sung wai] adj elderly; ความสูง [khwam sung] n height; สูงแค่ไหน? [sung khae nai] How high is it?

สูงที่สุด [sung thi sut] adj top

สูงสุด [sung sut] adj maximum; จำนวน สูงสุด [cham nuan sung sut] n maximum

สูญพันธุ์ [sun phan] adj extinct

สูญเสีย [sun sia] vt lose; การสูญเสียโดย

เปล่าประโยชน์ [kan sun sia doi plao pra yot] n waste; ความสูญเสีย [khwam sun sia] n loss; ที่สูญเสียน้ำจากร่างกาย [thii sun sia nam chak rang kai] adj dehydrated

สูญหาย [sun hai] adj lost

สูดจมูก [sut cha muk] สูดจมูกฟุดฟิต [sut cha muk fut fit] v sniff

สูตร [sut] n formula

สูตินารีแพทย์ [su ti na ri phaet] n gynaecologist

สูท [sut] ชุดสูท [chut sut] v suit

สูบ [sup] v pump, smoke; เครื่องสูบอากาศ หรือยาเข้าปอด [khrueang sup a kat rue ya khao pot] n inhaler; สูบขึ้นมา [sup khuen ma] v pump up; ที่สูบรถจักรยาน [thii sup rot chak kra yan] n bicycle pump; คุณมีเครื่องสูบลมไหม? [khun mii khrueang sup lom mai] Do you have a pump?

สูบบุหรี่ [sup bu ri] การสูบบุหรี่ [kan sub bu rii] n smoking; ซึ่งไม่สูบบุหรี่ [sueng mai sup bu rii] adj non-smoking; ผู้ไม่ สูบบุหรี่ [phu mai sup bu rii] n non-smoker; มีที่ไม่สูบบุหรี่ไหม? [mii thii mai sup bu rii mai] Is there a non-smoking area?

สู้รบ [su rop] การสู้รบ [kan su rop] n battle

เสก็ต [sa ket] การเล่นสเก็ต [kan len sa ket] n rollerskating

เส้น [sen] เส้นแวง [sen waeng] n longitude; เส้นขวางขนานกับเส้นศูนย์สูตร ของโลก [sen khwang kha nan kap sen sun sut khong lok] n latitude; เส้นตาย [sen tai] n deadline

เส้นทาง [sen thang] n route; เส้นทางขี่ จักรยาน [sen thang khi chak kra yan] n cycle path; เส้นทางอ้อม [sen thang om] n detour; มีเส้นทางใดที่หลีกเลี่ยงรถติดได้? [mii sen thang dai thii lik liang rot tit dai] Is there a route that avoids the traffic?

เส้นประสาท [sen pra sat] n nerve (to/

from brain)

เส้นผ่าศูนย์กลาง [sen pha sun klang] *n* diameter

เส้นใย [sen yai] *n* fibre

เส้นเลือดแดง [sen lueat daeng] เส้นเลือดแดงที่นำเลือดแดงออกจากหัวใจ [sen lueat daeng thii nam lueat daeng ok chak hua jai] *n* artery

เส้นโลหิต [sen lo hit] เส้นโลหิตดำ [sen lo hit dam] *n* vein

เส้นศูนย์สูตร [sen sun sut] เส้นขวางขนานกับเส้นศูนย์สูตรของโลก [sen khwang kha nan kap sen sun sut khong lok] *n* latitude

เสน่ห์ [sa ne] *n* charm; มีเสน่ห์ [moii sa ne] *adj* charming; มีเสน่ห์ดึงดูด [mii sa ne dueng dut] *adj* attractive; ซึ่งมีเสน่ห์ [sueng mii sa ne] *adj* glamorous

เสนอ [sa noe] *v* propose; เสนอเพื่อให้พิจารณา [sa noe phuea hai phi ja ra na] *v* offer; เสนอข้อเสนอ [sa noe kho sa noe] *v* put forward; เสนอชื่อ [sa noe chue] *v* nominate

เส้นเอ็น [sen en] เส้นเอ็นที่ยึดกล้ามเนื้อและกระดูก [sen en thii yuet klam nuea lae kra duk] *n* tendon

เสบียง [sa biang] ตู้เสบียงบนรถไฟ [tu sa biang bon rot fai] *n* dining car

เสมอ [sa moe] *adv* always; เสมอกัน [sa moe kan] *v* draw (equal with)

เสมอภาค [sa moe phak] ความเสมอภาค [khwam sa moe phak] *n* equality

เสร็จ [set] เสร็จสิ้น [set sin] *adj* done; ทำให้เสร็จสมบูรณ์ [tham hai set som boon] *v* finalize; รูปภาพจะเสร็จเมื่อไร? [rup phap ja set muea rai] When will the photos be ready?

เสริฟ [soep] หญิงเสิร์ฟเครื่องดื่มในบาร์ [ying soep khrueang duem nai ba] *n* barmaid; ชายเสิร์ฟเครื่องดื่มในบาร์ [chai soep khrueang duem nai bar] *n* barman; เสิร์ฟอาหารเช้าที่ไหน? [soep a han chao thii nai] Where is breakfast served?

เสริม [soem] เสริมซึ่งกันและกัน [soem sueng kan lae kan] *adj* complementary; ส่วนเสริม [suan sem] *n* supplement; คนหรือสิ่งที่เป็นตัวเสริม [khon rue sing thii pen tua soem] *n* subsidiary

เสริมสวย [some suai] ร้านเสริมสวย [ran soem suai] *n* beauty salon

เสรีนิยม [se ri niyom] เกี่ยวกับลัทธิเสรีนิยม [kiao kap lat thi se ri ni yom] *adj* liberal

เสา [sao] เสาเรือ [sao ruea] *n* mast; เสาไฟฟ้า [sao fai fa] *n* lamppost; เสาหลัก [sao lak] *n* pillar, post (stake)

เสาค้ำ [sao kham] ไม้ค้ำ เสาค้ำ ไม้เท้า [mai kham, sao kham, mai thao] *n* staff (stick or rod)

เสาร์ [sao] วันเสาร์ [wan sao] *n* Saturday

เสาวรส [sao wa rot] *n* passion fruit

เสิร์ฟ [soep] การเสิร์ฟลูกเทนนิส [kan soep luk then nis] *n* serve

เสีย [sia] รถตู้เสีย [rot tu sia] *n* breakdown van; รถบรรทุกเสีย [rot ban thuk sia] *n* breakdown truck; การเสีย [kan sia] *n* breakdown; เนื้อนี้เสีย [nuea ni sia] This meat is off

เสียง [siang] *n* noise, sound; เสียงในฟิล์ม [siang nai film] *n* soundtrack; เสียงร้อง [siang rong] *n* cry; เสียงสัญญาณเตือนภัย [siang san yan tuean phai] *n* siren; โทนเสียงต่ำ [thon siang tam] *n* bass

เสี่ยง [siang] *v* risk; ความเสี่ยง [khwam siang] *n* risk; ที่เสี่ยง [thii siang] *adj* risky

เสี่ยงโชค [siang chok] *v* speculate

เสียงดัง [siang dang] *adj* noisy; อย่างเสียงดัง [yang siang dang] *adv* loudly; ห้องเสียงดังมากเกินไป [hong siang dang mak koen pai] The room is too noisy

เสียใจ [sia chai] *v* regret; ความเสียใจ [khwam sia jai] *n* regret

เสียดสี [siat si] ช่างเสียดสี [chang siat sii] *adj* sarcastic

เสียเปรียบ [sia priap] คนที่เสียเปรียบ [khon thii sia priap] *n* disadvantage

เสียสติ [sai sa ti] อย่างเสียสติ [yang sia sa ti] *adv* madly

เสียสละ [sia sa la] การเสียสละ [kan sia sa la] *n* sacrifice; ผู้ยอมเสียสละชีวิตเพื่อศาสนาหรือความเชื่อของตน [phu yom sia sa la chi wit phuea sat sa na rue khwam chuea khong ton] *n* martyr

เสียหาย [sia hai] สิ่งที่ถูกทำลายอย่างเสียหายยับเยิน [sing thii thuk tham lai yang sia hai yap yoen] *n* wreck; ความเสียหาย [khwam sia hai] *n* damage; ซึ่งก่อให้เกิดความเสียหายอย่างมาก [sueng ko hai koet khwam sia hai yang mak] *adj* devastating; กระเป๋าเดินทางของฉันเสียหายเมื่อมาถึง [kra pao doen thang khong chan sia hai muea ma thueng] My suitcase has arrived damaged

เสือ [suea] *n* tiger; เสือดำ [suea dam] *n* panther; เสือดาว [suea dao] *n* leopard

เสื่อ [suea] *n* mat; เสื่อน้ำมัน [suea nam man] *n* lino

เสื้อ [suea] เสื้อเกราะ [suea kro] *n* armour; เสื้อเชิ้ต [suea choet] *n* shirt; เสื้อแจ๊กเก็ต [suea chaek ket] *n* jacket; เสื้อชั้นในสตรี [suea chan nai sa trii] *n* bra; เสื้อที่ถักด้วยขนสัตว์ [suea thii thak duai khon sat] *n* sweater

เสื้อคลุม [suea khlum] เสื้อคลุมของสตรีส่วนมากมีชายทำด้วยลูกไม้ [suea khlum khong sa trii suan mak mii chai tham duai luk mai] *n* negligee; เสื้อคลุมที่สวมเพื่อกันเปื้อน [suea khlum thii suam phuea kan puean] *npl* overalls

เสื้อเชิ้ต [suea choet] เสื้อเชิ้ตแขนสั้นมีปกและกระดุมสามเม็ดตรงสาบคอ [suea choet khaen san mii pok lae kra dum met trong sap kho] *n* polo shirt

เสื้อผ้า [suea pha] *n* clothing, garment ▷ *npl* clothes; เสื้อผ้าชุดทำงาน [suea pha chut tham ngan] *npl* dungarees; เสื้อผ้าทั้งชุด [suea pha thang chut] *n* outfit; เสื้อผ้าที่กำลังจะซัก [suea pha thii kam lang ja sak] *n* laundry; เสื้อผ้าฉันชื้น [suea pha chan chuen] My clothes are

damp

เสื้อผ้าชั้นใน [suea pha chan nai] *n* underwear

เสื่อมโทรม [sueam som] *v* deteriorate; ที่เสื่อมโทรมได้ [thii sueam som dai] *adj* biodegradable

เสื้อหนาว [suea nao] เสื้อหนาวคอโปโล [suea nao kho po lo] *n* polo-necked sweater

แส่ [sae] *n* whip

แสง [saeng] แสงเลเซอร์ [saeng le soe] *n* laser; แสงสว่าง [saeng sa wang] *n* light; ที่แสงเข้าตา [thit saeng khao ta] *adj* glaring

แสงแดด [saeng daet] โรคแพ้แสงแดดจัด [rok pae saeng daet chat] *n* sunstroke; มีแสงแดดมาก [mii saeng daet mak] *adj* sunny; ครีมป้องกันแสงแดด [khrim pong kan saeng daet] *n* sunscreen

แสงอาทิตย์ [saeng a thit] *n* sunlight, sunshine; ครีมทากันแสงอาทิตย์ [khrim tha kan saeng a thit] *n* suncream; พลังงานแสงอาทิตย์ [pha lang ngan saeng a thit] *n* solar power

แสดง [sa daeng] *v* display, perform, show; แสดงให้เห็น [sa daeng hai hen] *v* demonstrate; แสดงความคิดเห็น [sa daeng khwam kit hen] *v* comment; แสดงความยินดี [sa daeng khwam yin dii] *v* congratulate

แสดงแบบ [sa daeng baep] *v* model

แสดงออก [sa daeng ok] การแสดงออก [kan sa daeng ok] *n* expression

แสตมป์ [sa taem] ร้านขายแสตมป์ที่ใกล้ที่สุดอยู่ที่ไหน? [ran khai sa taem thii klai thii sut yu thii nai] Where is the nearest shop which sells stamps?; คุณขายแสตมป์ไหม? [khun khai sa taem mai] Do you sell stamps?; ฉันขอซื้อแสตมป์สำหรับโปสการ์ดสี่ใบไป...ได้ไหม? [chan kho sue sa taem sam rap pos kart sii bai pai...dai mai] Can I have stamps for four postcards to...

แสวงบุญ [sa waeng bun] การเดินทางเพื่อ

ไปแสวงบุญ [kan doen thang phue pai sa waeng bun] n pilgrimage

แสวงหา [sa waeng ha] แสวงหาติดตาม [sa waeng ha tit tam] v go after

โสด [sot] ชายโสด [chai sot] n bachelor; ใช่ ฉันเป็นโสด [chai chan pen sot] Yes, I'm single; คุณเป็นโสดหรือเปล่า? [khun pen sot rue plao] Are you single?

โสเภณี [so pe ni] n prostitute

ใส่ [sai] ใส่เสื้อผ้า [sai suea pha] vi dress; ใส่ข้อมูลส่วนบุคคล [sai kho mun suan buk khon] v blog; ใส่น้ำมัน [sai nam man] v oil; ฉันควรจะใส่อะไรดี? [chan khuan ja sai a rai di] What should I wear?

ไส้กรอก [sai krok] n sausage; ไส้กรอกซา ลามี [sai krok sa la mi] n salami; ขนมปัง ประกอบไส้กรอก [kha nom pang pra kop sai krok] n hot dog

ไส้ติ่ง [sai ting] ไส้ติ่งอักเสบ [sai ting ak sep] n appendicitis

ไส้พุง [sai phung] n gut

ไส้เลื่อน [sai luean] โรคไส้เลื่อน [rok sai luean] n hernia

ห

หก [hok] number six; ที่หก [thii hok] adj sixth; ทำหก [tham hok] vt spill; เวลาหก โมง [we la hok mong] It's six o'clock

หกล้ม [hok lom] v fall down

หกสิบ [hok sip] number sixty

หงส์ [hong] n swan

หงาย [ngai] พลิกหงาย [phlik ngai] v turn up

หงุดหงิด [ngut ngit] adj moody; ท้อแท้ หงุดหงิด [tho thae, ngut ngit] adj frustrated

หญ้า [ya] n grass (plant); เครื่องตัดหญ้า [khrueang tat ya] n lawnmower, mower; หญ้าแห้ง [ya haeng] n hay; กอง หญ้า [kong ya] n haystack

หญิง [ying] เกี่ยวกับเพศหญิง [kiao kap phet ying] feminine; เพศหญิง [phet ying] n female; หญิงทำความสะอาด [ying tham khwam sa at] n cleaning lady

หด [hot] v shrink

หดลง [hot long] ที่หดลง [thii hot long] adj shrunk

หดหู่ [hot hu] adj depressed, dismal; ความหดหู่ [khwam hot hu] n depression; ทำให้หดหู่ใจ [tham hai hot hu jai] adj miserable

หนทาง [hon thang] *n* track

หนวก [nuak] หูหนวก [hu nuak] *adj* deaf

หนวด [nuat] *n* moustache; ที่เต็มไปด้วยหนวดเครา [thii tem pai duai nuat khrao] *adj* bearded

หน่วย [nuai] *n* unit; หน่วยเงินเซ็นต์ [nuai ngoen sen] *n* cent; หน่วยเงินตราของสหราชอาณาจักรอังกฤษ [nuai ngoen tra khong sa ha rat cha a na chak ang krit] *n* pound sterling; หน่วยรักษาการณ์ตามชายฝั่งทะเล [nuai rak sa kan tam chai fang tha le] *n* coastguard

หน่วยกู้ไฟ [nuai ku phai] กรุณาเรียกรถดับเพลิง [ka ru na riak rot dap ploeng] Please call the fire brigade

หน่วยความจำ [nuai khwam cham] หน่วยความจำของคอมพิวเตอร์ [nuai khwam cham khong khom phio toe] *n* ram

หน่วยงาน [nuai ngan] *n* institute

หน่วยบริการ [hnuai bo ri kan] หน่วยบริการช่วยเหลือใกล้ที่สุดอยู่ที่ไหน? [nuai bo ri kan chuai luea klai thii sut yu thii nai] Where is the nearest mountain rescue service post?

หน่วยวัด [nuai wat] หน่วยวัดกำลังกระแสไฟฟ้า [nuai wat kam lang kra sae fai fa] *n* amp

หนอง [nong] *n* pus

หนองน้ำ [hnong nam] *n* swamp

หนอน [non] *n* maggot; หนอนผีเสื้อ [non phi suea] *n* caterpillar

หน่อไม้ [no mai] หน่อไม้ฝรั่ง [no mai fa rang] *n* asparagus

หนัก [nak] *adj* heavy; งานหนักและน่าเบื่อ [ngan nak lae na buea] *n* fag; อย่างหนัก [yang nak] *adv* heavily; นี่หนักเกินไป [ni nak koen pai] This is too heavy

หนัง [nang] *n* leather; หนังแกะ [nang kae] *n* sheepskin; หนังกลับชนิดนิ่ม [nang klap cha nit nim] *n* suede; หนังที่น่ากลัว [nang thii na klua] *n* horror film

หนังสือ [nang sue] *n* book; ร้านหนังสือ [ran nang sue] *n* bookshop; หนังสือเล่มเล็ก [nang sue lem lek] *n* booklet; หนังสือโรงเรียน [nang sue rong rian] *n* schoolbook; ปกหนังสือ [pok nang sue] *n* cover; คุณมีหนังสือแนะนำเกี่ยวกับ... [khun mii nang sue nae nam kiao kap...] Do you have a guide book in...?

หนังสือเดินทาง [nang sue doen thang] *n* passport; หน่วยควบคุมหนังสือเดินทาง [nuai khuap khum nang sue doen thang] *n* passport control; วีซ่า เอกสารอนุมัติที่ประทับตราบนหนังสือเดินทาง [wi sa, ek ka san a nu mat thii pra thap tra bon nang sue doen thang] *n* visa; เด็ก ๆ อยู่ในหนังสือเดินทางเล่มนี้ [dek dek yu nai nang sue doen thang lem nii] The children are on this passport

หนังสือพิมพ์ [nang sue phim] *n* newspaper; เส้นทางส่งหนังสือพิมพ์ [sen thang song nang sue phim] *n* paper round; ร้านขายหนังสือพิมพ์ [ran khai nang sue phim] *n* newsagent; นักหนังสือพิมพ์ [nak nang sue phim] *n* journalist; ร้านขายหนังสือพิมพ์ที่ใกล้ที่สุดอยู่ที่ไหน? [ran khai nang sue phim thii klai thii sut yu thii nai] Where is the nearest shop which sells newspapers?

หนังสือรับรอง [nang sue rap rong] ฉันอยากได้หนังสือรับรองว่าฉันแข็งแรงที่จะบินได้ [chan yak dai nang sue rap rong wa chan khaeng raeng thii ja bin dai] I need a 'fit to fly' certificate

หนา [na] *adj* thick; ความหนา [khwam na] *n* thickness

หน้า [na] *n* page; โดยไปข้างหน้า [doi pai khang na] *adv* forward; ไปข้างหน้า [pai khang na] *v* forward; หน้าหรือผิวแดง [na rue phio daeng] *n* flush

หน้ากาก [na kak] *n* mask; ที่ใส่หน้ากาก [thii sai na kak] *adj* masked

หน้าตา [na ta] ลักษณะหน้าตา [lak sa na na ta] *n* feature; หน้าตาดี [na ta di] *adj* good-looking

หน้าต่าง [hna tang] *n* window; หน้าต่างตู้โชว์ของร้านค้า [na tang tu cho khong ran ka] *n* shop window; กระจกหน้าต่าง [kra jok na tang] *n* window pane; ขอบหน้าต่างส่วนล่าง [kop na tang suan lang] *n* windowsill

หน้าที่ [na thi] *n* duty; หน้าที่หรือบทบาท [na thii rue bot bat] *n* role; หน้าที่ของพระ [na thii khong phra] *n* ministry *(religion)*

หนาแน่น [hna naen] *adj* dense; ความหนาแน่น [khwam na naen] *n* density

หน้าปัด [na pat] แผงหน้าปัดรถยนต์ [phaeng na pat rot yon] *n* dashboard

หน้าผา [na pha] *n* cliff

หน้าผาก [na phak] *n* forehead

หนาม [nam] *n* thorn

หน้าร้อน [na ron] ในหน้าร้อน [nai na ron] in summer; ระหว่างหน้าร้อน [ra wang na ron] during the summer; หลังหน้าร้อน [lang na ron] after summer

หนาว [nao] หนาวเย็น [nao yen] *adj* chilly; ห้องหนาวเกินไป [hong nao koen pai] The room is too cold; หนาวเยือกเย็น [nao yueak yen] It's freezing cold

หน้าอก [na ok] *n* breast, chest *(body part)*; หน้าอก นม [na ok, nom] *n* bust; ฉันเจ็บหน้าอก [chan chep na ok] I have a pain in my chest

หนี [ni] *v* flee, get away; หนีโรงเรียน [nii rong rian] *v* play truant; หนีงาน [nii ngan] *v* skive; วิ่งหนีไป [wing nii pai] *v* run away

หนี้ [ni] *n* debt; ใบแจ้งหนี้ [bai chaeng nii] *n* bill *(account)*; จำนวนเงินที่เป็นหนี้ธนาคาร [cham nuan ngen thii pen nii tha na khan] *n* overdraft

หนีบ [nip] ไม้หนีบผ้า [mai nip pha] *n* clothes peg; การหนีบติดกัน [kan niip tit kan] *n* clip

หนึ่ง [nue] *art* a ▷ *number* one; คนหรือของที่เป็นอันดับหนึ่ง [khon rue khong thii pen an dap nueng] *n* first; ชั้นหนึ่ง [chan nueng] *adj* first-class; ที่หนึ่ง [thii nueng] *adj* first; เวลาหนึ่งโมง [we la nueng mong] It's one o'clock

หนุ่ม [num] เด็กหนุ่ม [dek num] *n* lad

หนุ่มสาว [num sao] วัยหนุ่มสาว [wai num sao] *n* youth

หนู [nu] *n* mouse, rat; สัตว์ชนิดหนึ่งคล้ายหนู [sat cha nit nueng khlai nu] *n* hamster; หนูตะเภา [nu ta phao] *n* guinea pig *(rodent)*; หนูตะเภาสำหรับทดลอง [nu ta phao sam rap thot long] *n* guinea pig *(for experiment)*

หมด [mot] ใช้จนหมด [chai chon mot] *v* use up; หมดเงิน [mot ngoen] *adj* hard up; ขายหมด [khai mot] *v* sell out; ฉันเงินหมด [chan ngoen mot] I have run out of money

หมดสติ [mot sa ti] *v* pass out

หมดอายุ [mot a yu] *v* expire

หมวก [muak] *n* hat; หมวกแก๊ปสำหรับเล่นเบสบอล [muak kaep sam rap len bes bal] *n* baseball cap; หมวกกันน็อก [muak kan nok] *n* helmet; หมวกกลม [muak klom] *n* beret

หมวด [muat] หมวดหมู่ [muat mu] *n* category

หมอ [mo] หมอสอนศาสนา [mo son sat sa na] *n* missionary; หมอที่รักษาโรคที่เกี่ยวกับมือหรือเท้า [mo thii rak sa rok thii kiao kap mue rue thao] *n* chiropodist; หมอฟัน [mo fan] *n* dentist; เรียกหมอ [riak mo] Call a doctor!

หมอ [mo] *n* pot; หม้อกาแฟ [mo ka fae] *n* coffeepot; หม้อที่มีฝาปิดและมีด้ามยาว [mo thii mii fa pit lae mii dam yao] *n* saucepan; อาหารอบจากหม้อที่มีฝาปิด [a han op chak mo thii mii fa pit] *n* casserole

หมอก [mok] *n* fog, mist; ไฟหมอก [fai mok] *n* fog light; ที่เป็นหมอก [thii pen mok] *adj* foggy; ที่ปกคลุมด้วยหมอก [thii pok khlum duai mok] *adj* misty

หมอน [mon] *n* pillow; หมอนอิง [mon ing] *n* cushion; ปลอกหมอน [plok mon] *n* pillowcase; ช่วยเอาหมอนมาให้ฉันอีกหนึ่งใบ [chuai ao mon ma hai chan ik nueng bai] Please bring me an extra pillow

หมอนรองกระดูกสันหลัง [mon rong kra duk san hlang] หมอนรองกระดูกสันหลังเลื่อน [mon rong kra duk san lang luean] n slipped disc

หมอน้ำ [mo nam] n boiler

หมอบ [mop] หมอบลง [mop long] v crouch down

หมอฟัน [mo fan] ฉันต้องการหมอฟัน [chan tong kan mo fan] I need a dentist

หมัก [mak] v marinade; การหมัก [kan mak] v marinade; ยีสต์ เชื้อหมัก [yis, chuea mak] n yeast

หมัด [mat] n flea

หมั้น [mun] แหวนหมั้น [waen man] n engagement ring; การหมั้น [kan man] n engagement; ฉันหมั้นแล้ว [chan man laeo] I'm engaged

หมั้นหมาย [man mai] ที่หมั้นหมาย [thii man mai] adj engaged

หมากฝรั่ง [mak fa rang] n bubble gum, chewing gum, gum

หมากรุก [mak ruk] n chess; ที่มีลายตาราง หมากรุก [thii mii lai ta rang mak ruk] adj checked

หมากฮอส [mak hot] npl draughts

หมาย [mai] ฉันเป็นหม้าย [chan pen mai] I'm widowed

หมายกำหนดการ [mai kam not kan] n program, programme

หมายความ [mai khwam] หมายความว่า [mai khwam wa] v mean

หมายเลข [mai lek] หมายเลขเอกสารอ้างอิง [mai lek ek ka san ang ing] n reference number; หมายเลขโทรศัพท์ [mai lek tho ra sap] n phone number; หมายเลข โทรศัพท์ของโทรศัพท์มือถือ [mai lek tho ra sap khong tho ra sap mue thue] n mobile number; หมายเลขสอบถามคือ หมายเลขอะไร? [mai lek sop tham khue mai lek a rai] What is the number for directory enquiries?

หมายเหตุ [mai het] abbr NB (notabene)

หมิ่นประมาท [min pra mat] การหมิ่น ประมาท [kan min pra mat] n contempt

หมี [mi] n bear; สัตว์คล้ายหมีแต่ตัวเล็กและมี หางเป็นพวง [sat khlai mii tae tua lek lae mii hang pen puang] n racoon; หมี แพนด้า [mii phaen da] n panda; หมีขั้ว โลก [mii khua lok] n polar bear

หมึก [muek] n ink

หมุด [mut] n stud; ตอกหมุดสำหรับเต็นท์ [tok mut sam rap tent] n tent peg

หมุน [mun] v dial; หมุนกลับ [mun klap] v turn round, turn around; การหมุน [kan mun] n roll

หมุนเวียน [mun wian] การหมุนเวียน [kan mun wian] n circulation

หมู [mu] n pig; เนื้อหมูที่ติดกระดูก [nuea mu thii tit kra duk] n pork chop; เนื้อ ด้านหลังและส่วนนอกของหมูที่ใส่เกลือรม ควัน [nuea dan lang lae suan nok khong mu thii sai kluea rom khwan] n bacon; ต้นขาหลังของหมู [ton kha lang khong mu] n ham

หมู่ [mu] หมวดหมู่ [muat mu] n category; กลุ่ม หมู่คณะ [klum, moo ka na] n collective

หมู่เกาะ [mu ko] เกี่ยวกับหมู่เกาะใน มหาสมุทรแปซิฟิกใต้ [kiao kap mu ko nai ma ha sa mut pae si fik tai] adj Polynesian; หมู่เกาะในมหาสมุทรแปซิฟิก ได้แก่ ฮาวาย ซามัวร์และหมู่เกาะคุก [mu kao nai ma ha sa mut pae si fik dai kae ha wai sa mua lae mu kao khuk] n Polynesia; หมู่เกาะทางแปซิฟิก [mu kao thang pae si fik] n Oceania

หมู่บ้าน [mu ban] n village

หยด [yot] หยดน้ำ [yot nam] n drip, drop; ทำให้หยด [tham hai yot] v drip

หยอกล้อ [yok lo] vt tease

หยอด [yot] น้ำยาหยอดตา [nam ya yot ta] npl eye drops

หยอดเหรียญ [yot rian] ตู้ขายสินค้าแบบ หยอดเหรียญ [tu khai sin ka baep yot rian] n vending machine

หย่อน [yon] adj slack

หยักศก [yak sok] หยักศก ที่เป็นลอน [yak

sok, thii pen lon] *adj* curly

หย่า [ya] การหย่า [kan ya] *n* divorce; ซึ่ง
หย่าแล้ว [sueng ya laeo] *adj* divorced;
ฉันหย่าแล้ว [chan ya laeo] I'm divorced

หยาบ [yap] *adj* crude, harsh, rough;
อย่างหยาบ [yang yap] *adv* coarse,
roughly

หยาบคาย [yap khai] *adj* rude, vulgar

หยิก [yik] *vt* pinch

หยิ่ง [ying] หยิ่งยโส [ying ya so] *adj*
arrogant

หยุด [yut] ไม่หยุด [mai yut] *adv*
non-stop; หยุด ระงับ ปิดกั้น [yut, ra
ngab, pit kan] *vt* stop; หยุด ยุติ เลิก
[yut, yu ti, loek] *vi* stop; เราจะหยุดจอด
ครั้งต่อไปเมื่อไร? [rao ja yut jot khrang
to pai muea rai] When do we stop
next?

หยุดงาน [yut ngan] หยุดงานประท้วง [yut
ngan pra thuang] strike *(suspend work)*

หรือ [rue] *conj* or

หรูหรา [ru ra] *adj* luxurious; ความหรูหรา
[khwam ru ra] *n* luxury

หลง [long] ซึ่งทำให้หลงเสน่ห์ [sueng
tham hai long sa ne] *adj* fascinating;
เราหลงทาง [rao long thang] We're lost;
ฉันหลงทาง [chan long thang] I'm lost

หลงทาง [long thang] สัตว์ที่หลงทาง [sat
thii long thang] *n* stray; ลูกสาวฉันหลง
ทาง [luk sao chan long thang] My
daughter is lost; ลูกชายฉันหลงทาง [luk
chai chan long thang] My son is lost

หลน [lon] *vi* fall; การหลนลงมา [kan lon
long ma] *n* fall

หลบ [lop] หลบ กำบัง ป้องกัน ปกปิดเหมือน
กับมีฉากกั้น [lop, kam bang, pong kan,
pok pit muean kap mii chak kan] *v*
screen *(off)*

หลบภัย [lop phai] ที่หลบภัย [thii lop
phai] *n* refuge

หลบหนี [lop ni] *vi* escape; การหลบหนี
[kan lop nii] *n* escape

หลบหลีก [lop lik] *v* dodge

หลวม [luam] *adj* loose

หล่อ [lo] *adj* handsome

หลอกลวง [lok luang] *v* deceive, fool;
การโกง การหลอกลวง การต้มตุ๋น [kan
kong, kan lok luang, kan tom tun] *n*
rip-off

หลอด [lot] *n* tube; หลอดทดลอง [lot thot
long] *n* test tube

หลอดไฟ [lot fai] *n* light bulb

หลอดไฟฟ้า [lot fai fa] bulb *(electricity)*

หลอดลม [lot lom] โรคหลอดลมอักเสบ [rok
lot lom ak sep] *n* bronchitis

หลอน [lon] หลอนเอง [lon eng] *pron*
herself

หลอมละลาย [hlom la lai] ละลาย ทำให้
หลอมละลาย [la lai, tham hai lom la lai]
vt melt; ละลาย ทำให้หลอมละลาย [la lai,
tham hai lom la lai] *vt* melt

หลัก [luk] *adj* main; หลักเสาหินใหญ่ [lak
sao hin yai] *n* column; หลักความ
ประพฤติ [lak khwam pra phruet] *npl*
morals; อาหารมื้อหลัก [a han mue lak] *n*
main course

หลักเกณฑ์ [lak ken] *n* rule

หลักฐาน [lak than] *n* evidence, proof
(evidence)

หลักปฏิบัติ [lak pa ti bat] *n* principle; ที่
เป็นหลักปฏิบัติ [thii pen lak pa ti bat] *adj*
principal

หลักสูตร [lak sut] *n* course, curriculum;
หลักสูตรการเรียน [lak sut kan rian] *n*
syllabus; หลักสูตรการศึกษา [lak sut kan
suek sa] *n* module; หลักสูตรอบรม [lak
sut op rom] *n* training course

หลัง [lung] *n* behind; หลัง ส่วนหลัง [lang,
suan lang] *n* back; ข้างหลัง [khang
lang] *adj* behind, rear; ซึ่งผ่านมาแล้ว ซึ่ง
อยู่ด้านหลัง [sueng phan ma laeo, sueng
yu dan lang] *adj* back

หลังคา [lang kha] *n* roof; ห้องใต้หลังคา
[hong tai lang kha] *n* attic; หลังคารถ
[lang kha rot] *n* roof rack; หลังคากันแสง
พระอาทิตย์ [lang kha kan saeng phra a
thit] *n* sunroof; หลังคารั่ว [lang kha rua]
The roof leaks

หลังจาก [lang chak] *conj* after ▷ *prep* behind

หลังจากนั้น [lang chak nan] *adv* afterwards ▷ *conj* then

หลับ [lap] นอนหลับ [non lap] *adj* asleep; ฉันนอนไม่หลับ [chan non mai lap] I can't sleep

หลา [la] *n* yard (*measurement*)

หลาน [lan] *n* grandchild; หลาน ๆ [lan lan] *npl* grandchildren; หลานสาว [lan sao] *n* granddaughter, niece; หลานชาย [lan chai] *n* grandson, nephew

หลาย [lai] *adj* several ▷ *pron* several

หลีกเลี่ยง [lik liang] *v* avoid; ไม่สามารถ หลีกเลี่ยงได้ [mai sa mat lik liang dai] *adj* inevitable; ที่หลีกเลี่ยงไม่ได้ [thii lik liang mai dai] *adj* unavoidable

หลุด [lut] ฟันที่อุดหลุดออกมา [fan thii ut lut ok ma] A filling has fallen out

หลุม [lum] หลุมทราย [lum sai] *n* sandpit; หลุมบ่อ [lum bo] *n* pothole, puddle; หลุม ฝังศพ [lum fang sop] *n* grave

ห่วง [huang] เป็นห่วงกังวล [pen huang kang won] *adj* worried

ห่วงใย [huang yai] ที่ห่วงใยผู้อื่น [thii huang yai phu uen] *adj* caring

ห้วย [huai] *n* bog

หวัง [wang] *v* hope; ไม่มีความหวัง [mai mii khwam wang] *adj* hopeless; มีความ หวัง [mii khwam wang] *adj* hopeful; ความหวัง [khwam wang] *n* hope; ฉัน หวังว่าอากาศคงจะดีขึ้น [chan wang wa a kaat khong ja di khuen] I hope the weather improves

หวัด [wat] โรคหวัดที่มีน้ำมูกไหลออกมา [rok wat thii mii nam muk lai ok ma] *n* catarrh; ฉันเป็นหวัด [chan pen wat] I have a cold; ฉันอยากได้อะไรสักอย่าง สำหรับป้องกันหวัด [chan yak dai a rai sak yang sam rap pong kan wat] I'd like something for a cold

หวั่นไหว [hwan hwai] สั่นสะเทือน หวั่น ไหว [san sa thuean, wan wai] *vi* shake

หวาดกลัว [wat klua] *v* scare; ความหวาด กลัว [khwam wat klua] *n* phobia, scare; ความหวาดกลัวหรือวิตกกังวล [khwam wat klua rue wi tok kang won] *n* panic; ทำให้หวาดกลัว [tham hai wat klua] *v* terrify

หวาน [wan] *adj* sweet (*taste*); ของหวาน [khong wan] *n* dessert

หวี [wi] *n* comb; การหวี [kan wii] *v* comb

หวีดร้อง [wit rong] *v* shriek

ห่อ [ho] *v* wrap; แกะห่อออก [kae ho ok] *v* unwrap; ห่อหุ้ม [ho hum] *v* wrap up; ห่อ ของเล็ก ๆ [ho khong lek lek] *n* packet; คุณช่วยห่อให้ฉันได้ไหม? [khun chuai ho hai chan dai mai] Could you wrap it up for me, please?

ห้อง [hong] *n* room; เพื่อนร่วมห้อง [phuean ruam hong] *n* roommate; ห้อง เล็กในห้องขัง [hong lek nai hong khang] *n* cell; ห้องเรียน [hong rian] *n* classroom; ห้องลองเสื้อผ้า [hong long suea pha] *n* fitting room; ห้องที่ใช้นั่งรอ [hong thii chai nang ro] *n* waiting room; ห้องนั่งเล่นในบ้าน [hong nang len nai baan] *n* lounge; ห้องลองอยู่ที่ไหน? [hong long yu thii nai] Where are the changing rooms?

ห้องครอบครัว [hong khrop khrua] ฉัน อยากจองห้องสำหรับครอบครัวหนึ่งห้อง [chan yak chong hong sam rap khrob khrua nueng hong] I'd like to book a family room

ห้องคู่ [hong khu] ฉันอยากจองห้องคู่หนึ่ง ห้อง [chan yak chong hong khu nueng hong] I want to reserve a double room

ห้องชุด [hong chut] *n* suite; ห้องชุดที่เป็น ห้องทำงาน [hong chut thii pen hong tham ngan] *n* studio flat

ห้องเดี่ยว [hong diao] ฉันอยากจองห้อง เดี่ยวหนึ่งห้อง [chan yak chong hong diao nueng hong] I'd like to book a single room

ห้องนอน [hong non] คุณมีห้องนอนอยู่ชั้น ล่างไหม? [khun mii hong non yu chan lang mai] Do you have any bedrooms on the ground floor?

ห้องน้ำ [hong nam] n bathroom, lavatory, loo, toilet; ห้องน้ำสตรี [hong nam sa trii] n ladies'; ห้องน้ำชาย [hong nam chai] n gents'; มีห้องน้ำส่วนตัวใน ห้องไหม? [mii hong nam suan tua nai hong mai] Does the room have a private bathroom?

ห้องปฏิบัติการ [hong pa ti bat kan] ห้อง ปฏิบัติการทางภาษา [hong pa ti bat kan thang pha sa] n language laboratory

ห้องรับแขก [hong rap khaek] เราจะดื่ม กาแฟในห้องรับแขกได้ไหม? [rao ja duem ka fae nai hong rap khaek dai mai] Could we have coffee in the lounge?

ห้องสมุด [hong sa mut] n library

หอพัก [ho phak] n dormitory; หอพัก นักเรียน [ho phak nak rian] n hostel, youth hostel

หอม [hom] กลิ่นหอม [klin hom] n aroma; การรักษาที่ใช้เครื่องหอมกับสมุนไพร [kan rak sa thii chai khrueang hom kap sa mun phrai] n aromatherapy

หอย [hoi] หอยแมลงภู่ [hoi ma laeng phu] n mussel; หอยนางรม [hoi nang rom] n oyster; หอยพัด [hoi phat] n scallop

หอยทาก [hoi thak] n snail

ห่อหุ้ม [ho hum] สิ่งห่อหุ้ม [sing ho hum] n muffler

หัก [hak] แตกหัก [taek hak] adj broke, broken; รายการของเงินที่หักบัญชี [rai kan khong ngoen thii hak ban chi] n debit; หักบัญชี [hak ban chi] v debit; ฉันทำฟันหักหนึ่งซี่ [chan tham fan hak nueng si] I've broken a tooth

หักเลี้ยว [hak kiao] v swerve

หักหลัง [hak lang] v blackmail; หักหลัง ขูดเลือด [hak lang, khut lueat] adj extortionate

หัด [hat] โรคหัด [rok hat] npl measles; หัดเยอรมัน [hat yoe ra man] n German measles

หันเห [han he] การหันเหความสนใจ [kan han he khwam son jai] n diversion

หัว [hua] หัวของต้นไม้ [hua khong ton mai] n bulb (plant); ปวดหัว [puat hua] n headache

หัวข้อ [hua kho] n subject, theme, topic; หัวข้อข่าว [hua kho khao] n lead (position); หัวข้อที่ถกเถียงกัน [hua kho thii thok thiang kan] n issue

หัวเข็มขัด [hua khem khat] n buckle

หัวเข่า [hua khao] กระดูกสะบ้าหัวเข่า [kra duk sa ba hua khao] n kneecap

หัวใจ [hua chai] n heart; เส้นเลือดแดงที่ นำเลือดแดงออกจากหัวใจ [sen lueat daeng thii nam lueat daeng ok chak hua jai] n artery; หัวใจวาย [hua jai wai] n heart attack; ฉันมีอาการทางหัวใจ [chan mii a kan thang hua jai] I have a heart condition

หัวฉีดน้ำ [hua chit nam] n sprinkler

หัวไชเท้า [hua chai thao] ผักมีลูกกลมสี แดงรสคล้ายหัวไชเท้าใช้ใส่ในสลัดผัก [phak mii luk klom sii daeng rot khlai hua chai thao chai sai nai sa lad phak] n radish

หัวเทียน [hua thian] หัวเทียนไฟ เครื่องยนต์ [hua thian fai khrueang yon] n spark plug

หัวผักกาด [hua phak kat] n turnip

หัวมุม [hua mum] อยู่ใกล้ ๆ หัวมุม [yu klai klai hua mum] It's round the corner; อยู่ที่หัวมุม [yu thii hua mum] It's on the corner

หัวเราะ [hua ro] v laugh; เสียงหัวเราะ [siang hua rao] n laughter; หัวเราะต่อ กระซิก [hua ro to kra sik] v giggle; การ หัวเราะ [kan hua rao] n laugh

หัวเราะเยาะ [hua ro yo] v snigger

หัวล้าน [hua lan] คนที่โกนผมหัวล้าน [khon thii kon phom hua lan] n skinhead

หัวสูง [hua sung] คนหัวสูง [khon hua sung] n snob

หัวหน้า [hua na] หัวหน้างานที่ควบคุมดูแล [hua na ngan thii khuap khum du lae] n supervisor; หัวหน้าพ่อครัว [hua na pho khrua] *n* chef

หัวหอม [hua hom] *n* onion

หา [ha] *v* find, seek; กลไกการหาข้อมูลบน
อินเตอร์เน็ต [kon kai kan ha kho mun
bon in toe net] *n* search engine

ห้า [ha] *number* five; ลำดับที่ห้า [lam dap
thii ha] *adj* fifth

หาง [hang] *n* tail

ห่าง [hang] ห่างไกล [hang klai] *adv*
distant, far; ห่างออกไป [hang ok pai]
adj further; ความห่างไกล [khwam hang
klai] *n* distance; เราอยู่ห่างจากใจกลาง
เมืองมากแค่ไหน? [rao yu hang chak jai
klang mueang mak khae nai] How far
are we from the town centre?

ห่างไกล [hang klai] *adv* remotely

หางเปีย [hang pia] *n* pigtail

ห้างสรรพสินค้า [hang sap pha sin kha]
n department store

หาดทราย [hat sai] มีรถโดยสารไปหาด
ทรายไหม? [mii rot doi san pai hat sai
mai] Is there a bus to the beach?

ห่าน [han] *n* goose

ห้าม [ham] *v* ban, forbid; ห้ามโดยกฎหมาย
[ham doi kot mai] *v* prohibit; การห้าม
ออกนอกบ้านยามวิกาล [kan ham ok nok
baan yam wi kan] *n* curfew; ข้อห้าม
[kho ham] *n* taboo

ห้ามล้อ [ham lo] *v* brake

หาย [hai] สำนักงานเก็บของหาย [sam nak
ngan kep khong hai] *n* lost-property
office; หาย ฟื้น [hai, fuen] *vi* recover;
ซึ่งหายไป [sueng hai pai] *adj* missing;
ลูกสาวฉันหาย [luk sao chan hai] My
daughter is missing

หายใจ [hai chai] *v* breathe; ลมหายใจ
[lom hai chai] *n* breath; หายใจเข้า [hai
jai khao] *v* breathe in; หายใจไม่ออก
[hai jai mai ok] *v* suffocate; เขาหายใจ
ไม่ได้ [khao hai jai mai dai] He can't
breathe

หายนะ [ha ya na] ก่อให้เกิดความหายนะ
[ko hai koet khwam ha ya na] *adj*
disastrous; ความหายนะ [khwam hai ya

na] *n* catastrophe, disaster

หายไป [hai pai] *v* disappear; หายไปอย่าง
รวดเร็ว [hai pai yang ruat reo] *v* vanish;
การหายไป [kan hai pai] *n*
disappearance

หารือ [ha rue] การปรึกษาหารือ [kan
pruek sa ha rue] *n* discussion; ปรึกษา
หารือ [pruek sa ha rue] *v* discuss

หาว [hao] *v* yawn

ห้าสิบ [ha sip] *number* fifty; ห้าสิบต่อห้าสิบ
[ha sip to ha sip] *adv* fifty-fifty

หาเสียง [ha siang] ออกเที่ยวฟังความเห็น
เที่ยวหาเสียง [ok thiao fang khwam
hen, thiao ha siang] *v* canvass

หิน [hin] *n* rock, stone; แผ่นเหล็กหรือหิน
สลัก [phaen lek rue hin sa lak] *n*
plaque; หินแกรนิต [hin krae nit] *n*
granite; หินสลักหน้าหลุมฝังศพ [hin sa
lak na lum fang sop] *n* gravestone

หินปูน [hin pun] *n* limestone

หินอ่อน [hin on] *n* marble

หิมะ [hi ma] *n* snow; แคร่เลื่อนยาวติดกับ
รองเท้าใช้เล่นหิมะ [krae luean yao tit
kap rong thao chai len hi ma] *n* ski; รูป
ปั้นมนุษย์หิมะ [rup pan ma nut hi ma] *n*
snowman; รถไถกวาดหิมะ [rot thai
kwat hi ma] *n* snowplough; สภาพหิมะ
เป็นอย่างไร? [sa phap hi ma pen yang
rai] What are the snow conditions?

หิว [hio] *adj* hungry; ความหิว [khwam
hio] *n* hunger; ฉันไม่หิว [chan mai hio]
I'm not hungry; ฉันหิว [chan hio] I'm
hungry

หิ้ว [hio] หิ้วได้ [hio dai] *adj* portable

หีบ [hip] หีบ ลัง กล่อง [hip, lang, klong] *n*
chest *(storage)*

หีบเพลง [hip phleng] *n* accordion; หีบ
เพลง ออร์แกน [hip phleng, o kaen] *n*
organ *(music)*; หีบเพลงปาก [hip phleng
pak] *n* mouth organ

หีบศพ [hip sop] *n* coffin

หีบห่อ [hip ho] *n* package, packaging

หืด [huet] โรคหืด [rok huet] *n* asthma

หุ่น [hun] หุ่นกระบอก [hun kra bok] *n*

puppet; หุ่นจำลอง [hun cham long] *n* dummy

หุ้น [hun] การซื้อขายหุ้นของบริษัท [kan sue khai hun khong bo ri sat] *n* buyout; นายหน้าขายหุ้น [nai na khai hun] *n* stockbroker; ผู้ถือหุ้น [phu thue hun] *n* stockholder

หุ่นยนต์ [hun yon] *n* robot

หุ่นไล่กา [hun lai ka] *n* scarecrow

หุบเขา [hup khao] *n* valley; หุบเขาลึก [hup khao luek] *n* ravine

หุบทราย [hup sai] *n* sand dune

หุบปาก [hup pak] *v* shut up

หุ้ม [hum] ห่อหุ้ม [ho hum] *v* wrap up

หู [hu] *n* ear; เยื่อแก้วหู [yuea kaew hu] *n* eardrum; หูเจ็บ [hu chep] *n* earache; หู หนวก [hu nuak] *adj* deaf

หูด [hut] ก้อนเล็ก ๆ ที่ขึ้นบนผิวหนัง เช่น ไฝ หรือหูด [kon lek lek thii khuen bon phio nang chen fai rue hut] *n* wart

หูฟัง [hu fang] *npl* headphones; มีหูฟัง ไหม? [mii hu fang mai] Does it have headphones?

หูหนวก [hu nuak] ฉันหูหนวก [chan hu nuak] I'm deaf

เหงา [ngao] หงอยเหงา [ngoi ngao] *adj* lonely; ความเหงา [khwam ngao] *n* loneliness

เหงื่อ [nguea] *n* perspiration, sweat; เปียกเหงื่อ [piak nguea] *adj* sweaty; ทำให้เหงื่อออก [tham hai nguea ok] *v* sweat; ยาลดการขับเหงื่อ [ya lot kan khap nguea] *n* antiperspirant

เหงือก [ngueak] *n* gum; เหงือกฉันเลือด ออก [ngueak chan lueat ok] My gums are bleeding; เหงือกฉันปวด [ngueak chan puat] My gums are sore

เห็ด [het] *n* mushroom; เห็ดมีพิษชนิดหนึ่ง [het mii phit cha nit nueng] *n* toadstool

เหตุ [het] เหตุบังเอิญ [het bang oen] *n* coincidence

เหตุการณ์ [het kan] เหตุการณ์สำคัญ [het kan sam khan] *n* event; เหตุการณ์ที่เกิด

ขึ้น [het kan thii koet khuen] *n* occurrence; เหตุการณ์ที่เกิดขึ้นตามลำดับ [het kan thii koet khuen tam lam dap] *n* sequence

เหตุจูงใจ [het chung chai] *n* motive

เหตุบังเอิญ [het bang oen] เป็นเหตุบังเอิญ [pen het bang oen] *adj* accidental

เหตุผล [het phon] *n* reason; เหตุผลที่ดี [het phon thii di] *n* cause *(reason)*; ให้ เหตุผลสำหรับ [hai het phon sam rap] *v* account for; มีเหตุผล [mii het phon] *adj* logical

เห็น [hen] *vt* see; มองไม่เห็น [mong mai hen] *adj* invisible; ที่เห็นได้ [thii hen dai] *adj* visual; ที่สามารถมองเห็นได้ [thii sa maat mong hen dai] *adj* visible; เรา ไม่อยากเห็นใครเลยทั้งวันนอกจากเราเอง เท่านั้น [rao mai yak hen khrai loei thang wan nok chak rao eng thao nan] We'd like to see nobody but us all day!

เห็นแก่ตัว [hen kae tua] *adj* selfish; ซึ่ง เห็นแก่ตัวเอง [sueng hen kae tua eng] *adj* self-centred

เห็นใจ [hen chai] *v* sympathize; ความ เห็นใจ [khwam hen jai] *n* sympathy

เห็นด้วย [hen duai] *v* agree; ไม่เห็นด้วย [mai hen duai] *v* disagree

เหน็ดเหนื่อย [net nueai] *adj* exhausted, tired; น่าเหน็ดเหนื่อย [na net nueai] *adj* tiring

เหน็บแนม [nep name] ที่ชอบเหน็บแนม [thii chop nep naem] *adj* ironic

เห็นอกเห็นใจ [hen ok hen chai] *adj* sympathetic; ที่เข้าใจ อย่างเห็นอกเห็นใจ [thii khao jai yang hen ok hen chai] *adj* understanding

เหนียว [niao] *adj* sticky; ดินเหนียว [din niao] *n* clay

เหนือ [nuea] *prep* over; เหนือกว่า [nuea kwa] *adj* above; เกี่ยวกับทิศเหนือ [kiao kap thit nuea] *adj* north; ไปทางด้าน เหนือ [pai thang dan nuea] *adv* north

เหนือกว่า [nuea kwa] *adj* superior

เหนื่อย [nueai] ฉันเหนื่อย [chan nueai]

I'm tired; ฉันเหนื่อยนิดหน่อย [chan
nueai nit noi] I'm a little tired

เหม็น [men] เหม็นเน่า [men nao] *adj* foul;
ส่งกลิ่นเหม็น [song klin men] *v* stink;
กลิ่นเหม็น [klin men] *n* stink

เหมาะ [mo] เหมาะกัน [mo kan] *n* match

เหมาะสม [mo som] *adj* appropriate,
decent, proper, relevant, suitable;
เหมาะสมกัน [mo som kan] *v* suit; เหมาะ
สมที่สุด [mo som thii sut] *adv* best; ซึ่ง
ไม่เหมาะสม [sueng mai mo som] *adj*
unsuitable

เหมือง [mueang] เหมืองถ่านหิน [mueang
than hin] *n* colliery; การทำเหมือง [kan
tham mueang] *n* mining; คนงานเหมือง
[khon ngan mueang] *n* miner

เหมืองแร่ [mueang rae] *n* mine

เหมือน [muean] ไม่เหมือน [mai muean]
prep unlike; ดูเหมือนว่า [du muean wa] *v*
appear

เหมือนกัน [muean kan] *adj* same,
twinned; เหมือนกันทุกอย่าง [muean kan
thuk yang] *adj* identical; สิ่งที่เหมือนกัน
ราวกับพิมพ์มาจากบล็อกเดียวกัน [sing thii
muean kan rao kap phim ma chak
blok diao kan] *n* stereotype; ฉันอยากได้
เครื่องดื่มเหมือนกัน [chan yak dai
khrueang duem muean kan] I'll have
the same

เหมือนกับ [muean kap] *prep* like

เหยียดเชื้อชาติ [yiat chuea chat] การ
เหยียดเชื้อชาติ [kan yiat chuea chat] *n*
racism

เหยียดผิว [yiat phio] ผู้เหยียดผิว [phu
yiat phio] *n* racist

เหยียดหยาม [yiat yam] *v* despise

เหยียบ [yiap] *v* tread; กระทืบ เหยียบ [kra
thuep, yiab] *vt* stamp

เหยื่อ [yuea] *n* prey

เหยือก [yueak] *n* jug; น้ำหนึ่งเหยือก [nam
nueng yueak] a jug of water

เหรัญญิก [he ran yik] *n* treasurer

เหรียญ [rian] *n* coin, medal; การประดับ
เหรียญให้ [kan pra dap rian hai] *n*

medallion; ฉันอยากได้เหรียญสำหรับ
โทรศัพท์ [chan yak dai rian sam rap tho
ra sap] I'd like some coins for the
phone, please

เหล็ก [hlek] *n* iron, steel; เหล็กที่ไม่เป็น
สนิม [lek thii mai pen sa nim] *n*
stainless steel; แผ่นเหล็กหรือหินสลัก
[phaen lek rue hin sa lak] *n* plaque

เหล็กเสียบ [hlek siap] เหล็กเสียบเนื้ออย่าง
[lek siap nuea yang] *n* spit

เหลวไหล [leo lai] เรื่องเหลวไหล [rueang
leo lai] *n* trash

เหลา [lao] ที่เหลาดินสอ [thii lao din so] *n*
pencil sharpener

เหล้า [lao] *n* alcohol, liqueur; เหล้าเชอรี่
[lao choe ri] *n* sherry; เหล้ารัม [lao ram]
n rum; เหล้าราคาถูก [lao ra kha thuk] *n*
table wine; คุณมีเหล้าหวานชนิดไหน?
[khun mii lao wan cha nit nai] What
liqueurs do you have?

เหล่านั้น [lao nan] *adj* those ▷ *pron* those

เหล่านี้ [lao ni] *adj* these ▷ *pron* these

เหลือ [luea] ส่วนที่เหลือ [suan thii luea] *n*
the rest; ส่วนที่เหลืออยู่ [suan thii luea
yu] *n* stub; สิ่งที่เหลืออยู่ [sing thii luea
yu] *npl* remains

เหลือง [lueang] สีเหลืองอำพัน [sii lueang
am phan] *n* amber; ที่เป็นสีเหลือง [thii
pen sii lueang] *adj* yellow

เหา [hao] *npl* lice

เห่า [hao] *v* bark

เหี่ยว [hiao] เหี่ยวเฉา [hiao chao] *v* wilt

แห้ง [haeng] *adj* dried ▷ *v* dry; เครื่องอบผ้า
ให้แห้ง [khrueang op pha hai haeng] *n*
tumble dryer; แห้งสนิท [haeng sa nit]
adj bone dry; ฉันมีผมแห้ง [chan mii
phom haeng] I have dry hair

แห้งแล้ง [haeng laeng] ความแห้งแล้ง
[khwam haeng laeng] *n* drought

แห้งแล้ง [haeng laeng] *adj* dry

แหนบ [naep] *npl* tweezers

แหย่ [yae] แหย่ด้วยข้อศอกหรือนิ้ว [yae
duai kho sok rue nio] *v* poke

แหล่งเสื่อมโทรม [laeng sueam som] *n*

slum

แหลม [laem] แหลม คม [laem, khom] *adj* sharp

แหวน [waen] *n* ring; แหวนแต่งงาน [waen taeng ngan] *n* wedding ring; แหวนหมั้น [waen man] *n* engagement ring

โหด [hot] โหดร้าย [hot rai] *adj* brutal

โหดร้าย [hot rai] *adj* cruel; ความโหดร้าย [khwam hot rai] *n* cruelty

โหนก [nok] โหนกแก้ม [nok kaem] *n* cheekbone

โหยหวน [hoi huan] ร้องโหยหวน [rong hoi huan] *v* howl

โห่ร้อง [ho rong] โห่ร้องอวยชัย [ho rong uai chai] *v* hail

โหระพา [ho ra pha] ใบโหระพา [bai ho ra pha] *n* basil

โหราศาสตร์ [ho ra sat] *n* astrology, horoscope

โหล [lo] *n* dozen

ให้ [hai] *vt* give; ให้คืน [hai khuen] *v* give back; ฉันควรให้เท่าไร? [chan khuan hai thao rai] How much should I give?

ให้การ [hai kan] การให้การเท็จ [kan hai kan tet] *n* perjury

ให้กู้ [hai ku] ให้กู้เงิน [hai ku ngoen] *v* loan

ใหญ่ [yai] *adj* big, large; ใหญ่โต [yai to] *adj* huge, massive; ใหญ่โตมาก [yai to mak] *adj* tremendous; ใหญ่กว่า [yai kwa] *adj* bigger; คุณมีห้องใหญ่กว่านี้ไหม? [khun mii hong yai kwa nii mai] Do you have a bigger one?

ให้นม [hai nom] ให้นมทารกด้วยนมแม่ [hai nom tha rok duai nom mae] *v* breast-feed; ฉันให้นมลูกที่นี่ได้ไหม? [chan hai nom luk thii ni dai mai] Can I breast-feed here?; ฉันจะให้นมลูกได้ที่ไหน? [chan ja hai nom luk dai thii nai] Where can I breast-feed the baby?

ใหม่ [mai] *adj* new; ใหม่เอี่ยม [mai iam] *adj* brand-new; การจัดการแข่งขันใหม่ [kan chat kan khaeng khan mai] *n* replay; ปีใหม่ [pi mai] *n* New Year

ให้ยืม [hai yuem] *v* lend

ให้สินบน [hai sin bon] *v* bribe

ให้อภัย [hai a phai] *v* forgive; การให้อภัยโทษ [kan hai a phai thot] *n* pardon

ให้อาหาร [hai a han] *vt* feed

ไหปลาร้า [hai pla ra] กระดูกไหปลาร้า [kra duk hai pla ra] *n* collarbone

ไหม [mai] *n* silk; ไหมขัดฟัน [mai khat fan] *n* dental floss

ไหม้ [mai] ไหม้ เผาไหม้ [mai, phao mai] *n* burn; การที่ถูกไหม้ [kan thii thuk mai] *n* burn; ไฟไหม้ [fai mai] Fire!

ไหม้เกรียม [mai kriam] สีไหม้เกรียมของผิวหนังจากการตากแดด [sii mai kriam khong phio nang chak kan tak daet] *n* tan

ไหมพรม [mai phrom] เสื้อไหมพรมติดกระดุมหน้า [suea mai phrom tit kra dum na] *n* cardigan

ไหล [lai] *v* flow; ไหลบ่า ไหลล้น [lai ba, lai lon] *vi* flood; ปลาไหล [pla lai] *n* eel

ไหล่ [lai] *n* shoulder; หัวไหล่ [hua lai] *n* shoulder blade; ฉันปวดไหล่ [chan puat lai] I've hurt my shoulder

ไหวพริบ [wai prip] มีไหวพริบดี [mii wai phrip di] *adj* tactful; การมีไหวพริบหรือปฏิภาณดี [kan mii wai phrip rue pa ti phan dii] *n* tact

อ

อกหัก [ok hak] *adj* heartbroken

อคติ [a kha ti] *n* prejudice; มีอคติ [mii a kha ti] *adj* prejudiced

องค์กร [ong kon] *n* organization

องค์การ [ong kan] ตัวย่อขององค์การนาโต้ [tua yo khong ong kan na to] *abbr* NATO

องค์การสหประชาชาติ [ong kan sa ha pra cha chat] *n* United Nations; ตัวย่อ ขององค์การสหประชาชาติ [tua yo khong ong kan sa ha pra cha chat] *abbr* UN

องค์ประกอบ [ong pra kop] *n* element; การจัดวางองค์ประกอบ [kan chat wang ong pra kop] *n* composition

องศา [ong sa] *n* degree; องศาเซ็นติเกรด [ong sa sen ti kret] *n* degree centigrade; องศาเซลเซียส [ong sa sel sias] *n* degree Celsius; องศาฟาห์เรนไฮต์ [ong sa fa ren hai] *n* degree Fahrenheit

องุ่น [a ngun] *n* grape; ไร่องุ่น [rai a ngun] *n* vineyard; ต้นองุ่น [ton a ngun] *n* vine

อด [ot] *v* starve

อดกลั้น [ot klan] ประสบ อดทน อดกลั้น [pra sop, ot thon, ot klan] *v* undergo

อดทน [ot thon] *adj* patient; ไม่อดทน [mai ot thon] *adj* impatient; ความไม่ อดทน [khwam mai ot thon] *n* impatience; ความทรหดอดทน ความ แข็งแกร่งที่ยืนหยัดอยู่ได้นาน [khwam tho ra hot ot thon, khwam khaeng kraeng thii yuen yat yu dai nan] *n* stamina

อดิเรก [a di rek] งานอดิเรก [ngan a di rek] *n* hobby

อดีต [a dit] สิ่งที่เกิดในอดีต [sing thii koet nai a dit] *n* past; อดีตภรรยา [a dit phan ra ya] *n* ex-wife

อธิบาย [a thi bai] *v* describe ▷ *vi* explain; คำอธิบาย [kham a thi bai] *n* description, explanation; คำอธิบาย อย่างคราว ๆ [kham a thi bai yang khrao khrao] *n* outline; ที่สามารถอธิบายได้ [thii sa maat a thi bai dai] *adj* accountable; คุณอธิบายได้ไหมว่าเกิด อะไรขึ้น? [khun a thi bai dai mai wa koet a rai khuen] Can you explain what the matter is?

อนาคต [a na khot] *n* future; ในอนาคต [nai a na khot] *adv* ahead; มีอนาคตดี [mii a na khot di] *adj* promising

อนามัย [a na mai] *n* hygiene; ผิดหลัก อนามัย [phit lak a na mai] *adj* unhealthy

อนุญาต [a nu yat] *n* permit ▷ *v* allow, let; ใบอนุญาต [bai a nu yat] *n* licence, pass (*permit*), permit; ใบอนุญาตให้ทำงาน [bai a nu yat hai tham ngan] *n* work permit; การอนุญาต [kan a nu yat] *n* permission

อนุภรรยา [a nu phan ra ya] *n* mistress

อนุมัติ [a nu mat] *v* approve; การอนุมัติ [kan a nu mat] *n* approval

อนุรักษ์ [a nu rak] การอนุรักษ์ธรรมชาติและ สภาพแวดล้อม [kan a nu rak tham ma chat lae sa phap waet lom] *n* conservation

อนุรักษ์นิยม [a nu rak ni yom] ที่เป็น อนุรักษ์นิยม [thii pen a nu rak ni yom] *adj* conservative; พรรคการเมืองอนุรักษ์ นิยม [phak kan mueang a nu rak ni yom] *adj* right-wing

อนุสรณ์ [a nu son] *n* memorial

อนุสาวรีย์ [a nu sao wa ri] *n* monument

อบ [op] *adj* baked ▷ *v* bake; ร้อนและอบ [ron lae op] *adj* stifling; การอบ [kan op] *n* baking; ที่อบ [thii op] *adj* roast

อบเชย [op choei] *n* cinnamon; ใบอบเชย [bai op choei] *n* bay leaf

อบรม [op rom] *vt* train; หลักสูตรอบรม [lak sut op rom] *n* training course; ที่ได้รับการอบรม [thii dai rap kan op rom] *adj* trained

อบอุ่น [op un] อบอุ่นและสะดวกสบาย [op un lae sa duak sa bai] *adj* cosy

อบไอน้ำ [op ai nam] การอบไอน้ำ [kan op ai nam] *n* sauna

อพยพ [op pha yop] *v* evacuate; การอพยพ [kan op pa yop] *n* migration; การอพยพจากต่างประเทศ [kan op pa yop chak tang pra tet] *n* immigration; ผู้อพยพ [phu op pha yop] *n* migrant

อพาร์ทเมนท์ [a phat men] *n* apartment; เรากำลังมองหาอพาร์ทเมนท์ [rao kam lang mong ha a part ment] We're looking for an apartment; คุณพาเราดูพาร์ทเมนท์ได้ไหม? [khun pha rao du a phat ment dai mai] Could you show us around the apartment?

อภิปราย [a phi prai] หัวเรื่องการอภิปราย [hua rueang kan a phi prai] *n* cause (*ideals*)

อภิสิทธิ์ [a phi sit] *n* privilege

อมยิ้ม [om yim] *n* lolly; ลูกอมยิ้ม [luk om yim] *n* lollipop

อเมริกัน [a me ri kan] *n* ชาวอเมริกัน [chao a me ri kan] *n* American

อเมริกา [a me ri ka] *adj* เกี่ยวกับอเมริกา [kiao kap a me ri ka] *adj* American; เกี่ยวกับอเมริกาเหนือ [kiao kap a me ri ka nuea] *adj* North American ▷ *n* ทวีปอเมริกาเหนือ [tha wip a me ri ka nuea] *n* North America

อเมริกาใต้ [a me ri ka tai] *adj* เกี่ยวกับอเมริกาใต้ [kiao kap a me ri ka tai] *adj* South American; ชาวอเมริกาใต้ [chao a me ri ka tai] *n* South American ▷ *n* ทวีปอเมริกาใต้ [tha wip a me ri ka tai] *n* South America

อยาก [yak] ทำให้อยาก [tham hai yak] *v* tempt; คืนนี้คุณอยากไปที่ไหน? [khuen nii khun yak pai thii nai] Where would you like to go tonight?; ฉันอยากเช่าจักรยานหนึ่งคัน [chan yak chao chak kra yan nueng khan] I want to hire a bike

อยากได้ [yak dai] ฉันอยากได้ตั๋วสองใบสำหรับคืนนี้ [chan yak dai tua song bai sam rap khuen nii] I'd like two tickets for tonight

อยากรู้อยากเห็น [yak ru yak hen] *adj* curious, nosy; ที่อยากรู้อยากเห็น [thii yak ru yak hen] *adj* inquisitive

อย่างงั้นๆ [yang ngan yang ngan] อย่างงั้น ๆ อย่างงั้นแหละ [yang ngan ngan, yang ngan lae] *adv* so-so

อย่างงั้นแหละ [yang ngan lae] อย่างงั้น ๆ อย่างงั้นแหละ [yang ngan ngan, yang ngan lae] *adv* so-so

อย่างใดอย่างหนึ่ง [yang dai yang nueng] อย่างใดอย่างหนึ่งในจำนวนสอง [yang dai yang nueng nai cham nuan song] *pron* either

อย่างนั้น [yang nan] อย่างนี้หรืออย่างนั้น [yang nii rue yang nan] *conj* either… or

อย่างนี้ [yang ni] อย่างนี้หรืออย่างนั้น [yang nii rue yang nan] *conj* either… or

อย่างไร [yang rai] *adv* how; คุณรู้ไหมว่าจะทำนี่ได้อย่างไร? [khun ru mai wa ja tham ni dai yang rai] Do you know how to do this?; ฉันจะไปที่…ได้อย่างไร? [chan ja pai thii…dai yang rai] How do I get to…?

อย่างไรก็ตาม [yang rai ko tam] *adv* anyway, however, though, yet (*nevertheless*); แต่อย่างไรก็ตาม [tae yang rai ko tam] *adv* nevertheless

อยู่ [yu] เป็น อยู่ คือ [pen, yu, khue] *v* be; มีชีวิตอยู่ต่อไป [mii chi wid yu to pai] *v* live on; การพักอยู่ [kan phak yu] n stay; เราอยู่ที่... [rao yu thii…] We live in...

อยู่รอด [yu rot] การอยู่รอด [kan yu rot] n survival; ผู้ที่อยู่รอด [phu thii yu rot] n survivor

อร่อย [a roi] adj delicious; นั่นอร่อยมาก [nan a roi mak] That was delicious; อาหารมื้อนี้อร่อยมาก [a han mue nii a roi mak] The meal was delicious

อรุณ [a run] รุ่งอรุณ [rung a run] n dawn อรุณสวัสดิ์ [a run sa wat] Good morning

อลูมิเนียม [a lu mi niam] n aluminium

อวกาศ [a wa kat] มนุษย์อวกาศ [ma nut a wa kat] n astronaut

อ้วน [uan] adj fat; อ้วนเกินไป [uan koen pai] adj obese; อ้วนกลม [uan klom] adj chubby

อวยพร [uai pon] v bless; การดื่มอวยพร [kan duem uai pon] n toast (tribute); บัตรอวยพร [bat uai phon] n card, greetings card

อวัยวะ [a wai ya wa] อวัยวะต่าง ๆ [a wai ya wa tang tang] n organ (body part)

อสุจิ [a su chi] ตัวอสุจิ [tua a su chi] n sperm

อ้อ [o] ต้นไม้จำพวกอ้อหรือกก [ton mai cham phuak o rue kok] n reed

ออก [ok] v leave; ไป เคลื่อนไป ออกไป [pai, khluean pai, ok pai] vi go; การออกเดินทาง [kan ok doen thang] n departure; ช่วยกันออกค่าใช้จ่าย [chuai kan ok kha chai jai] v club together; รถไฟจะออกจากสถานีเวลาอะไร? [rot fai ja ok chak sa tha ni we la a rai] What time does the train leave?

ออกกำลังกาย [ok kam lang kai] สถานที่ที่คนไปออกกำลังกายหรือพักผ่อน [sa than thii thii khon pai ok kam lang kai rue phak phon] n leisure centre; การออกกำลังกาย [kan ok kam lang kai] n exercise; การออกกำลังกายแบบวิดพื้น [kan ok kam lang kai baep wid phuen] n push-up

ออกจาก [ok chak] prep off

ออกซิเจน [ok si chen] n oxygen

ออกดอก [ok dok] v blossom

ออกแบบ [ok baep] v design; การออกแบบ [kan ok baep] n design; ความมีรสนิยมการออกแบบ [khwam mii rot ni yom, kan ok baep] n style; ผู้ออกแบบ [phu ok baep] n designer

ออกไป [ok pai] v get out, go out

ออกรายการ [ok rai kan] การออกรายการอากาศ [kan ok rai kan a kat] n broadcast

ออกเสียง [ok siang] v pronounce; การออกเสียงคำพูด [kan ok siang kham phut] n pronunciation; อ่านออกเสียง [an ok siang] v read out; คุณอ่านออกเสียงคำนี้อย่างไร? [khun aan ok siang kham nii yang rai] How do you pronounce it?

อ่อน [on] สีอ่อน [sii on] adj fair (light colour); ซึ่งมีรสชาติอ่อน [sueng mii rot chat on] adj mild; อ่อนนุ่ม [on num] adj soft

ออนซ์ [on] หน่วยวัดน้ำหนักเป็นออนซ์ [nuai wat nam nak pen on] n ounce

อ่อนนุ่ม [on num] adj tender

อ่อนโยน [on yon] ความสุภาพอ่อนโยน [khwam su phap on yon] n politeness; อย่างอ่อนโยน [yang on yon] adj gentle

อ่อนวัย [on wai] adj young

อ่อนหวาน [on wan] adj sweet (pleasing)

อ่อนหัด [on hat] คนอ่อนหัด [khon on hat] adj green (inexperienced)

อ่อนไหว [on wai] มีอารมณ์อ่อนไหวมากเกินไป [mii a rom on wai mak koen pai] adj soppy

อ่อนแอ [on ae] adj weak; เจือจาง อ่อนแอ [chuea chang, on ae] v faint; ความอ่อนแอ [khwam on ae] n weakness

ออฟฟิศ [op fit] ฉันทำงานในออฟฟิศ [chan tham ngan nai op fit] I work in an office

อูม [om] เงินออม [ngoen om] npl savings

อ้อม [om] เส้นทางอ้อม [sen thang om] n detour; ทางอ้อม [thang om] n bypass

ออร์แกน [o kan] หีบเพลง ออร์แกน [hip phleng, o kaen] n organ (music)

ออริกาโน [o ri ka no] ต้นออริกาโนเป็นสมุนไพรใช้ทำอาหาร [ton o ri ka no pen sa mun phrai chai tham a han] n oregano

ออสเตรเลีย [os tre lia] n Australasia; ที่เกี่ยวกับออสเตรเลีย [thii kiao kap os tre lia] adj Australian; ประเทศออสเตรเลีย [pra tet os tre lia] n Australia

ออสเตรีย [os tria] ชาวออสเตรีย [chao os tria] n Austrian; ที่เกี่ยวกับออสเตรีย [thii kiao kap os tria] adj Austrian; ประเทศออสเตรีย [pra tet os tria] n Austria

ออสเตรียน [ot sa trian] ชาวออสเตรียน [chao os trian] n Austrian

อะตอม [a tom] n atom

อะไร [a rai] adj what; ไม่มีอะไร [mai mii a rai] n nothing; อะไรก็ได้ [a rai ko dai] pron anything; เป็นอะไรหรือเปล่า? [pen a rai rue plao] What's the matter?

อะลูมิเนียม [a lu mi niam] แผ่นอะลูมิเนียมที่ใช้ในครัว [phaen a lu mi niam thii chai nai khrua] n tinfoil

อะโวคาโด [a wo ka do] ผลอะโวคาโด [phon a vo kha do] n avocado

อะไหล่ [a lai] n spare part; ล้ออะไหล่ [lo a lai] n spare wheel; ยางอะไหล่ [yang a lai] n spare tyre

อักษร [ak son] ตัวอักษร [tua ak son] n alphabet, letter (a, b, c); ปริศนาอักษรไขว้ [prit sa na ak son khwai] n crossword; อักษรแรก ๆ ของชื่อ [ak son raek raek khong chue] npl initials

อักเสบ [ak sep] เยื่อหุ้มสมองอักเสบ [yuea hum sa mong ak sep] n meningitis; โรคไขข้ออักเสบ [rok khai kho ak sep] n rheumatism; โรคหลอดลมอักเสบ [rok lot lom ak sep] n bronchitis; ฉันทุกข์ทรมานด้วยข้อต่ออักเสบ [chan thuk tho ra man duai kho to ak sep] I suffer from arthritis

อังกฤษ [ang krit] adj เกี่ยวกับชาวอังกฤษ [kiao kap chao ang krit] adj English; เกี่ยวกับประเทศสหราชอาณาจักรอังกฤษ [kiao kap pra thet sa ha rat cha a na chak ang krit] adj British ▷ n สกุลเงินของสหราชอาณาจักรอังกฤษ [sa kun ngoen khong sa ha rat cha a na chak ang krit] n sterling; มีใครพูดภาษาอังกฤษได้ไหม? [mii khrai phut pha sa ang krit dai mai] Does anyone speak English?

อังคาร [ang kan] วันอังคาร [wan ang khan] n Tuesday

อัจฉริยะ [at cha ri ya] อัจฉริยบุคคล [at cha ri ya buk khon] n genius

อัญประกาศ [an ya pra kat] npl quotation marks

อัฒภาค [at tha phak] เครื่องหมายอัฒภาค [khrueang mai at ta phak] n semicolon

อัณฑะ [an tha] ลูกอัณฑะ [luk an tha] n testicle

อัดไฟ [at fai] v charge (electricity)

อัดสำเนา [at sam nao] v photocopy

อัตชีวประวัติ [at ta chi wa pra wat] n autobiography, biography

อัตโนมัติ [at ta no mat] adj automatic; โดยอัตโนมัติ [doi at ta no mat] adv automatically; การกระทำโดยอัตโนมัติ [kan kra tham doi at ta no mat] n reflex; เป็นรถขับแบบอัตโนมัติหรือเปล่า? [pen rot khap baep at ta no mat rue plao] Is it an automatic car?

อัตรา [at tra] n rate; แผงที่บอกอัตราความเร็ว [phaeng thii bok at tra khwam reo] n speedometer; อัตราแลกเปลี่ยน [at tra laek plian] n exchange rate; อัตราแลกเปลี่ยนเงิน [at tra laek plian ngoen] n rate of exchange; อัตราแลกคือเท่าไร? [at tra laek khue thao rai] What's the exchange rate?

อัตราส่วน [at tra suan] n ratio

อันดับ [an dap] ประเมินค่า จัดอันดับ [pra moen kha, chat an dap] v rate

อันตราย [an ta rai] n danger; เป็นอันตราย [pen an ta rai] adj harmful; ไม่มีอันตราย

[mai mii an ta rai] *adj* harmless; ไฟ
เตือนอันตราย [fai tuean an ta rai] *npl*
hazard warning lights; มีอันตรายเกี่ยว
กับหิมะถล่มไหม? [mii an ta rai kiao kap
hi ma tha lom mai] Is there a danger of
avalanches?

อันที่ [an thi] สิ่งที่ อันที่ [sing thii, an
thii] *pron* which

อันธพาล [an tha pan] *n* bully, thug; พวก
อันธพาล [phuak an tha phan] *n*
gangster

อันไหน [an nai] *adj* which; อันไหน สิ่ง
ไหน [an nai, sing nai] *pron* what

อับปาง [ap pang] ทำให้เรืออับปาง [tham
hai ruea ap pang] *adj* shipwrecked

อับอาย [ap ai] *adj* ashamed; ความอับอาย
[khwam ap ai] *n* shame; ซึ่งอับอาย
[sueng ap ai] *adj* embarrassed; น่า
อับอาย [na ap ai] *adj* disgraceful,
embarrassing

อัปลักษณ์ [ap pa lak] *adj* hideous

อัฟกานิสถาน [ap ka nit sa than] เกี่ยวกับ
อัฟกานิสถาน [kiao kap af ka ni sa than]
adj Afghan; ชาวอัฟกานิสถาน [chao af ka
ni sa than] *n* Afghan; ประเทศ
อัฟกานิสถาน [pra tet af ka ni sa than]
Afghanistan

อัฟริกัน [ap fri kan] ชาวอัฟริกัน [chao af
ri kan] *n* African, Afrikaner; ชาวอัฟริกัน
ตอนเหนือ [chao af ri kan ton nuea] *n*
North African

อัฟริกา [ap fri ka] เกี่ยวกับอัฟริกา [kiao
kap af ri ka] *adj* African; เกี่ยวกับอัฟริกา
เหนือ [kiao kap af ri ka nuea] *adj* North
African; ชื่อภาษาราชการของอัฟริกาใต้
[chue pha sa rat cha kan khong af ri ka
tai] *n* Afrikaans

อัฟริกาใต้ [ap fri ka tai] เกี่ยวกับอัฟริกาใต้
[kiao kap af ri ka tai] *adj* South African;
ชาวอัฟริกาใต้ [chao af ri kan tai] *n*
South African; ประเทศอัฟริกาใต้ [pra tet
af ri ka tai] *n* South Africa

อัมพาต [am ma phat] อัมพาตเนื่องจากเส้น
โลหิตในสมองแตก [am ma phat nueang

chak sen lo hit nai sa mong taek] *v*
stroke *(apoplexy)*

อัลจีเรีย [an chi ria] ชาวอัลจีเรีย [chao al
chi ria] *n* Algerian; ที่เกี่ยวกับอัลจีเรีย
[thii kiao kap al chi ria] *adj* Algerian;
ประเทศอัลจีเรีย [pra tet al chi ria] *n*
Algeria

อัลไซเมอร์ [an sai moe] โรคลืม อัลไซเมอร์
[rok luem, al sai moe] *n* Alzheimer's
disease

อัลบั้ม [al bam] อัลบั้ม [al bam] *n* album;
อัลบั้มใส่รูป [al bam sai rup] *n* photo
album

อัลเบเนีย [an be nia] ประเทศอัลเบเนีย [pra
tet al be nia] *n* Albania

อัลเบเนีย [an be nia] ชาวอัลเบเนียน [chao
al be nian] *n* Albanian *(person)*; ซึ่งเกี่ยว
กับอัลเบเนียน [sueng kiao kap al be
nian] *adj* Albanian; ภาษาอัลเบเนียน [pha
sa al be nian] *n* Albanian *(language)*

อัลมอนด์ [an mon] เมล็ดอัลมอนด์ [ma let
a mon] *n* almond; ส่วนผสมของอัลมอนด์
น้ำตาลและไข่ขาวใส่บนหน้าเค้ก [suan pha
som khong a mon nam tan lae khai
khao sai bon na khek] *n* marzipan;
ต้นไม้ในตระกูลอัลมอนด์ [ton mai nai tra
kun an mon] *n* elm

อัศเจรีย์ [at sa che ri] เครื่องหมายอัศเจรีย์
[khrueang mai at sa je ri] *n*
exclamation mark

อา [a] ป้า น้า อาผู้หญิง [pa na a phu ying]
n auntie; ป้า น้า อาผู้หญิง [pa na a phu
ying] *n* aunt

อาการ [a kan] อาการแพ้ [a kan phae] *n*
allergy; อาการของโรค [a kan khong
rok] *n* symptom; อาการชักของลมบ้าหมู
[a kan chak khong lom ba mu] *n*
epileptic fit

อากาศ [a kat] *n* air, climate, weather;
เครื่องปรับอากาศ [khrueang prap a kat]
n air conditioning; การเปลี่ยนแปลงของ
อากาศ [kan plian plaeng khong a kat] *n*
climate change; การพยากรณ์อากาศ
[kan pha ya kon a kat] *n* weather

forecast; จะใช้เวลานานเท่าไรถ้าส่งทางอากาศ? [ja chai we la nan thao rai tha song thang a kat] How long will it take by air?

อาคาร [a kan] ตึก อาคาร [tuek, a khan] *n* building

อ่าง [ang] อ่างล้างหน้าและมือ [ang lang na lae mue] *n* washbasin; อ่างสำหรับล้าง [ang sam rap lang] *n* sink; อ่างอาบน้ำ [ang aap nam] *n* bathtub

อ้าง [ang] คำอ้างว่าอยู่ที่อื่นขณะที่เกิดเหตุ [kham ang wa yu thii uen kha na thii koet het] *n* alibi

อ่างน้ำ [ang nam] *n* basin

อ่างล้างหน้า [ang lang na] อ่างล้างหน้าสกปรก [ang lang na sok ka prok] The washbasin is dirty

อ้างว้าง [ang wang] *adj* bleak; ความรู้สึกหรือสภาพเปล่าเปลี่ยวอ้างว้าง [khwam ru suek rue sa phap plao pliao ang wang] *n* void

อ้างอิง [ang ing] *v* quote, refer; เครื่องหมายอ้างอิง [khrueang mai ang ing] *npl* inverted commas; เอกสารอ้างอิง [ek ka san ang ing] *n* reference; หมายเลขเอกสารอ้างอิง [mai lek ek ka san ang ing] *n* reference number

อาจ [at] อาจจะ [at cha] *adv* maybe

อาจจะ [at cha] *adv* possibly

อาจารย์ [a chan] รองอาจารย์ใหญ่ [rong a chan yai] *n* deputy head

อาเจียน [a chian] *v* throw up, vomit

อาชญากรรม [at cha ya kam] *n* crime; เกี่ยวกับอาชญากรรม [kiao kap at cha ya kam] *adj* criminal; อาชญากรรมที่เกิดขึ้นบนอินเตอร์เน็ต [at cha ya kam thii koet khuen bon in ter net] *n* cybercrime

อาชีพ [a chip] *n* occupation (work), profession; เกี่ยวกับอาชีพ [kiao kap a chip] *adj* professional; ผู้ที่ได้ทำงานในอาชีพใดอาชีพหนึ่งมานาน [phu thii dai tham ngan nai a chip dai a chip nueng ma nan] *n* veteran; อาชีพการทำงาน [a chiip kan tham ngan] *n* career

อาเซอร์ไบจาน [a soe bai chan] เกี่ยวกับอาเซอร์ไบจาน [kiao kap a soe bai chan] *adj* Azerbaijani; ชาวอาเซอร์ไบจาน [chao a soe bi chan] *n* Azerbaijani; ประเทศอาเซอร์ไบจาน [pra tet a soe bi chan] *n* Azerbaijan

อาณาเขต [a na khet] *n* territory

อาณาจักร [a na chak] *n* empire

อาทิตย์ [a thit] สองอาทิตย์ [song a thit] *n* fortnight; วันอาทิตย์ [wan a thit] *n* Sunday; ราคาเท่าไรที่จะจอดหนึ่งอาทิตย์? [ra kha thao rai thii ja jot nueng a thit] How much is it for a week?

อาน [an] *n* saddle

อ่าน [an] *v* read; แปลคำพูดด้วยการอ่านริมฝีปาก [plae kham phut duai kan an rim fi pak] *v* lip-read; ไม่สามารถอ่านและเขียนได้ [mai sa mat an lae khian dai] *adj* illiterate; การอ่าน [kan an] *n* reading; ฉันอ่านไม่ได้ [chan an mai dai] I can't read it

อาบแดด [ap daet] *v* sunbathe; เตียงอาบแดด [tiang aap daet] *n* sunbed; โลชั่นหลังอาบแดด [lo chan lang aap daet] *n* after sun lotion

อาบน้ำ [ap nam] *v* bathe; เสื้อคลุมอาบน้ำ [suea khlum aap nam] *n* bathrobe; เจลอาบน้ำ [chen aap nam] *n* shower gel; หมวกอาบน้ำ [muak aap nam] *n* shower cap

อาบูดาบี [a bu da bi] *n* Abu Dhabi

อาย [ai] ขี้อาย [khii ai] *adj* shy

อายแชโดว์ [ai chae do] *n* eye shadow

อายุ [a yu] *n* age; สูงอายุ [sung a yu] *adj* aged; ชั่วอายุคน [chua a yu khon] *n* generation; ต่ำกว่ากำหนดอายุ [tam kwa kam not a yu] *adj* underage

อายุน้อย [a yu noi] อ้ายุน้อยกว่า [mii a yu noi kwa] *adj* younger; อายุน้อยที่สุด [a yu noi thii sut] *adj* youngest

อาร์เจนตินา [a chen ti na] เกี่ยวกับประเทศอาร์เจนตินา [kiao kap pra thet a chen ti na] *n* Argentinian; ชาวอาร์เจนตินา [chao a chen ti na] *n* Argentinian (*person*);

ประเทศอาร์เจนตินา [pra tet ar chen ti na] n Argentina

อารมณ์ [a rom] n mood, temper ▷ npl spirits; เกี่ยวกับอารมณ์ [kiao kap a rom] adj emotional; ไม่แสดงอารมณ์และความรู้สึก [mai sa daeng a rom lae khwam ru suek] adj reserved; ซึ่งไม่สามารถควบคุมอารมณ์ได้ [sueng mai sa maat khuap khum a rom dai] adj frantic

อารมณ์ขัน [a rom khan] การมีอารมณ์ขัน [kan mii a rom khan] n sense of humour

อารมณ์เสีย [a rom sia] ทำให้อารมณ์เสีย [tham hai a rom sia] v upset

อาร์มีเนีย [a mi nia] เกี่ยวกับประเทศอาร์มีเนีย [kiao kap pra thet a mii nia] adj Armenian; ประเทศอาร์มีเนีย [pra tet ar mii nia] n Armenia

อาร์มีเนียน [a mi nian] ชาวอาร์มีเนียน [chao a mii nian] n Armenian (person); ภาษาอาร์มีเนียน [pha sa ar mii nian] n Armenian (language)

อารยธรรม [a ra ya tham] n civilization; ซึ่งไร้อารยธรรม [sueng rai a ra ya tham] adj uncivilized

อาระเบีย [a ra bia] ประเทศต่าง ๆ ในคาบสมุทรอาระเบีย [pra tet tang tang nai khap sa mut a ra bia] npl Gulf States

อาราม [a ram] อารามเปิดให้สาธารณชนเข้าชมไหม? [a ram poet hai sa tha ra na chon khao chom mai] Is the monastery open to the public?

อ่าว [ao] n bay

อาวุธ [a wut] n weapon; ติดอาวุธ [tit a wut] adj armed; อาวุธยุทธภัณฑ์ [a wut yut tha phan] n ammunition

อาวุโส [a wu so] ผู้อาวุโส [phu a wu so] adj senior; พลเมืองอาวุโส [phon la mueang a wu so] n senior citizen

อาศัย [a sai] เขตที่มีคนอยู่อาศัย [khet thii mii khon yu a sai] n neighbourhood; ไม่มีคนอาศัยอยู่ [mai mii khon a sai yu] adj uninhabited; ที่พักอาศัย [thii phak a sai] n accommodation

อาสาสมัคร [a sa sa mak] n volunteer

อาหรับ [a rup] เกี่ยวกับชาวอาหรับ [kiao kap chao a rap] adj Arab; ชาวอาหรับ [chao a rap] n Arab; ที่เกี่ยวกับอาหรับ [thii kiao kap a rap] adj Arabic

อาหาร [a han] n diet, food; เกี่ยวกับการทานอาหารไม่ได้ [kiao kap kan than a han mai dai] adj anorexic; เครื่องทำอาหาร [khrueang tham a han] n food processor; เวลาอาหาร [we la a han] n mealtime; ความอยากอาหาร [khwam yak a han] n appetite; ภาวะไม่อยากหรือทานอาหารไม่ได้ [pha wa mai yak rue than a han mai dai] n anorexia; อาหารเย็น [a han yen] n dinner; อาหารย่าง [a han yang] n grill; คุณมีอาหารไหม? [khun mii a han mai] Do you have food?

อาหารกลางวัน [a han klang wan] n lunch; เวลาอาหารกลางวัน [we la a han klang wan] n lunchtime; ช่วงหยุดพักอาหารกลางวัน [chuang yut phak a han klang wan] n lunch break; อาหารกลางวันเตรียมจากบ้านไปทานที่อื่น [a han klang wan triam chak baan pai than thii uen] n packed lunch; อาหารกลางวันจะพร้อมเมื่อไร? [a han klang wan ja phrom muea rai] When will lunch be ready?

อาหารเจ [a han che] คุณมีอาหารเจไหม? [khun mii a han je mai] Do you have any vegan dishes?

อาหารเช้า [a han chao] อาหารเช้าที่ทำจากข้าวโอ๊ตที่ใส่น้ำหรือนม [a han chao thii tham chak khao ot thii sai nam rue nom] n porridge; เวลาอาหารเช้ากี่โมง? [we la a han chao ki mong] What time is breakfast?; ไม่มีอาหารเช้า [mai mii a han chao] without breakfast

อาหารทะเล [a han tha le] คุณช่วยทำอาหารที่ไม่มีอาหารทะเลได้ไหม? [khun chuai tham a han thii mai mii a han tha le dai mai] Could you prepare a meal without seafood?; คุณชอบอาหาร

ทะเลไหม? [khun chop a han tha le mai]
Do you like seafood?

อาหารเย็น [a han yen] *n* supper

อาหารว่าง [a han wang] *n* snack; ห้อง
ทานอาหารว่าง [hong than a han wang]
n snack bar

อาหารฮาลาล [a han ha lan] คุณมีอาหาร
ฮาลาล? [khun mii a han ha lal] Do you
have halal dishes?

อำนวยการ [am nuai kan] ผู้อำนวยการ
[phu am nuai kan] *n* director

อำนวยความสะดวก [am nuai khwam sa
duak] สิ่งอำนวยความสะดวกต่าง ๆ [sing
am nuai khwam sa duak tang tang]
npl facilities

อำนาจ [am nat] *n* power; ให้อำนาจ [hai
am nat] *v* authorize; ใช้อำนาจเหนือ
[chai am nat nuea] *v* overrule; อำนาจ
ในการยับยั้ง [am nat nai kan yap yang]
n veto

อำพัน [am pan] สีเหลืองอำพัน [sii lueang
am phan] *n* amber

อิจฉา [it cha] *adj* envious, jealous; ความ
อิจฉา [khwam it cha] *n* envy

อิฐ [it] *n* brick

อิตาลี [it ta li] *adj* เกี่ยวกับอิตาลี [kiao kap i
ta li] *adj* Italian ▷ *n* ชาวอิตาเลียน [chao i
ta lian] *n* Italian *(person)*; ประเทศอิตาลี
[pra tet i ta li] *n* Italy

อิทธิพล [it thi phon] *n* influence; มี
อิทธิพล [mii it thi phon] *v* influence; ที่มี
อิทธิพล [thii mii it ti pon] powerful

อินเดีย [in dia] *adj* เกี่ยวกับชาวอินเดีย
[kiao kap chao in dia] *adj* Indian ▷ *n*
มหาสมุทรอินเดีย [ma ha sa mut in dia] *n*
Indian Ocean; หมู่เกาะอินเดียตะวันตกใน
ทะเลคาริบเบียน [mu kao in dia ta wan
tok nai tha le kha rip bian] *npl* West
Indies

อินโดนีเซีย [in do ni sia] เกี่ยวกับ
อินโดนีเซีย [kiao kap in do ni sia] *adj*
Indonesian; ชาวอินโดนีเซีย [chao in do
ni sia] *n* Indonesian *(person)*; ประเทศ
อินโดนีเซีย [pra tet in do ni sia] *n*

Indonesia

อินเตอร์เน็ต [in toe net] หนังสือที่อ่านได้
จากอินเตอร์เนต [nang sue thii an dai
chak in toe net] *n* e-book; ข้อมูลของ
บุคคลในอินเตอร์เนต [kho mun khong
buk khon nai in toe net] *n* blog; ธุรกิจ
การค้าที่ทำบนอินเตอร์เนต [thu ra kit kan
kha thii tham bon in toe net] *n*
e-commerce

อินเตอร์เน็ต [in toe net] *n* Internet; เชื่อม
ต่อกับอินเตอร์เน็ตแบบไร้สาย [chueam to
kap in toe net baep rai sai] *n* WiFi; ร้าน
ที่ให้บริการอินเตอร์เน็ต [ran thii hai bo ri
kan in toe net] *n* Internet café; ระบบ
เครือข่ายที่ใช้ประโยชน์ของเทคโนโลยีของ
อินเตอร์เน็ต [ra bop khruea khai thii
chai pra yot khong thek no lo yii
khong in toe net] *n* intranet; มี
อินเตอร์เน็ตในห้องไหม? [mii in toe net
nai hong mai] Is there an Internet
connection in the room?

อินทรี [in si] นกอินทรีย์ [nok in sii] *n*
eagle

อิ่ม [im] ฉันอิ่ม [chan im] I'm full

อิรัก [i rak] เกี่ยวกับอิรัก [kiao kap i rak]
adj Iraqi; ชาวอิรัก [chao i rak] *n* Iraqi;
ประเทศอิรัก [pra tet i rak] *n* Iraq

อิเล็กทรอนิกส์ [i lek tho nik] เกี่ยวกับระบบ
อิเล็กทรอนิกส์ [kiao kap ra bop i lek tro
nik] *adj* electronic; วิชาอิเล็กทรอนิกส์ [wi
cha i lek tro nik] *npl* electronics

อิสรภาพ [it sa ra phap] *n* independence

อิสระ [it sa ra] *adj* free *(no restraint)*,
independent; การปลดปล่อยให้เป็นอิสระ
[kan plot ploi hai pen it sa ra] *n*
liberation; ความเป็นอิสระ [khwam pen
it sa ra] *n* freedom; ซึ่งทำงานเป็นอิสระไม่ได้
รับเงินเดือนประจำ [sueng tham ngan it
sa ra mai dai rap ngoen duean pra
cham] *adv* freelance

อิสราเอล [it sra el] เกี่ยวกับอิสราเอล [kiao
kap is sa ra el] *adj* Israeli; ชาวอิสราเอล
[chao is sa ra el] *n* Israeli; ประเทศ
อิสราเอล [pra tet is sa ra el] *n* Israel

อิสลาม [it sa lam] *n* Islam; ของอิสลาม [khong is sa lam] *adj* Islamic; พระเจ้า ศาสนาอิสลาม [phra chao sat sa na is sa lam] *n* Allah

อิหร่าน [i ran] เกี่ยวกับอิหร่าน [kiao kap i ran] *adj* Iranian; ชาวอิหร่าน [chao i ran] *n* Iranian *(person)*; ประเทศอิหร่าน [pra tet i ran] *n* Iran

อีก [ik] อีกครั้ง [ik khrang] *adv* again; อีก อันหนึ่ง [ik an nueng] *adj* another; เบียร์ อีกแก้ว [bia ik kaew] another beer

อีกด้วย [ik duai] *adv* too

อีกนัยหนึ่ง [ik nai nueng] อีกนัยหนึ่งเรียก ว่า [ik nai nueng riak wa] *prep* alias

อีเมลล [i mel] *n* email; ส่งอีเมลล [song e mail] *v* email *(a person)*; ที่อยู่อีเมลล [thi yu e mail] *n* email address; ฉันขออีเมลล ของคุณได้ไหม? [chan kho ii mail khong khun dai mai] Can I have your email?

อียิปต์ [i yip] เกี่ยวกับประเทศอียิปต์ [kiao kap pra thet i yip] *adj* Egyptian; ชาว อียิปต์ [chao i yip] *n* Egyptian; ประเทศ อียิปต์ [pra tet i yip] *n* Egypt

อีสเตอร [is toe] ไข่อีสเตอร [khai is toe] *n* Easter egg; วันอีสเตอร [wan is toe] *n* Easter

อีสุกอีใส [i suk i sai] โรคอีสุกอีใส [rok i suk i sai] *n* chickenpox

อีเห็น [i hen] *n* weasel

อึกทึก [uek ka thuek] เสียงอึกทึก [siang uek ka tuek] *n* din

อื่น [uen] มาจากประเทศอื่น [ma chak pra tet uen] *adj* exotic; ที่อื่น [thii uen] *adv* elsewhere; อื่น ๆ [uen uen] *adv* else, other; คุณมีห้องอื่น ๆ ไหม? [khun mii hong uen uen mai] Do you have any others?

อื้อฉาว [ue chao] เรื่องอื้อฉาว [rueang ue chao] *n* scandal

อุกกาบาต [uk ka bat] *n* meteorite

อุซเบกิสถาน [ut be kit sa than] ประเท ศอุซเบกิสถาน [pra tet us be ki sa than] *n* Uzbekistan

อุณหภูมิ [un na ha phum] *n* temperature; อุณหภูมิความร้อนของโลกที่ เพิ่มขึ้น [un ha phum khwam ron khong lok thii poem khuen] *n* global warming; เธอมีอุณหภูมิ [thoe mii un ha phum] She has a temperature; อุณหภูมิ เท่าไร? [un ha phum thao rai] What is the temperature?

อุด [ut] สิ่งที่ใช้อุดรู [sing thii chai ut ru] *n* plug; คุณอุดฟันชั่วคราวให้ได้ไหม? [khun ut fan chua khrao hai dai mai] Can you do a temporary filling?; ฟันที่อุดหลุด ออกมา [fan thii ut lut ok ma] A filling has fallen out

อุดตัน [ut tan] ที่อุดตัน [thii ut tan] *adj* jammed

อุดมการณ์ [u dom kan] ผู้ยึดถืออุดมการณ์ [phu yuet thue u dom kan] *n* chauvinist

อุดมสมบูรณ์ [u dom som bun] ไม่อุดม สมบูรณ์ [mai u dom som bun] *adj* infertile; ซึ่งมีดินอุดมสมบูรณ์ [sueng mii din u dom som bun] *adj* fertile

อุตสาหกรรม [ut sa ha kam] *n* industry; เกี่ยวกับอุตสาหกรรม [kiao kap ut sa ha kram] *adj* industrial; เขตอุตสาหกรรม [khet ut sa ha kam] *n* industrial estate

อุทธรณ์ [ut thon] ขออุทธรณ์ [kho ut thon] *v* appeal

อุทยาน [ut tha yan] อุทยานแห่งชาติ [ut tha yan haeng chat] *n* national park

อุทาน [u than] คำอุทานแสดงความรำคาญ [kham u than sa daeng khwam ram khan] *adj* damn

อุทิศ [u thit] การอุทิศให้ [kan u thit hai] *n* dedication; ซึ่งอุทิศตัวเพื่อ [sueng u thit tua phuea] *adj* dedicated

อุ่น [un] *adj* lukewarm, warm ▷ *v* heat up; การทำให้อุ่น [kan tham hai un] *n* heating; ทำให้อุ่นขึ้น [tham hai un khuen] *v* warm up; คุณช่วยอุ่นอันนี้ได้ ไหม? [khun chuai un an nii dai mai] Can you warm this up, please?

อุบัติเหตุ [u bat ti het] *n* accident; ประกัน

อุบัติเหตุ [pra kan u bat ti het] *n* accident insurance; อุบัติเหตุเล็ก ๆ [u bat ti het lek lek] *n* mishap; อุบัติเหตุและหน่วยฉุกเฉิน [u bat ti het lae nuai chuk choen] *n* accident & emergency department; มีอุบัติเหตุเกิดขึ้น [mii u bat ti het koet khuen] There's been an accident!

อุบาย [u bai] เล่ห์อุบาย [le u bai] *n* scam

อุปกรณ์ [up pa kon] *n* device; อุปกรณ์ในเครื่องคอมพิวเตอร์แบบกระเป๋าหิ้วที่ใช้แทนเมาส์เพื่อแสดงตัวชี้ตำแหน่ง [up pa kon nai khrueang khom phio toe baep kra pao hio thii chai thaen mao phuea sa daeng tua chii tam naeng] *n* touchpad; อุปกรณ์ไฟฟ้าที่ช่วยให้อัตราการเต้นของหัวใจสม่ำเสมอ [up pa kon fai fa thii chuai hai at tra kan ten khong hua jai sa mam sa moe] *n* pacemaker; อุปกรณ์รับและส่งสัญญาณ [up pa kon rap lae song san yan] *n* scanner

อุปถัมภ์ [up pa tham] แม่อุปถัมภ์ [mae up pa tham] *n* godmother; ลูกของพ่อแม่อุปถัมภ์ [luk khong pho mae up pa tham] *n* godchild

อุปถัมภ์ [up pa tham] *v* sponsor; ลูกสาวอุปถัมภ์ [luk sao up pa tham] *n* goddaughter; ลูกชายอุปถัมภ์ [luk chai up pa tham] *n* godson; การอุปถัมภ์ [kan op pa tham] *n* sponsorship

อุปนิสัย [up pa ni sai] *n* characteristic

อุปสรรค [up pa sak] *n* obstacle

อุ้มท้อง [um thong] ผู้หญิงที่รับอุ้มท้องแทน [phu ying thii rap um thong taen] *n* surrogate mother

อุโมงค์ [u mong] *n* tunnel

อุรุกวัย [u ru kwai] เกี่ยวกับอุรุกวัย [kiao kap u ru kwai] *adj* Uruguayan; ชาวอุรุกวัย [chao u ru kwai] *n* Uruguayan; ประเทศอุรุกวัย [pra tet u ru kwai] *n* Uruguay

อุลตราซาวด์ [un tra sao] การบำบัดโดยใช้อุลตราซาวด์ [kan bam bat doi chai ul tra sao] *n* ultrasound

อู่ [u] อู่เรือ [u ruea] *n* dock; อู่ซ่อมและต่อเรือ [u som lae to ruea] *n* shipyard; มีอู่อยู่ใกล้ที่นี่ไหม? [mii u yu klai thii ni mai] Is there a garage near here?

อูกันดา [u kan da] เกี่ยวกับประเทศอูกันดา [kiao kap pra thet u kan da] *adj* Ugandan; ชาวอูกันดา [chao u kan da] *n* Ugandan; ประเทศอูกันดาอยู่ในทวีปอัฟริกา [pra tet u kan da yu nai tha wip af ri ka] *n* Uganda

อูฐ [ut (uut)] *n* camel

เอกฉันท์ [ek ka chan] เป็นเอกฉันท์ [pen ek ka chan] *adj* unanimous

เอกชน [ek ka chon] แปรรูปหน่วยราชการและรัฐวิสาหกิจให้เป็นเอกชน [prae rup nuai rat cha kan lae rat wi sa ha kit hai pen ek ka chon] *v* privatize

เอกพจน์ [ek ka pot] *n* singular

เอกลักษณ์ [ek ka lak] *n* identity; การขโมยเอกลักษณ์ [kan kha moi ek ka lak] *n* identity theft

เอกสาร [ek ka san] *n* document; เอกสารต่าง ๆ [ek ka san tang tang] *npl* documents; แฟ้มเอกสาร [faem ek ka san] *n* file (*folder*); สถานที่เก็บเอกสารสำคัญ [sa than thii kep ek ka san som khan] *n* archive; นี่คือเอกสารต่าง ๆ ของรถฉัน [ni khue ek ka san tang tang khong rot chan] Here are my vehicle documents

เอกอัครราชทูต [ek ak khra rat cha thut] *n* ambassador

เอควาดอร์ [e khwa do] ประเทศเอควาดอร์ [pra tet e kwa do] *n* Ecuador

เอควาทอเรียลกินี [e khwa tho rian ki ni] ประเทศเอควาทอเรียลกินี [pra thet a khwa to rial ki ni] *n* Equatorial Guinea

เอเคอร์ [e koe] หน่วยวัดเนื้อที่เป็นเอเคอร์ [nuai wat nuea thii pen e khoe] *n* acre

เอเชีย [e chia] *adj* Asiatic; เกี่ยวกับประเทศในเอเชีย [kiao kap pra thet nai e chia] *adj* Asian; กลุ่มประเทศในเอเชียตะวันออก [klum pra tet nai e chia ta wan ok] *n* Far East; ชาวเอเชีย [chao e chia] *n*

Asian

เอเชียตะวันออก [e chia ta wan ok] *n*
Orient

เอดส์ [et] โรคเอดส์ [rok aid] *n* AIDS; ไม่มี
เชื้อไวรัสที่ทำให้เกิดโรคเอดส์ [mai mii
chuea vai ras thii tham hai koet rok
aid] *adj* HIV-negative; มีเชื้อไวรัสที่ทำให้
เกิดโรคเอดส์ [mii chuea vai ras thii
tham hai koet rok aid] *adj* HIV-positive

เอเดรียติค [e dria tik] *adj* Adriatic; ทะเลเอ
เดรียติค [tha le e dria tik] *n* Adriatic Sea

เอธิโอเปีย [e thi o pia] เกี่ยวกับเอธิโอเปียน
[kiao kap e thi o pia] *adj* Ethiopian; ชาว
เอธิโอเปียน [chao e thi o pian] *n*
Ethiopian; ประเทศเอธิโอเปีย [pra tet e
thi o pia] *n* Ethiopia

เอน [en] เอนไปข้างหน้า [en pai khang na]
v lean forward

เอ็มพี ๓ [em pi sam] เครื่องฟังดนตรีเอ็มพี
๓ [khrueang fang don trii em phi sam]
n MP3 player

เอ็มพี ๔ [em pi si] เครื่องฟังดนตรีเอ็มพี ๔
[khrueang fang don trii em phi si] *n*
MP4 player

เอริเทรีย [e ri thria] ประเทศเอริเทรีย [pra
tet e ri tria] *n* Eritrea

เอว [eo] *n* waist

เอสโตเนีย [es to nia] เกี่ยวกับเอสโตเนีย
[kiao kap es to nia] *adj* Estonian; ชาวเอ
สโตเนียน [chao es to nian] *n* Estonian
(*person*); ประเทศเอสโตเนีย [pra tet es to
nia] *n* Estonia

เอา [ao] เอาไป [ao pai] *vt* take; เอาของ
ออก [ao khong ok] *v* unpack; เอาออกไป
[ao ok pai] *v* take away; ฉันควรเอาไป
เท่าไร? [chan khuan ao pai thao rai]
How much should I take?

เอาใจใส่ [ao chai sai] ไม่เอาใจใส่ [mai ao
jai sai] *adj* unattended; ที่เอาใจใส่อย่าง
มาก [thii ao jai sai yang mak] *adj*
obsessed

เอาชนะ [ao cha na] *v* overcome

เอาตัวรอด [ao tua rot] ซึ่งเอาตัวรอดได้ใน
สังคมเมือง [sueng ao tua rot dai nai

sang khom mueang] *adj* streetwise

เอาเปรียบ [ao priap] *v* exploit; การเอา
เปรียบ [kan ao priap] *n* exploitation

เอาออก [ao ok] เอาออกไป [ao ok pai] *v*
clear off

เอียง [iang] ทำให้เอียง [tham hai iang] *v*
tip (*incline*)

เอื้ออำนวย [uea am nuai] ไม่เอื้ออำนวย
ประโยชน์ [mai uea am nuai pra yot] *adj*
unfavourable

แองโกลา [ang ko la] ชาวแองโกล่า [chao
aeng ko la] *n* Angolan; ซึ่งเกี่ยวกับแองโก
ล่า [sueng kiao kap aeng ko la] *adj*
Angolan; ประเทศแองโกลา [pra tet aeng
ko la] *n* Angola

แอตแลนติก [at laen tik] มหาสมุทร
แอตแลนติก [ma ha sa mut at laen tik] *n*
Atlantic

แอนโชวี [an cho wi] ปลาแอนโชวี [pla an
cho vi] *n* anchovy

แอนดอรา [an do ra] ประเทศแอนดอร่า
[pra tet aen do ra] *n* Andorra

แอนดีส [aen dit] เทือกเขาแอนดีส [thueak
khao aen dis] *npl* Andes

แอปเปิ้ล [aep poen] *n* apple; ขนมแอปเปิ้ล
พาย [kha nom ap poen phai] *n* apple
pie; น้ำแอปเปิ้ลที่มีแอลกอฮอล์ [nam ap
poen thii mii aen ko ho] *n* cider

แอปริคอท [aep pri cot] ลูกแอปริคอท [luk
ae pri kot] *n* apricot

แอร์ [ae] มีแอร์ไหม? [mii ae mai] Does it
have air conditioning?

แอร์คอนดิชั่น [ae khon di chan] มีแอร์
คอนดิชั่นในห้องไหม? [mii ae khon di
chan nai hong mai] Does the room
have air conditioning?

แอโรบิค [ae ro bik] การเต้นแอโรบิค
[kan ten ae ro bik] *npl* aerobics

แอร์โฮสเตส [ae hot sa tet] แอร์โฮสเตส
[ae hot sa tet] *n* air hostess

แอลกอฮอล์ [aen ko ho] เครื่องวัดปริมาณ
แอลกอฮอล์จากลมหายใจ [khrueang wat
pa ri man aen ko ho chak lom hai jai]
n Breathalyser®; แอลกอฮอล์ต่ำ [aen ko

ho tam] *adj* low-alcohol; คุณมีเครื่องดื่ม
ไม่มีแอลกอฮอล์อะไรบ้าง? [khun mii
khrueang duem mai mii aen ko ho a
rai bang] What non-alcoholic drinks do
you have?

แอลป์ [aelp] เทือกเขาแอลป์ [thueak khao
aelp] *npl* Alps

แอสไพริน [aes phai rin] ยาแอสไพริน [ya
as phai rin] *n* aspirin; ฉันกินแอสไพรินไม่
ได้ [chan kin as phai rin mai dai] I
can't take aspirin; ฉันอยากได้แอสไพริน
[chan yak dai as phai rin] I'd like some
aspirin

แออัด [ae at] *vi* cram; ความแออัด [khwam
ae at] *n* congestion; อย่างแออัด [yang ae
at] *adj* crammed

โอ๊ก [ok] ผลต้นโอ๊ก [phon ton oak] *n*
acorn

โอกาส [o kat] *n* chance, occasion,
opportunity, prospect

โอ๊ค [ok] ต้นโอ๊ค [ton ok] *n* oak

โอโซน [o son] ก๊าซโอโซน [kas o son] *n*
ozone; ชั้นก๊าซโอโซนล้อมรอบโลก [chan
kas o son lom rop lok] *n* ozone layer

โอน [on] จะใช้เวลานานเท่าไรในการโอน?
[ja chai we la nan thao rai nai kan on]
How long will it take to transfer?; ฉัน
อยากโอนเงินจากบัญชีของฉัน [chan yak
on ngoen chak ban chii khong chan] I
would like to transfer some money
from my account; ฉันอยากโอนเงินบาง
ส่วนจากธนาคารของฉันที่... [chan yak on
ngoen bang suan chak tha na khan
khong chan thii…] I would like to
transfer some money from my bank
in...

โอเปร่า [o pe ra] *n* opera

โอมาน [o man] ประเทศโอมาน [pra tet o
man] *n* Oman

โอวาท [o wat] การเทศนา การให้โอวาท
[kan ted sa na, kan hai o wat] *n*
sermon

โอ้อวด [o uat] คนที่ชอบโอ้อวด [khon thii
chop o uad] *n* show-off

ไอ [ai] *vi* cough; ส่วนผสมสำหรับแก้ไอ
[suan pha som sam rap kae ai] *n* cough
mixture; การไอ [kan ai] *n* cough; ฉันไอ
[chan ai] I have a cough

ไอคิว [ai khio] *abbr* IQ

ไอซ์แลนด์ [ais laen] *adj* เกี่ยวกับไอซ์แลนด์
[kiao kap ai laen] *n* Icelandic ▷ *n* ชาว
ไอซ์แลนด์ [chao ai laen] *n* Icelandic; ประ
เทศไอซ์แลนด์ [pra tet ai laen] *n* Iceland

ไอซียู [ai si yu] ห้องไอซียู [hong ai si u] *n*
intensive care unit

ไอติม [ai tim] ไอติมรสผลไม้ [ai tim rot
phon la mai] *n* ice lolly

ไอน้ำ [ai nam] *n* steam

ไอพอต [ai phot] *n* iPod®

ไอร์แลนด์ [ai laen] *adj* เกี่ยวกับไอร์แลนด์
[kiao kap ai laen] *adj* Irish ▷ *n* ประเทศ
ไอร์แลนด์ [pra tet ai laen] *n* Eire,
Ireland; ประเทศไอร์แลนด์เหนือ [pra tet ai
laen nuea] *n* Northern Ireland

ไอริช [ai rit] ชาวไอริช [chao ai rit] *n*
Irish; ผู้หญิงไอริช [phu ying ai rit] *n*
Irishwoman; ผู้ชายไอริช [phu chai ai
rit] *n* Irishman

ไอวี่ [ai wi] ไม้เลื้อยชื่อต้นไอวี่ [mai lueai
chue ton ai vi] *n* ivy

ไอศกรีม [ai sa khrim] *n* ice cream; เรา
อยากได้ไอศกรีม [rao yak dai ai sa krim]
I'd like an ice cream

ฮ

ฮอกกี้ [hok ki] กีฬาไอซ์ฮอกกี้ [ki la ai hok ki] n ice hockey

ฮ็อคกี้ [hok ki] กีฬาฮ็อคกี้ [ki la hok ki] n hockey

ฮอธอน [ho thon] ต้นฮอธอน [ton ho thon] n hawthorn

ฮอนดูรัส [hon du ras] ประเทศฮอนดูรัส [pra tet hon du ras] n Honduras

ฮอร์โมน [ho mon] n hormone

ฮอลลี่ [hon li] ต้นฮอลลี่ [ton hol li] n holly

ฮอลแลนด์ [hon laen] ประเทศฮอลแลนด์ [pra tet hol laen] n Holland

ฮังการี [hang ka ri] เกี่ยวกับประเทศฮังการี [kiao kap pra thet hang ka ri] adj Hungarian; ชาวฮังการี [chao hang ka ri] n Hungarian; ประเทศฮังการี [pra tet hang ka ri] n Hungary

ฮินดู [hin du] แขกที่นับถือศาสนาฮินดู [khaek thii nap thue sat sa na hin du] n Hindu; ชาวฮินดู [chao hin du] adj Hindu; ศาสนาฮินดู [sat sa na hin du] n Hinduism

ฮิปปี้ [hip pi] พวกฮิปปี้ [phuak hip pi] n hippie

ฮิปโป [hip po] n hippo, hippopotamus

ฮูเร [hu re] excl hooray!

เฮชไอวี [het ai wi] ฉันเป็นเฮชไอวีบวก [chan pen het ai wii buak] I am HIV-positive

เฮเซลนัท [he sel nat] ถั่วเฮเซลนัท [thua he sel nat] n hazelnut

เฮโรอิน [he ro in] n heroin

เฮลิคอปเตอร์ [he li kop toe] n helicopter

เฮอร์เซโกวีนา [hoe se ko wi na] ประเทศ บอสเนียและเฮอร์เซโกวีนา [pra tet bos nia lae hoe se ko vi na] n Bosnia and Herzegovina

เฮอริเคน [hoe ri khen] พายุเฮอริเคน [pha yu hoe ri khen] n hurricane

เฮอริ่ง [hoe ring] ปลาเฮอริ่ง [pla hoe ring] n herring

เฮฮา [he ha] สนุกสนานเฮฮา [sa nuk sa nan he ha] adj hilarious

แฮดดอค [haet dot] ปลาแฮดดอค [pla haed dot] n haddock

แฮมเบอร์เกอร์ [haem boe koe] n hamburger; แฮมเบอร์เกอร์เนื้อ [haem boe koe nuea] n beefburger

ไฮโดรเจน [hai dro chen] แก๊สไฮโดรเจน [kas hai dro chen] n hydrogen

ไฮติ [hai ti] ประเทศไฮติ [pra tet hai ti] n Haiti

ไฮไฟ [hai fai] เครื่องไฮไฟ [khrueang hai fai] n hifi

ไฮไลท์ [hai lait] ผมฉันทำไฮไลท์ [phom chan tham hai lai] My hair is highlighted

Thai Grammar

Introduction

This is a guide to some of the basic concepts and rules of Thai Grammar. To start with, there is no shortened or contracted form of verb or noun in the Thai language. For this reason, words, affixes (prefixes and suffixes) and word order are very important in delivering the meaning, as will be illustrated below.

Note on romanization of Thai: There are different systems of romanization. The romanized Thai used in this chapter follows the system used in this dictionary, which is one of the simplest.

Sentence structure

For affirmative sentences, the basic Thai sentence structure is the same as English: Subject + Verb + Object.

> ฉันกินข้าว [chan kin khao]
> *I eat rice*

For negative sentences, the word **ไม่ [mai]** is added before the verb:

> ฉันไม่กินข้าว [chan mai kin khao]
> *I don't eat rice*

For interrogative sentences, the question word is generally placed at the end of the sentence.

> คุณกินข้าวเมื่อไร [khun gin khao muea rai]
> *When did you eat rice?*

Please note that the Thai word for 'rice' can also be used as a more general word meaning 'food' or 'meal'.

Pronouns

There are many pronouns in Thai. The usage of each pronoun varies
according to gender, age, social status, the relationship between
speakers, the formality of the situation and individual personality.
The following are the basic pronouns in Thai:

Pronoun	Meaning
ผม [pom]	I/me (male)
ฉัน [chan]	I/me (female; informal)
ดิฉัน [dichan]	I/me (female; formal)
เรา [rao]	we/us
คุณ [khun]	you (singular and plural)
ท่าน [thaan]	you (formal; singular and plural)
เขา [khao]/เธอ [ter]	he/him; she/her; they/them
มัน [mun]	it

Possessive pronouns

In Thai, by adding the word ของ [khong] in front of a pronoun, that
pronoun will turn into a possessive, hence:

Possessive pronoun	Meaning
ของผม [khongpom]	my/mine (male)
ของฉัน [khongchan]	my/mine (female; informal)
ของดิฉัน [khongdichan]	my/mine (female; formal)
ของเรา [khongrao]	our/ours
ของคุณ [khongkhun]	your/yours (singular and plural)
ของท่าน [khongthaan]	your/yours (formal; singular and plural)

| ของเขา [**khong**khao] | his; her/hers; their/theirs |
| ของมัน [**khong**mun] | its |

In Thai, the possessive pronoun comes after the noun it modifies:

> รถของฉัน [rod khong chan]
> *my car*

> รถของคุณ [rod khong khun]
> *your car*

Nouns

There is no gender in Thai nouns. When nouns are used with numbers or words implying numbers, such as **some** or **many**, a **classifier** is needed. The word order for this is: noun + number/word implying number + classifier:

> บ้านสามหลัง [bann saam lung]
> *three houses*

> รถหลายคัน [rod laay kun]
> *many cars*

For uncountable nouns such as water or rice, the words used for measurement of them, for example, words like bottle or kilo, are considered as classifiers:

> น้ำสามขวด [naam saam kuad]
> *three bottles of water*

> ข้าวสามกิโล [khaao saam kilo]
> *three kilos of rice*

Certain words have certain classifiers. There are approximately 300 classifiers in Thai. Here are the most common ones:

Classifier	Nouns to use with the Classifiers
อัน [an]	small objects
คน [khon]	people (except monks and royalty)
หลัง [lung]	houses
คัน [kun]	vehicles, spoons, forks
ห้อง [hong]	rooms
ลูก [look]	fruits (generally of round shape), balls
ใบ [bai]	fruits, eggs, leaves, cups, plates, cards, documents, handbags, suitcases
ต้น [dton]	trees, plants
อย่าง [yaang]	types, kinds, sorts (of things)

Here are the most common words used for measuring uncountable nouns. They are treated as classifiers:

Words used for measuring uncountable nouns	Meaning
คู่ [koo]	pairs (e.g. shoes, socks but not trousers)
ขวด [kuad]	bottles (e.g. water, beer)
แก้ว [kaew]	glass (e.g. water, beer)
จาน [jaan]	plate (e.g. rice, food served in a plate)
ชาม [chaam]	bowl (e.g. soup, food served in a bowl)

Here are some examples of sentences with noun phrases containing classifiers:

> ฉันมีบ้านสามหลัง [chan mii baan saam lung]
> *I have three houses.*

> เขาสั่งน้ำสามขวด [khao sung naam saam kuad]
> *He orders three bottles of water.*

> ขอข้าวผัดสองจาน [khor khaao pud song jaan]
> *I'd like two (plates of) fried rice please.*

Adjectives

In Thai, adjectives always come after nouns: noun + adjective

> บ้านสวย [baan suay]
> *Beautiful house*

> บ้านสวยสามหลัง [baan suay saam lung]
> *Three beautiful houses*

In English, if an adjective follows the verb 'to be' without a noun afterwards, there is no need to translate 'to be' เป็น **[bpen]** into Thai:

> *She is beautiful* (i.e. no noun after the adjective 'beautiful')
> =เธอสวย [<u>ter</u>-suay]

However, if there is a noun after the adjective in English, 'to be' เป็น **[bpen]** does need to be translated:

> *She is a beautiful **woman***
> =เธอเป็นผู้หญิงสวย [<u>ter</u>-bpen phoo-ying suay]

Modification of adjectives

Adjective + modifier

The majority of adjective modifiers in Thai come after the adjective. Here are some of them:

Adjective Modifier	Meaning
มาก [maak]	very
จัง [jung]	really, so
จริง ๆ [jing jing]	really, truly
กว่า [kwua]	more
ที่สุด [tii sud]	the most
เกินไป [kern bpai]	too
นิดหน่อย [nid-noi]	a little bit
ไปหน่อย [bpai noi]	a little bit too

เธอสวยมาก [ter-suay maak]
She is very beautiful.

นี่เผ็ดเกินไป [nii phed kern bpai]
This is too spicy.

Modifier + adjective

Some adjective modifiers precede the adjective. Here are some of them:

ค่อนข้าง [khon khaang]   *rather*

ไม่ [mai]   *not* ไม่

ไม่ค่อย... เท่าไหร่ [mai khoi...tao rai]   *not very*

นี่ไม่ค่อยแพงเท่าไร [nii **mai khoi**paeng**tao rai**]
*This is **not very** expensive*

Comparison of adjectives

Modifiers for comparison such as **กว่า [kwua]** (*more than*) or **น้อยกว่า
[noi kwua]** (*less than*) are placed after the adjective:

> นี่อร่อย<u>กว่า</u> [nii aroi **kwua**]
> *This is **more** delicious.*

When comparing two nouns with an adjective, like in English the
second noun comes after **กว่า [kwua]** (*more than*) or **น้อยกว่า [noi
kwua]** (*less than*):

> คุณรวย<u>กว่า</u>ฉัน [khun ruay <u>**kwua**</u> chan]
> *You are **richer than** me.*

> ฉันสวย<u>กว่า</u>คุณ [chan suay <u>**kwua**</u> khun]
> *I am **more beautiful than** you.*

To make the adjective negative, simply put **ไม่ [mai]** (*not*) in front
of it:

> ฉันไม่รวย [chan <u>**mai**</u> ruay]
> *I am **not** rich.*

Here are some useful adjectives:

Adjective	Meaning
สวย [suay]	beautiful
แพง [paeng]	expensive
ถูก [thuk]	cheap

สูง [sung]	tall
เตี้ย [tia]	short (with height and not length)
อร่อย [a roi]	delicious, tasty
รวย [ruay]	rich
จน [chon]	poor
ร้อน [ron]	hot
เย็น [yen]	cool
หนาว [nao]	cold

Adverbs

In Thai, the adverb is always placed after the verb it modifies: verb + adverb

> เขาพูด**เร็ว** [khao pood **rew**]
> *He speaks **fast**.*

> เขาเดิน**ช้า** [khao dern **chaa**]
> *He walks **slowly**.*

If there is/are object(s) after the verb, the adverb is placed after the object(s):

> เขาพูดภาษาไทย**เก่ง** [khao pood phasa-Thai **keng**]
> *He speaks Thai **well**.*

Like the modification of adjectives, modifiers of adverbs also come after the adverb:

> เขาพูดเร็ว**มาก** [khao pood rew **maak**]
> *He speaks **very** fast.*

เขาพูดภาษาไทยเก่ง**มาก** [khao pood phasa-Thai **keng** maak.
*He speaks Thai **very** well.*

Like adjectives, modifiers for comparison such as **กว่า [kwua]** (*more than*) or **น้อยกว่า [noi kwua]** (*less than*) are placed after the adverb:

เขาพูดเร็ว**กว่า** [khao pood rew **kwua**]
*He speaks **faster**.*

คุณพูดภาษาไทยเก่ง**กว่า**ฉัน [khun pood phasa-Thai keng **kwua** chan]
*You speak (Thai) better **than** me.*

To make the adverb negative, simply place **ไม่ [mai]** (*not*) in front of the verb:

ฉันพูดภาษาไทย**ไม่**เก่ง [chan pood phasa-Thai **mai** keng]
*I **can't** speak Thai well.*

Here are some useful adverbs

Adverb	Meaning
เร็ว [reo]	fast, quickly
ช้า [cha]	slowly
เก่ง [keng]	well, fluently, skilfully
คล่อง [klong]	fluently
ดัง [dung]	loudly
ค่อย [koi]	softly

Verbs

Thai verbs cannot be shortened or contracted. They retain the same form no matter what form of noun they are used with or tense they imply. There are 'tense indicators' in Thai but often we need to depend on context and/or words expressing time in order to understand the tense of a verb.

The verb 'to be'

In Thai, there is no verb that functions as the English verb 'to be'. However, the verb 'to be' can be translated as: **เป็น [bpen]**, **อยู่ [yuu]** and **คือ [khue]**.

เป็น [bpen] and **คือ [khue]** are always followed by a noun or noun phrase and cannot be followed by an adjective (see above under 'Adjectives'). They are used when giving explanations, clarifications, and definitions. However, **คือ [khue]** is also used to convey the meaning of 'is equal to' or 'namely'.

> เขา**เป็น**ครูของฉัน [khao **bpen** krue khong chan]
> เขา**คือ**ครูของฉัน [khao **khue** krue khong chan]
> *He **is** my teacher.*

Note: In some cases, **เป็น [bpen]** and **คือ [khue]** can be substituted for each other as their meanings are similar. However, it depends on the context.

อยู่ [yuu] is used to describe the location of a noun or noun phrase.

> ห้องน้ำ**อยู่**ทางซ้าย [hong naam **yuu** taang saai]
> *The bathroom **is** on the left.*

There are many negative forms and ways to form negative sentences in Thai. For the verb 'to be', the negative forming words ไม่ [mai] or ไม่ได้ [mai dai], meaning 'not', are usually added in front of the main verb. However, this depends on the context.

ห้องน้ำไม่อยู่ทางซ้าย [hong naam **mai** yuu taang saai]
ห้องน้ำไม่ได้อยู่ทางซ้าย [hong naam **mai dai** yuu taang saai]
*The bathroom is **not** on the left.*

Finally, the word ไม่ใช่ [mai chai] is sometimes used to negate เป็น [bpen] and คือ [khue].

เขาไม่ใช่ครูของฉัน
*He is **not** my teacher.* [khao **mai chai** krue khong chan]

Future tense

The word จะ [ja] is used as the 'future tense indicator' to mean 'will, shall, would'. It is placed before the verb: จะ [ja] + verb

ฉันจะไปทำงาน [chan **ja**bpai tum ngarn]
*I **will** go to work.*

However, จะ is sometimes omitted. In such cases, the tense of the verb depends on the context.

ฉันไปทำงานพรุ่งนี้ [chan bpai tum ngarn prung nii]
I (will) go to work tomorrow.

To negate จะ [ja] simply add ไม่ [mai] in front.

ฉันจะไม่ไปทำงาน [chan**ja mai**bpai tum ngarn]
*I **will not** go to work.*

Past tense

There is no 'past tense indicator' in Thai: generally, you can tell the tense from the verb's context. However, the word **แล้ว [laew]** (*already*) is used to indicate that the action has been done 'already'. In this case, **แล้ว [laew]** is placed after the verb or verb phrase: **แล้ว [laew]** +verb/verb phrase:

> ฉันไปทำงานเมื่อวาน [chan bpai tum ngarn muea waan]
> *I went to work yesterday.*

> ฉันกินข้าวเช้า**แล้ว** [chan kin khaao chao **laew**]
> *I have **already** had breakfast.*

To make a verb in the past negative, **ไม่ได้ [mai dai]** is placed before the verb to mean 'did not':

> ฉัน**ไม่ได้**ไปทำงานเมื่อวาน [chan **mai dai** bpai tum ngarn muea waan]
> *I **did not** go to work yesterday.*

> ฉัน**ไม่ได้**กินข้าวเช้า [chan **mai dai** kin khaao chao]
> *I **did not** have breakfast.*

Continuous verbs

The pattern **กำลัง [kum lung]** + verb/verb phrase + **อยู่ [yuu]** is used to indicate that the action is/was being done. Its English equivalent is 'V+ing'. In Thai, this pattern can be used to indicate the continuous verbs in present, past and future tenses. Either **กำลัง [kum lung]** or **อยู่ [yuu]** can be omitted, but one of them does need to be there:

> เขา**กำลัง**ดูทีวี**อยู่**
> *He **is** watch**ing** TV.*

To make this negative, place **ไม่ได้ [mai dai]** in front of **กำลัง [kum lung]**. In the case of **กำลัง [kum lung]** being omitted, place **ไม่ได้** in front of the verb:

> เขา**ไม่ได้**ดูทีวี**อยู่** [khao **mai dai** doo TV **yuu**]
> *He **is not** watching TV.*

Here are some useful expressions of time to help understand the tense of the verb:

Expression of time	Meaning
เมื่อวาน [muea waan]	yesterday
วันนี้ [wan nii]	today
พรุ่งนี้ [prung nii]	tomorrow
เมื่อวานซืน(นี้) [muea waan suen (nii)]	the day before yesterday
มะรืน(นี้) [ma ruen (nii)]	the day after tomorrow
อาทิตย์ที่แล้ว [athit tii laew]	last week
เดือนที่แล้ว [duan tii laew]	last month
อาทิตย์นี้ [athit nii]	this week
เดือนนี้ [duan nii]	this month
อาทิตย์หน้า [athit naa]	next week
เดือนหน้า [duan naa]	next month

Question words

The majority of question words in Thai are placed at the end of the sentence.

Here are some common examples:

Question word	Meaning
ไหม [mai]	This question word is used when a 'yes or no' answer is required (e.g. Do you..?, does he/she...?)
อะไร [a-rai]	What
เมื่อไร [muea rai]	When
ที่ไหน [tii nai]	Where
อย่างไร [yaang rai]	How
เท่าไร [tao-rai]	How much

คุณทำงาน**ที่ไหน** [khun tum ngarn tii nai]
Where *do you work?*

นี่ราคา**เท่าไร** [nii raakaa **tao-rai**]
How much *does this cost?*

The question word 'why' or **ทำไม [tum-mai]** is normally placed at the beginning of the sentence:

ทำไมคุณเรียนภาษาไทย [tum-mai khun rian phasa-Thai]
Why *do you study Thai?*

The question word 'who' or **ใคร [krai]** is placed at the beginning of the sentence when it is the subject of the sentence:

ใครกำลังพูดกับคุณ [krai kum lung pood kub khun]
Who *is speaking to you?*

When **ใคร** is not the subject of the sentence, but the object (direct or indirect) – in other words, when **ใคร [krai]** can be translated as 'whom' in English, it is placed at the end of the sentence:

คุณจะไปหา**ใคร** [khun ja bpai haa krai]
Who (Whom) *are you going to see?*

Polite particles

In Thai, polite particles are often used at the end of the utterance to show respect to the addressee. The most common polite particle for a male speaker is **ครับ [krub]**. For a female speaker, **ค่ะ [kha]** (pronounced with low tone) is used at the end of statements, and **คะ [kha]** (pronounced with high tone) is used at the end of questions:

> ผมชื่ออาทิตย์**ครับ** [**pom chue Athit krub**]
> *My name is Athit*

> คุณชื่ออะไร**คะ** [khun chue a-rai kha]
> *What is your name?*

ไวยากรณ์ภาษาอังกฤษ

ไวยากรณ์ภาษาอังกฤษ

คำกริยาหลัก (Main verbs)

คำกริยาหลัก คือ คำกริยาที่ให้ความหมายหลักในประโยค ซึ่งใช้บอกการกระทำ สภาพ หรือสภาวะต่างๆ คำกริยาในประโยคภาษาอังกฤษอาจเป็นคำกริยาคำเดียว หรือกลุ่มของคำกริยาช่วย และกริยาหลักที่เรียงต่อกัน คำกริยาในภาษาอังกฤษ แบ่ง ออกเป็นสองประเภท คือ
คำกริยาที่ต้องการกรรม หรือสกรรมกริยา (Transitive verbs) คือ คำกริยาที่ ต้องมีกรรมตามหลังจึงจะให้ความหมายที่สมบูรณ์ ตัวอย่าง เช่น
กริยา like (ชอบ):

> She likes cheese.
> เธอชอบเนยแข็ง

คำกริยาที่ไม่ต้องการกรรม หรืออกรรมกริยา (Intransitive verbs) คือ คำกริยา ที่มีความหมายสมบูรณ์ในตัวเองไม่ต้องการกรรมตามหลัง ตัวอย่าง เช่น
กริยา sneeze (จาม):

> I sneezed loudly.
> ฉันจามเสียงดัง

โดยปกติแล้ว คำกริยาในภาษาอังกฤษจะมีการเปลี่ยนรูปเพื่อให้สอดคล้องกับ ประธาน (เอกพจน์ หรือพหูพจน์) หรือกาลของประโยค (อดีต ปัจจุบัน หรืออนาคต) แต่บางครั้งคำกริยาอาจอยู่ในรูปกริยาที่ไม่ได้ผัน หรือไม่เปลี่ยนแปลงรูป ซึ่งเรียกว่า **รูปกริยาแท้** (infinitive) ซึ่งเป็นรูปกริยาเดียวกับที่ปรากฏในพจนานุกรม รูปกริยา แท้ หรือกริยาที่ไม่ได้เปลี่ยนแปลงรูปเหล่านี้มีสองประเภท คือ **รูปกริยาที่มี 'to' นำ หน้า** และ**รูปคำกริยาที่ไม่มี 'to'นำหน้า** ซึ่งเรียกว่า 'bare infinitive'

คำกริยาช่วย (Auxiliary และ modal verbs)

คำกริยาช่วยที่ทำหน้าที่เป็นได้ทั้งคำกริยาหลัก และคำกริยาช่วยของประโยค (Auxiliary verbs) ใช้คู่กับคำกริยาหลักของประโยคเพื่อบอกเล่าการกระทำที่เกิดขึ้น ในช่วงเวลาที่แตกต่างกัน หรือเปลี่ยนรูปประโยคให้เป็นคำถาม หรือปฏิเสธ คำกริยา ช่วยประเภทนี้มีสองกลุ่มคือ คำกริยาช่วยหลัก (primary auxiliaries) และคำกริยา ช่วยเสริม (supporting auxiliary)
คำกริยาช่วยหลัก (Primary auxiliaries) ได้แก่ กริยา **'Be'** และ **'Have'** กริยา **'Be'** ใช้บอกปัจจุบัน (present continuous tense) หรืออดีต (past continuous tense) เพื่อให้ความหมายว่า กริยาของประโยคนั้นกำลังดำเนินอยู่ หรือใช้ใน ประโยคที่ประธานเป็นผู้ถูกกระทำ (passive) ตัวอย่าง เช่น

I am working.
ฉันกำลังทำงาน

Martin was arrested and held overnight.
มาร์ตินถูกจับ และขังตลอดทั้งคืน

กริยา **'Have'** ใช้บอกอดีต เพื่อให้ความหมายว่า กริยา หรือผลของกริยานั้นเกี่ยว
เนื่องกับปัจจุบัน (past perfect and present perfect tenses) ตัวอย่าง เช่น

Sara has finished fixing the car.
ซาร่าเพิ่งซ่อมรถเสร็จ

คำกริยาช่วยเสริม (Supporting auxiliary) ได้แก่ กริยา **'Do'** ใช้เปลี่ยนประโยค
บอกเล่าให้เป็นประโยคปฏิเสธ และประโยคคำถาม หรือตั้งคำถามในส่วนท้าย
ประโยคเพื่อเน้นความหมายของประโยค ตัวอย่าง เช่น

I do not like sausages at all.
ฉันไม่ชอบไส้กรอกที่สุดเลย

Do you like prawns?
คุณชอบกุ้งหรือไม่

You do like prawns, don't you?
คุณชอบกุ้งใช่ไหม

คำกริยาช่วยที่ต้องใช้คู่กับคำกริยาหลัก ไม่สามารถทำหน้าที่เป็นคำกริยาหลัก
ของประโยคได้ (Modal verbs) คำกริยาประเภทนี้จะใช้นำหน้าคำกริยาหลักของ
ประโยค เพื่อขยายความหมายคำกริยาหลัก เช่น บอกความสามารถ ความเป็นไปได้
หรือความจำเป็น ได้แก่

can	could	may	might
สามารถ	สามารถ (อดีต)	อาจจะ	อาจจะ (อดีต)
must	ought	shall	will
ต้อง	ควรจะ	ควร	จะ
would			
จะ (อดีต)			

คำกริยาช่วยประเภทนี้จะไม่มีการผันรูปตามประธานเมื่ออยู่ในประโยค ตัวอย่าง เช่น

She can ride a horse.
เธอขี่ม้าเป็น

รูปปฏิเสธของคำกริยาช่วยจะเขียน ดังนี้

รูปกริยา	รูปปฏิเสธ	รูปย่อ
can	cannot	can't
could	could not	couldn't
may	may not	mayn't (ไม่ค่อยมีผู้ใช้)
might	might not	mightn't
must	must not	mustn't
ought	ought not	oughtn't
shall	shall not	shan't
will	will not	won't
would	would not	wouldn't

กริยาวลี (Phrasal verbs) ใช้เรียกกลุ่มคำกริยาซึ่งประกอบด้วยคำกริยาหลักของ
ประโยค กับคำประเภทอื่นๆ เช่น
คำวิเศษณ์

> take off
> ถอด, นำ (เครื่องบิน) ขึ้น
>
> blow up
> โกรธ, ระเบิด

คำบุพบท

> pick on (weaker children)
> ตำหนิ, ลงโทษ

หรือคำวิเศษณ์ + คำบุพบท

> get out of (doing something)
> หลีกเลี่ยง, บ่ายเบี่ยง

คำนาม (Nouns)

คือคำที่ใช้เรียกสิ่งต่างๆทั่วไป เช่น คน สัตว์ สิ่งของ สถานที่ คำนามแบ่งเป็นประเภท
ต่างๆดังนี้
คำนามเฉพาะ หรือวิสามานยนาม (Proper nouns) คือ คำนามที่เป็นชื่อเฉพาะ
ของคนสัตว์ สิ่งของ และเขียนขึ้นต้นด้วยตัวอักษรพิมพ์ใหญ่ (Capital letter)
ตัวอย่าง เช่น

John Lennon	China	Thursday
จอห์น เลนนอน	ประเทศจีน	วันพฤหัส

คำนามทั่วไป หรือสามานยนาม (Common nouns) คำนามทั่วๆไปที่ไม่ได้เป็นชื่อเฉพาะ แบ่งเป็นประเภทต่างๆ ดังนี้

คำนามที่เป็นนามธรรม (Abstract nouns) คือ คำนามที่ไม่มีรูปร่าง ไม่สามารถมองเห็น หรือสัมผัสได้ ตัวอย่าง เช่น

honesty	idea	time
ความซื่อสัตย์	ความคิด	เวลา

คำนามที่เป็นรูปธรรม (Concrete nouns) คือ คำนามที่มีรูปร่าง สามารถมองเห็น หรือสัมผัสได้ คำนามที่เป็นรูปธรรมอาจหมายถึงสิ่งที่มีชีวิต (animate nouns) หรือสิ่งที่ไม่มีชีวิต(inanimate nouns) ตัวอย่าง เช่น

dog	teacher	stone
สุนัข	ครู	หิน

คำนามบอกหมวดหมู่ หรือสมุหนาม (Collective nouns) คือ คำนามที่เป็นกลุ่ม หรือหมวดหมู่ของสิ่งต่างๆ ตัวอย่าง เช่น

a herd of cows
วัวหนึ่งฝูง

คำนามประสม (Compound nouns) คือ คำนามที่เกิดจากการประสมคำนาม ตั้งแต่สองคำขึ้นไปเข้าด้วยกัน อาจเขียนติดกันเป็นหนึ่งคำ แยกออกจากกันเป็นสอง คำ หรือมีเครื่องหมาย hyphen (-) คั่นกลาง ตัวอย่าง เช่น

washing machine
เครื่องซักผ้า

คำนามนับได้ และคำนามนับไม่ได้ (Countable and uncountable nouns)
คำนามนับได้ (Countable nouns) คือ คำนามที่เราสามารถใส่จำนวนนับได้ เช่น one cat (แมวหนึ่งตัว), two cats (แมวสองตัว) เป็นต้น คำนามนับได้มีทั้งรูป เอกพจน์ และพหูพจน์ ถ้าเป็นรูปเอกพจน์ จะมีคำบ่งชี้นามนำหน้า ตัวอย่าง เช่น

We've bought six new chairs.
เราซื้อเก้าอี้ใหม่หกตัว

คำนามนับไม่ได้ (Uncountable nouns) คือ คำนามที่เราไม่สามารถใส่จำนวนนับ หรือบอกเป็นจำนวนได้ คำนามนับไม่ได้จะไม่มีรูปพหูพจน์ ตามหลังด้วยคำกริยา เอกพจน์ และไม่ใช้กับคำนำหน้านาม ('a' หรือ 'an') ตัวอย่าง คำนามนับไม่ได้ เช่น

Anna gave us some more information about her work.
แอนนาให้ข้อมูลเราเกี่ยวกับงานของเธอ

คำนามที่สามารถแบ่ง หรือวัดเป็นปริมาณได้ แต่ไม่สามารถใส่จำนวนนับได้

(Mass nouns) คำนามเหล่านี้จะไม่ใช้กับคำนำหน้านาม และอาจอยู่ในรูปพหูพจน์ได้ เมื่อมีความหมายเฉพาะถึง ประเภท ชนิด หรือปริมาณของสิ่งต่างๆ ตัวอย่าง เช่น ตัวอย่าง เช่น

> Sugar is quite cheap.
> น้ำตาลมีราคาค่อนข้างถูก

> The principal sugars are glucose, sucrose, and fructose.
> น้ำตาลชนิดหลัก ได้แก่ กลูโคส ซูโครส และฟรุคโตส

คำสรรพนาม (Pronouns)

คำสรรพนาม คือ คำที่ใช้แทนคำนาม หรือนามวลี เมื่อไม่ต้องการกล่าวถึงคำนามคำ เดิมซ้ำๆในประโยค หรือย่อหน้าเดียวกัน คำสรรพนามแบ่งเป็นประเภทต่างๆได้เจ็ด ประเภท ดังนี้

บุรุษสรรพนาม (Personal pronouns) คือ สรรพนามที่ใช้แทนคน หรือสิ่งของใน ประโยค บุรุษสรรพนาม มีสองรูป คือ รูปประธานใช้ในตำแหน่งประธานของประโยค ได้แก่

I	you	he	she	it	we	they
ฉัน	คุณ	เขา(ผู้ชาย)	เขา(ผู้หญิง)	มัน	เรา	พวกเขา

และรูปกรรมใช้ในตำแหน่งกรรมของประโยค ได้แก่

me	you	him	her	it	us	them
ฉัน	คุณ	เขา(ผู้ชาย)	เขา(ผู้หญิง)	มัน	เรา	พวกเขา

เมื่อต้องเลือกใช้สรรพนามสองคำในประโยคเดียวกัน มีข้อสังเกต ดังต่อไปนี้ ถ้าคำสรรพนามอยู่ในตำแหน่งประธานของประโยค สรรพนามทั้งสองคำนั้นจะอยู่ใน รูปประธาน ตัวอย่าง เช่น

> Manee and I are going shopping.
> มานีกับฉันกำลังจะไปซื้อของ

แต่หากสรรพนามนั้นอยู่ในตำแหน่งกรรมของประโยค สรรพนามนั้นจะอยู่ในรูป กรรม ตัวอย่าง เช่น

> They decided to help Jane and me.
> เขาตัดสินใจช่วยเหลือเจนกับฉัน

หมายเหตุ ระวังข้อผิดพลาดที่เกิดจากการใช้รูปประธาน และกรรมร่วมกัน ตัวอย่าง เช่น 'They decided to help Jane and I.' ลองสมมุติว่าตัดสรรพนามออกไปรูปหนึ่ง จะเห็นว่าเราจะไม่ใช้ 'They decided to help I.' เนื่องจาก 'I' เป็นรูปประธาน แต่ ตำแหน่งหลังคำกริยาเป็นตำแหน่งของกรรม ดังนั้น เราจะใช้ 'They decided to help Jane and me.'

สรรพนามที่ประธานเป็นผู้กระทำกริยานั้นเอง (Reflexive pronouns) คือ สรรพนามที่มีความหมายสะท้อนถึงตัวประธานเอง เพื่อเน้นย้ำการกระทำของ ประธานของประโยค ตัวอย่าง เช่น

> Never mind. I'll do it myself.
> ไม่เป็นไร ฉันจะทำเอง

สรรพนามแสดงความเป็นเจ้าของ (Possessive pronouns) คือ สรรพนามที่บอก ความเป็นเจ้าของสิ่งต่างๆในประโยค ตัวอย่าง เช่น

> Give it back, it's mine.
> ส่งของของฉันคืนมา

คำสรรพนามชี้เฉพาะ หรือนิยมสรรพนาม (Demonstrative pronouns) คือ สรรพนามที่ใช้ระบุถึงสิ่งที่อยู่ใกล้ หรือไกลจากตัวเรา ตัวอย่าง เช่น

> This is Betty's and that is Peter's.
> นี่ของเบตตี้ และนั่นของปีเตอร์

สรรพนามใช้เชื่อมความ หรือประพันธสรรพนาม (Relative pronouns) คือ สรรพนามที่ใช้แทนคำนามในประโยคย่อย หรืออนุประโยค เพื่อเชื่อมประโยค หรือ ให้ความหมายเพิ่มเติมกับประโยค ตัวอย่าง เช่น

> That's the girl who always comes top.
> เด็กผู้หญิงคนนั้นเธอเป็นที่หนึ่งเสมอ

สรรพนามคำถาม หรือปฤจฉาสรรพนาม (Interrogative pronouns) คือ สรรพนามที่ใช้ในการตั้งคำถาม ตัวอย่าง เช่น

> What would you like for lunch?
> คุณจะกินอะไรเป็นอาหารกลางวัน

สรรพนามไม่ชี้เฉพาะ หรืออนิยมสรรพนาม (Indefinite pronouns) คือ คำ สรรพนามที่ใช้ในความหมายกว้างๆ แทนคำนามทั่วไปที่ไม่จำเป็นต้องการบุรุษ สรรพนาม ตัวอย่าง เช่น

> Much needs to be done.
> ยังมีงานอีกมากที่ต้องทำให้เสร็จ

คำคุณศัพท์ (Adjectives)

คำคุณศัพท์ คือคำที่นำหน้าคำนาม เพื่อให้ความหมายเพิ่มเติม ทำให้เราสามารถระบุ
ได้ว่า เรากำลังกล่าวถึงอะไร คำคุณศัพท์สามารถใช้ร่วมกันหลายๆคำได้โดยไม่จำเป็น
ต้องมีเครื่องหมาย 'comma' (,) คั่นระหว่างคำคุณศัพท์

คุณศัพท์เปรียบเทียบขั้นกว่า (comparative form) ใช้เปรียบเทียบระหว่าง คน
หรือ สิ่งของ จำนวนสองสิ่ง ตัวอย่าง เช่น

> Anna is taller than Mary, but Mary is older.
> แอนนาตัวสูงกว่าแมรี่ แต่แมรี่มีอายุมากกว่า

คุณศัพท์เปรียบเทียบขั้นสูงสุด (superlative form) ใช้เปรียบเทียบคน หรือ
สิ่งของ จำนวนตั้งแต่สองสิ่งขึ้นไป ตัวอย่าง เช่น

> That is the smallest camera I have ever seen.
> กล้องตัวนี้คือ กล้องที่มีขนาดเล็กที่สุดเท่าที่ฉันเคยเห็นมา

การสร้างคำคุณศัพท์เพื่อใช้เปรียบเทียบขั้นกว่า และขั้นสูงสุดมีสองวิธี ดังนี้
คำคุณศัพท์ที่มีหนึ่งพยางค์จะเพิ่มหน่วยเติมท้าย **'-er'** (รูปขั้นกว่า) หรือ **'-est'** (รูป
ขั้นสูงสุด) ที่ท้ายคำคุณศัพท์ เช่น

> bright สว่าง – brighter สว่างกว่า – the brightest สว่างที่สุด
> long ยาว – longer ยาวกว่า – the longest ยาวที่สุด

คำคุณศัพท์ที่ลงท้ายด้วยอักษร '-e' เราสามารถเติม '-r' หรือ '-st' ที่ท้ายคำคุณศัพท์
ได้เลย ส่วนคำคุณศัพท์ที่ลงท้ายด้วยตัวอักษร '-y' ต้องเปลี่ยน '-y' เป็น '-i' แล้วจึงจะ
เติม '-er' หรือ '-est' เช่น

> wise ฉลาด – wiser ฉลาดกว่า – the wisest ฉลาดที่สุด
> pretty สวย – prettier สวยกว่า – the prettiest สวยที่สุด

หมายเหตุ คำคุณศัพท์ที่มีพยางค์เดียว คือ ประกอบด้วยพยัญชนะ และสระเสียงสั้น
จะต้องเพิ่มพยัญชนะตัวสุดท้ายอีกหนึ่งตัวก่อนที่จะเติม '-er' หรือ '-est' ท้ายคำ
คุณศัพท์ เช่น big – bigger (ใหญ่ – ใหญ่กว่า) เป็นต้น

คำคุณศัพท์ที่มีสามพยางค์ หรือมากกว่าสามพยางค์ขึ้นไป เราจะใช้ **'more'**
หรือ **'most'** นำหน้าคำคุณศัพท์เหล่านั้น ตัวอย่าง เช่น

> fortunate โชคดี – more fortunate โชคดีกว่า –
> the most fortunate โชคดีที่สุด

คำคุณศัพท์ที่มีสองพยางค์ รวมถึงคำคุณศัพท์ที่ลงท้ายด้วย '-er' สามารถเลือกใช้รูป
เปรียบเทียบรูปใดรูปหนึ่ง หากไม่แน่ใจ ให้เลือกใช้รูป 'more' และ 'most' เป็นหลัก
ตัวอย่าง เช่น

> polite สุภาพ – politer / more polite สุภาพกว่า – the politest /
> the most polite สุภาพที่สุด

คำคุณศัพท์จำนวนหนึ่งเมื่ออยู่ในรูปขั้นกว่า และขั้นสูงสุด จะมีรูปแตกต่างไปจาก

เดิม ตัวอย่าง เช่น

good ดี – better ดีกว่า – the best ดีที่สุด

bad เลว – worse เลวกว่า – the worst เลวที่สุด

far ไกล – further ไกลกว่า – the furthest ไกลที่สุด

เมื่อต้องการเปรียบเทียบของสองสิ่งในความหมายว่า น้อยกว่า หรือน้อยที่สุด เราจะ
ใช้ 'less' หรือ 'least' ตัวอย่าง เช่น interesting น่าสนใจ

less interesting น่าสนใจน้อยกว่า –

the least interesting น่าสนใจน้อยที่สุด

หมายเหตุ

ควรระวังข้อผิดพลาดที่เกิดจากการใช้ 'more' และ '-er' หรือ 'most' และ '-est'
ร่วมกันในประโยค เช่น 'the most cleverest person' ควรเลือกใช้รูปคุณศัพท์รูป
ใดรูปหนึ่ง เช่น 'the cleverest person' หรือ 'the most clever person' เป็นต้น

คำกริยาวิเศษณ์ หรือคำวิเศษณ์ (Adverbs)

คำกริยาวิเศษณ์ หรือคำวิเศษณ์ คือ คำที่ทำหน้าที่ขยายคำกริยา ว่ากริยานั้นเกิดขึ้น
อย่างไร เมื่อไหร่ และที่ไหน คำวิเศษณ์ส่วนใหญ่เกิดจากการเติมหน่วยเติมท้าย **'-ly'**
ที่ท้ายคำคุณศัพท์ ตัวอย่าง เช่น

slow ช้า

slowly อย่างช้าๆ

คำวิเศษณ์กลุ่มที่มาจากคำคุณศัพท์ที่ลงท้ายด้วย '-ble' ให้ตัด '-e' ท้ายคำออกก่อนที่
จะเติม '-ly' ทั้งนี้ รวมถึงคำว่า 'true' และ 'due' ด้วย ตัวอย่าง เช่น

suitable เหมาะสม

suitably อย่างเหมาะสม

หมายเหตุ เมื่อคำวิเศษณ์นั้นมีที่มาจากคำคุณศัพท์ที่ลงท้ายด้วย '-e' ควรระวังข้อผิด
พลาดจากการสะกด '-ly' เป็น '-ley' ตัวอย่าง เช่น

extreme รุนแรง

extremely อย่างรุนแรง

คำคุณศัพท์ที่ลงท้ายด้วย '-y' ต้องเปลี่ยน '-y' เป็น '-i' ก่อนเติม '-ly' ยกเว้นคำว่า
'sly' หรือ **'dry'** ซึ่งมีพยางค์เดียวสามารถเติม '-ly' ได้เลย ตัวอย่าง เช่น

happy มีความสุข

happily อย่างมีความสุข

เราอาจไม่สามารถบอกได้ว่า คำๆนั้นเป็นคำคุณศัพท์ หรือคำวิเศษณ์ เนื่องจากคำ
วิเศษณ์บางคำมีรูปสะกดเดียวกับคำคุณศัพท์ โดยทั่วไป ข้อสังเกตคือ ให้ดูที่บริบท

หรือคำแวดล้อม ถ้าคำนั้นตามด้วยคำนามให้สันนิษฐานว่าเป็นคำคุณศัพท์ ตัวอย่าง
เช่น

| a late meeting | การประชุมตอนสาย |
| an early lecture | การบรรยายแต่เช้า |

แต่หากคำนั้นทำหน้าที่ขยายคำกริยา หรือคำคุณศัพท์ในประโยค คำนั้นอาจเป็นคำ
วิเศษณ์ ตัวอย่าง เช่น

The lesson was cut short.
บทเรียนถูกตัดทอนให้สั้นลง

He came in early.
เขามาถึงแต่เช้า

คำวิเศษณ์ทำหน้าที่เชื่อมประโยค (Sentence adverbs) ใช้ในตำแหน่งต้น
ประโยค คำวิเศษณ์เหล่านี้อาจอยู่ในรูปที่ลงท้ายด้วย '-ly' หรือ รูปอื่นๆ เช่น
'nevertheless' หรือ 'however' เป็นต้น ตัวอย่างคำวิเศษณ์รูปอื่นๆ ได้แก่

Nevertheless, we must give him an answer.
อย่างไรก็ตาม เราต้องให้คำตอบเขา

คำวิเศษณ์เพื่อบอกระดับ หรือปริมาณ (Adverbs of degree) คำวิเศษณ์กลุ่มนี้
ได้แก่ rather (ค่อนข้าง), quite (ค่อนข้าง), too (ด้วย) หรือ almost (เกือบจะ)
เป็นต้น คำวิเศษณ์กลุ่มนี้จะนำหน้าคำคุณศัพท์ หรือคำวิเศษณ์ด้วยกัน ตัวอย่าง เช่น

Ann is a very good tennis player.
แอนเป็นนักเทนนิสที่เก่งมาก

คำวิเศษณ์บอกตำแหน่ง (Adverbs of place) คำวิเศษณ์กลุ่มนี้จะมีรูปสะกด
เหมือนกับคำบุพบท (prepositions) แต่ถ้าเป็นคำวิเศษณ์จะไม่มีกรรมตามหลัง
และมักอยู่ในตำแหน่งท้ายประโยค ตัวอย่าง เช่น

He rushed in.
เขารีบร้อนเข้ามา

The two friends fell out.
เพื่อนสองคนนั้นขัดแย้งกัน

คำวิเศษณ์บางคำอาจมีรูปเปรียบเทียบขั้นกว่า และขั้นสูงสุดเช่นเดียวกับคำคุณศัพท์
โดยปกติจะใช้คู่กับ 'more' หรือ 'most' ตัวอย่าง เช่น

Could you speak more slowly, please?
กรุณาพูดช้ากว่านี้ได้ไหม

รูปคำวิเศษณ์ของคำว่า 'good' และ 'bad' มีดังนี้

good ดี	well ดี	better ดีกว่า	best ดีที่สุด
bad เลว	badly เลว	worse เลวกว่า	worst เลวที่สุด

คำบ่งชี้คำนาม (Determiners)

คำบ่งชี้คำนาม คือ คำที่ใช้นำหน้าคำนาม เพื่อระบุว่าคำนามนั้นคือ คน สิ่งของ หรือ อะไรที่กำลังพูดถึง คำบ่งชี้คำนามใช้ระบุถึงคำนามที่ถูกกล่าวถึง เพื่อให้ความหมาย ชัดเจนยิ่งขึ้น คำบ่งชี้คำนาม ได้แก่

หน่วยนำหน้าคำนามไม่ชี้เฉพาะ (indefinite articles เช่น 'a' หรือ 'an') และ **หน่วยนำหน้าคำนามชี้เฉพาะ** (definite article เช่น 'the')

คำแสดงตำแหน่งคำนาม (demonstratives) คือ คำแสดงตำแหน่งคำนามว่าอยู่ ใกล้ หรือไกลจากตำแหน่งของผู้พูด หรือผู้เขียน เช่น this (นี่), that (นั่น), these (เหล่านี้), those (เหล่านั้น) เป็นต้น

คำแสดงความเป็นเจ้าของ (possessives) เพื่อบอกว่าคำนามต่างๆเป็นของใคร เช่น my (ของฉัน), your (ของคุณ), his (ของเขา), its (ของมัน), our (ของเรา), their (ของพวกเขา) เป็นต้น

คำบอกปริมาณ (quantifiers) คือ คำบอก หรือแสดงปริมาณของสิ่งต่างๆ เช่น some (จำนวนหนึ่ง), any (จำนวนหนึ่ง), few (บ้าง), enough (เพียงพอ), much (มาก) เป็นต้น

คำบอกจำนวน (cardinal numbers) เช่น one (หนึ่ง), two (สอง), three (สาม) เป็นต้น และคำบอกลำดับที่ (ordinal numbers) เช่น first (ที่หนึ่ง), second (ที่ สอง), third (ที่สาม) เป็นต้น

คำแบ่งจำนวน (distributes) เช่น each (แต่ละ), every (ทุกๆ), either (ทั้ง), neither (ไม่ทั้ง) เป็นต้น

คำอุทาน (exclamatives) ซึ่งคำเหล่านี้จะใช้กับเครื่องหมายอัศเจรีย์ (exclamations) เช่น what (อะไร), such (เช่นนั้น) เป็นต้น

คำบุพบท (Prepositions)

คำบุพบท (Prepositions) คือหน่วยคำที่ใช้เชื่อมคำต่างๆในประโยคเข้าด้วยกัน คำ บุพบทในภาษาอังกฤษมีสองประเภท ได้แก่

บุพบทคำเดียว (Simple prepositions) เช่น in (ใน), on (บน), under (ใต้) เป็นต้น และ **บุพบทหลายคำ** (complex prepositions) เช่น due to (เนื่องจาก), together with (ด้วยกันกับ), on top of (เหนือสิ่งอื่นใด), in spite of (นอกจาก), out of (จาก) เป็นต้น

คำบุพบทคำเดียวบางคำสามารถทำหน้าที่เป็นทั้งคำบุพบท หรือวิเศษณ์ ขึ้นอยู่กับว่า คำบุพบทนั้นจะใช้ร่วมกับคำประเภทใด นอกจากนี้คำบุพบทจะต้องมีกรรมตามหลัง

เช่นเดียวกับคำกริยาประเภทที่ต้องการกรรม ปัจจุบันเราสามารถลงท้ายประโยค
ด้วยคำบุพบทได้ แต่ในงานเขียนที่เป็นทางการเราควรจะหลีกเลี่ยง ตัวอย่าง เช่น

> That's the girl we were talking about.　　(งานเขียนทั่วไป)
>
> That's the girl about whom we were talking.　　(งานเขียนที่เป็นทางการ)
>
> เด็กผู้หญิงคนนั้นคนที่เรากำลังพูดถึง

คำสันธาน (Conjunctions)

คำสันธาน (Conjunctions) คือ คำที่ทำหน้าที่เชื่อมคำนาม หรือประโยคเข้าด้วย
กัน ตัวอย่าง เช่น

> I went to the shop and bought some bread.
> ฉันไปร้านขายขนมปัง และซื้อขนมปังมาจำนวนหนึ่ง

กาล (Tenses)

คือ การผัน หรือเปลี่ยนแปลงรูปคำกริยาของประโยค ทำหน้าที่บอกความสัมพันธ์
ระหว่างกริยา และเวลา ว่า กริยานั้น เกิดขึ้นใน อดีต ปัจจุบัน หรืออนาคต คำกริยาที่
ผันรูปตามช่วงเวลาต่างๆ มีสองประเภท คือ
กริยาคำเดียว (simple tense) คือ การใช้คำกริยาคำเดียวเป็นกริยาหลักของ
ประโยค
กริยาประสม (compound tense) คือ การใช้คำกริยามากกว่าหนึ่งคำขึ้นไปเป็น
กริยาหลักของประโยค ประกอบด้วยกริยาช่วย 'Be' หรือ 'Have' ในรูปกาลปัจจุบัน
หรืออดีต กับกริยาที่ลงท้ายด้วย '-ing' หรือ '-ed'
ตัวอย่างต่อไปนี้แสดงกาล หรือการผันรูปกริยาตามช่วงเวลาต่างๆ ในภาษาอังกฤษ

ปัจจุบัน (Present simple)

I/we/you/they	play	
he/she/it	plays	ตัวอย่าง เช่น

> I go to college in London.
> ฉันไปเรียนหนังสือที่วิทยาลัยในลอนดอน

อดีต (Past simple)

I/we/you/they	played	
he/she/it	played	ตัวอย่าง เช่น

> I cooked a meal.
> ฉันทำกับข้าว (เหตุการณ์จบแล้ว)

อนาคต (Future simple)

| I/we/you/they | will play | |
| he/she/it | will play | ตัวอย่าง เช่น |

> Louis will phone you later.
> หลุยส์จะโทรศัพท์ติดต่อคุณภายหลัง

อดีตสืบเนื่องปัจจุบัน (Present perfect)

| I/we/you/they | have played | |
| he/she/it | has played | ตัวอย่าง เช่น |

> This illness has ruined my life.
> ความเจ็บป่วยทำลายชีวิตของฉัน

กริยาที่เกิดขึ้น และสิ้นสุดแล้วในอดีต (Past perfect)

| I/we/you/they | had played | |
| he/she/it | had played | ตัวอย่าง เช่น |

> She had visited Paris before.
> เธอเคยไปปารีสมาแล้ว (กริยาเกิด และจบแล้วในอดีต)

กริยาบอกเหตุการณ์ในอนาคต (Future perfect)

| I/we/you/they | will have played | |
| he/she/it | will have played | ตัวอย่าง เช่น |

> We will have finished before dark.
> เราจะทำงานให้เสร็จก่อนมืด

กริยากำลังดำเนินอยู่ในปัจจุบัน (Present continuous)

I	am playing	
we/you/they	are playing	
he/she/it	is playing	ตัวอย่าง เช่น

> I am waiting for Jack.
> ฉันกำลังรอแจ็ค

กริยากำลังดำเนินอยู่ในอดีต (Past continuous)

I	was playing	
we/you/they	were playing	
he/she/it	was playing	ตัวอย่าง เช่น

> We were trying to see the queen.
> เราพยายามที่จะได้เห็นสมเด็จพระราชินี (เหตุการณ์จบแล้ว)

กริยากำลังดำเนินอยู่ในอนาคต (Future continuous)

I/we/you/they	will be playing
he/she/it	will be playing ตัวอย่าง เช่น

> Our choir will be performing in the cathedral.
> การร้องเพลงประสานเสียงของเราจะมีขึ้นในโบสถ์

กริยาดำเนินอยู่อย่างต่อเนื่องจากอดีตถึงปัจจุบัน (Present Perfect Continuous)

I/we/you/they	have been playing
he/she/it	has been playing ตัวอย่าง เช่น

> The snow has been falling all night.
> หิมะตกลงมาตลอดทั้งคืน

กริยาเกิดขึ้น และกำลังดำเนินอยู่ในอดีต (Past Perfect Continuous)

I/we/you/they	had been playing
he/she/it	had been playing ตัวอย่าง เช่น

> Anna had been sitting there all day.
> แอนนานั่งอยู่ตรงนี้ตลอดทั้งวัน

กริยาบอกเหตุการณ์ในอนาคต (Future Perfect Continuous)

I/we/you/they	will have been playing
he/she/it	will have been playing ตัวอย่าง เช่น

> On Sunday, we will have been living here for 10 years.
> วันอาทิตย์นี้เราจะอยู่ที่นี่มาครบสิบปี

คำกริยาที่เปลี่ยนรูปตามปกติ และไม่เปลี่ยนรูปตามปกติ (Regular and irregular verbs) โดยปกติ คำกริยาทั่วไปจะมีรูปอดีตที่ลงท้ายด้วย **'-ed'** แต่จะมีคำกริยาบางคำที่ไม่ได้เปลี่ยนแปลงรูปตามปกติ เช่น

cost > cost > cost	(ราคา)
leave > left > left	(ทิ้ง)
take > took > taken	(เอาไป, ยึด)

สรรพนามประธาน กรรมตรง และกรรมรองของประโยค (Subject, object and indirect object)

สรรพนามประธาน (Subject) คือ ส่วนที่นำหน้าคำกริยา และเป็นตัวกำหนดรูปกริยา ประโยคทุกประโยคจะต้องมีส่วนประธาน ตัวอย่าง เช่น

> The man in the red coat asked me some questions.
> ผู้ชายคนที่ใส่เสื้อโค้ทสีแดงถามคำถามฉัน

สรรพนามกรรม (Object) คือ คำนาม นามวลี หรือสรรพนามที่ตามหลังคำกริยาของประโยค ตัวอย่าง เช่น

> She saw a large, black bird.
> ฉันเห็นนกสีดำตัวใหญ่

สรรพนามกรรมมีสองประเภท คือ กรรมตรง และกรรมรอง กริยาบางคำอาจต้องการทั้งกรรมตรง และกรรมรองตามหลังกริยา จึงจะให้ความหมายที่สมบูรณ์ กริยาเหล่านี้ ได้แก่ give, find หรือ owe เป็นต้น ตัวอย่าง เช่น

> Natee gave me a box of chocolates.
> นทีให้ช็อคโกแลตฉันหนึ่งกล่อง

การเปลี่ยนรูปคำกริยาในประโยคให้สอดคล้องกับประธาน (Agreement)

ความสอดคล้องของประธาน และกริยา (Subject/verb agreement) ในประโยคที่มีความยาวมาก มักจะเกิดข้อผิดพลาดได้ง่าย เนื่องจากประธาน และกริยาของประโยคอยู่ห่างจากกัน ดังนั้น มีข้อสังเกต ต่อไปนี้ ถ้าประธานเอกพจน์สองตัวอยู่ร่วมกัน และเชื่อมด้วย 'and' ประโยคนั้นต้องการกริยาพหูพจน์ ตัวอย่าง เช่น

> Prem and Arnat are going on holiday.
> เปรม และอานัตกำลังจะไปเที่ยววันหยุด

ถ้าประธานสองตัวเชื่อมด้วย 'and' แต่ตามความหมายถือว่าประธานทั้งสองเป็นสิ่งเดียวกัน ประโยคต้องการกริยาเอกพจน์ ตัวอย่าง เช่น

> Bed and breakfast is the cheapest form of accommodation.
> ที่พักประเภทที่รวมอาหารเช้าด้วยถือเป็นที่พักที่ราคาถูกที่สุด

ประธานเอกพจน์นำหน้าด้วย 'each', 'every', no' หรือ 'any' กริยาควรอยู่ในรูปเอกพจน์ ตัวอย่าง เช่น

Every seat was taken already.
ที่นั่งทุกที่มีคนนั่งเรียบร้อยแล้ว

ประธานเอกพจน์สองตัวเชื่อมด้วย 'or', 'nor', 'neither/ nor', 'either/ or' หรือ 'not only/ but also' กริยาจะอยู่ในรูปเอกพจน์ ตัวอย่าง เช่น

Neither Ben nor Jane was available for comment.
ทั้งเบน และเจน ไม่ว่างที่จะรับฟังความคิดเห็น

ชื่อหนังสือ ภาพยนตร์ และเพลง จะใช้กริยาเอกพจน์ แม้ว่าความหมายของชื่อสิ่ง ต่างๆเหล่านั้นจะเป็นพหูพจน์ ตัวอย่าง เช่น

'The Birds' is a really scary film.
'เดอะ เบิร์ด' เป็นภาพยนตร์ที่น่ากลัวมาก

ความสอดคล้องของคำสรรพนาม (Pronoun agreement)
คำสรรพนามที่จะแทนคำนามในประโยคต้องอยู่ในรูปที่สอดคล้องกับคำนามคำที่ สรรพนามนั้นมาแทนที่ ตัวอย่าง เช่น

The car started fine, but it broke down half way to Manchester.
รถติดเครื่องได้ปกติ แต่เมื่อขับไปแมนเชสเตอร์ได้ครึ่งทางเครื่องก็ขัดข้อง

การใช้สรรพนามพหูพจน์แทนประธานที่เป็นคำนามเอกพจน์ ปัจจุบันการใช้ สรรพนามพหูพจน์นั้นยอมรับใช้กันอย่างแพร่หลาย เช่น แทนที่จะใช้ 'he/ she' หรือ 'he or she' แทนคำนามเอกพจน์ตามที่ใช้กันในอดีต การใช้ 'their' ทำให้ประโยค กระชับ

Any pupil who is going on the school trip should hand in their payment at the office.
นักเรียนคนไหนที่ต้องการจะไปทัศนศึกษากับทางโรงเรียน ต้องไปจ่ายเงิน ที่สำนักงาน

ความสอดคล้องของกาล หรือการผันรูปคำกริยา เพื่อแสดงเวลาของการกระทำที่ เกิดขึ้นในประโยค (Tense agreement) ปกติอาจพบประโยคที่ใช้คำกริยาช่วย (modal หรือ auxiliary) ตั้งแต่สองคำขึ้นไปร่วมกัน เช่น

I can and I have done it.

แต่รูปประโยคเช่นนี้ไม่ถูกต้อง เนื่องจาก 'can' ไม่สามารถใช้ร่วมกับ 'done' ได้ ดัง นั้น เพื่อความถูกต้องประโยคนี้ควรใช้ว่า

I can do it and I have done it.
ฉันทำได้ และฉันก็ได้ทำไปแล้ว

ENGLISH–THAI
อังกฤษ–ไทย

a

a [eɪ] *art* หนึ่ง [nue]

abandon [əˈbændən] *v* ละทิ้ง [la thing]

abbey [ˈæbɪ] *n* สำนักสงฆ์ [sam nak song]

abbreviation [əˌbriːvɪˈeɪʃən] *n* อักษรย่อ [ak sorn yor]

abdomen [ˈæbdəmən; æbˈdəʊ-] *n* ท้อง [thong]

abduct [æbˈdʌkt] *v* ลักพาตัว [lak pha tua]

ability [əˈbɪlɪtɪ] *n* ความสามารถ [khwam sa mat]

able [ˈeɪbəl] *adj* สามารถ [sa mat]

abnormal [æbˈnɔːməl] *adj* ผิดปรกติ [phit prok ka ti]

abolish [əˈbɒlɪʃ] *v* ยกเลิก [yok loek]

abolition [ˌæbəˈlɪʃən] *n* การล้มเลิก [kan lom loek]

abortion [əˈbɔːʃən] *n* การทำแท้ง [kan tham thang]

about [əˈbaʊt] *adv* ใกล้ [klai] ▷ *prep* เกี่ยวกับ [kiao kap]; **Do you have any leaflets about...?** คุณมีใบปลิวเกี่ยวกับ...บ้างไหม? [khun mii bai plio kiao kap... bang mai]; **I want to complain about the service** ฉันอยากร้องเรียนเกี่ยวกับการบริการ [chan yak rong rian kiao kap kan bo ri kan]

above [əˈbʌv] *prep* เหนือ [nuea]

abroad [əˈbrɔːd] *adv* ต่างประเทศ [tang pra thet]

abrupt [əˈbrʌpt] *adj* ทันทีทันใด [than thii than dai]

abruptly [əˈbrʌptlɪ] *adv* อย่างทันทีทันใด [yang than thee than dai]

abscess [ˈæbsɛs; -sɪs] *n* ฝี [fi]; **I have an abscess** ฉันมีฝี [chan mii fii]

absence [ˈæbsəns] *n* การขาด, ช่วงเวลาที่ไม่อยู่ [kan khat, chuang we la thii mai yu]

absent [ˈæbsənt] *adj* ขาด [khat]

absent-minded [ˌæbsənˈtˈmaɪndɪd] *adj* ใจลอย [chai loi]

absolutely [ˌæbsəˈluːtlɪ] *adv* อย่างแน่นอน [yang nae norn]

abstract [ˈæbstrækt] *adj* ที่เป็นนามธรรม [thii pen nam ma tham]

absurd [əbˈsɜːd] *adj* ไร้สาระ [rai sa ra]

Abu Dhabi [ˈæbuː ˈdɑːbɪ] *n* อาบูดาบี้ [a bu da bi]

abuse *n* [əˈbjuːs] การข่มเหง [kan khom heng] ▷ *v* [əˈbjuːz] ข่มเหง [khom heng]; **child abuse** *n* การกระทำทารุณต่อเด็ก [kan kra tham tha run to dek]

abusive [əˈbjuːsɪv] *adj* ซึ่งเป็นอันตราย [sueng pen an tra lai]

academic [ˌækəˈdɛmɪk] *adj* ด้านวิชาการ [dan wi cha kan]; **academic year** *n* ปีการศึกษา [pi kan suek sa]

academy [əˈkædəmɪ] *n* สถาบันศึกษา [sa tha ban suek sa]

accelerate [ækˈsɛləˌreɪt] *v* เร่งความเร็ว [reng khwam reo]

acceleration [ækˌsɛləˈreɪʃən] *n* การเพิ่มความเร็ว [kan poem khwam reo]

accelerator [ækˈsɛləˌreɪtə] *n* คันเร่ง [khan reng]

accept [əkˈsɛpt] *v* ยอมรับ [yom rap]

acceptable [əkˈsɛptəbəl] *adj* ที่ยอมรับได้ [thii yorm rab dai]

access [ˈæksɛs] *n* ทางเข้า [thang khao]

▷ v เข้าไปได้ [khao pai dai]; **Do you provide access for the disabled?** คุณจัดให้มีทางเข้าออกสำหรับคนพิการไหม? [khun chat hai mii thang khao ok sam rap khon phi kan mai]

accessible [ək'sɛsəbᵊl] adj ที่สามารถเข้าได้ [thii sa mart khao dai]

accessory [ək'sɛsərɪ] n เครื่องประดับ [khrueang pra dap]

accident ['æksɪdənt] n อุบัติเหตุ [u bat ti het]; **accident & emergency department** n อุบัติเหตุและหน่วยฉุกเฉิน [u bat ti het lae nuai chuk choen]; **I'd like to arrange personal accident insurance** ฉันอยากให้มีประกันชีวิตจากอุบัติเหตุ [chan yak hai mii pra kan chi vid chak u bat ti het]; **I've had an accident** ฉันเคยได้รับอุบัติเหตุ [chan khoei dai rap u bat ti het]; **There's been an accident!** มีอุบัติเหตุเกิดขึ้น [mii u bat ti het koet khuen]

accidental [ˌæksɪ'dɛntᵊl] adj เป็นเหตุบังเอิญ [pen het bang oen]

accidentally [ˌæksɪ'dɛntəlɪ] adv โดยบังเอิญ [doi bang oen]

accommodate [ə'kɒmədeɪt] v จัดที่อยู่ให้ [chad thii yu hai]

accommodation [əˌkɒmə'deɪʃən] n ที่พักอาศัย [thii phak a sai]

accompany [ə'kʌmpənɪ; ə'kʌmpnɪ] v ไปเป็นเพื่อน [pai pen phuean]

accomplice [ə'kɒmplɪs; ə'kʌm-] n ผู้สมรู้ร่วมคิด [phu som ru ruam kit]

according [ə'kɔːdɪŋ] prep **according to** prep ตามที่ [tan thi]

accordingly [ə'kɔːdɪŋlɪ] adv ตามนั้น [tam nan]

accordion [ə'kɔːdɪən] n หีบเพลง [hip phleng]

account [ə'kaʊnt] n (in bank) บัญชีเงินฝาก [ban chi ngoen fak], (report) รายงาน การบรรยาย [rai ngan, kan ban yai]; **account number** n หมายเลขบัญชี [mai lek ban chi]; **bank account** n บัญชีธนาคาร [ban chi tha na khan]; **current account** n บัญชีกระแสรายวัน [ban chi kra sae rai wan]

accountable [ə'kaʊntəbᵊl] adj ที่สามารถอธิบายได้ [thii sa maat a thi bai dai]

accountancy [ə'kaʊntənsɪ] n การบัญชี [kan ban chi]

accountant [ə'kaʊntənt] n นักบัญชี [nak ban chi]

account for [ə'kaʊnt fɔː] v ให้เหตุผลสำหรับ [hai het phon sam rap]

accuracy ['ækjʊrəsɪ] n ความแม่นยำ [khwam maen yam]

accurate ['ækjərɪt] adj แม่นยำ [maen yam]

accurately ['ækjərɪtlɪ] adv อย่างแม่นยำ [yang maen yam]

accusation [ˌækjʊ'zeɪʃən] n การกล่าวหา [kan klao ha]

accuse [ə'kjuːz] v กล่าวหา [klao ha]

accused [ə'kjuːzd] n ผู้ถูกกล่าวหา [phu thuk klao ha]

ace [eɪs] n แต้มเอหรือเลขหนึ่งในการเล่นไพ่ [taem e rue lek nueng nai kan len pai]

ache [eɪk] n ความเจ็บปวด [khwam chep puat] ▷ v เจ็บปวด [chep puat]

achieve [ə'tʃiːv] v ประสบผลสำเร็จ [pra sop phon sam ret]

achievement [ə'tʃiːvmənt] n การบรรลุผลสำเร็จ [kan ban lu phon sam ret]

acid ['æsɪd] n กรด [krot]; **acid rain** n ฝนที่เป็นกรด [fon thii pen krot]

acknowledgement [ək'nɒlɪdʒmənt] n การยอมรับ [kan yom rap]

acne ['æknɪ] n สิว [sio]

acorn ['eɪkɔːn] n ผลต้นโอ๊ก [phon ton oak]

acoustic [ə'kuːstɪk] adj ซึ่งเกี่ยวข้องกับเสียง [sueng kiao khong kab siang]

acre ['eɪkə] n หน่วยวัดเนื้อที่เป็นเอเคอร์ [nuai wat nuea thii pen e khoe]

acrobat ['ækrəˌbæt] n นักกายกรรม [nak kai ya kam]

acronym ['ækrənɪm] *n* ตัวย่อ [tua yo]

across [ə'krɒs] *prep* ข้าม [kham]

act [ækt] *n* การกระทำ [kan kra tham] ▷ *v* กระทำ [kra tham]

acting ['æktɪŋ] *adj* รักษาการแทน [rak sa kan thaen] ▷ *n* การแสดง [kan sa daeng]

action ['ækʃən] *n* การกระทำ [kan kra tham]

active ['æktɪv] *adj* คล่องแคล่ว [khlong khlaeo]

activity [æk'tɪvɪtɪ] *n* กระตือรือร้น [kra tue rue ron]; **activity holiday** *n* วันหยุด ท่องเที่ยวที่มีกิจกรรม [wan yut thong thiao thii mii kit cha kam]

actor ['æktə] *n* นักแสดงชาย [nak sa daeng chai]

actress ['æktrɪs] *n* นักแสดงหญิง [nak sa daeng hying]

actual ['æktʃʊəl] *adj* ที่จริง [thii chring]

actually ['æktʃʊəlɪ] *adv* อย่างที่เกิดขึ้น ตามจริง [yang thii koed khuen tam chring]

acupuncture ['ækjʊˌpʌŋktʃə] *n* การฝัง เข็ม [kan fang khem]

ad [æd] *abbr* ตัวย่อของโฆษณา [tua yor khong kho sa na]; **small ads** *npl* โฆษณาเล็ก ๆ [khot sa na lek lek]

AD [eɪ diː] *abbr* คริสต์ศักราช [khrit sak ka rat]

adapt [ə'dæpt] *v* ปรับตัว [prap tua]

adaptor [ə'dæptə] *n* ตัวแปลงไฟ [tua plaeng fai]

add [æd] *v* รวม [ruam]

addict ['ædɪkt] *n* ผู้ติดยาเสพติด [phu tit ya sep tit]; **drug addict** *n* ผู้ติดยา [phu tit ya]

addicted [ə'dɪktɪd] *adj* ทำให้ติดยาเสพติด [tham hai tit ya sep tit]

additional [ə'dɪʃənəl] *adj* ที่เพิ่มขึ้น [thii perm khuen]

additive ['ædɪtɪv] *n* สิ่งที่เพิ่มเข้าไป [sing thii perm khao pai]

address [ə'drɛs] *n* (*location*) ที่อยู่ [thi yu], (*speech*) คำปราศรัย [kham pra sai];

address book *n* สมุดที่อยู่ [sa mut thii yu]; **Please send my mail on to this address** ช่วยส่งจดหมายฉันไปตามที่อยู่ที่นี่ [chuai song chot mai chan pai tam thii yu thii ni]; **The website address is...** ที่อยู่ของเว็บไซต์คือ... [thii yu khong web sai khue...]; **Will you write down the address, please?** คุณจะช่วย เขียนที่อยู่ได้ไหม? [khun ja chuai khian thii yu dai mai]

add up [æd ʌp] *v* คิดผลรวม [kid phon ruam]

adjacent [ə'dʒeɪsʰnt] *adj* ติดกัน [tid kan]

adjective ['ædʒɪktɪv] *n* คำคุณศัพท์ [kham khun na sab]

adjust [ə'dʒʌst] *v* ปรับตัว [prap tua]

adjustable [ə'dʒʌstəbʰl] *adj* ปรับตัวได้ [prap tua dai]

adjustment [ə'dʒʌstmənt] *n* การปรับ เปลี่ยน [kan prap plian]

administration [ədˌmɪnɪ'streɪʃən] *n* การบริหาร [kan bo ri han]

administrative [ədˈmɪnɪˌstrətɪv] *adj* เกี่ยวกับการบริหาร [kiao kap kan bo ri han]

admiration [ˌædməˈreɪʃən] *n* ความ ชื่นชม [khwam chuen chom]

admire [əd'maɪə] *v* ชื่นชม [chuen chom]

admission [əd'mɪʃən] *n* การอนุญาตให้ เข้า [kan ar nu yard hai khao]; **admission charge** *n* ค่าธรรมเนียมใน การเข้า [kha tham niam nai kan khao]

admit [əd'mɪt] *v* (*allow in*) ยอมให้เข้า [yom hai khao], (*confess*) สารภาพ [sa ra phap]

admittance [əd'mɪtʰns] *n* การอนุญาต ให้เข้าได้ [kan ar nu yard hai khao dai]

adolescence [ˌædə'lɛsəns] *n* ช่วงวัยรุ่น [chuang wai run]

adolescent [ˌædə'lɛsʰnt] *n* วัยรุ่น [wai run]

adopt [ə'dɒpt] *v* รับเอามา [rap ao ma]

adopted [ə'dɒptɪd] *adj* รับเลี้ยงเป็นลูก

[rap liang pen luk]

adoption [ə'dɒpʃən] *n* การรับเลี้ยงบุตร
บุญธรรม [kan rap liang but bun tham]

adore [ə'dɔː] *v* บูชา [bu cha]

Adriatic [ˌeɪdrɪ'ætɪk] *adj* เอเดรียติค [e
dria tik]

Adriatic Sea [ˌeɪdrɪ'ætɪk siː] *n* ทะเลเอ
เดรียติค [tha le e dria tik]

adult ['ædʌlt; ə'dʌlt] *n* ผู้ใหญ่ [phu yai];
adult education *n* การศึกษาผู้ใหญ่
[kan suek sa phu yai]

advance [əd'vɑːns] *n* ความก้าวหน้า
[khwam kao na] ▷ *v* ก้าวหน้า [kao na];
advance booking *n* จองล่วงหน้า
[chong luang na]

advanced [əd'vɑːnst] *adj* ขั้นสูง [khan
sung]

advantage [əd'vɑːntɪdʒ] *n* ความได้
เปรียบ [khwam dai priap]

advent ['ædvɛnt; -vənt] *n* การปรากฏตัว
ของคนหรือสิ่งสำคัญ [kan pra kot tua
khong khon rue sing sam khan]

adventure [əd'vɛntʃə] *n* การผจญภัย
[kan pha chon phai]

adventurous [əd'vɛntʃərəs] *adj* ชอบ
ผจญภัย [chop pha chon phai]

adverb ['ædˌvɜːb] *n* คำวิเศษณ์ [kham vi
sed]

adversary ['ædvəsərɪ] *n* คู่ต่อสู้ [khu to
su]

advert ['ædvɜːt] *n* โฆษณา [kho sa na]

advertise ['ædvəˌtaɪz] *v* ลงโฆษณา [long
kho sa na]

advertisement [əd'vɜːtɪsmənt; -tɪz-]
n การโฆษณา [kan kho sa na]

advertising ['ædvəˌtaɪzɪŋ] *n* ธุรกิจ
โฆษณา [thu ra kid kho sa na]

advice [əd'vaɪs] *n* คำแนะนำ [kham nae
nam]

advisable [əd'vaɪzəbəl] *adj* ควรแก่การ
แนะนำ [khua kae kan nae nam]

advise [əd'vaɪz] *v* แนะนำ [nae nam]

aerial ['ɛərɪəl] *n* การตีลังกาโดยไม่ใช้มือ
[kan ti lang ka doi mai chai mue]

aerobics [ɛə'rəʊbɪks] *npl* การเต้นแอร์โร
บิค [kan ten ae ro bik]

aerosol ['ɛərəˌsɒl] *n* ละอองของเหลว [la
ong khong leo]

affair [ə'fɛə] *n* สถานการณ์ที่ได้รับการ
จัดการ [sa tha na kan thii dai rap kan
chat kan]

affect [ə'fɛkt] *v* กระทบ [kra thop]

affectionate [ə'fɛkʃənɪt] *adj* ซึ่งรักใคร่
[sueng rak khrai]

afford [ə'fɔːd] *v* สามารถจ่ายได้ [sa maat
chai dai]

affordable [ə'fɔːdəbəl] *adj* สามารถซื้อได้
[sa maat sue dai]

Afghan ['æfgæn; -gən] *adj* เกี่ยวกับ
อัฟกานิสถาน [kiao kap af ka ni sa than]
▷ *n* ชาวอัฟกานิสถาน [chao af ka ni sa
than]

Afghanistan [æf'gænɪˌstɑːn; -ˌstæn]
n ประเทศอัฟกานิสถาน [pra tet af ka ni sa
than]

afraid [ə'freɪd] *adj* กลัว [klua]

Africa ['æfrɪkə] *n* ทวีปอัฟริกา [tha vip af
ri ka]; **North Africa** *n* อัฟริกาเหนือ [af ri
ka nuea]; **South Africa** *n* ประเทศอัฟริกา
ใต้ [pra tet af ri ka tai]

African ['æfrɪkən] *adj* เกี่ยวกับอัฟริกา
[kiao kap af ri ka] ▷ *n* ชาวอัฟริกัน [chao
af ri kan]; **Central African Republic** *n*
ประเทศสาธารณรัฐอัฟริกันกลาง [pra tet sa
tha ra na rat af ri kan klang]; **North
African** *n* เกี่ยวกับอัฟริกาเหนือ [kiao kap
af ri ka nuea], ชาวอัฟริกันตอนเหนือ [kiao
kap af ri ka nuea, chao af ri kan ton
nuea]; **South African** *n* เกี่ยวกับอัฟริกา
ใต้ [kiao kap af ri ka tai], ชาวอัฟริกาใต้
[kiao kap af ri ka tai, chao af ri ka tai]

Afrikaans [ˌæfrɪ'kɑːns; -'kɑːnz] *n* ชื่อ
ภาษาราชการของอัฟริกาใต้ [chue pha sa
rat cha kan khong af ri ka tai]

Afrikaner [afrɪ'kɑːnə; ˌæfrɪ'kɑːnə] *n*
ชาวอัฟริกัน [chao af ri kan]

after ['ɑːftə] *conj* หลังจาก [lang chak] ▷
prep ภายหลัง [phai lang]

afternoon [ˌɑ:ftəˈnu:n] *n* ตอนบ่าย [ton bai]; **Good afternoon** สวัสดีตอนบ่าย [sa wat di ton bai]; **in the afternoon** ใน ตอนบ่าย [nai ton bai]

afters [ˈɑ:ftəz] *npl* ของหวาน [khong wan]

aftershave [ˈɑ:ftəˌʃeɪv] *n* น้ำหอมปรับผิว หลังโกนหนวด [nam hom prap phio lang kon nuat]

afterwards [ˈɑ:ftəwədz] *adv* หลังจากนั้น [lang chak nan]

again [əˈɡɛn; əˈɡeɪn] *adv* อีกครั้ง [ik khrang]

against [əˈɡɛnst; əˈɡeɪnst] *prep* ต่อต้าน [to tan]

age [eɪdʒ] *n* อายุ [a yu]; **age limit** *n* อายุ ขั้นต่ำ [a yu khan tam]; **Middle Ages** *npl* ยุคกลาง [yuk klang]

aged [eɪdʒd] *adj* สูงอายุ [sung a yu]

agency [ˈeɪdʒənsɪ] *n* บริษัทตัวแทน [bor ri sat tua tan]; **travel agency** *n* สำนักงาน ท่องเที่ยว [sam nak ngan thong thiao]

agenda [əˈdʒɛndə] *n* กำหนดการ [kam not kan]

agent [ˈeɪdʒənt] *n* ตัวแทน [tua thaen]; **estate agent** *n* คนที่ทำงานเกี่ยวกับขาย บ้านและที่ดิน [khon thii tham ngan kiao kap khai baan lae thii din]; **travel agent** *n* ตัวแทนสำนักงานท่องเที่ยว [tua thaen sam nak ngan thong thiao]

aggressive [əˈɡrɛsɪv] *adj* ก้าวร้าว [kao rao]

AGM [eɪ dʒi: ɛm] *abbr* การประชุมประจำปี [kan pra chum pra cham pi]

ago [əˈɡəʊ] *adv* **a month ago** หนึ่งเดือน มาแล้ว [nueng duean ma laeo]; **a week ago** อาทิตย์หนึ่งมาแล้ว [a thit nueng ma laeo]

agony [ˈæɡənɪ] *n* ความทรมาน [khwam tho ra man]

agree [əˈɡri:] *v* เห็นด้วย [hen duai]

agreed [əˈɡri:d] *adj* ยินยอม [yin yom]

agreement [əˈɡri:mənt] *n* ข้อตกลง [kho tok long]

agricultural [ˈæɡrɪˌkʌltʃərəl] *adj* ที่เกี่ยว กับเกษตรกรรม [thii kiao kap ka set tra kam]

agriculture [ˈæɡrɪˌkʌltʃə] *n* การเกษตร กรรม [kan ka set tra kam]

ahead [əˈhɛd] *adv* ในอนาคต [nai a na khot]

aid [eɪd] *n* ความช่วยเหลือ [khwam chuai luea]; **first aid** *n* การปฐมพยาบาลเบื้องต้น [kan pa thom pa ya baan bueang ton]; **first-aid kit** *n* ชุดปฐมพยาบาล [chut pa thom pha ya baan]; **hearing aid** *n* เครื่องช่วยฟัง [khrueang chuai fang]

AIDS [eɪdz] *n* โรคเอดส์ [rok aid]

aim [eɪm] *n* จุดหมาย [chut mai] ▷ *v* ตั้ง เป้า [tang pao]

air [eə] *n* อากาศ [a kat]; **air hostess** *n* พนักงานหญิงบริการบนเครื่องบิน [pha nak ngan ying], แอร์โฮสเตส [pha nak ngan ying bo ri kan bon khrueang bin, ae hos tes]; **air-traffic controller** *n* ผู้ ควบคุมเส้นทางการบิน [phu khuap khum sen thang kan bin]; **Air Force** *n* กองทัพ อากาศ [kong thap a kat]; **How long will it take by air?** จะใช้เวลานานเท่าไร ถ้าส่งทางอากาศ? [ja chai we la nan thao rai tha song thang a kat]

airbag [ɛəbæɡ] *n* ถุงอากาศนิรภัย [thung a kaat ni ra phai]

air-conditioned [ɛəkənˈdɪʃənd] *adj* ซึ่ง ได้ปรับอากาศ [sueng dai prap a kaat]

air conditioning [ɛə kənˈdɪʃənɪŋ] *n* เครื่องปรับอากาศ [khrueang prap a kat]; **The air conditioning doesn't work** เครื่องปรับอากาศไม่ทำงาน [khrueang prap a kat mai tham ngan]

aircraft [ˈɛəˌkrɑ:ft] *n* เครื่องบิน [khrueang bin]

airline [ˈɛəˌlaɪn] *n* สายการบิน [sai kan bin]

airmail [ˈɛəˌmeɪl] *n* จดหมายทางอากาศ [chod mai thang ar kard]

airport [ˈɛəˌpɔ:t] *n* สนามบิน [sa nam bin]; **How do I get to the airport?** ฉัน

จะไปสนามบินได้อย่างไร? [chan ja pai sa nam bin dai yang rai]; **How much is the taxi to the airport?** แท็กซี่ไปสนามบินราคาเท่าไร? [thaek si pai sa nam bin ra kha thao rai]; **Is there a bus to the airport?** มีรถโดยสารไปสนามบินไหม? [mii rot doi san pai sa nam bin mai]

airsick [ˈɛəˌsɪk] *adj* เมาเครื่องบิน [mao khrueang bin]

airspace [ˈɛəˌspeɪs] *n* น่านฟ้า [nan fa]

airtight [ˈɛəˌtaɪt] *adj* ที่ผนึกแน่นไม่ให้อากาศเข้า [thii pha nuek naen mai hai ar kard khao]

aisle [aɪl] *n* ทางเดินระหว่างที่นั่ง [thang doen ra wang thii nang]

alarm [əˈlɑːm] *n* สัญญาณเตือนภัย [san yan tuean phai]; **alarm call** *n* การโทรปลุก [kan to pluk]; **alarm clock** *n* นาฬิกาปลุก [na li ka pluk]; **false alarm** *n* สัญญาณเตือนภัยปลอม [san yan tuean phai plom]

alarming [əˈlɑːmɪŋ] *adj* ซึ่งน่าตกใจ [sueng na tok jai]

Albania [ælˈbeɪnɪə] *n* ประเทศอัลเบเนีย [pra tet al be nia]

Albanian [ælˈbeɪnɪən] *adj* ซึ่งเกี่ยวกับอัลเบเนี่ยน [sueng kiao kap al be nian] ▷ *n (language)* ภาษาอัลเบเนี่ยน [pha sa al be nian], *(person)* ชาวอัลเบเนี่ยน [chao al be nian]

album [ˈælbəm] *n* สมุดภาพ [sa mut phap], อัลบั้ม [al bam]; **photo album** *n* อัลบั้มใส่รูป [al bam sai rup]

alcohol [ˈælkəˌhɒl] *n* เหล้า [lao]

alcohol-free [ˈælkəˌhɒlfriː] *adj* ไม่มีเหล้า [mai mee lao]

alcoholic [ˌælkəˈhɒlɪk] *adj* ซึ่งติดเหล้า [sueng tid lao] ▷ *n* ผู้ติดเหล้า [phu tid lao]

alert [əˈlɜːt] *adj* ตื่นตัว [tuen tua] ▷ *v* เตือน [tuean]

Algeria [ælˈdʒɪərɪə] *n* ประเทศอัลจีเรีย [pra tet al chi ria]

Algerian [ælˈdʒɪərɪən] *adj* ที่เกี่ยวกับอัลจีเรีย [thii kiao kap al chi ria] ▷ *n* ชาวอัลจีเรีย [chao al chi ria]

alias [ˈeɪlɪəs] *adv* ฉายา [cha ya] ▷ *prep* อีกนัยหนึ่งเรียกว่า [ik nai nueng riak wa]

alibi [ˈælɪˌbaɪ] *n* คำอ้างว่าอยู่ที่อื่นขณะที่เกิดเหตุ [kham ang wa yu thii uen kha na thii koet het]

alien [ˈeɪljən; ˈeɪlɪən] *n* คนต่างด้าว [khon tang dao]

alive [əˈlaɪv] *adj* มีชีวิต [mii chi wit]

all [ɔːl] *adj* ทั้งหมด [thang mot] ▷ *pron* ทุกคน [thuk khon]

Allah [ˈælə] *n* พระเจ้าศาสนาอิสลาม [phra chao sat sa na is sa lam]

allegation [ˌælɪˈɡeɪʃən] *n* ข้อกล่าวหา [kho klao ha]

alleged [əˈlɛdʒd] *adj* ซึ่งถูกกล่าวหา [sueng thuk klao ha]

allergic [əˈlɜːdʒɪk] *adj* แพ้ [phae]; **I'm allergic to penicillin** ฉันแพ้เพ็นนิซิลิน [chan phae phen ni si lin]

allergy [ˈælədʒɪ] *n* อาการแพ้ [a kan phae]; **peanut allergy** *n* อาการแพ้ถั่วลิสง [a kan phae thua li song]

alley [ˈælɪ] *n* ตรอก [trok]

alliance [əˈlaɪəns] *n* พันธมิตร [phan tha mit]

alligator [ˈælɪˌɡeɪtə] *n* จระเข้ [cha ra ke]

allow [əˈlaʊ] *v* อนุญาต [a nu yat]

all right [ɔːl raɪt] *adv* อย่างน่าพอใจ [yang na phor jai]

ally [ˈælaɪ; əˈlaɪ] *n* สัมพันธมิตร [sam phan tha rat]

almond [ˈɑːmənd] *n* เมล็ดอัลมอนด์ [ma let a mon]

almost [ˈɔːlməʊst] *adv* เกือบจะ [kueap cha]

alone [əˈləʊn] *adj* โดยลำพัง [doi lam phang]

along [əˈlɒŋ] *prep* ไปตาม [pai tam]

aloud [əˈlaʊd] *adv* อย่างดัง [yang dang]

alphabet [ˈælfəˌbɛt] *n* ตัวอักษร [tua ak son]

Alps [ælps] *npl* เทือกเขาแอลป์ [thueak khao aelp]

already [ɔːl'rɛdɪ] *adv* แล้ว [laeo]

alright [ɔːl'raɪt] *adv* **Are you alright?** คุณตกลงไหม? [khun tok long mai]

also ['ɔːlsəʊ] *adv* เช่นกัน [chen kan]

altar ['ɔːltə] *n* แท่นบูชา [thaen bu cha]

alter ['ɔːltə] *v* ปรับเปลี่ยน [prap plian]

alternate [ɔːl'tɜːnɪt] *adj* ซึ่งสลับกัน [sueng sa lap kan]

alternative [ɔːl'tɜːnətɪv] *adj* ที่มีตัวเลือก [thii mii tua lueak] ▷ *n* ทางเลือก [thang lueak]

alternatively [ɔːl'tɜːnətɪvlɪ] *adv* ซึ่งมีตัวเลือก [sueng mii tua lueak]

although [ɔːl'ðəʊ] *conj* ถึงแม้ว่า [thueng mae wa]

altitude ['æltɪˌtjuːd] *n* ความสูงเหนือพื้นดินหรือเหนือน้ำทะเล [khwam sung nuea phuen din rue nuea nam tha le]

altogether [ˌɔːltə'gɛðə; 'ɔːltəˌgɛðə] *adv* ทั้งหมด [thang mot]

aluminium [ˌæljʊ'mɪnɪəm] *n* อลูมิเนียม [a lu mi niam]

always ['ɔːlweɪz; -wɪz] *adv* เสมอ [sa moe]

a.m. [eɪɛm] *abbr* เวลาหลังเที่ยงคืนถึงเที่ยงวัน [we la lang thiang khuen thueng thiang wan]

amateur ['æmətə; -tʃə; -ˌtjʊə; ˌæmə'tɜː] *n* มือสมัครเล่น [mue sa mak len]

amaze [ə'meɪz] *v* ทำให้ประหลาดใจ [tham hai pra lat jai]

amazed [ə'meɪzd] *adj* น่าทึ่ง [na thueng]

amazing [ə'meɪzɪŋ] *adj* น่าประหลาดใจ [na pra hlad jai]

ambassador [æm'bæsədə] *n* เอกอัครราชทูต [ek ak khra rat cha thut]

amber ['æmbə] *n* สีเหลืองอำพัน [sii lueang am phan]

ambition [æm'bɪʃən] *n* ความทะเยอทะยาน [khwam tha yoe tha yan]

ambitious [æm'bɪʃəs] *adj* ทะเยอทะยาน [tha yoe tha yan]

ambulance ['æmbjʊləns] *n* รถพยาบาล [rot pha ya ban]; **Call an ambulance** เรียกรถพยาบาล [riak rot pha ya baan]

ambush ['æmbʊʃ] *n* การซุ่มโจมตี [kan sum chom ti]

amenities [ə'miːnɪtɪz] *npl* สิ่งอำนวยความสะดวก [sing am nuai khwam sa duak]

America [ə'mɛrɪkə] *n* ประเทศอเมริกา [pra ted a me ri ka]; **Central America** *n* อเมริกากลาง [a me ri ka klang]; **North America** *n* ทวีปอเมริกาเหนือ [tha wip a me ri ka nuea]; **South America** *n* ทวีปอเมริกาใต้ [tha wip a me ri ka tai]

American [ə'mɛrɪkən] *adj* เกี่ยวกับอเมริกา [kiao kap a me ri ka] ▷ *n* ชาวอเมริกัน [chao a me ri kan]; **American football** *n* ฟุตบอลอเมริกัน [fut bal a me ri kan]; **North American** *n* เกี่ยวกับอเมริกาเหนือ [kiao kap a me ri ka nuea], ผู้อาศัยอยู่ในทวีปอเมริกาเหนือ [kiao kap a me ri ka nuea, phu a sai yu nai tha wip a me ri ka nuea]; **South American** *n* เกี่ยวกับอเมริกาใต้ [kiao kap a me ri ka tai], ชาวอเมริกาใต้ [kiao kap a me ri ka tai, chao a me ri ka tai]

ammunition [ˌæmjʊ'nɪʃən] *n* อาวุธยุทธภัณฑ์ [a wut yut tha phan]

among [ə'mʌŋ] *prep* ท่ามกลาง [tham klang]

amount [ə'maʊnt] *n* จำนวนรวม [cham nuan ruam]

amp [æmp] *n* หน่วยวัดกำลังกระแสไฟฟ้า [nuai wat kam lang kra sae fai fa]

amplifier ['æmplɪˌfaɪə] *n* เครื่องขยายเสียง [khrueang kha yai siang]

amuse [ə'mjuːz] *v* ทำให้หัวเราะ [tham hai hua rao]; **amusement arcade** *n* บริเวณที่มีตู้เกมส์ให้เล่น [bo ri wen thii mii tu kem hai len]

an [ɑːn] *art* คำกำกับนามที่ขึ้นต้นด้วยสระ [kham kam kap nam thii khuen ton duai sa ra]

anaemic [ə'niːmɪk] *adj* ที่เกี่ยวกับโรคโลหิตจาง [thii kiao kap rok lo hit chang]

anaesthetic [ˌænɪsˈθɛtɪk] n ยาชา [ya cha]; **general anaesthetic** n การวางยาสลบ [kan wang ya sa lop]; **local anaesthetic** n ยาชาเฉพาะแห่ง [ya chaa cha pho haeng]

analyse [ˈænəˌlaɪz] v วิเคราะห์ [wi khro]

analysis [əˈnælɪsɪs] n ผลการวิเคราะห์ [phon kan wi khrao]

ancestor [ˈænsɛstə] n บรรพบุรุษ [ban pha bu rut]

anchor [ˈæŋkə] n สมอเรือ [sa mo ruea]

anchovy [ˈæntʃəvɪ] n ปลาแอนโชวี่ [pla an cho vi]

ancient [ˈeɪnʃənt] adj โบราณ [bo ran]

and [ænd; ənd; ən] conj และ [lae]

Andes [ˈændiːz] npl เทือกเขาแอนดีส [thueak khao aen dis]

Andorra [ænˈdɔːrə] n ประเทศแอนดอร่า [pra tet aen do ra]

angel [ˈeɪndʒəl] n นางฟ้า [nang fa]

anger [ˈæŋɡə] n ความโกรธ [khwam krot]

angina [ænˈdʒaɪnə] n โรคอักเสบที่ลำคอจากโรคหัวใจ [rok ak seb thii lam kor chak rok hua jai]

angle [ˈæŋɡ°l] n มุม [mum]; **right angle** n มุมที่ถูกต้อง [mum thii thuk tong]

angler [ˈæŋɡlə] n นักตกปลา [nak tok pla]

angling [ˈæŋɡlɪŋ] n การตกปลา [kan tok pla]

Angola [æŋˈɡəʊlə] n ประเทศแองโกล่า [pra tet aeng ko la]

Angolan [æŋˈɡəʊlən] adj ซึ่งเกี่ยวกับแองโกล่า [sueng kiao kap aeng ko la] ▷ n ชาวแองโกล่า [chao aeng ko la]

angry [ˈæŋɡrɪ] adj โกรธ [krot]

animal [ˈænɪməl] n สัตว์ [sat]

aniseed [ˈænɪˌsiːd] n เมล็ดพืชชนิดหนึ่งใช้เป็นตัวแต่งกลิ่นแต่งรส [ma led phuet cha nit hueng chai pen tua taeng klin taeng rot]

ankle [ˈæŋk°l] n ข้อเท้า [kho thao]

anniversary [ˌænɪˈvɜːsərɪ] n การฉลองครบรอบปี [kan cha long khrop rob pi];

wedding anniversary n ปีครบรอบแต่งงาน [pi khrop rop taeng ngan]

announce [əˈnaʊns] v ประกาศ [pra kat]

announcement [əˈnaʊnsmənt] n การประกาศ [kan pra kat]

annoy [əˈnɔɪ] v ทำให้รำคาญ [tham hai ram khan]

annoying [əˈnɔɪɪŋ] adj น่ารำคาญ [na ram khan]

annual [ˈænjʊəl] adj ประจำปี [pra cham pi]

annually [ˈænjʊəlɪ] adv ซึ่งเกิดปีละครั้ง [sueng koet pi la khrang]

anonymous [əˈnɒnɪməs] adj นิรนาม [ni ra nam]

anorak [ˈænəˌræk] n เสื้อแจ็คเกตตัวใหญ่และหนา [suea chaek ket tua yai lae hna]

anorexia [ˌænɒˈrɛksɪə] n ภาวะไม่อยากหรือทานอาหารไม่ได้ [pha wa mai yak rue than a han mai dai]

anorexic [ˌænɒˈrɛksɪk] adj เกี่ยวกับการทานอาหารไม่ได้ [kiao kap kan than a han mai dai]

another [əˈnʌðə] adj อีกอันหนึ่ง [ik an nueng]

answer [ˈɑːnsə] n คำตอบ [kham top] ▷ v ตอบ [top]

answerphone [ˈɑːnsəfəʊn] n เครื่องตอบรับโทรศัพท์ [khrueang top rap tho ra sap]

ant [ænt] n มด [mot]

antagonize [ænˈtæɡəˌnaɪz] v ทำให้กลายเป็นศัตรู [tham hai klai pen sa tru]

Antarctic [æntˈɑːktɪk] adj บริเวณขั้วโลกใต้ [bor ri ven khua lok tai]; **the Antarctic** n ที่ใกล้บริเวณขั้วโลกใต้ [thii klai bo ri wen khua lok tai]

Antarctica [æntˈɑːktɪkə] n ที่ใกล้บริเวณขั้วโลกใต้ [thii klai bo ri wen khua lok tai]

antelope [ˈæntɪˌləʊp] n ละมั่ง [la mang]

antenatal [ˌæntɪˈneɪt°l] adj ก่อนเกิด [kon koed]

anthem [ˈænθəm] n เพลงชาติ [phleng

chat]

anthropology [ˌænθrəˈpɒlədʒɪ] *n* มนุษยศาสตร์ [ma nut sa ya sat]

antibiotic [ˌæntɪbaɪˈɒtɪk] *n* ยาปฏิชีวนะ [ya pa ti chi wa na]

antibody [ˈæntɪˌbɒdɪ] *n* โปรตีนต่อต้าน เชื้อโรคในร่างกาย [pro tin to tan chuea rok nai rang kai]

anticlockwise [ˌæntɪˈklɒkˌwaɪz] *adv* ที่ ทวนเข็มนาฬิกา [thii thuan khem na li ka]

antidepressant [ˌæntɪdɪˈprɛsᵊnt] *n* ยา ต้านอาการเศร้าซึม [ya tan a kan sao suem]

antidote [ˈæntɪˌdəʊt] *n* ยาถอนพิษ [ya thon phit]

antifreeze [ˈæntɪˌfriːz] *n* สารต้านการ เยือกแข็ง [san tan kan yueak khaeng]

antihistamine [ˌæntɪˈhɪstəˌmiːn; -mɪn] *n* ยาแก้แพ้ชนิดหนึ่ง [ya kae pae cha nit nueng]

antiperspirant [ˌæntɪˈpɜːspərənt] *n* ยา ลดการขับเหงื่อ [ya lot kan khap nguea]

antique [ænˈtiːk] *n* ของเก่า [khong kao]; **antique shop** *n* ร้านขายของเก่า [ran khai khong kao]

antiseptic [ˌæntɪˈsɛptɪk] *n* ยาฆ่าเชื้อโรค [ya kha chuea rok]

antivirus [ˈæntɪˌvaɪrəs] *n* ยาต่อต้านไวรัส [ya to tan vai ras]

anxiety [æŋˈzaɪɪtɪ] *n* ความวิตกกังวล [khwam wi tok kang won]

any [ˈɛnɪ] *pron* จำนวนหนึ่ง [cham nuan nueng], บาง [bang]; **Is there any garlic in it?** มีกระเทียมอยู่ในนี้บ้างไหม? [mii kra thiam yu nai nii bang mai]

anybody [ˈɛnɪˌbɒdɪ; -bədɪ] *pron* ใคร ก็ได้ [khrai ko dai]

anyhow [ˈɛnɪˌhaʊ] *adv* กรณีใด ๆ [ko ra nii dai dai]

anyone [ˈɛnɪˌwʌn; -wən] *pron* ใครสัก คน [khrai sak khon]

anything [ˈɛnɪˌθɪŋ] *pron* อะไรก็ได้ [a rai ko dai]

anyway [ˈɛnɪˌweɪ] *adv* อย่างไรก็ตาม [yang rai ko tam]

anywhere [ˈɛnɪˌwɛə] *adv* ที่ไหนก็ตาม [thii nai ko tam]

apart [əˈpɑːt] *adv* แยกจาก [yaek chak]

apart from [əˈpɑːt frɒm] *prep* นอกจาก [nok chak]

apartment [əˈpɑːtmənt] *n* อพาร์ทเมนท์ [a phat men]; **We're looking for an apartment** เรากำลังมองหาอพาร์ทเมนท์ [rao kam lang mong ha a part ment]; **We've booked an apartment in the hame of...** เราจองอพาร์ทเมนท์ในนาม ของ... [rao chong a part ment nai nam khong...]

aperitif [ɑːˌpɛrɪˈtiːf] *n* การดื่มเหล้าก่อน อาหาร [kan duem lao kon a han]

aperture [ˈæpətʃə] *n* ช่อง [chong]

apologize [əˈpɒləˌdʒaɪz] *v* ขอโทษ [kho thot]

apology [əˈpɒlədʒɪ] *n* คำขอโทษ [kham kho thot]

apostrophe [əˈpɒstrəfɪ] *n* เครื่องหมาย วรรคตอน [khrueang mai wak ton]

appalling [əˈpɔːlɪŋ] *adj* ซึ่งทำให้ตกใจ [sueng tham hai tok jai]

apparatus [ˌæpəˈreɪtəs; -ˈrɑːtəs; ˈæpəˌreɪtəs] *n* เครื่องมือ [khrueang mue]

apparent [əˈpærənt; əˈpɛər-] *adj* ชัดเจน [chat chen]

apparently [əˈpærəntlɪ; əˈpɛər-] *adv* อย่างชัดเจน [yang chat chen]

appeal [əˈpiːl] *n* คำขอร้อง [kham kho rong] ▷ *v* ขออุทธรณ์ [kho ut thon]

appear [əˈpɪə] *v* ดูเหมือนว่า [du muean wa]

appearance [əˈpɪərəns] *n* การปรากฏตัว [kan pra kot tua]

appendicitis [əˌpɛndɪˈsaɪtɪs] *n* ไส้ติ่ง อักเสบ [sai ting ak sep]

appetite [ˈæpɪˌtaɪt] *n* ความอยากอาหาร [khwam yak a han]

applaud [əˈplɔːd] *v* ปรบมือ [prop mue]

applause [əˈplɔːz] *n* การปรบมือแสดง ความชื่นชม [kan prop mue sa daeng khwam chuen chom]

apple ['æpᵊl] *n* แอปเปิ้ล [aep poen];
apple pie *n* ขนมแอปเปิ้ลพาย [kha nom
ap poen phai]

appliance [ə'plaɪəns] *n* เครื่องใช้
[khrueang chai]

applicant ['æplɪkənt] *n* ผู้สมัคร [phu sa
mak]

application [,æplɪ'keɪʃən] *n* ใบสมัคร
[bai sa mak]; **application form** *n* แบบ
ฟอร์มใบสมัคร [baep fom bai sa mak]

apply [ə'plaɪ] *v* ประยุกต์ใช้ [pra yuk chai]

appoint [ə'pɔɪnt] *v* แต่งตั้ง [taeng tang]

appointment [ə'pɔɪntmənt] *n* การแต่ง
ตั้ง [kan taeng tang]

appreciate [ə'priːʃɪˌeɪt; -sɪ-] *v* ยกย่อง
[yok yong]

apprehensive [,æprɪ'hɛnsɪv] *adj*
ตระหนก [tra nak]

apprentice [ə'prɛntɪs] *n* ผู้ฝึกงาน [phu
fuek ngan]

approach [ə'prəʊtʃ] *v* เข้าใกล้ [khao klai]

appropriate [ə'prəʊprɪɪt] *adj* เหมาะสม
[mo som]

approval [ə'pruːvᵊl] *n* การอนุมัติ [kan a
nu mat]

approve [ə'pruːv] *v* อนุมัติ [a nu mat]

approximate [ə'prɒksɪmɪt] *adj*
ประมาณ [pra man]

approximately [ə'prɒksɪmɪtlɪ] *adv*
โดยประมาณ [doi pra man]

apricot ['eɪprɪˌkɒt] *n* ลูกแอปริคอท [luk
ae pri kot]

April ['eɪprəl] *n* เดือนเมษายน [duean me
sa yon]; **April Fools' Day** *n* วันที่เล่น
แกล้งกันหรือล้อเลียน [wan thii len
klaeng kan rue lo lian]

apron ['eɪprən] *n* ผ้ากันเปื้อน [pha kan
puean]

aquarium [ə'kwɛərɪəm] *n* ตู้ปลา [tu
phla]

Aquarius [ə'kwɛərɪəs] *n* ราศีกุมภ์ [ra si
kum]

Arab ['ærəb] *adj* เกี่ยวกับชาวอาหรับ [kiao
kap chao a rap] ▷ *n* ชาวอาหรับ [chao a
rap]; **United Arab Emirates** *npl*
ประเทศยูไนเต็ดอาหรับเอมเรซ [pra tet yu
nai tet a rab e me ret]

Arabic ['ærəbɪk] *adj* ที่เกี่ยวกับอาหรับ
[thii kiao kap a rap] ▷ *n* (*language*)
ภาษาหรืออักขระอาหรับ [pha sa hue ak
kha ra ar hrab]

arbitration [,ɑːbɪ'treɪʃən] *n* การตัดสิน
[kan tat sin]

arch [ɑːtʃ] *n* โครงสร้างที่มีรูปโค้ง [khrong
sang thii mii rup khong]

archaeologist [,ɑːkɪ'ɒlədʒɪst] *n* นัก
โบราณคดี [nak bo ran kha di]

archaeology [,ɑːkɪ'ɒlədʒɪ] *n* วิชา
โบราณคดี [wi cha bo ran kha di]

archbishop ['ɑːtʃ'bɪʃəp] *n* หัวหน้าของ
บิชอพ [hua na khong bi chop]

architect ['ɑːkɪˌtɛkt] *n* สถาปนิก [sa tha
pa nik]

architecture ['ɑːkɪˌtɛktʃə] *n*
สถาปัตยกรรม [sa tha pat ta ya kam]

archive ['ɑːkaɪv] *n* สถานที่เก็บเอกสาร
สำคัญ [sa than thii kep ek ka san som
khan]

Arctic ['ɑːktɪk] *adj* ที่อยู่ใกล้บริเวณขั้วโลก
เหนือ [thii yu klai bo ri wen khua lok
nuea]; **Arctic Circle** *n* วงเขตขั้วโลกเหนือ
[wong khet khua lok nuea]; **Arctic
Ocean** *n* มหาสมุทรขั้วโลกเหนือ [ma ha
sa mut khua lok nuea]; **the Arctic** *n* ที่
อยู่ใกล้บริเวณขั้วโลกเหนือ [thii yu klai bo
ri wen khua lok nuea]

area ['ɛərɪə] *n* บริเวณ [bo ri wen];
service area *n* พื้นที่บริการ [phuen thii
bo ri kan]

Argentina [,ɑːdʒən'tiːnə] *n* ประเทศ
อาร์เจนตินา [pra tet ar chen ti na]

Argentinian [,ɑːdʒən'tɪnɪən] *adj* เกี่ยว
กับประเทศอาร์เจนตินา [kiao kap pra thet
a chen ti na] ▷ *n* (*person*) ชาวอาร์เจนตินา
[chao a chen ti na]

argue ['ɑːgjuː] *v* โต้เถียง [to thiang]

argument ['ɑːgjʊmənt] *n* การโต้เถียง
[kan to thiang]

Aries ['εəriːz] *n* ราศีเมษ [ra si met]

arm [ɑːm] *n* แขน [khaen]; **I can't move my arm** ฉันขยับแขนไม่ได้ [chan kha yap khaen mai dai]

armchair ['ɑːmˌtʃɛə] *n* เก้าอี้มีที่วางแขน [kao ee mee thii wang khaen]

armed [ɑːmd] *adj* ติดอาวุธ [tit a wut]

Armenia [ɑːˈmiːnɪə] *n* ประเทศอาร์มีเนีย [pra tet ar mii nia]

Armenian [ɑːˈmiːnɪən] *adj* เกี่ยวกับประเทศอาร์มีเนีย [kiao kap pra thet a mii nia] ▷ *n (language)* ภาษาอาร์มีเนียน [pha sa ar mii nian], *(person)* ชาวอาร์มีเนียน [chao a mii nian]

armour ['ɑːmə] *n* เสื้อเกราะ [suea kro]

armpit ['ɑːmˌpɪt] *n* รักแร้ [rak rae]

army ['ɑːmɪ] *n* กองทัพ [kang thap]

aroma [əˈrəʊmə] *n* กลิ่นหอม [klin hom]

aromatherapy [əˌrəʊməˈθerəpɪ] *n* การรักษาที่ใช้เครื่องหอมกับสมุนไพร [kan rak sa thii chai khrueang hom kap sa mun phrai]

around [əˈraʊnd] *adv* รอบๆ [rop rop] ▷ *prep* ประมาณ [pra man]; **Could you show us around?** คุณพาเราดูรอบ ๆ ได้ไหม? [khun pha rao du rop rop dai mai]

arrange [əˈreɪndʒ] *v* จัดเตรียม [chat triam]

arrangement [əˈreɪndʒmənt] *n* การจัดเตรียม [kan chat triam]

arrears [əˈrɪəz] *npl* เงินค้างชำระ [ngoen kang cham ra]

arrest [əˈrɛst] *n* การจับกุม [kan chap kum] ▷ *v* จับกุม [chap khum]

arrival [əˈraɪvəl] *n* การมาถึง [kan ma thueng]

arrive [əˈraɪv] *v* มาถึง [ma thueng]; **I've just arrived** ฉันเพิ่งมาถึง [chan phoeng ma thueng]; **My suitcase has arrived damaged** กระเป๋าเดินทางของฉันเสียหายเมื่อมาถึง [kra pao doen thang khong chan sia hai muea ma thueng]; **We arrived early/late** เรามาถึงก่อนเวลา/ช้า [rao ma thueng kon we la / cha]

arrogant ['ærəgənt] *adj* หยิ่งยโส [ying ya so]

arrow ['ærəʊ] *n* ลูกธนู [luk tha nu]

arson ['ɑːsən] *n* การลอบวางเพลิง [kan lop wang phloeng]

art [ɑːt] *n* ศิลป์ [sin]; **art gallery** *n* ห้องแสดงงานศิลปะ [hong sa daeng ngan sin la pa]; **art school** *n* โรงเรียนศิลปะ [rong rian sin la pa]; **work of art** *n* งานศิลปะ [ngan sin la pa]

artery ['ɑːtərɪ] *n* เส้นเลือดแดงที่นำเลือดแดงออกจากหัวใจ [sen lueat daeng thii nam lueat daeng ok chak hua jai]

arthritis [ɑːˈθraɪtɪs] *n* โรคข้อต่ออักเสบ [rok kho to ak sep]

artichoke ['ɑːtɪˌtʃəʊk] *n* พันธุ์ไม้ชนิดหนึ่งใช้ดอกทำอาหาร [phan mai cha nit nueng chai dok tham a han]

article ['ɑːtɪkəl] *n* บทความ [bot khwam]

artificial [ˌɑːtɪˈfɪʃəl] *adj* เทียม [thiam]

artist ['ɑːtɪst] *n* ศิลปิน [sin la pin]

artistic [ɑːˈtɪstɪk] *adj* เกี่ยวกับศิลปะ [kiao kap sin la pa]

as [əz] *adv* อย่างพอ ๆ กัน [yang pho pho kan] ▷ *conj* ขณะที่ ดังที่ เนื่องจาก [kha na thii, dang thii, nueang chak] ▷ *prep* ในฐานะ [nai tha na]

asap [eɪsæp] *abbr* ตัวย่อของเร็วที่สุดเท่าที่จะเป็นไปได้ [tua yo khong reo thii sut thao thii ja pen pai dai]

ascent [əˈsɛnt] *n* **When is the last ascent?** ปีนขึ้นทางชันครั้งสุดท้ายเมื่อไร? [pin khuen thang chan khrang sut thai muea rai]

ashamed [əˈʃeɪmd] *adj* อับอาย [ap ai]

ashore [əˈʃɔː] *adv* **Can we go ashore now?** เราขึ้นฝั่งตอนนี้ได้ไหม? [rao khuen fang ton nii dai mai]

ashtray ['æʃˌtreɪ] *n* ที่เขี่ยบุหรี่ [thi khia bu ri]; **May I have an ashtray?** ฉันขอที่เขี่ยบุหรี่ได้ไหม? [chan kho thii khia bu ri dai mai]

Asia ['eɪʃə; 'eɪʒə] *n* ทวีปเอเชีย [tha wip e

chia]

Asian ['eɪʃən; 'eɪʒən] *adj* เกี่ยวกับประเทศ
ในเอเชีย [kiao kap pra thet nai e chia]
▷ *n* ชาวเอเชีย [chao e chia]

Asiatic [ˌeɪʃɪ'ætɪk; -zɪ-] *adj* เอเชีย [e chia]

ask [ɑːsk] *v* ถาม [tham]

ask for [ɑːsk fɔː] *v* ขอให้ทำ [kho hai
tham]

asleep [ə'sliːp] *adj* นอนหลับ [non lap]

asparagus [ə'spærəgəs] *n* หน่อไม้ฝรั่ง
[no mai fa rang]

aspect ['æspɛkt] *n* มุมมอง [mum mong]

aspirin ['æsprɪn] *n* ยาแอสไพริน [ya as
phai rin]

assembly [ə'sɛmblɪ] *n* การรวมกลุ่ม [kan
ruam klum]

asset ['æsɛt] *n* ประโยชน์ [pra yot];
assets *npl* สินทรัพย์ [sin sap]

assignment [ə'saɪnmənt] *n* งานที่ได้รับ
มอบหมาย [ngan thii dai rap mop mai]

assistance [ə'sɪstəns] *n* ความช่วยเหลือ
[khwam chuai luea]

assistant [ə'sɪstənt] *n* ผู้ช่วย [phu
chuai]; **personal assistant** *n* ผู้ช่วยส่วน
ตัว [phu chuai suan tua]; **sales
assistant** *n* พนักงานขาย [pha nak
ngan khai]; **shop assistant** *n* พนักงาน
ขายของ [pha nak ngan khai khong]

associate *adj* [ə'səʊʃɪɪt] ที่เกี่ยวเนื่อง [thii
kiao nueang] ▷ *n* [ə'səʊʃɪɪt] ผู้มีความ
สัมพันธ์กัน เช่น ผู้ร่วมงาน เพื่อน หุ้นส่วน
[phu mee khwam sam phan kan chen
phu ruam ngan phuean hun suan]

association [əˌsəʊsɪ'eɪʃən; -ʃɪ-] *n* กลุ่ม
สมาคม [klum, sa ma khom]

assortment [ə'sɔːtmənt] *n* การจัด
ประเภท [kan chat pra phet]

assume [ə'sjuːm] *v* ทึกทักเอา [thuek
thak ao]

assure [ə'ʃʊə] *v* ให้ความมั่นใจ [hai
khwam man jai]

asthma ['æsmə] *n* โรคหืด [rok huet]

astonish [ə'stɒnɪʃ] *v* ทำให้แปลกใจ
[tham hai plaek jai]

astonished [ə'stɒnɪʃt] *adj* ที่ประหลาดใจ
[thii pra lat jai]

astonishing [ə'stɒnɪʃɪŋ] *adj* น่า
ประหลาดใจ [na pra hlad jai]

astrology [ə'strɒlədʒɪ] *n* โหราศาสตร์
[ho ra sat]

astronaut ['æstrəˌnɔːt] *n* มนุษย์อวกาศ
[ma nut a wa kat]

astronomy [ə'strɒnəmɪ] *n* ดาราศาสตร์
[da ra sat]

asylum [ə'saɪləm] *n* ที่ลี้ภัย [thii lii
phai]; **asylum seeker** *n* ผู้แสวงหาที่ลี้ภัย
[phu sa waeng ha thii lii phai]

at [æt] *prep* ที่ [thi]; **Do we stop at...?**
เราหยุดจอดที่...หรือเปล่า? [rao yut jot
thii...rue plao]; **I'm delighted to
meet you at last** ฉันดีใจที่ได้พบคุณใน
ท้ายที่สุด [chan di jai thii dai phop
khun nai thai thii sut]; **I'm staying at
a hotel** ฉันพักที่โรงแรม [chan phak thii
rong raem]

atheist ['eɪθɪˌɪst] *n* ผู้เชื่อว่าพระเจ้าไม่มี
จริง [phu chuea wa phra chao mai mii
ching]

athlete ['æθliːt] *n* นักกีฬา [nak ki la]

athletic [æθ'lɛtɪk] *adj* ในด้านกีฬา [nai
dan ki la]

athletics [æθ'lɛtɪks] *npl* การเล่นกีฬาทั้ง
ทางลู่และลาน [kan len ki la thang thang
lu lae lan]

Atlantic [ət'læntɪk] *n* มหาสมุทร
แอตแลนติก [ma ha sa mut at laen tik]

atlas ['ætləs] *n* สมุดแผนที่ [sa mut phaen
thii]

atmosphere ['ætməsˌfɪə] *n* บรรยากาศ
[ban ya kat]

atom ['ætəm] *n* อะตอม [a tom]; **atom
bomb** *n* ระเบิดปรมาณู [ra boet pa ra ma
nu]

atomic [ə'tɒmɪk] *adj* เกี่ยวกับปรมาณู
[kiao kap pa ra ma nu]

attach [ə'tætʃ] *v* ติดกัน [tid kan]

attached [ə'tætʃt] *adj* ที่ติดกัน [thii tid
kan]

attachment [ə'tætʃmənt] *n* การผูกติด สิ่งที่แนบมา [kan phuk tit, sing thii naep ma]

attack [ə'tæk] *n* การโจมตี [kan chom ti] ▷ *v* โจมตี [chom ti]; **heart attack** *n* หัวใจ วาย [hua jai wai]; **terrorist attack** *n* การถูกโจมตีจากผู้ก่อการร้าย [kan thuk chom ti chak phu ko kan rai]

attempt [ə'tɛmpt] *n* ความพยายาม [khwam pha ya yam] ▷ *v* พยายาม [pha ya yom]

attend [ə'tɛnd] *v* เข้าร่วม [khao ruam]

attendance [ə'tɛndəns] *n* การเข้าชั้น เรียน [kan khao chan rian]

attendant [ə'tɛndənt] *n* **flight attendant** *n* เจ้าหน้าที่ตอนรับบนเครื่องบิน [chao na thii ton rap bon khrueang bin]

attention [ə'tɛnʃən] *n* ความตั้งใจ [khwam tang jai]

attic ['ætɪk] *n* ห้องใต้หลังคา [hong tai lang kha]

attitude ['ætɪˌtjuːd] *n* ทัศนคติ ความเห็น [that sa na kha ti, khwam hen]

attorney [ə'tɜːnɪ] *n* ทนาย นิติกร [tha nai, ni ti kon]

attract [ə'trækt] *v* ดึงดูดความสนใจ [dueng dut khwam son jai]

attraction [ə'trækʃən] *n* การดึงดูดความ สนใจ [kan dueng dud khwam son jai]

attractive [ə'træktɪv] *adj* มีเสน่ห์ดึงดูด [mii sa ne dueng dut]

aubergine ['əʊbəˌʒiːn] *n* มะเขือฝรั่งมีสี ม่วงผลยาวใหญ่ [ma khuea fa rang mii sii muang phon yao yai]

auburn ['ɔːbən] *adj* สีน้ำตาลอมแดง [see nam tan om daeng]

auction ['ɔːkʃən] *n* การประมูล [kan pra mun]

audience ['ɔːdɪəns] *n* ผู้ชม [phu chom]

audit ['ɔːdɪt] *n* การตรวจสอบบัญชี [kan truat sob ban chii] ▷ *v* ตรวจสอบบัญชี [truat sop ban chii]

audition [ɔː'dɪʃən] *n* การทดสอบการแสดง [kan thot sop kan sa daeng]

auditor ['ɔːdɪtə] *n* ผู้สอบบัญชี [phu sob ban che]

August ['ɔːgəst] *n* เดือนสิงหาคม [duean sing ha khom]

aunt [ɑːnt] *n* ป้า น้า อาผู้หญิง [pa na a phu ying]

auntie ['ɑːntɪ] *n* ป้า น้า อาผู้หญิง [pa na a phu ying]

au pair [əʊ 'pɛə; o pɛr] *n* คนเลี้ยงดูเด็ก [khon liang du dek]

austerity [ɒ'stɛrɪtɪ] *n* ความเคร่งครัด [khwam khreng khrat]

Australasia [ˌɒstrə'leɪzɪə] *n* ออสเตรเลีย [os tre lia]

Australia [ɒ'streɪlɪə] *n* ประเทศ ออสเตรเลีย [pra tet os tre lia]

Australian [ɒ'streɪlɪən] *adj* ที่เกี่ยวกับ ออสเตรเลีย [thii kiao kap os tre lia] ▷ *n* ชาวออสเตรเลีย [chao os tre lia]

Austria ['ɒstrɪə] *n* ประเทศออสเตรีย [pra tet os tria]

Austrian ['ɒstrɪən] *adj* ที่เกี่ยวกับ ออสเตรีย [thii kiao kap os tria] ▷ *n* ชา วออสเตรเรียน [chao os trian]

authentic [ɔː'θɛntɪk] *adj* ของแท้ [khong thae]

author, authoress ['ɔːθə, 'ɔːθəˌrɛs] *n* นักประพันธ์ [nak pra phan]

authorize ['ɔːθəˌraɪz] *v* ให้อำนาจ [hai am nat]

autobiography [ˌɔːtəʊbaɪ'ɒgrəfɪ; ˌɔːtəbaɪ-] *n* อัตชีวประวัติ [at ta chi wa pra wat]

autograph ['ɔːtəˌgrɑːf; -ˌgræf] *n* ลาย เซ็น [lai sen]

automatic [ˌɔːtə'mætɪk] *adj* อัตโนมัติ [at ta no mat]; **An automatic, please** ขอ ค้นขับแบบอัตโนมัติ [kho khan khap baep at ta no mat]; **Is it an automatic car?** เป็นรถขับแบบอัตโนมัติหรือเปล่า? [pen rot khap baep at ta no mat rue plao]

automatically [ˌɔːtə'mætɪklɪ] *adv* โดย อัตโนมัติ [doi at ta no mat]

autonomous [ɔː'tɒnəməs] *adj* ซึ่ง

ปกครองตนเอง [sueng pok khrong ton ang]

autonomy [ɔː'tɒnəmɪ] *n* การปกครอง ตนเอง [kan pok khrong ton eng]

autumn ['ɔːtəm] *n* ฤดูใบไม้ร่วง [rue du bai mai ruang]

availability [ə'veɪləbɪlɪtɪ] *n* มีผลใช้ได้ [mii phon chai dai]

available [ə'veɪləbəl] *adj* มีอยู่ [mii yu]

avalanche ['ævəˌlɑːntʃ] *n* หิมะถล่ม [hi ma tha lom]; **Is there a danger of avalanches?** มีอันตรายเกี่ยวกับหิมะถล่ม ไหม? [mii an ta rai kiao kap hi ma tha lom mai]

avenue ['ævɪˌnjuː] *n* ถนนสายใหญ่ [tha non sai yai]

average ['ævərɪdʒ; 'ævrɪdʒ] *adj* โดย เฉลี่ย [doi cha lia] ▷ *n* ค่าเฉลี่ย [kha cha lia]

avocado, avocados [ˌævəˈkɑːdəʊ, ˌævəˈkɑːdəʊs] *n* ผลอะโวคาโด้ [phon a vo kha do]

avoid [ə'vɔɪd] *v* หลีกเลี่ยง [lik liang]

awake [ə'weɪk] *adj* ตื่น [tuen] ▷ *v* ปลุก ทำให้ตื่น [pluk, tham hai tuen]

award [ə'wɔːd] *n* รางวัล [rang wan]

aware [ə'wɛə] *adj* ตระหนักรู้ [tra nak ru]

away [ə'weɪ] *adv* ไปที่อื่น [pai thii aue]; **away match** *n* การแข่งขันที่ไปเล่นที่อื่น [kan khaeng khan thii pai len thii uen]

awful ['ɔːfʊl] *adj* แย่มาก [yae mak]; **What awful weather!** อากาศแย่มาก [a kaat yae mak]

awfully ['ɔːfəlɪ; 'ɔːflɪ] *adv* อย่างเลวร้าย [yang leo rai]

awkward ['ɔːkwəd] *adj* งุ่มง่าม [ngum ngam]

axe [æks] *n* ขวาน [khwan]

axle ['æksəl] *n* แกน เพลา [kaen, phlao]

Azerbaijan [ˌæzəbaɪ'dʒɑːn] *n* ประเทศอา เซอร์ไบจาน [pra tet a soe bi chan]

Azerbaijani [ˌæzəbaɪ'dʒɑːnɪ] *adj* เกี่ยวกับ อาเซอร์ไบจาน [kiao kap a soe bai chan] ▷ *n* ชาวอาเซอร์ไบจาน [chao a soe bi chan]

B&B [biː ænd biː] *n* ตัวย่อของเตียงนอน และอาหารเช้า [tua yo khong tiang non lae a han chao]

BA [bɑː] *abbr* ปริญญาตรี [pa rin ya tree]

baby ['beɪbɪ] *n* เด็กทารก [dek tha rok]; **baby milk** *n* นมสำหรับเด็กทารก [nom sam rap dek tha rok]; **baby wipe** *n* กระดาษหรือผ้าเช็ดตัวเด็ก [kra dat rue pha chet tua dek]; **baby's bottle** *n* ขวดนม เด็ก [khaut nom dek]

babysit ['beɪbɪsɪt] *v* ช่วยดูแลเด็ก [chuai du lae dek]

babysitter ['beɪbɪsɪtə] *n* ผู้ช่วยเลี้ยงเด็ก [phu chuai liang dek]

babysitting ['beɪbɪsɪtɪŋ] *n* การเป็นผู้ ช่วยเลี้ยงเด็ก [kan pen phu chuai liang dek]

bachelor ['bætʃələ; 'bætʃlə] *n* ชายโสด [chai sot]

back [bæk] *adj* ซึ่งผ่านมาแล้ว ซึ่งอยู่ด้าน หลัง [sueng phan ma laeo, sueng yu dan lang] ▷ *adv* กลับไปสภาพเดิม [klap pai sa phap doem] ▷ *n* หลัง ส่วนหลัง [lang, suan lang] ▷ *v* ถอยหลัง [thoi lang]; **back pain** *n* ปวดหลัง [puat lang]

backache ['bæk,eɪk] n อาการปวดหลัง [a kan puad hlang]

backbone ['bæk,bəʊn] n กระดูกสันหลัง [kra duk san lang]

backfire [,bæk'faɪə] v ให้ผลตรงข้ามกับที่ตั้งใจไว้ [hai phon trong kham kap thii tang jai wai]

background ['bæk,graʊnd] n ภูมิหลัง [phum hlang]

backing ['bækɪŋ] n ความช่วยเหลือ ผู้ช่วยเหลือ [khwam chuai hluea phu chuai hluea]

back out [bæk aʊt] v กลับคำ [klab kham]

backpack ['bæk,pæk] n กระเป๋าสะพายหลัง [kra pao sa phai lang]

backpacker ['bæk,pækə] n ผู้ใส่กระเป๋าสะพายหลัง [phu sai kra pao sa phai hlang]

backpacking ['bæk,pækɪŋ] n การใส่กระเป๋าสะพายหลัง [kan sai kra pao sa phai lang]

backside [,bæk'saɪd] n ด้านหลัง [dan hlang]

backslash ['bæk,slæʃ] n เครื่องหมาย มักใช้ในคอมพิวเตอร์ [khrueang mai mak chai nai khom phio toe]

backstroke ['bæk,strəʊk] n ท่าว่ายน้ำแบบตีกรรเชียง [tha wai nam baep ti kan chiang]

back up [bæk ʌp] v สนับสนุน [sa nap sa nun]

backup [bæk,ʌp] n สนับสนุน [sa nap sa nun]

backwards ['bækwədz] adv ถอยหลัง [thoi lang]

bacon ['beɪkən] n เนื้อด้านหลังและส่วนนอกของหมูที่ใส่เกลือรมควัน [nuea dan lang lae suan nok khong mu thii sai kluea rom khwan]

bacteria [bæk'tɪərɪə] npl เชื้อแบคทีเรีย [chuea baek thi ria]

bad [bæd] adj เลว [leo]

badge [bædʒ] n เข็มเครื่องหมาย [khem khrueang mai]

badger ['bædʒə] n สัตว์สี่เท้ามีขนสีเทาหัวมีลายเส้นสีขาวตัดกับขนสีเทา [sat si thao mee khon see thao hua mee lai sen see khao tad kab khon see thao]

badly ['bædlɪ] adv เลว [leo]

badminton ['bædmɪntən] n แบดมินตัน [bat min tan]

bad-tempered [bæd'tɛmpəd] adj อารมณ์เสีย [a rom sia]

baffled ['bæf°ld] adj ทำให้งงงวย [tham hai ngong nguai]

bag [bæg] n กระเป๋า ถุง [kra pao, thung]; **bum bag** n กระเป๋าเล็กที่ติดเข็มขัดสวมรอบเอว [kra pao lek thii tit khem khat suam rop eo]; **carrier bag** n ถุงใส่ของ [thung sai khong]; **overnight bag** n กระเป๋าเดินทางใบเล็กใช้เพื่อค้างคืน [kra pao doen thang bai lek chai phuea khang khuen]

baggage ['bægɪdʒ] n กระเป๋าเดินทาง [kra pao doen thang]; **baggage allowance** n การอนุญาตให้มีกระเป๋าเดินทางตามที่กำหนด [kan a nu yat hai mii kra pao doen thang tam thii kam not]; **baggage reclaim** n ที่เรียกเก็บกระเป๋าเดินทาง [thii riak kep kra pao doen thang]; **excess baggage** n กระเป๋าที่มีน้ำหนักเกิน [kra pao thii mii nam nak koen]; **What is the baggage allowance?** อนุญาตน้ำหนักกระเป๋าเดินทางเท่าไร? [a nu yaat nam nak kra pao doen thang thao rai]

baggy ['bægɪ] adj โป่งหรือพองเหมือนถุง [pong rue phong muean thung]

bagpipes ['bæg,paɪps] npl ปี่สก๊อต [pi sa kot]

Bahamas [bə'hɑːməz] npl ประเทศบาฮามาส [pra tet ba ha mas]

Bahrain [bɑː'reɪn] n ประเทศบาร์เรน [pra tet bar ren]

bail [beɪl] n การประกันตัว [kan pra kan tua]

bake [beɪk] v อบ [op]

baked [beɪkt] *adj* อบ [op]; **baked potato** *n* มันอบ [man op]

baker ['beɪkə] *n* คนทำขนมปัง [kon tham kha nom pang]

bakery ['beɪkərɪ] *n* ร้านขายขนมปัง [ran khai kha nom pang]

baking ['beɪkɪŋ] *n* การอบ [kan op]; **baking powder** *n* ผงฟู [phong fu]

balance ['bæləns] *n* ความสมดุล [khwam som dun]; **balance sheet** *n* งบดุล [ngop dun]; **bank balance** *n* งบดุลธนาคาร [ngop dun tha na khan]

balanced ['bælənst] *adj* ที่สมดุล [thii som dun]

balcony ['bælkənɪ] *n* ระเบียง [ra biang]; **Do you have a room with a balcony?** คุณมีห้องที่มีระเบียงไหม? [khun mii hong thii mii ra biang mai]

bald [bɔːld] *adj* ล้าน [lan]

Balkan ['bɔːlkən] *adj* ประเทศในคาบสมุทรบอลข่าน [pra tet nai khap sa mut bon khan]

ball [bɔːl] *n (dance)* งานบอล [ngan bon], *(toy)* ลูกบอล [luk bon]

ballerina [ˌbælə'riːnə] *n* นักเต้นบัลเลต์หญิง [nak ten bal le ying]

ballet ['bæleɪ; bæ'leɪ] *n* ระบำปลายเท้า [ra bam plai thao]; **ballet dancer** *n* นักเต้นระบำปลายเท้า [nak ten ra bam plai thao]; **ballet shoes** *npl* รองเท้าบัลเลต์ [rong thao ban le]

balloon [bə'luːn] *n* ลูกโป่ง [luk pong]

bamboo [bæm'buː] *n* ต้นไผ่ [ton phai]

ban [bæn] *n* คำสั่งห้าม [kham sang ham] ▷ *v* ห้าม [ham]

banana [bə'nɑːnə] *n* กล้วย [kluai]

band [bænd] *n (musical group)* วงดนตรี [wong don tri], *(strip)* สายคาด [sai khat]; **brass band** *n* วงดนตรีเครื่องเป่า [wong don tree khrueang pao]; **elastic band** *n* ยางยืด [yang yuet]; **rubber band** *n* ยางรัด [yang rat]

bandage ['bændɪdʒ] *n* ผ้าพันแผล [pha phan phae] ▷ *v* พันแผล [phan phae]; **I'd like a bandage** ฉันอยากได้ผ้าพันแผล [chan yak dai pha phan phlae]; **I'd like a fresh bandage** ฉันอยากได้ผ้าพันแผลใหม่ [chan yak dai pha phan phlae mai]

Band-Aid® ['bændeɪd] *n* ผ้าพลาสเตอร์ [pha plas toe]

bang [bæŋ] *n* เสียงดังมาก [siang dang mak] ▷ *v* ตีอย่างแรง ปิดอย่างแรง [ti yang raeng pid yang raeng]

Bangladesh [ˌbɑːŋglə'dɛʃ; ˌbæŋ-] *n* ประเทศบังคลาเทศ [pra tet bang khla tet]

Bangladeshi [ˌbɑːŋglə'dɛʃɪ; ˌbæŋ-] *adj* ที่เกี่ยวกับประเทศบังคลาเทศ [thii kiao kap pra tet bang khla tet] ▷ *n* ชาวบังคลาเทศ [chao bang khla tet]

banister ['bænɪstə] *n* ราวระเบียง [rao ra biang]

banjo ['bændʒəʊ] *n* แบนโจ เครื่องดนตรี [baen jo khrueang don trii]

bank [bæŋk] *n (finance)* ธนาคาร [tha na kan], *(ridge)* ตลิ่ง [ta ling]; **bank account** *n* บัญชีธนาคาร [ban chi tha na khan]; **How far is the bank?** ธนาคารอยู่ไกลแค่ไหน? [tha na khan yu klai khae nai]; **I would like to transfer some money from my bank in...** ฉันอยากโอนเงินบางส่วนจากธนาคารของฉันที่... [chan yak on ngoen bang suan chak tha na khan khong chan thii...]; **Is the bank open today?** วันนี้ธนาคารเปิดไหม? [wan nii tha na khan poet mai]

banker ['bæŋkə] *n* นายธนาคาร [nai tha na khan]

banknote ['bæŋkˌnəʊt] *n* ธนบัตร [tha na bat]

bankrupt ['bæŋkrʌpt; -rəpt] *adj* ล้มละลาย [lom la lai]

banned [bænd] *adj* ถูกห้าม [thuk ham]

Baptist ['bæptɪst] *n* ผู้ทำพิธีล้างบาป [phu tham phi thi lang bap]

bar [bɑː] *n (alcohol)* บาร์ ที่จำหน่ายเครื่องดื่ม [baa thii cham nai khrueang duem], (strip) แถบ เส้น ริ้ว [thaep, sen, rio]; **snack bar** n ห้องทานอาหารว่าง [hong than a han wang]

Barbados [bɑːˈbeɪdəʊs; -dəʊz; -dɒs] n ประเทศบาร์เบโดส [pra tet bar be dos]

barbaric [bɑːˈbærɪk] adj ป่าเถื่อน [pa thuean]

barbecue [ˈbɑːbɪˌkjuː] n บาร์บีคิว [ba bi kio]

barber [ˈbɑːbə] n ช่างตัดผม [chang tad phom]

bare [beə] adj เปลือยเปล่า [pluea plao] ▷ v ทำให้โล่ง เปิดเผยออกมา [tham hai long, poet phoei ok ma]

barefoot [ˈbeəˌfʊt] adj เท้าเปล่า [thao plao] ▷ adv เท้าเปล่า [thao plao]

barely [ˈbeəlɪ] adv เกือบไม่พอ [kueap mai pho]

bargain [ˈbɑːgɪn] n การต่อรอง [kan to rong]

barge [bɑːdʒ] n เรือบรรทุก เรือที่ใช้ในพิธี [ruea ban thuk ruea thii chai nai phi ti]

bark [bɑːk] v เห่า [hao]

barley [ˈbɑːlɪ] n ข้าวบาร์เล่ย์ [khao ba le]

barmaid [ˈbɑːˌmeɪd] n หญิงเสริฟเครื่อง ดื่มในบาร์ [ying soep khrueang duem nai ba]

barman, barmen [ˈbɑːmən, ˈbɑːmɛn] n ชายเสิร์ฟเครื่องดื่มในบาร์ [chai soep khrueang duem nai bar]

barn [bɑːn] n โรงนา [rong na]

barrel [ˈbærəl] n ถังใส่ของเหลว [thang sai khong leo]

barrier [ˈbærɪə] n สิ่งกีดขวาง [sing kit khwang]; **ticket barrier** n เครื่องกีดกั้นที่ ต้องแสดงตั๋วก่อนผ่านเข้าไป [khrueang kit kan thii tong sa daeng tua kon phan khao pai]

bartender [ˈbɑːˌtɛndə] n บาร์เทนเดอร์ [ba ten doe]

base [beɪs] n พื้นฐาน ฐานทัพ [phuen than, than thap]

baseball [ˈbeɪsˌbɔːl] n กีฬาเบสบอล [ki la

bes bal]; **baseball cap** n หมวกแก๊บ สำหรับเล่นเบสบอล [muak kaep sam rap len bes bal]

based [beɪst] adj ซึ่งเป็นรากฐาน [sueng pen rak than]

basement [ˈbeɪsmənt] n ห้องใต้ดิน [hong tai din]

bash [bæʃ] n ชนอย่างแรง [chon yang raeng] ▷ v ตีอย่างรุนแรง [ti yang run raeng]

basic [ˈbeɪsɪk] adj พื้นฐาน ธรรมดา [phuen than, tham ma da]

basically [ˈbeɪsɪklɪ] adv โดยพื้นฐาน [doi phuen than]

basics [ˈbeɪsɪks] npl สิ่งที่เป็นพื้นฐาน [sing thii pen phuen than]

basil [ˈbæzˀl] n ใบโหระพา [bai ho ra pha]

basin [ˈbeɪsˀn] n อ่างน้ำ [ang nam]

basis [ˈbeɪsɪs] n รากฐาน [rak than]

basket [ˈbɑːskɪt] n ตระกร้า [tra kra]; **wastepaper basket** n ตะกร้าใส่ขยะ [ta kra sai kha ya]

basketball [ˈbɑːskɪtˌbɔːl] n กีฬา บาสเกตบอล [ki la bas ket bal]

Basque [bæsk; bɑːsk] adj เกี่ยวกับชาว บาสค์ [kiao kap chao bas] ▷ n (language) ภาษาบาสค์ [pha sa bas], (person) ชาว บาสค์ [chao bas]

bass [beɪs] n โทนเสียงต่ำ [thon siang tam]; **bass drum** n กลองที่มีเสียงต่ำ [klong thii mii siang tam]; **double bass** n ดนตรีเครื่องสายชนิดหนึ่ง [don tree khrueang sai cha nit nueng]

bassoon [bəˈsuːn] n ปี่ใหญ่ [pi yai]

bat [bæt] n (mammal) ค้างคาว [khang khao], (with ball) ไม้ตีลูกบอล [mai ti luk bon]

bath [bɑːθ] n **bubble bath** n ฟองอาบน้ำ [fong aap nam]

bathe [beɪð] v อาบน้ำ [ap nam]

bathrobe [ˈbɑːθˌrəʊb] n เสื้อคลุมอาบน้ำ [suea khlum aap nam]

bathroom [ˈbɑːθˌruːm; -ˌrʊm] n ห้องน้ำ [hong nam]; **Are there support**

railings in the bathroom? มีราวช่วย
พยุงในห้องน้ำไหม? [mii rao chuai pha
yung nai hong nam mai]; **Does the
room have a private bathroom?** มี
ห้องน้ำส่วนตัวในห้องไหม? [mii hong
nam suan tua nai hong mai]; **The
bathroom is flooded** ห้องน้ำมีน้ำท่วม
[hong nam mii nam thuam]

baths [bɑːθz] npl สระว่ายน้ำ [sa wai
nam]

bathtub [ˈbɑːθˌtʌb] n อ่างอาบน้ำ [ang
aap nam]

batter [ˈbætə] n ส่วนผสมที่ทำจากแป้งนม
และไข่ [suan pha som thii tham chak
paeng num lae khai]

battery [ˈbætərɪ] n แบตเตอรี่ [bat toe ri];
Do you have any batteries? คุณมี
แบตเตอรี่ไหม? [khun mii baet toe ri
mai]; **Do you have batteries for this
camera?** คุณมีแบตเตอรี่สำหรับกล้องนี้
ไหม? [khun mii baet toe ri sam rap
klong nii mai]; **I need a new battery**
ฉันอยากได้แบตเตอรี่ใหม่ [chan yak dai
baet toe ri mai]

battle [ˈbætəl] n การสู้รบ [kan su rop]

battleship [ˈbætəlˌʃɪp] n เรือรบ [ruea
rob]

bay [beɪ] n อ่าว [ao]; **bay leaf** n ใบอบเชย
[bai op choei]

BC [biː siː] abbr ตัวย่อของก่อนคริสต์ศักราช
[tua yo khong kon khrit sak ka rat]

be [biː; bɪ] v เป็น อยู่ คือ [pen, yu, khue]

beach [biːtʃ] n ชายหาด [chai hat]; **Are
there any good beaches near here?**
มีชายหาดดีๆ ใกล้ที่นี่ไหม? [mee chai had
di di kai thii ni mai]; **How far is the
beach?** ชายหาดอยู่ไกลแค่ไหน? [chai
hat yu klai khae nai]; **I'm going to the
beach** ฉันจะไปที่ชายหาด [chan ja pai
thii chai hat]

bead [biːd] n ลูกปัด [luk pat]

beak [biːk] n จะงอยปากนก [cha ngoi pak
nok]

beam [biːm] n ลำแสง คานรับน้ำหนัก รอย

ยิ้มกว้าง [lam saeng, khan rap nam
nak, roi yim kwang]

bean [biːn] n ถั่ว [thua]; **broad bean** n
ถั่วชนิดหนึ่งเป็นผัก [thua cha nit nueng
pen phak]; **coffee bean** n เมล็ดกาแฟ
[ma let ka fae]; **French beans** npl ถั่ว
คล้ายถั่วฝักยาว [thua khlai thua fak
yao]

beansprout [ˈbiːnspraʊt] n
beansprouts npl ถั่วงอก [thua ngok]

bear [bɛə] n หมี [mi] ▷ v ทน [thon];
polar bear n หมีขั้วโลก [mii khua lok];
teddy bear n ตุ๊กตาหมี [tuk ka ta mii]

beard [bɪəd] n เครา [khrao]

bearded [bɪədɪd] adj ที่เต็มไปด้วยหนวด
เครา [thii tem pai duai nuat khrao]

bear up [bɛə ʌp] v ยังแข็งแรง [yang
khaeng raeng]

beat [biːt] n การตี [kan ti] ▷ v (outdo)
ทำให้พ่ายแพ้ [tham hai phai phae],
(strike) ตี [ti]

beautiful [ˈbjuːtɪfʊl] adj สวยงาม [suai
ngam]

beautifully [ˈbjuːtɪflɪ] adv อย่างสวยงาม
[yang suai ngam]

beauty [ˈbjuːtɪ] n ความงาม [khwam
ngam]; **beauty salon** n ร้านเสริมสวย
[ran soem suai]; **beauty spot** n สถานที่
สวยงาม [sa than thii suai ngam]

beaver [ˈbiːvə] n สัตว์ครึ่งบกครึ่งน้ำคล้าย
นาก [sat khrueng bok khrueng nam
khlai nak]

because [bɪˈkɒz; -ˈkəz] conj เพราะว่า
[phro wa]

become [bɪˈkʌm] v กลายเป็น [klai pen]

bed [bɛd] n เตียงนอน [tiang norn]; **bed
and breakfast** n ที่พักค้างแรมที่ให้อาหาร
เช้า [thii phak kang raem thii hai a
han chao]; **bunk beds** npl เตียงชั้น
[tiang chan]; **camp bed** n เตียงผ้าใบน้ำ
หนักเบา [tiang pha bai nam nak bao]

bedclothes [ˈbɛdˌkləʊðz] npl ของใช้บน
เตียงนอน เช่น ผ้าห่ม ฟูก [khong chai bon
tiang non chen pha hom fuk]

bedding ['bɛdɪŋ] *n* เครื่องนอน [khrueang non]

bedroom ['bɛd,ruːm; -,rʊm] *n* ห้องนอน [hong non]; **Do you have any bedrooms on the ground floor?** คุณมีห้องนอนอยู่ชั้นล่างไหม? [khun mii hong non yu chan lang mai]

bedsit ['bɛd,sɪt] *n* ห้องเดี่ยวที่รวมเป็นทั้งห้องนอนและนั่งเล่น [hong diao thii ruam pen thang hong norn lae nang len]

bedspread ['bɛd,sprɛd] *n* ผ้าคลุมเตียง [pha khlum tiang]

bedtime ['bɛd,taɪm] *n* เวลานอน [we la non]

bee [biː] *n* ผึ้ง [phueng]

beech [biːtʃ] *n* **beech (tree)** *n* ต้นบีช [ton bit]

beef [biːf] *n* เนื้อวัว [nuea wua]

beefburger ['biːf,bɜːgə] *n* แฮมเบอร์เกอร์เนื้อ [haem boe koe nuea]

beer [bɪə] *n* เบียร์ [bia]; **another beer** เบียร์อีกแก้ว [bia ik kaew]; **A draught beer, please** ขอเบียร์สด [kho bia sot]

beetle ['biːtəl] *n* แมลงปีกแข็ง เช่นตัวด้วง [ma laeng pik khaeng chen tua duang]

beetroot ['biːt,ruːt] *n* หัวบีทรูต [hua bit rut]

before [bɪ'fɔː] *adv* ก่อน [kon] ▷ *conj* ก่อนที่ [kon thii]; **before five o'clock** ก่อนห้าโมง [kon ha mong]; **Do we have to clean the house before we leave?** เราต้องทำความสะอาดบ้านก่อนออกไปไหม? [rao tong tham khwam sa at baan kon ok pai mai]; **the week before last** อาทิตย์ก่อนอาทิตย์ที่แล้ว [a thit kon a thit thii laeo]

beforehand [bɪ'fɔː,hænd] *adv* ล่วงหน้า [luang na]

beg [bɛg] *v* ขอร้อง [kho rong]

beggar ['bɛgə] *n* ขอทาน [kho than]

begin [bɪ'gɪn] *v* เริ่ม [roem]; **When does it begin?** จะเริ่มเมื่อไร? [ja roem muea rai]

beginner [bɪ'gɪnə] *n* ผู้เริ่มใหม่ [phu roem mai]

beginning [bɪ'gɪnɪŋ] *n* การเริ่มต้น [kan roem ton]

behave [bɪ'heɪv] *v* ปฏิบัติ [pa ti bat]

behaviour [bɪ'heɪvjə] *n* พฤติกรรม [phrue ti kam]

behind [bɪ'haɪnd] *adv* ข้างหลัง [khang lang] ▷ *n* หลัง [lung] ▷ *prep* หลังจาก [lang chak]; **lag behind** *v* เคลื่อนไหวช้ากว่าผู้อื่น [khluean wai cha kwa phu uen]; **I've been left behind** ฉันถูกทิ้งให้อยู่ข้างหลัง [chan thuk thing hai yu khang lang]

beige [beɪʒ] *adj* สีน้ำตาลอ่อน [sii nam tan on]

Beijing ['beɪ'dʒɪŋ] *n* กรุงปักกิ่ง [krung pak king]

Belarus ['bɛlə,rʌs; -,rʊs] *n* ประเทศเบลารุส [pra tet be ra rus]

Belarussian [,bɛləʊ'rʌʃən; ,bjɛl-] *adj* เกี่ยวกับชาวเบลารุส [kiao kap chao be ra rus] ▷ *n* *(language)* ภาษาเบลารัสเซี่ยน [pha sa be ra ras sian], *(person)* ชาวเบลารัสเซี่ยน [chao be ra ras sian]

Belgian ['bɛldʒən] *adj* เกี่ยวกับชาวเบลเยี่ยม [kiao kap chao bel yiam] ▷ *n* ชาวเบลเยี่ยม [chao bel yiam]

Belgium ['bɛldʒəm] *n* ประเทศเบลเยี่ยม [pra tet bel yiam]

belief [bɪ'liːf] *n* ความเชื่อมั่น [khwam chuea man]

believe [bɪ'liːv] *vi* เลื่อมใส ศรัทธา [lueam sai, sat tha] ▷ *vt* เชื่อ [chuea]

bell [bɛl] *n* ระฆัง [ra khang]

belly ['bɛlɪ] *n* ท้อง [thong]; **belly button** *n* สะดือ [sa due]

belong [bɪ'lɒŋ] *v* เป็นของ [pen khong]; **belong to** *v* เป็นสมาชิกของ [pen sa ma chik khong]

belongings [bɪ'lɒŋɪŋz] *npl* สมบัติส่วนตัว [som bat suan tua]

below [bɪ'ləʊ] *adv* อยู่ข้างล่าง [yu khang lang] ▷ *prep* อยู่ตอนใต้ [yu torn tai]

belt [bɛlt] *n* เข็มขัด [khem khat];

conveyor belt *n* สายพานการขนส่ง [sai phan kan khon song]; **money belt** *n* กระเป๋าใส่เงินคาดที่เอว [kra pao sai ngoen khat thii eo]; **safety belt** *n* เข็มขัดนิรภัย [khem khat ni ra phai]

bench [bɛntʃ] *n* ม้านั่ง [ma nang]

bend [bɛnd] *n* ทางโค้ง [thang khong] ▷ *v* งอ [ngo]; **bend down** *v* ย่อตัว [yo tua]; **bend over** *v* โค้งตัว [khong tua]

beneath [bɪˈniːθ] *prep* ข้างล่าง [khang laang]

benefit [ˈbɛnɪfɪt] *n* ผลประโยชน์ [phon pra yot] ▷ *v* มีประโยชน์ต่อ [mii pra yot to]

bent [bɛnt] *adj (dishonest)* โกงกิน [kong kin], *(not straight)* คดงอ [khot ngo]

beret [ˈbɛreɪ] *n* หมวกกลม [muak klom]

berry [ˈbɛrɪ] *n* ลูกเบอร์รี่เป็นลูกไม้ส่วนใหญ่กินได้และมีลักษณะกลม [luk boe ri pen luk mai suan yai kin dai lae mii lak sa na klom]

berth [bɜːθ] *n* ที่นอนในเรือหรือรถไฟ [thii non nai ruea rue rot fai]

beside [bɪˈsaɪd] *prep* ข้างๆ [khang khang]

besides [bɪˈsaɪdz] *adv* นอกจากนี้ [nak chak ni]

best [bɛst] *adj* ดีที่สุด [di thii sut] ▷ *adv* เหมาะสมที่สุด [mo som thii sut]; **best man** *n* เพื่อนเจ้าบ่าว [phuean chao bao]; **What's the best way to get to the city centre?** วิธีไหนที่ดีที่สุดที่จะไปใจกลางเมือง? [wi thi nai thii di thii sut thii ja pai jai klang mueang]

bestseller [ˌbɛstˈsɛlə] *n* ขายดีที่สุด [khai dee thii sud]

bet [bɛt] *n* การพนัน [kan pha nan] ▷ *v* พนัน [pha nan]

betray [bɪˈtreɪ] *v* ทรยศ [tho ra yot]

better [ˈbɛtə] *adj* ดีกว่า [di kwa] ▷ *adv* มาตรฐานที่ดีกว่า [mat tra than thii di kwa]

betting [bɛtɪŋ] *n* การพนัน [kan pha nan]; **betting shop** *n* ร้านรับพนัน [ran rap pha nan]

between [bɪˈtwiːn] *prep* ระหว่าง [ra wang]

bewildered [bɪˈwɪldəd] *adj* งุนงงอย่างที่สุด [ngun ngong yang thii sut]

beyond [bɪˈjɒnd] *prep* เลยออกไป [loei ok pai]

biased [ˈbaɪəst] *adj* ซึ่งลำเอียง [sueng lam iang]

bib [bɪb] *n* ผ้ากันเปื้อนเด็ก [pha kan puean dek]

Bible [ˈbaɪbəl] *n* คัมภีร์ไบเบิล [kham phii bai boen]

bicarbonate [baɪˈkɑːbənɪt; -,neɪt] *n* **bicarbonate of soda** *n* สารโซเดียมไบคาร์บอเนต [san so diam bi kha bo net]

bicycle [ˈbaɪsɪkəl] *n* จักรยาน [chak kra yan]; **bicycle pump** *n* ที่สูบรถจักรยาน [thii sup rot chak kra yan]

bid [bɪd] *n* การประมูล [kan pra mun] ▷ *v* *(at auction)* ประมูล [pra mun]

bifocals [baɪˈfəʊkəlz] *npl* แว่นสองเลนส์ [waen song len]

big [bɪg] *adj* ใหญ่ [yai]; **It's too big** มันใหญ่เกินไป [man yai koen pai]; **The house is quite big** บ้านค่อนข้างใหญ่ [baan khon khang yai]

bigger [bɪgə] *adj* ใหญ่กว่า [yai kwa]; **Do you have a bigger one?** คุณมีห้องใหญ่กว่านี้ไหม? [khun mii hong yai kwa nii mai]

bigheaded [ˈbɪgˌhɛdɪd] *adj* หัวดื้อ [hua due]

bike [baɪk] *n* จักรยาน [chak kra yan]; **Can I keep my bike here?** ฉันจอดจักรยานที่นี่ได้ไหม? [chan jot chak kra yan thii ni dai mai]; **Does the bike have brakes?** จักรยานคันนี้มีเบรคไหม? [chak kra yan khan nii mii brek mai]; **Does the bike have gears?** จักรยานคันนี้มีเกียร์ไหม? [chak kra yan khan nii mii kia mai]

bikini [bɪˈkiːnɪ] *n* บิกินี่ [bi ki ni]

bilingual [baɪˈlɪŋgwəl] *adj* สามารถเขียน

หรือพูดได้สองภาษา [sa maat khian rue phut dai song pha sa]

bill [bɪl] n (account) ใบแจ้งหนี้ [bai chaeng nii], (legislation) ร่างกฎหมาย [rang kot mai]; **phone bill** n บิลเก็บเงินค่าโทรศัพท์ [bil kep ngoen kha tho ra sap]

billiards ['bɪljədz] npl บิลเลียด [bin liat]

billion ['bɪljən] n พันล้าน [phan lan]

bin [bɪn] n ถังขยะ [thang kha ya]; **litter bin** n ถังใส่ขยะ [thang sai kha ya]

binding ['baɪndɪŋ] n **Can you adjust my bindings, please?** คุณช่วยปรับที่ผูกข้อมือให้ฉันได้ไหม [khun chuai prap thii phuk kho mue hai chan dai mai]; **Can you tighten my bindings, please?** คุณช่วยผูกที่ผูกข้อมือฉันให้แน่นขึ้นได้ไหม? [khun chuai phuk thii phuk kho mue chan hai naen khuen dai mai]

bingo ['bɪŋɡəʊ] n เกมบิงโก [kem bing ko]

binoculars [bɪ'nɒkjʊləz; baɪ-] npl กล้องส่องทางไกล [klong song thang klai]

biochemistry [ˌbaɪəʊ'kɛmɪstrɪ] n ชีวเคมี [chi wa ke mi]

biodegradable [ˌbaɪəʊdɪ'ɡreɪdəbəl] adj ที่เสื่อมโทรมได้ [thii sueam som dai]

biography [baɪ'ɒɡrəfɪ] n อัตชีวประวัติ [at ta chi wa pra wat]

biological [ˌbaɪə'lɒdʒɪkəl] adj ทางชีววิทยา [thang chi wa wit tha ya]

biology [baɪ'ɒlədʒɪ] n ชีววิทยา [chi wa wit tha ya]

biometric [ˌbaɪəʊ'mɛtrɪk] adj เกี่ยวกับชีวสถิติวิทยา [kiao kap chi wa sa thi ti wit tha ya]

birch [bɜːtʃ] n ต้นไม้ชนิดหนึ่งชื่อต้นเบิร์ช [ton mai cha nit nueng chue ton birch]

bird [bɜːd] n นก [nok]; **bird flu** n ไข้หวัดนก [khai wat nok]; **bird of prey** n นกล่าสัตว์หรือนกเล็ก ๆ เป็นอาหาร [nok la sat rue nok lek lek pen a han]

birdwatching [bɜːdwɒtʃɪŋ] n การดูนก [kan du nok]

Biro® ['baɪrəʊ] n ปากกาลูกลื่นกลม [pak ka luk luen klom]

birth [bɜːθ] n การเกิด [kan koed]; **birth certificate** n ใบเกิด [bai koet]; **birth control** n การคุมกำเนิด [kan khum kam noet]; **place of birth** n สถานที่เกิด [sa than thii koet]

birthday ['bɜːˌdeɪ] n วันเกิด [wan koet]; **Happy birthday!** สุขสันต์วันเกิด [suk san wan koet]

birthplace ['bɜːθˌpleɪs] n สถานที่เกิด [sa than thii koet]

biscuit ['bɪskɪt] n ขนมปังกรอบ [kha nom pang krob]

bishop ['bɪʃəp] n ตำแหน่งบาทหลวงที่ปกครองบาทหลวงอื่น ๆ [tam naeng bat luang thii pok khrong bat luang uen uen]

bit [bɪt] n เล็ก ๆ น้อย ๆ [lek lek noi noi]

bitch [bɪtʃ] n สุนัขตัวเมีย [su nak tua mia]

bite [baɪt] n รอยกัด [roi kat] ▷ v กัด [kat]; **I have been bitten** ฉันถูกกัด [chan thuk kat]; **This bite is infected** ที่ถูกกัดนี้ติดเชื้อโรค [thii thuk kat nii tit chuea rok]

bitter ['bɪtə] adj ขม [khom]

black [blæk] adj ดำ [dam]; **black ice** n น้ำแข็งสีดำ [nam khaeng sii dam]; **in black and white** เป็นขาวกับดำ [pen khao kap dam]

blackberry ['blækbərɪ] n ลูกแบรี่สีดำ [luk bae ri see dam]

blackbird ['blækˌbɜːd] n นกดุเหว่า [nok du wao]

blackboard ['blækˌbɔːd] n กระดานดำ [kra dan dam]

blackcurrant [ˌblæk'kʌrənt] n ผลแบลคเคอแรนต์ [phon blaek koe raen]

blackmail ['blækˌmeɪl] n การขู่ว่าจะเปิดโปงความลับ [kan ku wa ja poet pong khwam lap] ▷ v หักหลัง [hak lang]

blackout ['blækaʊt] *n* การดับไฟ [kan dap fai]

bladder ['blædə] *n* กระเพาะปัสสาวะ [kra pho pat sa wa]; **gall bladder** *n* ถุงน้ำดี [thung nam di]

blade [bleɪd] *n* ใบมีด [bai mit]; **razor blade** *n* ใบมีดโกน [bai mit kon]; **shoulder blade** *n* หัวไหล่ [hua lai]

blame [bleɪm] *n* การตำหนิ คำติเตียน [kan tam hni, kham ti tian] ▷ *v* ตำหนิ [tam ni]

blank [blæŋk] *adj* ว่าง [wang] ▷ *n* ช่อง ว่าง [chong wang]; **blank cheque** *n* เช็ค เปล่า [chek plao]

blanket ['blæŋkɪt] *n* ผ้าห่ม [pha hom]; **electric blanket** *n* ผ้าห่มไฟฟ้า [pha hom fai fa]; **Please bring me an extra blanket** ช่วยเอาผ้าห่มมาให้ฉันอีกผืน [chuai ao pha hom ma hai chan ik phuen]; **We need more blankets** เรา ต้องการผ้าห่มเพิ่มอีก [rao tong kan pha hom poem ik]

blast [blɑːst] *n* การระเบิด [kan ra boed]

blatant ['bleɪtᵊnt] *adj* ชัดแจ้ง [chat chen]

blaze [bleɪz] *n* เปลวไฟ [pleo fai]

blazer ['bleɪzə] *n* เสื้อแจ็กเก็ตกีฬาหรือ โรงเรียน [suea chaek ket ki la rue rong rian]

bleach [bliːtʃ] *n* ฟอก [fok]

bleached [bliːtʃt] *adj* ถูกฟอก [thuk fok]

bleak [bliːk] *adj* อางว้าง [ang wang]

bleed [bliːd] *v* เลือดออก [lueat ok]; **My gums are bleeding** เหงือกฉันเลือดออก [ngueak chan lueat ok]

bleeper ['bliːpə] *n* เครื่องส่งสัญญาณ ติดตามตัว [khrueang song san yan tit tam tua]

blender ['blɛndə] *n* เครื่องปั่น [khrueang pan]

bless [blɛs] *v* อวยพร [uai pon]

blind [blaɪnd] *adj* บังตา [bang ta] ▷ *n* ตาบอด [ta bot]; **Venetian blind** *n* ม่าน เกล็ดไม้รูดขึ้นลงได้ [man klet mai rut

khuen long dai]; **I'm blind** ฉันตาบอด [chan ta bot]

blindfold ['blaɪnd‚fəʊld] *n* สิ่งที่ใช้ปิดตา [sing thii chai pit ta] ▷ *v* เอาผ้าปิดตา [ao pha pit ta]

blink [blɪŋk] *v* กะพริบตา [ka prip ta]

bliss [blɪs] *n* ความสุขอันสุดยอด [khwam suk an sut yot]

blister ['blɪstə] *n* แผลพุพอง [phlae phu phong]

blizzard ['blɪzəd] *n* พายุหิมะ [pha yu hi ma]

block [blɒk] *n* (*buildings*) ช่วงตึก [chuang tuek], (*obstruction*) สิ่งกีดขวาง [sing kit khwang], (*solid piece*) ชิ้นหรือ ของหรือวัสดุที่เป็นของแข็ง [chin rue khong rue wat sa du thii pen khong khaeng] ▷ *v* กีดขวาง [kit khwang]

blockage ['blɒkɪdʒ] *n* การปิดล้อม [kan pit lom]

blocked [blɒkt] *adj* ที่กีดขวาง [thii kit khwang]

blog [blɒg] *n* ข้อมูลของบุคคลในอินเตอร์ เน็ต [kho mun khong buk khon nai in toe net] ▷ *v* ใส่ข้อมูลส่วนบุคคล [sai kho mun suan buk khon]

bloke [bləʊk] *n* ผู้ชาย [phu chai]

blonde [blɒnd] *adj* เป็นสีทอง [pen sii thong]

blood [blʌd] *n* เลือด [lueat]; **blood group** *n* กลุ่มเลือด [klum lueat]; **blood poisoning** *n* เลือดเป็นพิษ [lueat pen phit]; **blood pressure** *n* ความดันโลหิต [khwam dan lo hit]; **My blood group is O positive** เลือดฉันกลุ่มโอ [lueat chan klum o]

bloody ['blʌdɪ] *adj* เต็มไปด้วยเลือด [tem pai duai lueat]

blossom ['blɒsəm] *n* ดอกไม้ [dok mai] ▷ *v* ออกดอก [ok dok]

blouse [blaʊz] *n* เสื้อสตรี [suea sa tree]

blow [bləʊ] *n* การเป่า [kan pao] ▷ *v* เป่า [pao]

blow-dry [bləʊdraɪ] *n* การเป่าให้แห้ง

[kan pao hai haeng]

blow up [bləʊ ʌp] v เป่าให้ไฟลุก [pao hai fai luk]

blue [bluː] adj สีฟ้า [sii fa]

blueberry ['bluːbərɪ; -brɪ] n ผลบลูเบอร์รี่ [phon blu boe ri]

blues [bluːz] npl ความเศร้าใจ [khwam sao jai]

bluff [blʌf] n การแกล้งตั้งใจทำบางสิ่ง [kan klaeng tang jai tham bang sing] ▷ v แกล้งตั้งใจทำ [klaeng tang jai tham]

blunder ['blʌndə] n การทำผิดเพราะสะเพร่า [kan tham phit phro sa phrao]

blunt [blʌnt] adj ทื่อ [thue]

blush [blʌʃ] v เขินอาย [khoen ai]

blusher ['blʌʃə] n ครีมหรือแป้งสีทาแก้ม [khrim rue paeng sii tha kaem]

board [bɔːd] n (meeting) คณะกรรมการ [kha na kram ma kan], (wood) กระดาน [kra dan] ▷ v (go aboard) ไปต่างประเทศ [pai tang pra tet]; **board game** n เกมส์ที่เล่นบนกระดาน [kem thii len bon kra dan]; **boarding card** n บัตรขึ้นเครื่องบินหรือยานพาหนะ [bat khuen khrueang bin rue yan pha ha na]; **boarding pass** n บัตรผ่านขึ้นเครื่องบิน [bat phan khuen khrueang bin]

boarder ['bɔːdə] n เด็กประจำ [dek pra cham]

boast [bəʊst] v พูดยกย่องตัวเองจนเกินไป [phud yok yong tua eng chon koen pai]

boat [bəʊt] n เรือ [ruea]; **fishing boat** n เรือตกปลา [rua tok pla]; **Are there any boat trips on the river?** มีเรือท่องเที่ยวในแม่น้ำไหม? [mii ruea thong thiao nai mae nam mai]; **When is the first boat?** เรือลำแรกมาเมื่อไร? [ruea lam raek ma muea rai]; **When is the last boat?** เรือลำสุดท้ายมาเมื่อไร? [ruea lam sut thai ma muea rai]

body ['bɒdɪ] n ร่างกาย [rang kai]

bodybuilding ['bɒdɪˌbɪldɪŋ] n การเพาะกาย [kan po kai]

bodyguard ['bɒdɪˌgɑːd] n คนคุ้มกัน [khon khum kan]

bog [bɒg] n ห้วย [huai]

boil [bɔɪl] vi ทำให้เดือด [tham hai duead] ▷ vt ต้ม [tom]

boiled [bɔɪld] adj เดือดแล้ว [dueat laeo]; **boiled egg** n ไข่ต้ม [khai tom]

boiler ['bɔɪlə] n หม้อน้ำ [mo nam]

boiling ['bɔɪlɪŋ] adj กำลังเดือด [kam lang dueat]

boil over [bɔɪl 'əʊvə] v เดือดจนล้น [dueat chon lon]

Bolivia [bə'lɪvɪə] n ประเทศโบลิเวีย [pra thet bo li wia]

Bolivian [bə'lɪvɪən] adj เกี่ยวกับประเทศโบลิเวีย [kiao kap pra thet bo li via] ▷ n ชาวโบลิเวีย [chao bo li wia]

bolt [bəʊlt] n กลอนประตู [klon pra tu]

bomb [bɒm] n ลูกระเบิด [luk ra boet] ▷ v ทิ้งระเบิด [thing ra boed]; **atom bomb** n ระเบิดปรมาณู [ra boet pa ra ma nu]

bombing [bɒmɪŋ] n กำลังทิ้งระเบิด [kam lang thing ra boed]

bond [bɒnd] n ข้อผูกมัด [kho phuk mat]

bone [bəʊn] n กระดูก [kra duk]; **bone dry** adj แห้งสนิท [haeng sa nit]

bonfire ['bɒnˌfaɪə] n กองไฟจุดกลางแจ้ง [kong fai chut klang chaeng]

bonnet ['bɒnɪt] n (car) ฝากระโปรงรถยนต์ [fa kra prong rot yon]

bonus ['bəʊnəs] n เงินโบนัส [ngoen bo nas]

book [bʊk] n หนังสือ [nang sue] ▷ v จอง [chong]; **Can you book me into a hotel?** คุณจองโรงแรมให้ฉันได้ไหม? [khun chong rong raem hai chan dai mai]; **Can you book the tickets for us?** คุณจองตั๋วให้เราได้ไหม? [khun chong tua hai rao dai mai]; **I booked a room in the name of...** ฉันจองห้องในนาม... [chan chong hong nai nam…]

bookcase ['bʊkˌkeɪs] n ตู้หนังสือ [tu hnang sue]

booking ['bʊkɪŋ] n การจองล่วงหน้า [kan chong luang na]; **advance booking** n

จองล่วงหน้า [chong luang na]; **booking office** n สำนักงานจอง [sam nak ngan chong]

booklet ['bʊklɪt] n หนังสือเล่มเล็ก [nang sue lem lek]

bookmark ['bʊkˌmɑːk] n ที่คั่นหนังสือ [thii khan nang sue]

bookshelf ['bʊkˌʃɛlf] n ชั้นวางหนังสือ [chan wang hnang sue]

bookshop ['bʊkˌʃɒp] n ร้านหนังสือ [ran nang sue]

boost [buːst] v ส่งเสริม [song some]

boot [buːt] n รองเท้าบูท [rong thao but]

booze [buːz] n เครื่องดื่มที่มีแอลกอฮอล์ [khrueang duem thii mii aen ko ho]

border ['bɔːdə] n ขอบเขต [khop khet]

bore [bɔː] v (be dull) เบื่อ [buea], (drill) เจาะรู [jo ru]

bored [bɔːd] adj ทำให้เบื่อ [tham hai buea]

boredom ['bɔːdəm] n ความเบื่อ [khwam buea]

boring ['bɔːrɪŋ] adj น่าเบื่อ [na buea]

born [bɔːn] adj ที่เป็นมาโดยกำเนิด [thii pen ma doi kam noet]

borrow ['bɒrəʊ] v ยืม [yuem]; **Do you have a pen I could borrow?** คุณมีปากกาให้ฉันยืมไหม? [khun mii pak ka hai chan yuem mai]

Bosnia ['bɒznɪə] n ประเทศบอสเนีย [pra tet bos nia]; **Bosnia and Herzegovina** n ประเทศบอสเนียและเฮอร์เซโกวีน่า [pra tet bos nia lae hoe se ko vi na]

Bosnian ['bɒznɪən] adj เกี่ยวกับประเทศบอสเนีย [kiao kap pra thet bos nia] ▷ n (person) ชาวบอสเนีย [chao bos nia]

boss [bɒs] n เจ้านาย [chao nai]

boss around [bɒs əˈraʊnd] v บงการ [bong kan]

bossy ['bɒsɪ] adj จู้จี้ [chu chi]

both [bəʊθ] adj ทั้งสอง [thang song] ▷ pron ทั้งสอง [thang song]

bother ['bɒðə] v ทำให้ยุ่งยาก [tham hai yung yak]

Botswana [bʊˈtʃwɑːnə; bʊtˈswɑːnə; bɒt-] n ประเทศบอสซาวาน่า [pra tet bos sa wa na]

bottle ['bɒtªl] n ขวด [khuat]; **baby's bottle** n ขวดนมเด็ก [khaut nom dek]; **a bottle of mineral water** น้ำแร่หนึ่งขวด [nam rae nueng khaut]; **a bottle of red wine** ไวน์แดงหนึ่งขวด [wine daeng nueng khaut]; **Please bring another bottle** ขออีกหนึ่งขวด [kho ik nueng khaut]

bottle-opener ['bɒtªlˌəʊpənə] n ที่เปิดขวด [thii poed khaud]

bottom ['bɒtəm] adj ต่ำสุด [tam sut] ▷ n ก้น [kan]

bought [bɔːt] adj ได้ซื้อ [dai sue]

bounce [baʊns] v เด้ง [deng]

bouncer ['baʊnsə] n คนเฝ้าหน้าบาร์ที่กันไม่ให้คนเข้า [khon fao na bar thii kan mai hai khon khao]

boundary ['baʊndərɪ; -drɪ] n ขอบเขต [khop khet]

bouquet ['buːkeɪ] n ช่อดอกไม้ [cho dok mai]

bow n [bəʊ] (weapon) คันธนู [khan tha nu] ▷ v [baʊ] คำนับ [kham nap]

bowels ['baʊəlz] npl ลำไส้ [lam sai]

bowl [bəʊl] n ชาม [cham]

bowling ['bəʊlɪŋ] n โบว์ลิ่ง [bo ling]; **bowling alley** n เลนเล่นโบว์ลิ่ง [len len bo ling]; **tenpin bowling** n โบว์ลิ่งแบบตัวตั้งสิบตัว [bo ling baep tua tang sip tua]

bow tie [bəʊ] n bow tie โบว์หูกระต่าย [bo hu kra tai]

box [bɒks] n กล่อง [klong]; **box office** n ที่ขายตั๋วหนังหรือละคร [thii khai tua nang rue la khon]; **call box** n ตู้โทรศัพท์ [tu tho ra sap]; **fuse box** n กล่องใส่สายชนวน [klong sai sai cha nuan]

boxer ['bɒksə] n นักมวย [nak muai]; **boxer shorts** npl กางเกงขาสั้น [kang keng kha san]

boxing ['bɒksɪŋ] n การชกมวย [kan chok

muai]

boy [bɔɪ] n เด็กชาย [dek chai]

boyfriend ['bɔɪˌfrɛnd] n เพื่อนชาย [phuean chai]; **I have a boyfriend** ฉันมีเพื่อนชาย [chan mii phuean chai]

bra [brɑː] n เสื้อชั้นในสตรี [suea chan nai sa trii]

bracelet ['breɪslɪt] n กำไลหรือสร้อยข้อมือ [kam lai rue soi kho mue]

braces ['breɪsɪz] npl สายโยงกางเกง [sai yong kang keng]

brackets ['brækɪts] npl ในวงเล็บ [nai wong lep]

brain [breɪn] n สมอง [sa mong]

brainy ['breɪnɪ] adj ฉลาดมาก [cha lat mak]

brake [breɪk] n เบรคหรือเครื่องห้ามล้อ [brek rue khrueang ham lo] ▷ v ห้ามล้อ [ham lo]; **brake light** n ไฟเบรค [fai brek]

bran [bræn] n รำข้าว [ram khao]

branch [brɑːntʃ] n สาขา [sa kha]

brand [brænd] n ตรา [tra]; **brand name** n ยี่ห้อ [yi ho]

brand-new [brænd'njuː] adj ใหม่เอี่ยม [mai iam]

brandy ['brændɪ] n เหล้าบรั่นดี [lao bran di]

brass [brɑːs] n ทองเหลือง [thong lueang]; **brass band** n วงดนตรีเครื่องเป่า [wong don tree khrueang pao]

brat [bræt] n คนเลว [khon leo]

brave [breɪv] adj กล้าหาญ [kla han]

bravery ['breɪvərɪ] n ความกล้าหาญ [khwam kla han]

Brazil [brə'zɪl] n ประเทศบราซิล [pra tet bra sil]

Brazilian [brə'zɪljən] adj เกี่ยวกับประเทศบราซิล [kiao kap pra thet bra sil] ▷ n ชาวบราซิล [chao bra sin]

bread [brɛd] n ขนมปัง [kha nom pang]; **bread roll** n ขนมปังกลม [kha nom pang klom]; **brown bread** n ขนมปังสีน้ำตาล [kha nom pang sii nam tan]; **Please**

bring more bread ช่วยเอาขนมปังมาอีก [chuai ao kha nom pang ma ik]

bread bin [brɛdbɪn] n ที่เก็บขนมปัง [thii kep kha nom pang]

breadcrumbs ['brɛdˌkrʌmz] npl ขนมปังป่น [kha nom pang pon]

break [breɪk] n การแตกหัก [kan taek hak] ▷ v ทำให้เสีย [tham hai sia]; **lunch break** n ช่วงหยุดพักอาหารกลางวัน [chuang yut phak a han klang wan]

break down [breɪk daʊn] v ใช้งานไม่ได้ [chai ngan mai dai]

breakdown ['breɪkdaʊn] n การเสีย [kan sia]; **breakdown truck** n รถบรรทุกเสีย [rot ban thuk sia]; **breakdown van** n รถตู้เสีย [rot tu sia]; **nervous breakdown** n ช่วงเวลาที่เจ็บป่วยทางจิต [chuang we la thii chep puai thang chit]

breakfast ['brɛkfəst] n อาหารเช้า [a han chao]; **Can I have breakfast in my room?** ฉันทานอาหารเช้าในห้องฉันได้ไหม? [chan than a han chao nai hong chan dai mai]; **Is breakfast included?** รวมอาหารเช้าหรือไม่? [ruam a han chao rue mai]; **with breakfast** มีอาหารเช้า [mii a han chao]

break in [breɪk ɪn] v บุกเข้าไป [buk khao pai]; **break in (on)** v บุกเข้าไป [buk khao pai]

break-in ['breɪkɪn] n การบุกรุกเข้าไป [kan buk ruk khao pai]

break up [breɪk ʌp] v แตกแยก [taek yaek]

breast [brɛst] n หน้าอก [na ok]

breast-feed ['brɛstˌfiːd] v ให้นมทารกด้วยนมแม่ [hai nom tha rok duai nom mae]

breaststroke ['brɛstˌstrəʊk] n การว่ายน้ำท่าผีเสื้อ [kan wai nam tha phii suea]

breath [brɛθ] n ลมหายใจ [lom hai chai]

Breathalyser® ['brɛθəˌlaɪzə] n เครื่องวัดปริมาณแอลกอฮอล์จากลมหายใจ [khrueang wat pa ri man aen ko ho chak lom hai jai]

breathe [bri:ð] v หายใจ [hai chai]; **He can't breathe** เขาหายใจไม่ได้ [khao hai jai mai dai]

breathe in [bri:ð ɪn] v หายใจเข้า [hai jai khao]

breathe out [bri:ð aʊt] v หายใจออก [hai jai ork]

breathing [ˈbri:ðɪŋ] n การหายใจ [kan hai jai]

breed [bri:d] n พันธุ์ [phan] ▷ v เลี้ยง [liang], ผสมพันธุ์ [pha som phan]

breeze [bri:z] n สายลมที่พัดเบาๆ [sai lom thii phad bao bao]

brewery [ˈbrʊərɪ] n โรงงานต้มและกลั่น เหล้า [rong ngan tom lae klan lao]

bribe [braɪb] v ให้สินบน [hai sin bon]

bribery [ˈbraɪbərɪ] n การให้สินบน [kan hai sin bon]

brick [brɪk] n อิฐ [it]

bricklayer [ˈbrɪkˌleɪə] n ช่างปูน [chang pun]

bride [braɪd] n เจ้าสาว [chao sao]

bridegroom [ˈbraɪdˌgru:m; -ˌgrʊm] n เจ้าบ่าว [chao bao]

bridesmaid [ˈbraɪdzˌmeɪd] n เพื่อนเจ้า สาว [phuean chao sao]

bridge [brɪdʒ] n สะพาน [sa phan]; **suspension bridge** n สะพานแขวน [sa phan khwaen]

brief [bri:f] adj สั้น [san]

briefcase [ˈbri:fˌkeɪs] n กระเป๋าเอกสาร [kra pao aek san]

briefing [ˈbri:fɪŋ] n การสรุปแบบสั้นๆ [kan sa rup baeb san san]

briefly [ˈbri:flɪ] adv อย่างสั้น [yang san]

briefs [bri:fs] npl การสรุปอย่างสั้น [kan sa rup yang san]

bright [braɪt] adj สว่างจ้า [sa wang cha]

brilliant [ˈbrɪljənt] adj พรายแสง ฉลาด เยี่ยม [phrai saeng, cha lat yiam]

bring [brɪŋ] v นำมา [nam ma]

bring back [brɪŋ bæk] v นำกลับมา [nam klap ma]

bring forward [brɪŋ ˈfɔ:wəd] v ทำให้ เจริญก้าวหน้า [tham hai cha roen kao na]

bring up [brɪŋ ʌp] v เลี้ยงดู [liang du]

Britain [ˈbrɪtᵊn] n ประเทศสหราช อาณาจักรอังกฤษ [pra tet sa ha rat cha a na chak ang krit]

British [ˈbrɪtɪʃ] adj เกี่ยวกับประเทศสหราช อาณาจักรอังกฤษ [kiao kap pra thet sa ha rat cha a na chak ang krit] ▷ n ชาว สหราชอาณาจักร [chao sa ha rat cha a na chak]

broad [brɔ:d] adj กว้าง [kwang]

broadband [ˈbrɔ:dˌbænd] n บรอดแบน [brot baen]

broadcast [ˈbrɔ:dˌkɑ:st] n การออก รายการอากาศ [kan ok rai kan a kat] ▷ v กระจายเสียง เผยแพร่ [kra jai siang phoei prae]

broad-minded [brɔ:dˈmaɪndɪd] adj ใจ กว้าง [chai kwang]

broccoli [ˈbrɒkəlɪ] n ผักบร๊อคคอรี่ [phak brok koe ri]

brochure [ˈbrəʊʃjʊə; -ʃə] n แผ่นพับ โฆษณา [phaen phap khot sa na]

broke [brəʊk] adj แตกหัก [taek hak]

broken [ˈbrəʊkən] adj แตกหัก [taek hak]; **broken down** adj ทำให้แตกหัก [tham hai taek hak]

broker [ˈbrəʊkə] n นายหน้า [nai na]

bronchitis [brɒŋˈkaɪtɪs] n โรคหลอดลม อักเสบ [rok lot lom ak sep]

bronze [brɒnz] n ทองสัมฤทธิ์ [thong sam rit]

brooch [brəʊtʃ] n เข็มกลัด [khem klat]

broom [bru:m; brʊm] n ไม้กวาด [mai kwat]

broth [brɒθ] n ซุป [sup]

brother [ˈbrʌðə] n พี่ชายหรือน้องชาย [phi chai rue nong chai]

brother-in-law [ˈbrʌðə ɪn lɔ:] n พี่เขย หรือน้องเขย [phi khoei rue nong khoei]

brown [braʊn] adj สีน้ำตาล [see nam tan]; **brown bread** n ขนมปังสีน้ำตาล

[kha nom pang sii nam tan]; **brown rice** n ข้าวซ้อมมือ [khao som mue]

browse [braʊz] v ดูคร่าว ๆ [du khrao khrao]

browser [ˈbraʊzə] n โปรแกรมที่ใช้สำหรับเปิดดูเว็บไซต์ต่าง ๆ ที่ใช้ภาษาไฮเปอร์เท็กซ์ [pro kraem thii chai sam rap poet du web sai tang tang thii chai pha sa hai poe thek]

bruise [bruːz] n แผลฟกช้ำ [phlae fok cham]

brush [brʌʃ] n ไม้แปรง [mai praeng] ▷ v แปรง [plraeng]

brutal [ˈbruːtªl] adj โหดร้าย [hot rai]

bubble [ˈbʌbªl] n ฟอง [fong]; **bubble bath** n ฟองอาบน้ำ [fong aap nam]; **bubble gum** n หมากฝรั่ง [mak fa rang]

bucket [ˈbʌkɪt] n ถัง [thang]

buckle [ˈbʌkªl] n หัวเข็มขัด [hua khem khat]

Buddha [ˈbʊdə] n พระพุทธรูป [phra phut tha rup]

Buddhism [ˈbʊdɪzəm] n ศาสนาพุทธ [sat sa na phut]

Buddhist [ˈbʊdɪst] adj เกี่ยวกับชาวพุทธ [kiao kap chao phut] ▷ n ชาวพุทธ [chao phut]

budgerigar [ˈbʌdʒərɪˌgɑː] n นกขนาดเล็กตระกูลเดียวกับนกแก้ว [nok kha nard lek tra kul diao kab nok kaew]

budget [ˈbʌdʒɪt] n งบประมาณ [ngop pra man]

budgie [ˈbʌdʒɪ] n นกขนาดเล็ก [nok kha nard lek]

buffalo [ˈbʌfəˌləʊ] n กระบือ [kra bue]

buffet [ˈbʊfeɪ] n อาหารที่ลูกค้าบริการตัวเอง [a han thii luk ka bor ri kan tua eng]; **buffet car** n รถมีอาหารที่ลูกค้าบริการตัวเอง [rot mii a han thii luk kha bo ri kan tua eng]

bug [bʌg] n แมลง [ma leng]; **There are bugs in my room** มีแมลงในห้องฉัน [mii ma laeng nai hong chan]

bugged [ˈbʌgd] adj ดักฟัง [dak fung]

buggy [ˈbʌgɪ] n รถเล็กไม่มีประตู [rot lek mai mii pra tu]

build [bɪld] v สร้าง [sang]

builder [ˈbɪldə] n ช่างก่อสร้าง [chang ko sang]

building [ˈbɪldɪŋ] n ตึก อาคาร [tuek, a khan]; **building site** n บริเวณที่ก่อสร้าง [bo ri wen thii ko sang]

bulb [bʌlb] n (electricity) หลอดไฟฟ้า [lot fai fa], (plant) หัวของต้นไม้ [hua khong ton mai]

Bulgaria [bʌlˈgɛərɪə; bʊl-] n ประเทศบัลกาเรีย [pra tet bul ka ria]

Bulgarian [bʌlˈgɛərɪən; bʊl-] adj ที่เกี่ยวกับบัลกาเรีย [thii kiao kap bul ka ria] ▷ n (language) ภาษาบัลกาเรีย [pha sa bul ka ria], (person) ชาวบัลกาเรีย [chao bul ka ria]

bulimia [bjuːˈlɪmɪə] n โรคผิดปรกติทางอารมณ์ที่กินมากไปแล้วอาเจียรออก [rok phid prok ka ti thang ar rom thii kin mak pai laeo a chian ork]

bull [bʊl] n วัวตัวผู้ [vua tua phu]

bulldozer [ˈbʊlˌdəʊzə] n รถแทรกเตอร์เกลี่ยดิน [rot traek toe klia din]

bullet [ˈbʊlɪt] n กระสุน [kra sun]

bully [ˈbʊlɪ] n อันธพาล [an tha pan] ▷ v กดขี่รังแก [kot khii rang kae]

bum [bʌm] n ก้น [kan]; **bum bag** n กระเป๋าเล็กที่ติดเข็มขัดสวมรอบเอว [kra pao lek thii tit khem khat suam rop eo]

bumblebee [ˈbʌmbªlˌbiː] n ผึ้งมีขนตัวใหญ่ [phueng mii khon tua yai]

bump [bʌmp] n การชน [kan chon]; **bump into** v ชนกับ [chon kap]

bumper [ˈbʌmpə] n กันชน [kan chon]

bumpy [ˈbʌmpɪ] adj ขรุขระ [khru khra]

bun [bʌn] n ขนมปังนุ่ม [kha nom pang num]

bunch [bʌntʃ] n กลุ่ม พวง รวง เครือ [klum, phuang, ruang, khruea]

bungalow [ˈbʌŋgəˌləʊ] n บังกาโล [bang ka lo]

bungee jumping [ˈbʌndʒɪ] n การกระ

โดดจากสะพานหรือหน้าผาสูง [kan kra dod chak sa pan hue na pa sung]

bunion ['bʌnjən] *n* ตาปลาบนเท้า [ta pla bon thao]

bunk [bʌŋk] *n* ที่นอนในเรือ [thii non nai ruea]; **bunk beds** *npl* เตียงชั้น [tiang chan]

buoy [bɔɪ; 'buːɪ] *n* ทุ่น [thun]

burden ['bɜːdən] *n* ภาระ [pha ra]

bureaucracy [bjʊəˈrɒkrəsɪ] *n* ระบบ ราชการ [ra bop rat cha kan]

bureau de change ['bjʊərəʊ də 'ʃɒnʒ] *n* **I need to find a bureau de change** ฉันต้องหาที่แลกเงิน [chan tong ha thii laek ngoen]; **Is there a bureau de change here?** ที่นี่มีสำนักงานแลกเงิน ไหม? [thii ni mii sam nak ngan laek ngoen mai]; **When is the bureau de change open?** สำนักงานแลกเงินจะเปิด เมื่อไร? [sam nak ngan laek ngoen ja poet muea rai]

burger ['bɜːgə] *n* เบอร์เกอร์ [boe koe]

burglar ['bɜːglə] *n* ขโมย [kha moi]; **burglar alarm** *n* เครื่องกันขโมย [khrueang kan kha moi]

burglary ['bɜːglərɪ] *n* การบุกเข้ามาขโมย ของในอาคารหรือบ้าน [kan buk khao ma kha moi khlong nai ar khan hue baan]

burgle ['bɜːgəl] *v* บุกเข้ามาขโมยของ [buk khao ma kha moi khong]

Burma ['bɜːmə] *n* ประเทศพม่า [pra tet pha ma]

Burmese [bɜːˈmiːz] *adj* เกี่ยวกับประเทศ พม่า [kiao kap pra thet pha ma] ▷ *n (language)* ภาษาพม่า [pha sa pha ma], *(person)* ชาวพม่า [chao pha ma]

burn [bɜːn] *n* การที่ถูกไหม้ [kan thii thuk mai] ▷ *v* ไหม้ เผาไหม้ [mai, phao mai]

burn down [bɜːn daʊn] *v* เผาไหม้ทำลาย ลง [phao mai tham lai long]

burp [bɜːp] *n* การเรอ [kan roe] ▷ *v* เรอ [roe]

burst [bɜːst] *v* ระเบิด [ra boet]

bury ['bɛrɪ] *v* ฝัง [fang]

bus [bʌs] *n* รถประจำทาง [rot pra cham thang]; **airport bus** *n* รถโดยสารประจำ สนามบิน [rot doi san pra cham sa nam bin]; **bus station** *n* สถานีรถโดยสาร ประจำทาง [sa tha ni rot doi san pra cham thang]; **bus stop** *n* ป้ายรถโดยสาร ประจำทาง [pai rot doi san pra cham thang]

bush [bʊʃ] *n (shrub)* ไม้พุ่ม [mai phum], *(thicket)* พุ่มไม้ [phum mai]

business ['bɪznɪs] *n* ธุรกิจ [thu ra kit]; **business class** *n* ชั้นธุรกิจ [chan thu ra kit]; **business trip** *n* การเดินทางไปทำ ธุรกิจ [kan doen thang pai tham thu ra kit]; **show business** *n* ธุรกิจการบันเทิง [thu ra kit kan ban thoeng]; **I run my own business** ฉันทำงานธุรกิจของตัวเอง [chan tham ngan thu ra kit khong tua eng]

businessman, businessmen ['bɪznɪsˌmæn; -mən, 'bɪznɪsˌmɛn] *n* นักธุรกิจชาย [nak thu ra kit chai]

businesswoman, businesswomen ['bɪznɪsˌwʊmən, 'bɪznɪsˌwɪmɪn] *n* นัก ธุรกิจหญิง [nak thu ra kid hying]; **I'm a businesswoman** ฉันเป็นนักธุรกิจหญิง [chan pen nak thu ra kit ying]

busker ['bʌskə] *n* นักร้องรำทำกินเร่ตาม ถนน [nak rong ram tham kin re tam tha non]

bust [bʌst] *n* หน้าอก นม [na ok, nom]

busy ['bɪzɪ] *adj* ยุ่ง [yung]; **busy signal** *n* สัญญาณไม่ว่าง [san yan mai wang]

but [bʌt] *conj* แต่ [tae]

butcher ['bʊtʃə] *n* คนขายเนื้อ [kon khai nuea]

butcher's ['bʊtʃəz] *n* ที่ร้านคนขายเนื้อ [thii ran khon khai nuea]

butter ['bʌtə] *n* เนย [noei]; **peanut butter** *n* เนยผสมถั่วลิสงบด [noei pha som thua li song bod]

buttercup ['bʌtəˌkʌp] *n* ดอกไม้ป่าดอก เล็กสีเหลือง [dok mai pa dok lek see hlueang]

butterfly ['bʌtəˌflaɪ] *n* ผีเสื้อ [phi suea]

buttocks ['bʌtəkz] *npl* บั้นท้าย [ban thai]

button ['bʌtᵊn] *n* กระดุม [kra dum]; **belly button** *n* สะดือ [sa due]

buy [baɪ] *v* ซื้อ [sue]; **Where can I buy a map of the area?** ฉันจะซื้อแผนที่ของเขตนี้ได้ที่ไหน? [chan ja sue phaen thii khong khet nii dai thii nai]; **Where can I buy stamps?** ฉันจะซื้อแสตมป์ได้ที่ไหน? [chan ja sue sa taem dai thii nai]; **Where do I buy a ticket?** ฉันจะซื้อตั๋วได้ที่ไหน? [chan ja sue tua dai thii nai]

buyer ['baɪə] *n* ผู้ซื้อ [phu sue]

buyout ['baɪˌaʊt] *n* การซื้อขายหุ้นของบริษัท [kan sue khai hun khong bo ri sat]

by [baɪ] *prep* โดย [doi]; **Can you take me by car?** คุณพาฉันไปโดยรถยนต์ได้ไหม? [khun pha chan pai doi rot yon dai mai]

bye [baɪ] *excl* ลาก่อน [la kon]

bye-bye [baɪbaɪ] *excl* ลาก่อน [la kon]

bypass ['baɪˌpɑːs] *n* ทางอ้อม [thang om]

cab [kæb] *n* รถรับจ้าง [rot rap chang]

cabbage ['kæbɪdʒ] *n* กะหล่ำ [ka lam]

cabin ['kæbɪn] *n* ห้องเคบิน [hong khe bin]; **cabin crew** *n* ลูกเรือ [luk ruea]; **Where is cabin number five?** ห้องเคบินหมายเลข 5 อยู่ที่ไหน? [hong khe bin mai lek ha yu thii nai]

cabinet ['kæbɪnɪt] *n* คณะรัฐมนตรี [kha na rat tha mon tree]

cable ['keɪbᵊl] *n* สายเคเบิ้ล [sai khe boel]; **cable car** *n* รถที่เคลื่อนที่โดยสายเคเบิล [rot thii khluean thii doi sai khe boen]; **cable television** *n* โทรทัศน์ที่รับระบบการส่งสัญญาณด้วยสายเคเบิล [tho ra tat thii rap ra bop kan song san yan duai sai khe boen]

cactus ['kæktəs] *n* กระบองเพชร [kra bong phet]

cadet [kə'dɛt] *n* นักเรียนทหาร [nak rian tha han]

café ['kæfeɪ; 'kæfɪ] *n* ร้านกาแฟ [ran ka fae]; **Internet café** *n* ร้านที่ให้บริการอินเตอร์เน็ต [ran thii hai bo ri kan in toe net]

cafeteria [ˌkæfɪ'tɪərɪə] *n* ร้านอาหาร

บริการตนเอง [ran a han bor ri kan ton ang]

caffeine [ˈkæfiːn; ˈkæfɪˌiːn] n สารคาเฟ อีน [san kha fe in]

cage [keɪdʒ] n กรง [krong]

cagoule [kəˈguːl] n เสื้อแจ็คเก็ตมีหมวก คลุมหัวกันลมและฝน [sua chaek ket mii muak khlum hua kan lom lae fon]

cake [keɪk] n ขนมเค้ก [kha nom khek]

calcium [ˈkælsɪəm] n แคลเซี่ยม [khaen siam]

calculate [ˈkælkjʊˌleɪt] v คำนวณ [kham nuan]

calculation [ˌkælkjʊˈleɪʃən] n การ คำนวณ [kan kham nuan]

calculator [ˈkælkjʊˌleɪtə] n เครื่องคิดเลข [khrueang kit lek]; **pocket calculator** n เครื่องคิดเลขฉบับกระเป๋า [khrueang kit lek cha bap kra pao]

calendar [ˈkælɪndə] n ปฏิทิน [pa ti thin]

calf, calves [kɑːf, kɑːvz] n ลูกวัว [luk wua]

call [kɔːl] n การเรียก การโทรศัพท์ [kan riak, kan tho ra sap] ▷ v เรียก [riak]; **alarm call** n การโทรปลุก [kan to pluk]; **call box** n ตู้โทรศัพท์ [tu tho ra sap]; **call centre** n ศูนย์โทรศัพท์ [sun tho ra sap]; **Call a doctor!** เรียกหมอ [riak mo]

call back [kɔːl bæk] v โทรกลับ [tho klap]; **I'll call back later** ฉันจะโทรกลับ หาคุณอีก [chan ja tho klap ha khun ik]; **I'll call back tomorrow** ฉันจะโทรกลับ หาคุณพรุ่งนี้ [chan ja tho klap ha khun phrung nii]; **Please call me back** กรุณาโทรกลับหาฉัน [ka ru na tho klap ha chan]

call for [kɔːl fɔː] v เรียกหา [riak ha]

call off [kɔːl ɒf] v ยุติ [yu ti]

calm [kɑːm] adj ที่มีอารมณ์สงบ [thii mii a rom sa ngop]

calm down [kɑːm daʊn] v ทำให้สงบ [tham hai sa ngob]

calorie [ˈkælərɪ] n หน่วยพลังงานความ ร้อน [nuai pha lang ngan khwam ron]

Cambodia [kæmˈbəʊdɪə] n ประเทศ กัมพูชา [pra tet kam phu cha]

Cambodian [kæmˈbəʊdɪən] adj เกี่ยว กับประเทศกัมพูชา [kiao kap pra thet kam phu cha] ▷ n (person) ชาวกัมพูชา [chao kam phu cha]

camcorder [ˈkæmˌkɔːdə] n กล้องถ่าย วีดีโอที่สามารถนำติดตัวได้ [klong thai vi di o thii sa maad nam tid tua dai]

camel [ˈkæməl] n อูฐ [ut (uut)]

camera [ˈkæmərə; ˈkæmrə] n กล้องถ่าย รูป [klong thai lup]; **camera phone** n โทรศัพท์ที่มีกล้องถ่ายรูปในตัว [tho ra sap thii mii klong thai rup nai tua]; **digital camera** n กล้องดิจิตัล [klong di chi tan]; **video camera** n กล้องถ่าย วิดีโอ [klong thai vi di o]

cameraman, cameramen [ˈkæmərəˌmæn; ˈkæmrə-, ˈkæmərəˌmɛn] n ช่างภาพ [chang phap]

Cameroon [ˌkæməˈruːn; ˈkæməˌruːn] n ประเทศแคเมอรูน [pra tet khaem moe run]

camp [kæmp] n ค่าย [khai] ▷ v ไปค่าย [pai khai]; **camp bed** n เตียงผ้าใบน้ำ หนักเบา [tiang pha bai nam nak bao]; **Can we camp here overnight?** เราตั้ง ค่ายค้างคืนที่นี่ได้ไหม? [rao tang khai khang khuen thii ni dai mai]

campaign [kæmˈpeɪn] n การรณรงค์ [kan ron na rong]

camper [ˈkæmpə] n ชาวค่าย [chao khai]

camping [ˈkæmpɪŋ] n การไปค่าย [kan pai khai]; **camping gas** n ก๊าซที่บรรจุใน ภาชนะเล็ก ๆ ใช้เมื่อไปตั้งแคมป์ [kas thii ban chu nai pha cha na lek lek chai muea pai tang khaem]

campsite [ˈkæmpˌsaɪt] n บริเวณที่ตั้งค่าย [bor ri ven thii tang khai]

campus [ˈkæmpəs] n วิทยาเขต [wit tha ya khet]

can [kæn] n บรรจุกระป๋อง สามารถ [ban

chu kra pong sa mart]; **watering can**
n ฝักบัวรดน้ำต้นไม้ [fak bua rot nam ton
mai)

Canada ['kænədə] n ประเทศแคนาดา
[pra tet khae na da]

Canadian [kə'neɪdɪən] adj เกี่ยวกับ
ประเทศแคนาดา [kiao kap pra thet khae
na da] ▷ n ชาวแคนาดา [chao khae na
da]

canal [kə'næl] n คลอง [khlong]

Canaries [kə'nɛərɪːz] npl หมู่เกาะแคนารี่
[mu kao khae na ri]

canary [kə'nɛərɪ] n ไวน์จากหมู่เกาะแคนา
รี่ [wine chak mu ko khae na ri]

cancel ['kænsəl] v ยกเลิก [yok loek]; **I
want to cancel my booking** ฉันอยาก
ยกเลิกการจองของฉัน [chan yak yok loek
kan chong khong chan]; **I'd like to
cancel my flight** ฉันอยากยกเลิกเที่ยวบิน
ของฉัน [chan yak yok loek thiao bin
khong chan]

cancellation [ˌkænsɪ'leɪʃən] n การ
ยกเลิก [kan yok loek]; **Are there any
cancellations?** มีการยกเลิกเที่ยวบิน
ไหม? [mii kan yok loek thiao bin mai]

cancer ['kænsə] n (illness) มะเร็ง [ma
reng]

Cancer ['kænsə] n (horoscope) ราศีกรกฎ
[ra si ko ra kot]

candidate ['kændɪˌdeɪt; -dɪt] n ผู้สมัคร
[phu sa mak]

candle ['kændəl] n เทียน [thian]

candlestick ['kændəlˌstɪk] n เชิงเทียน
[choeng thian]

candyfloss ['kændɪˌflɒs] n ขนมสายไหม
[kha nom sai mai]

canister ['kænɪstə] n กระป๋องสเปรย์ [kra
pong sa pre]

cannabis ['kænəbɪs] n กัญชา [kan cha]

canned [kænd] adj ที่บรรจุในกระป๋อง
[thii ban chu nai kra pong]

canoe [kə'nuː] n เรือแคนู [ruea khae nu]

canoeing [kə'nuːɪŋ] n การเล่นเรือแคนู
[kan len ruea khae nu]

can-opener ['kæn'əʊpənə] n ที่เปิด
กระป๋อง [thii poet kra pong]

canteen [kæn'tiːn] n โรงอาหาร [rong a
han]

canter ['kæntə] v วิ่งเร็วกว่าวิ่งเหยาะ
[wing reo kwa wing hyao]

canvas ['kænvəs] n ผ้าหนาและหยาบใช้
วาดภาพ [pha hna lae hyab chai vad
phap]

canvass ['kænvəs] v ออกเที่ยวฟังความ
เห็น เที่ยวหาเสียง [ok thiao fang khwam
hen, thiao ha siang]

cap [kæp] n หมวกที่มีกระบังหน้า [hmuak
thii mee kra bang na]; **baseball cap** n
หมวกแก็บสำหรับเล่นเบสบอล [muak kaep
sam rap len bes bal]

capable ['keɪpəbəl] adj ที่สามารถทำได้
[thii sa maat tham dai]

capacity [kə'pæsɪtɪ] n ปริมาณสูงสุดที่รับ
ได้ [pa ri man sung sut thii rap dai]

capital ['kæpɪtəl] n เมืองหลวง [muang
luang]

capitalism ['kæpɪtəˌlɪzəm] n ระบบ
ทุนนิยม [ra bop thun ni yom]

Capricorn ['kæprɪˌkɔːn] n ราศีมังกร [ra
si mang kon]

capsize [kæp'saɪz] v คว่ำ [khwam]

capsule ['kæpsjuːl] n ยาที่อยู่ในหลอดเล็ก
ๆ [ya thii yu nai lot lek lek]

captain ['kæptɪn] n กัปตัน [kap tan]

caption ['kæpʃən] n คำบรรยายใต้ภาพ
[kham ban yai tai phap]

capture ['kæptʃə] v จับกุม [chap khum]

car [kɑː] n รถยนต์ [rot yon]; **buffet car** n
รถมีอาหารที่ลูกค้าบริการตัวเอง [rot mii a
han thii luk kha bo ri kan tua eng];
cable car n รถที่เคลื่อนที่โดยสายเคเบิล
[rot thii khluean thii doi sai khe boen];
car hire n รถเช่า [rot chao]; **Can you
take me by car?** คุณพาฉันไปโดยรถยนต์
ได้ไหม? [khun pha chan pai doi rot yon
dai mai]

carafe [kə'ræf; -'rɑːf] n ขวดชนิดหนึ่งที่
ใส่น้ำดื่มหรือไวน์เพื่อเสิร์ฟที่โต๊ะอาหาร

[khaut cha nit nueng thii sai nam duem rue wai phuea soep thii to a han]

caramel ['kærəməl; -ˌmɛl] n คาราเมล [ka ra mel]

carat ['kærət] n กะรัต [ka rat]

caravan ['kærəˌvæn] n รถคาราวาน [rot kha ra van]; **caravan site** n ที่จอดรถคาราวาน [thii jot rot kha ra wan]; **Can we park our caravan here?** เราจะจอดรถคาราวานของเราที่นี่ได้ไหม? [rao jot rot kha ra van khong rao thii ni dai mai]; **We'd like a site for a caravan** เราอยากได้บริเวณที่จอดรถคาราวาน [rao yak dai bo ri wen thii jot rot kha ra van]

carbohydrate [ˌkɑːbəʊˈhaɪdreɪt] n คาร์โบไฮเดรท [ka bo hai dret]

carbon ['kɑːbˀn] n คาร์บอน [kha bon]; **carbon footprint** n คาร์บอนที่แต่ละคนใช้ในชีวิตประจำวันส่งไปในบรรยากาศของโลก [kha bon thii tae la khon chai nai chi wid pra cham wan song pai nai ban ya kat khong lok]

carburettor [ˌkɑːbjʊˈrɛtə; 'kɑːbjʊˌrɛtə; -bə-] n ตัวดูดอากาศเข้าลูกสูบ [tua dut a kaat khao luk sup]

card [kɑːd] n บัตรอวยพร [bat uai phon]; **boarding card** n บัตรขึ้นเครื่องบินหรือยานพาหนะ [bat khuen khrueang bin rue yan pha ha na]; **credit card** n บัตรเครดิต [bat khre dit]; **debit card** n บัตรที่หักบัญชี [bat thii hak ban chi]

cardboard ['kɑːdˌbɔːd] n กระดาษแข็ง [kra dat khaeng]

cardigan ['kɑːdɪgən] n เสื้อไหมพรมติดกระดุมหน้า [suea mai phrom tit kra dum na]

cardphone ['kɑːdfəʊn] n บัตรโทรศัพท์ [bat tho ra sab]

care [kɛə] n การดูแล [kan du lae] ▷ v ดูแล [du lae]; **intensive care unit** n ห้องไอซียู [hong ai si u]; **Take care** ดูแล [du lae]

career [kəˈrɪə] n อาชีพการทำงาน [a chiip kan tham ngan]

careful ['kɛəfʊl] adj ระมัดระวัง [ra mat ra wang]

carefully ['kɛəfʊlɪ] adv อย่างระมัดระวัง [yang ra mat ra wang]

careless ['kɛəlɪs] adj ไม่ระมัดระวัง [mai ra mat ra wang]

caretaker ['kɛəˌteɪkə] n ผู้รับจ้างดูแล [phu rab chang du lae]

car-ferry ['kɑːfɛrɪ] n เรือแฟร์รี่บรรทุกรถต่าง ๆ [ruea fae ri ban thuk rot tang tang]

cargo ['kɑːgəʊ] n สินค้า [sin kha]

Caribbean [ˌkærɪˈbiːən; kəˈrɪbɪən] adj เกี่ยวกับประเทศในทะเลแคริเบียน [kiao kap pra thet nai tha le khae ri bian] ▷ n ชาวแคริเบียน [chao khae ri bian]

caring ['kɛərɪŋ] adj ที่ห่วงใยผู้อื่น [thii huang yai phu uen]

carnation [kɑːˈneɪʃən] n ดอกคาร์เนชั่น [dok kha ne chan]

carnival ['kɑːnɪvˀl] n งานฉลองของมวลชน [ngan cha long khong muan chon]

carol ['kærəl] n เพลงสวดหรือเพลงร้องเพื่อความสนุกสนาน [phleng suad hue phleng rong phue khwam sa nuk sa nan]

carpenter ['kɑːpɪntə] n ช่างไม้ [chang mai]

carpentry ['kɑːpɪntrɪ] n ที่เกี่ยวกับช่างไม้ [thii kiao kap chang mai]

carpet ['kɑːpɪt] n พรม [phrom]; **fitted carpet** n พรมที่ปูติดแน่น [phrom thii pu tit naen]

carriage ['kærɪdʒ] n ตู้โดยสารรถไฟ [tu doi san rot fai]

carriageway ['kærɪdʒˌweɪ] n **dual carriageway** n ทางรถคู่ [thang rot khu]

carrot ['kærət] n แครอท [kae rot]

carry ['kærɪ] v ขนส่ง [khon song]

carrycot ['kærɪˌkɒt] n ที่นอนเด็กที่หิ้วไปไหน ๆ ได้ [thii non dek thii hio pai nai nai dai]

carry on ['kærɪ ɒn] v ดำเนินต่อไป [dam noen to pai]

carry out ['kærɪ aʊt] v ทำให้สำเร็จ [tham hai sam ret]

cart [kɑːt] n เกวียน รถเข็น [kwian, rot khen]

carton ['kɑːtᵊn] n กล่องบรรจุกระดาษหรือ พลาสติก [klong ban chu kra dart hue phlas tik]

cartoon [kɑːˈtuːn] n การ์ตูน [ka tun]

cartridge ['kɑːtrɪdʒ] n ปลอกกระสุนปืน [plok kra sun puen]

carve [kɑːv] v แกะสลัก [kae sa lak]

case [keɪs] n คดี กรณี [kha di, ko ra nii]; **pencil case** n กล่องใส่ดินสอ [klong sai din so]

cash [kæʃ] n เงินสด [ngoen sot]; **Can I get a cash advance with my credit card?** ฉันจะเบิกเงินสดล่วงหน้าจากบัตร เครดิตของฉันได้ไหม? [chan ja boek ngoen sot luang na chak bat khre dit khong chan dai mai]; **Do you offer a discount for cash?** คุณมีส่วนลดสำหรับ เงินสดไหม? [khun mii suan lot sam rap ngoen sot mai]; **I don't have any cash** ฉันไม่มีเงินสด [chan mai mii ngoen sot]

cashew ['kæʃuː; kæˈʃuː] n เมล็ด มะม่วงหิมพานต์ [ma let ma muang him ma phan]

cashier [kæˈʃɪə] n เจ้าหน้าที่การเงิน [chao na thii kan ngoen]

cashmere ['kæʃmɪə] n ขนสัตว์นุ่มที่ได้ จากแพะ [khon sat num thii dai chak phae]

casino [kəˈsiːnəʊ] n บ่อนการพนัน [bon kan pha nan]

casserole ['kæsəˌrəʊl] n อาหารอบจาก หม้อที่มีฝาปิด [a han op chak mo thii mii fa pit]

cassette [kæˈsɛt] n ตลับเทป [ta lap thep]

cast [kɑːst] n การขว้าง [kan khwang]

castle ['kɑːsᵊl] n ปราสาท [pra sat]

casual ['kæʒjʊəl] adj โดยบังเอิญ [doi bang oen]

casually ['kæʒjʊəlɪ] adv อย่างบังเอิญ [yang bang oen]

casualty ['kæʒjʊəltɪ] n จำนวนคนเสีย ชีวิตหรือได้รับบาดเจ็บ [cham nuan kon sia chi vid hue dai rab bad chep]

cat [kæt] n แมว [maeo]

catalogue ['kætəˌlɒg] n บัญชีรายการ สินค้า [ban chi rai kan sin ka]

cataract ['kætəˌrækt] n (eye) ต้อ [to], (waterfall) น้ำตกที่สูงชัน [nam tok thii sung chan]

catarrh [kəˈtɑː] n โรคหวัดที่มีน้ำมูกไหล ออกมา [rok wat thii mii nam muk lai ok ma]

catastrophe [kəˈtæstrəfɪ] n ความ หายนะ [khwam hai ya na]

catch [kætʃ] v จับไว้ได้ ฉวยจับ [chap dai, chuai chap]

catching ['kætʃɪŋ] adj ที่ติดต่อได้ง่าย [thii tid tor dai ngai]

catch up [kætʃ ʌp] v ตามทัน [tam than]

category ['kætɪgərɪ] n หมวดหมู่ [muat mu]

catering ['keɪtərɪŋ] n การจัดอาหาร [kan chad a han]

caterpillar ['kætəˌpɪlə] n หนอนผีเสื้อ [non phi suea]

cathedral [kəˈθiːdrəl] n มหาวิหาร [ma ha wi han]

Catholic ['kæθəlɪk; 'kæθlɪk] adj นิกาย คาทอลิค [ni kai kha tho lik] ▷ n ผู้นับถือ นิกายคาทอลิค [phu nap thue ni kai kha tho lik]; **Roman Catholic** n ที่เกี่ยวกับ ศาสนาโรมันคาทอลิค [thii kiao kap sat sa na ro man kha tho lik], ผู้นับถือนิกาย โรมันคาทอลิค [thii kiao kap sat sa na ro man kha tho lik, phu nap thue ni kai ro man kha tho lik]

cattle ['kætᵊl] npl วัวควาย [vua khwai]

Caucasus ['kɔːkəsəs] n เทือกเขาในคอเค เซีย [thueak khao nai kho khe chia]

cauliflower ['kɒlɪˌflaʊə] n กะหล่ำดอก [ka lam dok]

cause [kɔːz] n (ideals) หัวเรื่องการอภิปราย [hua rueang kan a phi prai], (reason) เหตุผลที่ดี [het phon thii di] ▷ v ทำให้เกิด [tham hai koed]

caution ['kɔːʃən] n การตักเตือน [kan tak tuean]

cautious ['kɔːʃəs] adj ระมัดระวัง [ra mat ra wang]

cautiously ['kɔːʃəslɪ] adv อย่างระมัดระวัง [yang ra mat ra wang]

cave [keɪv] n ถ้ำ [tham]

CCTV [siː siː tiː viː] abbr ตัวย่อของกล้อง โทรทัศน์วงจรภายใน [tua yor khong klong tho ra tat wong chorn phai nai]

CD [siː diː] n ซีดี [si di]; **CD burner** n ซอฟแวร์ที่บันทึกดนตรีลงในซีดี [sop wae thii ban thuek don tree long nai si di]; **CD player** n เครื่องเล่นซีดี [khrueang len si di]; **Can I make CDs at this computer?** ฉันทำซีดีกับเครื่อง คอมพิวเตอร์นี้ได้ไหม? [chan tham si di kap khrueang khom phio toe nii dai mai]

CD-ROM [-'rɒm] n ซีดี-รอม [si di -rom]

ceasefire ['siːsˈfaɪə] n การหยุดรบ [kan yut rop]

ceiling ['siːlɪŋ] n เพดาน [phe dan]

celebrate ['sɛlɪˌbreɪt] v ฉลอง [cha long]

celebration ['sɛlɪˌbreɪʃən] n การฉลอง [kan cha long]

celebrity [sɪˈlɛbrɪtɪ] n ผู้มีชื่อเสียง [phu mee chue siang]

celery ['sɛlərɪ] n ผักคื่นช่าย [phak khuen chai]

cell [sɛl] n ห้องเล็กในห้องขัง [hong lek nai hong khang]

cellar ['sɛlə] n ห้องใต้ดิน [hong tai din]

cello ['tʃɛləʊ] n ไวโอลินเซโล [vi o lin che lo]

cement [sɪˈmɛnt] n ซีเมนต์ [si men]

cemetery ['sɛmɪtrɪ] n สุสาน [su san]

census ['sɛnsəs] n การสำรวจจำนวน ประชากร [kan sam ruat cham nuan pra cha kon]

cent [sɛnt] n หน่วยเงินเซ็นต์ [nuai ngoen sen]

centenary [sɛnˈtiːnərɪ] n การครบรอบ หนึ่งร้อยปี [kan khrop rop nueng roi pi]

centimetre ['sɛntɪˌmiːtə] n เซนติเมตร [sen ti met]

central ['sɛntrəl] adj ที่เป็นศูนย์กลาง [thii pen sun klang]; **central heating** n ระบบทำความร้อน [ra bop tham khwam ron]; **Central America** n อเมริกากลาง [a me ri ka klang]

centre ['sɛntə] n ศูนย์กลาง [sun klang]; **call centre** n ศูนย์โทรศัพท์ [sun tho ra sap]; **city centre** n ใจกลางเมือง [jai klang mueang]; **job centre** n หน่วย จัดหางาน [nuai chat ha ngan]

century ['sɛntʃərɪ] n ศตวรรษ [sa ta wat]

CEO [siː iː əʊ] abbr ตัวย่อของเจ้าหน้าที่ ระดับสูง [tua yor khong chao na thii ra dab sung]

ceramic [sɪˈræmɪk] adj เซรามิค [se ra mik]

cereal ['sɪərɪəl] n อาหารเช้าที่ทำจาก ธัญพืช [a han chao thii tham chak than ya phuet]

ceremony ['sɛrɪmənɪ] n พิธีการ [phi thi kon]

certain ['sɜːtən] adj แน่นอน [nae non]

certainly ['sɜːtənlɪ] adv อย่างแน่นอน [yang nae norn]

certainty ['sɜːtəntɪ] n ความแน่นอน [khwam nae non]

certificate [səˈtɪfɪkɪt] n ประกาศนียบัตร [pra ka sa ni ya bat]; **birth certificate** n ใบเกิด [bai koet]; **marriage certificate** n ใบทะเบียนสมรส [bai tha bian som rot]; **medical certificate** n ใบรับรองแพทย์ [bai rap rong phaet]

Chad [tʃæd] n ประเทศชาดในอัฟริกา [pra tet chad nai af ri ka]

chain [tʃeɪn] n โซ่ [so]; **Do I need snow chains?** ฉันต้องใส่โซ่กันหิมะหรือไม่? [chan tong sai so kan hi ma rue mai]

chair [tʃɛə] n (furniture) เก้าอี้ [kao i];

easy chair *n* เก้าอี้ที่มีที่วางแขน [kao ii thii mii thii wang khaen]; **rocking chair** *n* เก้าอี้โยก [kao ii yok]; **Do you have a high chair?** คุณมีเก้าอี้สำหรับเด็ก ไหม? [khun mii kao ii sam rap dek mai]

chairlift ['tʃɛə,lɪft] *n* เก้าอี้ยกคนขึ้นไปเล่น สกี [kao ee yok kon khuen pai len sa ki]

chairman, chairmen ['tʃɛəmən, 'tʃɛəmɛn] *n* ประธานกรรมการ [pra than kam ma kan]

chalk [tʃɔːk] *n* ชอล์ก [chok]

challenge ['tʃælɪndʒ] *n* การท้าทาย [kan tha thai] ▷ *v* ท้าทาย [tha thai]

challenging ['tʃælɪndʒɪŋ] *adj* ที่ท้าทาย [thii tha thai]

chambermaid ['tʃeɪmbə,meɪd] *n* สาว ใช้ทำความสะอาดห้องนอน [sao chai tham khwam sa at hong non]

champagne [ʃæm'peɪn] *n* แชมเปญ [chaem pen]

champion ['tʃæmpɪən] *n* ผู้ชนะเลิศ [phu cha na loet]

championship ['tʃæmpɪən,ʃɪp] *n* ตำแหน่งชนะเลิศ [tam naeng cha na loet]

chance [tʃɑːns] *n* โอกาส [o kat]; **by chance** *adv* โดยบังเอิญ [doi bang oen]

change [tʃeɪndʒ] *n* การเปลี่ยนแปลง [kan plian plaeng] ▷ *vi* เปลี่ยน [plian] ▷ *vt* เปลี่ยน แลกเปลี่ยน [plian, laek plian]; **Do I have to change?** ฉันต้องเปลี่ยนหรือ ไม่? [chan tong plian rue mai]; **I want to change my ticket** ฉันอยากเปลี่ยนตั๋ว ของฉัน [chan yak plian tua khong chan]; **I'd like to change my flight** ฉัน อยากเปลี่ยนเที่ยวบินของฉัน [chan yak plian thiao bin khong chan]

changeable ['tʃeɪndʒəbəl] *adj* ที่ เปลี่ยนแปลงได้ [thii plian plang dai]

channel ['tʃænəl] *n* ช่อง [chong]

chaos ['keɪɒs] *n* ความสับสน [khwam sap son]

chaotic ['keɪ'ɒtɪk] *adj* ยุ่งเหยิง [yung yoeng]

chap [tʃæp] *n* ผู้ชาย [phu chai]

chapel ['tʃæpəl] *n* โบสถ์เล็ก ๆ [bot lek lek]

chapter ['tʃæptə] *n* บทของหนังสือหรือ งานเขียน [bot khong nang sue rue ngan khian]

character ['kærɪktə] *n* คุณลักษณะ [khun na lak sa na]

characteristic [,kærɪktə'rɪstɪk] *n* อุปนิสัย [up pa ni sai]

charcoal ['tʃɑː,kəʊl] *n* ถ่าน [than]

charge [tʃɑːdʒ] *n* (accusation) ข้อกล่าวหา [kho klao ha], (electricity) ประจุไฟฟ้า [pra chu fai fa], (price) ค่าใช้จ่าย [kha chai chai] ▷ *v* (accuse) ฟ้องร้อง [fong rong], (electricity) อัดไฟ [at fai], (price) เรียกเก็บเงิน [riak kep ngoen]; **admission charge** *n* ค่าธรรมเนียมใน การเข้า [kha tham niam nai kan khao]; **cover charge** *n* ค่าบริการเพิ่มจากค่า อาหาร [kha bo ri kan poem chak kha a han]; **service charge** *n* ค่าบริการ [kha bo ri kan]

charger ['tʃɑːdʒə] *n* เครื่องอัดไฟ [khrueang at fai]

charity ['tʃærɪtɪ] *n* การกุศล [kan ku son]; **charity shop** *n* ร้านการกุศล [ran kan ku son]

charm [tʃɑːm] *n* เสน่ห์ [sa ne]

charming ['tʃɑːmɪŋ] *adj* มีเสน่ห์ [moii sa ne]

chart [tʃɑːt] *n* ตาราง [ta rang]; **pie chart** *n* ภาพแสดงสถิติรูปพาย [phap sa daeng sa thi ti rup phai]

chase [tʃeɪs] *n* การไล่ตาม [kan lai tam] ▷ *v* ไล่ตาม [lai tam]

chat [tʃæt] *n* การพูดคุยกันเล่น ๆ [kan phut khui kan len len] ▷ *v* คุยเล่น [khui len]; **chat show** *n* รายการทีวีที่มีการพูด คุยกับแขกรับเชิญ [rai kan thii wii thii mii kan phut khui kap khaek rap choen]

chatroom ['tʃæt,ruːm; -,rʊm] *n* ห้องคุย [hong khui]

chauffeur ['ʃəʊfə; ʃəʊ'fɜ:] *n* คนขับรถ [kon khab rot]

chauvinist ['ʃəʊvɪ,nɪst] *n* ผู้ยึดถือ อุดมการณ์ [phu yuet thue u dom kan]

cheap [tʃi:p] *adj* อย่างถูก [yang thuk]

cheat [tʃi:t] *n* การคดโกง [kan khot kong] ▷ *v* ทุจริต [thut cha rit]

Chechnya ['tʃɛtʃnjə] *n* ประเทศเชสเนีย [pra tet ches nia]

check [tʃɛk] *n* การตรวจ [kan truat] ▷ *v* ตรวจ [truat]; **Can you check the water, please?** คุณช่วยตรวจดูน้ำได้ ไหม? [khun chuai truat du nam dai mai]

checked [tʃɛkt] *adj* ที่มีลายตารางหมากรุก [thii mii lai ta rang mak ruk]

check in [tʃɛk ɪn] *v* ลงทะเบียนเพื่อเข้าพัก [long tha bian phuea khao phak]

check-in [tʃɛkɪn] *n* ลงทะเบียนเข้าพักใน โรงแรมหรือก่อนขึ้นรถ, เครื่องบิน [long tha bian khao phak nai rong raeng hue kon khuen rot, khueang bin]

check out [tʃɛk aʊt] *v* แจ้งออก [chaeng ok]

checkout ['tʃɛkaʊt] *n* การแจ้งออกจาก ที่พักหรือห้องของโรงแรม [kan chaeng ork chak thii phak hue hong khong rong raeng]

check-up ['tʃɛkʌp] *n* การตรวจสุขภาพ [kan truat suk kha phap]

cheek [tʃi:k] *n* แก้ม [kaem]

cheekbone ['tʃi:k,bəʊn] *n* โหนกแก้ม [nok kaem]

cheeky ['tʃi:kɪ] *adj* ที่ไม่เคารพ [thii mai khao rop]

cheer [tʃɪə] *n* การส่งเสียงเชียร์ [kan song siang chia] ▷ *v* เปล่งเสียงแสดงความยินดี [pleng siang sa daeng khwam yin dii]

cheerful ['tʃɪəfʊl] *adj* ที่ทำให้รู้สึกสดชื่น [thii tham hai ru suek sot chuen]

cheerio [,tʃɪərɪ'əʊ] *excl* ลาก่อน [la kon]

cheers [tʃɪəz] *excl* ไชโย ชนแก้ว [chai yo chon kaew]

cheese [tʃi:z] *n* เนยแข็ง [noei khaeng];

cottage cheese *n* เนยเหลวชนิดหนึ่ง [noei leo cha nit nueng]; **What sort of cheese?** คุณมีเนยแข็งแบบไหน? [khun mii noei khaeng baep nai]

chef [ʃɛf] *n* หัวหน้าพ่อครัว [hua na pho khrua]; **What is the chef's speciality?** อาหารพิเศษของหัวหน้าพ่อ ครัวคืออะไร? [a han phi set khong hua na pho khrua khue a rai]

chemical ['kɛmɪkəl] *n* สารเคมี [san khe mi]

chemist ['kɛmɪst] **chemist('s)** *n* ที่ร้าน ขายยาหรือเครื่องสำอาง [thii ran khai ya rue khrueang sam ang]; **Where is the nearest chemist?** ร้านขายยาที่ใกล้ที่สุด อยู่ที่ไหน? [ran khai ya thii klai thii sut yu thii nai]

chemistry ['kɛmɪstrɪ] *n* วิชาเคมี [wi cha ke mii]

cheque [tʃɛk] *n* ใบสั่งจ่ายเช็ค [bai sang chai chek]; **blank cheque** *n* เช็คเปล่า [chek plao]; **traveller's cheque** *n* เช็ค เดินทาง [chek doen thang]

chequebook ['tʃɛk,bʊk] *n* สมุดเช็ค [sa mud chek]

cherry ['tʃɛrɪ] *n* ผลเชอร์รี่ [phon choe ri]

chess [tʃɛs] *n* หมากรุก [mak ruk]

chest [tʃɛst] *n* (*body part*) หน้าอก [na ok], (*storage*) หีบ ลัง กล่อง [hip, lang, klong]; **chest of drawers** *n* ตู้ที่มีลิ้นชัก [tu thii mii lin chak]; **I have a pain in my chest** ฉันเจ็บหน้าอก [chan chep na ok]

chestnut ['tʃɛs,nʌt] *n* ลูกเกาลัด [luk kao lat]

chew [tʃu:] *v* เคี้ยว [khiao]; **chewing gum** *n* หมากฝรั่ง [mak fa rang]

chick [tʃɪk] *n* ลูกไก่ ลูกนก [luk kai, luk nok]

chicken ['tʃɪkɪn] *n* ไก่ [kai]

chickenpox ['tʃɪkɪn,pɒks] *n* โรคอีสุกอีใส [rok i suk i sai]

chickpea ['tʃɪk,pi:] *n* ถั่วจำพวกหนึ่งมีรูป กลมเล็กสีน้ำตาลอ่อนใช้ทำอาหาร [thua cham phua khueng mee rup klom lek see nam tan on chai tham a han]

chief [tʃiːf] *adj* สำคัญ [sam khan] ▷ *n* ผู้นำ [phu nam]

child, children [tʃaɪld, 'tʃɪldrən] *n* เด็ก [dek]; **Do you have a children's menu?** คุณมีรายการอาหารเด็กไหม? [khun mii rai kan a han dek mai]; **I need someone to look after the children tonight** ฉันอยากได้คนดูแลเด็ก ๆ คืนนี้ [chan yak dai khon du lae dek dek khuen nii]; **I'd like a child seat for a two-year-old child** ฉันอยากได้ที่นั่ง เด็กอายุสองขวบ [chan yak dai thii nang dek a yu song khuap]

childcare ['tʃaɪld,kɛə] *n* การดูแลเลี้ยงเด็ก [kan du lae liang dek]

childhood ['tʃaɪldhʊd] *n* วัยเด็ก [wai dek]

childish ['tʃaɪldɪʃ] *adj* ไร้เดียงสาอย่างเด็ก [rai diang sa yang dek]

childminder ['tʃaɪld,maɪndə] *n* คนดูแล เด็ก [kon du lae dek]

Chile ['tʃɪlɪ] *n* ประเทศชิลี [pra tet chi li]

Chilean ['tʃɪlɪən] *adj* เกี่ยวกับประเทศชิลี [kiao kap pra thet chi li] ▷ *n* ชาวชิลี [chao chi li]

chill [tʃɪl] *v* ทำให้เย็น [tham hai yen]

chilli ['tʃɪlɪ] *n* พริก [phrik]

chilly ['tʃɪlɪ] *adj* หนาวเย็น [nao yen]

chimney ['tʃɪmnɪ] *n* ปล่องไฟ [plong fai]

chimpanzee [,tʃɪmpæn'ziː] *n* ลิง ชิมแปนซี [ling chim paen si]

chin [tʃɪn] *n* คาง [khang]

china ['tʃaɪnə] *n* เครื่องเคลือบดินเผา [khrueang khlueap din phao]

China ['tʃaɪnə] *n* ประเทศจีน [pra tet chin]

Chinese [tʃaɪ'niːz] *adj* ที่เกี่ยวกับชาติจีน [thii kiao kap chat chin] ▷ *n* (*language*) ภาษาจีน [pha sa chin], (*person*) ชาวจีน [chao chin]

chip [tʃɪp] *n* (*electronic*) แผ่นไมโครชิป [phaen mai khro chip], (*small piece*)

เศษที่แตกออกไป [sed thii taek ork pai]; **silicon chip** *n* การฝังไมโครชิป [kan fang mai khro chip]

chips [tʃɪps] *npl* มันฝรั่งทอด [man fa rang thot]

chiropodist [kɪ'rɒpədɪst] *n* หมอที่รักษา โรคที่เกี่ยวกับมือหรือเท้า [mo thii rak sa rok thii kiao kap mue rue thao]

chisel ['tʃɪzᵊl] *n* สิ่ว [sio]

chives [tʃaɪvz] *npl* พืชคล้ายหัวหอมมีก้าน ยาวสีเขียว [phuet khlai hua hom mii kan yao sii khiao]

chlorine ['klɔːriːn] *n* คลอรีน [khlo rin]

chocolate ['tʃɒkəlɪt; 'tʃɒklɪt; -lət] *n* ช็อกโกแลต [chok ko laet]; **milk chocolate** *n* ช็อกโกแลตนม [chok ko laet nom]; **plain chocolate** *n* ช็อกโกแลตที่รสคนข้างขมและมีสีดำ [chok ko laet thii rot khon khang khom lae mii sii dam]

choice [tʃɔɪs] *n* การเลือก [kan lueak]

choir [kwaɪə] *n* คณะร้องเพลงประสานเสียง [kha na rong phleng pra san siang]

choke [tʃəʊk] *v* ทำให้หายใจไม่ออก [tham hai hai jai mai ork]

cholesterol [kə'lɛstəˌrɒl] *n* ไขมันใน เส้นเลือด [khai man nai sen lueat]

choose [tʃuːz] *v* เลือก [lueak]

chop [tʃɒp] *n* การสับ [kan sap] ▷ *v* สับ [sap]; **pork chop** *n* เนื้อหมูที่ติดกระดูก [nuea mu thii tit kra duk]

chopsticks ['tʃɒpstɪks] *npl* ตะเกียบ [ta kiap]

chosen ['tʃəʊzᵊn] *adj* ที่เลือกแล้ว [thii lueak laeo]

Christ [kraɪst] *n* พระเยซูคริสต์ [phra ye su khris]

christening ['krɪsᵊnɪŋ] *n* การทำพิธีล้าง บาปและตั้งชื่อ [kan tham phi thii lang bap lae tang chue]

Christian ['krɪstʃən] *adj* เกี่ยวกับชาว คริสต์ [kiao kap chao khris] ▷ *n* คริสต์ ศาสนิกชน [khrit sat sa nik ka chon]; **Christian name** *n* ชื่อที่ตั้งในพิธีชำระ

บาป [chue thii tang nai phi tii cham ra bap]

Christianity [ˌkrɪstɪˈænɪtɪ] *n* ศาสนา คริสต์ [sad sa na khris]

Christmas [ˈkrɪsməs] *n* คริสต์มาส [kris mat]; **Christmas card** *n* บัตรคริสต์มาส [bat khris mas]; **Christmas Eve** *n* คืน ก่อนวันคริสต์มาส [khuen kon wan khris mas]; **Christmas tree** *n* ต้นคริสต์มาส [ton khris mas]; **Merry Christmas!** เม อรี่คริสต์มาส [moe ri khris mas]

chrome [krəʊm] *n* แผ่นโครเมียม [phaen khro miam]

chronic [ˈkrɒnɪk] *adj* เรื้อรัง [rue rang]

chrysanthemum [krɪˈsænθəməm] *n* ดอกเบญจมาศ [dok ben cha mat]

chubby [ˈtʃʌbɪ] *adj* อ้วนกลม [uan klom]

chunk [tʃʌŋk] *n* เนื้อหรือไม้ชิ้นหนาสั้น [nuea rue mai chin na san]

church [tʃɜːtʃ] *n* โบสถ์ [bot]

cider [ˈsaɪdə] *n* น้ำแอปเปิ้ลที่มีแอลกอฮอล์ [nam ap poen thii mii aen ko ho]

cigar [sɪˈɡɑː] *n* ซิการ์ [si ka]

cigarette [ˌsɪɡəˈrɛt] *n* บุหรี่ [bu ri]; **cigarette lighter** *n* ไฟที่จุดบุหรี่ [fai thii chut bu ri]

cinema [ˈsɪnɪmə] *n* โรงภาพยนตร์ [rong phap pha yon]

cinnamon [ˈsɪnəmən] *n* อบเชย [op choei]

circle [ˈsɜːkᵊl] *n* วงกลม [wong klom]; **Arctic Circle** *n* วงเขตขั้วโลกเหนือ [wong khet khua lok nuea]

circuit [ˈsɜːkɪt] *n* ขอบเขต [khop khet]

circular [ˈsɜːkjʊlə] *adj* ที่เป็นวงกลม [thii pen wong klom]

circulation [ˌsɜːkjʊˈleɪʃən] *n* การ หมุนเวียน [kan mun wian]

circumstances [ˈsɜːkəmstənsɪz] *npl* สถานการณ์ [sa tha na kan]

circus [ˈsɜːkəs] *n* โรงละครสัตว์ [rong la khon sat]

citizen [ˈsɪtɪzᵊn] *n* พลเมือง [phon la muang]; **senior citizen** *n* พลเมืองอาวุโส [phon la mueang a wu so]

citizenship [ˈsɪtɪzənˌʃɪp] *n* ความเป็น พลเมือง [khwam pen phon la mueang]

city [ˈsɪtɪ] *n* เมือง [mueang]; **Is there a bus to the city?** มีรถโดยสารไปในเมือง ไหม? [mii rot doi san pai nai mueang mai]; **Please take me to the city centre** ช่วยพาฉันไปใจกลางเมือง [chuai pha chan pai jai klang mueang]; **Where can I buy a map of the city?** ฉันจะซื้อแผนที่ของเมืองนี้ได้ที่ไหน? [chan ja sue phaen thii khong mueang nii dai thii nai]

civilian [sɪˈvɪljən] *adj* เกี่ยวกับพลเรือน [kiao kap phon la ruean] ▷ *n* พลเรือน [phon la ruan]

civilization [ˌsɪvɪlaɪˈzeɪʃən] *n* อารยธรรม [a ra ya tham]

claim [kleɪm] *n* การเรียกร้อง [kan riak rong] ▷ *v* เรียกร้อง [riak rong]; **claim form** *n* แบบฟอร์มการเรียกร้อง [baep fom kan riak rong]

clap [klæp] *v* ปรบมือ [prop mue]

clarify [ˈklærɪˌfaɪ] *v* ทำให้ใสสะอาด [tham hai sai sa ad]

clarinet [ˌklærɪˈnɛt] *n* เครื่องดนตรี ประเภทเป่าชนิดหนึ่ง [khrueang don tri pra phet pao cha nit nueng]

clash [klæʃ] *v* ชน [chon]

clasp [klɑːsp] *n* เข็มกลัด [khem klat]

class [klɑːs] *n* ชั้นเรียน [chan rian]; **business class** *n* ชั้นธุรกิจ [chan thu ra kit]; **economy class** *n* ชั้นประหยัด [chan pra yat]; **second class** *n* ชั้นที่สอง [chan thii song]

classic [ˈklæsɪk] *adj* คลาสสิก [klat sik] ▷ *n* นักประพันธ์ นักศิลปะหรืองานทางศิลปะ ที่ยอดเยี่ยมที่สุด [nak pra phan, nak sin la pa rue ngan thang sin la pa thii yot yiam thii sut]

classical [ˈklæsɪkᵊl] *adj* เกี่ยวกับแบบกรีก และโรมัน [kiao kap baep krik lae ro man]

classmate [ˈklɑːsˌmeɪt] *n* เพื่อนร่วมชั้น

เรียน [phuean ruam chan rian]

classroom ['klɑːsˌruːm; -ˌrʊm] *n*
ห้องเรียน [hong rian]; **classroom
assistant** *n* ครูผู้ช่วยในห้องเรียน [khru
phu chuai nai hong rian]

clause [klɔːz] *n* มาตรา [mat tra]

claustrophobic [ˌklɔːstrəˈfəʊbɪk;
ˌklɒs-] *adj* การกลัวที่อยู่ในที่แคบ [kan
klua thii yu nai thii khaep]

claw [klɔː] *n* กรงเล็บ [krong lep]

clay [kleɪ] *n* ดินเหนียว [din niao]

clean [kliːn] *adj* สะอาด [sa ad] ▷ *v*
ทำความสะอาด [tham khwam sa ad];
Can you clean the room, please? คุณ
ช่วยทำความสะอาดห้องได้ไหม? [khun
chuai tham khwam sa at hong dai
mai]; **I'd like to get these things
cleaned** ฉันอยากทำความสะอาดเสื้อผ้า
พวกนี้ [chan yak tham khwam sa aat
suea pha phuak nii]; **The room isn't
clean** ห้องไม่สะอาด [hong mai sa at]

cleaner ['kliːnə] *n* คนทำความสะอาด
[kon tham khwam sa ad]; **When does
the cleaner come?** คนทำความสะอาดจะ
มาเมื่อไร? [khon tham khwam sa at ja
ma muea rai]

cleaning ['kliːnɪŋ] *n* การทำความสะอาด
[kan tham khwam sa ad]; **cleaning
lady** *n* หญิงทำความสะอาด [ying tham
khwam sa at]

cleanser ['klɛnzə] *n* สิ่งที่ใช้ทำความ
สะอาดผิวหน้า [sing thii chai tham
khwam sa at phio na]

clear [klɪə] *adj* ชัดเจน [chat chen]

clearly ['klɪəlɪ] *adv* อย่างชัดเจน [yang
chat chen]

clear off [klɪə ɒf] *v* เอาออกไป [ao ok pai]

clear up [klɪə ʌp] *v* ทำความสะอาดจนหมด
[tham khwam sa aat chon mot]

clementine ['klɛmənˌtiːn; -ˌtaɪn] *n* ส้ม
ชนิดหนึ่ง [som cha nit nueng]

clever ['klɛvə] *adj* เฉลียวฉลาด [cha liao
cha lat]

click [klɪk] *n* เสียงดังกริ๊ก [siang dang

krik] ▷ *v* เกิดเสียงดังกริ๊ก [koet siang
dang krik]

client ['klaɪənt] *n* ลูกค้า [lik kha]

cliff [klɪf] *n* หน้าผา [na pha]

climate ['klaɪmɪt] *n* อากาศ [a kat];
climate change *n* การเปลี่ยนแปลงของ
อากาศ [kan plian plaeng khong a kat]

climb [klaɪm] *v* ปีน [pin]; **I'd like to go
climbing** ฉันอยากไปปีนเขา [chan yak
pai pin khao]

climber ['klaɪmə] *n* คนปีน [khon pin]

climbing ['klaɪmɪŋ] *n* การปีน [kan pin]

clinic ['klɪnɪk] *n* คลินิค [kli nik]

clip [klɪp] *n* การหนีบติดกัน [kan niip tit
kan]

clippers ['klɪpəz] *npl* กรรไกร [kan krai]

cloakroom ['kləʊkˌruːm; -ˌrʊm] *n* ห้อง
เก็บเสื้อโค้ท [hong keb suea khot]

clock [klɒk] *n* นาฬิกา [na li ka]; **alarm
clock** *n* นาฬิกาปลุก [na li ka pluk]

clockwise ['klɒkˌwaɪz] *adv* ตามเข็ม
นาฬิกา [tam khem na li ka]

clog [klɒg] *n* รองเท้าไม้ [rong thao mai]

clone [kləʊn] *n* สิ่งมีชีวิตที่เกิดมาจากเซลล์
เดียวกัน [sing mii chi wit thii koet ma
chak sel diao kan] ▷ *v* ทำให้กำเนิดมาจาก
เซลล์เดียวกัน [tham hai kam noet ma
chak sel diao kan]

close *adj* [kləʊs] ใกล้ [klai] ▷ *adv* [kləʊs]
ชิดกัน [chit kan] ▷ *v* [kləʊz] ปิด [pit];
May I close the window? ฉันขอปิด
หน้าต่างได้ไหม? [chan kho pit na tang
dai mai]; **The door won't close** ปิด
ประตูไม่ได้ [pit pra tu mai dai]; **What
time do you close?** คุณปิดเวลาอะไร?
[khun pit we la a rai]

closed [kləʊzd] *adj* ปิดไม่รับสิ่งใหม่ [pid
mai rab sing mai]

closely [kləʊslɪ] *adv* อย่างใกล้ชิด [yang
klai chit]

closure ['kləʊʒə] *n* การปิด [kan pit]

cloth [klɒθ] *n* ผ้า [pha]

clothes [kləʊðz] *npl* เสื้อผ้า [suea pha];
clothes line *n* ราวตากผ้า [rao tak pha];

clothes peg n ไม้หนีบผ้า [mai nip pha]; **My clothes are damp** เสื้อผ้าฉันชื้น [suea pha chan chuen]

clothing ['kləʊðɪŋ] n เสื้อผ้า [suea pha]

cloud [klaʊd] n เมฆ [mek]

cloudy ['klaʊdɪ] adj ที่ปกคลุมด้วยเมฆ [thii pok khlum duai mek]

clove [kləʊv] n กานพลู [kan phlu]

clown [klaʊn] n ตัวตลก [tua ta lok]

club [klʌb] n (group) สมาคม สโมสร [sa ma khom, sa mo son], (weapon) ไม้ พลอง [mai phlong]; **golf club** n (game) ไม้ตีกอล์ฟ [mai ti kolf], (society) สโมสร กอล์ฟ [sa mo son kolf]

club together [klʌb tə'gɛðə] v ช่วยกัน ออกค่าใช้จ่าย [chuai kan ok kha chai jai]

clue [kluː] n เงื่อนงำ [nguean ngam]

clumsy ['klʌmzɪ] adj งุ่มง่าม [ngum ngam]

clutch [klʌtʃ] n คลัทช์ในรถยนต์ [khlat nai rot yon]

clutter ['klʌtə] n กองระเกะระกะ [kong ra ke ra ka]

coach [kəʊtʃ] n (trainer) ครูฝึกกีฬา [khru fuek ki la], (vehicle) รถโค้ช [rot khoch]

coal [kəʊl] n ถ่านหิน [than hin]

coarse [kɔːs] adj อย่างหยาบ [yang yap]

coast [kəʊst] n ชายฝั่ง [chai fang]

coastguard ['kəʊst,gɑːd] n หน่วยรักษา การณ์ตามชายฝั่งทะเล [nuai rak sa kan tam chai fang tha le]

coat [kəʊt] n เสื้อโค้ท [suea knot]; **fur coat** n เสื้อโค้ทที่ทำจากขนสัตว์ [suea khot tham chak khon sat]

coathanger ['kəʊt,hæŋə] n ไม้แขวนเสื้อ [mai khwaen suea]

cobweb ['kɒb,wɛb] n ใยแมงมุม [yai maeng mum]

cocaine [kə'keɪn] n ยาเสพติดชนิดหนึ่ง [ya sep tit cha nit nueng]

cock [kɒk] n ไก่ตัวผู้ [kai tua phu]

cockerel ['kɒkərəl; 'kɒkrəl] n ไก่ที่มีอายุ น้อยกว่าหนึ่งปี [kai thii mii a yu noi kwa nueng pi]

cockpit ['kɒk,pit] n ที่นั่งคนขับเครื่องบิน หรือรถแข่ง [thii nang kon khab khueang bin hue rot khaeng]

cockroach ['kɒk,rəʊtʃ] n แมลงสาบ [ma laeng sap]

cocktail ['kɒk,teɪl] n เครื่องดื่มเหล้าผสม น้ำผลไม้ [khrueang duem lao pha som nam phon la mai]

cocoa ['kəʊkəʊ] n ผงโกโก้ [phong ko ko]

coconut ['kəʊkə,nʌt] n มะพร้าว [ma phrao]

cod [kɒd] n ปลาคอด [pla khot]

code [kəʊd] n รหัส [ra hat]; **dialling code** n รหัสหมุนโทรศัพท์ [ra hat mun tho ra sap]; **Highway Code** n กฎจราจร ว่าด้วยการใช้ทางหลวง [kod ja ra jon wa duai kan chai thang luang]; **What is the dialling code for the UK?** รหัส หมุนไปสหราชอาณาจักรคืออะไร? [ra hat mun pai sa ha rat cha a na chak khue a rai]

coeliac ['siːlɪ,æk] adj ช่องท้อง [chong thong]

coffee ['kɒfɪ] n กาแฟ [ka fae]; **black coffee** n กาแฟดำ [ka fae dam]; **A white coffee, please** ขอกาแฟใส่นมหนึ่งที่ [kho ka fae sai nom nueng thii]; **Could we have another cup of coffee, please?** ขอกาแฟให้พวกเราอีกถ้วยได้ไหม? [kho ka fae hai phuak rao ik thuai dai mai]; **Have you got fresh coffee?** คุณมีกาแฟ สดไหม? [khun mii ka fae sot mai]

coffeepot ['kɒfɪ,pɒt] n หม้อกาแฟ [mo ka fae]

coffin ['kɒfɪn] n หีบศพ [hip sop]

coin [kɔɪn] n เหรียญ [rian]; **I'd like some coins for the phone, please** ฉันอยากได้เหรียญสำหรับโทรศัพท์ [chan yak dai rian sam rap tho ra sap]

coincide [,kəʊɪn'saɪd] v สอดคล้องกัน พอดี [sot khlong kan pho dii]

coincidence [kəʊ'ɪnsɪdəns] n เหตุ บังเอิญ [het bang oen]

Coke® [kəʊk] *n* โค้ก [khok]

colander ['kɒləndə; 'kʌl-] *n* กระชอน [kra chon]

cold [kəʊld] *adj* เย็น [yen] ▷ *n* ความเย็น [khwam yen]; **cold sore** *n* แผลเปื่อย [phlae pueai]; **it's freezing cold** หนาว เยือกเย็น [nao yueak yen]; **The food is too cold** อาหารเย็นเกินไป [a han yen koen pai]

coleslaw ['kəʊlˌslɔː] *n* สลัดกะหล่ำปลีใส่ มายองเนส [sa lat ka lam plii sai ma yong nes]

collaborate [kəˈlæbəˌreɪt] *v* ร่วมมือ [ruam mue]

collapse [kəˈlæps] *v* พังทลาย [phang tha lai]

collar ['kɒlə] *n* ปกเสื้อ [pok suea]

collarbone ['kɒləˌbəʊn] *n* กระดูก ไหปลาร้า [kra duk hai pla ra]

colleague ['kɒliːɡ] *n* เพื่อนร่วมงาน [phuean ruam ngan]

collect [kəˈlɛkt] *v* สะสม [sa som]

collection [kəˈlɛkʃən] *n* สิ่งที่สะสมไว้ [sing thii sa som wai]

collective [kəˈlɛktɪv] *adj* ซึ่งเป็นกลุ่ม [sueng pen klum] ▷ *n* กลุ่ม หมู่คณะ [klum, moo ka na]

collector [kəˈlɛktə] *n* นักสะสม [nak sa som]; **ticket collector** *n* ผู้เก็บตั๋ว [phu kep tua]

college ['kɒlɪdʒ] *n* วิทยาลัย [wit tha ya lai]

collide [kəˈlaɪd] *v* ปะทะกัน [pa tha kan]

collie ['kɒlɪ] *n* สุนัขใหญ่ขนยาวที่ใช้เลี้ยง แกะ [su nak yai khon yao thii chai liang kae]

colliery ['kɒljərɪ] *n* เหมืองถ่านหิน [mueang than hin]

collision [kəˈlɪʒən] *n* การชนกัน [kan chon kan]

Colombia [kəˈlɒmbɪə] *n* ประเทศ โคลัมเบีย [pra tet kho lam bia]

Colombian [kəˈlɒmbɪən] *adj* เกี่ยวกับ ประเทศโคลัมเบีย [kiao kap pra thet kho lam bia] ▷ *n* ชาวโคลัมเบีย [chao kho lam bia]

colon ['kəʊlən] *n* เครื่องหมาย [khrueang mai]

colonel ['kɜːnˀl] *n* พันเอก [phan ek]

colour ['kʌlə] *n* สี [si]; **A colour film, please** ขอฟิลมสี [kho fim sii]; **Do you have this in another colour?** คุณมีตัว นี้เป็นสีอื่นไหม? [khun mii tua nii pen sii uen mai]; **in colour** เป็นสี [pen sii]

colour-blind ['kʌləˈblaɪnd] *adj* ตาบอดสี [ta bot sii]

colourful ['kʌləfʊl] *adj* เต็มไปด้วยสีสัน [tem pai duai sii san]

colouring ['kʌlərɪŋ] *n* การให้สี [kan hai see]

column ['kɒləm] *n* หลักเสาหินใหญ่ [lak sao hin yai]

coma ['kəʊmə] *n* สภาพไม่รู้สึกตัวของผู้ ป่วย [sa phap mai ru suek tua khong phu puai]

comb [kəʊm] *n* หวี [wi] ▷ *v* การหวี [kan wii]

combination [ˌkɒmbɪˈneɪʃən] *n* การ รวมกัน [kan ruam kan]

combine [kəmˈbaɪn] *v* รวมกัน [ruam kan]

come [kʌm] *v* มา [ma]; **I'm not coming** ฉันจะไม่มา [chan ja mai ma]

come back [kʌm bæk] *v* กลับมา [klap ma]; **Shall I come back later?** ฉันกลับ มาทีหลังดีไหม? [chan klap ma thi lang di mai]

comedian [kəˈmiːdɪən] *n* ตัวตลก [tua ta lok]

come down [kʌm daʊn] *v* ลงมา [long ma]

comedy ['kɒmɪdɪ] *n* ละครตลก [la khon ta lok]

come from [kʌm frəm] *v* มาจาก [ma chak]

come in [kʌm ɪn] *v* เข้ามา [khao ma]; **Come in!** เข้ามา [khao ma]

come off [kʌm ɒf] *v* **The handle has**

come off ที่จับหลุดออกมา [thii chap lut ok ma]

come out [kʌm aʊt] v ออกมา [ork ma]

come round [kʌm raʊnd] v ฟื้นขึ้นมา [fuen khuen ma]

comet ['kɒmɪt] n ดาวหาง [dao hang]

come up [kʌm ʌp] v ถูกนำเสนอ [thuk nam sa noe]

comfortable ['kʌmftəbᵊl; 'kʌmfətəbᵊl] adj สะดวกสบาย [sa duak sa bai]

comic ['kɒmɪk] n ตัวละครตลก [tua la khon ta lok]; **comic book** n หนังสือตลก [nang sue ta lok]; **comic strip** n หนังสือการ์ตูน [nang sue ka tun]

coming ['kʌmɪŋ] adj ที่กำลังจะมาถึง [thii kam lang ja ma thueng]

comma ['kɒmə] n เครื่องหมายลูกน้ำ [khueang mai luk nam]; **inverted commas** npl เครื่องหมายอ้างอิง [khrueang mai ang ing]

command [kə'mɑ:nd] n คำสั่ง [kham sang]

comment ['kɒmɛnt] n ข้อคิดเห็น [kho khit hen] ▷ v แสดงความคิดเห็น [sa daeng khwam kit hen]

commentary ['kɒməntərɪ; -trɪ] n การแสดงความคิดเห็น คำวิจารณ์ [kan sa daeng khwam kit hen, kham wi chan]

commentator ['kɒmənˌteɪtə] n ผู้แสดงความคิดเห็นหรือผู้วิจารณ์ [phu sa daeng khwam kid hen hue phu vi chan]

commercial [kə'mɜ:ʃəl] n โฆษณาทางทีวีหรือวิทยุ [kho sa na thang tee vee hue wit tha yu]; **commercial break** n โฆษณาคั่นรายการ [khot sa na khan rai kan]

commission [kə'mɪʃən] n งานที่ได้รับสั่งให้ทำ [ngan thii dai rab sang hai tham]

commit [kə'mɪt] v ให้คำมั่นสัญญา [hai kham man san ya]

committee [kə'mɪtɪ] n คณะกรรมการ [kha na kram ma kan]

common ['kɒmən] adj ที่เกิดขึ้นทุกวัน [thii koed khuen thuk wan]; **common sense** n สามัญสำนึก [sa man sam nuek]

communicate [kə'mju:nɪˌkeɪt] v ติดต่อสื่อสาร [tit to sue san]

communication [kəˌmju:nɪ'keɪʃən] n การติดต่อสื่อสาร [kan tit to sue san]

communion [kə'mju:njən] n การมีส่วนร่วม [kan mii suan ruam]

communism ['kɒmjʊˌnɪzəm] n ระบบคอมมิวนิสต์ [ra bop khom mio nis]

communist ['kɒmjʊnɪst] adj เกี่ยวกับคอมมิวนิสต์ [kiao kap khom mio nis] ▷ n คอมมิวนิสต์ [khom mio nit]

community [kə'mju:nɪtɪ] n ชุมชน [chum chon]

commute [kə'mju:t] v เดินทาง [doen thang]

commuter [kə'mju:tə] n ผู้เดินทาง [phu doen thang]

compact [kəm'pækt] adj กระชับ [kra chap]; **compact disc** n แผ่นดิสก์ [phaen dis]

companion [kəm'pænjən] n เพื่อนเดินทาง [phuean doen thang]

company ['kʌmpənɪ] n บริษัท [bo ri sat]; **company car** n รถบริษัท [rot bo ri sat]; **I would like some information about the company** ฉันอยากได้ข้อมูลเกี่ยวกับบริษัทคุณ [chan yak dai kho mun kiao kap bo ri sat khun]

comparable ['kɒmpərəbᵊl] adj ที่สามารถเปรียบเทียบได้ [thii sa mart priab thiab dai]

comparatively [kəm'pærətɪvlɪ] adv ที่เปรียบเทียบได้ [thii priap thiap dai]

compare [kəm'pɛə] v เปรียบเทียบ [priap thiap]

comparison [kəm'pærɪsᵊn] n การเปรียบเทียบ [kan priap thiap]

compartment [kəm'pɑ:tmənt] n ห้องในรถไฟ [hong nai rot fai]

compass ['kʌmpəs] n เข็มทิศ [khem thit]

compatible [kəm'pætəbᵊl] adj ที่อยู่ร่วม

กันได้ [thii yu ruam kan dai]

compensate ['kɒmpɛnˌseɪt] *v* ชดเชย [chot choei]

compensation [ˌkɒmpɛn'seɪʃən] *n* การชดเชย [kan chot choei]

compere ['kɒmpɛə] *n* พิธีกร [phi thi kon]

compete [kəm'piːt] *v* แข่งขัน [khaeng khan]

competent ['kɒmpɪtənt] *adj* ที่มีความสามารถ [thii mee khwam sa mart]

competition [ˌkɒmpɪ'tɪʃən] *n* การแข่งขัน [kan khaeng khan]

competitive [kəm'pɛtɪtɪv] *adj* ที่เกี่ยวกับการแข่งขัน [thii kiao kab kan khaeng khan]

competitor [kəm'pɛtɪtə] *n* ผู้แข่งขัน [phu khaeng khan]

complain [kəm'pleɪn] *v* ร้องทุกข์ [rong thuk]

complaint [kəm'pleɪnt] *n* ความไม่พอใจ [khwam mai phor jai]

complementary [ˌkɒmplɪ'mɛntərɪ; -trɪ] *adj* เสริมซึ่งกันและกัน [soem sueng kan lae kan]

complete [kəm'pliːt] *adj* ทั้งหมด [thang mot]

completely [kəm'pliːtlɪ] *adv* อย่างทั้งหมด [yang thang mot]

complex ['kɒmplɛks] *adj* ซับซ้อน [sap son] ▷ *n* ความคิดหรือกิจกรรมที่สัมพันธ์กัน [khwam kit rue kit cha kam thii sam phan kan]

complexion [kəm'plɛkʃən] *n* ผิว [phio]

complicated ['kɒmplɪˌkeɪtɪd] *adj* ยากที่จะเข้าใจ [yak thii ja khao jai]

complication [ˌkɒmplɪ'keɪʃən] *n* การทำให้ยุ่งยาก [kan tham hai yung yak]

compliment *n* ['kɒmplɪmənt] คำชมเชย [kham chom choei] ▷ *v* ['kɒmplɪˌmɛnt] ชมเชย [chom choei]

complimentary [ˌkɒmplɪ'mɛntərɪ; -trɪ] *adj* ที่ชมเชย [thii chom choei]

component [kəm'pəʊnənt] *adj* เกี่ยว

กับส่วนประกอบ [kiao kap suan pra kop] ▷ *n* ส่วนประกอบ [suan pra kop]

composer [kəm'pəʊzə] *n* นักแต่งเพลง [nak taeng phleng]

composition [ˌkɒmpə'zɪʃən] *n* การจัดวางองค์ประกอบ [kan chat wang ong pra kop]

comprehension [ˌkɒmprɪ'hɛnʃən] *n* ความเข้าใจ [khwam khao jai]

comprehensive [ˌkɒmprɪ'hɛnsɪv] *adj* ที่ครอบคลุม [thii khrop khlum]

compromise ['kɒmprəˌmaɪz] *n* การประนีประนอม [kan pra nii pra nom] ▷ *v* ประนีประนอม [pra ni pra nom]

compulsory [kəm'pʌlsərɪ] *adj* ที่บังคับ [thii bang khap]

computer [kəm'pjuːtə] *n* เครื่องคอมพิวเตอร์ [khrueang khom phio toe]; **computer game** *n* เกมส์คอมพิวเตอร์ [kem khom phio toe]; **computer science** *n* วิทยาศาสตร์คอมพิวเตอร์ [wit tha ya saat khom phio toe]; **May I use your computer?** ฉันขอใช้เครื่องคอมพิวเตอร์คุณได้ไหม? [chan kho chai khrueang khom phio toe khun dai mai]

computing [kəm'pjuːtɪŋ] *n* งานคอมพิวเตอร์และเขียนโปรแกรม [ngan khom pio ter lae khian pro kraem]

concentrate ['kɒnsənˌtreɪt] *v* เพ่งความสนใจ [pheng khwam son jai]

concentration [ˌkɒnsən'treɪʃən] *n* การตั้งใจ [kan tang jai]

concern [kən'sɜːn] *n* ความกังวล [khwam kang won]

concerned [kən'sɜːnd] *adj* กังวล [kang won]

concerning [kən'sɜːnɪŋ] *prep* เกี่ยวกับ [kiao kap]

concert ['kɒnsət] *n* คอนเสิร์ต [kon soet]; **Are there any good concerts on?** มีการแสดงคอนเสิร์ตดี ๆ บ้างไหม? [mii kan sa daeng khon soet di di bang mai]; **What's on tonight at the**

concert hall? คืนนี้มีการแสดงอะไรที่หอแสดงคอนเสิร์ต? [khuen nii mii kan sa daeng a rai thii ho sa daeng khon soet]; **Where can I buy tickets for the concert?** ฉันจะซื้อตั๋วคอนเสิร์ตได้ที่ไหน? [chan ja sue tua khon soet dai thii nai]

concerto, concerti [kən'tʃɛətəʊ, kən'tʃɛətɪ] n การเล่นเพลงคลาสสิคที่มีนักร้องเดี่ยวหนึ่งหรือมากกว่าหนึ่งคน [kan len phleng khlas sik thii mee nak rong diao hueng hue mak kwa hueng kon]

concession [kən'sɛʃən] n สัมปทาน การยินยอม [sam pa than, kan yin yom]

concise [kən'saɪs] adj สั้นกระชับ [san kra chap]

conclude [kən'kluːd] v สรุป [sa rup]

conclusion [kən'kluːʒən] n การสรุป [kan sa rup]

concrete ['kɒnkriːt] n คอนกรีต [khon krit]

concussion [kən'kʌʃən] n การสั่นอย่างแรง [kan san yang raeng]

condemn [kən'dɛm] v ประณาม [pra nam]

condensation [ˌkɒndɛn'seɪʃən] n การทำให้มีความเข้มข้นมากขึ้น การย่อความ [kan tham hai mii khwam khem khon mak khuen, kan yo khwam]

condition [kən'dɪʃən] n สภาวะ เงื่อนไข [sa pha wa, nguean khai]

conditional [kən'dɪʃənªl] adj ที่เป็นเงื่อนไข [thii pen nguean khai]

conditioner [kən'dɪʃənə] n น้ำยาปรับให้นุ่ม [nam ya prap hai num]

condom ['kɒndɒm; 'kɒndəm] n ถุงยางอนามัย [thung yang a na mai]

conduct [kən'dʌkt] v จัดการ [chat kan]

conductor [kən'dʌktə] n ผู้ควบคุมวงดนตรี [phu khuab khum wong don tree]; **bus conductor** n คนเก็บเงินบนรถประจำทาง [khon kep ngen bon rot pra cham thang]

cone [kəʊn] n กรวย [kruai]

conference ['kɒnfərəns; -frəns] n การสัมมนา [kan sam ma na]; **press conference** n การแถลงข่าว [kan tha laeng khao]

confess [kən'fɛs] v สารภาพ [sa ra phap]

confession [kən'fɛʃən] n คำสารภาพ [kham sa ra phap]

confetti [kən'fɛtɪ] npl เศษกระดาษสีสันที่ใช้โปรยในงานแต่งงาน [sed kra dart see san thii chai proi nai ngan taeng ngan]

confidence ['kɒnfɪdəns] n (secret) ความเชื่อใจ [khwam chuea jai], (self-assurance) ความมั่นใจ [khwam man jai], (trust) ความไว้เนื้อเชื่อใจ [khwam wai nuea chuea jai]

confident ['kɒnfɪdənt] adj ที่มั่นใจ [thii man jai]

confidential [ˌkɒnfɪ'dɛnʃəl] adj ที่เป็นความลับ [thii pen khwam lap]

confirm [kən'fɜːm] v ยืนยัน [yuen yan]; **I confirmed my booking by letter** ฉันยืนยันการจองด้วยจดหมาย [chan yuen yan kan chong duai chot mai]

confirmation [ˌkɒnfə'meɪʃən] n การยืนยัน [kan yuen yan]

confiscate ['kɒnfɪˌskeɪt] v ยึดทรัพย์ [yuet sap]

conflict ['kɒnflɪkt] n ความขัดแย้ง [khwam khat yaeng]

confuse [kən'fjuːz] v สับสน [sap son]

confused [kən'fjuːzd] adj ที่สับสน [thii sab son]

confusing [kən'fjuːzɪŋ] adj น่าสับสน [na sab son]

confusion [kən'fjuːʒən] n ความสับสน [khwam sap son]

congestion [kən'dʒɛstʃən] n ความแออัด [khwam ae at]

Congo ['kɒŋgəʊ] n ประเทศคองโก [pra tet khong ko]

congratulate [kən'grætjʊˌleɪt] v แสดงความยินดี [sa daeng khwam yin dii]

congratulations [kənˌgrætjʊ'leɪʃənz] npl การแสดงความยินดี [kan sa daeng khwam yin dii]

conifer ['kəʊnɪfə; 'kɒn-] *n* ต้นสน [ton son]

conjugation [ˌkɒndʒʊˈɡeɪʃən] *n* การ รวมกัน [kan ruam kan]

conjunction [kənˈdʒʌŋkʃən] *n* การเกิด ขึ้นรวมกัน [kan koet khuen ruam kan]

conjurer ['kʌndʒərə] *n* นักแสดงมายากล [nak sa daeng ma ya kon]

connect [kəˈnɛkt] *v* ต่อ [to]

connection [kəˈnɛkʃən] *n* ความสัมพันธ์ กัน [khwam sam phan kan]

conquer ['kɒŋkə] *v* ชนะ [cha na]

conscience ['kɒnʃəns] *n* ความรู้สึกผิด ชอบชั่วดี [khwam ru suek phit chop chua dii]

conscientious [ˌkɒnʃɪˈɛnʃəs] *adj* ที่ทำ ด้วยความรู้สึกในด้านดี [thii tham duai khwam ru suek nai dan di]

conscious ['kɒnʃəs] *adj* รู้สึกตัว [ru suek tua]

consciousness ['kɒnʃəsnɪs] *n* การรู้สึก ตัว [kan ru suk tua]

consecutive [kənˈsɛkjʊtɪv] *adj* ที่ต่อ เนื่องตามลำดับ [thii to nueang tam lam dap]

consensus [kənˈsɛnsəs] *n* ความคิดเห็น ของคนส่วนใหญ่ [khwam kid hen khong kon suan yai]

consequence ['kɒnsɪkwəns] *n* ผลลัพธ์ [phon lap]

consequently ['kɒnsɪkwəntlɪ] *adv* ดัง นั้น [dang nan]

conservation [ˌkɒnsəˈveɪʃən] *n* การ อนุรักษ์ธรรมชาติและสภาพแวดล้อม [kan a nu rak tham ma chat lae sa phap waet lom]

conservative [kənˈsɜːvətɪv] *adj* ที่เป็น อนุรักษ์นิยม [thii pen a nu rak ni yom]

conservatory [kənˈsɜːvətrɪ] *n* เรือน กระจกสำหรับเก็บต้นไม้ [ruean kra chok sam rap kep ton mai]

consider [kənˈsɪdə] *v* พิจารณา [phi cha ra na]

considerate [kənˈsɪdərɪt] *adj* ที่คิดถึง ความคิดของผู้อื่น [thii kit thueng khwam kit khong phu uen]

considering [kənˈsɪdərɪŋ] *prep* ในความ คิดของ [nai khwam kit khong]

consist [kənˈsɪst] *v* **consist of** *v* ประกอบ ด้วย [pra kop duai]

consistent [kənˈsɪstənt] *adj* ที่สอดคล้อง กัน [thii sot khlong kan]

consonant ['kɒnsənənt] *n* ตัวพยัญชนะ [tua pha yan cha na]

conspiracy [kənˈspɪrəsɪ] *n* การวางแผน การอย่างลับ ๆ [kan wang phaen kan yang lap lap]

constant ['kɒnstənt] *adj* ที่เกิดขึ้นตลอด เวลา [thii koet khuen ta lot we la]

constantly ['kɒnstəntlɪ] *adv* เกิดขึ้น ตลอดเวลา [koet khuen ta lot we la]

constipated ['kɒnstɪˌpeɪtɪd] *adj* ท้อง ผูก [thong phuk]; **I'm constipated** ฉัน ท้องผูก [chan thong phuk]

constituency [kənˈstɪtjʊənsɪ] *n* เขต เลือกตั้ง [khet lueak tang]

constitution [ˌkɒnstɪˈtjuːʃən] *n* รัฐธรรมนูญ [rat tha tham ma nun]

construct [kənˈstrʌkt] *v* สร้าง [sang]

construction [kənˈstrʌkʃən] *n* การ ก่อสร้าง [kan ko sang]

constructive [kənˈstrʌktɪv] *adj* ที่เกี่ยว กับโครงสร้าง [thii kiao kap khrong sang]

consul ['kɒnsəl] *n* กงสุล [kong sun]

consulate ['kɒnsjʊlɪt] *n* สถานกงสุล [sa than kong sun]

consult [kənˈsʌlt] *v* ปรึกษา [pruek sa]

consultant [kənˈsʌltənt] *n* (*adviser*) ผู้ ให้คำปรึกษา [phu hai kham pruek sa]

consumer [kənˈsjuːmə] *n* ผู้บริโภค [phu bo ri phok]

contact *n* ['kɒntækt] การติดต่อ [kan tit to] ▷ *v* ['kɒntækt] ติดต่อ [tit to]; **contact lenses** *npl* คอนแท็คเลนส์ [khon taek len]; **Where can I contact you?** ฉันจะติดต่อคุณได้ที่ไหน? [chan ja tit to khun dai thii nai]; **Who do we contact if there are problems?** เราจะต้องติดต่อใครถ้าเกิดปัญหา? [rao ja tong tit to khrai tha koet pan ha]

contagious [kən'teɪdʒəs] *adj* ซึ่งแพร่กระจายได้ [sueng phrae kra jai dai]

contain [kən'teɪn] *v* ควบคุม [khuap khum]

container [kən'teɪnə] *n* ภาชนะใส่ของ [pha cha na sai khong]

contemporary [kən'tɛmprərɪ] *adj* ทันสมัย [than sa mai]

contempt [kən'tɛmpt] *n* การหมิ่นประมาท [kan min pra mat]

content ['kɒntɛnt] *n* ความพึงพอใจ [khwam phueng phor jai]; **contents** (list) *npl* จำนวนสิ่งของที่บรรจุอยู่ [cham nuan sing khong thii ban chu yu]

contest ['kɒntɛst] *n* การแข่งขัน [kan khaeng khan]

contestant [kən'tɛstənt] *n* ผู้แข่งขัน [phu khaeng khan]

context ['kɒntɛkst] *n* บริบท [bo ri bot]

continent ['kɒntɪnənt] *n* ทวีป [tha wip]

continual [kən'tɪnjʊəl] *adj* ต่อเนื่อง [to nueang]

continually [kən'tɪnjʊəlɪ] *adv* อย่างต่อเนื่อง [yang tor nueang]

continue [kən'tɪnjuː] *vi* เริ่มอีกครั้ง [roem ik khrang] ▷ *vt* ดำเนินต่อไป [dam noen to pai]

continuous [kən'tɪnjʊəs] *adj* ซึ่งต่อเนื่องกัน [sueng to nueang kan]

contraception [ˌkɒntrə'sɛpʃən] *n* การคุมกำเนิด [kan khum kam noet]

contraceptive [ˌkɒntrə'sɛptɪv] *n* ยาหรือสิ่งที่ใช้คุมกำเนิด [ya rue sing thii chai khum kham noet]

contract ['kɒntrækt] *n* สัญญา [san ya]

contractor ['kɒntræktə; kən'træk-] *n* ผู้ทำสัญญา [phu tham san ya]

contradict [ˌkɒntrə'dɪkt] *v* ขัดแย้ง [khat yaeng]

contradiction [ˌkɒntrə'dɪkʃən] *n* ความขัดแย้ง [khwam khat yaeng]

contrary ['kɒntrərɪ] *n* การตรงกันข้าม [kan trong kan kham]

contrast ['kɒntrɑːst] *n* ความแตกต่าง [khwam taek tang]

contribute [kən'trɪbjuːt] *v* มีส่วนทำให้ [mi suan tham hai]

contribution [ˌkɒntrɪ'bjuːʃən] *n* การบริจาค [kan bo ri chak]

control [kən'trəʊl] *n* การควบคุมดูแล [kan khuap khum du lae] ▷ *v* ควบคุม [khuap khum]; **birth control** *n* การคุมกำเนิด [kan khum kam noet]; **passport control** *n* หน่วยควบคุมหนังสือเดินทาง [nuai khuap khum nang sue doen thang]; **remote control** *n* อุปกรณ์ควบคุมระยะห่างหรือไกลที่ไม่ต้องมีสาย เช่น ที่ใช้กับทีวีหรือเครื่องเสียง [up pa kon khuap khum ra ya hang rue klai thii mai tong mii sai chen thii chai kap tii wii rue khrueang siang]

controller [kən'trəʊlə] *n* **air-traffic controller** *n* ผู้ควบคุมเส้นทางการบิน [phu khuap khum sen thang kan bin]

controversial [ˌkɒntrə'vɜːʃəl] *adj* ซึ่งก่อให้เกิดการโต้แย้ง [sueng ko hai koet kan to yaeng]

convenient [kən'viːnɪənt] *adj* สะดวก [sa duak]

convent ['kɒnvənt] *n* สำนักแม่ชี [sam nak mae chi]

conventional [kən'vɛnʃənʳl] *adj* เกี่ยวกับประเพณีนิยม [kiao kap pra phe ni ni yom]

conversation [ˌkɒnvə'seɪʃən] *n* บทสนทนา [bot son tha na]

convert [kən'vɜːt] *v* เปลี่ยน [plian]; **catalytic converter** *n* อุปกรณ์ที่ช่วยลดสารเป็นพิษในท่อไอเสีย [up pa kon thii chuai lot san pen phit nai tho ai sia]

convertible [kən'vɜːtəbʳl] *adj* ที่สามารถเปลี่ยนแปลงได้ [thii sa mart plian plang dai] ▷ *n* การเปลี่ยนแปลงได้ [kan plian plang dai]

convict [kən'vɪkt] v พิสูจน์ว่ามีความผิด [phi sut wa mii khwam phit]

convince [kən'vɪns] v โน้มน้าว [nom nao]

convincing [kən'vɪnsɪŋ; con'vincing] adj ซึ่งโน้มน้าว [sueng nom nao]

convoy ['kɒnvɔɪ] n ยานพาหนะที่เดินทางไปด้วยกัน [yan pha ha na thii doen thang pai duai kan]

cook [kʊk] n พ่อครัว [pho khrua] ▷ v ทำอาหาร [tham a han]; **How do you cook this dish?** คุณทำอาหารจานนี้อย่างไร? [khun tham a han chan nii yang rai]

cookbook ['kʊkˌbʊk] n ตำราอาหาร [tam ra a han]

cooker ['kʊkə] n เตาหุงอาหาร [tao hung a han]; **gas cooker** n เตาทำอาหารที่ใช้แก๊ส [tao tham a han thii chai kaes]

cookery ['kʊkərɪ] n การปรุงอาหาร [kan prung a han]; **cookery book** n หนังสือการปรุงอาหาร [nang sue kan prung a han]

cooking ['kʊkɪŋ] n การทำอาหาร [kan tham a han]

cool [kuːl] adj (cold) เย็น [yen], (stylish) ทันสมัย [than sa mai]

cooperation [kəʊˌɒpəˈreɪʃən] n การร่วมมือกัน [kan ruam mue kan]

cop [kɒp] n ตำรวจ [tam ruat]

cope [kəʊp] v **cope (with)** v รับมือได้ [rap mue dai]

copper ['kɒpə] n ทองแดง [thong daeng]

copy ['kɒpɪ] n (reproduction) ทำสำเนา [tham sam nao], (written text) ฉบับสำเนา [cha bap sam nao] ▷ v ถ่ายสำเนา [thai sam nao]

copyright ['kɒpɪˌraɪt] n ลิขสิทธิ์ [lik kha sit]

coral ['kɒrəl] n หินปะการัง [hin pa ka rang]

cord [kɔːd] n **spinal cord** n ไขสันหลัง [khai san lang]

cordless ['kɔːdlɪs] adj ที่ไร้สาย [thii rai sai]

corduroy ['kɔːdəˌrɔɪ; ˌkɔːdəˈrɔɪ] n สักหลาดที่เป็นริ้ว [sak ka lat thii pen rio]

core [kɔː] n ส่วนสำคัญ [suan sam khan]

coriander [ˌkɒrɪˈændə] n ผักชี [phak chi]

cork [kɔːk] n จุกไม้ก๊อก [chuk mai kok]

corkscrew ['kɔːkˌskruː] n สว่านเปิดจุกขวด [sa wan poet chuk khaut]

corn [kɔːn] n ข้าวโพด [khao pot]

corner ['kɔːnə] n มุม [mum]; **It's on the corner** อยู่ที่หัวมุม [yu thii hua mum]; **It's round the corner** อยู่ใกล้ ๆ หัวมุม [yu klai klai hua mum]

cornet ['kɔːnɪt] n แตรทองเหลืองขนาดเล็ก [trae thong lueang kha nat lek]

cornflakes ['kɔːnˌfleɪks] npl อาหารเช้าที่ทำจากพืชพันธุ์ธัญญาหาร [a han chao thii tham chak phuet phan than ya han]

cornflour ['kɔːnˌflaʊə] n แป้งข้าวโพด [paeng khao phot]

corporal ['kɔːpərəl; -prəl] n สิบโท จ่าอากาศโท [sip tho, cha a kaat tho]

corpse [kɔːps] n ซากศพ [saak sop]

correct [kəˈrɛkt] adj ถูกต้อง [tuk tong] ▷ v แก้ไขให้ถูกต้อง [kae khai hai thuk tong]

correction [kəˈrɛkʃən] n การแก้ไขให้ถูกต้อง [kan kae khai hai thuk tong]

correctly [kəˈrɛktlɪ] adv อย่างถูกต้อง [yang thuk tong]

correspondence [ˌkɒrɪˈspɒndəns] n การติดต่อกันทางจดหมาย [kan tit to kan thang chot mai]

correspondent [ˌkɒrɪˈspɒndənt] n นักข่าว [nak khao]

corridor ['kɒrɪˌdɔː] n ทางเดินยาว [thang doen yao]

corrupt [kəˈrʌpt] adj ทุจริต [thut cha rit]

corruption [kəˈrʌpʃən] n การทุจริต [kan thut cha rit]

cosmetics [kɒz'mɛtiks] *npl* เครื่องสำอาง [khrueang sam ang]

cost [kɒst] *n* ค่าใช้จ่าย [kha chai chai] ▷ *v* มีมูลค่า [mii mun kha]; **cost of living** *n* ค่าครองชีพ [kha khrong chiip]

Costa Rica ['kɒstə 'riːkə] *n* ประเทศคอสตาริก้า [pra tet kos ta ri ka]

costume ['kɒstjuːm] *n* เครื่องแต่งกาย [khrueang taeng kai]; **swimming costume** *n* ชุดว่ายน้ำ [chut wai nam]

cosy ['kəʊzɪ] *adj* อบอุ่นและสะดวกสบาย [op un lae sa duak sa bai]

cot [kɒt] *n* เตียงสำหรับเด็ก [tiang sam rap dek]

cottage ['kɒtɪdʒ] *n* กระท่อม [kra thom]; **cottage cheese** *n* เนยเหลวชนิดหนึ่ง [noei leo cha nit nueng]

cotton ['kɒtᵊn] *n* ผ้าฝ้าย [pha fai]; **cotton bud** *n* สำลีแคะหู [sam lii khae hu]; **cotton wool** *n* สำลี [sam lii]

couch [kaʊtʃ] *n* เก้าอี้ยาว [kao ee yao]

couchette [kuːˈʃɛt] *n* เตียงนอนบนรถไฟ [tiang non bon rot fai]

cough [kɒf] *n* การไอ [kan ai] ▷ *v* ไอ [ai]; **cough mixture** *n* ส่วนผสมสำหรับแก้ไอ [suan pha som sam rap kae ai]; **I have a cough** ฉันไอ [chan ai]

council ['kaʊnsəl] *n* สภาท้องถิ่น [sa pha thong thin]; **council house** *n* บ้านของเทศบาล [baan khong tet sa ban]

councillor ['kaʊnsələ] *n* สมาชิกสภาเทศบาล [sa ma chik sa pha tet sa ban]

count [kaʊnt] *v* นับ [nap]

counter ['kaʊntə] *n* เคาน์เตอร์ [kao toe]

count on [kaʊnt ɒn] *v* พึ่งพาได้ [phueng pha dai]

country ['kʌntrɪ] *n* ประเทศ [pra thet]; **developing country** *n* ประเทศที่กำลังพัฒนา [pra tet thii kam lang phat ta na]; **Where can I buy a map of the country?** ฉันจะซื้อแผนที่ของประเทศนี้ได้ที่ไหน? [chan ja sue phaen thii khong pra tet nii dai thii nai]

countryside ['kʌntrɪˌsaɪd] *n* ชนบท [chon na bot]

couple ['kʌpᵊl] *n* คู่ [khu]

courage ['kʌrɪdʒ] *n* ความกล้าหาญ [khwam kla han]

courageous [kə'reɪdʒəs] *adj* กล้าหาญ [kla han]

courgette [kʊə'ʒɛt] *n* บวบ [buap]

courier ['kʊərɪə] *n* คนเดินหนังสือ [kon doen nang sue]

course [kɔːs] *n* หลักสูตร [lak sut]; **golf course** *n* สนามกอล์ฟ [sa nam kop]; **main course** *n* อาหารมื้อหลัก [a han mue lak]; **refresher course** *n* วิชาที่ปรับปรุงใหม่ [wi cha thii prap prung mai]

court [kɔːt] *n* ศาล [san]; **tennis court** *n* สนามเทนนิส [sa nam then nis]

courtyard ['kɔːtˌjɑːd] *n* สนามรอบบ้าน [sa nam rob baan]

cousin ['kʌzᵊn] *n* ลูกพี่ลูกน้อง [luk pi luk nong]

cover ['kʌvə] *n* ปกหนังสือ [pok nang sue] ▷ *v* คลุม [khlum]; **cover charge** *n* ค่าบริการเพิ่มจากค่าอาหาร [kha bo ri kan poem chak kha a han]; **How much extra is comprehensive insurance cover?** ต้องจ่ายเพิ่มเท่าไรสำหรับประกันแบบครอบคลุมทุกอย่าง? [tong jai poem thao rai sam rap pra kan baep khrop khlum thuk yang]

cow [kaʊ] *n* วัวตัวเมีย [vua tua mia]

coward ['kaʊəd] *n* คนขี้ขลาด [khon khii khlat]

cowardly ['kaʊədlɪ] *adj* อย่างขี้ขลาด [yang khii khlad]

cowboy ['kaʊˌbɔɪ] *n* คาวบอย [khao boi]

crab [kræb] *n* ปู [pu]

crack [kræk] *n* (cocaine) โคเคน [kho khen], (fracture) รอยแตก [roi taek] ▷ *v* แตกร้าว [taek rao]; **crack down on** *v* จำกัด [cham kat]

cracked [krækt] *adj* ร้าว [rao]

cracker ['krækə] *n* ขนมปังกรอบไม่หวาน [kha nom pang krob mai hwan],

ประทัด [pra that]

cradle ['kreɪdəl] *n* เปลเด็ก [ple dek]

craft [krɑːft] *n* งานศิลปะที่ทำด้วยมือ [ngan sin la pa thii tham duai mue]

craftsman ['krɑːftsmən] *n* ช่างฝีมือ [chang fi mue]

cram [kræm] *v* แออัด [ae at]

crammed [kræmd] *adj* อย่างแออัด [yang ae at]

cranberry ['krænbərɪ; -brɪ] *n* ลูกแครน เบอร์รี่ [luk khraen boe ri]

crane [kreɪn] *n* (*bird*) นกกระสา [nok kra sa], (*for lifting*) ปั้นจั่นยกของหนัก [pan chan yok khong nak]

crash [kræʃ] *n* การชน [kan chon] ▷ *vi* เคลื่อนที่อย่างเสียงดัง [khluean thii yang siang dang] ▷ *vt* ชนอย่างแรง [chon yang raeng]

crawl [krɔːl] *v* คลาน [khlan]

crayfish ['kreɪ̩fɪʃ] *n* กุ้งชนิดหนึ่งคล้ายกุ้ง ก้ามกราม [kung cha nit nueng khlai kung kam kram]

crayon ['kreɪən; -ɒn] *n* ดินสอสี [din so sii]

crazy ['kreɪzɪ] *adj* บ้า [ba]

cream [kriːm] *adj* เป็นสีนวล [pen sii nuan] ▷ *n* ส่วนที่เป็นไขมันของนมซึ่งลอย ขึ้นมาบนผิวนม [suan thii pen khai man khong nom sueng loi khuen ma bon phio nom], ครีม [khrim]; **ice cream** *n* ไอศครีม [ai sa khrim]; **shaving cream** *n* ครีมโกนหนวด [khrim kon nuat]; **whipped cream** *n* ครีมที่ตีจนเบาและฟู [khrim thii ti chon bao lae fu]

crease [kriːs] *n* รอยยับ [roi yon]

creased [kriːst] *adj* อย่างยับ [yang yon]

create [kriːˈeɪt] *v* สร้าง [sang]

creation [kriːˈeɪʃən] *n* การสร้าง [kan sang]

creative [kriːˈeɪtɪv] *adj* ซึ่งมีความคิดริเริ่ม [sueng mii khwam kit ri roem]

creature ['kriːtʃə] *n* สิ่งมีชีวิต [sing mi chi wit]

crèche [krɛʃ] *n* สถานที่ดูแลเด็ก [sa than thii du lae dek]

credentials [krɪˈdɛnʃəlz] *npl* หนังสือ รับรอง [nang sue rap rong]

credible ['krɛdɪbəl] *adj* น่าเชื่อถือ [na chuea thue]

credit ['krɛdɪt] *n* การซื้อเชื่อ [kan sue chuea], ความน่าเชื่อถือ [khwam na chuea thue]; **credit card** *n* บัตรเครดิต [bat khre dit]

crematorium, crematoria [ˌkrɛməˈtɔːrɪəm, ˌkrɛməˈtɔːrɪə] *n* เมรุ [men]

cress [krɛs] *n* ใบพืชที่มีรสแรงใช้ทำสลัด และสำหรับตกแต่งอาหาร [bai phuet thii mii rot raeng chai tham sa lat lae sam rap tok taeng a han]

crew [kruː] *n* ลูกเรือ [luk ruea]; **crew cut** *n* ทรงผมของผู้ชายที่สั้นมาก [song phom khong phu chai thii san mak]

cricket ['krɪkɪt] *n* (*game*) กีฬาคริกเก็ต [ki la khrik ket], (*insect*) จิ้งหรีด [ching rit]

crime [kraɪm] *n* อาชญากรรม [at cha ya kam]

criminal ['krɪmɪnəl] *adj* เกี่ยวกับ อาชญากรรม [kiao kap at cha ya kam] ▷ *n* ผู้ทำผิดกฎหมาย [phu tham phid kod mai]

crisis ['kraɪsɪs] *n* ช่วงวิกฤต [chuang wi krit]

crisp [krɪsp] *adj* กรอบ [krop]

crisps [krɪsps] *npl* มันฝรั่งหั่นบางทอด กรอบ [man fa rang han bang thot krop]

crispy ['krɪspɪ] *adj* อย่างกรอบ [yang krop]

criterion, criteria [kraɪˈtɪərɪən, kraɪˈtɪərɪə] *n* เกณฑ์ [ken]

critic ['krɪtɪk] *n* นักวิจารณ์ [nak vi chan]

critical ['krɪtɪkəl] *adj* เกี่ยวกับการวิจารณ์ สำคัญ [kiao kap kan wi chan, sam khan]

criticism ['krɪtɪˌsɪzəm] *n* การวิจารณ์ [kan wi chan]

criticize ['krɪtɪˌsaɪz] *v* วิจารณ์ [wi chan]

Croatia [krəʊ'eɪʃə] n ประเทศโครเอเชีย [pra tet khro e chia]

Croatian [krəʊ'eɪʃən] adj เกี่ยวกับประเทศโครเอเชีย [kiao kap pra thet khro e chia] ▷ n (language) ภาษาโครเอเชียน [pha sa khro e chian], (person) ชาวโครเอเชียน [chao khro e chian]

crochet ['krəʊʃeɪ; -ʃɪ] v การถักโครเชต์ [kan thak kro chae]

crockery ['krɒkərɪ] n **We need more crockery** เราอยากได้เครื่องถ้วยชามเพิ่มอีก [rao yak dai khrueang thuai cham poem ik]

crocodile ['krɒkəˌdaɪl] n จระเข้ [cha ra ke]

crocus ['krəʊkəs] n ไม้ดอกชนิดหนึ่งนิยมปลูกในสวนใบเหมือนหญ้าดอกเล็ก [mai dok cha nit nueng ni yom pluk nai suan bai muean ya dok lek]

crook [krʊk] n ของที่มีรูปร่างโค้งเหมือนตะขอ [khong thii mii rup rang khong muean ta kho], (swindler) คนทุจริต [khon thut cha rit]

crop [krɒp] n ผลผลิต [phon pha lit]

cross [krɒs] adj โกรธฉุนเฉียว [krot chun chiao] ▷ n ไม้กางเขน [mai kang khen] ▷ v ข้าม [kham]; **Red Cross** n สภากาชาด [sa pha ka chat]

cross-country ['krɒs'kʌntrɪ] n ข้ามประเทศ [kham pra tet]

crossing ['krɒsɪŋ] n การข้าม [kan kham]; **level crossing** n จุดที่ทางรถไฟและถนนตัดผ่านกัน [chut thii thang rot fai lae tha non tad phan kan]; **pedestrian crossing** n ทางเดินข้าม [thang doen kham]; **pelican crossing** n ทางข้ามไฟฟ้าที่มีสัญญาณโดยผู้ข้ามเป็นผู้กดปุ่ม [thang kham fai thii mii san yan doi phu kham pen phu kot pum]; **The crossing was rough** การข้ามฝั่งเจอพายุทะเล [kan kham fang choe pha yu tha le]

cross out [krɒs aʊt] v ขีดฆ่า [khid kha]

crossroads ['krɒsˌrəʊdz] n ทางข้าม [thang kham]

crossword ['krɒsˌwɜːd] n ปริศนาอักษรไขว้ [prit sa na ak son khwai]

crouch down [kraʊtʃ daʊn] v หมอบลง [mop long]

crow [krəʊ] n นกกา [nok ka]

crowd [kraʊd] n ฝูงชน [fung chon]

crowded [kraʊdɪd] adj ซึ่งเต็มไปด้วยฝูงชน [sueng tem pai duai fung chon]

crown [kraʊn] n มงกุฎ [mong kut]

crucial ['kruːʃəl] adj สำคัญมาก [sam khan mak]

crucifix ['kruːsɪfɪks] n ไม้กางเขนที่พระเยซูถูกตรึง [mai kang khen thii phra ye su thuk trueng]

crude [kruːd] adj หยาบ [yap]

cruel ['kruːəl] adj โหดร้าย [hot rai]

cruelty ['kruːəltɪ] n ความโหดร้าย [khwam hot rai]

cruise [kruːz] n การล่องเรือ [kan long ruea]

crumb [krʌm] n เศษเล็กเศษน้อย [set lek set noi]

crush [krʌʃ] v บดละเอียด [bot la iat]

crutch [krʌtʃ] n ไม้เท้าใช้พยุง [mai thao chai pha yung]

cry [kraɪ] n เสียงร้อง [siang rong] ▷ v ร้องไห้ [rong hai]

crystal ['krɪstəl] n แก้วเจียรนัย [kaew chia ra nai]

cub [kʌb] n ลูกของสัตว์ [luk khong sat]

Cuba ['kjuːbə] n ประเทศคิวบา [pra tet khio ba]

Cuban ['kjuːbən] adj เกี่ยวกับประเทศคิวบา [kiao kap pra thet khio ba] ▷ n ชาวคิวบา [chao khio ba]

cube [kjuːb] n ลูกบาศก์ [luk bat]; **ice cube** n ก้อนน้ำแข็ง [kon nam khaeng]; **stock cube** n ก้อนสต๊อค [kon sa tok]

cubic ['kjuːbɪk] adj ที่เป็นลูกบาศก์ [thii pen luk baat]

cuckoo ['kʊkuː] n นกชนิดหนึ่งที่วางไข่ในรังนกอื่น [nok cha nit hueng thii wang khai nai rang nok aue]

cucumber ['kjuː,kʌmbə] n แตงกวา
[taeng kwa]

cuddle ['kʌdªl] n การกอดด้วยความรักใคร่
[kan kot duai khwam ruk kai] ▷ v กอด
ด้วยความรักใคร่ [kot duai khwam ruk
khrai]

cue [kjuː] n (billiards) ไม้แทงบิลเลียด [mai
thaeng bil liad]

cufflinks ['kʌflɪŋks] npl กระดุมข้อมือเสื้อ
เชิ้ต [kra dum kho mue suea shoet]

culprit ['kʌlprɪt] n ผู้กระทำความผิด [phu
kra tham khwam phit]

cultural ['kʌltʃərəl] adj ทางวัฒนธรรม
[thang wat tha na tham]

culture ['kʌltʃə] n วัฒนธรรม [wat tha na
tham]

cumin ['kʌmɪn] n ขมิ้น [kha min]

cunning ['kʌnɪŋ] adj เจ้าเล่ห์ [chao le]

cup [kʌp] n ถ้วย [tuai]; **World Cup** n การ
แข่งขันกีฬานานาชาติโดยเฉพาะกีฬา
ฟุตบอล [kan khaeng khan ki la na na
chat doi cha po ki la fut ball]; **Could
we have another cup of tea, please?**
ขอชาให้พวกเราอีกถ้วยได้ไหม? [kho cha
hai phuak rao ik thuai dai mai]

cupboard ['kʌbəd] n ตู้ [tu]

curb [kɜːb] n การควบคุม [kan khuap
khum]

cure [kjʊə] n การรักษา [kan rak sa] ▷ v
รักษา [rak sa]

curfew ['kɜːfjuː] n การห้ามออกนอกบ้าน
ยามวิกาล [kan ham ok nok baan yam
wi kan]

curious ['kjʊərɪəs] adj อยากรู้อยากเห็น
[yak ru yak hen]

curl [kɜːl] n ผมเป็นลอน [phom pen lon]

curler ['kɜːlə] n โรลม้วนผม [rol muan
phom]

curly ['kɜːlɪ] adj หยักศก ที่เป็นลอน [yak
sok, thii pen lon]

currant ['kʌrənt] n ลูกเกด [luk ket]

currency ['kʌrənsɪ] n เงินตรา [ngen tra]

current ['kʌrənt] adj ที่ใช้กันในปัจจุบัน
[thii chai kan nai pad chu ban] ▷ n
(electricity) กระแสไฟ [kra sae fai], (flow)
กระแสน้ำ [kra sae nam]; **current
account** n บัญชีกระแสรายวัน [ban chi
kra sae rai wan]; **current affairs** npl
เหตุการณ์ปัจจุบัน [het kan pat chu ban];
Are there currents? มีกระแสน้ำไหม?
[mii kra sae nam mai]

currently ['kʌrəntlɪ] adv ในปัจจุบัน [nai
pat chu ban]

curriculum [kə'rɪkjʊləm] n หลักสูตร
[lak sut]; **curriculum vitae** n ประวัติ
ส่วนตัว [pra wat suan tua]

curry ['kʌrɪ] n แกง [kaeng]; **curry
powder** n เครื่องแกงที่เป็นผง [khrueang
kaeng thii pen phong]

curse [kɜːs] n คำสาปแช่ง [kham sap
chaeng]

cursor ['kɜːsə] n สัญลักษณ์บนคอมพิวเตอร์
แสดงให้เห็นจุดที่พิมพ์ได้ [san ya lak bon
khom phio toe sa daeng hai hen chut
thii phim dai]

curtain ['kɜːtªn] n ผ้าม่าน [pha man]

cushion ['kʊʃən] n หมอนอิง [mon ing]

custard ['kʌstəd] n คัสตาร์ด [cus tat]

custody ['kʌstədɪ] n การคุ้มครอง [kan
khum khrong]

custom ['kʌstəm] n ศุลกากร [sun la ka
kon]

customer ['kʌstəmə] n ลูกค้า [lik kha]

customized ['kʌstə,maɪzd] adj ที่สั่งทำ
[thii sang tham]

customs ['kʌstəmz] npl ภาษีนำสินค้าเข้า
หรือส่งออก [pha si nam sin ka khao rue
song ok]; **customs officer** n เจ้าหน้าที่
ศุลกากร [chao na thii sun la ka kon]

cut [kʌt] n การลดลง [kan lod long] ▷ v
ตัด [tat]; **crew cut** n ทรงผมของผู้ชายที่
สั้นมาก [song phom khong phu chai
thii san mak]; **power cut** n การตัดไฟ
ชั่วคราว [kan tat fai chua khrao]; **A cut
and blow-dry, please** ช่วยตัดและเป่าให้
แห้ง [chuai tat lae pao hai haeng];
Don't cut too much off อย่าตัดออกมาก

เกินไป [ya tat ok mak koen pai]

cutback [ˈkʌtˌbæk] n การลดจำนวนลง [kan lod cham nuan long]

cut down [kʌt daʊn] v โค่นต้นไม้ [khon ton mai]

cute [kjuːt] adj น่ารัก [na rak]

cutlery [ˈkʌtləri] n มีด ช้อนและส้อม [miit chon lae som]

cutlet [ˈkʌtlɪt] n เนื้อจากส่วนคอหรือ บริเวณซี่โครง [nuea chak suan khor hue bor ri ven si khrong]

cut off [kʌt ɒf] v ตัดทิ้ง [tad thing]

cutting [ˈkʌtɪŋ] n การตัด [kan tat]

cut up [kʌt ʌp] v ตัดเป็นชิ้นๆ [tad pen chin chin]

CV [siː viː] abbr ตัวย่อของประวัติส่วนตัว [tua yo khong pra wat suan tua]

cybercafé [ˈsaɪbəˌkæfeɪ; -ˌkæfɪ] n อินเตอร์เน็ตคาเฟ่ [in toe net ka fae]

cybercrime [ˈsaɪbəˌkraɪm] n อาชญากรรมที่เกิดขึ้นบนอินเตอร์เน็ต [at ya kam thii koet khuen bon in toe net]

cycle [ˈsaɪkəl] n (bike) จักรยาน [chak kra yan], (recurring period) ระยะเวลายาวนาน [ra ya we la yao nan] ▷ v ขี่จักรยาน [khi chak ka yan]; **cycle lane** n ทางขี่ จักรยาน [thang khi chak ka yan]; **cycle path** n เส้นทางขี่จักรยาน [sen thang khi chak ka yan]; **Where is the cycle path to…?** ทางรถจักรยานที่จะ ไป…อยู่ที่ไหน? [thang rot chak kra yan thii ja pai…yu thii nai]

cycling [ˈsaɪklɪŋ] n การขี่จักรยาน [kan khi chak kra yan]

cyclist [ˈsaɪklɪst] n ผู้ขี่จักรยาน [phu khi chak ka yan]

cyclone [ˈsaɪkləʊn] n พายุหมุนไซโคลน [pha yu mun sai khlon]

cylinder [ˈsɪlɪndə] n กระบอกสูบ [kra bok sub]

cymbals [ˈsɪmbəlz] npl ฉิ่ง [ching]

Cypriot [ˈsɪpriət] adj เกี่ยวกับประเทศ ไซปรัส [kiao kap pra thet sai bras] ▷ n (person) ชาวไซปรัส [chao sai pras]

Cyprus [ˈsaɪprəs] n ประเทศไซปรัส [pra tet sai pras]

cyst [sɪst] n ถุงน้ำที่เกิดในร่างกายคนหรือ สัตว์ [thung nam thii koet nai rang kai khon rue sat]

cystitis [sɪˈstaɪtɪs] n โรคกระเพาะปัสสาวะ [rok kra phao pat sa wa]

Czech [tʃɛk] adj เกี่ยวกับสาธารณรัฐเช็ก [kiao kap sa tha ra na rat chek] ▷ n (language) ภาษาเช็ค [pha sa chek], (person) ชาวเช็ก [chao chek]; **Czech Republic** n สาธารณรัฐเช็ก [sa tha ra na rat chek]

d

dad [dæd] *n* พ่อ [pho]

daddy ['dædɪ] *n* พ่อ [pho]

daffodil ['dæfədɪl] *n* ดอกแดฟโฟดีลมีสี
เหลือง [dok daef fo dil mii sii lueang]

daft [dɑːft] *adj* โง่ [ngo]

daily ['deɪlɪ] *adj* ทุกวัน [thuk wan] ▷ *adv*
แต่ละวัน [tae la wan]

dairy ['dɛərɪ] *n* ผลิตภัณฑ์ที่ทำจากนม [pha
lit ta phan thii tham chak nom]; **dairy
produce** *n* ผลผลิตจากนม [phon pha lit
chak nom]; **dairy products** *npl* ผลผลิต
ต่าง ๆ จากนม [phon pha lit tang tang
chak nom]

daisy ['deɪzɪ] *n* ดอกเดซี่ [dok de si]

dam [dæm] *n* เขื่อน [khuean]

damage ['dæmɪdʒ] *n* ความเสียหาย
[khwam sia hai] ▷ *v* การทำร้าย [kan
tham rai]

damaged ['dæmɪdʒd] *adj* **My luggage
has been damaged** กระเป๋าเดินทางฉัน
เสียหาย [kra pao doen thang chan sia
hai]; **My suitcase has arrived
damaged** กระเป๋าเดินทางของฉันเสียหาย
เมื่อมาถึง [kra pao doen thang khong
chan sia hai muea ma thueng]

damn [dæm] *adj* คำอุทานแสดงความ
รำคาญ [kham u than sa daeng khwam
ram khan]

damp [dæmp] *adj* ชื้น [chuen]

dance [dɑːns] *n* การเต้นรำ [kan ten ram]
▷ *v* เต้นรำ [ten ram]; **I don't really
dance** ที่จริงฉันไม่เต้นรำ [thii ching chan
mai ten ram]; **I feel like dancing** ฉันรู้สึก
อยากเต้นรำ [chan ru suek yak ten ram];
Would you like to dance? คุณอยาก
เต้นรำไหม? [khun yak ten ram mai]

dancer ['dɑːnsə] *n* นักเต้นรำ [nak ten
ram]

dancing ['dɑːnsɪŋ] *n* การเต้นรำ [kan ten
ram]; **ballroom dancing** *n* การเต้นรำ
จังหวะบอลรูม [kan ten ram chang wa
ball room]

dandelion ['dændɪˌlaɪən] *n* พันธุ์ไม้ชนิด
หนึ่งใบหยักมีสีเหลือง [phan mai cha nit
hueng bai hyik mee see hlueang]

dandruff ['dændrəf] *n* รังแค [rang
khae]

Dane [deɪn] *n* ชาวเดนมาร์ก [chao den
mak]

danger ['deɪndʒə] *n* อันตราย [an ta rai];
Is there a danger of avalanches? มี
อันตรายเกี่ยวกับหิมะถล่มไหม? [mii an ta
rai kiao kap hi ma tha lom mai]

dangerous ['deɪndʒərəs] *adj* ซึ่งเป็น
อันตราย [sueng pen an tra lai]

Danish ['deɪnɪʃ] *adj* เกี่ยวกับชาวเดนมาร์ก
[kiao kap chao den mak] ▷ *n (language)*
ภาษาเดนมาร์ก [pha sa den mak]

dare [dɛə] *v* กล้า [kla]

daring ['dɛərɪŋ] *adj* กล้าหาญ [kla han]

dark [dɑːk] *adj* มืด [muet] ▷ *n* ความมืด
[khwam mued]; **It's dark** มืด [muet]

darkness ['dɑːknɪs] *n* ความมืด [khwam
mued]

darling ['dɑːlɪŋ] *n* ที่รัก [thi rak]

dart [dɑːt] *n* ลูกดอก [luk dok]

darts [dɑːts] *npl* ลูกดอกหลายลูก [luk dok
lai luk]

dash [dæʃ] *v* ถลาไปอย่างรวดเร็ว [tha la

pai yang ruat reo]

dashboard ['dæʃ,bɔːd] *n* แผงหน้าปัด
รถยนต์ [phaeng na pat rot yon]

data ['deɪtə; 'dɑːtə] *npl* สถิติ ข้อมูล [sa
thi ti, kho mun]

database ['deɪtə,beɪs] *n* ฐานข้อมูล [tan
kho mun]

date [deɪt] *n* วันที่ [wan thi];
best-before date *n* วันหมดอายุ [wan
mot a yu]; **expiry date** *n* วันที่หมดอายุ
[wan thii mot a yu]; **sell-by date** *n*
ขายก่อนหมดวันที่กำหนด [khai kon mot
wan thii kam nod]; **What is the date?**
วันที่อะไร? [wan thii a rai]

daughter ['dɔːtə] *n* ลูกสาว [luk sao]; **My
daughter is lost** ลูกสาวฉันหลงทาง [luk
sao chan long thang]; **My daughter is
missing** ลูกสาวฉันหาย [luk sao chan hai]

daughter-in-law ['dɔːtə ɪn lɔː] (*pl*
daughters-in-law) *n* ลูกสะใภ้ [luk sa
phai]

dawn [dɔːn] *n* รุ่งอรุณ [rung a run]

day [deɪ] *n* วัน [wan]; **Do you run day
trips to...?** คุณจัดเที่ยวแบบหนึ่งวันไป...
ไหม? [khun chat thiao baep nueng
wan pai...mai]; **I want to hire a car
for five days** ฉันอยากเช่ารถคันหนึ่งสักห้า
วัน [chan yak chao rot khan nueng sak
ha wan]; **Is the museum open every
day?** พิพิธภัณฑ์เปิดทุกวันไหม? [phi phit
tha phan poet thuk wan mai]

daytime ['deɪ,taɪm] *n* เวลากลางวัน [we
la klang wan]

dead [dɛd] *adj* ตายแล้ว [tai laeo] ▷ *adv*
อย่างแน่นอน [yang nae norn]; **dead end**
n ทางตัน [thang ton]

deadline ['dɛd,laɪn] *n* เส้นตาย [sen tai]

deaf [dɛf] *adj* หูหนวก [hu nuak]; **I'm
deaf** ฉันหูหนวก [chan hu nuak]

deafening ['dɛfᵊnɪŋ] *adj* เสียงดังมาก
[siang dang mak]

deal [diːl] *n* การซื้อขาย [kan sue khai]

dealer ['diːlə] *n* ผู้ทำธุรกิจ [phu tham
thu ra kid]; **drug dealer** *n* คนขายยา

[khon khai ya]

deal with [diːl wɪθ] *v* จัดการ [chat kan]

dear [dɪə] *adj (expensive)* มีราคาสูง [mii
ra kha sung], (*loved*) ซึ่งเป็นที่รักยิ่ง
[sueng pen thii rak ying]

death [dɛθ] *n* ความตาย [khwam tai]

debate [dɪ'beɪt] *n* การโต้วาที [kan to wa
tii] ▷ *v* โต้วาที [to wa thi]

debit ['dɛbɪt] *n* รายการของเงินที่หักบัญชี
[rai kan khong ngoen thii hak ban chi]
▷ *v* หักบัญชี [hak ban chi]; **debit card** *n*
บัตรที่หักบัญชี [bat thii hak ban chi];
direct debit *n* การหักบัญชีโดยตรง [kan
hak ban chii doi trong]

debt [dɛt] *n* หนี้ [ni]

decade ['dɛkeɪd; dɪ'keɪd] *n* ทศวรรษ
[thot sa wat]

decaffeinated [dɪ'kæfɪ,neɪtɪd] *adj* ที่
ไม่มีคาเฟอีน [thii mai mii kha fe in];
decaffeinated coffee *n* กาแฟที่ไม่มี
คาเฟอีน [ka fae thii mai mii kha fe in]

decay [dɪ'keɪ] *v* เน่าเปื่อย [nao pueai]

deceive [dɪ'siːv] *v* หลอกลวง [lok luang]

December [dɪ'sɛmbə] *n* เดือนธันวาคม
[duean than wa khom]

decent ['diːsᵊnt] *adj* เหมาะสม [mo som]

decide [dɪ'saɪd] *v* ตัดสินใจ [tat sin chai]

decimal ['dɛsɪməl] *adj* เลขทศนิยม [lek
thot sa ni yom]

decision [dɪ'sɪʒən] *n* การตัดสินใจ [kan
tat sin jai]

decisive [dɪ'saɪsɪv] *adj* ซึ่งลงความเห็น
แล้ว [sueng long khwam hen laeo]

deck [dɛk] *n* ดาดฟ้าเรือ [dat fa ruea];
Can we go out on deck? เราขึ้นไปบน
ดาดฟ้าเรือได้ไหม? [rao khuen pai bon
dat fa ruea dai mai]

deckchair ['dɛk,tʃɛə] *n* เก้าอี้ผ้าใบ [kao ii
pha bai]

declare [dɪ'klɛə] *v* ประกาศ [pra kat]

decorate ['dɛkə,reɪt] *v* ประดับ [pra dap]

decorator ['dɛkə,reɪtə] *n* ช่างตกแต่ง
[chang tok taeng]

decrease *n* ['diːkriːs] การลดลง [kan lod

long] ▷ v [dɪ'kriːs] ลดลง [lot long]

dedicated ['dɛdɪ.keɪtɪd] *adj* ซึ่งอุทิศตัว เพื่อ [sueng u thit tua phuea]

dedication [.dɛdɪ'keɪʃən] *n* การอุทิศให้ [kan u thit hai]

deduct [dɪ'dʌkt] *v* ลบออก [lop ok]

deep [diːp] *adj* ลึก [luek]

deep-fry [diːpfraɪ] *v* ทอดอาหารที่มีน้ำมัน มาก [thot a han thii mii nam man mak]

deeply ['diːplɪ] *adv* อย่างลึกมาก [yang luek mak]

deer [dɪə] (*pl* **deer**) *n* กวาง [kwang]

defeat [dɪ'fiːt] *n* ความพ่ายแพ้ [khwam phai phae] ▷ v ทำให้พ่ายแพ้ [tham hai phai phae]

defect [dɪ'fɛkt] *n* ข้อบกพร่อง [kho bok phrong]

defence [dɪ'fɛns] *n* การป้องกัน [kan pong kan]

defend [dɪ'fɛnd] *v* แก้ตัว [kae tua]

defendant [dɪ'fɛndənt] *n* จำเลย [cham loei]

defender [dɪ'fɛndə] *n* ผู้ปกป้อง [phu pok pong]

deficit ['dɛfɪsɪt; dɪ'fɪsɪt] *n* ปริมาณที่ขาด การขาดดุล [pa ri man thii khat, kan khat dun]

define [dɪ'faɪn] *v* นิยาม [ni yam]

definite ['dɛfɪnɪt] *adj* แน่นอน [nae non]

definitely ['dɛfɪnɪtlɪ] *adv* อย่างแน่นอน [yang nae norn]

definition [.dɛfɪ'nɪʃən] *n* คำจำกัดความ [kham cham kad khwam]

degree [dɪ'griː] *n* องศา [ong sa]; **degree centigrade** *n* องศาเซนติเกรด [ong sa sen ti kret]; **degree Celsius** *n* องศา เซลเซียส [ong sa sel sias]; **degree Fahrenheit** *n* องศาฟาห์เรนไฮต์ [ong sa fa ren hai]

dehydrated [diːhaɪ'dreɪtɪd] *adj* ที่สูญ เสียน้ำจากร่างกาย [thii sun sia nam chak rang kai]

de-icer [diː'aɪsə] *n* ขจัดน้ำแข็ง [kha chat nam khaeng]

delay [dɪ'leɪ] *n* ความล่าช้า [khwam la cha] ▷ v ล่าช้า [la cha]

delayed [dɪ'leɪd] *adj* ทำให้ล่าช้า [tham hai la cha]

delegate *n* ['dɛlɪ.geɪt] ตัวแทน [tua thaen] ▷ v ['dɛlɪ.geɪt] มอบให้ทำแทน [mop hai tham thaen]

delete [dɪ'liːt] *v* ลบ [lop]

deliberate [dɪ'lɪbərɪt] *adj* ซึ่งทำอย่าง รอบคอบ [sueng tham yang rop khop]

deliberately [dɪ'lɪbərətlɪ] *adv* อย่าง รอบคอบ [yang rop khop]

delicate ['dɛlɪkɪt] *adj* ละเอียดอ่อน [la iat on]

delicatessen [.dɛlɪkə'tɛsən] *n* ร้าน อาหารที่นำเข้าจากต่างประเทศเช่น ไส้กรอก เนื้อรมควันและอื่น ๆ [ran a han thii nam khao chak tang pra tet chen sai krok nuea rom khwan lae uen uen]

delicious [dɪ'lɪʃəs] *adj* อร่อย [a roi]; **That was delicious** นั่นอร่อยมาก [nan a roi mak]; **The meal was delicious** อาหารมื้อนี้อร่อยมาก [a han mue nii a roi mak]

delight [dɪ'laɪt] *n* ความยินดี [khwam yin dee]

delighted [dɪ'laɪtɪd] *adj* น่าชื่นชมยินดี [na chuen chom yin dii]

delightful [dɪ'laɪtfʊl] *adj* น่าปีติยินดี [na pi ti yin dii]

deliver [dɪ'lɪvə] *v* ส่งมอบ [song mop]

delivery [dɪ'lɪvərɪ] *n* การส่ง [kan song]; **recorded delivery** *n* ลงทะเบียน [long tha bian]

demand [dɪ'mɑːnd] *n* ความต้องการ [khwam tong kan] ▷ v ต้องการ [tong kan]

demanding [dɪ'mɑːndɪŋ] *adj* ต้องการ อย่างมาก [tong kan yang mak]

demo, demos ['dɛməʊ, 'diːmɒs] *n* การ สาธิต [kan sa thit]

democracy [dɪ'mɒkrəsɪ] *n* ประชาธิปไตย [pra cha thi pa tai]

democratic [.dɛmə'krætɪk] *adj* เกี่ยวกับ

ประชาธิปไตย [kiao kap pra cha thip pa tai]

demolish [dɪ'mɒlɪʃ] v รื้อถอน [rue thon]

demonstrate ['dɛmən,streɪt] v แสดงให้เห็น [sa daeng hai hen]

demonstration [,dɛmən'streɪʃən] n การประท้วง [kan pra thuang]

demonstrator ['dɛmən,streɪtə] n ผู้ประท้วง [phu pra thuang]

denim ['dɛnɪm] n ผ้ายีนส์ [pha yin]

denims ['dɛnɪmz] npl ผ้ายีนส์ [pha yin]

Denmark ['dɛnmɑːk] n ประเทศเดนมาร์ก [pra tet den mak]

dense [dɛns] adj หนาแน่น [hna naen]

density ['dɛnsɪtɪ] n ความหนาแน่น [khwam na naen]

dent [dɛnt] n รอยบุ๋ม [roi bum] ▷ v ทำให้เป็นรอยบุ๋ม [tham hai pen roi bum]

dental ['dɛntᵊl] adj เกี่ยวกับฟัน [kiao kap fan]; **dental floss** n ไหมขัดฟัน [mai khat fan]; **I don't know if I have dental insurance** ฉันไม่รู้ว่าฉันมีประกันเกี่ยวกับฟันไหม? [chan mai ru wa chan mii pra kan kiao kap fan mai]

dentist ['dɛntɪst] n หมอฟัน [mo fan]; **I need a dentist** ฉันต้องการหมอฟัน [chan tong kan mo fan]

dentures ['dɛntʃəz] npl ฟันปลอม [fan plom]; **Can you repair my dentures?** คุณซ่อมฟันปลอมฉันได้ไหม? [khun som fan plom chan dai mai]

deny [dɪ'naɪ] v ปฏิเสธ [pa ti set]

deodorant [diː'əʊdərənt] n ยาดับกลิ่น [ya dap klin]

depart [dɪ'pɑːt] v ออกเดินทาง [ork doen thang]

department [dɪ'pɑːtmənt] n แผนก [pha naek]; **accident & emergency department** n อุบัติเหตุและหน่วยฉุกเฉิน [u bat ti het lae nuai chuk choen]; **department store** n ห้างสรรพสินค้า [hang sap pha sin kha]; **Where is the lingerie department?** แผนกชุดชั้นในอยู่ที่ไหน? [pha naek chut chan nai yu thii nai]

departure [dɪ'pɑːtʃə] n การออกเดินทาง [kan ok doen thang]; **departure lounge** n ห้องพักผู้โดยสารที่จะเดินทางออก [hong phak phu doi san thii ja doen thang ok]

depend [dɪ'pɛnd] v ขึ้นอยู่กับ [khuen yu kap]

deport [dɪ'pɔːt] v เนรเทศออกจากประเทศ [ne ra thet ok chak pra thet]

deposit [dɪ'pɒzɪt] n เงินฝาก [ngoen fak]

depressed [dɪ'prɛst] adj หดหู่ [hot hu]

depressing [dɪ'prɛsɪŋ] adj หมดกำลังใจ [mot kam lang jai]

depression [dɪ'prɛʃən] n ความหดหู่ [khwam hot hu]

depth [dɛpθ] n ความลึก [khwam luek]

descend [dɪ'sɛnd] v ลงมา [long ma]

describe [dɪ'skraɪb] v อธิบาย [a thi bai]

description [dɪ'skrɪpʃən] n คำอธิบาย [kham a thi bai]

desert ['dɛzət] n ทะเลทราย [tha le sai]; **desert island** n เกาะกลางทะเลทราย [ko klang tha le sai]

deserve [dɪ'zɜːv] v สมควรได้รับ [som khuan dai rap]

design [dɪ'zaɪn] n การออกแบบ [kan ok baep] ▷ v ออกแบบ [ok baep]

designer [dɪ'zaɪnə] n ผู้ออกแบบ [phu ok baep]; **interior designer** n นักตกแต่งภายใน [nak tok taeng phai nai]

desire [dɪ'zaɪə] n ความปรารถนา [khwam prat tha na] ▷ v ปรารถนา [prat tha na]

desk [dɛsk] n โต๊ะ [to]; **enquiry desk** n โต๊ะสอบถาม [to sop tham]; **May I use your desk?** ฉันขอใช้โต๊ะหนังสือคุณได้ไหม? [chan kho chai to nang sue khun dai mai]

despair [dɪ'spɛə] n ความสิ้นหวัง [khwam sin wang]

desperate ['dɛspərɪt; -prɪt] adj ซึ่งสิ้นหวัง [sueng sin wang]

desperately ['dɛspərɪtlɪ] adv อย่างสิ้นหวัง [yang sin wang]

despise [dɪ'spaɪz] v เหยียดหยาม [yiat yam]

despite [dɪ'spaɪt] prep ทั้งๆ ที่ [thang thang thii]

dessert [dɪ'zɜːt] n ของหวาน [khong wan]; **dessert spoon** n ช้อนของหวาน [chon khong wan]; **The dessert menu, please** ขอรายการของหวาน [kho rai kan khong wan]; **We'd like a dessert** เราอยากได้ของหวาน [rao yak dai khong wan]

destination [ˌdɛstɪ'neɪʃən] n จุดหมาย ปลายทาง [chut mai plai thang]

destiny ['dɛstɪnɪ] n ชะตากรรม [cha ta kam]

destroy [dɪ'strɔɪ] v ทำลาย [tham lai]

destruction [dɪ'strʌkʃən] n การทำลาย [kan tham lai]

detail ['diːteɪl] n รายละเอียด [rai la iad]; **Here are my insurance details** นี่คือ รายละเอียดการประกันของฉัน [ni khue rai la iat kan pra kan khong chan]

detailed ['diːteɪld] adj ซึ่งมีรายละเอียด มาก [sueng mii rai la iat mak]

detective [dɪ'tɛktɪv] n นักสืบ [nak suep]

detention [dɪ'tɛnʃən] n การควบคุมตัว [kan khuab khum tua]

detergent [dɪ'tɜːdʒənt] n ผงซักฟอก [phong sak fok]

deteriorate [dɪ'tɪərɪəˌreɪt] v เสื่อมโทรม [sueam som]

determined [dɪ'tɜːmɪnd] adj เด็ดเดี่ยว [det diao]

detour ['diːtʊə] n เส้นทางอ้อม [sen thang om]

devaluation [diːˌvæljuː'eɪʃən] n การลด ค่าเงิน [kan lot kha ngen]

devastated ['dɛvəˌsteɪtɪd] adj ทำให้ ท่วมท้นด้วยความรู้สึก ที่เสียหาย [tham hai thuam thon duai khwam ru suk thii sia hai]

devastating ['dɛvəˌsteɪtɪŋ] adj ซึ่งก่อให้ เกิดความเสียหายอย่างมาก [sueng ko hai koet khwam sia hai yang mak]

develop [dɪ'vɛləp] vi พัฒนา เจริญ เติบโต [phat ta na, cha roen, toep to] ▷ vt พัฒนา ทำให้เติบโต ทำให้ดีขึ้น [phat ta na tham hai toep to tham hai di khuen]; **developing country** n ประเทศที่กำลัง พัฒนา [pra tet thii kam lang phat ta na]

development [dɪ'vɛləpmənt] n การ พัฒนา [kan phat ta na]

device [dɪ'vaɪs] n อุปกรณ์ [up pa kon]

devil ['dɛvəl] n ภูต [phut]

devise [dɪ'vaɪz] v คิดขึ้นใหม่ [kid khuen mai]

devoted [dɪ'vəʊtɪd] adj คลั่งไคล้ [khlang khlai]

diabetes [ˌdaɪə'biːtɪs; -tiːz] n โรคเบา หวาน [rok bao wan]

diabetic [ˌdaɪə'bɛtɪk] adj ซึ่งเป็นเบาหวาน [sueng pen bao wan] ▷ n คนเป็นเบาหวาน [khon pen bao wan]

diagnosis [ˌdaɪəg'nəʊsɪs] n การวินิจฉัย โรค [kan wi nit chai rok]

diagonal [daɪ'ægənəl] adj ทแยงมุม [tha yaeng mum]

diagram ['daɪəˌgræm] n แผนภาพ [phaen phap]

dial ['daɪəl; daɪl] v หมุน [mun]; **dialling code** n รหัสหมุนโทรศัพท์ [ra hat mun tho ra sap]; **dialling tone** n เสียงหมุน โทรศัพท์ [siang mun tho ra sap]

dialect ['daɪəˌlɛkt] n ภาษาท้องถิ่น [pha sa thong thin]

dialogue ['daɪəˌlɒg] n การสนทนา [kan son tha na]

diameter [daɪ'æmɪtə] n เส้นผ่าศูนย์กลาง [sen pha sun klang]

diamond ['daɪəmənd] n เพชร [pet]

diarrhoea [ˌdaɪə'rɪə] n อาการท้องร่วง [a kan thong ruang]

diary ['daɪərɪ] n สมุดบันทึกประจำวัน [sa mud ban thuek pra cham wan]

dice, die [daɪs, daɪ] npl ลูกเต๋า [luk tao]

dictation [dɪk'teɪʃən] n การเขียนตามคำ บอก [kan khian tam kham bork]

dictator [dɪk'teɪtə] n ผู้เผด็จการ [phu

pha det kan]

dictionary ['dɪkʃənərɪ; -ʃənrɪ] *n*
พจนานุกรม [phot cha na nu krom]

die [daɪ] *v* ตาย [tai]

diesel ['di:zəl] *n* น้ำมันดีเซล [nam man di
sel]

diet ['daɪət] *n* อาหาร [a han] ▷ *v* ควบคุม
อาหารเพื่อลดน้ำหนัก [khuap khum a
han phuea lot nam nak]; **I'm on a diet**
ฉันกำลังควบคุมอาหารเพื่อลดน้ำหนัก [chan
kam lang khum a han phuea lot nam
nak]

difference ['dɪfərəns; 'dɪfrəns] *n* ความ
แตกต่าง [khwam taek tang]

different ['dɪfərənt; 'dɪfrənt] *adj* ต่าง
กัน [tang kan]

difficult ['dɪfɪkəlt] *adj* ยาก [yak]

difficulty ['dɪfɪkəltɪ] *n* ความยากลำบาก
[khwam yak lam bak]

dig [dɪg] *v* ขุด [khut]

digest [dɪ'dʒɛst; daɪ-] *v* ย่อย [yoi]

digestion [dɪ'dʒɛstʃən; daɪ-] *n* การย่อย
[kan yoi]

digger ['dɪgə] *n* เครื่องมือที่ใช้ในการขุด
[khrueang mue thii chai nai kan khut]

digital ['dɪdʒɪtəl] *adj* ซึ่งส่งรับข้อมูลโดยใช้
ตัวเลข [sueng song rap kho mun doi
chai tua lek]; **digital camera** *n* กล้องดิ
จิตัล [klong di chi tan]; **digital radio** *n*
วิทยุดิจิตัล [wit tha yu di chi tal]; **digital
television** *n* โทรทัศน์ดิจิตัล [tho ra tat di
chi tal]

dignity ['dɪgnɪtɪ] *n* ความมีเกียรติ
[khwam mii kiat]

dilemma [dɪ'lɛmə; daɪ-] *n* สภาวะลำบาก
[sa pha wa lam bak]

dilute [daɪ'lu:t] *v* เจือจาง [chue chang]

diluted [daɪ'lu:tɪd] *adj* ทำให้เจือจาง
[tham hai chuea chang]

dim [dɪm] *adj* สลัว [sa lua]

dimension [dɪ'mɛnʃən] *n* การวัดขนาด
[kan wat kha nat]

diminish [dɪ'mɪnɪʃ] *v* ทำให้ลดลง [tham
hai lot long]

din [dɪn] *n* เสียงอึกทึก [siang uek ka tuek]

diner ['daɪnə] *n* คนที่มารับประทานในร้าน
อาหาร [khon thii ma rap pra than nai
ran a han]

dinghy ['dɪŋɪ] *n* เรือขนาดเล็ก [ruea kha
nard lek]

dinner ['dɪnə] *n* อาหารเย็น [a han yen];
dinner jacket *n* เสื้อนอกที่ใส่ไปงานเลี้ยง
อาหารค่ำ [suea nok thii sai pai ngan
liang a han kham]; **The dinner was
delicious** อาหารเย็นที่อร่อยมาก [a han
yen thii a roi mak]; **What time is
dinner?** อาหารเย็นเวลาใด? [a han yen
we la dai]; **Would you like to go out
for dinner?** คุณอยากออกไปทานอาหาร
เย็นไหม? [khun yak ok pai than a han
yen mai]

dinosaur ['daɪnə,sɔ:] *n* ไดโนเสาร์ [dai
no sao]

dip [dɪp] *n* (food/sauce) การจิ้มน้ำจิ้ม [kan
chim nam chim] ▷ *v* จุ่ม [chum]

diploma [dɪ'pləʊmə] *n* ประกาศนียบัตร
[pra ka sa ni ya bat]

diplomat ['dɪplə,mæt] *n* นักการทูต [nak
kan thut]

diplomatic [,dɪplə'mætɪk] *adj* เกี่ยวกับ
การทูต [kiao kap kan thut]

dipstick ['dɪp,stɪk] *n* ก้านโลหะที่ใช้ตรวจ
วามน้ำมันอยู่ในแท่งค่าเท่าไหร่ [kan lo ha
thii chai truat wa mii nam man yu nai
thaeng thao rai]

direct [dɪ'rɛkt; daɪ-] *adj* ตรง [trong] ▷ *v*
จัดการ [chat kan]; **direct debit** *n* การหัก
บัญชีโดยตรง [kan hak ban chii doi
trong]; **I'd prefer to go direct** ฉัน
ต้องการเดินทางสายตรง [chan tong kan
doen thang sai trong]; **Is it a direct
train?** มีรถไฟสายตรงไหม? [mii rot fai
sai trong mai]

direction [dɪ'rɛkʃən; daɪ-] *n* ทิศทาง
[thit thang]; **Can you draw me a map
with directions?** คุณวาดแผนที่บอก
ทิศทางให้ฉันได้ไหม? [khun wat phaen
thii bok thit thang hai chan dai mai]

directions [dɪˈrekʃənz; daɪ-] *npl* ทิศทาง
ต่าง ๆ [thit thang tang tang]

directly [dɪˈrektlɪ; daɪ-] *adv* โดยตรง
[doi trong]

director [dɪˈrektə; daɪ-] *n* ผู้อำนวยการ
[phu am nuai kan]; **managing
director** *n* กรรมการผู้จัดการ [kam ma
kan phu chat kan]

directory [dɪˈrektərɪ; -trɪ; daɪ-] *n* สมุด
รายชื่อ [sa mut rai chue]; **directory
enquiries** *npl* การสอบถามข้อมูลรายชื่อ
[kan sop tham kho mun rai chue];
telephone directory *n* สมุดโทรศัพท์
[sa mut tho ra sap]

dirt [dɜːt] *n* ดิน [din]

dirty [ˈdɜːtɪ] *adj* สกปรก [sok ka prok];
It's dirty มันสกปรก [man sok ka prok];
My sheets are dirty ผ้าปูที่นอนฉัน
สกปรก [pha pu thii non chan sok ka
prok]

disability [ˌdɪsəˈbɪlɪtɪ] *n* ความพิการ
[khwam phi kan]

disabled [dɪˈseɪbˀld] *adj* พิการ [phi kan]
▷ *npl* คนพิการ [khon phi kan]; **Are
there any toilets for the disabled?** มี
ห้องน้ำสำหรับคนพิการไหม? [mii hong
nam sam rap khon phi kan mai]; **Do
you provide access for the disabled?**
คุณจัดให้มีทางเข้าออกสำหรับคนพิการไหม?
[khun chat hai mii thang khao ok sam
rap khon phi kan mai]; **Is there a
reduction for disabled people?** มี
ส่วนลดให้คนพิการไหม? [mii suan lot hai
khon phi kan mai]

disadvantage [ˌdɪsədˈvɑːntɪdʒ] *n* คนที่
เสียเปรียบ [khon thii sia priap]

disagree [ˌdɪsəˈɡriː] *v* ไม่เห็นด้วย [mai
hen duai]

disagreement [ˌdɪsəˈɡriːmənt] *n* ความ
ขัดแย้งกัน [khwam khat yaeng kan]

disappear [ˌdɪsəˈpɪə] *v* หายไป [hai pai]

disappearance [ˌdɪsəˈpɪərəns] *n* การ
หายไป [kan hai pai]

disappoint [ˌdɪsəˈpɔɪnt] *v* ทำให้ผิดหวัง

[tham hai phid hwang]

disappointed [ˌdɪsəˈpɔɪntɪd] *adj* ที่ผิด
หวัง [thii phit hwang]

disappointing [ˌdɪsəˈpɔɪntɪŋ] *adj* ซึ่ง
ผิดหวัง [sueng phit wang]

disappointment [ˌdɪsəˈpɔɪntmənt] *n*
ความผิดหวัง [khwam phit wang]

disaster [dɪˈzɑːstə] *n* ความหายนะ
[khwam hai ya na]

disastrous [dɪˈzɑːstrəs] *adj* ก่อให้เกิดความ
หายนะ [ko hai koet khwam ha ya na]

disc [dɪsk] *n* แผ่นดิสค์ [phaen dis];
compact disc *n* แผ่นดิสก์ [phaen dis];
disc jockey *n* ผู้จัดรายการดนตรีแผ่นเสียง
[phu chat rai kan don tree phaen
siang]; **slipped disc** *n* หมอนรองกระดูก
สันหลังเลื่อน [mon rong kra duk san
lang luean]

discharge [dɪsˈtʃɑːdʒ] *v* **When will I be
discharged?** ฉันจะออกจากโรงพยาบาล
ได้เมื่อไร? [chan ja ok chak rong pha ya
baan dai muea rai]

discipline [ˈdɪsɪplɪn] *n* ข้อบังคับ [kho
bang khap]

disclose [dɪsˈkləʊz] *v* เปิดเผย [poet phoei]

disco [ˈdɪskəʊ] *n* การเต้นดิสโก้ [kan ten
dis ko]

disconnect [ˌdɪskəˈnekt] *v* ตัดขาดจาก
กัน [tat khat chak kan]

discount [ˈdɪskaʊnt] *n* การลดราคา [kan
lod ra kha]; **student discount** *n* ราคา
ลดสำหรับนักเรียน [ra kha lot sam rap
nak rian]

discourage [dɪsˈkʌrɪdʒ] *v* ทำให้หมด
กำลังใจ [tham hai hmod kam lang jai]

discover [dɪˈskʌvə] *v* ค้นพบ [khon phop]

discretion [dɪˈskreʃən] *n* การใช้ดุลยพินิจ
[kan chai dun la ya phi nit]

discrimination [dɪˌskrɪmɪˈneɪʃən] *n*
การแบ่งแยก [kan baeng yaek]

discuss [dɪˈskʌs] *v* ปรึกษาหารือ [pruek
sa ha rue]

discussion [dɪˈskʌʃən] *n* การปรึกษา
หารือ [kan pruek sa ha rue]

disease [dɪˈziːz] *n* โรค [rok];
Alzheimer's disease *n* โรคคลืม อัลไซเม
อร์ [rok luem, al sai moe]

disgraceful [dɪsˈɡreɪsfʊl] *adj* น่าอับอาย
[na ap ai]

disguise [dɪsˈɡaɪz] *v* ปลอมตัว [plom tua]

disgusted [dɪsˈɡʌstɪd] *adj* ซึ่งน่า
ขยะแขยง [sueng na kha ya kha yaeng]

disgusting [dɪsˈɡʌstɪŋ] *adj* น่าขยะแขยง
[na kha ya kha yaeng]

dish [dɪʃ] *n (food)* กับข้าว [kap khao],
(plate) จาน [chan]; **dish towel** *n* ผ้าเช็ด
จาน [pha chet chan]; **Can you
recommend a local dish?** คุณแนะนำ
อาหารจานท้องถิ่นได้ไหม? [khun nae
nam a han chan thong thin dai mai];
How do you cook this dish? คุณทำ
อาหารจานนี้อย่างไร? [khun tham a han
chan nii yang rai]; **How is this dish
served?** เสิร์ฟอาหารจานนี้อย่างไร? [serf
a han chan nee yang rai]

dishcloth [ˈdɪʃˌklɒθ] *n* ผ้าเช็ดจาน [pha
chet chan]

dishonest [dɪsˈɒnɪst] *adj* ไม่ซื่อสัตย์
[mai sue sat]

dishwasher [ˈdɪʃˌwɒʃə] *n* เครื่องล้างจาน
[khrueang lang chan]

disinfectant [ˌdɪsɪnˈfɛktənt] *n* สารที่ใช้
ฆ่าเชื้อโรค [san thii chai kha chuea rok]

disk [dɪsk] *n* แผ่นดิสก์ [phaen dis]; **disk
drive** *n* หน่วยจานบันทึก [nuai chan ban
thuek]

diskette [dɪsˈkɛt] *n* จานบันทึก [chan
ban thuek]

dislike [dɪsˈlaɪk] *v* ไม่ชอบ [mai chop]

dismal [ˈdɪzməl] *adj* หดหู่ [hot hu]

dismiss [dɪsˈmɪs] *v* ปลดออกจากตำแหน่ง
[plot ok chak tam naeng]

disobedient [ˌdɪsəˈbiːdɪənt] *adj* ซึ่งไม่
เชื่อฟัง [sueng mai chuea fang]

disobey [ˌdɪsəˈbeɪ] *v* ไม่เชื่อฟัง [mai
chuea fang]

dispenser [dɪsˈpɛnsə] *n* ผู้จ่าย [phu
chai]; **cash dispenser** *n* เครื่องกดเงินสด

จากธนาคาร [khrueang kot ngoen sot
chak tha na khan]

display [dɪˈspleɪ] *n* การแสดง การจัดวาง
[kan sa daeng, kan chat wang] ▷ *v*
แสดง [sa daeng]

disposable [dɪˈspəʊzəbəl] *adj* ซึ่ง
ออกแบบมาให้ใช้แล้วทิ้ง [sueng ok baep
ma hai chai laeo thing]

disqualify [dɪsˈkwɒlɪˌfaɪ] *v* ตัดสิทธิ
เพราะฝ่าฝืนกฎหรือไม่มีคุณสมบัติ [tad sid
khro fa fuen kod hue mai mee khun
som bat]

disrupt [dɪsˈrʌpt] *v* ทำให้ยุ่งเหยิง [tham
hai yung yoeng]

dissatisfied [dɪsˈsætɪsˌfaɪd] *adj* ซึ่งไม่
พอใจ [sueng mai phor jai]

dissolve [dɪˈzɒlv] *v* ละลาย [la lai]

distance [ˈdɪstəns] *n* ความห่างไกล
[khwam hang klai]

distant [ˈdɪstənt] *adj* ห่างไกล [hang
klai]

distillery [dɪˈstɪlərɪ] *n* โรงกลั่นสุรา [rong
klan su ra]

distinction [dɪˈstɪŋkʃən] *n* การแบ่งแยก
[kan baeng yaek]

distinctive [dɪˈstɪŋktɪv] *adj* เด่น [den]

distinguish [dɪˈstɪŋɡwɪʃ] *v* จำแนกความ
แตกต่าง [cham naek khwam taek tang]

distract [dɪˈstrækt] *v* ทำให้ไขว้เขว
[tham hai khwai khwe]

distribute [dɪˈstrɪbjuːt] *v* แจกจ่าย
[chaek chai]

distributor [dɪˈstrɪbjʊtə] *n* ผู้แทน
จำหน่าย [phu thaen cham nai]

district [ˈdɪstrɪkt] *n* เขต [khet]

disturb [dɪˈstɜːb] *v* รบกวน [rop kuan]

ditch [dɪtʃ] *n* คูน้ำ [khu nam] ▷ *v* ทิ้ง
[thing]

dive [daɪv] *n* การดำน้ำ [kan dam nam]
▷ *v* ดำน้ำ [dam nam]; **I'd like to go
diving** ฉันอยากไปดำน้ำ [chan yak pai
dam nam]; **Where is the best place
to dive?** ที่ไหนเป็นที่ดำน้ำที่ดีที่สุด? [thii
nai pen thii dam nam thii di thii sut]

diver ['daɪvə] n นักดำน้ำ [nak dam nam]

diversion [daɪ'vɜːʃən] n การหันเหความ สนใจ [kan han he khwam son jai]

divide [dɪ'vaɪd] v แบ่ง [baeng]

diving ['daɪvɪŋ] n การดำน้ำ [kan dam nam]; **diving board** n กระดานกระโดด น้ำ [kra dan kra dot nam]; **scuba diving** n การดำน้ำด้วยถังออกซิเจน [kan dam nam duai thang ok si chen]

division [dɪ'vɪʒən] n การแบ่ง [kan baeng]

divorce [dɪ'vɔːs] n การหย่า [kan ya] ▷ v การหย่า [kan ya]

divorced [dɪ'vɔːst] adj ซึ่งหย่าแล้ว [sueng ya laeo]

DIY [diː aɪ waɪ] abbr ตัวย่อของทำด้วยตัว เอง [tua yo khong tham duai tua eng]

dizzy ['dɪzɪ] adj เวียนศีรษะ [wian si sa]

DJ [diː dʒeɪ] abbr ดีเจ [di che]

DNA [diː ɛn eɪ] n รหัสทางพันธุกรรม [ra hat thang phan tu kam]

do [duː] v ทำ [tham]; **Can you do it straightaway?** คุณทำทันทีเลยได้ไหม? [khun tham than thii loei dai mai]; **What are you doing this evening?** คุณทำอะไรเย็นนี้? [khun tham a rai yen nii]; **What do I do?** ฉันจะทำอย่างไร? [chan ja tham yang rai]

dock [dɒk] n อู่เรือ [u ruea]

doctor ['dɒktə] n แพทย์ [phaet]

document ['dɒkjʊmənt] n เอกสาร [ek ka san]; **Here are my vehicle documents** นี่คือเอกสารต่าง ๆ ของรถฉัน [ni khue ek ka san tang tang khong rot chan]; **I want to copy this document** ฉันอยากถ่ายเอกสารใบนี้ [chan yak thai ek ka san bai nii]

documentary [ˌdɒkjʊ'mɛntərɪ; -trɪ] n สารคดี [sa ra kha di]

documentation [ˌdɒkjʊmɛn'teɪʃən] n การเตรียมเอกสาร [kan triam ek ka sarn]

documents [ˌdɒkjʊmɛnts] npl เอกสาร ต่าง ๆ [ek ka san tang tang]

dodge [dɒdʒ] v หลบหลีก [lop lik]

dog [dɒg] n สุนัข [su nak]; **guide dog** n สุนัขนำทาง [su nak nam thang]; **hot dog** n ขนมปังประกอบไส้กรอก [kha nom pang pra kop sai krok]

dole [dəʊl] n เงินที่รัฐบาลให้กับคนว่างงาน ทุกเดือน [ngoen thii rat tha ban hai kap khon wang ngan thuk duean]

doll [dɒl] n ตุ๊กตา [tuk ka ta]

dollar ['dɒlə] n เงินดอลล่าร์ [ngoen don la]

dolphin ['dɒlfɪn] n ปลาโลมา [pla lo ma]

domestic [də'mɛstɪk] adj ในประเทศ [nai pra tet]

Dominican Republic [də'mɪnɪkən rɪ'pʌblɪk] n ประเทศโดมินิกันรีพับบลิค [pra tet do mi ni kan ri phap lik]

domino ['dɒmɪˌnəʊ] n เกมโดมิโน [kem do mi no]

dominoes ['dɒmɪˌnəʊz] npl เกมโดมิโน [kem do mi no]

donate [dəʊ'neɪt] v บริจาค [bo ri chak]

done [dʌn] adj เสร็จสิ้น [set sin]

donkey ['dɒŋkɪ] n ลา [la (laa)]

donor ['dəʊnə] n ผู้บริจาค [phu bo ri chak]

door [dɔː] n ประตู [pra tu]; **Keep the door locked** ล็อคประตู [lok pra tu]; **The door handle has come off** ที่จับประตู หลุดออกมา [thii chap pra tu lut ok ma]; **The door won't close** ปิดประตูไม่ได้ [pit pra tu mai dai]

doorbell ['dɔːˌbɛl] n กริ่งประตู [kring pra tu]

doorman, doormen ['dɔːˌmæn; -mən, 'dɔːˌmɛn] n คนเปิดประตูหน้า โรงแรมหรืออาคารต่าง ๆ [khon poet pra tu na rong raeng rue a khan tang tang]

doorstep ['dɔːˌstɛp] n ธรณีประตู [tho ra nee pra tu]

dorm [dɔːm] n **Do you have any single sex dorms?** คุณมีหอพักสำหรับ เพศเดียวกันไหม? [khun mii ho phak sam rap phet diao kan mai]

dormitory ['dɔːmɪtərɪ; -trɪ] n หอพัก [ho phak]

dose [dəʊs] n ปริมาณยาที่ให้แต่ละครั้ง [pa

ri man ya thii hai tae la khrang]

dot [dɒt] *n* จุด [chut]

double ['dʌbəl] *adj* สองเท่า [song thao] ▷ *v* ทำเป็นสองเท่า [tham pen song thao]; **double bass** *n* ดนตรีเครื่องสายชนิดหนึ่ง [don tree khrueang sai cha nit nueng]; **double bed** *n* เตียงคู่ [tiang khu]; **double glazing** *n* การติดตั้งกระจกหนา สองชั้น [kan tit tang kra chok na song chan]

doubt [daʊt] *n* ความสงสัย [khwam song sai] ▷ *v* สงสัย [song sai]

doubtful ['daʊtfʊl] *adj* ที่เป็นที่สงสัย [thii pen thii song sai]

dough [dəʊ] *n* ส่วนผสมของแป้ง น้ำและอื่น ๆ เช่นน้ำมัน น้ำตาลเพื่อทำขนมปัง [suan pha som khong paeng nam lae uen uen chen nam man nam tan phuea tham kha nom pang]

doughnut ['dəʊnʌt] *n* ขนมโดนัท [kha nom do nat]

do up [du ʌp] *v* ห่อทำให้เป็นก้อน [hor tham hai pen kon]

dove [dʌv] *n* นกพิราบ [nok phi rap]

do without [du wɪ'ðaʊt] *v* ทำโดย ปราศจาก [tham doi prad sa chak]

down [daʊn] *adv* น้อยลง [noi long]

download ['daʊnˌləʊd] *n* การบรรจุลง [kan ban chu long] ▷ *v* บรรจุลง [ban chu long]

downpour ['daʊnˌpɔː] *n* ฝนตกหนักมาก [fon tok nak mak]

downstairs ['daʊn'stɛəz] *adj* ข้างล่าง [khang laang] ▷ *adv* ข้างล่าง [khang laang]

downtown ['daʊn'taʊn] *adv* ตัวเมือง [tua mueang]

doze [dəʊz] *v* งีบหลับ [ngip lap]

dozen ['dʌzən] *n* โหล [lo]

doze off [dəʊz ɒf] *v* งีบหลับไป [ngip lap pai]

drab [dræb] *adj* ไม่มีชีวิตชีวา [mai mii chi wit chi wa]

draft [drɑːft] *n* ตั๋วแลกเงิน [tua laek ngoen]

drag [dræg] *v* ลาก [lak]

dragon ['drægən] *n* มังกร [mang kon]

dragonfly ['drægənˌflaɪ] *n* แมลงปอ [ma laeng po]

drain [dreɪn] *n* ท่อระบายน้ำ [tho ra bai nam] ▷ *v* ระบายออก [ra bai ok]; **draining board** *n* กระดานที่ใช้วางเครื่อง ใช้ในครัวให้แห้ง [kra dan thii chai wang khrueang chai nai khrua hai haeng]; **The drain is blocked** ท่อระบายน้ำตัน [tho ra bai nam tan]

drainpipe ['dreɪnˌpaɪp] *n* ท่อระบายน้ำ [tho ra bai nam]

drama ['drɑːmə] *n* ละคร [la kon]

dramatic [drə'mætɪk] *adj* ที่เกี่ยวกับ ละคร [thii kiao kab la khon]

drastic ['dræstɪk] *adj* รุนแรงมาก [run raeng mak]

draught [drɑːft] *n* กระแสลม [kra sae lom]

draughts [drɑːfts] *npl* หมากฮอส [mak hot]

draw [drɔː] *n* (lottery) สลาก [sa lak], (tie) คะแนนเท่ากัน [kha naen thao kan] ▷ *v* (equal with) เสมอกัน [sa moe kan], (sketch) วาดภาพ [wat phap]

drawback ['drɔːˌbæk] *n* ข้อเสียเปรียบ [kho thii sia priap]

drawer ['drɔːə] *n* ลิ้นชัก [lin chak]; **The drawer is jammed** ลิ้นชักติด [lin chak tit]

drawers [drɔːz] *n* **chest of drawers** *n* ตู้ ที่มีลิ้นชัก [tu thii mii lin chak]

drawing ['drɔːɪŋ] *n* รูปวาด [rup wat]

drawing pin ['drɔːɪŋ pɪn] *n* **drawing pin** *n* เข็มหมุด [khem mut]

dreadful ['drɛdfʊl] *adj* น่าสะพรึงกลัว [na sa phrueng klau]

dream [driːm] *n* ความฝัน [khwam fan] ▷ *v* ฝัน [fan]

drench [drɛntʃ] *v* ทำให้เปียกชุ่ม [tham hai piak chum]

dress [drɛs] *n* เครื่องแต่งกาย [khrueang taeng kai] ▷ *v* ใส่เสื้อผ้า [sai suea pha];

evening dress n ชุดกลางคืน [chut klang khuen]; **wedding dress** n ชุดแต่งงาน [chut taeng ngan]

dressed [drɛst] adj ได้แต่งตัวแล้ว [dai taeng tua laeo]

dresser ['drɛsə] n ตู้ที่ลิ้นชักสำหรับใส่เสื้อผ้า [tu thii lin chak sam hrab sai suea pha]

dressing ['drɛsɪŋ] n **salad dressing** n น้ำสลัด [nam sa lat]

dressing gown ['drɛsɪŋ gaʊn] n **dressing gown** n เสื้อคลุม [suea khluim]

dressing table ['drɛsɪŋ 'teɪbᵊl] n **dressing table** n โต๊ะแต่งตัว [to taeng tua]

dress up [drɛs ʌp] v แต่งตัวอย่างสวยงาม [taeng tua yang suai ngam]

dried [draɪd] adj แห้ง [haeng]

drift [drɪft] n กองดิน [kong din] ▷ v เร่ร่อน [re ron]

drill [drɪl] n การฝึกฝน [kan fuek fon] ▷ v เจาะ [cho]; **pneumatic drill** n สว่านชนิดที่ใช้กำลังอัดของอากาศ [sa wan cha nit thii chai kam lang at khong a kaat]

drink [drɪŋk] n เครื่องดื่ม [khrueang duem] ▷ v ดื่ม [duem]; **binge drinking** n การดื่มเหล้ามากเกินไป [kan duem lao mak koen pai]; **Can I get you a drink?** ฉันเอาเครื่องดื่มให้คุณได้ไหม? [chan ao khrueang duem hai khun dai mai]; **Do you drink milk?** คุณดื่มนมไหม? [khun duem nom mai]; **I don't drink alcohol** ฉันไม่ดื่มแอลกอฮอล์ [chan mai duem aen ko ho]

drink-driving ['drɪŋk'draɪvɪŋ] n ดื่มอัลกอฮอล์แล้วขับรถ [duem aen ko ho laeo khap rot]

drip [drɪp] n หยดน้ำ [yot nam] ▷ v ทำให้หยด [tham hai yot]

drive [draɪv] n การขับ [kan khap] ▷ v ขับ [khap]; **driving instructor** n ครูสอนขับรถ [khru son khap rot]; **four-wheel drive** n การขับทั้งสี่ล้อ [kan khap thang

si lo]; **left-hand drive** n การขับด้านซ้าย [kan khap dan sai]; **You were driving too fast** คุณขับรถเร็วเกินไป [khun khap rot reo koen pai]

driver ['draɪvə] n คนขับ [kon khab]; **learner driver** n นักเรียนเรียนขับรถ [nak rian rian khap rot]; **lorry driver** n คนขับรถบรรทุก [khon khap rot ban thuk]; **racing driver** n ผู้ขับรถแข่ง [phu khap rot khaeng]

driveway ['draɪv.weɪ] n ทางที่จอดรถส่วนบุคคล [thang thii jod rot suan bu kon]

driving lesson ['draɪvɪŋ 'lɛsᵊn] n บทเรียนสอนขับรถ [bot rian son khap rot]

driving licence ['draɪvɪŋ 'laɪsᵊns] n **Here is my driving licence** นี่คือใบขับขี่ของฉัน [ni khue bai khap khi khong chan]; **I don't have my driving licence on me** ฉันไม่มีใบขับขี่ในตอนนี้ [chan mai mii bai khap khii nai ton nii]; **My driving licence number is...** ใบขับขี่ของฉันหมายเลข... [bai khap khi khong chan mai lek...]

driving test ['draɪvɪŋ 'tɛst] n การสอบขับรถ [kan sop khap rot]

drizzle ['drɪzᵊl] n ฝนตกปรอย ๆ [fon tok proi proi]

drop [drɒp] n หยดน้ำ [yot nam]; **eye drops** npl น้ำยาหยอดตา [nam ya yot ta]

drought [draʊt] n ความแห้งแล้ง [khwam haeng laeng]

drown [draʊn] v จมน้ำ [chom nam]; **Someone is drowning!** มีคนกำลังจะจมน้ำ [mii khon kam lang ja chom nam]

drowsy ['draʊzɪ] adj ง่วงเงีย [ngua ngia]

drug [drʌɡ] n ยา [ya]; **drug addict** n ผู้ติดยา [phu tit ya]; **drug dealer** n คนขายยา [khon khai ya]

drum [drʌm] n กลอง [klong]

drummer ['drʌmə] n คนตีกลอง [khon ti klong]

drunk [drʌŋk] adj เมา [mao] ▷ n คนเมา [kon mao]

dry [draɪ] adj แห้งแล้ง [haeng laeng] ▷ v

แห้ง [haeng]; **bone dry** adj แห้งสนิท [haeng sa nit]; **I have dry hair** ฉันมีผม แห้ง [chan mii phom haeng]

dry-cleaner's ['draɪˈkliːnəz] n ที่ร้าน ซักแห้ง [thii ran sak haeng]

dry-cleaning ['draɪˈkliːnɪŋ] n การ ซักแห้ง [kan sak haeng]

dryer ['draɪə] n เครื่องเป่า [khrueang pao]; **spin dryer** n เครื่องปั่นผ้าให้แห้ง [khrueang pan pha hai haeng]; **tumble dryer** n เครื่องอบผ้าให้แห้ง [khrueang op pha hai haeng]

dual ['djuːəl] adj **dual carriageway** n ทางรถคู่ [thang rot khu]

dubbed [dʌbt] adj ที่แปลงเสียงเป็นภาษา อื่น [thii plang siang pen pha sa aue]

dubious ['djuːbɪəs] adj สงสัย [song sai]

duck [dʌk] n เป็ด [pet]

due [djuː] adj ถึงกำหนด [thueng kam not]

due to [djuː tʊ] prep เพราะ [phro]

dull [dʌl] adj น่าเบื่อ [na buea]

dumb [dʌm] adj โง่ [ngo]

dummy ['dʌmɪ] n หุ่นจำลอง [hun cham long]

dump [dʌmp] n ที่ทิ้งขยะ [thii thing kha ya] ▷ v ทิ้ง [thing]; **rubbish dump** n ที่ ทิ้งขยะ [thii thing kha ya]

dumpling ['dʌmplɪŋ] n ก้อนพุดดิ้ง [kon phut ding]

dune [djuːn] n **sand dune** n หุบทราย [hup sai]

dungarees [ˌdʌŋɡəˈriːz] npl เสื้อผ้าชุด ทำงาน [suea pha chut tham ngan]

dungeon ['dʌndʒən] n คุกใต้ดินใน ปราสาท [khuk tai din nai pra sat]

duration [djʊˈreɪʃən] n ช่วงเวลา [chuang we la]

during ['djʊərɪŋ] prep ในระหว่าง [nai ra wang]

dusk [dʌsk] n เวลาเย็นก่อนค่ำ [we la yen kon kham]

dust [dʌst] n ฝุ่น [fun] ▷ v ปัดฝุ่น [pat fun]

dustbin ['dʌstˌbɪn] n ที่ใส่ขยะ [thii sai kha ya]

dustman, dustmen ['dʌstmən, 'dʌstmɛn] n คนเก็บขยะ [khon kep kha ya]

dustpan ['dʌstˌpæn] n ที่ปัดฝุ่นพร้อม แปรง [thii pat fun phrom praeng]

dusty ['dʌstɪ] adj ซึ่งปกคลุมไปด้วยฝุ่น [sueng pok khlum pai duai fun]

Dutch [dʌtʃ] adj เกี่ยวกับดัช [kiao kap dat] ▷ n ชาวดัช [chao dat]

Dutchman, Dutchmen ['dʌtʃmən, 'dʌtʃmɛn] n ผู้ชายชาวดัช [phu chai chao dat]

Dutchwoman, Dutchwomen [ˌdʌtʃwʊmən, 'dʌtʃwɪmɪn] n ผู้หญิง ชาวดัช [phu ying chao dat]

duty ['djuːtɪ] n หน้าที่ [na thi]; **(customs) duty** n ภาษีนำสินค้าเข้าหรือ ส่งออก [pha si nam sin ka khao rue song ok]

duty-free ['djuːtɪˈfriː] adj ที่ปลอดภาษี [thii plot pha si] ▷ n สินค้าปลอดภาษี [sin kha plot pha si]

duvet ['duːveɪ] n ผ้าห่ม [pha hom]

DVD [diː viː diː] n ดีวีดี [di wi di]; **DVD burner** n ซอฟแวร์ที่ทำให้บันทึกลงในดีวีดี ได้ [sop wae thii tham hai ban thuek long nai di wi di dai]; **DVD player** n เครื่องเล่นดีวีดี [khrueang len di vi di]

dwarf, dwarves [dwɔːf, dwɔːvz] n คน แคระ [khon khrae]

dye [daɪ] n การย้อม [kan yom] ▷ v ย้อม [yom]; **Can you dye my hair, please?** คุณช่วยย้อมผมให้ฉันได้ไหม? [khun chuai yom phom hai chan dai mai]

dynamic [daɪˈnæmɪk] adj เต็มไปด้วย พลังและความคิดสร้างสรรค์ [tem pai duai pha lang lae khwam kit sang san]

dyslexia [dɪsˈlɛksɪə] n ความผิดปกติใน การอ่าน [khwam phid pok kha ti nai kan arn]

dyslexic [dɪsˈlɛksɪk] adj ที่ท่องอ่านเขียน ลำบาก [thii thong arn khian lam bak] ▷ n ผู้ที่ท่องอ่านเขียนลำบาก [phu thii thong arn khian lam bak]

e

each [iːtʃ] *adj* แต่ละ [tae la] ▷ *pron* แต่ละ [tae la]

eagle [ˈiːgᵊl] *n* นกอินทรีย์ [nok in sii]

ear [ɪə] *n* หู [hu]

earache [ˈɪərˌeɪk] *n* หูเจ็บ [hu chep]

eardrum [ˈɪəˌdrʌm] *n* เยื่อแก้วหู [yuea kaew hu]

earlier [ˈɜːlɪə] *adv* ก่อนหน้านั้น [kon na nan]

early [ˈɜːlɪ] *adj* ก่อนเวลาที่กำหนดไว้ [kon we la thii kam not wai] ▷ *adv* แต่แรก [tae raek]

earn [ɜːn] *v* ได้รับรายได้ [dai rap rai dai]

earnings [ˈɜːnɪŋz] *npl* รายได้ [rai dai]

earphones [ˈɪəˌfəʊnz] *npl* หูฟัง [hu fang]

earplugs [ˈɪəˌplʌgz] *npl* ที่ปิดหู [thii pid hu]

earring [ˈɪəˌrɪŋ] *n* ตุ้มหู [tum hu]

earth [ɜːθ] *n* โลก [lok]

earthquake [ˈɜːθˌkweɪk] *n* แผ่นดินไหว [phaen din wai]

easily [ˈiːzɪlɪ] *adv* อย่างสะดวก [yang sa duak]

east [iːst] *adj* เกี่ยวกับทิศตะวันออก [kiao kap thit ta wan ok] ▷ *adv* ที่อยู่ทางทิศตะวันออก [thii yu thang thid ta wan ork] ▷ *n* ทิศตะวันออก [thit ta wan ok]; **Far East** *n* กลุ่มประเทศในเอเชียตะวันออก [klum pra tet nai e chia ta wan ok]; **Middle East** *n* ตะวันออกกลาง [ta wan ok klang]

eastbound [ˈiːstˌbaʊnd] *adj* ซึ่งเดินทางไปทางด้านตะวันออก [sueng doen thang pai thang dan ta wan ok]

Easter [ˈiːstə] *n* วันอีสเตอร์ [wan is toe]; **Easter egg** *n* ไข่อีสเตอร์ [khai is toe]

eastern [ˈiːstən] *adj* เกี่ยวกับทิศตะวันออก [kiao kap thit ta wan ok]

easy [ˈiːzɪ] *adj* ง่าย [ngai]; **easy chair** *n* เก้าอี้ที่มีที่วางแขน [kao ii thii mii thii wang khaen]

easy-going [ˈiːzɪˈgəʊɪŋ] *adj* อย่างง่าย ๆ อย่างสบาย ๆ [yang ngai ngai, yang sa bai sa bai]

eat [iːt] *v* รับประทาน [rap pra than]

e-book [ˈiːˌbʊk] *n* หนังสือที่อ่านได้จากอินเตอร์เนต [nang sue thii an dai chak in toe net]

eccentric [ɪkˈsɛntrɪk] *adj* คนที่แปลกประหลาด [khon thii plaek pra lat]

echo [ˈɛkəʊ] *n* เสียงสะท้อน [siang sa thon]

ecofriendly [ˈiːkəʊˌfrɛndlɪ] *adj* ที่ไม่ทำความเสียหายกับสภาพแวดล้อม [thii mai tham khwam sia hai kap sa phap waet lom]

ecological [ˌiːkəˈlɒdʒɪkᵊl] *adj* เกี่ยวกับนิเวศน์วิทยา [kiao kap ni wet wit tha ya]

ecology [ɪˈkɒlədʒɪ] *n* นิเวศน์วิทยา [ni wet wit tha ya]

e-commerce [ˈiːkɒmɜːs] *n* ธุรกิจการค้าที่ทำบนอินเตอร์เนต [thu ra kit kan kha thii tham bon in toe net]

economic [ˌiːkəˈnɒmɪk; ˌɛkə-] *adj* เกี่ยวกับเศรษฐกิจ [kiao kap set tha kit]

economical [ˌiːkəˈnɒmɪkᵊl; ˌɛkə-] *adj* ประหยัด [pra yat]

economics [ˌiːkəˈnɒmɪks; ˌɛkə-] *npl*

วิชาเศรษฐศาสตร์ [wi cha set tha sat]

economist [ɪ'kɒnəmɪst] n นัก
เศรษฐศาสตร์ [nak set tha sat]

economize [ɪ'kɒnə,maɪz] v ประหยัด
[pra yat]

economy [ɪ'kɒnəmɪ] n เศรษฐกิจ [set
tha kit]; **economy class** n ชั้นประหยัด
[chan pra yat]

ecstasy ['ɛkstəsɪ] n ความปิติยินดีอย่าง
ล้นพ้น [khwam pi thi yin dee yang lon
phon]

Ecuador ['ɛkwə,dɔː] n ประเทศเอกวาดอร์
[pra tet e kwa do]

eczema ['ɛksɪmə; ɪg'ziːmə] n โรคเรื้อน
กวาง [rok ruean kwang]

edge [ɛdʒ] n ขอบ [khop]

edgy ['ɛdʒɪ] adj กระสับกระส่าย [kra sap
kra sai]

edible ['ɛdɪbəl] adj ซึ่งกินได้ [sueng kin
dai]

edition [ɪ'dɪʃən] n จำนวนพิมพ์ทั้งหมดต่อ
ครั้ง [cham nuan phim thang hmod tor
khrang]

editor ['ɛdɪtə] n บรรณาธิการ [ban na thi
kan]

educated ['ɛdjʊ,keɪtɪd] adj ซึ่งได้รับการ
ศึกษา [sueng dai rab kan suek sa]

education [,ɛdjʊ'keɪʃən] n การศึกษา
[kan suek sa]; **adult education** n การ
ศึกษาผู้ใหญ่ [kan suek sa phu yai];
higher education n การศึกษาระดับสูง
[kan suek sa ra dap sung]

educational [,ɛdjʊ'keɪʃənəl] adj ที่เกี่ยว
กับการเรียนการสอน [thii kiao kap kan
rian kan son]

eel [iːl] n ปลาไหล [pla lai]

effect [ɪ'fɛkt] n ผลกระทบ [phon kra
thop]; **side effect** n ผลข้างเคียง [phon
khang khiang]

effective [ɪ'fɛktɪv] adj ได้ผลดี [dai phon
di]

effectively [ɪ'fɛktɪvlɪ] adv อย่างได้ผล
[yang dai phon]

efficient [ɪ'fɪʃənt] adj ซึ่งมีประสิทธิภาพ

[sueng mii pra sit thi phap]

efficiently [ɪ'fɪʃəntlɪ] adv อย่างมี
ประสิทธิภาพ [yang mii pra sit thi phap]

effort ['ɛfət] n ความพยายาม [khwam
pha ya yam]

e.g. [iː dʒiː] abbr ตัวย่อของตัวอย่างเช่น
[tua yo khong tua yang chen]

egg [ɛg] n ไข่ [khai]; **boiled egg** n ไข่ต้ม
[khai tom]; **egg white** n ไข่ขาว [khai
khao]; **egg yolk** n ไข่แดง [khai daeng];
**Could you prepare a meal without
eggs?** คุณทำอาหารที่ไม่มีไข่ได้ไหม?
[khun tham a han thii mai mii khai
dai mai]

eggcup ['ɛg,kʌp] n ถ้วยใส่ไข่ [thuai sai
khai]

Egypt ['iːdʒɪpt] n ประเทศอียิปต์ [pra tet i
yip]

Egyptian [ɪ'dʒɪpʃən] adj เกี่ยวกับประเทศ
อียิปต์ [kiao kap pra thet i yip] ▷ n ชาว
อียิปต์ [chao i yip]

eight [eɪt] number แปด [plaet]; **two for
the eight o'clock showing** สองที่
สำหรับการแสดงรอบ แปดโมง [song thii
sam hrab kan sa daeng rob paed mong]

eighteen ['eɪ'tiːn] number สิบแปด [sip
paet]

eighteenth ['eɪ'tiːnθ] adj ที่สิบแปด [thii
sip paet]

eighth [eɪtθ] adj ที่แปด [thii paet] ▷ n ที่
แปด [thii paet]

eighty ['eɪtɪ] number แปดสิบ [paet sip]

Eire ['ɛərə] n ประเทศไอร์แลนด์ [pra tet ai
laen]

either ['aɪðə; 'iːðə] adv (with negative)
ไม่เช่นกัน [mai chen kan] ▷ conj (... or)
ถ้าไม่...ก็... [tha mai...ko...] ▷ pron อย่าง
ใดอย่างหนึ่งในจำนวนสอง [yang dai yang
nueng nai cham nuan song]; **either...
or** conj อย่างนี้หรืออย่างนั้น [yang nii rue
yang nan]

elastic [ɪ'læstɪk] n ความยืดหยุ่น [khwam
yuet yun]; **elastic band** n ยางยืด [yang
yuet]

Elastoplast® [ɪ'læstəˌplɑːst] *n* พลาส
เตอร์ [plas toe]

elbow ['ɛlbəʊ] *n* ข้อศอก [kho sok]

elder ['ɛldə] *adj* แก่กว่า [kae kwa]

elderly ['ɛldəlɪ] *adj* สูงวัย [sung wai]

eldest ['ɛldɪst] *adj* แก่ที่สุด [kae thii sut]

elect [ɪ'lɛkt] *v* คัดเลือก [khat lueak]

election [ɪ'lɛkʃən] *n* การเลือกตั้ง [kan
lueak tang]; **general election** *n* การ
เลือกตั้งทั่วไป [kan lueak tang thua pai]

electorate [ɪ'lɛktərɪt] *n* ประชาชนผู้เลือก
ตั้ง [pra cha chon phu lueak tang]

electric [ɪ'lɛktrɪk] *adj* เกี่ยวกับไฟฟ้า
[kiao kap fai fa]; **electric blanket** *n*
ผ้าห่มไฟฟ้า [pha hom fai fa]; **electric
shock** *n* กระแสไฟดูด [kra sae fai dut];
**There is something wrong with the
electrics** มีอะไรผิดปรกติเกี่ยวกับไฟฟ้า
[mii a rai phit prok ka ti kiao kap fai
fa]

electrical [ɪ'lɛktrɪkᵊl] *adj* เกี่ยวกับไฟฟ้า
[kiao kap fai fa]

electrician [ɪlɛk'trɪʃən; ˌiːlɛk-] *n*
ช่างไฟ [chang fai]

electricity [ɪlɛk'trɪsɪtɪ; ˌiːlɛk-] *n* ไฟฟ้า
[fai fa]; **There is no electricity** ไม่มี
ไฟฟ้า [mai mii fai fa]

electronic [ɪlɛk'trɒnɪk; ˌiːlɛk-] *adj*
เกี่ยวกับระบบอิเล็กทรอนิกส์ [kiao kap ra
bop i lek tro nik]

electronics [ɪlɛk'trɒnɪks; ˌiːlɛk-] *npl*
วิชาอิเล็กทรอนิกส์ [wi cha i lek tro nik]

elegant ['ɛlɪgənt] *adj* สวยงาม [suai
ngam]

element ['ɛlɪmənt] *n* องค์ประกอบ [ong
pra kop]

elephant ['ɛlɪfənt] *n* ช้าง [chang]

eleven [ɪ'lɛvᵊn] *number* สิบเอ็ด [sip et]

eleventh [ɪ'lɛvᵊnθ] *adj* ที่สิบเอ็ด [thii sip
et]

eliminate [ɪ'lɪmɪˌneɪt] *v* ขจัด [kha chat]

elm [ɛlm] *n* ต้นไม้ในตระกูลอัลมอนด์ [ton
mai nai tra kun an mon]

else [ɛls] *adj* อื่น ๆ [uen uen]

elsewhere [ˌɛls'wɛə] *adv* ที่อื่น [thii uen]

email ['iːmeɪl] *n* อีเมลล์ [i mel] ▷ *vt (a
person)* ส่งอีเมลล์ [song e mail]; **email
address** *n* ที่อยู่อีเมลล์ [thii yu e mail];
Can I have your email? ฉันขออีเมลล์
ของคุณได้ไหม? [chan kho ii mail
khong khun dai mai]; **Can I send an
email?** ฉันส่งอีเมลล์ได้ไหม? [chan song
e mail dai mai]; **Did you get my
email?** คุณได้รับอีเมลลฉันไหม? [khun
dai rap e mail chan mai]; **My email
address is...** อีเมลล์เอดเดรสของฉันคือ...
[e mail ad dres khong chan khue...];
What is your email address? อีเมลล์
เอดเดรสของคุณคืออะไร? [e mail ad dres
khong khun khue a rai]

embankment [ɪm'bæŋkmənt] *n* เขื่อน
[khuean]

embarrassed [ˌɪm'bærəst] *adj* ซึ่ง
อับอาย [sueng ap ai]

embarrassing [ɪm'bærəsɪŋ] *adj* น่า
อับอาย [na ap ai]

embassy ['ɛmbəsɪ] *n* สถานทูต [sa than
thut]

embroider [ɪm'brɔɪdə] *v* เย็บปักถักร้อย
[yep pak thak roi]

embroidery [ɪm'brɔɪdərɪ] *n* การเย็บปัก
ถักร้อย [kan yep pak thak roi]

emergency [ɪ'mɜːdʒənsɪ] *n* ภาวะฉุกเฉิน
[pha wa chuk choen]; **accident &
emergency department** *n* อุบัติเหตุ
และหน่วยฉุกเฉิน [u bat ti het lae nuai
chuk choen]; **emergency exit** *n*
ทางออกฉุกเฉิน [thang ok chuk choen];
emergency landing *n* การจอดลงอย่าง
ฉุกเฉินของเครื่องบิน [kan jod long yang
chuk choen khong khrueang bin]; **It's
an emergency!** เป็นสภาวะฉุกเฉิน [pen
sa pha wa chuk choen]

emigrate ['ɛmɪˌgreɪt] *v* อพยพย้ายถิ่นฐาน
[op pa yop yai thin tan]

emotion [ɪ'məʊʃən] *n* ความรู้สึก
[khwam ru suek]

emotional [ɪ'məʊʃənᵊl] *adj* เกี่ยวกับ

อารมณ์ [kiao kap a rom]

emperor, empress [ˈɛmpərə, ˈɛmprɪs] *n* จักรพรรดิ [chak kra phat]

emphasize [ˈɛmfəˌsaɪz] *v* เน้น [nen]

empire [ˈɛmpaɪə] *n* อาณาจักร [a na chak]

employ [ɪmˈplɔɪ] *v* ว่าจ้าง [wa chang]

employee [ɛmˈplɔɪiː; ˌɛmplɔɪˈiː] *n* ลูกจ้าง [luk chang]

employer [ɪmˈplɔɪə] *n* นายจ้าง [nai chang]

employment [ɪmˈplɔɪmənt] *n* การว่าจ้าง [kan wa chang]

empty [ˈɛmptɪ] *adj* ว่างเปล่า [wang plao] ▷ *v* ทำให้ว่างเปล่า [tham hai wang plao]

enamel [ɪˈnæməl] *n* สิ่งเคลือบ [sing khlueap]

encourage [ɪnˈkʌrɪdʒ] *v* ให้กำลังใจ [hai kam lang jai]

encouragement [ɪnˈkʌrɪdʒmənt] *n* การให้กำลังใจ [kan hai kam lang jai]

encouraging [ɪnˈkʌrɪdʒɪŋ] *adj* ที่ให้กำลังใจ [thii hai kam lang jai]

encyclopaedia [ɛnˌsaɪkləʊˈpiːdɪə] *n* สารานุกรม [sa ra nu krom]

end [ɛnd] *n* ตอนจบ [ton job] ▷ *v* ทำให้สิ้นสุด [tham hai sin sut]; **dead end** *n* ทางตัน [thang ton]

endanger [ɪnˈdeɪndʒə] *v* ทำให้อยู่ในอันตราย [tham hai yu nai an tra lai]

ending [ˈɛndɪŋ] *n* ตอนจบ [ton job]

endless [ˈɛndlɪs] *adj* ซึ่งไม่สิ้นสุด [sueng mai sin sut]

enemy [ˈɛnəmɪ] *n* ศัตรู [sat tru]

energetic [ˌɛnəˈdʒɛtɪk] *adj* กระตือรือร้น [kra tue rue ron]

energy [ˈɛnədʒɪ] *n* พลังงาน [pha lang ngan]

engaged [ɪnˈgeɪdʒd] *adj* ที่หมั้นหมาย [thii man mai]; **engaged tone** *n* เสียงสายไม่ว่างของโทรศัพท์ [siang sai mai wang khong tho ra sap]

engagement [ɪnˈgeɪdʒmənt] *n* การหมั้น [kan man]; **engagement ring** *n*

แหวนหมั้น [waen man]

engine [ˈɛndʒɪn] *n* เครื่องยนต์ [khruang yon]; **search engine** *n* กลไกการหาข้อมูลบนอินเตอร์เน็ต [kon kai kan ha kho mun bon in toe net]; **The engine is overheating** เครื่องยนต์ร้อนเกินไป [khruang yon ron koen pai]

engineer [ˌɛndʒɪˈnɪə] *n* วิศวกร [wit sa wa kon]

engineering [ˌɛndʒɪˈnɪərɪŋ] *n* วิศวกรรมศาสตร์ [wit sa wa kam ma sat]

England [ˈɪŋglənd] *n* ประเทศอังกฤษ [pra ted ang krid]

English [ˈɪŋglɪʃ] *adj* เกี่ยวกับชาวอังกฤษ [kiao kap chao ang krit] ▷ *n* ชาวอังกฤษ [chao ang krid]

Englishman, Englishmen [ˈɪŋglɪʃmən, ˈɪŋglɪʃmɛn] *n* ชายชาวอังกฤษ [chai chao ang krid]

Englishwoman, Englishwomen [ˈɪŋglɪʃwʊmən, ˈɪŋglɪʃwɪmɪn] *n* หญิงชาวอังกฤษ [hying chao ang krid]

engrave [ɪnˈgreɪv] *v* สลัก [sa lak]

enjoy [ɪnˈdʒɔɪ] *v* สนุกสนาน [sa nuk sa nan]

enjoyable [ɪnˈdʒɔɪəbᵊl] *adj* ที่สนุกสนาน [thii sa nuk sa nan]

enlargement [ɪnˈlɑːdʒmənt] *n* การขยาย [kan kha yai]

enormous [ɪˈnɔːməs] *adj* ที่ใหญ่มหึมา [thii yai ma hu ma]

enough [ɪˈnʌf] *adj* พอเพียง [pho phiang] ▷ *pron* จำนวนที่พอเพียง [cham nuan thii pho phiang]

enquire [ɪnˈkwaɪə] *v* ถามคำถาม [tham kham tham]

enquiry [ɪnˈkwaɪərɪ] *n* การไต่สวน [kan tai suan]; **enquiry desk** *n* โต๊ะสอบถาม [to sop tham]

ensure [ɛnˈʃʊə; -ˈʃɔː] *v* ทำให้แน่ใจว่า [tham hai nae jai wa]

enter [ˈɛntə] *v* เข้า [khao]

entertain [ˌɛntəˈteɪn] *v* ทำให้เพลิดเพลิน [tham hai phoet phloen]

entertainer [ˌɛntəˈteɪnə] n ผู้ให้ความ
บันเทิง [phu hai khwam ban thoeng]

entertaining [ˌɛntəˈteɪnɪŋ] adj ซึ่ง
สนุกสนานเพลิดเพลิน [sueng sa nuk sa
nan phloet ploen]

entertainment [ˌɛntəˈteɪnmənt] n
What entertainment is there? มี
ความบันเทิงอะไรบ้างที่นั่น? [mii khwam
ban thoeng a rai bang thii nan]

enthusiasm [ɪnˈθjuːzɪˌæzəm] n ความ
กระตือรือร้น [khwam kra tue rue ron]

enthusiastic [ɪnˌθjuːzɪˈæstɪk] adj
กระตือรือร้น [kra tue rue ron]

entire [ɪnˈtaɪə] adj ทั้งหมด [thang mot]

entirely [ɪnˈtaɪəlɪ] adv โดยทั้งหมด [doi
thang mot]

entrance [ˈɛntrəns] n ทางเข้า [thang
khao]; **entrance fee** n ค่าเข้า [kha
khao]

entry [ˈɛntrɪ] n การเข้า [kan khao];
entry phone n รายการเบอร์โทรศัพท์ [rai
kan boe tho ra sap]

envelope [ˈɛnvəˌləʊp; ˈɒn-] n ซอง
จดหมาย [song chot mai]

envious [ˈɛnvɪəs] adj อิจฉา [it cha]

environment [ɪnˈvaɪrənmənt] n สภาพ
แวดล้อม [sa phap waet lom]

environmental [ɪnˌvaɪrənˈmɛntəl]
adj สภาวะแวดล้อม [sa pha wa waet
lom]; **environmentally friendly** adj ที่
เป็นมิตรกับสภาพแวดล้อม [thii pen mit
kap sa phap waet lom]

envy [ˈɛnvɪ] n ความอิจฉา [khwam it cha]
▷ v ริษยา [rit sa ya]

epidemic [ˌɛpɪˈdɛmɪk] n การแพร่ระบาด
อย่างรวดเร็ว [kan prae ra bat yang ruat
reo]

epileptic [ˌɛpɪˈlɛptɪk] n โรคลมบ้าหมู [rok
lom ba mu]; **epileptic fit** n อาการชัก
ของลมบ้าหมู [a kan chak khong lom ba
mu]

episode [ˈɛpɪˌsəʊd] n ตอน [ton]

equal [ˈiːkwəl] adj ซึ่งเท่ากัน [sueng thao
kan] ▷ v ทำให้เท่าเทียมกัน [tham hai

thao thiam kan]

equality [ɪˈkwɒlɪtɪ] n ความเสมอภาค
[khwam sa moe phak]

equalize [ˈiːkwəˌlaɪz] v ทำคะแนนเท่ากัน
[tham kha naen thao kan]

equation [ɪˈkweɪʒən; -ʃən] n ความเท่า
เทียม [khwam thao thiam]

equator [ɪˈkweɪtə] n เส้นศูนย์สูตร [sen
sun sut]

Equatorial Guinea [ˌɛkwəˈtɔːrɪəl
ˈɡɪnɪ] n ประเทศเอควาทอเรียลกินี [pra thet
a khwa to rial ki ni]

equipment [ɪˈkwɪpmənt] n เครื่องมือ
[khrueang mue]

equipped [ɪˈkwɪpt] adj ครบครัน [khrop
khran]

equivalent [ɪˈkwɪvələnt] n เท่ากับ
[thao kap]

erase [ɪˈreɪz] v ลบออก [lop ok]

Eritrea [ˌɛrɪˈtreɪə] n ประเทศเอริเทรีย [pra
tet e ri tria]

erotic [ɪˈrɒtɪk] adj ซึ่งกระตุ้นความรู้สึกทาง
เพศ [sueng kra tun khwam ru suk
thang phed]

error [ˈɛrə] n ข้อผิดพลาด [kho phit phlat]

escalator [ˈɛskəˌleɪtə] n บันไดเลื่อน [ban
dai luean]

escape [ɪˈskeɪp] n การหลบหนี [kan lop
nii] ▷ v หลบหนี [lop ni]; **fire escape** n
ทางหนีไฟ [thang nii fai]

escort [ɪsˈkɔːt] v การคุ้มครอง [kan khum
khrong]

especially [ɪˈspɛʃəlɪ] adv โดยเฉพาะอย่าง
ยิ่ง [doi cha pho yang ying]

espionage [ˈɛspɪəˌnɑːʒ] n จารกรรม
[cha ra kam]

essay [ˈɛseɪ] n เรียงความ [riang khwam]

essential [ɪˈsɛnʃəl] adj ซึ่งสำคัญ [sueng
sam khan]

estate [ɪˈsteɪt] n ทรัพย์สินที่ดิน [sap sin
thii din]; **estate agent** n คนที่ทำงาน
เกี่ยวกับขายบ้านและที่ดิน [khon thii
tham ngan kiao kap khai baan lae thii
din]; **estate car** n รถเก๋งที่บรรทุกทั้งคน

และสินค้า [rot keng thii ban thuk thang khon lae sin kha]

estimate n ['ɛstɪmɪt] การตีราคา [kan ti ra kha] ▷ v ['ɛstɪˌmeɪt] ประมาณ [pra man]

Estonia [ɛ'stəʊnɪə] n ประเทศเอสโตเนีย [pra tet es to nia]

Estonian [ɛ'stəʊnɪən] adj เกี่ยวกับเอสโตเนีย [kiao kap es to nia] ▷ n (language) ภาษาเอสโตเนียน [pha sa es to nian], (person) ชาวเอสโตเนียน [chao es to nian]

etc [ɪt 'sɛtrə] abbr ตัวย่อของ และอื่น ๆ [tua yo khong lae uen uen]

eternal [ɪ'tɜːnªl] adj ที่อยู่ชั่วนิรันดร์ [thii yu chua ni ran]

eternity [ɪ'tɜːnɪtɪ] n นิรันดร [ni ran don]

ethical ['ɛθɪkªl] adj ตามหลักจริยธรรม [tam lak cha ri ya tham]

Ethiopia [ˌiːθɪ'əʊpɪə] n ประเทศเอธิโอเปีย [pra tet e thi o pia]

Ethiopian [ˌiːθɪ'əʊpɪən] adj เกี่ยวกับเอธิโอเปียน [kiao kap e thi o pia] ▷ n ชาวเอธิโอเปียน [chao e thi o pian]

ethnic ['ɛθnɪk] adj เกี่ยวกับเชื้อชาติ [kiao kap chuea chat]

e-ticket ['iː'tɪkɪt] n ตั๋วที่ซื้อจากเครื่องคอมพิวเตอร์ [tua thii sue chak khueang khom pio ter]

EU [iː juː] abbr ประเทศในกลุ่มสหภาพยุโรป [pra tet nai klum sa ha phap yu rop]

euro ['jʊərəʊ] n เงินยูโร [ngoen u ro]

Europe ['jʊərəp] n ทวีปยุโรป [tha wip yu rop]

European [ˌjʊərə'pɪən] adj เกี่ยวกับยุโรป [kiao kap yu rop] ▷ n ชาวยุโรป [chao yu rop]; **European Union** n สหภาพยุโรป [sa ha phap yu rop]

evacuate [ɪ'vækjʊˌeɪt] v อพยพ [op pha yop]

eve [iːv] n คืนวันก่อนวันเทศกาล [khuen wan kon wan tet sa kan]

even ['iːvªn] adj ราบเรียบ [rap riap] ▷ adv ยิ่งไปกว่านั้น [ying pai kwa nan]

evening ['iːvnɪŋ] n เวลาเย็น [we la yen]; **evening class** n ชั้นเรียนในเวลาเย็น [chan rian nai we la yen]; **evening dress** n ชุดกลางคืน [chut klang khuen]

event [ɪ'vɛnt] n เหตุการณ์สำคัญ [het kan sam khan]

eventful [ɪ'vɛntfʊl] adj เต็มไปด้วยเหตุการณ์ที่สำคัญ [tem pai duai hed kan thii sam khan]

eventually [ɪ'vɛntʃʊəlɪ] adv ในที่สุด [nai thi sut]

ever ['ɛvə] adv ตลอด [ta lot]

every ['ɛvrɪ] adj ทุก [thuk]; **The bus runs every twenty minutes** รถโดยสารวิ่งทุกยี่สิบนาที [rot doi san wing thuk yi sip na thi]

everybody ['ɛvrɪˌbɒdɪ] pron ทุกคน [thuk khon]

everyone ['ɛvrɪˌwʌn; -wən] pron ทุกคน [thuk khon]

everything ['ɛvrɪθɪŋ] pron ทุกสิ่งทุกอย่าง [thuk sing thuk yang]

everywhere ['ɛvrɪˌwɛə] adv ทุกที่ [thuk thi]

evidence ['ɛvɪdəns] n หลักฐาน [lak than]

evil ['iːvªl] adj ชั่วร้าย [chua rai]

evolution [ˌiːvə'luːʃən] n วิวัฒนาการ [wi wat tha na kan]

ewe [juː] n แกะตัวเมียที่โตเต็มที่ [kae tua mia thii to tem thii]

exact [ɪg'zækt] adj ถูกต้องแม่นยำ [thuk tong maen yam]

exactly [ɪg'zæktlɪ] adv อย่างถูกต้อง [yang thuk tong]

exaggerate [ɪg'zædʒəˌreɪt] v พูดเกินความจริง [phud koen khwam chring]

exaggeration [ɪg'zædʒəˌreɪʃən] n การพูดเกินความจริง [kan phut koen khwam ching]

exam [ɪg'zæm] n ข้อสอบ [kho sop]

examination [ɪgˌzæmɪ'neɪʃən] n (medical) การสอบ [kan sop], (school) การสอบ [kan sop]

examine [ɪgˈzæmɪn] v ตรวจสอบ [truat sop]

examiner [ɪgˈzæmɪnə] n ผู้ตรวจสอบ [phu truat sorb]

example [ɪgˈzɑːmpᵊl] n ตัวอย่าง [tua yang]

excellent [ˈɛksələnt] adj ดีเยี่ยม [di yiam]

except [ɪkˈsɛpt] prep นอกจาก [nok chak]

exception [ɪkˈsɛpʃən] n ข้อยกเว้น [kho yok wen]

exceptional [ɪkˈsɛpʃᵊnᵊl] adj ดีเป็นพิเศษ [di pen phi set]

excessive [ɪkˈsɛsɪv] adj ซึ่งมากเกินความจำเป็น [sueng mak koen khwam cham pen]

exchange [ɪksˈtʃeɪndʒ] v การแลกเปลี่ยน [kan laek plian]; **exchange rate** n อัตราแลกเปลี่ยน [at tra laek plian]; **rate of exchange** n อัตราแลกเปลี่ยนเงิน [at tra laek plian ngoen]; **stock exchange** n ตลาดหลักทรัพย์ [ta lad hlak sap]

excited [ɪkˈsaɪtɪd] adj ตื่นเต้นดีใจ [tuen ten di jai]

exciting [ɪkˈsaɪtɪŋ] adj ที่น่าตื่นเต้น [thii na tuen ten]

exclude [ɪkˈskluːd] v แยกออกไป [yaek ok pai]

excluding [ɪkˈskluːdɪŋ] prep ที่แยกออกไป [thii yaek ork pai]

exclusively [ɪkˈskluːsɪvlɪ] adv โดยเฉพาะ [doi cha pho]

excuse n [ɪkˈskjuːs] ข้อแก้ตัว [kho kae tua] ▷ v [ɪkˈskjuːz] แก้ตัว [kae tua]

execute [ˈɛksɪˌkjuːt] v ดำเนินการ [dam noen kan]

execution [ˌɛksɪˈkjuːʃən] n การประหารชีวิต [kan pra han chi wit]

executive [ɪgˈzɛkjʊtɪv] n ผู้บริหาร [phu bo ri han]

exercise [ˈɛksəˌsaɪz] n การออกกำลังกาย [kan ok kam lang kai]

exhaust [ɪgˈzɔːst] n The exhaust is broken ท่อไอเสียแตก [tho ai sia taek]

exhausted [ɪgˈzɔːstɪd] adj เหน็ดเหนื่อย [net nueai]

exhibition [ˌɛksɪˈbɪʃən] n งานแสดง [ngan sa daeng]

ex-husband [ɛksˈhʌzbənd] n อดีตสามี [a dit sa mii]

exile [ˈɛgzaɪl; ˈɛksaɪl] n การลี้ภัย [kan lii phai]

exist [ɪgˈzɪst] v มีชีวิต [mii chi wit]

exit [ˈɛgzɪt; ˈɛksɪt] n ทางออก [thang ok]; **emergency exit** n ทางออกฉุกเฉิน [thang ok chuk choen]; **Where is the exit?** ทางออกอยู่ที่ไหน? [thang ok yu thii nai]; **Which exit for...?** ทางออกทางไหนสำหรับ...? [thang ok thang nai sam rap...]

exotic [ɪgˈzɒtɪk] adj มาจากประเทศอื่น [ma chak pra tet uen]

expect [ɪkˈspɛkt] v คาดว่า [khat wa]

expedition [ˌɛkspɪˈdɪʃən] n คณะเดินทาง [kha na doen thang]

expel [ɪkˈspɛl] v ไล่ออก [lai ok]

expenditure [ɪkˈspɛndɪtʃə] n การใช้จ่ายเงิน [kan chai chai ngen]

expenses [ɪkˈspɛnsɪz] npl ค่าใช้จ่าย [kha chai chai]

expensive [ɪkˈspɛnsɪv] adj แพง [phaeng]; **It's quite expensive** ราคาค่อนข้างแพง [ra kha khon khang phaeng]; **It's too expensive for me** ราคาแพงเกินไปสำหรับฉัน [ra kha phaeng koen pai sam rap chan]

experience [ɪkˈspɪərɪəns] n ประสบการณ์ [phra sop kan]; **work experience** n ประสบการณ์การทำงาน [pra sop kan kan tham ngan]

experienced [ɪkˈspɪərɪənst] adj ที่มีประสบการณ์ [thii mii pra sop kan]

experiment [ɪkˈspɛrɪmənt] n การทดลอง [kan thod long]

expert [ˈɛkspɜːt] n ผู้เชี่ยวชาญ [phu chiao chan]

expire [ɪkˈspaɪə] v หมดอายุ [mot a yu]

explain [ɪk'spleɪn] v อธิบาย [a thi bai]; **Can you explain what the matter is?** คุณอธิบายได้ไหมว่าเกิดอะไรขึ้น? [khun a thi bai dai mai wa koet a rai khuen]

explanation [ˌɛkspləˈneɪʃən] n คำอธิบาย [kham a thi bai]

explode [ɪk'spləʊd] v ระเบิด [ra boet]

exploit [ɪk'splɔɪt] v เอาเปรียบ [ao priap]

exploitation [ˌɛksplɔɪˈteɪʃən] n การเอาเปรียบ [kan ao priap]

explore [ɪk'splɔː] v สำรวจ [sam ruat]

explorer [ɪk'splɔːrə] n นักสำรวจ [nak sam ruat]

explosion [ɪk'spləʊʒən] n การระเบิด [kan ra boed]

explosive [ɪk'spləʊsɪv] n ระเบิด [ra boet]

export n ['ɛkspɔːt] การส่งออก [kan song ok] ▷ v [ɪk'spɔːt] ส่งออก [song ok]

express [ɪk'sprɛs] v แสดงออก [sa daeng ok]

expression [ɪk'sprɛʃən] n การแสดงออก [kan sa daeng ok]

extension [ɪk'stɛnʃən] n การขยายออก [kan kha yai ok]; **extension cable** n ที่ต่อสายไฟ [thii to sai fai]

extensive [ɪk'stɛnsɪv] adj กว้างขวาง [kwang khwang]

extensively [ɪk'stɛnsɪvlɪ] adv อย่างกว้างขวาง [yang kwang khwang]

extent [ɪk'stɛnt] n ขอบเขต [khop khet]

exterior [ɪk'stɪərɪə] adj ภายนอก [phai nok]

external [ɪk'stɜːnºl] adj ที่ใช้ภายนอก [thii chai phai nok]

extinct [ɪk'stɪŋkt] adj สูญพันธุ์ [sun phan]

extinguisher [ɪk'stɪŋgwɪʃə] n เครื่องดับเพลิง [khrueang dap phloeng]

extortionate [ɪk'stɔːʃənɪt] adj หักหลังขูดเลือด [hak lang, khut lueat]

extra ['ɛkstrə] adj เป็นพิเศษ [pen phi set] ▷ adv อย่างพิเศษ [yang phi sed]

extraordinary [ɪk'strɔːd^ənrɪ; -d^ənərɪ] adj ผิดธรรมดา [phit tham ma da]

extravagant [ɪk'strævɪgənt] adj ฟุ่มเฟือย [fum fueai]

extreme [ɪk'striːm] adj ที่สุด [thi sut]

extremely [ɪk'striːmlɪ] adv อย่างที่สุด [yang thii sut]

extremism [ɪk'striːmɪzəm] n พวกหัวรุนแรง [phuak hua run raeng]

extremist [ɪk'striːmɪst] n คนที่มีหัวรุนแรง [khon thii mii hua run raeng]

ex-wife [ɛks'waɪf] n อดีตภรรยา [a dit phan ra ya]

eye [aɪ] n ตา [ta]; **eye drops** npl น้ำยาหยอดตา [nam ya yot ta]; **eye shadow** n อายแชโดว์ [ai chae do]; **I have something in my eye** มีบางอย่างอยู่ในลูกตาฉัน [mii bang yang yu nai luk ta chan]

eyebrow ['aɪˌbraʊ] n คิ้ว [khwio]

eyelash ['aɪˌlæʃ] n ขนตา [khon ta]

eyelid ['aɪˌlɪd] n เปลือกตา [plueak ta]

eyeliner ['aɪˌlaɪnə] n ที่วาดขอบตา [thii wat kop ta]

eyesight ['aɪˌsaɪt] n สายตา [sai ta]

f

fabric ['fæbrɪk] *n* ผ้าหรือสิ่งทอ [pha rue sing tho]

fabulous ['fæbjʊləs] *adj* เยี่ยม [yiam]

face [feɪs] *n* ใบหน้า [bai na] ▷ *v* เผชิญหน้า [pha choen na]; **face cloth** *n* ผ้าขนหนูผืนเล็กใช้เช็ดหน้า [pha khon nu phuen lek chai chet na]

facial ['feɪʃəl] *adj* เกี่ยวกับใบหน้า [kiao kap bai na] ▷ *n* การบำรุงผิวหน้า [kan bam rung phio na]

facilities [fə'sɪlɪtɪz] *npl* สิ่งอำนวยความสะดวกต่าง ๆ [sing am nuai khwam sa duak tang tang]

fact [fækt] *n* ความจริง [khwam ching]

factory ['fæktərɪ] *n* โรงงาน [rong ngan]; **I work in a factory** ฉันทำงานในโรงงาน [chan tham ngan nai rong ngan]

fade [feɪd] *v* เลือน [luean]

fag [fæg] *n* งานหนักและน่าเบื่อ [ngan nak lae na buea]

fail [feɪl] *v* ล้มเหลว [lom leo]

failure ['feɪljə] *n* ความล้มเหลว [khwam lom leo]

faint [feɪnt] *adj* เจือจาง อ่อนแอ [chuea chang, on ae] ▷ *v* เป็นลม [pen lom]; **She has fainted** เธอเป็นลม [thoe pen lom]

fair [fɛə] *adj (light colour)* สีอ่อน [sii on], *(reasonable)* สมเหตุสมผล [som het som phon] ▷ *n* งานแสดงสินค้า [ngan sa daeng sin ka]

fairground ['fɛə,graʊnd] *n* สวนสนุก [suan sa nuk]

fairly ['fɛəlɪ] *adv* อย่างยุติธรรม [yang yu ti tham]

fairness ['fɛənɪs] *n* ความยุติธรรม [khwam yut ti tham]

fairy ['fɛərɪ] *n* นางฟ้า [nang fa]

fairytale ['fɛərɪ,teɪl] *n* นิทานเทพนิยาย [ni than thep ni yai]

faith [feɪθ] *n* ความศรัทธา [khwam sat tha]

faithful ['feɪθfʊl] *adj* เชื่อถือได้ [chuea thue dai]

faithfully ['feɪθfʊlɪ] *adv* อย่างเชื่อถือได้ [yang chuea thue dai]

fake [feɪk] *adj* ปลอม [plom] ▷ *n* ของปลอม [khong plom]

fall [fɔːl] *n* การหล่นลงมา [kan lon long ma] ▷ *v* หล่น [lon]

fall down [fɔːl daʊn] *v* หกล้ม [hok lom]

fall for [fɔːl fɔː] *v* ตกหลุมรัก [tok lum rak]

fall out [fɔːl aʊt] *v* ทะเลาะกัน [tha lao kan]

false [fɔːls] *adj* ปลอม [plom]; **false alarm** *n* สัญญาณเตือนภัยปลอม [san yan tuean phai plom]

fame [feɪm] *n* ชื่อเสียง [chue siang]

familiar [fə'mɪlɪə] *adj* คุ้นเคย [khun khoei]

family ['fæmɪlɪ; 'fæmlɪ] *n* ครอบครัว [khrop khrua]; **I want to reserve a family room** ฉันอยากจองห้องสำหรับครอบครัวหนึ่งห้อง [chan yak chong hong sam rap khrob khrua nueng hong]; **I'd like to book a family room** ฉันอยากจองห้องสำหรับครอบครัวหนึ่งห้อง [chan yak chong hong sam rap khrob khrua nueng hong]; **I'm here with my family** ฉันมาที่นี่กับครอบครัว [chan ma thii ni kap khrob khrua]

famine ['fæmɪn] n ความขาดแคลนอาหาร [khwam khaat khlaen a han]

famous ['feɪməs] adj มีชื่อเสียง [mii chue siang]

fan [fæn] n พัดลม [phat lom]; **fan belt** n สายพานในเครื่องยนต์ [sai phan nai khrueang yon]; **Does the room have a fan?** มีพัดลมในห้องไหม? [mii phat lom nai hong mai]

fanatic [fə'nætɪk] n ผู้คลั่งไคล้ [phu khlang khlai]

fancy ['fænsɪ] v ปรารถนา [prat tha na]; **fancy dress** n ชุดแฟนซี [chut faen si]

fantastic [fæn'tæstɪk] adj วิเศษ [wi set]

FAQ [ɛf ɛɪ kjuː] abbr ตัวย่อของคำถามที่ถามบ่อย ๆ [tua yo khong kham tham thii tham boi boi]

far [fɑː] adj ห่างไกล [hang klai] ▷ adv ไกล [klai]; **How far is it?** อยู่ไกลแค่ไหน? [yu klai khae nai]; **How far is the bank?** ธนาคารอยู่ไกลแค่ไหน? [tha na khan yu klai khae nai]; **Is it far?** อยู่ไกลไหม? [yu klai mai]

fare [fɛə] n ค่าโดยสาร [kha doi san]

farewell [ˌfɛə'wɛl] excl ลาก่อน [la kon]

farm [fɑːm] n ที่เพาะปลูกและเลี้ยงสัตว์ [thii pho pluk lae liang sat]

farmer ['fɑːmə] n ชาวนา [chao na]

farmhouse ['fɑːmˌhaʊs] n บ้านไร่ [baan rai]

farming ['fɑːmɪŋ] n การเกษตรกรรม [kan ka set tra kam]

Faroe Islands ['fɛərəʊ 'aɪləndz] npl หมู่เกาะฟาโรห์ [mu kao fa ro]

fascinating ['fæsɪˌneɪtɪŋ] adj ซึ่งทำให้หลงเสน่ห์ [sueng tham hai long sa ne]

fashion ['fæʃən] n แฟชั่น [fae chan]

fashionable ['fæʃənəbəl] adj ทันสมัย [than sa mai]

fast [fɑːst] adj เร็ว [reo] ▷ adv อย่างรวดเร็ว [yang ruat reo]; **He was driving too fast** เขาขับรถเร็วเกินไป [khao khap rot reo koen pai]; **I think my watch is fast** ฉันคิดว่านาฬิกาฉันเดินเร็ว [chan kit wa na li ka chan doen reo]

fat [fæt] adj อ้วน [uan] ▷ n ไขมัน [khai man]

fatal ['feɪtəl] adj ซึ่งทำให้ถึงตาย [sueng tham hai thueng tai]

fate [feɪt] n โชคชะตา [chok cha ta]

father ['fɑːðə] n พ่อ [pho]

father-in-law ['fɑːðə ɪn lɔː] (pl **fathers-in-law**) n พ่อของสามีหรือภรรยา [phor khong sa mee hue phan ra ya]

fault [fɔːlt] n (defect) ตำหนิ [tam ni], (mistake) ข้อผิดพลาด [kho phit phlat]

faulty ['fɔːltɪ] adj ซึ่งมีข้อผิดพลาด [sueng mee khor phid phlad]

fauna ['fɔːnə] npl สัตว์ในท้องถิ่นหนึ่งๆ [sat nai thong thin hueng hueng]

favour ['feɪvə] n ความช่วยเหลือ [khwam chuai luea]

favourite ['feɪvərɪt; 'feɪvrɪt] adj ที่ชอบที่สุด [thii chop thiisud] ▷ n คนหรือสิ่งของที่ชอบเป็นพิเศษ [khon rue sing khong thii chop pen phi set]

fax [fæks] n โทรสาร [tho ra san] ▷ v ส่งแฟ็กซ์ [song fak]; **Do you have a fax?** คุณมีเครื่องโทรสารไหม? [khun mii khrueang tho ra san mai]; **How much is it to send a fax?** ค่าส่งโทรสารราคาเท่าไร? [kha song tho ra san ra kha thao rai]; **I want to send a fax** ฉันอยากส่งโทรสาร [chan yak song tho ra san]

fear [fɪə] n ความกลัว [khwam klua] ▷ v กลัว [klua]

feasible ['fiːzəbəl] adj ซึ่งเป็นไปได้ [sueng pen pai dai]

feather ['fɛðə] n ขนนก [khon nok]

feature ['fiːtʃə] n ลักษณะหน้าตา [lak sa na na ta]

February ['fɛbrʊərɪ] n เดือนกุมภาพันธ์ [duean kum pha phan]

fed up [fɛd ʌp] *adj* เบื่อ [buea]

fee [fiː] *n* ค่าธรรมเนียม [kha tham niam]; **entrance fee** *n* ค่าเข้า [kha khao]; **tuition fees** *npl* ค่าเล่าเรียน [kha lao rian]

feed [fiːd] *v* ให้อาหาร [hai a han]

feedback ['fiːdˌbæk] *n* ผลตอบรับ [phon top rab]

feel [fiːl] *v* รู้สึก [ru suek]; **How are you feeling now?** คุณรู้สึกอย่างไรตอนนี้? [khun ru suek yang rai ton nii]; **I feel cold** ฉันรู้สึกหนาว [chan ru suek nao]; **I feel dizzy** ฉันรู้สึกเวียนศีรษะ [chan ru suek wian sii sa]

feeling ['fiːlɪŋ] *n* ความรู้สึก [khwam ru suek]

feet [fiːt] *npl* เท้า [thao]; **My feet are a size six** เท้าฉันเบอร์หก [thao chan boe hok]; **My feet are sore** เท้าฉันเจ็บ [thao chan chep]

felt [fɛlt] *n* ผ้าขนสัตว์ [pha khon sat]

female ['fiːmeɪl] *adj* เกี่ยวกับสตรี [kiao kap sa tree] ▷ *n* เพศหญิง [phet ying]

feminine ['fɛmɪnɪn] *adj* เกี่ยวกับเพศหญิง [kiao kap phet ying]

feminist ['fɛmɪnɪst] *n* ผู้สนับสนุนสิทธิสตรี [phu sa nab sa nun sit thi sa tree]

fence [fɛns] *n* รั้ว [rua]

fennel ['fɛnəl] *n* เม็ดยี่หร่า [met yi ra]

fern [fɜːn] *n* ต้นเฟิร์น [ton foen]

ferret ['fɛrɪt] *n* สัตว์คล้ายพังพอน [sat khlai phang phon]

ferry ['fɛrɪ] *n* เรือข้ามฟาก [ruea kham fak]

fertile ['fɜːtaɪl] *adj* ซึ่งมีดินอุดมสมบูรณ์ [sueng mii din u dom som bun]

fertilizer ['fɜːtɪˌlaɪzə] *n* ปุ๋ย [pui]

festival ['fɛstɪvəl] *n* เทศกาล [thet sa kan]

fetch [fɛtʃ] *v* ไปเอามา [pai ao ma]

fever ['fiːvə] *n* การเป็นไข้ [kan pen khai]; **hay fever** *n* ไข้ละอองฟาง [khai la ong fang]

few [fjuː] *adj* น้อย [noi] ▷ *pron* จำนวนน้อย [cham nuan noi]

fewer [fjuːə] *adj* น้อยกว่า [noi kwa]

fiancé [fɪˈɒnseɪ] *n* คู่หมั้นชาย [khu man chai]

fiancée [fɪˈɒnseɪ] *n* คู่หมั้นหญิง [khu man ying]

fibre ['faɪbə] *n* เส้นใย [sen yai]

fibreglass ['faɪbəˌglɑːs] *n* ใยไหมแก้ว [yai mai kaew]

fiction ['fɪkʃən] *n* นวนิยาย [na wa ni yai]; **science fiction** *n* นวนิยายวิทยาศาสตร์ [na wa ni yai wit tha ya saat]

field [fiːld] *n* สนาม [sa nam]; **playing field** *n* สนามกีฬา [sa nam ki la]

fierce [fɪəs] *adj* ดุร้าย [du rai]

fifteen ['fɪf'tiːn] *number* สิบห้า [sip ha]

fifteenth ['fɪf'tiːnθ] *adj* ลำดับที่สิบห้า [lam dap thii sip ha]

fifth [fɪfθ] *adj* ลำดับที่ห้า [lam dap thii ha]

fifty ['fɪftɪ] *number* ห้าสิบ [ha sip]

fifty-fifty ['fɪftɪˌfɪftɪ] *adj* ห้าสิบต่อห้าสิบ [ha sip to ha sip] ▷ *adv* ห้าสิบต่อห้าสิบ [ha sip to ha sip]

fig [fɪg] *n* ต้นหรือผลตระกูลมะเดื่อ [ton rue phon tra kun ma duea]

fight [faɪt] *n* การต่อสู้ [kan to su] ▷ *v* ต่อสู้ [to su]

fighting [faɪtɪŋ] *n* การต่อสู้ [kan to su]

figure ['fɪgə; 'fɪgjər] *n* ตัวเลข [tua lek]

figure out ['fɪgə aʊt] *v* คิดคำนวณ [khit kham nuan]

Fiji ['fiːdʒiː; fiːˈdʒiː] *n* ประเทศฟิจิ [pra tet fi chi]

file [faɪl] *n* (folder) แฟ้มเอกสาร [faem ek ka san], (tool) ตะไบ [ta bai] ▷ *v* (folder) จัดเข้าแฟ้ม [chat khao faem], (smoothing) ตะไบ [ta bai]

Filipino, Filipina [ˌfɪlɪˈpiːnəʊ, ˌfɪlɪˈpiːna] *adj* เกี่ยวกับชาวฟิลิปปินส์ [kiao kap chao fi lip pin] ▷ *n* หญิงชาวฟิลิปปินส์ [ying chao fi lip pin]

fill [fɪl] *v* เติม [toem]

fillet ['fɪlɪt] n ชิ้นปลาหรือเนื้อที่ไม่มีกระดูก [chin pla rue nuea thii mai mii kra duk] ▷ v ตัดชิ้นเนื้อโดยไม่มีกระดูกติด [tad chin nuea doi mai mee kra duk tid]

fill in [fɪl ɪn] v กรอก [krok]

filling ['fɪlɪŋ] n **A filling has fallen out** ฟันที่อุดหลุดออกมา [fan thii ut lut ok ma]; **Can you do a temporary filling?** คุณอุดฟันชั่วคราวให้ได้ไหม? [khun ut fan chua khrao hai dai mai]

fill up [fɪl ʌp] v เติมให้เต็ม [toem hai tem]; **Fill it up, please** ช่วยเติมให้เต็ม ด้วย [chuai toem hai tem duai]

film [fɪlm] n ภาพยนตร์ [phap pha yon]; **film star** n ดาราภาพยนตร์ [da ra phap pha yon]; **horror film** n หนังที่น่ากลัว [nang thii na klua]

filter ['fɪltə] n เครื่องกรอง [khrueang krong] ▷ v กรอง [krong]

filthy ['fɪlθɪ] adj สกปรกที่สุด [sok ka prok thii sut]

final ['faɪnᵊl] adj สุดท้าย [sut thai] ▷ n อัน สุดท้าย [an sut thai]

finalize ['faɪnəˌlaɪz] v ทำให้เสร็จสมบูรณ์ [tham hai set som boon]

finally ['faɪnəlɪ] adv ในที่สุด [nai thi sut]

finance [fɪ'næns; 'faɪnæns] n การเงิน [kan ngoen] ▷ v จัดหาเงินทุนให้ [chat ha ngen thun hai]

financial [fɪ'nænʃəl; faɪ-] adj ทางการ เงิน [thang kan ngoen]; **financial year** n ปีงบประมาณ [pi ngop pra man]

find [faɪnd] v หา [ha]; **I can't find the at sign** ฉันหาเครื่องหมาย@ ไม่ได้ [chan ha khrueang mai mai dai]; **I need to find a supermarket** ฉันต้องมองหา ซุปเปอร์มาเก็ต [chan tong mong ha sup poe ma ket]

find out [faɪnd aʊt] v ค้นพบ [khon phop]

fine [faɪn] adj ดี [di] ▷ adv น่าพึงพอใจ [na phueng phor jai] ▷ n ค่าปรับ [kha prup]; **Fine, thanks** สบายดี ขอบคุณ [sa bai di, kop khun]; **How much is the fine?** ค่า ปรับเท่าไร? [kha prap thao rai]; **Is it going to be fine?** อากาศจะดีหรือไม่? [a kaat ja di rue mai]

finger ['fɪŋgə] n นิ้วมือ [nio mue]; **index finger** n นิ้วชี้ [nio chii]

fingernail ['fɪŋgəˌneɪl] n เล็บมือ [lep mue]

fingerprint ['fɪŋgəˌprɪnt] n ลายพิมพ์นิ้ว มือ [lai phim nio mue]

finish ['fɪnɪʃ] n ตอนจบ [ton job] ▷ v จบ [chop]

finished ['fɪnɪʃt] adj ยุติ [yu ti]

Finland ['fɪnlənd] n ประเทศฟินแลนด์ [pra tet fin laen]

Finn ['fɪn] n ชาวฟินแลนด์ [chao fin laen]

Finnish ['fɪnɪʃ] adj เกี่ยวกับประเทศ ฟินแลนด์ [kiao kap pra thet fin laen] ▷ n ชาวฟินแลนด์ [chao fin laen]

fir [fɜː] n **fir (tree)** n ต้นเฟอร์ [ton foe]

fire [faɪə] n ไฟ [fai]; **fire alarm** n สัญญาณเตือนไฟไหม้ [san yan tuean fai mai]; **fire brigade** n หน่วยดับเพลิง [nuai dap phloeng]; **fire escape** n ทางหนีไฟ [thang nii fai]; **Fire!** ไฟไหม้ [fai mai]

fireman, firemen ['faɪəmən, 'faɪəmɛn] n เจ้าหน้าที่ดับเพลิง [chao na thii dap phloeng]

fireplace ['faɪəˌpleɪs] n เตาผิง [tao phing]

firewall ['faɪəˌwɔːl] n ระบบความปลอดภัย ที่กั้นไม่ให้เข้าถึงเครือข่ายของคอมพิวเตอร์ จากอินเตอร์เน็ต [ra bob khwam plod phai thiikan mai hai khao thueng khruea khai khong khom pio ter chak in toe net]

fireworks ['faɪəˌwɜːks] npl ดอกไม้ไฟ [dok mai fai]

firm [fɜːm] adj แข็ง [khaeng] ▷ n บริษัท [bo ri sat]

first [fɜːst] adj ที่หนึ่ง [thii nueng] ▷ adv อย่างแรก [yang raek] ▷ n คนหรือของที่ เป็นอันดับหนึ่ง [khon rue khong thii pen an dap nueng]; **first aid** n การ ปฐมพยาบาลเบื้องต้น [kan pa thom pa ya baan bueang ton]; **first name** *n* ชื่อจริง [chue chring]

first-class ['fɜːst'klɑːs] *adj* ชั้นหนึ่ง [chan nueng]

firstly ['fɜːstlɪ] *adv* อันดับแรก [an dab raek]

fiscal ['fɪskəl] *adj* เกี่ยวกับการเงิน [kiao kap kan ngoen]; **fiscal year** *n* ปีงบประมาณ [pi ngop pra man]

fish [fɪʃ] *n* ปลา [pla] ▷ *v* ตกปลา [tok pla]; **Am I allowed to fish here?** อนุญาตให้ ฉันตกปลาที่นี่ได้ไหม? [a nu yaat hai chan tok pla thii ni dai mai]; **Can we fish here?** ขอเราตกปลาที่นี่ได้ไหม? [kho rao tok pla thii nii dai mai]; **Could you prepare a meal without fish?** คุณทำอาหารที่ไม่มีปลาได้ไหม? [khun tham a han thii mai mii pla dai mai]

fisherman, fishermen ['fɪʃəmən, 'fɪʃəmɛn] *n* ชาวประมง [chao pra mong]

fishing ['fɪʃɪŋ] *n* การตกปลา [kan tok pla]; **fishing boat** *n* เรือตกปลา [ruea tok pla]; **fishing rod** *n* คันเบ็ด [khan bet]; **fishing tackle** *n* อุปกรณ์ตกปลา [up pa kon tok pla]

fishmonger ['fɪʃˌmʌŋɡə] *n* คนขายปลา [khon khai pla]

fist [fɪst] *n* กำปั้น [kam pan]

fit [fɪt] *adj* ที่มีสุขภาพดี [thii mee su kha phap di] ▷ *n* ความพอดี [khwam pho dii] ▷ *v* พอดี [pho di]; **epileptic fit** *n* อาการ ชักของลมบ้าหมู [a kan chak khong lom ba mu]; **fitted kitchen** *n* ครัวสำเร็จรูปที่ สร้างติดไว้กับที่ [khrua sam ret rup thii sang tit wai kap thii]; **fitted sheet** *n* ผ้าปูที่นอน [pha pu thi non]; **It doesn't fit me** ฉันใส่ไม่พอดี [chan sai mai pho dii]

fit in [fɪt ɪn] *v* บรรจุลงใน [ban chu long nai]

five [faɪv] *number* ห้า [ha]

fix [fɪks] *v* ซ่อมแซม [som saem]

fixed [fɪkst] *adj* ติดแน่น [tit naen]

fizzy ['fɪzɪ] *adj* ออกเสียงฟู่ [ok siang fu]

flabby ['flæbɪ] *adj* หย่อนยาน [yon yan]

flag [flæg] *n* ธง [thong]

flame [fleɪm] *n* เปลวไฟ [pleo fai]

flamingo [fləˈmɪŋɡəʊ] *n* นกฟลามิงโก [nok fla ming ko]

flammable ['flæməbəl] *adj* ซึ่งไวไฟ [sueng vai fai]

flan [flæn] *n* ขนมน้ำผลไม้ [kha nom nam phon la mai]

flannel ['flænəl] *n* ผ้าสักหลาดอ่อน [pha sak ka lat on]

flap [flæp] *v* กระพือปีก [kra phue piik]

flash [flæʃ] *n* ไฟแฟลชของกล้องถ่ายรูป [fai flaet khong klong thai rup] ▷ *v* ส่อง แสงวาบขึ้นมา [song saeng wab khuen ma]

flashlight ['flæʃˌlaɪt] *n* ไฟฉาย [fai chai]

flask [flɑːsk] *n* กระติกน้ำร้อนหรือน้ำเย็น [kra tik nam ron rue nam yen]

flat [flæt] *adj* ราบ [rap] ▷ *n* ที่ราบ [thii rap]; **studio flat** *n* ห้องชุดที่เป็นห้อง ทำงาน [hong chut thii pen hong tham ngan]

flat-screen ['flætˌskriːn] *adj* จอภาพ แบน [cho phap baen]

flatter ['flætə] *v* ยกยอ [yok yo]

flattered ['flætəd] *adj* ที่ได้รับการยกยอ [thii dai rap kan yok yo]

flavour ['fleɪvə] *n* รสชาติ [rot chat]

flavouring ['fleɪvərɪŋ] *n* การปรุงรส [kan prung rot]

flaw [flɔː] *n* ข้อบกพร่อง [kho bok phrong]

flea [fliː] *n* หมัด [mat]; **flea market** *n* ตลาดขายของที่ใช้แล้ว [ta lat khai khong thii chai laeo]

flee [fliː] *v* หนี [ni]

fleece [fliːs] *n* ผ้าขนแกะ [pha khon kae]

fleet [fliːt] *n* กองเรือรบ [kong ruea rob]

flex [flɛks] *n* สายไฟ [sai fai]

flexible ['flɛksɪbəl] *adj* ที่ปรับตัวเข้ากับ สถานการณ์ [thii prap tua khao kap sa tha na kan]

flexitime ['flɛksɪˌtaɪm] *n* เวลาที่ยืดหยุ่น

ได้ [we la thii yuet yun dai]

flight [flaɪt] n เที่ยวบิน [thiao bin]; **charter flight** n เครื่องบินเช่า [khrueang bin chao]; **Are there any cheap flights?** มีเที่ยวบินราคาถูกไหม? [mii thiao bin ra kha thuk mai]; **I would prefer an earlier flight** ฉันอยากได้เที่ยวบินก่อนหน้านี้ [chan yak dai thiao bin kon na nii]; **I'd like to cancel my flight** ฉันอยากยกเลิกเที่ยวบินของฉัน [chan yak yok loek thiao bin khong chan]

fling [flɪŋ] v ขว้าง [khwang]

flip-flops ['flɪpˌflɒpz] npl รองเท้าแตะ [rong thao tae]

flippers ['flɪpəz] npl รองเท้านักดำน้ำ [rong thao nak dam nam]

flirt [flɜːt] n คนเจ้าชู้ [khon chao chu] ▷ v เกี้ยวพาราสี [kiao pha ra si]

float [fləʊt] n สิ่งที่ลอยได้เช่นแพ [sing thii loi dai chen phae] ▷ v ลอยบนผิวน้ำหรือในอากาศ [loi bon phio nam rue nai a kaat]

flock [flɒk] n ฝูงสัตว์ [fung sat]

flood [flʌd] n น้ำท่วม [nam thuam] ▷ vi ไหลบ่า ไหลล้น [lai ba, lai lon] ▷ vt ท่วม [thuam]

flooding ['flʌdɪŋ] n น้ำท่วม [nam thuam]

floodlight ['flʌdˌlaɪt] n แสงไฟสว่างจ้าที่ใช้ในสนามกีฬาหรือนอกอาคาร [saeng fai sa wang cha thii chai nai sa nam ki la rue nok a khan]

floor [flɔː] n พื้น [phuen]; **ground floor** n ชั้นล่าง [chan lang]

flop [flɒp] n ความล้มเหลว [khwam lom leo]

floppy ['flɒpɪ] adj **floppy disk** n แผ่นบันทึก [phaen ban thuek]

flora ['flɔːrə] npl พืชที่ขึ้นในเฉพาะพื้นที่ [phuet thii khuen nai cha pau phuen thii]

florist ['flɒrɪst] n ร้านดอกไม้ [ran dok mai]

flour ['flaʊə] n แป้ง [paeng]

flow [fləʊ] v ไหล [lai]

flower ['flaʊə] n ดอกไม้ [dok mai] ▷ v ผลิดอก [phli dok]

flu [fluː] n ไข้หวัดใหญ่ [khai wat yai]; **bird flu** n ไข้หวัดนก [khai wat nok]; **I had flu recently** ฉันเป็นไข้หวัดใหญ่เมื่อเร็ว ๆ นี้ [chan pen khai wat yai muea reo reo nii]; **I've got flu** ฉันเป็นไข้หวัดใหญ่ [chan pen khai wat yai]

fluent ['fluːənt] adj พูดหรือเขียนได้อย่างคล่องแคล่ว [phut rue khian dai yang klong khaeo]

fluorescent [ˌfluəˈrɛsᵊnt] adj ไฟนีออน [fai ni on]

flush [flʌʃ] n หน้าหรือผิวแดง [na rue phio daeng] ▷ v ชักโครก [chak khrok]

flute [fluːt] n ขลุ่ย [khlui]

fly [flaɪ] n การบิน [kan bin] ▷ v บิน [bin]; **I need a 'fit to fly' certificate** ฉันอยากได้หนังสือรับรองว่าฉันแข็งแรงที่จะบินได้ [chan yak dai nang sue rap rong wa chan khaeng raeng thii ja bin dai]

fly away [flaɪ əˈweɪ] v บินไป [bin pai]

foal [fəʊl] n ลูกม้า [luk ma]

foam [fəʊm] n **shaving foam** n โฟมโกนหนวด [fom kon nuat]

focus ['fəʊkəs] n จุดเน้น [chut nen] ▷ v มุ่งเน้น [mung nen]

foetus ['fiːtəs] n ทารกในครรภ์ [tha rok nai khan]

fog [fɒg] n หมอก [mok]; **fog light** n ไฟหมอก [fai mok]

foggy ['fɒgɪ] adj ที่เป็นหมอก [thii pen mok]

foil [fɔɪl] n โลหะแผ่น [lo ha phaen]

fold [fəʊld] n รอยพับ [roi phap] ▷ v พับ [phap]

folder ['fəʊldə] n ที่เก็บเอกสาร [thii keb ek ka sarn]

folding [fəʊldɪŋ] adj ที่พับเก็บได้ [thii phap kep dai]

folklore ['fəʊkˌlɔː] n เรื่องราวประเพณีและความเชื่อของผู้คน [rueang rao pra phe ni lae khwam chuea khong phu kon]

follow ['fɒləʊ] v ตาม [tam]

following ['fɒləʊɪŋ] adj ถัดไป [that pai]

food [fuːd] n อาหาร [a han]; **Do you have food?** คุณมีอาหารไหม? [khun mii a han mai]; **The food is too hot** อาหารร้อนเกินไป [a han ron koen pai]; **The food is very greasy** อาหารมันมาก [a han man mak]

fool [fuːl] n คนโง่ [khon ngo] ▷ v หลอกลวง [lok luang]

foot, feet [fʊt, fiːt] n เท้า [thao]; **My feet are a size six** เท้าฉันเบอร์หก [thao chan boe hok]

football ['fʊtˌbɔːl] n ฟุตบอล [fut bon]; **American football** n ฟุตบอลอเมริกัน [fut bal a me ri kan]; **football match** n กีฬาแข่งขันฟุตบอล [ki la khaeng khan fut bal]; **football player** n นักเล่นฟุตบอล [nak len fut bal]; **I'd like to see a football match** ฉันอยากดูการแข่งฟุตบอล [chan yak du kan khaeng fut bal]

footballer ['fʊtˌbɔːlə] n นักฟุตบอล [nak fut bal]

footpath ['fʊtˌpɑːθ] n ทางเดิน [thang doen]

footprint ['fʊtˌprɪnt] n รอยเท้า [roi thao]

footstep ['fʊtˌstɛp] n ก้าวเดิน [kao doen]

for [fɔː; fə] prep เพื่อ [phuea]

forbid [fə'bɪd] v ห้าม [ham]

forbidden [fə'bɪdᵊn] adj ที่ไม่ได้รับอนุญาต [thii mai dai rab ar nu yard]

force [fɔːs] n กำลัง [kam lang] ▷ v บังคับ [bang khap]; **Air Force** n กองทัพอากาศ [kong thap a kat]

forecast ['fɔːˌkɑːst] n การพยากรณ์ [kan pha ya kon]

foreground ['fɔːˌɡraʊnd] n ทัศนียภาพที่อยู่ใกล้ที่สุด [that sa nii ya phap thii yu klai thii sut]

forehead ['fɒrɪd; 'fɔːˌhɛd] n หน้าผาก [na phak]

foreign ['fɒrɪn] adj เกี่ยวกับต่างประเทศ [kiao kap tang pra thet]

foreigner ['fɒrɪnə] n ชาวต่างชาติ [chao tang chat]

foresee [fɔː'siː] v รู้ล่วงหน้า [ru luang na]

forest ['fɒrɪst] n ป่า [pa]

forever [fɔː'rɛvə; fə-] adv ตลอดไป [ta lot pai]

forge [fɔːdʒ] v ปลอมแปลง [plom plaeng]

forgery ['fɔːdʒərɪ] n การปลอมแปลง [kan plom plaeng]

forget [fə'ɡɛt] v ลืม [luem]

forgive [fə'ɡɪv] v ให้อภัย [hai a phai]

forgotten [fə'ɡɒtᵊn] adj ที่ถูกลืม [thii thuk luem]

fork [fɔːk] n ส้อมทานอาหาร [som than a han]

form [fɔːm] n รูปทรง [rup song]; **application form** n แบบฟอร์มใบสมัคร [baep fom bai sa mak]; **order form** n แบบฟอร์มสั่งซื้อ [baep fom sang sue]

formal ['fɔːməl] adj ตามธรรมเนียมปฏิบัติ [tam tham niam pa ti bat]

formality [fɔː'mælɪtɪ] n ความเป็นทางการ [khwam pen thang kan]

format ['fɔːmæt] n รูปแบบ [rup baep] ▷ v การจัด [kan chat]

former ['fɔːmə] adj ก่อนหน้านี้ [kon na nee]

formerly ['fɔːməlɪ] adv เมื่อก่อนนี้ [muea kon nii]

formula ['fɔːmjʊlə] n สูตร [sut]

fort [fɔːt] n ป้อม [pom]

fortnight ['fɔːtˌnaɪt] n สองอาทิตย์ [song a thit]

fortunate ['fɔːtʃənɪt] adj โชคดี [chok di]

fortunately ['fɔːtʃənɪtlɪ] adv อย่างโชคดี [yang chok di]

fortune ['fɔːtʃən] n ทรัพย์สมบัติมากมาย [sap som bat mak mai]

forty ['fɔːtɪ] number สี่สิบ [si sip]

forward ['fɔːwəd] adv โดยไปข้างหน้า [doi pai khang na] ▷ v ไปข้างหน้า [pai khang na]; **forward slash** n ทับ [thap]; **lean forward** v เอนไปข้างหน้า [en pai khang na]

foster ['fɒstə] v เลี้ยงดูเด็ก [liang du dek]; **foster child** n ลูกเลี้ยง [luk liang]

foul [faʊl] adj เหม็นเน่า [men nao] ▷ n การทำผิดกติกา [kan tham phit ka ti ka]

foundations [faʊn'deɪʃənz] npl รากฐานสิ่งก่อสร้าง [rak than sing ko sang]

fountain ['faʊntɪn] n น้ำพุ [nam phu]; **fountain pen** n ปากกาหมึกซึม [pak ka muek suem]

four [fɔː] number สี่ [si]

fourteen ['fɔː'tiːn] number สิบสี่ [sip si]

fourteenth ['fɔː'tiːnθ] adj อันดับที่สิบสี่ [an dap thii sip si]

fourth [fɔːθ] adj อันดับที่สี่ [an dap thii si]

fox [fɒks] n สุนัขจิ้งจอก [su nak ching chok]

fracture ['fræktʃə] n การแตกโดยเฉพาะกระดูก [kan taek doi cha pau kra duk]

fragile ['frædʒaɪl] adj เปราะบาง [pro bang]

frail [freɪl] adj แบบบาง [baep bang]

frame [freɪm] n โครงสร้าง [khrong sang], กรอบรูป [krop rup]; **picture frame** n กรอบรูป [krop rup]; **Zimmer® frame** n อุปกรณ์ช่วยเดิน [up pa kon chuai doen]

France [frɑːns] n ประเทศฝรั่งเศส [pra ted fa rang set]

frankly ['fræŋklɪ] adv อย่างตรงไปตรงมา [yang trong pai trong ma]

frantic ['fræntɪk] adj ซึ่งไม่สามารถควบคุมอารมณ์ได้ [sueng mai sa maat khuap khum a rom dai]

fraud [frɔːd] n การโกง [kan kong]

freckles ['frɛkᵊlz] npl ตกกระ [tok kra]

free [friː] adj (no cost) ฟรี [fri], (no restraint) อิสระ [it sa ra] ▷ v ทำให้อิสระ [tham hai is sa ra]; **free kick** n เตะฟรีในฟุตบอล [te frii nai fut bal]

freedom ['friːdəm] n ความเป็นอิสระ [khwam pen it sa ra]

freelance ['friːˌlɑːns] adj ที่ทำงานอิสระ [thii tham ngan is sa ra] ▷ adv ซึ่งทำงานอิสระไม่ได้รับเงินเดือนประจำ [sueng tham ngan it sa ra mai dai rap ngoen duean pra cham]

freeze [friːz] v กลายเป็นน้ำแข็ง [klai pen nam khaeng]

freezer ['friːzə] n ตู้แช่แข็ง [tu chae khaeng]

freezing ['friːzɪŋ] adj เย็นเฉียบ [yen chiap]

freight [freɪt] n สินค้าที่ขนส่ง [sin kha thii khon song]

French [frɛntʃ] adj เกี่ยวกับชาวฝรั่งเศส [kiao kap chao fa rang set] ▷ n ชาวฝรั่งเศส [chao fa rang set]; **French beans** npl ถั่วคล้ายถั่วฝักยาว [thua khlai thua fak yao]; **French horn** n แตรทองเหลืองรูปร่างโค้งงอ [trae thong lueang rup rang khong ngo]

Frenchman, Frenchmen ['frɛntʃmən, 'frɛntʃmɛn] n ชายฝรั่งเศส [chai fa rang set]

Frenchwoman, Frenchwomen ['frɛntʃwʊmən, 'frɛntʃwɪmɪn] n หญิงฝรั่งเศส [ying fa rang set]

frequency ['friːkwənsɪ] n ความถี่ [khwam thi]

frequent ['friːkwənt] adj บ่อย ๆ [boi boi]

fresh [frɛʃ] adj สด [sot]

fret [frɛt] v กลัดกลุ้ม [klat klum]

Friday ['fraɪdɪ] n วันศุกร์ [wan suk]; **Good Friday** n วันทางศาสนาคริสต์ วันที่พระเยซูถูกตรึงไม้กางเขน [wan thang sat sa na khris, wan thii phra ye su thuk trueng mai kang khen]; **on Friday the thirty first of December** วันศุกร์ที่สามสิบเอ็ด ธันวาคม [wan suk thii sam sip et than wa khom]; **on Friday** วันศุกร์ [wan suk]

fridge [frɪdʒ] n ตู้เย็น [tu yen]

fried [fraɪd] adj ซึ่งทอดในน้ำมัน [sueng thot nai nam man]

friend [frɛnd] n เพื่อน [phuean]; **I'm here with my friends** ฉันมาที่นี่กับเพื่อน ๆ [chan ma thii ni kap phuean phuean]

friendly ['frɛndlɪ] adj เป็นมิตร [pen mit]

friendship ['frɛndʃɪp] n มิตรภาพ [mit

tra phap]

fright [fraɪt] *n* ความตกใจ [khwam tok jai]

frighten ['fraɪt°n] *v* ตระหนกตกใจ [tra hnok tok jai]

frightened ['fraɪtənd] *adj* น่าตกใจ [na tok jai]

frightening ['fraɪt°nɪŋ] *adj* ที่น่าตกใจ [thii na tok jai]

fringe [frɪndʒ] *n* ระบาย ขอบ [ra bai khop]

frog [frɒg] *n* กบ [kop]

from [frɒm; frəm] *prep* จาก [chak]; **How far are we from the beach?** เราอยู่ห่างจากชายหาดมากแค่ไหน? [rao yu hang chak chai hat mak khae nai]; **I'm from...** ฉันมาจาก... [chan ma chak...]; **Where are you from?** คุณมาจากไหน? [khun ma chak nai]

front [frʌnt] *adj* ข้างหน้า [khang na] ▷ *n* ด้านหน้า [dan na]; **Facing the front, please** ขอนั่งที่หันหน้าไปด้านหน้า [kho nang thii han na pai dan na]

frontier ['frʌntɪə; frʌn'tɪə] *n* เขตพรมแดน [khet phrom daen]

frost [frɒst] *n* ความเย็น [khwam yen]

frosting ['frɒstɪŋ] *n* น้ำตาลไอซิ่งบนขนมเค้ก [nam tan ai sing bon kha nom khek]

frosty ['frɒstɪ] *adj* เย็นจัด [yen chat]

frown [fraʊn] *v* ทำหน้าบึ้ง [tham na bueng]

frozen ['frəʊz°n] *adj* ซึ่งเป็นน้ำแข็ง [sueng pen nam khaeng]

fruit [fruːt] *n (botany)* ผลไม้ [phon la mai], *(collectively)* ผลไม้ [phon la mai]; **fruit juice** *n* น้ำผลไม้ [nam phon la mai]; **fruit machine** *n* เครื่องหยอดเหรียญสำหรับเล่นการพนัน [khrueang yot rian sam rap len kan pha nan]; **fruit salad** *n* สลัดผลไม้ [sa lat phon la mai]

frustrated [frʌ'streɪtɪd] *adj* ท้อแท้ หงุดหงิด [tho thae, ngut ngit]

fry [fraɪ] *v* ทอด [thot]; **frying pan** *n* กระทะทอด [kra tha thot]

fuel [fjʊəl] *n* เชื้อเพลิง [chuea phloeng]

fulfil [fʊl'fɪl] *v* สมหวัง [som wang]

full [fʊl] *adj* เต็ม [tem]; **full moon** *n* พระจันทร์เต็มดวง [phra chan tem duang]; **full stop** *n* มหัพภาค จุด [ma hup phak chut]

full-time ['fʊl‚taɪm] *adj* ซึ่งเต็มเวลา [sueng tem we la] ▷ *adv* อย่างเต็มเวลา [yang tem we la]

fully ['fʊlɪ] *adv* อย่างเต็มที่ [yang tem thii]

fumes [fjuːmz] *npl* ควันพิษ [khwan phit]; **exhaust fumes** *npl* ควันจากท่อไอเสีย [khwan chak tho ai sia]

fun [fʌn] *adj* น่าสนุก [na sa nuk] ▷ *n* ความขบขัน [khwam khop khan]

funds [fʌndz] *npl* กองทุน [kong thun]

funeral ['fjuːnərəl] *n* งานศพ [ngan sop]; **funeral parlour** *n* โรงงานประกอบพิธีฌาปนกิจศพ [rong ngan pra kop phi ti cha pa na kit sop]

funfair ['fʌn‚fɛə] *n* สวนสนุก [suan sa nuk]

funnel ['fʌn°l] *n* กรวย [kruai]

funny ['fʌnɪ] *adj* ตลก [ta lok]

fur [fɜː] *n* ขนสัตว์ [khon sat]; **fur coat** *n* เสื้อโค้ททำจากขนสัตว์ [suea khot tham chak khon sat]

furious ['fjʊərɪəs] *adj* โกรธ [krot]

furnished ['fɜːnɪʃt] *adj* ซึ่งมีเครื่องเรือนพร้อม [sueng mii khrueang ruean phrom]

furniture ['fɜːnɪtʃə] *n* เครื่องเรือน [khrueang ruean]

further ['fɜːðə] *adj* ห่างออกไป [hang ok pai] ▷ *adv* ไกลกว่า [klai kwa]; **further education** *n* การศึกษาระดับสูง [kan suek sa ra dap sung]

fuse [fjuːz] *n* สายชนวน [sai cha nuan]; **fuse box** *n* กล่องใส่สายชนวน [klong sai sai cha nuan]

fusebox ['fjuːz‚bɒks] *n* **Where is the fusebox?** กล่องฟิวส์อยู่ที่ไหน? [klong fio yu thii nai]

fuss [fʌs] *n* ความวุ่นวาย [khwam wun wai]

fussy ['fʌsɪ] *adj* จู้จี้ [chu chi]

future ['fjuːtʃə] *adj* ภายหน้า [phai na] ▷ *n* อนาคต [a na khot]

g

Gabon [gə'bɒn] n ประเทศกาบอน [pra tet ka bon]

gain [geɪn] n ผลกำไร [phon kam rai] ▷ v ได้กำไร [dai kam rai]

gale [geɪl] n ลมพายุ [lom pha yu]

gallery ['gælərɪ] n ห้องแสดงภาพ [hong sa daeng phap]; **art gallery** n ห้องแสดงงานศิลปะ [hong sa daeng ngan sin la pa]

gallop ['gæləp] n การควบม้า [kan khuap ma] ▷ v ควบม้า [khuap ma]

gallstone ['gɔːlˌstəʊn] n นิ่วในถุงน้ำดี [nio nai thung nam di]

Gambia ['gæmbɪə] n ประเทศแกมเบีย [pra tet kaem bia]

gamble ['gæmbʰl] v เล่นพนัน [len pha nan]

gambler ['gæmblə] n นักพนัน [nak pha nan]

gambling ['gæmblɪŋ] n การพนัน [kan pha nan]

game [geɪm] n เกมส์ [kem]; **board game** n เกมส์ที่เล่นบนกระดาน [kem thii len bon kra dan]; **games console** n เครื่องที่ต่อกับทีวีใช้เล่นวิดีโอเกมส์ [khrueang thii to kap thii wii chai len vi di o kem]; **Can I play video games?** ฉันเล่นวีดีโอเกมส์ได้ไหม? [chan len wi di o kem dai mai]

gang [gæŋ] n สมัครพรรคพวก [sa mak phak phuak]

gangster ['gæŋstə] n พวกอันธพาล [phuak an tha phan]

gap [gæp] n ช่องว่าง [chong wang]

garage ['gærɑːʒ; -rɪdʒ] n โรงรถ [rong rot]; **Which is the key for the garage?** กุญแจดอกไหนเป็นกุญแจโรงรถ? [kun jae dok nai pen kun jae rong rot]

garbage ['gɑːbɪdʒ] n ขยะ [kha ya]

garden ['gɑːdʰn] n สวน [suan]; **garden centre** n ศูนย์ขายต้นไม้และเครื่องมือในการทำสวน [sun khai ton mai lae khrueang mue nai kan tham suan]; **Can we visit the gardens?** เราไปเยี่ยมชมสวนได้ไหม? [rao pai yiam chom suan dai mai]

gardener ['gɑːdnə] n คนทำสวน [kon tham suan]

gardening ['gɑːdʰnɪŋ] n การทำสวน [kan tham suan]

garlic ['gɑːlɪk] n กระเทียม [kra thiam]; **Is there any garlic in it?** มีกระเทียมอยู่ในนี้บ้างไหม? [mii kra thiam yu nai nii bang mai]

garment ['gɑːmənt] n เสื้อผ้า [suea pha]

gas [gæs] n ก๊าซ [kas]; **gas cooker** n เตาทำอาหารที่ใช้แก๊ส [tao tham a han thii chai kaes]; **natural gas** n ก๊าซธรรมชาติ [kas tham ma chat]; **I can smell gas** ฉันได้กลิ่นก๊าซ [chan dai klin kas]

gasket ['gæskɪt] n วงแหวนอัดลูกสูบ [wong waen at luk sup]

gate [geɪt] n ประตู [pra tu]; **Please go to gate...** กรุณาไปที่ประตูโดยสารที่... [ka ru na pai thii pra tu doi san thii...]; **Which gate for the flight to...?** ประตูไหนสำหรับเที่ยวบินไป...? [pra tu nai sam rap thiao bin pai...]

gateau, gateaux ['gætəʊ, 'gætəʊz] *n* เค้กชั้นก้อนใหญ่ [khek chan kon yai]

gather ['gæðə] *v* จัดรวม [chad ruam]

gauge [geɪdʒ] *n* เครื่องวัด [khrueang wat] ▷ *v* วัด [wat]

gaze [geɪz] *v* จ้องมอง [chong mong]

gear [gɪə] *n (equipment)* เกียร์ [kia], *(mechanism)* เกียร์รถ [kia rot]; **gear box** *n* กระปุกเกียร์ [kra puk kia]; **gear lever** *n* ที่เปลี่ยนเกียร์ [thii plian kia]; **gear stick** *n* กระปุกเกียร์ [kra puk kia]; **Does the bike have gears?** จักรยานคันนี้มีเกียร์ไหม? [chak kra yan khan nii mii kia mai]

gearbox ['gɪəˌbɒks] *n* **The gearbox is broken** กระปุกเกียร์เสีย [kra puk kia sia]

gearshift ['gɪəˌʃɪft] *n* การเปลี่ยนเกียร์ [kan plian kia]

gel [dʒɛl] *n* เจลสำหรับแต่งผม [chen sam rap taeng phom]; **hair gel** *n* เจลใส่ผม [chen sai phom]

gem [dʒɛm] *n* เพชรพลอย [pet ploi]

Gemini ['dʒɛmɪˌnaɪ; -ˌniː] *n* ราศีมิถุน [ra si mi thun]

gender ['dʒɛndə] *n* เพศ [phet]

gene [dʒiːn] *n* สายพันธุ์ [sai phan]

general ['dʒɛnərəl; 'dʒɛnrəl] *adj* โดยทั่วไป [doi thua pai] ▷ *n* นายพล [nai phon]; **general anaesthetic** *n* การวางยาสลบ [kan wang ya sa lop]; **general election** *n* การเลือกตั้งทั่วไป [kan lueak tang thua pai]; **general knowledge** *n* ความรู้ทั่วไป [khwam ru thua pai]

generalize ['dʒɛnrəˌlaɪz] *v* พูดคลุมทั่ว ๆ ไป [phut khlum thua thua pai]

generally ['dʒɛnrəlɪ] *adv* โดยทั่วไป [doi thua pai]

generation [ˌdʒɛnəˈreɪʃən] *n* ชั่วอายุคน [chua a yu khon]

generator ['dʒɛnəˌreɪtə] *n* เครื่องกำเนิดไฟฟ้า [khrueang kam noet fai fa]

generosity [ˌdʒɛnəˈrɒsɪtɪ] *n* ความมีใจกว้าง [khwam mii jai kwang]

generous ['dʒɛnərəs; 'dʒɛnrəs] *adj* ใจกว้าง [chai kwang]

genetic [dʒɪˈnɛtɪk] *adj* เกี่ยวกับพันธุศาสตร์ [kiao kap phan thu sat]

genetically-modified [dʒɪˈnɛtɪklɪˈmɒdɪˌfaɪd] *adj* ซึ่งเปลี่ยนแปลงทางพันธุศาสตร์ [sueng plian plang thang phan tu sat]

genetics [dʒɪˈnɛtɪks] *n* พันธุศาสตร์ [pan thu sat]

genius ['dʒiːnɪəs; -njəs] *n* อัจฉริยบุคคล [at cha ri ya buk khon]

gentle ['dʒɛntˀl] *adj* อย่างอ่อนโยน [yang on yon]

gentleman, gentlemen ['dʒɛntˀlmən; 'dʒɛntˀlmɛn] *n* สุภาพบุรุษ [su phap bu rut]

gently ['dʒɛntlɪ] *adv* อย่างนุ่มนวล [yang num nuan]

gents' [dʒɛnts] *n* ห้องน้ำชาย [hong nam chai]

genuine ['dʒɛnjʊɪn] *adj* จริง [ching]

geography [dʒɪˈɒgrəfɪ] *n* ภูมิศาสตร์ [phu mi sat]

geology [dʒɪˈɒlədʒɪ] *n* ธรณีวิทยา [tho ra ni wit ta ya]

Georgia ['dʒɔːdʒjə] *n (country)* ประเทศจอร์เจีย [pra tet chor chia], *(US state)* รัฐจอร์เจียในอเมริกา [rat chor chia nai a me ri ka]

Georgian ['dʒɔːdʒjən] *adj* เกี่ยวกับจอร์เจีย [kiao kap cho chia] ▷ *n (inhabitant of Georgia)* ชาวจอร์เจียน [chao chor chian]

geranium [dʒɪˈreɪnɪəm] *n* ต้นเจอเรเนียมมีดอกสีชมพูหรือสีม่วง [ton choe re niam mii dok sii chom phu rue sii muang]

gerbil ['dʒɜːbɪl] *n* สัตว์ทะเลทรายขนาดเล็กคล้ายหนู [sat tha le srai kha nard lek khlai nu]

geriatric [ˌdʒɛrɪˈætrɪk] *adj* เกี่ยวกับคนชรา [kiao kap khon cha ra] ▷ *n* คนชรา [khon cha ra]

germ [dʒɜːm] *n* เชื้อโรค [chue rok]

German ['dʒɜːmən] *adj* เกี่ยวกับเยอรมัน [kiao kap yoe ra man] ▷ *n (language)* ภาษาเยอรมัน [pha sa yoe ra man], *(person)* ชาวเยอรมัน [chao yoe ra man]; **German measles** *n* หัดเยอรมัน [hat yoe ra man]

Germany ['dʒɜːmənɪ] *n* ประเทศเยอรมัน [pra tet yoe ra man]

gesture ['dʒɛstʃə] *n* ท่าทาง [tha thang]

get [gɛt] *v* ได้ [dai], *(to a place)* ได้ [dai]; **Can I get you a drink?** ฉันเอาเครื่องดื่มให้คุณได้ไหม? [chan ao khrueang duem hai khun dai mai]; **Did you get my email?** คุณได้รับอีเมลล์ฉันไหม? [khun dai rap e mail chan mai]; **How do I get to the airport?** ฉันจะไปสนามบินได้อย่างไร? [chan ja pai sa nam bin dai yang rai]

get away [gɛt ə'weɪ] *v* หนี [ni]

get back [gɛt bæk] *v* กลับมา [klap ma]; **When do we get back?** เราจะกลับมาเมื่อไร? [rao ja klap ma muea rai]

get in [gɛt ɪn] **How much does it cost to get in?** ต้องเสียค่าเข้าเท่าไรเพื่อเข้าข้างใน? [tong sia kha khao thao rai phuea khao khang nai]

get into [gɛt 'ɪntə] *v* เข้าไปใน [khao pai nai]

get off [gɛt ɒf] *v* ลงรถ [long rot]; **Please tell me when to get off** ช่วยบอกฉันด้วยว่าจะต้องลงรถเมื่อไร [chuai bok chan duai wa ja tong long rot muea rai]

get on [gɛt ɒn] *v* ขึ้น [khuen]; **Can you help me get on, please?** คุณช่วยพาฉันลุกขึ้นได้ไหม? [khun chuai pha chan luk khuen dai mai]

get out [gɛt aʊt] *v* ออกไป [ok pai]

get over [gɛt 'əʊvə] *v* รู้แล้วรู้รอด [ru laeo ru rot]

get through [gɛt θruː] *v* **I can't get through** ฉันต่อสายไม่ติด [chan to sai mai tit]

get together [gɛt tə'gɛðə] *v* สังสรรค์ [sang san]

get up [gɛt ʌp] *v* ลุกขึ้น [luk khuen]

Ghana ['gɑːnə] *n* ประเทศกานา [pra tet ka na]

Ghanaian [gɑːˈneɪən] *adj* เกี่ยวกับชาวกานา [kiao kap chao ka na] ▷ *n* ชาวกานา [chao ka na]

ghost [gəʊst] *n* ผี [phi]

giant ['dʒaɪənt] *adj* สูงใหญ่ [sung yai] ▷ *n* ยักษ์ [yak]

gift [gɪft] *n* ของขวัญ [khong khwan]; **gift shop** *n* ร้านขายของขวัญ [ran khai khong khwan]; **gift voucher** *n* บัตรของขวัญ [bat khong khwan]; **Please can you gift-wrap it?** คุณห่อของขวัญให้ได้ไหม? [khun ho khong khwan hai dai mai]

gifted ['gɪftɪd] *adj* มีพรสวรรค์ [mii phon sa wan]

gigantic [dʒaɪˈgæntɪk] *adj* มโหฬาร [ma ho lan]

giggle ['gɪgəl] *v* หัวเราะต่อกระซิก [hua ro to kra sik]

gin [dʒɪn] *n* เหล้ายิน [lao yin]

ginger ['dʒɪndʒə] *adj* แดงน้ำตาล [daeng nam tan] ▷ *n* ขิง [khing]

giraffe [dʒɪˈrɑːf; -ˈræf] *n* ยีราฟ [yi rap]

girl [gɜːl] *n* เด็กผู้หญิง [dek phu hying]

girlfriend ['gɜːlˌfrɛnd] *n* เพื่อนผู้หญิง [phuean phu hying]

give [gɪv] *v* ให้ [hai]; **Can you give me something for the pain?** คุณให้อะไรฉันสักอย่างเพื่อแก้ปวดได้ไหม? [khun hai a rai chan sak yang phue kae puat dai mai]; **Could you give me change of...?** คุณให้เงินทอนฉันเป็น...ได้ไหม? [khun hai ngen thon chan pen...dai mai]; **Give me your insurance details, please** ขอให้คุณให้รายละเอียดการประกันของคุณ [kho hai khun hai rai la iad kan pra kan khong khun]

give back [gɪv bæk] *v* ให้คืน [hai khuen]

give in [gɪv ɪn] *v* ยอมแพ้ [yom phae]

give out [gɪv aʊt] *v* แจกจ่าย [chaek]

chai]

give up [gɪv ʌp] v ยกเลิก [yok loek]

glacier ['glæsɪə; 'gleɪs-] n ธารน้ำแข็ง [than nam khaeng]

glad [glæd] adj ดีใจ [di chai]

glamorous ['glæmərəs] adj ซึ่งมีเสน่ห์ [sueng mii sa ne]

glance [glɑːns] n การชำเลือง [kan cham lueang] ▷ v ชำเลืองดู [cham lueang du]

gland [glænd] n ต่อม [tom]

glare [glɛə] v ส่องแสงเจิดจ้า [song saeng chet cha]

glaring ['glɛərɪŋ] adj ที่แสงเข้าตา [thit saeng khao ta]

glass [glɑːs] n แก้ว [kaeo], (vessel) แก้วน้ำ [kaew nam]; **a glass of water** น้ำหนึ่งแก้ว [nam nueng kaew]; **A glass of lemonade, please** ขอน้ำมะนาวหนึ่งแก้ว [kho nam ma nao nueng kaew]; **Can I have a clean glass, please?** ฉันขอแก้วสะอาดหนึ่งใบได้ไหม? [chan kho kaew sa aat nueng bai dai mai]

glasses ['glɑːsɪz] npl แว่นตา [waen ta]; **Can you repair my glasses?** คุณซ่อมแว่นตาฉันได้ไหม? [khun som waen ta chan dai mai]

glazing ['gleɪzɪŋ] n **double glazing** n การติดตั้งกระจกหนาสองชั้น [kan tit tang kra chok na song chan]

glider ['glaɪdə] n เครื่องร่อน [khrueang ron]

gliding ['glaɪdɪŋ] n การร่อน [kan ron]

global ['gləʊbəl] adj ทั่วโลก [thua lok]; **global warming** n อุณหภูมิความร้อนของโลกที่เพิ่มขึ้น [un ha phum khwam ron khong lok thii poem khuen]

globalization [ˌgləʊbəlaɪ'zeɪʃən] n การกระจายไปทั่วโลก [kan kra chai pai thua lok]

globe [gləʊb] n ลูกโลก [luk lok]

gloomy ['gluːmɪ] adj เศร้าใจ [sao chai]

glorious ['glɔːrɪəs] adj เกียรติยศ [kiat ti yot]

glory ['glɔːrɪ] n ความทรงเกียรติ [khwam

song kiat]

glove [glʌv] n ถุงมือ [thung mue]; **glove compartment** n ที่ใส่ถุงมือในรถ [thii sai thung mue nai rot]; **oven glove** n ถุงมือจับภาชนะร้อนจากเตาอบ [thung mue chap pha cha na ron chak tao op]; **rubber gloves** npl ถุงมือยาง [thung mue yang]

glucose ['gluːkəʊz; -kəʊs] n กลูโคส [klu khos]

glue [gluː] n กาว [kao] ▷ v ใช้กาวติด [chai kao tit]

gluten ['gluːtən] n โปรตีนเหนียวที่พบในธัญพืช [pro tin niao thii phop nai than ya phuet]

GM [dʒiː ɛm] abbr ตัวย่อของแก้ไขเปลี่ยนแปลงเกี่ยวกับพันธุศาสตร์ [tua yo khong kae khai plian plang kiao kap phan thu sat]

go [gəʊ] v ไป เคลื่อนไป ออกไป [pai, khluean pai, ok pai]

go after [gəʊ 'ɑːftə] v แสวงหาติดตาม [sa waeng ha tit tam]

go ahead [gəʊ ə'hɛd] v ทำต่อไปโดยไม่รีรอ [tham tor pai doi mai ri ror]

goal [gəʊl] n เป้าหมาย [pao mai]

goalkeeper ['gəʊlˌkiːpə] n ผู้รักษาประตู [phu rak sa pra tu]

goat [gəʊt] n แพะ [phae]

go away [gəʊ ə'weɪ] v ไปให้พ้น [pai hai phon]

go back [gəʊ bæk] v กลับไป [klap pai]

go by [gəʊ baɪ] v ผ่านไป [phan pai]

god [gɒd] n พระเจ้า [phra chao]

godchild, godchildren ['gɒdˌtʃaɪld, 'gɒdˌtʃɪldrən] n ลูกของพ่อแม่อุปถัมภ์ [luk khong pho mae up pa tham]

goddaughter ['gɒdˌdɔːtə] n ลูกสาวอุปถัมภ์ [luk sao up pa tham]

godfather ['gɒdˌfɑːðə] n (baptism) พ่ออุปถัมภ์ [phor op pa tam], (criminal leader) เจ้าพ่อ [chao pho]

godmother ['gɒdˌmʌðə] n แม่อุปถัมภ์ [mae up pa tham]

go down [gəʊ daʊn] v ลงไป [long pai]

godson ['gɒd,sʌn] n ลูกชายอุปถัมภ์ [luk chai up pa tham]

goggles ['gɒg²lz] npl แว่นตากันลม/ ฝุ่น/ น้ำ [waen ta kan lom/ fun/ nam]

go in [gəʊ ɪn] v เข้าไป [khao pai]

gold [gəʊld] n ทอง [thong]

golden ['gəʊldən] adj เหมือนทอง [muean thong]

goldfish ['gəʊld,fɪʃ] n ปลาทอง [pla thong]

gold-plated ['gəʊld'pleɪtɪd] adj เคลือบ ทอง [khlueap thong]

golf [gɒlf] n กีฬากอล์ฟ [ki la kolf]; **golf club** n (game) ไม้ตีกอล์ฟ [mai ti kolf], (society) สโมสรกอล์ฟ [sa mo son kolf]; **golf course** n สนามกอล์ฟ [sa nam kop]

gone [gɒn] adj จากไป [chak pai]

good [gʊd] adj ดี [di]; **Good afternoon** สวัสดีตอนบ่าย [sa wat di ton bai]; **Good evening** สวัสดีตอนเย็น [sa wat di ton yen]; **It's quite good** ค่อนข้างดี [khon khang di]

goodbye [,gʊd'baɪ] excl ลาก่อน [la kon]

good-looking ['gʊd'lʊkɪŋ] adj หน้าตาดี [na ta di]

good-natured ['gʊd'neɪtʃəd] adj คน ใจดี [khon jai dii]

goods [gʊdz] npl สินค้า [sin kha]

go off [gəʊ ɒf] v จากไป [chak pai]

Google® ['guː,gᵊl] v หาข้อมูลบน อินเตอร์เน็ต [ha khor mun bon in toe net]

go on [gəʊ ɒn] v ดำเนินการต่อไป [dam noen kan to pai]

goose, geese [guːs, giːs] n ห่าน [han]; **goose pimples** npl ขนลุก [khon luk]

gooseberry ['gʊzbərɪ; -brɪ] n ผลไม้ ชนิดหนึ่งมีลูกสีเขียว [phon la mai cha nit hueng mee luk see khiao]

go out [gəʊ aʊt] v ออกไป [ok pai]

go past [gəʊ pɑːst] v เดินผ่านไป [doen phan pai]

gorgeous ['gɔːdʒəs] adj สวยงาม [suai ngam]

gorilla [gə'rɪlə] n ลิงกอริลล่า [ling ko ril la]

go round [gəʊ raʊnd] v วนไปวนมา [won pai won ma]

gospel ['gɒspᵊl] n คำสอนของพระเยซู [kham son khong phra ye su]

gossip ['gɒsɪp] n การนินทา [kan nin tha] ▷ v นินทา [nin tha]

go through [gəʊ θruː] v ผ่านไป [phan pai]

go up [gəʊ ʌp] v ขึ้นไป [khuen pai]

government ['gʌvənmənt; 'gʌvəmənt] n รัฐบาล [rat tha ban]

gown [gaʊn] n **dressing gown** n เสื้อ คลุม [suea khlum]

GP [dʒiː piː] abbr ตัวย่อของแพทย์ทั่วไป [tua yor khong phaet thua pai]

GPS [dʒiː piː ɛs] abbr ระบบการค้นหาทาง โดยใช้ดาวเทียม [ra bop kan khon ha thang doi chai dao thiam]

grab [græb] v จับฉวย [chap chuai]

graceful ['greɪsfʊl] adj อย่างสง่างาม [yang sa ngan gam]

grade [greɪd] n ระดับชั้น [ra dap chan]

gradual ['grædjʊəl] adj ค่อยเป็นค่อยไป [khoi pen phoi pai]

gradually ['grædjʊəlɪ] adv อย่างค่อยเป็น ค่อยไป [yang khoi pen khoi pai]

graduate ['grædjʊɪt] n ผู้จบปริญญา [phu job pa rin ya]

graduation [,grædjʊ'eɪʃən] n การจบ ปริญญา [kan job pa rin ya]

graffiti, graffito [græ'fiːtiː, græ'fiːtəʊ] npl ภาพวาดหรือคำต่างๆที่วาด หรือสเปรย์ลงบนกำแพงหรือโปสเตอร์ [phap vad hue kham tang tang thii vad hue sa prey long bon kom phaeng hue pos toe]

grain [greɪn] n เมล็ดพืช [ma let phuet]

grammar ['græmə] n ไวยากรณ์ [wai ya kon]

grammatical [grə'mætɪkᵊl] adj ที่เกี่ยว กับไวยากรณ์ [thii kiao kap wai ya kon]

gramme [græm] n น้ำหนักเป็นกรัม [nam nak pen kram]

grand [grænd] adj ยิ่งใหญ่ [ying yai]

grandchild ['græn,tʃaɪld] n หลาน [lan]; **grandchildren** npl หลาน ๆ [lan lan]

granddad ['græn,dæd] n ปู่ ตา [pu ta]

granddaughter ['græn,dɔːtə] n หลาน สาว [lan sao]

grandfather ['græn,fɑːðə] n ปู่ ตา [pu ta]

grandma ['græn,mɑː] n ย่า ยาย [ya, yai]

grandmother ['græn,mʌðə] n ย่า ยาย [ya, yai]

grandpa ['græn,pɑː] n ตา [ta]

grandparents ['græn,pɛərəntz] npl ปู่ ย่า ตา ยาย [pu ya ta yai]

grandson ['grænsʌn; 'grænd-] n หลาน ชาย [lan chai]

granite ['grænɪt] n หินแกรนิต [hin krae nit]

granny ['grænɪ] n ยาย ย่า [yai, ya]

grant [grɑːnt] n เงินทุน [ngoen thun]

grape [greɪp] n องุ่น [a ngun]

grapefruit ['greɪp,fruːt] n ส้มโอฝรั่ง [som o fa rang]

graph [grɑːf; græf] n กราฟ [krap]

graphics ['græfɪks] npl ภาพกราฟฟิก [phap kraf fik]

grasp [grɑːsp] v คว้า [khwa]

grass [grɑːs] n (informer) คนที่ส่งข้อมูลให้ ตำรวจ [kon thiisong khor mun hai tam ruad], (marijuana) กัญชา [kan cha], (plant) หญ้า [ya]

grasshopper ['grɑːs,hɒpə] n ตั๊กแตน [tak ka taen]

grate [greɪt] v ขูดออก [khud ok]

grateful ['greɪtfʊl] adj ซึ่งสำนึกในบุญคุณ [sueng sam nuek nai bun khun]

grave [greɪv] n หลุมฝังศพ [lum fang sop]

gravel ['grævəl] n ก้อนกรวด [kon kraut]

gravestone ['greɪv,stəʊn] n หินสลักหน้า หลุมฝังศพ [hin sa lak na lum fang sop]

graveyard ['greɪv,jɑːd] n สุสาน [su san]

gravy ['greɪvɪ] n น้ำที่หยดออกมาจากเนื้อ [nam thii yot ok ma chak nuea]

grease [griːs] n น้ำมัน [nam man]

greasy ['griːzɪ; -sɪ] adj เป็นไขมันลื่น [pen khai man luen]

great [greɪt] adj ยิ่งใหญ่ [ying yai]

Great Britain ['greɪt 'brɪtən] n ประเทศ สหราชอาณาจักร [pra tet sa ha rat cha a na chak]

great-grandfather ['greɪt'græn,fɑːðə] n ทวด [thuat]

great-grandmother ['greɪt'græn,mʌðə] n ทวด [thuat]

Greece [griːs] n ประเทศกรีก [pra ted krik]

greedy ['griːdɪ] adj โลภ [lop]

Greek [griːk] adj แห่งประเทศกรีก [haeng pra tet krik] ▷ n (language) ภาษากรีก [pha sa krik], (person) ชาวกรีก [chao kriik]

green [griːn] adj (colour) สีเขียว [sii khiao], (inexperienced) คนอ่อนหัด [khon on hat] ▷ n สีเขียว [sii khiao]; **green salad** n สลัดผักสีเขียว [sa lat phak sii khiao]

greengrocer's ['griːn,grəʊsəz] n ร้าน ขายผักและผลไม้สด [ran khai phak lae phon la mai sot]

greenhouse ['griːn,haʊs] n เรือนกระจก สำหรับปลูกต้นไม้ [ruean kra chok sam rap pluk ton mai]

Greenland ['griːnlənd] n ประเทศ กรีนแลนด์ [pra tet krin laen]

greet [griːt] v ทักทาย [thak thai]

greeting ['griːtɪŋ] n คำทักทาย [kham thak thai]; **greetings card** n บัตร อวยพร [bat uai phon]

grey [greɪ] adj สีเทา [sii thao]

grey-haired [,greɪ'hɛəd] adj ที่มีผมสีเทา [thii mii phom sii thao]

grid [grɪd] n ตะแกรง [ta klaeng]

grief [griːf] n ความเศร้าโศก [khwam sao sok]

grill [grɪl] n อาหารย่าง [a han yang] ▷ v

ย่าง [yang]

grilled [grɪld] *adj* ซึ่งถูกย่าง [sueng thuk yang]

grim [grɪm] *adj* เคร่งขรึม [khreng khruem]

grin [grɪn] *n* การยิ้มอย่างเปิดเผย [kan yim yang poet phoei] ▷ *v* ยิ้มยิงฟัน [yim ying fan]

grind [graɪnd] *v* บด [bot]

grip [grɪp] *v* จับอย่างแน่น [chab yang naen]

gripping ['grɪpɪŋ] *adj* น่าติดใจ [na tit jai]

grit [grɪt] *n* กรวดทราย [kraut sai]

groan [grəʊn] *v* คราง [khrang]

grocer ['grəʊsə] *n* คนขายของชำ [khon khai khong cham]

groceries ['grəʊsərɪz] *npl* อาหารและสิ่งอื่น ๆ ขายที่ร้านขายของชำ [a han lae sing uen uen khai thii ran khai khong cham]

grocer's ['grəʊsəz] *n* ร้านขายของชำ [ran khai khong cham]

groom [gruːm; grʊm] *n* คนเลี้ยงม้า [kon liang ma], *(bridegroom)* เจ้าบ่าว [chao bao]

grope [grəʊp] *v* คลำ [khlam]

gross [grəʊs] *adj (fat)* ที่มีมันเยอะ [thii mee man yuea], *(income etc.)* เบื้องต้น [bueang ton]

grossly [grəʊslɪ] *adv* มากเกินไป [mak koen pai]

ground [graʊnd] *n* พื้นดิน [phuen din] ▷ *v* วางลงบนพื้น [wang long bon phuen]; **ground floor** *n* ชั้นล่าง [chan lang]

group [gruːp] *n* กลุ่ม [klum]; **Are there any reductions for groups?** มีส่วนลดสำหรับกลุ่มต่าง ๆ หรือไม่? [mii suan lot sam rap klum tang tang rue mai]

grouse [graʊs] *n (complaint)* การบ่น [kan bon], *(game bird)* ไก่ป่า [kai pa]

grow [grəʊ] *vi* เติบโต งอกงาม [toep to, ngok ngam] ▷ *vt* ปลูก ทำให้เจริญเติบโต [pluk, tham hai cha roen toep to]

growl [graʊl] *v* บ่นด้วยความโกรธ [bon duai khwam krot]

grown-up [grəʊnʌp] *n* ผู้ใหญ่ [phu yai]

growth [grəʊθ] *n* ความเติบโต [khwam toep to]

grow up [grəʊ ʌp] *v* เจริญเติบโต [cha roen toep to]

grub [grʌb] *n* ตัวอ่อนของแมลง [tua on khong ma laeng]

grudge [grʌdʒ] *n* ความไม่เต็มใจ [khwam mai tem jai]

gruesome ['gruːsəm] *adj* น่ากลัว [na klua]

grumpy ['grʌmpɪ] *adj* อารมณ์บูดบึ้ง [a rom but bueng]

guarantee [ˌgærən'tiː] *n* การรับประกัน [kan rap pra kan] ▷ *v* รับประกัน [rap pra kan]

guard [gɑːd] *n* ยาม [yam] ▷ *v* เฝ้า [fao]; **security guard** *n* ผู้คุ้มกันความปลอดภัย [phu khum kan khwam plot phai]; **Have you seen the guard?** คุณเห็นคนเฝ้ารถไฟไหม? [khun hen khon fao rot fai mai]

Guatemala [ˌgwɑːtə'mɑːlə] *n* ประเทศกัวเตมาลา [pra tet kua te ma la]

guess [gɛs] *n* การคาดคะเน [kan khat kha ne] ▷ *v* คาดคะเน [khat kha ne]

guest [gɛst] *n* แขกที่มาเยี่ยม [khaek thii ma yiam]

guesthouse ['gɛstˌhaʊs] *n* บ้านรับรองแขก [baan rab rong khaek]

guide [gaɪd] *n* คนนำทาง [khon nam thang] ▷ *v* นำทาง [nam thang]; **guide dog** *n* สุนัขนำทาง [su nak nam thang]; **guided tour** *n* กรุ๊ปทัวร์ [krup thua]; **tour guide** *n* มัคคุเทศก์ [mak khu thet]; **Can you guide me, please?** คุณช่วยนำทางให้ฉันด้วยได้ไหม? [khun chuai nam thang hai chan duai dai mai]; **Do you have a guide to local walks?** คุณมีไกด์นำทางเดินเส้นทางท้องถิ่นไหม? [khun mii kai nam thang doen sen thang thong thin mai]; **I have a guide**

dog ฉันมีสุนัขนำทาง [chan mii su nak nam thang]

guidebook ['gaɪdˌbʊk] *n* หนังสือที่ให้ข้อมูลกับนักท่องเที่ยว [nang sue thii hai kho mun kap nak thong thiao]

guilt [gɪlt] *n* ความผิด [khwam phit]

guilty ['gɪltɪ] *adj* เกี่ยวกับความผิด [kiao kap khwam phit]

Guinea ['gɪnɪ] *n* ประเทศกินี [pra tet ki ni]; **guinea pig** *n* (for experiment) หนูตะเภาสำหรับทดลอง [nu ta phao sam rap thot long], (rodent) หนูตะเภา [nu ta phao]

guitar [gɪ'tɑː] *n* กีตาร์ [ki ta]

gum [gʌm] *n* เหงือก [ngueak], หมากฝรั่ง [mak fa rang]; **chewing gum** *n* หมากฝรั่ง [mak fa rang]; **My gums are bleeding** เหงือกฉันเลือดออก [ngueak chan lueat ok]; **My gums are sore** เหงือกฉันปวด [ngueak chan puat]

gun [gʌn] *n* ปืน [puen]; **machine gun** *n* ปืนกล [puen kon]

gust [gʌst] *n* ลมแรงพัดกะทันหัน [lom raeng phat kra tan han]

gut [gʌt] *n* ไส้พุง [sai phung]

guy [gaɪ] *n* ผู้ชาย [phu chai]

Guyana [gaɪ'ænə] *n* ประเทศกูยาน่า [pra tet ku ya na]

gym [dʒɪm] *n* โรงยิม [rong yim]

gymnast ['dʒɪmnæst] *n* นักกายบริหาร [nak kai bo ri han]

gymnastics [dʒɪm'næstɪks] *npl* กายบริหาร [kai bo ri han]

gynaecologist [ˌgaɪnɪ'kɒlədʒɪst] *n* สูตินารีแพทย์ [su ti na ri phaet]

gypsy ['dʒɪpsɪ] *n* ชาวยิปซี [chao yip si]

habit ['hæbɪt] *n* ความเคยชิน [khwam khoei chin]

hack [hæk] *v* ฟัน [fan]

hacker ['hækə] *n* ผู้ที่ชำนาญในการใช้เครื่องคอมพิวเตอร์ในทางที่ผิดกฎหมาย [phu thii cham nan nai kan chai khueang khom pio ter nai thang thii phid kod mai]

haddock ['hædək] *n* ปลาแฮดดอค [pla haed dok]

haemorrhoids ['hɛməˌrɔɪdz] *npl* ริดสีดวงทวาร [rit si duang tha wan]

haggle ['hægᵊl] *v* ต่อรองราคา [to rong ra kha]

hail [heɪl] *n* ลูกเห็บ [luk hep] ▷ *v* โห่ร้องอวยชัย [ho rong uai chai]

hair [hɛə] *n* ผม [phom]; **Can you dye my hair, please?** คุณช่วยย้อมผมให้ฉันได้ไหม? [khun chuai yom phom hai chan dai mai]; **Can you straighten my hair?** คุณยืดผมฉันให้ตรงได้ไหม? [khun yuet phom chan hai trong dai mai]; **I have greasy hair** ฉันมีผมมัน [chan mii phom man]

hairband ['hɛəˌbænd] *n* ยางรัดผม [yang

rat phom]

hairbrush ['hɛə,brʌʃ] *n* แปรงแปรงผม [praeng praeng phom]

haircut ['hɛə,kʌt] *n* การตัดผม [kan tat phom]

hairdo ['hɛə,duː] *n* ทรงผม [song phom]

hairdresser ['hɛə,drɛsə] *n* ช่างทำผม [chang tham phom]

hairdresser's ['hɛə,drɛsəz] *n* ที่ร้านช่าง ทำผม [thii ran chang tham phom]

hairdryer ['hɛə,draɪə] *n* เครื่องเป่าผม [khrueang pao phom]

hairgrip ['hɛəgrɪp] *n* กิ๊บติดผม [kip tit phom]

hairstyle ['hɛəstaɪl] *n* ทรงผม [song phom]

hairy ['hɛərɪ] *adj* เต็มไปด้วยขน [tem pai duai khon]

Haiti ['heɪtɪ; hɑː'iːtɪ] *n* ประเทศไฮติ [pra tet hai ti]

half [hɑːf] *adj* ครึ่ง [khrueng] ▷ *adv* ครึ่ง [khrueng] ▷ *n* ครึ่งหนึ่ง [khrueng hueng]; **half board** *n* ที่พักอาหารเช้าและ เย็น [thii phak a han chao lae yen]; **It's half past two** เวลาสองโมงครึ่ง [we la song mong khrueng]

half-hour ['hɑːf,aʊə] *n* ครึ่งชั่วโมง [khrueng chau mong]

half-price ['hɑːf,praɪs] *adj* ครึ่งราคา [khrueng ra kha] ▷ *adv* อย่างครึ่งราคา [yang khrueng ra kha]

half-term ['hɑːf,tɜːm] *n* ครึ่งเทอม [khrueng thoem]

half-time ['hɑːf,taɪm] *n* ครึ่งเวลา [khrueng we la]

halfway [,hɑːf'weɪ] *adv* ครึ่งทาง [khrueng thang]

hall [hɔːl] *n* ห้องโถง [hong thong]; **town hall** *n* ศาลากลางจังหวัด [sa la klang changhwat]

hallway ['hɔːl,weɪ] *n* ทางเดินห้องโถง [thang doen hong thong]

halt [hɔːlt] *n* การหยุด [kan yud]

ham [hæm] *n* ต้นขาหลังของหมู [ton kha

lang khong mu]

hamburger ['hæm,bɜːgə] *n* แฮมเบอร์เกอร์ [haem boe koe]

hammer ['hæmə] *n* ค้อน [khon]

hammock ['hæmək] *n* เปล [ple]

hamster ['hæmstə] *n* สัตว์ชนิดหนึ่งคล้าย หนู [sat cha nit nueng khlai nu]

hand [hænd] *n* มือ [mue] ▷ *v* ส่งให้ [song hai]; **hand luggage** *n* กระเป๋าเดินทางใบ เล็กที่ถือขึ้นเครื่องบิน [kra pao doen thang bai lek thii thue khuen khrueang bin]; **Where can I wash my hands?** ฉันล้าง มือได้ที่ไหน? [chan lang mue dai thii nai]

handbag ['hænd,bæg] *n* กระเป๋าถือ [kra pao thue]

handball ['hænd,bɔːl] *n* กีฬาเล่นโดยใช้ ลูกบอลโยนกับกำแพง [ki la len doi chai luk bal yon kap kam phaeng]

handbook ['hænd,bʊk] *n* หนังสือคู่มือ [nang sue khu mue]

handbrake ['hænd,breɪk] *n* เบรคมือ [brek mue]

handcuffs ['hænd,kʌfs] *npl* ที่ใส่ กุญแจมือ [thii sai kun jae mue]

handicap ['hændɪ,kæp] *n* **My handicap is...** แต้มต่อของฉันคือ... [taem to khong chan khue...]; **What's your handicap?** แต้มต่อของคุณเท่าไร? [taem to khong khun thao rai]

handicapped ['hændɪ,kæpt] *adj* พิการ [phi kan]

handkerchief ['hæŋkətʃɪf; -tʃiːf] *n* ผ้าเช็ดหน้า [pha chet na]

handle ['hændəl] *n* ด้าม [dam] ▷ *v* จัดการ [chat kan]

handlebars ['hændəl,bɑːz] *npl* มือถือ สำหรับเลี้ยวรถจักรยาน [mue thue sam rap liao rot chak kra yan]

handmade [,hænd'meɪd] *adj* ที่ทำด้วย มือ [thii tham duai mue]; **Is this handmade?** เป็นของที่ทำด้วยมือหรือ เปล่า? [pen khong thii tham duai mue rue plao]

hands-free ['hændz‚friː] *adj* ไม่ใช้มือ [mai chai mue]; **hands-free kit** *n* อุปกรณ์ที่ไม่ต้องใช้มือ [up pa kon thii mai tong chai mue]

handsome ['hændsəm] *adj* หล่อ [lo]

handwriting ['hænd‚raitiŋ] *n* ลายมือ [lai mue]

handy ['hændi] *adj* ใช้สะดวก [chai sa duak]

hang [hæŋ] *vi* แขวน [khwaen]

hanger ['hæŋə] *n* ไม้แขวนเสื้อ [mai khwaen suea]

hang-gliding ['hæŋ'glaidiŋ] *n* เครื่องร่อน [khrueang ron]

hang on [hæŋ ɒn] *v* คอย [khoi]

hangover ['hæŋ‚əʊvə] *n* การเมาค้าง [kan mao kang]

hang up [hæŋ ʌp] *v* วางหูโทรศัพท์ [wang hu tho ra sap]

hankie ['hæŋki] *n* ผ้าเช็ดหน้า [pha chet na]

happen ['hæpən] *v* เกิดขึ้น [koet khuen]; **When did it happen?** เกิดขึ้นเมื่อไร? [koet khuen muea rai]

happily ['hæpili] *adv* อย่างมีความสุข [yang mee khwam suk]

happiness ['hæpinis] *n* ความสุข [khwam suk]

happy ['hæpi] *adj* เป็นสุข [pen suk]

harassment ['hærəsmənt] *n* การรังควาน [kan rang khwan]

harbour ['hɑːbə] *n* ท่าเรือ [tha rue]

hard [hɑːd] *adj* (difficult) ยาก [yak], (firm, rigid) แข็ง [khaeng] ▷ *adv* ยากเย็น [yak yen]; **hard disk** *n* แผ่นบันทึก [phaen ban thuek]; **hard shoulder** *n* ไหล่ทาง [lai thang]

hardboard ['hɑːd‚bɔːd] *n* ไม้อัด [mai at]

hardly ['hɑːdli] *adv* เกือบจะไม่ [kueap ja mai]

hard up [hɑːd ʌp] *adj* หมดเงิน [mot ngoen]

hardware ['hɑːd‚wɛə] *n* เครื่องใช้ที่ทำด้วยโลหะ [khrueang chai thii tham duai lo ha]

hare [hɛə] *n* กระต่ายป่า [kra tai pa]

harm [hɑːm] *v* ทำอันตราย [tham an tra lai]

harmful ['hɑːmfʊl] *adj* เป็นอันตราย [pen an ta rai]

harmless ['hɑːmlis] *adj* ไม่มีอันตราย [mai mii an ta rai]

harp [hɑːp] *n* พิณตั้ง [phin tang]

harsh [hɑːʃ] *adj* หยาบ [yap]

harvest ['hɑːvist] *n* การเก็บเกี่ยว [kan kep kiao] ▷ *v* เก็บเกี่ยว [kep kiao]

hastily [heistili] *adv* อย่างรีบเร่ง [yang rip reng]

hat [hæt] *n* หมวก [muak]

hatchback ['hætʃ‚bæk] *n* รถยนต์ที่มีประตูหลัง [rot yon thii mii pra tu lang]

hate [heit] *v* เกลียด [kliat]; **I hate...** ฉันเกลียด... [chan kliat...]

hatred ['heitrid] *n* ความเกลียด [khwam kliat]

haunted ['hɔːntid] *adj* ซึ่งสิงอยู่ [sueng sing yu]

have [hæv] *v* มี [mi]; **Do you have a room?** คุณมีห้องว่างสักห้องไหม? [khun mii hong wang sak hong mai]; **I don't have any children** ฉันไม่มีลูก [chan mai mii luk]; **I have a child** ฉันมีลูกหนึ่งคน [chan mii luk nueng khon]

have to [hæv tʊ] *v* ต้อง [tong]; **Do you have to be a member?** คุณต้องเป็นสมาชิกหรือไม่? [khun tong pen sa ma chik rue mai]; **We will have to report it to the police** เราต้องแจ้งกับตำรวจ [rao tong chaeng kap tam ruat]; **Will I have to pay?** ฉันต้องจ่ายไหม? [chan tong chai mai]

hawthorn ['hɔː‚θɔːn] *n* ต้นฮอธอน [ton ho thon]

hay [hei] *n* หญ้าแห้ง [ya haeng]; **hay fever** *n* ไข้ละอองฟาง [khai la ong fang]

haystack ['hei‚stæk] *n* กองหญ้า [kong ya]

hazelnut ['heizəl‚nʌt] *n* ถั่วเฮเซลนัท

[thua he sel nat]

he [hiː] *pron* เขาผู้ชาย [khao phu chai]

head [hɛd] *n (body part)* ศีรษะ [si sa], *(principal)* ครูใหญ่ [khru yai] ▷ *v* นำ [nam]; **deputy head** *n* รองอาจารย์ใหญ่ [rong a chan yai]; **head office** *n* สำนักงานใหญ่ [sam nak ngan yai]

headache [ˈhɛdˌeɪk] *n* ปวดหัว [puat hua]; **I'd like something for a headache** ฉันอยากได้อะไรสักอย่างเพื่อแก้ปวดหัว [chan yak dai a rai sak yang phuea kae puat hua]

headlamp [ˈhɛdˌlæmp] *n* ไฟหน้าของรถยนต์ [fai na khong rot yon]

headlight [ˈhɛdˌlaɪt] *n* ไฟหน้าของรถยนต์ [fai na khong rot yon]

headline [ˈhɛdˌlaɪn] *n* หัวข่าว [hua khao]

headphones [ˈhɛdˌfəʊnz] *npl* หูฟัง [hu fang]; **Does it have headphones?** มีหูฟังไหม? [mii hu fang mai]

headquarters [ˌhɛdˈkwɔːtəz] *npl* กองบัญชาการ [kong ban cha kaan]

headroom [ˈhɛdˌrʊm; -ˌruːm] *n* ที่ว่างเหนือศีรษะ [thii wang nuea si sa]

headscarf, headscarves [ˈhɛdˌskɑːf, ˈhɛdˌskɑːvz] *n* ผ้าพันศีรษะ [pha phan sri sa]

headteacher [ˈhɛdˌtiːtʃə] *n* ครูใหญ่ [khru yai]

heal [hiːl] *v* รักษา [rak sa]

health [hɛlθ] *n* สุขภาพ [suk kha phap]; **I don't have health insurance** ฉันไม่มีประกันสุขภาพส่วนตัว [chan mai mii pra kan suk kha phap suan tua]; **I have private health insurance** ฉันมีประกันสุขภาพส่วนตัว [chan mii pra kan suk kha phap suan tua]

healthy [ˈhɛlθɪ] *adj* มีสุขภาพดี [mii suk kha phap di]

heap [hiːp] *n* กอง [kong]

hear [hɪə] *v* ได้ยิน [dai yin]

hearing [ˈhɪərɪŋ] *n* การได้ยิน [kan dai yin]; **hearing aid** *n* เครื่องช่วยฟัง

[khrueang chuai fang]

heart [hɑːt] *n* หัวใจ [hua chai]; **heart attack** *n* หัวใจวาย [hua jai wai]; **I have a heart condition** ฉันมีอาการทางหัวใจ [chan mii a kan thang hua jai]

heartbroken [ˈhɑːtˌbrəʊkən] *adj* อกหัก [ok hak]

heartburn [ˈhɑːtˌbɜːn] *n* ร้อนใน [ron nai]

heat [hiːt] *n* ความร้อน [khwam ron] ▷ *v* ทำให้ร้อน [tham hai ron]

heater [ˈhiːtə] *n* เครื่องทำความร้อน [khrueang tham khwam ron]

heather [ˈhɛðə] *n* เครื่องทำความร้อน [khrueang tham khwam ron]

heating [ˈhiːtɪŋ] *n* การทำให้อุ่น [kan tham hai un]; **central heating** *n* ระบบทำความร้อน [ra bop tham khwam ron]

heat up [hiːt ʌp] *v* อุ่น [un]

heaven [ˈhɛvˀn] *n* สวรรค์ [sa wan]

heavily [ˈhɛvɪlɪ] *adv* อย่างหนัก [yang nak]

heavy [ˈhɛvɪ] *adj* หนัก [nak]; **This is too heavy** นี่หนักเกินไป [ni nak koen pai]

hedge [hɛdʒ] *n* รั้ว [rua]

hedgehog [ˈhɛdʒˌhɒg] *n* เม่น [men]

heel [hiːl] *n* ส้นเท้า [son thao]; **high heels** *npl* รองเท้าส้นสูง [rong thao son sung]

height [haɪt] *n* ความสูง [khwam sung]

heir [ɛə] *n* ทายาท [tha yat]

heiress [ˈɛərɪs] *n* ทายาทหญิง [tha yat ying]

helicopter [ˈhɛlɪˌkɒptə] *n* เฮลิคอปเตอร์ [he li kop toe]

hell [hɛl] *n* นรก [na rok]

hello [hɛˈləʊ] *excl* สวัสดี [sa wat di]

helmet [ˈhɛlmɪt] *n* หมวกกันน็อก [muak kan nok]

help [hɛlp] *n* ความช่วยเหลือ [khwam chuai luea] ▷ *v* ช่วย [chuai]; **Can you help me?** คุณช่วยฉันได้ไหม? [khun chuai chan dai mai]; **Fetch help quickly!** ขอคนมาช่วยเร็วหน่อย [kho khon ma chuai reo noi]; **Help!** ช่วยด้วย

[chuai duai]

helpful ['hɛlpfʊl] *adj* เป็นประโยชน์ [pen pra yot]

helpline ['hɛlpˌlaɪn] *n* การให้ความช่วยเหลือทางโทรศัพท์ [kan hai khwam chuai luea thang tho ra sap]

hen [hɛn] *n* แม่ไก่ [mae kai]; **hen night** *n* งานปาร์ตี้ที่หญิงสาวฉลองคืนก่อนวันแต่งงาน [ngan pa tii thii ying sao cha long khuen kon wan taeng ngan]

hepatitis [ˌhɛpəˈtaɪtɪs] *n* โรคตับอักเสบ [rok tap ak sep]

her [hɜː; hə; ə] *pron* เธอ [thoe], ของหล่อน [khong hlon]; **She has hurt her leg** เธอทำขาเธอเจ็บ [thoe tham kha thoe chep]

herbs [hɜːbz] *npl* สมุนไพร [sa mun phrai]

herd [hɜːd] *n* ฝูงสัตว์ [fung sat]

here [hɪə] *adv* ที่นี่ [thi ni]; **I'm here for work** ฉันมาทำงานที่นี่ [chan ma tham ngan thii ni]; **I'm here on my own** ฉันมาที่นี่คนเดียว [chan ma thii ni khon diao]

hereditary [hɪˈrɛdɪtərɪ; -trɪ] *adj* เป็นกรรมพันธุ์ [pen kam ma phan]

heritage ['hɛrɪtɪdʒ] *n* มรดก [mo ra dok]

hernia ['hɜːnɪə] *n* โรคไส้เลื่อน [rok sai luean]

hero ['hɪərəʊ] *n* วีรบุรุษ [wi ra bu rut]

heroin ['hɛrəʊɪn] *n* เฮโรอิน [he ro in]

heroine ['hɛrəʊɪn] *n* วีรสตรี [wi ra sa tri]

heron ['hɛrən] *n* นกกระสา [nok kra sa]

herring ['hɛrɪŋ] *n* ปลาเฮอริง [pla hoe ring]

hers [hɜːz] *pron* ของหล่อน [khong hlon]

herself [həˈsɛlf] *pron* หล่อนเอง [lon eng]

hesitate ['hɛzɪˌteɪt] *v* ลังเลใจ [lang le jai]

heterosexual [ˌhɛtərəʊˈsɛksjʊəl] *adj* เกี่ยวกับเพศตรงข้าม [kiao kap phet trong kham]

HGV [eɪtʃ dʒiː viː] *abbr* ตัวย่อของยานพาหนะที่สามารถบรรทุกของหนัก [tua yo khong yan pha ha na thii sa maat ban thuk khong nak]

hi [haɪ] *excl* สวัสดี [sa wat di]

hiccups ['hɪkʌps] *npl* สะอึก [sa uek]

hidden ['hɪdᵊn] *adj* ซึ่งปิดบัง [sueng pit bang]

hide [haɪd] *vi* ซ่อน ปกปิด [son, pok pit] ▷ *vt* ซ่อน ซุกซ่อน [son, suk son]

hide-and-seek [ˌhaɪdændˈsiːk] *n* การเล่นซ่อนหา [kan len saun ha]

hideous ['hɪdɪəs] *adj* อัปลักษณ์ [ap pa lak]

hifi ['haɪˈfaɪ] *n* เครื่องไฮไฟ [khrueang hai fai]

high [haɪ] *adj* สูง [sung] ▷ *adv* อย่างสูง [yang sung]; **high heels** *npl* รองเท้าส้นสูง [rong thao son sung]; **high jump** *n* กระโดดสูง [kra dot sung]; **high season** *n* ฤดูกาลที่มีธุรกิจมาก [rue du kan thii mii thu ra kit mak]; **How high is it?** สูงแค่ไหน? [sung khae nai]

highchair ['haɪˌtʃɛə] *n* เก้าอี้เด็ก [kao ee dek]

high-heeled ['haɪˌhiːld] *adj* ที่มีส้นสูง [thii mii son sung]

highlight ['haɪˌlaɪt] *n* จุดเด่น [chut den] ▷ *v* เน้น [nen]

highlighter ['haɪˌlaɪtə] *n* ปากกาสะท้อนแสงที่ใช้เน้นข้อความให้เด่นชัด [pak ka sa thon saeng thii chai nen kho khwam hai den chat]

high-rise ['haɪˌraɪz] *n* ตึกสูง [tuek sung]

hijack ['haɪˌdʒæk] *v* ปล้น [plon]

hijacker ['haɪˌdʒækə] *n* โจรปล้นจี้ [chon plon chi]

hike [haɪk] *n* การเดินทางไกลด้วยเท้า [kan doen thang kai duai thao]

hiking [haɪkɪŋ] *n* การเดินทางไกลในชนบท [kan doen thang kai nai chon na bot]

hilarious [hɪˈlɛərɪəs] *adj* สนุกสนานเฮฮา [sa nuk sa nan he ha]

hill [hɪl] *n* เขาเตี้ย ๆ [khao tia tia]

hill-walking ['hɪlˌwɔːkɪŋ] n เดินเขา [doen khao]

him [hɪm; ɪm] pron เขาผู้ชาย [khao phu chai]

himself [hɪm'sɛlf; ɪm'sɛlf] pron ตัวเขาเอง [tua khao eng]

Hindu ['hɪnduː; hɪn'duː] adj ชาวฮินดู [chao hin du] ▷ n แขกที่นับถือศาสนาฮินดู [khaek thii nap thue sat sa na hin du]

Hinduism ['hɪnduˌɪzəm] n ศาสนาฮินดู [sat sa na hin du]

hinge [hɪndʒ] n บานพับ [ban phap]

hint [hɪnt] n การบอกใบ้ [kan bok bai] ▷ v บอกใบ้ [bok bai]

hip [hɪp] n สะโพก [sa phok]

hippie ['hɪpɪ] n พวกฮิปปี้ [phuak hip pi]

hippo ['hɪpəʊ] n ฮิปโป [hip po]

hippopotamus, hippopotami [ˌhɪpə'pɒtəməs, ˌhɪpə'pɒtəmaɪ] n ฮิปโป [hip po]

hire ['haɪə] n การให้เช่า [kan hai chao] ▷ v เช่า [chao]; **Can we hire the equipment?** เราจะเช่าอุปกรณ์ได้ที่ไหน? [rao ja chao up pa kon dai thii nai]; **Do they hire out rackets?** เขามีไม้เล่นเทนนิสให้เช่าไหม? [khao mii mai len then nis hai chao mai]; **Do you hire push-chairs?** คุณมีรถเข็นเด็กให้เช่าไหม? [khun mii rot khen dek hai chao mai]

his [hɪz; ɪz] adj ของเขา [khong khao] ▷ pron ของเขาผู้ชาย [khong khao phu chai]

historian [hɪ'stɔːrɪən] n นักประวัติศาสตร์ [nak pra wat ti saat]

historical [hɪ'stɒrɪkəl] adj ที่เกี่ยวกับประวัติศาสตร์ [thii kiao kap pra wat ti saat]

history ['hɪstərɪ; 'hɪstrɪ] n ประวัติศาสตร์ [pra wat ti sat]

hit [hɪt] n การตี [kan ti] ▷ v ตี [ti]

hitch [hɪtʃ] n การหยุดชะงัก [kan yut cha ngak]

hitchhike ['hɪtʃˌhaɪk] v โบกรถเพื่อนเดินทาง [bok rot phuean doen thang]

hitchhiker ['hɪtʃˌhaɪkə] n คนที่เดินทางโดยการขออาศัยรถคนอื่น [kon thii doen thang doi kan khor a sai rot kon aue]

hitchhiking ['hɪtʃˌhaɪkɪŋ] n เดินทางโดยอาศัยรถของผู้อื่น [doen thang doi a sai rot khong phu aue]

HIV-negative [eɪtʃ aɪ viː 'nɛgətɪv] adj ไม่มีเชื้อไวรัสที่ทำให้เกิดโรคเอดส์ [mai mii chuea vai ras thii tham hai koet rok aid]

HIV-positive [eɪtʃ aɪ viː 'pɒzɪtɪv] adj มีเชื้อไวรัสที่ทำให้เกิดโรคเอดส์ [mii chuea wai ras thii tham hai koet rok aid]

hobby ['hɒbɪ] n งานอดิเรก [ngan a di rek]

hockey ['hɒkɪ] n กีฬาฮ็อคกี้ [ki la hok ki]; **ice hockey** n กีฬาไอซ์ฮอกกี้ [ki la ai hok ki]

hold [həʊld] v ถือ [thue]; **Could you hold this for me?** คุณช่วยถือนี้ให้ฉันได้ไหม? [khun chuai thue nii hai chan dai mai]

holdall ['həʊldˌɔːl] n กระเป๋าเดินทางที่พับเก็บได้ [kra pao doen thang thii phap kep dai]

hold on [həʊld ɒn] v ยึดแน่น [yuet naen]

hold up [həʊld ʌp] v ทำให้ชักช้า [tham hai chak cha]

hold-up [həʊldʌp] n การหยุดชะงัก [kan yut cha ngak]

hole [həʊl] n รู [ru]; **I have a hole in my shoe** รองเท้าฉันมีรู [rong thao chan mii ru]

holiday ['hɒlɪˌdeɪ; -dɪ] n วันหยุด [wan yut]; **activity holiday** n วันหยุดท่องเที่ยวที่มีกิจกรรม [wan yut thong thiao thii mii kit cha kam]; **bank holiday** n วันหยุดธนาคาร [wan yut tha na khan]; **holiday home** n บ้านที่ใช้ในระหว่างเวลาหยุดงานหรือหยุดเรียน [baan thii chai nai ra wang we la yut ngan rue yut rian]

Holland ['hɒlənd] n ประเทศฮอลแลนด์ [pra tet hol laen]

hollow ['hɒləʊ] adj เป็นโพรง [pen phrong]

holly ['hɒlɪ] n ต้นฮอลลี่ [ton hol li]

holy ['həʊlɪ] *adj* เป็นที่เคารพบูชา [pen thii khao rop bu cha]

home [həʊm] *adv* ที่บ้าน [thii baan] ▷ *n* บ้าน [ban]; **home address** *n* ที่อยู่ [thi yu]; **I'd like to go home** ฉันอยากกกลับบ้าน [chan yak klap baan]; **Please come home by 11p.m.** กรุณากลับบ้านภายในห้าทุ่ม [ka ru na klap baan pai nai ha tum]; **When do you go home?** คุณจะกลับบ้านเมื่อไร? [khun ja klap baan muea rai]

homeland ['həʊm,lænd] *n* บ้านเกิดเมืองนอน [baan koed mueang norn]

homeless ['həʊmlɪs] *adj* ไม่มีบ้าน [mai mii baan]

home-made ['həʊm'meɪd] *adj* ที่ทำเองในครอบครัว [thii tham eng nai khrop khrua]

homeopathic [,həʊmɪəʊ'pæθɪk] *adj* ที่เกี่ยวกับการรักษาที่ใช้ยาจำนวนเล็กน้อยสร้างระบบเชื้อโรคในร่างกายคนที่แข็งแรง [thii kiao kab kan rak sa thii chai ya cham nuan lek noi srang ra bob chuea rok nai rang kai kon thii khaeng raeng]

homeopathy [,həʊmɪ'ɒpəθɪ] *n* วิธีการรักษาโดยใช้ยาจำนวนเล็กน้อยที่จะสร้างระบบเชื้อโรคในคนที่ร่างกายแข็งแรง [vi thi kan rak sa doi chai ya cham nuan lek noi thii ja srang ra bob chuea rok nai kon thii mee rang kai khaeng raeng]

homesick ['həʊm,sɪk] *adj* คิดถึงบ้าน [khit thueng baan]

homework ['həʊm,wɜːk] *n* การบ้าน [kan ban]

Honduras [hɒn'djʊərəs] *n* ประเทศฮอนดูรัส [pra tet hon du ras]

honest ['ɒnɪst] *adj* ซื่อสัตย์ [sue sat]

honestly ['ɒnɪstlɪ] *adv* อย่างซื่อสัตย์ [yang sue sat]

honesty ['ɒnɪstɪ] *n* ความซื่อสัตย์ [khwam sue sat]

honey ['hʌnɪ] *n* น้ำผึ้ง [nam khueng]

honeymoon ['hʌnɪ,muːn] *n* น้ำผึ้งพระจันทร์ [nam phueng phra chan]; **We are on our honeymoon** เรามาดื่มน้ำผึ้งพระจันทร์ที่นี่ [rao ma duem nam phueng phra chan thii ni]

honeysuckle ['hʌnɪ,sʌkᵊl] *n* ต้นไม้เลื้อยชนิดหนึ่งมีกลิ่นหอม [ton mai lueai cha nit nueng mii klin hom]

honour ['ɒnə] *n* เกียรติยศ [kiat ti yot]

hood [hʊd] *n* หมวกครอบ [hmuak khrob]

hook [hʊk] *n* ตะขอ [ta kho]

hooray [huː'reɪ] *excl* ฮูเร [hu re]

Hoover® ['huːvə] *n* ยี่ห้อเครื่องดูดฝุ่น [yi ho khrueang dut fun]; **hoover** *v* ดูดฝุ่น [dud fun]

hope [həʊp] *n* ความหวัง [khwam wang] ▷ *v* หวัง [wang]; **I hope the weather improves** ฉันหวังว่าอากาศคงจะดีขึ้น [chan wang wa a kaat khong ja di khuen]

hopeful ['həʊpfʊl] *adj* มีความหวัง [mii khwam wang]

hopefully ['həʊpfʊlɪ] *adv* ด้วยความหวังว่าจะสมหวัง [duai khwam hwang wa ja som hwang]

hopeless ['həʊplɪs] *adj* ไม่มีความหวัง [mai mii khwam wang]

horizon [hə'raɪzᵊn] *n* ขอบฟ้า [khop fa]

horizontal [,hɒrɪ'zɒntᵊl] *adj* แนวนอน [naeo non]

hormone ['hɔːməʊn] *n* ฮอร์โมน [ho mon]

horn [hɔːn] *n* เขา [khao]; **French horn** *n* แตรทองเหลืองรูปร่างโค้งงอ [trae thong lueang rup rang khong ngo]

horoscope ['hɒrə,skəʊp] *n* โหราศาสตร์ [ho ra sat]

horrendous [hɒ'rɛndəs] *adj* น่ากลัว [na klua]

horrible ['hɒrəbᵊl] *adj* เลวร้าย [leo rai]

horrifying ['hɒrɪ,faɪɪŋ] *adj* ที่ทำให้ขยะแขยง [thii tham hai kha ya kha yaeng]

horror ['hɒrə] *n* ความน่ากลัว [khwam na

klua]; **horror film** *n* หนังที่น่ากลัว [nang thii na klua]

horse [hɔːs] *n* ม้า [ma]; **horse racing** *n* การแข่งม้า [kan khaeng ma]; **Can we go horse riding?** เราไปขี่ม้าได้ไหม? [rao pai khi ma dai mai]; **I'd like to see a horse race** ฉันอยากดูแข่งม้า [chan yak du khaeng ma]; **Let's go horse riding** ไปขี่ม้ากันเถอะ [pai khi ma kan thoe]

horseradish ['hɔːsˌrædɪʃ] *n* สมุนไพรอย่างหนึ่งเป็นหัวมีรสเผ็ด [sa mun phrai yang nueng pen hua mii rot phet]

horseshoe ['hɔːsˌʃuː] *n* เกือกม้า [kueak ma]

hose [həʊz] *n* ข้อต่อสำหรับเครื่องอัดน้ำมันหรือน้ำ [kho to sam rap khrueang at nam man rue nam]

hosepipe ['həʊzˌpaɪp] *n* สายยาง [sai yang]

hospital ['hɒspɪtəl] *n* โรงพยาบาล [rong pha ya ban]; **How do I get to the hospital?** ฉันจะไปโรงพยาบาลได้อย่างไร? [chan ja pai rong pha ya baan dai yang rai]; **I work in a hospital** ฉันทำงานในโรงพยาบาล [chan tham ngan nai rong pha ya baan]; **We must get him to hospital** เราต้องพาเขาไปโรงพยาบาล [rao tong pha khao pai rong pha ya baan]

hospitality [ˌhɒspɪ'tælɪtɪ] *n* การรับรองแขก [kan rap rong khaek]

host [həʊst] *n* (*entertains*) เจ้าภาพ [chao phap], (*multitude*) จำนวนมาก [cham nuan mak]

hostage ['hɒstɪdʒ] *n* ตัวประกัน [tua pra kan]

hostel ['hɒstəl] *n* หอพักนักเรียน [ho phak nak rian]; **Is there a youth hostel nearby?** มีหอพักนักเรียนใกล้ๆ บ้างไหม? [mee hor phak nak rian kai kai bang mai]

hostess ['həʊstɪs] *n* **air hostess** *n* พนักงานหญิงบริการบนเครื่องบิน [pha nak ngan ying], แอร์โฮสเตส [pha nak ngan

ying bo ri kan bon khrueang bin, ae hos tes]

hostile ['hɒstaɪl] *adj* ไม่เป็นมิตร [mai pen mit]

hot [hɒt] *adj* ร้อน [ron]; **I feel hot** ฉันรู้สึกร้อน [chan ru suek ron]; **I'm too hot** ฉันร้อนเกินไป [chan ron koen pai]; **It's very hot** ร้อนมาก [ron mak]

hotel [həʊ'tɛl] *n* โรงแรม [rong raem]; **Can you book me into a hotel?** คุณจองโรงแรมให้ฉันได้ไหม? [khun chong rong raem hai chan dai mai]; **Can you recommend a hotel?** คุณแนะนำโรงแรมให้ได้ไหม? [khun nae nam rong raem hai dai mai]; **He runs the hotel** เขาดำเนินกิจการโรงแรม [khao dam noen kit cha kan rong raeng]

hour [aʊə] *n* ชั่วโมง [chua mong]; **office hours** *npl* ชั่วโมงทำงาน [chau mong tham ngan]; **opening hours** *npl* ชั่วโมงที่เปิด [chau mong thii poet]; **peak hours** *npl* ชั่วโมงที่มีผู้ใช้ถนนมาก [chau mong thii mii phu chai tha non mak]; **How much is it per hour?** ชั่วโมงละเท่าไร? [chau mong la thao rai]

hourly ['aʊəlɪ] *adj* ที่เกิดประจำทุกชั่วโมง [thii koed pra cham thuk chau mong] ▷ *adv* ทุกชั่วโมง [thuk chau mong]

house [haʊs] *n* บ้าน [ban]; **council house** *n* บ้านของเทศบาล [baan khong tet sa ban]; **detached house** *n* บ้านเดี่ยว [baan diao]; **semi-detached house** *n* บ้านที่อยู่ติดกัน [baan thii yu tit kan]; **Do we have to clean the house before we leave?** เราต้องทำความสะอาดบ้านก่อนออกไปไหม? [rao tong tham khwam sa at baan kon ok pai mai]

household ['haʊsˌhəʊld] *n* ครอบครัว [khrop khrua]

housewife, housewives ['haʊsˌwaɪf, 'haʊsˌwaɪvz] *n* แม่บ้าน [mae ban]

housework ['haʊsˌwɜːk] *n* งานบ้าน [ngan baan]

hovercraft ['hɒvəˌkrɑːft] *n* เรือที่แล่นได้

อย่างรวดเร็วบนน้ำ [ruea thii laen dai yang ruad reo bon nam]

how [haʊ] *adv* อย่างไร [yang rai]; **Do you know how to do this?** คุณรู้ไหมว่าจะทำนี่ได้อย่างไร? [khun ru mai wa ja tham ni dai yang rai]; **How do I get to...?** ฉันจะไปที่...ได้อย่างไร? [chan ja pai thii...dai yang rai]; **How does this work?** นี่ทำงานอย่างไร? [ni tham ngan yang rai]

however [haʊˈɛvə] *adv* อย่างไรก็ตาม [yang rai ko tam]

howl [haʊl] *v* ร้องโหยหวน [rong hoi huan]

HQ [eɪtʃ kjuː] *abbr* ตัวย่อของสำนักงานใหญ่ [tua yor khong sam nak ngan yai]

hubcap [ˈhʌbˌkæp] *n* หมวกครอบศรีษะ [hmuak khrob sri sa]

hug [hʌɡ] *n* การกอด [kan kot] ▷ *v* กอด [kot]

huge [hjuːdʒ] *adj* ใหญ่โต [yai to]

hull [hʌl] *n* ตัวเรือ [tua ruea]

hum [hʌm] *v* ร้องเพลงในคอ [rong phleng nai kho]

human [ˈhjuːmən] *adj* เกี่ยวกับมนุษย์ [kiao kap ma nut]; **human being** *n* คน [khon]; **human rights** *npl* สิทธิของมนุษย์ [sit thi khong ma nut]

humanitarian [hjuːˌmænɪˈtɛərɪən] *adj* มีมนุษยธรรม [mii ma nut sa ya tham]

humble [ˈhʌmbəl] *adj* ถ่อมตัว [thom tua]

humid [ˈhjuːmɪd] *adj* ชื้น [chuen]

humidity [hjuːˈmɪdɪtɪ] *n* ความชื้น [khwam chuen]

humorous [ˈhjuːmərəs] *adj* ตลกขบขัน [ta lok khop khan]

humour [ˈhjuːmə] *n* อารมณ์ขัน [a rom khan]; **sense of humour** *n* การมีอารมณ์ขัน [kan mii a rom khan]

hundred [ˈhʌndrəd] *number* ที่หนึ่งร้อย [thii nueng roi]

Hungarian [hʌŋˈɡɛərɪən] *adj* เกี่ยวกับประเทศฮังการี [kiao kap pra thet hang ka ri] ▷ *n* ชาวฮังการี [chao hang ka ri]

Hungary [ˈhʌŋɡərɪ] *n* ประเทศฮังการี [pra tet hang ka ri]

hunger [ˈhʌŋɡə] *n* ความหิว [khwam hio]

hungry [ˈhʌŋɡrɪ] *adj* หิว [hio]; **I'm hungry** ฉันหิว [chan hio]; **I'm not hungry** ฉันไม่หิว [chan mai hio]

hunt [hʌnt] *n* ล่าสัตว์ [la sat] ▷ *v* ล่าสัตว์ [la sat]

hunter [ˈhʌntə] *n* นายพราน [nai phran]

hunting [ˈhʌntɪŋ] *n* การล่าสัตว์ [kan la sat]

hurdle [ˈhɜːdəl] *n* รั้วสำหรับแข่งกระโดดข้าม [rua sam rap khaeng kra dot kham]

hurricane [ˈhʌrɪkən; -keɪn] *n* พายุเฮอริเคน [pha yu hoe ri khen]

hurry [ˈhʌrɪ] *n* ความเร่งรีบ [khwam reng rip] ▷ *v* เร่งรีบ [reng rip]

hurry up [ˈhʌrɪ ʌp] *v* เร่งรีบ [reng rip]

hurt [hɜːt] *adj* ได้รับบาดเจ็บ [dai rap bat chep] ▷ *v* ทำให้บาดเจ็บ [bat chep]

husband [ˈhʌzbənd] *n* สามี [sa mi]; **This is my husband** นี่สามีดิฉันค่ะ [ni sa mii di chan kha]

hut [hʌt] *n* กระท่อม [kra thom]; **Where is the nearest mountain hut?** กระท่อมที่ใกล้ที่สุดบนเขาอยู่ที่ไหน? [kra thom thii klai thii sud bon khao yu thii nai]

hyacinth [ˈhaɪəsɪnθ] *n* ชื่อพันธุ์ไม้ชนิดหนึ่ง [chue phan mai cha nit nueng]

hydrogen [ˈhaɪdrɪdʒən] *n* แก๊สไฮโดรเจน [kas hai dro chen]

hygiene [ˈhaɪdʒiːn] *n* อนามัย [a na mai]

hymn [hɪm] *n* เพลงศาสนา [phleng sad da na]

hypermarket [ˈhaɪpəˌmɑːkɪt] *n* ร้านขายของขนาดใหญ่มากมักอยู่นอกเมือง [ran khai khong kha nard yai mak mak yu nork mueang]

hyphen [ˈhaɪfən] *n* เครื่องหมายขีดสั้นกลางระหว่างคำ [khueang mai khid san klang ra wang kham]

I [aɪ] *pron* ฉัน [chan]; **I am HIV-positive** ฉันเป็นเฮชไอวีบวก [chan pen het ai wii buak]; **I don't like…** ฉันไม่ชอบ… [chan mai chop…]; **I have an appointment with…** ฉันมีนัดกับ… [chan mii nat kap…]

ice [aɪs] *n* น้ำแข็ง [nam khaeng]; **black ice** *n* น้ำแข็งสีดำ [nam khaeng sii dam]; **ice cube** *n* ก้อนน้ำแข็ง [kon nam khaeng]; **ice hockey** *n* กีฬาไอซ์ฮอกกี้ [ki la ai hok ki]; **With ice, please** ขอน้ำแข็งด้วย [kho nam khaeng duai]

iceberg ['aɪsbɜːg] *n* ภูเขาน้ำแข็งลอยอยู่กลางทะเล [phu khao nam khaeng loi yu klang tha le]

icebox ['aɪsˌbɒks] *n* ช่องน้ำแข็งในตู้เย็น [chong nam khaeng nai tu yen]

ice cream ['aɪs 'kriːm] *n* ไอศกรีม [ai sa krim]; **I'd like an ice cream** เราอยากได้ไอศกรีม [rao yak dai ai sa krim]

Iceland ['aɪslənd] *n* ประเทศไอซ์แลนด์ [pra tet ai laen]

Icelandic [aɪs'lændɪk] *adj* เกี่ยวกับไอซ์แลนด์ [kiao kap ai laen] ▷ *n* ชาวไอซ์แลนด์ [chao ai laen]

ice-skating ['aɪsˌskeɪtɪŋ] *n* การเล่นสเก็ตน้ำแข็ง [kan len sa ket nam khaeng]

icing ['aɪsɪŋ] *n* น้ำตาลไอซิ่งบนหน้าขนมเค้ก [nam tan ai sing bon na kha nom khek]; **icing sugar** *n* น้ำตาลผง [nam tan phong]

icon ['aɪkɒn] *n* สัญลักษณ์ภาพ [san ya lak phap]

icy ['aɪsɪ] *adj* เย็นจัด [yen chat]

idea [aɪ'dɪə] *n* ความคิด [khwam khit]

ideal [aɪ'dɪəl] *adj* ดีเลิศ [di loet]

ideally [aɪ'dɪəlɪ] *adv* อย่างดีเลิศ [yang di loet]

identical [aɪ'dɛntɪkəl] *adj* เหมือนกันทุกอย่าง [muean kan thuk yang]

identification [aɪˌdɛntɪfɪ'keɪʃən] *n* การชี้ตัว [kan chii tua]

identify [aɪ'dɛntɪˌfaɪ] *v* ชี้ตัว [chi tua]

identity [aɪ'dɛntɪtɪ] *n* เอกลักษณ์ [ek ka lak]; **identity card** *n* บัตรประจำตัว [bat pra cham tua]; **identity theft** *n* การขโมยเอกลักษณ์ [kan kha moi ek ka lak]

ideology [ˌaɪdɪ'ɒlədʒɪ] *n* มโนคติวิทยา [ma no kha ti wit tha ya]

idiot ['ɪdɪət] *n* คนโง่ [khon ngo]

idiotic [ˌɪdɪ'ɒtɪk] *adj* ที่โง่เขลา [thii ngo khlao]

idle ['aɪdəl] *adj* เกียจคร้าน [kiat khran]

i.e. [aɪ iː] *abbr* ตัวย่อของคือ [tua yo khong khue]

if [ɪf] *conj* ถ้า [tha]; **Do you mind if I smoke?** คุณจะว่าอะไรไหมถ้าฉันสูบบุหรี่? [khun ja wa a rai mai tha chan sup bu rii]; **Please call us if you'll be late** ช่วยโทรบอกเราถ้าคุณจะมาช้า [chuai tho bok rao tha khun ja ms cha]

ignition [ɪg'nɪʃən] *n* การติดเครื่อง [kan tit khrueang]

ignorance ['ɪgnərəns] *n* ความโง่เขลา [khwam ngo khlao]

ignorant ['ɪgnərənt] *adj* เขลา [khlao]

ignore [ɪg'nɔː] *v* ละเลย [la loei]

ill [ɪl] *adj* ป่วย [puai]; **I feel ill** ฉันรู้สึกป่วย [chan ru suek puai]

illegal [ɪˈliːgᵊl] *adj* ผิดกฎหมาย [phit kot mai]

illegible [ɪˈlɛdʒɪbᵊl] *adj* อ่านออกได้ยาก [arn ork dai yak]

illiterate [ɪˈlɪtərɪt] *adj* ไม่สามารถอ่านและเขียนได้ [mai sa mat an lae khian dai]

illness [ˈɪlnɪs] *n* ความเจ็บป่วย [khwam chep puai]

ill-treat [ɪlˈtriːt] *v* ปฏิบัติต่ออย่างไม่ดี [pa ti bat to yang mai di]

illusion [ɪˈluːʒən] *n* ภาพลวงตา [phap luang ta]

illustration [ˌɪləˈstreɪʃən] *n* ภาพประกอบ [phap pra kop]

image [ˈɪmɪdʒ] *n* ภาพพจน์ [phap phot]

imaginary [ɪˈmædʒɪnərɪ; -dʒɪnrɪ] *adj* มีอยู่ในความนึกคิด [mii yu tae nai khwam nuek kit]

imagination [ɪˌmædʒɪˈneɪʃən] *n* จินตนาการ [chin ta na kan]

imagine [ɪˈmædʒɪn] *v* วาดมโนภาพ [wad ma no phap]

imitate [ˈɪmɪˌteɪt] *v* เลียนแบบ [lian baep]

imitation [ˌɪmɪˈteɪʃən] *n* การลอกเลียนแบบ [kan lok lian baep]

immature [ˌɪməˈtjʊə; -ˈtʃʊə] *adj* ยังเยาว์วัย [yang yao wai]

immediate [ɪˈmiːdɪət] *adj* ทันที [than thi]

immediately [ɪˈmiːdɪətlɪ] *adv* โดยทันที [doi than thi]

immigrant [ˈɪmɪgrənt] *n* ผู้อพยพเข้าประเทศ [phu op pa yop khao pra ted]

immigration [ˌɪmɪˈgreɪʃən] *n* การอพยพจากต่างประเทศ [kan op pa yop chak tang pra tet]

immoral [ɪˈmɒrəl] *adj* ผิดศีลธรรม [phit sin la tham]

impact [ˈɪmpækt] *n* ผลกระทบ [phon kra thop]

impaired [ɪmˈpɛəd] *adj* **I'm visually impaired** สายตาของฉันแย่ลง [sai ta khong chan yae long]

impartial [ɪmˈpɑːʃəl] *adj* ไม่ลำเอียง [mai lam iang]

impatience [ɪmˈpeɪʃəns] *n* ความไม่อดทน [khwam mai ot thon]

impatient [ɪmˈpeɪʃənt] *adj* ไม่อดทน [mai ot thon]

impatiently [ɪmˈpeɪʃəntlɪ] *adv* อย่างไม่อดทน [yang mai od thon]

impersonal [ɪmˈpɜːsənᵊl] *adj* ไม่ใช่ส่วนตัว [mai chai suan tua]

import *n* [ˈɪmpɔːt] การนำเข้า [kan nam khao] ▷ *v* [ɪmˈpɔːt] นำเข้า [nam khao]

importance [ɪmˈpɔːtəns] *n* ความสำคัญ [khwam sam khan]

important [ɪmˈpɔːtᵊnt] *adj* สำคัญ [sam khan]

impossible [ɪmˈpɒsəbᵊl] *adj* ที่เป็นไปไม่ได้ [thii pen pai mai dai]

impractical [ɪmˈpræktɪkᵊl] *adj* ที่ปฏิบัติไม่ได้ [thii pa ti bat mai dai]

impress [ɪmˈprɛs] *v* ประทับใจ [pra thap chai]

impressed [ɪmˈprɛst] *adj* อย่างประทับใจ [yang pra thap jai]

impression [ɪmˈprɛʃən] *n* สิ่งที่ประทับใจ [sing thii pra thap jai]

impressive [ɪmˈprɛsɪv] *adj* น่าประทับใจ [na pra thap jai]

improve [ɪmˈpruːv] *v* ทำให้ดีขึ้น [tha hai di khuen]

improvement [ɪmˈpruːvmənt] *n* การทำให้ดีขึ้น [kan tham hai di khuen]

in [ɪn] *prep* ใน [nai]; **in a month's time** ภายในเวลาหนึ่งเดือน [phai nai we la nueng duean]; **in summer** ในหน้าร้อน [nai na ron]; **in the evening** ในตอนเย็น [nai ton yen]

inaccurate [ɪnˈækjʊrɪt] *adj* ไม่เที่ยงตรง [mai thiang trong]

inadequate [ɪnˈædɪkwɪt] *adj* ไม่เพียงพอ [mai phiang pho]

inadvertently [ˌɪnədˈvɜːtᵊntlɪ] *adv* ไม่ได้ตั้งใจ [mai dai tang jai]

inbox [ˈɪnbɒks] *n* แฟ้มในเครื่อง

คอมพิวเตอร์ใช้เก็บข้อความที่ส่งทางอิเล็กโท
รนิค [faem nai khrueang khom phio
toe chai kep kho khwam thii song
thang i lek tro nik]

incentive [ɪnˈsɛntɪv] n สิ่งกระตุ้น [sing
kra tun]

inch [ɪntʃ] n นิ้ว [nio]

incident [ˈɪnsɪdənt] n เหตุการณ์ที่บังเกิด
ขึ้น [hed kan thii bang koed khuen]

include [ɪnˈkluːd] v นับรวมเข้าด้วย [nab
ruam khao duai]

included [ɪnˈkluːdɪd] adj ประกอบด้วย
[pra kop duai]

including [ɪnˈkluːdɪŋ] prep รวมทั้ง
[ruam thang]

inclusive [ɪnˈkluːsɪv] adj รวมทุกอย่าง
[ruam thuk yang]

income [ˈɪnkʌm; ˈɪnkəm] n รายได้ [rai
dai]; **income tax** n ภาษีเงินได้ [pha si
ngoen dai]

incompetent [ɪnˈkɒmpɪtənt] adj ไม่มี
ความสามารถ [mai mii khwam sa mat]

incomplete [ˌɪnkəmˈpliːt] adj ไม่
สมบูรณ์ [mai som boon]

inconsistent [ˌɪnkənˈsɪstənt] adj ไม่
สม่ำเสมอ [mai sa mam sa moe]

inconvenience [ˌɪnkənˈviːnjəns;
-ˈviːnɪəns] n อย่างไม่สะดวก [yang mai
sa duak]

inconvenient [ˌɪnkənˈviːnjənt;
-ˈviːnɪənt] adj ไม่สะดวก [mai sa duak]

incorrect [ˌɪnkəˈrɛkt] adj ไม่ถูกต้อง [mai
thuk tong]

increase n [ˈɪnkriːs] การเพิ่มขึ้น [kan
poem khuen] ▷ v [ɪnˈkriːs] เพิ่มขึ้น
[phoem khuen]

increasingly [ɪnˈkriːsɪŋli] adv เพิ่มมาก
ขึ้นทุกที [poem mak khuen thuk thi]

incredible [ɪnˈkrɛdəbəl] adj ไม่น่าเชื่อ
[mai na chuea]

indecisive [ˌɪndɪˈsaɪsɪv] adj ลังเล [lang
le]

indeed [ɪnˈdiːd] adv โดยแท้จริง [doi thae
ching]

independence [ˌɪndɪˈpɛndəns] n
อิสรภาพ [it sa ra phap]

independent [ˌɪndɪˈpɛndənt] adj อิสระ
[it sa ra]

index [ˈɪndɛks] n (list) สารบัญ [sa ra
ban], (numerical scale) ดัชนี [dut cha ni];
index finger n นิ้วชี้ [nio chii]

India [ˈɪndɪə] n ประเทศอินเดีย [pra ted in
dia]

Indian [ˈɪndɪən] adj เกี่ยวกับชาวอินเดีย
[kiao kap chao in dia] ▷ n ชาวอินเดีย
[chao in dia]; **Indian Ocean** n
มหาสมุทรอินเดีย [ma ha sa mut in dia]

indicate [ˈɪndɪˌkeɪt] v ชี้บอก [chi bok]

indicator [ˈɪndɪˌkeɪtə] n เครื่องชี้นำ
[khrueang chii nam]

indigestion [ˌɪndɪˈdʒɛstʃən] n การไม่
ย่อยของอาหาร [kan mai yoi khong a
han]

indirect [ˌɪndɪˈrɛkt] adj ไม่ตรง [mai
trong]

indispensable [ˌɪndɪˈspɛnsəbəl] adj ที่
ขาดไม่ได้ [thii khat mai dai]

individual [ˌɪndɪˈvɪdjʊəl] adj เฉพาะ
บุคคล [cha pho buk khon]

Indonesia [ˌɪndəʊˈniːzɪə] n ประเทศ
อินโดนีเซีย [pra tet in do ni sia]

Indonesian [ˌɪndəʊˈniːzɪən] adj เกี่ยว
กับอินโดนีเซีย [kiao kap in do ni sia] ▷ n
(person) ชาวอินโดนีเซีย [chao in do ni
sia]

indoor [ˈɪnˌdɔː] adj ในร่ม [nai rom];
What indoor activities are there? มี
กิจกรรมในร่มอะไรบ้าง? [mii kit cha kam
nai rom a rai bang]

indoors [ˌɪnˈdɔːz] adv ในบ้าน [nai baan]

industrial [ɪnˈdʌstrɪəl] adj เกี่ยวกับ
อุตสาหกรรม [kiao kap ut sa ha kram];
industrial estate n เขตอุตสาหกรรม
[khet ut sa ha kam]

industry [ˈɪndəstri] n อุตสาหกรรม [ut sa
ha kam]

inefficient [ˌɪnɪˈfɪʃənt] adj ไร้
ประสิทธิภาพ [rai pra sit thi phap]

inevitable [ɪn'ɛvɪtəbᵊl] *adj* ไม่สามารถหลีกเลี่ยงได้ [mai sa mat lik liang dai]

inexpensive [ˌɪnɪk'spɛnsɪv] *adj* ไม่แพง [mai phaeng]

inexperienced [ˌɪnɪk'spɪərɪənst] *adj* ไม่มีประสบการณ์ [mai mii pra sop kan]

infantry ['ɪnfəntrɪ] *n* กองทหารราบ [kong tha haan raap]

infection [ɪn'fɛkʃən] *n* การติดเชื้อโรค [kan tit chuea rok]

infectious [ɪn'fɛkʃəs] *adj* ติดเชื้อโรค [tid chuea rok]

inferior [ɪn'fɪərɪə] *adj* ด้อยกว่า [doi kwa] ▷ *n* ผู้ด้อยกว่า [phu doi kwa]

infertile [ɪn'fɜːtaɪl] *adj* ไม่อุดมสมบูรณ์ [mai u dom som bun]

infinitive [ɪn'fɪnɪtɪv] *n* รูปกริยาที่ตั้งต้นด้วย [rup ka ri ya thii tang ton duai to]

infirmary [ɪn'fɜːmərɪ] *n* โรงพยาบาล [rong pha ya ban]

inflamed [ɪn'fleɪmd] *adj* ทำให้อักเสบ [tham hai ak seb]

inflammation [ˌɪnflə'meɪʃən] *n* การอักเสบ [kan ak seb]

inflatable [ɪn'fleɪtəbᵊl] *adj* ที่ทำให้พองได้ [thii tham hai phong dai]

inflation [ɪn'fleɪʃən] *n* ภาวะเงินเฟ้อ [pha wa ngoen foe]

inflexible [ɪn'flɛksəbᵊl] *adj* ไม่ยืดหยุ่น [mai yuet yun]

influence ['ɪnflʊəns] *n* อิทธิพล [it thi phon] ▷ *v* มีอิทธิพล [mii it thi phon]

influenza [ˌɪnflʊ'ɛnzə] *n* ไข้หวัดใหญ่ [khai wat yai]

inform [ɪn'fɔːm] *v* แจ้งให้ทราบ [chaeng hai sap]

informal [ɪn'fɔːməl] *adj* ไม่เป็นทางการ [mai pen thang kan]

information [ˌɪnfə'meɪʃən] *n* ข้อมูล [kho mun]; **information office** *n* สำนักงานข้อมูล [sam nak ngan kho mun]; **Here's some information about my company** นี่เป็นข้อมูลเกี่ยวกับบริษัทฉัน? [ni pen kho mun kiao kap bo ri sat chan]; **I'd like some information about...** ฉันอยากได้ข้อมูลเกี่ยวกับ... [chan yak dai kho mun kiao kap...]

informative [ɪn'fɔːmətɪv] *adj* ให้ความรู้ [hai khwam ru]

infrastructure ['ɪnfrəˌstrʌktʃə] *n* โครงสร้างพื้นฐานเช่น ถนน สะพาน [khrong sang phuen than chen tha non sa phan]

infuriating [ɪn'fjʊərɪeɪtɪŋ] *adj* ทำให้โกรธเป็นไฟ [tham hai kod pen fai]

ingenious [ɪn'dʒiːnjəs; -nɪəs] *adj* เฉลียวฉลาด [cha liao cha lat]

ingredient [ɪn'griːdɪənt] *n* ส่วนผสม [suan pha som]

inhabitant [ɪn'hæbɪtənt] *n* ผู้อยู่อาศัย [phu yu a sai]

inhaler [ɪn'heɪlə] *n* เครื่องสูบอากาศหรือยาเข้าปอด [khrueang sup a kat rue ya khao pot]

inherit [ɪn'hɛrɪt] *v* รับมรดก [rap mo ra dok]

inheritance [ɪn'hɛrɪtəns] *n* มรดก [mo ra dok]

inhibition [ˌɪnɪ'bɪʃən; ˌɪnhɪ-] *n* การขัดขวาง [kan khat khwang]

initial [ɪ'nɪʃəl] *adj* แรก [raek] ▷ *v* เขียนอักษรยอ [khian ak son yo]

initially [ɪ'nɪʃəlɪ] *adv* ตั้งแต่แรก [tang tae raek]

initials [ɪ'nɪʃəlz] *npl* อักษรแรก ๆ ของชื่อ [ak son raek raek khong chue]

initiative [ɪ'nɪʃɪətɪv; -'nɪʃətɪv] *n* การริเริ่ม [kan ri roem]

inject [ɪn'dʒɛkt] *v* ฉีด [chit]

injection [ɪn'dʒɛkʃən] *n* การฉีดยา [kan chit ya]

injure ['ɪndʒə] *v* ทำให้ได้รับบาดเจ็บ [tham hai dai rab bad chep]

injured ['ɪndʒəd] *adj* ที่ได้รับบาดเจ็บ [thii dai rab bad chep]

injury ['ɪndʒərɪ] *n* ความบาดเจ็บ [khwam bat chep]; **injury time** *n* การทดเวลาบาด

เจ็บ [kan thot we la bat chep]

injustice [ɪn'dʒʌstɪs] n ความไม่ยุติธรรม [khwam mai yut ti tham]

ink [ɪŋk] n หมึก [muek]

in-laws [ɪnlɔːz] npl ญาติพี่น้องที่มาจาก การแต่งงาน [yat phi nong thii ma chak kan taeng ngan]

inmate ['ɪn,meɪt] n ผู้ถูกกักขังในคุก [phu thuk kak khang nai khuk]

inn [ɪn] n โรงแรมเล็ก ๆ [rong raeng lek lek]

inner ['ɪnə] adj ข้างใน [khang nai]; **inner tube** n ยางในของรถ [yang nai khong rot]

innocent ['ɪnəsənt] adj ไร้เดียงสา [rai diang sa]

innovation [,ɪnə'veɪʃən] n ความคิด สร้างสรรค์ [khwam kit sang san]

innovative ['ɪnəˌveɪtɪv] adj สร้างสรรค์ [sang san]

inquest ['ɪn,kwɛst] n การสอบสวนสาเหตุ ที่เสียชีวิต [kan sop suan sa het thii sia chi wid]

inquire [ɪn'kwaɪə] v ไต่ถาม [tai tham]

inquiry [ɪn'kwaɪərɪ] n การสอบสวน [kan sop suan]; **inquiries office** n สำนักงาน ที่คนไปสอบถาม [sam nak ngan thii khon pai sop tham]

inquisitive [ɪn'kwɪzɪtɪv] adj ที่อยากรู้ อยากเห็น [thii yak ru yak hen]

insane [ɪn'seɪn] adj ที่วิกลจริต [thii wi kon ja rit]

inscription [ɪn'skrɪpʃən] n ข้อความที่ จารึก [kho khwam thii cha ruek]

insect ['ɪnsɛkt] n แมลง [ma leng]; **insect repellent** n ยากันแมลง [ya kan ma laeng]; **stick insect** n ที่ดักแมลง [thii dak ma laeng]; **Do you have insect repellent?** คุณมียากันแมลงไหม? [khun mii ya kan ma laeng mai]

insecure [,ɪnsɪ'kjʊə] adj ไม่มั่นคง [mai man khong]

insensitive [ɪn'sɛnsɪtɪv] adj ที่ไม่ไวต่อ ความรู้สึกของผู้อื่น [thii mai wai to khwam ru suek khong phu uen]

inside adv [,ɪn'saɪd] ภายใน [phai nai] ▷ n ['ɪn'saɪd] ด้านใน [dan nai] ▷ prep ข้างใน [khang nai]; **It's inside** อยู่ข้างใน [yu khang nai]

insincere [,ɪnsɪn'sɪə] adj ไม่จริงใจ [mai ching jai]

insist [ɪn'sɪst] v ยืนยัน [yuen yan]

insomnia [ɪn'sɒmnɪə] n โรคนอนไม่หลับ [rok norn mai hlap]

inspect [ɪn'spɛkt] v ตรวจสอบอย่าง ละเอียด [truat sop yang la iad]

inspector [ɪn'spɛktə] n ผู้ตรวจสอบ [phu truat sorb]; **ticket inspector** n ผู้ตรวจ ตั๋ว [phu truat tua]

instability [,ɪnstə'bɪlɪtɪ] n ความไม่ แน่นอน [khwam mai nae non]

instalment [ɪn'stɔːlmənt] n เงินที่จ่าย เป็นงวด [ngoen thii chai pen nguat]

instance ['ɪnstəns] n ตัวอย่าง [tua yang]

instant ['ɪnstənt] adj ทันทีทันใด [than thii than dai]

instantly ['ɪnstəntlɪ] adv อย่างทันที ทันใด [yang than thee than dai]

instead [ɪn'stɛd] adv แทนที่ [thaen thi]; **instead of** prep แทนที่จะ [thaen thi cha]

instinct ['ɪnstɪŋkt] n สัญชาตญาณ [san chat ta yan]

institute ['ɪnstɪˌtjuːt] n หน่วยงาน [nuai ngan]

institution [,ɪnstɪ'tjuːʃən] n สถาบัน [sa tha ban]

instruct [ɪn'strʌkt] v แนะนำ [nae nam]

instructions [ɪn'strʌkʃənz] npl คำ แนะนำสั่งสอน [kham nae nam sang son]

instructor [ɪn'strʌktə] n ผู้แนะนำสั่งสอน [phu nae nam sang son]; **driving instructor** n ครูสอนขับรถ [khru son khap rot]

instrument ['ɪnstrəmənt] n เครื่อง ดนตรี [khrueang don tri]; **musical instrument** n เครื่องดนตรี [khrueang don tri]

insufficient [ˌɪnsəˈfɪʃənt] *adj* ไม่เพียงพอ [mai phiang pho]

insulation [ˌɪnsjʊˈleɪʃən] *n* ฉนวนกัน ความร้อน [cha nuan kan khwam ron]

insulin [ˈɪnsjʊlɪn] *n* สารชนิดหนึ่งสกัดจาก ตับอ่อน [san cha nit nueng sa kat chak tap on]

insult *n* [ˈɪnsʌlt] การดูถูก [kan du thuk] ▷ *v* [ɪnˈsʌlt] ดูถูก [du thuk]

insurance [ɪnˈʃʊərəns; -ˈʃɔː-] *n* การ ประกัน [kan pra kan]; **accident insurance** *n* ประกันอุบัติเหตุ [pra kan u bat ti het]; **Give me your insurance details, please** ขอให้คุณให้รายละเอียด การประกันของคุณ [kho hai khun hai rai la iad kan pra kan khong khun]; **Here are my insurance details** นี่คือราย ละเอียดการประกันของฉัน [ni khue rai la iat kan pra kan khong chan]; **Is fully comprehensive insurance included in the price?** การประกันแบบครอบคลุมทุก อย่างรวมอยู่ในราคาหรือไม่? [kan pra kan baep khrop khlum thuk yang ruam yu nai ra kha rue mai]

insure [ɪnˈʃʊə; -ˈʃɔː-] *v* ประกัน [pra kan]; **Can I insure my luggage?** ฉันขอ ประกันกระเป๋าเดินทางของฉันได้ไหม? [chan kho pra kan kra pao doen thang khong chan dai mai]

insured [ɪnˈʃʊəd; -ˈʃɔːd] *adj* ที่ได้ประกัน [thii dai pra kan]

intact [ɪnˈtækt] *adj* คงอยู่ [khong yu]

intellectual [ˌɪntɪˈlɛktʃʊəl] *adj* ซึ่งมี ปัญญาสูง [sueng mii pan ya sung] ▷ *n* ผู้ มีปัญญาสูง [phu mii pan ya sung]

intelligence [ɪnˈtɛlɪdʒəns] *n* สติปัญญา [sa ti pan ya]

intelligent [ɪnˈtɛlɪdʒənt] *adj* ฉลาด [cha lat]

intend [ɪnˈtɛnd] *v* **intend to** *v* ตั้งใจที่จะ [tang jai thii ja]

intense [ɪnˈtɛns] *adj* แรงกล้า [raeng kla]

intensive [ɪnˈtɛnsɪv] *adj* คร่ำเคร่ง [khlam khleng]; **intensive care unit** *n* ห้องไอซียู [hong ai si u]

intention [ɪnˈtɛnʃən] *n* ความตั้งใจ [khwam tang jai]

intentional [ɪnˈtɛnʃənᵊl] *adj* เจตนา [chet ta na]

intercom [ˈɪntəˌkɒm] *n* การติดต่อทาง โทรศัพท์ภายในอาคาร [kan tid tor thang tho ra sab phai nai ar khan]

interest [ˈɪntrɪst; -tərɪst] *n* (curiosity) ความสนใจ [khwam son jai], (income) ดอกเบี้ย [dok bia] ▷ *v* สนใจ [son chai]; **interest rate** *n* อัตราดอกเบี้ย [at tra dok bia]

interested [ˈɪntrɪstɪd; -tərɪs-] *adj* มี ความสนใจ [mii khwam son jai]

interesting [ˈɪntrɪstɪŋ; -tərɪs-] *adj* น่า สนใจ [na son chai]; **Are there any interesting walks nearby?** มีที่เดินที่น่า สนใจใกล้ ๆ บ้างไหม? [mii thii doen thii na son jai klai klai bang mai]; **Can you suggest somewhere interesting to go?** คุณแนะนำที่ที่น่าสนใจที่จะไปได้ไหม? [khun nae nam thii thii na son jai thii ja pai dai mai]

interior [ɪnˈtɪərɪə] *n* ภายใน [phai nai]; **interior designer** *n* นักตกแต่งภายใน [nak tok taeng phai nai]

intermediate [ˌɪntəˈmiːdɪɪt] *adj* ระหว่างกลาง [ra wang klang]

internal [ɪnˈtɜːnᵊl] *adj* ภายใน [phai nai]

international [ˌɪntəˈnæʃənᵊl] *adj* ระหว่างประเทศ [ra wang pra thet]

Internet [ˈɪntəˌnɛt] *n* อินเตอร์เน็ต [in toe net]; **Are there any Internet cafés here?** ที่นี่มีร้านอินเตอร์เน็ตไหม? [thii ni mii ran in toe net mai]; **Does the room have wireless Internet access?** มีอินเตอร์เน็ตไร้สายในห้องไหม? [mii in toe net rai sai nai hong mai]; **Is there an Internet connection in the room?** มีอินเตอร์เน็ตในห้องไหม? [mii in toe net nai hong mai]

interpret [ɪnˈtɜːprɪt] *v* แปล [plae]

interpreter [ɪnˈtɜːprɪtə] n ล่าม [lam]; **Could you act as an interpreter for us, please?** คุณช่วยเป็นล่ามแปลให้เราได้ไหม? [khun chuai pen laam plae hai rao dai mai]; **I need an interpreter** ฉันต้องการล่าม [chan tong kan lam]

interrogate [ɪnˈtɛrəˌgeɪt] v สอบปากคำ [sop pak kham]

interrupt [ˌɪntəˈrʌpt] v ทำให้หยุดชะงัก [tham hai yut cha ngak]

interruption [ˌɪntəˈrʌpʃən] n การหยุดชะงัก [kan yut cha ngak]

interval [ˈɪntəvəl] n ช่วงเวลาพัก [chuang we la phak]

interview [ˈɪntəˌvjuː] n การสัมภาษณ์ [kan sam phat] ▷ v สัมภาษณ์ [sam pat]

interviewer [ˈɪntəˌvjuːə] n ผู้สัมภาษณ์ [phu sam phat]

intimate [ˈɪntɪmɪt] adj ใกล้ชิด [klai chit]

intimidate [ɪnˈtɪmɪˌdeɪt] v ข่มขู่คุกคาม [khom khu khuk kham]

into [ˈɪntuː; ˈɪntə] prep เข้าไปข้างใน [khao pai khang nai]; **bump into** v ชนกับ [chon kap]

intolerant [ɪnˈtɒlərənt] adj ซึ่งทนไม่ได้ [sueng thon mai dai]

intranet [ˈɪntrəˌnɛt] n ระบบเครือข่ายที่ใช้ประโยชน์ของเทคโนโลยีของอินเตอร์เน็ต [ra bop khruea khai thii chai pra yot khong thek no lo yii khong in toe net]

introduce [ˌɪntrəˈdjuːs] v แนะนำ [nae nam]

introduction [ˌɪntrəˈdʌkʃən] n การแนะนำ [kan nae nam]

intruder [ɪnˈtruːdə] n ผู้บุกรุก [phu buk ruk]

intuition [ˌɪntjʊˈɪʃən] n การรู้โดยสัญชาตญาณ [kan ru doi san chat ta yan]

invade [ɪnˈveɪd] v บุกรุก [buk ruk]

invalid [ˈɪnvəˌlɪd] n คนเจ็บ [khon chep]

invent [ɪnˈvɛnt] v ประดิษฐ์ [pra dit]

invention [ɪnˈvɛnʃən] n การประดิษฐ์ [kan pra dit]

inventor [ɪnˈvɛntə] n ผู้ประดิษฐ์ [phu pra dit]

inventory [ˈɪnvəntərɪ; -trɪ] n รายการสิ่งของ [rai kan sing khong]

invest [ɪnˈvɛst] v ลงทุน [long thun]

investigation [ɪnˌvɛstɪˈgeɪʃən] n การสืบสวน [kan suep suan]

investment [ɪnˈvɛstmənt] n การลงทุน [kan long thun]

investor [ɪnˈvɛstə] n นักลงทุน [nak long thun]

invigilator [ɪnˈvɪdʒɪˌleɪtə] n ผู้คุมสอบ [phu khum sob]

invisible [ɪnˈvɪzəbᵊl] adj มองไม่เห็น [mong mai hen]

invitation [ˌɪnvɪˈteɪʃən] n การเชื้อเชิญ [kan chuea choen]

invite [ɪnˈvaɪt] v เชิญ [choen]; **It's very kind of you to invite me** คุณใจดีมากที่เชิญฉัน [khun jai di mak thii choen chan]

invoice [ˈɪnvɔɪs] n ใบรายการส่งสินค้าที่แสดงราคา [bai rai kan song sin ka thii sa daeng ra kha] ▷ v ทำใบส่งของ [tham bai song khong]

involve [ɪnˈvɒlv] v เข้าไปมีส่วนร่วม [khao pai mii suan ruam]

iPod® [ˈaɪˌpɒd] n ไอพอด [ai phot]

IQ [aɪ kjuː] abbr ไอคิว [ai khio]

Iran [ɪˈrɑːn] n ประเทศอิหร่าน [pra tet i ran]

Iranian [ɪˈreɪnɪən] adj เกี่ยวกับอิหร่าน [kiao kap i ran] ▷ n (person) ชาวอิหร่าน [chao i ran]

Iraq [ɪˈrɑːk] n ประเทศอิรัก [pra tet i rak]

Iraqi [ɪˈrɑːkɪ] adj เกี่ยวกับอิรัก [kiao kap i rak] ▷ n ชาวอิรัก [chao i rak]

Ireland [ˈaɪələnd] n ประเทศไอร์แลนด์ [pra tet ai laen]; **Northern Ireland** n ประเทศไอร์แลนด์เหนือ [pra tet ai laen nuea]

iris [ˈaɪrɪs] n ม่านตา [man ta]

Irish [ˈaɪrɪʃ] adj เกี่ยวกับไอร์แลนด์ [kiao

kap ai laen] ▷ *n* ชาวไอริช [chao ai rit]

Irishman, Irishmen [ˈaɪrɪʃmən, ˈaɪrɪʃmɛn] *n* ผู้ชายไอริช [phu chai ai rit]

Irishwoman, Irishwomen [ˈaɪrɪʃwʊmən, ˈaɪrɪʃwɪmɪn] *n* ผู้หญิงไอริช [phu ying ai rit]

iron [ˈaɪən] *n* เหล็ก [hlek] ▷ *v* รีดด้วยเตารีด [riit duai tao riit]

ironic [aɪˈrɒnɪk] *adj* ที่ชอบเหน็บแนม [thii chop nep naem]

ironing [ˈaɪənɪŋ] *n* การรีดผ้า [kan rit pha]; **ironing board** *n* ที่รีดผ้า [thii riit pha]

ironmonger's [ˈaɪənˌmʌŋgəz] *n* ร้านขายเครื่องใช้ที่ทำด้วยโลหะ [ran khai khrueang chai thii tham duai lo ha]

irony [ˈaɪrənɪ] *n* การประชด [kan pra chot]

irregular [ɪˈrɛgjʊlə] *adj* ไม่สม่ำเสมอ [mai sa mam sa moe]

irrelevant [ɪˈrɛləvənt] *adj* ไม่เกี่ยวข้องกัน [mai kiao khong kan]

irresponsible [ˌɪrɪˈspɒnsəbəl] *adj* ไม่รับผิดชอบ [mai rap phit chop]

irritable [ˈɪrɪtəbəl] *adj* โกรธง่าย [krot ngai]

irritating [ˈɪrɪˌteɪtɪŋ] *adj* ทำให้รำคาญ [tham hai ram khan]

Islam [ˈɪzlɑːm] *n* อิสลาม [it sa lam]

Islamic [ɪzˈlɑːmɪk] *adj* ของอิสลาม [khong is sa lam]

island [ˈaɪlənd] *n* เกาะ [ko]; **desert island** *n* เกาะกลางทะเลทราย [ko klang tha le sai]

isolated [ˈaɪsəˌleɪtɪd] *adj* โดดเดี่ยว [dot diao]

ISP [aɪ ɛs piː] *abbr* ตัวย่อของธุรกิจจัดหาการเชื่อมต่อกับอินเตอร์เน็ตให้กับลูกค้า [tua yor khong thu ra kid chad ha kan chueam tor kab in toe net hai kab luk ka]

Israel [ˈɪzreɪəl; -rɪəl] *n* ประเทศอิสราเอล [pra tet is sa ra el]

Israeli [ɪzˈreɪlɪ] *adj* เกี่ยวกับอิสราเอล [kiao kap is sa ra el] ▷ *n* ชาวอิสราเอล [chao is sa ra el]

issue [ˈɪʃjuː] *n* หัวข้อที่ถกเถียงกัน [hua kho thii thok thiang kan] ▷ *v* แถลงข้อความต่อสาธารณชน [tha laeng kho khwam to sa tha ra na chon]

it [ɪt] *pron* มัน [man]; **It hurts** มันเจ็บ [man chep]; **It won't turn on** มันเปิดไม่ได้ [man poet mai dai]

IT [aɪ tiː] *abbr* ตัวย่อของเทคโนโลยีสารสนเทศ [tua yo khong thek no lo yii sa ra son tet]

Italian [ɪˈtæljən] *adj* เกี่ยวกับอิตาลี [kiao kap i ta li] ▷ *n* (*language*) ภาษาอิตาเลียน [pha sa i ta lian], (*person*) ชาวอิตาเลียน [chao i ta lian]

Italy [ˈɪtəlɪ] *n* ประเทศอิตาลี [pra tet i ta li]

itch [ɪtʃ] *v* คัน [khan]; **My leg itches** ขาฉันคัน [kha chan khan]

itchy [ˈɪtʃɪ] *adj* มีอาการคัน [mii a kan khan]

item [ˈaɪtəm] *n* สิ่งของในรายการ [sing khong nai rai kan]

itinerary [aɪˈtɪnərərɪ; ɪ-] *n* กำหนดการเดินทาง [kam not kan doen thang]

its [ɪts] *adj* ของมัน [khong man]

itself [ɪtˈsɛlf] *pron* ตัวมันเอง [tua man eng]

ivory [ˈaɪvərɪ; -vrɪ] *n* งาช้าง [nga chang]

ivy [ˈaɪvɪ] *n* ไม้เลื้อยชื่อต้นไอวี่ [mai lueai chue ton ai vi]

J

jab [dʒæb] *n* การแย็บ [kan yaep]

jack [dʒæk] *n* ปั้นจั่น [pan chan]

jacket ['dʒækɪt] *n* เสื้อแจ็กเก็ต [suea chaek ket]; **jacket potato** *n* มันฝรั่งอบ ทั้งลูก [man fa rang op thang luk]; **life jacket** *n* เสื้อชูชีพ [suea chu chip]

jackpot ['dʒæk,pɒt] *n* เงินกองกลางก้อน ใหญ่จากการเล่นการพนัน [ngen kong klang kon yai chak kan len kan pha nan]

jail [dʒeɪl] *n* คุก [khuk] ▷ *v* เอาเข้าคุก [ao khao khuk]

jam [dʒæm] *n* แยม [yaem]; **jam jar** *n* ขวดแยม [khaut yaem]; **traffic jam** *n* การจราจรติดขัด [kan cha ra chorn tit khat]

Jamaican [dʒə'meɪkən] *adj* เกี่ยวกับจา ไมก้า [kiao kap cha mai ka] ▷ *n* ชาวจา ไมก้า [chao cha mai ka]

jammed [dʒæmd] *adj* ที่อุดตัน [thii ut tan]

janitor ['dʒænɪtə] *n* ภารโรง [phan rong]

January ['dʒænjʊərɪ] *n* เดือนมกราคม [duean mok ka ra khom]

Japan [dʒə'pæn] *n* ประเทศญี่ปุ่น [pra tet yii pun]

Japanese [,dʒæpə'niːz] *adj* เกี่ยวกับญี่ปุ่น [kiao kap yi pun] ▷ *n (language)* ภาษา ญี่ปุ่น [pha sa yib pun], *(person)* ชาวญี่ปุ่น [chao yi pun]

jar [dʒɑː] *n* ขวด [khuat]; **jam jar** *n* ขวด แยม [khaut yaem]

jaundice ['dʒɔːndɪs] *n* โรคดีซ่าน [rok di san]

javelin ['dʒævlɪn] *n* กีฬาพุ่งหลาว [ki la phung lao]

jaw [dʒɔː] *n* ขากรรไกร [kha kan krai]

jazz [dʒæz] *n* ดนตรีแจ๊ส [don tree jas]

jealous ['dʒɛləs] *adj* อิจฉา [it cha]

jeans [dʒiːnz] *npl* กางเกงยีนส์ [kang keng yin]

jelly ['dʒɛlɪ] *n* เยลลี่ [yen li]

jellyfish ['dʒɛlɪ,fɪʃ] *n* แมงกระพรุน [maeng kra phrun]; **Are there jellyfish here?** ที่นี่มีแมงกะพรุนไหม? [thii ni mii maeng ka prun mai]

jersey ['dʒɜːzɪ] *n* เสื้อถักไหมพรม [suea thak mai phrom]

Jesus ['dʒiːzəs] *n* พระเยซูคริสต์ [phra ye su khris]

jet [dʒɛt] *n* เครื่องบินเจ็ท [khrueang bin chet]; **jumbo jet** *n* เครื่องบินเจ็ทขนาด ใหญ่มาก [khrueang bin chet kha nat yai mak]

jetty ['dʒɛtɪ] *n* ท่าเรือ [tha rue]

Jew [dʒuː] *n* ชาวยิว [chao yio]

jewel ['dʒuːəl] *n* เพชรพลอย [pet ploi]

jeweller ['dʒuːələ] *n* คนขายซื้อและซ่อม เครื่องเพชรพลอย [khon khai sue lae som khrueang phet ploi]

jeweller's ['dʒuːələz] *n* ที่ร้านขายเครื่อง เพชรพลอย [thii ran khai khrueang phet ploy]

jewellery ['dʒuːəlrɪ] *n* เครื่องเพชรพลอย [khrueang phet ploy]

Jewish ['dʒuːɪʃ] *adj* เกี่ยวกับยิว [kiao kap yio]

jigsaw ['dʒɪg,sɔː] *n* ตัวต่อสำหรับสร้างเป็น ภาพ [tua to sam rap sang pen phap]

job [dʒɒb] *n* งาน [ngan]; **job centre** *n* หน่วยจัดหางาน [nuai chat ha ngan]

jobless [ˈdʒɒblɪs] *adj* ไม่มีงาน [mai mii ngan]

jockey [ˈdʒɒkɪ] *n* คนขี่ม้าแข่ง [kon khi ma khaeng]

jog [dʒɒg] *v* วิ่งเหยาะ [wing yo]

jogging [ˈdʒɒgɪŋ] *n* การวิ่งเหยาะ [kan wing yo]

join [dʒɔɪn] *v* เข้าร่วม [khao ruam]; **Can I join you?** ฉันเข้าร่วมกับคุณได้ไหม? [chan khao ruam kap khun dai mai]

joiner [ˈdʒɔɪnə] *n* ผู้เข้าร่วม [phu khao ruam]

joint [dʒɔɪnt] *adj* สัมพันธ์กัน [sam phan kan] ▷ *n (junction)* ทางแยก [thang yaek], *(meat)* ข้อต่อ [kho to]; **joint account** *n* บัญชีร่วม [ban chi ruam]

joke [dʒəʊk] *n* เรื่องตลก [rueang ta lok] ▷ *v* พูดตลก [phud ta lok]

jolly [ˈdʒɒlɪ] *adj* รื่นเริง [ruen roeng]

Jordan [ˈdʒɔːdən] *n* ประเทศจอร์แดน [pra tet chor daen]

Jordanian [dʒɔːˈdeɪmɪən] *adj* เกี่ยวกับ ประเทศจอร์แดน [kiao kap pra thet cho daen] ▷ *n* ชาวจอร์แดน [chao cho daen]

jot down [dʒɒt daʊn] *v* จดลง [chot long]

jotter [ˈdʒɒtə] *n* สมุดโน๊ตเล่มเล็ก [sa mud nod lem lek]

journalism [ˈdʒɜːnəˌlɪzəm] *n* วารสารศาสตร์ [wa ra san sat]

journalist [ˈdʒɜːnəˈlɪst] *n* นักหนังสือพิมพ์ [nak nang sue phim]

journey [ˈdʒɜːnɪ] *n* การเดินทาง [kan doen thang]; **How long is the journey?** การ เดินทางใช้เวลานานแค่ไหน? [kan doen thang chai we la nan khae nai]

joy [dʒɔɪ] *n* ความยินดี [khwam yin dee]

joystick [ˈdʒɔɪˌstɪk] *n* คันบังคับเครื่องบิน [khan bang khap khrueang bin]

judge [dʒʌdʒ] *n* ผู้พิพากษา [phu phi phak sa] ▷ *v* ตัดสิน [tat sin]

judo [ˈdʒuːdəʊ] *n* กีฬายูโด [ki la yu do]

jug [dʒʌg] *n* เหยือก [yueak]; **a jug of water** น้ำหนึ่งเหยือก [nam nueng yueak]

juggler [ˈdʒʌglə] *n* นักเล่นกล [nak len kon]

juice [dʒuːs] *n* น้ำผลไม้ [nam phon la mai]; **orange juice** *n* น้ำส้ม [nam som]

July [dʒuːˈlaɪ; dʒə-; dʒʊ-] *n* เดือน กรกฎาคม [duean ka ra ka da khom]

jump [dʒʌmp] *n* กระโดดยาว [kra dot yao] ▷ *v* กระโดด [kra dot]; **high jump** *n* กระโดดสูง [kra dot sung]; **long jump** *n* กระโดดยาว [kra dot yao]

jumper [ˈdʒʌmpə] *n* เสื้อถักด้วยไหมพรม [suea thak duai mai phrom]

jumping [dʒʌmpɪŋ] *n* **show-jumping** *n* การแสดงการขี่ม้าวิ่งข้ามสิ่งกีดขวาง [kan sa daeng kan khi ma wing kham sing kit khwang]

junction [ˈdʒʌŋkʃən] *n* ทางแยก [thang yaek]; **Go right at the next junction** เลี้ยวขวาที่ทางแยก [liao khwa thii thang yaek]; **Which junction is it for...?** ทาง แยกใดที่ไป...? [thang yaek dai thii pai...]

June [dʒuːn] *n* เดือนมิถุนายน [duean mi thu na yon]; **at the beginning of June** ต้นเดือนมิถุนายน [ton duean mi thu na yon]; **for the whole of June** ตลอดเดือน มิถุนายน [ta lot duen mi thu na yon]

jungle [ˈdʒʌŋgəl] *n* ป่าทึบ [pa thuep]

junior [ˈdʒuːnjə] *adj* ที่อายุน้อยกว่า [thii a yu noi kwa]

junk [dʒʌŋk] *n* ของเก่าที่ไม่ต้องการแล้ว [khong kao thii mai tong kan laeo]

jury [ˈdʒʊərɪ] *n* คณะลูกขุน [kha na luk khun]

just [dʒəst] *adv* เพิ่ง [phoeng]; **I've just arrived** ฉันเพิ่งมาถึง [chan phoeng ma thueng]

justice [ˈdʒʌstɪs] *n* ความยุติธรรม [khwam yut ti tham]

justify [ˈdʒʌstɪˌfaɪ] *v* พิสูจน์ว่าถูกต้อง [phi sut wa thuk tong]

K

kangaroo [ˌkæŋɡəˈruː] *n* จิงโจ้ [ching cho]

karaoke [ˌkɑːrəˈəʊkɪ] *n* การร้องเพลงไป กับทำนองเพลงที่มีเนื้อร้องบนจอทีวี [kan rong phleng pai kap tham nong phleng thii mii nuea rong bon jo tii wii]

karate [kəˈrɑːtɪ] *n* มวยคาราเต้ [muai kha ra te]

Kazakhstan [ˌkɑːzɑːkˈstæn; -ˈstɑːn] *n* ประเทศคาซัคสถาน [pra tet kha sak sa than na]

kebab [kəˈbæb] *n* เนื้อและผักชิ้นเล็กเสียบ ด้วยไม้เสียบแล้วย่าง [nuea lae phak chin lek siap duai mai siap laeo yang]

keen [kiːn] *adj* กระตือรือร้น [kra tue rue ron]

keep [kiːp] *v* เก็บ [kep]; **Keep the change** คุณเก็บเงินทอนไว้ [khun kep ngen thon wai]; **May I keep it?** ขอฉัน เก็บไว้ได้ไหม? [kho chan kep wai dai mai]

keep-fit [ˈkiːpˌfɪt] *n* การออกกำลังกาย อย่างสม่ำเสมอ [kan ork kam lang kai yang sa mom sa moe]

keep out [kiːp aʊt] *v* ให้อยู่ข้างนอก [hai yu khang nok]

keep up [kiːp ʌp] *v* รักษาไว้ที่ระดับปัจจุบัน [rak sa wai thii ra dap pat chu ban]; **keep up with** *v* รักษาไว้ที่ระดับปัจจุบัน [rak sa wai thii ra dap pat chu ban]

kennel [ˈkɛnəl] *n* บ้านสุนัข [baan su nak]

Kenya [ˈkɛnjə; ˈkiːnjə] *n* ประเทศเคนยา [pra tet ken ya]

Kenyan [ˈkɛnjən; ˈkiːnjən] *adj* จาก เคนยา [chak ken ya] ▷ *n* ชาวเคนยา [chao ken ya]

kerb [kɜːb] *n* ขอบถนน [kop tha non]

kerosene [ˈkɛrəˌsiːn] *n* น้ำมันก๊าด [nam man kad]

ketchup [ˈkɛtʃəp] *n* ซ้อสมะเขือเทศ [sos ma khuea tet]

kettle [ˈkɛtəl] *n* กาต้มน้ำ [ka tom nam]

key [kiː] *n* (for lock) กุญแจ [kun chae], (music/computer) ระดับเสียง รหัสผ่านที่ เข้าไปในแฟ้มข้อมูล [ra dab siang ra has phan thii khao pai nai faem khor mun]; **Can I have a key?** ฉันขอกุญแจ ได้ไหม? [chan kho kun jae dai mai]; **I left the keys in the car** ฉันลืมกุญแจไว้ ในรถ [chan luem kun jae wai nai rot]

keyboard [ˈkiːˌbɔːd] *n* แผงแป้นอักขระ [phaeng paen ak kha ra]

keyring [ˈkiːˌrɪŋ] *n* พวงกุญแจ [phuang kun jae]

kick [kɪk] *n* การเตะ [kan te] ▷ *v* เตะ [te]

kick off [kɪk ɒf] *v* เตะเริ่ม [te roem]

kick-off [kɪkɒf] *n* การเตะลูกครั้งแรก [kan te luk khrang raek]

kid [kɪd] *n* เด็ก [dek] ▷ *v* ล้อเล่น [lo len]

kidnap [ˈkɪdnæp] *v* ลักพาตัว [lak pha tua]

kidney [ˈkɪdnɪ] *n* ไต [tai]

kill [kɪl] *v* ฆ่า [kha]

killer [ˈkɪlə] *n* ผู้ฆ่า [phu kha]

kilo [ˈkiːləʊ] *n* กิโล [ki lo]

kilometre [kɪˈlɒmɪtə; ˈkɪləˌmiːtə] *n* กิโลเมตร [ki lo met]

kilt [kɪlt] *n* กระโปรงสั้นแค่เข่าจับจีบลายตา ใส่ทั้งชายและหญิงในสก๊อตแลนด์ [kra prong san khae khao chap chip lai ta sai thang chai lae ying nai sa kot land]

kind [kaɪnd] *adj* ใจดี [chai di] ▷ *n* จำพวก [cham phuak]; **It's very kind of you to invite me** คุณใจดีมากที่เชิญฉัน [khun jai di mak thii choen chan]

kindly ['kaɪndlɪ] *adv* อย่างใจดี [yang jai di]

kindness ['kaɪndnɪs] *n* ความเมตตากรุณา [khwam met ta ka ru na]

king [kɪŋ] *n* พระเจ้าแผ่นดิน [phra chao phaen din]

kingdom ['kɪŋdəm] *n* ราชอาณาจักร [rat cha a na chak]

kingfisher ['kɪŋˌfɪʃə] *n* นกกินปลา [nok kin pla]

kiosk ['kiːɒsk] *n* ร้านที่เป็นบูทเล็ก ๆ [ran thii pen but lek lek]

kipper ['kɪpə] *n* ปลาคิปเปอร์ [pla khip poe]

kiss [kɪs] *n* การจูบ [kan chup] ▷ *v* จูบ [chup]

kit [kɪt] *n* ชุดเครื่องมือ [chut khrueang mue]; **hands-free kit** *n* อุปกรณ์ที่ไม่ต้องใช้มือ [up pa kon thii mai tong chai mue]; **repair kit** *n* ชุดสำหรับการซ่อม [chut sam rap kan som]

kitchen ['kɪtʃɪn] *n* ครัว [khrua]; **fitted kitchen** *n* ครัวสำเร็จรูปที่สร้างติดไว้กับที่ [khrua sam ret rup thii sang tit wai kap thii]

kite [kaɪt] *n* ว่าว [wao]

kitten ['kɪtən] *n* ลูกแมว [luk maeo]

kiwi ['kiːwiː] *n* ผลกีวี [phon ki wi]

knee [niː] *n* เข่า [khao]

kneecap ['niːˌkæp] *n* กระดูกสะบ้าหัวเข่า [kra duk sa ba hua khao]

kneel [niːl] *v* คุกเข่า [khuk khao]

kneel down [niːl daʊn] *v* คุกเข่าลง [khuk khao long]

knickers ['nɪkəz] *npl* กางเกงในสตรี [kang keng nai sa tree]

knife [naɪf] *n* มีด [mit]

knit [nɪt] *v* ถัก [thak]

knitting ['nɪtɪŋ] *n* การถัก [kan thak]; **knitting needle** *n* เข็มถัก [khem thak]

knob [nɒb] *n* ลูกบิด [luk bit]

knock [nɒk] *n* การเคาะ [kan kho] ▷ *v* เคาะ [kho], (on the door etc.) เคาะ [kho]

knock down [nɒk daʊn] *v* ลดราคา [lot ra kha]

knock out [nɒk aʊt] *v* ต่อยจนล้มลุกไม่ขึ้น [toi chon lom luk mai khuen]

knot [nɒt] *n* เงื่อน [nguean]

know [nəʊ] *v* รู้ [ru]; **Do you know him?** คุณรู้จักเขาไหม? [khun ru chak khao mai]; **Do you know how to do this?** คุณรู้ไหมว่าจะทำนี้ได้อย่างไร? [khun ru mai wa ja tham ni dai yang rai]; **I'm very sorry, I didn't know the regulations** ฉันเสียใจมาก ฉันไม่รู้กฎข้อบังคับ [chan sia jai mak chan mai ru kot kho bang khap]

know-all ['nəʊɔːl] *n* คนที่แกล้งทำเป็นรู้มากกว่าคนอื่น [khon thii klaeng tham pen ru mak kwa khon uen]

know-how ['nəʊˌhaʊ] *n* ความชำนาญในการทำสิ่งที่ยาก [khwam cham nan nai kan tham sing thii yak]

knowledge ['nɒlɪdʒ] *n* ความรู้ [khwam ru]

knowledgeable ['nɒlɪdʒəbºl] *adj* มีความรู้ [mii khwam ru]

known [nəʊn] *adj* เป็นที่รู้จัก [pen thii ru chak]

Koran [kɔːˈrɑːn] *n* คัมภีร์โกหร่าน [kham phii ko ran]

Korea [kəˈriːə] *n* ประเทศเกาหลี [pra ted kao hlee]; **North Korea** *n* เกาหลีเหนือ [kao lii nuea]; **South Korea** *n* ประเทศเกาหลีใต้ [pra tet kao lii tai]

Korean [kəˈriːən] *adj* เกี่ยวกับเกาหลี [kiao kap kao lii] ▷ *n* (language) ภาษาเกาหลี [pha sa kao hlee], (person) ชาวเกาหลี [chao kao lii]

kosher ['kəʊʃə] *adj* สะอาดและดีพอที่จะกินได้ตามกฎของอาหารยิว [sa at lae di pho thii ja kin dai tam kot khong a han yio]

Kosovo [ˈkɔsɔvɔ; ˈkɒsəvəʊ] *n* ประเทศคอสโซโว [pra tet kos so vo]

Kuwait [kʊˈweɪt] *n* ประเทศคูเวต [pra tet khu wet]

Kuwaiti [kʊˈweɪtɪ] *adj* เกี่ยวกับคูเวต [kiao kap khu wet] ▷ *n* ชาวคูเวต [chao khu wet]

Kyrgyzstan [ˈkɪəgɪzˌstɑːn; -ˌstæn] *n* ประเทศไครกิสถาน [pra tet khai ki sa than]

lab [læb] *n* ตัวย่อของห้องทดลองทางวิทยาศาสตร์ [tua yo khong hong thot long thang wit ta ya saat]

label [ˈleɪbəl] *n* ป้ายชื่อ [pai chue]

laboratory [ləˈbɒrətərɪ; -trɪ; ˈlæbrəˌtɔːrɪ] *n* ห้องทดลองทางวิทยาศาสตร์ [hong thot long thang wit tha ya sart]; **language laboratory** *n* ห้องปฏิบัติการทางภาษา [hong pa ti bat kan thang pha sa]

labour [ˈleɪbə] *n* แรงงาน [raeng ngan]

labourer [ˈleɪbərə] *n* กรรมกร [kam ma kan]

lace [leɪs] *n* ลูกไม้ [luk mai]

lack [læk] *n* การขาด [kan khat]

lacquer [ˈlækə] *n* น้ำมันแล็กเกอร์ [nam man laek koe]

lad [læd] *n* เด็กหนุ่ม [dek num]

ladder [ˈlædə] *n* บันได [ban dai]

ladies [ˈleɪdɪz] *n* **ladies'** *n* ห้องน้ำสตรี [hong nam sa trii]; **Where is the ladies?** ห้องน้ำผู้หญิงอยู่ที่ไหน? [hong nam phu ying yu thii nai]

ladle [ˈleɪdəl] *n* ทัพพี [thap phi]

lady [ˈleɪdɪ] *n* สุภาพสตรี [su phap sa tri]

ladybird ['leɪdɪ,bɜːd] n แมลงปีกแข็ง [ma laeng pik khaeng]

lag [læg] n **jet lag** n ความรู้สึกหมดแรงและสูญเสียทิศทางเพราะการเดินทางระหว่างเวลาที่ต่างกัน [khwam ru suek mot raeng lae sun sia thit thang phro kan doen thang ra wang we la thii tang kan]; **I'm suffering from jet lag** ฉันรู้สึกทรมานจากการเดินทางโดยเครื่องบิน [chan ru suek tho ra man chak kan doen thang doi khrueang bin]

lager ['lɑːgə] n เบียร์สีอ่อนเก็บไว้ในถังบ่ม [bia sii on kep wai nai thang bom]

lagoon [ləˈguːn] n บึงน้ำเค็ม [bueng nam khem]

laid-back ['leɪdbæk] adj อาการผ่อนคลาย [a kan phon khlai]

lake [leɪk] n ทะเลสาบ [tha le sap]

lamb [læm] n แกะ [kae]

lame [leɪm] adj พิการที่ขา [phi kan thii kha]

lamp [læmp] n ตะเกียง [ta kiang]; **bedside lamp** n โคมไฟข้างเตียงนอน [khom fai khang tiang non]

lamppost ['læmp,pəʊst] n เสาไฟฟ้า [sao fai fa]

lampshade ['læmp,ʃeɪd] n โคมไฟ [khom fai]

land [lænd] n ที่ดิน [thi din] ▷ v น่าร่อนลง [nam ron long]

landing ['lændɪŋ] n การนำเครื่องบินลงจอด [kan nam khrueang bin long jod]

landlady ['lænd,leɪdɪ] n เจ้าของบ้านหญิง [chao khong baan hying]

landlord ['lænd,lɔːd] n เจ้าของบ้านชาย [chao khong baan chai]

landmark ['lænd,mɑːk] n สิ่งที่เป็นลักษณะเด่นของภูมิประเทศ [sing thii pen lak sa na den khong phu mi pra tet]

landowner ['lænd,əʊnə] n เจ้าของที่ดิน [chao khong thii din]

landscape ['lænd,skeɪp] n ภูมิประเทศ [phu mi prathet]

landslide ['lænd,slaɪd] n แผ่นดินถล่ม [phaen din tha lom]

lane [leɪn] n ตรอก [trok], (driving) ตรอก [trok]; **cycle lane** n ทางขี่จักรยาน [thang khi chak kra yan]

language ['læŋgwɪdʒ] n ภาษา [pha sa]; **language laboratory** n ห้องปฏิบัติการทางภาษา [hong pa ti bat kan thang pha sa]; **language school** n โรงเรียนสอนภาษา [rong rian son pha sa]; **sign language** n ภาษาสัญลักษณ์ [pha sa san ya lak]; **What languages do you speak?** คุณพูดภาษาอะไรบ้าง? [khun phut pha sa a rai bang]

lanky ['læŋkɪ] adj ผอมโย่ง [phom yong]

Laos [laʊz; laʊs] n ประเทศลาว [pra tet lao]

lap [læp] n ตัก [tak]

laptop ['læp,tɒp] n คอมพิวเตอร์พกพา [khom pio ter phok pha]

larder ['lɑːdə] n ตู้เก็บอาหาร [tu kep a han]

large [lɑːdʒ] adj ใหญ่ [yai]; **Do you have a large?** คุณมีขนาดใหญ่ไหม? [khun mi kha nat yai mai]; **Do you have an extra large?** คุณมีขนาดใหญ่พิเศษไหม? [khun mii kha nat yai phi set mai]

largely ['lɑːdʒlɪ] adv อย่างมาก [yang mak]

laryngitis [,lærɪn'dʒaɪtɪs] n โรคกล่องเสียงอักเสบ [rok klong siang ak sep]

laser ['leɪzə] n แสงเลเซอร์ [saeng le soe]

lass [læs] n เด็กผู้หญิง [dek phu hying]

last [lɑːst] adj สุดท้าย [sut thai] ▷ adv ล่าสุด [la sut] ▷ v ยืนหยัด [yuen yan]; **When does the last chair-lift go?** เก้าอี้ลิฟต์คันสุดท้ายจะขึ้นไปเมื่อไร? [kao ii lift khan sut thai ja khuen pai muea rai]; **When is the last bus to...?** รถโดยสารคันสุดท้ายที่จะไป...เดินทางเมื่อไร? [rot doi san khan sut thai thii ja pai... doen thang muea rai]

lastly ['lɑːstlɪ] adv ที่สุดท้าย [thii sut thai]

late [leɪt] *adj (dead)* เพิ่งตาย [phoeng tai], *(delayed)* ช้า [cha] ▷ *adv* สาย [sai]; **Is the train running late?** รถไฟมาสาย ใช่ไหม? [rot fai ma sai chai mai]; **It's too late** ช้าเกินไป [cha koen pai]; **Please call us if you'll be late** ช่วยโทร บอกเราถ้าคุณจะมาช้า [chuai tho bok rao tha khun ja ms cha]

lately ['leɪtlɪ] *adv* เมื่อเร็วๆนี้ [muea reo reo ni]

later ['leɪtə] *adv* ตอนหลัง [ton lang]

Latin ['lætɪn] *n* ภาษาละติน [pha sa la tin]

Latin America ['lætɪn ə'mɛrɪkə] *n* ละตินอเมริกา [la tin a me ri ka]

Latin American ['lætɪn ə'mɛrɪkən] *adj* อเมริกากลางและใต้ที่ภาษาทางการคือเอส ปนและโปรตุเกส [a me ri ka klang lae tai thii pha sa thang kan khue sa pen lae pro tu ked]

latitude ['lætɪˌtjuːd] *n* เส้นขวางขนานกับ เส้นศูนย์สูตรของโลก [sen khwang kha nan kap sen sun sut khong lok]

Latvia ['lætvɪə] *n* ประเทศแลตเวีย [pra tet laet via]

Latvian ['lætvɪən] *adj* เกี่ยวกับประเทศ แลตเวีย [kiao kap pra thet laet via] ▷ *n (language)* ภาษาแลตเวีย [pha sa laet via], *(person)* ชาวแลตเวีย [chao laet wia]

laugh [lɑːf] *n* การหัวเราะ [kan hua rao] ▷ *v* หัวเราะ [hua ro]

laughter ['lɑːftə] *n* เสียงหัวเราะ [siang hua rao]

launch [lɔːntʃ] *v* ปล่อยเรือลงน้ำเป็นครั้ง แรก [ploi ruea long nam pen khrang raek]

Launderette® [ˌlɔːndə'rɛt; lɔːn'drɛt] *n* ร้านซักผ้าด้วยเครื่องโดยใช้เหรียญหยอด [ran sak pha duai khueang doi chai lian hyod]

laundry ['lɔːndrɪ] *n* เสื้อผ้าที่กำลังจะซัก [suea pha thii kam lang ja sak]

lava ['lɑːvə] *n* หินลาวา [hin la va]

lavatory ['lævətərɪ; -trɪ] *n* ห้องน้ำ [hong nam]

lavender ['lævəndə] *n* ต้นลาเวนเดอร์ดอก มีสีฟ้าม่วง [ton la wen doe dok mii sii fa muang]

law [lɔː] *n* กฎหมาย [kot mai]; **law school** *n* คณะรัฐศาสตร์ [kha na rat tha sat]

lawn [lɔːn] *n* สนามหญ้า [sa nam ya]

lawnmower ['lɔːnˌməʊə] *n* เครื่องตัด หญ้า [khrueang tat ya]

lawyer ['lɔːjə; 'lɔɪə] *n* ทนายความ [tha nai khwam]

laxative ['læksətɪv] *n* ยาระบาย [ya ra bai]

lay [leɪ] *v* วางลง [wang long]

layby ['leɪˌbaɪ] *n* ข้างทาง [khang thang]

layer ['leɪə] *n* ชั้น [chan]; **ozone layer** *n* ชั้นก๊าซโอโซนล้อมรอบโลก [chan kas o son lom rop lok]

lay off [leɪ ɒf] *v* เลิกจ้างงาน [loek chang ngan]

layout ['leɪˌaʊt] *n* โครงงาน [khrong ngan]

lazy ['leɪzɪ] *adj* ขี้เกียจ [khi kiat]

lead¹ [liːd] *n (in play/film)* ตัวเอก [tua ek], *(position)* หัวข้อข่าว [hua kho khao] ▷ *v* นำ [nam]; **jump leads** *npl* สายต่อหม้อ แบตเตอรี่ [sai to mo baet toe ri]; **lead singer** *n* นักร้องนำ [nak rong nam]

lead² [lɛd] *n (metal)* ตะกั่ว [ta kua]

leader ['liːdə] *n* ผู้นำ [phu nam]

lead-free [ˌlɛd'friː] *adj* ไร้สารตะกั่ว [rai san ta kua]

leaf [liːf] *n* ใบไม้ [bai mai]; **bay leaf** *n* ใบ อบเชย [bai op choei]

leaflet ['liːflɪt] *n* แผ่นใบปลิว [phaen bai plio]

league [liːg] *n* สหพันธ์ [sa ha phan]

leak [liːk] *n* การรั่ว [kan rua] ▷ *v* รั่ว [rua]; **The petrol tank is leaking** แท็งค์น้ำมัน รั่ว [thang nam man rua]; **The roof leaks** หลังคารั่ว [lang kha rua]; **There is a leak in the radiator** เครื่องทำความ ร้อนรั่ว [khrueang tham khwam ron rua]

lean [liːn] v พิง [phing]; **lean forward** v เอนไปข้างหน้า [en pai khang na]

lean on [liːn ɒn] v พึ่งพา [phueng pha]

lean out [liːn aʊt] v ชะโงกออกไป [cha ngok ok pai]

leap [liːp] v กระโดด [kra dot]; **leap year** n ปีที่มีวันที่ ๒๙ กุมภาพันธ์ [pi thii mii wan thii yi sip kao kum pha phan]

learn [lɜːn] v เรียน [rian]

learner ['lɜːnə] n ผู้เรียน [phu rian]; **learner driver** n นักเรียนเรียนขับรถ [nak rian rian khap rot]

lease [liːs] n สัญญาเช่า [san ya chao] ▷ v เช่า [chao]

least [liːst] adj น้อยที่สุด [noi thii sud]; **at least** adv อย่างน้อยที่สุด [yang noi thii sut]

leather ['lɛðə] n หนัง [nang]

leave [liːv] n การลาหยุด [kan la yut] ▷ v ทอดทิ้ง [thot thing], ออก [ok]; **maternity leave** n การลาหยุดหลังคลอด [kan la yut lang khlot]; **Do we have to clean the house before we leave?** เราต้องทำความสะอาดบ้านก่อนออกไปไหม? [rao tong tham khwam sa at baan kon ok pai mai]; **My plane leaves at…** เครื่องบินฉันออกจาก… [khrueang bin chan ok chak…]; **Where do we hand in the key when we're leaving?** เราจะคืนกุญแจได้ที่ไหนเวลาเราออกไป [rao ja khuen kun jae dai thii nai we la rao ok pai]; **Which platform does the train for… leave from?** รถไฟที่จะไป…จะออกจากชานชาลาไหน? [rot fai thii ja pai… ja ok chak chan cha la nai]

leave out [liːv aʊt] v ลบออกไป [lop ok pai]

leaves [liːvz] npl ใบไม้หลายใบ [bai mai lai bai]

Lebanese [ˌlɛbə'niːz] adj เกี่ยวกับเลบานอน [kiao kap le ba non] ▷ n ชาวเลบานอน [chao le ba non]

Lebanon ['lɛbənɒn] n ประเทศเลบานอน [pra tet le ba non]

lecture ['lɛktʃə] n การบรรยาย [kan ban yai], บรรยาย [ban yai]

lecturer ['lɛktʃərə] n ผู้บรรยาย [phu ban yai]

leek [liːk] n ผักลีค [phak lik]

left [lɛft] adj ทางซ้ายมือ [thang sai mue] ▷ adv ไปทางซ้าย [pai thang sai] ▷ n ด้านซ้าย [dan sai]

left-hand [ˌlɛft'hænd] adj มือซ้าย [mue sai]; **left-hand drive** n การขับด้านซ้าย [kan khap dan sai]

left-handed [ˌlɛft'hændɪd] adj ถนัดมือซ้าย [tha nat mue sai]

left-luggage [ˌlɛft'lʌgɪdʒ] n ที่ฝากกระเป๋า [thii fak kra pao]; **left-luggage locker** n ตู้ล็อคเกอร์เก็บกระเป๋าเดินทาง [tu lok koe kep kra pao doen thang]; **left-luggage office** n สำนักงานที่เก็บกระเป๋าที่ถูกทิ้งไว้ [sam nak ngan thii kep kra pao thii thuk thing wai]

leftovers ['lɛftˌəʊvəz] npl อาหารเหลือ [a han hluea]

left-wing [ˌlɛft'wɪŋ] adj พรรคการเมืองฝ่ายซ้าย [phak kan mueang fai sai]

leg [lɛg] n ขา [kha]; **I can't move my leg** ฉันขยับขาไม่ได้ [chan kha yap kha mai dai]; **I've got cramp in my leg** ฉันเป็นตะคิวที่ขา [chan pen ta khio thii kha]; **My leg itches** ขาฉันคัน [kha chan khan]

legal ['liːgᵊl] adj ที่ถูกกฎหมาย [thii thuk kot mai]

legend ['lɛdʒənd] n ตำนาน [tam nan]

leggings ['lɛgɪŋz] npl กางเกงรัดรูป [kang keng rat rup]

legible ['lɛdʒəbᵊl] adj อ่านออกได้ [arn ork dai]

legislation [ˌlɛdʒɪs'leɪʃən] n การออกกฎหมาย [kan ok kot mai]

leisure ['lɛʒə; 'liːʒər] n เวลาว่าง [we la wang]; **leisure centre** n สถานที่ที่คนไปออกกำลังกายหรือพักผ่อน [sa than thii thii khon pai ok kam lang kai rue phak phon]

lemon ['lɛmən] n มะนาว [ma nao]; **with lemon** ใส่มะนาว [sai ma nao]

lemonade [,lɛmə'neɪd] n น้ำมะนาว [nam ma nao]

lend [lɛnd] v ให้ยืม [hai yuem]

length [lɛŋkθ; lɛŋθ] n ความยาว [khwam yao]

lens [lɛnz] n เลนส์ตา [len to]; **contact lenses** npl คอนแท็คเลนส์ [khon taek len]; **zoom lens** n เลนส์ของกล้องที่ขยายปรับภาพโดยรักษาโฟกัสเดิมไว้ [len khong klong thii kha yai prab phap doi rak sa fo kas doem wai]

Lent [lɛnt] n ฤดูถือบวชโดยอดอาหารประจำปีก่อนวันอีสเตอร์ของชาวคริสต์ [rue du thue buat doi ot a han pra cham pi kon wan is toe khong chao khris]

lentils ['lɛntɪlz] npl เมล็ดพืชขนาดเล็กของเอเซียที่กินได้ [ma led phuet kha nard lek khong e sia thii kin dai]

Leo ['liːəʊ] n ราศีสิงห์ [ra si sing]

leopard ['lɛpəd] n เสือดาว [suea dao]

leotard ['liə̯tɑːd] n เสื้อชุดติดกันแนบเนื้อ [suea chud tid kan naep nuea]

less [lɛs] adv น้อยกว่า [noi kwa] ▷ pron น้อยลง [noi long]

lesson ['lɛsˀn] n บทเรียน [bot rian]; **driving lesson** n บทเรียนสอนขับรถ [bot rian son khap rot]

let [lɛt] v อนุญาต [a nu yat]

let down [lɛt daʊn] v ทำให้ผิดหวัง [tham hai phid hwang]

let in [lɛt ɪn] v ให้เข้ามา [hai khao ma]

letter ['lɛtə] n (a, b, c) ตัวอักษร [tua ak son], (message) จดหมาย [chot mai]; **I'd like to send this letter** ฉันอยากส่งจดหมายฉบับนี้ [chan yak song chot mai cha bap nii]

letterbox ['lɛtə,bɒks] n ตู้จดหมาย [tu chod mai]

lettuce ['lɛtɪs] n ผักกาดที่ใส่ในสลัด [phak kaat thii sai nai sa lad]

leukaemia [luː'kiːmɪə] n โรคที่มีเม็ด

โลหิตขาวมากเกินไป [rok thii mii met lo hit khao mak koen pai]

level ['lɛvˀl] adj ระดับตามแนวราบ [ra dap tam naeo rap] ▷ n ระดับ [ra dap]; **level crossing** n จุดที่ทางรถไฟและถนนตัดผ่านกัน [chut thii thang rot fai lae tha non tad phan kan]; **sea level** n ระดับน้ำทะเล [ra dap nam tha le]

lever ['liːvə] n ชะแลง [cha laeng]

liar ['laɪə] n คนโกหก [khon ko hok]

liberal ['lɪbərəl; 'lɪbrəl] adj เกี่ยวกับลัทธิเสรีนิยม [kiao kap lat thi se ri ni yom]

liberation [,lɪbə'reɪʃən] n การปลดปล่อยให้เป็นอิสระ [kan plot ploi hai pen it sa ra]

Liberia [laɪ'bɪərɪə] n ประเทศไลบีเรีย [pra tet lai bi ria]

Liberian [laɪ'bɪərɪən] adj เกี่ยวกับไลบีเรีย [kiao kap lai bi ria] ▷ n ชาวไลบีเรีย [chao lai bi ria]

Libra ['liːbrə] n ราศีตุล [ra si tun]

librarian [laɪ'brɛərɪən] n บรรณารักษ์ [ban na rak]

library ['laɪbrərɪ] n ห้องสมุด [hong sa mut]

Libya ['lɪbɪə] n ประเทศลิเบีย [pra tet li bia]

Libyan ['lɪbɪən] adj เกี่ยวกับลิเบีย [kiao kap li bia] ▷ n ชาวลิเบีย [chao li bia]

lice [laɪs] npl เหา [hao]

licence ['laɪsəns] n ใบอนุญาต [bai a nu yat]; **driving licence** n ใบขับขี่ [bai khap khi]

lick [lɪk] v เลีย [lia]

lid [lɪd] n ฝาปิด [fa pit]

lie [laɪ] n การโกหก [kan ko hok] ▷ v โกหก [ko hok]

Liechtenstein ['lɪktən,staɪn; 'lɪçtənʃtain] n ประเทศลิคเตนสไตน์ [pra tet lik ten sa tai]

lie down [laɪ daʊn] v นอนลง [non long]

lie in [laɪ ɪn] v การนอนตื่นสายในตอนเช้า [kan non tuen sai nai ton chao]

lie-in ['laɪɪn] n **have a lie-in** v การนอนตื่นสายในตอนเช้า [kan non tuen sai nai ton chao]

lieutenant [lɛf'tɛnənt; luː'tɛnənt] *n* นายร้อยโท [nai roi tho]

life [laɪf] *n* ชีวิต [chi wit]; **life insurance** *n* การประกันชีวิต [kan pra kan chi wit]; **life jacket** *n* เสื้อชูชีพ [suea chu chip]

lifebelt ['laɪf,bɛlt] *n* เข็มขัดชูชีพ [khem khat chu chip]

lifeboat ['laɪf,bəʊt] *n* เรือชูชีพ [rua chu chip]; **Call out the lifeboat!** เรียกเรือ ชูชีพ [riak ruea chu chip]

lifeguard ['laɪf,gɑːd] *n* เจ้าหน้าที่ช่วยคน ตกน้ำ [chao na thii chuai kon tok nam]; **Get the lifeguard!** เรียกเจ้าหน้าที่ ช่วยคนตกน้ำ [riak chao na thii chuai khon tok nam]

life-saving ['laɪf,seɪvɪŋ] *adj* ซึ่งช่วยชีวิต [sueng chuai chi wit]

lifestyle ['laɪf,staɪl] *n* วิถีทางการดำเนิน ชีวิต [wi thi thang kan dam noen chi wit]

lift [lɪft] *n (free ride)* การโดยสารไปด้วย [kan doi san pai duai], *(up/down)* ลิฟต์ [lip] ▷ *v* ยกขึ้น [yok khuen]; **ski lift** *n* กระเช้าไฟฟ้า [kra chao fai fa]; **Do you have a lift for wheelchairs?** คุณมีลิฟต์ สำหรับเก้าอี้เข็นคนพิการไหม? [khun mii lift sam rap kao ii khen khon phi kan mai]; **Where is the lift?** ลิฟต์อยู่ที่ไหน? [lift yu thii nai]

light [laɪt] *adj (not dark)* สว่าง [sa wang], *(not heavy)* เบา [bao] ▷ *n* แสงสว่าง [saeng sa wang] ▷ *v* จุดไฟ [chut fai]; **brake light** *n* ไฟเบรค [fai brek]; **hazard warning lights** *npl* ไฟเตือนอันตราย [fai tuean an ta rai]; **light bulb** *n* หลอดไฟ [lot fai]; **May I take it over to the light?** ฉันเอาไปดูตรงที่สว่างได้ไหม? [chan ao pai du trong thii sa wang dai mai]

lighter ['laɪtə] *n* ไฟแช็ก [fai cheak]

lighthouse ['laɪt,haʊs] *n* ประภาคาร [pra pha khan]

lighting ['laɪtɪŋ] *n* การจัดแสง [kan chat saeng]

lightning ['laɪtnɪŋ] *n* สายฟ้าแลบ [sai fa laep]

like [laɪk] *prep* เหมือนกับ [muean kap] ▷ *v* ชอบ [chop]; **I don't like...** ฉันไม่ชอบ... [chan mai chop...]; **I like...** ฉันชอบ... [chan chop...]; **I like you very much** ฉันชอบคุณมาก [chan chop khun mak]

likely ['laɪklɪ] *adj* เป็นไปได้ [pen pai dai]

lilac ['laɪlək] *adj* ที่มีสีม่วงอ่อน [thii mii sii muang on] ▷ *n* ดอกไลแลคมีสีม่วงแดงหรือ ขาวมีกลิ่นหอม [dok lai laek mii sii muang daeng rue khao mii klin hom]

Lilo® ['laɪləʊ] *n* เบาะพลาสติกที่เป่าให้พอง ลมได้ [bo phas tik thii pao hai phong lom dai]

lily ['lɪlɪ] *n* ดอกลิลลี่ [dok lil li]; **lily of the valley** *n* ดอกไม้ชื่อลิลลี่ออฟเดอะแวลลี่ มีสี ขาวมีกลิ่นหอม [dok mai chue lil li of doe vael li mii sii khao mii klin hom]

lime [laɪm] *n (compound)* ปูนขาว [pun khao], *(fruit)* มะนาว [ma nao]

limestone ['laɪm,stəʊn] *n* หินปูน [hin pun]

limit ['lɪmɪt] *n* ขีดจำกัด [khit cham kat]; **age limit** *n* อายุขั้นต่ำ [a yu khan tam]; **speed limit** *n* อัตราความเร็ว [at tra khwam reo]

limousine ['lɪmə,ziːn; ,lɪmə'ziːn] *n* รถ คันใหญ่ที่หรูหราโอ่อ่า [rot khan yai thii ru ra o a]

limp [lɪmp] *v* เดินโขยกเขยก [doen kha yok kha yek]

line [laɪn] *n* เส้นบรรทัด [sen ban that]; **washing line** *n* ราวตากผ้า [rao tak pha]

linen ['lɪnɪn] *n* ผ้าลินิน [pha li nin]; **bed linen** *n* ผ้าปูที่นอน [pha pu thi non]

liner ['laɪnə] *n* เรือหรือเครื่องบินที่เดินทาง ประจำเส้นทาง [ruea rue khrueang bin thii doen thang pra cham sen thang]

lingerie ['lænʒərɪ] *n* ชุดชั้นในของสตรี [chut chan nai khong sa tree]

linguist ['lɪŋgwɪst] *n* นักภาษาศาสตร์ [nak pha sa saat]

linguistic [lɪŋ'gwɪstɪk] *adj* เกี่ยวกับ ภาษาศาสตร์ [kiao kap pha sa sat]

lining ['laɪnɪŋ] n ผ้าซับใน [pha sab nai]

link [lɪŋk] n ข้อลูกโซ่ [kho luk so]; **link (up)** v เชื่อม [chueam]

lino ['laɪnəʊ] n เสื่อน้ำมัน [suea nam man]

lion ['laɪən] n สิงโต [sing to]

lioness ['laɪənɪs] n สิงโตตัวเมีย [sing to tua mia]

lip [lɪp] n ริมฝีปาก [rim fi pak]; **lip salve** n ครีมทากันริมฝีปากแตก [khrim tha kan rim fi pak taek]

lip-read ['lɪp,riːd] v แปลคำพูดด้วยการอ่านริมฝีปาก [plae kham phut duai kan an rim fi pak]

lipstick ['lɪp,stɪk] n ลิปสติก [lip sa tik]

liqueur [lɪ'kjʊə] n เหล้า [lao]; **What liqueurs do you have?** คุณมีเหล้าหวานชนิดไหน? [khun mii lao wan cha nit nai]

liquid ['lɪkwɪd] n ของเหลว [khong leo]; **washing-up liquid** n น้ำยาล้างจาน [nam ya lang chan]

liquidizer ['lɪkwɪ,daɪzə] n เครื่องทำให้เป็นของเหลว [khrueang tham hai pen khong leo]

list [lɪst] n รายการ [rai kan] ▷ v ลงรายการ [long rai kan]; **mailing list** n รายชื่อและที่อยู่ของคนที่ได้รับข่าวสาร โฆษณาและข้อมูลเป็นประจำ [rai chue lae thii yu khong khon thii dai rap khao san khot sa na lae kho mun pen pra cham]; **price list** n รายการราคา [rai kan ra kha]; **waiting list** n รายชื่อของคนที่รอคิวอยู่ [rai chue khong khon thii ro khio yu]; **The wine list, please** ขอรายการไวน์ [khor rai kan wine]

listen ['lɪsən] v ฟัง [fang]; **listen to** v ฟัง [fang]

listener ['lɪsnə] n ผู้ฟัง [phu fang]

literally ['lɪtərəlɪ] adv อย่างแท้จริง [yang thae ching]

literature ['lɪtərɪtʃə; 'lɪtrɪ-] n วรรณคดี [wan na kha di]

Lithuania [,lɪθjʊ'eɪnɪə] n ประเทศลิทัวเนีย [pra tet li thua nia]

Lithuanian [,lɪθjʊ'eɪnɪən] adj เกี่ยวกับลิทัวเนีย [kiao kap li thua nia] ▷ n (language) ภาษาลิทัวเนีย [pha sa li thua nia], (person) ชาวลิทัวเนีย [chao li thua nia]

litre ['liːtə] n หน่วยวัดปริมาณ ๑ ลิตร [nuai wat pa ri man nueng lit]

litter ['lɪtə] n ขยะ [kha ya], (offspring) ลูกสัตว์ [luk sat]; **litter bin** n ถังใส่ขยะ [thang sai kha ya]

little ['lɪtəl] adj เล็ก [lek]

live¹ [lɪv] v ดำเนินชีวิต [dam noen chi wit]

live² [laɪv] adj ที่มีชีวิตชีวา [thii mii chi wit chi wa]

lively ['laɪvlɪ] adj มีชีวิตชีวา [mi chi wit chi wa]

live on [lɪv ɒn] v มีชีวิตอยู่ต่อไป [mii chi wid yu to pai]

liver ['lɪvə] n ตับ [tap]

live together [lɪv] v อยู่ด้วยกัน [yu duai kan]

living ['lɪvɪŋ] n ความเป็นอยู่ [kham pen yu]; **cost of living** n ค่าครองชีพ [kha khrong chiip]; **living room** n ห้องนั่งเล่น [hong nang len]; **standard of living** n มาตรฐานการครองชีพ [mat tra than kan khrong chip]

lizard ['lɪzəd] n สัตว์เลื้อยคลานเช่นจิ้งจกหรือตุ๊กแก [sat lueai khlan chen ching chok rue tuk kae]

load [ləʊd] n น้ำหนักบรรทุก [nam nak ban thuk] ▷ v บรรทุกสินค้า [ban thuk sin kha]

loaf, loaves [ləʊf, ləʊvz] n ก้อนขนมปัง [kon kha nom pang]

loan [ləʊn] n เงินกู้ [ngoen ku] ▷ v ให้กู้เงิน [hai ku ngoen]

loathe [ləʊð] v เกลียดชัง [kliat chang]

lobby ['lɒbɪ] n **I'll meet you in the lobby** ฉันจะไปพบคุณที่ล็อบบี้ [chan ja pai phop khun thii lop bi]

lobster ['lɒbstə] n กุ้งทะเลขนาดใหญ่ [kung tha le kha nat yai]

local ['ləʊkᵊl] *adj* ประจำท้องถิ่น [pra cham thong thin]; **local anaesthetic** *n* ยาชาเฉพาะแห่ง [ya chaa cha pho haeng]

location [ləʊ'keɪʃən] *n* สถานที่ [sa than thi]

lock [lɒk] *n* (door) กุญแจ [kun chae], (hair) ปอยผม [poi phom] ▷ *v* ใส่กุญแจ [sai kun jae]; **Can I have a lock?** ฉันขอกุญแจล็อคได้ไหม? [chan kho kun jae lok dai mai]; **The door won't lock** ใส่กุญแจประตูไม่ได้ [sai kun jae pra tu mai dai]; **The lock is broken** กุญแจเสีย [kun jae sia]

locker ['lɒkə] *n* ตู้ล็อคเกอร์ [tu lok koe]; **left-luggage locker** *n* ตู้ล็อคเกอร์เก็บกระเป๋าเดินทาง [tu lok koe kep kra pao doen thang]; **Where are the clothes lockers?** ตู้ล็อคเกอร์เสื้อผ้าอยู่ที่ไหน? [tu lok koe suea pha yu thii nai]

locket ['lɒkɪt] *n* จี้ห้อยคอ [chi hoi kho]

lock out [lɒk aʊt] *v* ปิดประตูทางเข้า [pid pra tu thang khao]

locksmith ['lɒkˌsmɪθ] *n* ช่างทำกุญแจ [chang tham kun jae]

lodger ['lɒdʒə] *n* ผู้พักอาศัย [phu phak a sai]

loft [lɒft] *n* ห้องเพดาน [hong phe dan]

log [lɒg] *n* ไม้เป็นท่อน [mai pen thon]

logical ['lɒdʒɪkᵊl] *adj* มีเหตุผล [mii het phon]

log in [lɒg ɪn] *v* ลงบันทึกเข้า [long ban thuek khao]

logo ['ləʊgəʊ; 'lɒg-] *n* โลโก้ [lo ko]

log off [lɒg ɒf] *v* ลงบันทึกปิด [long ban thuek pit]

log on [lɒg ɒn] *v* ลงบันทึกเปิด [long ban thuek poet]

log out [lɒg aʊt] *v* บันทึกออกไป [ban thuek ork pai]

lollipop ['lɒlɪˌpɒp] *n* ลูกอมยิ้ม [luk om yim]

lolly ['lɒlɪ] *n* อมยิ้ม [om yim]

London ['lʌndən] *n* ลอนดอน [lon don]

loneliness ['ləʊnlɪnɪs] *n* ความเหงา [khwam ngao]

lonely ['ləʊnlɪ] *adj* หงอยเหงา [ngoi ngao]

lonesome ['ləʊnsəm] *adj* เดียวดาย [diao dai]

long [lɒŋ] *adj* ยาว [yao] ▷ *adv* ยาวนาน [yao nan] ▷ *v* รอคอย [ro khoi]; **long jump** *n* กระโดดยาว [kra dot yao]

longer [lɒŋə] *adv* ยาวกว่า [yao kwa]

longitude ['lɒndʒɪˌtjuːd; 'lɒŋg-] *n* เส้นแวง [sen waeng]

loo [luː] *n* ห้องน้ำ [hong nam]

look [lʊk] *n* การมอง [kan morng] ▷ *v* มองดู [morng du]; **look at** *v* ดูที่ [du thii]

look after [lʊk ɑːftə] *v* ดูแล [du lae]; **I need someone to look after the children tonight** ฉันอยากได้คนดูแลเด็ก ๆ คืนนี้ [chan yak dai khon du lae dek dek khuen nii]

look for [lʊk fɔː] *v* มองหา [mong ha]; **We're looking for...** เรากำลังมองหา... [rao kam lang mong ha...]

look round [lʊk raʊnd] *v* มองไปรอบ ๆ [mong pai rop rop]

look up [lʊk ʌp] *v* ค้นหาศัพท์หรือข้อมูล [khon ha sap rue kho mun]

loose [luːs] *adj* หลวม [luam]

lorry ['lɒrɪ] *n* รถบรรทุก [rot ban thuk]; **lorry driver** *n* คนขับรถบรรทุก [khon khap rot ban thuk]

lose [luːz] *vi* พ่ายแพ้ [phai phae] ▷ *vt* สูญเสีย [sun sia]

loser ['luːzə] *n* ผู้สูญเสีย [phu sun sia]

loss [lɒs] *n* ความสูญเสีย [khwam sun sia]

lost [lɒst] *adj* สูญหาย [sun hai]; **lost-property office** *n* สำนักงานเก็บของหาย [sam nak ngan kep khong hai]

lost-and-found ['lɒstænd'faʊnd] *n* ที่เก็บของหาย [thii keb khong hai]

lot [lɒt] *n* **a lot** *n* จำนวนทั้งหมด [cham nuan thang mot]

lotion ['ləʊʃən] *n* โลชั่น [lo chan]; **after sun lotion** *n* โลชั่นหลังอาบแดด [lo chan lang aap daet]; **cleansing lotion** *n*

โลชั่นทำความสะอาด [lo chan tham khwam sa at]; **suntan lotion** n ครีมที่ทำให้ผิวเป็นสีน้ำตาล [khrim thii tham hai phio pen sii nam tan]

lottery ['lɒtərɪ] n สลากกินแบ่ง [sa lak kin baeng]

loud [laʊd] adj ดัง [dang]; **Could you speak louder, please?** คุณกรุณาพูดดังกว่านี้ได้ไหม? [khun ka ru na phut dang kwa nii dai mai]; **It's too loud** เสียงดังเกินไป [siang dang koen pai]

loudly [laʊdlɪ] adv อย่างเสียงดัง [yang siang dang]

loudspeaker [,laʊd'spi:kə] n เครื่องกระจายเสียง [khrueang kra jai siang]

lounge [laʊndʒ] n ห้องนั่งเล่นในบ้าน [hong nang len nai baan]; **departure lounge** n ห้องพักผู้โดยสารที่จะเดินทางออก [hong phak phu doi san thii ja doen thang ok]; **transit lounge** n ห้องพักสำหรับผู้โดยสารที่เปลี่ยนเครื่องบิน [hong phak sam rap phu doi san thii ja plian khrueang bin]

lousy ['laʊzɪ] adj น่ารังเกียจ [na rang kiat]

love [lʌv] n ความรัก [khwam rak] ▷ v รัก [rak]; **I love...** ฉันรัก... [chan rak...]; **I love you** ฉันรักคุณ [chan rak khun]; **Yes, I'd love to** ใช่ ฉันรักที่จะ... [chai chan rak thii ja...]

lovely ['lʌvlɪ] adj น่ารัก [na rak]

lover ['lʌvə] n คู่รัก [khu rak]

low [ləʊ] adj ต่ำ [tam] ▷ adv ต่ำ [tam]; **low season** n ฤดูท่องเที่ยวที่มีนักท่องเที่ยวน้อย [rue du thong thiao thii mii nak thong thiao noi]

low-alcohol ['ləʊˌælkəˌhɒl] adj แอลกอฮอล์ต่ำ [aen ko ho tam]

lower ['ləʊə] adj ที่ต่ำกว่า [thii tam kwa] ▷ v ต่ำกว่า [tam kwa]

low-fat ['ləʊˌfæt] adj ที่ไขมันต่ำ [thii khai man tam]

loyalty ['lɔɪəltɪ] n ความจงรักภักดี [khwam chong rak phak dii]

luck [lʌk] n โชค [chok]

luckily ['lʌkɪlɪ] adv โชคดี [chok di]

lucky ['lʌkɪ] adj โชคดี [chok di]

lucrative ['lu:krətɪv] adj มีกำไรงาม [mii kam rai ngam]

luggage ['lʌgɪdʒ] n กระเป๋าเดินทาง [kra pao doen thang]; **hand luggage** n กระเป๋าเดินทางใบเล็กที่ถือขึ้นเครื่องบิน [kra pao doen thang bai lek thii thue khuen khrueang bin]; **Are there any luggage trolleys?** มีรถเข็นกระเป๋าเดินทางไหม? [mii rot khen kra pao doen thang mai]; **Can I insure my luggage?** ฉันขอประกันกระเป๋าเดินทางของฉันได้ไหม? [chan kho pra kan kra pao doen thang khong chan dai mai]; **My luggage has been damaged** กระเป๋าเดินทางฉันเสียหาย [kra pao doen thang chan sia hai]

lukewarm [,lu:k'wɔ:m] adj อุ่น [un]

lullaby ['lʌləˌbaɪ] n เพลงร้องกล่อมเด็ก [phleng rong klom dek]

lump [lʌmp] n ก้อน [kon]

lunatic ['lu:ˌnætɪk] n คนบ้า [khon ba]

lunch [lʌntʃ] n อาหารกลางวัน [a han klang wan]; **Can we meet for lunch?** เราพบกันตอนอาหารกลางวันได้ไหม? [rao phop kan ton a han klang wan dai mai]; **I'm free for lunch** ฉันว่างตอนอาหารกลางวัน [chan wang ton a han klang wan]; **The lunch was excellent** อาหารกลางวันที่ยอดเยี่ยม [a han klang wan thii yot yiam]

lunchtime ['lʌntʃˌtaɪm] n เวลาอาหารกลางวัน [we la a han klang wan]

lung [lʌŋ] n ปอด [pot]

lush [lʌʃ] adj เขียวชอุ่ม [kheo cha um]

lust [lʌst] n ตัณหา [tan ha]

Luxembourg ['lʌksəmˌbɜːg] n ประเทศลักเซมเบิร์ก [pra tet lak sem boek]

luxurious [lʌg'zjʊərɪəs] adj หรูหรา [ru ra]

luxury ['lʌkʃərɪ] n ความหรูหรา [khwam ru ra]

lyrics ['lɪrɪks] npl เนื้อเพลง [nuea phleng]

mac [mæk] *abbr* ตัวย่อของเสื้อคลุมกันฝน [tua yor khong suea khlum kan fon]

macaroni [ˌmækəˈrəʊnɪ] *npl* มะกะโรนี [ma ka ro ni]

machine [məˈʃiːn] *n* เครื่องจักร [khrueang chak]; **answering machine** *n* เครื่องตอบรับโทรศัพท์ [khrueang top rap tho ra sap]; **machine gun** *n* ปืนกล [puen kon]; **machine washable** *adj* ซักด้วยเครื่องซักผ้าได้ [sak duai khrueang sak pha dai]

machinery [məˈʃiːnərɪ] *n* เครื่องจักร [khrueang chak]

mackerel [ˈmækrəl] *n* ปลาแม็กเคอเรล [pla mak koe rel]

mad [mæd] *adj (angry)* โกรธ [krot], *(insane)* วิกลจริต [wi kon cha rit]

Madagascar [ˌmædəˈgæskə] *n* เกาะมาดากัสการ์ในมหาสมุทรอินเดีย [ko ma da kas ka nai ma ha sa mut in dia]

madam [ˈmædəm] *n* คุณผู้หญิง [khun phu ying]

madly [ˈmædlɪ] *adv* อย่างเสียสติ [yang sia sa ti]

madman [ˈmædmən] *n* คนบ้า [khon ba]

madness [ˈmædnɪs] *n* ความวิกลจริต [khwam wi kon ja rit]

magazine [ˌmægəˈziːn] *n (ammunition)* ที่ใส่กระสุน [thii sai kra sun], *(periodical)* นิตยสาร [nit ta ya san]; **Where can I buy a magazine?** ฉันจะซื้อนิตยสารได้ที่ไหน? [chan ja sue nit ta ya san dai thii nai]

maggot [ˈmægət] *n* หนอน [non]

magic [ˈmædʒɪk] *adj* วิเศษ [wi set] ▷ *n* เวทมนตร์ [wet mon]

magical [ˈmædʒɪkəl] *adj* ซึ่งมีเวทมนตร์ [sueng mii wet mon]

magician [məˈdʒɪʃən] *n* นักเล่นกล [nak len kon]

magistrate [ˈmædʒɪˌstreɪt; -strɪt] *n* เจ้าหน้าที่ฝ่ายปกครอง [chao na thii fai pok khrong]

magnet [ˈmægnɪt] *n* แม่เหล็ก [mae lek]

magnetic [mægˈnɛtɪk] *adj* ซึ่งมีคุณสมบัติเป็นแม่เหล็ก [sueng mii khun som bat pen mae lek]

magnificent [mægˈnɪfɪsənt] *adj* สง่างาม [sa nga ngam]

magpie [ˈmægˌpaɪ] *n* นกแมกไพ [nok maek phai]

mahogany [məˈhɒgənɪ] *n* ต้นมะฮอกกานี [ton ma hok ka ni]

maid [meɪd] *n* สาวใช้ [sao chai]

maiden [ˈmeɪdən] *n* **maiden name** *n* ชื่อสกุลของหญิงก่อนแต่งงาน [chue sa kun khong ying kon taeng ngan]

mail [meɪl] *n* จดหมาย [chot mai] ▷ *v* ส่งจดหมาย [song chod mai]; **junk mail** *n* จดหมายที่ไม่ต้องการส่วนมากเป็นการโฆษณาขายสินค้า [chot mai thii mai tong kan suan mak pen kan khot sa na khai sin ka]; **Is there any mail for me?** มีจดหมายถึงฉันบ้างไหม? [mii chot mai thueng chan bang mai]; **Please send my mail on to this address** ช่วยส่งจดหมายฉันไปตามที่อยู่ที่นี่ [chuai song chot mai chan pai tam thii yu thii ni]

mailbox ['meɪlˌbɒks] *n* ตู้จดหมาย [tu chod mai]

mailing list ['meɪlɪŋ 'lɪst] *n* รายชื่อและที่อยู่ของคนที่ได้รับข่าวสาร โฆษณาและข้อมูลเป็นประจำ [rai chue lae thii yu khong khon thii dai rap khao san khot sa na lae kho mun pen pra cham]

main [meɪn] *adj* หลัก [luk]; **main course** *n* อาหารมื้อหลัก [a han mue lak]; **main road** *n* ถนนสายหลัก [tha non sai lak]

mainland ['meɪnlənd] *n* แผ่นดินใหญ่ [phaen din yai]

mainly ['meɪnlɪ] *adv* โดยส่วนใหญ่ [doi suan yai]

maintain [meɪn'teɪn] *v* ดูแลรักษา [du lae rak sa]

maintenance ['meɪntɪnəns] *n* การดูแลรักษา [kan du lae rak sa]

maize [meɪz] *n* ข้าวโพด [khao pot]

majesty ['mædʒɪstɪ] *n* ความสงผาเผย [khwam sa nga pha phoei]

major ['meɪdʒə] *adj* ส่วนมาก [suan mak]

majority [mə'dʒɒrɪtɪ] *n* ส่วนใหญ่ [suan yai]

make [meɪk] *v* ทำ [tham]; **Is it made with unpasteurised milk?** นี่ทำจากนมที่ไม่ได้ผ่านการฆ่าเชื้อโรคด้วยความร้อนสูงหรือเปล่า? [ni tham chak nom thii mai dai phan kan kha chuea rok duai khwam ron sung rue plao]; **Where can I make a phone call?** ฉันจะโทรศัพท์ได้ที่ไหน? [chan ja tho ra sap dai thii nai]

makeover ['meɪkˌəʊvə] *n* การเปลี่ยนแปลง [kan plian plaeng]

maker ['meɪkə] *n* ผู้ผลิต [phu pha lit]

make up [meɪk ʌp] *v* ทำขึ้น [tham khuen]

make-up [meɪkʌp] *n* เครื่องสำอางค์ [khrueang sam ang]

malaria [mə'lɛərɪə] *n* ไข้มาลาเรีย [khai ma la ria]

Malawi [mə'lɑːwɪ] *n* ประเทศมาลาวี [pra tet ma la wi]

Malaysia [mə'leɪzɪə] *n* ประเทศมาเลเซีย [pra tet ma le sia]

Malaysian [mə'leɪzɪən] *adj* เกี่ยวกับประเทศมาเลเซีย [kiao kap pra thet ma le sia] ▷ *n* ชาวมาเลเซีย [chao ma le sia]

male [meɪl] *adj* ซึ่งเป็นของผู้ชาย [sueng pen khong phu chai] ▷ *n* ผู้ชาย [phu chai]

malicious [mə'lɪʃəs] *adj* มุ่งร้าย [mung rai]

malignant [mə'lɪgnənt] *adj* ที่มุ่งร้าย [thii mung rai]

malnutrition [ˌmælnjuː'trɪʃən] *n* การขาดอาหาร [kan khat a han]

Malta ['mɔːltə] *n* ประเทศมอลตา [pra tet mol ta]

Maltese [mɔːl'tiːz] *adj* เกี่ยวกับมอลตา [kiao kap mol ta] ▷ *n (language)* ภาษามอลตา [pha sa mol ta], *(person)* ชาวมอลตา [chao mol ta]

mammal ['mæməl] *n* สัตว์เลี้ยงลูกด้วยนม [sat liang luk duai nom]

mammoth ['mæməθ] *adj* มหึมา [ma hue ma] ▷ *n* สัตว์ขนาดใหญ่คล้ายช้างขนยาว งาโค้งยาวสูญพันธุ์ไปแล้ว [sat kha nat yai khlai chang khon yao nga khong yao sun phan pai laeo]

man, men [mæn, mɛn] *n* ผู้ชาย [phu chai]; **best man** *n* เพื่อนเจ้าบ่าว [phuean chao bao]

manage ['mænɪdʒ] *v* จัดการ [chat kan]

manageable ['mænɪdʒəbˀl] *adj* ที่จัดการได้ [thii chat kan dai]

management ['mænɪdʒmənt] *n* คณะผู้บริหาร [kha na phu bo ri han]

manager ['mænɪdʒə] *n* ผู้จัดการ [phu chat kan]; **I'd like to speak to the manager, please** ฉันขอพูดกับผู้จัดการ [chan kho phut kap phu chat kan]

manageress [ˌmænɪdʒə'rɛs; 'mænɪdʒəˌrɛs] *n* ผู้จัดการหญิง [phu chat kan ying]

mandarin ['mændərɪn] *n (fruit)* ส้ม

[som], *(official)* ภาษาจีนกลาง [pha sa chin klang]

mangetout ['mɑ̃ʒ'tuː] *n* ถั่วผักชนิดหนึ่ง [thua phak cha nit hueng]

mango ['mæŋgəʊ] *n* มะม่วง [ma muang]

mania ['meɪnɪə] *n* ความคลั่งไคล้ [khwam khlang khlai]

maniac ['meɪnɪˌæk] *n* คนคลั่ง [khon khlang]

manicure ['mænɪˌkjʊə] *n* การทำเล็บ [kan tham leb] ▷ *v* ทำเล็บ [tham leb]

manipulate [məˈnɪpjʊˌleɪt] *v* ควบคุมบงการ [khuap khum bong kan]

mankind [ˌmænˈkaɪnd] *n* มนุษยชาติ [ma nut sa ya chat]

man-made ['mænˌmeɪd] *adj* ซึ่งสร้างขึ้นมา [sueng sang khuen ma]

manner ['mænə] *n* ลักษณะท่าทาง [lak sa na tha thang]

manners ['mænəz] *npl* มรรยาท [ma ra yat]

manpower ['mænˌpaʊə] *n* กำลังคน [kam lang kon]

mansion ['mænʃən] *n* บ้านหลังใหญ่ [baan hlang yai]

mantelpiece ['mæntˀlˌpiːs] *n* ชั้นที่อยู่เหนือเตาผิง [chan thii yu nuea tao phing]

manual ['mænjʊəl] *n* หนังสือคู่มือ [nang sue khu mue]

manufacture [ˌmænjʊˈfæktʃə] *v* ผลิต [pha lit]

manufacturer [ˌmænjʊˈfæktʃərə] *n* ผู้ผลิต [phu pha lit]

manure [məˈnjʊə] *n* มูลสัตว์ [mun sat]

manuscript ['mænjʊˌskrɪpt] *n* หนังสือที่เขียนด้วยลายมือ [hnang sue thii khian duai lai mue]

many ['mɛnɪ] *adj* มากมาย [mak mai] ▷ *pron* คนหรือสิ่งของจำนวนมาก [khon rue ma sing khong cham nuan mak]

Maori ['maʊrɪ] *adj* เกี่ยวกับเมารี [kiao kap mao ri] ▷ *n (language)* ภาษาเมารี [pha sa mao ri], *(person)* ชาวเมารี [chao mao ri]

map [mæp] *n* แผนที่ [phaen thi]; **Can I have a map?** ฉันขอแผนที่ได้ไหม? [chan kho phaen thii dai mai]; **Can you draw me a map with directions?** คุณวาดแผนที่บอกทิศทางให้ฉันได้ไหม? [khun wat phaen thii bok thit thang hai chan dai mai]; **Can you show me where it is on the map?** คุณบอกฉันได้ไหมว่ามันอยู่ที่ใดบนแผนที่ [khun bok chan dai mai wa man yu thii dai bon phaen thii]

maple ['meɪpˀl] *n* ต้นเมเปิล [ton me poel]

marathon ['mærəθən] *n* การวิ่งแข่งมาราธอน [kan wing khaeng ma ra thon]

marble ['mɑːbˀl] *n* หินอ่อน [hin on]

march [mɑːtʃ] *n* การเดินขบวน [kan doen kha buan] ▷ *v* เดิน [doen]

March [mɑːtʃ] *n* เดือนกุมภาพันธ์ [duean kum pha phan]

mare [mɛə] *n* ม้าหรือม้าลายตัวเมีย [ma rue ma lai tua mia]

margarine [ˌmɑːdʒəˈriːn; ˌmɑːgə-] *n* เนยเทียม [noei thiam]

margin ['mɑːdʒɪn] *n* ขอบ [khop]

marigold ['mærɪˌgəʊld] *n* ต้นไม้ประเภทดาวเรือง [ton mai pra phet dao rueang]

marijuana [ˌmærɪˈhwɑːnə] *n* กัญชา [kan cha]

marina [məˈriːnə] *n* ท่าจอดเรือ [tha jot ruea]

marinade *n* [ˌmærɪˈneɪd] การหมัก [kan mak] ▷ *v* ['mærɪˌneɪd] หมัก [mak]

marital ['mærɪtˀl] *adj* **marital status** *n* สถานภาพการแต่งงาน [sa tha na phap kan taeng ngan]

maritime ['mærɪˌtaɪm] *adj* ทางทะเล [thang tha le]

marjoram ['mɑːdʒərəm] *n* ต้นมาจอรั่มมีใบหอมใช้ปรุงอาหารและใส่ในสลัด [ton ma cho ram mii bai hom chai prung a han lae sai nai sa lat]

mark [mɑːk] *n* คะแนน [kha naen] ▷ *v* (*grade*) การให้คะแนน [kan hai kha naen], (*make sign*) ทำเครื่องหมาย [tham khueang mai]; **exclamation mark** *n* เครื่องหมายอัศเจรีย์ [khrueang mai at sa je ri]; **question mark** *n* เครื่องหมายคำถาม [khrueang mai kham tham]; **quotation marks** *npl* อัญประกาศ [an ya pra kat]

market ['mɑːkɪt] *n* ตลาด [ta lat]; **market research** *n* การวิจัยตลาด [kan wi jai ta lad]; **stock market** *n* ตลาดหุ้น [ta lad hun]; **When is the market on?** มีตลาดเมื่อไร? [mii ta lat muea rai]

marketing ['mɑːkɪtɪŋ] *n* การทำการตลาด [kan tham kan ta lat]

marketplace ['mɑːkɪtˌpleɪs] *n* ตลาดสินค้า [ta lat sin kha]

marmalade ['mɑːməˌleɪd] *n* แยมส้ม [yam som]

maroon [məˈruːn] *adj* ซึ่งมีสีแดงม่วงเข้มอมน้ำตาล [sueng mee see daeng muang khem om nam tan]

marriage ['mærɪdʒ] *n* การแต่งงาน [kan taeng ngan]; **marriage certificate** *n* ใบทะเบียนสมรส [bai tha bian som rot]

married ['mærɪd] *adj* ได้แต่งงานแล้ว [dai taeng ngan laeo]

marrow ['mærəʊ] *n* บวบฝรั่งขนาดใหญ่ [buap fa rang kha naat yai]

marry ['mærɪ] *v* แต่งงาน [taeng ngan]

marsh [mɑːʃ] *n* บึง [bueng]

martyr ['mɑːtə] *n* ผู้ยอมเสียสละชีวิตเพื่อศาสนาหรือความเชื่อของตน [phu yom sia sa la chi wit phuea sat sa na rue khwam chuea khong ton]

marvellous ['mɑːvˡəs] *adj* ดีเยี่ยม [di yiam]

Marxism ['mɑːksɪzəm] *n* ลัทธิมาร์กซ์ [lat thi mark]

marzipan ['mɑːzɪˌpæn] *n* ส่วนผสมของอัลมอนด์น้ำตาลและไข่ขาวใส่บนหน้าเค้ก [suan pha som khong a mon nam tan lae khai khao sai bon na khek]

mascara [mæˈskɑːrə] *n* เครื่องสำอางค์ใช้ทาขนตา [khrueang sam ang chai tha khon ta]

masculine ['mæskjʊlɪn] *adj* อย่างผู้ชาย [yang phu chai]

mask [mɑːsk] *n* หน้ากาก [na kak]

masked [mɑːskt] *adj* ที่ใส่หน้ากาก [thii sai na kak]

mass [mæs] *n* (*amount*) จำนวนมาก [cham nuan mak], (*church*) พิธีแมสในโบถส์ [phi ti maes nai bot]

massacre ['mæsəkə] *n* การฆ่าหมู่ [kan kha mu]

massage ['mæsɑːʒ, -sɑːdʒ] *n* การนวด [kan nuat]

massive ['mæsɪv] *adj* ใหญ่โต [yai to]

mast [mɑːst] *n* เสาเรือ [sao ruea]

master ['mɑːstə] *n* เจ้านาย [chao nai] ▷ *v* เข้าใจถ่องแท้ [khao jai thong thae]

masterpiece ['mɑːstəˌpiːs] *n* งานชิ้นเอก [ngan chin ek]

mat [mæt] *n* เสื่อ [suea]; **mouse mat** *n* แผ่นรองเมาส์ [phaen rong mao]

match [mætʃ] *n* (*partnership*) คู่ที่เหมือนกัน [khu thiihmuean kan], (*sport*) การแข่งขัน [kan khaeng khan] ▷ *v* เหมาะกัน [mo kan]; **away match** *n* การแข่งขันที่ไปเล่นที่อื่น [kan khaeng khan thii pai len thii uen]; **home match** *n* การแข่งขันที่เล่นที่สนามกีฬาของเจ้าถิ่น [kan khaeng khan thii len thii sa nam ki la khong chao thin]

matching [mætʃɪŋ] *adj* เข้ากัน [khao kan]

mate [meɪt] *n* เพื่อน [phuean]

material [məˈtɪərɪəl] *n* วัสดุ [wat sa du]; **What is the material?** วัสดุอะไร? [wat sa du a rai]

maternal [məˈtɜːnˡl] *adj* เกี่ยวกับมารดา [kiao kap man da]

mathematical [ˌmæθəˈmætɪkˡl; ˌmæθˈmæt-] *adj* เกี่ยวกับคณิตศาสตร์ [kiao kap kha nit ta sat]

mathematics [ˌmæθəˈmætɪks;

,mæθ'mæt-] *npl* คณิตศาสตร์ [kha nit ta sat]

maths [mæθs] *npl* วิชาคณิตศาสตร์ [wi cha kha nit ta sat]

matter ['mætə] *n* สิ่งที่ต้องทำ [sing thii tong tham] ▷ *v* เป็นเรื่องสำคัญ [pen rueang sam khan]

mattress ['mætrɪs] *n* ที่นอน [thi non]

mature [mə'tjʊə; -'tʃʊə] *adj* เป็นผู้ใหญ่ [pen phu yai]; **mature student** *n* นักเรียนผู้ใหญ่ [nak rian phu yai]

Mauritania [ˌmɒrɪ'teɪnɪə] *n* ประเทศมอริ ทาเนีย [pra tet mo ri tha nia]

Mauritius [mə'rɪʃəs] *n* ชาวมอริชัส [chao mo ri chas]

mauve [məʊv] *adj* สีม่วงอ่อน [sii muang on]

maximum ['mæksɪməm] *adj* สูงสุด [sung sut] ▷ *n* จำนวนสูงสุด [cham nuan sung sut]

may [meɪ] *v* **May I call you tomorrow?** ฉันโทรหาคุณพรุ่งนี้ได้ไหม? [chan tho ha khun phrung nii dai mai]; **May I open the window?** ฉันขอเปิดหน้าต่างได้ไหม? [chan kho poet na tang dai mai]

May [meɪ] *n* เดือนพฤษภาคม [duean phruet sa pha khom]

maybe ['meɪˌbiː] *adv* อาจจะ [at cha]

mayonnaise [ˌmeɪə'neɪz] *n* มายองเนส [ma yong net]

mayor, mayoress [mɛə, 'mɛərɪs] *n* นายกเทศมนตรี [na yok tet sa mon tree]

maze [meɪz] *n* ทางวกวน [thang wok won]

me [miː] *pron* ฉัน [chan]; **Can you show me where it is on the map?** คุณบอกฉันได้ไหมว่ามันอยู่ที่ใดบนแผนที่ [khun bok chan dai mai wa man yu thii dai bon phaen thii]; **Please let me off** ขอให้ฉันลงจากรถ [kho hai chan long chak rot]

meadow ['mɛdəʊ] *n* ทุ่งหญ้า [thung ya]

meal [miːl] *n* มื้ออาหาร [mue a han]

mealtime ['miːlˌtaɪm] *n* เวลาอาหาร [we la a han]

mean [miːn] *adj* ค่าเฉลี่ย [kha cha lia] ▷ *v* หมายความว่า [mai khwam wa]

meaning ['miːnɪŋ] *n* ความหมาย [khwam mai]

means [miːnz] *npl* วิธี [wi thi]

meantime ['miːnˌtaɪm] *adv* ในระหว่าง นั้น [nai ra wang nan]

meanwhile ['miːnˌwaɪl] *adv* ขณะที่ [kha na thi]

measles ['miːzəlz] *npl* โรคหัด [rok hat]; **German measles** *n* หัดเยอรมัน [hat yoe ra man]; **I had measles recently** ฉัน เป็นโรคหัดเมื่อเร็ว ๆ นี้ [chan pen rok hat muea reo reo nii]

measure ['mɛʒə] *v* วัด [wat]; **tape measure** *n* สายวัด [sai wat]; **Can you measure me, please?** คุณช่วยวัดตัวฉัน ได้ไหม? [khun chuai wat tua chan dai mai]

measurements ['mɛʒəmənts] *npl* การ วัด [kan wat]

meat [miːt] *n* เนื้อ [nuea]; **Do you eat meat?** คุณทานเนื้อไหม? [khun than nuea mai]; **I don't eat meat** ฉันไม่กิน เนื้อ [chan mai kin nuea], ฉันไม่ทานเนื้อ [chan mai kin nuea, chan mai than nuea]; **I don't eat red meat** ฉันไม่กิน เนื้อแดง [chan mai kin nuea daeng]

meatball ['miːtˌbɔːl] *n* ลูกชิ้น [luk chin]

Mecca ['mɛkə] *n* กรุงเมกกะ [krung mek ka]

mechanic [mɪ'kænɪk] *n* ช่างเครื่อง [chang khrueang]

mechanical [mɪ'kænɪkᵊl] *adj* เกี่ยวกับ เครื่องจักรกล [kiao kap khrueang chak kon]

mechanism ['mɛkəˌnɪzəm] *n* กลไกการ ทำงานของเครื่องจักร [kon kai kan tham ngan khong khrueang chak]

medal ['mɛdᵊl] *n* เหรียญ [rian]

medallion [mɪ'dæljən] *n* การประดับ เหรียญให้ [kan pra dap rian hai]

media ['miːdɪə] *npl* สื่อมวลชน [sue

muan chon]

mediaeval [ˌmɛdɪˈiːvəl] *adj* เกี่ยวกับยุค กลาง [kiao kap yuk klang]

medical [ˈmɛdɪkəl] *adj* ทางการแพทย์ [thang kan phaet] ▷ *n* การตรวจร่างกาย [kan truat rang kai]; **medical certificate** *n* ใบรับรองแพทย์ [bai rap rong phaet]

medication [ˌmɛdɪˈkeɪʃən] *n* **I'm on this medication** ฉันกำลังใช้ยานี้ [chan kam lang chai ya nii]

medicine [ˈmɛdɪsɪn; ˈmɛdsɪn] *n* ยา [ya]; **I'm already taking this medicine** ฉันได้รับยานี้ไปแล้ว [chan dai rap ya nii pai laeo]

meditation [ˌmɛdɪˈteɪʃən] *n* การนั่ง สมาธิ [kan nang sa ma thi]

Mediterranean [ˌmɛdɪtəˈreɪnɪən] *adj* เกี่ยวกับทะเลเมดิเตอร์เรเนียน [kiao kap tha le me di toe re nian] ▷ *n* ทะเล เมดิเตอร์เรเนียน [tha le me di toe re nian]

medium [ˈmiːdɪəm] *adj (between extremes)* ซึ่งอยู่ระหว่างกลาง [sueng yu ra wang klang]

medium-sized [ˈmiːdɪəmˌsaɪzd] *adj* ขนาดกลาง [kha nat klang]

meet [miːt] *vi* ชุมนุม จัดให้พบกัน [chum num, chat hai phop kan] ▷ *vt* พบโดย บังเอิญ ต้อนรับ [phop doi bang oen, ton rab]

meeting [ˈmiːtɪŋ] *n* การประชุม [kan pra chum]; **I'd like to arrange a meeting with...** ฉันอยากจัดให้การประชุมกับ... [chan yak chat hai kan pra chum kap...]

meet up [miːt ʌp] *v* พบกัน [phob kan]

mega [ˈmɛgə] *adj* ยิ่งใหญ่ [ying yai]

melody [ˈmɛlədɪ] *n* เสียงดนตรี [siang don trii]

melon [ˈmɛlən] *n* เมลอนเป็นผลไม้พวก แตง [me lon pen phon la mai cham phuak taeng]

melt [mɛlt] *vi* ละลาย ทำให้หลอมละลาย

[la lai, tham hai lom la lai]

=2*vt* ละลาย ทำให้หลอมละลาย [la lai, tham hai lom la lai]

member [ˈmɛmbə] *n* สมาชิก [sa ma chik]; **Do I have to be a member?** ฉัน ต้องเป็นสมาชิกไหม? [chan tong pen sa ma chik mai]

membership [ˈmɛmbəˌʃɪp] *n* การเป็น สมาชิก [kan pen sa ma chik]; **membership card** *n* บัตรสมาชิก [bat sa ma chik]

memento [mɪˈmɛntəʊ] *n* ของที่ระลึก [khong thi ra luek]

memo [ˈmɛməʊ] *n* กระดาษจดบันทึก [kra dart chod ban thuek]

memorial [mɪˈmɔːrɪəl] *n* อนุสรณ์ [a nu son]

memorize [ˈmɛməˌraɪz] *v* ท่องจำ [thong cham]

memory [ˈmɛmərɪ] *n* ความจำ [khwam cham]; **memory card** *n* การ์ดบันทึก ความจำของคอมพิวเตอร์ [kat ban thuek khwam cham khong khom pio toe]

mend [mɛnd] *v* ซ่อมแซม [som saem]

meningitis [ˌmɛnɪnˈdʒaɪtɪs] *n* เยื่อหุ้ม สมองอักเสบ [yuea hum sa mong ak sep]

menopause [ˈmɛnəʊˌpɔːz] *n* ช่วงวัย หมดประจำเดือน [chuang wai mot pra cham duen]

menstruation [ˌmɛnstrʊˈeɪʃən] *n* การ มีประจำเดือน [kan mii pra cham duen]

mental [ˈmɛntəl] *adj* เป็นโรคจิต [pen rok chit]; **mental hospital** *n* โรงพยาบาล โรคจิต [rong pha ya baan rok chit]

mentality [mɛnˈtælɪtɪ] *n* ความสามารถ ทางจิต [khwam sa mat thang chit]

mention [ˈmɛnʃən] *v* กล่าวถึง [klao thueng]

menu [ˈmɛnjuː] *n* รายการอาหาร [rai kan a han]; **Do you have a children's menu?** คุณมีรายการอาหารเด็กไหม? [khun mii rai kan a han dek mai]; **Do you have a set-price menu?** คุณมี รายการอาหารที่ตั้งราคาเป็นชุดไหม?

[khun mii rai kan a han thii tang ra kha pen chut mai]; **The menu, please** ขอรายการอาหาร [kho rai kan a han]

mercury ['mɜːkjʊrɪ] n ธาตุปรอท [that pa rot]

mercy ['mɜːsɪ] n ความเมตตา [khwam met ta]

mere [mɪə] adj เพียงเท่านั้น [phiang thao nan]

merge [mɜːdʒ] v รวมเข้าด้วยกัน [ruam khao duai kan]

merger ['mɜːdʒə] n การควบรวม [kan khuap ruam]

meringue [mə'ræŋ] n ขนมอบที่ใช้ไข่ขาวตีจนฟูแล้วอบ [kha nom op thii chai khai khao ti chon fu laeo op]

mermaid ['mɜːˌmeɪd] n นางเงือก [nang ngueak]

merry ['mɛrɪ] adj รื่นเริง [ruen roeng]

merry-go-round ['mɛrɪgəʊ'raʊnd] n ม้าหมุน [ma mun]

mess [mɛs] n สภาพรกรุงรัง [sa phap rok rung rang]

mess about [mɛs ə'baʊt] v ฆ่าเวลาโดยการทำอะไรที่ไม่สำคัญ [kha we la doi kan tham a rai thii mai sam khan]

message ['mɛsɪdʒ] n ข่าวสาร [khao san]; **text message** n ข้อความที่ส่งทางโทรศัพท์มือถือ [kho khwam thii song thang tho ra sap mue thue]

messenger ['mɛsɪndʒə] n คนส่งข่าว [khon song khao]

mess up [mɛs ʌp] v ทำให้สกปรก [tham hai sok ka prok]

messy ['mɛsɪ] adj ซึ่งไม่เรียบร้อยและสกปรก [sueng mai riap roi lae sok ka prok]

metabolism [mɪ'tæbəˌlɪzəm] n กระบวนการเผาผลาญอาหาร [kra buan kan phao phlan a han]

metal ['mɛtᵊl] n โลหะ [lo ha]

meteorite ['miːtɪəˌraɪt] n อุกกาบาต [uk ka bat]

meter ['miːtə] n หน่วยวัดความยาวเป็น เมตร [nuai wat khwam yao pen met]; **parking meter** n มิเตอร์จอดรถ [mi toe jot rot]

method ['mɛθəd] n วิธีการ [wi thi kan]

Methodist ['mɛθədɪst] adj ที่เกี่ยวกับนิกายโปรเตสแตนส์ [thii kiao kap ni kai pro tes taen]

metre ['miːtə] n เมตร [met]

metric ['mɛtrɪk] adj ซึ่งวัดเป็นเมตร [sueng wat pen met]

Mexican ['mɛksɪkən] adj เกี่ยวกับเม็กซิกัน [kiao kap mex si kan] ▷ n ชาวเม็กซิกัน [chao mex si kan]

Mexico ['mɛksɪˌkəʊ] n ประเทศเม็กซิโก [pra tet mex si ko]

microchip ['maɪkrəʊˌtʃɪp] n ไมโครชิฟ [maek phai]

microphone ['maɪkrəˌfəʊn] n ไมโครโฟน [mai khro fon]; **Does it have a microphone?** มีไมโครโฟนไหม? [mii mai khro fon mai]

microscope ['maɪkrəˌskəʊp] n กล้องจุลทรรศน์ [klong chun la that]

mid [mɪd] adj ตรงกลาง [trong klang]

midday ['mɪd'deɪ] n เที่ยงวัน [thiang wan]; **at midday** ตอนเที่ยงวัน [ton thiang wan]; **It's twelve midday** เวลาเที่ยงวัน [we la thiang wan]

middle ['mɪdᵊl] n จุดกลาง [chud klang]; **Middle Ages** npl ยุคกลาง [yuk klang]; **Middle East** n ตะวันออกกลาง [ta wan ok klang]

middle-aged ['mɪdᵊlˌeɪdʒɪd] adj ซึ่งมีวัยกลางคน [sueng mii wai klang khon]

middle-class ['mɪdᵊlˌklɑːs] adj ชนชั้นกลาง [chon chan klang]

midge [mɪdʒ] n แมลงตัวเล็กคล้ายยุงกัดคนและสัตว์ [ma laeng tua lek khlai yung kat khon lae sat]

midnight ['mɪdˌnaɪt] n เที่ยงคืน [thiang khuen]; **at midnight** เวลาเที่ยงคืน [we la thiang khuen]

midwife, midwives ['mɪdˌwaɪf, 'mɪdˌwaɪvz] n นางพยาบาลผดุงครรภ์

[nang pha ya baan pa dung khan]

migraine ['mi:greın; 'maɪ-] n อาการ
ปวดศรีษะเพียงข้างเดียว [a kan puad sri
sa phiang khang diao]

migrant ['maɪgrənt] adj เคลื่อนย้ายจาก
ที่หนึ่งไปอีกที่หนึ่ง [khluean yai chak thii
nueng pai ik thii nueng] ▷ n ผู้อพยพ
[phu op pha yop]

migration [maɪ'greɪʃən] n การอพยพ
[kan op pa yop]

mike [maɪk] n ไมโครโฟน [mai khro fon]

mild [maɪld] adj ซึ่งมีรสชาติอ่อน [sueng
mii rot chat on]

mile [maɪl] n ไมล์ [mai]

mileage ['maɪlɪdʒ] n ระยะทางเป็นไมล์ [ra
ya thang pen mai]

mileometer [maɪ'lɒmɪtə] n เครื่องวัด
จำนวนไมล์ [khrueang wat cham nuan
mai]

military ['mɪlɪtərɪ; -trɪ] adj ทางทหาร
[thang tha han]

milk [mɪlk] n นม [nom] ▷ v รีดนม [rit
nom]; **baby milk** n นมสำหรับเด็กทารก
[nom sam rap dek tha rok]; **Do you
drink milk?** คุณดื่มนมไหม? [khun
duem nom mai]; **Have you got real
milk?** คุณมีนมสดไหม? [khun mii nom
sot mai]; **Is it made with
unpasteurised milk?** นี่ทำจากนมที่ไม่
ได้ผ่านการฆ่าเชื้อโรคด้วยความร้อนสูงหรือ
เปล่า? [ni tham chak nom thii mai dai
phan kan kha chuea rok duai khwam
ron sung rue plao]

milkshake ['mɪlk,ʃeɪk] n นมปั่น [nom
pan]

mill [mɪl] n โรงสี [rong si]

millennium [mɪ'lɛnɪəm] n ระยะเวลา
หนึ่งพันปี [ra ya we la nueng phan pi]

millimetre ['mɪlɪ,mi:tə] n มิลลิเมตร
[min li met]

million ['mɪljən] n หนึ่งล้าน [nueng lan]

millionaire [,mɪljə'nɛə] n เศรษฐีเงินล้าน
[set thi ngoen lan]

mimic ['mɪmɪk] v ล้อเลียน [lo lian]

mince [mɪns] v บด [bot]

mind [maɪnd] n จิตใจ [chit chai] ▷ v
ระมัดระวัง [ra mat ra wang]

mine [maɪn] n เหมืองแร่ [mueang rae]
▷ pron ของฉัน [khong chan]

miner ['maɪnə] n คนงานเหมือง [khon
ngan mueang]

mineral ['mɪnərəl; 'mɪnrəl] adj ที่มีแร่
[thii mii rae] ▷ n แร่ธาตุ [rae that];
mineral water n น้ำแร่ [nam rae]

miniature ['mɪnɪtʃə] adj เล็กมาก [lek
mak] ▷ n สิ่งที่มีขนาดเล็กมาก [sing thii
mii kha naat lek mak]

minibar ['mɪnɪ,bɑ:] n ตู้เย็นขนาดเล็กใน
ห้องพักโรงแรม [tu yen kha naat lek nai
hong phak rong raeng]

minibus ['mɪnɪ,bʌs] n รถเมล์เล็ก [rot me
lek]

minicab ['mɪnɪ,kæb] n รถขับที่ใช้เป็น
แท็กซี่ [rot khap thii chai pen thaek si]

minimal ['mɪnɪməl] adj น้อยที่สุด [noi
thii sud]

minimize ['mɪnɪ,maɪz] v ทำให้เล็กลง
ที่สุด [tham hai lek long thii sut]

minimum ['mɪnɪməm] adj ต่ำที่สุด [tam
thii sud] ▷ n จำนวนน้อยที่สุด [cham
nuan noi thii sut]

mining ['maɪnɪŋ] n การทำเหมือง [kan
tham mueang]

miniskirt ['mɪnɪ,skɜ:t] n กระโปรงสั้น
[kra prong san]

minister ['mɪnɪstə] n (clergy) พระผู้สอน
ศาสนา [phra phu sorn sad sa na],
(government) รัฐมนตรี [rat tha mon tri];
prime minister n นายกรัฐมนตรี [na yok
rat tha mon tri]

ministry ['mɪnɪstrɪ] n (government)
กระทรวง [kra suang], (religion) หน้าที่
ของพระ [na thii khong phra]

mink [mɪŋk] n ตัวมิงค์ ขนใช้ทำเสื้อกัน
หนาว [tua ming khon chai tham suea
kan nao]

minor ['maɪnə] adj เป็นรอง [pen rong]
▷ n ผู้เยาว์ [phu yao]

minority [maɪˈnɒrɪtɪ; mɪ-] *n* คนกลุ่ม
น้อย [khon klum noi]

mint [mɪnt] *n* (coins) โรงกษาปณ์ [rong
ka sap], (herb/sweet) ใบสะระแหน่ [bai sa
ra nae]

minus [ˈmaɪnəs] *prep* ลบ [lop]

minute *adj* [maɪˈnjuːt] เล็กมาก [lek
mak] ▷ *n* [ˈmɪnɪt] นาที [na thi]; **Can
you wait here for a few minutes?**
คุณรอที่นี่สักสองสามนาทีได้ไหม? [khun ro
thii nii sak song sam na thii dai mai];
We are ten minutes late เรามาช้าสิบ
นาที [rao ma cha sip na thi]

miracle [ˈmɪrəkəl] *n* เรื่องมหัศจรรย์
[rueang ma hat sa chan]

mirror [ˈmɪrə] *n* กระจก [kra chok];
rear-view mirror *n* กระจกส่องหลัง [kra
jok song lang]; **wing mirror** *n* กระจก
ส่องข้าง [kra jok song khang]

misbehave [ˌmɪsbɪˈheɪv] *v* ประพฤติตัว
ไม่เหมาะสม [pra phruet tua mai mo
som]

miscarriage [mɪsˈkærɪdʒ] *n* การแท้ง
บุตร [kan thang but]

miscellaneous [ˌmɪsəˈleɪnɪəs] *adj*
เบ็ดเตล็ด [bet ta let]

mischief [ˈmɪstʃɪf] *n* การก่อกวน [kan ko
kuan]

mischievous [ˈmɪstʃɪvəs] *adj* เกเร [ke
re]

miser [ˈmaɪzə] *n* คนตระหนี่ [khon tra
nii]

miserable [ˈmɪzərəbəl; ˈmɪzrə-] *adj*
ทำให้หดหู่ใจ [tham hai hot hu jai]

misery [ˈmɪzərɪ] *n* ความทุกข์ยาก
[khwam thuk yak]

misfortune [mɪsˈfɔːtʃən] *n* ความโชค
ร้าย [khwam chok rai]

mishap [ˈmɪshæp] *n* อุบัติเหตุเล็ก ๆ [u
bat ti het lek lek]

misjudge [ˌmɪsˈdʒʌdʒ] *v* ตัดสินใจผิด [tat
sin jai phit]

mislay [mɪsˈleɪ] *v* วางผิดที่ [wang phid
thii]

misleading [mɪsˈliːdɪŋ] *adj* ซึ่งทำให้
เข้าใจผิด [sueng tham hai khao jai
phit]

misprint [ˈmɪsˌprɪnt] *n* การพิมพ์ผิด [kan
phim phit]

miss [mɪs] *v* พลาด ไม่เห็น ไม่เข้าใจ ไม่
ได้ยิน [phlat, mai hen, mai khao jai,
mai dai yin]

Miss [mɪs] *n* นางสาว [nang sao]

missile [ˈmɪsaɪl] *n* ขีปนาวุธ [khi pa na
wut]

missing [ˈmɪsɪŋ] *adj* ซึ่งหายไป [sueng
hai pai]

missionary [ˈmɪʃənərɪ] *n* หมอสอน
ศาสนา [mo son sat sa na]

mist [mɪst] *n* หมอก [mok]

mistake [mɪˈsteɪk] *n* ความผิดพลาด
[khwam phit phlat] ▷ *v* ทำผิด [tham
phit]

mistaken [mɪˈsteɪkən] *adj* ซึ่งเข้าใจผิด
[sueng khao jai phit]

mistakenly [mɪˈsteɪkənlɪ] *adv* อย่าง
เข้าใจผิด [yang khao jai phid]

mistletoe [ˈmɪsəlˌtəʊ] *n* ไม้จำพวกกาฝาก
ขึ้นตามต้นไม้ [mai cham phuak ka fak
khuen tam ton mai]

mistress [ˈmɪstrɪs] *n* อนุภรรยา [a nu
phan ra ya]

misty [ˈmɪstɪ] *adj* ที่ปกคลุมด้วยหมอก
[thii pok khlum duai mok]

misunderstand [ˌmɪsʌndəˈstænd] *v*
เข้าใจผิด [khao chao phit]

misunderstanding
[ˌmɪsʌndəˈstændɪŋ] *n* การเข้าใจผิด
[kan khao jai phit]; **There's been a
misunderstanding** มีการเข้าใจผิด [mii
kan khao jai phit]

mitten [ˈmɪtən] *n* ถุงมือแบบมีสี่นิ้วรวมกัน
แต่นิ้วโป้งแยกออก [thung mue baep mii
si nio ruam kan tae nio pong yaek ok]

mix [mɪks] *n* การผสม [kan pha som] ▷ *v*
ผสม [pha som]

mixed [mɪkst] *adj* ที่ผสมกัน [thii pha
som kan]; **mixed salad** *n* สลัดรวม [sa

lat ruam]

mixer ['mɪksə] *n* เครื่องผสม [khrueang pha som]

mixture ['mɪkstʃə] *n* ส่วนผสม [suan pha som]

mix up [mɪks ʌp] *v* รวม [ruam]

mix-up [mɪksʌp] *n* ส่วนผสม [suan pha som]

MMS [ɛm ɛm ɛs] *abbr* ระบบการส่ง ข้อความทางโทรศัพท์ [ra bop kan song kho khwam thang tho ra sap]

moan [məʊn] *v* บ่น [bon]

moat [məʊt] *n* คูน้ำรอบปราสาทหรือเมือง [khu nam rop pra saat rue mueang]

mobile ['məʊbaɪl] **mobile home** *n* บ้าน เคลื่อนที่ [baan khluean thii]; **Do you have a mobile?** คุณมีโทรศัพท์มือถือ ไหม? [khun mii tho ra sap mue thue mai]; **My mobile number is...** เบอร์มือ ถือฉันเบอร์... [boe mue thue chan boe...]; **What is the number of your mobile?** เบอร์มือถือคุณเบอร์อะไร? [boe mue thue khun boe a rai]

mock [mɒk] *adj* ที่จำลองขึ้น [thii cham long khuen] ▷ *v* เยาะเย้ย [yo yoei]

mod cons ['mɒd kɒnz] *npl* ความสะดวก สบายสมัยใหม่ [khwam sa duak sa bai sa mai mai]

model ['mɒdəl] *adj* ทำให้เป็นแบบอย่าง [tham hai pen baep yang] ▷ *n* นางแบบ [nang baep] ▷ *v* แสดงแบบ [sa daeng baep]

modem ['məʊdɛm] *n* โมเด็ม [mo dem]

moderate ['mɒdərɪt] *adj* ปานกลาง [pan klang]

moderation [ˌmɒdə'reɪʃən] *n* ความพอ ประมาณ [khwam pho pra man]

modern ['mɒdən] *adj* สมัยใหม่ [sa mai mai]; **modern languages** *npl* ภาษา สมัยใหม่ต่าง ๆ [pha sa sa mai mai tang tang]

modernize ['mɒdəˌnaɪz] *v* ทำให้ทันสมัย [tham hai tan sa mai]

modest ['mɒdɪst] *adj* ถ่อมตัว [thom

tua]

modification [ˌmɒdɪfɪ'keɪʃən] *n* การ เปลี่ยนแปลงแก้ไข [kan pian plang kae khai]

modify ['mɒdɪˌfaɪ] *v* เปลี่ยนแปลงแก้ไข [plian plaeng kae khai]

module ['mɒdjuːl] *n* หลักสูตรการศึกษา [lak sut kan suek sa]

moist [mɔɪst] *adj* ชื้น [chuen]

moisture ['mɔɪstʃə] *n* ความชื้น [khwam chuen]

moisturizer ['mɔɪstʃəˌraɪzə] *n* ครีมทา ให้ผิวนุ่ม [khrim tha hai phio num]

Moldova [mɒl'dəʊvə] *n* ประเทศมอลโด วาอยู่ในทวีปอัฟริกา [pra tet mol do va yu nai tha wip af ri ka]

Moldovan [mɒl'dəʊvən] *adj* เกี่ยวกับ มอลโดวา [kiao kap mol do va] ▷ *n* ชาว มอลโดวัน [chao mol do wan]

mole [məʊl] *n (infiltrator)* ผู้แทรกซึม [phu saek suem], *(mammal)* ตัวตุ่น [tua tun], *(skin)* ไฝ [fai]

molecule ['mɒlɪˌkjuːl] *n* โมเลกุล [mo le kun]

moment ['məʊmənt] *n* ชั่วขณะ [chua kha na]

momentarily ['məʊməntərəlɪ; -trɪlɪ] *adv* ในเวลาอันใกล้ [nai we la an kai]

momentary ['məʊməntərɪ; -trɪ] *adj* ชั่วครู่ [chua khru]

momentous [məʊ'mɛntəs] *adj* ซึ่งมี ความสำคัญมาก [sueng mee khwam sam khan mak]

Monaco ['mɒnəˌkəʊ; mə'nɑːkəʊ; mɒnako] *n* ประเทศโมนาโค [pra tet mo na kho]

monarch ['mɒnək] *n* เจ้าแผ่นดิน [chao phaen din]

monarchy ['mɒnəkɪ] *n* การปกครองโดย มีพระมหากษัตริย์เป็นประมุข [kan pok khrong doi mii phra ma ha ka sat pen pra muk]

monastery ['mɒnəstərɪ; -strɪ] *n* ที่อยู่ ของพระ [thii yu khong phra]

Monday ['mʌndɪ] *n* วันจันทร์ [wan chan]; **It's Monday fifteenth June** วันจันทร์ที่สิบห้า มิถุนายน [wan chan thii sip ha mi thu na yon]; **on Monday** วันจันทร์ [wan chan]

monetary ['mʌnɪtərɪ; -trɪ] *adj* เกี่ยวกับเงินตรา [kiao kap ngoen tra]

money ['mʌnɪ] *n* เงิน [ngoen]; **Can I have my money back?** ฉันขอเงินคืนได้ไหม? [chan kho ngen khuen dai mai]; **Can you arrange to have some money sent over urgently?** คุณจัดการให้มีเงินส่งมาด่วนได้ไหม? [khun chat kan hai mii ngoen song ma duan dai mai]; **Could you lend me some money?** คุณให้ฉันยืมเงินได้ไหม? [khun hai chan yuem ngen dai mai]

Mongolia [mɒŋ'ɡəʊlɪə] *n* ประเทศมองโกเลีย [pra tet mong ko lia]

Mongolian [mɒŋ'ɡəʊlɪən] *adj* เกี่ยวกับมองโกเลีย [kiao kap mong ko lia] ▷ *n (language)* ภาษามองโกเลีย [pha sa morng ko lia], *(person)* ชาวมองโกเลีย [chao mong ko lia]

mongrel ['mʌŋɡrəl] *n* คนสัตว์หรือพืชที่เป็นพันธุ์ผสม [khon sat rue phuet thii pen phan pha som]

monitor ['mɒnɪtə] *n* เครื่องโทรทัศน์วงจรปิด [khrueang tho ra tat wong chon pit]

monk [mʌŋk] *n* พระ [phra]

monkey ['mʌŋkɪ] *n* ลิง [ling]

monopoly [mə'nɒpəlɪ] *n* ระบบผูกขาด [ra bop phuk khat]

monotonous [mə'nɒtənəs] *adj* น่าเบื่อหน่ายเพราะซ้ำซาก [na buea nai phro sam sak]

monsoon [mɒn'suːn] *n* ฤดูมรสุม [rue du mo ra sum]

monster ['mɒnstə] *n* สัตว์ประหลาด [sat pra lat]

month [mʌnθ] *n* เดือน [duean]; **a month ago** หนึ่งเดือนมาแล้ว [nueng duean ma laeo]; **in a month's time** ภายในเวลาหนึ่งเดือน [phai nai we la nueng duean]

monthly ['mʌnθlɪ] *adj* ทุกเดือน [thuk duean]

monument ['mɒnjʊmənt] *n* อนุสาวรีย์ [a nu sao wa ri]

mood [muːd] *n* อารมณ์ [a rom]

moody ['muːdɪ] *adj* หงุดหงิด [ngut ngit]

moon [muːn] *n* พระจันทร์ [phra chan]; **full moon** *n* พระจันทร์เต็มดวง [phra chan tem duang]

moor [mʊə; mɔː] *n* ทุ่งโล่ง [thung long] ▷ *v* จอดเรือ [jot ruea]

mop [mɒp] *n* ไม้ถูพื้น [mai thu phuen]

moped ['məʊpɛd] *n* มอเตอร์ไซค์ขนาดเล็ก [mo toe sai kha naat lek]

mop up [mɒp ʌp] *v* เช็ดทำความสะอาดด้วยไม้ถูพื้น [chet tham khwam sa at duai mai thu phuen]

moral ['mɒrəl] *adj* เกี่ยวกับศีลธรรม [kiao kap sin la tham] ▷ *n* เรื่องสอนใจ [rueang son jai]

morale [mɒ'rɑːl] *n* กำลังใจ [kam lang chai]

morals ['mɒrəlz] *npl* หลักความประพฤติ [lak khwam pra phruet]

more [mɔː] *adj* มากกว่า [mak kwa] ▷ *adv* บ่อยขึ้น [boi khuen] ▷ *pron* จำนวนที่มากกว่า [cham nuan thii mak kwa]

morgue [mɔːɡ] *n* ห้องเก็บศพ [hong kep sop]

morning ['mɔːnɪŋ] *n* เวลาเช้า [we la chao]; **morning sickness** *n* แพ้ท้อง [phae thong]

Moroccan [mə'rɒkən] *adj* เกี่ยวกับโมร็อคโค [kiao kap mo rok kho] ▷ *n* ชาวโมร็อคโค [chao mo rok kho]

Morocco [mə'rɒkəʊ] *n* ประเทศโมร็อคโค [pra thet mo rok ko]

morphine ['mɔːfiːn] *n* มอร์ฟีน [mo fin]

Morse [mɔːs] *n* รหัสมอร์ส [ra hat mos]

mortar ['mɔːtə] *n (military)* ปืนใหญ่ขนาดเล็ก [puen yai kha nat lek], *(plaster)* ส่วนผสมของปูนขาวหรือซีเมนต์กับ

น้ำและทราย [suan pha som khong pun khao rue si men kap nam lae sai]

mortgage ['mɔːgɪdʒ] n การจำนอง [kan cham nong] ▷ v จำนอง [cham nong]

mosaic [mə'zeɪɪk] n ลวดลายที่ทำด้วยกระจกสี [luat lai thii tham duai kra chok sii]

Moslem ['mɒzləm] adj เกี่ยวกับมุสลิม [kiao kap mus sa lim] ▷ n ชาวมุสลิม [chao mus sa lim]

mosque [mɒsk] n สุเหร่า [su rao]; **Where is there a mosque?** มีสุเหร่าอยู่ที่ไหน? [mii su rao yu thii nai]

mosquito [mə'skiːtəʊ] n ยุง [yung]

moss [mɒs] n พืชตะไคร่น้ำ [phuet ta khrai nam]

most [məʊst] adj มากที่สุด [mak thii sut] ▷ adv (superlative) ที่สุด [thi sut] ▷ n (majority) จำนวนมากที่สุด [cham nuan mak thii sud]

mostly ['məʊstlɪ] adv ส่วนมาก [suan mak]

MOT [ɛm əʊ tiː] abbr ตัวย่อของการตรวจเช็ครถประจำปี [tua yor khong kan truat chek rot pra cham pi]

motel [məʊ'tɛl] n โมเต็ล [mo ten]

moth [mɒθ] n ผีเสื้อราตรีออกหากินกลางคืน [phi suea ra tree ok ha kin klang khuen]

mother ['mʌðə] n แม่ [mae]; **mother tongue** n ภาษาแม่ [pha sa mae]; **surrogate mother** n ผู้หญิงที่รับอุ้มท้องแทน [phu ying thii rap um thong taen]

mother-in-law ['mʌðə ɪn lɔː] (pl **mothers-in-law**) n แม่สามี [mae sa mii]

motionless ['məʊʃənlɪs] adj ไม่มีการเคลื่อนไหว [mai mii kan khluean wai]

motivated ['məʊtɪˌveɪtɪd] adj ซึ่งมีแรงบันดาลใจ [sueng mii raeng ban dan jai]

motivation [ˌməʊtɪ'veɪʃən] n แรงบันดาลใจ [raeng ban dan chai]

motive ['məʊtɪv] n เหตุจูงใจ [het chung chai]

motor ['məʊtə] n เครื่องยนต์ [khrueang yon]; **motor mechanic** n ช่างเครื่องยนต์ [chang khrueang yon]; **motor racing** n การแข่งรถยนต์ [kan khaeng rot yon]

motorbike ['məʊtəˌbaɪk] n รถจักรยานยนต์ [rot chak kra yan yon]

motorboat ['məʊtəˌbəʊt] n เรือยนต์ [ruea yon]

motorcycle ['məʊtəˌsaɪkəl] n รถมอเตอร์ไซด์ [rot mo toe sai]

motorcyclist ['məʊtəˌsaɪklɪst] n นักขับมอเตอร์ไซด์ [nak khap mo toe sai]

motorist ['məʊtərɪst] n คนขับรถยนต์ [khon khap rot yon]

motorway ['məʊtəˌweɪ] n ทางหลวง [thang luang]; **How do I get to the motorway?** ฉันจะขึ้นทางหลวงได้อย่างไร? [chan ja khuen thang luang dai yang rai]; **Is there a toll on this motorway?** มีด่านเก็บทางบนทางหลวงนี้ไหม? [mii dan kep thang bon thang luang nii mai]

mould [məʊld] n (fungus) รา [ra], (shape) แม่พิมพ์ [mae phim]

mouldy ['məʊldɪ] adj ซึ่งปกคลุมด้วยรา [sueng pok khlum duai ra]

mount [maʊnt] v ขึ้นม้า ไต่เขา [khuen ma, tai khao]

mountain ['maʊntɪn] n ภูเขา [phu khao]; **mountain bike** n จักรยานขี่บนทางขรุขระ [chak kra yan khi bon thang khru khra]

mountaineer [ˌmaʊntɪ'nɪə] n นักไต่เขา [nak tai khao]

mountaineering [ˌmaʊntɪ'nɪərɪŋ] n การไต่เขา [kan tai khao]

mountainous ['maʊntɪnəs] adj เต็มไปด้วยภูเขา [tem pai duai phu khao]

mount up [maʊnt ʌp] v ค่อยๆเพิ่มขึ้น [khoi khoi perm khuen]

mourning ['mɔːnɪŋ] n การไว้ทุกข์ [kan wai thuk]

mouse, mice [maʊs, maɪs] n หนู [nu]; **mouse mat** n แผ่นรองเมาส์ [phaen rong mao]

mousse [muːs] n มูสใส่ผมให้อยู่ทรง [mus sai phom hai yu song]

moustache [məˈstɑːʃ] n หนวด [nuat]

mouth [maʊθ] n ปาก [pak]; **mouth organ** n หีบเพลงปาก [hip phleng pak]

mouthwash [ˈmaʊθˌwɒʃ] n น้ำยาล้าง ปาก [nam ya lang pak]

move [muːv] n การย้ายที่อยู่ [kan yai thii yu] ▷ vi เคลื่อน เปลี่ยนตำแหน่ง [khluean plian tam naeng] ▷ vt ย้าย ขยับ [yai, kha yap]

move back [muːv bæk] v ย้ายกลับ [yai klap]

move forward [muːv ˈfɔːwəd] v เคลื่อน ไปข้างหน้า [khluean pai khang na]

move in [muːv ɪn] v ย้ายเข้า [yai khao]

movement [ˈmuːvmənt] n การ เคลื่อนไหว [kan khluean wai]

movie [ˈmuːvɪ] n ภาพยนตร์ [phap pha yon]

moving [ˈmuːvɪŋ] adj ซึ่งดลใจ [sueng don jai]

mow [məʊ] v ตัดหญ้า [tat ya]

mower [ˈmaʊə] n เครื่องตัดหญ้า [khrueang tat ya]

Mozambique [ˌməʊzəmˈbiːk] n ประเทศโมซัมบิก [pra tet mo sam bik]

mph [maɪlz pə aʊə] abbr ตัวย่อของไมล์ ต่อชั่วโมง [tua yo khong mai to chau mong]

Mr [ˈmɪstə] n นาย [nai]

Mrs [ˈmɪsɪz] n นาง [nang]

Ms [mɪz; məs] n ตัวย่อรวมของคำที่ใช้ เรียกหญิงที่แต่งงานและไม่ได้แต่งงาน [tua yor ruam khong kham thii chai riak hying thii taeng ngan lae mai dai taeng ngan]

MS [ˈɛmɛs] abbr ตัวย่อของแม่น้ำมิสซิสซิปปี้ ในอเมริกา [tua yo khong mae nam mis sis sip pi nai a me ri ka]

much [mʌtʃ] adj มาก [mak] ▷ adv จำนวน มาก [cham nuan mak], อย่างมาก [yang mak]; **I like you very much** ฉันชอบคุณ มาก [chan chop khun mak]; **Thank you very much** ขอบคุณมาก [kop khun mak]; **There's too much... in it** มี...ใน นี้มากเกินไป [mii...nai nii mak koen pai]

mud [mʌd] n โคลน [khlon]

muddle [ˈmʌdˀl] n ความไม่เป็นระเบียบ [khwam mai pen ra biap]

muddy [ˈmʌdɪ] adj เต็มไปด้วยโคลน [tem pai duai khlon]

mudguard [ˈmʌdˌɡɑːd] n บังโคลนรถ [bang khlon rot]

muesli [ˈmjuːzlɪ] n อาหารที่ประกอบด้วย ธัญพืชถั่วและผลไม้แห้ง [a han thii pra kop duai than ya phuet thua lae phon la mai haeng]

muffler [ˈmʌflə] n สิ่งห่อหุ้ม [sing ho hum]

mug [mʌɡ] n ถ้วยใหญ่มีหู [thuai yai mii hu] ▷ v ทำร้ายเพื่อชิงทรัพย์ [tham rai phuea ching sap]

mugger [ˈmʌɡə] n คนข่มขู่เพื่อชิงทรัพย์ [khon khom khu phuea ching sap]

mugging [ˈmʌɡɪŋ] n การทำร้ายเพื่อปล้น ทรัพย์ [kan tham rai phuea plon sab]

muggy [ˈmʌɡɪ] adj **It's muggy** ร้อน อบอ้าว [ron op oa]

mule [mjuːl] n ล่อ [lo]

multinational [ˌmʌltɪˈnæʃənˀl] adj เกี่ยวกับหลายประเทศ [kiao kap lai pra tet] ▷ n บริษัทระหว่างประเทศ [bo ri sat ra wang pra tet]

multiple [ˈmʌltɪpˀl] adj **multiple sclerosis** n โรคเลือดคั่งในสมอง [rok lueat khang nai sa mong]

multiplication [ˌmʌltɪplɪˈkeɪʃən] n การคูณ [kan khun]

multiply [ˈmʌltɪˌplaɪ] v คูณ [khun]

mum [mʌm] n แม่ [mae]

mummy [ˈmʌmɪ] n (body) มัมมี่ [mam mi], (mother) แม่ [mae]

mumps [mʌmps] n โรคคางทูม [rok khang thum]

murder [ˈmɜːdə] n การฆาตกรรม [kan

khat ta kam] ⊳ v ฆาตกรรม [ka ta kam]

murderer ['mɜːdərə] n ฆาตกร [kha ta kon]

muscle ['mʌsəl] n กล้ามเนื้อ [klam nuea]

muscular ['mʌskjʊlə] adj เกี่ยวกับกล้ามเนื้อ [kiao kap klam nuea]

museum [mjuːˈzɪəm] n พิพิธภัณฑ์ [phi phit tha phan]; **Is the museum open every day?** พิพิธภัณฑ์เปิดทุกวันไหม? [phi phit tha phan poet thuk wan mai]; **When is the museum open?** พิพิธภัณฑ์จะเปิดเมื่อไร? [phi phit tha phan ja poet muea rai]

mushroom ['mʌʃruːm; -rʊm] n เห็ด [het]

music ['mjuːzɪk] n ดนตรี [don tri]; **folk music** n ดนตรีลูกทุ่ง [don tree luk thung]; **music centre** n ศูนย์ดนตรี [sun don tree]; **Where can we hear live music?** เราจะฟังดนตรีสดได้ที่ไหน? [rao ja fang don trii sot dai thii nai]

musical ['mjuːzɪkᵊl] adj เกี่ยวกับดนตรี [kiao kap don tree] ⊳ n ละครเพลง [la khon phleng]; **musical instrument** n เครื่องดนตรี [khrueang don tri]

musician [mjuːˈzɪʃən] n นักดนตรี [nak don tri]; **Where can we hear local musicians play?** เราจะฟังนักดนตรีท้องถิ่นเล่นได้ที่ไหน? [rao ja fang nak don trii thong thin len dai thii nai]

Muslim ['mʊzlɪm; 'mʌz-] adj มุสลิม [mut sa lim] ⊳ n ชาวมุสลิม [chao mus sa lim]

mussel ['mʌsᵊl] n หอยแมลงภู่ [hoi ma laeng phu]

must [mʌst] v ต้อง [tong]

mustard ['mʌstəd] n ผงมัสตาร์ดใช้ปรุงอาหาร [phong mas tat chai prung a han]

mutter ['mʌtə] v บ่น [bon]

mutton ['mʌtᵊn] n เนื้อแกะ [nuea kae]

mutual ['mjuːtʃʊəl] adj ซึ่งมีส่วนร่วมกัน [sueng mii suan ruam kan]

my [maɪ] pron ของฉัน [khong chan];

Here are my insurance details นี่คือรายละเอียดการประกันของฉัน [ni khue rai la iat kan pra kan khong chan]

Myanmar ['maɪænmɑː; 'mjænmɑː] n ประเทศพม่า [pra tet pha ma]

myself [maɪˈsɛlf] pron ตัวของฉัน [tua khong chan]

mysterious [mɪˈstɪərɪəs] adj ที่ลึกลับ [thii luek lap]

mystery ['mɪstərɪ] n ความลึกลับ [khwam luek lap]

myth [mɪθ] n นิทานปรัมปรา [ni than pa ram pa ra]

mythology [mɪˈθɒlədʒɪ] n ตำนาน [tam nan]

n

naff [næf] *adj* ซึ่งขาดรสนิยม [sueng khat rot ni yom]

nag [næg] *v* จ้องจับผิด [chong chap phit]

nail [neɪl] *n* เล็บ [lep], ตะปู [ta pu]; **nail polish** *n* น้ำยาทาเล็บ [nam ya tha lep]; **nail scissors** *npl* กรรไกรตัดเล็บ [kan krai tat lep]; **nail varnish** *n* น้ำยาทาเล็บ [nam ya tha lep]

nailbrush ['neɪlˌbrʌʃ] *n* แปรงทำความ สะอาดเล็บ [praeng tham khwam sa at lep]

nailfile ['neɪlˌfaɪl] *n* ตะไบขัดเล็บ [ta bai khat lep]

naive [nɑːˈiːv; naɪˈiːv] *adj* ไม่มีเล่ห์เหลี่ยม ไม่มีมารยา [mai mii le liam, mai mii man ya]

naked ['neɪkɪd] *adj* เปลือยกาย [plueai kai]

name [neɪm] *n* ชื่อ [chue]; **brand name** *n* ยี่ห้อ [yi ho]; **first name** *n* ชื่อจริง [chue chring]; **maiden name** *n* ชื่อสกุล ของหญิงก่อนแต่งงาน [chue sa kun khong ying kon taeng ngan]; **My name is...** ฉันชื่อ... [chan chue...]

nanny ['nænɪ] *n* พี่เลี้ยงดูแลเด็ก [phi liang du lae dek]

nap [næp] *n* การงีบหลับ [kan ngib lap]

napkin ['næpkɪn] *n* ผ้าเช็ดปาก [pha ched pak]

nappy ['næpɪ] *n* ผ้าอ้อมเด็ก [pha om dek]

narrow ['nærəʊ] *adj* แคบ [khaep]

narrow-minded ['nærəʊˈmaɪndɪd] *adj* ใจแคบ [chai khaep]

nasty ['nɑːstɪ] *adj* น่ารังเกียจ [na rang kiat]

nation ['neɪʃən] *n* ประเทศ [pra thet]; **United Nations** *n* องค์การสหประชาชาติ [ong kan sa ha pra cha chat]

national ['næʃənəl] *adj* ประจำชาติ [pra cham chad]; **national anthem** *n* เพลง ชาติ [phleng chat]; **national park** *n* อุทยานแห่งชาติ [ut tha yan haeng chat]

nationalism ['næʃənəˌlɪzəm; 'næʃnə-] *n* ชาตินิยม [chat ni yom]

nationalist ['næʃənəlɪst] *n* คนรักชาติ [khon rak chat]

nationality [ˌnæʃəˈnælɪtɪ] *n* สัญชาติ [san chat]

nationalize ['næʃənəˌlaɪz; 'næʃnə-] *v* กำกับดูแลโดยรัฐ [kam kap du lae doi rat]

native ['neɪtɪv] *adj* พื้นเมือง [phuen mueang]; **native speaker** *n* เจ้าของ ภาษา [chao khong pha sa]

NATO ['neɪtəʊ] *abbr* ตัวย่อขององค์การนา โต้ [tua yo khong ong kan na to]

natural ['nætʃrəl; -tʃərəl] *adj* ธรรมชาติ [tham ma chat]; **natural gas** *n* ก๊าซ ธรรมชาติ [kas tham ma chat]; **natural resources** *npl* ทรัพยากรธรรมชาติ [sap pha ya kon tham ma chaat]

naturalist ['nætʃrəlɪst; -tʃərəl-] *n* นัก ธรรมชาตินิยม [nak tham ma chard ni yom]

naturally ['nætʃrəlɪ; -tʃərə-] *adv* อย่าง เป็นธรรมชาติ [yang pen tham ma chard]

nature ['neɪtʃə] *n* ธรรมชาติ [tham ma chat]

naughty ['nɔːtɪ] *adj* ซุกซน [suk son]

nausea ['nɔːzɪə; -sɪə] *n* อาการคลื่นไส้ [a kan khluen sai]

naval ['neɪvᵊl] *adj* เกี่ยวกับเรือ [kiao kab ruea]

navel ['neɪvᵊl] *n* สะดือ [sa due]

navy ['neɪvɪ] *n* กองทัพเรือ [kong thap ruea]

navy-blue ['neɪvɪ'bluː] *adj* น้ำเงินเข้ม [nam ngoen khem]

NB [ɛn biː] *abbr (notabene)* หมายเหตุ [mai het]

near [nɪə] *adj* ใกล้ [klai] ▷ *adv* ในระยะเวลาอันใกล้ [nai ra ya we la an klai] ▷ *prep* เร็วๆนี้ [reo reo ni]; **Are there any good beaches near here?** มีชายหาดดีๆ ใกล้ที่นี่ไหม? [mee chai had di di kai thii ni mai]; **How do I get to the nearest tube station?** ฉันจะไปสถานีรถไฟใต้ดินที่ใกล้ที่สุดได้อย่างไร? [chan ja pai sa tha ni rot fai tai din thii klai thii sut dai yang rai]; **It's very near** อยู่ใกล้มาก [yu klai mak]

nearby *adj* ['nɪəbaɪ] แค่เอื้อม [khae ueam] ▷ *adv* ['nɪə‚baɪ] ใกล้เคียง [klai khiang]

nearly ['nɪəlɪ] *adv* เกือบ [kueap]

near-sighted [‚nɪə'saɪtɪd] *adj* สายตาสั้น [sai ta san]

neat [niːt] *adj* เรียบร้อย [riap roi]

neatly [niːtlɪ] *adv* อย่างเรียบร้อย [yang riab roi]

necessarily ['nɛsɪsərɪlɪ; ‚nɛsɪ'sɛrɪlɪ] *adv* อย่างจำเป็น [yang cham pen]

necessary ['nɛsɪsərɪ] *adj* จำเป็น [cham pen]

necessity [nɪ'sɛsɪtɪ] *n* ความจำเป็น [khwam cham pen]

neck [nɛk] *n* คอ [kho]

necklace ['nɛklɪs] *n* สร้อยคอ [soi kho]

nectarine ['nɛktərɪn] *n* ผลไม้สีเหลืองแดงคล้ายลูกพีช [phon la mai see hlueang daeng khlai luk phit]

need [niːd] *n* ความต้องการ [khwam tong kan] ▷ *v* ต้องการ [tong kan]; **Do you need anything?** คุณต้องการอะไรบ้างไหม? [khun tong kan a rai bang mai]; **I don't need a bag, thanks** ฉันไม่ต้องการถุง ขอบคุณ [chan mai tong kan thung kop khun]; **I need assistance** ฉันต้องการผู้ช่วย [chan tong kan phu chuai]

needle ['niːdᵊl] *n* เข็ม [khem]; **knitting needle** *n* เข็มถัก [khem thak]; **Do you have a needle and thread?** คุณมีเข็มกับด้ายไหม? [khun mii khem kap dai mai]

negative ['nɛgətɪv] *adj* ที่เป็นด้านลบ [thii pen dan lop] ▷ *n* คำปฏิเสธ [kham pa ti set]

neglect [nɪ'glɛkt] *n* การละเลย [kan la loei] ▷ *v* ทอดทิ้ง [thot thing]

neglected [nɪ'glɛktɪd] *adj* ถูกทอดทิ้ง [thuk thot thing]

negligee ['nɛglɪ‚ʒeɪ] *n* เสื้อคลุมของสตรีส่วนมากมีชายทำด้วยลูกไม้ [suea khlum khong sa trii suan mak mii chai tham duai luk mai]

negotiate [nɪ'gəʊʃɪ‚eɪt] *v* ต่อรอง [to rong]

negotiations [nɪ‚gəʊʃɪ'eɪʃnz] *npl* การต่อรอง [kan to rong]

negotiator [nɪ'gəʊʃɪ‚eɪtə] *n* ผู้ต่อรอง [phu to rong]

neighbour ['neɪbə] *n* เพื่อนบ้าน [phuean ban]

neighbourhood ['neɪbə‚hʊd] *n* เขตที่มีคนอยู่อาศัย [khet thii mii khon yu a sai]

neither ['naɪðə; 'niːðə] *adv* ต่างก็ไม่ [tang ko mai] ▷ *conj* ไม่ใช่ทั้งสอง [mai chai thang song] ▷ *pron* ต่างก็ไม่ [tang ko mai]

neon ['niːɒn] *n* ไฟนีออน [fai ni on]

Nepal [nɪ'pɔːl] *n* ประเทศเนปาล [pra tet ne pan]

nephew ['nɛvjuː; 'nɛf-] *n* หลานชาย [lan chai]

nerve [nɜːv] *n (boldness)* ความกล้าหาญ

[khwam kla han], *(to/from brain)* เส้น
ประสาท [sen pra sat]

nerve-racking ['nɜːv'rækɪŋ] *adj* น่า
เขย่าขวัญ [na kha yao khwan]

nervous ['nɜːvəs] *adj* กระวนกระวาย [kra
won kra wai]; **nervous breakdown** *n*
ช่วงเวลาที่เจ็บป่วยทางจิต [chuang we la
thii chep puai thang chit]

nest [nɛst] *n* รัง [rang]

Net [nɛt] *n* เครือข่าย [khruea khai]

net [nɛt] *n* ตาข่ายดักสัตว์ [ta khai dak
sat]

netball ['nɛt,bɔːl] *n* กีฬาเน็ตบอลมีสองทีม
ๆ ละเจ็ดคน [ki la net bal mii song thim
thim la chet kon]

Netherlands ['nɛðələndz] *npl* ประเทศ
เนเธอร์แลนด์ [pra tet ne thoe laen]

nettle ['nɛtl] *n* ต้นไม้ป่าเป็นขนที่ทำให้
ระคายเคือง [ton mai pa bai pen khon
thii tham hai ra khai khueng]

network ['nɛt,wɜːk] *n* เครือข่าย [khruea
khai]; **I can't get a network** ฉันไม่ได้
รับเครือข่าย [chan mai dai rap khruea
khai]

neurotic [njʊˈrɒtɪk] *adj* เกี่ยวกับ
โรคประสาท [kiao kap rok pra sat]

neutral ['njuːtrəl] *adj* ที่เป็นกลาง [thii
pen klang] ▷ *n* ความเป็นกลาง [khwam
pen klang]

never ['nɛvə] *adv* ไม่มีทาง [mai mi
thang]

nevertheless [,nɛvəðə'lɛs] *adv* แต่
อย่างไรก็ตาม [tae yang rai ko tam]

new [njuː] *adj* ใหม่ [mai]; **New Year** *n* ปี
ใหม่ [pi mai]; **New Zealand** *n* ประเทศ
นิวซีแลนด์ [pra tet nio si laen]; **New
Zealander** *n* ชาวนิวซีแลนด์ [chao nio si
laen]; **Happy New Year!** สวัสดีปีใหม่ [sa
wat di pii mai]

newborn ['njuː,bɔːn] *adj* แรกเกิด [raek
koet]

newcomer ['njuː,kʌmə] *n* ผู้มาใหม่
[phu ma mai]

news [njuːz] *npl* ข่าว [khao]; **When is**
the news? จะมีข่าวเมื่อไร? [ja mii khao
muea rai]

newsagent ['njuːz,eɪdʒənt] *n* ร้านขาย
หนังสือพิมพ์ [ran khai nang sue phim]

newspaper ['njuːz,peɪpə] *n* หนังสือพิมพ์
[nang sue phim]; **Do you have**
newspapers? คุณมีหนังสือพิมพ์ไหม?
[khun mii nang sue phim mai]; **I**
would like a newspaper ฉันอยากได้
หนังสือพิมพ์หนึ่งฉบับ [chan yak dai nang
sue phim nueng cha bap]; **Where can I**
buy a newspaper? ฉันจะซื้อหนังสือพิมพ์
ได้ที่ไหน? [chan ja sue nang sue phim
dai thii nai]

newsreader ['njuːz,riːdə] *n* ผู้อ่านข่าว
[phu arn khao]

newt [njuːt] *n* สัตว์ประเภทจิ้งจกอาศัยได้
ทั้งบนบกและในน้ำ [sat pra phet ching
chok a sai dai thang bon bok lae nai
nam]

next [nɛkst] *adj* ต่อไป [to pai] ▷ *adv* ที่จะ
ตามมา [thii ja tam ma]; **next to** *prep*
ข้างๆ [khang khang]; **When do we**
stop next? เราจะหยุดจอดครั้งต่อไป
เมื่อไร? [rao ja yut jot khrang to pai
muea rai]; **When is the next bus**
to...? รถโดยสารคันต่อไปที่จะไป...เดินทาง
เมื่อไร? [rot doi san khan to pai thii ja
pai...doen thang muea rai]

next-of-kin ['nɛkstɒv'kɪn] *n* ญาติที่ใกล้
ที่สุด [yat thii klai thii sut]

Nicaragua [,nɪkə'rægjʊə;
nika'raɣwa] *n* ประเทศนิคารากัว [pra tet
ni kha ra kua]

Nicaraguan [,nɪkə'rægjʊən; -gwən]
adj เกี่ยวกับนิคารากัว [kiao kap ni kha ra
kua] ▷ *n* ชาวนิคารากัว [chao ni kha ra
kua]

nice [naɪs] *adj* ดี [di]; **It doesn't taste**
very nice รสไม่ค่อยดี [rot mai khoi di];
Where is there a nice bar? มีบาร์ดีๆ อยู่
ที่ไหน? [mee bar di di yu thii nai]

nickname ['nɪk,neɪm] *n* ชื่อเล่น [chue
len]

nicotine ['nɪkəˌtiːn] n สารนิโคตินใน ยาสูบหรือบุหรี่ [san ni kho tin nai ya sup rue bu ri]

niece [niːs] n หลานสาว [lan sao]

Niger ['naɪdʒɪər] n คนดำ [khon dam]

Nigeria [naɪˈdʒɪərɪə] n ประเทศไนจีเรีย [pra tet nai chi ria]

Nigerian [naɪˈdʒɪərɪən] adj เกี่ยวกับ ไนจีเรีย [kiao kap nai chi ria] ▷ n ชาว ไนจีเรีย [chao nai chi ria]

night [naɪt] n กลางคืน [klang khuen]; **hen night** n งานปาร์ตี้ที่หญิงสาวฉลองคืน ก่อนวันแต่งงาน [ngan pa tii thii ying sao cha long khuen kon wan taeng ngan]; **night school** n โรงเรียนในตอนเย็นหรือ กลางคืน [rong rian nai ton yen rue klang khuen]; **stag night** n งานเลี้ยง ของหนุ่มโสดก่อนวันแต่งงาน [ngan liang khong num sot kon wan taeng ngan]; **at night** ตอนกลางคืน [ton klang khuen]

nightclub ['naɪtˌklʌb] n ไนท์คลับ [nait khlap]

nightdress ['naɪtˌdrɛs] n ชุดนอน [chut non]

nightie ['naɪtɪ] n ชุดนอน [chut non]

nightlife ['naɪtˌlaɪf] n สถานบันเทิงเวลา กลางคืน [sa than ban thoeng we la klang khuen]

nightmare ['naɪtˌmɛə] n ฝันร้าย [fan rai]

nightshift ['naɪtˌʃɪft] n กะกลางคืน [ka klang khuen]

nil [nɪl] n ศูนย์ [sun]

nine [naɪn] number เก้า [kao]

nineteen [ˌnaɪnˈtiːn] number สิบเก้า [sip kao]

nineteenth [ˌnaɪnˈtiːnθ] adj ที่สิบเก้า [thii sip kao]

ninety ['naɪntɪ] number เก้าสิบ [kao sip]

ninth [naɪnθ] adj ที่เก้า [thii kao] ▷ n ลำดับที่เก้า [lam dap thii kao]

nitrogen ['naɪtrədʒən] n ไนโตรเจน [nai tro chen]

no [nəʊ] pron ไม่แม้แต่หนึ่ง [mai mae tae nueng]; **no!** excl ไม่ [mai]; **no one** pron ไม่มีใคร [mai mii khrai]

nobody ['nəʊbədɪ] pron ไม่มีใคร [mai mii khrai]

nod [nɒd] v พยักหน้า [pha yak na]

noise [nɔɪz] n เสียง [siang]; **I can't sleep for the noise** ฉันนอนไม่หลับ เพราะเสียง [chan non mai lap phro siang]

noisy ['nɔɪzɪ] adj เสียงดัง [siang dang]; **It's noisy** เสียงดัง [siang dang]; **My dorm-mates are very noisy** เพื่อนร่วม ห้องพักฉันเสียงดังมาก [phuean ruam hong phak chan siang dang mak]; **The room is too noisy** ห้องเสียงดังมากเกิน ไป [hong siang dang mak koen pai]

nominate ['nɒmɪˌneɪt] v เสนอชื่อ [sa noe chue]

nomination [ˌnɒmɪˈneɪʃən] n การเสนอ ชื่อ [kan sa noe chue]

none [nʌn] pron ไม่มีสักสิ่ง [mai mii sak sing]

nonsense ['nɒnsəns] n เรื่องไร้สาระ [rueang rai sa ra]

non-smoker [nɒnˈsməʊkə] n ผู้ไม่สูบ บุหรี่ [phu mai sup bu rii]

non-smoking [nɒnˈsməʊkɪŋ] adj ซึ่ง ไม่สูบบุหรี่ [sueng mai sup bu rii]

non-stop ['nɒnˈstɒp] adv ไม่หยุด [mai yut]

noodles ['nuːdəlz] npl เส้นก๋วยเตี๋ยว [sen kuai tiao]

noon [nuːn] n เที่ยงวัน [thiang wan]

nor [nɔː; nə] conj ไม่ มักใช้คู่กับ neither [mai mak chai khu kap neither]

normal ['nɔːməl] adj ปรกติ [prok ka ti]

normally ['nɔːməlɪ] adv โดยปรกติ [doi prok ka ti]

north [nɔːθ] adj เกี่ยวกับทิศเหนือ [kiao kap thit nuea] ▷ adv ไปทางด้านเหนือ [pai thang dan nuea] ▷ n ทิศเหนือ [thit nuea]; **North Africa** n อัฟริกาเหนือ [af ri ka nuea]; **North African** n เกี่ยวกับอัฟ

ริกาเหนือ [kiao kap af ri ka nuea], ชา
วอัฟริกันตอนเหนือ [kiao kap af ri ka
nuea, chao af ri kan ton nuea]; **North
America** n ทวีปอเมริกาเหนือ [tha wip a
me ri ka nuea]

northbound ['nɔːθˌbaʊnd] adj ซึ่งไป
ทางเหนือ [sueng pai thang hnuea]

northeast [ˌnɔːθˈiːst; ˌnɔːrˈiːst] n ทิศ
ตะวันออกเฉียงเหนือ [thid ta wan ork
chiang hnuea]

northern ['nɔːðən] adj ทางภาคเหนือ
[thang phak hnuea]; **Northern
Ireland** n ประเทศไอร์แลนด์เหนือ [pra tet
ai laen nuea]

northwest [ˌnɔːθˈwɛst; ˌnɔːˈwɛst] n
ทิศตะวันตกเฉียงเหนือ [thid ta wan tok
chiang hnuea]

Norway ['nɔːˌweɪ] n ประเทศนอร์เวย์ [pra
tet nor we]

Norwegian [nɔːˈwiːdʒən] adj เกี่ยวกับ
นอร์เวย์ [kiao kap no we] ▷ n (language)
ภาษานอร์เวย์ [pha sa nor we], (person)
ชาวนอร์เวย์ [chao no we]

nose [nəʊz] n จมูก [cha muk]

nosebleed ['nəʊzˌbliːd] n เลือดกำเดา
ออก [lueat kam dao ok]

nostril ['nɒstrɪl] n รูจมูก [ru cha muk]

nosy ['nəʊzɪ] adj อยากรู้อยากเห็น [yak ru
yak hen]

not [nɒt] adv ไม่ [mai]; **I'm not
drinking** ฉันไม่ดื่ม [chan mai duem];
This wine is not chilled ไวน์ไม่เย็น
[wine mai yen]

note [nəʊt] n (banknote) ธนบัตร [tha na
bat], (message) ข้อความ [kho khwam],
(music) โน้ตเพลง [not phleng]; **sick
note** n จดหมายลาป่วยที่แพทย์เป็นผู้เขียน
[chot mai la puai thii phaet pen phu
khian]; **Do you have change for this
note?** คุณมีเงินทอนสำหรับธนบัตรใบนี้
ไหม? [khun mii ngen thon sam rap
tha na bat bai nii mai]

notebook ['nəʊtˌbʊk] n สมุดบันทึก [sa
mud ban thuek]

note down [nəʊt daʊn] v จดลงไป
[chot long pai]

notepad ['nəʊtˌpæd] n กระดาษจดบันทึก
[kra dart chod ban thuek]

notepaper ['nəʊtˌpeɪpə] n กระดาษจด
[kra dart chod]

nothing ['nʌθɪŋ] pron ไม่มีอะไร [mai
mii a rai]

notice ['nəʊtɪs] n (note) การสังเกต [kan
sang ket], (termination) การแจ้งล่วงหน้า
[kan chaeng luang na] ▷ v ประกาศ [pra
kat]; **notice board** n ป้ายประกาศ [pai
pra kaat]

noticeable ['nəʊtɪsəbəl] adj ที่สังเกตเห็น
ได้ [thii sang ket hen dai]

notify ['nəʊtɪˌfaɪ] v บอกกล่าว [bok klao]

nought [nɔːt] n ศูนย์ [sun]

noun [naʊn] n คำนาม [kham nam]

novel ['nɒvəl] n นิยาย [ni yai]

novelist ['nɒvəlɪst] n นักแต่งนวนิยาย
[nak taeng na wa ni yai]

November [nəʊˈvɛmbə] n เดือน
พฤศจิกายน [duean phruet sa chi ka
yon]

now [naʊ] adv เดี๋ยวนี้ [diao ni]; **I need
to pack now** ฉันต้องจัดกระเป๋าเดี๋ยวนี้
[chan tong chat kra pao diao nii]

nowadays ['naʊəˌdeɪz] adv ปัจจุบันนี้
[pad chu ban nee]

nowhere ['nəʊˌwɛə] adv ไม่มีที่ไหน [mai
mii thii nai]

nuclear ['njuːklɪə] adj เกี่ยวกับนิวเคลียร์
[kiao kap nio khlia]

nude [njuːd] adj เปลือยกาย [plueai kai]
▷ n คนเปลือยกาย [khon plueai kai]

nudist ['njuːdɪst] n คนเปลือยกาย [khon
plueai kai]

nuisance ['njuːsəns] n การก่อให้เกิด
ความรำคาญ [kan ko hai koed khwam
ram khan]

numb [nʌm] adj ชา [cha]

number ['nʌmbə] n ตัวเลข [tua lek];
account number n หมายเลขบัญชี [mai
lek ban chi]; **mobile number** n

หมายเลขโทรศัพท์ของโทรศัพท์มือถือ [mai lek tho ra sap khong tho ra sap mue thue]; **number plate** n ป้ายทะเบียนรถ [pai tha bian rot]

numerous ['njuːmərəs] *adj* มากมาย [mak mai]

nun [nʌn] n แม่ชี [mae chi]

nurse [nɜːs] n นางพยาบาล [nang pha ya ban]

nursery ['nɜːsrɪ] n สถานรับเลี้ยงเด็ก [sa than rap liang dek]; **nursery rhyme** n กลอนหรือเพลงง่าย ๆ สำหรับเด็ก [klon rue pleng ngai ngai sam rup dek]; **nursery school** n โรงเรียนเด็กเล็กอายุ ๒ ถึง ๕ ปี [rong rian dek lek a yu song thueng ha pi]

nursing home ['nɜːsɪŋ həʊm] n สถานดูแลคนชรา [sa than du lae khon cha ra]

nut [nʌt] n (device) แป้นเกลียวของสลัก [paen kliao khong sa lak], (food) ถั่ว [thua]; **nut allergy** n การแพ้ถั่ว [kan phae thua]; **Could you prepare a meal without nuts?** คุณทำอาหารที่ไม่มีถั่วได้ไหม? [khun tham a han thii mai mii thua dai mai]

nutmeg ['nʌtmɛg] n ต้นจันทร์เทศ [ton chan tet]

nutrient ['njuːtrɪənt] n สารอาหาร [san a han]

nutrition [njuːˈtrɪʃən] n โภชนาการ [pho cha na kan]

nutritious [njuːˈtrɪʃəs] *adj* ซึ่งบำรุงสุขภาพ [sueng bam rung su kha phap]

nutter ['nʌtə] n คนเพี้ยน [khon phian]

nylon ['naɪlɒn] n เส้นใยไนลอน [sen yai nai lon]

O

oak [əʊk] n ต้นโอ๊ค [ton ok]

oar [ɔː] n ไม้พาย [mai phai]

oasis, oases [əʊˈeɪsɪs, əʊˈeɪsiːz] n บริเวณอุดมสมบูรณ์ในทะเลทราย [bo ri wen u dom som bun nai tha le sai]

oath [əʊθ] n คำปฏิญาณ [kham pa ti yan]

oatmeal ['əʊtˌmiːl] n ข้าวโอ๊ตบดหยาบ ๆ [khao oat bot yab yab]

oats [əʊts] *npl* ข้าวโอ๊ต [khao ot]

obedient [əˈbiːdɪənt] *adj* เชื่อฟัง [chue fung]

obese [əʊˈbiːs] *adj* อ้วนเกินไป [uan koen pai]

obey [əˈbeɪ] v เชื่อฟัง [chue fung]

obituary [əˈbɪtjʊərɪ] n การประกาศข่าวมรณกรรม [kan pra kat khao mo ra na kam]

object ['ɒbdʒɪkt] n วัตถุสิ่งของ [wat thu sing khong]

objection [əbˈdʒɛkʃən] n ความรู้สึกคัดค้าน [khwam ru suek khat khan]

objective [əbˈdʒɛktɪv] n เป้าหมาย [pao mai]

oblong ['ɒbˌlɒŋ] *adj* รูปสี่เหลี่ยมผืนผ้า

[rup si liam phuen pha]

obnoxious [əbˈnɒkʃəs] *adj* น่ารังเกียจ [na rang kiat]

oboe [ˈəʊbəʊ] *n* เครื่องดนตรีประเภทเป่า ชนิดหนึ่ง [khrueang don tri pra phet pao cha nit nueng]

obscene [əbˈsiːn] *adj* ลามก [la mok]

observant [əbˈzɜːvənt] *adj* ช่างสังเกต [chang sang ket]

observatory [əbˈzɜːvətərɪ; -trɪ] *n* หอ สังเกตการณ์ [ho sang ket kan]

observe [əbˈzɜːv] *v* สังเกต [sang ket]

observer [əbˈzɜːvə] *n* ผู้สังเกตการณ์ [phu sang ket kan]

obsessed [əbˈsɛst] *adj* ที่เอาใจใส่อย่าง มาก [thii ao jai sai yang mak]

obsession [əbˈsɛʃən] *n* การครอบงำจิตใจ [kan khrop ngam jit jai]

obsolete [ˈɒbsəˌliːt; ˌɒbsəˈliːt] *adj* ที่ล้า สมัย [thii la sa mai]

obstacle [ˈɒbstəkˀl] *n* อุปสรรค [up pa sak]

obstinate [ˈɒbstɪnɪt] *adj* ดื้อดึง [due dueng]

obstruct [əbˈstrʌkt] *v* ขวางทาง [khwang thang]

obtain [əbˈteɪn] *v* ได้รับ [dai rap]

obvious [ˈɒbvɪəs] *adj* เห็นได้ชัด [hen dai chat]

obviously [ˈɒbvɪəslɪ] *adv* อย่างเห็นได้ชัด [yang hen dai chat]

occasion [əˈkeɪʒən] *n* โอกาส [o kat]

occasional [əˈkeɪʒənˀl] *adj* ซึ่งเป็นครั้ง คราว [sueng pen khrang khrao]

occasionally [əˈkeɪʒənlɪ] *adv* บางครั้ง บางคราว [bang khang bang khrao]

occupation [ˌɒkjʊˈpeɪʃən] *n* (invasion) การยึดครอง [kan yuet khrong], (work) อาชีพ [a chip]

occupy [ˈɒkjʊˌpaɪ] *v* ยึดครอง [yuet khrong]

occur [əˈkɜː] *v* เกิดขึ้น [koet khuen]

occurrence [əˈkʌrəns] *n* เหตุการณ์ที่เกิด ขึ้น [het kan thii koet khuen]

ocean [ˈəʊʃən] *n* มหาสมุทร [ma ha sa mut]; **Arctic Ocean** *n* มหาสมุทรขั้วโลก เหนือ [ma ha sa mut khua lok nuea]; **Indian Ocean** *n* มหาสมุทรอินเดีย [ma ha sa mut in dia]

Oceania [ˌəʊʃɪˈɑːnɪə] *n* หมู่เกาะทาง แปซิฟิก [mu kao thang pae si fik]

o'clock [əˈklɒk] *adv* **after eight o'clock** หลังแปดโมง [lang paet mong]; **at three o'clock** เวลาสามโมง [we la sam mong]; **I'd like to book a table for four people for tonight at eight o'clock** ฉันอยากจองโต๊ะสำหรับ 4 คนคืนนี้เวลาแปด โมง [chan yak chong to sam hrab si kon khuen nee we la paed mong]

October [ɒkˈtəʊbə] *n* เดือนตุลาคม [duean tu la khom]

octopus [ˈɒktəpəs] *n* ปลาหมึกยักษ์ [pla muek yak]

odd [ɒd] *adj* แปลก [plaek]

odour [ˈəʊdə] *n* กลิ่น [klin]

of [ɒv; əv] *prep* ของ [khong]; **Could I have a map of the tube, please?** ฉัน ขอแผนที่ของรถไฟใต้ดินได้ไหม? [chan kho phaen thii khong rot fai tai din dai mai]; **How do I get to the centre of...?** ฉันจะไปที่ศูนย์กลางของ...ได้ อย่างไร? [chan ja pai thii sun klang khong...dai yang rai]

off [ɒf] *adv* ไม่ทำงาน [mai tham ngan] ▷ *prep* ออกจาก [ok chak]; **time off** *n* ช่วงวันหยุดหรือไม่ไปทำงาน [chuang wan yut rue mai pai tham ngan]

offence [əˈfɛns] *n* การกระทำผิดกฏหมาย [kan kra tham pit kot mai]

offend [əˈfɛnd] *v* ทำให้ขุ่นเคือง [tham hai khun khueang]

offensive [əˈfɛnsɪv] *adj* ซึ่งทำให้ขุ่นเคือง [sueng tham hai khun khueang]

offer [ˈɒfə] *n* ข้อเสนอ [khor sa noe] ▷ *v* เสนอเพื่อให้พิจารณา [sa noe phuea hai phi ja ra na]; **special offer** *n* การขาย สินค้าราคาพิเศษ [kan khai sin kha ra kha phi set]

office [ˈɒfɪs] *n* สำนักงาน [sam nak ngan]; **booking office** *n* สำนักงานจอง [sam nak ngan chong]; **box office** *n* ที่ขายตั๋วหนังหรือละคร [thii khai tua nang rue la khon]; **head office** *n* สำนักงานใหญ่ [sam nak ngan yai]; **Do you have a press office?** คุณมีสำนักงานแถลงข่าวไหม? [khun mii sam nak ngan tha laeng khao mai]

officer [ˈɒfɪsə] *n* นายทหาร [nai tha han]; **customs officer** *n* เจ้าหน้าที่ศุลกากร [chao na thii sun la ka kon]; **police officer** *n* นายพลตำรวจ [nai pon tam ruat]; **prison officer** *n* เจ้าหน้าที่เรือนจำ [chao na thii ruean cham]

official [əˈfɪʃəl] *adj* เจ้าหน้าที่ [chao na thii]

off-licence [ˈɒfˌlaɪsəns] *n* ร้านขายสุรา [ran khai su ra]

off-peak [ˈɒfˌpiːk] *adv* ซึ่งมีราคาถูกและไม่ใช่ช่วงที่นิยม [sueng mii ra kha thuk lae mai chai chuang thii ni yom]

off-season [ˈɒfˌsiːzən] *adj* ที่มีกิจกรรมที่เกิดขึ้นน้อย [thii mii kit cha kam thii koet khuen noi] ▷ *adv* ในระหว่างเวลาที่มีกิจกรรมน้อย [nai ra wang we la thii mii kit cha kam noi]

offside [ˈɒfˈsaɪd] *adj* ที่อยู่ในตำแหน่งล้ำหน้า [thii yu nai tam naeng lam na]

often [ˈɒfən; ˈɒftən] *adv* บ่อย [boi]; **How often are the buses to…?** รถโดยสารไป…บ่อยแค่ไหน? [rot doi san pai…boi khae nai]

oil [ɔɪl] *n* น้ำมัน [nam man] ▷ *v* ใส่น้ำมัน [sai nam man]; **olive oil** *n* น้ำมันมะกอก [nam man ma kok]; **The oil warning light won't go off** ไฟเตือนน้ำมันปิดไม่ได้ [fai tuean nam man pit mai dai]; **This stain is oil** นี่คือคราบน้ำมัน [ni khue khrap nam man]

oil refinery [ɔɪl rɪˈfaɪnərɪ] *n* โรงกลั่นน้ำมัน [rong klan nam man]

oil rig [ɔɪl rɪg] *n* ฐานโครงสร้างใช้เจาะหาบ่อน้ำมัน [tan khrong sang chai jo ha bo nam man]

oil slick [ɔɪl slɪk] *n* คราบน้ำมันที่ลอยบนผิวน้ำ [khrap nam man thii loi bon phio nam]

oil well [ɔɪl wɛl] *n* บ่อน้ำมัน [bo nam man]

ointment [ˈɔɪntmənt] *n* ขี้ผึ้ง [khi phueng]

OK [ˌəʊˈkeɪ] *excl* โอ เค [o khe]

okay [ˌəʊˈkeɪ] *adj* พอใช้ได้ [pho chai dai]; **okay!** *excl* โอ เค [o khe]

old [əʊld] *adj* แก่ [kae]; **old-age pensioner** *n* คนชราเกษียณผู้รับบำนาญ [khon cha ra ka sian phu rap bam nan]

old-fashioned [ˈəʊldˈfæʃənd] *adj* สมัยเก่า [sa mai kao]

olive [ˈɒlɪv] *n* มะกอก [ma kok]; **olive oil** *n* น้ำมันมะกอก [nam man ma kok]; **olive tree** *n* ต้นมะกอก [ton ma kok]

Oman [əʊˈmɑːn] *n* ประเทศโอมาน [pra tet o man]

omelette [ˈɒmlɪt] *n* ไข่เจียว [khai chiao]

on [ɒn] *adv* กำลังดำเนินอยู่ [kam lang dam noen yu] ▷ *prep* บน [bon]; **on behalf of** *n* ในนามของ [nai nam khong]; **on time** *adj* ตรงเวลา [trong we la]

once [wʌns] *adv* ครั้งหนึ่ง [khrang nueng]

one [wʌn] *number* หนึ่ง [nue] ▷ *pron* คนหรือสิ่งที่ไม่เจาะจง [kon hue sing thii mai jo chong]; **no one** *pron* ไม่มีใคร [mai mii khrai]

one-off [ˈwʌnˌɒf] *n* สิ่งที่เกิดขึ้นหรือทำขึ้นเพียงครั้งเดียว [sing thii koet khuen rue tham khuen phiang khrang diao]

onion [ˈʌnjən] *n* หัวหอม [hua hom]; **spring onion** *n* ต้นหอม [ton hom]

online [ˈɒnˌlaɪn] *adj* ที่เชื่อมตรงกับอินเตอร์เน็ต [thii chueam trong kap in toe net] ▷ *adv* ขณะเชื่อมต่อกับอินเตอร์เน็ต [kha na chueam to kap in toe net]

onlooker [ˈɒnˌlʊkə] *n* ผู้เห็นเหตุการณ์

[phu hen het kan]

only ['əʊnlɪ] *adj* เพียงเท่านั้น [phiang thao nan] ▷ *adv* เท่านั้น [thao nan]

open ['əʊpᵊn] *adj* เปิดออก [poet ok] ▷ *v* เปิด [poet]; **Are you open?** คุณเปิดหรือ ไม่? [khun poet rue mai]; **Is it open today?** เปิดวันนี้ไหม? [poet wan nii mai]; **Is the castle open to the public?** ปราสาทเปิดให้สาธารณะชนเข้าชม ไหม? [pra saat poet hai sa tha ra na chon khao chom mai]

opera ['ɒpərə] *n* โอเปร่า [o pe ra]; **soap opera** *n* ละครน้ำเน่า [la khon nam nao]; **What's on tonight at the opera?** คืน นี้มีการแสดงโอเปร่าอะไร? [khuen nii mii kan sa daeng o pe ra a rai]

operate ['ɒpəˌreɪt] *v (to function)* ปฏิบัติ [pa ti bat], *(to perform surgery)* ผ่าตัด [pha tat]

operating theatre ['ɒpəˌreɪtɪŋ 'θɪətə] *n* ห้องผ่าตัด [hong pha tat]

operation [ˌɒpə'reɪʃən] *n (surgery)* ศัลยกรรม [san ya kam], *(undertaking)* การดำเนินการ [kan dam noen kan]

operator ['ɒpəˌreɪtə] *n* ผู้ควบคุม เครื่องจักร [phu khuap khum khrueang chak]

opinion [ə'pɪnjən] *n* ความคิดเห็น [khwam kit hen]; **opinion poll** *n* การ สำรวจความคิดเห็น [kan sam ruat khwam kit hen]; **public opinion** *n* ความคิดเห็นของสาธารณชน [khwam kit hen khong sa tha ra na chon]

opponent [ə'pəʊnənt] *n* ฝ่ายตรงข้าม [fai trong kham]

opportunity [ˌɒpə'tjuːnɪtɪ] *n* โอกาส [o kat]

oppose [ə'pəʊz] *v* ต่อต้าน [to tan]

opposed [ə'pəʊzd] *adj* ถูกต่อต้าน [thuk tor tan]

opposing [ə'pəʊzɪŋ] *adj* ซึ่งต่อต้าน [sueng to tan]

opposite ['ɒpəzɪt; -sɪt] *adj* ที่อยู่ตรงกัน ข้าม [thii yu trong kan kham] ▷ *adv* ที่ อยู่คนละด้าน [thii yu khon la dan] ▷ *prep* ตรงข้าม [trong kham]

opposition [ˌɒpə'zɪʃən] *n* ฝ่ายตรงข้าม [fai trong kham]

optician [ɒp'tɪʃən] *n* ผู้มีคุณสมบัติที่จะ ตรวจ ออกใบวัดและขายอุปกรณ์เกี่ยวกับ สายตา [phu mii khun na som bat thii ja truat ok bai wat lae khai ub pa kon kiao kap sai ta]

optimism ['ɒptɪˌmɪzəm] *n* การมองในแง่ ดี [kan mong nai ngae dii]

optimist ['ɒptɪˌmɪst] *n* ผู้มองโลกในแง่ดี [phu mong lok nai ngae di]

optimistic [ˌɒptɪ'mɪstɪk] *adj* โดยคาด หวังสิ่งที่ดี [doi khat wang sing thii di]

option ['ɒpʃən] *n* การเลือก [kan lueak]

optional ['ɒpʃənᵊl] *adj* ซึ่งเป็นทางเลือก [sueng pen thang lueak]

opt out [ɒpt aʊt] *v* เลือกที่จะไม่เกี่ยวข้อง ด้วย [lueak thii ja mai kiao khong duai]

or [ɔː] *conj* หรือ [rue]; **either... or** *conj* อย่างนี้หรืออย่างนั้น [yang nii rue yang nan]; **Do I pay now or later?** ฉันจ่าย ตอนนี้หรือจ่ายทีหลัง? [chan chai ton nii rue chai thii lang]

oral ['ɔːrəl; 'ɒrəl] *adj* ที่ใช้การพูด [thii chai kan phud] ▷ *n* การสอบปากเปล่า [kan sorb pak plao]

orange ['ɒrɪndʒ] *adj* ที่มีสีส้ม [thii mii sii som] ▷ *n* ต้นส้ม [ton som]; **orange juice** *n* น้ำส้ม [nam som]

orchard ['ɔːtʃəd] *n* สวนผลไม้ [suan phon la mai]

orchestra ['ɔːkɪstrə] *n* วงดนตรีขนาด ใหญ่ที่เล่นเพลงคลาสสิค [wong don tree kha naat yai thii len phleng khlas sik]

orchid ['ɔːkɪd] *n* ต้นกล้วยไม้ [ton kluai mai]

ordeal [ɔː'diːl] *n* ประสบการณ์ที่ทารุณ [pra sob kan thii tha run]

order ['ɔːdə] *n* คำสั่ง [kham sang], ความ เป็นระเบียบ [khwam pen ra biap] ▷ *v (command)* สั่ง [sang], *(request)* สั่ง

[sang]; **order form** *n* แบบฟอร์มสั่งซื้อ [baep fom sang sue]; **postal order** *n* เช็คไปรษณีย์ [chek prai sa ni]; **standing order** *n* เงินเฉพาะจำนวนที่ให้ธนาคารจ่าย [ngoen cha pho cham nuan thii hai tha na khan chai]; **Can I order now, please?** ฉันขอสั่งตอนนี้ได้ไหม? [chan kho sang ton nii dai mai]; **I'd like to order something local** ฉันอยากสั่งอะไรสักอย่างที่เป็นของท้องถิ่น [chan yak sang a rai sak yang thii pen khong thong thin]; **This isn't what I ordered** ฉันไม่ได้สั่ง [chan mai dai sang]

ordinary ['ɔːdənrɪ] *adj* อย่างธรรมดา [yang tham ma da]

oregano [ˌɒrɪˈɡɑːnəʊ] *n* ต้นออริกาโนเป็นสมุนไพรใช้ทำอาหาร [ton o ri ka no pen sa mun phrai chai tham a han]

organ ['ɔːɡən] *n (body part)* อวัยวะต่าง ๆ [a wai ya wa tang tang], *(music)* หีบเพลง ออร์แกน [hip phleng, o kaen]; **mouth organ** *n* หีบเพลงปาก [hip phleng pak]

organic [ɔːˈɡænɪk] *adj* ซึ่งมาจากสิ่งมีชีวิต [sueng ma chak sing mii chi wit]

organism ['ɔːɡəˌnɪzəm] *n* สิ่งมีชีวิตเช่นพืชและสัตว์ [sing mii chi wit chen phuet lae sat]

organization [ˌɔːɡənaɪˈzeɪʃən] *n* องค์กร [ong kon]

organize ['ɔːɡəˌnaɪz] *v* จัดการ [chat kan]

organizer ['ɔːɡəˌnaɪzə] *n* **personal organizer** *n* ไดอารี่เล่มใหญ่ [dai a ri lem yai]

orgasm ['ɔːɡæzəm] *n* จุดสุดยอดของความรู้สึกทางเพศ [chut sut yot khong khwam ru suek thang phet]

Orient ['ɔːrɪənt] *n* เอเชียตะวันออก [e chia ta wan ok]

oriental [ˌɔːrɪˈɛntəl] *adj* ซึ่งเกี่ยวกับประเทศเอเชีย [sueng kiao kab pra ted e chia]

origin ['ɒrɪdʒɪn] *n* จุดกำเนิด [chut kam noet]

original [əˈrɪdʒɪnəl] *adj* ซึ่งเป็นแบบฉบับ [sueng pen baep cha bap]

originally [əˈrɪdʒɪnəlɪ] *adv* โดยแรกเริ่ม [doi raek roem]

ornament ['ɔːnəmənt] *n* เครื่องประดับ [khrueang pra dap]

orphan ['ɔːfən] *n* ลูกกำพร้า [luk kam phra]

ostrich ['ɒstrɪtʃ] *n* นกกระจอกเทศ [nok kra chok thet]

other ['ʌðə] *adj* อื่น ๆ [uen uen]; **Do you have any others?** คุณมีห้องอื่น ๆ ไหม? [khun mii hong uen uen mai]

otherwise ['ʌðəˌwaɪz] *adv* ไม่เช่นนั้น [mai chen nan] ▷ *conj* มิฉะนั้น [mi cha nan]

otter ['ɒtə] *n* ตัวนาก [tua nak]

ounce [aʊns] *n* หน่วยวัดน้ำหนักเป็นออนซ์ [nuai wat nam nak pen on]

our [aʊə] *adj* ของเรา [khong rao]

ours [aʊəz] *pron* ของเราเอง [khong rao eng]

ourselves [aʊəˈsɛlvz] *pron* ตัวของพวกเราเอง [tua khong phuak rao eng]

out [aʊt] *adj* ข้างนอก [khang nok] ▷ *adv* ภายนอก [phai nok]

outbreak ['aʊtˌbreɪk] *n* การเกิดขึ้นอย่างรุนแรงและทันทีทันใด [kan koed khuen yang run raeng lae than thee than dai]

outcome ['aʊtˌkʌm] *n* ผลลัพธ์ [phon lap]

outdoor ['aʊtˌdɔː] *adj* ที่อยู่กลางแจ้ง [thii yu klang chaeng]

outdoors [ˌaʊtˈdɔːz] *adv* ข้างนอก [khang nok]

outfit ['aʊtˌfɪt] *n* เสื้อผ้าทั้งชุด [suea pha thang chut]

outgoing ['aʊtˌɡəʊɪŋ] *adj* ที่กำลังออกไป [thii kam lang ork pai]

outing ['aʊtɪŋ] *n* การเดินทางท่องเที่ยวระยะสั้น [kan doen thang thong thiao ra ya san]

outline ['aʊtˌlaɪn] n คำอธิบายอย่างคร่าว ๆ [kham a thi bai yang khrao khrao]

outlook ['aʊtˌlʊk] n ทัศนคติ [that sa na kha ti]

out-of-date ['aʊtɒv'deɪt] adj ล้าสมัย [la sa mai]

out-of-doors ['aʊtɒv'dɔːz] adv กลาง แจ้ง [klang chaeng]

outrageous [aʊt'reɪdʒəs] adj ผิดปรกติ และน่าตกใจ [phit prok ka ti lae na tok jai]

outset ['aʊtˌsɛt] n การเริ่มต้น [kan roem ton]

outside adj ['aʊtˌsaɪd] ข้างนอก [khang nok] ▷ adv [ˌaʊt'saɪd] ภายนอก [phai nok] ▷ n ['aʊt'saɪd] ข้างนอก [khang nok] ▷ prep นอกจาก [nok chak]; **I want to make an outside call, can I have a line?** ฉันอยากโทรศัพท์ออกข้างนอก ขอ สายนอก? [chan yak tho ra sap ok khang nok kho sai nok]

outsize ['aʊtˌsaɪz] adj ที่ใหญ่เป็นพิเศษ [thii yai pen phi sed]

outskirts ['aʊtˌskɜːts] npl ชานเมือง [chan mueang]

outspoken [ˌaʊt'spəʊkən] adj พูดจาเปิด เผย [phud cha poet phoei]

outstanding [ˌaʊt'stændɪŋ] adj ที่ดี เยี่ยม [thii di yiam]

oval ['əʊvᵊl] adj ซึ่งเป็นรูปไข่ [sueng pen rup khai]

ovary ['əʊvərɪ] n รังไข่ของสตรี [rang khai khong sa tree]

oven ['ʌvᵊn] n เตาอบ [tao op]; **microwave oven** n เตาอบไมโครเวฟ [tao op mai khro wep]; **oven glove** n ถุงมือจับภาชนะร้อนจากเตาอบ [thung mue chap pha cha na ron chak tao op]

ovenproof ['ʌvᵊnˌpruːf] adj เหมาะกับการ ใช้ในเตาอบ [mo kap kan chai nai tao op]

over ['əʊvə] adj ที่จบสิ้น [thii job sin] ▷ prep เหนือ [nuea]

overall [ˌəʊvər'ɔːl] adv ทั้งหมด [thang mot]

overalls [ˌəʊvə'ɔːlz] npl เสื้อคลุมที่สวมเพื่อ กันเปื้อน [suea khlum thii suam phuea kan puean]

overcast ['əʊvəˌkɑːst] adj มีเฆมมาก [mii mek mak]

overcharge [ˌəʊvə'tʃɑːdʒ] v คิดเกินราคา [khit koen ra kha]

overcoat ['əʊvəˌkəʊt] n เสื้อโค้ทกันหนาว [suea khot kan nao]

overcome [ˌəʊvə'kʌm] v เอาชนะ [ao cha na]

overdone [ˌəʊvə'dʌn] adj ที่สุกมากเกินไป [thii suk mak koen pai]

overdose ['əʊvəˌdəʊs] n ปริมาณยาที่มาก เกินไป [po ri man ya thii mak koen pai]

overdraft ['əʊvəˌdrɑːft] n จำนวนเงินที่ เป็นหนี้ธนาคาร [cham nuan ngen thii pen nii tha na khan]

overdrawn [ˌəʊvə'drɔːn] adj ถอนเงินเกิน [thon ngoen koen]

overdue [ˌəʊvə'djuː] adj พ้นกำหนดเวลา [phon kam not we la]

overestimate [ˌəʊvər'ɛstɪˌmeɪt] v ประเมินมากเกินไป [pra moen mak koen pai]

overheads ['əʊvəˌhɛdz] npl ค่าใช้จ่ายใน การดำเนินธุรกิจ [kha chai chai nai kan dam noen thu ra kit]

overlook [ˌəʊvə'lʊk] v มองข้าม [mong kham]

overnight ['əʊvəˌnaɪt] adv **Can I park here overnight?** ฉันจอดค้างคืนที่นี่ได้ ไหม? [chan jot khang khuen thii ni dai mai]; **Can we camp here overnight?** เราตั้งค่ายค้างคืนที่นี่ได้ไหม? [rao tang khai khang khuen thii ni dai mai]; **Do I have to stay overnight?** ฉันต้องนอนค้างคืนไหม? [chan tong non khang khuen mai]

overrule [ˌəʊvə'ruːl] v ใช้อำนาจเหนือ [chai am nat nuea]

overseas [ˌəʊvə'siːz] adv เกี่ยวกับต่าง ประเทศ [kiao kap tang pra thet]

oversight [ˈəʊvəˌsaɪt] n (mistake) ความ
ผิดพลาดเพราะละเลยหรือไม่สังเกต
[khwam phit phlat phro la loei rue
mai sang ket], (supervision) การดูแล
ตรวจตรา [kan du lae truat tra]

oversleep [ˌəʊvəˈsliːp] v นอนเกินเวลา
[norn koen we la]

overtake [ˌəʊvəˈteɪk] v ไล่ตามทัน [lai
tam than]

overtime [ˈəʊvəˌtaɪm] n ล่วงเวลา [luang
we la]

overweight [ˌəʊvəˈweɪt] adj ที่มีน้ำหนัก
มากเกินไป [thii mii nam nak koen
pai]

owe [əʊ] v เป็นหนี้ [pen ni]

owing to [ˈəʊɪŋ tuː] prep เนื่องจาก
[nueang chak]

owl [aʊl] n นกเค้าแมว [nok khao maeo]

own [əʊn] adj ที่เป็นของตัวเอง [thii pen
khong tua eng] ▷ v เป็นเจ้าของ [pen
chao khong]

owner [ˈəʊnə] n เจ้าของ [chao khong];
Could I speak to the owner, please?
ฉันขอพูดกับเจ้าของได้ไหม? [chan kho
phut kap chao khong dai mai]

own up [əʊn ʌp] v สารภาพ [sa ra phap]

oxygen [ˈɒksɪdʒən] n ออกซิเจน [ok si
chen]

oyster [ˈɔɪstə] n หอยนางรม [hoi nang
rom]

ozone [ˈəʊzəʊn; əʊˈzəʊn] n ก๊าซโอโซน
[kas o son]; **ozone layer** n ชั้นก๊าซ
โอโซนล้อมรอบโลก [chan kas o son lom
rop lok]

P

PA [pi: eɪ] abbr ตัวย่อของเลขาส่วนตัว [tua
yo khong le kha suan tua]

pace [peɪs] n ก้าวเดิน [kao doen]

pacemaker [ˈpeɪsˌmeɪkə] n อุปกรณ์
ไฟฟ้าที่ช่วยให้อัตราการเต้นของหัวใจ
สม่ำเสมอ [up pa kon fai fa thii chuai
hai at tra kan ten khong hua jai sa
mam sa moe]

Pacific [pəˈsɪfɪk] n มหาสมุทรแปซิฟิก [ma
ha sa mut pae si fik]

pack [pæk] n สิ่งของ [sing khong] ▷ v
บรรจุ [ban chu]

package [ˈpækɪdʒ] n หีบห่อ [hip ho];
package holiday n การท่องเที่ยวกับ
บริษัททัวร์จัดบริการแบบครบวงจร [kan
thong thiao kap bo ri sat tua chad bo ri
kan baep khrop wong chon]; **package
tour** n ทัวร์ที่จัดแบบครบวงจร [thua thii
chat baep khrop wong chon]

packaging [ˈpækɪdʒɪŋ] n หีบห่อ [hip
ho]

packed [pækt] adj แน่น [naen]; **packed
lunch** n อาหารกลางวันเตรียมจากบ้านไป
ทานที่อื่น [a han klang wan triam chak
baan pai than thii uen]

packet [ˈpækɪt] *n* ห่อของเล็ก ๆ [ho khong lek lek]

pad [pæd] *n* เบาะรอง [bo rong]

paddle [ˈpædᵊl] *n* ไม้พายเรือ [mai phai ruea] ▷ *v* พายเรือ [phai ruea]

padlock [ˈpædˌlɒk] *n* กุญแจแบบคล้อง สายยู [kun jae baeb khlong sai u]

paedophile [ˈpiːdəʊˌfaɪl] *n* ผู้ที่ชอบร่วม เพศกับเด็ก [phu thii chop ruam phet kap dek]

page [peɪdʒ] *n* หน้า [na] ▷ *v* เรียกโดยใช้ เครื่องขยายเสียงหรือเครื่องส่งสัญญาณ ติดตามตัว [riak doi chai khrueang kha yai siang rue khrueang song san yan tit tam tua]; **home page** *n* หน้าแรกของ ข่าวสารขององค์การหรือบุคคล [na raek khong khao san khong ong kan rue buk khon]; **Yellow Pages®** *npl* สมุด โทรศัพท์ฉบับโฆษณาสินค้า [sa mut tho ra sap cha bap khot sa na sin ka]

pager [ˈpeɪdʒə] *n* วิทยุหรือเครื่องส่ง สัญญาณติดตามตัว [wit tha yu hue khueang song san yan tid tam tua]

paid [peɪd] *adj* ได้จ่ายแล้ว [dai chai laeo]

pail [peɪl] *n* ถัง [thang]

pain [peɪn] *n* ความเจ็บปวด [khwam chep puat]; **back pain** *n* ปวดหลัง [puat lang]

painful [ˈpeɪnfʊl] *adj* เจ็บปวด [chep puat]

painkiller [ˈpeɪnˌkɪlə] *n* ยาแก้ปวด [ya kae puad]

paint [peɪnt] *n* สี [si] ▷ *v* ทาสี [tha si]

paintbrush [ˈpeɪntˌbrʌʃ] *n* แปรงทาสี [praeng tha sii]

painter [ˈpeɪntə] *n* จิตรกร [chit ta kon]

painting [ˈpeɪntɪŋ] *n* ภาพวาด [phap wat]

pair [peə] *n* คู่ [khu]

Pakistan [ˌpɑːkɪˈstɑːn] *n* ประเทศ ปากีสถาน [pra tet pa ki sa than]

Pakistani [ˌpɑːkɪˈstɑːnɪ] *adj* เกี่ยวกับ ปากีสถาน [kiao kap pa ki sa than] ▷ *n* ชาวปากีสถาน [chao pa ki sa than]

pal [pæl] *n* เพื่อนสนิท [phuean sa nit]

palace [ˈpælɪs] *n* พระราชวัง [phra rat cha wang]; **Is the palace open to the public?** พระราชวังเปิดให้สาธารณะชนเข้า ชมไหม? [phra rat cha wang poet hai sa tha ra na chon khao chom mai]; **When is the palace open?** พระราชวังจะเปิด เมื่อไร? [phra rat cha wang ja poet muea rai]

pale [peɪl] *adj* ซีดเผือด [sid phueat]

Palestine [ˈpælɪˌstaɪn] *n* ประเทศ ปาเลสไตน์ [pra tet pa les tai]

Palestinian [ˌpælɪˈstɪnɪən] *adj* เกี่ยวกับ ปาเลสไตน์ [kiao kap pa les tai] ▷ *n* ชาว ปาเลสไตน์ [chao pa les tai]

palm [pɑːm] *n* *(part of hand)* ฝ่ามือ [fa mue], *(tree)* ต้นปาล์ม [ton palm]

pamphlet [ˈpæmflɪt] *n* แผ่นพับ [phaen phap]

pan [pæn] *n* กระทะ [kra tha]; **frying pan** *n* กระทะทอด [kra tha thot]

Panama [ˌpænəˈmɑː; ˈpænəˌmɑː] *n* ประเทศปานามา [pra tet pa na ma]

pancake [ˈpænˌkeɪk] *n* ขนมแพนเค้ก [kha nom phaen khek]

panda [ˈpændə] *n* หมีแพนด้า [mii phaen da]

panic [ˈpænɪk] *n* ความหวาดกลัวหรือวิตก กังวล [khwam wat klua rue wi tok kang won] ▷ *v* ทำให้ตื่นตกใจ [tham hai tuen tok jai]

panther [ˈpænθə] *n* เสือดำ [suea dam]

panties [ˈpæntɪz] *npl* กางเกงในของสตรี หรือเด็ก [kang keng nai khong sa tee hue dek]

pantomime [ˈpæntəˌmaɪm] *n* ละครที่มี พื้นฐานมาจากเทพนิยายแสดงช่วงคริสต์มาส [la khon thii mii phuen than chak thep ni yai sa daeng chuang khris mas]

pants [pænts] *npl* กางเกงขายาว [kang keng kha yao]

paper [ˈpeɪpə] *n* กระดาษ [kra dat]; **paper round** *n* เส้นทางส่งหนังสือพิมพ์ [sen thang song nang sue phim];

scrap paper n กระดาษทด [kra dat thot]; **toilet paper** n กระดาษชำระ [kra dat cham ra]; **There is no toilet paper** ไม่มีกระดาษชำระ [mai mii kra dat cham ra]

paperback ['peɪpə,bæk] n หนังสือปกอ่อน [hnang sue pok on]

paperclip ['peɪpə,klɪp] n คลิปติดกระดาษ [khlip tit kra dat]

paperweight ['peɪpə,weɪt] n ที่วางกระดาษ [thii wang kra dart]

paperwork ['peɪpə,wɜːk] n งานเอกสาร [ngan ek ka sarn]

paprika ['pæprɪkə; pæ'priː-] n เครื่องเทศสีแดงออนใส่อาหาร [khrueang tet sii daeng on sai a han]

paracetamol [,pærə'siːtə,mɒl; -'sɛtə-] n **I'd like some paracetamol** ฉันอยากได้พาราเซตตามอล [chan yak dai pha ra set ta mon]

parachute ['pærə,ʃuːt] n ร่มชูชีพ [rom chu chip]

parade [pə'reɪd] n ขบวนแห่ [kha buan hae]

paradise ['pærə,daɪs] n สวรรค์ [sa wan]

paraffin ['pærəfɪn] n พาราฟิน [pha ra fin]

paragraph ['pærə,grɑːf; -,græf] n ย่อหน้า [yo na]

Paraguay ['pærə,gwaɪ] n ประเทศปารากวัย [pra tet pa ra kwai]

Paraguayan [,pærə'gwaɪən] adj เกี่ยวกับปารากวัย [kiao kap pa ra kwai] ▷ n ชาวปารากวัย [chao pa ra kwai]

parallel ['pærə,lɛl] adj ขนาน [kha nan]

paralysed ['pærə,laɪzd] adj เคลื่อนไหวไม่ได้ [khluean wai mai dai]

paramedic [,pærə'mɛdɪk] n เจ้าหน้าที่ทางการแพทย์ [chao na thii thang kan phaet]

parcel ['pɑːsəl] n พัสดุ [phat sa du]; **How much is it to send this parcel?** ราคาส่งกล่องพัสดุใบนี้เท่าไร? [ra kha song klong phat sa du bai nii thao rai]; **I'd**

like to send this parcel ฉันอยากส่งกล่องพัสดุใบนี้ [chan yak song klong phat sa du bai nii]

pardon ['pɑːdᵊn] n การให้อภัยโทษ [kan hai a phai thot]

parent ['pɛərənt] n พ่อหรือแม่ [pho rue mae]; **parents** npl พ่อแม่ [pho mae]; **single parent** n พ่อหรือแม่ที่เลี้ยงลูกคนเดียว [pho rue mae thii liang luk khon diao]

parish ['pærɪʃ] n เขตศาสนาที่มีโบสถ์และพระ [khet sat sa na thii mii bot lae phra]

park [pɑːk] n สวนสาธารณะ [suan sa tha ra na] ▷ v จอด [chot]; **car park** n ที่จอดรถ [thi chot rot]; **Can I park here?** ฉันจอดที่นี่ได้ไหม? [chan jot thii ni dai mai]; **Can we park our caravan here?** เราจอดรถคาราวานของเราที่นี่ได้ไหม? [rao jot rot kha ra van khong rao thii ni dai mai]; **How long can I park here?** ฉันจอดได้นานแค่ไหน? [chan jot dai nan khae nai]

parking [pɑːkɪŋ] n ที่จอดรถ [thi chot rot]; **parking meter** n มิเตอร์จอดรถ [mi toe jot rot]; **parking ticket** n ใบสั่ง [bai sang]

parliament ['pɑːləmənt] n รัฐสภา [rat tha sa pha]

parole [pə'rəʊl] n การพ้นโทษอย่างมีเงื่อนไขหรือทำทัณฑ์เบ่นบนไว้ [kan phon thot yang mii nguean khai rue tham than bon wai]

parrot ['pærət] n นกแก้ว [nok kaew]

parsley ['pɑːslɪ] n พาสลี่ ผักใช้ปรุงอาหาร [phas li phak chai prung a han]

parsnip ['pɑːsnɪp] n พืชจำพวกมีหัวตระกูลเดียวกับแครอทมีสีขาว [phuet cham phuak mee hua tra kul diao kab kae rot mee see khao]

part [pɑːt] n ส่วนหนึ่ง [suan nueng]; **spare part** n อะไหล่ [a lai]

partial ['pɑːʃəl] adj ซึ่งเป็นบางส่วน [sueng pen bang suan]

participate [pɑː'tɪsɪˌpeɪt] v มีส่วนร่วม [mi suan ruam]

particular [pə'tɪkjʊlə] adj โดยเฉพาะ [doi cha pho]

particularly [pə'tɪkjʊləlɪ] adv โดยเฉพาะอย่างยิ่ง [doi cha pho yang ying]

parting ['pɑːtɪŋ] n การจากกัน [kan chak kan]

partly ['pɑːtlɪ] adv บางส่วน [bang suan]

partner ['pɑːtnə] n คู่สมรส [khu som rot]

partridge ['pɑːtrɪdʒ] n นกกระทา [nok kra tha]

part-time ['pɑːtˌtaɪm] adj ซึ่งไม่เต็มเวลา [sueng mai tem we la] ▷ adv นอกเวลา [nok we la]

part with [pɑːt wɪð] v ยอมสละ [yom sa la]

party ['pɑːtɪ] n (group) คณะ [kha na], (social gathering) งานเลี้ยง [ngan liang] ▷ v จัดงานเลี้ยง [chat ngan liang]; **dinner party** n งานเลี้ยงอาหารค่ำ [ngan liang a han kham]; **search party** n คณะผู้สำรวจผู้สูญหาย [kha na phu sam ruat phu sun hai]

pass [pɑːs] n (in mountains) ช่องแคบ [chong khaep], (meets standard) การสอบผ่าน [kan sorb phan], (permit) ใบอนุญาต [bai a nu yat] ▷ v (an exam) สอบผ่าน สอบไล่ได้ [sop phan, sop lai dai] ▷ vi ส่งต่อไป ส่งผ่าน ส่งให้ [song to pai, song phan, song hai] ▷ vt ผ่านไป แล่นผ่าน ส่งผ่าน [phan pai doen phan song phan]; **boarding pass** n บัตรผ่านขึ้นเครื่องบิน [bat phan khuen khrueang bin]; **ski pass** n บัตรเล่นสกี [bat len sa ki]

passage ['pæsɪdʒ] n (musical) บทเพลง [bod phleng], (route) ทางเดิน [thang doen]

passenger ['pæsɪndʒə] n ผู้โดยสาร [phu doi san]

passion ['pæʃən] n อารมณ์อันเร่าร้อน [ar rom an rao ron]; **passion fruit** n เสาวรส [sao wa rot]

passive ['pæsɪv] adj เฉื่อยชา [chueai cha]

pass out [pɑːs aʊt] v หมดสติ [mot sa ti]

Passover ['pɑːsˌəʊvə] n วันหยุดเพื่อระลึกถึงการอพยพของชาวอียิปต์ [wan yut phuea ra luek thueng kan op pha yop khong chao i yip]

passport ['pɑːspɔːt] n หนังสือเดินทาง [nang sue doen thang]; **Here is my passport** นี่คือหนังสือเดินทางของฉัน [ni khue nang sue doen thang khong chan]; **I've forgotten my passport** ฉันลืมหนังสือเดินทาง [chan luem nang sue doen thang]; **I've lost my passport** ฉันทำหนังสือเดินทางหาย [chan tham nang sue doen thang hai]

password ['pɑːsˌwɜːd] n รหัสผ่าน [ra had phan]

past [pɑːst] adj ที่ผ่านไปแล้ว [thii phan pai laeo] ▷ n สิ่งที่เกิดในอดีต [sing thii koet nai a dit] ▷ prep เลยผ่าน [loei phan]

pasta ['pæstə] n พาสต้า อาหารจำพวกแป้ง [phas ta a han cham phuak paeng]

paste [peɪst] n ส่วนผสมที่มีลักษณะเหนียว [suan pha som thii mee lak sa na hniao]

pasteurized ['pæstəˌraɪzd] adj ที่ผ่านการฆ่าเชื้อโรค [thii phan kan kha chuea rok]

pastime ['pɑːsˌtaɪm] n งานอดิเรก [ngan a di rek]

pastry ['peɪstrɪ] n ขนมอบ [kha nom op]; **puff pastry** n แป้งผสมฟูที่มีแผ่นบางหลายชั้นซ้อนกัน [paeng pha som fu thii mii phaen bang lai chan son kan]; **shortcrust pastry** n แป้งที่ใช้เป็นฐานของขนมพาย [paeng thii chai pen than khong kha nom phai]

patch [pætʃ] n แผ่นผ้าปะรุในเสื้อผ้า [phaen pha pa ru nai suea pha]

patched [pætʃt] adj ที่ได้รับการปะ [thii dai rap kan pa]

path [pɑːθ] n ทางเดิน [thang doen];

cycle path n เส้นทางขี่จักรยาน [sen thang khi chak kra yan]; **Keep to the path** เดินบนทางเดิน [doen bon thang doen]; **Where does this path lead?** ทางเดินนี้จะพาไปที่ไหน? [thang doen nii ja pha pai thii nai]

pathetic [pə'θɛtɪk] adj น่าสงสาร [na song san]

patience ['peɪʃəns] n ความอดทน [khwam od thon]

patient ['peɪʃənt] adj อดทน [ot thon] ▷ n คนป่วย [khon puai]

patio ['pætɪ,əʊ] n นอกชาน [nok chan]

patriotic ['pætrɪə,tɪk] adj มีใจรักชาติ [mii jai rak chat]

patrol [pə'trəʊl] n การลาดตระเวน [kan lat tra wen]; **patrol car** n รถลาดตระเวน [rot lay tra wen]

pattern ['pætᵊn] n แบบ [baep]

pause [pɔːz] n การหยุด [kan yud]

pavement ['peɪvmənt] n ทางเดินเท้า [thang doen thao]

pavilion [pə'vɪljən] n พลับพลา [phlap phla]

paw [pɔː] n อุ้งเท้า [ung thao]

pawnbroker ['pɔːn,brəʊkə] n โรงรับจำนำ [rong rap cham nam]

pay [peɪ] n การจ่าย [kan chai] ▷ v จ่าย [chai]; **Can I pay by cheque?** ฉันจ่ายด้วยเช็คได้ไหม? [chan chai duai chek dai mai]; **Do I have to pay duty on this?** ฉันต้องจ่ายภาษีอันนี้ไหม? [chan tong chai pha sii an nii mai]; **Do I have to pay it straightaway?** ฉันต้องจ่ายทันทีหรือไม่? [chan tong chai than thi rue mai]

payable ['peɪəbᵊl] adj ซึ่งสามารถจ่ายได้ [sueng sa mart chai dai]

pay back [peɪ bæk] v จ่ายคืน [chai khuen]

payment ['peɪmənt] n การจ่ายเงิน [kan chai ngen]

payphone ['peɪ,fəʊn] n ตู้โทรศัพท์สาธารณะที่ต้องหยอดเหรียญ [tu tho ra sab sa ta ra na thii tong hyod lian]

PC [piː siː] n เครื่องคอมพิวเตอร์ส่วนตัว [khrueang khom phio toe suan tua]

PDF [piː diː ɛf] n พีดีเอฟไฟล์ [phi di ef fim]

peace [piːs] n ความสงบเรียบร้อย [khwam sa ngob riap roi]

peaceful ['piːsfʊl] adj อย่างสงบ [yang sa ngob]

peach [piːtʃ] n ลูกพีช [luk phiit]

peacock ['piː,kɒk] n นกยูง [nok yung]

peak [piːk] n จุดสูงสุด [chud sung sud]; **peak hours** npl ชั่วโมงที่มีผู้ใช้ถนนมาก [chau mong thii mii phu chai tha non mak]

peanut ['piː,nʌt] n ถั่วลิสง [thua li song]; **peanut allergy** n อาการแพ้ถั่วลิสง [a kan phae thua li song]; **peanut butter** n เนยผสมถั่วลิสงบด [noei pha som thua li song bod]; **Does that contain peanuts?** นั่นมีถั่วลิสงไหม? [nan mii thua li song mai]

pear [pɛə] n ลูกแพร์ [luk pae]

pearl [pɜːl] n ไข่มุก [khai muk]

peas [piːs] npl พืชตระกูลถั่ว [phuet tra kul thua]

peat [piːt] n ถ่านหินเลน [than hin len]

pebble ['pɛbᵊl] n กรวด [kruat]

peculiar [pɪ'kjuːlɪə] adj ประหลาด [pra lat]

pedal ['pɛdᵊl] n กลีบดอกไม้ [klip dok mai]

pedestrian [pɪ'dɛstrɪən] n คนเดินถนน [kon doen tha non]; **pedestrian crossing** n ทางเดินข้าม [thang doen kham]; **pedestrian precinct** n บริเวณที่คนข้าม [bo ri wen thii khon kham]

pedestrianized [pɪ'dɛstrɪə,naɪzd] adj ที่สำหรับคนเดินโดยไม่มีรถ [thii sam hrab kon doen doi mai mee rot]

pedigree ['pɛdɪ,griː] adj เชื้อสายวงศ์ตระกูล [chuea sai wong tra kun]

peel [piːl] n การปอก [kan pok] ▷ v ปลอก [plok]

peg [pɛg] *n* ไม้หนีบผ้า [mai nip pha]

Pekinese [ˌpiːkɪŋˈiːz] *n* ชาวปักกิ่ง [chao pak king]

pelican [ˈpɛlɪkən] *n* นกกระทุง [nok kra thung]; **pelican crossing** *n* ทางข้ามไฟ ที่มีสัญญาณโดยผู้ข้ามเป็นผู้กดปุ่ม [thang kham fai thii mii san yan doi phu kham pen phu kot pum]

pellet [ˈpɛlɪt] *n* ก้อนกลมเล็ก ๆ [kon klom lek lek]

pelvis [ˈpɛlvɪs] *n* กระดูกเชิงกราน [kra duk choeng kran]

pen [pɛn] *n* ปากกา [pak ka]; **ballpoint pen** *n* ปากกาลูกลื่น [pak ka luk luen]; **felt-tip pen** *n* ปากกาที่ใช้ทำเครื่องหมาย [pak ka thii chai tham khrueang mai]; **fountain pen** *n* ปากกาหมึกซึม [pak ka muek suem]; **Do you have a pen I could borrow?** คุณมีปากกาให้ฉันยืม ไหม? [khun mii pak ka hai chan yuem mai]

penalize [ˈpiːnəˌlaɪz] *v* ลงโทษ [long thot]

penalty [ˈpɛnəltɪ] *n* โทษทัณฑ์ทางกฎ หมาย [thot than thang kot mai]

pencil [ˈpɛnsəl] *n* ดินสอ [din so]; **pencil case** *n* กล่องใส่ดินสอ [klong sai din so]; **pencil sharpener** *n* ที่เหลาดินสอ [thii lao din so]

pendant [ˈpɛndənt] *n* จี้ห้อยคอ [chi hoi kho]

penfriend [ˈpɛnˌfrɛnd] *n* เพื่อนทาง จดหมาย [phuean thang chot mai]

penguin [ˈpɛŋgwɪn] *n* นกเพ็นกวิน [nok phen kwin]

penicillin [ˌpɛnɪˈsɪlɪn] *n* ยาปฏิชีวนะชื่อ เพนนิซิลิน [ya pa ti chi wa na chue pen ni si lin]

peninsula [pɪˈnɪnsjʊlə] *n* คาบสมุทร [khap sa mut]

penknife [ˈpɛnˌnaɪf] *n* มีดเล็กที่พับได้ [miit lek thii phap dai]

penny [ˈpɛnɪ] *n* เพนนี [pen ni]

pension [ˈpɛnʃən] *n* บำนาญ [bam nan]

pensioner [ˈpɛnʃənə] *n* ผู้รับบำนาญ [phu rap bam nan]; **old-age pensioner** *n* คนชราเกษียณผู้รับบำนาญ [khon cha ra ka sian phu rap bam nan]

pentathlon [pɛnˈtæθlən] *n* การแข่งขัน กรีฑาห้าประเภท [kan khaeng khan krii tha ha pra phet]

penultimate [pɪˈnʌltɪmɪt] *adj* ที่สอง จากที่สุดท้าย [thii song chak thii sut thai]

people [ˈpiːpəl] *npl* ผู้คน [phu kon]

pepper [ˈpɛpə] *n* พริกไทยป่น [phrik thai pon]

peppermill [ˈpɛpəˌmɪl] *n* กระปุกบดพริก ไทย [kra puk bod prik thai]

peppermint [ˈpɛpəˌmɪnt] *n* สะระแหน่ [sa ra nae]

per [pɜː; pə] *prep* ต่อ [to]; **per cent** *adv* เปอร์เซ็นต์ [poe sen]

percentage [pəˈsɛntɪdʒ] *n* อัตราร้อยละ [at tra roi la]

percussion [pəˈkʌʃən] *n* การตี [kan ti]

perfect [ˈpɜːfɪkt] *adj* ถูกต้อง [tuk tong]

perfection [pəˈfɛkʃən] *n* ความสมบูรณ์ แบบ [khwam som boon baep]

perfectly [ˈpɜːfɪktlɪ] *adv* อย่างสมบูรณ์ แบบ [yang som boon baeb]

perform [pəˈfɔːm] *v* แสดง [sa daeng]

performance [pəˈfɔːməns] *n* (*functioning*) ผลงาน [phon ngan]

perfume [ˈpɜːfjuːm] *n* น้ำหอม [nam hom]

perhaps [pəˈhæps; præps] *adv* บางที [bang thi]

period [ˈpɪərɪəd] *n* ระยะเวลา [ra ya we la]; **trial period** *n* ระยะเวลาทดลอง [ra ya we la thot long]

perjury [ˈpɜːdʒərɪ] *n* การให้การเท็จ [kan hai kan tet]

perm [pɜːm] *n* การดัดผม [kan dat phom]

permanent [ˈpɜːmənənt] *adj* ถาวร [tha won]

permanently [ˈpɜːmənəntlɪ] *adv* อย่าง ถาวร [yang tha won]

permission [pə'mɪʃən] *n* การอนุญาต [kan a nu yat]

permit *n* ['pɜːmɪt] ใบอนุญาต [bai a nu yat] ▷ *v* [pə'mɪɪt] อนุญาต [a nu yat]; **work permit** *n* ใบอนุญาตให้ทำงาน [bai a nu yat hai tham ngan]; **Do you need a fishing permit?** คุณต้องมีใบอนุญาตตก ปลาไหม? [khun tong mii bai a nu yat tok pla mai]

persecute ['pɜːsɪ,kjuːt] *v* จับมาลงโทษ [chab ma long thod]

persevere [,pɜːsɪ'vɪə] *v* ยืนหยัดถึงที่สุด [yuen yat thueng thii sut]

Persian ['pɜːʃən] *adj* เกี่ยวกับเปอร์เซีย [kiao kap poe sia]

persistent [pə'sɪstənt] *adj* ที่ยังคงอยู่ [thii yang khong yu]

person ['pɜːsən] **(people** [piːpᵊl]**)** *n* บุคคล [bu khon]

personal ['pɜːsənəl] *adj* ส่วนบุคคล [suan bu khon]; **personal assistant** *n* ผู้ช่วยส่วนตัว [phu chuai suan tua]; **personal organizer** *n* ไดอารีเล่มใหญ่ [dai a ri lem yai]; **personal stereo** *n* สเตอริโอส่วนตัว [sa toe ri o suan tua]

personality [,pɜːsə'nælɪtɪ] *n* บุคลิกลักษณะ [buk kha lik lak sa na]

personally ['pɜːsənəlɪ] *adv* โดยส่วนตัว [doi suan tua]

personnel [,pɜːsə'nɛl] *n* ฝ่ายบุคคล [fai buk khon]

perspective [pə'spɛktɪv] *n* ทัศนคติ [that sa na kha ti]

perspiration [,pɜːspə'reɪʃən] *n* เหงื่อ [nguea]

persuade [pə'sweɪd] *v* ชักจูง [chak chung]

persuasive [pə'sweɪsɪv] *adj* ซึ่งชักจูงได้ [sueng chak chung dai]

Peru [pə'ruː] *n* ประเทศเปรู [pra tet pe ru]

Peruvian [pə'ruːvɪən] *adj* เกี่ยวกับเปรู [kiao kap pe ru] ▷ *n* ชาวเปรู [chao pe ru]

pessimist ['pɛsɪ,mɪst] *n* คนมองโลกในแง่ ร้าย [khon mong lok nai ngae rai]

pessimistic ['pɛsɪ,mɪstɪk] *adj* ที่มองโลก ในแง่ร้าย [thii mong lok nai ngae rai]

pest [pɛst] *n* สัตว์ที่รบกวน [sat thii rob kuan]

pester ['pɛstə] *v* รบกวน [rop kuan]

pesticide ['pɛstɪ,saɪd] *n* ยาฆ่าแมลง [ya kha ma laeng]

pet [pɛt] *n* สัตว์เลี้ยง [sat liang]

petition [pɪ'tɪʃən] *n* การร้องเรียน [kan rong rian]

petrified ['pɛtrɪ,faɪd] *adj* ทำให้ตกตะลึง เพราะความกลัว [tham hai tok ta lueng phro khwam klua]

petrol ['pɛtrəl] *n* น้ำมันเติมรถ [nam man toem rot]; **petrol station** *n* ปั๊มน้ำมัน [pam nam man]; **petrol tank** *n* ถัง น้ำมัน [thang nam man]; **unleaded petrol** *n* น้ำมันไร้สารตะกั่ว [nam man rai san ta kua]

pewter ['pjuːtə] *n* ตะกั่ว [ta kua]

pharmacist ['fɑːməsɪst] *n* เภสัชกร [phe sat cha kon]

pharmacy ['fɑːməsɪ] *n* ร้านขายยา [ran khai ya]; **Which pharmacy provides emergency service?** ร้านขายยาร้าน ไหนมีบริการขายฉุกเฉิน? [ran khai ya ran nai mii bo ri kan khai chuk choen]

PhD [piː eɪtʃ diː] *n* ตัวย่อของปริญญาเอก [tua yo khong pa rin yaa ek]

pheasant ['fɛzᵊnt] *n* ไก่ฟ้า [kai fa]

philosophy [fɪ'lɒsəfɪ] *n* ปรัชญา [plat cha ya]

phobia ['fəʊbɪə] *n* ความหวาดกลัว [khwam wat klua]

phone [fəʊn] *n* โทรศัพท์ [tho ra thap] ▷ *v* โทร [tho]; **camera phone** *n* โทรศัพท์ที่มีกล้องถ่ายรูปในตัว [tho ra sap thii mii klong thai rup nai tua]; **Can I have your phone number?** ฉันขอเบอร์ โทรศัพท์คุณได้ไหม? [chan kho boe tho ra sap khun dai mai]; **Can I phone from here?** ฉันโทรศัพท์จากที่นี่ได้ไหม? [chan tho ra sap chak thii ni dai mai]; **Can I phone internationally from**

here? ฉันโทรศัพท์ไปต่างประเทศจากที่นี่ได้
ไหม? [chan tho ra sap pai tang pra tet
chak thii ni dai mai]

phonebook ['fəʊn,bʊk] n สมุดโทรศัพท์
[sa mut tho ra sap]

phonebox ['fəʊn,bɒks] n ตู้โทรศัพท์ [tu
tho ra sap]

phonecall ['fəʊn,kɔːl] n โทรศัพท์หา [tho
ra sab ha]

phonecard ['fəʊn,kɑːd] n บัตรโทรศัพท์
[bat tho ra sab]

photo ['fəʊtəʊ] n ภาพถ่าย [phap thai];
photo album n อัลบั้มใส่รูป [al bam sai
rup]

photocopier ['fəʊtəʊ,kɒpɪə] n เครื่อง
ถ่ายเอกสาร [khrueang thai ek ka san]

photocopy ['fəʊtəʊ,kɒpɪ] n การถ่าย
สำเนา [kan thai sam nao] ▷ v อัดสำเนา
[at sam nao]

photograph ['fəʊtəgrɑːf; -,græf] n
ภาพถ่าย [phap thai] ▷ v ถ่ายภาพ [thai
phap]

photographer [fə'tɒgrəfə] n ช่างถ่าย
ภาพ [chang thai phap]

photography [fə'tɒgrəfɪ] n การถ่าย
ภาพ [kan thai phap]

phrase [freɪz] n วลี [wa li]

phrasebook ['freɪz,bʊk] n หนังสือที่เกี่ยว
กับวลี [nang sue thii kiao kap wa li]

physical ['fɪzɪkəl] adj เกี่ยวกับร่างกาย
[kiao kap rang kai] ▷ n ร่างกาย [rang
kai]

physicist ['fɪzɪsɪst] n นักฟิสิกส์ [nak fi
sik]

physics ['fɪzɪks] npl วิชาฟิสิกส์ [wi cha
phi sik]

physiotherapist [,fɪzɪəʊ'θɛrəpɪst] n
นักกายภาพบำบัด [nak kai ya phap bam
bat]

physiotherapy [,fɪzɪəʊ'θɛrəpɪ] n การ
ทำกายภาพบำบัด [kan tham kai ya phap
bam bat]

pianist ['pɪənɪst] n นักเปียโน [nak pia
no]

piano [pɪ'ænəʊ] n เปียโน [pia no]

pick [pɪk] n การเลือก [kan lueak] ▷ v เลือก
[lueak]

pick on [pɪk ɒn] v กลั่นแกล้ง [klan
klaeng]

pick out [pɪk aʊt] v เลือกออก [lueak ok]

pickpocket ['pɪk,pɒkɪt] n นักล้วงกระเป๋า
[nak luang kra pao]

pick up [pɪk ʌp] v ขับรถไปรับ [khab rot
pai rab]

picnic ['pɪknɪk] n การไปเที่ยวนอกบ้านและ
นำอาหารไปรับประทาน [kan pai thiao
nok baan lae nam a han pai rap pra
than]

picture ['pɪktʃə] n รูปภาพ [rup phap];
picture frame n กรอบรูป [krop rup]

picturesque [,pɪktʃə'rɛsk] adj สวย
งดงาม [suai ngot ngam]

pie [paɪ] n ขนมพาย [kha nom phai];
apple pie n ขนมแอปเปิ้ลพาย [kha nom
ap poen phai]; **pie chart** n ภาพแสดง
สถิติรูปพาย [phap sa daeng sa thi ti rup
phai]

piece [piːs] n ชิ้นส่วน [chin suan]

pier [pɪə] n สะพานที่ยื่นออกไปในน้ำ [sa
phan thii yuen ok pai nai nam]

pierce [pɪəs] v เจาะ [cho]

pierced [pɪəst] adj ที่ถูกเจาะ [thii thuk
jo]

piercing ['pɪəsɪŋ] n การเจาะ [kan jo]

pig [pɪg] n หมู [mu]; **guinea pig** n (for
experiment) หนูตะเภาสำหรับทดลอง [nu ta
phao sam rap thot long], (rodent) หนู
ตะเภา [nu ta phao]

pigeon ['pɪdʒɪn] n นกพิราบ [nok phi
rap]

piggybank ['pɪgɪ,bæŋk] n กระปุกใส่
สตางค์ที่เป็นรูปหมู [kra puk sai sa tang
thii pen rup mu]

pigtail ['pɪg,teɪl] n หางเปีย [hang pia]

pile [paɪl] n กอง [kong]

piles [paɪlz] npl โรคริดสีดวงทวาร [rok rit
sii duang tha wan]

pile-up [paɪlʌp] n กองขึ้นมา [kong

khuen ma]

pilgrim ['pɪlgrɪm] *n* ผู้ที่เดินทางไปสถานที่ ศักดิ์สิทธิ์ [phu thii doen thang pai sa than thii sak sit]

pilgrimage ['pɪlgrɪmɪdʒ] *n* การเดินทาง เพื่อไปแสวงบุญ [kan doen thang phue pai sa waeng bun]

pill [pɪl] *n* ยา [ya]; **sleeping pill** *n* ยานอน หลับ [ya non lap]; **I'm not on the pill** ฉันไม่รับยานี้ [chan mai rap ya nii]; **I'm on the pill** ฉันกำลังรับยานี้ [chan kam lang rap ya nii]

pillar ['pɪlə] *n* เสาหลัก [sao lak]

pillow ['pɪləʊ] *n* หมอน [mon]; **Please bring me an extra pillow** ช่วยเอา หมอนมาให้ฉันอีกหนึ่งใบ [chuai ao mon ma hai chan ik nueng bai]

pillowcase ['pɪləʊˌkeɪs] *n* ปลอกหมอน [plok mon]

pilot ['paɪlət] *n* นักบิน [nak bin]; **pilot light** *n* เปลวไฟที่จุดเตาแก๊ซ [pheo fai thii chut tao kaes]

pimple ['pɪmpəl] *n* สิว [sio]

pin [pɪn] *n* เข็มหมุด [khem mut]; **drawing pin** *n* เข็มหมุด [khem mut]; **rolling pin** *n* ไม้นวดแป้ง [mai nuat paeng]; **safety pin** *n* เข็มกลัด [khem klat]

PIN [pɪn] *npl* เลขรหัสลับส่วนตัว [lek ra hat lap suan tua]

pinafore ['pɪnəˌfɔː] *n* ผ้ากันน้ำลายของ เด็ก [pha kan nam lai khong dek]

pinch [pɪntʃ] *v* หยิก [yik]

pine [paɪn] *n* ต้นสน [ton son]

pineapple ['paɪnˌæpəl] *n* สับปะรด [sap pa rot]

pink [pɪŋk] *adj* ซึ่งมีสีชมพู [sueng mii sii chom phu]

pint [paɪnt] *n* หน่วยวัดความจุของเหลวที่มี ค่าเท่ากับครึ่งควอร์ต [hnuai wat khwam chu khong hleo thii mee kha thao kab khrueng kvot]

pip [pɪp] *n* เมล็ดในของผลไม้ [ma let nai khong phon la mai]

pipe [paɪp] *n* ท่อ [tho]; **exhaust pipe** *n* ท่อไอเสีย [tho ai sia]

pipeline ['paɪpˌlaɪn] *n* ท่อยาวส่งผ่าน น้ำมัน น้ำหรือแก๊ซ [tho yao song phan nam man nam hue kaes]

pirate ['paɪrɪt] *n* โจรสลัด [chon sa lat]

Pisces ['paɪsiːz; 'pɪ-] *n* ราศีมีน [ra si miin]

pistol ['pɪstəl] *n* ปืน [puen]

piston ['pɪstən] *n* ลูกสูบ [luk sup]

pitch [pɪtʃ] *n* (sound) ระดับเสียง [ra dap siang], (sport) สนามเด็กเล่น [sa nam dek len] ▷ *v* ขว้าง [khwang]

pity ['pɪtɪ] *n* ความสงสาร [khwam song san] ▷ *v* สงสาร [song san]

pixel ['pɪksəl] *n* จุดที่เล็กที่สุดที่รวมกันเป็น ภาพ [chut thii lek thii sut thii ruam kan pen phap]

pizza ['piːtsə] *n* พิซซ่า [phit sa]

place [pleɪs] *n* สถานที่ [sa than thi] ▷ *v* วางไว้ในตำแหน่ง [wang wai nai tam naeng]; **place of birth** *n* สถานที่เกิด [sa than thii koet]

placement ['pleɪsmənt] *n* ตำแหน่ง [tam naeng]

plain [pleɪn] *adj* ราบเรียบ [rap riap] ▷ *n* ที่ราบ [thii rap]; **plain chocolate** *n* ช็อกโกแลตที่รสค่อนข้างขมและมีสีดำ [chok ko laet thii rot khon khang khom lae mii sii dam]

plait [plæt] *n* รอยจีบ [roi chip]

plan [plæn] *n* แผนการ [phaen kan] ▷ *v* วางแผน [wang phen]; **street plan** *n* แผนที่ถนน [phaen thii tha non]

plane [pleɪn] *n* (aeroplane) เครื่องบิน [khrueang bin], (surface) พื้นราบ [phuen rap], (tool) กบไสไม้ [kop sai mai]; **My plane leaves at...** เครื่องบิน ฉันออกจาก... [khrueang bin chan ok chak...]

planet ['plænɪt] *n* ดาวเคราะห์เก้าดวง [dao khrao kao duang]

planning ['plænɪŋ] *n* การวางแผน [kan wang phaen]

plant [plɑːnt] *n* พืช [phuet], *(site/equipment)* โรงงาน [rong ngan] ▷ *v* ปลูก [pluk]; **plant pot** *n* กระถางต้นไม้ [kra thang ton mai]; **pot plant** *n* ต้นไม้ที่ปลูกในกระถาง [ton mai thii pluk nai kra thang]; **We'd like to see local plants and trees** เราอยากเห็นพืชของท้องถิ่น [rao yak hen phuet khong thong thin]

plaque [plæk; plɑːk] *n* แผ่นเหล็กหรือหินสลัก [phaen lek rue hin sa lak]

plaster ['plɑːstə] *n* *(for wall)* ปูนฉาบผนัง [pun chap pha nang], *(for wound)* พลาสเตอร์ปิดแผล [phlas toe pit phlae]

plastic ['plæstɪk; 'plɑːs-] *adj* ซึ่งทำด้วยพลาสติก [sueng tham duai phlat sa tik] ▷ *n* วัตถุพลาสติก [wat thu phlas tik]; **plastic bag** *n* ถุงพลาสติก [thung phas tik]; **plastic surgery** *n* ศัลยกรรมตกแต่ง [san la ya kam tok taeng]

plate [pleɪt] *n* จาน [chan]; **number plate** *n* ป้ายทะเบียนรถ [pai tha bian rot]

platform ['plætfɔːm] *n* เวทีที่ยกพื้น [we thi thii yok phuen]

platinum ['plætɪnəm] *n* ทองคำขาว [thong kham khao]

play [pleɪ] *n* การแสดง [kan sa daeng] ▷ *v* *(in sport)* เล่น [len], *(music)* เล่นดนตรี [len don trii]; **play truant** *v* หนีโรงเรียน [nii rong rian]; **playing card** *n* การเล่นไพ่ [kan len pai]; **playing field** *n* สนามกีฬา [sa nam ki la]; **Can I play video games?** ฉันเล่นวีดีโอเกมส์ได้ไหม? [chan len wi di o kem dai mai]; **We'd like to play tennis** เราอยากเล่นเทนนิส [rao yak len then nis]

player ['pleɪə] *n* *(instrumentalist)* นักดนตรี [nak don tri], *(of sport)* นักกีฬา [nak ki la]; **CD player** *n* เครื่องเล่นซีดี [khrueang len si di]; **MP3 player** *n* เครื่องฟังดนตรีเอ็มพี ๓ [khrueang fang don trii em phi sam]; **MP4 player** *n* เครื่องฟังดนตรีเอ็มพี ๔ [khrueang fang

don trii em phi si]

playful ['pleɪfʊl] *adj* ชอบเล่นสนุกสนาน [chop len sa nuk sa nan]

playground ['pleɪˌɡraʊnd] *n* สนามเด็กเล่น [sa nam dek len]

playgroup ['pleɪˌɡruːp] *n* กลุ่มเล่นของเด็ก [klum len khong dek]

PlayStation® ['pleɪˌsteɪʃən] *n* เกมส์คอมพิวเตอร์ [kem khom phio toe]

playtime ['pleɪˌtaɪm] *n* เวลาเล่น [we la len]

playwright ['pleɪˌraɪt] *n* ผู้เขียนบทละคร [phu khian bot la khon]

pleasant ['plɛzᵊnt] *adj* น่าพอใจ [na phor jai]

please [pliːz] *excl* กรุณา [ka ru na]; **I'd like to check in, please** ฉันต้องการเช็คอิน [chan tong kan chek in]

pleased [pliːzd] *adj* พอใจ [pho chai]

pleasure ['plɛʒə] *n* ความปีติยินดี [khwam pi ti yin dii]

plenty ['plɛntɪ] *n* จำนวนมากมาย [cham nuan mak mai]

pliers ['plaɪəz] *npl* คีม [khim]

plot [plɒt] *n* *(piece of land)* ที่ดิน [thi din], *(secret plan)* วางแผน [wang phen] ▷ *v* *(conspire)* วางแผน [wang phen]

plough [plaʊ] *n* การไถ [kan thai] ▷ *v* ไถ [thai]

plug [plʌɡ] *n* สิ่งที่ใช้อุดรู [sing thii chai ut ru], ปลั๊กไฟ [plak fai]; **spark plug** *n* หัวเทียนไฟเครื่องยนต์ [hua thian fai khrueang yon]

plughole ['plʌɡˌhəʊl] *n* รูที่ให้น้ำไหลออก [ru thii hai nam lai ok]

plug in [plʌɡ ɪn] *v* เสียบปลั๊ก [siap pluk]

plum [plʌm] *n* ลูกพลัม [luk phlam]

plumber ['plʌmə] *n* ช่างประปา [chang pra pa]

plumbing ['plʌmɪŋ] *n* ท่อประปา [tho pra pa]

plump [plʌmp] *adj* เจ้าเนื้อ [chao nuea]

plunge [plʌndʒ] *v* พุ่งไปอย่างรวดเร็ว [phung pai yang ruat reo]

plural ['pluərəl] *n* พหูพจน์ [pha hu phot]

plus [plʌs] *prep* เพิ่มอีก [perm ik]

plywood ['plaɪˌwʊd] *n* ไม้อัด [mai at]

p.m. [piː ɛm] *abbr* ตัวย่อของเวลาตั้งแต่หลังเที่ยงวันถึงเที่ยงคืน [tua yor khong we la tang tae hlang thiang wan thueng thiang khuen]

pneumonia [njuː'məʊnɪə] *n* โรคปอดบวม [rok pot buam]

poached [pəʊtʃt] *adj* (caught illegally) รุกล้ำ [ruk lam], (simmered gently) เคี่ยวอาหาร [khiao a han]

pocket ['pɒkɪt] *n* กระเป๋า [kra pao]; **pocket calculator** *n* เครื่องคิดเลขฉบับกระเป๋า [khrueang kit lek cha bap kra pao]; **pocket money** *n* เงินติดกระเป๋า [ngoen tit kra pao]

podcast ['pɒdˌkɑːst] *n* การส่งกระจายเสียงทางอินเตอร์เน็ต [kan song kra jai siang thang in toe net]

poem ['pəʊɪm] *n* บทกวี [bot ka wi]

poet ['pəʊɪt] *n* กวี [ka wi]

poetry ['pəʊɪtrɪ] *n* บทกวี [bot ka wi]

point [pɔɪnt] *n* ความคิดเห็น [khwam kit hen] ▷ *v* ชี้ [chi]

pointless ['pɔɪntlɪs] *adj* ไร้จุดหมาย [rai chut mai]

point out [pɔɪnt aʊt] *v* มุ่งไปที่ [mung pai thii]

poison ['pɔɪzᵊn] *n* ยาพิษ [ya phit] ▷ *v* วางยาพิษ [wang ya phit]

poisonous ['pɔɪzənəs] *adj* ซึ่งเป็นพิษ [sueng pen phit]

poke [pəʊk] *v* แหย่ด้วยข้อศอกหรือนิ้ว [yae duai kho sok rue nio]

Poland ['pəʊlənd] *n* ประเทศโปแลนด์ [pra tet po laen]

polar ['pəʊlə] *adj* เกี่ยวกับขั้วโลก [kiao kap khua lok]; **polar bear** *n* หมีขั้วโลก [mii khua lok]

pole [pəʊl] *n* ไม้หรือโลหะหรือวัสดุอื่นที่กลมยาว [mai hue lo ha hue wat sa du aue thii klom yao], ขั้วโลก [khua lok]; **North Pole** *n* ขั้วโลกเหนือ [khua lok nuea]; **pole vault** *n* กีฬากระโดดค้ำถ่อ [ki la kra dot kham tho]; **South Pole** *n* ขั้วโลกใต้ [khua lok tai]

Pole [pəʊl] *n* ชาวโปแลนด์ [chao po laen]

police [pə'liːs] *n* ตำรวจ [tam ruat]; **Call the police** เรียกตำรวจ [riak tam ruat]; **I need a police report for my insurance** ฉันจำเป็นต้องมีรายงานของตำรวจสำหรับการประกัน [chan cham pen tong mii rai ngan khong tam ruat sam rap kan pra kan]; **We will have to report it to the police** เราต้องแจ้งกับตำรวจ [rao tong chaeng kap tam ruat]

policeman, policemen [pə'liːsmən, pə'liːsmɛn] *n* ตำรวจชาย [tam ruat chai]

policewoman, policewomen [pə'liːswʊmən, pə'liːswɪmɪn] *n* ตำรวจหญิง [tam ruat ying]

policy ['pɒlɪsɪ] *n* **insurance policy** *n* กรมธรรม์ประกัน [krom ma than pra kan]

polio ['pəʊlɪəʊ] *n* โรคโปลิโอ [rok po li o]

polish ['pɒlɪʃ] *n* การขัดให้ขึ้นเงา [kan khat hai khuen ngao] ▷ *v* ขัดให้ขึ้นเงา [khat hai khuen ngao]; **nail polish** *n* น้ำยาทาเล็บ [nam ya tha lep]; **shoe polish** *n* ยาขัดรองเท้า [ya khat rong thao]

Polish ['pəʊlɪʃ] *adj* ที่เกี่ยวกับโปแลนด์ [thii kiao kap po laen] ▷ *n* ชาวโปแลนด์ [chao po laen]

polite [pə'laɪt] *adj* สุภาพ [su phap]

politely [pə'laɪtlɪ] *adv* อย่างสุภาพ [yang su phap]

politeness [pə'laɪtnɪs] *n* ความสุภาพอ่อนโยน [khwam su phap on yon]

political [pə'lɪtɪkᵊl] *adj* ที่เกี่ยวกับพรรคการเมืองหรือรัฐบาล [thii kiao kap phak kan mueang rue rat tha ban]

politician [ˌpɒlɪ'tɪʃən] *n* นักการเมือง [nak kan mueang]

politics ['pɒlɪtɪks] *npl* หลักการและข้อคิดเห็นทางการเมือง [lak kan lae kho kit hen thang kan mueang]

poll [pəʊl] *n* การสำรวจความคิดเห็นจากคนส่วนมาก [kan sam ruat khwam kit hen chak kon suan mak]; **opinion poll** *n* การสำรวจความคิดเห็น [kan sam ruat khwam kit hen]

pollen ['pɒlən] *n* ละอองเกสรดอกไม้ [la ong ke son dok mai]

pollute [pə'luːt] *v* ทำให้เป็นมลพิษ [tham hai pen mon la phit]

polluted [pə'luːtɪd] *adj* ที่เป็นมลพิษ [thii pen mon la phit]

pollution [pə'luːʃən] *n* การทำให้เป็นมลพิษ [kan tham hai pen mon la phit]

Polynesia [ˌpɒlɪ'niːʒə; -ʒɪə] *n* หมู่เกาะในมหาสมุทรแปซิฟิกได้แก่ ฮาวาย ซามัวร์และหมู่เกาะคุก [mu kao nai ma ha sa mut pae si fik dai kae ha wai sa mua lae mu kao khuk]

Polynesian [ˌpɒlɪ'niːʒən; -ʒɪən] *adj* เกี่ยวกับหมู่เกาะในมหาสมุทรแปซิฟิกใต้ [kiao kap mu ko nai ma ha sa mut pae si fik tai] ▷ *n* (*language*) ภาษาของหมู่เกาะในมหาสมุทรแปซิฟิกใต้ [pha sa khong mu kao nai ma ha sa mut pae si fik tai], (*person*) ชาวหมู่เกาะในมหาสมุทรแปซิฟิกใต้ [chao mu kao nai ma ha sa mut pae si fik tai]

pomegranate ['pɒmɪˌgrænɪt; 'pɒmˌgrænɪt] *n* ผลทับทิม [phon thap thim]

pond [pɒnd] *n* สระน้ำ [sa nam]

pony ['pəʊnɪ] *n* ม้าพันธุ์เล็ก [ma phan lek]; **pony trekking** *n* การขี่ม้าขึ้นไปในระยะทางชันและลำบาก [kan khi ma khuen pai nai ra ya thang chan lae lam bak]

ponytail ['pəʊnɪˌteɪl] *n* ทรงผมหางม้าของเด็กผู้หญิง [song phom hang ma khong dek phu ying]

poodle ['puːdəl] *n* สุนัขพันธุ์พุดเดิ้ล [su nak phan put doen]

pool [puːl] *n* (*resources*) เงินกองกลาง [ngen kong klang], (*water*) สระน้ำ [sa nam]; **paddling pool** *n* สระน้ำตื้น ๆ สำหรับเด็กเล็ก [sa nam tuen tuen sam rap dek lek]; **swimming pool** *n* สระว่ายน้ำ [sa wai nam]

poor [pʊə; pɔː] *adj* ยากจน [yak chon]

poorly ['pʊəlɪ; 'pɔː-] *adj* ไม่ค่อยสบาย [mai khoi sa bai]

popcorn ['pɒpˌkɔːn] *n* ข้าวโพดคั่ว [khao phot khua]

pope [pəʊp] *n* พระสันตปาปาหัวหน้าบิชชอปและผู้นำของนิกายโรมันคาทอลิค [phra san ta pa pa hua na bis chop lae phu nam khong ni kai ro man kha tho lik]

poplar ['pɒplə] *n* ต้นพอปล่า [ton phop la]

poppy ['pɒpɪ] *n* ดอกป๊อปปี้ [dok pop pi]

popular ['pɒpjʊlə] *adj* เป็นที่นิยม [pen thii ni yom]

popularity ['pɒpjʊlærɪtɪ] *n* ความนิยม [khwam ni yom]

population [ˌpɒpjʊ'leɪʃən] *n* ประชากร [pra cha kon]

pop-up [pɒpʌp] *n* ซึ่งโผล่อย่างฉับพลัน [sueng phlo yang chap phlan]

porch [pɔːtʃ] *n* ชานบ้าน [chaan baan]

pork [pɔːk] *n* สุกร [su kon]; **pork chop** *n* เนื้อหมูที่ติดกระดูก [nea mu thii tit kra duk]

porn [pɔːn] *n* ตัวย่อของหนังสือ ภาพ เรื่องเขียน หนังและศิลปะที่ลามก [tua yo khong nang sue phap rueang khian nang lae sin la pa thii la mok]

pornographic [pɔː'nɒgræfɪk] *adj* ที่ลามก [thii la mok]

pornography [pɔː'nɒgrəfɪ] *n* หนังสือ ภาพ เรื่องเขียน หนังและศิลปะที่ลามก [nang sue phap rueang khian nang lae sin la pa thii la mok]

porridge ['pɒrɪdʒ] *n* อาหารเช้าที่ทำจากข้าวโอ๊ตที่ใส่น้ำหรือนม [a han chao thii tham chak khao ot thii sai nam rue nom]

port [pɔːt] *n* (*ships*) ท่าเรือ [tha rue], (*wine*) เหล้าองุ่นแดง [lao a ngun daeng]

portable ['pɔːtəbəl] *adj* หิ้วได้ [hio dai]

porter ['pɔːtə] *n* พนักงานยกกระเป๋า [pha nak ngan yok kra pao]

portfolio [pɔːt'fəʊlɪəʊ] *n* กระเป๋าใส่เอกสาร [kra pao sai aek san]

portion ['pɔːʃən] *n* ส่วนแบ่ง [suan baeng]

portrait ['pɔːtrɪt; -treɪt] *n* รูปวาดของคน [rup wat khong khon]

Portugal ['pɔːtjʊɡəl] *n* ประเทศโปรตุเกส [pra tet pro tu ket]

Portuguese [ˌpɔːtjʊ'ɡiːz] *adj* เกี่ยวกับชาวโปรตุเกส [kiao kap chao pro tu ket] ▷ *n (language)* ภาษาโปรตุเกส [pha sa pro tu ked], *(person)* ชาวโปรตุเกส [chao pro tu ket]

position [pə'zɪʃən] *n* ตำแหน่ง [tam naeng]

positive ['pɒzɪtɪv] *adj* ซึ่งมองในแง่ดี [sueng mong nai ngae di]

possess [pə'zɛs] *v* เป็นเจ้าของ [pen chao khong]

possession [pə'zɛʃən] *n* ความเป็นเจ้าของ [khwam pen chao khong]

possibility [ˌpɒsɪ'bɪlɪtɪ] *n* ความเป็นไปได้ [khwam pen pai dai]

possible ['pɒsɪbəl] *adj* ซึ่งเป็นไปได้ [sueng pen pai dai]

possibly ['pɒsɪblɪ] *adv* อาจจะ [at cha]

post [pəʊst] *n (mail)* จดหมาย [chot mai], *(position)* ตำแหน่ง [tam naeng], *(stake)* เสาหลัก [sao lak] ▷ *v* ส่งจดหมาย [song chod mai]; **post office** *n* ไปรษณีย์ [prai sa ni]

postage ['pəʊstɪdʒ] *n* ค่าส่งของทางไปรษณีย์ [kha song khong thang pai ra sa ni]

postbox ['pəʊstˌbɒks] *n* ตู้ไปรษณีย์ [tu pai ra sa ni]

postcard ['pəʊstˌkɑːd] *n* ไปรษณียบัตร [prai sa ni ya bat]

postcode ['pəʊstˌkəʊd] *n* รหัสไปรษณีย์ [ra hat prai sa ni]

poster ['pəʊstə] *n* ป้ายโฆษณา [pai khot sa na]

postgraduate [pəʊst'ɡrædjʊɪt] *n* นักศึกษาที่เรียนต่อจากปริญญาตรี [nak suek sa thii rian to chak pa rin ya tree]

postman, postmen ['pəʊstmən, 'pəʊstmɛn] *n* บุรุษไปรษณีย์ [bu rud pai ra sa ni]

postmark ['pəʊstˌmɑːk] *n* ตราประทับบนไปรษณียภัณฑ์ [tra pra thap bon prai sa ni phan]

postpone [pəʊst'pəʊn; pə'spəʊn] *v* เลื่อนออกไป [luean ok pai]

postwoman, postwomen ['pəʊstˌwʊmən, 'pəʊstˌwɪmɪn] *n* ไปรษณีย์หญิง [prai sa ni ying]

pot [pɒt] *n* หม้อ [mo]; **plant pot** *n* กระถางต้นไม้ [kra thang ton mai]; **pot plant** *n* ต้นไม้ที่ปลูกในกระถาง [ton mai thii pluk nai kra thang]

potato, potatoes [pə'teɪtəʊ, pə'teɪtəʊz] *n* มันฝรั่ง [man fa rang]; **baked potato** *n* มันอบ [man op]; **jacket potato** *n* มันฝรั่งอบทั้งลูก [man fa rang op thang luk]; **mashed potatoes** *npl* มันบด [man bot]

potential [pə'tɛnʃəl] *adj* ที่อาจเกิดขึ้นได้ [thii at koed khuen dai] ▷ *n* ความเป็นไปได้ [khwam pen pai dai]

pothole ['pɒtˌhəʊl] *n* หลุมบ่อ [lum bo]

pottery ['pɒtərɪ] *n* เครื่องปั้นดินเผา [khrueang pan din phao]

potty ['pɒtɪ] *n* กระโถนสำหรับเด็กเล็ก [kra thon sam rap dek lek]

pound [paʊnd] *n* เงินปอนด์ [ngoen pon]; **pound sterling** *n* หน่วยเงินตราของสหราชอาณาจักรอังกฤษ [nuai ngoen tra khong sa ha rat cha a na chak ang krit]

pour [pɔː] *v* เท [the]

poverty ['pɒvətɪ] *n* ความยากจน [khwam yak chon]

powder ['paʊdə] *n* ผง [phong]; **baking powder** *n* ผงฟู [phong fu]; **soap powder** *n* ผงสบู่ [phong sa bu]; **talcum powder** *n* แป้งฝุ่น [paeng fun]; **Do you**

have washing powder? คุณมีผง
ซักฟอกไหม? [khun mii phong sak fok
mai]

power ['paʊə] *n* อำนาจ [am nat]; **power
cut** *n* การตัดไฟชั่วคราว [kan tat fai chua
khrao]; **solar power** *n* พลังงานแสง
อาทิตย์ [pha lang ngan saeng a thit]

powerful ['paʊəfʊl] *adj* ที่มีอิทธิพล [thii
mii it ti pon]

practical ['præktɪkᵊl] *adj* เหมาะสมที่จะ
ปฏิบัติ [mo som thii ja pa ti bat]

practically ['præktɪkəlɪ; -klɪ] *adv* อย่าง
เหมาะสมที่จะปฏิบัติ [yang hmo som thii
ja pa ti bat]

practice ['præktɪs] *n* การฝึกซ้อมที่ทำเป็น
ประจำ [kan fuek som thii tham pen pra
cham]

practise ['præktɪs] *v* ฝึกซ้อม [fuek som]

praise [preɪz] *v* การสรรเสริญ [kan san
sen]

pram [præm] *n* รถเข็นเด็ก [rot khen
dek]

prank [præŋk] *n* การเล่นตลก [kan len ta
lok]

prawn [prɔːn] *n* กุ้ง [kung]

pray [preɪ] *v* สวดมนต์ [suat mon]

prayer [preə] *n* ผู้สวดมนต์ [phu suat
mon]

precaution [prɪ'kɔːʃən] *n* การระมัดระวัง
ไว้ก่อน [kan ra mat ra wang wai kon]

preceding [prɪ'siːdɪŋ] *adj* เป็นอันดับแรก
[pen an dab raek]

precinct ['priːsɪŋkt] *n* เขต [khet];
pedestrian precinct *n* บริเวณที่คนข้าม
[bo ri wen thii khon kham]

precious ['preʃəs] *adj* ล้ำค่า [lam kha]

precise [prɪ'saɪs] *adj* แม่นย่ำ [maen
yam]

precisely [prɪ'saɪslɪ] *adv* อย่างแม่นย่ำ
[yang maen yam]

predecessor ['priːdɪˌsɛsə] *n* คนที่อยู่มา
ก่อน [kon thii yu ma kon]

predict [prɪ'dɪkt] *v* ทำนาย [tham nai]

predictable [prɪ'dɪktəbᵊl] *adj* พอที่จะ

ทำนายได้ [pho thii ja tham nai dai]

prefect ['priːfɛkt] *n* นักเรียนที่ดูแลควบคุม
นักเรียนที่เด็กกว่า [nak rian thii du lae
khuab khum nak rian thii dek kwa]

prefer [prɪ'fɜː] *v* ชอบมากกว่า [chop mak
kwa]

preferably ['prɛfərəblɪ; 'prɛfrəblɪ] *adv*
ที่ชอบมากกว่า [thii chop mak kwa]

preference ['prɛfərəns; 'prɛfrəns] *n*
การชอบมากกว่า [kan chop mak kwa]

pregnancy ['prɛgnənsɪ] *n* การตั้งท้อง
[kan tang thong]

pregnant ['prɛgnənt] *adj* ตั้งครรภ์ [tang
khan]

prehistoric [ˌpriːhɪ'stɒrɪk] *adj* ก่อน
ประวัติศาสตร์ [kon pra wat ti sat]

prejudice ['prɛdʒʊdɪs] *n* อคติ [a kha ti]

prejudiced ['prɛdʒʊdɪst] *adj* มีอคติ [mii
a kha ti]

premature [ˌprɛmə'tjʊə; 'prɛməˌtjʊə]
adj ยังไม่โตเต็มที่ [yang mai to tem thii]

premiere ['prɛmɪˌɛə; 'prɛmɪə] *n* อันดับ
หนึ่ง [an dab hueng]

premises ['prɛmɪsɪz] *npl* ที่ดินและสิ่งปลูก
สร้าง [thii din lae sing pluk sang]

premonition [ˌprɛmə'nɪʃən] *n* การเตือน
ล่วงหน้า [kan tuean luang na]

preoccupied [priː'ɒkjʊˌpaɪd] *adj* ใจจด
ใจจ่อ [chai chot chai cho]

prepaid [priː'peɪd] *adj* จ่ายล่วงหน้า [chai
luang na]

preparation [ˌprɛpə'reɪʃən] *n* การตระ
เตรียม [kan tra triam]

prepare [prɪ'pɛə] *v* เตรียม [triam];
Please prepare the bill ช่วยเตรียมบิล
ให้ด้วย [chuai triam bin hai duai]

prepared [prɪ'pɛəd] *adj* ที่เตรียมไว้ [thii
triam wai]

Presbyterian [ˌprɛzbɪ'tɪərɪən] *adj* เกี่ยว
กับนิกายหนึ่งของโปรแตสแตนต์ [kiao kap
ni kai nueng khong pro tes taen] ▷ *n*
สมาชิกของนิกายหนึ่งในศาสนาคริสต์ [sa
ma chik khong ni kai nueng nai sat sa
na kris]

prescribe [prɪˈskraɪb] v สั่งจ่ายยา [sang chai ya]

prescription [prɪˈskrɪpʃən] n ใบสั่งจ่ายยา [bai sang chai ya]

presence [ˈprɛzəns] n การอยู่ในสถานที่หนึ่ง [kan yu nai sa than thii hueng]

present adj [ˈprɛznt] ที่เกิดในปัจจุบัน [thii koed nai pad chu ban] ▷ n [ˈprɛznt] (gift) ของขวัญ [khong khwan], (time being) ณ ที่นี้ [na thi ni] ▷ v [prɪˈzɛnt] แนะนำให้รู้จัก [nae nam hai ru chak]; **I'm looking for a present for my husband** ฉันกำลังหาของขวัญสักชิ้นหนึ่งให้สามี [chan kam lang ha khong khwan sak chin nueng hai sa mii]

presentation [ˌprɛzənˈteɪʃən] n การเสนอ [kan sa noe]

presenter [prɪˈzɛntə] n ผู้นำเสนอ [phu nam sa noe]

presently [ˈprɛzəntlɪ] adv ในไม่ช้า [nai mai cha]

preservative [prɪˈzɜːvətɪv] n สารกันบูด [san khan but]

president [ˈprɛzɪdənt] n ประธานาธิบดี [pra tha na thi bo di]

press [prɛs] n เครื่องบีบอัด [khrueang bip at] ▷ v กด [kot]; **press conference** n การแถลงข่าว [kan tha laeng khao]

press-up [prɛsʌp] n การวิดพื้น [kan wit phuen]

pressure [ˈprɛʃə] n ความกดดัน [khwam kot dan] ▷ v กดดันให้ทำ [kot dan hai tham]; **blood pressure** n ความดันโลหิต [khwam dan lo hit]

prestige [prɛˈstiːʒ] n ความเคารพนบนอบที่เป็นผลมาจากความสำเร็จ [khwam khao rop nop nop thii pen phon ma chak khwam sam ret]

prestigious [prɛˈstɪdʒəs] adj ซึ่งเป็นที่เคารพนับถือ [sueng pen thii khao rop nap thue]

presumably [prɪˈzjuːməblɪ] adv ที่น่าเป็นไปได้ [thii na pen pai dai]

presume [prɪˈzjuːm] v สันนิษฐาน [san ni than]

pretend [prɪˈtɛnd] v แกล้ง [klaeng]

pretext [ˈpriːtɛkst] n ข้ออ้าง [kho ang]

prettily [ˈprɪtɪlɪ] adv อย่างสวยงาม [yang suai ngam]

pretty [ˈprɪtɪ] adj สวย [suai] ▷ adv พอใช้ได้ [pho chai dai]

prevent [prɪˈvɛnt] v ป้องกัน [pong kan]

prevention [prɪˈvɛnʃən] n การป้องกัน [kan pong kan]

previous [ˈpriːvɪəs] adj เมื่อก่อน [muea kon]

previously [ˈpriːvɪəslɪ] adv แต่ก่อน [tae kon]

prey [preɪ] n เหยื่อ [yuea]

price [praɪs] n ราคา [ra kha]; **price list** n รายการราคา [rai kan ra kha]; **Do you have a set-price menu?** คุณมีรายการอาหารที่ตั้งราคาเป็นชุดไหม? [khun mii rai kan a han thii tang ra kha pen chut mai]; **Does the price include boots?** ราคานี้รวมรองเท้าบู๊ทไหม? [ra kha nii ruam rong thao but mai]; **Please write down the price** คุณช่วยเขียนราคาให้ด้วย [khun chuai khian ra kha hai duai]

prick [prɪk] v เจาะ [cho]

pride [praɪd] n ความภาคภูมิใจ [khwam phak phum jai]

priest [priːst] n พระ [phra]

primarily [ˈpraɪmərəlɪ] adv อย่างที่เป็นพื้นฐาน [yang thii pen phuen tan]

primary [ˈpraɪmərɪ] adj ที่สำคัญที่สุด [thii sam khan thiisud]; **primary school** n โรงเรียนชั้นประถม [rong rian chan pra thom]

primitive [ˈprɪmɪtɪv] adj แบบดั้งเดิม [baep dang doem]

primrose [ˈprɪmˌrəʊz] n ต้นไม้ป่าที่มีดอกสีเหลือง [ton mai pa thii mee dok see hluea]

prince [prɪns] n เจ้าชาย [chao chai]

princess [prɪnˈsɛs] n เจ้าหญิง [chao

ying]

principal ['prɪnsɪpᵊl] *adj* ที่เป็นหลักปฏิบัติ [thii pen lak pa ti bat] ▷ *n* สำคัญมากกว่าอย่างอื่น [sam khan mak kwa yang aue]

principle ['prɪnsɪpᵊl] *n* หลักปฏิบัติ [lak pa ti bat]

print [prɪnt] *n* สิ่งพิมพ์ [sing phim] ▷ *v* พิมพ์ [phim]

printer ['prɪntə] *n (machine)* เครื่องพิมพ์ [khrueang phim], *(person)* ผู้พิมพ์ [phu phim]; **Is there a colour printer?** มีเครื่องพิมพ์สีไหม? [mii khrueang phim sii mai]

printing ['prɪntɪŋ] *n* **How much is printing?** ค่าพิมพ์ราคาเท่าไร? [kha phim ra kha thao rai]

printout ['prɪntaʊt] *n* ข้อมูลที่พิมพ์ออกจากเครื่องคอมพิวเตอร์ [kho mun thii phim ok chak khrueang khom pio toe]

priority [praɪˈɒrɪtɪ] *n* สิ่งสำคัญที่สุดที่ต้องจัดการก่อน [sing sam kan thii sud thii tong chad kan kon]

prison ['prɪzᵊn] *n* เรือนจำ [ruan cham]; **prison officer** *n* เจ้าหน้าที่เรือนจำ [chao na thii ruean cham]

prisoner ['prɪzənə] *n* ผู้ถูกขัง [phu thuk khang]

privacy ['praɪvəsɪ; 'prɪvəsɪ] *n* ความเป็นส่วนตัว [khwam pen suan tua]

private ['praɪvɪt] *adj* ที่เป็นส่วนตัว [thii pen suan tua]; **private property** *n* ทรัพย์สมบัติส่วนตัว [sap som bat suan tua]

privatize ['praɪvɪ.taɪz] *v* แปรรูปหน่วยราชการและรัฐวิสาหกิจให้เป็นเอกชน [prae rup nuai rat cha kan lae rat wi sa ha kit hai pen ek ka chon]

privilege ['prɪvɪlɪdʒ] *n* อภิสิทธิ์ [a phi sit]

prize [praɪz] *n* รางวัล [rang wan]

prize-giving ['praɪz.gɪvɪŋ] *n* การให้รางวัล [kan hai rang wan]

prizewinner ['praɪz.wɪnə] *n* ผู้ชนะรางวัล [phu cha na rang wan]

probability [.prɒbəˈbɪlɪtɪ] *n* ความน่าจะเป็นไปได้ [khwam na ja pen pai dai]

probable ['prɒbəbᵊl] *adj* ที่น่าจะเป็นไปได้ [thii na ja pen pai dai]

probably ['prɒbəblɪ] *adv* อย่างน่าจะเป็นไปได้ [yang na ja pen pai dai]

problem ['prɒbləm] *n* ปัญหา [pan ha]; **No problem** ไม่มีปัญหา [mai mii pan ha]; **There's a problem with the room** ห้องนี้มีปัญหา [hong nii mii pan ha]; **Who do we contact if there are problems?** เราจะต้องติดต่อใครถ้าเกิดปัญหา? [rao ja tong tit to khrai tha koet pan ha]

proceedings [prəˈsiːdɪŋz] *npl* การดำเนินการ [kan dam noen kan]

proceeds ['prəʊsiːdz] *npl* รายได้ [rai dai]

process ['prəʊsɛs] *n* การพัฒนาต่อเนื่อง [kan phat ta na to nueang]

procession [prəˈsɛʃən] *n* ขบวนที่เคลื่อนที่ไป [kha buan thii khluean thii pai]

produce [prəˈdjuːs] *v* ผลิต [pha lit]

producer [prəˈdjuːsə] *n* ผู้ผลิต [phu pha lit]

product ['prɒdʌkt] *n* ผลผลิต [phon pha lit]

production [prəˈdʌkʃən] *n* การผลิต [kan pha lit]

productivity [.prɒdʌkˈtɪvɪtɪ] *n* ความสามารถในการผลิต [khwam sa mat nai kan pha lit]

profession [prəˈfɛʃən] *n* อาชีพ [a chip]

professional [prəˈfɛʃənᵊl] *adj* เกี่ยวกับอาชีพ [kiao kap a chip] ▷ *n* ผู้เชี่ยวชาญในวิชาชีพ [phu chiao chan nai wi cha chip]

professionally [prəˈfɛʃənəlɪ] *adv* อย่างมืออาชีพ [yang mue a chip]

professor [prəˈfɛsə] *n* ศาสตราจารย์ [sat tra chan]

profit ['prɒfɪt] *n* ผลกำไร [phon kam rai]

profitable ['prɒfɪtəbᵊl] *adj* ที่ได้ผลกำไร [thii dai phon kam rai]

program ['prəʊɡræm] *n* หมาย

กำหนดการ [mai kam not kan] ▷ v วางวิธี
การให้ [wang wi thi kan hai]

programme ['prəʊɡræm] n หมาย
กำหนดการ [mai kam not kan]

programmer ['prəʊɡræmə] n นักเขียน
โปรแกรมคอมพิวเตอร์ [nak khian pro
kraem khom pio ter]

programming ['prəʊɡræmɪŋ] n การ
เขียนโปรแกรมคอมพิวเตอร์ [kan khian
pro kraem khom pio ter]

progress ['prəʊɡrɛs] n ความก้าวหน้า
[khwam kao na]

prohibit [prə'hɪbɪt] v ห้ามโดยกฎหมาย
[ham doi kot mai]

prohibited [prə'hɪbɪtɪd] adj ที่ถูกห้ามโด
ยกฎหมาย [thii thuk ham doi kod mai]

project ['prɒdʒɛkt] n โครงการ [khrong
kan]

projector [prə'dʒɛktə] n เครื่องฉายแผ่น
ไสลด์ [khrueang chai phaen sa lai];
overhead projector n เครื่องฉายภาพ
บนผนังหรือจอ [khrueang chai phap bon
pha nang rue cho]

promenade [ˌprɒmə'nɑːd] n ทางเดิน
เลียบชายทะเลที่สถานพักผ่อนชายทะเล
[thang doen liap chai tha le thii sa
than phak phon chai tha le]

promise ['prɒmɪs] n คำมั่นสัญญา [kham
man san ya] ▷ v สัญญา [san ya]

promising ['prɒmɪsɪŋ] adj มีอนาคตดี
[mii a na khot di]

promote [prə'məʊt] v ส่งเสริม [song
some]

promotion [prə'məʊʃən] n การส่งเสริม
สนับสนุน [kan song sem sa nab sa nun]

prompt [prɒmpt] adj ที่ตรงเวลา [thii
trong we la]

promptly [prɒmptlɪ] adv อย่างตรงเวลา
[yang trong we la]

pronoun ['prəʊˌnaʊn] n สรรพนาม [sap
pha nam]

pronounce [prə'naʊns] v ออกเสียง [ok
siang]; **How do you pronounce it?**
คุณอ่านออกเสียงคำนี้อย่างไร? [khun aan

ok siang kham nii yang rai]

pronunciation [prəˌnʌnsɪ'eɪʃən] n การ
ออกเสียงคำพูด [kan ok siang kham
phut]

proof [pruːf] n (evidence) หลักฐาน [lak
than], (for checking) ข้อพิสูจน์ [kho phi
sut]

propaganda [ˌprɒpə'ɡændə] n การ
โฆษณาชวนเชื่อ [kan kho sa na chuan
chuea]

proper ['prɒpə] adj เหมาะสม [mo som]

properly ['prɒpəlɪ] adv อย่างถูกต้อง
[yang thuk tong]

property ['prɒpətɪ] n ทรัพย์สมบัติ [sap
som bat]; **private property** n ทรัพย์
สมบัติส่วนตัว [sap som bat suan tua]

proportion [prə'pɔːʃən] n สัดส่วน [sat
suan]

proportional [prə'pɔːʃənəl] adj ทำให้ได้
สัดส่วนกัน [tham hai dai sat suan kan]

proposal [prə'pəʊzəl] n ข้อเสนอ [khor
sa noe]

propose [prə'pəʊz] v เสนอ [sa noe]

prosecute ['prɒsɪˌkjuːt] v ฟ้องร้อง [fong
rong]

prospect ['prɒspɛkt] n โอกาส [o kat]

prospectus [prə'spɛktəs] n หนังสือ
โครงการ [nang sue khrong kan]

prosperity [prɒ'spɛrɪtɪ] n ความเจริญ
รุ่งเรือง [khwam cha roen rung rueang]

prostitute ['prɒstɪˌtjuːt] n โสเภณี [so
pe ni]

protect [prə'tɛkt] v ป้องกัน [pong kan]

protection [prə'tɛkʃən] n การป้องกัน
[kan pong kan]

protein ['prəʊtiːn] n โปรตีน [pro tin]

protest n ['prəʊtɛst] การประท้วง [kan
pra thuang] ▷ v [prə'tɛst] ประท้วง [pra
thuang]

Protestant ['prɒtɪstənt] adj เกี่ยวกับ
นิกายโปรเตสแตนต์ [kiao kab ni kai pro
taes taen] ▷ n นิกายโปรเตสแตนต์ [ni kai
pro tes taen]

proud [praʊd] adj ภูมิใจ [phum chai]

prove [pruːv] v พิสูจน์ [phi sut]

proverb ['prɒvɜːb] n คติพจน์ [kha ti phot]

provide [prə'vaɪd] v จัดหา [chat ha]; **provide for** v จัดหาให้ [chat ha hai]

provided [prə'vaɪdɪd] conj ภายใต้เงื่อนไขว่า [phai tai nguean khai wa]

providing [prə'vaɪdɪŋ] conj ภายใต้เงื่อนไขว่า [phai tai nguean khai wa]

provisional [prə'vɪʒənºl] adj ชั่วคราว [chua khrao]

proximity [prɒk'sɪmɪtɪ] n บริเวณที่ใกล้เคียง [bo ri wen thii klai khiang]

prune [pruːn] n ลูกพรุน [luk phrun]

pry [praɪ] v สอดรู้สอดเห็น [sot ru sot hen]

pseudonym ['sjuːdənɪm] n นามแฝง [nam faeng]

psychiatric [ˌsaɪkɪ'ætrɪk] adj ที่เกี่ยวกับจิตวิทยา [thii kiao kap chit ta wit ta ya]

psychiatrist [saɪ'kaɪətrɪst] n จิตแพทย์ [chit ta phaet]

psychological [ˌsaɪkə'lɒdʒɪkºl] adj เกี่ยวกับจิต [kiao kap chit]

psychologist [saɪ'kɒlədʒɪst] n นักจิตวิทยา [nak chit ta wit tha ya]

psychology [saɪ'kɒlədʒɪ] n จิตวิทยา [chit wit tha ya]

psychotherapy [ˌsaɪkəʊ'θɛrəpɪ] n วิธีการรักษาจิต [vi thi kan rak sa chit]

PTO [piː tiː əʊ] abbr ตัวย่อของกรุณาเปิดหน้าถัดไป [tua yor khong ka ru na poed na tad pai]

pub [pʌb] n บาร์ [ba]

public ['pʌblɪk] adj ที่สาธารณะ [thii sa tha ra na] ⊳ n สาธารณะ [sa tha ra na]; **public holiday** n วันหยุดของประเทศ [wan yut khong pra tet]; **public opinion** n ความคิดเห็นของสาธารณชน [khwam kit hen khong sa tha ra na chon]; **public relations** npl ประชาสัมพันธ์ [pra cha sam phan]; **Is the castle open to the public?** ปราสาทเปิดให้สาธารณะชนเข้าชมไหม? [pra saat poet hai sa tha ra na chon khao chom mai]

publican ['pʌblɪkən] n เจ้าของและผู้จัดการบาร์ [chao khong lae phu chat kan ba]

publication [ˌpʌblɪ'keɪʃən] n สิ่งตีพิมพ์ [sing ti phim]

publish ['pʌblɪʃ] v พิมพ์จำหน่าย [phim cham hnai]

publisher ['pʌblɪʃə] n ผู้พิมพ์จำหน่าย [phu phim cham hnai]

pudding ['pʊdɪŋ] n ของหวาน [khong wan]

puddle ['pʌdºl] n หลุมบ่อ [lum bo]

Puerto Rico ['pwɜːtəʊ 'riːkəʊ; 'pwɛə-] n ประเทศเปอร์โตริโก [pra tet poe to ri ko]

pull [pʊl] v ดึง [dueng]

pull down [pʊl daʊn] v ดึงลง [dueng long]

pull out [pʊl aʊt] vi ออกไป [ok pai] ⊳ vt ดึงออก [dueng ork]

pullover ['pʊlˌəʊvə] n เสื้อกันหนาวแบบสวมหัว [suea kan hnao baeb suam hua]

pull up [pʊl ʌp] v ดึงขึ้น [dueng khuen]

pulse [pʌls] n ชีพจร [chip pha chon]

pulses [pʌlsɪz] npl ถั่วต่างๆ [thua tang tang]

pump [pʌmp] n เครื่องปั้ม [khrueang pum] ⊳ v สูบ [sup]; **bicycle pump** n ที่สูบรถจักรยาน [thii sup rot chak kra yan]; **Do you have a pump?** คุณมีเครื่องสูบลมไหม? [khun mii khrueang sup lom mai]

pumpkin ['pʌmpkɪn] n ฟักทอง [fak thong]

pump up [pʌmp ʌp] v สูบขึ้นมา [sup khuen ma]

punch [pʌntʃ] n (blow) การชก [kan chok], (hot drink) เครื่องดื่มผสมที่มีน้ำผลไม้และเหล้า [khueang duem pha som thii mee nam phon la mai lae lao] ⊳ v ชก [chok]

punctual ['pʌŋktjʊəl] adj ที่ตรงต่อเวลา [thii trong to we la]

punctuation [ˌpʌŋktjʊ'eɪʃən] n

เครื่องหมายวรรคตอน [khrueang mai wak ton]

puncture [ˈpʌŋktʃə] n การเจาะ [kan jo]

punish [ˈpʌnɪʃ] v ลงโทษ [long thot]

punishment [ˈpʌnɪʃmənt] n การลงโทษ [kan long thot]; **capital punishment** n การลงโทษประหารชีวิต [kan long thot pra han chi wit]; **corporal punishment** n การลงโทษทางร่างกายของผู้กระทำผิด [kan long thot thang rang kai khong phu kra tham phit]

punk [pʌŋk] n คนที่ไม่มีคุณค่า [khon thii mai mii khun kha]

pupil [ˈpjuːpl] n (eye) ช่องตาดำ [chong ta dam], (learner) นักเรียน [nak rian]

puppet [ˈpʌpɪt] n หุ่นกระบอก [hun kra bok]

puppy [ˈpʌpɪ] n ลูกสุนัข [luk su nak]

purchase [ˈpɜːtʃɪs] v ซื้อ [sue]

pure [pjʊə] adj บริสุทธิ์ [bo ri sut]

purple [ˈpɜːpl] adj ที่มีสีม่วง [thii mii sii muang]

purpose [ˈpɜːpəs] n วัตถุประสงค์ [wat thu pra song]

purr [pɜː] v ร้องแสดงความพอใจ [rong sa daeng khwam pho jai]

purse [pɜːs] n ถุงเงิน [thung ngoen]

pursue [pəˈsjuː] v ติดตาม [tit tam]

pursuit [pəˈsjuːt] n การติดตาม [kan tit tam]

pus [pʌs] n หนอง [nong]

push [pʊʃ] v ผลัก [phlak]

pushchair [ˈpʊʃˌtʃɛə] n รถเข็นเด็ก [rot khen dek]

push-up [pʊʃʌp] n การออกกำลังกายแบบวิดพื้น [kan ok kam lang kai baep wid phuen]

put [pʊt] v วาง [wang]; **I would like to put my jewellery in the safe** ฉันอยากวางเครื่องประดับไว้ในตู้นิรภัย [chan yak wang khrueang pra dap wai nai tu ni ra phai]; **Put it down over there, please** ช่วยวางมันลงที่นั่น [chuai wang man long thii nan]

put aside [pʊt əˈsaɪd] v วางไว้ข้างหนึ่ง [wang wai khang hueng]

put away [pʊt əˈweɪ] v เอาเก็บไว้ [ao keb wai]

put back [pʊt bæk] v เก็บไว้ที่เดิม [kep wai thii doem]

put forward [pʊt ˈfɔːwəd] v เสนอข้อเสนอ [sa noe kho sa noe]

put in [pʊt ɪn] v วางเข้าไปใน [wang khao pai nai]

put off [pʊt ɒf] v เลื่อนออกไป [luean ok pai]

put up [pʊt ʌp] v ตั้งขึ้น [tang khuen]

puzzle [ˈpʌzl] n ปัญหายุ่งยาก [pan ha yung yak]

puzzled [ˈpʌzld] adj ที่ยุ่งยาก [thii yung yak]

puzzling [ˈpʌzlɪŋ] adj ทำให้งงงวย [tham hai ngong nguai]

pyjamas [pəˈdʒɑːməz] npl ชุดนอน [chut non]

pylon [ˈpaɪlən] n เสาทำด้วยเหล็กสำหรับติดสายไฟฟ้า [sao tham duai hlek sam hrab tid sai fai fa]

pyramid [ˈpɪrəmɪd] n ปิรามิด [pi ra mit]

Qatar [kæˈtɑː] n ประเทศกาตาร์ [pra tet ka ta]

quail [kweɪl] n นกกระทา [nok kra tha]

quaint [kweɪnt] adj แบบโบราณ [baep bo ran]

Quaker [ˈkweɪkə] n นิกายหนึ่งของศาสนาคริสต์ซึ่งเคร่งมาก [ni kai nueng khong sat sa na khris sueng khreng mak]

qualification [ˌkwɒlɪfɪˈkeɪʃən] n คุณสมบัติ [khun na som bat]

qualified [ˈkwɒlɪˌfaɪd] adj ที่มีคุณสมบัติ [thii mii khun na som bat]

qualify [ˈkwɒlɪˌfaɪ] v มีคุณสมบัติ [mii khun som bat]

quality [ˈkwɒlɪtɪ] n คุณภาพ [khun na phap]

quantify [ˈkwɒntɪˌfaɪ] v ค้นพบจำนวนที่แน่นอน [khon phop cham nuan thii nae non]

quantity [ˈkwɒntɪtɪ] n จำนวนที่แน่นอน [cham nuan thii nae norn]

quarantine [ˈkwɒrənˌtiːn] n สถานกักกันเพื่อป้องกันการแพร่ของเชื้อโรค [sa than kak kan phuea pong kan kan prae khong chuea rok]

quarrel [ˈkwɒrəl] n การทะเลาะวิวาท [kan tha lo wi wat] ▷ v ทะเลาะ [tha lo]

quarry [ˈkwɒrɪ] n สถานที่ที่ขุดเอาหินออกมา [sa than thii thii khut ao hin ok ma]

quarter [ˈkwɔːtə] n เศษหนึ่งส่วนสี่ [set nueng suan si]

quartet [kwɔːˈtɛt] n กลุ่มนักร้องหรือนักดนตรีสี่คน [klum nak rong rue nak don tree sii khon]

quay [kiː] n ท่าเรือ [tha rue]

queen [kwiːn] n พระราชินี [phra ra chi ni]

query [ˈkwɪərɪ] n คำถาม [kham tham] ▷ v ซักถาม [sak tham]

question [ˈkwɛstʃən] n คำถาม [kham tham] ▷ v ไต่ถาม [tai tham]; **question mark** n เครื่องหมายคำถาม [khrueang mai kham tham]

questionnaire [ˌkwɛstʃəˈnɛə; ˌkɛs-] n แบบสอบถาม [baep sop tham]

queue [kjuː] n แถว [thaeo] ▷ v เข้าคิว [khao khio]; **Is this the end of the queue?** นี่เป็นตอนท้ายของแถวใช่ไหม? [ni pen ton thai khong thaeo chai mai]

quick [kwɪk] adj รวดเร็ว [ruat reo]

quickly [ˈkwɪklɪ] adv อย่างรวดเร็ว [yang ruat reo]

quiet [ˈkwaɪət] adj เงียบ [ŋgiap]; **I'd like a quiet room** ฉันอยากได้ห้องเงียบ ๆ [chan yak dai hong ngiap ngiap]

quietly [ˈkwaɪətlɪ] adv อย่างเงียบ [yang ngiap]

quilt [kwɪlt] n ผ้าบุคลุมเตียง [pha bu khlum tiang]

quit [kwɪt] v เลิก [loek]

quite [kwaɪt] adv ค่อนข้างจะ [khon khang cha]

quiz, quizzes [kwɪz, ˈkwɪzɪz] n การสอบความรู้รอบตัว [kan sorb khwam ru rob tua]

quotation [kwəʊˈteɪʃən] n ข้อความอ้างอิง [khor khwam ang eng]; **quotation marks** npl อัญญประกาศ [an ya pra kat]

quote [kwəʊt] n ข้อความอ้างอิง [khor khwam ang eng] ▷ v อ้างอิง [ang ing]

r

rabbi ['ræbaɪ] *n* พระในศาสนายิว [phra nai sat sa na yio]

rabbit ['ræbɪt] *n* กระต่าย [kra tai]

rabies ['reɪbiːz] *n* โรคพิษสุนัขบ้า [rok phit su nak ba]

race [reɪs] *n (contest)* การวิ่งแข่ง [kan wing khaeng], *(origin)* เชื้อชาติ [chuea chat] ▷ *v* วิ่งแข่ง [wing khaeng]

racecourse ['reɪsˌkɔːs] *n* สนามแข่ง [sa nam khaeng]

racehorse ['reɪsˌhɔːs] *n* สนามแข่งม้า [sa nam khaeng ma]

racer ['reɪsə] *n* ผู้เข้าร่วมการแข่งขัน [phu khao ruam kan khaeng khan]

racetrack ['reɪsˌtræk] *n* ลู่ที่ใช้แข่งขัน ความเร็ว [lu thii chai khaeng khan khwam reo]

racial ['reɪʃəl] *adj* ที่เกี่ยวกับเชื้อชาติ [thii kiao kap chuea chat]

racing ['reɪsɪŋ] *n* **horse racing** *n* การ แข่งม้า [kan khaeng ma]; **motor racing** *n* การแข่งรถยนต์ [kan khaeng rot yon]; **racing car** *n* รถแข่ง [rot khaeng]

racism ['reɪsɪzəm] *n* การเหยียดเชื้อชาติ [kan yiat chuea chat]

racist ['reɪsɪst] *adj* เกี่ยวกับลัทธิชนชาติ [kiao kap lat thi chon chat] ▷ *n* ผู้เหยียด ผิว [phu yiat phio]

rack [ræk] *n* ชั้นวางของ [chan wang khong]; **luggage rack** *n* ชั้นวางกระเป๋า เดินทาง [chan wang kra pao doen thang]

racket ['rækɪt] *n (racquet)* เสียงหนวกหู [siang hnuak hu]; **tennis racket** *n* ไม้ตี เทนนิส [mai ti then nis]

racoon [rə'kuːn] *n* สัตว์คล้ายหมีแต่ตัวเล็ก และมีหางเป็นพวง [sat khlai mii tae tua lek lae mii hang pen puang]

racquet ['rækɪt] *n* ไม้ตีลูกในการเล่นกีฬา [mai ti luk nai kan len ki la]

radar ['reɪdɑː] *n* เรดาห์ [re da]

radiation [ˌreɪdɪ'eɪʃən] *n* รังสี [rang si]

radiator ['reɪdɪˌeɪtə] *n* เครื่องทำความร้อน [khrueang tham khwam ron]; **There is a leak in the radiator** เครื่องทำความร้อน รั่ว [khrueang tham khwam ron rua]

radio ['reɪdɪəʊ] *n* วิทยุ [wit tha yu]; **digital radio** *n* วิทยุดิจิตัล [wit tha yu di chi tal]; **radio station** *n* สถานีวิทยุ [sa tha ni wit tha yu]; **Can I switch the radio off?** ฉันปิดวิทยุได้ไหม? [chan pit wit tha yu dai mai]

radioactive [ˌreɪdɪəʊ'æktɪv] *adj* เกี่ยว กับกัมมันตภาพรังสี [kiao kap kam man ta phap rang sii]

radio-controlled ['reɪdɪəʊ'kən'trəʊld] *adj* ที่ควบคุมด้วยวิทยุ [thii khuap khum duai wit tha yu]

radish ['rædɪʃ] *n* ผักมีลูกกลมสีแดงรสคล้าย หัวไชเท้าใช้ใส่ในสลัดผัก [phak mii luk klom sii daeng rot khlai hua chai thao chai sai nai sa lad phak]

raffle ['ræfªl] *n* การขายตั๋วจับฉลากที่มี สิ่งของเป็นรางวัลมากกว่าเงิน [kan khai tua chab cha lak thii mii sing khong pen rang wan mak kwa ngen]

raft [rɑːft] *n* แพ [phae]

rag [ræg] *n* ผ้าขี้ริ้ว [pha khi rio]

rage [reɪdʒ] *n* ความเดือดดาล [khwam

dueat dan]; **road rage** *n* ความโกรธที่เกิด
จากสภาพการจราจรบนท้องถนน [khwam
krot thii koet chak sa phap kan cha ra
chon bon thong tha non]

raid [reɪd] *n* การจู่โจม [kan chu chom]
▷ *v* จู่โจม [chu chom]

rail [reɪl] *n* ราง [rang], ราว [rao]

railcard ['reɪlˌkɑːd] *n* บัตรรถไฟ [bat rot
fai]

railings ['reɪlɪŋz] *npl* ราว [rao]

railway ['reɪlˌweɪ] *n* รถไฟ [rot fai];
railway station *n* สถานีรถไฟ [sa tha
ni rot fai]

rain [reɪn] *n* ฝน [fon] ▷ *v* ฝนตก [fon tok];
acid rain *n* ฝนที่เป็นกรด [fon thii pen
krot]; **Do you think it's going to rain?**
คุณคิดว่าฝนจะตกไหม? [khun kit wa fon
ja tok mai]; **It's raining** ฝนกำลังตก [fon
kam lang tok]

rainbow ['reɪnˌbəʊ] *n* รุ้งกินน้ำ [rung kin
nam]

raincoat ['reɪnˌkəʊt] *n* เสื้อกันฝน [suea
kan fon]

rainforest ['reɪnˌfɒrɪst] *n* ป่าหนาทึบใน
เขตร้อนซึ่งมีฝนตกมาก [pa na thuep nai
khet ron sueng mii fon tok mak]

rainy ['reɪnɪ] *adj* ซึ่งมีฝนตก [sueng mii
fon tok]

raise [reɪz] *v* ยกขึ้น [yok khuen]

raisin ['reɪzən] *n* ลูกเกด [luk ket]

rake [reɪk] *n* คราด [khrat]

rally ['rælɪ] *n* การชุมนุม [kan chum num]

ram [ræm] *n* หน่วยความจำของ
คอมพิวเตอร์ [nuai khwam cham khong
khom phio toe] ▷ *v* ชนอย่างแรง [chon
yang raeng]

Ramadan [ˌræməˈdɑːn] *n* เดือนถือศีลอด
ของชาวมุสลิม [duean thue sin ot khong
chao mus sa lim]

rambler ['ræmblə] *n* คนที่ไปเดินในชนบท
[khon thii pai doen nai chon na bot]

ramp [ræmp] *n* ทางลาด [thang lat
(thang laat)]

random ['rændəm] *adj* โดยการสุ่ม [doi

range [reɪndʒ] *n* (limits) ขอบเขต [khop
khet], (mountains) ทิวเขา [thio khao]
▷ *v* ลำดับ [lam dap]

rank [ræŋk] *n* (line) แถว [thaeo], (status)
ตำแหน่ง [tam naeng] ▷ *v* จัดแถว [chat
thaeo]

ransom ['rænsəm] *n* ค่าไถ่ตัว [kha thai
tua]

rape [reɪp] *n* (plant) พืชชนิดหนึ่งที่ใช้เลี้ยง
สัตว์หรือสกัดน้ำมัน [phuet cha nit hueng
thiichai liang sat hue sa kad nam
man], (sexual attack) ข่มขืน [khom
khuen] ▷ *v* ข่มขืน [khom khuen]; **I've
been raped** ฉันถูกข่มขืน [chan thuk
khom khuen]

rapids ['ræpɪdz] *npl* ส่วนของแม่น้ำที่ไหล
แรงและเร็ว [suan khong mae nam thii
lai raeng lae reo]

rapist ['reɪpɪst] *n* คนที่ข่มขืน [khon thii
khom khuen]

rare [rɛə] *adj* (uncommon) ที่พบได้น้อย
[thii phop dai noi], (undercooked) ไม่สุก
[mai suk]

rarely ['rɛəlɪ] *adv* นาน ๆ ครั้ง [nan nan
khrang]

rash [ræʃ] *n* ผื่นคัน [phuen khan]; **I have
a rash** ฉันมีผื่นคัน [chan mii phuen
khan]

raspberry ['rɑːzbərɪ; -brɪ] *n* ลูกราสเบอรี่
[luk ras boe ri]

rat [ræt] *n* หนู [nu]

rate [reɪt] *n* อัตรา [at tra] ▷ *v* ประเมินค่า
จัดอันดับ [pra moen kha, chat an dap];
What are your rates per day? อัตรา
ค่าเช่าของคุณวันละเท่าไร? [at tra kha
chao khong khun wan la thao rai];
What is the rate for...to...? อัตราแลก
จาก...เป็น...เท่าไร? [at tra laek chak...
pen...thao rai]; **What's the exchange
rate?** อัตราแลกคือเท่าไร? [at tra laek
khue thao rai]

rather ['rɑːðə] *adv* ค่อนข้าง [khon khang]

ratio ['reɪʃɪˌəʊ] *n* อัตราส่วน [at tra suan]

rational ['ræʃənᵊl] *adj* ซึ่งมีเหตุผล [sueng mee hed phon]

rattle ['rætᵊl] *n* ของเล่นเด็กที่เขย่ามีเสียงรัว [khong len dek thii kha yao mii siang rua]

rattlesnake ['rætᵊl,sneɪk] *n* งูกะปะ [ngu ka pa]

rave [reɪv] *n* การชมเชย [kan chom choei] ▷ *v* พูดเพ้อเจ้อ [phut phoe choe]

raven ['reɪvᵊn] *n* นกขนาดใหญ่จำพวกกา [nok kha nard yai cham phuak ka]

ravenous ['rævənəs] *adj* ซึ่งตะกละมาก [sueng ta kla mak]

ravine [rə'viːn] *n* หุบเขาลึก [hup khao luek]

raw [rɔː] *adj* ดิบ [dip]; **I can't eat raw eggs** ฉันทานไข่ดิบไม่ได้ [chan than khai dip mai dai]

razor ['reɪzə] *n* มีดโกน [mit kon]; **razor blade** *n* ใบมีดโกน [bai mit kon]

reach [riːtʃ] *v* ไปถึง [pai thueng]

react [rɪ'ækt] *v* มีปฏิกิริยา [mii pa ti ki ri ya]

reaction [rɪ'ækʃən] *n* ปฏิกิริยา [pa ti ki ri ya]

reactor [rɪ'æktə] *n* เครื่องปฏิกรณ์นิวเคลียร์ [khrueang pa ti kon nio khlia]

read [riːd] *v* อ่าน [an]; **I can't read it** ฉันอ่านไม่ได้ [chan an mai dai]

reader ['riːdə] *n* ผู้อ่าน [phu arn]

readily ['rɛdɪlɪ] *adv* อย่างไม่ลังเล [yang mai lang le]

reading ['riːdɪŋ] *n* การอ่าน [kan an]

read out [riːd] *v* อ่านออกเสียง [an ok siang]

ready ['rɛdɪ] *adj* พร้อม [phrom]; **Are you ready?** คุณพร้อมหรือยัง? [khun phrom rue yang]; **I'm not ready** ฉันยังไม่พร้อม [chan yang mai phrom]; **I'm ready** ฉันพร้อมแล้ว [chan phrom laeo]

ready-cooked ['rɛdɪ'kʊkt] *adj* ที่สุกแล้ว [thii suk laeo]

real ['rɪəl] *adj* แท้จริง [thae ching]

realistic [,rɪə'lɪstɪk] *adj* ใกล้เคียงความจริง [klai khiang khwam ching]

reality [rɪ'ælɪtɪ] *n* ความจริง [khwam ching]; **reality TV** *n* รายการทีวีที่แสดงสภาพความเป็นจริง [rai kan thii wii thii sa daeng sa phap khwam pen ching]; **virtual reality** *n* สภาวะเหมือนจริงที่จำลองโดยทางเทคนิคคอมพิวเตอร์ [sa pha wa muean ching thii cham long doi thang tek nik khom phio toe]

realize ['rɪə,laɪz] *v* ตระหนัก [tra nak]

really ['rɪəlɪ] *adv* โดยแท้จริง [doi thae ching]

rear [rɪə] *adj* ข้างหลัง [khang lang] ▷ *n* ด้านหลัง [dan hlang]; **rear-view mirror** *n* กระจกส่องหลัง [kra jok song lang]

reason ['riːzᵊn] *n* เหตุผล [het phon]

reasonable ['riːzənəbᵊl] *adj* ที่มีเหตุผล [thii mee hed phon]

reasonably ['riːzənəblɪ] *adv* อย่างมีเหตุผล [yang mee hed phon]

reassure [,riːə'ʃʊə] *v* ทำให้วางใจ [tham hai wang jai]

reassuring [,riːə'ʃʊəɪŋ] *adj* ที่ให้ความมั่นใจ [thii hai khwam man jai]

rebate ['riːbeɪt] *n* เงินที่ต้องจ่ายคืนมา [ngen thii tong chai khuen ma]

rebellious [rɪ'bɛljəs] *adj* ยากที่จะควบคุม [yak thii ja khuab khum]

rebuild [riː'bɪld] *v* สร้างใหม่ [sang mai]

receipt [rɪ'siːt] *n* ใบเสร็จรับเงิน [bai set rap ngoen]; **I need a receipt, please** ฉันขอใบเสร็จรับเงิน [chan kho bai set rap ngoen]

receive [rɪ'siːv] *v* ได้รับ [dai rap]

receiver [rɪ'siːvə] *n* (*electronic*) อุปกรณ์รับสัญญาณเสียงหรือภาพ [ub pa korn rab san yan siang hue phap], (*person*) ผู้ได้รับ [phu dai rap]

recent ['riːsᵊnt] *adj* เร็วๆนี้ [reo reo ni]

recently ['riːsəntlɪ] *adv* เมื่อเร็วๆนี้ [muea reo reo ni]

reception [rɪ'sɛpʃən] *n* การรับไว้ [kan rap wai]

receptionist [rɪ'sɛpʃənɪst] *n* พนักงาน

ต้อนรับ [pha nak ngan ton rap]

recession [rɪ'sɛʃən] n การตกต่ำทาง
เศรษฐกิจ [kan tok tam thang set tha kit]

recharge [ri:'tʃɑːdʒ] v บรรจุใหม่ [ban
chu mai]

recipe ['rɛsɪpɪ] n ตำรากับข้าว [tam ra
kap khao]

recipient [rɪ'sɪpɪənt] n ผู้ได้รับ [phu dai
rap]

reckon ['rɛkən] v คิดว่า พิจารณาว่า [khit
wa, phi cha ra na wa]

reclining [rɪ'klaɪnɪŋ] adj แนวนอน [naeo
non]

recognizable ['rɛkəg,naɪzəbªl] adj ซึ่ง
สามารถจำได้ [sueng sa maat cham dai]

recognize ['rɛkəg,naɪz] v จำได้ [cham
dai]

recommend [,rɛkə'mɛnd] v แนะนำ
[nae nam]; **Can you recommend a
good restaurant?** คุณแนะนำร้านอาหาร
ดีๆ ให้ได้ไหม? [khun nae nam ran a
han di di hai dai mai]; **Can you
recommend a hotel?** คุณแนะนำโรงแรม
ให้ได้ไหม? [khun nae nam rong raem
hai dai mai]; **Can you recommend a
paediatrician?** คุณแนะนำหมอเด็กให้ได้
ไหม? [khun nae nam mo dek hai dai
mai]

recommendation [,rɛkəmɛn'deɪʃən]
n การแนะนำ [kan nae nam]

reconsider [,ri:kən'sɪdə] v พิจารณาใหม่
[phi cha ra na mai]

record n ['rɛkɔːd] การบันทึก [kan ban
thuek] ▷ v [rɪ'kɔːd] บันทึก [ban thuek]

recorded delivery [rɪ'kɔːdɪd dɪ'lɪvərɪ]
n **recorded delivery** n ลงทะเบียน [long
tha bian]

recorder [rɪ'kɔːdə] n (music) ผู้บันทึกหรือ
เครื่องมือที่ใช้บันทึก เช่นวีดีโอ เทปบันทึก
หรือตลับเทป [phu ban thuek hue
khueang mue thii chai ban thuek
chen vi di o thep ban thuek hue ta lap
thep], (scribe) ผู้บันทึก [phu ban thuek]

recording [rɪ'kɔːdɪŋ] n การบันทึกเสียง

[kan ban thuek siang]

recover [rɪ'kʌvə] v หาย ฟื้น [hai, fuen]

recovery [rɪ'kʌvərɪ] n พื้นจากการเจ็บป่วย
[fuen chak kan chep puai]

recruitment [rɪ'kruːtmənt] n การรับ
สมาชิกใหม่ [kan rap sa ma chik mai]

rectangle ['rɛk,tæŋgªl] n สี่เหลี่ยมผืนผ้า
[si liam phuen pha]

rectangular [rɛk'tæŋgjulə] adj ที่เป็น
สี่เหลี่ยมผืนผ้า [thii pen si liam phuen
pha]

rectify ['rɛktɪ,faɪ] v แก้ไขให้ถูกต้อง [kae
khai hai thuk tong]

recurring [rɪ'kʌrɪŋ] adj เกิดซ้ำ ๆ [koet
sam sam]

recycle [ri:'saɪkªl] v นำกลับมาใช้อีก
[nam klap ma chai ik]

recycling [ri:'saɪklɪŋ] n การนำกลับมาใช้
อีก [kan nam klap ma chai ik]

red [rɛd] adj แดง [daeng]; **red meat** n
เนื้อสีแดง [nuea sii daeng]; **red wine** n
ไวน์แดง [wine daeng]; **Red Cross** n
สภากาชาด [sa pha ka chat]; **a bottle of
red wine** ไวน์แดงหนึ่งขวด [wine daeng
nueng khaut]

redcurrant ['rɛd'kʌrənt] n ลูกไม้สีแดง
ขนาดเล็กปลูกเป็นพุ่ม [luk mai see daeng
kha nard lek pluk pen phum]

redecorate [ri:'dɛkə,reɪt] v ตกแต่งใหม่
[tok taeng mai]

red-haired ['rɛd,hɛəd] adj ที่มีผมสีแดง
[thii mee phom see daeng]

redhead ['rɛd,hɛd] n คนที่มีผมสีแดง [kon
thii mee phom see daeng]

redo [ri:'duː] v ทำใหม่ [tham mai]

reduce [rɪ'djuːs] v ทำให้ลดลง [tham hai
lot long]

reduction [rɪ'dʌkʃən] n การทำให้ลดลง
[kan tham hai lot long]

redundancy [rɪ'dʌndənsɪ] n การมีมาก
เกินไป [kan mee mak koen pai]

redundant [rɪ'dʌndənt] adj การมีมาก
เกินไป [kan mee mak koen pai]

reed [riːd] n ต้นไม้จำพวกอ้อหรือกก [ton

mai cham phuak o rue kok]

reel [ri:l; rɪəl] *n* เครื่องม้วน [khrueang muan]

refer [rɪ'fɜ:] *v* อ้างอิง [ang ing]

referee [ˌrɛfə'ri:] *n* กรรมการ [kam ma kan]

reference ['rɛfərəns; 'rɛfrəns] *n* เอกสารอ้างอิง [ek ka san ang ing]; **reference number** *n* หมายเลขเอกสารอ้างอิง [mai lek ek ka san ang ing]

refill [ri:'fɪl] *v* เติมให้เต็ม [toem hai tem]

refinery [rɪ'faɪnərɪ] *n* โรงกลั่น [rong klan]; **oil refinery** *n* โรงกลั่นน้ำมัน [rong klan nam man]

reflect [rɪ'flɛkt] *v* สะท้อนกลับ [sa thon klap]

reflection [rɪ'flɛkʃən] *n* การสะท้อนกลับ [kan sa thon klap]

reflex ['ri:flɛks] *n* การกระทำโดยอัตโนมัติ [kan kra tham doi at ta no mat]

refreshing [rɪ'frɛʃɪŋ] *adj* ซึ่งทำให้สดชื่น [sueng tham hai sot chuen]

refreshments [rɪ'frɛʃmənts] *npl* การทำให้สดชื่น [kan tham hai sot chuen]

refrigerator [rɪ'frɪdʒəˌreɪtə] *n* ตู้เย็น [tu yen]

refuel [ri:'fju:əl] *v* เติมเชื้อเพลิง [toem chuea phloeng]

refuge ['rɛfju:dʒ] *n* ที่หลบภัย [thii lop phai]

refugee [ˌrɛfjʊ'dʒi:] *n* ผู้ลี้ภัย [phu lee phai]

refund *n* ['ri:ˌfʌnd] เงินที่คืนให้ [ngen thii khuen hai] ▷ *v* [rɪ'fʌnd] คืนเงินให้ [khuen ngen hai]

refusal [rɪ'fju:zəl] *n* การปฏิเสธ [kan pa ti set]

refuse¹ [rɪ'fju:z] *v* ปฏิเสธ [pa ti set]

refuse² ['rɛfju:s] *n* ขยะ [kha ya]

regain [rɪ'geɪn] *v* ได้คืนมาอีก [dai khuen ma ik]

regard [rɪ'gɑ:d] *n* ความนับถือ [khwam nap thue] ▷ *v* พิจารณา [phi cha ra na]

regarding [rɪ'gɑ:dɪŋ] *prep* เกี่ยวกับ [kiao kap]

regiment ['rɛdʒɪmənt] *n* กองทหาร [kong tha haan]

region ['ri:dʒən] *n* เขต [khet]; **Do you have anything typical of this region?** คุณมีอะไรที่เป็นของพื้นเมืองของเขตนี้ไหม? [khun mii a rai thii pen khong phuen mueang khong khet nii mai]

regional ['ri:dʒənᵊl] *adj* เกี่ยวกับเขตนั้น ๆ [kiao kap khet nan nan]

register ['rɛdʒɪstə] *n* การลงทะเบียน [kan long tha bian] ▷ *v* ลงทะเบียน [long tha bian]; **cash register** *n* เครื่องคิดเงิน [khrueang kit ngoen]; **Where do I register?** ฉันจะลงทะเบียนได้ที่ไหน? [chan ja long tha bian dai thii nai]

registered ['rɛdʒɪstəd] *adj* ที่ได้ลงทะเบียน [thii dai long tha bian]

registration [ˌrɛdʒɪ'streɪʃən] *n* การขึ้นทะเบียน [kan khuen tha bian]

regret [rɪ'grɛt] *n* ความเสียใจ [khwam sia jai] ▷ *v* เสียใจ [sia chai]

regular ['rɛgjʊlə] *adj* เป็นประจำ [pen pra cham]

regularly ['rɛgjʊləlɪ] *adv* โดยปรกติ [doi prok ka ti]

regulation [ˌrɛgjʊ'leɪʃən] *n* กฎระเบียบ [kot ra biap]

rehearsal [rɪ'hɜ:sᵊl] *n* การฝึกซ้อม [kan fuek som]

rehearse [rɪ'hɜ:s] *v* ฝึกซ้อม [fuek som]

reimburse [ˌri:ɪm'bɜ:s] *v* ใช้เงินคืน [chai ngoen khuen]

reindeer ['reɪnˌdɪə] *n* กวางขนาดใหญ่แถบขั้วโลกเหนือ [kwang kha nat yai thaep khua lok nuea]

reins [reɪnz] *npl* เชือกบังเหียน [chueak bang hian]

reject [rɪ'dʒɛkt] *v* ปฏิเสธ [pa ti set]

relapse ['ri:ˌlæps] *n* อาการที่โรคกำเริบอีก [a kan thii rok kam roep ik]

related [rɪ'leɪtɪd] *adj* เป็นญาติกัน [pen yat kan]

relation [rɪ'leɪʃən] *n* ความเกี่ยวข้องกัน ของสิ่งของหรือบุคคล [khwam kiao khong kan khong sing khong rue buk kon]; **public relations** *npl* ประชาสัมพันธ์ [pra cha sam phan]

relationship [rɪ'leɪʃənʃɪp] *n* ความ สัมพันธ์ [khwam sam phan]

relative ['rɛlətɪv] *n* เครือญาติ [khruea yat]

relatively ['rɛlətɪvlɪ] *adv* โดยเปรียบเทียบ กับสิ่งอื่น [doi priap thiap kap sing uen]

relax [rɪ'læks] *v* พักผ่อน [phak phon]

relaxation [ˌriːlæk'seɪʃən] *n* การพักผ่อน [kan phak phon]

relaxed [rɪ'lækst] *adj* ซึ่งผ่อนคลาย [sueng phon khlai]

relaxing [rɪ'læksɪŋ] *adj* ซึ่งช่วยให้ผ่อน คลาย [sueng chuai hai phon khlai]

relay ['riːleɪ] *n* การถ่ายทอด [kan thai thot]

release [rɪ'liːs] *n* การปลดปล่อย การปลด ปล่อยเป็นอิสระ [kan plot ploi, kan plot ploi pen it sa ra] ▷ *v* ปลดปล่อย [plot ploi]

relegate ['rɛlɪˌgeɪt] *v* ลดตำแหน่ง [lot tam naeng]

relevant ['rɛlɪvənt] *adj* เหมาะสม [mo som]

reliable [rɪ'laɪəbᵊl] *adj* เชื่อถือได้ [chuea thue dai]

relief [rɪ'liːf] *n* การผ่อนคลาย [kan phon khlai]

relieve [rɪ'liːv] *v* ผ่อนคลาย [phon khlai]

relieved [rɪ'liːvd] *adj* ที่ผ่อนคลาย [thii phon khlai]

religion [rɪ'lɪdʒən] *n* ศาสนา [sat sa na]

religious [rɪ'lɪdʒəs] *adj* เกี่ยวกับศาสนา [kiao kap sat sa na]

reluctant [rɪ'lʌktənt] *adj* ไม่เต็มใจ [mai tem jai]

reluctantly [rɪ'lʌktəntlɪ] *adv* อย่างไม่ เต็มใจ [yang mai tem jai]

rely [rɪ'laɪ] *v* **rely on** *v* ขึ้นอยู่กับ [khuen yu kap]

remain [rɪ'meɪn] *v* คงอยู่ [khong yu]

remaining [rɪ'meɪnɪŋ] *adj* ที่ยังคงอยู่ [thii yang khong yu]

remains [rɪ'meɪnz] *npl* สิ่งที่เหลืออยู่ [sing thii luea yu]

remake ['riːˌmeɪk] *n* ทำใหม่ [tham mai]

remark [rɪ'mɑːk] *n* การให้ข้อคิดเห็น [kan hai kho kit hen]

remarkable [rɪ'mɑːkəbᵊl] *adj* มีคุณค่าที่ น่าสังเกต [mii khun kha thii na sang ket]

remarkably [rɪ'mɑːkəblɪ] *adv* อย่าง พิเศษ [yang phi sed]

remarry [riː'mærɪ] *v* แต่งงานใหม่ [taeng ngan mai]

remedy ['rɛmɪdɪ] *n* ยาและการรักษา [ya lae kan rak sa]

remember [rɪ'mɛmbə] *v* จำ [cham]

remind [rɪ'maɪnd] *v* เตือน [tuean]

reminder [rɪ'maɪndə] *n* สิ่งเตือนความ หลัง [sing tuean khwam lang]

remorse [rɪ'mɔːs] *n* การสำนึกผิด [kan sam nuek phit]

remote [rɪ'məʊt] *adj* ไกล [klai]; **remote control** *n* อุปกรณ์ควบคุมระยะ ห่างหรือไกลที่ไม่ต้องมีสาย เช่น ที่ใช้กับทีวี หรือเครื่องเสียง [up pa kon khuap khum ra ya hang rue klai thii mai tong mii sai chen thii chai kap tii wii rue khrueang siang]

remotely [rɪ'məʊtlɪ] *adv* ห่างไกล [hang klai]

removable [rɪ'muːvəbᵊl] *adj* ที่เคลื่อนที่ ได้ [thii khluean thii dai]

removal [rɪ'muːvᵊl] *n* การเคลื่อนย้าย [kan khluean yai]; **removal van** *n* รถที่ ใช้ในการขนย้าย [rot thii chai nai kan khon yai]

remove [rɪ'muːv] *v* เคลื่อนย้าย [khluean yai]

remover [rɪ'muːvə] *n* **nail-polish remover** *n* น้ำยาล้างเล็บ [nam ya lang lep]

rendezvous ['rɒndɪˌvuː] *n* การนัดพบ ตามเวลาที่นัดไว้ [kan nat phop tam we la thii nat wai]

renew [rɪ'njuː] v เริ่มใหม่ [roem mai]

renewable [rɪ'njuːəbªl] adj ซึ่งต่ออายุ
ใหม่ได้ [sueng to a yu mai dai]

renovate ['rɛnəveɪt] v ปรับปรุงใหม่
[prap prung mai]

renowned [rɪ'naʊnd] adj มีชื่อเสียง [mii
chue siang]

rent [rɛnt] n ค่าเช่า [kha chao] ▷ v เช่า
[chao]; **Do you rent DVDs?** คุณเช่าดีวีดี
ไหม? [khun chao di vi di mai]; **I'd like
to rent a room** ฉันอยากเช่าห้องหนึ่งห้อง
[chan yak chao hong nueng hong]

rental ['rɛntªl] n ค่าเช่า [kha chao]; **car
rental** n รถเช่า [rot chao]; **rental car** n
รถเช่า [rot chao]

reorganize [riː'ɔːgənaɪz] v จัดระบบใหม่
ให้ดีขึ้น [chad ra bob mai hai di khuen]

rep [rɛp] n บริษัททละคร [bo ri sat la khon]

repair [rɪ'pɛə] n การซ่อม [kan som] ▷ v
ซ่อมแซม [som saem]; **repair kit** n ชุด
สำหรับการซ่อม [chut sam rap kan som];
How long will it take to repair? ใช้
เวลานานเท่าไรในการซ่อม? [chai we la
nan thao rai nai kan som]

repay [rɪ'peɪ] v จ่ายเงินคืน [chai ngen
khuen]

repayment [rɪ'peɪmənt] n เงินที่จ่ายคืน
[ngoen thii chai khuen]

repeat [rɪ'piːt] n การกระทำซ้ำ [kan kra
tham sam] ▷ v พูด เขียนทำซ้ำ [phut
khian tham som]

repeatedly [rɪ'piːtɪdlɪ] adv อย่างซ้ำๆ
[yang som som]

repellent [rɪ'pɛlənt] adj ทำให้เป็นที่
รังเกียจ [tham hai pen thii rang kiat];
insect repellent n ยากันแมลง [ya kan
ma laeng]

repercussions [ˌriːpə'kʌʃənz] npl ผล
ของการกระทำ [phon khong kan kra
tham]

repetitive [rɪ'pɛtɪtɪv] adj ที่ทำซ้ำซาก
[thii tham sam sak]

replace [rɪ'pleɪs] v แทนที่ [thaen thi]

replacement [rɪ'pleɪsmənt] n การทำ
หน้าที่แทน [kan tham na thii thaen]

replay n ['riːˌpleɪ] การจัดการแข่งขันใหม่
[kan chat kan khaeng khan mai] ▷ v
[riːˈpleɪ] เล่นใหม่ [len mai]

replica ['rɛplɪkə] n ของจำลอง [khong
cham long]

reply [rɪ'plaɪ] n คำตอบ [kham top] ▷ v
ให้คำตอบ [hai kham top]

report [rɪ'pɔːt] n การรายงาน [kan rai
ngan] ▷ v รายงาน [rai ngan]; **report
card** n บัตรรายงาน [bat rai ngan]; **I
need a police report for my
insurance** ฉันจำเป็นต้องมีรายงานของ
ตำรวจสำหรับการประกัน [chan cham pen
tong mii rai ngan khong tam ruat sam
rap kan pra kan]

reporter [rɪ'pɔːtə] n ผู้รายงาน [phu rai
ngan]

represent [ˌrɛprɪ'zɛnt] v เป็นตัวแทน
[pen tua taen]

representative [ˌrɛprɪ'zɛntətɪv] adj
เป็นตัวแทน [pen tua taen]

reproduction [ˌriːprə'dʌkʃən] n การ
ผลิตใหม่ [kan pha lit mai]

reptile ['rɛptaɪl] n สัตว์เลื้อยคลาน [sat
lueai khlan]

republic [rɪ'pʌblɪk] n สาธารณรัฐ [sa tha
ra na rat]

repulsive [rɪ'pʌlsɪv] adj น่าขยะแขยง [na
kha ya kha yaeng]

reputable ['rɛpjʊtəbªl] adj น่าเชื่อถือ [na
chuea thue]

reputation [ˌrɛpjʊ'teɪʃən] n ชื่อเสียง
[chue siang]

request [rɪ'kwɛst] n การเรียกร้อง [kan
riak rong] ▷ v เรียกร้อง [riak rong]

require [rɪ'kwaɪə] v ต้องการ [tong kan]

requirement [rɪ'kwaɪəmənt] n ความ
ต้องการ [khwam tong kan]

rescue ['rɛskjuː] n การช่วยชีวิต [kan
chuai chi wit] ▷ v ช่วยเหลือ [chuai
luea]; **Where is the nearest
mountain rescue service post?**

หน่วยบริการช่วยเหลือใกล้ที่สุดอยู่ที่ไหน?
[nuai bo ri kan chuai luea klai thii sut
yu thii nai]

research [rɪ'sɜːtʃ; 'riːsɜːtʃ] *n* การค้นคว้า
[kan khon khwa]; **market research** *n*
การวิจัยตลาด [kan wi jai ta lad]

resemblance [rɪ'zɛmbləns] *n* ความ
คล้ายคลึง [khwam khlai khlueng]

resemble [rɪ'zɛmbᵊl] *v* คล้าย [khlai]

resent [rɪ'zɛnt] *v* รู้สึกขมขื่น [ru suk
khom khuen]

resentful [rɪ'zɛntfʊl] *adj* ซึ่งไม่พอใจ
[sueng mai phor jai]

reservation [ˌrɛzə'veɪʃən] *n* การจอง
[kan chong]

reserve [rɪ'zɜːv] *n* (land) เขตสงวน
[khet sa nguan], (retention) การเก็บรักษา [kan
kep rak sa] ▷ *v* สำรอง [sam rong]

reserved [rɪ'zɜːvd] *adj* ไม่แสดงอารมณ์
และความรู้สึก [mai sa daeng a rom lae
khwam ru suek]

reservoir ['rɛzəˌvwɑː] *n* ที่เก็บน้ำ [thii
kep nam]

resident ['rɛzɪdənt] *n* ผู้พักอาศัย [phu
phak a sai]

residential [ˌrɛzɪ'dɛnʃəl] *adj* เขตที่มีที่พัก
อาศัย [khet thii mii thii phak a sai]

resign [rɪ'zaɪn] *v* ลาออก [la ok]

resin ['rɛzɪn] *n* ยางไม้ [yang mai]

resist [rɪ'zɪst] *v* ต่อต้าน [to tan]

resistance [rɪ'zɪstəns] *n* การต่อต้าน
[kan to tan]

resit [riː'sɪt] *v* สอบใหม่ [sop mai]

resolution [ˌrɛzə'luːʃən] *n* ความเด็ดเดี่ยว
แน่นอน [khwam det diao nae non]

resort [rɪ'zɔːt] *n* สถานที่ตากอากาศ [sa
than thii tak a kaat]; **resort to** *v* ขอ
ความช่วยเหลือ [kho khwam chuai luea]

resource [rɪ'zɔːs; -'sɔːs] *n* ทรัพยากร
[pha ya kon]; **natural resources** *npl*
ทรัพยากรธรรมชาติ [sap pha ya kon
tham ma chaat]

respect [rɪ'spɛkt] *n* ความเคารพ [khwam
khao rop] ▷ *v* เคารพ [khao rop]

respectable [rɪ'spɛktəbᵊl] *adj* น่านับถือ
[na nap thue]

respectively [rɪ'spɛktɪvlɪ] *adv* ตาม
ลำดับ [tam lam dap]

respond [rɪ'spɒnd] *v* ตอบ [top]

response [rɪ'spɒns] *n* คำตอบ [kham top]

responsibility [rɪˌspɒnsə'bɪlɪtɪ] *n*
ความรับผิดชอบ [khwam rap phit chop]

responsible [rɪ'spɒnsəbᵊl] *adj* อย่างรับ
ผิดชอบ [yang rap phit chop]

rest [rɛst] *n* การพักผ่อน [kan phak phon]
▷ *v* พักผ่อน [phak phon]; **the rest** *n* ส่วน
ที่เหลือ [suan thii luea]

restaurant ['rɛstəˌrɒŋ; 'rɛstrɒŋ;
-rɒnt] *n* ร้านอาหาร [ran a han]; **Are
there any vegetarian restaurants
here?** มีร้านอาหารมังสวิรัติที่นี่ไหม? [mii
ran a han mang sa wi rat thii ni mai]

restful ['rɛstfʊl] *adj* ซึ่งเงียบสงบและผ่อน
คลาย [sueng ngiap sa ngob lae phon
khlai]

restless ['rɛstlɪs] *adj* เบื่อและไม่พอใจ
[buea lae mai pho jai]

restore [rɪ'stɔː] *v* ซ่อมแซมให้สู่สภาพเดิม
[som saem hai su sa phap doem]

restrict [rɪ'strɪkt] *v* จำกัด [cham kat]

restructure [riː'strʌktʃə] *v* เปลี่ยน
โครงสร้างใหม่ [plian khrong sang mai]

result [rɪ'zʌlt] *n* ผลลัพธ์ [phon lap];
result in *v* เป็นผล [pen phon]

resume [rɪ'zjuːm] *v* ดำเนินต่อไปใหม่
[dam noen to pai mai]

retail ['riːteɪl] *n* การขายปลีก [kan khai
plik] ▷ *v* ขายปลีก [khai phlik]; **retail
price** *n* ราคาขายปลีก [ra kha khai plik]

retailer ['riːteɪlə] *n* ผู้ขายปลีก [phu khai
plik]

retire [rɪ'taɪə] *v* เกษียณ [ka sian]

retired [rɪ'taɪəd] *adj* ปลดเกษียณ [plot ka
sian]

retirement [rɪ'taɪəmənt] *n* การปลด
เกษียณ [kan plot ka sian]

retrace [rɪ'treɪs] *v* ย้อนรอยเดิม [yon roi
doem]

return [rɪˈtɜːn] n (coming back) การกลับ
คืนมา [kan klap khuen ma], (yield)
ผลผลิต ปริมาณผลผลิต [phon pha lit, pa
ri man phon pha lit] ▷ vi กลับคืน กลับมา
[klab khuen klab ma] ▷ vt ส่งคืน [song
khuen]; **day return** n ไปกลับในหนึ่งวัน
[pai klap nai nueng wan]; **return
ticket** n ตั๋วไปกลับ [tua pai klap]; **tax
return** n ภาษีคืน [pha si khuen]

reunion [riːˈjuːnjən] n การกลับมารวมกัน
ใหม่ [kan klap ma ruam kan mai]

reuse [riːˈjuːz] v ใช้อีก [chai ik]

reveal [rɪˈviːl] v เปิดเผย [poet phoei]

revenge [rɪˈvɛndʒ] n การแก้แค้น [kan
kae khaen]

revenue [ˈrɛvɪˌnjuː] n รายได้ของรัฐที่ได้
จากการเก็บภาษีอากรและธรรมเนียม [rai
dai khong rat thii dai chak kan kep
pha si a kon lae tham niam]

reverse [rɪˈvɜːs] n ด้านตรงข้าม [dan
trong kham] ▷ v ถอยกลับ [thoi klap]

review [rɪˈvjuː] n บทเขียนวิจารณ์ [bot
khian wi chan]

revise [rɪˈvaɪz] v ทบทวน [thop thuan]

revision [rɪˈvɪʒən] n การทบทวน [kan
thop thuan]

revive [rɪˈvaɪv] v มีชีวิตชีวา [mi chi wit
chi wa]

revolting [rɪˈvəʊltɪŋ] adj น่ารังเกียจ [na
rang kiat]

revolution [ˌrɛvəˈluːʃən] n การปฏิวัติ
[kan pa ti wat]

revolutionary [ˌrɛvəˈluːʃənərɪ] adj เกี่ยว
กับการปฏิวัติ [kiao kap kan pa ti wat]

revolver [rɪˈvɒlvə] n ปืนพกลูกโม่ [puen
phok luk mo]

reward [rɪˈwɔːd] n รางวัล [rang wan]

rewarding [rɪˈwɔːdɪŋ] adj ซึ่งให้รางวัล
[sueng hai rang wan]

rewind [riːˈwaɪnd] v กรอเทปกลับ [kro
thep klap]

rheumatism [ˈruːməˌtɪzəm] n โรค
ไขข้ออักเสบ [rok khai kho ak sep]

rhubarb [ˈruːbɑːb] n พืชใบใหญ่มีก้านยาว

สีเขียวและแดงใช้ทำอาหารได้ [phuet bai
yai mee kan yao see khiao lae daeng
chai tham a han dai]

rhyme [raɪm] n **nursery rhyme** n กลอน
หรือเพลงง่ายๆสำหรับเด็ก [klorn huen
pleng ngai ngai sam rub dek]

rhythm [ˈrɪðəm] n จังหวะ [chang wa]

rib [rɪb] n เนื้อติดซี่โครง [nuea tit si
khrong]

ribbon [ˈrɪbʰn] n ริบบิ้น เส้นหรือแถบผ้ายาว
ที่ใช้ผูกเพื่อประดับตกแต่ง [rip bin, sen
rue thaep pha yao thii chai phuk
phuea pra dap tok taeng]

rice [raɪs] n ข้าว [khao]; **brown rice** n
ข้าวซ้อมมือ [khao som mue]

rich [rɪtʃ] adj รวย [ruai]

ride [raɪd] n การเดินทางโดยยานพาหนะ
หรือหลังม้า [kan doen thang doi yan
pha ha na hue hlang ma] ▷ v ขี่ เช่นขี่ม้า
ขี่จักรยานหรือจักรยานยนต์ [khi chen khi
ma khi chak kra yan rue chak kra yan
yon]

rider [ˈraɪdə] n ผู้ขับขี่ [phu khap khi]

ridiculous [rɪˈdɪkjʊləs] adj น่าหัวเราะ
[na hua rao]

riding [ˈraɪdɪŋ] n การขี่ม้า [kan khi ma];
horse riding n การขี่ม้า [kan khi ma]

rifle [ˈraɪfʰl] n ปืนเล็กยาว [puen lek yao]

rig [rɪɡ] n เครื่องขุดเจาะ [khueang khud
jo]; **oil rig** n ฐานโครงสร้างใช้เจาะหาบ่อน้ำ
มัน [tan khrong sang chai jo ha bo nam
man]

right [raɪt] adj (correct) ถูกต้อง [tuk
tong], (not left) ทางขวา [thang khwa]
▷ adv อย่างถูกต้อง [yang thuk tong] ▷ n
สิทธิ [sit thi]; **civil rights** npl สิทธิที่เท่า
กันของพลเมือง [sit thi thii thao kan
khong phon la mueang]; **human
rights** npl สิทธิของมนุษย์ [sit thi khong
ma nut]; **right angle** n มุมที่ถูกต้อง
[mum thii thuk tong]

right-hand [ˈraɪtˌhænd] adj ด้านขวามือ
[dan khwa mue]; **right-hand drive** n
ขับทางด้านขวามือ [khap thang dan

khwa mue]

right-handed ['raɪt,hændɪd] *adj* ทาง
ด้านขวามือ [thang dan khwua mue]

rightly ['raɪtlɪ] *adv* อย่างถูกต้องและ
ยุติธรรม [yang thuk tong lae yu thi
tham]

right-wing ['raɪt,wɪŋ] *adj* พรรคการเมือง
อนุรักษ์นิยม [phak kan mueang a nu rak
ni yom]

rim [rɪm] *n* ขอบ [khop]

ring [rɪŋ] *n* แหวน [waen] ▷ *v* ส่งเสียงดัง
กังวาน [song siang dang kang wan];
engagement ring *n* แหวนหมั้น [waen
man]; **ring binder** *n* ตาไก่ [ta kai]; **ring
road** *n* ถนนวงแหวน [tha non wong
waen]

ring back [rɪŋ bæk] *v* โทรกลับ [tho
klap]

ringtone ['rɪŋ,təʊn] *n* เสียงดังของ
โทรศัพท์ [siang dang khong tho ra sab]

ring up [rɪŋ ʌp] *v* โทรศัพท์หา [tho ra sab
ha]

rink [rɪŋk] *n* ลานเล่นสเก็ตน้ำแข็ง [lan len
sa ket nam khaeng]; **ice rink** *n* ลานน้ำ
แข็งเล่นสเก็ต [lan nam khaeng len sa
ket]; **skating rink** *n* ลานเล่นสเก็ต [lan
len sa ket]

rinse [rɪns] *n* การชำระล้าง [kan cham ra
lang] ▷ *v* ชำระล้าง [cham ra lang]

riot ['raɪət] *n* การจลาจล [kan cha la chon]
▷ *v* ก่อการจลาจล [ko kan cha la chon]

rip [rɪp] *v* ฉีก [chik]

ripe [raɪp] *adj* สุก [suk]

rip off [rɪp ɒf] *v* คิดราคามากเกินไป [kid
ra kha mak koen pai]

rip-off ['rɪpɒf] *n* การโกง การหลอกลวง
การต้มตุ๋น [kan kong, kan lok luang,
kan tom tun]

rip up [rɪp ʌp] *v* ดึงขึ้นอย่างแรง [dueng
khuen yang raeng]

rise [raɪz] *n* การลุกขึ้น [kan luk khuen]
▷ *v* ลุกขึ้น [luk khuen]

risk [rɪsk] *n* ความเสี่ยง [khwam siang]
▷ *vt* เสี่ยง [siang]

risky ['rɪskɪ] *adj* ที่เสี่ยง [thii siang]

ritual ['rɪtjʊəl] *adj* เกี่ยวกับพิธีกรรม [kiao
kap phi thi kam] ▷ *n* พิธีกรรมทางศาสนา
[phi ti kam thang sat sa na]

rival ['raɪvəl] *adj* ที่เป็นคู่แข่งกัน [thii pen
khu khaeng kan] ▷ *n* คู่แข่ง [khu
khaeng]

rivalry ['raɪvəlrɪ] *n* การแข่งขัน [kan
khaeng khan]

river ['rɪvə] *n* แม่น้ำ [mae nam]; **Can
one swim in the river?** เราว่ายน้ำใน
แม่น้ำได้ไหม? [rao wai nam nai mae
nam dai mai]

road [rəʊd] *n* ถนน [tha non]; **main
road** *n* ถนนสายหลัก [tha non sai lak];
Are the roads icy? ถนนมีน้ำแข็งเกาะ
ไหม? [tha non mii nam khaeng kao
mai]; **Do you have a road map of
this area?** คุณมีแผนที่ถนนของบริเวณนี้
ไหม? [khun mii phaen thii tha non
khong bo ri wen nii mai]; **I need a
road map of...** ฉันอยากได้แผนที่ถนน
ของ... [chan yak dai phaen thii tha
non khong...]

roadblock ['rəʊd,blɒk] *n* สิ่งกีดขวาง
[sing kit khwang]

roadworks ['rəʊd,wɜːks] *npl* การซ่อม
ถนน [kan som tha non]

roast [rəʊst] *adj* ที่อบ [thii op]

rob [rɒb] *v* ปล้น [plon]; **I've been
robbed** ฉันถูกปล้น [chan thuk plon]

robber ['rɒbə] *n* โจร [chon]

robbery ['rɒbərɪ] *n* การปล้น [kan plon]

robin ['rɒbɪn] *n* นกสีน้ำตาลขนาดเล็กมือกสี
แดง [nok see nam tan kha nard lek
mee ok see daeng]

robot ['rəʊbɒt] *n* หุ่นยนต์ [hun yon]

rock [rɒk] *n* หิน [hin] ▷ *v* โยก แกว่ง เขย่า
[yok, kwaeng, kha yao]; **rock
climbing** *n* การไต่เขา [kan tai khao]

rocket ['rɒkɪt] *n* จรวด [cha ruat]

rod [rɒd] *n* ไม้หรือแท่งโลหะยาวๆ [mai hue
thaeng lo ha yao yao]

rodent ['rəʊdᵊnt] *n* สัตว์เลี้ยงลูกด้วยนมที่

ใช้ฟันแทะ [sat liang luk duai nom thii chai fan thae]

role [rəʊl] *n* หน้าที่หรือบทบาท [na thii rue bot bat]

roll [rəʊl] *n* การหมุน [kan mun] ▷ *v* กลิ้ง [kling]; **bread roll** *n* ขนมปังกลม [kha nom pang klom]; **roll call** *n* การขานชื่อ [kan khan chue]

roller ['rəʊlə] *n* เครื่องบดถนน [khrueang bot tha non]

rollercoaster ['rəʊlə,kəʊstə] *n* ลานรถ ลื่นไถลสำหรับการเล่นของเด็กในสวนสนุก [lan rot luen tha lai sam rap kan len khong dek nai suan sa nuk]

rollerskates ['rəʊlə,skeɪts] *npl* รองเท้าส เก็ตที่มีล้อเลื่อนสี่ล้อ [rong thao sa ket thii mee lor luean si lor]

rollerskating ['rəʊlə,skeɪtɪŋ] *n* การเล่น สเก็ต [kan len sa ket]

Roman ['rəʊmən] *adj* ที่เกี่ยวกับโรม [thii kiao kap rom]; **Roman Catholic** *n* ที่ เกี่ยวกับศาสนาโรมันคาทอลิค [thii kiao kap sat sa na ro man kha tho lik], ผู้ นับถือนิกายโรมันคาทอลิค [thii kiao kap sat sa na ro man kha tho lik, phu nap thue ni kai ro man kha tho lik]

romance ['rəʊmæns] *n* เรื่องรักใคร่ [rueang rak khrai]

Romanesque [,rəʊmə'nɛsk] *adj* ซึ่งเป็น สถาปัตยกรรมที่แพร่ในยุโรปตะวันตกตั้งแต่ ศตวรรษที่ ๙ ถึง ๑๒ [sueng pen sa ta pat ta ya kam thii phrae nai yu rop ta wan tok tang tae sat ta wat thii thueng]

Romania [rəʊ'meɪnɪə] *n* ประเทศ โรมาเนีย [pra tet ro ma nia]

Romanian [rəʊ'meɪnɪən] *adj* เกี่ยวกับ โรมาเนีย [kiao kap ro ma nia] ▷ *n* (language) ภาษาโรมาเนีย [pha sa ro ma nia], (person) ชาวโรมาเนีย [chao ro ma nia]

romantic [rəʊ'mæntɪk] *adj* เกี่ยวกับเรื่อง รักใคร่ [kiao kap rueang rak khrai]

roof [ru:f] *n* หลังคา [lang kha]; **The roof leaks** หลังคารั่ว [lang kha rua]

roof rack ['ru:f,ræk] *n* หลังคารถ [lang kha rot]

room [ru:m; rʊm] *n* ห้อง [hong]; **changing room** *n* ห้องเปลี่ยนเสื้อผ้า [hong plian suea pha]; **Can I see the room?** ฉันขอดูห้องได้ไหม? [chan kho du hong dai mai]; **Can I switch rooms?** ฉันเปลี่ยนห้องได้ไหม? [chan plian hong dai mai]; **Can you clean the room, please?** คุณช่วยทำความ สะอาดห้องได้ไหม [khun chuai tham khwam sa at hong dai mai]

roommate ['ru:m,meɪt; 'rʊm-] *n* เพื่อน ร่วมห้อง [phuean ruam hong]

root [ru:t] *n* ราก [rak]; **Can you dye my roots, please?** คุณช่วยย้อมรากผมให้ฉัน ได้ไหม? [khun chuai yom rak phom hai chan dai mai]

rope [rəʊp] *n* เชือก [chueak]

rope in [rəʊp ɪn] *v* ชักชวนให้เข้าร่วม [chak chuan hai khao ruam]

rose [rəʊz] *n* ต้นกุหลาบ [ton ku lap]

rosé ['rəʊzeɪ] *n* ไวน์สีชมพู [vine see chom phu]

rosemary ['rəʊzmərɪ] *n* ไม้พุ่มสมุนไพร [mai phum sa mun phrai]

rot [rɒt] *v* เน่า [nao]

rotten ['rɒtᵊn] *adj* เน่าเปื่อย [nao pueai]

rough [rʌf] *adj* หยาบ [yap]

roughly ['rʌflɪ] *adv* อย่างหยาบ [yang yap]

roulette [ru:'lɛt] *n* เกมส์พนันรูเลทท [kem pha nan ru let]

round [raʊnd] *adj* กลม [klom] ▷ *n* (circle) วงกลม [wong klom], (series) รูปทรงกลม [rup song klom] ▷ *prep* ล้อมรอบ [lom rop]; **paper round** *n* เส้นทางส่ง หนังสือพิมพ์ [sen thang song nang sue phim]; **round trip** *n* การเดินทางไปและ กลับ [kan doen thang pai lae klap]; **You have to turn round** คุณต้องเลี้ยวกลับ [khun tong liao klap]

roundabout ['raʊndə,baʊt] *n* วงเวียนที่ ต้องขับรถรอบ [wong wian thii tong khap rot rop]

round up [raʊnd ʌp] v รวมตัวกัน [ruam tua kan]

route [ruːt] n เส้นทาง [sen thang]; **Is there a route that avoids the traffic?** มีเส้นทางใดที่หลีกเลี่ยงรถติดได้? [mii sen thang dai thii lik liang rot tit dai]

routine [ruːˈtiːn] n กิจวัตรประจำ [kit ja wat pra cham]

row¹ [rəʊ] n (line) แถว [thaeo] ▷ v (in boat) พาย [phai]

row² [raʊ] n (argument) การทะเลาะวิวาท [kan tha lo wi wat] ▷ v (to argue) ทะเลาะ วิวาท [tha lo wi wat]

rowing [ˈrəʊɪŋ] n การพายเรือ [kan phai ruea]; **rowing boat** n เรือขนาดเล็กที่ใช้ ไม้พาย [ruea kha nat lek thii chai mai phai]

royal [ˈrɔɪəl] adj เกี่ยวกับราชวงศ์ [kiao kap rat cha wong]

rub [rʌb] v ถู [thu]

rubber [ˈrʌbə] n ยาง [yang]; **rubber band** n ยางรัด [yang rat]; **rubber gloves** npl ถุงมือยาง [thung mue yang]

rubbish [ˈrʌbɪʃ] adj ที่ไร้สาระ [thii rai sa ra] ▷ n ขยะ [kha ya]; **rubbish dump** n ที่ ทิ้งขยะ [thii thing kha ya]; **Where do we leave the rubbish?** เราจะทิ้งขยะ ได้ที่ไหน? [rao ja thing kha ya dai thii nai]

rucksack [ˈrʌkˌsæk] n เป้สะพายหลัง [pe sa phai lang]

rude [ruːd] adj หยาบคาย [yap khai]

rug [rʌg] n พรมผืนเล็ก [phrom phuen lek]

rugby [ˈrʌgbɪ] n กีฬารักบี้ [ki la rak bii]

ruin [ˈruːɪn] n ซากปรักหักพัง [sak prak hak phang] ▷ v ทำให้พินาศ [tham hai phi nat]

rule [ruːl] n หลักเกณฑ์ [lak ken]

rule out [ruːl aʊt] v ไม่ยอมรับ [mai yom rap]

ruler [ˈruːlə] n (commander) ผู้ควบคุม [phu khuab khum], (measure) ไม้บรรทัด [mai ban that]

rum [rʌm] n เหล้ารัม [lao ram]

rumour [ˈruːmə] n ข่าวลือ [khao lue]

run [rʌn] n การวิ่ง [kan wing] ▷ vi วิ่ง วิ่งหนี เปิดเครื่อง เดินเครื่อง [wing, wing nii, poet khrueang, doen khrueang] ▷ vt วิ่งแข่ง รีบไป เคลื่อนไปอย่างรวดเร็ว [wing khaeng, rip pai, khluean pai yang ruat reo]

run away [rʌn əˈweɪ] v วิ่งหนีไป [wing nii pai]

runner [ˈrʌnə] n นักวิ่ง [nak wing]; **runner bean** n ถั่วฝักชนิดหนึ่ง [thua fak cha nit nueng]

runner-up [ˈrʌnəʌp] n ผู้รองชนะเลิศ [phu rong cha na loet]

running [ˈrʌnɪŋ] n การบริหาร [kan bo ri han], การวิ่ง [kan wing]

run out [rʌn aʊt] v **The towels have run out** ผ้าเช็ดตัวหมด [pha chet tua mot]

run out of [rʌn aʊt ɒv] v ไม่มีสำรอง [mai mii sam rong]

run over [rʌn ˈəʊvə] v ชนล้มและบาดเจ็บ [chon lom lae bat chep]

runway [ˈrʌnˌweɪ] n ลานบิน [lan bin]

rural [ˈrʊərəl] adj ในชนบท [nai chon na bot]

rush [rʌʃ] n การเร่ง [kan reng] ▷ v เคลื่อน หรือทำอย่างเร่งรีบ [khluean rue tham yang reng rip]; **rush hour** n ชั่วโมงเร่ง ด่วน [chau mong reng duan]

rusk [rʌsk] n ขนมปังกรอบที่ใช้เลี้ยงเด็ก [kha nom pang krob thiichai liang dek]

Russia [ˈrʌʃə] n ประเทศรัสเซีย [pra tet ras sia]

Russian [ˈrʌʃən] adj เกี่ยวกับรัสเซีย [kiao kap ras sia] ▷ n (language) ภาษารัสเซีย [pha sa ras sia], (person) ชาวรัสเซีย [chao ras sia]

rust [rʌst] n สนิม [sa nim]

rusty [ˈrʌstɪ] adj ที่เป็นสนิม [thii pen sa nim]

ruthless [ˈruːθlɪs] adj ไร้ความเมตตา ปราณี [rai khwam met ta pra nii]

rye [raɪ] n ธัญพืชคล้ายข้าวสาลี [than ya phuet khlai khao sa lii]

Sabbath ['sæbəθ] *n* วันประกอบพิธีทาง
ศาสนาและพักผ่อนของชาวคริสต์ [wan pra
kop phi ti thang sad sa na lae phak
phon khong chao khris]

sabotage ['sæbə͵tɑːʒ] *n* การก่อ
วินาศกรรม [kan ko wi nat sa kam] ▷ *v*
ก่อวินาศกรรม [ko wi nat sa kam]

sachet ['sæʃeɪ] *n* ซอง [song]

sack [sæk] *n* (container) กระสอบ [kra
sop], (dismissal) ไล่ออก [lai ok] ▷ *v*
ทำลาย [tham lai]

sacred ['seɪkrɪd] *adj* ซึ่งเป็นที่สักการะทาง
ศาสนา [sueng pen thii sak ka ra thang
sat sa na]

sacrifice ['sækrɪ͵faɪs] *n* การเสียสละ [kan
sia sa la]

sad [sæd] *adj* เศร้า [sao]

saddle ['sædᵊl] *n* อาน [an]

saddlebag ['sædᵊl͵bæg] *n* ถุงที่บรรจุหลัง
สัตว์ [thung thii ban chu hlang sat]

sadly [sædlɪ] *adv* อย่างเศร้าใจ [yang sao
jai]

safari [sə'fɑːrɪ] *n* การเดินทางเพื่อล่าสัตว์
และท่องเที่ยว [kan doen thang phue la
sad lae thong thiao]

safe [seɪf] *adj* ปลอดภัย [plot phai] ▷ *n* ตู้
นิรภัย [tu ni ra phai]; **I have some
things in the safe** ฉันมีของในตู้นิรภัย
[chan mii khong nai tu ni ra phai]; **I
would like to put my jewellery in
the safe** ฉันอยากวางเครื่องประดับไว้ในตู้
นิรภัย [chan yak wang khrueang pra
dap wai nai tu ni ra phai]; **Is it safe for
children?** ปลอดภัยสำหรับเด็กไหม? [plot
phai sam rap dek mai]

safety ['seɪftɪ] *n* ความปลอดภัย [khwam
plot phai]; **safety belt** *n* เข็มขัดนิรภัย
[khem khat ni ra phai]; **safety pin** *n*
เข็มกลัด [khem klat]

saffron ['sæfrən] *n* ผงสีเหลืองอมส้มทำ
จากดอกโครคัส [phong sii lueang om
som tham chak dok khro khas]

Sagittarius [͵sædʒɪ'tɛərɪəs] *n* ราศีธนู
[ra si tha nu]

Sahara [sə'hɑːrə] *n* ทะเลทรายซาฮารา
[tha le sai sa ha ra]

sail [seɪl] *n* ใบเรือ [bai rua] ▷ *v* แล่นเรือ
[laen rua]

sailing ['seɪlɪŋ] *n* การเดินเรือ [kan doen
rua]; **sailing boat** *n* เรือใบ [rua bai]

sailor ['seɪlə] *n* ลูกเรือ [luk rua]

saint [seɪnt; sənt] *n* นักบุญ [nak bun]

salad ['sæləd] *n* สลัด [sa lat]; **mixed
salad** *n* สลัดรวม [sa lat ruam]; **salad
dressing** *n* น้ำสลัด [nam sa lat]

salami [sə'lɑːmɪ] *n* ไส้กรอกซาลามิ [sai
krok sa la mi]

salary ['sælərɪ] *n* เงินเดือน [ngoen
duean]

sale [seɪl] *n* การขาย [kan khai]; **sales
assistant** *n* พนักงานขาย [pha nak
ngan khai]; **sales rep** *n* ผู้แทนการขาย
[phu thaen kan khai]

salesman, salesmen ['seɪlzmən,
'seɪlzmɛn] *n* พนักงานขายชาย [pha nak
ngan khai chai]

salesperson ['seɪlzpɜː͵sᵊn] *n* พนักงาน
ขาย [pha nak ngan khai]

saleswoman, saleswomen

['seɪzwʊmən, 'seɪzwɪmɪn] *n* พนักงานขายหญิง [pha nak ngan khai ying]

saliva [sə'laɪvə] *n* น้ำลาย [nam lai]

salmon ['sæmən] *n* ปลาแซลมอน [pla sael mon]

salon ['sælɒn] *n* **beauty salon** *n* ร้านเสริมสวย [ran soem suai]

saloon [sə'luːn] *n* บาร์คุณภาพสูง [bar khun na phap sung]; **saloon car** *n* รถเก๋งที่มีสองหรือสี่ประตู [rot keng thii mii song rue si pra tu]

salt [sɔːlt] *n* เกลือ [kluea]; **Pass the salt, please** ช่วยส่งเกลือให้หน่อย [chuai song kluea hai noi]

saltwater ['sɔːlt,wɔːtə] *adj* เกี่ยวกับน้ำเค็ม [kiao kap nam khem]

salty ['sɔːltɪ] *adj* ซึ่งมีรสเค็ม [sueng mii rot khem]

salute [sə'luːt] *v* คำนับ [kham nap]

salve [sælv] *n* **lip salve** *n* ครีมทากันริมฝีปากแตก [khrim tha kan rim fi pak taek]

same [seɪm] *adj* เหมือนกัน [muean kan]; **I'll have the same** ฉันอยากได้เครื่องดื่มเหมือนกัน [chan yak dai khrueang duem muean kan]

sample ['sɑːmpəl] *n* ตัวอย่าง [tua yang]

sand [sænd] *n* ทราย [sai]; **sand dune** *n* หุบทราย [hup sai]

sandal ['sændəl] *n* รองเท้าแตะ [rong thao tae]

sandcastle [sændkɑːsəl] *n* ปราสาททราย [pra saat sai]

sandpaper ['sænd,peɪpə] *n* กระดาษทราย [kra dart sai]

sandpit ['sænd,pɪt] *n* หลุมทราย [lum sai]

sandstone ['sænd,stəʊn] *n* หินทราย [hin sai]

sandwich ['sænwɪdʒ; -wɪtʃ] *n* ขนมปังแซนด์วิช [kha nom pang saen wit]; **What kind of sandwiches do you have?** คุณมีขนมปังแซนด์วิชอะไรบ้าง? [khun mii kha nom pang saen wit a rai bang]

San Marino [ˌsæn mə'riːnəʊ] *n* ประเทศซานมาริโน [pra tet san ma ri no]

sapphire ['sæfaɪə] *n* ไพลินสีน้ำเงินหรือสีฟ้าเข้ม [phai lin sii nam ngoen rue sii fa khem]

sarcastic [sɑː'kæstɪk] *adj* ช่างเสียดสี [chang siat sii]

sardine [sɑː'diːn] *n* ปลาซาร์ดีน [pla sa din]

satchel ['sætʃəl] *n* กระเป๋าหนังสือ [kra pao nang sue]

satellite ['sætəlaɪt] *n* ดาวเทียม [dao thiam]; **satellite dish** *n* จานดาวเทียม [chan dao thiam]

satisfaction [ˌsætɪs'fækʃən] *n* ความพอใจ [khwam phor jai]

satisfactory [ˌsætɪs'fæktərɪ; -trɪ] *adj* ที่พึงพอใจ [thii phueng phor jai]

satisfied ['sætɪs,faɪd] *adj* พอใจ [pho chai]; **I'm not satisfied with this** ฉันไม่พอใจกับสิ่งนี้ [chan mai pho jai kap sing nii]

sat nav ['sæt næv] *n* เครื่องนำทาง นาวิเกเตอร์ [khrueang nam thang, na wi ke toe]

Saturday ['sætədɪ] *n* วันเสาร์ [wan sao]; **every Saturday** ทุกวันเสาร์ [thuk wan sao]; **last Saturday** วันเสาร์ที่แล้ว [wan sao thii laeo]; **next Saturday** วันเสาร์หน้า [wan sao na]

sauce [sɔːs] *n* น้ำปรุงรส [nam prung rot]; **soy sauce** *n* น้ำซีอิ๊ว [nam si io]; **tomato sauce** *n* ซอสมะเขือเทศ [sos ma khuea tet]

saucepan ['sɔːspən] *n* หม้อที่มีฝาปิดและมีด้ามยาว [mo thii mii fa pit lae mii dam yao]

saucer ['sɔːsə] *n* จานรอง [chan rong]

Saudi ['sɔːdɪ; 'saʊ-] *adj* เกี่ยวกับประเทศซาอุดิอาระเบีย [kiao kap pra thet sa u di a ra bia] ▷ *n* ชาวซาอุดิอาระเบีย [chao sa u di a ra bia]

Saudi Arabia ['sɔːdɪ; 'saʊ-] n ประเทศ
ซาอุดีอาระเบีย [pra tet sa u di a ra bia]

Saudi Arabian ['sɔːdɪ əˈreɪbɪən] adj
เกี่ยวกับประเทศซาอุดิอาระเบีย [kiao kap
pra thet sa u di a ra bia] ▷ n ชาวซาอุดี
อาศัยอยู่ในประเทศซาอุดิอาระเบีย [chao sa u
thii a sai yu nai pra ted su di a ra bia]

sauna ['sɔːnə] n การอบไอน้ำ [kan op ai
nam]

sausage ['sɒsɪdʒ] n ไส้กรอก [sai krok]

save [seɪv] v ช่วยชีวิต [chuai chi wit]

save up [seɪv ʌp] v เก็บเงิน [kep ngoen]

savings ['seɪvɪŋz] npl เงินออม [ngoen
om]

savoury ['seɪvərɪ] adj ที่เป็นของคาว [thii
pen khong khao]

saw [sɔː] n เลื่อย [lueai]

sawdust ['sɔːˌdʌst] n ขี้เลื่อย [khi lueai]

saxophone ['sæksəˌfəʊn] n แซ็กโซโฟน
[saek so fon]

say [seɪ] v พูด [phut]

saying ['seɪɪŋ] n การพูด [kan phut]

scaffolding ['skæfəldɪŋ] n โครงยกพื้นที่
ใช้สำหรับสร้างหรือซ่อมตึกหรือสถานที่ต่าง ๆ
[khrong yok phuen thii chai sam rap
sang rue som tuek rue sa than thii
tang tang]

scale [skeɪl] n (measure) การวัด [kan
wat], (tiny piece) เกล็ด [klet]

scales [skeɪlz] npl เครื่องชั่ง [khrueang
chang]

scallop ['skɒləp; 'skæl-] n หอยพัด [hoi
phat]

scam [skæm] n เล่ห์อุบาย [le u bai]

scampi ['skæmpɪ] npl กุ้งชุบแป้งทอด
[kung chup paeng thot]

scan [skæn] n การตรวจรายละเอียด [kan
truat rai la iad] ▷ v ตรวจรายละเอียด
[truat rai la iad]

scandal ['skændəl] n เรื่องอื้อฉาว
[rueang ue chao]

Scandinavia [ˌskændɪˈneɪvɪə] n กลุ่ม
ประเทศสแกนดิเนเวีย [klum pra tet sa
kaen di ne via]

Scandinavian [ˌskændɪˈneɪvɪən] adj
เกี่ยวกับดินแดนในยุโรปเหนือ [kiao kap
din daen nai yu rop nuea]

scanner ['skænə] n อุปกรณ์รับและส่ง
สัญญาณ [up pa kon rap lae song san
yan]

scar [skɑː] n แผลเป็น [phlae pen]

scarce [skɛəs] adj ไม่ค่อยพบ [mai khoi
phop]

scarcely ['skɛəslɪ] adv อย่างไม่พอเพียง
[yang mai pho phiang]

scare [skɛə] n ความหวาดกลัว [khwam
wat klua] ▷ v หวาดกลัว [wat klua]

scarecrow ['skɛəˌkrəʊ] n หุ่นไล่กา [hun
lai ka]

scared [skɛəd] adj ที่น่ากลัว [thii na
klua]

scarf, scarves [skɑːf, skɑːvz] n ผ้าพัน
คอ [pha phan kho]

scarlet ['skɑːlɪt] adj สีแดงสด [sii daeng
sot]

scary ['skɛərɪ] adj น่าตกใจ [na tok jai]

scene [siːn] n สถานที่เกิดเหตุ [sa than
thii koet het]

scenery ['siːnərɪ] n ทิวทัศน์ [thio that]

scent [sɛnt] n กลิ่น [klin]

sceptical ['skɛptɪkəl] adj น่าสงสัย [na
song sai]

schedule ['ʃɛdjuːl; 'skɛdʒʊəl] n ตาราง
เวลา [ta rang we la]

scheme [skiːm] n แผนการ [phaen kan]

schizophrenic [ˌskɪtsəʊˈfrɛnɪk] adj
โรคจิตชนิดหนึ่งที่มีสองบุคคลิกในคนคน
เดียว [rok chit cha nit nueng thii mii
song buk kha lik nai khon khon diao]

scholarship ['skɒləʃɪp] n ทุนเล่าเรียน
[thun lao rian]

school [skuːl] n โรงเรียน [rong rian]; **art
school** n โรงเรียนศิลปะ [rong rian sin la
pa]; **boarding school** n โรงเรียนประจำ
[rong rian pra cham]; **elementary
school** n โรงเรียนระดับประถมศึกษา [rong
rian ra dap pra thom suek sa]

schoolbag ['skuːlˌbæg] n กระเป๋านักเรียน

[kra pao nak rian]

schoolbook ['sku:l,bʊk] *n* หนังสือ โรงเรียน [nang sue rong rian]

schoolboy ['sku:l,bɔɪ] *n* เด็กนักเรียนชาย [dek nak rian chai]

schoolchildren ['sku:l,tʃɪldrən] *npl* เด็กนักเรียน [dek nak rian]

schoolgirl ['sku:l,gɜːl] *n* เด็กนักเรียนหญิง [dek nak rian hying]

schoolteacher ['sku:l,ti:tʃə] *n* ครูสอน นักเรียน [khru son nak rian]

science ['saɪəns] *n* วิชาวิทยาศาสตร์ [vi cha wit ta ya sard]; **science fiction** *n* นวนิยายวิทยาศาสตร์ [na wa ni yai wit tha ya saat]

scientific [,saɪən'tɪfɪk] *adj* ตามหลัก วิทยาศาสตร์ [tam lak wit ta ya sard]

scientist ['saɪəntɪst] *n* นักวิทยาศาสตร์ [nak wit ta ya sard]

scifi ['saɪ,faɪ] *n* นวนิยายวิทยาศาสตร์เรื่อง สั้น [na wa ni yai wit tha ya saat rueang san]

scissors ['sɪzəz] *npl* กรรไกร [kan krai]; **nail scissors** *npl* กรรไกรตัดเล็บ [kan krai tat lep]

sclerosis [sklɪə'rəʊsɪs] *n* **multiple sclerosis** *n* โรคเลือดคั่งในสมอง [rok lueat khang nai sa mong]

scoff [skɒf] *v* พูดเยาะเย้ย [put yo yoei]

scold [skəʊld] *v* ด่าว่า [du wa]

scooter ['sku:tə] *n* รถของเด็กเล่นที่ใช้เท้า ถีบ [rot khong dek len thii chai thao thip]

score [skɔ:] *n* (*game/match*) คะแนน [kha naen], (*of music*) โน้ตเพลง [not phleng] ▷ *v* ทำคะแนน [tham kha naen]

Scorpio ['skɔ:pɪ,əʊ] *n* ราศีพิจิก [ra si phi chik]

scorpion ['skɔ:pɪən] *n* แมลงป่อง [ma laeng pong]

Scot [skɒt] *n* ชาวสก็อตแลนด์ [chao sa kot laen]

Scotland ['skɒtlənd] *n* ประเทศสก็อต แลนด์ [pra ted sa kot laen]

Scots [skɒts] *adj* ชาวสก็อตแลนด์ [chao sa kot laen]

Scotsman, Scotsmen ['skɒtsmən, 'skɒtsmɛn] *n* ชายชาวสก็อตแลนด์ [chai chao sa kot laen]

Scotswoman, Scotswomen ['skɒts,wʊmən, 'skɒts,wɪmɪn] *n* หญิง ชาวสก็อตแลนด์ [ying chao sa kot laen]

Scottish ['skɒtɪʃ] *adj* เกี่ยวกับสก็อตแลนด์ [kiao kap sa kot laen]

scout [skaʊt] *n* ลูกเสือ [luk suea]

scrap [skræp] *n* (*dispute*) การต่อสู้ [kan to su], (*small piece*) เศษชิ้นเล็กชิ้นน้อย [set chin lek chin noi] ▷ *v* ต่อสู้ [to su]; **scrap paper** *n* กระดาษทด [kra dat thot]

scrapbook ['skræp,bʊk] *n* สมุดติดรูป หรือข่าวที่ตัดจากสื่อสิ่งตีพิมพ์ต่างๆ [sa mud tid rup hue khao thii tad chak sue sing ti phim tang tang]

scratch [skrætʃ] *n* รอยข่วน [roi khuan] ▷ *v* ขูดออก [khud ok]

scream [skri:m] *n* การกรีดร้อง [kan krit rong] ▷ *v* กรีดร้อง [krit rong]

screen [skri:n] *n* จอภาพ เช่นจอภาพยนตร์ จอทีวี [chor phap chen chor phap pa yon chor tee vee]; **plasma screen** *n* จอภาพแบน [cho phap baen]; **screen (off)** *v* หลบ กำบัง ป้องกัน ปกปิดเหมือนกับ มีฉากกัน [lop, kam bang, pong kan, pok pit muean kap mii chak kan]

screen-saver ['skri:n,seɪvə] *n* โปรแกรมรักษาจอภาพ [pro kraem rak sa cho phap]

screw [skru:] *n* ตะปูควง [ta pu khuang]

screwdriver ['skru:,draɪvə] *n* ไขควง [khai khuang]

scribble ['skrɪbəl] *v* เขียนหวัด ๆ [khian wat wat]

scrub [skrʌb] *v* ถูทำความสะอาดอย่างแรง [thu tham khwam sa aat yang raeng]

sculptor ['skʌlptə] *n* นักปั้น [nak pan]

sculpture ['skʌlptʃə] *n* รูปปั้น [rup pan]

sea [si:] *n* ทะเล [tha le]; **North Sea** *n* ทะเลเหนือ [tha le nuea]; **Red Sea** *n*

ทะเลแดง [tha le daeng]; **sea level** *n* ระดับน้ำทะเล [ra dap nam tha le]; **Is the sea rough today?** วันนี้มีพายุทะเลไหม? [wan nii mii pha yu tha le mai]

seafood ['siːˌfuːd] *n* อาหารทะเล [a han tha le]; **Could you prepare a meal without seafood?** คุณช่วยทำอาหารที่ไม่มีอาหารทะเลได้ไหม? [khun chuai tham a han thii mai mii a han tha le dai mai]; **Do you like seafood?** คุณชอบอาหารทะเลไหม? [khun chop a han tha le mai]

seagull ['siːˌɡʌl] *n* นกนางนวล [nok nang nuan]

seal [siːl] *n* (*animal*) แมวน้ำ [maeo nam], (*mark*) ตราประทับ [tra pra thap] ▷ *v* ปิดผนึก [pit pha nuek]

seam [siːm] *n* ตะเข็บ [ta khep]

seaman, seamen ['siːmən, 'siːmɛn] *n* ลูกเรือ [luk ruea]

search [sɜːtʃ] *n* การค้นหา [kan khon ha] ▷ *v* ค้นหา [khon ha]; **search engine** *n* กลไกการหาข้อมูลบนอินเตอร์เน็ต [kon kai kan ha kho mun bon in toe net]; **search party** *n* คณะผู้สำรวจผู้สูญหาย [kha na phu sam ruat phu sun hai]

seashore ['siːˌʃɔː] *n* ชายฝั่งทะเล [chai fang tha le]

seasick ['siːˌsɪk] *adj* เมาคลื่น [mao khluen]

seaside ['siːˌsaɪd] *n* ชายทะเล [chai tha le]

season ['siːzən] *n* ฤดู [rue du]; **high season** *n* ฤดูกาลที่มีธุรกิจมาก [rue du kan thii mii thu ra kit mak]; **low season** *n* ฤดูท่องเที่ยวที่มีนักท่องเที่ยวน้อย [rue du thong thiao thii mii nak thong thiao noi]; **season ticket** *n* ตั๋วทั้งฤดู [tua thang rue du]

seasonal ['siːzənˀl] *adj* ตามฤดูกาล [tam rue du kan]

seasoning ['siːzənɪŋ] *n* การปรุงรส [kan prung rot]

seat [siːt] *n* (*constituency*) ที่นั่งในรัฐสภา [thii nang nai rat tha sa pha], (*furniture*) เก้าอี้นั่ง [kao ee nang]; **aisle seat** *n* ที่นั่งระหว่างทางเดินในเครื่องบิน [thii nang ra wang thang doen nai khrueang bin]; **window seat** *n* ที่นั่งใกล้หน้าต่าง [thii nang klai na tang]

seatbelt ['siːtˌbɛlt] *n* เข็มขัดนิรภัย [khem khat ni ra phai]

seaweed ['siːˌwiːd] *n* สาหร่ายทะเล [sa rai tha le]

second ['sɛkənd] *adj* ที่สอง [thii song] ▷ *n* ลำดับที่สอง [lam dap thii song]; **second class** *n* ชั้นที่สอง [chan thii song]

second-class ['sɛkəndˌklɑːs] *adj* อันดับสอง [an dab song]

secondhand ['sɛkəndˌhænd] *adj* มือสอง [mue song]

secondly ['sɛkəndlɪ] *adv* ในลำดับที่สอง [nai lam dap thii song]

second-rate ['sɛkəndˌreɪt] *adj* ชั้นรอง [chan rong]

secret ['siːkrɪt] *adj* เป็นความลับ [pen khwam lap] ▷ *n* ความลับ [khwam lap]; **secret service** *n* หน่วยสืบราชการลับ [nuai suep rat cha kan lap]

secretary ['sɛkrətrɪ] *n* เลขานุการ [le kha nu kan]

secretly ['siːkrɪtlɪ] *adv* อย่างลับ ๆ [yang lap lap]

sect [sɛkt] *n* นิกายทางศาสนาที่แยกออกมา [ni kai thang sad sa na thii yaek ork ma]

section ['sɛkʃən] *n* ส่วนที่ตัดออก [suan thii tat ok]

sector ['sɛktə] *n* ภาคหรือกลุ่ม [phak rue klum]

secure [sɪ'kjʊə] *adj* ปลอดภัย [plot phai]

security [sɪ'kjʊərɪtɪ] *n* ความปลอดภัย [khwam plot phai]; **security guard** *n* ผู้คุ้มกันความปลอดภัย [phu khum kan khwam plot phai]; **social security** *n* การประกันสังคม [kan pra kan sang khom]

sedative [ˈsɛdətɪv] n ยาระงับประสาท [ya ra ngap pra saat]

see [siː] v เห็น [hen]; **Have you seen the guard?** คุณเห็นคนเฝ้ารถไฟไหม? [khun hen khon fao rot fai mai]

seed [siːd] n เมล็ดพืช [ma let phuet]

seek [siːk] v หา [ha]

seem [siːm] v ที่ปรากฏ [thii pra kot]

seesaw [ˈsiːˌsɔː] n แผนกระดานหก [phaen kra dan hok]

see-through [ˈsiːˌθruː] adj โปร่งใส [prong sai]

seize [siːz] v ฉกฉวย [chok chuai]

seizure [ˈsiːʒə] n การจับ การยึด [kan chap, kan yued]

seldom [ˈsɛldəm] adv ไม่ค่อยจะ [mai khoi ja]

select [sɪˈlɛkt] v เลือก [lueak]

selection [sɪˈlɛkʃən] n การคัดเลือก [kan khat lueak]

self-assured [ˈsɛlfəˈʃʊəd] adj ซึ่งเชื่อมั่นในตัวเอง [sueng chuea man nai tua eng]

self-catering [ˈsɛlfˌkeɪtərɪŋ] n อาหารของตนเอง [a han khong ton ang]

self-centred [ˈsɛlfˌsɛntəd] adj ซึ่งเห็นแก่ตัวเอง [sueng hen kae tua eng]

self-conscious [ˈsɛlfˈkɒnʃəs] adj มีสติรู้ตัว [mii sa ti ru tua]

self-contained [ˈsɛlfˌkənˈteɪnd] adj ซึ่งมีทุกอย่างพร้อมในตัว [sueng mii thuk yang prom nai tua]

self-control [ˈsɛlfˌkənˈtrəʊl] n การข่มใจตัวเอง [kan khom jai tua eng]

self-defence [ˈsɛlfˌdɪˈfɛns] n การป้องกันตัวเอง [kan pong kan tua eng]

self-discipline [ˈsɛlfˌdɪsɪplɪn] n การทำให้มีระเบียบวินัย [kan tham hai mii ra biap wi nai]

self-employed [ˈsɛlɪmˈplɔɪd] adj การทำงานด้วยตัวเอง [kan tham ngan duai tua eng]

selfish [ˈsɛlfɪʃ] adj เห็นแก่ตัว [hen kae tua]

self-service [ˈsɛlfˌsɜːvɪs] adj แบบบริการตัวเอง [baep bo ri kan tua eng]

sell [sɛl] v ขาย [khai]; **sell-by date** n ขายก่อนหมดวันที่กำหนด [khai kon mot wan thii kam nod]; **selling price** n ราคาขาย [ra kha khai]; **Do you sell phone cards?** คุณขายการ์ดโทรศัพท์ไหม? [khun khai kaat tho ra sap mai]

sell off [sɛl ɒf] v ขายในราคาถูก [khai nai ra kha thuk]

Sellotape® [ˈsɛləˌteɪp] n เทปใส [thep sai]

sell out [sɛl aʊt] v ขายหมด [khai mot]

semester [sɪˈmɛstə] n เทอม [thoem]

semi [ˈsɛmɪ] n ครึ่งหนึ่ง [khrueng hueng]

semicircle [ˈsɛmɪˌsɜːk[l] n ครึ่งวงกลม [khueng wong klom]

semicolon [ˌsɛmɪˈkəʊlən] n เครื่องหมายอัฒภาค [khrueang mai at ta phak]

semifinal [ˌsɛmɪˈfaɪnᵊl] n การแข่งขันกีฬารอบรองชนะเลิศ [kan khaeng khan ki la rop rong cha na loet]

send [sɛnd] v ส่ง [song]; **Can I send a fax from here?** ฉันส่งโทรสารจากที่นี่ได้ไหม? [chan song tho ra san chak thii ni dai mai]; **Can I send an email?** ฉันส่งอีเมลล์ได้ไหม? [chan song e mail dai mai]; **How much is it to send this parcel?** ราคาส่งกล่องพัสดุใบนี้เท่าไร? [ra kha song klong phat sa du bai nii thao rai]

send back [sɛnd bæk] v ส่งกลับ [song klap]

sender [ˈsɛndə] n ผู้ส่ง [phu song]

send off [sɛnd ɒf] v ส่งออกไป [song ork pai]

send out [sɛnd aʊt] v ส่งออกไป [song ork pai]

Senegal [ˌsɛnɪˈgɔːl] n สาธารณรัฐเซเนกัลในอัฟริกา [sa tha ra na rat se ne kal nai af ri ka]

Senegalese [ˌsɛnɪgəˈliːz] adj เกี่ยวกับสาธารณรัฐเซเนกัล [kiao kap sa tha ra na rat se ne kal] ▷ n ชาวเซเนกัล [chao se ne kal]

senior ['siːnjə] *adj* ผู้อาวุโส [phu a wu
so]; **senior citizen** *n* พลเมืองอาวุโส
[phon la mueang a wu so]

sensational [sɛnˈseɪʃənˀl] *adj* น่าเร้าใจ
[na rao jai]

sense [sɛns] *n* ความรู้สึก [khwam ru
suek]; **sense of humour** *n* การมีอารมณ์
ขัน [kan mii a rom khan]

senseless ['sɛnslɪs] *adj* โง่เขลา [ngo
khlao]

sensible ['sɛnsɪbˀl] *adj* มีความน่าเชื่อ
[mii khwam na chuea]

sensitive ['sɛnsɪtɪv] *adj* ซึ่งไวต่อสิ่ง
กระตุ้น [sueng wai to sing kra tun]

sensuous ['sɛnsjʊəs] *adj* กระตุ้นให้เกิด
ความรู้สึกในทางสวยงาม [kra tun hai
koed khwam ru suk nai thang suai
ngam]

sentence ['sɛntəns] *n (punishment)* การ
พิพากษา [kan phi phak sa], *(words)*
ประโยค [pra yok] ▷ *v* ตัดสินลงโทษ [tat
sin long thot]

sentimental [ˌsɛntɪˈmɛntˀl] *adj* ซึ่ง
สะเทือนอารมณ์ [sueng sa thuean ar
rom]

separate *adj* ['sɛpərɪt] ซึ่งแยกออกจากกัน
[sueng yaek ork chak kan] ▷ *v*
['sɛpəˌreɪt] แยกออกจาก [yaek ork chak]

separately ['sɛpərətlɪ] *adv* อย่างแยก
ออกจากกัน [yang yaek ork chak kan]

separation [ˌsɛpəˈreɪʃən] *n* การแยกจาก
กัน [kan yaek chak kan]

September [sɛpˈtɛmbə] *n* เดือนกันยายน
[duean kan ya yon]

sequel ['siːkwəl] *n* เรื่องราวที่ติดตามมา
[rueang rao thii tit tam ma]

sequence ['siːkwəns] *n* เหตุการณ์ที่เกิด
ขึ้นตามลำดับ [het kan thii koet khuen
tam lam dap]

Serbia ['sɜːbɪə] *n* ประเทศเซอร์เบีย [pra tet
soe bia]

Serbian ['sɜːbɪən] *adj* เกี่ยวกับเซอร์เบีย
[kiao kap soe bia] ▷ *n (language)* ภาษา

เซอร์เบีย [pha sa soe bia], *(person)* ชาว
เซอร์เบีย [chao soe bia]

sergeant ['sɑːdʒənt] *n* จ่า [cha]

serial ['sɪərɪəl] *n* ที่เป็นตอน ๆ [thii pen
ton ton]

series ['sɪəriːz; -rɪz] *n* สิ่งที่ต่อเนื่องกัน
[sing thii to nueang kan]

serious ['sɪərɪəs] *adj* เคร่งขรึม [khreng
khruem]

seriously ['sɪərɪəslɪ] *adv* อย่างจริงจัง
[yang ching chang]

sermon ['sɜːmən] *n* การเทศนา การให้
โอวาท [kan ted sa na, kan hai o wat]

servant ['sɜːvˀnt] *n* คนรับใช้ [khon rap
chai]; **civil servant** *n* ข้าราชการพลเรือน
[kha rat cha kan phon la ruean]

serve [sɜːv] *n* การเสิร์ฟลูกเทนนิส [kan
soep luk then nis] ▷ *v* บริการ [bo ri kan];
We are still waiting to be served เรา
ยังรอให้คุณมาบริการเรา [rao yang ro hai
khun ma bo ri kan rao]

server ['sɜːvə] *n (computer)* บริการของ
คอมพิวเตอร์ [bor ri kan khong khom pio
ter], *(person)* คนที่คอยบริการ [kon thii
khoi bor ri kan]

service ['sɜːvɪs] *n* การบริการ [kan bor ri
kan] ▷ *v* การให้ความช่วยเหลือ [kan hai
khwam chuai hluea]; **room service** *n*
บริการรับใช้ในห้องของโรงแรม [bo ri kan
rap chai nai hong khong rong raeng];
secret service *n* หน่วยสืบราชการลับ
[nuai suep rat cha kan lap]; **service
area** *n* พื้นที่บริการ [phuen thii bo ri
kan]; **I want to complain about the
service** ฉันอยากร้องเรียนเกี่ยวกับการ
บริการ [chan yak rong rian kiao kap
kan bo ri kan]

serviceman, servicemen
['sɜːvɪsˌmæn; -mən, 'sɜːvɪsˌmɛn] *n* ผู้
ที่รับราชการทหาร [phu thii rab rat cha
kan tha han]

servicewoman, servicewomen
['sɜːvɪsˌwʊmən, 'sɜːvɪsˌwɪmɪn] *n* สตรี
ที่รับราชการทหาร [sa tree thii rap rat

cha kan tha han]

serviette [ˌsɜːvɪˈɛt] n ผ้าเช็ดปากบนโต๊ะอาหาร [pha ched pak bon to a han]

session [ˈsɛʃən] n ระยะเวลา [ra ya we la]

set [sɛt] n ชุด [chut] ▷ v วาง จัดเตรียม ตั้งเวลา ตั้งระบบ [wang, chat triam, tang we la, tang ra bop]

setback [ˈsɛtbæk] n ทำให้ช้า [tham hai cha]

set menu [sɛt ˈmɛnjuː] n รายการอาหารเป็นชุด [rai kan a han pen chut]

set off [sɛt ɒf] v เริ่มเดินทาง [roem doen thang]

set out [sɛt aʊt] v เริ่มออกเดินทาง [roem ok doen thang]

settee [sɛˈtiː] n ที่นั่งมีพนักพิงและที่วางแขน [thii nang mii pha nak phing lae thii wang khaen]

settle [ˈsɛtəl] v แก้ปัญหา [kae pan ha]

settle down [ˈsɛtəl daʊn] v ตั้งหลักฐาน [tang lak than]

seven [ˈsɛvən] number เจ็ด [chet]

seventeen [ˈsɛvənˈtiːn] number สิบเจ็ด [sip chet]

seventeenth [ˈsɛvənˈtiːnθ] adj ที่สิบเจ็ด [thii sip chet]

seventh [ˈsɛvənθ] adj ที่เจ็ด [thii chet] ▷ n ลำดับที่เจ็ด [lam dap thii chet]

seventy [ˈsɛvəntɪ] number เจ็ดสิบ [chet sip]

several [ˈsɛvrəl] adj หลาย [lai] ▷ pron หลาย [lai]

sew [səʊ] v เย็บ [yep]

sewer [ˈsuːə] n ท่อน้ำเสีย [tho nam sia]

sewing [ˈsəʊɪŋ] n การเย็บ [kan yep]; **sewing machine** n จักรเย็บผ้า [chak yep pha]

sew up [səʊ ʌp] v ซ่อมแซมโดยการเย็บ [som saem doi kan yep]

sex [sɛks] n เพศ [phet]; **Do you have any single sex dorms?** คุณมีหอพักสำหรับเพศเดียวกันไหม? [khun mii ho phak sam rap phet diao kan mai]

sexism [ˈsɛksɪzəm] n การกีดกันทางเพศ

[kan kit kan thang phet]

sexist [ˈsɛksɪst] adj การแบ่งแยกเพศ [kan baeng yaek phet]

sexual [ˈsɛksjʊəl] adj เกี่ยวกับเพศ [kiao kap phet]; **sexual intercourse** n การมีความสัมพันธ์ทางเพศ [kan mii khwam sam phan thang phet]

sexuality [ˌsɛksjʊˈælɪtɪ] n เรื่องทางเพศ [rueang thang phet]

sexy [ˈsɛksɪ] adj ที่ดึงดูดทางเพศ [thii dueng dud thang phed]

shabby [ˈʃæbɪ] adj มองดูเก่า [mong du kao]

shade [ʃeɪd] n ร่ม ที่ร่ม [rom, thii rom]

shadow [ˈʃædəʊ] n เงา [ngao]; **eye shadow** n อายแชร์โดว์ [ai chae do]

shake [ʃeɪk] vi สั่นสะเทือน หวั่นไหว [san sa thuean, wan wai] ▷ vt สั่น ทำให้สั่น ทำให้ตกใจและสะเทือนใจ [san, tham hai san, tham hai tok jai lae sa thuean jai]

shaken [ˈʃeɪkən] adj ที่ทำให้ว้าวุ่นใจ [thii tham hai wa wun jai]

shaky [ˈʃeɪkɪ] adj สั่นคลอน [san khlon]

shallow [ˈʃæləʊ] adj ตื้น [tuen]

shambles [ˈʃæmbəlz] npl ความยุ่งเหยิง ความโกลาหล สถานการณ์สับสนวุนวาย [khwam yung yoeng, khwam ko la hon, sa than na kan sap son wun wai]

shame [ʃeɪm] n ความอับอาย [khwam ap ai]

shampoo [ʃæmˈpuː] n ยาสระผม [ya sa phom]; **Do you sell shampoo?** คุณขายยาสระผมไหม? [khun khai ya sa phom mai]

shape [ʃeɪp] n รูปร่าง [rup rang]

share [ʃɛə] n ส่วนแบ่ง [suan baeng] ▷ v แบ่งส่วน [baeng suan]

shareholder [ˈʃɛəˌhəʊldə] n ผู้ถือหุ้น [phu thue hun]

share out [ʃɛə aʊt] v แบ่งออก [baeng ok]

shark [ʃɑːk] n ฉลาม [cha lam]

sharp [ʃɑːp] adj แหลม คม [laem, khom]

shave [ʃeɪv] v โกน [kon]; **shaving cream** n ครีมโกนหนวด [khrim kon nuat]; **shaving foam** *n* โฟมโกนหนวด [fom kon nuat]

shaver ['ʃeɪvə] *n* มีดโกนไฟฟ้า [miit kon fai fa]

shawl [ʃɔːl] *n* ผ้าคลุมไหล่ [pha khlum lai]

she [ʃiː] *pron* เธอ [thoe]

shed [ʃɛd] *n* เพิงเก็บของ [phoeng kep khong]

sheep [ʃiːp] *n* แกะ [kae]

sheepdog ['ʃiːpˌdɒg] *n* สุนัขที่ไล่ต้อนแกะ [su nak thii lai ton kae]

sheepskin ['ʃiːpˌskɪn] *n* หนังแกะ [nang kae]

sheer [ʃɪə] *adj* เต็มที่ [tem thi]

sheet [ʃiːt] *n* ผ้าปูที่นอน [pha pu thi non]; **My sheets are dirty** ผ้าปูที่นอนฉันสกปรก [pha pu thii non chan sok ka prok]; **The sheets are dirty** ผ้าปูที่นอนสกปรก [pha pu thii non sok ka prok]; **We need more sheets** เราอยากได้ผ้าปูที่นอนเพิ่มอีก [rao yak dai pha pu thii non poem ik]

shelf, shelves [ʃɛlf, ʃɛlvz] *n* ชั้นวาง [chan wang]

shell [ʃɛl] *n* เปลือก [plueak]; **shell suit** *n* ชุดกีฬาในลอน [chut ki la nai lon]

shellfish ['ʃɛlˌfɪʃ] *n* สัตว์น้ำประเภทมีเปลือก [sat nam pra phet mii plueak]

shelter ['ʃɛltə] *n* ที่กำบัง [thii kam bang]

shepherd ['ʃɛpəd] *n* คนเลี้ยงแกะ [khon liang kae]

sherry ['ʃɛrɪ] *n* เหล้าเชอร์รี่ [lao choe ri]

shield [ʃiːld] *n* โล่ห์ [lo]

shift [ʃɪft] *n* การเคลื่อนย้าย การย้าย [kan khluean yai, kan yai] ▷ *v* เคลื่อนย้าย [khluean yai]

shifty ['ʃɪftɪ] *adj* ซึ่งมีกลอุบาย [sueng mii kon u bai]

Shiite ['ʃiːaɪt] *adj* นิกายชีอะ [ni kai chi a]

shin [ʃɪn] *n* คาง [khang]

shine [ʃaɪn] *v* ทำให้ส่องแสง [tham hai song saeng]

shiny ['ʃaɪnɪ] *adj* ซึ่งเป็นมันเงา [sueng pen man ngao]

ship [ʃɪp] *n* เรือ [ruea]

shipbuilding ['ʃɪpˌbɪldɪŋ] *n* การสร้างเรือ [kan srang ruea]

shipment ['ʃɪpmənt] *n* จำนวนสินค้าที่ขนส่งทางเรือ [cham nuan sin ka thii khon song thang ruea]

shipwreck ['ʃɪpˌrɛk] *n* เรือแตก [ruea taek]

shipwrecked ['ʃɪpˌrɛkt] *adj* ทำให้เรืออับปาง [tham hai ruea ap pang]

shipyard ['ʃɪpˌjaːd] *n* อู่ซ่อมและต่อเรือ [u som lae to ruea]

shirt [ʃɜːt] *n* เสื้อเชิ้ต [suea choet]; **polo shirt** *n* เสื้อเชิ้ตแขนสั้นมีปกและกระดุมสามเม็ดตรงสาบคอ [suea choet khaen san mii pok lae kra dum sam met trong sap kho]

shiver ['ʃɪvə] *v* สั่นเพราะหนาวหรือความกลัว [san phro nao rue khwam klua]

shock [ʃɒk] *n* ความตกใจ [khwam tok jai] ▷ *v* ตกใจ [tok chai]; **electric shock** *n* กระแสไฟดูด [kra sae fai dut]

shocking ['ʃɒkɪŋ] *adj* ซึ่งตกใจสุดขีด [sueng tok jai sut khit]

shoe [ʃuː] *n* รองเท้า [rong thao]; **Can you re-heel these shoes?** คุณใส่ส้นรองเท้านี้ได้ไหม? [khun sai son rong thao nii dai mai]; **Can you repair these shoes?** คุณซ่อมรองเท้านี้ได้ไหม? [khun som rong thao nii dai mai]; **I have a hole in my shoe** รองเท้าฉันนี้มีรู [rong thao chan mii ru]

shoelace ['ʃuːˌleɪs] *n* เชือกผูกรองเท้า [chueak phuk rong thao]

shoot [ʃuːt] *v* ยิง [ying]

shooting ['ʃuːtɪŋ] *n* การยิง [kan ying]

shop [ʃɒp] *n* ร้าน [ran]; **antique shop** *n* ร้านขายของเก่า [ran khai khong kao]; **gift shop** *n* ร้านขายของขวัญ [ran khai khong khwan]; **shop assistant** *n* พนักงานขายของ [pha nak ngan khai khong]; **What time do the shops close?** ร้านต่างๆ ปิดเมื่อไร? [ran tang

tang pid muea rai]

shopkeeper ['ʃɒpˌkiːpə] n เจ้าของร้าน [chao khong ran]

shoplifting ['ʃɒpˌlɪftɪŋ] n การลักขโมยของในร้าน [kan lak ka moi khong nai ran]

shopping ['ʃɒpɪŋ] n การซื้อของ [kan sue khong]; **shopping bag** n ถุงใส่ของ [thung sai khong]; **shopping centre** n ศูนย์การค้า [sun kan kha]; **shopping trolley** n รถเข็นในห้างสรรพสินค้า [rot khen nai hang sap pha sin ka]

shore [ʃɔː] n ชายฝั่ง [chai fang]

short [ʃɔːt] adj สั้น [san]; **short story** n เรื่องสั้น [rueang san]

shortage ['ʃɔːtɪdʒ] n การขาดแคลน [kan khat khlaen]

shortcoming ['ʃɔːtˌkʌmɪŋ] n ข้อบกพร่อง [kho bok phrong]

shortcut ['ʃɔːtˌkʌt] n ทางลัด [thang lat]

shortfall ['ʃɔːtˌfɔːl] n จำนวนที่ขาดไป [cham nuan thii khat pai]

shorthand ['ʃɔːtˌhænd] n ชวเลข [cha wa lek]

shortlist ['ʃɔːtˌlɪst] n รายการที่สั้นลง [rai kan thii san long]

shortly ['ʃɔːtlɪ] adv ในเร็ว ๆ นี้ [nai reo reo nii]

shorts [ʃɔːts] npl กางเกงขาสั้น [kang keng kha san]

short-sighted ['ʃɔːt'saɪtɪd] adj ซึ่งมีสายตาสั้น [sueng mii sai ta san]

short-sleeved ['ʃɔːtˌsliːvd] adj แขนสั้น [khaen san]

shot [ʃɒt] n การยิง [kan ying]

shotgun ['ʃɒtˌgʌn] n ปืนล่าสัตว์ [puen la sat]

shoulder ['ʃəʊldə] n ไหล่ [lai]; **hard shoulder** n ไหล่ทาง [lai thang]; **shoulder blade** n หัวไหล่ [hua lai]; **I've hurt my shoulder** ฉันปวดไหล่ [chan puat lai]

shout [ʃaʊt] n การตะโกน [kan ta khon] ▷ v ตะโกน [ta kon]

shovel ['ʃʌvəl] n พลั่ว [phlua]

show [ʃəʊ] n การแสดง [kan sa daeng] ▷ v แสดง [sa daeng]; **show business** n ธุรกิจการบันเทิง [thu ra kit kan ban thoeng]; **two for the eight o'clock showing** สองที่สำหรับการแสดงรอบ แปดโมง [song thii sam hrab kan sa daeng rob paed mong]

shower ['ʃaʊə] n การอาบน้ำฝักบัว [kan aab nam fak bua]; **shower cap** n หมวกอาบน้ำ [muak aap nam]; **shower gel** n เจลอาบน้ำ [chen aap nam]

showerproof ['ʃaʊəˌpruːf] adj ที่ป้องกันน้ำได้ [thii pong kan nam dai]

showing ['ʃəʊɪŋ] n การแสดง [kan sa daeng]

show off [ʃəʊ ɒf] v แสดงออก [sa daeng ok]

show-off [ʃəʊɒf] n คนที่ชอบโอ้อวด [khon thii chop o uad]

show up [ʃəʊ ʌp] v เปิดเผยให้เห็น [poet phoei hai hen]

shriek [ʃriːk] v หวีดร้อง [wit rong]

shrimp [ʃrɪmp] n กุ้ง [kung]

shrine [ʃraɪn] n แทนบูชา [thaen bu cha]

shrink [ʃrɪŋk] v หด [hot]

shrub [ʃrʌb] n พุ่มไม้ [phum mai]

shrug [ʃrʌg] v ยักไหล่เพื่อแสดงความไม่สนใจหรือไม่ทราบ [yak lai phuea sa daeng khwam mai son jai rue mai sap]

shrunk [ʃrʌŋk] adj ที่หดลง [thii hot long]

shudder ['ʃʌdə] v สั่นระริกด้วยความกลัว [san ra rik duai khwam klua]

shuffle ['ʃʌfəl] v เดินลากเท้า [doen lak thao]

shut [ʃʌt] v ปิด [pit]

shut down [ʃʌt daʊn] v ปิดลง [pid long]

shutters ['ʃʌtəz] n บานเกล็ดหน้าต่าง [baan klet na tang]

shuttle ['ʃʌtəl] n พาหนะขนส่งสาธารณะ [pha ha na khon song sa tha ra na]

shuttlecock ['ʃʌtəlˌkɒk] n ลูกขนไก่ [luk khon kai]

shut up [ʃʌt ʌp] v หุบปาก [hup pak]

shy [ʃaɪ] adj ขี้อาย [khii ai]

Siberia [saɪˈbɪərɪə] n ประเทศไซบีเรีย [pra tet sai bi ria]

siblings [ˈsɪblɪŋz] npl พี่น้อง [phi nong]

sick [sɪk] adj คลื่นไส้ [khluen sai]; **sick leave** n การลาป่วย [kan la puai]; **sick note** n จดหมายลาป่วยที่แพทย์เป็นผู้เขียน [chot mai la puai thii phaet pen phu khian]; **sick pay** n ค่าจ้างในระหว่างที่ลาป่วย [kha chang nai ra wang thii la puai]

sickening [ˈsɪkənɪŋ] adj น่าสะอิดสะเอียน [na sa it sa ian]

sickness [ˈsɪknɪs] n ความเจ็บป่วย [khwam chep puai]; **morning sickness** n แพ้ท้อง [phae thong]; **travel sickness** n อาการเมารถ เรือหรือเครื่องบิน [a kan mao rot ruea rue khrueang bin]

side [saɪd] n ด้าน [dan]; **side effect** n ผลข้างเคียง [phon khang khiang]; **side street** n ทางแยกจากถนนใหญ่ [thang yaek chak tha non yai]

sideboard [ˈsaɪdˌbɔːd] n ตู้เก็บเครื่องใช้หรือภาชนะที่ใช้ในการรับประทานอาหาร [tu kep khrueang chai rue pha cha na thii chai nai kan rap pra than a han]

sidelight [ˈsaɪdˌlaɪt] n ไฟข้าง [fai khang]

sideways [ˈsaɪdˌweɪz] adv เคลื่อนไปด้านข้าง [khluean pai dan khang]

sieve [sɪv] n ที่กรอง [thii krong]

sigh [saɪ] n การถอนหายใจ [kan thon hai jai] ▷ v ถอนหายใจ [thon hai chai]

sight [saɪt] n การมองเห็น [kan mong hen]

sightseeing [ˈsaɪtˌsiːɪŋ] n การเยี่ยมชม [kan yiam chom]

sign [saɪn] n ป้าย [pai] ▷ v เซ็นต์ชื่อ [sen chue]; **road sign** n ป้ายจราจร [pai cha ra chon]; **sign language** n ภาษาสัญลักษณ์ [pha sa san ya lak]

signal [ˈsɪgnəl] n สัญญาณ [san yan] ▷ v ให้สัญญาณ [hai san yan]; **busy signal** n สัญญาณไม่ว่าง [san yan mai wang]

signature [ˈsɪgnɪtʃə] n ลายเซ็น [lai sen]

significance [sɪgˈnɪfɪkəns] n ผลที่ตามมา [phon thii tam ma]

significant [sɪgˈnɪfɪkənt] adj ซึ่งสำคัญ [sueng sam khan]

sign on [saɪn ɒn] v เซ็นต์ลงทะเบียนเพื่อรับเงินสวัสดิการ [sen long tha bian phuea rap ngoen sa wat sa di kan]

signpost [ˈsaɪnˌpəʊst] n เสาติดป้ายบอกทางตามถนน [sao tid pai bork thang tam tha non]

Sikh [siːk] adj เกี่ยวกับศาสนาซิกซ์ [kiao kap sat sa na sik] ▷ n ชาวศาสนาซิกซ์ [chao sat sa na sik]

silence [ˈsaɪləns] n ความเงียบ [khwam ngiap]

silencer [ˈsaɪlənsə] n เครื่องกำจัดเสียงในรถ [khueang kam chad siang nai rot]

silent [ˈsaɪlənt] adj เงียบ [ngiap]

silk [sɪlk] n ไหม [mai]

silly [ˈsɪlɪ] adj โง่ [ngo]

silver [ˈsɪlvə] n เงิน [ngoen]

similar [ˈsɪmɪlə] adj คล้ายคลึง [khlai khlueng]

similarity [ˈsɪmɪˈlærɪtɪ] n ความคล้ายคลึง [khwam khlai khlueng]

simmer [ˈsɪmə] v ตุ๋น [tun]

simple [ˈsɪmpªl] adj ง่าย [ngai]

simplify [ˈsɪmplɪˌfaɪ] v ทำให้ง่ายขึ้น [tham hai ngai khuen]

simply [ˈsɪmplɪ] adv อย่างง่าย ๆ [yang ngai ngai]

simultaneous [ˌsɪməlˈteɪnɪəs; ˌsaɪməlˈteɪnɪəs] adj ที่พร้อมกัน [thii phrom kan]

simultaneously [ˌsɪməlˈteɪnɪəslɪ] adv โดยเกิดขึ้นพร้อมกัน [doi koet khuen phrom kan]

sin [sɪn] n บาป [bap]

since [sɪns] adv จากนั้นมา [chak nan ma] ▷ conj เนื่องจาก [nueang chak] ▷ prep ตั้งแต่ [tang tae]; **I've been sick since Monday** ฉันป่วยตั้งแต่วันจันทร์

[chan puai tang tae wan chan]

sincere [sɪn'sɪə] *adj* จริงใจ [ching chai]

sincerely [sɪn'sɪəlɪ] *adv* อย่างจริงใจ [yang ching jai]

sing [sɪŋ] *v* ร้องเพลง [rong phleng]

singer ['sɪŋə] *n* นักร้อง [nak rong]; **lead singer** *n* นักร้องนำ [nak rong nam]

singing ['sɪŋɪŋ] *n* การร้องเพลง [kan rong phleng]

single ['sɪŋgəl] *adj* เดี่ยว [diao] ▷ *n* ห้องเดี่ยว [hong diao]; **single bed** *n* เตียงเดี่ยว [tiang diao]; **single parent** *n* พ่อหรือแม่ที่เลี้ยงลูกคนเดียว [pho rue mae thii liang luk khon diao]; **single room** *n* ห้องเดี่ยว [hong diao]; **I want to reserve a single room** ฉันอยากจองห้องเดี่ยวหนึ่งห้อง [chan yak chong hong diao nueng hong]

singles ['sɪŋgəlz] *npl* การเล่นเดี่ยว [kan len diao]

singular ['sɪŋgjʊlə] *n* เอกพจน์ [ek ka pot]

sinister ['sɪnɪstə] *adj* ชั่วร้าย [chua rai]

sink [sɪŋk] *n* อ่างสำหรับล้าง [ang sam rap lang] ▷ *v* จม [chom]

sinus ['saɪnəs] *n* โพรงกระดูกในศีรษะ [phrong kra duk nai si sa]

sir [sɜː] *n* คำสุภาพสำหรับเรียกผู้ชาย [kham su phap sam rap riak phu chai]

siren ['saɪərən] *n* เสียงสัญญาณเตือนภัย [siang san yan tuean phai]

sister ['sɪstə] *n* พี่สาวหรือน้องสาว [phi sao rue nong sao]

sister-in-law ['sɪstə ɪn lɔː] *n* น้องสะใภ้หรือพี่สะใภ้ [nong sa phai rue phii sa phai]

sit [sɪt] *v* นั่ง [nang]; **Can I sit here?** ฉันนั่งที่นี่ได้ไหม? [chan nang thii ni dai mai]

sitcom ['sɪtˌkɒm] *n* ตลกที่เกิดจากการสร้างสถานการณ์ [ta lok thii koed chak kan srang sa than na kan]

sit down [sɪt daʊn] *v* นั่งลง [nang long]

site [saɪt] *n* สถานที่ตั้ง [sa than thii tang]; **building site** *n* บริเวณที่ก่อสร้าง [bo ri wen thii ko sang]; **caravan site** *n* ที่จอดรถคาราวาน [thii jot rot kha ra wan]

situated ['sɪtjʊˌeɪtɪd] *adj* ซึ่งตั้งอยู่ [sueng tang yu]

situation [ˌsɪtjʊ'eɪʃən] *n* สถานการณ์ [sa tha na kan]

six [sɪks] *number* หก [hok]; **It's six o'clock** เวลาหกโมง [we la hok mong]

sixteen ['sɪks'tiːn] *number* สิบหก [sip hok]

sixteenth ['sɪks'tiːnθ] *adj* ที่สิบหก [thii sip hok]

sixth [sɪksθ] *adj* ที่หก [thii hok]

sixty ['sɪkstɪ] *number* หกสิบ [hok sip]

size [saɪz] *n* ขนาด [kha nat]; **Do you have this in a bigger size?** คุณมีขนาดใหญ่กว่าตัวนี้ไหม? [khun mii kha nat yai kwa tua nii mai]; **Do you have this in a smaller size?** คุณมีขนาดเล็กกว่าตัวนี้ไหม? [khun mii kha nat lek kwa tua nii mai]; **I'm a size 16** ฉันขนาดเบอร์สิบหก [chan kha nat boe sip hok]

skate [skeɪt] *v* เล่นสเก็ต [len sa ket]; **Where can we go ice-skating?** เราจะไปเล่นสเก็ตน้ำแข็งได้ที่ไหน? [rao ja pai len sa ket nam khaeng dai thii nai]; **Where can we go roller skating?** เราจะไปเล่นสเก็ตกระดานได้ที่ไหน? [rao ja pai len sa ket kra dan dai thii nai]

skateboard ['skeɪtˌbɔːd] *n* กระดานเล่นสเก็ตซึ่งมีล้อเล็กๆช่วยให้เคลื่อนที่ [kra dan len sa ket sueng mee lor lek lek chuai hai khluean tee]

skateboarding ['skeɪtˌbɔːdɪŋ] *n* การเล่นกระดานสเก็ต [kan len kra dan sa ket]

skates [skeɪts] *npl* รองเท้าสเก็ต [rong thao sa ket]

skating ['skeɪtɪŋ] *n* กีฬาการเล่นสเก็ต [ki la kan len sa ket]; **skating rink** *n* ลานเล่นสเก็ต [lan len sa ket]

skeleton ['skɛlɪtən] *n* โครงกระดูก [khlong kra duk]

sketch [skɛtʃ] *n* ภาพร่าง [phap rang] ▷ *v* ร่างภาพ [rang phap]

skewer ['skjʊə] *n* ไม้เสียบ [mai siap]

ski [ski:] *n* แคร่เลื่อนยาวติดกับรองเท้าใช้ เล่นหิมะ [krae luean yao tit kap rong thao chai len hi ma] ▷ *v* เคลื่อนไปบนสกี [khluean pai bon sa ki]; **ski lift** *n* กระเช้าไฟฟ้า [kra chao fai fa]; **ski pass** *n* บัตรเล่นสกี [bat len sa ki]

skid [skɪd] *v* ลื่น [luen]; **The car skidded** รถลื่น [rot luen]

skier ['ski:ə] *n* ผู้เล่นสกี [phu len sa ki]

skiing ['ski:ɪŋ] *n* การเล่นสกี [kan len sa ki]; **Do you organise skiing lessons?** คุณจัดสอนการเล่นสกีไหม? [khun chat son kan len sa ki mai]

skilful ['skɪlfʊl] *adj* ซึ่งมีความชำนาญ [sueng mee khwam cham nan]

skill [skɪl] *n* ความเชี่ยวชาญ [khwam chiao chan]

skilled [skɪld] *adj* ซึ่งมีความชำนาญ [sueng mee khwam cham nan]

skimpy ['skɪmpɪ] *adj* ไม่พอเพียง [mai pho phiang]

skin [skɪn] *n* ผิวหนัง [phio nang]

skinhead ['skɪnˌhɛd] *n* คนที่โกนผมหัว ล้าน [khon thii kon phom hua lan]

skinny ['skɪnɪ] *adj* ผอมมาก [phom mak]

skin-tight ['skɪnˈtaɪt] *adj* รัดรูป [rat rup]

skip [skɪp] *v* กระโดดโลดเต้น [kra dot lot ten]

skirt [skɜ:t] *n* กระโปรง [kra prong]

skive [skaɪv] *v* หนีงาน [nii ngan]

skull [skʌl] *n* กะโหลกศีรษะ [ka lok sii sa]

sky [skaɪ] *n* ท้องฟ้า [thong fa]

skyscraper ['skaɪˌskreɪpə] *n* ตึกระฟ้า [tuek ra fa]

slack [slæk] *adj* หย่อน [yon]

slam [slæm] *v* ปิดดังปัง [pid dang pang]

slang [slæŋ] *n* ภาษาสแลง [pha sa sa laeng]

slap [slæp] *v* ตบ [top]

slash [slæʃ] *n* **forward slash** *n* ทับ [thap]

slate [sleɪt] *n* กระเบื้องหินชนวน [kra bueang hin cha nuan]

slave [sleɪv] *n* ทาส [that] ▷ *v* ทำงานอย่าง หนัก [tham ngan yang hnak]

sledge [slɛdʒ] *n* เลื่อนหิมะขนาดใหญ่ [luean hi ma kha nat yai]

sledging ['slɛdʒɪŋ] *n* การเล่นเลื่อนหิมะ [kan len luean hi ma]

sleep [sli:p] *n* การนอนหลับ [kan non lap] ▷ *v* นอน [non]; **sleeping bag** *n* ถุงนอน [thung non]; **sleeping car** *n* ตู้นอน [tu non]; **sleeping pill** *n* ยานอนหลับ [ya non lap]; **Did you sleep well?** คุณนอน หลับดีไหม? [khun non lap di mai]; **I can't sleep** ฉันนอนไม่หลับ [chan non mai lap]; **I can't sleep for the heat** ฉันนอนไม่หลับเพราะร้อน [chan non mai lap phro ron]

sleep around [sli:p əˈraʊnd] *v* มีเพศ สัมพันธ์กับคนหลายคน [mii phet sam phan kap khon lai khon]

sleeper ['sli:pə] *n* **Can I reserve a sleeper?** ฉันจองตั๋วนอนได้ไหม? [chan chong tua non dai mai]; **I want to book a sleeper to...** ฉันต้องการจองตั๋ว นอนหนึ่งที่ไป... [chan tong kan chong tua non nueng thii pai...]

sleep in [sli:p ɪn] *v* นอนนานกว่าปรกติ [non nan kwa prok ka ti]

sleep together [sli:p təˈgɛðə] *v* นอน ห้องเดียวกัน [non hong diao kan]

sleepwalk ['sli:pˌwɔ:k] *v* เดินละเมอ [doen la moe]

sleepy ['sli:pɪ] *adj* ง่วงนอน [nguang non]

sleet [sli:t] *n* ฝนที่ปนหิมะตกลงปกคลุมพื้น ดินหรือต้นไม้ [fon thii pon hi ma tok long pok khlum phuen din hue ton mai] ▷ *v* หิมะที่แทรกด้วยฝน [hi ma thii thraek duai fon]

sleeve [sli:v] *n* แขนเสื้อ [khaen suea]

sleeveless ['sli:vlɪs] *adj* ไม่มีแขนเสื้อ

[mai mii khaen suea]

slender ['slɛndə] *adj* ผอมเพรียว [phom phriao]

slice [slaɪs] *n* ชิ้น [chin] ▷ *v* ตัดเป็นแผ่นบาง [tad pen phaen bang]

slick [slɪk] *n* **oil slick** *n* คราบน้ำมันที่ลอยบนผิวน้ำ [khrap nam man thii loi bon phio nam]

slide [slaɪd] *n* การลื่นไถล [kan luen tha lai] ▷ *v* ทำให้ลื่นถลา [tham hai luen tha la]

slight [slaɪt] *adj* เล็กน้อยมาก [lek noi mak]

slightly ['slaɪtlɪ] *adv* อย่างเล็กน้อย [yang lek noi]

slim [slɪm] *adj* ผอมเพรียว [phom phriao]

sling [slɪŋ] *n* แถบผ้าคล้องคอสำหรับแขวนมือหรือแขนที่บาดเจ็บ [thaep pha khlong kho sam rap khwaen mue rue khaen thii bat chep]

slip [slɪp] *n* (mistake) พลาด [phlat], (paper) กระดาษชิ้นเล็กๆ [kra dart chin lek lek], (underwear) ชุดชั้นในของผู้หญิง [chut chan nai khong phu ying] ▷ *v* ลื่นไถลไป [luen tha lai pai]; **slip road** *n* ถนนเชื่อมทางหลวง [tha non chueam thang luang]; **slipped disc** *n* หมอนรองกระดูกสันหลังเลื่อน [mon rong kra duk san lang luean]

slipper ['slɪpə] *n* รองเท้าสวมเดินในบ้าน [rong thao suam doen nai baan]

slippery ['slɪpərɪ; -prɪ] *adj* ลื่นไถล [luen tha lai]

slip up [slɪp ʌp] *v* ทำผิดพลาด [tham phid phlad]

slip-up [slɪpʌp] *n* ความผิดพลาด [khwam phit phlat]

slope [sləʊp] *n* พื้นที่ลาดเอียง [phuen thii lat iang]; **nursery slope** *n* ที่ลาดชันสำหรับฝึกเล่นสกี [thii lat chan sam rap fuek len sa ki]

sloppy ['slɒpɪ] *adj* ซึ่งไม่เป็นระเบียบ [sueng mai pen ra biap]

slot [slɒt] *n* ช่องที่แคบและยาว [chong thii khaep lae yao]; **slot machine** *n* เครื่องหยอดเหรียญสำหรับเล่นพนัน [khrueang yot rian sam rap len pha nan]

Slovak ['sləʊvæk] *adj* เกี่ยวกับสาธารณรัฐสโลวาเกีย [kiao kap sa tha ra na rat sa lo va kia] ▷ *n* (language) ภาษาสโลวาเกีย [pha sa sa lo va kia], (person) ชาวสโลวาเกีย [chao sa lo wa kia]

Slovakia [sləʊ'vækɪə] *n* ประเทศสโลวาเกีย [pra tet sa lo va kia]

Slovenia [sləʊ'viːnɪə] *n* สาธารณรัฐสโลเวเนีย [sa tha ra na rat sa lo ve nia]

Slovenian [sləʊ'viːnɪən] *adj* เกี่ยวกับสาธารณรัฐสโลเวเนีย [kiao kap sa tha ra na rat sa lo ve nia] ▷ *n* (language) ภาษาสโลเวเนียน [pha sa sa lo ve nian], (person) ชาวสโลเวเนียน [chao sa lo we nian]

slow [sləʊ] *adj* ช้า [cha]; **I think my watch is slow** ฉันคิดว่านาฬิกาฉันเดินช้า [chan kit wa na li ka chan doen cha]; **The connection seems very slow** การติดต่อเชื่อมกันค่อนข้างช้า [kan tit to chueam kan khon khang cha]

slow down [sləʊ daʊn] *v* แล่นช้าลง [laen cha long]

slowly ['sləʊlɪ] *adv* อย่างช้า ๆ [yang cha cha]

slug [slʌg] *n* ตัวทากกินใบไม้ [tua thak kin bai mai]

slum [slʌm] *n* แหล่งเสื่อมโทรม [laeng sueam som]

slush [slʌʃ] *n* หิมะหรือน้ำแข็งที่กำลังละลาย [hi ma hue nam khaeng thii kam lang la lai]

sly [slaɪ] *adj* ซึ่งมีเล่ห์เหลี่ยม อย่างฉลาดแกมโกง [sueng mii le liam, yang cha lat kaem kong]

smack [smæk] *v* ตีดังผัวะ [ti dang phau]

small [smɔːl] *adj* เล็ก [lek]; **Do you have a small?** คุณมีขนาดเล็กไหม? [khun mii kha nat lek mai]; **Do you have this in a smaller size?** คุณมีขนาดเล็กกว่าตัวนี้ไหม? [khun mii kha nat lek kwa tua nii mai]; **I don't have anything smaller** ฉันไม่มีอะไรที่เล็กกว่านี้ [chan mai mii a rai thii lek kwa nii]

smart [smɑːt] *adj* สะอาดและประณีต [sa at lae pra nit]; **smart phone** *n* โทรศัพท์มือถือที่มีปฏิทิน อีเมลล์ [tho ra sap mue thue thii mii pa ti thin i mail]

smash [smæʃ] *v* ทำให้แตกเป็นเสียงๆ [tham hai taek pen siang siang]

smashing [ˈsmæʃɪŋ] *adj* ดีเยี่ยม [di yiam]

smell [smɛl] *n* กลิ่น [klin] ▷ *vi* ดมกลิ่น [dom klin] ▷ *vt* ได้กลิ่น [dai klin]; **I can smell gas** ฉันได้กลิ่นก๊าซ [chan dai klin kas]; **My room smells of smoke** ห้องฉันมีกลิ่นบุหรี่ [hong chan mii klin bu ri]; **There's a funny smell** มีกลิ่นแปลก ๆ [mii klin plaek plaek]

smelly [ˈsmɛlɪ] *adj* มีกลิ่น [mii klin]

smile [smaɪl] *n* รอยยิ้ม [roi yim] ▷ *v* ยิ้ม [yim]

smiley [ˈsmaɪlɪ] *n* หน้าที่มีรอยยิ้ม [na thii mii roi yim]

smoke [sməʊk] *n* ควัน [khwan] ▷ *v* สูบ [sup]; **smoke alarm** *n* เครื่องสัญญาณเตือนภัย [khrueang san yan tuean phai]; **Do you mind if I smoke?** คุณจะว่าอะไรไหมถ้าฉันสูบบุหรี่? [khun ja wa a rai mai tha chan sup bu rii]; **Do you smoke?** คุณสูบบุหรี่ไหม? [khun sup bu rii mai]; **Where can I smoke?** ฉันสูบบุหรี่ได้ที่ไหน? [chan sup bu rii dai thii nai]

smoked [ˈsməʊkt] *adj* รมควัน [rom khwan]

smoker [ˈsməʊkə] *n* ผู้สูบบุหรี่ [phu sub bu hree]

smoking [ˈsməʊkɪŋ] *n* การสูบบุหรี่ [kan sub bu rii]

smoky [ˈsməʊkɪ] *adj* **It's too smoky here** ที่นี่ควันบุหรี่มากไป [thii ni khwan bu ri mak pai]

smooth [smuːð] *adj* เรียบ [riap]

SMS [ɛs ɛm ɛs] *n* ข้อความสั้นส่งจาก

โทรศัพท์มือถืออันหนึ่งไปอีกอันหนึ่ง [khor khwam san song chak tho ra sab mue thue an hueng pai ik an hueng]

smudge [smʌdʒ] *n* รอยเปื้อน [roi puean]

smug [smʌg] *adj* สบายใจ [sa bai chai]

smuggle [ˈsmʌgəl] *v* ลักลอบนำเข้า [lak lop nam khao]

smuggler [ˈsmʌglə] *n* ผู้ลักลอบนำเข้า [phu lak lop nam khao]

smuggling [ˈsmʌglɪŋ] *n* การลักลอบนำเข้า [kan lak lop nam khao]

snack [snæk] *n* อาหารว่าง [a han wang]; **snack bar** *n* ห้องทานอาหารว่าง [hong than a han wang]

snail [sneɪl] *n* หอยทาก [hoi thak]

snake [sneɪk] *n* งู [ngu]

snap [snæp] *v* ขาดหรือแตกอย่างฉับพลัน [khat rue taek yang chap phlan]

snapshot [ˈsnæp.ʃɒt] *n* การถ่ายภาพอย่างรวดเร็ว [kan thai phap yang ruad reo]

snarl [snɑːl] *v* แยกเขี้ยว [yaek khiao]

snatch [snætʃ] *v* คว้า [khwa]

sneakers [ˈsniːkəz] *npl* รองเท้าผ้าใบ [rong thao pha bai]

sneeze [sniːz] *v* จาม [cham]

sniff [snɪf] *v* สูดจมูกฟุดฟิต [sut cha muk fut fit]

snigger [ˈsnɪgə] *v* หัวเราะเยาะ [hua ro yo]

snob [snɒb] *n* คนหัวสูง [khon hua sung]

snooker [ˈsnuːkə] *n* สนุกเกอร์ [sa nuk koe]

snooze [snuːz] *n* การงีบหลับ [kan ngib lap] ▷ *v* งีบหลับ [ngip lap]

snore [snɔː] *v* กรน [kron]

snorkel [ˈsnɔːkəl] *n* ท่อช่วยหายใจในน้ำ [tho chuai hai jai nai nam]

snow [snəʊ] *n* หิมะ [hi ma] ▷ *v* หิมะตก [hi ma tok]; **Do I need snow chains?** ฉันต้องใส่โซ่กันหิมะหรือไม่? [chan tong sai so kan hi ma rue mai]; **Do you think it will snow?** คุณคิดว่าจะมีหิมะตกหรือไม่? [khun kit wa ja mii hi ma tok rue mai]; **It's snowing** หิมะกำลังตก [hi ma kam lang tok]

snowball ['snəʊ,bɔːl] n หิมะก้อนที่ปั้นไว้ ขว้างเล่น [hi ma kon thii pan wai khwang len]

snowboard ['snəʊ,bɔːd] n **I want to hire a snowboard** ฉันอยากเช่ากระดาน เล่นหิมะ [chan yak chao kra dan len hi ma]

snowflake ['snəʊ,fleɪk] n เกล็ดหิมะ [klet hi ma]

snowman ['snəʊ,mæn] n รูปปั้นมนุษย์ หิมะ [rup pan ma nut hi ma]

snowplough ['snəʊ,plaʊ] n รถไถกวาด หิมะ [rot thai kwat hi ma]

snowstorm ['snəʊ,stɔːm] n พายุหิมะ [pha yu hi ma]

so [səʊ] adv มาก [mak]; **so (that)** conj ดัง นั้น [dang nan]

soak [səʊk] v แช่ [chae]

soaked [səʊkt] adj ทำให้เปียก [tham hai piak]

soap [səʊp] n สบู่ [sa bu]; **soap dish** n จานสบู่ [chan sa bu]; **soap opera** n ละครน้ำเน่า [la khon nam nao]; **soap powder** n ผงสบู่ [phong sa bu]; **There is no soap** ไม่มีสบู่ [mai mii sa bu]

sob [sɒb] v ร้องไห้สะอึกสะอื้น [rong hai sa uek sa uen]

sober ['səʊbə] adj ไม่เมา [mai mao]

sociable ['səʊʃəb³l] adj เป็นมิตร [pen mit]

social ['səʊʃəl] adj อยู่ร่วมกันในสังคม [yu ruam kan nai sang khom]; **social security** n การประกันสังคม [kan pra kan sang khom]; **social services** npl การ บริการสังคมสงเคราะห์ [kan bo ri kan sang khom song khro]; **social worker** n นักสังคมสงเคราะห์ [nak sang khom song khro]

socialism ['səʊʃə,lɪzəm] n ระบบ สังคมนิยม [ra bop sang khom ni yom]

socialist ['səʊʃəlɪst] adj ที่เป็นแบบ สังคมนิยม [thii pen baep sang khom ni

yom] ▷ n นักสังคมนิยม [nak sang khom ni yom]

society [sə'saɪətɪ] n สังคม [sang khom]

sociology [,səʊsɪ'ɒlədʒɪ] n สังคมวิทยา [sang khom wit tha ya]

sock [sɒk] n ถุงเท้า [thung thao]

socket ['sɒkɪt] n ปลั๊กตัวเมีย [plak tua mia]

sofa ['səʊfə] n เก้าอี้นวม [kao ee nuam]; **sofa bed** n เก้าอี้นวมที่นั่งในเวลากลางวัน และเป็นเตียงเวลากลางคืน [kao ii nuam thii nang nai we la klang wan lae pen tiang we la klang khuen]

soft [sɒft] adj อ่อนนุ่ม [on num]; **soft drink** n เครื่องดื่มซึ่งไม่ใช่เหล้า [khrueang duem sueng mai chai lao]

softener ['sɒfnə] n **Do you have softener?** คุณมีน้ำยาปรับผ้านุ่มไหม? [khun mii nam ya prab pha num mai]

software ['sɒft,wɛə] n โปรแกรม คอมพิวเตอร์ [pro kraem khom phio toe]

soggy ['sɒgɪ] adj เปียกโชก [piak chok]

soil [sɔɪl] n ดิน [din]

solar ['səʊlə] adj เกี่ยวกับดวงอาทิตย์ [kiao kap duang a thit]; **solar power** n พลังงานแสงอาทิตย์ [pha lang ngan saeng a thit]; **solar system** n ระบบ สุริยะจักรวาล [ra bop su ri ya chak kra wan]

soldier ['səʊldʒə] n ทหาร [tha han]

sold out [səʊld aʊt] adj ขายหมดแล้ว [khai hmod laeo]

solicitor [sə'lɪsɪtə] n ทนายความ [tha nai khwam]

solid ['sɒlɪd] adj แข็ง [khaeng]

solo ['səʊləʊ] n เพลงร้องเดี่ยว [phleng rong diao]

soloist ['səʊləʊɪst] n นักร้องเดี่ยว [nak rong diao]

soluble ['sɒljʊb³l] adj ซึ่งสามารถละลาย ได้ [sueng sa maat la lai dai]

solution [sə'luːʃən] n คำตอบที่แก้ปัญหา [kham top thii kae pan ha]

solve [sɒlv] v แก้ปัญหา [kae pan ha]

solvent ['sɒlvənt] n ตัวทำละลาย [tua tham la lai]

Somali [sɒʊ'mɑːlɪ] adj เกี่ยวกับประเทศโซมาเลีย [kiao kap pra thet so ma lia] ▷ n (language) ภาษาโซมาเลีย [pha sa so ma lia], (person) ชาวโซมาเลีย [chao so ma lia]

Somalia [sɒʊ'mɑːlɪə] n ประเทศโซมาเลีย [pra tet so ma lia]

some [sʌm; səm] adj เล็กน้อย [lek noi] ▷ pron บางส่วน [bang suan]

somebody ['sʌmbədɪ] pron บางคน [bang khon]

somehow ['sʌm,haʊ] adv เนื่องด้วยเหตุผลบางอย่าง [nueang duai het phon bang yang]

someone ['sʌm,wʌn; -wən] pron บางคน [bang khon]

someplace ['sʌm,pleɪs] adv บางแห่ง [bang haeng]

something ['sʌmθɪŋ] pron บางสิ่ง [bang sing]

sometime ['sʌm,taɪm] adv บางเวลา [bang we la]

sometimes ['sʌm,taɪmz] adv บางครั้งบางคราว [bang khang bang khrao]

somewhere ['sʌm,wɛə] adv ที่ใดที่หนึ่ง [thi dai thi nueng]

son [sʌn] n ลูกชาย [luk chai]; **My son is lost** ลูกชายฉันหลงทาง [luk chai chan long thang]; **My son is missing** ลูกชายฉันหาย [luk chai chan hai]

song [sɒŋ] n เพลง [phleng]

son-in-law [sʌn ɪn lɔː] (pl **sons-in-law**) n ลูกเขย [luk khoei]

soon [suːn] adv ไม่นาน [mai nan]

sooner ['suːnə] adv ในไม่ช้า [nai mai cha]

soot [sʊt] n เขม่า เขม่าถ่านหิน [kha mao, kha mao than hin]

sophisticated [sə'fɪstɪ,keɪtɪd] adj ที่ดูมีรสนิยมสูง [thii du mee rot ni yom sung]

soppy ['sɒpɪ] adj มีอารมณ์อ่อนไหวมากเกินไป [mii a rom on wai mak koen pai]

soprano [sə'prɑːnəʊ] n นักร้องหญิงที่ร้องเสียงสูงสุด [nak rong hying thii rong siang sung sud]

sorbet ['sɔːbeɪ; -bɪt] n น้ำแข็งที่ผสมน้ำผลไม้ [nam khaeng thii pha som nam phon la mai]

sorcerer ['sɔːsərə] n พ่อมด [pho mot]

sore [sɔː] adj เจ็บปวด [chep puat] ▷ n ความเจ็บ [khwam chep]; **cold sore** n แผลเปื่อย [phlae pueai]

sorry ['sɒrɪ] interj **I'm sorry** ฉันเสียใจด้วย [chan sia jai duai]; **I'm sorry to trouble you** ฉันขอโทษที่ทำความลำบากให้คุณ [chan kho thot thii tham khwam lam bak hai khun]; **I'm very sorry, I didn't know the regulations** ฉันเสียใจมาก ฉันไม่รู้กฎข้อบังคับ [chan sia jai mak chan mai ru kot kho bang khap]

sort [sɔːt] n การจัดประเภท [kan chat pra phet]

sort out [sɔːt aʊt] v แยกออก [yaek ok]

SOS [ɛs əʊ ɛs] n สัญญาณขอความช่วยเหลือ [san yan kho khwam chuai luea]

so-so [sɒʊsəʊ] adv อย่างนั้น ๆ อย่างนั้นแหละ [yang ngan ngan, yang ngan lae]

soul [səʊl] n วิญญาณ [win yan]

sound [saʊnd] adj ที่ไม่เสียหาย [thii mai sia hai] ▷ n เสียง [siang]

soundtrack ['saʊnd,træk] n เสียงในฟิล์ม [siang nai film]

soup [suːp] n ซุป [sup]; **What is the soup of the day?** ซุปประจำวันคืออะไร? [sup pra cham wan khuea a rai]

sour ['saʊə] adj มีรสเปรี้ยว [mee rot priao]

south [saʊθ] adj ทิศใต้ [thid tai] ▷ adv ทางใต้ [thang tai] ▷ n ภาคใต้ [phak tai]; **South Africa** n ประเทศอัฟริกาใต้ [pra tet af ri ka tai]; **South African** n เกี่ยวกับอัฟริกาใต้ [kiao kap af ri ka tai], ชาวอัฟริกาใต้ [kiao kap af ri ka tai, chao af ri ka tai]; **South America** n ทวีปอเมริกาใต้ [tha wip a me ri ka tai]

southbound ['saʊθ,baʊnd] *adj* ที่มุ่งไปทางใต้ [thii mung pai thang tai]

southeast [,saʊθ'i:st; ,saʊ'i:st] *n* ตะวันออกเฉียงใต้ [ta wan ork chiang tai]

southern ['sʌðən] *adj* ในทางภาคใต้ [nai thang phak tai]

southwest [,saʊθ'wɛst; ,saʊ'wɛst] *n* ตะวันตกเฉียงใต้ [ta wan tok chiang tai]

souvenir [,su:və'nɪə; 'su:və,nɪə] *n* ของที่ระลึก [khong thi ra luek]; **Do you have souvenirs?** คุณมีของที่ระลึกไหม? [khun mii khong thii ra luek mai]

soya ['sɔɪə] *n* ถั่วเหลือง [thua lueang]

spa [spɑ:] *n* สถานบำรุงสุขภาพ [sa than bam rung suk kha phap]

space [speɪs] *n* ที่ว่าง [thi wang]

spacecraft ['speɪs,krɑ:ft] *n* ยานอวกาศ [yan a wa kat]

spade [speɪd] *n* พลั่ว [phlua]

spaghetti [spə'gɛtɪ] *n* สปาเก็ตตี้ [sa pa ket ti]

Spain [speɪn] *n* ประเทศสเปน [pra tet sa pen]

spam [spæm] *n* ขยะไปรษณีย์อิเล็กทรอนิกส์ [kha ya prai sa nii i lek thro nik]

Spaniard ['spænjəd] *n* ชาวสเปน [chao sa pen]

spaniel ['spænjəl] *n* สุนัขพันธุ์หนึ่ง [su nak phan hueng]

Spanish ['spænɪʃ] *adj* เกี่ยวกับสเปน [kiao kap sa pen] ▷ *n* ประเทศสเปน [pra tet sa pen]

spank [spæŋk] *v* ตีก้นเพื่อลงโทษ [ti kon phue long thod]

spanner ['spænə] *n* กุญแจเลื่อน [kun jae luean]

spare [spɛə] *adj* ที่สำรองไว้ [thii sam rong wai] ▷ *v* ซึ่งสำรองไว้ [sueng sam rong wai]; **spare part** *n* อะไหล่ [a lai]; **spare room** *n* ห้องว่างหรือห้องสำรอง [hong wang rue hong sam rong]; **spare time** *n* เวลาว่าง [we la wang]

spark [spɑ:k] *n* ประกายไฟ [pra kai phai]; **spark plug** *n* หัวเทียนไฟเครื่องยนต์ [hua thian fai khrueang yon]

sparrow ['spærəʊ] *n* นกกระจอก [nok kra chok]

spasm ['spæzəm] *n* การชักกระตุกของกล้ามเนื้อ [kan chak kra tuk khong klam nuea]

spatula ['spætjʊlə] *n* ไม้พายที่ใช้ทำอาหาร [mai phai thii chai tham a han]

speak [spi:k] *v* พูด [phut]; **Can I speak to...?** ฉันขอพูดกับ...ได้ไหม? [chan kho phut kap...dai mai]; **Can I speak to you in private?** ฉันพูดกับคุณเป็นการส่วนตัวได้ไหม? [chan phut kap khun pen kan suan tua dai mai]; **Could you speak louder, please?** คุณกรุณาพูดดังกว่านี้ได้ไหม? [khun ka ru na phut dang kwa nii dai mai]

speaker ['spi:kə] *n* ผู้พูด [phu phud]; **native speaker** *n* เจ้าของภาษา [chao khong pha sa]

speak up [spi:k ʌp] *v* พูดเสียงดัง [phud siang dang]

special ['spɛʃəl] *adj* พิเศษ [phi set]; **special offer** *n* การขายสินค้าราคาพิเศษ [kan khai sin kha ra kha phi set]

specialist ['spɛʃəlɪst] *n* ผู้เชี่ยวชาญ [phu chiao chan]

speciality [,spɛʃɪ'ælɪtɪ] *n* ความชำนาญพิเศษ [khwam cham nan phi set]

specialize ['spɛʃə,laɪz] *v* ศึกษาเป็นพิเศษ [suek sa pen phi sed]

specially ['spɛʃəlɪ] *adv* อย่างพิเศษ [yang phi sed]

species ['spi:ʃi:z; 'spi:ʃɪ,i:z] *n* ชนิด [cha nit]

specific [spɪ'sɪfɪk] *adj* โดยเฉพาะ [doi cha pho]

specifically [spɪ'sɪfɪklɪ] *adv* อย่างพิเศษ [yang phi sed]

specify ['spɛsɪ,faɪ] *v* ระบุ [ra bu]

specs [spɛks] *npl* แว่นตา [waen ta]

spectacles ['spɛktək°lz] *npl* แว่นตา

[waen ta]

spectacular [spɛk'tækjʊlə] *adj* ซึ่ง
ปรากฏที่ยิ่งใหญ่ [sueng pra kot thii ying
yai]

spectator [spɛk'teɪtə] *n* ผู้ชม [phu
chom]

speculate ['spɛkjʊ,leɪt] *v* เสี่ยงโชค
[siang chok]

speech [spi:tʃ] *n* คำบรรยาย [kham ban
yai]

speechless ['spi:tʃlɪs] *adj* ไม่สามารถพูด
ได้ [mai sa mat phut dai]

speed [spi:d] *n* ความเร็ว [khwam reo];
speed limit *n* อัตราความเร็ว [at tra
khwam reo]; **What is the speed limit
on this road?** ความเร็วสูงสุดบนถนนนี้
เท่าไร? [khwam reo sung sut bon tha
non nii thao rai]

speedboat ['spi:d,bəʊt] *n* เรือเร็ว [ruea
reo]

speeding ['spi:dɪŋ] *n* อัตราความเร็ว [at
tra khwam reo]

speedometer [spɪ'dɒmɪtə] *n* แผงที่บอก
อัตราความเร็ว [phaeng thii bok at tra
khwam reo]

speed up [spi:d ʌp] *v* เร่งให้เร็วขึ้น [reng
hai reo khuen]

spell [spɛl] *n* (*magic*) มนตร์คาถา [mon
kha tha], (*time*) ช่วงเวลา [chuang we la]
▷ *v* อ่านสะกดคำ [arn sa kot kham]

spellchecker ['spɛl,tʃɛkə] *n* ซอฟแวร์ของ
คอมพิวเตอร์ที่ใช้สำหรับตรวจคำศัพท์ [sop
wae khong khom phio toe thii chai
sam rap truat kham sap]

spelling ['spɛlɪŋ] *n* การสะกดคำ [kan sa
kot kham]

spend [spɛnd] *v* ใช้ [chai]

sperm [spɜ:m] *n* ตัวอสุจิ [tua a su chi]

spice [spaɪs] *n* เครื่องเทศ [khrueang
thet]

spicy ['spaɪsɪ] *adj* ที่มีรสจัด [thii mii rot
chat]

spider ['spaɪdə] *n* แมงมุม [maeng mum]

spill [spɪl] *v* ทำหก [tham hok]

spinach ['spɪnɪdʒ; -ɪtʃ] *n* ผักโขม [phak
khom]

spine [spaɪn] *n* กระดูกสันหลัง [kra duk
san lang]

spinster ['spɪnstə] *n* สตรีที่ไม่ได้แต่งงาน
[sa tree thii mai dai taeng ngan]

spire [spaɪə] *n* สิ่งก่อสร้างสูงรูปกรวยที่เป็น
ส่วนหนึ่งของโบสถ์ [sing ko sang sung
rup kruai thii pen suan nueng khong
bot]

spirit ['spɪrɪt] *n* วิญญาณ [win yan]

spirits ['spɪrɪts] *npl* อารมณ์ [a rom]

spiritual ['spɪrɪtjʊəl] *adj* เกี่ยวกับศาสนา
[kiao kap sat sa na]

spit [spɪt] *n* เหล็กเสียบเนื้อย่าง [lek siap
nuea yang] ▷ *v* ถ่มน้ำลาย [thom nam
lai]

spite [spaɪt] *n* เจตนาร้าย [chet ta na rai]
▷ *v* มุ่งร้าย [mung rai]

spiteful ['spaɪtfʊl] *adj* ซึ่งมีเจตนาร้าย
[sueng mii chet ta na rai]

splash [splæʃ] *v* สาดกระเด็น [sat kra
den]

splendid ['splɛndɪd] *adj* ยอดเยี่ยม [yod
yiam]

splint [splɪnt] *n* เฝือก [fueak]

splinter ['splɪntə] *n* เศษเล็ก ๆ ที่แตกออก
[set lek lek thii taek ok]

split [splɪt] *v* แยก [yaek]

split up [splɪt ʌp] *v* แยกออกจากกัน [yaek
ork chak kan]

spoil [spɔɪl] *v* ทำให้เสียหาย ตามใจจน
เสียคน [tham hai sia hai, tam jai chon
sia khon]

spoilsport ['spɔɪl,spɔ:t] *n* ผู้รบกวนความ
สุขของผู้อื่น [phu rop kuan khwam suk
khong phu uen]

spoilt [spɔɪlt] *adj* ทำให้เสียหาย [tham
hai sia hai]

spoke [spəʊk] *n* ซี่ล้อรถ [si lo rot]

spokesman, spokesmen
['spəʊksmən, 'spəʊksmɛn] *n* โฆษก
[kho sok]

spokesperson ['spəʊks,pɜːsən] *n*

โฆษก [kho sok]

spokeswoman, spokeswomen ['spəʊks,wʊmən, 'spəʊks,wɪmɪn] n โฆษกหญิง [kho sok ying]

sponge [spʌndʒ] n (cake) เค้กที่ฟู [khek thii fu], (for washing) ฟองน้ำ [fong nam]; **sponge bag** n กระเป๋าใส่เครื่องใช้ในการอาบน้ำ เช่น สบู่ ยาสระผม ยาสีฟัน เป็นต้น [kra pao sai khrueang chai nai kan ap nam chen sa bu ya sa phom ya sii fan pen ton]

sponsor ['spɒnsə] n ผู้อุปถัมภ์ [phu op pa tam] ▷ v อุปถัมภ์ [up pa tham]

sponsorship ['spɒnsəʃɪp] n การอุปถัมภ์ [kan op pa tham]

spontaneous [spɒn'teɪnɪəs] adj ซึ่งกระทำเองโดยทันที [sueng kra tham eng doi than thi]

spooky ['spuːkɪ; 'spooky] adj น่ากลัว [na klua]

spoon [spuːn] n ช้อน [chon]; **Could I have a clean spoon, please?** ฉันขอช้อนสะอาดหนึ่งคันได้ไหม? [chan kho chon sa aat nueng khan dai mai]

spoonful ['spuːn,fʊl] n เต็มช้อน [tem chon]

sport [spɔːt] n กีฬา [ki la]; **winter sports** npl กีฬาฤดูหนาว [ki la rue du nao]; **What sports facilities are there?** มีอุปกรณ์กีฬาอะไรบ้าง? [mii up pa kon ki la a rai bang]; **Which sporting events can we go to?** มีกิจกรรมกีฬาอะไรที่เราจะไปดูได้ [mii kit cha kam ki la a rai thii rao ja pai du dai]

sportsman, sportsmen ['spɔːtsmən, 'spɔːtsmɛn] n นักกีฬา [nak ki la]

sportswear ['spɔːts,wɛə] n ชุดกีฬา [chud ki la]

sportswoman, sportswomen ['spɔːts,wʊmən, 'spɔːts,wɪmɪn] n นักกีฬาหญิง [nak ki la ying]

sporty ['spɔːtɪ] adj มีน้ำใจเป็นนักกีฬา

[mii nam jai pen nak ki la]

spot [spɒt] n (blemish) จุดด่างพร้อย [chut dang phroi], (place) สถานที่ [sa than thi] ▷ v พบเห็น [phop hen]

spotless ['spɒtlɪs] adj สะอาดไม่มีตำหนิ [sa at mai mii tam ni]

spotlight ['spɒt,laɪt] n ไฟฉายที่มีแสงสว่างจ้ามาก [fai chai thii mii saeng sa wang cha mak]

spotty ['spɒtɪ] adj เต็มไปด้วยสิว [tem pai duai sio]

spouse [spaʊs] n สามีหรือภรรยา [sa mii rue phan ra ya]

sprain [spreɪn] n อาการเคล็ด [a kan khlet] ▷ v ทำให้เคล็ด [tham hai khlet]

spray [spreɪ] n ละอองน้ำ [la ong nam] ▷ v พ่น [phon]; **hair spray** n สเปรย์ฉีดผม [sa pre chit phom]

spread [sprɛd] n การกระจาย [kan kra chai] ▷ v กระจาย [kra chai]

spread out [sprɛd aʊt] v แผ่ออกไป [phae ok pai]

spreadsheet ['sprɛd,ʃiːt] n ตารางจัดการหมายถึงโปรแกรมคอมพิวเตอร์ประเภทหนึ่ง [ta rang chat kan mai thueng pro kraem khom phio toe pra pet nueng]

spring [sprɪŋ] n (coil) ลวดสปริง [luat sa pring], (season) ฤดูใบไม้ผลิ [rue du bai mai phli]; **spring onion** n ต้นหอม [ton hom]

spring-cleaning ['sprɪŋ,kliːnɪŋ] n ทำความสะอาดบ้านทั่วทั้งหลัง [tham khwam sa aat baan thua thang lang]

springtime ['sprɪŋ,taɪm] n ฤดูใบไม้ผลิ [rue du bai mai phli]

sprinkler ['sprɪŋklə] n หัวฉีดน้ำ [hua chit nam]

sprint [sprɪnt] n การแข่งวิ่งเร็วในระยะสั้น [kan khaeng wing reo nai ra ya san] ▷ v วิ่งเต็มฝีเท้า [wing tem fi thao]

sprinter ['sprɪntə] n นักวิ่งเร็ว [nak wing reo]

sprouts [spraʊts] npl ต้นอ่อน [ton on]; **Brussels sprouts** npl ลูกกะหล่ำเล็ก [luk ka lam lek]

spy [spaɪ] *n* นักสืบ [nak suep] ▷ *v* สืบ [suep]

spying ['spaɪɪŋ] *n* การสอดแนม [kan sot naem]

squabble ['skwɒbəl] *v* ทะเลาะกัน [tha lao kan]

squander ['skwɒndə] *v* ใช้จ่ายสุรุ่ยสุร่าย [chai chai su rui su rai]

square [skwɛə] *adj* เป็นสี่เหลี่ยมจัตุรัส [pen si liam chat tu rat] ▷ *n* สี่เหลี่ยมจตุรัส [si liam chat tu rat]

squash [skwɒʃ] *n* เครื่องดื่มน้ำผลไม้ผสมด้วยน้ำให้เจือจางลง [khueang duem nam phon la mai pha som duai nam hai chuea chang long] ▷ *v* เบียดเสียด [biat siat]

squeak [skwiːk] *v* พูดเสียงแหลม [phud siang hlaem]

squeeze [skwiːz] *v* บีบ [bip]

squeeze in [skwiːz ɪn] *v* เบียดเข้าไป [biat khao pai]

squid [skwɪd] *n* ปลาหมึก [pla muek]

squint [skwɪnt] *v* ตาเหล่ [ta le]

squirrel ['skwɪrəl; 'skwɜːrəl; 'skwʌr-] *n* กระรอก [kra rok]

Sri Lanka [ˌsriː 'læŋkə] *n* ประเทศศรีลังกา [pra tet sri lang ka]

stab [stæb] *v* แทง [thaeng]

stability [stə'bɪlɪtɪ] *n* ความมั่นคง [khwam man khong]

stable ['steɪbəl] *adj* มั่นคง [man khong] ▷ *n* คอกม้า [khok ma]

stack [stæk] *n* กองที่ซ้อนกัน [kong thii sorn kan]

stadium, stadia ['steɪdɪəm, 'steɪdɪə] *n* สนามกีฬาที่มีอัฒจันทร์โดยรอบ [sa nam ki la thii mii at tha chan doi rop]

staff [stɑːf] *n* (stick or rod) ไม้ค้ำ เสาค้ำ ไม้เท้า [mai kham, sao kham, mai thao], (workers) พนักงาน [pha nak ngan]

staffroom ['stɑːfˌruːm] *n* ห้องสำหรับคณะผู้ทำงาน [hong sam hrab kha na phu tham ngan]

stage [steɪdʒ] *n* เวทีการแสดง [we thi kan sa daeng]

stagger ['stægə] *v* เซ [se]

stain [steɪn] *n* รอยเปื้อน [roi puean] ▷ *v* เป็นคราบ [pen khrap]; **stain remover** *n* น้ำยากำจัดคราบเปื้อน [nam ya kam chat khrab puean]

staircase ['stɛəˌkeɪs] *n* บันไดทอดหนึ่ง [ban dai thot nueng]

stairs [stɛəz] *npl* บันได [ban dai]

stale [steɪl] *adj* ไม่สด [mai sot]

stalemate ['steɪlˌmeɪt] *n* สภาพที่จนมุม [sa phap thii chon mum]

stall [stɔːl] *n* แผงขายของ [phaeng khai khong]

stamina ['stæmɪnə] *n* ความทรหดอดทน ความแข็งแกร่งที่ยืนหยัดอยู่ได้นาน [khwam tho ra hot ot thon, khwam khaeng kraeng thii yuen yat yu dai nan]

stammer ['stæmə] *v* พูดติดอ่าง [put tit ang]

stamp [stæmp] *n* ดวงตราไปรษณียกร [duang tra prai sa ni] ▷ *v* กระทืบ เหยียบ [kra thuep, yiab]

stand [stænd] *v* ยืน [yuen]

standard ['stændəd] *adj* ซึ่งเป็นมาตรฐาน [sueng pen mat tra than] ▷ *n* มาตรฐาน [mat tra than]; **standard of living** *n* มาตรฐานการครองชีพ [mat tra than kan khrong chip]

stand for [stænd fɔː] *v* แทน [thaen]

stand out [stænd aʊt] *v* เห็นชัด [hen chat]

standpoint ['stændˌpɔɪnt] *n* ทัศนคติ [that sa na kha ti]

stands ['stændz] *npl* เคาน์เตอร์ที่ขายของ [khao toe thii khai khong]

stand up [stænd ʌp] *v* ยืนขึ้น [yuen khuen]

staple ['steɪpəl] *n* (commodity) อาหารหลัก [a han lak], (wire) ลวดเย็บกระดาษ [luat yep kra dat] ▷ *v* ติดด้วยลวดเย็บกระดาษ [tit duai luat yep kra daat]

stapler ['steɪplə] *n* ที่เย็บกระดาษ [thi yep kra dat]

star [stɑ:] *n (person)* คนที่มีชื่อเสียงในด้านใดด้านหนึ่ง [khon thii mii chue siang nai dan dai dan nueng], *(sky)* ดาว [dao] ▷ *v* เป็นดาราน่าแสดง [pen da ra nam sa daeng]; **film star** *n* ดาราภาพยนตร์ [da ra phap pha yon]

starch [stɑ:tʃ] *n* แป้ง [paeng]

stare [stɛə] *v* จ้อง [chong]

stark [stɑ:k] *adj* เคร่งครัด [khreng khrat]

start [stɑ:t] *n* การเริ่ม [kan roem] ▷ *vi* เริ่มลงมือ ทำให้เกิด [roem, long mue, tham hai koet] ▷ *vt* เริ่ม เริ่มทำ เริ่มต้น [roem, roem tham, roem ton]

starter ['stɑ:tə] *n* อาหารจานแรก [a han chan raek]

startle ['stɑ:tᵊl] *v* สะดุ้ง [sa dung]

start off [stɑ:t ɒf] *v* เริ่มเดินทาง [roem doen thang]

starve [stɑ:v] *v* อด [ot]

state [steɪt] *n* สภาพแวดล้อม [sa phap waet lom] ▷ *v* บอกกล่าว [bok klao]; **Gulf States** *npl* ประเทศต่าง ๆ ในคาบสมุทรอาระเบีย [pra tet tang tang nai khap sa mut a ra bia]

statement ['steɪtmənt] *n* แถลงการณ์ [tha laeng kan]; **bank statement** *n* รายการเงินฝากถอน [rai kan ngoen fak thon]

station ['steɪʃən] *n* สถานี [sa tha ni]; **bus station** *n* สถานีรถโดยสารประจำทาง [sa tha ni rot doi san pra cham thang]; **How far are we from the bus station?** เราอยู่ห่างจากสถานีรถโดยสารมากแค่ไหน? [rao yu hang chak sa tha ni rot doi san mak khae nai]; **I need to find a police station** ฉันมองต้องหาสถานีตำรวจ [chan mong tong ha sa tha ni tam ruat]; **Where is the nearest tube station?** สถานีรถไฟใต้ดินที่ใกล้ที่สุดอยู่ที่ไหน? [sa tha ni rot fai tai din thii klai thii sut yu thii nai]

stationer's ['steɪʃənəz] *n* ร้านขายเครื่องเขียน [ran khai khrueang khian]

stationery ['steɪʃənərɪ] *n* เครื่องเขียน [khrueang khian]

statistics [stə'tɪstɪks] *npl* วิชาสถิติ [vi cha sa thi ti]

statue ['stætju:] *n* รูปปั้น [rup pan]

status ['steɪtəs] *n* **marital status** *n* สถานภาพการแต่งงาน [sa tha na phap kan taeng ngan]

status quo ['steɪtəs kwəʊ] *n* สถานภาพปัจจุบัน [sa tha na phap pat chu ban]

stay [steɪ] *n* การพักอยู่ [kan phak yu] ▷ *v* พักอยู่ [phak yu]

stay in [steɪ ɪn] *v* อยู่ในบ้าน [yu nai baan]

stay up [steɪ ʌp] *v* อยู่ดึก [yu duek]

steady ['stɛdɪ] *adj* มั่นคง [man khong]

steak [steɪk] *n* เนื้อสเต็ค [nua sa tek]; **rump steak** *n* เนื้อสะโพกของสัตว์ [nua sa phok khong sat]

steal [sti:l] *v* ลักขโมย [lak kha moi]

steam [sti:m] *n* ไอน้ำ [ai nam]

steel [sti:l] *n* เหล็ก [hlek]; **stainless steel** *n* เหล็กที่ไม่เป็นสนิม [lek thii mai pen sa nim]

steep [sti:p] *adj* สูงชัน [sung chan]

steeple ['sti:pᵊl] *n* ยอดหลังคา [yot lang kha]

steering ['stɪərɪŋ] *n* การขับ [kan khap]; **steering wheel** *n* พวงมาลัยรถ [phuang ma lai rot]

step [stɛp] *n* ก้าว [kao]

stepbrother ['stɛp,brʌðə] *n* พี่ชายน้องชายต่างบิดา [phi chai nong chai tang bi da]

stepdaughter ['stɛp,dɔ:tə] *n* ลูกเลี้ยงหญิง [luk liang ying]

stepfather ['stɛp,fɑ:ðə] *n* พ่อเลี้ยง [pho liang]

stepladder ['stɛp,lædə] *n* บันไดพับได้ [ban dai phap dai]

stepmother ['stɛp,mʌðə] *n* แม่เลี้ยง [mae liang]

stepsister ['stɛp,sɪstə] *n* พี่สาวน้องสาว

ต่างบิดา [phi sao nong sao tang bi da]

stepson ['stɛp,sʌn] *n* ลูกเลี้ยงที่เป็นชาย [luk liang thii pen chai]

stereo ['stɛrɪəʊ; 'stɪər-] *n* ระบบเสียงแบบ สเตอริโอ [ra bop siang baep sa toe ri o]; **personal stereo** *n* สเตอริโอส่วนตัว [sa toe ri o suan tua]

stereotype ['stɛrɪə,taɪp; 'stɪər-] *n* สิ่งที่ เหมือนกันราวกับพิมพ์มาจากบล็อกเดียวกัน [sing thii muean kan rao kap phim ma chak blok diao kan]

sterile ['stɛraɪl] *adj* ปราศจากเชื้อ [prat sa chak chuea]

sterilize ['stɛrɪ,laɪz] *v* ทำให้ปราศจากเชื้อ [tham hai prat sa chak chuea]

sterling ['stɜːlɪŋ] *n* สกุลเงินของสหราช อาณาจักรอังกฤษ [sa kun ngoen khong sa ha rat cha a na chak ang krit]

steroid ['stɪərɔɪd; 'stɛr-] *n* สเตอรอยด์ [sa toe roi]

stew [stjuː] *n* สตูว์ [sa tu]

steward ['stjʊəd] *n* บริกรบนเครื่องบิน [bo ri kon bon khrueang bin]

stick [stɪk] *n* ไม้เท้า [mai thao] ▷ *v* แทง [thaeng]; **stick insect** *n* ที่ดักแมลง [thii dak ma laeng]; **walking stick** *n* ไม้เท้า [mai thao]

sticker ['stɪkə] *n* ฉลากติด สติ๊กเกอร์ [cha lak tid sa tik koe]

stick out [stɪk aʊt] *v* ยื่นออกมา [yuen ok ma]

sticky ['stɪkɪ] *adj* เหนียว [niao]

stiff [stɪf] *adj* แข็ง [khaeng]

stifling ['staɪflɪŋ] *adj* ร้อนและอบ [ron lae op]

still [stɪl] *adj* นิ่ง [ning] ▷ *adv* ยังคง [yang khong]

sting [stɪŋ] *n* แผลถูกแมลงกัดต่อย [phlae thuk ma laeng kat toi] ▷ *v* กัด [kat]

stingy ['stɪndʒɪ] *adj* ขี้เหนียว [khi niao]

stink [stɪŋk] *n* กลิ่นเหม็น [klin men] ▷ *v* ส่งกลิ่นเหม็น [song klin men]

stir [stɜː] *v* คน [khon]

stitch [stɪtʃ] *n* รอยเย็บ [roi yep] ▷ *v* เย็บ [yep]

stock [stɒk] *n* คลังสินค้า [khlang sin kha] ▷ *v* เก็บ [kep]; **stock cube** *n* ก้อน สต๊อด [kon sa tok]; **stock exchange** *n* ตลาดหลักทรัพย์ [ta lad hlak sap]; **stock market** *n* ตลาดหุ้น [ta lad hun]

stockbroker ['stɒk,brəʊkə] *n* นายหน้า ขายหุ้น [nai na khai hun]

stockholder ['stɒk,həʊldə] *n* ผู้ถือหุ้น [phu thue hun]

stocking ['stɒkɪŋ] *n* ถุงน่อง [thung nong]

stock up [stɒk ʌp] *v* **stock up on** *v* เก็บ สำรองไว้ [kep sam rong wai]

stomach ['stʌmək] *n* ท้อง [thong]

stomachache ['stʌmək,eɪk] *n* ปวดท้อง [puat thong]

stone [stəʊn] *n* หิน [hin]

stool [stuːl] *n* ม้านั่งไม่มีพนัก [ma nang mai mii pha nak]

stop [stɒp] *n* การหยุด [kan yud] ▷ *vi* หยุด ยุติ เลิก [yut, yu ti, loek] ▷ *vt* หยุด ระงับ ปิดกั้น [yut, ra ngab, pit kan]; **bus stop** *n* ป้ายรถโดยสารประจำทาง [pai rot doi san pra cham thang]; **full stop** *n* มหัพ ภาค จุด [ma hup phak chut]

stopover ['stɒp,əʊvə] *n* การหยุดพัก ระหว่างทาง [kan yut phak ra wang thang]

stopwatch ['stɒp,wɒtʃ] *n* นาฬิกาจับเวลา [na li ka chab we la]

storage ['stɔːrɪdʒ] *n* ที่เก็บ [thi kep]

store [stɔː] *n* ร้านค้า [ran kha] ▷ *v* เก็บ [kep]; **department store** *n* ห้างสรรพ สินค้า [hang sap pha sin kha]

storm [stɔːm] *n* พายุ [pha yu]; **Do you think there will be a storm?** คุณคิดว่า จะมีพายุหรือไม่? [khun kit wa ja mii pha yu rue mai]

stormy ['stɔːmɪ] *adj* ราวกับพายุ [rao kap pha yu]

story ['stɔːrɪ] *n* เรื่องราว [rueang rao]; **short story** *n* เรื่องสั้น [rueang san]

stove [stəʊv] *n* เตาทำอาหาร [tao tham a

han]

straight [streɪt] *adj* ที่ตรงไป [thii trong pai]; **straight on** *adv* อย่างตรงไป [yang trong pai]

straighteners ['streɪtᵊnəz] *npl* เครื่อง ทำผมให้ตรง [khrueang tham phom hai trong]

straightforward [ˌstreɪtˈfɔːwəd] *adj* ตรงไปตรงมา [trong pai trong ma]

strain [streɪn] *n* ความตึงเครียด [khwam tueng khriat] ▷ *v* ทำงานหนักเกินไป [tham ngan hnak koen pai]

strained [streɪnd] *adj* ที่ไม่เป็นธรรมชาติ [thii mai pen tham ma chaat]

stranded ['strændɪd] *adj* โดดเดี่ยว [dot diao]

strange [streɪndʒ] *adj* แปลก [plaek]

stranger ['streɪndʒə] *n* คนแปลกหน้า [khon plaek na]

strangle ['stræŋgᵊl] *v* ฆ่าโดยการบีบคอ [kha doi kan bip kho]

strap [stræp] *n* สายรัด [sai rat]; **watch strap** *n* สายนาฬิกา [sai na li ka]

strategic [strəˈtiːdʒɪk] *adj* เกี่ยวกับ ยุทธวิธีหรือกลยุทธ์ [kiao kap yut tha wi thi rue kon la yut]

strategy ['strætɪdʒɪ] *n* ยุทธวิธี [yut tha wi thi]

straw [strɔː] *n* ฟางข้าว [fang khao]

strawberry ['strɔːbərɪ; -brɪ] *n* ผลสตรอ เบอรี่ [phon sa tro boe ri]

stray [streɪ] *n* สัตว์ที่หลงทาง [sat thii long thang]

stream [striːm] *n* ลำธาร [lam than]

street [striːt] *n* ถนน [tha non]; **street map** *n* แผนที่ถนน [phaen thii tha non]; **street plan** *n* แผนที่ถนน [phaen thii tha non]; **I want a street map of the city** ฉันอยากได้แผนที่ถนนของเมืองนี้ [chan yak dai phaen thii tha non khong mueang nii]

streetlamp ['striːtˌlæmp] *n* ไฟถนน [fai tha non]

streetwise ['striːtˌwaɪz] *adj* ซึ่งเอาตัว รอดได้ในสังคมเมือง [sueng ao tua rot dai nai sang khom mueang]

strength [strɛŋθ] *n* ความเข้มแข็ง [khwam khem khaeng]

strengthen ['strɛŋθən] *v* แข็งแรงขึ้น [khaeng raeng khuen]

stress [strɛs] *n* ความเครียด [khwam khriat] ▷ *v* เครียด [khriat]

stressed ['strɛst] *adj* ภาวะถูกกดดัน [pha wa thuk kot dan]

stressful ['strɛsfʊl] *adj* ตึงเครียด [tueng khriat]

stretch [strɛtʃ] *v* ขยายออก [kha yai ork]

stretcher ['strɛtʃə] *n* เปลหาม [phle ham]

stretchy ['strɛtʃɪ] *adj* ซึ่งยืดหยุ่นได้ [sueng yued hyun dai]

strict [strɪkt] *adj* เข้มงวด [khem nguat]

strictly [strɪktlɪ] *adv* อย่างเคร่งครัด [yang khreng khrat]

strike [straɪk] *n* ประท้วง [pra thuang] ▷ *vi* ตี ตีด ปะทะ [ti, diit, pa tha], *(suspend work)* หยุดงานประท้วง [yut ngan pra thuang] ▷ *vt* ตี ตีด ปะทะ [ti, diit, pa tha]; **because of a strike** เพราะมีการประท้วง [khro mii kan pra thuang]

striker ['straɪkə] *n* คนที่หยุดงานประท้วง [khon thii yut ngan pra thuang]

striking ['straɪkɪŋ] *adj* ซึ่งโดดเด่น [sueng dot den]

string [strɪŋ] *n* เชือก [chueak]

strip [strɪp] *n* การเต้นระบำเปลื้องผ้า [kan ten ra bam plueang pha] ▷ *v* แก้ผ้า [khae pha]

stripe [straɪp] *n* แถบสี [thaep si]

striped [straɪpt] *adj* ซึ่งเป็นแถบ [sueng pen thaep]

stripper ['strɪpə] *n* นักเต้นระบำเปลื้องผ้า [nak ten ra bam plueang pha]

stripy ['straɪpɪ] *adj* ซึ่งมีลาย [sueng mii lai]

stroke [strəʊk] *n* *(apoplexy)* อัมพาต เนื่องจากเส้นโลหิตในสมองแตก [am ma

phat nueang chak sen lo hit nai sa
mong taek], (hit) การลูบหรือการสัมผัส
[kan lub rue kan sam phat] ▷ v สัมผัส
หรือลูบคลำ [sam phat rue lup khlam]

stroll [strəʊl] n การเดินทอดน่อง [kan
doen thod nong]

strong [strɒŋ] adj แข็งแรง [khaeng
raeng]

strongly [strɒŋlɪ] adv อย่างมีกำลัง [yang
mii kam lang]

structure [ˈstrʌktʃə] n โครงสร้าง
[khrong sang]

struggle [ˈstrʌgəl] v พยายาม [pha ya
yom]

stub [stʌb] n ส่วนที่เหลืออยู่ [suan thii
luea yu]

stubborn [ˈstʌbən] adj ดื้อ [due]

stub out [stʌb aʊt] v ขยี้ให้ดับ [kha yii
hai dab]

stuck [stʌk] adj ติดชะงัก [tit cha ngak]

stuck-up [stʌkʌp] adj เยอหยิ่ง [yoe ying]

stud [stʌd] n หมุด [mut]

student [ˈstjuːdənt] n นักเรียน [nak
rian]; **student discount** n ราคาลด
สำหรับนักเรียน [ra kha lot sam rap nak
rian]; **Are there any reductions for
students?** มีส่วนลดสำหรับนักเรียนหรือ
ไม่? [mii suan lot sam rap nak rian rue
mai]; **I'm a student** ฉันเป็นนักเรียน
[chan pen nak rian]

studio [ˈstjuːdɪˌəʊ] n ห้องทำงานของช่าง
ถ่ายภาพ ศิลปินและนักดนตรี [hong tham
ngan khong chang thai phap sil la pin
lae nak don tree]; **studio flat** n ห้องชุด
ที่เป็นห้องทำงาน [hong chut thii pen
hong tham ngan]

study [ˈstʌdɪ] v เรียน [rian]; **I'm still
studying** ฉันยังเรียนหนังสืออยู่ [chan
yang rian nang sue yu]

stuff [stʌf] n สิ่งต่างๆ [sing tang tang]

stuffy [ˈstʌfɪ] adj อากาศไม่ถ่ายเท [a kaat
mai thai the]

stumble [ˈstʌmbəl] v สะดุด [sa dut]

stunned [stʌnd] adj ตกตะลึง [tok ta

lueng]

stunning [ˈstʌnɪŋ] adj น่าทึ่ง [na
thueng]

stunt [stʌnt] n การแสดงเสี่ยงอันตราย
[kan sa daeng siang an tra lai]

stuntman, stuntmen [ˈstʌntmən,
ˈstʌntmɛn] n ผู้แสดงแทนในฉากเสี่ยง
อันตราย [phu sa daeng thaen nai chak
siang an ta rai]

stupid [ˈstjuːpɪd] adj โง่ [ngo]

stutter [ˈstʌtə] v ติดอ่าง [tit ang]

style [staɪl] n ความมีรสนิยม การออกแบบ
[khwam mii rot ni yom, kan ok baep]

styling [ˈstaɪlɪŋ] n **Do you sell styling
products?** คุณขายสินค้าแฟชั่นทำผม
ไหม? [khun khai sin ka fae chan tham
phom mai]

stylist [ˈstaɪlɪst] n ช่างทำผมที่เป็นนัก
ออกแบบ [chang tham phom thii pen
nak ork baeb]

subject [ˈsʌbdʒɪkt] n หัวข้อ [hua kho]

submarine [ˈsʌbməˌriːn; ˌsʌbməˈriːn]
n เรือดำน้ำ [ruea dam nam]

subscription [səbˈskrɪpʃən] n การสั่งซื้อ
เป็นประจำ [kan sang sue pen pra cham]

subsidiary [səbˈsɪdɪərɪ] n คนหรือสิ่งที่
เป็นตัวเสริม [khon rue sing thii pen tua
soem]

subsidize [ˈsʌbsɪˌdaɪz] v ให้ความช่วย
เหลือในด้านการเงิน [hai khwam chuai
luea nai dan kan ngoen]

subsidy [ˈsʌbsɪdɪ] n เงินช่วยเหลือ [ngoen
chuai luea]

substance [ˈsʌbstəns] n เนื้อหาสาระ
[nuea ha sa ra]

substitute [ˈsʌbstɪˌtjuːt] n คนหรือสิ่งที่
เข้าแทนที่ [khon rue sing thii khao taen
thii] ▷ v แทนที่ [thaen thi]

subtitled [ˈsʌbˌtaɪtəld] adj ที่มีคำแปล
เขียนไว้ข้างล่างในภาพยนตร์ [thii mii
kham plae khian wai khang lang nai
phap pha yon]

subtitles [ˈsʌbˌtaɪtəlz] npl คำแปลที่เขียน
ไว้ข้างล่างในภาพยนตร์ [kham plae thii

khian wai khang lang nai phap pa yon]

subtle ['sʌt°l] *adj* ซึ่งบอกเป็นนัย ๆ [sueng bok pen nai nai]

subtract [səb'trækt] *v* ลบออกไป [lop ok pai]

suburb ['sʌbɜ:b] *n* ชานเมือง [chan mueang]

suburban [sə'bɜ:bʰn] *adj* นอกเมือง [nok mueang]

subway ['sʌb,weɪ] *n* รถไฟใต้ดิน [rot fai tai din]

succeed [sək'si:d] *v* ประสบความสำเร็จ [pra sop khwam sam ret]

success [sək'sɛs] *n* ความสำเร็จ [khwam sam ret]

successful [sək'sɛsfʊl] *adj* ประสบผลสำเร็จ [pra sop phon sam ret]

successfully [sək'sɛsfʊlɪ] *adv* อย่างประสบผลสำเร็จ [yang pra sop phon sam ret]

successive [sək'sɛsɪv] *adj* อย่างต่อเนื่องกัน [yang tor nueang kan]

successor [sək'sɛsə] *n* ผู้สืบตำแหน่ง [phu suep tam naeng]

such [sʌtʃ] *adj* เช่นนี้ [chen ni] ▷ *adv* อย่างมาก [yang mak]

suck [sʌk] *v* ดูด [dud]

Sudan [su:'dɑːn; -'dæn] *n* ประเทศซูดาน [pra tet su dan]

Sudanese [,su:dʰ'ni:z] *adj* เกี่ยวกับประเทศซูดาน [kiao kap pra thet su dan] ▷ *n* ชาวซูดาน [chao su dan]

sudden ['sʌdʰn] *adj* ทันทีทันใด [than thii than dai]

suddenly ['sʌdʰnlɪ] *adv* อย่างกะทันหัน [yang ka than han]

sue [sjuː; suː] *v* ฟ้องร้อง [fong rong]

suede [sweɪd] *n* หนังกลับชนิดนิ่ม [nang klap cha nit nim]

suffer ['sʌfə] *v* ทนทุกข์ทรมาน [thon thuk tho ra man]

sufficient [sə'fɪʃʰnt] *adj* เพียงพอ [phiang pho]

suffocate ['sʌfə,keɪt] *v* หายใจไม่ออก [hai jai mai ok]

sugar ['ʃʊgə] *n* น้ำตาล [nam tan]; **icing sugar** *n* น้ำตาลผง [nam tan phong]; **no sugar** ไม่ใส่น้ำตาล [mai sai nam tan]

sugar-free ['ʃʊgəfriː] *adj* ไม่มีน้ำตาล [mai mii nam tan]

suggest [sə'dʒɛst; səg'dʒɛst] *v* แนะนำ [nae nam]

suggestion [sə'dʒɛstʃən] *n* คำแนะนำ [kham nae nam]

suicide ['su:ɪ,saɪd; 'sju:-] *n* การฆ่าตัวตาย [kan kha tua tai]; **suicide bomber** *n* ผู้วางระเบิดโดยการฆ่าตัวเอง [phu wang ra boet doi kan kha tua eng]

suit [su:t; sju:t] *n* ชุดสูท [chut sut] ▷ *v* เหมาะสมกัน [mo som kan]; **bathing suit** *n* ชุดอาบน้ำ [chut aap nam]; **shell suit** *n* ชุดกีฬาไนลอน [chut ki la nai lon]

suitable ['su:təbʰl; 'sju:t-] *adj* เหมาะสม [mo som]

suitcase ['su:t,keɪs; 'sju:t-] *n* กระเป๋าเดินทาง [kra pao doen thang]

suite [swi:t] *n* ห้องชุด [hong chut]

sulk [sʌlk] *v* อารมณ์บูดบึ้งไม่พูดไม่จา [a rom but bueng mai phut mai cha]

sulky ['sʌlkɪ] *adj* ที่โกรธขึ้งไม่พูดไม่จา [thii kod khueng mai phud mai cha]

sultana [sʌl'tɑːnə] *n* ลูกเกดชนิดไม่มีเมล็ด [luk ket cha nit mai mii ma let]

sum [sʌm] *n* ผลรวม [phon ruam]

summarize ['sʌmə,raɪz] *v* สรุป [sa rup]

summary ['sʌmərɪ] *n* ใจความสรุป [jai khwam sa rup]

summer ['sʌmə] *n* ฤดูร้อน [rue du ron]; **summer holidays** *npl* วันหยุดในฤดูร้อน [wan yut nai rue du ron]

summertime ['sʌmə,taɪm] *n* เวลาในฤดูร้อน [we la nai rue du ron]

summit ['sʌmɪt] *n* ยอดสุดของภูเขา [yot sut khong phu khao]

sum up [sʌm ʌp] *v* สรุปสาระ [sa rup sa ra]

sun [sʌn] *n* พระอาทิตย์ [phra a thit]

sunbathe ['sʌn,beɪð] v อาบแดด [ap daet]

sunbed ['sʌn,bɛd] n เตียงอาบแดด [tiang aap daet]

sunblock ['sʌn,blɒk] n ครีมกันแสงอาทิตย์ [khrim kan saeng a thit]

sunburn ['sʌn,bɜːn] n ผิวเกรียมจากการถูกแดดมากเกินไป [phio kriam chak kan thuk daet mak koen pai]

sunburnt ['sʌn,bɜːnt] adj เกรียมจากการถูกแดดมากเกินไป [kriam chak kan thuk daet mak koen pai]

suncream ['sʌn,kriːm] n ครีมทากันแสงอาทิตย์ [khrim tha kan saeng a thit]

Sunday ['sʌndɪ] n วันอาทิตย์ [wan a thit]; **Is the museum open on Sundays?** พิพิธภัณฑ์เปิดวันอาทิตย์ไหม? [phi phit tha phan poet wan a thit mai]; **on Sunday** วันอาทิตย์ [wan a thit]

sunflower ['sʌn,flauə] n ดอกทานตะวัน [dok than ta wan]

sunglasses ['sʌn,glɑːsɪz] npl แว่นตากันแดด [waen ta kan daet]

sunlight ['sʌnlaɪt] n แสงอาทิตย์ [saeng a thit]

sunny ['sʌnɪ] adj มีแสงแดดมาก [mii saeng daet mak]

sunrise ['sʌn,raɪz] n พระอาทิตย์ขึ้น [phra a thit khuen]

sunroof ['sʌn,ruːf] n หลังคากันแสงพระอาทิตย์ [lang kha kan saeng phra a thit]

sunscreen ['sʌn,skriːn] n ครีมป้องกันแสงแดด [khrim pong kan saeng daet]

sunset ['sʌn,sɛt] n พระอาทิตย์ตก [phra a thit tok]

sunshine ['sʌn,ʃaɪn] n แสงอาทิตย์ [saeng a thit]

sunstroke ['sʌn,strəʊk] n โรคแพ้แสงแดดจัด [rok pae saeng daet chat]

suntan ['sʌn,tæn] n ผิวหนังเป็นสีน้ำตาลเนื่องจากตากแดด [phio nang pen sii nam tan nueang chak tak daet];

suntan lotion n ครีมที่ทำให้ผิวเป็นสีน้ำตาล [khrim thii tham hai phio pen sii nam tan]; **suntan oil** n น้ำมันที่ทำให้ผิวเป็นสีน้ำตาล [nam man thii tham hai phio pen sii nam tan]

super ['suːpə] adj ดีเยี่ยม [di yiam]

superb [sʊ'pɜːb; sjʊ-] adj วิเศษ [wi set]

superficial [,suːpə'fɪʃəl] adj ผิวเผิน ไม่ลึกซึ้ง ไม่สำคัญ [phio phoen, mai luek sueng, mai sam khan]

superior [suː'pɪərɪə] adj เหนือกว่า [nuea kwa] ▷ n ผู้บังคับบัญชา [phu bang khap ban cha]

supermarket ['suːpə,mɑːkɪt] n ซุปเปอร์มาร์เก็ต [sup poe ma ket]

supernatural [,suːpə'nætʃrəl; -'nætʃərəl] adj เหนือธรรมชาติ [nuea tham ma chat]

superstitious [,suːpə'stɪʃəs] adj ซึ่งเชื่อโชคลาง [sueng chuea chok lang]

supervise ['suːpə,vaɪz] v ตรวจตรา [truat tra]

supervisor ['suːpə,vaɪzə] n หัวหน้างานที่ควบคุมดูแล [hua na ngan thii khuap khum du lae]

supper ['sʌpə] n อาหารเย็น [a han yen]

supplement ['sʌplɪmənt] n ส่วนเสริม [suan sem]

supplier [sə'plaɪə] n ผู้จัดหาสิ่งของให้ [phu chad ha sing khong hai]

supplies [sə'plaɪz] npl สิ่งที่จัดหาให้ [sing thii chat ha hai]

supply [sə'plaɪ] n สิ่งที่จัดหาให้ [sing thii chat ha hai] ▷ v จัดหา [chat ha]; **supply teacher** n ครูตัวแทน [khru tua tan]

support [sə'pɔːt] n การสนับสนุน [kan sa nap sa nun] ▷ v สนับสนุน [sa nap sa nun]

supporter [sə'pɔːtə] n ผู้สนับสนุน [phu sa nap sa nun]

suppose [sə'pəʊz] v สมมติ [som mut]

supposedly [sə'pəʊzɪdlɪ] adv ตามที่สมมติ [tam thii som mut]

supposing [sə'pəʊzɪŋ] conj ถ้าสมมติว่า

[tha som mut wa]

surcharge ['sɜː.tʃɑːdʒ] *n* การเก็บเงินเพิ่ม [kan keb ngen perm]

sure [ʃʊə; ʃɔː] *adj* แน่นอน [nae non]

surely ['ʃʊəlɪ; 'ʃɔː-] *adv* อย่างแน่นอน [yang nae norn]

surf [sɜːf] *n* คลื่นที่ซัดฝั่ง [khluen thii sat fang] ▷ *v* เล่นกระดานโต้คลื่น [len kra dan to khuen]

surface ['sɜːfɪs] *n* ผิวหน้า [phio na]

surfboard ['sɜːfbɔːd] *n* กระดานโต้คลื่น [kra dan to khluen]

surfer ['sɜːfə] *n* ผู้เล่นกระดานโต้คลื่น [phu len kra dan to khluen]

surfing ['sɜːfɪŋ] *n* การเล่นกระดานโต้คลื่น [kan len kra dan to khuen]

surge [sɜːdʒ] *n* การเพิ่มขึ้นอย่างรวดเร็ว [kan perm khuen yang ruad reo]

surgeon ['sɜːdʒən] *n* แพทย์ผ่าตัด [phaet pha tat]

surgery ['sɜːdʒərɪ] *n* (doctor's) ห้องแพทย์ [hong phaet], (operation) การผ่าตัด [kan pha tat]; **cosmetic surgery** *n* การผ่าตัดศัลยกรรมเสริมความงาม [kan pha tat san la ya kam soem khwam ngam]; **plastic surgery** *n* ศัลยกรรมตกแต่ง [san la ya kam tok taeng]

surname ['sɜːˌneɪm] *n* นามสกุล [nam sa kun]

surplus ['sɜːpləs] *adj* เป็นส่วนเกิน [pen suan koen] ▷ *n* จำนวนที่เกิน [cham nuan thii koen]

surprise [sə'praɪz] *n* ความประหลาดใจ [khwam pra lat jai]

surprised [sə'praɪzd] *adj* ทำให้ประหลาดใจ [tham hai pra lat jai]

surprising [sə'praɪzɪŋ] *adj* น่าประหลาดใจ [na pra hlad jai]

surprisingly [sə'praɪzɪŋlɪ] *adv* อย่างประหลาดใจ [yang pra hlad jai]

surrender [sə'rɛndə] *v* ยอมแพ้ [yom phae]

surround [sə'raʊnd] *v* ล้อมรอบ [lom rop]

surroundings [sə'raʊndɪŋz] *npl* บริเวณที่รอบล้อม [bo ri wen thii rop lom]

survey ['sɜːveɪ] *n* การสำรวจ [kan sam ruat]

surveyor [sɜː'veɪə] *n* ผู้สำรวจ [phu sam ruat]

survival [sə'vaɪv°l] *n* การอยู่รอด [kan yu rot]

survive [sə'vaɪv] *v* มีชีวิตรอด [mi chi wit rot]

survivor [sə'vaɪvə] *n* ผู้ที่อยู่รอด [phu thii yu rot]

suspect *n* ['sʌspɛkt] ผู้ต้องสงสัย [phu tong song sai] ▷ *v* [sə'spɛkt] สงสัย [song sai]

suspend [sə'spɛnd] *v* แขวน [khwaen]

suspenders [sə'spɛndəz] *npl* สายที่แขวนกางเกง [sai thii khwaen kang keng]

suspense [sə'spɛns] *n* ความไม่แน่นอนใจ [khwam mai nae non jai]

suspension [sə'spɛnʃən] *n* การหยุดชั่วคราว [kan yut chua khrao]; **suspension bridge** *n* สะพานแขวน [sa phan khwaen]

suspicious [sə'spɪʃəs] *adj* สงสัย [song sai]

swallow ['swɒləʊ] *n* การกลืนน้ำลาย [kan kluen nam lai] ▷ *vi* กล้ำกลืน [klam kluen] ▷ *vt* กลืน ดูดกลืน ฝืนทน [kluen, dut kluen, fuen thon]

swamp [swɒmp] *n* หนองน้ำ [hnong nam]

swan [swɒn] *n* หงส์ [hong]

swap [swɒp] *v* แลกเปลี่ยน [laek plian]

swat [swɒt] *v* ตีอย่างแรง [ti yang raeng]

sway [sweɪ] *v* แกว่งไปมา [kwaeng pai ma]

Swaziland ['swɑːzɪˌlænd] *n* ประเทศสวาซิแลนด์ [pra tet sa wa si laen]

swear [swɛə] *v* สบถ [sa bot]

swearword ['swɛəˌwɜːd] *n* คำสบถ [kham sa bot]

sweat [swɛt] *n* เหงื่อ [nguea] ▷ *v* ทำให้

เหงื่อออก [tham hai nguea ok]

sweater ['swɛtə] n เสื้อที่ถักด้วยขนสัตว์ [suea thii thak duai khon sat]; **polo-necked sweater** n เสื้อหนาวคอ โปโล [suea nao kho po lo]

sweatshirt ['swɛt,ʃɜːt] n เสื้อกีฬาแขน ยาวที่ใช้สวมทับกันหนาวหรือให้เหงื่อออก [suea ki la khaen yao thii chai suam thap kan hnao hue hai hnguea ork]

sweaty ['swɛtɪ] adj เปียกเหงื่อ [piak nguea]

swede [swiːd] n ผักสวิดิเป็นหัว [phak sa wi di pen hua]

Swede [swiːd] n ชาวสวีเดน [chao sa wi den]

Sweden ['swiːdºn] n ประเทศสวีเดน [pra tet sa wi den]

Swedish ['swiːdɪʃ] adj เกี่ยวกับประเทศ สวีเดน [kiao kap pra thet sa wi den] ▷ n ภาษาสวีเดน [pha sa sa vi den]

sweep [swiːp] v กวาด [kwat]

sweet [swiːt] adj (pleasing) อ่อนหวาน [on wan], (taste) หวาน [wan] ▷ n ของ หวาน [khong wan]

sweetcorn ['swiːt,kɔːn] n ข้าวโพดหวาน [khao phot wan]

sweetener ['swiːtºnə] n น้ำตาลเทียม [nam tan thiam]; **Do you have any sweetener?** คุณมีน้ำตาลเทียมไหม? [khun mii nam tan thiam mai]

sweets ['swiːtz] npl ลูกกวาด [luk kwat]

sweltering ['swɛltərɪŋ] adj ร้อนมาก [ron mak]

swerve [swɜːv] v หักเลี้ยว [hak kiao]

swim [swɪm] v ว่ายน้ำ [wai nam]; **Can you swim here?** คุณว่ายน้ำที่นี่ได้ไหม? [khun wai nam thii ni dai mai]; **Let's go swimming** ไปว่ายน้ำกันเถอะ [pai wai nam kan thoe]; **Where can I go swimming?** ฉันจะไปว่ายน้ำได้ที่ไหน? [chan ja pai wai nam dai thii nai]

swimmer ['swɪmə] n นักว่ายน้ำ [nak kwai nam]

swimming ['swɪmɪŋ] n การว่ายน้ำ [kan wai nam]; **swimming costume** n ชุด ว่ายน้ำ [chut wai nam]; **swimming pool** n สระว่ายน้ำ [sa wai nam]; **swimming trunks** npl กางเกงว่ายน้ำ ชาย [kang keng wai nam chai]

swimsuit ['swɪm,suːt; -,sjuːt] n ชุดว่าย น้ำ [chut wai nam]

swing [swɪŋ] n การแกว่งไปมา [kan kwaeng pai ma] ▷ v แกว่ง [kwaeng]

Swiss [swɪs] adj เกี่ยวกับชาวสวิตเซอร์ แลนด์ [kiao kap chao sa wis soe laen] ▷ n ประเทศสวิตเซอร์แลนด์ [pra tet sa vis soe laen]

switch [swɪtʃ] n เครื่องปิดและเปิดไฟฟ้า [khueang pid lae poed fai fa] ▷ v เปลี่ยน [plian]; **Can I switch rooms?** ฉันเปลี่ยน ห้องได้ไหม? [chan plian hong dai mai]

switchboard ['swɪtʃbɔːd] n แผงสาย โทรศัพท์ [phaeng sai tho ra sab]

switch off [swɪtʃ ɒf] v ปิด [pit]; **Can I switch the light off?** ฉันปิดไฟได้ไหม? [chan pit fai dai mai]

switch on [swɪtʃ ɒn] v เปิด [poet]; **Can I switch the radio on?** ฉันเปิดวิทยุได้ ไหม? [chan poet wit tha yu dai mai]; **How do you switch it on?** คุณเปิด โทรทัศน์ได้อย่างไร? [khun poet tho ra tat dai yang rai]

Switzerland ['swɪtsələnd] n ประเทศส วิตเซอร์แลนด์ [pra tet sa vis soe laen]

swollen ['swəʊlən] adj บวม [buam]

sword [sɔːd] n ดาบ [dap]

swordfish ['sɔːd,fɪʃ] n ปลาทะเลขนาด ใหญ่มีขากรรไกรยาวคล้ายกระบี่ [pla tha le kha nard yai mee kha kan kai yao khai kra bi]

swot [swɒt] v เรียนอย่างหนัก [rian yang nak]

syllable ['sɪləbºl] n พยางค์ [pha yang]

syllabus ['sɪləbəs] n หลักสูตรการเรียน [lak sut kan rian]

symbol ['sɪmbºl] n สัญญลักษณ์ [san ya lak]

symmetrical [sɪ'mɛtrɪkºl] adj ซึ่งมี

สัดส่วนสมดุลกัน [sueng mii sat suan som dun kan]

sympathetic [ˌsɪmpəˈθɛtɪk] *adj* เห็นอก เห็นใจ [hen ok hen chai]

sympathize [ˈsɪmpəˌθaɪz] *v* เห็นใจ [hen chai]

sympathy [ˈsɪmpəθɪ] *n* ความเห็นใจ [khwam hen jai]

symphony [ˈsɪmfənɪ] *n* เพลงสำหรับวง ดนตรีประสานเสียงขนาดใหญ่ [phleng sam rap wong don trii pra san siang kha nat yai]

symptom [ˈsɪmptəm] *n* อาการของโรค [a kan khong rok]

synagogue [ˈsɪnəˌɡɒɡ] *n* โบสถ์ของ ศาสนายิว [bot khong sat sa na yio]

syndrome [ˈsɪndrəʊm] *n* **Down's syndrome** *n* โรคอาการพิการทางสมอง [rok a kan phi kan thang sa mong]

Syria [ˈsɪrɪə] *n* ประเทศซีเรีย [pra tet si ria]

Syrian [ˈsɪrɪən] *adj* เกี่ยวกับประเทศซีเรีย [kiao kap pra thet si ria] ▷ *n* ชาวซีเรีย [chao si ria]

syringe [ˈsɪrɪndʒ; sɪˈrɪndʒ] *n* กระบอกฉีด [kra bok chit]

syrup [ˈsɪrəp] *n* น้ำเชื่อม [nam chueam]

system [ˈsɪstəm] *n* ระบบ [ra bop]; **immune system** *n* ระบบต่อต้านเชื้อโรค [ra bop to tan chuea rok]; **solar system** *n* ระบบสุริยะจักรวาล [ra bop su ri ya chak kra wan]; **systems analyst** *n* นักวิเคราะห์ระบบ [nak wi khrao ra bop]

systematic [ˌsɪstɪˈmætɪk] *adj* ซึ่งเป็น ระบบ [sueng pen ra bob]

t

table [ˈteɪbəl] *n (chart)* ตารางรายการ [ta rang rai kan], *(furniture)* โต๊ะ [to]; **bedside table** *n* โต๊ะข้างเตียงนอน [to khang tiang non]; **A table for four people, please** ขอโต๊ะสำหรับสี่คน [kho to sam rap si kon]; **I'd like to book a table for three people for tonight** ฉันอยากจองโต๊ะสำหรับสามคนคืนนี้ [chan yak chong to sam rap sam khon khuen nii]; **I'd like to book a table for two people for tomorrow night** ฉันอยาก จองโต๊ะสำหรับสองคนคืนพรุ่งนี้ [chan yak chong to sam rap song khon khuen phrung nii]

tablecloth [ˈteɪbəlˌklɒθ] *n* ผ้าปูโต๊ะ [pha pu to]

tablespoon [ˈteɪbəlˌspuːn] *n* ช้อนโต๊ะ [chon to]

tablet [ˈtæblɪt] *n* ยาเม็ดแบน [ya med baen]

taboo [təˈbuː] *adj* ซึ่งต้องห้าม [sueng tong ham] ▷ *n* ข้อห้าม [kho ham]

tackle [ˈtækəl; ˈteɪkəl] *n* การยื้อยุดหยุด ฝ่ายตรงข้ามในการครองลูกฟุตบอลหรือรักบี้ [kan yue yut fai trong kham nai kan

khrong luk fut bon rue rak bii] ▷ v
รับมือ [rap mue]; **fishing tackle** n
อุปกรณ์ตกปลา [up pa kon tok pla]

tact [tækt] n การมีไหวพริบหรือปฏิภาณดี
[kan mii wai phrip rue pa ti phan dii]

tactful ['tæktful] adj มีไหวพริบดี [mii
wai phrip di]

tactics ['tæktɪks] npl ยุทธวิธี [yut tha wi
thi]

tactless ['tæktlɪs] adj ปราศจากยุทธวิธี
[prat sa chak yut tha wi thii]

tadpole ['tæd,pəʊl] n ลูกกบ [luk kop]

tag [tæg] n แถบป้ายบอกข้อมูล [thaep pai
bok kho mun]

Tahiti [tə'hiːtɪ] n เกาะตาฮิติทางตอนใต้
ของมหาสมุทรแปซิฟิก [ko ta hi ti thang
ton tai khong ma ha sa mut pae si fik]

tail [teɪl] n หาง [hang]

tailor ['teɪlə] n ช่างตัดเสื้อ [chang tat
suea]

Taiwan ['taɪ'wɑːn] n ประเทศไต้หวัน [pra
tet tai wan]

Taiwanese [ˌtaɪwɑː'niːz] adj ที่เกี่ยวกับ
ประเทศไต้หวัน [thii kiao kap pra tet tai
wan] ▷ n ชาวไต้หวัน [chao tai wan]

Tajikistan [tɑːˌdʒɪkɪ'stɑːn; -stæn] n
ประเทศทาเจคิสถาน [pra tet tha chek ki
sa than]

take [teɪk] v เอาไป [ao pai], (time) ใช้
เวลา [chai we la]; **How long will it
take to get there?** ใช้เวลานานแค่ไหนที่
จะไปที่นั่น? [chai we la nan khae nai
thii ja pai thii nan]; **How long will it
take?** จะใช้เวลานานเท่าไร? [ja chai we
la nan thao rai]; **How much should I
take?** ฉันควรเอาไปเท่าไร? [chan khuan
ao pai thao rai]

take after [teɪk 'ɑːftə] v เจริญรอยตาม
[cha roen roi tam]

take apart [teɪk ə'pɑːt] v ทำให้แยกเป็น
ส่วน [tham hai yaek pen suan]

take away [teɪk ə'weɪ] v เอาออกไป [ao
ok pai]

takeaway ['teɪkə,weɪ] n ร้านที่ขายอาหาร
หรืออาหารที่ซื้อกลับไปทานที่บ้าน [ran thii
khai a han hue a han thii sue klap pai
than thii baan]

take back [teɪk bæk] v นำไปคืน [nam
pai khuen]

taken ['teɪkən] adj **Is this seat taken?**
มีคนนั่งที่นี่ไหม? [mii khon nang thii ni
mai]

take off [teɪk ɒf] v ถอด [thot]

takeoff ['teɪk,ɒf] n การบินขึ้น [kan bin
khuen]

take over [teɪk 'əʊvə] v เข้าควบคุม
[khao khuap khum]

takeover ['teɪk,əʊvə] n การครอบครอง
[kan khrop khrong]

takings ['teɪkɪŋz] npl รายได้ [rai dai]

tale [teɪl] n เรื่องเล่า [rueang lao]

talent ['tælənt] n ความสามารถพิเศษ
[khwam sa mat phi set]

talented ['tæləntɪd] adj ซึ่งมีความ
สามารถพิเศษ [sueng mii khwam sa
maat phi set]

talk [tɔːk] n การแสดงปาฐกถา [kan sa
daeng pa tha ka tha] ▷ v พูดคุย [phud
khui]; **talk to** v พูดกับ [phut kap]

talkative ['tɔːkətɪv] adj ช่างพูด [chang
phut]

tall [tɔːl] adj สูง [sung]; **How tall are
you?** คุณสูงเท่าไร? [khun sung thao
rai]

tame [teɪm] adj เชื่อง [chueang]

tampon ['tæmpɒn] n ผ้าอนามัยแบบสอด
[pha a na mai baep sot]

tan [tæn] n สีไหม้เกรียมของผิวหนังจากการ
ตากแดด [sii mai kriam khong phio
nang chak kan tak daet]

tandem ['tændəm] n จักรยานสองที่นั่ง
[chak ka yan song thii nang]

tangerine [ˌtændʒə'riːn] n ผลส้มจีน
[phon som chin]

tank [tæŋk] n (combat vehicle) รถถัง [rot
thang], (large container) ถังขนาดใหญ่
บรรจุน้ำหรือก๊าซ [thang kha naat yai
ban chu nam rue kas]; **petrol tank** n

ถังน้ำมัน [thang nam man]; **septic tank** n ถังปุ๋ยหมัก [thang pui mak]

tanker ['tæŋkə] n เรือหรือรถที่บรรทุกน้ำมันหรือของเหลวอื่น ๆ [ruea rue rot thii ban thuk nam man rue khong leo uen uen]

tanned [tænd] adj ที่มีผิวสีแทน [thii mii phio sii taen]

tantrum ['tæntrəm] n การมีอารมณ์เกรี้ยวกราด [kan mii a rom kriao krat]

Tanzania [ˌtænzə'nɪə] n ประเทศแทนซาเนีย [pra tet taen sa nia]

Tanzanian [ˌtænzə'nɪən] adj เกี่ยวกับประเทศแทนซาเนีย [kiao kap pra thet thaen sa nia] ▷ n ชาวแทนซาเนีย [chao taen sa nia]

tap [tæp] n การตบเบา ๆ การเคาะเบา ๆ การตีเบา ๆ [kan top bao bao, kan kho bao bao, kan ti bao bao]

tap-dancing ['tæpˌdɑːnsɪŋ] n การเต้นรำโดยใช้รองเท้าเคาะพื้นเป็นจังหวะ [kan ten ram doi chai rong thao kho phuen pen chang wa]

tape [teɪp] n สายผูกและสายมัด [sai phuk lae sai mad] ▷ v บันทึกเสียง [ban thuek siang]; **tape measure** n สายวัด [sai wat]; **tape recorder** n เครื่องอัดเทป [khrueang at thep]

target ['tɑːgɪt] n เป้าหมาย [pao mai]

tariff ['tærɪf] n อัตราภาษีขาเข้า [ad tra pha si kha khao]

tarmac ['tɑːmæk] n ยางมะตอย [yang ma toi]

tarpaulin [tɑː'pɔːlɪn] n ผ้าใบอาบน้ำมันใช้ทำผ้าคลุมกันฝน [pha bai aap nam man chai tham pha khlum kan fon]

tarragon ['tærəgən] n สมุนไพรชนิดหนึ่งมีกลิ่นหอมใช้อาหาร [sa mun phrai cha nit nueng mii klin hom chai a han]

tart [tɑːt] n ขนมพายไส้ต่าง ๆ [kha nom phai sai tang tang]

tartan ['tɑːtⁿn] adj ลายสก็อต [lai sa kot]

task [tɑːsk] n ภารกิจ [pha ra kit]

Tasmania [tæz'meɪnɪə] n รัฐทัสเมเนียใน ประเทศออสเตรเลีย [rat tas me nia nai pra tet os tre lia]

taste [teɪst] n รสชาติ [rot chat] ▷ v ชิม [chim]; **Can I taste it?** ขอฉันชิมได้ไหม? [kho chan chim dai mai]

tasteful ['teɪstfʊl] adj ซึ่งมีรสนิยม [sueng mii rot ni yom]

tasteless ['teɪstlɪs] adj ไม่มีรสนิยม [mai mii rot ni yom]

tasty ['teɪstɪ] adj อร่อรส [ok rot]

tattoo [tæ'tuː] n รอยสัก [roi sak]

Taurus ['tɔːrəs] n ราศีพฤษภ [ra si phrue sop]

tax [tæks] n ภาษี [pha si]; **income tax** n ภาษีเงินได้ [pha si ngoen dai]; **road tax** n ภาษีการใช้ถนน [pha si kan chai tha non]; **tax payer** n ผู้เสียภาษี [phu sia pha si]

taxi ['tæksɪ] n รถแท็กซี่ [rot thaek si]; **taxi driver** n คนขับรถแท็กซี่ [khon khap rot thaek si]; **taxi rank** n ที่ที่แท็กซี่จอดรอรับผู้โดยสาร [thii thii thaek si jot ro rap phu doi san]

TB [tiː biː] n โรควัณนาโรค [rok wan na rok]

tea [tiː] n น้ำชา [nam cha]; **herbal tea** n ชาสมุนไพร [cha sa mun phrai]; **tea bag** n ถุงชา [thung cha]; **tea towel** n ผ้าเช็ดมือ [pha chet mue]

teach [tiːtʃ] v สอน [son]

teacher ['tiːtʃə] n ครู [khru]; **supply teacher** n ครูตัวแทน [khru tua tan]; **I'm a teacher** ฉันเป็นครู [chan pen khru]

teaching ['tiːtʃɪŋ] n การสอน [kan son]

teacup ['tiːˌkʌp] n ถ้วยชา [thuai cha]

team [tiːm] n กลุ่มคนทำงานหรือเล่นกีฬาในกลุ่มเดียวกัน [klum kon tam ngan hue len kee la nai klum diaw kan]

teapot ['tiːˌpɒt] n กาน้ำชา [ka nam cha]

tear¹ [tɪə] n (from eye) น้ำตา [nam ta]

tear² [tɛə] n (split) รอยฉีก [roi chik] ▷ v ฉีก [chik]; **tear up** v ฉีกออก [chiik ok]

teargas ['tɪəˌgæs] n แก๊ซน้ำตา [kaet nam ta]

tease [tiːz] v หยอกล้อ [yok lo]

teaspoon ['tiːˌspuːn] n ช้อนชา [chorn cha]

teatime ['tiːˌtaɪm] n เวลาดื่มน้ำชา [we la duem nam cha]

technical ['tɛknɪkəl] adj เกี่ยวกับวิชาช่าง [kiao kap wi cha chang]

technician [tɛk'nɪʃən] n ผู้ที่มีความ ชำนาญเฉพาะด้าน [phu thii mee khwam cham nan cha pau dan]

technique [tɛk'niːk] n กลวิธี [kon wi thi]

techno ['tɛknɒʊ] n ดนตรีดิสโก้ที่เล่นเร็ว โดยใช้เสียงอิเล็กทรอนิกส์ [don tree dis ko thii len reo doi chai siang e lek tro nik]

technological [tɛk'nɒlədʒɪkəl] adj ทาง เทคโนโลยี [thang thek no lo yii]

technology [tɛk'nɒlədʒɪ] n การนำเอา วิทยาศาสตร์มาใช้ในการปฏิบัติ [kan nam ao wit ta ya sat ma chai nai kan pa ti bat]

tee [tiː] n เป้ารองรับลูกกอล์ฟในการตี [pao rong rap luk kolf nai kan ti]

teenager ['tiːnˌeɪdʒə] n วัยรุ่น [wai run]

teens [tiːnz] npl ช่วงวัยรุ่น [chuang wai run]

tee-shirt ['tiːˌʃɜːt] n เสื้อยืด [suea yued]

teethe [tiːð] v ฟันน้ำนมขึ้น [fan nam num khuen]

teetotal [tiː'təʊtəl] adj เกี่ยวกับเลิกเหล้า อย่างสิ้นเชิง [kiao kab loek lao yang sin cheng]

telecommunications [ˌtɛlɪkəˌmjuːnɪ'keɪʃənz] npl การสื่อสาร ทางไกลโดยใช้เทคโนโลยี [kan sue san thang klai doi chai thek no lo yii]

telegram ['tɛlɪˌɡræm] n โทรเลข [tho ra lek]; **Can I send a telegram from here?** ฉันส่งโทรเลขจากที่นี่ได้ไหม? [chan song tho ra lek chak thii ni dai mai]

telephone ['tɛlɪˌfəʊn] n โทรศัพท์ [tho ra thap]; **telephone directory** n สมุด โทรศัพท์ [sa mut tho ra sap]; **What's the telephone number?** โทรศัพท์เบอร์ อะไร? [tho ra sap boe a rai]

telesales ['tɛlɪˌseɪlz] npl การขายทาง โทรศัพท์ [kan khai tang to ra sab]

telescope ['tɛlɪˌskəʊp] n กล้องส่องทาง ไกล [klong song thang klai]

television ['tɛlɪˌvɪʒən] n โทรทัศน์ [tho ra that]; **cable television** n โทรทัศน์ที่ รับระบบการส่งสัญญาณด้วยสายเคเบิล [tho ra tat thii rap ra bop kan song san yan duai sai khe boen]; **colour television** n โทรทัศน์สี [tho ra tat sii]; **digital television** n โทรทัศน์ดิจิตัล [tho ra tat di chi tal]; **Where is the television?** โทรทัศน์อยู่ที่ไหน? [tho ra tat yu thii nai]

tell [tɛl] v บอก [bok]

teller ['tɛlə] n ผู้เล่านิทาน [phu lao ni than]

tell off [tɛl ɒf] v ด่าว่า [du wa]

telly ['tɛlɪ] n ทีวี [thi wi]

temp [tɛmp] n พนักงานชั่วคราว [pha nak ngan chua khrao]

temper ['tɛmpə] n อารมณ์ [a rom]

temperature ['tɛmprɪtʃə] n อุณหภูมิ [un na ha phum]; **She has a temperature** เธอมีอุณหภูมิ [thoe mii un ha phum]; **What is the temperature?** อุณหภูมิเท่าไร? [un ha phum thao rai]

temple ['tɛmpəl] n วัด [wat]; **Is the temple open to the public?** วัดเปิดให้ สาธารณะชนเข้าชมไหม? [wat poet hai sa tha ra na chon khao chom mai]; **When is the temple open?** วัดจะเปิดเมื่อไร? [wat ja poet muea rai]

temporary ['tɛmpərərɪ; 'tɛmprərɪ] adj ชั่วคราว [chua khrao]

tempt [tɛmpt] v ทำให้อยาก [tham hai yak]

temptation [tɛmp'teɪʃən] n การล่อใจ [kan lo jai]

tempting ['tɛmptɪŋ] adj ล่อใจ [lo chai]

ten [tɛn] number สิบ [sip]; **It's ten o'clock** เวลาสิบโมง [we la sip mong]

tenant ['tɛnənt] n ผู้เช่า [phu chao]

tend [tɛnd] v โน้มเอียง [nom iang]

tendency ['tɛndənsɪ] n ความโน้มเอียง [khwam nom iang]

tender ['tɛndə] adj อ่อนนุ่ม [on num]

tendon ['tɛndən] n เส้นเอ็นที่ยึดกล้ามเนื้อ และกระดูก [sen en thii yuet klam nuea lae kra duk]

tennis ['tɛnɪs] n เทนนิส [then nis]; **table tennis** n การเล่นปิงปอง [kan len ping pong]; **tennis player** n ผู้เล่น เทนนิส [phu len then nis]; **tennis racket** n ไม้ตีเทนนิส [mai ti then nis]; **How much is it to hire a tennis court?** ค่าเช่าสนามเทนนิสเป็นจำนวน เท่าใด? [kha chao sa nam then nis pen cham nuan thao dai]

tenor ['tɛnə] n เสียงสูงรองลงมาจากเสียง สูงสุด [siang sung rong long ma chak siang sung sud]

tense [tɛns] adj ตึง [tueng] ▷ n ตึงเครียด [tueng khriat]

tension ['tɛnʃən] n ความตึงเครียด [khwam tueng khriat]

tent [tɛnt] n เต็นท์ [ten]; **Can we pitch our tent here?** เราเลือกที่ตั้งเต็นท์ที่นี่ได้ ไหม? [rao lueak thii tang tent thii ni dai mai]; **How much is it per night for a tent?** เต็นท์ราคาคืนละเท่าไร? [tent ra kha khuen la thao rai]; **How much is it per week for a tent?** เต็นท์ราคา อาทิตย์ละเท่าไร? [tent ra kha a thit la thao rai]

tenth [tɛnθ] adj ที่สิบ [thii sip] ▷ n อันดับ ที่สิบ [an dap thii sip]

term [tɜːm] n (description) ระยะเวลาที่ กำหนด [ra ya we la thii kam not], (division of year) ภาคเรียน [phak rian]

terminal ['tɜːmɪnəl] adj อยู่ในขั้นร้ายแรง [yu nai khan rai raeng] ▷ n สถานีปลาย ทาง [sa tha ni plai thang]

terminally ['tɜːmɪnəlɪ] adv ไม่สามารถ รักษาได้ [mai sa mat rak sa dai]

terrace ['tɛrəs] n ระเบียง [ra biang]

terraced ['tɛrəst] adj ทำให้ลดหลั่นเป็นชั้น [tham hai lot lan pen chan]

terrible ['tɛrəbəl] adj ซึ่งแย่มาก [sueng yae mak]

terribly ['tɛrəblɪ] adv อย่างน่ากลัว [yang na klua]

terrier ['tɛrɪə] n สุนัขขนาดเล็กพันธุ์หนึ่ง เมื่อก่อนใช้เป็นสุนัขล่าเนื้อ [su nak kha naat lek phan nueng muea kon chai pen su nak la nuea]

terrific [tə'rɪfɪk] adj อย่างมาก [yang mak]

terrified ['tɛrɪˌfaɪd] adj ทำให้น่ากลัวมาก [tham hai na klua mak]

terrify ['tɛrɪˌfaɪ] v ทำให้หวาดกลัว [tham hai wat klua]

territory ['tɛrɪtərɪ; -trɪ] n อาณาเขต [a na khet]

terrorism ['tɛrəˌrɪzəm] n ลัทธิก่อการร้าย [lat thi ko kan rai]

terrorist ['tɛrərɪst] n ผู้ก่อการร้าย [phu ko kan rai]; **terrorist attack** n การถูก โจมตีจากผู้ก่อการร้าย [kan thuk chom ti chak phu ko kan rai]

test [tɛst] n การทดสอบ [kan thot sob] ▷ v ทดสอบ [thot sop]; **driving test** n การ สอบขับรถ [kan sop khap rot]; **smear test** n การตรวจภายใน [kan truat phai nai]; **test tube** n หลอดทดลอง [lot thot long]

testicle ['tɛstɪkəl] n ลูกอัณฑะ [luk an tha]

tetanus ['tɛtənəs] n โรคบาดทะยัก [rok bat tha yak]

text [tɛkst] n ต้นฉบับ [ton cha bap] ▷ v ส่งข้อความทางโทรศัพท์มือถือ [song khor khwam thang tho ra sab mue thue]; **text message** n ข้อความที่ส่งทาง โทรศัพท์มือถือ [kho khwam thii song thang tho ra sap mue thue]

textbook ['tɛkstˌbʊk] n ตำราเรียน [tam ra rian]

textile ['tɛkstaɪl] n วัตถุดิบที่นำมาทำสิ่ง ทอ [wat thu dip thii nam ma tham sing tho]

Thai [taɪ] *adj* เกี่ยวกับประเทศไทย [kiao kap pra thet thai] ▷ *n* (*language*) ภาษาไทย [pha sa thai], (*person*) ชาวไทย [chao thai]

Thailand ['taɪˌlænd] *n* ประเทศไทย [pra tet thai]

than [ðæn; ðən] *conj* เกินกว่า [koen kwa]

thank [θæŋk] *v* ขอบคุณ [khop khun]; **Thank you** ขอบคุณ [khop khun]; **Thank you very much** ขอบคุณมาก [kop khun mak]

thanks [θæŋks] *excl* ขอบคุณ [khop khun]; **Fine, thanks** สบายดี ขอบคุณ [sa bai di, kop khun]

that [ðæt; ðət] *adj* นั้น [nan] ▷ *conj* เพราะว่า [phro wa] ▷ *pron* นั้น [nan], อันนั้น [an nan]

thatched [θætʃt] *adj* ที่มุงด้วยจาก [thii mung duai chak]

thaw [θɔː] *v* **It's thawing** หิมะกำลังละลาย [hi ma kam lang la lai]

the [ðə] *art* คำนำหน้านามชี้เฉพาะ [kham nam na nam chii cha pho]

theatre ['θɪətə] *n* โรงละคร [rong la kon]; **operating theatre** *n* ห้องผ่าตัด [hong pha tat]; **What's on at the theatre?** มีการแสดงอะไรที่โรงละคร? [mii kan sa daeng a rai thii rong la khon]

theft [θɛft] *n* การโขมย [kan kha moi]; **identity theft** *n* การขโมยเอกลักษณ์ [kan kha moi ek ka lak]

their [ðɛə] *pron* ของพวกเขา [khong phuak khao]

theirs [ðɛəz] *pron* ของพวกเขา [khong phuak khao]

them [ðɛm; ðəm] *pron* พวกเขา [phuak khao]

theme [θiːm] *n* หัวข้อ [hua kho]; **theme park** *n* สวนสนุก [suan sa nuk]

themselves [ðəm'sɛlvz] *pron* ด้วยตัวของพวกเขาเอง [duai tua khong phuak khao eng]

then [ðɛn] *adv* ในขณะนั้น [nai kha na nan] ▷ *conj* หลังจากนั้น [lang chak nan]

theology [θɪ'blədʒɪ] *n* ศาสนศาสตร์ [sat sa na]

theory ['θɪərɪ] *n* ทฤษฎี [thrit sa di]

therapy ['θɛrəpɪ] *n* การบำบัดโรค [kan bam bat rok]

there [ðɛə] *adv* ที่นั่น [thi nan]; **How do I get there?** ฉันจะไปที่นั่นได้อย่างไร? [chan ja pai thii nan dai yang rai]

therefore ['ðɛəˌfɔː] *adv* เพราะฉะนั้น [phro cha nan]

thermometer [θə'mɒmɪtə] *n* ปรอทวัดอุณหภูมิ [pa rot wat un ha phum]

Thermos® ['θɜːməs] *n* กระติกน้ำร้อนหรือน้ำเย็น [kra tik nam ron rue nam yen]

thermostat ['θɜːməˌstæt] *n* เครื่องอัตโนมัติสำหรับควบคุมความร้อน [khrueang at ta no mat sam rap khuap khum khwam ron]

these [ðiːz] *adj* เหล่านี้ [lao ni] ▷ *pron* เหล่านี้ [lao ni]

they [ðeɪ] *pron* พวกเขา [phuak khao]

thick [θɪk] *adj* หนา [na]

thickness ['θɪknɪs] *n* ความหนา [khwam na]

thief [θiːf] *n* ขโมย [kha moi]

thigh [θaɪ] *n* ต้นขา [ton kha]

thin [θɪn] *adj* ผอม [phom]

thing [θɪŋ] *n* สิ่งของ [sing khong]

think [θɪŋk] *v* คิด [khit]

third [θɜːd] *adj* ซึ่งเป็นลำดับที่สาม [sueng pen lam dap thii sam] ▷ *n* เศษหนึ่งส่วนสาม [set nueng suan sam]; **third-party insurance** *n* การประกันสำหรับบุคคลที่สาม [kan pra kan sam rap buk khon thii sam]; **Third World** *n* ประเทศที่ด้อยพัฒนา [pra tet thii doi phat ta na]

thirdly [θɜːdlɪ] *adv* ในลำดับสาม [nai lam dap sam]

thirst [θɜːst] *n* ความกระหายน้ำ [khwam kra hai nam]

thirsty ['θɜːstɪ] *adj* ที่กระหายน้ำ [thii kra hai nam]

thirteen ['θɜː'tiːn] *number* สิบสาม [sip

sam]

thirteenth ['θɜːˈtiːnθ] *adj* ลำดับที่สิบสาม [lam dap thii sip sam]

thirty ['θɜːtɪ] *number* สามสิบ [sam sip]

this [ðɪs] *adj* นี้ [ni] ▷ *pron* อันนี้ [an nii]; **I'll have this** ฉันจะสั่งอันนี้ [chan ja sang an nii]; **What is in this?** มีอะไรอยู่ ในนี้ [mii a rai yu nai nii]

thistle ['θɪsᵊl] *n* พันธุ์ไม้มีหนามจำพวกหนึ่ง [phan mai mii nam cham phuak nueng]

thorn [θɔːn] *n* หนาม [nam]

thorough ['θʌrə] *adj* ละเอียดถี่ถ้วน [la iat thi thuan]

thoroughly ['θʌrəlɪ] *adv* อย่างละเอียด รอบคอบ [yang la iat rop khop]

those [ðəʊz] *adj* เหล่านั้น [lao nan] ▷ *pron* เหล่านั้น [lao nan]

though [ðəʊ] *adv* อย่างไรก็ตาม [yang rai ko tam] ▷ *conj* ถึงแม้ว่า [thueng mae wa]

thought [θɔːt] *n* ความคิด [khwam khit]

thoughtful ['θɔːtfʊl] *adj* อย่างมีความคิด [yang mee khwam kid]

thoughtless ['θɔːtlɪs] *adj* อย่างไม่มีความ คิด [yang mai mee khwam kid]

thousand ['θaʊzənd] *number* หนึ่งพัน [nueng phan]

thousandth ['θaʊzənθ] *adj* ที่หนึ่งพัน [thii nueng phan] ▷ *n* เศษหนึ่งส่วนพัน [set nueng suan phan]

thread [θrɛd] *n* ด้าย [dai]

threat [θrɛt] *n* การขู่เข็ญ [kan ku khen]

threaten ['θrɛtᵊn] *v* ขู่เข็ญ [khu khen]

threatening ['θrɛtᵊnɪŋ] *adj* ที่ขู่เข็ญ [thii khu khen]

three [θriː] *number* สาม [sam]; **It's three o'clock** เวลาสามโมง [we la sam mong]

three-dimensional [ˌθriːdɪˈmɛnʃənᵊl] *adj* สามมิติ [sam mi ti]

thrifty ['θrɪftɪ] *adj* ตระหนี่ [tra ni]

thrill [θrɪl] *n* ความตื่นเต้น [khwam tuen ten]

thrilled [θrɪld] *adj* ที่รู้สึกตื่นเต้น [thii ru

suek tuen ten]

thriller ['θrɪlə] *n* เรื่องเขย่าขวัญ [rueang kha yao khwan]

thrilling ['θrɪlɪŋ] *adj* เขย่าขวัญ [kha yao khwan]

throat [θrəʊt] *n* คอ [kho]

throb [θrɒb] *v* เต้นเป็นจังหวะ [ten pen chang wa]

throne [θrəʊn] *n* บัลลังก์ [ban lang]

through [θruː] *prep* ผ่านไป [phan pai]

throughout [θruːˈaʊt] *prep* ทุกหนทุก แห่ง [thuk hon thuk haeng]

throw [θrəʊ] *v* โยน [yon]

throw away [θrəʊ əˈweɪ] *v* โยนทิ้ง [yon thing]

throw out [θrəʊ aʊt] *v* โยนออกไป [yon ok pai]

throw up [θrəʊ ʌp] *v* อาเจียน [a chian]

thrush [θrʌʃ] *n* นกขนาดเล็กมีเสียงไพเราะ [nok kha nard lek mee siang phai rao]

thug [θʌg] *n* อันธพาล [an tha pan]

thumb [θʌm] *n* นิ้วโป้ง [nio pong]

thumb tack ['θʌmˌtæk] *n* เข็มหัวใหญ่ [khem hua yai]

thump [θʌmp] *v* ทุบ [thup]

thunder ['θʌndə] *n* เสียงฟ้าร้อง [siang fa rong]

thunderstorm ['θʌndəˌstɔːm] *n* พายุ ฝนฟ้าคะนอง [pha yu fon fa kha norng]

thundery ['θʌndərɪ] *adj* เสียงและลักษณะ แบบฟ้าร้อง [siang lae lak sa na baep fa rong]

Thursday ['θɜːzdɪ] *n* วันพฤหัสบดี [wan pha rue hat sa bo di]; **on Thursday** วัน พฤหัสบดี [wan pha rue hat sa bo di]

thyme [taɪm] *n* ต้นไม้พันธุ์เตี้ยใช้เป็น เครื่องเทศ [ton mai phan tia chai pen khueang tet]

Tibet [tɪˈbɛt] *n* ประเทศทิเบต [pra tet thi bet]

Tibetan [tɪˈbɛtᵊn] *adj* ที่เกี่ยวกับประเทศ ทิเบต [thii kiao kab pra ted thi bet] ▷ *n* (*language*) ภาษาทิเบต [pha sa thi bet], (*person*) ชาวทิเบต [chao thi bet]

tick [tɪk] *n* เครื่องหมาย [khrueang mai] ▷ *v* ทำเครื่องหมาย [tham khueang mai]

ticket ['tɪkɪt] *n* ตั๋ว [tua]; **bus ticket** *n* ตั๋วรถโดยสารประจำทาง [tua rot doi san pra cham thang]; **a child's ticket** ตั๋วเด็กหนึ่งใบ [tua dek nueng bai]; **Can I buy the tickets here?** ฉันซื้อตั๋วที่นี่ได้ไหม? [chan sue tua thii ni dai mai]; **Can you book the tickets for us?** คุณจองตั๋วให้เราได้ไหม? [khun chong tua hai rao dai mai]

tickle ['tɪkᵊl] *v* ทำให้จั๊กจี้ [tham hai chak ka chi]

ticklish ['tɪklɪʃ] *adj* จั๊กจี้ได้ง่าย [chak ka chi dai ngai]

tick off [tɪk ɒf] *v* ทำเครื่องหมายขีดออก [tham khrueang mai khit ok]

tide [taɪd] *n* ปรากฏการณ์น้ำขึ้นน้ำลง [pra kot kan nam khuen nam long]

tidy ['taɪdɪ] *adj* ที่เป็นระเบียบ [thii pen ra biap] ▷ *v* จัดให้เป็นระเบียบ [chad hai pen ra biap]

tidy up ['taɪdɪ ʌp] *v* จัดให้เป็นระเบียบเรียบร้อย [chat hai pen ra biap riap roi]

tie [taɪ] *n* เนคไท [nek thai] ▷ *v* ผูกให้แน่น [phuk hai naen]; **bow tie** *n* โบว์หูกระต่าย [bo hu kra tai]

tie up [taɪ ʌp] *v* มัดให้แน่น [mat hai naen]

tiger ['taɪɡə] *n* เสือ [suea]

tight [taɪt] *adj* คับแน่น [khap naen]

tighten ['taɪtᵊn] *v* ทำให้แน่นหรือตึงขึ้น [tham hai naen rue tueng khuen]

tights [taɪts] *npl* ถุงน่อง [thung nong]

tile [taɪl] *n* กระเบื้อง [kra bueang]

tiled ['taɪld] *adj* ที่ปูด้วยกระเบื้อง [thii pu duai kra bueang]

till [tɪl] *conj* จนกระทั่ง [chon kra thang] ▷ *prep* จนกว่า จนกระทั่ง [chon kwa, chon kra thang] ▷ *n* กล่องหรือลิ้นชักเก็บเงิน [klong rue lin chak kep ngen]

timber ['tɪmbə] *n* ไม้ที่ใช้ในการก่อสร้าง [mai thii chai nai kan kor srang]

time [taɪm] *n* เวลา [we la]; **closing time** *n* เวลาปิด [we la pit]; **By what time?** ภายในเวลากี่โมง? [phai nai we la ki mong]; **in a month's time** ภายในเวลาหนึ่งเดือน [phai nai we la nueng duean]; **in a week's time** ภายในเวลาหนึ่งอาทิตย์ [phai nai we la nueng a thit]

time bomb ['taɪm‚bɒm] *n* ระเบิดที่ตั้งเวลาได้ [ra boet thii tang we la dai]

timer ['taɪmə] *n* เครื่องจับเวลา [khrueang chap we la]

timeshare ['taɪm‚ʃɛə] *n* ที่พักที่คนซื้อและใช้ตามเวลาที่กำหนดในแต่ละปี [thii phak thii khon sue lae chai tam we la thii kam not nai tae la pi]

timetable ['taɪm‚teɪbᵊl] *n* ตารางเวลา [ta rang we la]; **Can I have a timetable, please?** ฉันขอตารางเวลาได้ไหม? [chan kho ta rang we la dai mai]

tin [tɪn] *n* ดีบุก [di buk]; **tin-opener** *n* ที่เปิดกระป๋อง [thii poet kra pong]

tinfoil ['tɪn‚fɔɪl] *n* แผ่นอะลูมิเนียมที่ใช้ในครัว [phaen a lu mi niam thii chai nai khrua]

tinned [tɪnd] *adj* ที่บรรจุกระป๋อง [thii ban chu kra pong]

tinsel ['tɪnsəl] *n* สิ่งประดับแวววาว [sing pra dap waeo wao]

tinted ['tɪntɪd] *adj* ทำให้สีเข้มขึ้น [tham hai sii khem khuen]

tiny ['taɪnɪ] *adj* เล็กมาก [lek mak]

tip [tɪp] *n* (end of object) จุดปลายสุด [chut plai sut], (reward) การให้เงินรางวัล [kan hai ngen rang wan], (suggestion) ข้อคิดเห็นที่มีประโยชน์ [kho kit hen thii mii pra yot] ▷ *v* (incline) ทำให้เอียง [tham hai iang], (reward) ให้เงินรางวัล [hai ngoen rang wan]

tipsy ['tɪpsɪ] *adj* มึนเมา [muen mao]

tiptoe ['tɪp‚təʊ] *n* เดินด้วยปลายเท้า [doen duai plai thao]

tired ['taɪəd] *adj* เหนื่อยเหนื่อย [net nueai]

tiring ['taɪərɪŋ] *adj* น่าเหนื่อยเหนื่อย [na net nueai]

tissue ['tɪʃjuː; 'tɪʃuː] n (anatomy) เนื้อเยื่อ
ของคน สัตว์และพืช [nuea yuea khong
khon sat lae phuet], (paper) กระดาษ
ทิชชู [kra dat thit chu]

title ['taɪtᵊl] n ชื่อเรื่อง [chue rueang]

to [tuː; tʊ; tə] prep ถึง [thueng]

toad [təʊd] n คางคก [khang khok]

toadstool ['təʊdˌstuːl] n เห็ดมีพิษชนิด
หนึ่ง [het mii phit cha nit nueng]

toast [təʊst] n (grilled bread) ขนมปังปิ้ง
[kha nom pang ping], (tribute) การดื่ม
อวยพร [kan duem uai por]

toaster ['təʊstə] n เครื่องปิ้งขนมปัง
[khrueang ping kha nom pang]

tobacco [tə'bækəʊ] n ต้นยาสูบ [ton ya
sup]

tobacconist's [tə'bækənɪsts] n พ่อค้า
ขายผลิตภัณฑ์ประเภทยาสูบ [pho kha
khai pha lit ta phan pra phet ya sup]

tobogganing [tə'bɒɡənɪŋ] n การเล่น
เลื่อนหิมะ [kan len luean hi ma]

today [tə'deɪ] adv วันนี้ [wan ni]; **What
day is it today?** วันนี้วันอะไร? [wan nii
wan a rai]; **What is today's date?** วันนี้
วันที่เท่าไร? [wan nii wan thii thao rai]

toddler ['tɒdlə] n เด็กวัยหัดเดิน [dek vai
had doen]

toe [təʊ] n นิ้วเท้า [nio thao]

toffee ['tɒfɪ] n ลูกอม [luk om]

together [tə'ɡɛðə] adv ร่วมกัน [ruam
kan]

Togo ['təʊɡəʊ] n สาธารณรัฐโทโก [sa tha
ra na rat tho ko]

toilet ['tɔɪlɪt] n ห้องน้ำ [hong nam];
toilet bag n กระเป๋าใส่เครื่องอาบน้ำเช่น
สบู่ ยาสีฟัน ผมเป็นต้น [kra pao sai
khrueang ap nam chen sa bu ya sii
fan]; **Are there any toilets for the
disabled?** มีห้องน้ำสำหรับคนพิการไหม?
[mii hong nam sam rap khon phi kan
mai]; **Can I use the toilet?** ขอฉันใช้
ห้องน้ำได้ไหม? [kho chan chai hong
nam dai mai]; **Is there a toilet on
board?** มีห้องน้ำบนรถไหม? [mii hong

nam bon rot mai]

toiletries ['tɔɪlɪtriːs] npl เครื่องใช้ใน
ห้องน้ำ เช่น สบู่ ยาสระผม ยาสีฟัน เป็นต้น
[khrueang chai nai hong nam chen sa
bu ya sa phom ya sii fan pen ton]

token ['təʊkən] n สิ่งที่ใช้เป็นสัญลักษณ์
[sing thii chai pen san ya lak]

tolerant ['tɒlərənt] adj ที่มีความอดทน
[thii mee khwam od thon]

toll [təʊl] n การตีระฆัง [kan ti ra khang]

tomato, tomatoes [tə'mɑːtəʊ,
tə'mɑːtəʊz] n มะเขือเทศ [ma khuea
thet]; **tomato sauce** n ซอสมะเขือเทศ
[sos ma khuea tet]

tomb [tuːm] n สุสานฝังศพ [su san fang
sop]

tomboy ['tɒmˌbɔɪ] n เด็กผู้หญิงที่มี
พฤติกรรมคล้ายเด็กผู้ชาย [dek phu ying
thii mii phruet ti kam khlai dek phu
chai]

tomorrow [tə'mɒrəʊ] adv พรุ่งนี้
[phrung ni]; **Is it open tomorrow?** เปิด
พรุ่งนี้ไหม? [poet phrung nii mai];
tomorrow morning พรุ่งนี้เช้า [phrung
nii chao]

ton [tʌn] n หน่วยน้ำหนักเท่ากับสองพันสอง
ร้อยสี่สิบปอนด์ [nuai nam nak thao kap
song phan song roi si sip pond]

tone [təʊn] n **dialling tone** n เสียงหมุน
โทรศัพท์ [siang mun tho ra sap];
engaged tone n เสียงสายไม่ว่างของ
โทรศัพท์ [siang sai mai wang khong
tho ra sap]

Tonga ['tɒŋɡə] n สาธารณรัฐทองกา [sa
tha ra na rat thong ka]

tongue [tʌŋ] n ลิ้น [lin]; **mother
tongue** n ภาษาแม่ [pha sa mae]

tonic ['tɒnɪk] n ยาบำรุง [ya bam rung]

tonight [tə'naɪt] adv คืนนี้ [khuen ni];
Two tickets for tonight, please ขอตั๋ว
สองใบสำหรับคืนนี้ [kho tua song bai sam
rap khuen nii]; **What's on tonight at
the cinema?** คืนนี้โรงหนังมีหนังอะไร
ฉาย? [khuen nii rong nang mii nang a

rai chai]; **Where would you like to go tonight?** คืนนี้คุณอยากจะไปที่ไหน? [khuen nii khun yak pai thii nai]

tonsillitis [ˌtɒnsɪˈlaɪtɪs] *n* ภาวะต่อมทอนซิลอักเสบ [pha wa tom thon sil ak sep]

tonsils [ˈtɒnsəlz] *npl* ต่อมทอนซิล [tom thon sin]

too [tuː] *adv* อีกด้วย [ik duai]

tool [tuːl] *n* เครื่องมือ [khrueang mue]

tooth, teeth [ˈtuːθ, tiːθ] *n* ฟัน [fan]; **wisdom tooth** *n* ฟันกราม [fan kram]; **I've broken a tooth** ฉันทำฟันหักหนึ่งซี่ [chan tham fan hak nueng si]; **This tooth hurts** ปวดฟันซี่นี้ [puat fan si nii]

toothache [ˈtuːθˌeɪk] *n* การปวดฟัน [kan puat fan]

toothbrush [ˈtuːθˌbrʌʃ] *n* แปรงสีฟัน [praeng si fan]

toothpaste [ˈtuːθˌpeɪst] *n* ยาสีฟัน [ya si fan]

toothpick [ˈtuːθˌpɪk] *n* ไม้จิ้มฟัน [mai chim fan]

top [tɒp] *adj* สูงที่สุด [sung thi sut] ▷ *n* ลูกข่าง [luk khang]

topic [ˈtɒpɪk] *n* หัวข้อ [hua kho]

topical [ˈtɒpɪkəl] *adj* เกี่ยวกับเรื่องที่ได้รับความสนใจในขณะนั้น [kiao kap rueang thii dai rap khwam son jai nai kha na nan]

top-secret [ˈtɒpˈsiːkrɪt] *adj* ลับสุดยอด [lap sut yot]

top up [tɒp ʌp] *v* **Can you top up the windscreen washers?** คุณเติมน้ำยาล้างกระจกได้ไหม? [khun toem nam ya lang kra chok dai mai]; **Where can I buy a top-up card?** คุณซื้อการ์ดเติมได้ที่ไหน? [khun sue kat toem dai thii nai]

torch [tɔːtʃ] *n* ไฟฉาย [fai chai]

tornado [tɔːˈneɪdəʊ] *n* พายุทอร์นาโด [pha yu tho na do]

tortoise [ˈtɔːtəs] *n* เต่า [tao]

torture [ˈtɔːtʃə] *n* การทรมาน [kan tho ra man] ▷ *v* ทรมาน [to ra man]

toss [tɒs] *v* โยนเหรียญ [yon lian]

total [ˈtəʊtəl] *adj* โดยสมบูรณ์ [doi som bun] ▷ *n* ผลรวม [phon ruam]

totally [ˈtəʊtəlɪ] *adv* โดยสิ้นเชิง [doi sin choeng]

touch [tʌtʃ] *v* สัมผัส [sam phat]

touchdown [ˈtʌtʃˌdaʊn] *n* การบินลงแตะพื้น [kan bin long tae phuen]

touched [tʌtʃt] *adj* ที่ถูกสัมผัส [thii thuk sam phat]

touching [ˈtʌtʃɪŋ] *adj* ที่สามารถกระตุ้นความรู้สึกออนโยน [thii sa mart kra tun khwam ru suk on yon]

touchline [ˈtʌtʃˌlaɪn] *n* ขอบเขตของการเล่นกีฬาบางอย่าง [kop khet khong kan len ki la bang yang]

touchpad [ˈtʌtʃˌpæd] *n* อุปกรณ์ในเครื่องคอมพิวเตอร์แบบกระเป๋าหิ้วที่ใช้แทนเมาส์เพื่อแสดงตัวชี้ตำแหน่ง [up pa kon nai khrueang khom phio toe baep kra pao hio thii chai thaen mao phuea sa daeng tua chii tam naeng]

touchy [ˈtʌtʃɪ] *adj* ฉุนเฉียวโกรธง่าย [chun chiao krot ngai]

tough [tʌf] *adj* ที่ทนทาน [thii thon than]

toupee [ˈtuːpeɪ] *n* ผมปลอมของชาย [phom plom khong chai]

tour [tʊə] *n* การท่องเที่ยวไปชมสถานที่ต่างๆ [kan thong thiao pai chom sa than thii tang tang] ▷ *v* ท่องเที่ยวไปชมสถานที่ต่างๆ [thong thiao pai chom sa than thii tang tang]; **guided tour** *n* กรุ๊ปทัวร์ [krup thua]; **package tour** *n* ทัวร์ที่จัดแบบครบวงจร [thua thii chat baep khrop wong chon]; **tour guide** *n* มัคคุเทศก์ [mak khu thet]

tourism [ˈtʊərɪzəm] *n* การท่องเที่ยว [kan thong thiao]

tourist [ˈtʊərɪst] *n* นักท่องเที่ยว [nak thong thiao]; **tourist office** *n* สำนักงานการท่องเที่ยว [sam nak ngan kan thong thiao]; **I'm here as a tourist** ฉันมาที่นี่

อย่างนักท่องเที่ยว [chan ma thii ni yang nak thong thiao]

tournament ['tʊənəmənt; 'tɔː-; 'tɜː-] *n* การแข่งขัน [kan khaeng khan]

towards [təˈwɔːdz; tɔːdz] *prep* ไปทาง [pai thang]

tow away [təʊ əˈweɪ] *v* ลากไป [lak pai]

towel ['taʊəl] *n* ผ้าขนหนู [pha khon nu]; **bath towel** *n* ผ้าขนหนูเช็ดตัว [pha khon nu chet tua]; **dish towel** *n* ผ้าเช็ดจาน [pha chet chan]; **sanitary towel** *n* ผ้าอนามัย [pha a na mai]

tower ['taʊə] *n* ตึกสูง [tuek sung]

town [taʊn] *n* เขตเมือง [khet mueang]; **town centre** *n* ใจกลางเมือง [jai klang mueang]; **town hall** *n* ศาลากลางจังหวัด [sa la klang changhwat]; **town planning** *n* การวางผังเมือง [kan wang phang mueang]

toxic ['tɒksɪk] *adj* มีพิษ [mii phit]

toy [tɔɪ] *n* ของเล่น [khong len]

trace [treɪs] *n* ร่องรอย [rong roi]

tracing paper ['treɪsɪŋ 'peɪpə] *n* กระดาษลอกลาย [kra dat lok lai]

track [træk] *n* หนทาง [hon thang]

track down [træk daʊn] *v* ติดตามจนพบ [tit tam chon phop]

tracksuit ['trækˌsuːt; -ˌsjuːt] *n* ชุดกีฬา [chud ki la]

tractor ['træktə] *n* รถแทรกเตอร์ [rot traek toe]

trade [treɪd] *n* การค้าขาย [kan ka khai]; **trade union** *n* สหภาพแรงงาน [sa ha phap raeng ngan]; **trade unionist** *n* สมาชิกสหภาพแรงงาน [sa ma chik sa ha phap raeng ngan]

trademark ['treɪdˌmɑːk] *n* เครื่องหมายการค้า [khrueang mai kan kha]

tradition [trəˈdɪʃən] *n* ประเพณี [pra phe ni]

traditional [trəˈdɪʃənᵊl] *adj* โบราณ แบบดั้งเดิม แบบเก่าแก่ [bo ran, baep dang doem, baep kao kae]

traffic ['træfɪk] *n* การจราจร [kan cha ra chorn]; **traffic jam** *n* การจราจรติดขัด [kan cha ra chorn tit khat]; **traffic lights** *npl* สัญญาณจราจร [san yan cha ra chon]; **traffic warden** *n* เจ้าหน้าที่การจัดการจราจร [chao na thii kan chat kan cha ra chon]

tragedy ['trædʒɪdɪ] *n* โศกนาฏกรรม [sok ka nat ta kam]

tragic ['trædʒɪk] *adj* น่าสลดใจ [na sa lot jai]

trailer ['treɪlə] *n* รถพ่วง [rot phuang]

train [treɪn] *n* รถไฟ [rot fai] ▷ *v* อบรม [op rom]; **Does the train stop at…?** รถไฟคันนี้จอดที่…หรือไม่? [rot fai khan nii jot thii…rue mai]; **How frequent are the trains to…?** รถไฟไป…มาบ่อยแค่ไหน? [rot fai pai…ma boi khae nai]; **I've missed my train** ฉันพลาดรถไฟ [chan phlat rot fai]

trained ['treɪnd] *adj* ที่ได้รับการอบรม [thii dai rap kan op rom]

trainee [treɪˈniː] *n* ผู้ได้รับการฝึก [phu dai rap kan fuek]

trainer ['treɪnə] *n* ผู้ฝึก [phu fuek]

trainers ['treɪnəz] *npl* รองเท้าผ้าใบ [rong thao pha bai]

training ['treɪnɪŋ] *n* การฝึก [kan fuek]; **training course** *n* หลักสูตรอบรม [lak sut op rom]

tram [træm] *n* รถราง [rot rang]

tramp [træmp] *n* (*beggar*) คนจรจัด [khon chon chat], (*long walk*) การเดินทางไกล [kan doen thang kai]

trampoline ['træmpəlɪn; -ˌliːn] *n* เตียงที่ใช้ตีลังกาของคณะกายกรรม [tiang thii chai ti lang ka khong kha na kai ya kram]

tranquillizer ['træŋkwɪˌlaɪzə] *n* ยาที่ทำให้จิตใจสงบ [ya thii tham hai chit jai sa ngop]

transaction [trænˈzækʃən] *n* การติดต่อทางธุรกิจ การดำเนินการทางธุรกิจ [kan tit to thang thu ra kit, kan dam noen kan thang thu ra kit]

transcript ['trænskrɪpt] *n* ใบรับรองผล
การศึกษา [bai rap rong phon kan suek
sa]

transfer *n* ['trænsfɜː] การย้ายโอน [kan
yai on] ▷ *v* [træns'fɜː] ย้ายโอน [yai on]

transform [træns'fɔːm] *v* ทำให้
เปลี่ยนแปลง [tham hai plian plang]

transfusion [træns'fjuːʒən] *n* การถ่าย
เลือด [kan thai luead]; **blood
transfusion** *n* การถ่ายเลือด [kan thai
luead]

transistor [træn'zɪstə] *n* อุปกรณ์กึ่ง
ตัวนำช่วยขยายสัญญาณทางอิเล็กทรอนิกส์
[ub pa korn kueng tua nam chuai kha
yai san yanthang e lek thro nik]

transit ['trænsɪt; 'trænz-] *n* การขนส่ง
[kan khon song]; **transit lounge** *n* ห้อง
พักสำหรับผู้โดยสารที่จะเปลี่ยนเครื่องบิน
[hong phak sam rap phu doi san thii ja
plian khrueang bin]

transition [træn'zɪʃən] *n* การ
เปลี่ยนแปลง [kan plian plaeng]

translate [træns'leɪt; trænz-] *v* แปล
[plae]; **Can you translate this for
me?** คุณกรุณาแปลนี่ให้ได้ไหม? [khun ka
ru na plae ni hai dai mai]

translation [træns'leɪʃən; trænz-] *n*
การแปล [kan plae]

translator [træns'leɪtə; trænz-] *n* ผู้
แปล [phu plae]

transparent [træns'pærənt; -'pɛər-]
adj โปร่งใส [prong sai]

transplant ['træns,plɑːnt] *n* การปลูก
ถ่ายอวัยวะ [kan pluk thai a wai ya wa]

transport *n* ['træns,pɔːt] การขนส่ง
[kan khon song] ▷ *v* [træns'pɔːt] ขนส่ง
[khon song]; **public transport** *n*
การขนส่งมวลชน [kan khon song muan
chon]

transvestite [trænz'vɛstaɪt] *n* ผู้ชายที่
แต่งตัวเป็นเพศตรงกันข้าม [phu chai thii
taeng tua pen phet trong kan kham]

trap [træp] *n* กับดัก [kap dak]

trash [træʃ] *n* เรื่องเหลวไหล [rueang leo
lai]

traumatic ['trɔːmətɪk] *adj* ซึ่งบอบช้ำ
ทางจิตใจ [sueng bop cham thang chit
jai]

travel ['trævəl] *n* การเดินทาง [kan doen
thang] ▷ *v* เดินทาง [doen thang]; **travel
agency** *n* สำนักงานท่องเที่ยว [sam nak
ngan thong thiao]; **travel agent's** *n* ที่
สำนักงานตัวแทนท่องเที่ยว [thii sam nak
ngan tua taen thong thiao]; **travel
sickness** *n* อาการเมารถ เรือหรือเครื่องบิน
[a kan mao rot ruea rue khrueang bin];
I don't have travel insurance ฉันไม่มี
ประกันการเดินทาง [chan mai mii pra
kan kaan doen thang]; **I get
travel-sick** ฉันรู้สึกป่วยเวลาเดินทาง
[chan ru suek puai we la doen thang];
I'm travelling alone ฉันเดินทางคนเดียว
[chan doen thang khon diao]

traveller ['trævələ; 'trævlə] *n* ผู้เดินทาง
[phu doen thang]; **traveller's cheque**
n เช็คเดินทาง [chek doen thang]

travelling ['trævəlɪŋ] *n* การเดินทาง [kan
doen thang]

tray [treɪ] *n* ถาด [that]

treacle ['triːkəl] *n* น้ำเชื่อม [nam
chueam]

tread [trɛd] *v* เหยียบ [yiap]

treasure ['trɛʒə] *n* สมบัติ [som bat]

treasurer ['trɛʒərə] *n* เหรัญญิก [he ran
yik]

treat [triːt] *n* เลี้ยงให้ของ [liang hai
khong] ▷ *v* ปฏิบัติ [pa ti bat]

treatment ['triːtmənt] *n* การดูแลรักษา
[kan du lae rak sa]

treaty ['triːtɪ] *n* สนธิสัญญา [son thi san
ya]

treble ['trɛbəl] *v* เพิ่มเป็นสามเท่า [poem
pen sam thao]

tree [triː] *n* ต้นไม้ [ton mai]

trek [trɛk] *n* การเดินทางระยะยาวด้วยความ
ยากลำบาก [kan doen thang ra ya yao
duai khwam yak lam bak] ▷ *v* เดินอย่าง

ช้าๆ [doen yang cha cha]

trekking ['trɛkɪŋ] n I'd like to go pony
trekking ฉันอยากไปขี่ม้าช้าๆ ตามทางที่
ขรุขระ [chan yak pai khi ma cha cha
tam thang thii khru khra]

tremble ['trɛmbəl] v สั่นสะเทือน [san sa
thuean]

tremendous [trɪ'mɛndəs] adj ใหญ่โต
มาก [yai to mak]

trench [trɛntʃ] n คู [khu]

trend [trɛnd] n แนวทาง [naeo thang]

trendy ['trɛndɪ] adj ซึ่งเป็นที่นิยม [sueng
pen thii ni yom]

trial ['traɪəl] n การทดลอง [kan thod
long], การพิจารณาคดี [kan phi cha ra
na kha di]; **trial period** n ระยะเวลา
ทดลอง [ra ya we la thot long]

triangle ['traɪˌæŋgəl] n สามเหลี่ยม [sam
liam]

tribe [traɪb] n เผ่า [phao]

tribunal [traɪ'bjuːnəl; trɪ-] n ศาล
ยุติธรรม [san yu ti tham]

trick [trɪk] n เล่ห์เหลี่ยม [le liam] ▷ v ใช้
เล่ห์เหลี่ยม [chai le liam]

tricky ['trɪkɪ] adj ที่มีเล่ห์เหลี่ยม [thii mee
le hliam]

tricycle ['traɪsɪkəl] n รถสามล้อ [rot sam
lo]

trifle ['traɪfəl] n เรื่องเล็ก ๆ น้อย ๆ [rueang
lek lek noi noi]

trim [trɪm] v ขลิบ [khlip]

Trinidad and Tobago ['trɪnɪˌdæd
ænd tə'beɪgəʊ] n สาธารณรัฐทรินิแดดและ
โทบาโก [sa tha ra na rat thri ni daet lae
tho ba ko]

trip [trɪp] n การเดินทาง [kan doen
thang]; **business trip** n การเดินทางไป
ทำธุรกิจ [kan doen thang pai tham thu
ra kit]; **round trip** n การเดินทางไปและ
กลับ [kan doen thang pai lae klap]; **trip
(up)** v สะดุด [sa dut]; **This is my first
trip to..** นี่เป็นการเดินทางครั้งแรกของฉัน
ที่จะไป... [ni pen kan doen thang
khrang raek khong chan thii ja pai…]

triple ['trɪpəl] adj ประกอบด้วยสามส่วน
[pra kop duai sam suan]

triplets ['trɪplɪts] npl แฝดสาม [faer
sam]

triumph ['traɪəmf] n ความยินดีจาก
ชัยชนะ [khwam yin dii chak chai cha
na] ▷ v ประสบความสำเร็จ [pra sop
khwam sam ret]

trivial ['trɪvɪəl] adj ไม่สำคัญ [mai sam
khan]

trolley ['trɒlɪ] n รถเข็น [rot khen];
luggage trolley n รถเข็นกระเป๋าเดินทาง
[rot khen kra pao doen thang];
shopping trolley n รถเข็นในห้างสรรพ
สินค้า [rot khen nai hang sap pha sin
ka]

trombone [trɒm'bəʊn] n แตรยาว [trae
yao]

troops ['truːps] npl กองทหาร [kong tha
haan]

trophy ['trəʊfɪ] n ถ้วยรางวัล [thuai rang
wan]

tropical ['trɒpɪkəl] adj เกี่ยวกับเขตร้อน
[kiao kap khet ron]

trot [trɒt] v วิ่งเหยาะๆ [wing hyao hyao]

trouble ['trʌbəl] n ปัญหา [pan ha]

troublemaker ['trʌbəlˌmeɪkə] n ผู้ก่อ
ปัญหา [phu kor pan ha]

trough [trɒf] n รางอาหารหรือน้ำสำหรับ
สัตว์ [rang a han rue nam sam rap sat]

trousers ['traʊzəz] npl กางเกง [kang
keng]; **Can I try on these trousers?**
ฉันลองกางเกงตัวนี้ได้ไหม? [chan long
kang keng tua nii dai mai]

trout [traʊt] n ปลาจำพวกหนึ่งมีลักษณะ
คล้ายปลาแซลมอน [pla cham phuak
hueng mee lak sa na khlai pla sael
mon]

trowel ['traʊəl] n เกรียง [kriang]

truant ['truːənt] n play truant v หนี
โรงเรียน [nii rong rian]

truce [truːs] n การสงบศึกชั่วคราว [kan sa
ngob suek chua khrao]

truck [trʌk] n รถสินค้าในขบวนรถไฟ [rot

sin ka nai kha buan rot fai];
breakdown truck *n* รถบรรทุกเสีย [rot ban thuk sia]; **truck driver** *n* คนขับรถบรรทุก [khon khap rot ban thuk]

true [truː] *adj* ที่เป็นเรื่องจริง [thii pen rueang chring]

truly ['truːlɪ] *adv* อย่างแท้จริง [yang thae ching]

trumpet ['trʌmpɪt] *n* แตร [trae]

trunk [trʌŋk] *n* ลำต้น [lam ton];
swimming trunks *npl* กางเกงว่ายน้ำชาย [kang keng wai nam chai]

trunks [trʌŋks] *npl* กางเกงว่ายน้ำชาย [kang keng wai nam chai]

trust [trʌst] *n* ความเชื่อใจ [khwam chuea jai] ▷ *v* ไว้วางใจ [wai wang chai]

trusting ['trʌstɪŋ] *adj* ที่ไว้วางใจ [thii wai wang jai]

truth [truːθ] *n* ความจริง [khwam ching]

truthful ['truːθfʊl] *adj* ซื่อสัตย์ [sue sat]

try [traɪ] *n* ความพยายาม [khwam pha ya yam] ▷ *v* พยายาม [pha ya yom]

try on [traɪ ɒn] *v* ลองสวมใส่ [long suam sai]

try out [traɪ aʊt] *v* ลองดู [long du]

T-shirt ['tiːˌʃɜːt] *n* เสื้อยืด [suea yued]

tsunami [tsʊˈnæmɪ] *n* คลื่นซึนามิเกิดจากแผ่นดินไหวใต้ทะเล [khluen sue na mi koet chak phaen din wai tai tha le]

tube [tjuːb] *n* หลอด [lot]; **inner tube** *n* ยางในของรถ [yang nai khong rot]; **test tube** *n* หลอดทดลอง [lot thot long]; **tube station** *n* สถานีรถไฟใต้ดิน [sa tha ni rot fai tai din]

tuberculosis [tjʊˌbɜːkjʊˈləʊsɪs] *n* วัณโรค [wan na rok]

Tuesday ['tjuːzdɪ] *n* วันอังคาร [wan ang khan]; **Shrove Tuesday** *n* วันเทศกาลสารภาพบาป [wan tet sa kan sa ra phap bap]; **on Tuesday** วันอังคาร [wan ang khan]

tug-of-war ['tʌgɒvˈwɔː] *n* ชักเย่อ [chak ka yoe]

tuition [tjuːˈɪʃən] *n* การสอนพิเศษ [kan son phi set]; **tuition fees** *npl* ค่าเล่าเรียน [kha lao rian]

tulip ['tjuːlɪp] *n* ดอกทิวลิป [dok thio lip]

tummy ['tʌmɪ] *n* ท้อง [thong]

tumour ['tjuːmə] *n* เนื้องอก [nue ngok]

tuna ['tjuːnə] *n* ปลาทูน่า [pla thu na]

tune [tjuːn] *n* ทำนอง [tham nong]

Tunisia [tjuːˈnɪzɪə; -ˈnɪsɪə] *n* ประเทศตูนิเซีย [pra tet tu ni sia]

Tunisian [tjuːˈnɪzɪən; -ˈnɪsɪən] *adj* เกี่ยวกับตูนิเซีย [kiao kap tu ni sia] ▷ *n* ชาวตูนิเซีย [chao tu ni sia]

tunnel ['tʌnəl] *n* อุโมงค์ [u mong]

turbulence ['tɜːbjʊləns] *n* ความปั่นป่วน [khwam pan puan]

Turk [tɜːk] *n* ชาวตุรกี [chao tu ra ki]

Turkey ['tɜːkɪ] *n* ประเทศตุรกี [pra tet tu ra ki]

turkey ['tɜːkɪ] *n* ไก่งวง [kai nguang]

Turkish ['tɜːkɪʃ] *adj* เกี่ยวกับตุรกี [kiao kap tu ra ki] ▷ *n* ภาษาตุรกี [pha sa tu ra ki]

turn [tɜːn] *n* การเลี้ยว [kan liao] ▷ *v* เลี้ยว [liao]; **Turn left** เลี้ยวซ้าย [liao sai]; **Turn right** เลี้ยวขวา [liao khwa]

turn around [tɜːn əˈraʊnd] *v* หมุนกลับ [mun klap]

turn back [tɜːn bæk] *v* เลี้ยวกลับ [liao klap]

turn down [tɜːn daʊn] *v* ทำให้ลดลง [tham hai lot long]

turning ['tɜːnɪŋ] *n* จุดเลี้ยว [chud liao]

turnip ['tɜːnɪp] *n* หัวผักกาด [hua phak kat]

turn off [tɜːn ɒf] *v* ปิด [pit]; **I can't turn the heating off** ฉันปิดเครื่องทำความร้อนไม่ได้ [chan pit khrueang tham khwam ron mai dai]; **It won't turn off** มันปิดไม่ได้ [man pit mai dai]; **Turn it off at the mains** ปิดที่สายเคเบิลใหญ่ [pit thii sai khe boen yai]

turn on [tɜːn ɒn] *v* เปิด [poet]; **I can't turn the heating on** ฉันเปิดเครื่องทำความร้อนไม่ได้ [chan poet khrueang tham khwam ron mai dai]; **It won't turn on** มันเปิดไม่ได้ [man poet mai dai]

turn out [tɜːn aʊt] v ปิด [pit]

turnover ['tɜːnˌəʊvə] n ยอดขาย [yot khai]

turn round [tɜːn raʊnd] v หมุนกลับ [mun klap]

turnstile ['tɜːnˌstaɪl] n ทางเข้าที่มีแกนหมุนให้ผ่านได้ทีละคน [thang khao thii mii kaen mun hai phan dai thi la khon]

turn up [tɜːn ʌp] v พลิกหงาย [phlik ngai]

turquoise ['tɜːkwɔɪz; -kwɑːz] adj สีน้ำเงินอมเขียว [sii nam ngoen om khiao]

turtle ['tɜːtəl] n เต่า [tao]

tutor ['tjuːtə] n ครูสอนพิเศษ [khru sorn phi sed]

tutorial [tjuːˈtɔːrɪəl] n การเรียนพิเศษแบบเข้ม [kan rian phi set baep khem]

tuxedo [tʌkˈsiːdəʊ] n ชุดทักซิโด [chut thak si do]

TV [tiː viː] n ทีวี [thi wi]; **plasma TV** n ทีวีที่มีจอภาพแบน [tii wii thii mii cho phap baen]; **reality TV** n รายการทีวีที่แสดงสภาพความเป็นจริง [rai kan thii wii thii sa daeng sa phap khwam pen ching]; **Does the room have a TV?** มีทีวีในห้องไหม? [mii thii wii nai hong mai]

tweezers ['twiːzəz] npl แหนบ [naep]

twelfth [twɛlfθ] adj ลำดับที่สิบสอง [lam dap thii sip song]

twelve [twɛlv] number สิบสอง [sip song]

twentieth ['twɛntɪɪθ] adj ลำดับที่ยี่สิบ [lam dap thii yi sip]

twenty ['twɛntɪ] number ยี่สิบ [yi sip]

twice [twaɪs] adv สองครั้ง [song khrang]

twin [twɪn] n คู่แฝด [khu faet]; **twin beds** npl เตียงคู่ [tiang khu]; **twin room** n ห้องคู่ [hong khu]; **twin-bedded room** n ห้องที่มีเตียงคู่ [hong thii mii tiang khu]

twinned ['twɪnd] adj เหมือนกัน [muean kan]

twist [twɪst] v บิดเป็นเกลียว [bit pen kliao]

twit [twɪt] n คนโง่ [khon ngo]

two [tuː] num สอง [song]; **I'd like two hundred...** ฉันอยากเบิกสองร้อย... [chan yak boek song roi...]

type ['taɪp] n รูปแบบ [rup baep] ▷ v พิมพ์ [phim]

typewriter ['taɪpˌraɪtə] n เครื่องพิมพ์ดีด [khrueang phim dit]

typhoid ['taɪfɔɪd] n ไข้รากสาดน้อย [khai rak sat noi]

typical ['tɪpɪkəl] adj ซึ่งเป็นตัวอย่าง [sueng pen tua yang]

typist ['taɪpɪst] n ผู้พิมพ์ดีด [phu phim did]

tyre ['taɪə] n ยางรถ [yang rot]; **spare tyre** n ยางอะไหล่ [yang a lai]; **The tyre has burst** ยางรถระเบิด [yang rot ra boet]

u

UFO [ˈjuːfəʊ] *abbr* ตัวย่อของจานบินของ
มนุษย์ต่างดาว [tua yo khong chan bin
khong ma nut tang dao]

Uganda [juːˈɡændə] *n* ประเทศอูกันดาอยู่
ในทวีปอัฟริกา [pra tet u kan da yu nai
tha wip af ri ka]

Ugandan [juːˈɡændən] *adj* เกี่ยวกับ
ประเทศอูกันดา [kiao kap pra thet u kan
da] ▷ *n* ชาวอูกันดา [chao u kan da]

ugh [ʊx; ʊh; ʌh] *excl* คำอุทานแสดงความ
รังเกียจหรือไม่พอใจ [kham u than sa
daeng khwam rang kiat rue mai pho
jai]

ugly [ˈʌɡlɪ] *adj* น่าเกลียด [na kliat]

UK [juː keɪ] *n* ตัวย่อของ สหราชอาณาจักร
อังกฤษ [tua yor khong sa ha rad cha a
na chak ang krid]

Ukraine [juːˈkreɪn] *n* ประเทศยูเครน [pra
tet yu khren]

Ukrainian [juːˈkreɪnɪən] *adj* เกี่ยวกับ
ประเทศยูเครน [kiao kap pra thet yu
khren] ▷ *n* (*language*) ภาษายูเครน [pha
sa u khren], (*person*) ชาวยูเครน [chao u
khren]

ulcer [ˈʌlsə] *n* แผลเปื่อย [phlae pueai]

Ulster [ˈʌlstə] *n* อีกชื่อหนึ่งของ
ไอร์แลนด์เหนือ [ik chue hueng khong ai
laen hnuea]

ultimate [ˈʌltɪmɪt] *adj* สุดท้าย [sut thai]

ultimately [ˈʌltɪmɪtlɪ] *adv* ท้ายที่สุด
[thai thi sut]

ultimatum [ˌʌltɪˈmeɪtəm] *n* คำขาด
[kham khat]

ultrasound [ˈʌltrəˌsaʊnd] *n* การบำบัด
โดยใช้อุลตราซาวด์ [kan bam bat doi
chai ul tra sao]

umbrella [ʌmˈbrɛlə] *n* ร่ม [rom]

umpire [ˈʌmpaɪə] *n* กรรมการตัดสิน [kam
ma kan tat sin]

UN [juː ɛn] *abbr* ตัวย่อขององค์การ
สหประชาชาติ [tua yo khong ong kan sa
ha pra cha chat]

unable [ʌnˈeɪbəl] *adj* **unable to** *adj* ไม่
สามารถที่จะ [mai sa mat thii ja]

unacceptable [ˌʌnəkˈsɛptəbəl] *adj* ซึ่ง
ไม่สามารถยอมรับได้ [sueng mai sa maat
yom rap dai]

unanimous [juːˈnænɪməs] *adj* เป็น
เอกฉันท์ [pen ek ka chan]

unattended [ˌʌnəˈtɛndɪd] *adj* ไม่เอาใจ
ใส่ [mai ao jai sai]

unavoidable [ˌʌnəˈvɔɪdəbəl] *adj* ที่หลีก
เลี่ยงไม่ได้ [thii lik liang mai dai]

unbearable [ʌnˈbɛərəbəl] *adj* ซึ่งไม่
สามารถทนได้ [sueng mai sa maat thon
dai]

unbeatable [ʌnˈbiːtəbəl] *adj* ทำให้พ่าย
แพ้ไม่ได้ [tham hai phai phae mai dai]

unbelievable [ˌʌnbɪˈliːvəbəl] *adj* ซึ่งไม่
น่าเชื่อว่าเป็นจริง [sueng mai na chuea
wa pen ching]

unbreakable [ʌnˈbreɪkəbəl] *adj* ซึ่งไม่
สามารถทำให้แตกได้ [sueng mai sa mart
tham hai taek dai]

uncanny [ʌnˈkænɪ] *adj* แปลกจนไม่
สามารถอธิบายได้ [plaek chon mai sa
mat a thi bai dai]

uncertain [ʌnˈsɜːtən] *adj* ที่ไม่แน่นอน
[thii mai nae norn]

uncertainty [ʌnˈsɜːt̯ntɪ] n ความไม่แน่นอน [khwam mai nae non]

unchanged [ʌnˈtʃeɪndʒd] adj ที่ไม่เปลี่ยนแปลงจากเดิม [thii mai plian plang chak doem]

uncivilized [ʌnˈsɪvɪˌlaɪzd] adj ซึ่งไร้อารยธรรม [sueng rai a ra ya tham]

uncle [ˈʌŋkəl] n ลุง [lung]

unclear [ʌnˈklɪə] adj ซึ่งไม่ชัดเจน [sueng mai chat chen]

uncomfortable [ʌnˈkʌmftəbəl] adj ไม่สะดวกสบาย [mai sa duak sa bai]

unconditional [ˌʌnkənˈdɪʃənəl] adj ที่ไม่มีเงื่อนไข [thii mai mii nguean khai]

unconscious [ʌnˈkɒnʃəs] adj ไม่รู้สึกตัว [mai ru suek tua]

uncontrollable [ˌʌnkənˈtrəʊləbəl] adj ที่ควบคุมไม่ได้ [thii khuab khum mai dai]

unconventional [ˌʌnkənˈvɛnʃənəl] adj ไม่เป็นไปตามกฎทั่วไป [mai pen pai tam kot thua pai]

undecided [ˌʌndɪˈsaɪdɪd] adj ไม่ตกลงใจ [mai tok long jai]

undeniable [ˌʌndɪˈnaɪəbəl] adj ซึ่งไม่อาจปฏิเสธได้ [sueng mai aat pa ti set dai]

under [ˈʌndə] prep ภายใต้ [phai tai]

underage [ˌʌndərˈeɪdʒ] adj ต่ำกว่ากำหนดอายุ [tam kwa kam not a yu]

underestimate [ˌʌndərˈɛstɪˌmeɪt] v ประเมินต่ำไป [pra moen tam pai]

undergo [ˌʌndəˈɡəʊ] v ประสบ อดทน อดกลั้น [pra sop, ot thon, ot klan]

undergraduate [ˌʌndəˈɡrædjʊɪt] n นักศึกษาระดับปริญญาตรี [nak suek sa ra dap pa ra ya tree]

underground adj [ˈʌndəˌɡraʊnd] ใต้ดิน [tai din] ▷ n [ˈʌndəˌɡraʊnd] ชั้นใต้ดิน [chan tai din]

underline [ˌʌndəˈlaɪn] v ขีดเส้นใต้ [khit sen tai]

underneath [ˌʌndəˈniːθ] adv ภายใต้ [phai tai] ▷ prep ข้างใต้ [khang tai]

underpaid [ˌʌndəˈpeɪd] adj ได้รับค่าจ้างน้อยไป [dai rap kha chang noi pai]

underpants [ˈʌndəˌpænts] npl กางเกงชั้นในของผู้ชาย [kang keng chan nai khong phu chai]

underpass [ˈʌndəˌpɑːs] n ทางข้างใต้ [thang khang tai]

underskirt [ˈʌndəˌskɜːt] n กระโปรงชั้นในผู้หญิง [kra prong chan nai phu ying]

understand [ˌʌndəˈstænd] v เข้าใจ [khao chai]; **Do you understand?** คุณเข้าใจไหม? [khun khao jai mai]; **I don't understand** ฉันไม่เข้าใจ [chan mai khao jai]; **I understand** ฉันเข้าใจ [chan khao jai]

understandable [ˌʌndəˈstændəbəl] adj เข้าใจได้ [khao jai dai]

understanding [ˌʌndəˈstændɪŋ] adj ที่เข้าใจ อย่างเห็นอกเห็นใจ [thii khao jai yang hen ok hen jai]

undertaker [ˈʌndəˌteɪkə] n ผู้จัดการศพ [phu chad kan sob]

underwater [ˈʌndəˈwɔːtə] adv ใต้น้ำ [tai nam]

underwear [ˈʌndəˌwɛə] n เสื้อผ้าชั้นใน [suea pha chan nai]

undisputed [ˌʌndɪˈspjuːtɪd] adj ไม่อาจจะโต้แย้งได้ [mai at ja to yaeng dai]

undo [ʌnˈduː] v แก้ [kae]

undoubtedly [ʌnˈdaʊtɪdlɪ] adv ไม่เป็นที่น่าสงสัยใด ๆ ทั้งสิ้น [mai pen thii na song sai dai dai thang sin]

undress [ʌnˈdrɛs] v ถอดเสื้อผ้า [thot suea pha]

unemployed [ˌʌnɪmˈplɔɪd] adj ไม่มีงานทำ [mai mii ngan tham]

unemployment [ˌʌnɪmˈplɔɪmənt] n การว่างงาน [kan wang ngan]

unexpected [ˌʌnɪkˈspɛktɪd] adj ไม่คาดคิดมาก่อน [mai khat kit ma kon]

unexpectedly [ˌʌnɪkˈspɛktɪdlɪ] adv อย่างไม่คาดคิดมาก่อน [yang mai khat kit ma kon]

unfair [ʌnˈfɛə] adj ไม่ยุติธรรม [mai yu ti

tham]

unfaithful [ʌn'feɪθfʊl] *adj* ไม่ซื่อสัตย์ [mai sue sat]

unfamiliar [ˌʌnfə'mɪljə] *adj* ไม่รู้จักคุ้นเคย [mai ru chak khun khoei]

unfashionable [ʌn'fæʃənəbªl] *adj* ไม่ทันสมัย [mai than sa mai]

unfavourable [ʌn'feɪvərəbªl; -'feɪvrə-] *adj* ไม่เอื้ออำนวยประโยชน์ [mai uea am nuai pra yot]

unfit [ʌn'fɪt] *adj* ไม่มีคุณสมบัติ [mai khun som bat]

unforgettable [ˌʌnfə'gɛtəbªl] *adj* ไม่สามารถที่จะลืมได้ [mai sa mat thii ja luem dai]

unfortunately [ʌn'fɔːtʃənɪtlɪ] *adv* อย่างเคราะห์ร้าย [yang khrao rai]

unfriendly [ʌn'frɛndlɪ] *adj* ไม่เป็นมิตร [mai pen mit]

ungrateful [ʌn'greɪtfʊl] *adj* ไม่สำนึกบุญคุณ [mai sam nuek bun khun]

unhappy [ʌn'hæpɪ] *adj* เศร้า [sao]

unhealthy [ʌn'hɛlθɪ] *adj* ผิดหลักอนามัย [phit lak a na mai]

unhelpful [ʌn'hɛlpfʊl] *adj* ไม่ช่วยเหลือ [mai chuai luea]

uni ['juːnɪ] *n* ตัวย่อของมหาวิทยาลัย [tua yo khong ma ha wit ta ya lai]

unidentified [ʌnaɪ'dɛntɪˌfaɪd] *adj* ไม่ปรากฏชื่อ [mai pra kot chue]

uniform ['juːnɪˌfɔːm] *n* เครื่องแบบ [khrueang baep]; **school uniform** *n* เครื่องแบบนักเรียน [khrueang baep nak rian]

unimportant [ˌʌnɪm'pɔːtªnt] *adj* ไม่สำคัญ [mai sam khan]

uninhabited [ˌʌnɪn'hæbɪtɪd] *adj* ไม่มีคนอาศัยอยู่ [mai mii khon a sai yu]

unintentional [ˌʌnɪn'tɛnʃənªl] *adj* ไม่ได้เจตนา [mai dai chet ta na]

union ['juːnjən] *n* การรวมกัน [kan ruam kan]; **European Union** *n* สหภาพยุโรป [sa ha phap yu rop]; **trade union** *n* สหภาพแรงงาน [sa ha phap raeng ngan]

unique [juː'niːk] *adj* ลักษณะเฉพาะ [lak sa na cha pho]

unit ['juːnɪt] *n* หน่วย [ŋuai]

unite [juː'naɪt] *v* ทำให้เป็นหนึ่ง [tham hai pen hueng]

United Kingdom [juː'naɪtɪd 'kɪŋdəm] *n* ประเทศสหราชอาณาจักรอังกฤษ [pra tet sa ha rat cha a na chak ang krit]

United States [juː'naɪtɪd steɪts] *n* ประเทศสหรัฐอเมริกา [pra tet sa ha rat a me ri ka]

universe ['juːnɪˌvɜːs] *n* จักรวาล [chak kra wan]

university [ˌjuːnɪ'vɜːsɪtɪ] *n* มหาวิทยาลัย [ma ha wit tha ya lai]

unknown [ʌn'nəʊn] *adj* ไม่มีใครรู้จัก [mai mii khrai ru chak]

unleaded [ʌn'lɛdɪd] *n* น้ำมันไร้สารตะกั่ว [nam man rai san ta kua]; **unleaded petrol** *n* น้ำมันไร้สารตะกั่ว [nam man rai san ta kua]; **...worth of premium unleaded, please** เติมน้ำมันไร้สารตะกั่วชั้นหนึ่งเป็นเงิน... [toem nam man rai san ta kua chan nueng pen ngoen...]

unless [ʌn'lɛs] *conj* ถ้าไม่ [tha mai]

unlike [ʌn'laɪk] *prep* ไม่เหมือน [mai muean]

unlikely [ʌn'laɪklɪ] *adj* ไม่น่าจะเกิดขึ้น [mai na ja koet khuen]

unlisted [ʌn'lɪstɪd] *adj* ไม่อยู่ในรายการ [mai yu nai rai kan]

unload [ʌn'ləʊd] *v* ถ่ายสินค้า [thai sin ka]

unlock [ʌn'lɒk] *v* ไขกุญแจ [khai kun jae]

unlucky [ʌn'lʌkɪ] *adj* โชคร้าย [chok rai]

unmarried [ʌn'mærɪd] *adj* ไม่แต่งงาน [mai taeng ngan]

unnecessary [ʌn'nɛsɪsərɪ; -ɪsrɪ] *adj* ไม่จำเป็น [mai cham pen]

unofficial [ˌʌnə'fɪʃəl] *adj* ไม่เป็นทางการ [mai pen thang kan]

unpack [ʌn'pæk] *v* เอาของออก [ao

khong ok]; **I have to unpack** ฉันต้องเอา
ของออกจากกระเป๋า [chan tong ao khong
ok chak kra pao]

unpaid [ʌnˈpeɪd] *adj* ไม่ได้ค่าจ้าง [mai
dai kha chang]

unpleasant [ʌnˈplɛzənt] *adj* ไม่สนุก ไม่
ราบรื่น [mai sa nuk, mai rap ruen]

unplug [ʌnˈplʌg] *v* ถอดปลั๊ก [thot pluk]

unpopular [ʌnˈpɒpjʊlə] *adj* ไม่เป็นที่
นิยม [mai pen thii ni yom]

unprecedented [ʌnˈprɛsɪˌdɛntɪd] *adj*
ไม่เคยมีมาก่อน [mai khoei ma kon]

unpredictable [ˌʌnprɪˈdɪktəbəl] *adj*
ทำนายไม่ได้ [tham nai mai dai]

unreal [ʌnˈrɪəl] *adj* อยู่ในจินตนาการ [yu
nai chin ta na kan]

unrealistic [ˌʌnrɪəˈlɪstɪk] *adj* ไม่มองดู
สภาพจริง [mai mong du sa phap ching]

unreasonable [ʌnˈriːznəbəl] *adj* ไม่สม
เหตุสมผล [mai som het som phon]

unreliable [ˌʌnrɪˈlaɪəbəl] *adj* ไว้ใจไม่ได้
[wai jai mai dai]

unroll [ʌnˈrəʊl] *v* ม้วนออก [muan ork]

unsatisfactory [ˌʌnsætɪsˈfæktəri;
-trɪ] *adj* ไม่น่าพอใจ [mai na pho jai]

unscrew [ʌnˈskruː] *v* คลายเกลียว [khlai
kliao]

unshaven [ʌnˈʃeɪvən] *adj* ไม่โกนหนวด
เครา [mai kon nuat khrao]

unskilled [ʌnˈskɪld] *adj* ไม่มีความชำนาญ
[mai mii khwam cham nan]

unstable [ʌnˈsteɪbəl] *adj* ไม่มั่นคง [mai
man khong]

unsteady [ʌnˈstɛdɪ] *adj* ไม่มั่นคง [mai
man khong]

unsuccessful [ˌʌnsəkˈsɛsfʊl] *adj* ไม่
ประสบความสำเร็จ [mai pra sop khwam
sam ret]

unsuitable [ʌnˈsuːtəbəl; ʌnˈsjuːt-] *adj*
ซึ่งไม่เหมาะสม [sueng mai mo som]

unsure [ʌnˈʃʊə] *adj* ไม่แน่ใจ [mai nae
jai]

untidy [ʌnˈtaɪdɪ] *adj* ไม่เป็นระเบียบ
เรียบร้อย [mai pen ra biap riap roi]

untie [ʌnˈtaɪ] *v* แก้ออก [kae ork]

until [ʌnˈtɪl] *conj* จนกระทั่ง [chon kra
thang] ▷ *prep* จนกว่า [chon kwa]

unusual [ʌnˈjuːʒʊəl] *adj* ผิดปรกติ [phit
prok ka ti]

unwell [ʌnˈwɛl] *adj* ไม่สบาย [mai sa bai]

unwind [ʌnˈwaɪnd] *v* คลี่ออก [khlii ok]

unwise [ʌnˈwaɪz] *adj* ไม่ฉลาด [mai cha
lat]

unwrap [ʌnˈræp] *v* แก้ห่อออก [kae ho
ok]

unzip [ʌnˈzɪp] *v* รูดซิปออก [rut sip ok]

up [ʌp] *adv* ในทิศทางขึ้น [nai thit thang
khuen]

upbringing [ˈʌpˌbrɪŋɪŋ] *n* การเลี้ยงดู
อบรมสั่งสอน [kan liang du op rom sang
son]

update *n* [ˈʌpˌdeɪt] ทำให้ทันสมัย [tham
hai tan sa mai] ▷ *v* [ʌpˈdeɪt] ทำให้ทัน
สมัย [tham hai tan sa mai]

upgrade [ʌpˈgreɪd] *n* **I want to
upgrade my ticket** ฉันอยากได้ตั๋วที่ดี
กว่านี้ [chan yak dai tua thii di kwa nii]

uphill [ˈʌpˈhɪl] *adv* ซึ่งเป็นเนิน [sueng pen
noen]

upper [ˈʌpə] *adj* สูงกว่า [sung kwa]

upright [ˈʌpˌraɪt] *adv* ที่ตั้งขึ้น [thii tang
khuen]

upset *adj* [ʌpˈsɛt] สับสนวุ่นวาย [sap son
wun wai] ▷ *v* [ʌpˈsɛt] ทำให้อารมณ์เสีย
[tham hai a rom sia]

upside down [ˈʌpˌsaɪd daʊn] *adv* พลิก
เอาด้านบนลงล่าง [phlik ao dan bon long
lang]

upstairs [ˈʌpˈstɛəz] *adv* ข้างบน [khang
bon]

uptight [ʌpˈtaɪt] *adj* ตึงเครียด [tueng
khriat]

up-to-date [ˈʌptʊˌdeɪt] *adj* ทันสมัย
[than sa mai]

upwards [ˈʌpwədz] *adv* ขึ้นไปทางเหนือ
[khuen pai thang nuea]

uranium [jʊˈreɪnɪəm] *n* ธาตุยูเรเนียม
[that u re niam]

urgency ['ɜːdʒənsɪ] *n* การเร่งรีบ [kan reng rip]

urgent ['ɜːdʒənt] *adj* ที่จำเป็นเร่งด่วน [thii cham pen reng duan]

urine ['jʊərɪn] *n* น้ำปัสสาวะ [nam pat sa wa]

URL [juː ɑː ɛl] *n* คำย่อของที่อยู่ของเว็บไซต์บนอินเตอร์เน็ต [kham yo khong thii yu khong web sai bon in toe net]

Uruguay ['jʊərəˌgwaɪ] *n* ประเทศอุรุกวัย [pra tet u ru kwai]

Uruguayan [ˌjʊərəˈgwaɪən] *adj* เกี่ยวกับอุรุกวัย [kiao kap u ru kwai] ▷ *n* ชาวอุรุกวัย [chao u ru kwai]

us [ʌs] *pron* เรา [rao]; **Could you show us around the apartment?** คุณพาเราดูพาร์ทเมนท์ได้ไหม? [khun pha rao du a phat ment dai mai]; **Please call us if you'll be late** ช่วยโทรบอกเราถ้าคุณจะมาช้า [chuai tho bok rao tha khun ja ms cha]; **We'd like to see nobody but us all day!** เราไม่อยากเห็นใครเลยทั้งวันนอกจากเราเองเท่านั้น [rao mai yak hen khrai loei thang wan nok chak rao eng thao nan]

US [juː ɛs] *n* สหรัฐอเมริกา [sa ha rat a me ri ka]

USA [juː ɛs eɪ] *n* ตัวย่อของประเทศสหรัฐอเมริกา [tua yo khong pra tet sa ha rat a me ri ka]

use *n* [juːs] วิธีการใช้ [vi thi kan chai] ▷ *v* [juːz] ใช้ [chai]; **How do I use the car wash?** ฉันจะใช้ที่ล้างรถอย่างไร? [chan ja chai thii lang rot yang rai]; **It is for my own personal use** นี่สำหรับใช้ส่วนตัว [ni sam rap chai suan tua]; **May I use your phone?** ฉันขอใช้โทรศัพท์ของคุณได้ไหม? [chan kho chai tho ra sap khong khun dai mai]

used [juːzd] *adj* ซึ่งถูกใช้ [sueng thuk chai]

useful ['juːsfʊl] *adj* ที่มีประโยชน์ [thii mee pra yot]

useless ['juːslɪs] *adj* ซึ่งไม่มีประโยชน์ [sueng mai mii pra yot]

user ['juːzə] *n* ผู้ใช้ [phu chai]; **Internet user** *n* ผู้ใช้อินเตอร์เน็ต [phu chai in toe net]

user-friendly ['juːzəˌfrɛndlɪ] *adj* ใช้สะดวก [chai sa duak]

use up [juːz ʌp] *v* ใช้จนหมด [chai chon mot]

usual ['juːʒʊəl] *adj* เป็นปรกติ [pen prok ka ti]

usually ['juːʒʊəlɪ] *adv* โดยปรกติ [doi prok ka ti]

U-turn ['juːˌtɜːn] *n* การเลี้ยวกลับที่ทางเลี้ยวเป็นรูปตัวยู [kan liao klap thii thang liao pen rup tua u]

Uzbekistan [ˌʌzbɛkɪˈstɑːn] *n* ประเทศอุซเบกิสถาน [pra tet us be ki sa than]

V

vacancy ['veɪkənsɪ] *n* ตำแหน่งว่าง [tam naeng wang]

vacant ['veɪkənt] *adj* ว่าง [wang]

vacate [vəˈkeɪt] *v* ปล่อยให้ว่าง [ploi hai wang]

vaccinate ['væksɪˌneɪt] *v* ฉีดวัคซีน [chiit wak sin]

vaccination [ˌvæksɪˈneɪʃən] *n* การฉีดวัคซีน [kan chit wak sin]

vacuum ['vækjʊəm] *v* ดูดฝุ่น [dud fun]; **vacuum cleaner** *n* เครื่องดูดฝุ่น [khrueang dut fun]

vague [veɪg] *adj* คลุมเครือ [khlum khluea]

vain [veɪn] *adj* หยิ่งแบบถือตัว [ying baep thue tua]

valid ['vælɪd] *adj* มีผลบังคับใช้ [mi phon bang khap]

valley ['vælɪ] *n* หุบเขา [hup khao]

valuable ['væljʊəbˀl] *adj* มีค่าเป็นเงินมาก [mii kha pen ngoen mak]

valuables ['væljʊəbˀlz] *npl* ของมีค่า [khong mi kha]; **I'd like to put my valuables in the safe** ฉันอยากวางของมีค่าไว้ในตู้นิรภัย [chan yak wang khong

mii kha wai nai tu ni ra phai]; **Where can I leave my valuables?** ฉันเก็บของมีค่าไว้ที่ไหนได้? [chan kep khong mii kha wai thii nai dai]

value ['vælju:] *n* คุณค่า [khun kha]

vampire ['væmpaɪə] *n* ผีที่สูบเลือดคน [phi thii sup lueat khon]

van [væn] *n* รถตู้ [rot tu]; **breakdown van** *n* รถตู้เสีย [rot tu sia]; **removal van** *n* รถที่ใช้ในการขนย้าย [rot thii chai nai kan khon yai]

vandal ['vændˀl] *n* ผู้ทำลายทรัพย์สิน [phu tham lai srab sin]

vandalism ['vændəˌlɪzəm] *n* การทำลายทรัพย์สิน [kan tham lai sap sin]

vandalize ['vændəˌlaɪz] *v* ทำลายทรัพย์สิน [tham lai srab sin]

vanilla [vəˈnɪlə] *n* กลิ่นหรือรสวนิลา [klin rue rot wa ni la]

vanish ['vænɪʃ] *v* หายไปอย่างรวดเร็ว [hai pai yang ruat reo]

variable ['vɛərɪəbˀl] *adj* เปลี่ยนแปลงได้ตลอดเวลา [plian plaeng dai ta lot we la]

varied ['vɛərɪd] *adj* ต่างต่างนานา [tang tang na na]

variety [vəˈraɪɪtɪ] *n* ประเภทต่าง ๆ [pra phet tang tang]

various ['vɛərɪəs] *adj* ต่างชนิด [tang cha nit]

varnish ['vɑːnɪʃ] *n* น้ำมันชักเงา [nam man chak ngao] ▷ *v* ใส่น้ำมันชักเงา [sai nam man chak ngao]; **nail varnish** *n* น้ำยาทาเล็บ [nam ya tha lep]

vary ['vɛərɪ] *v* เปลี่ยนแปลง [plian pleng]

vase [vɑːz] *n* แจกัน [chae kan]

VAT [væt] *abbr* ภาษีมูลค่าเพิ่ม [pha si munkha perm]; **Is VAT included?** รวมภาษีมูลค่าเพิ่มไหม? [ruam pha si mun kha poem mai]

Vatican ['vætɪkən] *n* สำนักวาติกันที่เป็นที่ประทับขององค์สันตะปาปาในกรุงโรม [sam nak wa ti kan thii pen thii pra thap khong ong san ta pa pa nai krung rom]

vault [vɔːlt] *n* **pole vault** *n* กีฬากระโดด

ค้าก่อ [ki la kra dot kham tho]

veal [viːl] *n* เนื้อลูกวัว [nuea luk wua]

vegan ['viːgən] *n* ผู้นับถือลัทธิมังสวิรัติ [phu nap thue lat thi mang sa wi rat]

vegetable ['vɛdʒtəbəl] *n* ผัก [phak]; **Are the vegetables fresh or frozen?** ผักต่าง ๆ สดหรือแช่แข็ง? [phak tang tang sot rue chae khaeng]; **Are the vegetables included?** มีผักรวมอยู่ในนี้ด้วยไหม? [mii phak ruam yu nai nii duai mai]

vegetarian [ˌvɛdʒɪ'tɛərɪən] *adj* มังสวิรัติ [mang sa wi rat] ▷ *n* คนที่กินแต่ผักเป็นอาหาร [kon thii kin tae phak pen a han]; **Do you have any vegetarian dishes?** คุณมีอาหารมังสวิรัติไหม? [khun mii a han mang sa wi rat mai]; **I'm vegetarian** ฉันเป็นมังสวิรัติ [chan pen mang sa wi rat]

vegetation [ˌvɛdʒɪ'teɪʃən] *n* พืชผัก [phuet phak]

vehicle ['viːɪkəl] *n* ยานพาหนะ [yan pha ha na]

veil [veɪl] *n* ผ้าคลุมหน้า [pha khlum na]

vein [veɪn] *n* เส้นโลหิตดำ [sen lo hit dam]

Velcro® ['vɛlkrəʊ] *n* เวลโคร ไนล่อนสองชิ้นที่ยึดสิ่งของให้ติดแน่น ใช้แทนซิป กระดุม และขอเกี่ยว [wel khro nai lon song chin thii yuet sing khong hai tit naen chai taen sip kra dum lae kho kiao]

velvet ['vɛlvɪt] *n* ผ้ากำมะหยี่ [pha kam ma yi]

vendor ['vɛndɔː] *n* คนขายของ [kon khai khong]

Venezuela [ˌvɛnɪ'zweɪlə] *n* ประเทศเวเนซุเอลา [pra tet ve ne su e la]

Venezuelan [ˌvɛnɪ'zweɪlən] *adj* ที่เกี่ยวกับเวเนซุเอลา [thii kiao kap we ne su e la] ▷ *n* ชาวเวเนซุเอลา [chao we ne su e la]

venison ['vɛnɪzən; -sən] *n* เนื้อกวาง [nuea kwang]

venom ['vɛnəm] *n* ความรู้สึกโกรธและขมขื่น [khwam ru suek krot lae khom khuen]

ventilation [ˌvɛntɪ'leɪʃən] *n* การระบายอากาศ [kan ra bai a kat]

venue ['vɛnjuː] *n* สถานที่ที่คนมาพบปะหรือชุมนุมกัน [sa than thii thii kon ma phob pa hue chum num kan]

verb [vɜːb] *n* คำกริยา [kham ka ri ya]

verdict ['vɜːdɪkt] *n* คำตัดสินของคณะลูกขุน [kham tat sin khong kha na luk khun]

versatile ['vɜːsəˌtaɪl] *adj* ซึ่งมีประโยชน์หลายอย่าง [sueng mee pra yot lai yang]

version ['vɜːʃən; -ʒən] *n* ฉบับ [cha bap]

versus ['vɜːsəs] *prep* ต่อสู้กับ [to su kap]

vertical ['vɜːtɪkəl] *adj* ซึ่งเป็นแนวดิ่ง [sueng pen naeo ding]

vertigo ['vɜːtɪˌgəʊ] *n* อาการเวียนศรีษะ ทำให้ทรงตัวลำบาก [a kan wian si sa tham hai song tua lam bak]

very ['vɛrɪ] *adv* อย่างมาก [yang mak]

vest [vɛst] *n* เสื้อกั๊ก [suea kak]

vet [vɛt] *n* สัตวแพทย์ [sat phaet]

veteran ['vɛtərən; 'vɛtrən] *adj* ซึ่งมีประสบการณ์ [sueng mii pra sop kan] ▷ *n* ผู้ที่ได้ทำงานในอาชีพใดอาชีพหนึ่งมานาน [phu thii dai tham ngan nai a chip dai a chip nueng ma nan]

veto ['viːtəʊ] *n* อำนาจในการยับยั้ง [am nat nai kan yap yang]

via ['vaɪə] *prep* โดยทาง [doi thang]

vicar ['vɪkə] *n* พระในคริสต์ศาสนา [phra nai khris sat sa na]

vice [vaɪs] *n* ความชั่วร้าย [khwam chua rai]

vice versa ['vaɪsɪ 'vɜːsə] *adv* ในทางกลับกัน [nai thang klap kan]

vicinity [vɪ'sɪnɪtɪ] *n* บริเวณใกล้เคียง [bo ri wen klai khiang]

vicious ['vɪʃəs] *adj* ที่ร้ายแรง [thii rai raeng]

victim ['vɪktɪm] *n* ผู้เคราะห์ร้าย [phu khrao rai]

victory ['vɪktərɪ] *n* ชัยชนะในการสงคราม [chai cha na nai kan song khram]

video ['vɪdɪˌəʊ] n ภาพหรือหนังในเทปวีดีโอ [phap rue nang nai thep wi di o]; **video camera** n กล้องถ่ายวิดีโอ [klong thai vi di o]

videophone ['vɪdɪəˌfəʊn] n เครื่องโทรศัพท์ที่เห็นภาพได้ [khueang tho ra sab thii hen phap dai]

Vietnam [ˌvjɛt'næm] n ประเทศเวียดนาม [pra tet viat nam]

Vietnamese [ˌvjɛtnə'miːz] adj เวียดนาม [wiat nam] ▷ n (language) เวียดนาม [wiat nam], (person) เวียดนาม [wiat nam]

view [vjuː] n ความคิดเห็น [khwam kit hen]

viewer ['vjuːə] n ผู้ดู ผู้ชมเช่น ผู้ชมรายการโทรทัศน์ [phu du, phu chom chen phu chom rai kan tho ra tat]

viewpoint ['vjuːˌpɔɪnt] n ทัศนคติ [that sa na kha ti]

vile [vaɪl] adj ชั่วร้าย [chua rai]

villa ['vɪlə] n บ้านขนาดใหญ่ที่มีสวน [baan kha nard yai thii mee suan]

village ['vɪlɪdʒ] n หมู่บ้าน [mu ban]

villain ['vɪlən] n ตัวชั่วร้าย [tua chua rai]

vinaigrette [ˌvɪneɪ'grɛt] n น้ำสลัดชนิดหนึ่งทำจากน้ำมัน น้ำส้มและเครื่องปรุงรส [nam sa lat cha nit nueng tham chak nam man nam som lae khrueang prung rot]

vine [vaɪn] n ต้นองุ่น [ton a ngun]

vinegar ['vɪnɪgə] n น้ำส้ม [nam som]

vineyard ['vɪnjəd] n ไร่องุ่น [rai a ngun]

viola [vɪ'əʊlə] n เครื่องดนตรีชนิดหนึ่งคล้ายไวโอลินแต่มีขนาดใหญ่กว่าและมีเสียงต่ำกว่า [khrueang don tri cha nit nueng khlai wai o lin tae mii kha naat yai kwa lae mii siang tam kwa]

violence ['vaɪələns] n ความรุนแรง [khwam run raeng]

violent ['vaɪələnt] adj ที่มีสาเหตุมาจากความรุนแรง [thii mee sa hed ma chak khwam run raeng]

violin [ˌvaɪə'lɪn] n เครื่องดนตรีประเภทสีชนิดหนึ่ง ไวโอลิน [khrueang don tri pra phet sii cha nit nueng vi o lin]

violinist [ˌvaɪə'lɪnɪst] n นักสีไวโอลิน [nak see vi o lin]

virgin ['vɜːdʒɪn] n หญิงพรหมจารีย์ [ying prom ma cha ri]

Virgo ['vɜːgəʊ] n ราศีกันย์ [ra si kan]

virtual ['vɜːtʃʊəl] adj โดยแท้จริง [doi thae ching]; **virtual reality** n สภาวะเหมือนจริงที่จำลองโดยทางเทคนิคคอมพิวเตอร์ [sa pha wa muean ching thii cham long doi thang tek nik khom phio toe]

virus ['vaɪrəs] n เชื้อไวรัส [chuea wai rat]

visa ['viːzə] n วีซ่า เอกสารอนุมัติที่ประทับตราบนหนังสือเดินทาง [wi sa, ek ka san a nu mat thii pra thap tra bon nang sue doen thang]

visibility [ˌvɪzɪ'bɪlɪtɪ] n ทัศนวิสัย [that sa na wi sai]

visible ['vɪzɪbəl] adj ที่สามารถมองเห็นได้ [thii sa maat mong hen dai]

visit ['vɪzɪt] n การไปเยี่ยม [kan pai yiam] ▷ v มาเยี่ยม [ma yiam]; **visiting hours** npl ชั่วโมงเยี่ยม [chau mong yiam]; **I'm here visiting friends** ฉันมาเยี่ยมเพื่อนที่นี่ [chan ma yiam phuean thii ni]

visitor ['vɪzɪtə] n ผู้เยี่ยม [phu yiam]; **visitor centre** n ศูนย์บริการข้อมูลนักท่องเที่ยว [sun bo ri kan kho mun nak thong thiao]

visual ['vɪzʊəl; -zjʊ-] adj ที่เห็นได้ [thii hen dai]

visualize ['vɪʒʊəˌlaɪz; -zjʊ-] v ทำให้จินตนาการจินตนาการเห็น [tham hai chin ta na kan chin ta na kan hen]

vital ['vaɪtəl] adj สำคัญมาก [sam khan mak]

vitamin ['vɪtəmɪn; 'vaɪ-] n วิตามิน [wi ta min]

vivid ['vɪvɪd] adj เจิดจ้า สว่างไสว [choet cha, sa wang sa wai]

vocabulary [və'kæbjʊlərɪ] n คำศัพท์ [kham sap]

vocational [vəʊ'keɪʃənəl] adj เกี่ยวกับวิชาชีพ [kiao kap wi cha chip]

vodka ['vɒdkə] *n* เหล้าวอดกาของรัสเซีย ไม่มีสี [lao vod ka khong ras sia mai mee see]

voice [vɔɪs] *n* เสียงพูด [siang phud]

voicemail ['vɔɪsˌmeɪl] *n* ระบบอีเล็คทรอ นิกส์ที่ส่งผ่านและเก็บข้อความทางโทรศัพท์ [ra bop e lek tro nik thii song phan lae kep kho khwam thang tho ra sap]

void [vɔɪd] *adj* ที่เป็นโมฆะ [thii pen mo kha] ▷ *n* ความรู้สึกหรือสภาพเปล่าเปลี่ยว อ้างว้าง [khwam ru suek rue sa phap plao pliao ang wang]

volcano, volcanoes [vɒl'keɪnəʊ, vɒl'keɪnəʊz] *n* ภูเขาไฟ [phu khao fai]

volleyball ['vɒlɪˌbɔːl] *n* กีฬาวอลเลย์บอล [ki la wal le bal]

volt [vəʊlt] *n* หน่วยแรงดันไฟฟ้า [nuai raeng dan fai fa]

voltage ['vəʊltɪdʒ] *n* แรงดันไฟฟ้าที่มี หน่วยเป็นโวลต์ [raeng dan fai fa thii mii nuai pen volt]

volume ['vɒljuːm] *n* ความจุ ปริมาตร [khwam ju, pa ri mat]

voluntarily ['vɒləntərɪlɪ] *adv* อย่าง สมัครใจ [yang sa mak jai]

voluntary ['vɒləntərɪ; -trɪ] *adj* โดย สมัครใจ [doi sa mak jai]

volunteer [ˌvɒlən'tɪə] *n* อาสาสมัคร [a sa sa mak] ▷ *v* เสนอตัวโดยสมัครใจ [sa noe tua doi sa mak jai]

vomit ['vɒmɪt] *v* อาเจียน [a chian]

vote [vəʊt] *n* การลงคะแนนเสียง [kan long kha naen siang] ▷ *v* ลงคะแนนเสียง [long kha naen siang]

voucher ['vaʊtʃə] *n* ตั๋วหรือบัตรที่ใช้แทน เงินในการซื้อสินค้าที่ระบุ [tua rue bat thii chai thaen ngoen nai kan sue sin kha thii ra bu]; **gift voucher** *n* บัตรของขวัญ [bat khong khwan]

vowel ['vaʊəl] *n* เสียงสระ [siang sa ra]

vulgar ['vʌlgə] *adj* หยาบคาย [yap khai]

vulnerable ['vʌlnərəbªl] *adj* ซึ่งบาดเจ็บ ได้ง่าย [sueng bad chep dai ngai]

vulture ['vʌltʃə] *n* นกแร้ง [nok raeng]

W

wafer ['weɪfə] *n* ขนมปังกรอบบางรสหวาน มักกินกับไอศกรีม [kha nom pang krob bang rot hwan mak kin kab ai sa krim]

waffle ['wɒfªl] *n* ขนมอบลักษณะคล้าย ตะแกรง [kha nom op lak sa na khlai ta kraeng] ▷ *v* พูดคลุมเครือ [phut khlum khruea]

wage [weɪdʒ] *n* ค่าจ้าง [kha chang]

waist [weɪst] *n* เอว [eo]

waistcoat ['weɪsˌkəʊt] *n* เสื้อกั๊ก [suea kak]

wait [weɪt] *v* รอ [ro]; **wait for** *v* รอคอย [ro khoi]; **Can you do it while I wait?** คุณทำให้ขณะที่ฉันรออยู่ได้ไหม? [khun tham hai kha na thii chan ro yu dai mai]; **Can you wait here for a few minutes?** คุณรอที่นี่สักสองสามนาทีได้ ไหม? [khun ro thii nii sak song sam na thii dai mai]; **Please wait for me** รอ ฉันด้วย [ro chan duai]

waiter ['weɪtə] *n* บริกรชาย [bo ri kon chai]

waitress ['weɪtrɪs] *n* บริกรหญิง [bo ri kon ying]

wait up [weɪt ʌp] *v* รอคอย [ro khoi]

waive [weɪv] v สละสิทธิ์ [sa la sit]

wake up [weɪk ʌp] v ตื่นขึ้น [tuen khuen]

Wales [weɪlz] n ประเทศเวลส์ที่รวมอยู่ใน สหราชอาณาจักรอังกฤษ [pra tet wel thii ruam yu nai sa ha rat cha na chak ang krit]

walk [wɔːk] n ท่องเที่ยวไปด้วยการเดินเท้า [thong thiao pai duai kan doen thao] ▷ v เดิน [doen]; **Are there any guided walks?** มีคนแนะนำเส้นทางเดินไหม? [mii khon nae nam sen thang doen mai]; **Can I walk there?** ฉันเดินไปได้ไหม? [chan doen pai dai mai]; **Do you have a guide to local walks?** คุณมีไกด์ นำทางเดินเส้นทางท้องถิ่นไหม? [khun mii kai nam thang doen sen thang thong thin mai]

walkie-talkie [ˌwɔːkɪˈtɔːkɪ] n เครื่องรับ ส่งวิทยุมือถือ [khrueang rap song wit tha yu mue thue]

walking [ˈwɔːkɪŋ] n การเดิน [kan doen]; **walking stick** n ไม้เท้า [mai thao]

walkway [ˈwɔːkˌweɪ] n ทางเดินเท้า [thang doen thao]

wall [wɔːl] n กำแพง [kam phaeng]

wallet [ˈwɒlɪt] n กระเป๋าใส่เงินผู้ชาย [kra pao sai ngen phu chai]

wallpaper [ˈwɔːlˌpeɪpə] n กระดาษบุผนัง หรือเพดาน [kra dat bu pha nang rue phe dan]

walnut [ˈwɔːlˌnʌt] n ถั่ววอลนัทมีเปลือก แข็ง รอยหยักและทานได้ [thua wal nat mii plueak khaeng roi yak lae than dai]

walrus [ˈwɔːlrəs; ˈwɒl-] n สัตว์ทะเลพวก เดียวกับสิงโตทะเลและแมวน้ำ [sat tha le phuak diao kap sing to tha le lae maeo nam]

waltz [wɔːls] n การเต้นรำจังหวะวอลทซ์ [kan ten ram chang wa walt] ▷ v เต้นรำ จังหวะวอลทซ์ [ten ram chang wa walt]

wander [ˈwɒndə] v เดินไปโดยไม่มีจุด หมาย [doen pai doi mai mii chut mai]

want [wɒnt] v ต้องการ [tong kan]

war [wɔː] n สงคราม [song khram]; **civil war** n สงครามกลางเมือง [song khram klang mueang]

ward [wɔːd] n (area) เขตเลือกตั้ง [khet lueak tang], (hospital room) ตึกคนไข้ [tuek khon khai]

warden [ˈwɔːdən] n เจ้าหน้าที่ดูแลสถาบัน เช่น หอพักเด็กนักเรียน [chao na thii du lae sa ta ban chen hor phak dek nak rian]; **traffic warden** n เจ้าหน้าที่การ จัดการจราจร [chao na thii kan chat kan cha ra chon]

wardrobe [ˈwɔːdrəʊb] n ตู้เสื้อผ้า [tu suea pha]

warehouse [ˈwɛəˌhaʊs] n โกดังสินค้า [ko dang sin ka]

warm [wɔːm] adj อุ่น [un]

warm up [wɔːm ʌp] v ทำให้อุ่นขึ้น [tham hai un khuen]

warn [wɔːn] v เตือน [tuean]

warning [ˈwɔːnɪŋ] n การเตือน [kan tuean]; **hazard warning lights** npl ไฟ เตือนอันตราย [fai tuean an ta rai]

warranty [ˈwɒrəntɪ] n การรับประกัน [kan rap pra kan]

wart [wɔːt] n ก้อนเล็ก ๆ ที่ขึ้นบนผิวหนัง เช่น ไฝหรือหูด [kon lek lek thii khuen bon phio nang chen fai rue hut]

wash [wɒʃ] v ล้างออกไป [lang ok pai]; **car wash** n ที่ล้างรถ [thii lang rot]

washable [ˈwɒʃəbəl] adj **machine washable** adj ซักด้วยเครื่องซักผ้าได้ [sak duai khrueang sak pha dai]; **Is it washable?** ซักได้ไหม? [sak dai mai]

washbasin [ˈwɒʃˌbeɪsən] n อ่างล้างหน้า และมือ [ang lang na lae mue]

washing [ˈwɒʃɪŋ] n การซักเสื้อผ้า [kan sak suea pha]; **washing line** n ราวตาก ผ้า [rao tak pha]; **washing machine** n เครื่องซักผ้า [khrueang sak pha]; **washing powder** n ผงซักฟอก [phong sak fok]

washing-up [ˈwɒʃɪŋʌp] n การล้างจาน

ซาม [kan lang jan cham]; **washing-up liquid** *n* น้ำยาล้างจาน [nam ya lang chan]

wash up [wɒʃ ʌp] *v* ล้างจาน [lang chan]

wasp [wɒsp] *n* ตัวแตน ตัวต่อ [tua taen, tua to]

waste [weɪst] *n* การสูญเสียโดยเปล่าประโยชน์ [kan sun sia doi plao pra yot] ▷ *v* ใช้ไปโดยเปล่าประโยชน์ [chai pai doi plao pra yot]

watch [wɒtʃ] *n* นาฬิกาข้อมือ [na li ka kho mue] ▷ *v* เฝ้าดู [fao du]; **digital watch** *n* นาฬิกาดิจิตัล [na li ka di chi tal]

watch out [wɒtʃ aʊt] *v* เฝ้าระวังดู [fao ra wang du]

water ['wɔːtə] *n* น้ำ [nam] ▷ *v* รดน้ำ [rot nam]; **drinking water** *n* น้ำดื่ม [nam duem]; **a glass of water** น้ำหนึ่งแก้ว [nam nueng kaew]; **Can you check the water, please?** คุณช่วยตรวจดูน้ำได้ไหม? [khun chuai truat du nam dai mai]; **How deep is the water?** น้ำลึกแค่ไหน? [nam luek khae nai]; **Is hot water included in the price?** รวมน้ำร้อนในราคานี้ไหม? [ruam nam ron nai ra kha nii mai]; **Please bring more water** ช่วยเอาน้ำมาอีก [chuai ao nam ma ik]

watercolour ['wɔːtə,kʌlə] *n* สีน้ำ [si nam]

watercress ['wɔːtə,krɛs] *n* พืชน้ำมีสีเขียวเข้มใส่ในสลัดหรือตกแต่งอาหาร [phuet nam mee see khiao khem sai nai sa lad hue tok taeng a han]

waterfall ['wɔːtə,fɔːl] *n* น้ำตก [nam tok]

watermelon ['wɔːtə,mɛlən] *n* แตงโม [taeng mo]

waterproof ['wɔːtə,pruːf] *adj* ที่กันน้ำได้ [thii kan nam dai]

water-skiing ['wɔːtə,skiːɪŋ] *n* การเล่นสกีน้ำ [kan len sa ki nam]

wave [weɪv] *n* คลื่น [khluen] ▷ *v* โบกมือ [bok mue]

wavelength ['weɪv,lɛŋθ] *n* ช่วงความยาวคลื่น [chuang khwam yao khluen]

wavy ['weɪvɪ] *adj* ที่เป็นคลื่น [thii pen khluen]

wax [wæks] *n* ขี้ผึ้ง [khi phueng]

way [weɪ] *n* วิธีหรือแนวทาง [wi thi rue naeo thang]; **right of way** *n* สิทธิผ่านทาง [sit thi phan thang]

way in [weɪ ɪn] *n* ทางเข้า [thang khao]

way out [weɪ aʊt] *n* ทางออก [thang ok]

we [wiː] *pron* พวกเรา [phuak rao]

weak [wiːk] *adj* อ่อนแอ [on ae]

weakness ['wiːknɪs] *n* ความอ่อนแอ [khwam on ae]

wealth [wɛlθ] *n* ความร่ำรวยมั่งคั่ง [khwam ram ruai mang khang]

wealthy ['wɛlθɪ] *adj* ร่ำรวยมั่งคั่ง [ram ruai mang khang]

weapon ['wɛpən] *n* อาวุธ [a wut]

wear [wɛə] *v* สวมใส่ [suam sai]

weasel ['wiːzəl] *n* อีเห็น [i hen]

weather ['wɛðə] *n* อากาศ [a kat]; **Is the weather going to change?** อากาศจะเปลี่ยนหรือไม่? [a kaat ja plian rue mai]; **What awful weather!** อากาศแย่มาก [a kaat yae mak]; **What will the weather be like tomorrow?** พรุ่งนี้อากาศจะเป็นอย่างไร? [phrung nii a kaat ja pen yang rai]

web [wɛb] *n* ใยแมงมุม [yai maeng mum]; **web address** *n* ที่อยู่ของข้อมูลที่เราจะหาได้ทางอินเตอร์เน็ต [thii yu khong kho mun thii rao ja ha dai thang in toe net]; **web browser** *n* โปรแกรมที่ทำให้เราสามารถอ่านไฮเปอร์เทกซ์บนเครือข่ายคอมพิวเตอร์ทั่วโลกได้ [pro kraem thii tham hai rao sa mat an hai poe thek bon khruea khai khom phio toe thua lok dai]

webcam ['wɛb,kæm] *n* กล้องวีดีโอที่เชื่อมต่อกับคอมพิวเตอร์และอินเตอร์เน็ต [klong vi di o thii chueam tor kap khom phiow ter lae in ter net]

webmaster ['wɛb,mɑːstə] *n* ผู้ดูแลเว็บ ไซต์ [phu du lae wep sai]

website ['wɛb,saɪt] *n* ที่อยู่ของเว็บบน ระบบค้นหาและเข้าถึงข้อมูลบนอินเตอร์เน็ต [thii yu khong web bon ra bop khon ha lae khao thueng kho mun bon in toe net]

webzine ['wɛb,ziːn] *n* นิตยสารใน คอมพิวเตอร์ [nit ta ya san nai khom phio toe]

wedding ['wɛdɪŋ] *n* การแต่งงาน [kan taeng ngan]; **wedding anniversary** *n* ปีครบรอบแต่งงาน [pi khrop rop taeng ngan]; **wedding dress** *n* ชุดแต่งงาน [chut taeng ngan]; **wedding ring** *n* แหวนแต่งงาน [waen taeng ngan]

Wednesday ['wɛnzdɪ] *n* วันพุธ [wan phut]; **Ash Wednesday** *n* วันทางศาสนา คริสต์ [wan thang sat sa na khris]; **on Wednesday** วันพุธ [wan phut]

weed [wiːd] *n* วัชพืช [wat cha phuet]

weedkiller ['wiːd,kɪlə] *n* ยากำจัดวัชพืช [ya kam chat wat cha phuet]

week [wiːk] *n* หนึ่งสัปดาห์ [nueng sap da]

weekday ['wiːk,deɪ] *n* วันธรรมดาตั้งแต่ วันจันทร์ถึงวันศุกร์ [wan tham ma da tang tae wan chan thueng wan suk]

weekend [,wiːk'ɛnd] *n* วันหยุดสุดสัปดาห์ [wan yud sud sap da]

weep [wiːp] *v* ร้องไห้ [rong hai]

weigh [weɪ] *v* ชั่งน้ำหนัก [chang nam nak]

weight [weɪt] *n* น้ำหนัก [nam nak]

weightlifter ['weɪt,lɪftə] *n* ผู้ยกน้ำหนัก [phu yok nam nak]

weightlifting ['weɪt,lɪftɪŋ] *n* การยกน้ำ หนัก [kan yok nam nak]

weird [wɪəd] *adj* แปลกประหลาด [plaek pra lat]

welcome ['wɛlkəm] *n* การต้อนรับ [kan ton rap] ▷ *v* ต้อนรับ [ton rap]; **welcome!** *excl* ยินดีต้อนรับ [yin di ton rap]

well [wɛl] *adj* ดี [di] ▷ *adv* อย่างชำนาญ [yang cham nan] ▷ *n* บ่อ เช่น บ่อแร่ บ่อน้ำ มัน บ่อน้ำ [bo chen bo rae bo nam man bo nam]; **oil well** *n* บ่อน้ำมัน [bo nam man]; **well done!** *excl* ทำดีมาก [tham dii mak]; **Did you sleep well?** คุณนอน หลับดีไหม? [khun non lap di mai]

well-behaved ['wɛl'bɪ'heɪvd] *adj* ที่มี ความประพฤติเรียบร้อย [thii mii khwam pra phruet riap roi]

wellies ['wɛlɪz] *npl* รองเท้าบู๊ทยาง [rong thao but yang]

wellingtons ['wɛlɪŋtənz] *npl* รองเท้า บู๊ทยาง [rong thao but yang]

well-known ['wɛl'nəʊn] *adj* ที่มีชื่อเสียง [thii mii chue siang]

well-off ['wɛl'ɒf] *adj* ซึ่งร่ำรวย [sueng ram ruai]

well-paid ['wɛl'peɪd] *adj* ซึ่งให้เงินเดือน สูง [sueng hai ngoen duean sung]

Welsh [wɛlʃ] *adj* เกี่ยวกับประชาชนและ วัฒนธรรมเวลส์ [kiao kap pra cha chon lae wat tha na tham wel] ▷ *n* ชาวเวลส์ [chao wel]

west [wɛst] *adj* ซึ่งเกี่ยวกับทางทิศตะวันตก [sueng kiao kap thang thit ta wan tok] ▷ *adv* อยู่ทางทิศตะวันตก [yu thang thid ta wan tok] ▷ *n* ทิศตะวันตก [thid ta wan tok]; **West Indian** *n* ชาวหมู่เกาะอินเดีย ตะวันตกในทะเลคาริเบียน [chao mu kao in dia ta wan tok nai tha le kha ri bian], ที่เกี่ยวกับหมู่เกาะอินเดียตะวันตกใน ทะเลคาริเบียน [chao mu kao in dia ta wan tok nai tha le kha ri bian, thii kiao kap mu kao in dia ta wan tok nai tha le kha ri bian]; **West Indies** *npl* หมู่ เกาะอินเดียตะวันตกในทะเลคาริบเบียน [mu kao in dia ta wan tok nai tha le kha rip bian]

westbound ['wɛst,baʊnd] *adj* ซึ่งเคลื่อน ไปทางตะวันตก [sueng khluean pai thang ta wan tok]

western ['wɛstən] *adj* ซึ่งอยู่ไปทางทิศ ตะวันตก [sueng yu pai thang thit ta

wan tok] ▷ *n* ภาพยนตร์หรือหนังสือที่เกี่ยว
กับดินแดนทางตะวันตกของอเมริกา [phap
pa yon hue hnang sue thiikiao kab din
daen thang ta wan tok khong a me ri
ka]

wet [wɛt] *adj* เปียก [piak]

wetsuit ['wɛtˌsuːt] *n* ชุดดำน้ำ [chut
dam nam]

whale [weɪl] *n* ปลาวาฬ [pla wan]

what [wɒt; wət] *adj* อะไร [a rai] ▷ *pron*
อันไหน สิ่งไหน [an nai, sing nai]; **What
do you do?** คุณทำอะไร? [khun tham a
rai]; **What is it?** นี่คืออะไร? [ni khue a
rai]; **What is the word for...?** คำนี้ใช้
เพื่ออะไร? [kham nii chai phuea a rai]

wheat [wiːt] *n* ข้าวสาลี [khao sa li];
wheat intolerance *n* คนที่แพ้อาหารที่
ทำจากข้าวสาลี [khon thii pae a han thii
tham chak khao sa lii]

wheel [wiːl] *n* ล้อ [lo]; **spare wheel** *n*
ล้ออะไหล่ [lo a lai]; **steering wheel** *n*
พวงมาลัยรถ [phuang ma lai rot]

wheelbarrow ['wiːlˌbærəʊ] *n* รถเข็นล้อ
เดียว [rot khen lor diao]

wheelchair ['wiːlˌtʃɛə] *n* เก้าอี้เข็นสำหรับ
คนป่วยหรือคนพิการ [kao ii khen sam rap
khon puai rue khon phi kan]

when [wɛn] *adv* เมื่อไหร่ [muea rai]
▷ *conj* เมื่อหรือขณะที่ [muea rue kha na
thii]

where [wɛə] *adv* ที่ไหน [thi nai] ▷ *conj*
ในที่ซึ่ง [nai thii sueng]; **Where are
we?** เราอยู่ที่ไหน? [rao yu thii nai];
Where are you staying? คุณพักที่ไหน?
[khun phak thii nai]; **Where can we
meet?** เราจะพบกันได้ที่ไหน? [rao ja
phop kan dai thii nai]

whether ['wɛðə] *conj* ไม่ว่าจะ...หรือไม่
[mai wa ja...rue mai]

which [wɪtʃ] *pron* สิ่งที่ อันที่ [sing thii,
an thii], อันไหน [an nai]

while [waɪls] *conj* ขณะที่ [kha na thi]
▷ *n* ชั่วขณะหนึ่ง [chua kha na nueng];
Can you do it while I wait? คุณทำให้

ขณะที่ฉันรออยู่ได้ไหม? [khun tham hai
kha na thii chan ro yu dai mai]

whip [wɪp] *n* แส้ [sae]; **whipped cream**
n ครีมที่ตีจนเบาและฟู [khrim thii ti chon
bao lae fu]

whiskers ['wɪskəz] *npl* เคราแข็งสองข้าง
ปาก [khrao khaeng song khang pak]

whisky ['wɪski] *n* วิสกี้ [wit sa ki]; **malt
whisky** *n* เหล้าวิสกี้ที่ทำจากข้าวมอลต์ [lao
wis ki thii tham chak khao malt
whisky]; **a whisky and soda** วิสกี้กับ
โซดาหนึ่งแก้ว [wis ki kap so da nueng
kaeo]; **I'll have a whisky** ฉันจะดื่มวิสกี้
[chan ja duem wis ki]

whisper ['wɪspə] *v* กระซิบ [kra sip]

whistle ['wɪsᵊl] *n* การผิวปาก [kan phio
pak] ▷ *v* ผิวปาก [phio pak]

white [waɪt] *adj* สีขาว [sii khao]; **egg
white** *n* ไข่ขาว [khai khao]

whiteboard ['waɪtˌbɔːd] *n* กระดานสีขาว
[kra dan sii kao]

whitewash ['waɪtˌwɒʃ] *v* ทาให้ขาว [tha
hai khao]

whiting ['waɪtɪŋ] *n* ปลาของยุโรปตระกูล
ปลาคอด [pla khong yu rop tra kul pla
khot]

who [huː] *pron* ใคร [khrai], บุคคลที่ [buk
khon thii]; **Who am I talking to?** ฉัน
กำลังพูดกับใคร? [chan kam lang phut
kap khrai]; **Who is it?** นี่คือใคร? [ni
khue khrai]; **Who's calling?** ใครโทร
มา? [khrai tho ma]

whole [həʊl] *adj* ทั้งหมด [thang mot] ▷ *n*
สิ่งที่ครบถ้วน [sing thii khrop thuan]

wholefoods ['həʊlˌfuːdz] *npl* อาหารที่
ผ่านขั้นตอนการผลิตและการขัดเกลาน้อย
ที่สุด [a han thii phan khan torn kan
pha lit lae kan khad klao noi thii sud]

wholemeal ['həʊlˌmiːl] *adj* ซึ่งไม่ได้เอา
รำข้าวสาลีออก [sueng mai dai ao ram
khao sa lii ok]

wholesale ['həʊlˌseɪl] *adj* โดยการขายส่ง
[doi kan khai song] ▷ *n* การขายส่ง [kan
khai song]

whom [hu:m] *pron* ใคร [khrai]

whose [hu:z] *adj* ของผู้ซึ่ง [khong phu sueng] ▷ *pron* ของใคร [khong khrai]

why [waɪ] *adv* ทำไม [tham mai]

wicked [ˈwɪkɪd] *adj* ชั่วร้าย [chua rai]

wide [waɪd] *adj* กว้าง [kwang] ▷ *adv* กว้างขวาง [kwang khwang]

widespread [ˈwaɪdˌsprɛd] *adj* แพร่ไปทั่ว [prae pai thua]

widow [ˈwɪdəʊ] *n* แม่ม่าย [mae mai]

widower [ˈwɪdəʊə] *n* พ่อหม้าย [pho mai]

width [wɪdθ] *n* ความกว้าง [khwam kwang]

wife, wives [waɪf, waɪvz] *n* ภรรยา [phan ra ya]; **This is my wife** นี่ภรรยาผมครับ [ni phan ra ya phom krap]

WiFi [waɪ faɪ] *n* เชื่อมต่อกับอินเตอร์เน็ตแบบไร้สาย [chueam to kap in toe net baep rai sai]

wig [wɪg] *n* ผมปลอม [phom plom]

wild [waɪld] *adj* ไม่เชื่อง [mai chueang]

wildlife [ˈwaɪldˌlaɪf] *n* สัตว์และพืชป่า [sat lae phuet pa]

will [wɪl] *n* (*document*) พินัยกรรม [phi nai kam], (*motivation*) แรงบันดาลใจ [raeng ban dan chai]

willing [ˈwɪlɪŋ] *adj* อย่างสมัครใจ [yang sa mak jai]

willingly [ˈwɪlɪŋlɪ] *adv* อย่างเต็มใจ [yang tem jai]

willow [ˈwɪləʊ] *n* ต้นวิลโลว์ปลูกใกล้น้ำ [ton vil lo pluk kai nam]

willpower [ˈwɪlˌpaʊə] *n* ความตั้งใจและความมีวินัยที่นำตัวเองไปสู่ความสำเร็จ [khwam tang jai lae khwam mii wi nai thii nam tua eng pai su khwam sam ret]

wilt [wɪlt] *v* เหี่ยวเฉา [hiao chao]

win [wɪn] *v* ชนะ [cha na]

wind¹ [wɪnd] *n* ลม [lom] ▷ *vt* (*with a blow etc.*) ระบายลม [ra bai lom]

wind² [waɪnd] *v* (*coil around*) พัน [phan]

windmill [ˈwɪndˌmɪl; ˈwɪnˌmɪl] *n* กังหันลม [kang han lom]

window [ˈwɪndəʊ] *n* หน้าต่าง [hna tang]; **shop window** *n* หน้าต่างตู้โชว์ของร้านค้า [na tang tu cho khong ran ka]; **I can't open the window** ฉันเปิดหน้าต่างไม่ได้ [chan poet na tang mai dai]; **I'd like a window seat** ฉันขอที่นั่งที่หน้าต่าง [chan kho thii nang thii na tang]; **May I close the window?** ฉันขอปิดหน้าต่างได้ไหม? [chan kho pit na tang dai mai]

windowsill [ˈwɪndəʊˌsɪl] *n* ขอบหน้าต่างส่วนล่าง [kop na tang suan lang]

windscreen [ˈwɪndˌskriːn] *n* กระจกหน้ารถ [kra jok na rot]; **windscreen wiper** *n* ที่ปัดกระจก [thii pat kra chok]; **Could you clean the windscreen?** คุณช่วยล้างกระจกหน้ารถได้ไหม? [khun chuai lang kra chok na rot dai mai]

windsurfing [ˈwɪndˌsɜːfɪŋ] *n* กีฬาวินด์เซิร์ฟ [ki la win serf]

windy [ˈwɪndɪ] *adj* ซึ่งมีลมแรง [sueng mee lom raeng]

wine [waɪn] *n* ไวน์ [wai]; **house wine** *n* ไวน์ของร้านอาหาร [wine khong ran a han]; **a bottle of white wine** ไวน์ขาวหนึ่งขวด [wine khao nueng khaut]; **Can you recommend a good wine?** คุณแนะนำไวน์ดี ๆ ได้ไหม? [khun nae nam wine di di dai mai]; **Is the wine chilled?** ไวน์เย็นไหม? [wine yen mai]

wineglass [ˈwaɪnˌglɑːs] *n* แก้วไวน์ [kaew wine]

wing [wɪŋ] *n* ปีก [pik]; **wing mirror** *n* กระจกข้าง [kra jok khang]

wink [wɪŋk] *v* ขยิบตา [kha yip ta]

winner [ˈwɪnə] *n* ผู้ชนะ [phu cha na]

winning [ˈwɪnɪŋ] *adj* ซึ่งมีชัยชนะ [sueng mii chai cha na]

winter [ˈwɪntə] *n* ฤดูหนาว [rue du nao]; **winter sports** *npl* กีฬาฤดูหนาว [ki la rue du nao]

wipe [waɪp] *v* เช็ดออก [chet ok]; **baby wipe** *n* กระดาษหรือผ้าเช็ดตัวเด็ก [kra dat rue pha chet tua dek]

wipe up [waɪp ʌp] v เช็ดให้สะอาด [chet hai sa at]

wire [waɪə] n ลวด [luat]; **barbed wire** n เส้นลวด [sen luat]

wisdom ['wɪzdəm] n สติปัญญา ความเฉลียวฉลาด [sa ti pan ya, khwam cha liao cha lat]; **wisdom tooth** n ฟันกราม [fan kram]

wise [waɪz] adj เฉลียวฉลาด [cha liao cha lat]

wish [wɪʃ] n ความต้องการ [khwam tong kan] ▷ v ปรารถนา [prat tha na]

wit [wɪt] n คำพูดหรือข้อเขียนที่แสดงเชาว์ปัญญา [kham phut rue kho khian thii sa daeng chao pan ya]

witch [wɪtʃ] n แม่มด [mae mot]

with [wɪð; wɪθ] prep ร่วมกับ [ruam kap]

withdraw [wɪð'drɔː] v ถอนคืน [thon khuen]

withdrawal [wɪð'drɔːəl] n ถอนตำแหน่ง [thon tam naeng]

within [wɪ'ðɪn] prep (space) ภายใน [phai nai], (term) ภายใน [phai nai]

without [wɪ'ðaʊt] prep ปราศจาก [prat sa chak]

witness ['wɪtnɪs] n พยาน [pha yan]; **Jehovah's Witness** n สมาชิกของนิกายยะโฮวาวิทเนส [sa ma chik khong ni kai ya ho va wit nes]; **Can you be a witness for me?** คุณเป็นพยานให้ฉันได้ไหม? [khun pen pha yan hai chan dai mai]

witty ['wɪtɪ] adj ซึ่งใช้คำพูดอย่างมีสติปัญญาและตลก [sueng chai kham phut yang mii sa ti pan ya lae ta lok]

wolf, wolves [wʊlf, wʊlvz] n สุนัขป่า [su nak pa]

woman, women ['wʊmən, 'wɪmɪn] n ผู้หญิง [phu ying]

wonder ['wʌndə] v สงสัย [song sai]

wonderful ['wʌndəfʊl] adj ดีเยี่ยม [di yiam]

wood [wʊd] n (forest) ป่าไม้ [pa mai],

(material) ไม้ [mai]

wooden ['wʊdᵊn] adj ที่ทำจากไม้ [thii tham chak mai]

woodwind ['wʊd,wɪnd] n เครื่องดนตรีประเภทเป่า [khrueang don tri pra phet pao]

woodwork ['wʊd,wɜːk] n สิ่งที่ทำจากไม้ สิ่งของภายในบ้าน เช่นกรอบประตู หน้าต่าง บันได [sing thii tham chak mai sing khong phai nai baan chen krob pra tu na tang ban dai]

wool [wʊl] n ขนสัตว์ เช่น ขนแกะและสัตว์อื่น ๆ [khon sat chen khon kae lae sat uen uen]; **cotton wool** n สำลี [sam lii]

woollen ['wʊlən] adj ทำจากขนสัตว์ [tham chak khon sat]

woollens ['wʊlənz] npl เสื้อผ้าที่ทำจากขนสัตว์ [suea pha thii tham chak khon sat]

word [wɜːd] n คำ [kham]; **all one word** คำเดียวทั้งหมด [kham diao thang mot]; **What is the word for...?** คำนี้ใช้เพื่ออะไร? [kham nii chai phuea a rai]

work [wɜːk] n การงาน [kan ngan] ▷ v ทำงาน [tham ngan]; **work experience** n ประสบการณ์การทำงาน [pra sop kan kan tham ngan]; **work of art** n งานศิลปะ [ngan sin la pa]; **work permit** n ใบอนุญาตให้ทำงาน [bai a nu yat hai tham ngan]; **How does the ticket machine work?** เครื่องขายตั๋วทำงานอย่างไร? [khrueang khai tua tham ngan yang rai]; **How does this work?** นี่ทำงานอย่างไร? [ni tham ngan yang rai]; **I hope we can work together again soon** ฉันหวังว่าเราจะทำงานด้วยกันอีกเร็วๆ นี้ [chan hwang wa rao ja tham ngan duai kan ik reo reo nee]; **Where do you work?** คุณทำงานที่ไหน? [khun tham ngan thii nai]

worker ['wɜːkə] n ผู้ทำงาน [phu tham ngan]; **social worker** n นักสังคมสงเคราะห์ [nak sang khom song khro]

workforce ['wɜːkˌfɔːs] n จำนวนคน
ทำงาน [cham nuan kon tham ngan]

working-class ['wɜːkɪŋklɑːs] adj
ชนชั้นผู้รับจ้าง [chon chan phu rap
chang]

workman, workmen ['wɜːkmən,
'wɜːkmɛn] n คนงาน [khon ngan]

work out [wɜːk aʊt] v แก้ปัญหาหรือ
วางแผนโดยการคิดไตร่ตรอง [kae pan ha
rue wang phaen doi kan kit trai trong]

workplace ['wɜːkˌpleɪs] n สถานที่ทำงาน
[sa than thii tham ngan]

workshop ['wɜːkˌʃɒp] n ห้องทำงานใน
โรงงาน [hong tham ngan nai rong
ngan]

workspace ['wɜːkˌspeɪs] n ที่ที่คนทำงาน
[thii thii khon tham ngan]

workstation ['wɜːkˌsteɪʃən] n สถานที่
ทำงาน [sa than thii tham ngan]

world [wɜːld] n โลก [lok]; **Third World**
n ประเทศที่ด้อยพัฒนา [pra tet thii doi
phat ta na]; **World Cup** n การแข่งขัน
กีฬานานาชาติโดยเฉพาะกีฬาฟุตบอล [kan
khaeng khan ki la na na chat doi cha
po ki la fut ball]

worm [wɜːm] n พยาธิ [pha yat]

worn [wɔːn] adj ซึ่งใช้จนเก่า [sueng chai
chon kao]

worried ['wʌrɪd] adj เป็นห่วงกังวล [pen
huang kang won]

worry ['wʌrɪ] v วิตกกังวล [wi tok kang
won]

worrying ['wʌrɪɪŋ] adj สาเหตุของความ
วิตกกังวล [sa het khong khwam wi tok
kang won]

worse [wɜːs] adj แย่ลง [yae long] ▷ adv
แย่กว่า [yae kwa]

worsen ['wɜːsən] v ทำให้แย่ลง [tham
hai yae long]

worship ['wɜːʃɪp] v บูชา [bu cha]

worst [wɜːst] adj เลวที่สุด [leo thii sut]

worth [wɜːθ] n มูลค่า [mun kha]

worthless ['wɜːθlɪs] adj ที่ไม่มีคุณค่า
[thii mai mii khun kha]

would [wʊd; wəd] v **I would like to
wash the car** ฉันอยากล้างรถ [chan yak
lang rot]; **We would like to go cycling**
ฉันอยากไปขี่จักรยาน [chan yak pai khi
chak kra yan]

wound [wuːnd] n บาดแผล [bat phlae]
▷ v บาดเจ็บ [bat chep]

wrap [ræp] v ห่อ [ho]; **wrapping paper**
n กระดาษห่อ [kra dat ho]

wrap up [ræp ʌp] v ห่อหุ้ม [ho hum]

wreck [rɛk] n สิ่งที่ถูกทำลายอย่างเสียหาย
ยับเยิน [sing thii thuk tham lai yang
sia hai yap yoen] ▷ v ทำให้เสียหายยับเยิน
[tham hai sia hai yak yoen]

wreckage ['rɛkɪdʒ] n ซากปรักหักพัง [sak
prak hak phang]

wren [rɛn] n นกขนาดเล็กสีน้ำตาลร้องเพลง
ไพเราะอยู่ในตระกูล Troglodytidae [nok
kha nard lek see nam tan rong phleng
pai rao yu nai tra kul troglodytidae]

wrench [rɛntʃ] n การดึงและบิดอย่างแรง
[kan dueng lae bit yang raeng] ▷ v ดึง
และบิดอย่างแรง [dueng lae bit yang
raeng]

wrestler ['rɛslə] n นักมวยปล้ำ [nak muai
plam]

wrestling ['rɛslɪŋ] n การแข่งขันมวยปล้ำ
[kan khaeng khan muai plam]

wrinkle ['rɪŋkəl] n รอยย่นบนผิว [roi yon
bon phio]

wrinkled ['rɪŋkəld] adj ซึ่งมีรอยย่น
[sueng mii roi yon]

wrist [rɪst] n ข้อมือ [kho mue]

write [raɪt] v เขียน [khian]

write down [raɪt daʊn] v เขียนลง
[khian long]

writer ['raɪtə] n นักเขียน [nak khian]

writing ['raɪtɪŋ] n งานเขียน [ngan
khian]; **writing paper** n กระดาษเขียน
[kra dat khian]

wrong [rɒŋ] adj อย่างไม่ถูกต้อง [yang
mai thuk tong] ▷ adv อย่างผิดพลาด
[yang phid phlad]; **wrong number** n
หมายเลขที่ผิด [mai lek thii phit]

X y

Xmas ['ɛksməs; 'krɪsməs] *n* คริสต์มาส [kris mat]

X-ray [ɛksreɪ] *n* รังสีแม่เหล็กไฟฟ้าชนิดหนึ่งผ่านสิ่งของบางประเภทได้ [rang sii mae lek fai fa cha nit nueng phan sing khong bang pra phet dai] ▷ *v* ถ่ายภาพด้วยรังสีเอ็กซ์ [thai phap duai rang sii ex]

xylophone ['zaɪləˌfəʊn] *n* ระนาดฝรั่ง [ra nat fa rang]

yacht [jɒt] *n* เรือใบสำหรับที่ใช้ท่องเที่ยวหรือแข่งเรือ [rua bai sam rap thii chai thong thiao rue khaeng ruea]

yard [jɑːd] *n* (*enclosure*) บริเวณบ้าน [bor ri ven baan], (*measurement*) หลา [la]

yawn [jɔːn] *v* หาว [hao]

year [jɪə] *n* ปี [pi]; **academic year** *n* ปีการศึกษา [pi kan suek sa]; **Happy New Year!** สวัสดีปีใหม่ [sa wat di pii mai]; **I'm fifty years old** ฉันอายุห้าสิบปี [chan a yu ha sib pi]

yearly ['jɪəlɪ] *adj* ประจำปี [pra cham pi] ▷ *adv* ปีละครั้ง [pi la khrang]

yeast [jiːst] *n* ยีสต์ เชื้อหมัก [yis, chuea mak]

yell [jɛl] *v* ตะโกน ร้อง [ta khon, rong]

yellow ['jɛləʊ] *adj* ที่เป็นสีเหลือง [thii pen sii lueang]; **Yellow Pages®** *npl* สมุดโทรศัพท์ฉบับโฆษณาสินค้า [sa mut tho ra sap cha bap khot sa na sin ka]

Yemen ['jɛmən] *n* ประเทศเยเมน [pra tet ye men]

yes [jɛs] *excl* ใช่ [chai]

yesterday ['jɛstədɪ; -ˌdeɪ] *adv* เมื่อวานนี้ [muea wan ni]

yet [jɛt] *adv (with negative)* ยัง [yang]
▷ *conj (nevertheless)* อย่างไรก็ตาม [yang
rai ko tam]

yew [juː] *n* ต้นไม้ที่เขียวตลอดปี [ton mai
thii khiao ta lod pi]

yield [jiːld] *v* ผลิต [pha lit]

yoga ['jəʊɡə] *n* โยคะ [yo kha]

yoghurt ['jəʊɡət; 'jɒɡ-] *n* นมเปรี้ยว
[num priao]

yolk [jəʊk] *n* ไข่แดง [khai daeng]

you [juː; jʊ] *pron (plural)* พวกคุณ
[phuak khun], *(singular polite)* ท่าน
[than], *(singular)* คุณ [khun]; **Are you
alright?** คุณตกลงไหม? [khun tok long
mai]; **How are you?** คุณสบายดีหรือ?
[khun sa bai di rue]

young [jʌŋ] *adj* อ่อนวัย [on wai]

younger [jʌŋə] *adj* มีอายุน้อยกว่า [mii a
yu noi kwa]

youngest [jʌŋɪst] *adj* อายุน้อยที่สุด [a yu
noi thii sut]

your [jɔː; jʊə; jə] *adj (plural)* ของพวกคุณ
[khong phuak khun], *(singular polite)*
ของพวกท่าน [khong phuak than],
(singular) ของคุณ [khong khun]; **May I
use your phone?** ฉันขอใช้โทรศัพท์ของ
คุณได้ไหม? [chan kho chai tho ra sap
khong khun dai mai]

yours [jɔːz; jʊəz] *pron (plural)* ของพวก
คุณ [khong phuak khun], *(singular
polite)* ของพวกท่าน [khong phuak
than], *(singular)* ของคุณ [khong khun]

yourself [jɔːˈsɛlf; jʊə-] *pron* ตัวคุณเอง
[tua khun eng], *(intensifier)* ตัวคุณเอง
[tua khun eng], *(polite)* ตัวท่านเอง [tua
than eng]

yourselves [jɔːˈsɛlvz] *pron (intensifier)*
ตัวพวกคุณเอง [tua phuak khun eng],
(polite) ตัวพวกท่านเอง [tua phuak than
eng], *(reflexive)* ตัวพวกคุณเอง [tua
phuak khun eng]

youth [juːθ] *n* วัยหนุ่มสาว [wai num
sao]; **youth club** *n* คลับวัยรุ่นที่จัดให้มี
กิจกรรมเพื่อความบันเทิง [khlap wai run
thii chat hai mii kit cha kam phuea
khwam ban thoeng]; **youth hostel** *n*
หอพักนักเรียน [ho phak nak rian]

Z

ra si]

zone [zəʊn] *n* โซน แถบ เขต [son, thaep, khet]; **time zone** *n* เขตเวลาของโลกซึ่งมี ๒๔ เขต [khet we la khong lok sueng mii yi sip sii khet]

zoo [zuː] *n* สวนสัตว์ [suan sat]

zoology [zəʊˈɒlədʒɪ; zuː-] *n* สัตววิทยา [sat ta wa wit tha ya]

zoom [zuːm] *n* **zoom lens** *n* เลนส์ของ กล้องที่ขยายปรับภาพโดยรักษาโฟกัสเดิมไว้ [len khong klong thii kha yai prab phap doi rak sa fo kas doem wai]

zucchini [tsuːˈkiːnɪ; zuː-] *n* บวบ [buap]

Zambia [ˈzæmbɪə] *n* ประเทศแซมเบีย [pra tet saem bia]

Zambian [ˈzæmbɪən] *adj* เกี่ยวกับประเทศ แซมเบีย [kiao kap pra thet saem bia] ▷ *n* ชาวแซมเบีย [chao saem bia]

zebra [ˈziːbrə; ˈzɛbrə] *n* ม้าลาย [ma lai]; **zebra crossing** *n* ทางม้าลาย [thang ma lai]

zero, zeroes [ˈzɪərəʊ, ˈzɪərəʊz] *n* ศูนย์ [sun]

zest [zɛst] *n* (excitement) ความสนุกสนาน [khwam sa nuk sa nan], (lemon-peel) เปลือกมะนาวหรือส้ม [plueak ma nao rue som]

Zimbabwe [zɪmˈbɑːbwɪ; -weɪ] *n* ประเทศซิมบับเว [pra tet sim bab we]

Zimbabwean [zɪmˈbɑːbwɪən; -weɪən] *adj* เกี่ยวกับประเทศซิมบับเว [kiao kap pra thet sim bap we] ▷ *n* ชาว ซิมบับเว [chao sim bap we]

zinc [zɪŋk] *n* สังกะสี [sang ka si]

zip [zɪp] *n* ซิป [sip]; **zip (up)** *v* รูดซิป [rut sip]

zit [zɪt] *n* สิว [sio]

zodiac [ˈzəʊdɪˌæk] *n* จักรราศี [chak kra